D0555787

Strategic Management
Text and Cases

SECOND EDITION

Peter Wright
Memphis State University

Charles D. Pringle
James Madison University

Mark J. Kroll
University of Texas at Tyler

with contributions by

John A. Parnell
Middle Tennessee State University

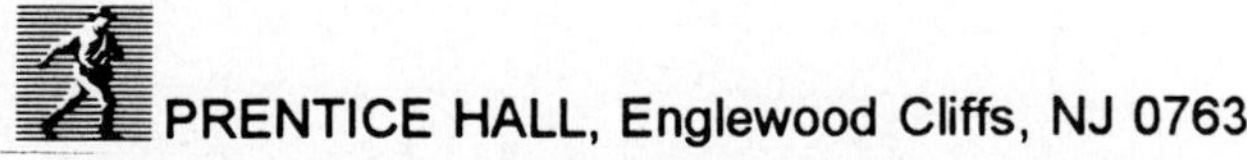

PRENTICE HALL, Englewood Cliffs, NJ 07632

Editor-in-Chief, Business and Economics: Rich Wohl
Senior Series Editor: Suzy Spivey
Cover Administrator: Linda Dickinson
Composition Buyer: Linda Cox
Manufacturing Buyer: Megan Cochran
Editorial-Production Service: Woodstock Publishers' Services
Text Designer: Nancy McJennett

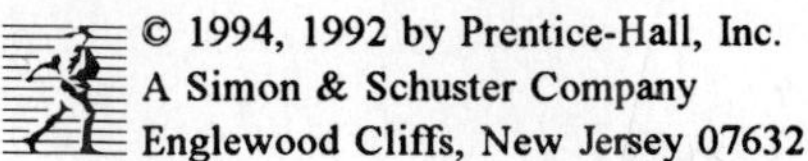

© 1994, 1992 by Prentice-Hall, Inc.
A Simon & Schuster Company
Englewood Cliffs, New Jersey 07632

All rights reserved. No part of the material protected by this copyright notice may be reproduced or utilized in any form or by any means, electronic or mechanical, including photocopying, recording, or by any information storage and retrieval system, without the written permission of the copyright holder.

With regard to the software disk accompanying this text, the publisher assumes no responsibility for damages, errors, or omissions, without any limitation, which may result from the use of the program or the text.

Library of Congress Cataloging-in-Publication Data

Wright, Peter
Strategic management: text and cases / Peter Wright, Charles D. Pringle, Mark J. Kroll, with contributions by John A. Parnell. 2nd ed.
p. cm.
Includes bibliographical references and index.
ISBN 0-205-14884-0
1. Strategic planning. 2. Strategic planning—Case studies.
I. Pringle, Charles D. II. Kroll, Mark J. III. Title.
Hd30.28.W75 1993
658.4'012—dc20 93-5124
CIP

ISBN 0-205-14884-0

Printed in the United States of America

10 9 8 7 6 5 4 3 2

Contents

Preface

This second edition reflects the truth of one of our book's basic tenets: environmental change is inevitable. In fact, changes in the business environment and developments in the academic field of strategic management drove us to begin revising *Strategic Management: Text and Cases* less than a year after it first appeared on the market. This new edition not only contains those changes, but it also benefits significantly from the perceptive feedback of our reviewers and the adopters of the first edition.

The text portion synthesizes and builds upon the most recent strategy-related literature from numerous fields. And virtually every concept, theory, or idea is illustrated with examples from real organizations. The cases represent the works of knowledgeable and discerning authors who have provided highly readable information on enterprises ranging from small, local businesses to huge, global corporations.

GOALS OF THE TEXT

Our purpose in writing this text was twofold: to provide students with the most current, comprehensive, state-of-the-art analysis of the field of strategic management, and to promote student understanding of the material with applied, innovative learning features.

To accomplish our first goal, we incorporated the most up-to-date coverage of the strategic management literature into the text in a clear, easy-to-read style. The coverage includes the most relevant and exciting multidisciplinary contributions to the field. Strategic management is a relatively young discipline that has borrowed from, built upon, and contributed to such business fields as economics, management, marketing, finance, operations management, and accounting, among others. In recent years, however, exciting developments from such diverse fields as psychology, sociology, and anthropology have also broadened and enriched the knowledge base of strategic management. Students will gain new insights from these cutting-edge, integrative developments.

The strategic management and business policy course is designed to help students integrate and apply what they have learned in their separate functional business courses and to help them gain experience in using the tools of strategic analysis. To facilitate this process and promote student learning—the second major goal of this text—we have developed a number of innovative learning tools. You will find this book rich with applied material—realistic business examples carefully woven throughout the text, provocative discussions of strategic management conducted by well-known companies, and experiential exercises to help students think strategically. And, since the core of the course is case analysis, our text provides an excellent, diverse collection of up-to-date cases depicting meaningful decision situations.

The book is comprised of two major parts. Part I, "The Concepts and Techniques of Strategic Management," consists of 12 chapters—carefully integrated from a conceptual perspective and by a consistent writing style—that introduce the major concepts and methodologies of strategic management. Part II, "Cases in Strategic Management," provides a broad selection of 40 cases that allows students to apply and integrate their knowledge of the strategic management process.

STATE-OF-THE-ART COVERAGE

Along with traditional coverage, this text incorporates a number of innovative topics and provides several unique chapters that give it a distinct competitive advantage over other textbooks in strategic management. Some of that coverage includes the following material:

- Chapter 3 presents not only the traditional viewpoint that a firm's strategy should be shareholder-driven, but also the competing perspectives that strategy should be customer-driven or, more broadly, stakeholder-driven.
- Chapter 6, a unique chapter on business unit strategies, relates generic strategies to such concepts as total quality management (TQM), product/process/system innovations, leverage through organizational expertise and image, market share, profitability, value analysis, and strategic groups.
- Unique coverage of how functional activities can be integrated to help a business attain superior product design, customer service, speed, and product/service guarantees is contained in Chapter 7.
- A framework is presented in Chapter 8 for helping top management assess the effectiveness of the organization's structure.
- Chapter 9 offers innovative discussion of how strategy is implemented through managerial leadership, the appropriate use of power, and the molding of organizational culture.
- A unique approach to strategic control in Chapter 10 presents multiple control standards and several different and useful ways of exerting strategic control.
- Global issues are not only integrated throughout the text but are comprehensively covered in Chapter 11. This unique chapter revisits the strategic management processes covered in Chapters 2 through 10 in the context of the world marketplace.
- Chapter 12 is devoted exclusively to strategic management in not-for-profit organizations.
- Differences in strategic management processes in large and small companies are examined in separate sections throughout the chapter portions of the text.

NEW TO THIS EDITION

New to the Second Edition is the coverage of the following material:

- Diverse theories that have influenced our approach to strategic management are briefly presented in Chapter 1. These include biological and Schumpeterian theories of evolution and revolution; theories based upon the fields of industrial organization and Chamberlinian economics; and contingency and resource-based theories.
- Coverage of corporate strategy has been expanded to two chapters (4 and 5) to reflect the increasing importance of this topic and to provide students with more guidelines for analysis. Resource-based theory is used to analyze a firm's strengths and weaknesses in Chapter 4. This chapter also presents a most comprehensive overview of corporate-level strategies.
- Our new S.W.O.T. portfolio framework is introduced in Chapter 5, along with more traditional approaches. New material analyzing corporate strategies and returns is also included in Chapter 5.

- In Chapter 6, a framework is presented for selecting a generic strategy within the context of industry life cycle.
- In Chapter 7, a new integrative framework that links business unit strategies to functional strategies is presented. Also in this chapter, new sections on human resource and information system strategies are provided.
- In Chapter 8, a new section is included on current trends in structuring organizations, such as the modular corporation.
- Many new and updated "Strategic Insight" boxes throughout the text portion of the book show successful and unsuccessful decision making by companies such as Boeing, American Airlines, and Compaq Computers.

CASES

Part II, "Cases in Strategic Management," includes a rich, wide-ranging collection of cases. A special introductory section preceding the cases, "Strategic Management Case Analysis," is designed to help students prepare written and oral case analyses by offering specific guidelines and methodologies. Concluding this section are several suggestions for enhancing student performance in the strategic management course and for working within a group.

We have selected 40 cases that students and instructors should find interesting and thought-provoking to read. Cases range from some of the largest, best-known businesses in the world to small, developing organizations. Company operations range from those of huge, multidivisional enterprises to smaller, single businesses.

The collection includes a broad cross section of industries and organizations, with operational settings ranging from the United States to China, Russia, Eastern Europe, and Western Europe. Students will read about enterprises as familiar as a neighborhood video rental store and as exotic as a joint venture in China. The case selection also reflects a conscious effort to expose students not only to a diversity of enterprises but also to the diversity of the individuals who manage those enterprises. The following are key features of case selection:

- In keeping with the increasing globalization of business and AACSB's concern for the internationalization of the business curriculum, we have selected cases that provide a more global perspective of business. These cases include enterprises based outside of the united States, as found in "Cadbury, Schweppes, PLC" and "The Swatch," and U.S. based firms with multinational operations, such as "Delta Airlines, Inc." and "Cognex Corporation."
- Students are also exposed to organizations that are attempting to make the transition from state control to private ownership in former communist countries. These cases include "Rimeda" and "Taurus Hungarian Rubber Works."
- A concerted effort was made to include cases that not only detail the history and present condition of an organization, but also present the future issues that management must face if the enterprise is to survive and prosper. Whether the issues involve exploiting new opportunities in the environment or taking fundamental steps to survive, the student analyzing the case must make critical decisions regarding the future of the organization.
- The extensive case selection gives students an opportunity to make strategic management decisions at the corporate level, the business unit level, and the functional level.
- Several small business cases are included, addressing such issues as new business startup, growth, and survival.
- Not-for-profit cases range from one that analyzes a major, world-famous museum ("The Metropolitan Museum of Art") to one that examines a community recreation and youth facility ("YWCA of Blackhawk County").
- Two superb business ethics cases address the controversial topics of abortion ("Hoechst-Roussel Pharmaceuticals, Inc.: RU 486") and the trade-off between economic development and the environment ("BASF's Proposed Paint Plant").

As in the first edition, the primary criterion for our case selection was the overall quality of the case. Special attention was also given to finding cases that were not only well-written and interesting but also contained ample information for analysis.

SPECIAL LEARNING FEATURES OF THIS TEXT

We have consistently integrated theory with practice throughout the chapter portion of the book. You will find that strategic management concepts are liberally illustrated with examples from actual, well-known organizations.

To promote student learning further, we built into the text a number of special features to help students understand and apply the concepts presented. Each chapter of the text provides the following learning features:

- A *strategic management model* helps to portray visually the important stages in the strategic management process. This model is introduced and explained in Chapter 1, then reappears at the beginning of each chapter, with the portion to be discussed in a given chapter highlighted. The model serves as a student's road map throughout each chapter of Part I.
- *Key concepts* are boldfaced in the text when first introduced and are immediately defined. A list of key concepts with definitions appears at the end of each chapter.
- *Strategic Insight boxes* throughout the chapter portion of the book illustrate successful and unsuccessful applications of strategic management concepts in such companies as Southwest Airlines, IBM, Coca-Cola, and Sears, Roebuck and Company. Each of the boxes illustrates a major point in the text.
- A *chapter summary* helps reinforce the major concepts that the student has learned in the chapter.
- End-of-chapter *discussion questions* test the student's retention and understanding of important chapter material and can be used as a tool for review and classroom discussion.
- *Strategic Management Exercises* unique to this text appear at the end of each chapter. These experiential exercises offer students the opportunity to apply their knowledge of the chapter material to realistic strategic business situations.

SUPPLEMENTS

Details of the comprehensive supplement package that accompanies the text can be found in the Instructor's Annotated Edition. The package includes the following:

- An Instructor's Annotated Edition
- An Instructor's Manual with test items and a set of extensive case notes containing a synopsis, a mini-S.W.O.T. analysis, and teaching notes for each case
- Transparency Masters
- A Case Analysis and Review Guide
- The Allyn & Bacon Test Manager, a computerized test bank
- CASE ANALYST, spreadsheet templates for case analysis
- *The Microcomputer Version of the Business Strategy and Policy Game* by David L. Eldredge and James R. Marshall, which works on all IBM PC-compatible computers
- Integrated CNN video programs including exclusive videos tied to the "Strategic Insight" boxes in the chapter portion of the text and CNN Video Industry Notes tied to specific cases
- A unique Just-in-Time Publishing Program, which allows instructors to create their own custom versions of the text, mixing and matching chapters and cases as well as adding their own lecture notes and materials or including cases from other sources.

ACKNOWLEDGMENTS

We are deeply indebted to many individuals for their assistance and support in this project. We especially wish to thank our manuscript reviewers for both the first and second editions. These colleagues were particularly able and deserve considerable credit for their helpful and extensive suggestions. They include:

William P. Anthony, *Florida State University*
B.R. Baliga, *Wake Forest University*
Robert B. Brown, *University of Virginia*
Peng Chan, *California State University, Fullerton*
Edward J. Conlon, *University of Notre Dame*
George B. Davis, *Cleveland State University*
Louis R. Desfosses, *State University of New York, Brockport*
Pierre E. Du Jardin, *Bentley College*
Lawrence K. Finley, *Western Kentucky University*
Philip C. Fisher, *University of South Dakota*
Joseph J. Geiger, *University of Idaho*
Manolete V. Gonzalez, *Oregon State University*
Donald Harvey, *California State University, Bakersfield*
Marilyn M. Helms, *University of Tennessee at Chattanooga*
Stevan R. Holmberg, *The American University*
Michael J. Keeffe, *Southwest Texas State University*
Daniel G. Kopp, *Southwest Missouri State University*
William Litzinger, *University of Texas, San Antonio*
James Logan, *University of New Orleans*
Michael Lubatkin, *University of Connecticut*
John E. Merchant, *California State University, Sacramento*
Hael Y. Sammour, *East Texas State*
Daniel A. Sauers, *Louisiana Tech University*
Charles W. Schilling, *University of Wisconsin, Platteville*
Jeffery C. Shuman, *Bentley College*
Carl L. Swanson, *University of North Texas*
James B. Thurman, *George Washington University*
Philip M. Van Auken, *Baylor University*
Robert P. Vichas, *Florida Atlantic University*
Richard J. Ward, *Bowling Green State University*
Marion White, *James Madison University*
Carolyn Y. Woo, *Purdue University*
David C. Wyld, *Southeastern Louisiana University*

We are deeply indebted to our colleagues who have so generously permitted us to use their excellent cases in this text. The selection process was lengthy and rigorous, and we take considerable pride in presenting these cases. The author(s) of each case is identified on the first page of the case. A list of case contributors appears below:

A.J. Almaney, *DePaul University*
Mary Astone, *Auburn University*
Jan Willem Bol, *Miami University of Ohio*
Gyula Bosnyak, *Taurus Hungarian Rubber Works*
James A. Brunner, *University of Toledo*
Gary J. Castrogiovanni, *Louisiana State University*
Cecil Chacon, *North Carolina Central University*
James J. Chrisman, *Louisiana State University*
James W. Clinton, *University of Northern Colorado*
Jeremy J. Coleman, *Fort Lewis College*
James Combs, *Louisiana State University*
Roy A. Cook, *Fort Lewis College*
Steven Cox, *University of Western Ontario*
Clifford E. Darden, *Pepperdine University*
Otto P. Dobnick, *Southeastern Wisconsin Regional Planning Commission*
Max E. Douglas, *Indiana State University*
W. Jack Duncan, *University of Alabama at Birmingham*
John Dunkelberg, *Wake Forest University*
Brentt Eads, *Loyola Marymount University*
S. Regena Farnsworth, *Texas A&M University*
Jeffery Foulk, *Vice President of an affiliated moving agency*
Peter M. Ginter, *University of Alabama at Birmingham*
Tom Goho, *Wake Forest University*
Juan J. Gonzalez, *University of Texas at San Antonio*
Lynda L. Goulet, *University of Northern Iowa*
Peter G. Goulet, *University of Northern Iowa*
Walter E. Greene, *University of Texas-Pan American*
Paula J. Haynes, *University of Tennessee at Chattanooga*
Marilyn M. Helms, *University of Tennessee at Chattanooga*
Fred Hendon, *Samford University*
Don Hopkins, *Temple University*
William C. House, *University of Arkansas at Fayetteville*
Mao Jianhua, *University of Toledo*
J.P. Kairys, *Jr., University of Western Ontario*
Michael J. Keefe, *Southwest Texas State University*
Mark J. Kroll, *University of Texas at Tyler*
Hooshang Kuklan, *North Carolina Central University*
Franz T. Lohrke, *Louisiana State University*
Jennings Marshall, *Samford University*
Michael D. Martin, *HEALTHSOUTH Rehabilitation Corporation*
John P. McCray, *University of Texas at San Antonio*
Robert N. McGrath, *Louisiana State University*
Bill J. Middlebrook, *Southwest Texas State University*
Bradley W. Miller, *University of Tulsa*
Stephanie Newport, *Creighton University*
Vickie Noble, *University of Texas Health Center at Tyler*
Sharon L. Oswald, *Auburn University*
Paul R. Reed, *Sam Houston State University*
Carol A. Reeves, *University of Arkansas*

David W. Rosenthal, *Miami University of Ohio*
John K. Ross III, *Southwest Texas State University*
Arthur Sharplin, *McNeese State University*
Sherry E. Sullivan, *Memphis State University*
Tammy L. Swenson, *University of Tennessee at Chattanooga*
Paul M. Swiercz, *Georgia State University*
Leslie A. Toombs, *University of Texas at Tyler*
Howard S. Tu, *Memphis State University*
Arieh A. Ullman, *SUNY–Binghamton*
Harold Valentine, *Louisiana State University*
Janos Vecsenyi, *International Management Center, Budapest*
Robert B. Welch, *University of Texas at Tyler*
Larry D. White, *University of Texas at Tyler*
Randall K. White, *University of Auburn at Montgomery*
Joseph Wolfe, *University of Tulsa*

Special thanks are due to our editor, Suzy Spivey, for overseeing this project from inception to completion and to Sarah Carter, senior editorial assistant, who so capably handled the myriad of details that accompany a project of this complexity. In addition, we thank Marshall Schminke and James Anderson of Creighton University for developing the superior CASE ANALYST software package that accompanies this text.

The impressive package of ancillary materials that accompanies the book would not be complete without the contributions of an essential member of our team—John Parnell of Middle Tennessee State University. John is responsible for the annotations in the Instructor's Annotated Edition, the Instructor's Manual, and the new Case Analysis and Review Guide created with the assistance of L. Michelle Kittrell. John also selected, arranged, and edited the CNN video tapes.

Administrators at each of our universities have been most supportive of our work. We particularly wish to thank Dean Howard Tuckman and Management Chairman Thomas R. Miller of Memphis State University; Dean Robert E. Holmes and Management Department Head Daniel G. Gallagher of James Madison University; and President George F. Hamm and Vice President of Academic Affairs Gerald Morris of the University of Texas at Tyler.

Finally, but certainly not least, the support, patience, and understanding of special family members—William, Mahin, and Teresa Wright; Anne Marie and Erin Pringle; and Nghi Kroll—were not only helpful but essential in making this book a reality.

About The Authors

Peter Wright is a Professor of Management who holds the Memphis State University Endowed Chair of Excellence in Free Enterprise Management. He received his M.B.A. and his Ph.D. in management from Louisiana State University. He has acted as a consultant to many business organizations and was president/owner of an international industrial trading firm. Professor Wright is widely published in journals such as the *Strategic Management Journal, Harvard Business Review, Journal of Management, Journal of Business Research, Long Range Planning, British Journal of Management, Journal of the Academy of Marketing Science, Business Horizons, Planning Review,* and *Managerial Planning.*

Charles D. Pringle is a Professor of Management who holds the CSX Endowed Professorship in Management at James Madison University in Harrisonburg, Virginia. He received his M.B.A. from Baylor University and a D.B.A. in management and organizational behavior from the University of Kentucky. Professor Pringle is the author of numerous articles on such topics as job performance and motivation, organizational effectiveness, leadership, ethics, and group decision making. His publications have appeared in such journals as the *Academy of Management Review* and *The Journal of Applied Behavioral Science.* In addition to his academic training, he has held managerial positions in both business and government and has worked as a consultant for profit and nonprofit organizations in several states.

Mark J. Kroll is Chairman of the Management and Marketing Department at the University of Texas at Tyler. He received his M.B.A. from Sam Houston State University and his D.B.A. in management from Mississippi State University. His articles on strategic management topics have appeared in many journals including the *Academy of Management Review, Journal of Business Research,* and *Journal of the Academy of Marketing Science.* He has also authored a number of cases, which have appeared in various strategic management textbooks and in the *Case Research Journal.* Professor Kroll consults for a wide variety of business organizations and teaches the capstone strategic management course at both the undergraduate and graduate levels.

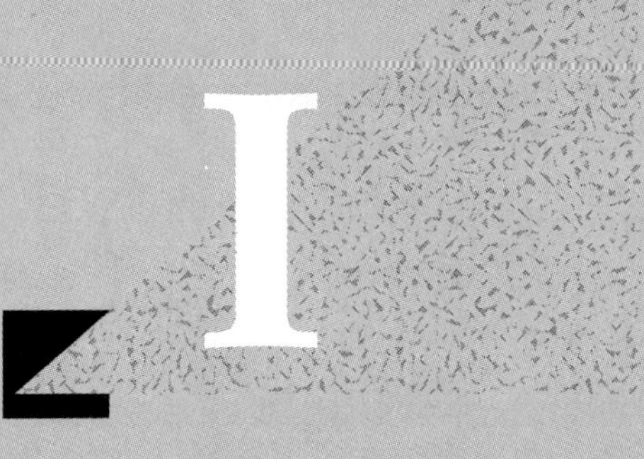

The Concepts and Techniques of Strategic Management

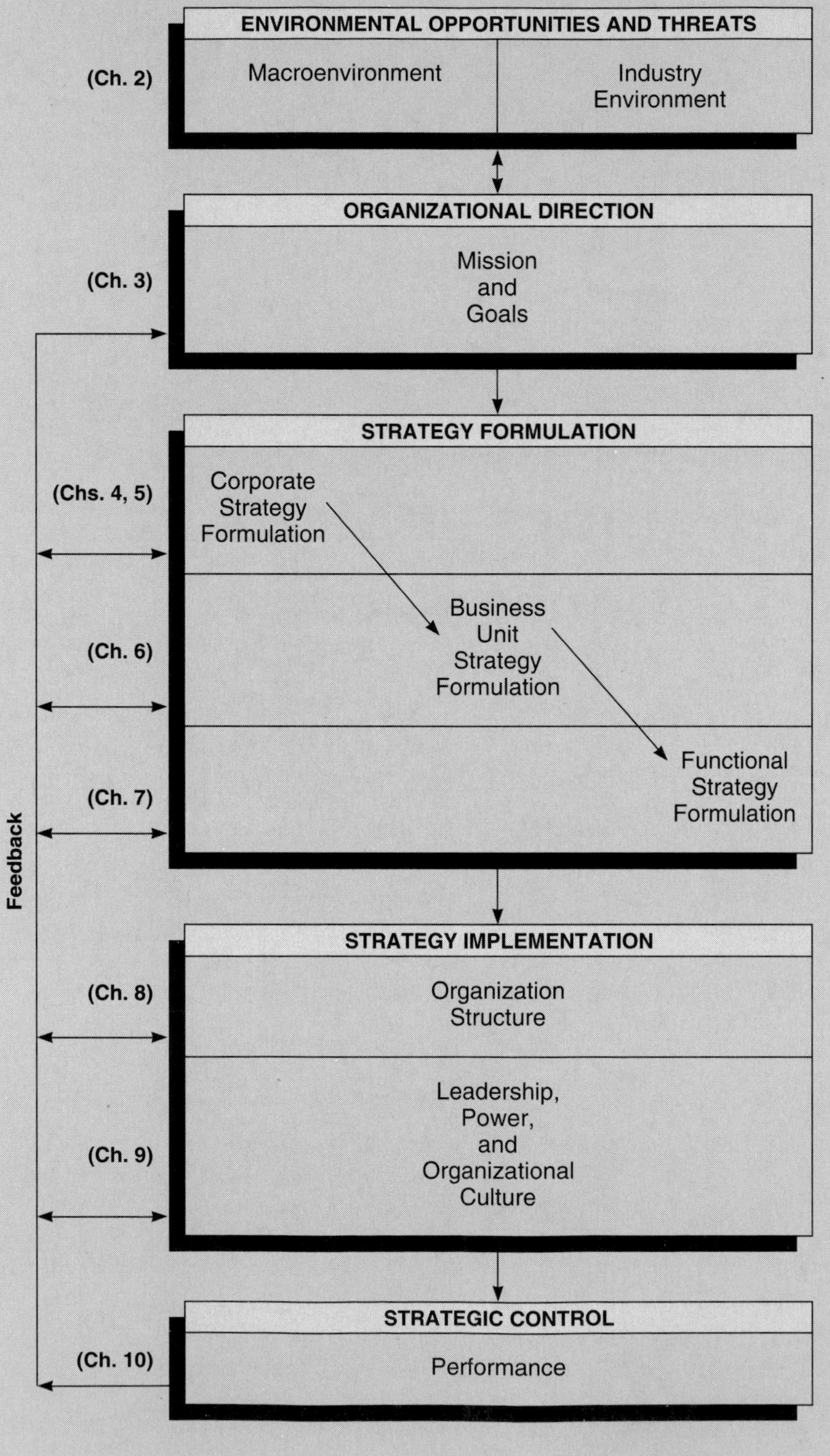
STRATEGIC MANAGEMENT MODEL
ENVIRONMENTAL OPPORTUNITIES AND THREATS
(Ch. 2)
Macroenvironment
Industry Environment
ORGANIZATIONAL DIRECTION
(Ch. 3)
Mission and Goals
STRATEGY FORMULATION
(Chs. 4, 5)
Corporate Strategy Formulation
(Ch. 6)
Business Unit Strategy Formulation
(Ch. 7)
Functional Strategy Formulation
Feedback
STRATEGY IMPLEMENTATION
(Ch. 8)
Organization Structure
(Ch. 9)
Leadership, Power, and Organizational Culture
STRATEGIC CONTROL
(Ch. 10)
Performance

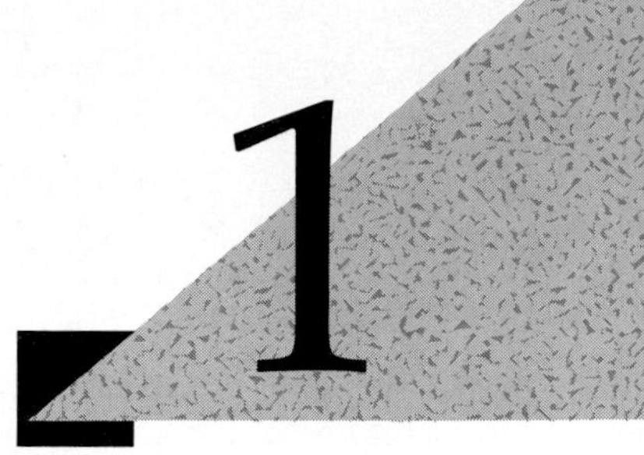

Introduction to Strategic Management

Managers face no greater challenge than that of strategic management. Guiding a complex organization through a dynamic, rapidly changing environment requires the best of judgment. Strategic management issues are invariably ambiguous and unstructured, and the way in which management responds to them determines whether an organization will succeed or fail.

Strategic management is challenging because it is far more than simply setting goals and then ordering organization members to attain those goals. An organization's strategic direction depends upon a variety of considerations. Among them are top management's assessment of the external environment's opportunities and threats, and management's analysis of the firm's internal strengths and weaknesses. Simultaneously, the top management team must take into account the competing desires and needs of the organization's various stakeholders (or interested parties) because their support is essential to successful strategy implementation. Stakeholders include not only the organization's managers and employees but also the firm's owners (stockholders), suppliers, customers, creditors, and community members.

This text focuses on strategic management. The issues and processes discussed are real ones that are directly relevant to all types of organizations—large or small, international or domestic, diversified or single-product, and profit or nonprofit. The material contained herein should provide keen insight into strategic management and an appreciation of its vital role in enhancing organizational effectiveness.

WHAT IS STRATEGIC MANAGEMENT?

■ Strategic Management Defined

Since the word *strategy* or some variation of it is used throughout the text, its definition should be clear. **Strategy** refers to top management's plans to attain outcomes consistent with the organization's mission and goals. One can look at strategy from three vantage points: (1) strategy formulation (developing the strategy), (2) strategy implementation (putting the strategy into action), and

(3) strategic control (modifying either the strategy or its implementation to ensure that the desired outcomes are attained).

Strategic management is a broader term that encompasses managing not only the stages already identified but also the earlier stages of determining the mission and goals of an organization within the context of its external environment. Hence, strategic management can be viewed as a series of steps in which top management should accomplish the following tasks:

1. Analyze the opportunities and threats or constraints that exist in the external environment.
2. Analyze the organization's internal strengths and weaknesses.
3. Establish the organization's mission and develop its goals.
4. Formulate strategies (at the corporate level, the business unit level, and the functional level) that will match the organization's strengths and weaknesses with the environment's opportunities and threats.
5. Implement the strategies.
6. Engage in strategic control activities to ensure that the organization's goals are attained.

Although the various steps in this process are discussed sequentially in this book, in reality they are highly related. Any single stage in the strategic management process must be considered in conjunction with the other stages because a change at any given point will affect other stages in the process. These stages are discussed sequentially throughout the text only to make them more understandable.

In its broadest sense, strategic management consists of managerial decisions and actions that help to ensure that the organization formulates and maintains a beneficial fit with its environment. Thus, strategic managers evaluate their company's evolving strengths and weaknesses in the context of changing opportunities and threats in the external environment. Maintaining a compatible fit between the business and its environment is necessary for competitive viability. Since both the environment and the organization change with the passage of time, this process is an ongoing concern for management.

■ Model of Strategic Management

As an aid in envisioning the strategic management process, a schematic model of this process is presented in Figure 1.1. At the top, the model begins with an analysis of environmental opportunities and threats. In the next stage, the organization's mission and goals are linked to the environment by a dual arrow. This arrow means that the mission and goals are set in the context of environmental opportunities and threats. The organization, in other words, is affected by environmental forces. But the organization can also have an impact upon its environment.[1]

> Federal legislation, for instance, can be influenced by lobbying activities; the ecological environment can be improved through corporate social responsibility actions; customer behavior can be swayed through advertising and sales promotion; large, economically powerful retailers can affect the actions of suppliers; and pricing strategy and product improvements certainly influence the activities of competitors.[2]

The mission and goals of the organization drive strategy formulation at the corporate, business unit, and functional levels, as demonstrated by the one-way arrow. At the corporate level, the decision makers are the chief executive officer (CEO), other top managers, and the board of directors. Most of the strategic decisions at the business unit level are made by the top manager of the business unit and his or her key executives, and the decision makers at the functional level are the heads of the functional areas (the managers of such departments as production, finance, marketing, and research and development).

The next arrow depicts the idea that strategy formulation sets strategy implementation in motion. Specifically, strategy is implemented through the organization's structure, its leadership, its distribution of power, and its culture. Then, the final downward arrow indicates that the actual strategic performance of the organization is evaluated. To the extent that performance fails to meet the organization's goals, strategic control is exerted to modify some or all of the stages in the model in order to improve performance. The control stage is demonstrated by the feedback line that connects strategic control to the other parts of the model.

More details on the strategic management model are provided in the next nine chapters. At the beginning of each chapter, the part of the model that is to be featured is highlighted. In Chapters 11 and 12, the entire model is revisited through a focus, respectively, on international and not-for-profit organizations.

■ Importance of Strategic Management

Most of the significant current events covered in such business publications as *Fortune, Business Week,* and *The Wall Street Journal* involve strategic management concepts. Hence, an understanding of the business world requires familiarity with the strategic management process. As domestic and foreign competition intensifies, and during those periods when government's influence on business operations expands, an understanding of strategic management becomes even more essential.

Employees, supervisors, and middle managers must also be familiar with strategic management. An appreciation of their organization's strategy helps them relate their work assignments more closely to the direction of the organization, thereby enhancing their job performance and opportunity for promotion and making their organization more effective.

■ Evolving Study of Strategic Management

During the 1950s, the Ford Foundation and the Carnegie Corporation funded an analysis of business school curricula and teaching. From this research came the Gordon-Howell report, which concluded that formal business education at universities should be broadened and should conclude with a capstone course that would integrate students' knowledge from such courses as accounting, finance, marketing, management, and economics.[3] Most business schools accepted the conclusions of this report and developed a capstone course that became known as "Business Policy."

The initial thrust of the business policy course was to integrate the functional areas within an enterprise so that it could attain a consistent direction.

Figure 1.1 **Strategic Management Model**

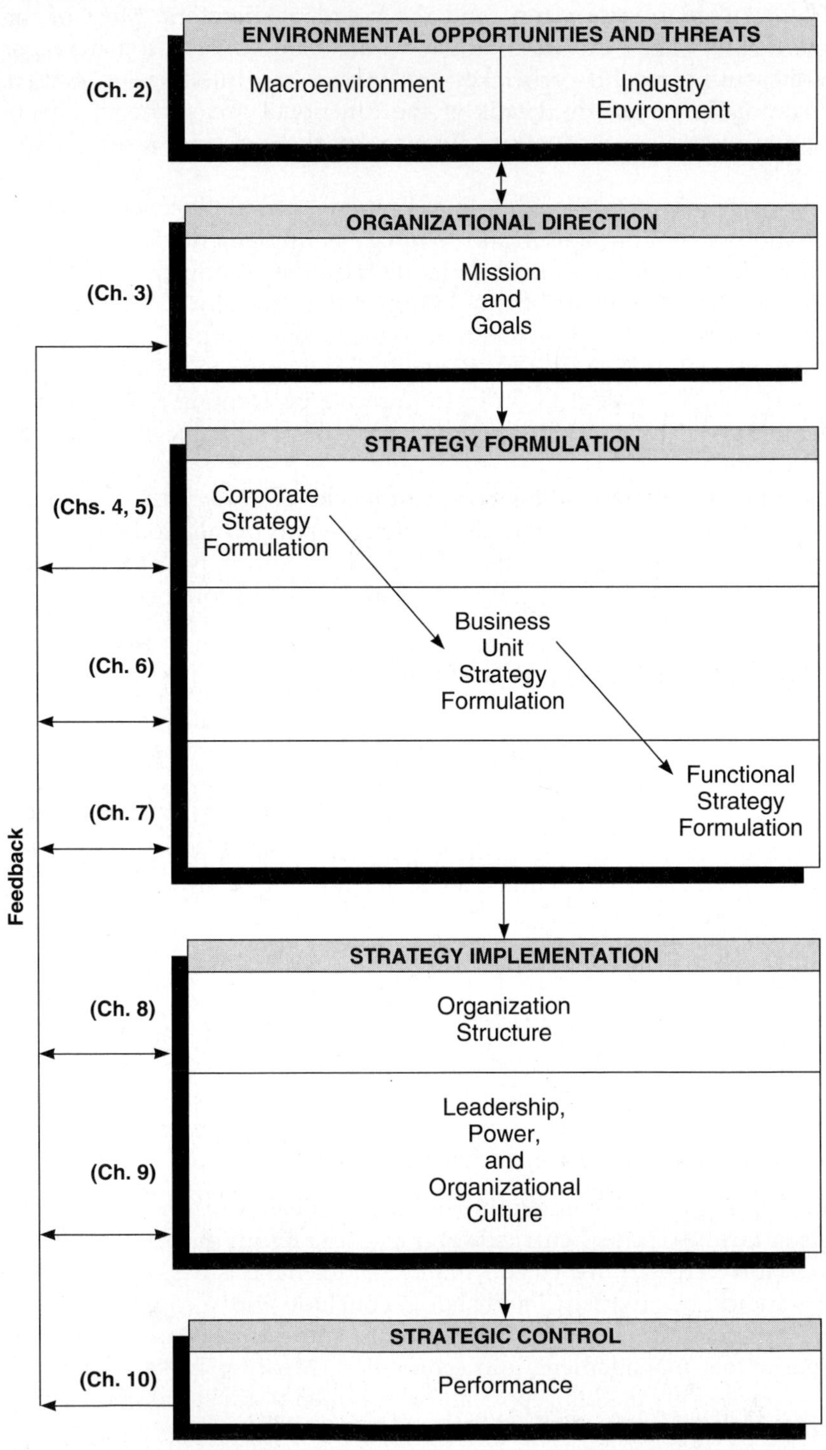

The direction would be one that capitalized upon its strengths while de-emphasizing its weaknesses, relative to the opportunities and threats presented by the organization's external environment.

Over time, the parameters of this capstone course expanded to include more formal analyses of the organization's macroenvironment, industry environment, mission and goals, strategy formulation, strategy implementation, and strategic control. This expanded conception of the field began to be referred to as *strategic management*, as opposed to the more narrow term *business policy*.[4]

INFLUENCES ON STRATEGIC MANAGEMENT

As a field of study, strategic management is eclectic, drawing upon a variety of theoretical frameworks. This section examines some of the diverse roots that have influenced our approach to strategic management.

■ Theories of Evolution and Revolution

Charles Darwin, the naturalist, proposed a theory of evolutionary change of biological species.[5] In its most basic form, Darwin's theory suggested that environmental change forces each species into incremental, but continuous, mutation or transformation. Through such a change, a living entity can adapt to its environment and survive. A species that cannot conform to its environmental requirements is doomed, eventually becoming extinct.

This perspective of evolutionary change has influenced many management thinkers.[6] As a result, they believe that organizations are influenced by the environment; that environmental change is gradual, requiring concomitant organizational change; and that effective organizations are those that conform most closely to environmental requirements. Firms that cannot or do not adapt to gradual external change eventually find themselves outpaced by their competitors and forced out of business.

A different view of environmental change was proposed by certain natural historians and by the economist Joseph Schumpeter.[7] According to this view, environmental change is not gradual but occurs in revolutionary and abrupt forms. Natural historians in this school of thought believe that species can exist in unaltered form for a lengthy period of time. Then, as a result of sudden, revolutionary environmental change, old species might be destroyed and novel species created. The resultant species then exist for many decades or centuries until the environment again changes abruptly, promoting the creation of still newer species.

Likewise in the field of social science, Schumpeter proposed that an economic environment is characterized by a relatively long period of stability, punctuated by brief periods of discontinuous and revolutionary change. These revolutions are generated by the advent of new entrepreneurial enterprises with novel technologies. The new industries created by these entrepreneurial ventures destroy existing firms by making them obsolete.

Some views of revolutionary change are more moderate, proposing that at least some of the existing firms would be able to adapt to the abrupt environmental change.[8] These adaptive organizations allow the innovative firms to absorb the costs and risks of creating new products and services and then imitate those successful innovations.[9] Even Schumpeter, in 1950, changed from his earlier (1934) position by arguing that some existing firms could survive revolutionary change.[10] Survival, he believed, could come reactively through imitating the revolutionary products or services of newer enterprises or proactively by originating new products or services.

▪ Industrial Organization Theory

Industrial organization, a branch of microeconomics, emphasizes the influence of industry environment upon the firm. Implicit in industrial organization theory is the premise of evolutionary change. A firm must adapt to its particular industry's forces to survive and prosper (these forces are discussed in detail in the following chapter), and thus its financial performance is determined by that industry in which it competes. Industries with favorable structures, or forces, offer the opportunity for high returns, while the opposite is true for firms operating in industries with less favorable forces.[11]

Industrial organization theory is deterministic because it assumes that an organization's survival depends upon its ability to adapt to industry forces. A firm's strategies, resources, and competencies are reflections of the industry environment.[12] Because the focus of this field is on industry forces, the organizations within an industry are viewed as possessing similar strategies, resources, and competencies. Hence, competing firms in an industry operate in relatively homogeneous ways. If one firm should develop a superior strategy or operating competency, its uniqueness would be short-lived. Less successful firms could imitate the higher-performing firm by purchasing the resources, competencies, or management talent that have made the leading firm so profitable.[13]

The areas that we have briefly examined—theories of evolution and revolution and industrial organization theory—enhance our understanding of how environmental forces can affect organizations. The following theories take a somewhat different perspective by looking not only at the environment but also at the competitive status of the firm. These ideas will complement those theories that we have just discussed.

▪ Chamberlin's Economic Theories

Economist Edward Chamberlin, representing another branch of microeconomics, presented his ideas within the context of evolutionary environmental change. He proposed that a single firm could clearly distinguish itself from its competitors:

> [A] general class of product is differentiated if any significant basis exists for distinguishing the goods (or services) of one seller from those of another. Where such differentiation exists, even though it might be slight, buyers will be paired with sellers, not by chance . . . but according to their preferences.[14]

Differentiation can exist for quite some time because of such legal protection as trademarks or patents or because a firm's unique strategies, competencies, and resources cannot be easily duplicated by its competitors.

The premise that buyers will be paired with sellers, not by chance but according to their preferences, emphasizes the need for the firm to structure a compatible fit between its competitive status (its strengths and weaknesses relative to those of its competitors) and the opportunities and threats within its environment. This emphasis on the fit between a firm and its environment is reflected in recent contingency theories.

■ Contingency Theory

Contingency theory also exists within the context of evolutionary environmental change. The basic premise of contingency theory is that higher financial returns are associated with those firms that most closely develop a beneficial fit with their environment. Unlike the earlier theories on evolutionary and revolutionary change and industrial organization, which were framed at a high level of abstraction, contingency theory can be used to view environment–organization interaction at any level of analysis—industry, strategic group (discussed in Chapter 6), or individual firm.[15] And, while those earlier theories were deterministic, contingency theorists view organizational performance as the joint outcome of environmental forces and the firm's strategic actions. Firms can become proactive by choosing to operate in environments in which the opportunities and threats match the firms' strengths and weaknesses.[16] Should the industry environment change in a way that is unfavorable to the firm, the firm could perhaps leave that industry and reallocate its resources and competencies to other, more favorable industries.

So both Chamberlin and contingency theorists view organizations as heterogeneous firms that can choose their own operating environments. Organizational performance is determined by the fit between the environment's opportunities and threats and the firm's strengths and weaknesses.

■ Resource-based Theory

Resource-based theory accords even more weight to the firm's proactive choices. Although environmental opportunities and threats are important considerations, a firm's unique resources comprise the key variables that allow it to develop and sustain a competitive strategic advantage. "Resources" include all of a firm's tangible and intangible assets (such as capital, equipment, employees, knowledge, and information).[17] As can be inferred, resource-based theory focuses primarily on individual firms rather than on the competitive environment.

If a firm is to use its resources for sustained competitive advantage, those resources must be valuable, rare, and subject to imperfect imitation, and they must have no strategically relevant substitutes.[18] Valuable resources are those that contribute significantly to the firm's effectiveness and efficiency. Rare resources are possessed by few competitors. Imperfectly imitable resources cannot be fully duplicated by rivals. And resources that have no strategically relevant substitutes enable the firm to operate in a matchless competitive fashion.

Resource-based theory can be framed in the context of either evolutionary or revolutionary change.[19] A firm that possesses unique advantages within an evolutionary environment can continue to compete effectively by making incremental improvements to its resource base. Alternatively, resources that give a firm a competitive advantage within a revolutionary environment do not become irrelevant in newly created settings.

The ideas that we have just examined have important philosophical influences on the field of strategic management. As will become evident, these theories form the basic conceptual underpinnings of the remainder of this textbook.

STRATEGIC DECISIONS

■ Who Makes the Decisions?

The chief executive officer is the individual ultimately responsible for the organization's strategic management. But except in the smallest companies, the CEO relies on a host of other individuals, including members of the board of directors, vice presidents, and various line and staff managers. Precisely who these individuals are depends upon the type of organization. For instance, businesses with centralized decision-making processes generally have fewer managers involved in strategic decisions than do companies that are decentralized. Businesses that are organized around functions (production, marketing, finance, personnel) generally involve the vice presidents of the functional departments in strategic decisions. Firms with product divisional structures (e.g., the home appliance division, the lawn mower division, the hand tool division) usually include the product division managers along with the CEO. Very large organizations often employ corporate-level strategic-planning staffs to assist the CEO and other top managers in making strategic management decisions.

Inputs to strategic decisions can be generated in a number of ways. For example, an employee in a company's research and development department may attend a conference where a new product or production process idea that seems relevant to the company may be discussed. Upon returning from the conference, the employee may relate the idea to his supervisor, who, in turn, may pass it along to her boss. Eventually, the idea may be discussed with the organization's marketing and production managers. As it moves from one area to another, the idea becomes increasingly clear and specific. Ultimately, it may be presented to top management in a formal report. The CEO will eventually decide to adopt or to reject the idea. But can we actually say that this strategic decision was made solely by the CEO? In a sense, the answer is yes because it is the CEO's responsibility to decide which alternative the company will adopt. But from a broader perspective, the answer is no because most strategic decisions result from the streams of inputs, decisions, and actions of many people. Top management is ultimately responsible for the final decision, but its decision is the culmination of the ideas, creativity, information, and analyses of others.

■ Characteristics of Strategic Decisions

In addition to involving more than one area of an organization, strategic decisions usually require obtaining and allocating sizable resources (human, financial, informational, and physical). Further, strategic decisions involve a lengthy time period, anywhere from several years to more than a decade. Consequently, strategic decisions are future-oriented with long-term ramifications. In other words, strategic decisions require commitment.[20]

STRATEGIC INSIGHT

Strategic Decisions

Strategic decisions, by their very nature, are characterized by considerable risk and uncertainty. Dynamic and largely unpredictable environmental changes can quickly transform even the most well-conceived plans into ineffectual strategies. Most strategic decision makers clearly recognize this danger and learn to live with it. Some examples:

- Designing and producing a large commercial aircraft costs as much as $5 billion before any sales revenue is realized. Boeing is taking this enormous risk with its new 777 airliner. With an introduction date planned for mid-1995, the 777 is designed to transport 328 passengers and has a range of 5,000 miles. The design phase began in 1986 when Boeing planners probed the ideas of numerous pilots, passengers, and mechanics about a new type of airliner. As Dean Thornton, head of Boeing's Commercial Airplane Group, puts it: "The 777 causes me to sit bolt upright in bed periodically. It's a . . . gamble. There's a big risk in doing things totally differently."
- American Airlines, the largest airline in the Western Hemisphere, faces—like all major airlines—a number of challenges: steadily rising costs, unstable national economies, stagnant or declining volumes of domestic traffic, and protectionist threats to international traffic. In the face of these threats, CEO Robert Crandall suggests that "you have to accept the notion that at the senior levels of any big company, you rarely know what the outcome of any decision is going to be. . . . Most people at big corporations are rarely certain of what they ought to do. . . . If it were clear what should be done, these jobs wouldn't be nearly so hard."
- Compaq Computer uses a strategic decision-making process designed to ensure that no one individual—even the chairman or the CEO—can unilaterally force his or her pet ideas on the organization. Each week, Compaq's top managers and engineers meet for eight to twelve hours to discuss strategies. Various individuals are required to argue one side or the other of each issue so that all facets of every idea can be aired thoroughly. Even the opinions of outsider suppliers and dealers may be sought. Once a new project is finally adopted or rejected by consensus, everyone is expected to support the decision.

SOURCES: J. Main, "Betting on the 21st Century Jet," *Fortune*, 20 April 1992, pp. 102–117 (quotation from p. 102); R. McGough, "Changing Course," *Financial World*, 23 July 1991, pp. 42–45 (quotation from pp. 43 and 45); M. Ivey and G. Lewis, "How Compaq Gets There Firstest with the Mostest," *Business Week*, 26 June 1989, pp. 146–150.

STRATEGIC MANAGEMENT: A CONTINUOUS PROCESS

Once a planned strategy is implemented, it often requires modification as environmental or organizational conditions change. These changes are often difficult or even impossible to forecast. In fact, it is a rare situation indeed in which top management is able to develop a long-range strategic plan and implement it over several years without any need for modification.

Hence, an **intended strategy** (what management originally planned) may be realized in its original form, in a modified form, or even in an entirely different form. Occasionally, of course, the strategy that management intends is actually realized, but usually, the intended strategy and the **realized strategy** (what management actually implements) differ.[21] The reason is that unforeseen environmental or organizational events occur that necessitate changes in the intended strategy. The full range of possibilities is illustrated in Table 1.1.

Table 1.1 **Intended Strategy, Realized Strategy, and Results: Range of Possibilities**

1. What is intended as a strategy is realized with desirable results.
2. What is intended as a strategy is realized, but with less than desirable results.
3. What is intended as a strategy is realized in some modified version because of an unanticipated environmental or internal requirement or change. The results are desirable.
4. What is intended as a strategy is realized in some modified version because of an unanticipated environmental or internal requirement or change. The results are less than desirable.
5. What is intended as a strategy is not realized. Instead, an unanticipated environmental or internal change requires an entirely different strategy. The different strategy is realized with desirable results.
6. What is intended as a strategy is not realized. Instead, an unanticipated environmental or internal change requires an entirely different strategy. The different strategy is realized with less than desirable results.

As an example of the difference between intended strategy and realized strategy, consider Honda's entry into the U.S. motorcycle market.[22] When Honda established an American subsidiary in Los Angeles in 1959, its intended strategy was to emphasize the sale of motorcycles with 250-cc and 305-cc engines despite the fact that its smaller 50-cc model was a big seller in Japan. Honda's top managers believed that American consumers would prefer larger models. But Honda's 250-cc and 305-cc bikes met a disappointing response from U.S. motorcyclists. The intended strategy failed.

During this time, Honda's executives were using their own 50-cc motorcycles to commute in traffic-congested Los Angeles. The convenience and appearance of the motorcycles were soon noticed by automobile drivers, pedestrians, and retailers. Orders for the 50-cc model began to come in from some motorcycle retailers, but Honda was reluctant to fill them because management did not wish to be associated with a no-frills motorcycle. When the huge retailer Sears, Roebuck expressed an interest in selling the 50-cc model, however, Honda executives changed their minds. The intended strategy of selling 250-cc and 305-cc motorcycles was modified to emphasize sales of the 50-cc machine. This modified strategy was realized with desirable results (alternative 3 in Table 1.1).

Honda's overwhelming success in selling its 50-cc motorcycle gradually convinced its executives to build upon that base by expanding into the larger-bike categories. This intended strategy was realized with desirable results (alternative 1 in Table 1.1) from the late 1960s through the mid-1980s.[23]

Honda's success during this time was partially based on its reliable, sturdy products. But Honda was also successful because of weak competition. With the exception of a lethargic Harley-Davidson, Honda did not face any competitive threat from American companies, and European and Japanese competitors had not matched Honda's investment in the U.S. market. This scenario began to change during the mid-1980s, however.

Foreign competitors became more assertive in the American market, particularly in the small and midsized lines. And following a management-led

STRATEGIC INSIGHT

Strategy in the Automobile Industry: Japanese Inroads

Contrary to popular belief, the world's first workable cars were not manufactured in the United States but in France and in Germany. In fact, automakers in those two countries dominated car manufacturing until Henry Ford began producing cars through assembly line techniques. By 1920, Ford alone produced almost half of the cars in the world. This U.S. leadership in car production continued for the next several decades.

By the 1950s, however, U.S. carmakers were becoming complacent. They routinely produced large, heavy cars with powerful engines. Following their policy of "planned obsolescence," U.S. manufacturers gave these cars annual cosmetic changes, designed to make it clear which consumers were driving the latest models. While U.S. car companies were concentrating on styling and sales, European producers were developing an impressive array of technological improvements, including disc brakes, rack-and-pinion steering, front-wheel drive, unitized bodies, and fuel injection systems. By 1970, European automobile exports were twenty-five times those of the United States.

When the first oil price shock hit the United States in 1974, American carmakers were virtually unprepared. American consumers began to turn to the more fuel-efficient European models and, increasingly, to Japan's small economical vehicles. Detroit's carmakers grudgingly began to manufacture smaller cars. But their attitude was best summed up by the comment of Henry Ford II: "Minicars mean miniprofits."

By the late 1970s, American consumers were turning to Japanese cars in record numbers. Not only were the cars more economical, but most buyers felt that they were of higher quality than American-made cars. Frightened, U.S. automakers sought government protection. At the behest of the U.S. government, the Japanese "voluntarily" agreed to import restrictions in the early 1980s.

Ironically, however, these restrictions provided Japanese automakers with the impetus to construct plants in the United States to avoid the restrictions. Although they originally only assembled cars in America, today Honda, Toyota, and Nissan have established research and development, engineering, and design centers in the United States. In fact, by 1990, Honda was producing cars that were totally planned and built in America—mostly by Americans. Over a million Japanese cars were produced in the United States by 1990, compared with about a thousand just eight years earlier. Honda's Accord even began to vie with Ford's Taurus for the title of best-selling car in the United States.

In 1991 and 1992, the U.S. auto industry declined to its lowest point, posting record losses. But the red ink masked the changes that were under way. Boards of directors replaced key top management figures at GM and Chrysler, Big Three cost-cutting programs began taking effect, attractive new models were released by U.S. companies, and the lower cost of capital that Japanese automakers had for so long enjoyed was erased. In 1992, U.S. carmakers recaptured 1.6 market share points (each point is worth $2 billion in sales) and, in some cases, equaled or exceeded their Japanese competitors in quality, production efficiency, fuel economy, and safety features.

Simultaneously, attention turned to the large and lucrative European market, where trade barriers were being torn down. Nissan, Toyota, and Honda followed the earlier lead of American companies by constructing assembly plants there. By 1992, Japanese cars accounted for 12 percent of the European market, compared to the 36 percent share held by the U.S. Big Three.

SOURCES: J. Mitchell and N. Templin, "Ford's Taurus Passes Honda's Accord As Bestselling Car in a Lackluster Year," *The Wall Street Journal*, 7 January 1993; P. Ingrassia and T. Aeppel, "Worried by Japanese, Thriving GM Europe Vows to Get Leaner," *The Wall Street Journal*, 27 July 1992; K. Kerwin, J.B. Treece, T. Peterson, L. Armstrong, and K.L. Miller, "Detroit's Big Chance," *Business Week*, 29 June 1992, pp. 82–90; A. Taylor III, "Japan's New U.S. Car Strategy," *Fortune*, 10 September 1990, pp. 65–80; D. Cordtz, "The First Hundred Years: How the U.S. Auto Companies Blew Their Stranglehold on the Industry," *Financial World*, 22 August 1989, pp. 54–56.

leveraged buyout in 1981, Harley-Davidson began to reassert its dominance in the large-motorcycle market. While Honda was busy battling competitors with product offerings in all sizes of bikes, Harley-Davidson increased its market share for the largest motorcycles from 23 percent in 1983 to 63 percent in 1992.[24] Honda's sales, meanwhile, dropped from $1.1 billion in 1985 to $230 million in 1990, and its share of the U.S. motorcycle market plunged from 58 to 28 percent during that period.[25] Hence, as the competitive situation changed rapidly after 1984, Honda's results deteriorated. The years from 1985 through 1992, therefore, can be characterized as an intended strategy that was realized with less than desirable results (i.e., alternative 2 in Table 1.1).

This text assumes that strategies need to be examined continuously in light of changing situations. Table 1.1 presents the range of outcomes that are possible as an organization implements its strategy. Therefore, whenever reference is made to plans for strategic formulation and implementation in the text, recall that management's intended strategy is rarely realized in its original, unchanged form.

OVERVIEW OF THE TEXTBOOK

This presentation of the strategic management process begins with an analysis of the environment in which a company operates. All businesses are concerned with two levels of environments. The broader of the two is the macroenvironment, which is comprised of political-legal, economic, technological, and social trends that affect all organizations. But each organization also has a more specific environment, known as an industry, in which it operates. The industry defines the company's set of customers and competitors. The first step in strategic management is analysis of these two levels of environments. Chapter 2 provides a framework for understanding and analyzing the macroenvironment and industry.

Since strategic management consists of structuring a compatible fit between the organization and its environment, the reason for the existence of the busi-

Figure 1.2 **Corporate- and Business Unit–Level Strategic Questions**

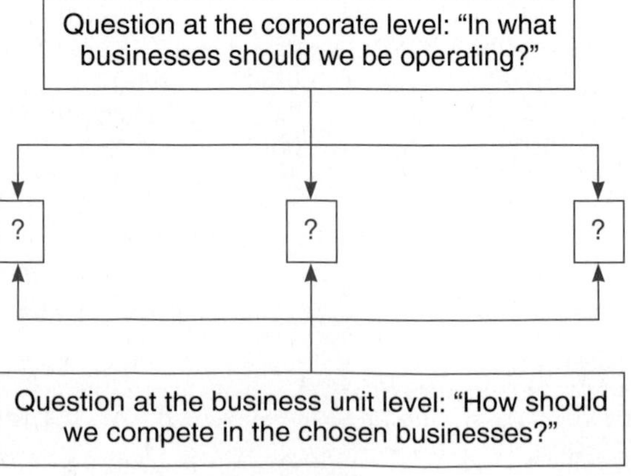

ness (i.e., its mission) must be defined within its environmental context. Once the company's identity is clearly understood, top management must formulate goals to give the organization direction within the opportunities, threats, and constraints of its environment. Establishing the organization's mission and goals is the subject of Chapter 3.

After its mission and goals are established, the organization's strategy must be addressed. Strategy formulation occurs at three organizational levels: corporate, business unit, and functional. Chapters 4 and 5 focus on corporate-level strategy formulation. At this level, the essential question is, In what businesses or industries should we be operating? Chapter 4 presents a framework for analyzing the firm's strengths and weaknesses and delineates the strategic alternatives that are available to top management. Chapter 5 introduces several analytical frameworks that may be used by corporations that operate multiple businesses.

At the business unit level, the question that must be answered is, How should we compete in each of the businesses or industries in which we have chosen to operate? (The difference between corporate-level and business unit strategies is illustrated in Figure 1.2.) Chapter 6 identifies the alternative generic business unit strategies that are available to management and explains under what circumstances each is appropriate.

Chapter 7 analyzes the formulation of functional strategies (strategies in production, marketing, research and development, finance, etc.). It emphasizes the interdependence of an organization's functional strategies and their relationship to the company's business unit strategies.

After the examination of strategy formulation at these three levels, the discussion turns to how these strategies can be implemented. The organizational structure adopted by a company plays a key role in strategy implementation. Chapter 8 identifies the structures available to management and discusses the circumstances under which each is likely to lead to effective implementation of the organization's strategies.

Other essential aspects of strategy implementation are presented in Chapter 9. How the CEO and the top management team secure the cooperation of the organization's members by exercising leadership and informal power is discussed in some detail. Then, the key role played by organizational culture in implementing strategy is analyzed.

As strategies are implemented, the process of strategic control begins. Strategic control consists of determining the extent to which the organization's goals are being attained. This process often requires management to modify its strategies or implementation in some fashion so that the company's ability to reach its goals will be improved. Strategic control is the subject of Chapter 10.

Strategic management is discussed in the context of the world marketplace in Chapter 11. Here, the contents of Chapters 2 through 10 are revisited through a distinctly international perspective.

The process of strategic management is applied to not-for-profit organizations in Chapter 12. Although the basic principles of strategic management apply equally to profit and not-for-profit organizations, there are some differences that require examination. A diagrammatic overview of Chapters 2 through 12 is shown in Figure 1.3.

Finally, the second section of the text begins by presenting an overview of strategic management case analysis. The methodology discussed will help in analyzing the cases contained in the latter part of the text.

Figure 1.3 **Overview of the Book**

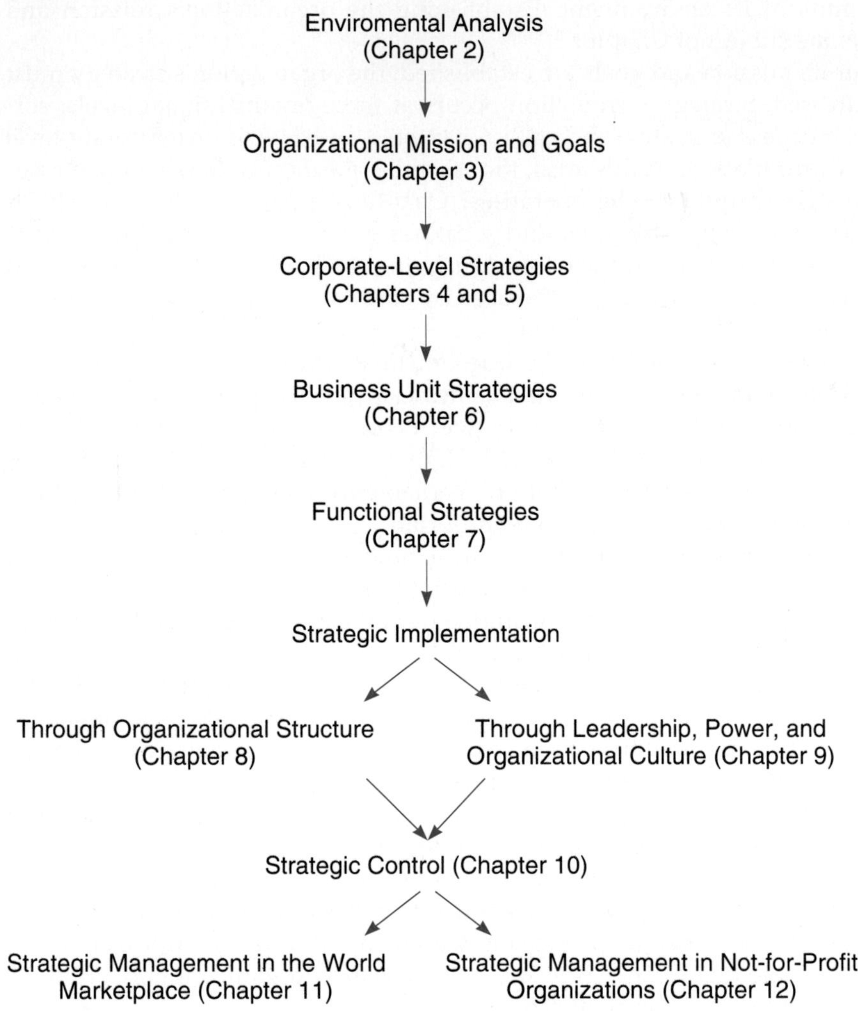

Cases, which present the strategies and operations of real companies, provide the opportunity to apply the knowledge gleaned from Chapters 1 through 12 to analyses of real situations. Case analysis encourages active, involved learning rather than passive recall of the book's contents.

Some of the cases are narrow, primarily involving single issues. These cases provide opportunities to apply knowledge to a specific issue, problem, or situation. Most, however, are broad, encompassing many different aspects of an organization and its environment. The advantages of such cases are several. First, they encourage the application and integration of what has been learned in this text with knowledge gained from other courses and even from one's work experience. Second, they provide a vehicle for analyzing a total organization versus one narrow aspect or functional area of that company. Third, they promote the awareness that varied aspects of the organization and its environment, and their interrelationships, must be examined to formulate and implement strategies effectively.

SUMMARY

Strategic management refers to the process that begins with determining the mission and goals of an organization within the context of its external environment. Appropriate strategies are then formulated and implemented. Finally, strategic control is exerted to ensure that the organization's strategies are successful in attaining its goals.

Strategic management, as a field of study, has been influenced by such diverse disciplines as biology (in theories of evolution and revolution) and economics (particularly the views of Schumpeter and Chamberlin and the perspective of industrial organization theory). More recently, the views of contingency theory (that high financial returns are associated with those firms that most closely develop a beneficial fit with their environment) and resource-based theory (that a firm's unique resources are the key variables that allow it to develop and sustain a competitive strategic advantage) have provided useful frameworks for analyzing strategic management.

Determining organizational strategy is the direct responsibility of the CEO, but he or she relies on a host of other individuals, including the board of directors, vice presidents, and various line and staff managers. In its final form, a strategic decision is molded from the streams of inputs, decisions, and actions of many people.

Strategic management is a continuous process. Once a strategy is implemented, it often requires modification as environmental or organizational conditions change. Because these changes are often difficult or even impossible to predict, a strategy may, over time, be modified so that it bears only a slight resemblance to the organization's intended strategy. This realized strategy is the result of unforeseen external or internal events that require changes in the organization's intended strategy. Thus, strategies need to be examined continuously in the light of changing situations.

KEY CONCEPTS

Intended strategy The original strategy that management plans and intends to implement.

Realized strategy The actual and eventual strategy that management implements. The realized strategy often differs from the intended strategy because unforeseen environmental or organizational events occur that necessitate modifications in the intended strategy.

Strategic management The continuous process of determining the mission and goals of an organization within the context of its external environment, formulating appropriate strategies, implementing those strategies, and exerting strategic control to ensure that the organization's strategies are successful in attaining its goals.

Strategy Top management's plans to attain outcomes consistent with the organization's mission and goals.

DISCUSSION QUESTIONS

1. In what sense does the CEO alone make the company's strategic decisions? In what sense does the CEO *not* make the company's strategic decisions alone?

2. Explain the difference between an intended strategy and a realized strategy. Relate an example of a company whose ultimate realized strategy differed from its original intended strategy.

3. How can an understanding of strategic management be beneficial to your career?

NOTES

1. See J.B. Barney, "Types of Competition and the Theory of Strategy: Toward an Integrative Framework," *Academy of Management Review* 11 (1986): 791–800; J. Child, "Organizational Structure, Environment, and Performance: The Role of Strategic Choice," *Sociology* 6 (1972): 1–22; J.A. Schumpeter, *The Theory of Economic Development* (New York: Oxford University Press, 1934).
2. J.G. Longenecker and C.D. Pringle, "The Illusion of Contingency Theory as a General Theory," *Academy of Management Review* 3 (1978): 682.
3. R.A. Gordon and J.E. Howell, *Higher Education for Business* (New York: Columbia University Press, 1959).
4. M. Leontiades, "The Confusing Words of Business Policy," *Academy of Management Review* 7 (1982): 46.
5. S.J. Gould, *Ever Since Darwin* (New York: Norton, 1977).
6. D.A. Gioia and E. Pitre, "Multiparadigm Perspectives on Theory Building," *Academy of Management Review* 15 (1990): 584–602.
7. N. Eldredge and S.J. Gould, "Punctuated Equilibria: An Alternative to Phyletic Gradualism," in T.J.M. Schopf, ed., *Models in Paleobiology* (San Francisco, Freeman, Cooper, 1972), pp. 82–115; Schumpeter, *The Theory of Economic Development*).
8. M.L. Tushman, W.H. Newman, and E. Romanelli, "Convergence and Upheaval: Managing the Unsteady Pace of Organizational Evolution," *California Management Review* 29, no. 1 (1986): 29–44; J.D. Utterback and W.J. Abernathy, "A Dynamic Model of Product and Process Innovation," *Omega* 3 (1975): 639–656.
9. Barney, "Types of Competition and the Theory of Strategy"; R.R. Nelson and S.G. Winter, *An Evolutionary Theory of Economic Change* (Cambridge, Mass.: Harvard University Press, 1982).
10. J.A. Schumpeter, *Capitalism, Socialism, and Democracy* (New York: Harper & Row, 1950).
11. M.E. Porter, "The Contributions of Industrial Organization to Strategic Management," *Academy of Management Review* 6 (1981): 609–620.
12. J.S. Bain, *Industrial Organization* (New York: Wiley, 1968); F.M. Scherer and D. Ross, *Industrial Market Structure and Economic Performance* (Boston: Houghton-Mifflin, 1990).
13. A. Lado, N. Boyd, and P. Wright, "A Competency-based Model of Sustainable Competitive Advantage: Toward a Conceptual Integration," *Journal of Management* 18 (1992): 77–91; J.B. Barney, "Strategic Factor Markets: Expectations, Luck, and Business Strategy," *Management Science* 42 (1986): 1231–1241; J.B. Barney, "Firm Resources and Sustained Competitive Advantage," *Journal of Management* 17 (1991): 99–120.

14. E.H. Chamberlin, *The Theory of Monopolistic Competition* (Cambridge, Mass.: Harvard University Press, 1956), p. 231.
15. A. Lado, P. Wright, M. Kroll, and J. Parnell, "Organizational Culture and Competitive Advantage: A Synthesis and a Dialectical Conceptualization," Unpublished manuscript, Cleveland State University, 1992; J. Parnell, A. Lado, and P. Wright, "Why Good Things Never Seem to Last: A Dialectic Perspective for Long-term Competitive Advantage," *Journal of Business Strategies* 9 (1992): 62–68.
16. L.G. Hrebiniak and W.F. Joyce, "Organizational Adaptation: Strategic Choice and Environmental Determinism," *Administrative Science Quarterly* 21 (1985): 41–65.
17. Barney, "Firm Resources and Sustained Competitive Advantage."
18. Ibid.
19. R. Rumelt, "Towards a Strategic Theory of the Firm," in R. Lamb, ed., *Competitive Strategic Management* (Englewood Cliffs, N.J.: Prentice-Hall, 1984), pp. 556–570; Nelson and Winter, *An Evolutionary Theory of Economic Change;* R. Rumelt and R. Wensley, "In Search of the Market Share Effect," in K. Chung, ed., *Academy of Management Proceedings* (1981): 2–6; S. Winter, "Schumpeterian Competition in Alternative Technological Regimes," *Journal of Economic Behavior and Organization* 5 (1984): 287–320.
20. P. Ghemawat, *Commitment: The Dynamic of Strategy* (New York: The Free Press, 1991).
21. H. Mintzberg, "Opening Up the Definition of Strategy," in J.B. Quinn, H. Mintzberg, and R.M. James, eds., *The Strategy Process* (Englewood Cliffs, N.J.: Prentice-Hall, 1988), pp. 14–15.
22. R.T. Pascale, "Perspectives on Strategy: The Real Story Behind Honda's Success," *California Management Review* 26 (1984): 47–72.
23. S. Phillips, "That 'Vroom!' You Hear Is Honda Motorcycles," *Business Week,* 3 September 1990, pp. 74–75.
24. C. Willis, "Wall Street," *Money,* April 1992, p. 72.
25. Phillips, "That 'Vroom!' You Hear."

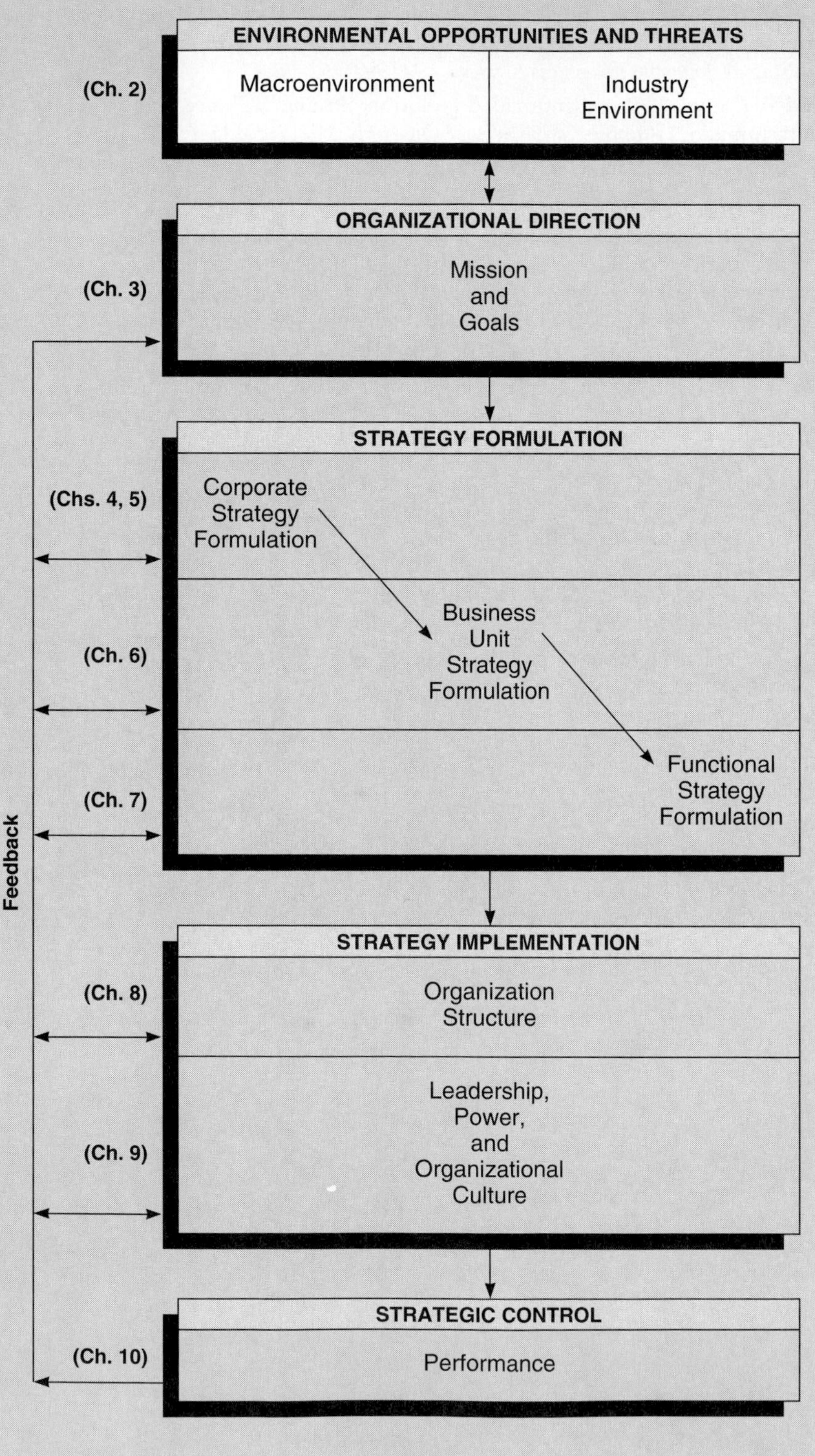
STRATEGIC MANAGEMENT MODEL
ENVIRONMENTAL OPPORTUNITIES AND THREATS
(Ch. 2)
Macroenvironment
Industry Environment
ORGANIZATIONAL DIRECTION
(Ch. 3)
Mission and Goals
STRATEGY FORMULATION
(Chs. 4, 5)
Corporate Strategy Formulation
(Ch. 6)
Business Unit Strategy Formulation
(Ch. 7)
Functional Strategy Formulation
Feedback
STRATEGY IMPLEMENTATION
(Ch. 8)
Organization Structure
(Ch. 9)
Leadership, Power, and Organizational Culture
STRATEGIC CONTROL
(Ch. 10)
Performance

2

Environmental Opportunities and Threats

Strategic management involves three levels of analysis: the organization's macroenvironment, the industry in which the organization operates, and the organization itself. These levels are portrayed in Figure 2.1. This chapter focuses upon the first two levels—the macroenvironment and industry. Then, Chapter 3 begins our analysis of the firm.

Every organization exists within a complex network of environmental forces. All firms are affected by political-legal, economic, technological, and social systems and trends. Together, these elements comprise the **macroenvironment** of business firms. Because these forces are so dynamic, their constant change presents a myriad of opportunities and threats or constraints to strategic managers.

Each business also operates within a more specific environment termed an **industry:** a group of companies that produce competing products or services. The structure of an industry influences the intensity of competition among the firms in the industry by placing certain restrictions upon their operations and by providing various opportunities for well-managed firms to seize the advantage over their competitors. As we shall see in this chapter, successful management depends upon forging a link between business and its environment through the activities of environmental analysis.

ANALYSIS OF THE MACROENVIRONMENT

All organizations are affected by four macroenvironmental forces: political-legal, economic, technological, and social. Although very large organizations (or several firms in association with one another) will occasionally attempt to influence legislation or, through research and development, will pioneer technological or social changes, these macroenvironmental forces are generally not under the direct control of business organizations. Hence, the purpose of strategic management is to enable the firm to operate effectively within environmental threats or constraints and to capitalize on the opportunities pro-

Figure 2.1 **Three Levels of Analysis**

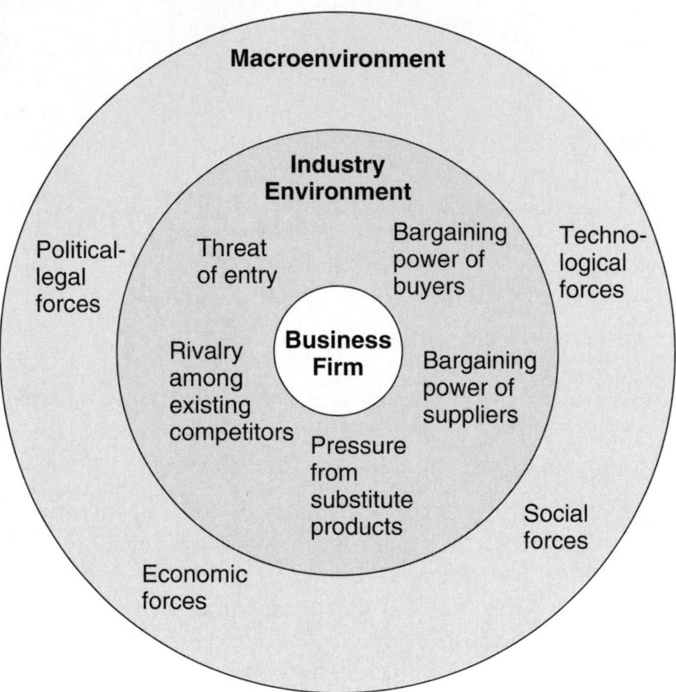

vided by the environment. To accomplish this purpose, strategic managers must identify and analyze these national and global macroenvironmental forces, which are described in the following sections.

■ Political-Legal Forces

Political-legal forces include the outcomes of elections, legislation, and court judgments, as well as the decisions rendered by various commissions and agencies at every level of government. As an example of the impact of these forces, consider the automobile industry. The U.S. government's insistence on legislating gradually increasing fuel economy standards for cars has affected the size and design of cars, their engine size, and their horsepower. Although American automakers have viewed these regulations as a constraint upon the types of models that they can make and sell, Japanese car manufacturers perceived it as an opportunity to make inroads into the prosperous American market.

On the other hand, the U.S. government's imposition of import fees on automobiles and its success in convincing Japanese manufacturers to restrict "voluntarily" their exports to the United States have provided opportunities for American firms to increase their car sales. Unfortunately, the U.S. car producers have not taken advantage of all of these opportunities to increase their market share. But some Japanese carmakers successfully adapted to these constraints by building manufacturing plants in the United States.

As another example, consider the U.S. defense industry. Both the Bush and Clinton administrations and the Congress recommended huge cuts in defense spending through 1997. These reductions resulted in massive layoffs and restructurings among some of the nation's largest corporations. Affected, to some extent, were such prominent firms as General Dynamics, Northrop, LTV, Martin Marietta, McDonnell Douglas, and Lockheed. But an even greater impact was felt by the thousands of small suppliers and subcontractors whose businesses depended almost entirely on defense contracts. We can see, then, that the U.S. political-legal system can have a major impact on business.

On a more global scale, the 1985 decision by the Commission of the European Community to form a single European market for the twelve-nation European community presents both opportunities and threats to U.S.-based firms. One of the major opportunities is the attractive nature of this large, affluent market, which some U.S. firms may have avoided up until now because they considered the market too fragmented and its trade regulations overly complicated. However, a possible threat is that a consolidated market may allow European firms to build a solid base upon which they can develop into much stronger world competitors.

A nation's political-legal system greatly influences its business operations and the standard of living of its citizens. Historically, higher standards of living have been associated with nations whose economic systems are probusiness. In the United States, capitalism has contributed significantly over the past two centuries to America's unparalleled economic growth. But even free enterprise has its weaknesses. By the beginning of the twentieth century, such undesirable social consequences as unsafe working conditions, child labor, low wages, monopolistic competition, deceptive advertising, and unsafe products made it clear that some degree of governmental regulation was necessary. Examples of some of the more significant regulations are shown in Table 2.1.

Not all of the legislative and judicial movement in American society, however, has been in the direction of greater regulation of business. In the late 1970s and the 1980s, a major shift in national policy occurred, which reversed this trend in several industries. This "deregulation" movement eliminated a number of legal constraints in such industries as airlines, trucking, and banking.

However, at the same time that some industries were being deregulated, overall regulation was increasing. In 1992, for instance, the federal government employed 122,400 regulators, an all-time high. And a study sponsored by the U.S. Chamber of Commerce predicted that business regulatory costs would increase by 25 percent in the 1990s.[1]

Deregulation presented both new opportunities and new threats to organizations in the affected industries. Airline deregulation, for instance, offered opportunities to entrepreneurs to start companies such as Southwest Airlines. For some established firms, though, like Eastern and Pan Am, the reduction of regulation posed a threat by creating intense cost and price competition, resulting in their eventual demise. In banking, deregulation presented vast opportunities for expansion in services and geographic scope. Banks began offering brokerage services, for example, and mergers across state lines became common. On the other hand, deregulation intensified competition for banks because nonbanking firms, such as money market funds and brokerage houses, began competing directly with banks for consumers' savings.

Table 2.1 **Examples of Government Regulation of Business**

Legislation	*Purpose*
Sherman Antitrust Act (1890)	Prohibit monopoly or conspiracy in restraint of trade
Pure Food and Drug Act (1906)	Outlaw production of unsanitary foods and drugs
Clayton Act (1914)	Forbid tying contracts, which tie the sale of some products to the sale of others
Federal Trade Commission Act (1914)	Stop unfair methods of competition, such as deceptive advertising, selling practices, and pricing
Fair Labor Standards Act (1938)	Set minimum-wage rates, regulations for overtime pay, and child labor standards
Wheeler–Lea Amendment (1938)	Outlaw deceptive packaging and advertising
Antimerger Act (1950)	Make the buying of competitors illegal when it lessens competition
Equal Pay Act (1963)	Prohibit discrimination in wages on the basis of sex when males and females are performing jobs requiring equal skill, effort, and responsibility under similar working conditions
Occupational Safety and Health Act (1970)	Require employer to provide a working environment free from hazards to health
Consumer Product Safety Act (1972)	Set standards on selected products, require warning labels, and order product recalls
Equal Employment Opportunity Act (1972)	Forbid discrimination in all areas of employer-employee relations
Magnuson–Moss Act (1975)	Require accuracy in product warranties
Americans with Disabilities Act (1992)	Protect the physically and mentally disabled from job discrimination
Family and Medical Leave Act (1993)	Offer workers up to 12 weeks of unpaid leave after childbirth or adoption, or to care for a seriously ill child, spouse, or parent

▪ Economic Forces

Like political-legal systems, economic forces also have a significant impact on business operations. As prime examples, we will consider the impact of growth or decline in gross national product and increases or decreases in interest rates, inflation, and the value of the dollar. These changes present both opportunities and threats or constraints to strategic managers.

Gross National Product

Gross national product (GNP) refers to the value of a nation's annual total production of goods and services and serves as a major indicator of economic growth. Moderate, consistent growth in GNP generally produces a healthy economy in which businesses find increasing demand for their outputs because of rising consumer expenditures. Opportunities abound for both established and new businesses during such prosperous times.

On the other hand, a decline in GNP normally reflects reduced consumer expenditures and lower demand for business outputs. When GNP declines for two consecutive quarters, the national economy is considered to be in a recession. During such times, competitive pressures on businesses increase dramatically; profitability suffers and business failure rates increase. However, even recessions provide opportunities for some firms. Movie theaters are normally strong performers during hard economic times, providing escape from financial worries for their patrons. Likewise, trade school enrollments often increase as unskilled laborers attempt to learn trades to improve their job marketability.

Interest Rates

Short- and long-term interest rates significantly affect the demand for products and services. Low short-term interest rates, for instance, are particularly beneficial for retailers such as Sears and Kmart because such rates encourage consumer spending. For other businesses, such as construction companies and automobile manufacturers, low longer-term rates are especially beneficial because they result in increased spending by consumers for durable goods.

Interest rate levels greatly affect strategic decisions. High rates, for instance, normally dampen business plans to raise funds to expand or to replace aging facilities. Lower rates, by contrast, are more conducive to capital expenditures and to mergers and acquisitions. But some businesses may buck these trends. For example, firms that own apartment buildings usually benefit when long-term interest rates rise, because potential home buyers find that they cannot qualify for mortgage loans and are forced to rent until rates decline significantly.

Inflation Rates

High inflation rates generally result in constraints on business organizations. High rates boost various costs of doing business, such as the purchases of raw materials and parts and the wages and salaries of employees. Consistent increases in inflation rates will constrict the expansion plans of businesses and cause the government to take action that slows the growth of the economy. The combination of government and business restraints can create an economic recession.

Of course, inflation can present opportunities for some firms. For instance, oil companies may benefit during inflationary times if the prices of oil and gas rise faster than the costs of exploration, refining, and transporting. Likewise, companies that mine or sell precious metals benefit since such metals serve as inflation hedges for consumers.

Value of the Dollar

As we have seen, the value of the dollar relative to other major world currencies can be affected by international agreements and the coordinated economic policies of governments. Currency exchange rates, however, can also be affected by international economic conditions. When economic conditions boost the value of the dollar, U.S. firms find themselves at a competitive disadvantage internationally. Foreign customers are less inclined to buy American-made goods because they are too expensive relative to goods produced in their own home markets. Likewise, U.S. consumers find that their strong dollars can be stretched by buying foreign-made products, which are less expensive than goods produced domestically.

For example, in 1990, Caterpillar was in the midst of a major cost-cutting program designed to maintain its position as the world leader in heavy machinery. Yet even as it reduced its cost structure, its efforts were being undermined by the rise in the value of the dollar vis-à-vis the Japanese yen. In a sixteen-month period alone, the dollar climbed 30 percent against the yen. The resultant difference in exchange rates gave Caterpillar's chief Japanese competitor, Komatsu, such a substantial price advantage in the U.S. market that it completely negated Caterpillar's extensive cost-cutting program. Komatsu even merged its U.S.-based manufacturing and engineering facilities with Dresser Industries, headquartered in Dallas, as a hedge against future currency fluctuations.[2]

The dollar's value affects the strategic decisions of managers. When it is strong, American manufacturers tend to locate more of their plants abroad, make purchases from foreign sources, and enter into strategic alliances with firms in other countries. However, when the dollar is relatively weak, less financial incentive exists for American companies to purchase from foreign sources or to build new plants overseas.

■ Technological Forces

Technological forces include scientific improvements and innovations that provide opportunities or threats for businesses. The rate of technological change varies considerably from one industry to another. In electronics, for example, change is rapid and constant, but in furniture manufacturing, change is slower and more gradual.

Changes in technology can affect a firm's operations as well as its products and services. Recent technological advances in computers, robotics, lasers, satellite networks, fiber optics, and other related areas have provided significant opportunities for operational improvements. Manufacturers, banks, and retailers, for example, have used advances in computer technology to perform their traditional tasks at lower costs and higher levels of customer satisfaction.

From another perspective, however, technological change can decimate existing businesses and even entire industries, since it shifts demand from one product to another. Examples of such change include the shifts from vacuum tubes to transistors, from steam locomotives to diesel and electric engines, from fountain pens to ballpoints, from propeller airplanes to jets, and from typewriters to computer-based word processors. Interestingly enough, these new technologies are often invented outside of the traditional industries that they eventually affect.

■ Social Forces

Social forces include traditions, values, societal trends, consumer psychology, and a society's expectations of business. Traditions, for instance, define societal practices that have lasted for decades or even centuries. For example, the celebration of Christmas in many countries in the Western Hemisphere provides significant financial opportunities for card companies, toy retailers, turkey processors, tree growers, mail-order catalog firms, and other related businesses.

Values refer to concepts that a society holds in high esteem. In the United States, for example, major values include individual freedom and equality of opportunity. In a business sense, these values translate into an emphasis on entrepreneurship and the belief that one's success is limited only by one's ambition, energy, and ability. These values, over the past century, have attracted millions of immigrants to the United States in search of economic and political freedom. We can expect, therefore, to find a more vibrant and dynamic business environment in the United States than in countries that place less value on the freedom of the individual and equality of opportunity.

Societal trends present various opportunities and threats or constraints to businesses. For example, the health-and-fitness trend that began several years ago has led to financial success for such companies as Nike (sport shoes) and Nautilus (exercise equipment) and the makers of diet soft drinks, light beer, and bottled water. This trend, however, has financially harmed businesses in other industries such as cattle raising, meat and dairy processing, tobacco, and liquor.

For example, over the past ten years, the consumption of beer and hard liquor by the 18-to-34-year-old segment of the U.S. population fell significantly. This trend is of considerable concern to brewers and distillers because that age group comprises 40 percent of the U.S. population and has traditionally accounted for 50 percent of beer consumption. The reasons include not only the health-and-fitness trend but also a growing nationwide revulsion toward drunk driving, the increased legal liability of hosts who serve alcohol to their guests, and a general increase in "sin taxes" (taxes on alcohol and tobacco products) at the federal and state levels. As a result, many alcohol makers are diversifying into nonalcoholic drinks.[3]

Societal trends also include demographic changes. Fast-food chains, for instance, are currently wrestling with a pressing problem. Teenagers, who comprise 85 percent of the fast-food work force, are declining in number by 5 million between 1981 and 1995, while the number of preteen children (primary customers for fast food) is increasing by 4 million. The result is more customers for fast-food restaurants with fewer people to serve them. These pressures are resulting in increased hiring of the elderly, attempts to reduce turnover among teenage employees, and improvements in productivity.[4]

Demographic trends can dramatically affect business opportunities. The baby boom, which lasted from 1945 through the mid-1960s, initially provided opportunities for such businesses as clothing and baby apparel manufacturers, private schools, record companies, candy and snack makers, and so on. Later, as the baby boomers entered the job market, businesses were blessed with a tremendous pool of job applicants. As they continue to age, the baby boomers will spend vast sums of money for health care needs, leisure activities, and vacation alternatives.

Finally, a society's expectations of business present other opportunities and constraints. These expectations emanate from diverse groups referred to as **stakeholders.** These groups affect and, in turn, are affected by the activities of companies. Stakeholders include a firm's owners (stockholders), members of the board of directors, managers and operating employees, suppliers, creditors, distributors, customers, and other interest groups.

At the broadest level, stakeholders include the general public. Increasingly, in recent decades, the general public has expected socially responsible behavior from business firms. Although social responsibility will be discussed in the

STRATEGIC INSIGHT

Capitalizing on Technological and Social Forces at Knight-Ridder

Environmental analysis helps a company take advantage of the changing technological and social forces. One such example is Miami-based Knight-Ridder, a firm that has achieved annual sales of $2.3 billion in the information industry.

Founded in 1903, Knight-Ridder was originally a newspaper company. Its first major newspapers were the *Miami Herald* and the *Akron Beacon Journal.* Since that time, it has purchased numerous newspapers and today owns such well-known publications as the *Detroit Free Press,* the *Philadelphia Inquirer,* and the *San Jose Mercury News.* Its newspaper business, which includes a news syndication service, a newsprint mill, and newspaper printing plants in twenty-nine cities, provides 86 percent of its sales revenue.

Increasingly, however, Knight-Ridder is taking advantage of technological innovations to expand its information network. The company owns an on-line newswire service for financial markets, a cable/pay television channel, and an electronic information retrieval service. Its various information services reach more than 100 million people in 129 countries.

The company has also been cognizant of changing social forces. According to its CEO, James Batten, the firm successfully capitalized upon an opportunity provided by demographic changes in Miami several years ago. Observing that the Miami area was becoming home to over two hundred fifty thousand residents of Cuban origin, management believed that the time was right to introduce a Spanish-language daily newspaper. The paper, *El Nuevo Herald,* became an instant success and is now the largest of its kind in the United States.

Knight-Ridder may go even further in taking advantage of the opportunities presented by demographics. Management is currently studying the feasibility of tailoring newspapers to specific groups of readers, such as the elderly, households with children, and so on.

following chapter, consider just one element of social responsibility—pollution. The public's concern about pollution has resulted in various forms of legislation that have constrained the operations of firms in such industries as automobiles, energy, and mining. On the other hand, this legislation has provided an opportunity for firms such as Waste Management to sell its services in reducing pollution.

In a more limited sense, stakeholder groups may hold conflicting expectations of business performance. For example, stockholders and unionized employees may have financial goals that clash. Chapter 3 will elaborate further on this topic.

■ Environmental Scanning

The preceding sections were able to examine only a few of the important macroenvironmental forces that affect organizations. Examples of other significant forces are identified in Table 2.2.

How do managers recognize the various opportunities or threats that arise from changes in the political-legal, economic, technological, and social arenas? They engage in **environmental scanning**—the gathering and analysis of information about relevant environmental trends.

Examples of Additional Macroenvironmental Forces **Table 2.2**

Political-Legal Forces	*Social Forces*	*Economic Forces*	*Technological Forces*
Tax laws	Attitudes toward product innovations, lifestyles, careers, and consumer activism	Money supply	Expenditures on research and development (government and industry)
International trade regulations	Concern with quality of life	Monetary policy	Focus of R&D expenditures
Consumer lending regulations	Expectations from the workplace	Unemployment rate	Rate of new-product introductions
Environmental protection laws	Shifts in the presence of women in the work force	Energy costs	Automation
Enforcement of antitrust regulations	Birth rates	Disposable personal income	Robotics
Laws on hiring, firing, promotion, and pay	Population shifts	Stage of economic cycle	
Wage/price controls	Life expectancies		

Responses to a survey of Fortune 500 firms that were asked to identify the major payoffs of their environmental-scanning activities included an increased general awareness of environmental changes, better strategic planning and decision making, greater effectiveness in governmental matters, better industry and market analysis, and sound diversification and resource allocation decisions. However, the respondents also indicated that the results of their environmental analyses were often too general or uncertain for specific interpretation.[5]

There is also some evidence that top managers may use "selective perception" in scanning the environment; that is, their scanning activities may be influenced by their organization's strategy. One study concluded that the heads of financial institutions that use a "low-cost" strategy (one that focuses upon being the low-cost provider of products or services) emphasize monitoring the activities of competitors and regulators. By contrast, scanning activities in financial institutions that use a "differentiation" strategy (one that emphasizes superior products or services) are likely to focus upon opportunities for growth and ways of satisfying customer needs.[6]

Although macroenvironmental forces influence the operations of all firms in a general fashion, a more specific set of forces within an industry directly and powerfully affects the strategic-planning activities of the firms within that industry. Figure 2.2 presents a diagrammatic representation of the impact of macroenvironmental and industry forces. These industry forces are discussed in the following section.

ANALYSIS OF THE INDUSTRY

Professor Michael E. Porter of Harvard University is the nation's leading authority on industry analysis; the following overview of industry forces is based on his work.[7] Porter contends that an industry's profit potential (the

Figure 2.2 **Macroenvironmental and Industry Forces That Present Opportunities and Threats to Firms**

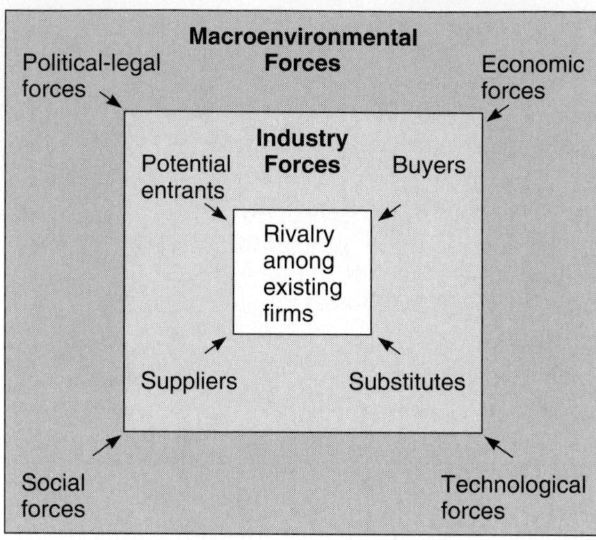

long-run return on invested capital) depends on five basic competitive forces within the industry:

1. The threat of new competitors entering the industry
2. The intensity of rivalry among existing competitors
3. The threat of substitute products or services
4. The bargaining power of buyers
5. The bargaining power of suppliers

These forces can be quite intense in industries such as tires or steel, where returns are generally low, but may be relatively mild in such industries as cosmetics and toiletries, where returns are often high.

The key to competing effectively is for the company to find a position in the industry where it can influence these five forces to its advantage or can effectively defend itself against them. Such a strategy requires an understanding of these competitive forces, which are described in the following sections.

■ Threat of Entry

As new competitors enter an industry, its productive capacity expands. Unless the market is growing rapidly, a new entry intensifies the fight for market share, thereby bidding prices down and lowering industry profitability. The likelihood that new firms will enter an industry rests on two factors: barriers to entry and the expected retaliation from existing competitors. Each factor is discussed in the sections that follow.

Barriers to Entry

High barriers and/or expectations of sharp retaliation reduce the threat of entry. There are seven major **barriers to entry,** that is, obstacles to entering an industry. Each barrier is described next.

Economies of Scale. Economies of scale refer to the decline in unit costs of a product or service (or an operation, or a function that goes into producing a product or service) that occurs as the absolute volume of production per period of time increases. Substantial economies of scale deter new entrants by forcing them either to come in at a large scale, thereby risking a strong reaction from existing firms, or to come in at a small scale, with its accompanying cost disadvantages. For example, Xerox and General Electric failed in their attempts to enter the mainframe computer industry some years back, probably because of scale economies in production, research, marketing, and service.

Product Differentiation. Established firms may enjoy strong brand identification and customer loyalties that are based on actual or perceived product differences, customer service, or advertising. New entrants must spend a great deal of money and time to overcome this barrier. Product differentiation is particularly important in baby care products, over-the-counter drugs, cosmetics, and public accounting. Large brewers, such as Anheuser-Busch, have gone even further by coupling their product differentiation with economies of scale in production, marketing, and distribution.

Capital Requirements. The need to invest large financial resources to compete creates a third type of entry barrier. Large amounts of capital may be necessary for production facility construction, research and development, advertising, customer credit, and inventories. Some years ago, Xerox cleverly created a capital barrier by renting its copiers rather than only selling them. This move increased the capital needs for new entrants.

Switching Costs. Switching costs refer to the one-time costs that buyers of the industry's outputs incur if they switch from one company's products to another's. Changing from an established supplier to a new supplier may require the buyer to retrain employees, purchase new ancillary equipment, and/or hire technical help. Most customers are reluctant to switch unless the new supplier offers a major improvement in cost or performance. For example, nurses in hospitals may resist buying from a new supplier of intravenous (IV) solutions and kits, since the procedures for attaching solutions to patients and the hardware for hanging the IV bottles differ from one supplier to another.

Access to Distribution Channels. To enter the distribution channels already being used by established firms, a new firm must often entice distributors through price breaks, cooperative advertising allowances, or sales promotions. Each of these actions, of course, reduces profits. Existing competitors often have distribution channel ties based on long-standing, or even exclusive, relationships, meaning that the new entrant must create a new channel of distribution. Timex was forced to do exactly that decades ago to circumvent the channels dominated by the Swiss watchmakers.

Cost Disadvantages Independent of Scale. Established firms may possess cost advantages that cannot be replicated by new entrants regardless of their size or economies of scale. These advantages include proprietary product technology (e.g., Polaroid's monopoly on instant photography), favorable access to raw materials (e.g., Texas Gulf Sulphur's control of large salt dome sulphur deposits), favorable locations (e.g., McDonald's locations at interstate highway exits), and the learning or experience curve (the tendency for unit costs to decline as a firm gains experience producing a product or service; an example is Federal Express's efficient operations or Toyota's production process).

Government Policy. Governments can control entry to certain industries with licensing requirements or other regulations. For instance, entry into the

STRATEGIC INSIGHT

Enormous Barriers to Entry in the Airline Industry

One of the major purposes of deregulating the airline industry in 1978 was to encourage new start-up ventures, thereby increasing the amount of competition in the industry. For a while, deregulation worked; new companies such as Southwest Airlines, Midway Airlines, and People Express helped to lower ticket prices significantly.

But over time, the major airlines have succeeded in erecting enormous barriers to entry. Consider the following obstacles:

- Major carriers hold twenty- to forty-year leases on almost all of the passenger-loading gates at big airports.
- They have 95 percent of the landing rights (i.e., permission to take off and land in certain time slots) at four key airports.
- They own the computer reservation systems, pay travel agents (who book 85 percent of all tickets) extra commissions for bringing business to them, and charge small carriers hefty fees for tickets sold through those systems.
- They operate frequent-flier programs that are far too costly for a new airline to offer and that encourage passengers to avoid switching airlines.
- Their computer-pricing systems enable them to selectively offer low fares on certain seats and to certain destinations, thereby wiping out a start-up airline's pricing edge.
- Most have a large number of U.S. hub airports, a feeder system to those hubs, and international routes that tie into the hubs. Such systems take decades and hundreds of millions of dollars to acquire.
- The dominant major carriers are willing to match or beat the ticket prices of smaller, niche airlines. Most have proved themselves capable of absorbing losses until weaker competitors are driven out of business.

As a result of these obstacles, less than fifteen years after deregulation, the airline industry's best routes and markets were concentrated in the hands of a few huge carriers. In fact, not one airline of significant size that was formed after deregulation has managed to avoid bankruptcy, merger, or failure.

SOURCES: W. Zellner, A. Rothman, and E. Schine, "The Airline Mess," *Business Week,* 6 July 1992, pp. 50–55; R. Thomas, J. Schwartz, T. Barrett, and H. Manly, " 'Death Struggle' in the Sky," *Newsweek,* 15 June 1992, pp. 43–45; B. O'Brian, "Airlines' Ailments Give Most of Their Suppliers Big Headaches as Well," *The Wall Street Journal,* 31 December 1991; M. Oneal, W. Zellner, and S. Payne, "Fly the Lucrative Skies of United American Delta," *Business Week,* 14 October 1991, pp. 90–91; R.L. Rose and J. Dahl, "Skies Are Deregulated, But Just Try Starting a Sizable New Airline," *The Wall Street Journal,* 19 July 1989.

taxicab business in most large cities is controlled by licensing, and entry into the liquor retail business is heavily regulated by states. Even pollution control requirements can serve as an entry barrier because of the need for a certain level of technological sophistication.

Expected Retaliation

Entry may well be deterred if the potential entering firm expects existing competitors to respond forcefully. These expectations are reasonable if the industry has a history of vigorous retaliation to new entrants or if the industry is growing slowly. Retaliation may also be expected if the established firms are committed to the industry and have specialized fixed assets that are not transferable to other industries, or if the firms have sufficient cash and productive capacity to meet customer needs in the future.

■ Intensity of Rivalry Among Existing Competitors

Competition intensifies when one—or more—of the firms in an industry sees the opportunity to improve its position or feels competitive pressure from others. It manifests itself in the form of price cutting, advertising battles, new-product introductions or modifications, and increased customer service or warranties. The intensity of competition depends on a number of interacting factors, as discussed in the following sections.

Numerous or Equally Balanced Competitors

One factor is the number of companies in the industry and how equally balanced they are in terms of size and power. Industries that are dominated by one or a few firms are less competitive because the dominant firm often acts as the price leader. But industries that contain only a few firms that are roughly equivalent in size and power are more likely to be highly competitive because each firm will fight for dominance. Competition is also likely to be intense in industries with large numbers of firms, since some of those companies believe that they can make competitive moves without being noticed.

Slow Industry Growth

Firms in industries that grow slowly are more likely to be highly competitive than companies in fast-growing industries. In slow-growth industries, one firm's increase in market share must come at the expense of other firms' shares.

High Fixed or Storage Costs

Companies with high fixed costs are under pressure to operate at near-capacity levels to spread their overhead expenses over more units of production. This pressure often leads to price cutting, thereby intensifying competition. The U.S. airline industry has experienced this problem over the past several years. The same is true of firms that have high storage costs. For that reason, profits tend to be low in industries such as lobster fishing and hazardous-chemical manufacturing.

Lack of Differentiation or Switching Costs

When products are differentiated, competition is less intense because buyers have preferences and loyalties to particular sellers. Switching costs have the same effect. But when products or services are less differentiated, purchase decisions are based on price and service considerations, resulting in greater competition.

STRATEGIC INSIGHT

Two Equally Balanced Competitors: PepsiCo and Coca-Cola

Consolidated industries that contain only a few companies can be highly competitive. One of the best examples is the soft-drink industry, where Coca-Cola and PepsiCo have been fighting for dominance for many years. Although most consumers probably consider these two fierce competitors to be similar types of firms, they are actually quite different.

PepsiCo, for instance, is considerably larger than Coca-Cola. The New York–based corporation's $22.1 billion in sales (placing it 15th on the 1992 Fortune 500) considerably overshadows Atlanta-based Coca-Cola's $13.2 billion in sales (34th on the 1992 Fortune 500). A second distinction is that most of Coca-Cola's sales come from the soft-drink market, but PepsiCo is more diversified. Over the past twenty years, Coca-Cola made several attempts at diversification (e.g., motion pictures, coffee, tea, and wine), but none was particularly successful. PepsiCo, on the other hand, consists of three major product divisions: soft drinks, snack foods (e.g., Frito-Lay), and fast-food restaurants (Pizza Hut, KFC, and Taco Bell).

The battle arena for the two firms is the soft-drink market. Most of their competition has taken the form of advertising, attempting to maximize shelf space in retail outlets, waging price wars, and introducing new products. Coke leads in the battle, holding around 41 percent of the total U.S. market share for soft-drink sales (sales in restaurants, grocery stores, vending machines, and convenience stores) to Pepsi's 31 percent. And Coca-Cola clearly dominates markets outside the United States by a 4-to-1 margin, accounting for almost half of the world's soft-drink sales.

As U.S. demand for cola drinks softens, and young drinkers turn increasingly to such "New Age" drinks as flavored seltzers, juice drinks, and "natural" soda pop, the Coke–Pepsi rivalry is intensifying. Perhaps the most ferocious battleground has been the restaurant industry. PepsiCo is aggressively expanding its restaurant business—and its soft-drink sales, since Coca-Cola products are prohibited in PepsiCo-owned restaurants. Coca-Cola, however, has used Pepsi's expansion to convince such major fast-food chains as Wendy's and Burger King to drop Pepsi products in favor of Coke's. Coca-Cola argued that selling Pepsi products would be tantamount to enriching the owner of three of Burger King's and Wendy's major competitors. The argument has been effective; Coke now controls 63 percent of U.S. restaurant soft-drink sales, compared to Pepsi's 21 percent.

SOURCES: M.J. McCarthy, "Soft-Drink Firms Search for Answers as Volumes Drop," *The Wall Street Journal,* 27 July 1992; W. Konrad, "The Cola Kings Are Feeling a Bit Jumpy," *Business Week,* 13 July 1992, p. 112; "The Fortune 500 Largest U.S. Industrial Corporations," *Fortune,* 19 April 1993, p. 184; W. Konrad and G. DeGeorge, "Sorry, No Pepsi. How 'Bout a Coke?" *Business Week,* 27 May 1991, pp. 71–72; M.J. McCarthy, "Coca-Cola Is Facing New Pepsi Challenge: Avoiding Signs of Age," *The Wall Street Journal,* 1 October 1991; W. Konrad, "The Real Thing is Getting Real Aggressive," *Business Week,* 26 November 1990, pp. 94–104; "The 'Stateless' World of Manufacturing," *Business Week,* 14 May 1990, p. 103; M.J. McCarthy, "As a Global Marketer, Coke Excels by Being Tough and Consistent," *The Wall Street Journal,* 19 December 1989.

Capacity Augmented in Large Increments

If economies of scale dictate that productive capacity must be added only in large increments, then capacity additions will lead to temporary overcapacity in the industry and resultant price cutting. This problem characterizes the manufacture of chlorine, vinyl chloride, and ammonium fertilizer.

Diverse Competitors

Companies that are diverse in their origins, cultures, and strategies will often have differing goals and differing ways of competing. These differences mean that competitors will have a difficult time agreeing on a set of "rules for the game." Industries with foreign competitors and industries with entrepreneurial owner-operators may, therefore, be particularly competitive.

High Strategic Stakes

Rivalry will be quite volatile if firms have high stakes in achieving success in a particular industry. For instance, Sony or Toyota may have perceived a strong need to establish a solid position in the U.S. market to enhance its global prestige or technological credibility. These desires can even involve the willingness to sacrifice profitability

High Exit Barriers

Exit barriers can be economic, strategic, or emotional factors that keep companies from leaving an industry even though they are earning a low—or possibly negative—return on their investment. Examples of exit barriers are fixed assets that have no alternative uses, labor agreements, strategic interrelationships between that business unit and other business units within the same company, management's unwillingness to leave an industry because of pride, and governmental pressure to continue operations to avoid adverse economic effects in a geographic region.

■ Pressure from Substitute Products

Firms in one industry may be competing with firms in other industries that produce **substitute products,** which are alternative products that satisfy similar consumer needs but differ in specific characteristics. Substitutes place a ceiling on the prices that firms can charge. For instance, the producers of fiberglass insulation were unable to raise their prices despite unprecedented demand during a severe winter because of the availability of insulation substitutes such as cellulose, rock wool, and Styrofoam. And movie theaters are coming under increasing competition from pay-per-view cable channels, which show first-run movies at less than half the theater ticket price. In contrast, firms that produce products that have no substitutes are likely to be highly profitable.

■ Bargaining Power of Buyers

The buyers of an industry's outputs can lower that industry's profitability by bargaining for higher quality or more services and playing one firm against another. Buyers are powerful under the following circumstances.

- Buyers are concentrated or purchase large volumes relative to total industry sales. If a few buyers purchase a substantial proportion of an industry's sales, then they will wield considerable power over prices.
- The products that the buyers purchase represent a significant percentage of the buyers' costs. If the products account for a large portion of the buyers' costs, then price is an important issue for the buyers. Hence, they will shop for a favorable price and will purchase selectively.
- The products that the buyers purchase are standard or undifferentiated. In such cases, buyers are prone to play one seller against another.
- The buyers face few switching costs. Switching costs, of course, lock buyers to particular sellers.
- The buyers earn low profits. Low profits create pressure for the buyers to reduce their purchasing costs.
- Buyers can engage in backward integration (they become their own suppliers). General Motors and Ford, for example, use the threat of self-manufacture as a powerful bargaining lever.
- The industry's product is relatively unimportant to the quality of the buyers' products or services. When the quality of the buyers' products is greatly affected by what they purchase from the industry, the buyers are less likely to have significant power over the suppliers.
- Buyers have full information. The more information buyers have regarding demand, actual market prices, and supplier costs, the greater their bargaining power.

■ Bargaining Power of Suppliers

Suppliers can squeeze the profitability out of an industry that is unable to recover cost increases in its own prices. The conditions that make suppliers powerful basically mirror those that make buyers powerful. Hence, suppliers are powerful under the following circumstances.

- The supplying industry is dominated by a few companies and is more concentrated than the industry to which it sells. Selling to fragmented buyers means that concentrated suppliers will be able to exert considerable control over prices, quality, and selling terms.
- There are no substitute products. If buyers have no alternative sources of supply, then they are weak in relation to the suppliers that exist.
- The buying industry is not an important customer of the suppliers. If a particular industry does not represent a significant percentage of the suppliers' sales, then the suppliers have considerable power. If the industry is an important customer, however, suppliers' fortunes will be closely tied to that industry and they will find that reasonable pricing and assistance in such areas as research and development are in their best interests.
- The suppliers' product is an important input of the buyers' business. If the product is a key element in the buyers' manufacturing process or product quality, the suppliers possess significant power.
- The suppliers' products are differentiated or they have built-in switching costs. Product differentiation or switching costs reduce the buyers' ability to play one supplier against another.
- The suppliers pose a credible threat of forward integration (they can become their own customers). If suppliers have the ability and resources

to operate their own manufacturing facilities, distribution channels, or retail outlets, they will possess considerable power over buyers.

We can see, then, that—at one extreme—a company could operate quite profitably in an industry with high entry barriers, low intensity of competition among member firms, no substitute products, weak buyers, and weak suppliers. On the other hand, a company doing business in an industry with low entry barriers, intense competition, many substitute products, and strong buyers and/or suppliers would be hard-pressed to generate an adequate profit. The key, of course, is for management to scan and understand the industry in

STRATEGIC INSIGHT

Supplier Power: The Case of NutraSweet

In 1901, John Francisco Queeny was unable to persuade the wholesale pharmaceutical company for which he worked to produce saccharin, the low-calorie sweetener, rather than to continue to import it from Germany. So he took $5,000 and started his own company in St. Louis, calling it Monsanto Chemical Works after his wife's family name.

Some eighty-four years later, Monsanto returned to its roots by acquiring G.D. Searle, the pharmaceutical company known for its extremely successful low-calorie sweetener, NutraSweet. Now a separate business unit of Monsanto, NutraSweet manufactures aspartame for beverages, dessert products, and tabletop sweeteners (under the brand name Equal). Its sales represented 10 percent of Monsanto's annual revenues of $9 billion, and, in 1992, it controlled 75 percent of the U.S. sweetener market. Furthermore, aspartame's operating margins were an impressive 20 percent.

The secret to this success was NutraSweet's patent protection on aspartame. In fact, for two decades, NutraSweet was the world's only supplier of this artificial sweetener. Its monopoly sometimes resulted in a reputation for high-handedness among its customers. For instance, NutraSweet insisted that its logo be displayed in a certain way on all products that contained aspartame. And its power was further demonstrated through its high prices.

But the days of unilateral power are over. NutraSweet's patent expired in 1992, opening the market for aspartame to numerous competitors. To adapt to its declining clout with customers, top management lowered prices by one-third and pledged its $20 million advertising budget to support customer products that contained NutraSweet.

Shortly before the patent expired, Coca-Cola and PepsiCo, NutraSweet's two largest customers, signed contracts to buy aspartame from NutraSweet for a few more years, although Coke also signed a similar contract with Holland Sweetener of The Netherlands. Industry observers suggested that neither of the soft-drink giants wanted to take the risk of replacing an ingredient that already had such high consumer acceptance.

NutraSweet's management, which had feared the patent expiration, used this reprieve to continue to test Sweetener 2000, an artificial sweetener that is hundreds of times sweeter than sugar and yet contains no calories.

SOURCES: L. Therrien, P. Oster, and C. Hawkins, "How Sweet It Isn't at NutraSweet," *Business Week*, 14 December 1992, p. 42; J. Seligmann and M. Hager, "Good News for Sweet Teeth," *Newsweek*, 11 May 1992, p. 69; M.J. McCarthy, "Pepsi, Coke Say They're Loyal To NutraSweet," *The Wall Street Journal*, 22 April 1992; L. Therrien, "NutraSweet Tries Being More of a Sweetie," *Business Week*, 8 April 1991, p. 88; "Monsanto," *International Directory of Company Histories*, Vol. I (Chicago: St. James Press, 1988), pp. 365–367.

which it operates and to position its company as favorably as possible within that industry. In fact, the next few chapters are devoted to an examination of this key issue in strategic management.

FORECASTING THE ENVIRONMENT

Macroenvironmental and industry scanning and analyses are only marginally useful if all they do is reveal current conditions. To be truly meaningful, such analyses must forecast future trends and changes. Although no form of forecasting is foolproof, several techniques can be helpful: time series analysis, judgmental forecasting, multiple scenarios, and the Delphi technique. Each method is described in the following sections.

■ Time Series Analysis

Time series analysis attempts to examine the effects of selected trends (such as population growth, technological innovations, changes in disposable personal income, or number of suppliers) on such variables as a firm's costs, sales, profitability, and market share over a number of years. This methodology also enables management to relate such factors as seasonal fluctuations, weather conditions, and holidays to the firm's performance. Likewise, time series analysis can reveal the effect of economic cycles on the organization's sales and profits. The purpose is to make a prediction about these variables.

Because time series analysis projects historical trends into the future, its validity depends upon the similarity between past trends and future conditions. Any significant departure from historical trends will weaken the forecast dramatically. Unfortunately, departures from historical trends seem to be occurring with increasing frequency.

A second potential weakness in time series analysis is that it provides quantitative answers. Managers must take care that they do not place too much confidence in these results. The use of numbers and equations often gives a misleading appearance of scientific accuracy.

■ Judgmental Forecasting

When the relationships between variables are less clear than they are in time series analysis or when they cannot be adequately quantified, judgmental forecasting may be used. In **judgmental forecasting,** an organization may use its own employees, customers, suppliers, or trade association as sources of qualitative information about future trends. For instance, sales representatives may be asked to forecast sales growth in various product categories from their knowledge of customers' expansion plans. Survey instruments may be mailed to customers, suppliers, or trade associations to obtain their judgments on specific trends.

For example, Allied Corporate Investments, a Los Angeles broker for buyers and sellers of businesses, originally specialized in relatively low-priced small businesses. In 1980, however, it conducted a judgmental forecast, asking its research staff, sales force, and outsiders (such as banks, customers, and the Chamber of Commerce) to forecast what business opportunities might be available in the future. The consensus of the forecast was that the Los Angeles economy would expand and the value of businesses would be substantially bid up. In response, Allied opened several more offices, contacted commercial sections of foreign embassies to inform them of business opportunities, and brokered more expensive businesses. As a result of its judgmental forecast, its volume of business increased by ten times.

■ Multiple Scenarios

The increasing unpredictability of environmental change makes it incredibly difficult to formulate dependable assumptions upon which forecasts can be based. One means of circumventing this troublesome state is to develop multiple scenarios about the future. In **multiple scenarios,** the manager formulates several alternative descriptions of future events and trends.[8]

One scenario, for example, may specify the economic conditions thought most likely to occur at some future point. Alternative scenarios may use a more optimistic assumption and a more pessimistic assumption. The same process can just as easily be used to express differing assumptions about technology, political elections, environmental regulation, oil prices, strikes, and other events.

For example, Royal Dutch/Shell Group, the world's second largest corporation, with annual sales exceeding $103 billion, currently uses two scenarios to formulate strategy. One assumes that European economic unification is successful, Japan and the United States avoid a trade war, and stable economic growth occurs throughout most of the world. In such a case, the physical environment will receive increasing attention, meaning governments will formulate additional emission restrictions and natural gas will take precedence over oil as a source of energy. The second scenario assumes international trade wars and widespread recession. Under such conditions, environmental regulations will be de-emphasized and oil consumption will increase dramatically. The point is not to predict which outcome will occur but to encourage managers to analyze a variety of "what if" possibilities.[9]

In formulating scenarios, strategic managers must identify the key forces in the macroenvironment and industry, assess their likely interrelationships, and estimate their influence upon future events. Contingency plans can then be prepared to cover the various conditions specified in the multiple scenarios. These plans may be general statements of action to be taken, without completely specifying the intended operational details. Contingency plans usually specify trigger points—events that call for implementing particular aspects of a plan.[10]

■ Delphi Technique

In certain cases, the **Delphi technique**[11] may be used to forecast the future. If the trend to be forecasted lies within a particular field of study, then experts in that field can be identified and questioned about the probability of the trend's occurring. For instance, if a home building firm would like to know when it will become feasible to build entire housing developments with solar energy as the sole source of electricity, heating, and cooling, the firm would compile a list of experts in the field of solar energy. Each expert would then be mailed a questionnaire asking for his or her judgments as to when knowledge of solar

Table 2.3 **Other Forecasting Techniques**

Technique	*Description*	*Weakness*
Econometric forecast	Simultaneous multiple regression systems	Assumes past relationships will continue into the future
Sales force forecast (judgmental)	Aggregate sales force estimate	Potential bias in opinions
Managerial forecast (judgmental)	Aggregation of estimates made by R&D, production, finance, and marketing managers	Potential bias in opinions
Consumer survey (judgmental)	Aggregate preferences of consumers	Potential bias in opinions
Brainstorming (judgmental)	Idea generation in supportive group interaction	Potential bias in opinions

energy will be sufficiently advanced to rely solely on it for home energy needs. The respondents will fill out the questionnaires, without communicating with one another, and return them to the home building company.

The company will compile a summary of the results and send it to each respondent along with a second questionnaire. After reviewing the summary and observing the other experts' judgments, each respondent will then fill out and mail in the second questionnaire. Some respondents may alter their judgments on this questionnaire after reviewing the judgments of the other members. This process of responding–receiving–feedback–responding continues until consensus is reached. The home builder will then rely, at least partially, on this consensus in formulating the firm's plans for the future.

In the previous paragraphs, several forecasting techniques were presented. Examples of others are shown in Table 2.3.

SUMMARY

Each organization exists within a complex network of environmental forces comprised of (1) the national and global macroenvironment and (2) the industry in which the organization competes. Because these forces are dynamic, their constant change presents numerous opportunities and threats to strategic managers.

Four macroenvironmental forces affect business strategy. Political-legal forces, in the broadest sense, include a government's basic stance toward business operations and, more narrowly, the outcomes of elections, legislation, and court judgments, as well as the decisions of various commissions and agencies at all levels of government. Economic forces comprise elements such as the impact of growth or decline in gross national product and increases or decreases in interest rates, inflation, and the value of the dollar. Technological forces include scientific improvements and innovations that affect a firm's operations and/or its products and services. Social forces include traditions, values, societal trends, consumer psychology, and a society's expectations of business. To identify and understand changes and trends in these forces, managers engage in environmental scanning.

A more specific set of forces within a firm's industry directly and powerfully affects management's strategic planning. Professor Michael Porter of Harvard University has identified five basic competitive industry forces: the threat of new entrants in the industry, the intensity of rivalry among existing competitors in the industry, the pressure from producers of substitute products or services, the bargaining power of buyers of the industry's outputs, and the bargaining power of suppliers to the industry's companies. The goal of a competitive strategy for a firm is to find a position in the industry from which it can best defend itself against these competitive forces or can influence them to its advantage.

Strategic planners must not only understand the current state of the macroenvironment and their industry but also be able to forecast its future states. Although forecasting is an inexact science, four techniques can be particularly helpful: time series analysis, judgmental forecasting, multiple scenarios, and the Delphi technique.

KEY CONCEPTS

Barriers to entry Obstacles to entering an industry. The major barriers to entry are economies of scale, product differentiation, capital requirements, switching costs, access to distribution channels, cost disadvantages independent of scale, and government policy.

Delphi technique A forecasting procedure in which experts in the appropriate field of study are independently questioned about the probability of some event's occurrence. The responses of all the experts are compiled, and a summary is sent to each expert, who, on the basis of this new information, responds again. Those responses are then compiled and a summary is again sent to each expert, with the cycle continuing until consensus is reached regarding the particular forecasted event.

Economies of scale The decline in unit costs of a product, an operation, or a function that goes into producing a product, which occurs as the absolute volume of production per period of time increases.

Environmental scanning The gathering and analysis of information about relevant environmental trends.

Exit barriers Obstacles to leaving an industry. Exit barriers can be economic, strategic, or emotional.

Industry A group of companies that produces products or services that are in competition.

Judgmental forecasting A forecasting procedure in which employees, customers, suppliers, and/or trade associations serve as sources of qualitative information regarding future trends.

Macroenvironment The general environment that affects all business firms. Its principal components are political-legal, economic, technological, and social systems and trends.

Multiple scenarios A forecasting procedure in which management formulates several plausible hypothetical descriptions of sequences of future events and trends.

Stakeholder An individual or group who is affected by—or can influence—an organization's operations.

Substitute products Alternative products that may satisfy similar consumer needs and wants but that differ somewhat in specific characteristics.

Switching costs One-time costs that buyers of an industry's outputs incur if they switch from one company's products to another's.

Time series analysis An empirical forecasting procedure in which certain historical trends are used to predict such variables as a firm's sales or market share.

DISCUSSION QUESTIONS

1. Give an example, other than those in the text, of how political-legal forces have presented an opportunity or a threat to a particular industry or business organization.

2. Explain how changes in the value of the dollar affect the domestic and international sales of U.S.-based companies.

3. Give an example, other than those in the text, of how technological forces have presented an opportunity or a threat to a particular industry or business organization.

4. Select a specific business organization and identify the stakeholders of that particular firm.

5. Using your university as an example, explain how political-legal, economic, technological, and social forces have affected its operations over the past decade.

6. Identify an industry that has low barriers to entry and one that has high barriers. Explain how these differences in barriers to entry affect the intensity and form of competition in those two industries.

7. Give some specific examples of exit barriers. How do they affect competition in those industries?

8. Aside from the examples given in the text, identify some products whose sales have been adversely affected by substitute products.

9. Identify an industry in which the suppliers have strong bargaining power and another industry in which the buyers have most of the bargaining power.

10. What are the strengths and weaknesses of time series analysis as a forecasting technique?

STRATEGIC MANAGEMENT EXERCISES

1. Select a specific company with which you are somewhat familiar. From your recollection of current events (events you may have read about in newspapers or magazines or have heard about on television or radio), identify some of the important macroenvironmental opportunities and threats for this company.

2. From your recollection of current events (events you may have read about in newspapers or magazines or have heard about on television or radio), identify and analyze the industry forces for an automobile company of your choice.

3. Select a major company for which there is considerable information available in your university library. Conduct a macroenvironmental analysis for that company. Your analysis should contain four sections: political-legal forces, economic forces, technological forces, and social forces. (See Appendix 2A for help in locating sources of macroenvironmental information.) Worksheet 1 may help to structure your analysis.

   You need not limit yourself to the terms listed under "Important Information." In some cases, other items that you discover in your research will be of equal or greater importance.

   Once you have identified the important components of each macroenvironmental force, you should determine whether each presents an opportunity or a threat to your company. You might assign a "+" to opportunities and a "–" to threats, or you might list each item under the subheadings "Opportunities" and "Threats." (You can refer to the beginning of the case section, "Strategic Management Case Analysis," for further details.)

4. Conduct an industry analysis for the company that you selected in Exercise 3. Your analysis should contain information in five areas: threat of entry, intensity of rivalry among existing competitors, pressure from substitute products, bargaining power of buyers, and bargaining power of suppliers. (See Appendix 2A for help in locating sources of industry information.) Worksheet 2 should help you to organize your work.

   Now, determine whether each component that you have identified constitutes an opportunity or a threat to your company.

5. Assume that you have been asked to develop an environmental forecast for the bookstore at your university, using the judgmental forecasting technique. Attempt to forecast the environment of the bookstore by writing a summary report based on questions that you ask several employees and customers of the bookstore. Since you may not have access to suppliers or trade associations, include your own judgment of what opportunities and threats the environment holds for the bookstore.

Worksheet 1

Macroenvironmental Analysis

Macroenvironmental Force	*Important Information*
Political-legal	Outcomes of elections, legislation, court judgments, and decisions rendered by various federal, state, and local agencies
Economic	GNP, short- and long-term interest rates, inflation, and value of the dollar
Technological	Scientific improvements, inventions, and the rate of technological change in the industry
Social	Traditions, values, societal trends, consumer psychology, and the public's expectations of business

Worksheet 2

Industry Analysis

Industry Sector	*Important Information*
Threat of entry	Extent to which the following factors prevent new companies from entering the industry: economies of scale, product differentiation, capital requirements, switching costs, access to distribution channels, cost disadvantages independent of scale, government policy, and expected retaliation
Intensity of rivalry among existing competitors	Number and relative balance of competitors, rate of industry growth, extent of fixed or storage costs, degree of product differentiation and switching costs, size of capacity augmentation, diversity of competitors, extent of strategic stakes, and height of exit barriers
Pressure from substitute products	Identification of substitute products, and analysis of the relative price and quality of those products
Bargaining power of buyers	Concentration of buyers, their purchase volume relative to industry sales and to the buyer's costs, product differentiation, buyers' switching costs, buyers' profits, possibility of buyers integrating backward, importance of the product to the quality of the buyer's product, and amount of information possessed by the buyer
Bargaining power of suppliers	Number and concentration of suppliers, availability of substitute products, importance of the buying industry to the suppliers, importance of the suppliers' product to the buyer's business, differentiation and switching costs associated with the suppliers' product, and possibility of suppliers integrating forward

NOTES

1. J. Saddler, "Small Businesses Complain That Jungle of Regulations Jeopardize Their Futures," *The Wall Street Journal*, 11 June 1992.
2. K. Kelly, "A Dream Marriage Turns Nightmarish," *Business Week*, 29 April 1991, pp. 94–95; R.L. Rose, "Caterpillar Sees Gains in Efficiency Imperiled by Strength of Dollar," *The Wall Street Journal*, 6 April 1990.
3. T.Y. Wiltz, "It's Enough to Drive the Distillers to Drink," *Business Week*, 25 June 1990, pp. 98–99; M. Charlier, "Youthful Sobriety Tests Liquor Firms," *The Wall Street Journal*, 14 June 1990.
4. A. Miller, "Burgers: The Heat Is On," *Newsweek*, 16 June 1986, p. 53.
5. J. Diffenbach, "Corporate Environmental Analysis in Large U.S. Corporations," *Long Range Planning* 16, no. 3 (June 1983):109, 112–113.
6. D.F. Jennings and J.R. Lumpkin, "Insights Between Environmental Scanning Activities and Porter's Generic Strategies: An Empirical Analysis," *Journal of Management* 18 (1992): 791–803.
7. M.E. Porter, *Competitive Strategy* (New York: Free Press, 1980), pp. 3–4, 7–14, 17–21, 23–28. Reprinted with permission of The Free Press, a Division of Macmillan, Inc., from *Competitive Strategy: Techniques for Analyzing Industries and Competitors*, by Michael E. Porter. Copyright © 1980 by The Free Press.
8. L. Fahey and V.K. Narayanan, *Macroenvironmental Analysis for Strategic Management* (St. Paul, Minn.: West, 1986), p. 215.
9. C. Knowlton, "Shell Gets Rich by Beating Risk," *Fortune*, 26 August 1991, p. 82.
10. C.D. Pringle, D.F. Jennings, and J.G. Longenecker, *Managing Organizations: Functions and Behaviors* (Columbus, Ohio: Merrill, 1988), p. 114.
11. N.C. Dalkey, *The Delphi Method: An Experimental Study of Group Opinion* (Santa Monica, Calif.: Rand Corporation, 1969).

APPENDIX 2A: SOURCES OF ENVIRONMENTAL AND INDUSTRY INFORMATION

Much valuable information on environmental and industry conditions and trends is available from published or other secondary sources. Managers should consult these sources prior to gathering expensive primary data.

Local libraries, for instance, contain introductory information on the political-legal, economic, technological, and social components of the macroenvironment in almanacs and encyclopedias. University libraries provide government publications that are rich with political-legal and economic data. Additional information can be obtained from business literature indexes, business periodicals, and reference services. Regularly published periodicals and newspapers such as *Business Week, The Wall Street Journal,* and *Fortune* provide excellent, timely macroenvironmental and industry information. More specific sources of information that may be found in many libraries are listed in Table 2A.l.

Other highly specific information may be obtained from the annual reports of companies, reports of major brokerage firms (such as Merrill Lynch), and trade publications (examples include *American Paints and Coatings Journal, Modern Brewery Age, Quick Frozen Foods,* and *The Retail Grocer*).

Information on the macroenvironment and industries may also be assimilated from radio business news, television shows (such as "Wall Street Week" and "Money Line"), suppliers, customers, and employees within the industry. And a visit to a branch office of the U.S. Commerce Department can be helpful. The Commerce Department has an extensive bibliography of its own publications, which is available at the branch offices.

Managers can use these sources of information along with assistance from consultants to forecast changes so that the firm can modify its strategy appropriately. Professional consulting firms are available in all major cities and many midsize locales. University professors in all areas of business administration and other disciplines such as sociology, psychology, engineering, and the sciences can also provide expert consulting in relevant areas.

Major Sources of Information on the Business Environment **Table 2A.1**

Name of Index	*Breadth of Information*	*Description*
Business Periodicals Index	Political-legal Economic Technological Social Industry	Identifies periodicals in all aspects of business and industry. Its "Book Reviews" covers publications on a variety of topics.
Funk & Scott Index of Corporations & Industries	Industry Economic Suppliers Competitors	Identifies periodicals and brokerage reports on all SIC (Standard Industrial Classification) industries. Its yellow pages provide weekly updates, its green pages provide lists of articles and dates, and its white pages list information on articles about specific companies.
New York Times Index	Political-legal Economic Technological Social Industry	Provides an index of articles published in the *New York Times.*
Public Affairs Information Service Bulletin	Social Economic Political-legal	Provides a subject listing on national and international journals, books, pamphlets, government publications, and reports of private and public agencies.
Reader's Guide to Periodical Literature	Political-legal Economic Technological Social Industry	Provides an author and subject index on periodicals and books.
Social Science Index	Political-legal Economic Social	Provides an author and subject index on periodicals and books.
Wall Street Journal/Barron's Index	Political-legal Economic Technological Social Industry	Provides an index of articles published in *The Wall Street Journal* and *Barron's.* Also includes a list of book reviews.
U.S. Industrial Outlook	Political-legal Economic Technological Social Industry	Gives the U.S. Department of Commerce's annual forecasts for over 350 industries.
Predicasts Forecasts	Political-legal Economic Technological Social Industry	Provides forecasts (as a quarterly service) of products, markets, and industry and economic aggregates for the United States and North America. Forecasts are grouped by SIC numbers and many go into the twenty-first century.
Standard and Poor's Industry Surveys	Political-legal Economic Technological Social Industry	Profiles and analyzes 33 basic industry groups. Trends and projections are detailed. Also contains analyses of each industry's leading performers.
Corporate & Industry Research Reports	Political-legal Economic Technological Social Industry	Provides analyses and forecasts of 8,000 U.S. companies and 600 industries from analytical research reports of 68 securities and institutional investment firms.

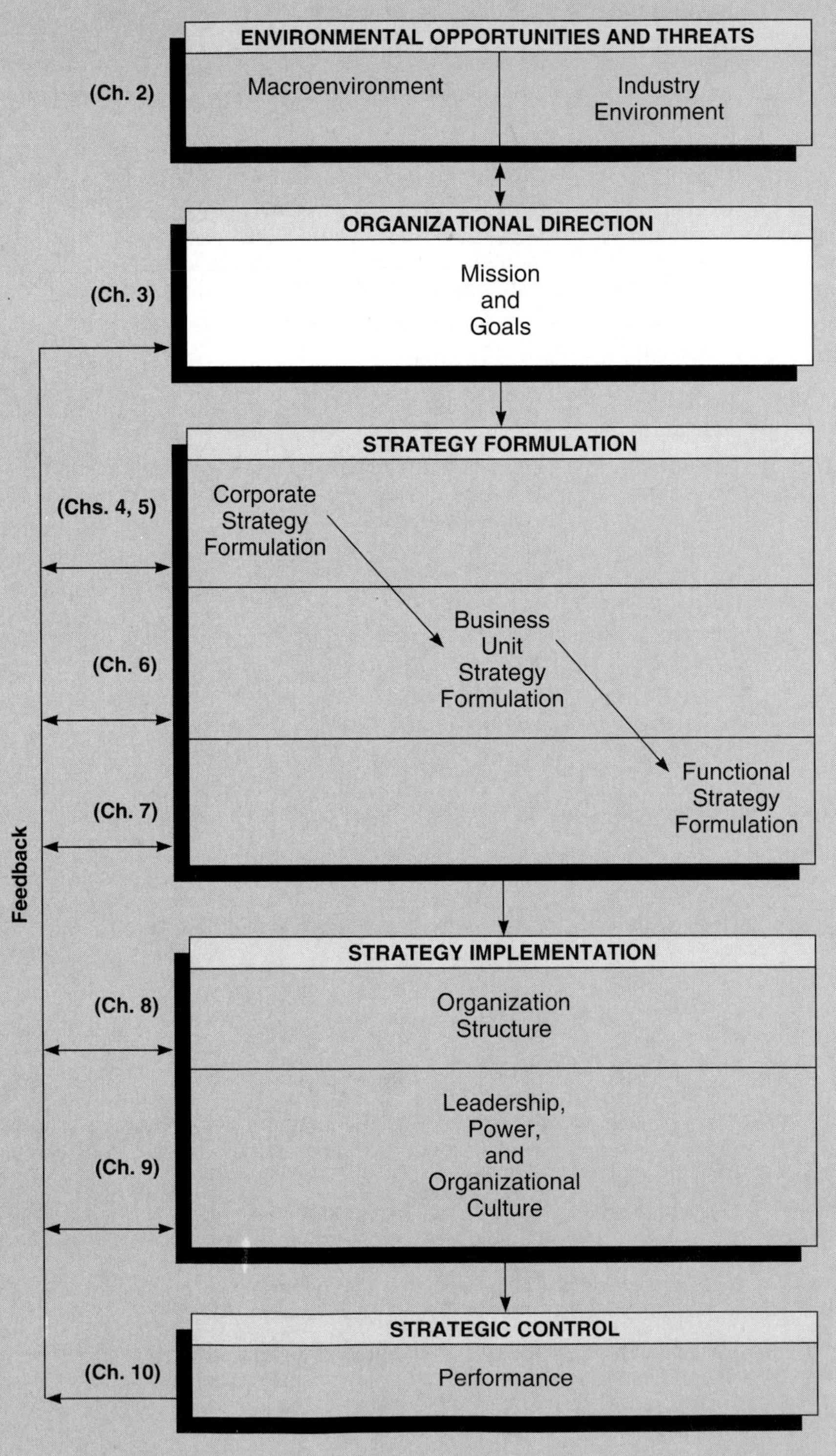
STRATEGIC MANAGEMENT MODEL
ENVIRONMENTAL OPPORTUNITIES AND THREATS
(Ch. 2)
Macroenvironment
Industry Environment
ORGANIZATIONAL DIRECTION
(Ch. 3)
Mission and Goals
STRATEGY FORMULATION
(Chs. 4, 5)
Corporate Strategy Formulation
(Ch. 6)
Business Unit Strategy Formulation
(Ch. 7)
Functional Strategy Formulation
Feedback
STRATEGY IMPLEMENTATION
(Ch. 8)
Organization Structure
(Ch. 9)
Leadership, Power, and Organizational Culture
STRATEGIC CONTROL
(Ch. 10)
Performance

3 Organizational Direction: Mission and Goals

As we saw in the preceding chapter, an assessment of the opportunities and constraints in the organization's environment is essential in formulating strategy. In this chapter, we turn from the environment to take an inward look at the firm. This step in the strategy process—establishing the organization's mission and goals—requires management to determine the direction in which the organization is to move within its environment.

Organizational direction is difficult to determine unless management and the board of directors, with inputs from diverse stakeholders, have clearly delineated the firm's purpose. Hence, this chapter begins with a discussion of the organization's *raison d'etre,* its reason for existing.

THE ORGANIZATION'S MISSION

Organizations are founded for a purpose. Although this purpose may change over time, it is essential that stakeholders understand the reason for the organization's existence, that is, the organization's **mission.** Often, the organization's mission is defined in a formal, written **mission statement**—a broadly defined but enduring statement of purpose[1] that identifies the scope of an organization's operations and its offerings to the various stakeholders.

This section examines the organization's mission at the corporate level and the business unit level. Changes in the organization's mission over time are then discussed, followed by an overview of the relationship between the organization's mission and its strategy.

■ Mission and Organizational Level

The mission of an organization, at the corporate level, is stated in fairly broad terms. For instance, the management of General Motors (GM) has stated the firm's overall mission as follows:

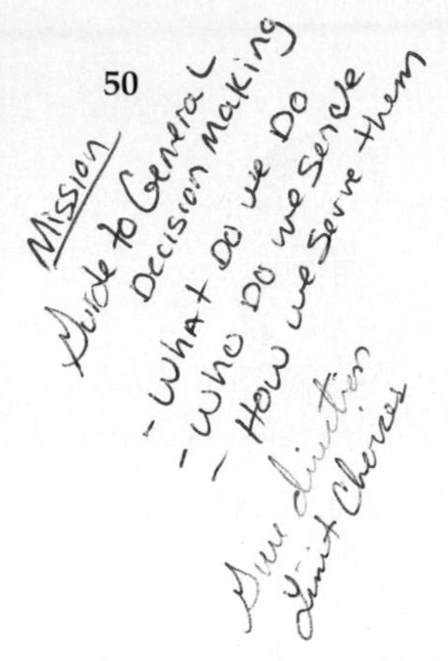

> The fundamental purpose of General Motors is to provide products and services of such quality that our customers will receive superior value, our employees and business partners will share in our success, and our stockholders will receive a sustained, superior return on their investment.[2]

Certainly, a large number of activities can be covered by such a broad statement. Such disparate GM undertakings as manufacturing vehicles, producing electronics and defense products, and providing information systems and technology can all be included in this mission statement. However, in each of these cases, the statement indicates that GM intends to furnish superior value to customers, to have employees and business partners share in the firm's success, and to provide a sustained, superior return to stockholders on their investment. So even though very broad, this corporate-level statement does provide direction to the company.

At the business unit level, the mission becomes narrower in scope and more clearly defined. For example, the mission of the Chevrolet business unit would include manufacturing safe and reliable economy cars, sports cars, sedans, and trucks. The Hughes Aircraft subsidiary's mission would be to produce electronic components and systems for defense and industrial customers. And the mission of the Electronic Data Systems business unit would encompass designing and operating information systems for both public and private organizations (including General Motors itself).

■ Mission and Change

Corporate and strategic business-level missions will generally change over time. In many cases, the change will be slow and gradual, but in some instances, the change may take place very rapidly. As an example of a firm whose mission changed gradually, consider Primerica. At one time, Primerica was known as American Can Company and was engaged in the container manufacturing and packaging businesses. Over the years, the company diversified into financial services and specialty retailing. When it finally sold its can and packaging operations, its name no longer fit its businesses, and it was renamed Primerica. Obviously, its mission had also gradually changed from manufacturing to services. Now its mission is to provide life insurance to individual consumers, originate home mortgages, provide mutual and pension fund management and brokerage services, and offer retail services for recorded music and audio and video products.

UAL, Inc. (United Airlines), serves as an example of a firm whose mission changed quickly. In 1987, UAL's chief executive officer, Richard Ferris, decided to broaden the company's mission. Rather than only provide air travel, UAL would become an integrated travel service company with operations encompassing the total service requirements of travelers. The firm would expand into rental cars (to provide customers transportation to and from airports) and hotels (where customers could stay while on trips). To reflect this broadened mission, the firm's name was changed from United Airlines to Allegis. The new mission was quite controversial, and various groups that had vested interests in the company believed that those interests would be better served by the

STRATEGIC INSIGHT

A Blurred Mission at Sears

Prior to 1975, Sears, Roebuck was the dominant national force in U.S. retailing. As a full-line general merchandiser with 850 stores, Sears was a regular shopping stop for most of America's families. That dominance ended abruptly, however, as the retail industry experienced rapid and dramatic changes. Sears' private-label business was eroded by the growing popularity of specialty retailers, such as Circuit City and The Limited, and its cost structure was successfully challenged by such low-overhead discounters as Wal-Mart and Kmart.

Initially, Sears reacted by attempting to emphasize fashion with such labels as Cheryl Tiegs sportswear. But high-fashion models did not mesh well with Sears' middle-America image. In fact, Sears allowed the key post of women's fashion director to remain vacant from 1980 until 1989. Turning next to diversification, Sears tried to convert its dowdy image into a "financial supermarket" by purchasing Dean Witter Financial Services and Coldwell Banker Real Estate. But in-store kiosks never caught on with customers, and the expected synergy between these two subsidiaries and Sears' Allstate Insurance business unit and its Discover Card failed to materialize. Eventually, Sears decided to spin off its Dean Witter Financial Services Group and its Coldwell Banker real estate holdings to permit the firm to sharpen its focus on its core retailing business.

Next, management modified the store's image to one that sold nationally branded merchandise along with private-label brands at "everyday low prices." The idea was to create individual "superstores" within each of the Sears outlets to compete more effectively with powerful niche competitors. Sears' original intent, which was widely publicized, was to depart from its traditional practice of holding weekly sales in order to save on advertising expenses and inventory handling while offering stable, everyday low prices. But the "everyday low prices" turned out to be, in some cases, higher than Sears' old sale prices, advertising expenses climbed rather than declined, and Sears continued to run special sales. By this time, customers were totally confused. Sears' response was to announce that, once again, it was going to emphasize women's fashions and would advertise them in such magazines as *Vogue* and *Mademoiselle*. But, in 1992 alone, Sears lost $3.9 billion, its worst performance ever.

Although Sears attempted to cut its costs significantly between 1990 and 1993 by eliminating over 93,000 jobs, its big catalog operation, and 113 stores, its inability to define a mission for itself and to establish a clear image in the customer's mind made it improbable that the store would ever again dominate the U.S. retailing landscape.

SOURCES: "Sears Loses $3.93 Billion in '92," *Harrisonburg (VA) Daily News-Record*, 10 February 1993; G.A. Patterson, "Sears Will Re-Establish Base in Malls, Target Middle-of-the-Road Merchants," *The Wall Street Journal*, 27 January 1993; G.A. Patterson and F. Schwadel, "Sears Suddenly Undoes Years of Diversifying Beyond Retailing Field," *The Wall Street Journal*, 30 September 1992; F. Schwadel, "Sears Plans More Cutbacks at Retail Unit," *The Wall Street Journal*, 11 April 1992; S. Caminiti, "Sears' Need: More Speed," *Fortune*, 15 July 1991; p. 89; K. Kelly, "At Sears, the More Things Change . . . ," *Business Week*, 12 November 1990; pp. 66–68; M. Oneal, "Shaking Sears Right Down to its Work Boots," *Business Week*, 17 October 1990, pp. 84–87; and F. Schwadel, "Sears' Glitzy Ads Target Affluent Fashion Market," *The Wall Street Journal*, 15 August 1990.

firm's original mission—passenger and cargo air transportation. Within four months, Ferris was fired and the company's name and mission reverted to their previous forms.

■ Mission and Strategy

An organization with a keen sense of its own identity is far more likely to be successful than one that has no clear understanding of its reason for existence. For example, Armco diversified widely more than a decade ago in an attempt to shelter itself from fluctuations in the steel industry. But it found itself in alien territory when it moved into financial services and insurance. After acquiring an insurance holding company, Armco's managers discovered that they "had very few people in [their] management group who could ask the right questions and trouble shoot in that part of [their] operations."[3] They determined to limit future diversification to markets with which they were familiar.

By contrast, Kmart Corporation identifies itself as a general merchandise retailer that distributes a wide range of merchandise through a chain of discount department stores. To satisfy its broad array of customers, the company sells staple merchandise at low prices, as well as a selective mix of national brands. This clear sense of mission has undoubtedly been influential in Kmart's success since the early 1960s.

Hence, effective management requires not only an understanding of the environment but also a focus on the organization's mission. A clear sense of purpose is necessary in establishing goals, because it is difficult to know where one is going if one does not first know who one is. Firms with a clear sense of their mission are able to determine which activities fit into their strategic direction and which ones do not.

Management consultant C. K. Prahalad emphasizes that organizations should spend more time understanding what proficiencies they possess. For instance, Sony has used its skills in miniaturizing audio, video, and electronics products as its particular strategic competence. Likewise, AT&T's diversification into the credit card field was an application of its strategic competence in transaction processing, based on its extensive billing experience in the telephone industry.[4] Figure 3.1 summarizes the discussion up to this point.

THE ORGANIZATION'S GOALS AND OBJECTIVES

This section focuses on organizational goals and objectives. On the surface, it appears that establishing organizational goals is a fairly straightforward process. As will become evident, however, this process is actually quite complex. Various stakeholder groups have different goals for the firm. The organizational goals that eventually emerge must balance the pressures from the different stakeholder groups so that the continuing participation of each is assured.

■ Goals and Objectives Defined

Whereas the mission is the reason for the existence of the firm, the organization's **goals** represent the desired general ends toward which efforts are directed. **Objectives** are specific, and often quantified, versions of goals. For example, management may establish a goal "to expand the size of the firm through internal growth." From this goal, a number of specific objectives may be derived, such as "to increase sales by 10 percent each year for the next eight years." As another example, management's goal may be "to become the innovative leader in the industry." On the basis of this goal, one of the specific

Figure 3.1 **The Role of the Organization's Mission**

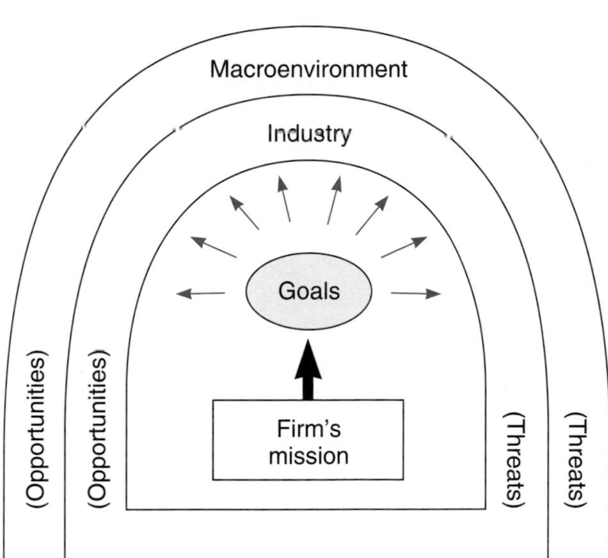

objectives will be "to have 25 percent of sales each year come from new products developed during the preceding three years."

As you can see, objectives are verifiable and specific. That is, with the objectives in the preceding paragraph, management will be able to answer the question: "Has this objective been attained?" Without verifiability and specificity, objectives will not provide a clear direction for managerial decision making, nor will they permit an assessment of organizational performance.

■ Goals and Stakeholders

Various stakeholders will have different goals for the firm. Each stakeholder group—owners (stockholders), members of the board of directors, managers, employees, suppliers, creditors, distributors, and customers—views the firm from a different perspective. To illustrate this point, Table 3.1 delineates the goals of selected stakeholders for Kellogg Company.

Rationality suggests that stakeholders establish goals from the perspective of their own interests. Because of the diversity of these interests, top management faces the difficult task of attempting to reconcile and satisfy each of the stakeholder groups while pursuing its own set of goals. Since the interests of various stakeholder groups are quite different, a close examination of some of their interests can be enlightening.

■ Influences on Goals

Who has the most influence on a firm's goals and who determines what the organization does? The traditional view is one of a shareholder-driven corporation. From this perspective, both top management and the board of directors

General Goals of Kellogg's Stakeholders **Table 3.1**

Stakeholders	*Goals*
Customers	Customers would likely want Kellogg's goals to include providing healthy, quality foods at reasonable prices.
General public	The general public would likely want Kellogg's goals to include providing goods and services with minimum costs (i.e., pollution), increasing employment opportunities, and contributing to charitable causes.
Suppliers	Suppliers would likely want Kellogg's goals to include remaining with them for the long term and purchasing from them at prices that allow the suppliers reasonable profit margins.
Employees	Employees would likely want Kellogg's goals to include providing good working conditions, equitable compensation, and promotion opportunities
Creditors	Creditors would likely want Kellogg's goals to include maintaining a healthy financial posture and a policy of on-time payment of debt.
Distributors	Wholesalers and retailers would likely want Kellogg's goals to include remaining with them for the long term and selling to them at prices that allow for reasonable profit margins.
Stockholders	Stockholders would likely want Kellogg's goals to be the maximization of returns on their equity.
Board of directors	Directors would likely want Kellogg's goals to be to keep them as directors and to satisfy the demands of the other stakeholders so that the directors would not be liable to lawsuits.
Managers	Managers would likely want to benefit personally from Kellogg. Other management goals are to expand Kellogg's market share in the cereal business, to make compatible growth-oriented acquisitions, to boost capacity, to improve productivity, and to launch new cereals worldwide.

are primarily accountable to the owners (the shareholders) of the corporation. Top management is responsible for enhancing the financial value of the firm, and the board of directors is charged with overseeing top management's decisions.

An argument exists, however, that if owners are to experience enhanced financial returns, the corporation must be customer-driven. Consumer advocate Ralph Nader, for instance, has argued for over thirty years that large corporations must be more responsive to customers' needs.[5] And the marketing strategy literature emphasizes the necessity for firms to maintain strategic adaptability based on changes in customer desires.[6]

A broader viewpoint recognizes that, because corporations are complex and depend upon environmental resources, they cannot maximize any single stakeholder group's interests. Rather corporations must be broadly stakeholder-driven, attempting to balance the desires of all stakeholders.[7] Maximizing any one stakeholder group's interests at the expense of other groups can seriously jeopardize the corporation's effectiveness. A firm cannot emphasize the financial interests of shareholders over the monetary needs of employees, for example, without alienating the employees and eventually harming the firm's financial returns. Likewise, raising prices to please stockholders will cause customers to take their business elsewhere.

Since various stakeholders' desires may conflict, management must resolve these opposing demands.[8] Fortunately, however, some stakeholders may have more than a unidimensional self-interest. For instance, although some stockholders may desire high financial returns, they may be unwilling to invest in corporations that operate in South Africa or produce tobacco products, even though higher returns may be associated with those investment opportunities. And some consumers may be willing to pay higher prices for products that do not harm the environment.

Ideally, top managers recognize that the corporation must be managed to balance the pluralistic demands of various stakeholder groups. Obviously, this requirement poses a considerable challenge. A careful reading of the goals in Table 3.1 illustrates this point. In the following paragraphs, select stakeholder groups are discussed in the context of their paramount goals.

■ Goals of Top Management

Ideally, the goals of top management should be to attempt to enhance the return to stockholders on their investment while simultaneously attempting to satisfy the interests of other stakeholders. Underlying the extensive research in this area is the assumption that stockholders are primarily interested in top management's maximizing profits in order to pay them dividends and increase the market value of their stock.

However, the motivation of top management to maximize profits has been questioned for many years. In fact, for as long as absentee owners (stockholders) have been hiring professional managers to operate their companies, questions have been raised concerning the extent to which these hired managers actually attempt to increase the wealth of the absentee owners. During this century, as larger and larger firms with ever more diffuse ownerships have emerged, the issue of whose interests the hired top executives actually serve has been widely examined.

Although researchers have studied this issue from a number of different perspectives, underlying many of the studies is one common philosophical premise: Top managers act primarily in their own interests. What remains to be resolved is whether top managers, by furthering their own self-interests, are also acting in the best interests of the firm's shareholders. From this research, three viewpoints have emerged, which are described in the sections that follow.

Management Serves Its Own Interests

The argument of researchers adhering to the first viewpoint is that hired top managers tend to pursue strategies that ultimately increase their own rewards.[9] In particular, top executives are likely to increase the size of their firms since larger rewards usually accompany larger organizational size and its greater responsibilities.

Perhaps the major work in this area can be traced to Herbert A. Simon,[10] who won the 1978 Nobel Prize in economics for his research on managerial decision-making behavior. Building on Roberts's[11] study of executive compensation, Simon suggests that a reward differential exists at each managerial level in an organizational hierarchy. That is, first-level supervisors receive the lowest managerial salaries, but salaries increase with each succeeding level in the organization up through the chief executive officer's salary. The larger the organization and the greater the number of levels in its hierarchy, the greater the rewards will be for top-level executives. Hence, top managers have a powerful incentive to increase the size of their firms. Other researchers have empirically demonstrated that larger firm size is positively associated with greater rewards.[12] One study concluded that "the size/pay relation is causal and . . . CEOs can increase their pay by increasing firm size, even when the increase in size reduces the firm's market value."[13]

Top managers may also be selfishly motivated to increase the size of their firms through diversification, by acquiring companies in other industries. Diversification not only increases a firm's size but may also reduce the top managers' job risks, for when an organization falters, its top managers often lose their jobs. Diversification should spread this risk and help upper-level managers preserve their positions. Although diversification can benefit top management, it may not similarly advance stockholders' interests. They can more effectively reduce their financial risks by diversifying their personal financial portfolios.[14]

This interest in organizational growth does not necessarily mean that top management is unconcerned with the firm's profitability or market value, but it does suggest to researchers that top managers are likely to emphasize business performance only to the extent that it discourages shareholder revolts and hostile takeovers. Simon suggests, for instance, that the difference between what a firm's profits can be and what its profits actually are represents "organizational slack," which will only be reduced if outside pressure is applied.[15]

Management Responds to Pressure from Significant Stockholders

A second viewpoint maintains that the degree to which top managers will implement strategies that benefit stockholders depends on the extent to which ownership of the firm is concentrated.[16] Significant stockholders (those holding 5 percent or more of a firm's stock) can force managers to act responsibly by demanding information from management, using their voting power, or threatening to sell their stock to permit a takeover.[17]

Evidence indicates that the top managers of corporations that have at least one significant stockholder have less self-seeking managerial discretion than managers of firms with more diffuse ownership.[18] The top executives of companies with a significant stockholder, then, are likely to be rewarded on the basis of the firm's performance; top managers of firms without a single major stockholder are more likely to be rewarded on the basis of nonperformance criteria, such as an increase in the size of the firm.[19] Parenthetically, the presence of a significant shareholder may also inhibit diversification through acquisition.

Management Shares the Same Interests as Stockholders

A third viewpoint contradicts both of the preceding views by proposing that the interests of top management are the same as those of the stockholders. Indeed, some studies do reveal positive associations between business performance and managerial rewards. One study, for example, found that profits, not the size of firms, determine top management rewards.[20] Another points to the existence of a significant relationship between common stock earnings and the rewards of top executives.[21]

STRATEGIC INSIGHT

CEO Compensation

See video:
CEO Compensation

Excessive CEO compensation has been roundly criticized in recent years. Although no firm standards exist for defining what is "excessive," a number of CEOs have come under fire for their annual compensation. Some examples:

- Over the past several years, Champion Paper's average annual return has been less than the average annual return on risk-free U.S. Treasury notes. Yet Champion's CEO, Andrew Sigler, receives more than $1 million in annual compensation and has been awarded a bonus for eighteen consecutive years.
- William Anders, former CEO of General Dynamics, raised his company's stock price by cutting costs through firing thousands of employees, slashing R&D expenses, and transferring manufacturing jobs from the United States to Mexico. As compensation, he received $3.75 million in salary and bonuses plus options on more than 325,000 shares of company stock.
- The CEO of Coca-Cola, Robert Goizueta, whose firm has returned an average of 35 percent a year to stockholders over the past decade, received total 1991 compensation valued at $81 million (almost $3 million in salary and bonuses plus a grant of one million shares of stock).

Whether any of these examples illustrates "excessive" CEO compensation depends upon one's perspective. But it is clear that U.S. CEOs are the highest paid in the world. For example, while the average CEO compensation among large U.S. companies is $3.2 million a year, it averages only $525,000 (plus housing and golf club expenses and other benefits) for Japanese CEOs. Additionally, compensation for Japanese CEOs generally declines when company performance deteriorates, while in the United States, compensation is likely to increase. There are exceptions, of course; Avon Products' annual salary payments to James Preston, its CEO, have been frozen at just over $600,000. But compensation expert Graef Crystal estimates that only 5 percent of firms link CEO pay directly to company performance.

Part of the reason for the lack of correlation between company performance and CEO compensation is the way the typical CEO's compensation is set. Determining that compensation is the responsibility of the compensation committee of the board of directors. This committee is usually appointed by the CEO and is guided by a compensation consultant hired by the CEO. Often, the CEO does not even leave the room when his or her compensation is discussed.

As a result of stockholder discontent, the Securities and Exchange Commission has granted shareholders the means to protest the salaries of top managers. Although the shareholders' resolutions are not binding on the board of directors, they are expected to make board members considerably more cautious in determining CEO compensation packages.

In a widely cited theoretical work, Eugene F. Fama argues that the self-interests of hired top managers require that they behave in ways that benefit the stockholders.[22] His argument is based on the premise that the market for managerial talent provides an effective disciplining force. If top managers do not promote the interests of stockholders, this information will result in a lowering of their value in the managerial labor market. This lowered value will adversely affect the managers' alternative employment opportunities.[23] Managerial performance may also be indirectly evaluated by the stock market, because it implicitly judges top management's performance by bidding the firm's stock price either up or down.[24]

From a different perspective, John Child proposes that stock option plans and high salaries bring the interests of top management and stockholders closer together.[25] According to his reasoning, top executives wish to protect their salaries and option plans and can do so only by striving for higher business performance.

This concept of congruent interests has gained support from other scholars, but for different reasons.[26] They suggest that managerial jobs contain "structural imperatives" that force managers to attempt to maximize profits.

> Before the rise of the large stock corporation, individuals who filled the roles of entrepreneur were probably motivated to realize profits. If they did not act as if they were so motivated, however, the failure of their firms would eventually remove them from their positions. . . . The behavior exhibited by entrepreneurs was a structural requirement of the position of entrepreneur itself rather than merely a function of the motivation of individuals who became entrepreneurs.[27]

Similarly, managers would be removed from their positions if they failed to maximize profits. Therefore, these scholars reason that top managers will be motivated to enhance profitability, and "even if they are not so motivated, they must act as if they are if they wish to remain in their positions of authority."[28]

As we can see from the preceding discussion, the issue of whether top managers will attempt to enhance their firms' returns or whether they will pursue a more narrow goal of self-enrichment has not been satisfactorily resolved. Compelling evidence and logic exist on both sides of the controversy. Also unresolved is how motivated top managers are to satisfy the interests of stakeholders beyond the owners of the firm. We turn now to another controversial area—the goals of the board of directors and stockholders.

■ Goals of the Board of Directors and Stockholders

Legally, boards of directors are responsible for such aspects of corporate leadership as selecting and replacing the chief executive officer, representing the interests of the firm's shareholders, advising top management, and monitoring managerial and company performance.[29] There is evidence, however, that board members have, in many cases, failed to fulfill their legal roles.[30] A common explanation for this failure is that boards have long been considered "creatures of the CEO."[31] Often, board members are nominated by the chief executive officer, who, in return, expects the directors to support his or her strategic decisions. For their support, the directors receive generous compensation. One British member of several corporate boards once described board membership as follows:

> No effort of any kind is called for. You go to a meeting once a month in a car supplied by the company. You look both grave and sage, and on two occasions say "I agree," say "I don't think so" once, and if all goes well, you get 500 [pounds] a year. If you have five of them, it is total heaven, like having a permanent hot bath.[32]

Directors sometimes behave in this fashion, not only because they wish to show their loyalty to the chief executive officer, who appoints and compensates them (average annual compensation is over $50,000 for serving on the board of a major corporation), but also because they often make decisions based primarily on information provided by the CEO.[33] As one CEO put it: "[My board members] often have to have blind faith in management. It would take them a month to really understand some of the decisions they make."[34]

In theory, the primary goal of the board is to safeguard the interests of the stockholders. Technically speaking, board members are elected by the stockholders. In reality, however, stockholders are limited to casting a yes or no vote for each individual nominated to the board by top management. Each nominee's credentials are briefly stated in management's mailed "notice of annual meeting of shareholders," and few stockholders will have much knowledge regarding the nominees beyond these basic facts. Hence, most stockholders will simply follow the recommendations of top management.

Therefore, it is not surprising to find that board members are often beholden to top management for their positions. In such cases, the directors' basic loyalties lie with the CEO rather than with the stockholders. Frequently, this loyalty takes the form of approval of lavish compensation packages for top management. In some cases, these packages may even conceal the actual amounts that top managers receive. For example, stockholders did not know that F. Ross Johnson was granted 40,000 shares of stock before RJR Nabisco was acquired by Kohlberg Kravis Roberts. One account described it as follows:

STRATEGIC INSIGHT

The Growing Responsiveness of Boards

The directors of several prominent corporations have become increasingly responsive to stockholder interests in recent years. In the most celebrated example, the outside members of the board of the world's largest corporation, General Motors, replaced Robert Stempel, chairman of the board's executive committee, with John Smale, retired chairman of Procter & Gamble, and promoted John F. Smith, Jr., head of GM's international operations, to CEO.

For years, GM's financial and market positions had been steadily deteriorating. Between 1981 and 1992, for instance, the company's market share declined from 44 to 33 percent, and its 1991 and 1992 losses were record-setting. As a result, shareholder pressure on the board of directors to make faster changes in company operations intensified. Among those shareholders was the huge California Public Employees' Retirement System (Calpers). Responding to this shareholder pressure, the eleven outside members of GM's board (a majority of the fifteen-person board) met privately to determine what direction to take. The "coup" was a surprise to most observers since GM has rarely demoted executives and no top manager had been demoted by the board since 1920.

But the message the shake-up sent to GM's management was unmistakable. As ex-president Reuss put it: "The board said: 'Hey, you weren't moving fast enough. You gotta move faster.' "

This incident illustrates that the system of corporate governance does not need overhauling; it simply needs to be made to work as intended. Fortunately for most small shareholders, huge institutional investors (such as pension funds, mutual funds, insurance companies, and bank trust departments) often hold stocks for lengthy periods of time. Hence, rather than selling the stock of a poor-performing company, they are more likely to press for improvements in the way the firm is managed.

SOURCES: A. Taylor III, "What's Ahead for GM's New Team," *Fortune*, 30 November 1992, pp. 58–61; M. Magnet, "Directors, WAKE UP!" *Fortune*, 15 June 1992, pp. 85–92; J.B. Treece, "The Board Revolt," *Business Week*, 20 April 1992, pp. 31–36 (source of quotation, p. 31); W. Brown and F. Swoboda, "An Outside Director's Coup Inside GM," *The Washington Post*, 12 April 1992; R. Norton, "Who Owns This Company, Anyhow?" *Fortune*, 29 July 1991, pp. 131–142.

> Johnson received around $20 million, most of which the shareholders didn't know he had coming until the takeover. . . . Shareholders may not always have a legal right to override the decisions of their own board of directors. But they surely have a right to know what their boards have decided.[35]

Ignoring the stockholders' interests has begun to diminish in recent years, however. The turning point was the 1985 decision by the Delaware Supreme Court that Trans Union Corporation's directors had accepted a takeover bid too quickly. They were accused of failing to read the sales contract before approving it, not soliciting an independent, outside opinion on the fairness of the sales price, and approving the sale of the company in a hasty, two-hour meeting dominated by the CEO. They were held personally liable for the difference between the offer they accepted and the price the company might have received in an open sale. The directors had to pay $13.5 million of the $23.5 million settlement—the excess over their liability insurance coverage.[36]

The pressure on directors to acknowledge stockholder wishes continues to increase. For instance, stockholder suits against directors rose by almost 70 percent over the past fifteen years.[37] But the major source of pressure in recent years has come from institutional investors. These stockholders—chiefly pension funds, mutual funds, and insurance companies—own $1 trillion of stock in U.S. corporations. By virtue of the size of their investments, they wield considerable power and are becoming more active in using it. For example, the California Public Employees' Retirement System and Pennsylvania Public School Employees' Retirement System recently launched a proxy battle that led Honeywell's management to restructure the company. Considering that institutional investors own large chunks of many major companies (e.g., 89 percent of Capital Cities/ABC, 82 percent of Lotus Development, 81 percent of Southwest Airlines, and 80 percent of Whirlpool), their potential power is quite impressive.[38]

On the other side, however, it should be emphasized that some board members have played effective stewardship roles. Many directors promote strongly the best interests of the firm's shareholders and various other stakeholder groups as well. Research indicates, for instance, that board members are invaluable sources of environmental information.[39] By conscientiously carrying out their duties, directors can ensure that management does not solely pursue its own interests by focusing management's attention on company performance.[40] Directors do exist who believe that their job is to represent shareholders. For example, the chairman of the board of Compaq Computer states that "the owners of the company should be represented by the directors. That has ceased to happen at lots of companies where management dominates the board."[41] Murray Weidenbaum, an economist who serves on three corporate boards, does not "view the director's role as helping the CEO. The role of the director, the legal obligation, is to represent the shareholders."[42]

■ Goals of Creditors

Creditors of a corporation include bondholders, banks, and other financial institutions. Their primary goal is to influence the firm to maintain a healthy financial posture in order to safeguard both the principal and interest on their loaned funds. Recent trends toward acquisitions and mergers that involve financial leverage have given creditors increasingly powerful roles in corporate America. In fact, should the trend toward heavy debt financing continue, an increasing number of business decisions may be transferred to creditors. Such decisions could include choices as crucial as the selection of top management, the identification of acquisition targets, and the determination of which products to produce and where and how to produce them. Furthermore, as mergers and acquisitions continue, fewer competitors will remain in the marketplace, and many of those who do remain will be heavily financed by creditors.

The increased power of creditors can result in market distortions. For example, now-defunct Pan Am Corporation, which operated one of the oldest fleets of airplanes in the airline industry, was on the brink of bankruptcy for years. Yet in 1989, after losing $2.5 billion over the preceding decade, it tried (but failed) to buy Northwest Airlines—a much larger and more profitable competitor. It could only attempt this through the strong support of a group of creditors—such as Bankers Trust, Morgan Guaranty, Citicorp, and Prudential-Bache—that was willing to provide financing of $2.7 billion.

■ Conflicting Goals

It is evident from the preceding discussion that the goals of top managers, boards of directors, and creditors are not always congruent with the goals of the firm's shareholders or other stakeholder groups. Broadly speaking, of course, the goals of all stakeholders are best served when the firm functions as a viable entity. It is then able to supply goods to customers, contribute to society's standard of living, provide employment, and channel financial benefits to all stakeholders.

We must realize, however, that a viable firm has the power to benefit each stakeholder group differentially. For instance, tough bargaining with suppliers will transfer benefits from suppliers to stockholders, managers, and customers. Shirking responsibility for controlling environmental pollution transfers benefits from society (because the general public bears the costs of pollution) to a number of stakeholders who benefit from the financial savings. Bestowing extremely generous compensation on top management transfers benefits from stockholders, employees, and customers to upper-level managers. In fact, a recent survey by a New York consulting firm reveals that 66 percent of employees and 73 percent of stockholders believe that senior managers receive too much compensation at the expense of other stakeholders.[43]

Perhaps the most common suggestion for making the goals of top management and stockholders more congruent is to award shares of stock or stock options to top management. The rationale is that significant stock ownership would align the interests of top management with the interests of shareholders. Attempts to align the interests of upper-level management with those of other stakeholder groups have also been negatively imposed through lawsuits—that is, fines imposed on the firm by various public agencies and court decisions.

STAKEHOLDERS AND TAKEOVERS

What happens when top managers of a firm with ineffective board members continue to mismanage the firm? In many cases, large numbers of shareholders will sell their shares, depressing the market price of the company's stock. Depressed prices often attract takeover attempts, as discussed in the following paragraphs.

■ An Overview

Any firm whose stock is publicly traded constantly faces the possibility of a takeover. Depending upon the form in which a takeover occurs, different groups of stakeholders will be affected in various ways.

A **takeover** refers to the purchase of a significant number of shares of a firm by an individual, a group of investors, or another organization. Takeovers may be attempted by outsiders or insiders.

Attempts to take over a company by an individual, group, or organization that is outside the organization may be friendly or unfriendly. A friendly takeover is one in which both the buyer and seller desire the transaction. In recent years, General Electric's takeover of RCA, Capital Cities' takeover of ABC, and Greyhound's takeover of Trailways illustrate friendly takeovers. An unfriendly takeover is one in which the target firm resists the sale. Recent examples of unfriendly takeovers include Carl Icahn's successful bid for TWA and Sir James Goldsmith's unsuccessful bid for Goodyear.

Unfriendly takeovers are sometimes precipitated by **raiders**—individuals who believe that the way a company is being managed can be significantly improved. Raiders purchase a large number of shares in the target firm either to force a change in top management personnel or to manage the firm themselves.

Other reasons for takeovers by outsiders include acquisitions by investors or creditors for financial purposes or acquisitions by another firm for strategic reasons. For example, Chrysler's takeover of American Motors several years ago provided Chrysler with immediate expansion of product lines, production capacity, and market share.

Transfer of ownership to organizational insiders, such as employees or top managers, may occur gradually through special types of takeovers known as **employee stock ownership plans (ESOPs).** Since the enactment of a tax law in 1974 that encouraged ESOPs, many closely held firms (those with only a few stockholders) have been partially turned over to their managers and employees. This process usually begins when the principal owner of the closely held firm retires or when an ESOP plan is developed as a benefit or motivational incentive for the firm's employees. As the employees receive more and more shares of stock over a period of time, the ownership of the firm is gradually turned over to them.

The transfer of ownership to insiders may also occur suddenly through a takeover by the firm's employees or top managers. In one of the most publicized takeover attempts in American business, F. Ross Johnson, the CEO of RJR Nabisco, and his top management group attempted to take the firm private (concentrate its ownership in their hands). However, their bids were topped by the investment firm of Kohlberg Kravis Roberts & Company, which paid about $25 billion for the firm.

Sudden takeover attempts often (but not always) rely heavily on borrowed funds to finance the acquisition. Borrowing funds to purchase a firm is referred to as a **leveraged buyout (LBO).** When a takeover is financed in this fashion, the company is burdened with heavy debt, which must be paid back either by funds generated from operations or by the sale of company assets, such as subsidiaries or product divisions.

■ Pros and Cons

Takeovers have been both defended and criticized. Their defense generally consists of pointing out the useful role that takeovers play in replacing ineffective management. For instance, T. Boone Pickens, Jr., a renowned corporate raider, has argued:

> After decades of sovereign autonomy, the professional managers of many large, publicly held corporations are finding themselves on the firing line. They are being asked to justify lackluster performance and questionable strategies. They are being called on to address the chronic undervaluation of their securities.[44]

Takeovers have been criticized from several perspectives. One argument is that the primary goal of some takeover attempts is for the raider to make short-term profits. Even the bidder who ultimately loses out to a higher bidder usually pockets a considerable profit because of the increase in the stock's price brought about by the bidding. Such a losing bidder is said to have engaged in "greenmail." In some cases, management will attempt to take the firm private, usually through a leveraged buyout, to prevent the unfriendly takeover. This action will limit the firm's future strategic options because it must make heavy interest payments on its newly acquired debt for many years. These payments make it difficult for the firm to finance research and development activities, to explore new markets, and to promote and advertise its goods and services.

Bondholders, too, suffer from LBOs. As company debt increases following an LBO, the firm's bonds become more risky to purchase since their ultimate redemption is less certain. This increase in risk results in a deterioration of the credit rating of the firm's bonds and a loss of value to the bondholders.

Finally, most takeovers are followed by layoffs of employees and managers. But more than those employees and their families are affected. For example, when Gulf Oil was taken over by Chevron, Gulf's Pittsburgh headquarters was closed. Nearly six thousand employees either were transferred from Pittsburgh or were fired. This move had a significant negative impact on the many Pittsburgh-area firms that supplied various products and services to Gulf. Additionally, the city suffered because of lower tax revenues, and the price of real estate throughout the city declined.

For these reasons, some states have passed laws that protect their firms from takeovers. For example, when T. Boone Pickens attempted, in 1987, an unfriendly takeover of Boeing, the largest employer in the state of Washington, a bill was passed by state legislators that put a five-year ban on the sale of Boeing's assets to pay off creditors. This act effectively nullified Pickens's bid, because his only way to repay the debt he would incur in buying the company was to sell off some of its assets.

SOCIAL RESPONSIBILITY AND ETHICS

One of an organization's primary goals is its obligation to operate in a socially responsible manner. This section examines corporate social responsibility and the related area of managerial ethics.

■ Corporate Social Responsibility

Our society grants considerable freedom to business organizations. In return, businesses are expected to operate in a manner consistent with society's interests. **Social responsibility** refers to the expectation that business firms should act in the public interest. Certainly, businesses have always been expected to provide employment for individuals and to provide goods and services for customers. But social responsibility implies more than that. Today, society expects business to help preserve the environment, to sell safe products, to treat its employees equitably, to be truthful with its customers, and, in some cases, to go even further by training the hard-core unemployed, contributing to education and the arts, and helping revitalize urban slum areas.

Some observers, ranging from Adam Smith to Milton Friedman, have argued that social responsibility should not be part of management's decision-making process.[45] Friedman has maintained that business functions best when it sticks to its primary mission—producing goods and services within society's legal restrictions. In other words, its sole responsibility is to attempt to maximize returns. When it goes further than that by tackling social problems, business is spending money that should more properly be returned to its stockholders. The stockholders, who have rightfully earned the money, should be able to spend that money as they see fit, and their spending priorities may differ from those of business.

In reality, however, business is part of society, and its actions have both economic and social ramifications. It would be practically impossible to isolate the business decisions of corporations from their economic and social consequences. For instance, Federal Express's insistence that its South African partner, XPS Services, employ a 50/50 ratio of minority and white managers and Microsoft's development of an internship program for South Africans at its U.S. headquarters advance the social aims of both the South African and the U.S. governments.[46]

In fact, top managers may find a number of areas where their interests, various stakeholders' interests, and society's interests are mutually compatible. For example, a firm that pollutes the atmosphere because it fails to purchase costly antipollution equipment is harming not only society but also, ultimately, its own stakeholders. With a polluted environment, the quality of life of the firm's stockholders, directors, managers, employees, suppliers, customers, and creditors suffers. As another example, if businesses do not contribute to the education of young people, their recruitment efforts will suffer and they will eventually experience a decline in the quality of their work force. This result benefits no group of stakeholders.

Many government regulations over business operations came into being because some firms refused to be socially responsible. Had organizations not damaged the environment, sold unsafe products, discriminated against some employees, and engaged in untruthful advertising, laws in these areas would not have been necessary. The threat of ever more government regulation exists unless companies operate in a manner consistent with society's well-being.

Ideally, then, firms that are socially responsible are those that are able to operate profitably while simultaneously benefiting society. But realistically, it is not always clear exactly what is good for society. For example, society's needs for high employment and the production of desired goods and services must be balanced against the pollution and industrial wastes that are generated by these operations. Despite these difficulties, however, many firms in

STRATEGIC INSIGHT

Social Responsibility at GM

Each year, General Motors publishes a *Public Interest Report* detailing its corporate activities in the area of social responsibility. Although describing all of these activities would require several pages, a few of the areas in which GM is involved are listed here.

- A corporationwide UAW–GM education program publishes *Straight Talk,* a magazine intended to educate teenagers about AIDS and HIV infection.
- GM offers hourly and salaried employees a Tuition Assistance Plan for improving specific skills or even for pursuing studies not related to their jobs.
- GM has presented a program called "Skilled Trades and Engineering: Explore the Possibilities" to over two hundred thousand junior and senior high school students, especially minorities and young women. The program attempts to enhance understanding of the rewards and opportunities in engineering and skilled trades.
- GM donates an average of $35 million annually in cash grants, scholarship assistance, and equipment to colleges and universities.
- Since 1978, the General Motors Cancer Research Foundation has recognized scientists throughout the world for their achievements in the detection, prevention, and treatment of cancer.
- GM was the sole sponsor of "The Civil War," a widely acclaimed (and widely watched) ten-hour special that appeared on PBS television stations in 1990 and 1991.
- Since 1970, GM has used its Motor Enterprises, Inc., subsidiary to provide start-up capital for new minority businesses.
- GM's Minority Supplier Development Program has been, since 1968, the largest of its kind in the nation. In 1989, for example, GM purchased $1.15 billion in materials and services from minority suppliers. As part of this program, GM provides consulting and training programs to aid potential minority suppliers in receiving GM's business.

SOURCES: *General Motors Public Interest Report 1990* (Detroit: General Motors Corporation, 1990).

their annual reports express, at least in general terms, how they are socially responsible. General Motors, for instance, has published an annual *Public Interest Report* for over twenty years. A recent issue described GM's efforts in such areas as clean air, ozone depletion, global warming, waste management, automotive safety, minority programs, philanthropic activities, higher-quality products, and greater operating efficiency.

■ Managerial Ethics

Closely related to issues of corporate social responsibility are the ethics of individual managers. **Ethics** refers to standards of conduct and moral judgment—that is, whether managers' decisions and behaviors are right or wrong. (Table 3.2 presents two companies' views of ethical behavior.) What is morally right or wrong, of course, has been argued since the beginning of civilization, and as we might expect, there are few generally accepted global standards of ethical behavior. Even in the same nation, various people may look at ethical issues from different perspectives. Over the past several years, for example, many American corporations have "restructured" to become more competitive. Part of the restructuring process inevitably involves mass layoffs of employees. Is it right to lay off employees so that a company can compete more effectively with foreign firms and—in essence—assure its survival, or is it

Table 3.2 **Codes of Ethics**

A Large Business: Electronic Data Systems (EDS)

We conduct EDS' business in accordance with both the letter and spirit of the applicable laws of the United States and of those foreign countries in which EDS does business. We will conduct our business in the center of the field of ethical behavior—not along the sidelines, skirting the boundaries. . . . We must be honest in all our relationships and must avoid even the appearance of illegal or unethical conduct. For example, no employee of EDS will give or receive bribes or kickbacks; make improper political contributions; abuse proprietary or trade secret information, whether EDS' or our suppliers', business partners' or customers'; or misuse the company's funds and assets. . . .

The success of EDS rests directly on the quality of our people and our services. The integrity of all our people is an essential part of this quality that we offer to our customers. If our integrity ever became suspect, the future of EDS would be in jeopardy. . . .

When in doubt, measure your conduct against this Golden Rule of Business Ethics: Could you do business in complete trust with someone who acts the way you do? The answer must be YES.

A Small Business: Schilling's Enterprises (operates automobile dealerships in Tennessee and Arkansas and a heating/air-conditioning distributorship in Alabama)

Schilling's Guiding Principles:

- Practice honesty, integrity and fairness in everything we do.
- Assure every customer receives value, quality, and satisfaction.
- Create an environment in which our employees can succeed.
- Return to the community a share of the success we experience.
- Consistently promote these principles through our Christian behavior.

*Excerpted from *EDS Code of Conduct,* copyright © 1990, EDS, Dallas, Texas. Reprinted with permission.

wrong to put people with family and financial responsibilities and obligations out of work?

Ethical behavior can be viewed in several different ways. First, it may be considered from the perspective of self-interest. Adam Smith proposed that if each individual pursued his or her own economic self-interests, society as a whole would benefit. Milton Friedman, as mentioned earlier, believed that firms that attempt to maximize their returns within the legal regulations of society behave ethically.

Smith and Friedman viewed ethics economically, but Charles Darwin approached the issue from a biological perspective. In this sense, ethics can be explained implicitly in terms of survival of the fittest. Some species survive at the expense of other species. The survivors are those who are either instinctively or deterministically able to structure compatible fits with their environments. Ethical behavior, in a Darwinian sense, then, may encompass survival of one at the expense of the destruction of another. Hence, self-interest is at the heart of the approaches of Darwin, Smith, and Friedman. It is ethical to take care of oneself.

A second way of viewing ethics also involves the concept of self-interest, but in a broader sense. From this perspective, if an individual always promotes his or her interests at the expense of others, eventually the individual will be isolated by others. Selfish children find themselves without playmates, just as selfish managers are unable to secure the cooperation of their peers or supervisor. Hence, individuals should be concerned with the welfare of others because it serves their own interests in the long run.

A third common perspective of ethics bases the concepts of right and wrong on religious beliefs. In the United States, the strongest religious tradition is the Judeo–Christian heritage, although other religious viewpoints also prevail. From this perspective, it is "God's will" for individuals to behave in ways that benefit others. Behaving in a correct manner involves treating other people as one would wish to be treated. The concept of selfishness is frowned upon, and individuals are cautioned against ignoring the plight of others who are less fortunate.

Another view of ethics differs from all of the preceding by holding that human beings are inherently concerned with others. This concern is not based on either selfish or religious reasons but is simply a natural condition of humankind. In wars, soldiers help the wounded at the expense of their own lives. In natural disasters, individuals sacrifice their own lives in attempts to save others. Such naturally unselfish behavior is not without precedent, for it also occurs outside the domain of human beings. Certain species of animals, such as elephants, dolphins, and bison, routinely show great concern for the welfare of their family members, even to the point of protecting them with their own lives.

However ethical behavior is viewed, evidence exists that ethical operations may be related to organizational success. For instance, in certain parts of the country, Quaker or Mennonite entrepreneurs are often successful because of their reputations for being conscientious, reliable, trustworthy, and willing to stand behind their firms' products or services. Some research also reveals that enterprises with high ethical and social standards tend to be more profitable than companies lacking in those areas.[47] For example, James Burke, CEO of Johnson & Johnson, compiled a list of major firms known for their high ethical standards. Included were such corporations as Coca-Cola, Deere, Gerber, IBM, Johnson & Johnson, Kodak, J. C. Penney, Xerox, and 3M. From 1950 to 1990, the market value of this group grew at an annual rate of 11.3 percent while the annual growth rate for Dow Jones Industrials during that same period was 6.2 percent.[48] Other evidence even suggests that investors shun companies that are not socially and ethically responsible because they consider them to be risky investments.[49] And some institutional investors invest only in stocks that represent firms known for their high social and ethical standards. In summary, behavior that is ethically considerate of other stakeholders and socially responsible makes good business sense.

SUMMARY

Organizations are founded for a particular purpose, known as the organization's mission. The mission, at the corporate level, is stated in fairly broad terms but is sufficiently precise to give direction to the organization. At the business unit level, the mission is narrower in scope and more clearly defined. It is essential that an organization carefully understand its mission, because a clear sense of purpose is necessary for an organization to establish appropriate goals.

Goals represent the desired general ends toward which organizational efforts are directed. From the organization's goals, management formulates objectives—specific, verifiable versions of goals. However, various stakeholder groups, because of their own interests, will desire different goals for the firm. Because of the diversity of these interests, top management faces the difficult task of attempting to reconcile and satisfy the interests of each of the stakeholder groups while pursuing its own set of goals.

Controversy exists over the extent to which top management actually attempts to maximize return on the stockholders' investment. One viewpoint argues that top managers pursue strategies, such as increasing the size of their firm, that ultimately increase their own rewards. Another proposes that top managers in firms in which ownership of the corporation is concentrated will attempt to maximize profits. A third school theorizes that top management's interests coincide with those of the firm's stockholders for various reasons.

Controversy also exists over the extent to which boards of directors serve as "creatures of the CEO" versus the degree to which they represent the interests of the stockholders. Certainly, recent legal trends have emphasized the boards' stewardship of the stockholders' interests.

Stakeholder groups are affected by corporate takeovers. Their impact differs, depending upon whether the takeover is friendly or unfriendly and whether it is engineered by outsiders or insiders. Takeovers, from a societal viewpoint, have both defenders and critics.

Of considerable concern in the strategic decision-making process are the concepts of corporate social responsibility and managerial ethics. Social responsibility refers to the extent to which business firms should act in the public interest while conducting their operations. Ethical considerations involve questions of moral judgment in managerial decision making and behavior. Society today demands that companies operate in a socially responsible manner and that managers exhibit high ethical behavior in their conduct.

KEY CONCEPTS

Employee stock ownership plan (ESOP) A formal program, administered by a trust, that transfers ownership of a corporation—through shares of stock—to its employees. The program is usually initiated by the organization's owners for financial, tax, and/or motivational reasons.

Ethics Standards of conduct and moral judgment.

Goals Desired general ends toward which efforts are directed.

Leveraged buyout (LBO) A takeover in which the acquiring party borrows funds to purchase the firm. The resulting interest payments and principal are paid back by funds generated from operations and/or the sale of company assets.

Mission The reason for an organization's existence.

Mission statement A broadly defined but enduring statement of purpose that identifies the scope of an organization's operations and its offerings to the various stakeholders.

Objective A specific, verifiable, and often quantified version of a goal.

Raider An individual who attempts to take over a company because he or she believes that its management can be significantly improved. Raiders purchase a large number of shares in the target firm either to force a change in top management personnel or to manage the firm themselves.

Social responsibility The expectation that business firms should act in the public interest.

Takeover The purchase of a significant number of shares in a firm by an individual, a group of investors, or another organization. Takeovers may be friendly—in which both the buyer and seller desire the transaction—or unfriendly—in which the target firm resists the sale.

DISCUSSION QUESTIONS

1. Do corporate-level missions and business unit missions usually change over time? Why or why not?

2. Explain the relationship between an organization's mission and its strategy.

3. Explain the difference between a goal and an objective. Give an example of each, different from those given in the text.

4. Why is it essential that objectives be verifiable?

5. Why do various groups that are stakeholders in the same organization have different goals? Should they not all be pulling together in the same direction?

6. How might the goals of top management differ from those of the firm's board of directors? How might they be similar?

7. What might be the impact of a takeover on such stakeholder groups as the acquired company's stockholders, top management, and operating employees?

8. What are the risks for the acquiring party in a leveraged buyout?

9. Explain the relationship between corporate strategy and social responsibility.

10. Explain the relationship between corporate strategy and managerial ethics.

STRATEGIC MANAGEMENT EXERCISES

1. Select a particular type of business that you may wish to start.
   a. Develop a written mission statement for that business.
   b. Construct a set of goals for the business.
   c. From the set of goals developed in part (b), formulate specific, verifiable objectives.
   d. Devise a statement of social responsibility for the business.

2. Select a company that has a written mission statement. Evaluate its mission statement along each of the following criteria:

    a. Is the mission statement all-encompassing yet relatively brief?
    b. Does the mission statement delineate, in broad terms, what products or services the firm is to offer?
    c. Does the mission statement define the company's geographical operating parameters (whether it will conduct business locally, regionally, nationally, or internationally)?
    d. Is the mission statement consistent as it moves from the corporate level to the business unit level?
    e. Is the mission statement consistent with the company's actual activities and competitive prospects at the corporate level? (For instance, Chrysler's mission of using its technology to operate both in the automobile industry and in the defense industry failed to match its competitive stance. Facing powerful international competition in the automobile industry required Chrysler to concentrate totally on that industry. As a result, it was forced to sell its nonvehicle businesses.)
    f. Is the mission statement consistent with the company's actual activities and competitive prospects at the business unit level? (For instance, General Motors' mission of providing quality outputs matches the operation of its Electronic Data Systems business unit, but the quality of its vehicle products has been questioned over the years by many industry observers and customers.)

NOTES

1. J.A. Pearce II, "The Company Mission as a Strategic Tool," *Sloan Management Review* 23 (Spring 1982):15.
2. J.K. Clemens, "A Lesson from 431 B.C.," *Fortune,* 13 October 1986, p. 164.
3. G. Brooks, "Some Concerns Find That the Push to Diversify Was a Costly Mistake," *The Wall Street Journal,* 2 October 1984.
4. M. Schrage, "Consultant's Maxim for Management: Ignore Markets, Build on Competence," *The Washington Post,* 17 May 1991.
5. For an example of his early work, see R. Nader, *Unsafe at Any Speed: Design and Dangers of the American Automobile* (New York: Grossman, 1964).
6. D.O. McKee, R. Varadarajan, and W.M. Pride, "Strategic Adaptability and Firm Performance: A Market Contingent Perspective," *Journal of Marketing* 53 (1989): 21–35.
7. H.A. Simon, "On the Concept of Organizational Goal," *Administrative Science Quarterly* 9 (1964): 1–22; J. Pfeffer and G. Salancik, *The External Control of Organizations* (New York: Harper & Row, 1978).
8. R.M. Cyert and J.G. March, *A Behavioral Theory of the Firm* (Englewood Cliffs, N.J.: Prentice-Hall, 1963); J.G. March and H.A. Simon, *Organizations* (New York: John Wiley & Sons, 1958).
9. M. Aoki, *The Co-Operative Game Theory of the Firm* (Oxford, England: Clarendon Press, 1984); W. Baumol, *Business Behavior, Value and Growth* (New York: Macmillan, 1967); J.K. Galbraith, *Economics and the Public Purpose* (Boston: Houghton Mifflin,

1973); H.A. Simon, "Theories of Decision Making in Economics and Behavioral Science," *American Economic Review* 49 (1959): 253–283; O.E. Williamson, "Dynamic Stochastic Theory of Managerial Behavior," in A. Phillips and O.E. Williams, eds., *Prices: Issues in Theory, Practice and Public Policy* (Philadelphia: University of Pennsylvania Press, 1967).

10. H.A. Simon, "The Compensation of Executives," *Sociometry* 20 (1957): 32–35.
11. D.R. Roberts, "A General Theory of Executive Compensation Based on Statistically Tested Propositions," *Quarterly Journal of Economics* 20 (1956): 270–294.
12. K.J. Murphy, "Corporate Performance and Managerial Remuneration: An Empirical Analysis," *Journal of Accounting and Economics* 7 (1985): 11–42; Aoki, *Co-Operative Game Theory;* A.A. Berle and G.C. Means, *The Modern Corporation and Private Property,* rev. ed. (New York: Harcourt, Brace & World, 1968).
13. G.P. Baker, M.C. Jensen, and K.J. Murphy, "Compensation and Incentives: Practice vs. Theory," *Journal of Finance* 43 (1988): 609.
14. D.J. Teece, "Towards an Economic Theory of the Multiproduct Firm," *Journal of Economic Behavior and Organization* 3 (1982): 39–63.
15. H.A. Simon, *Administrative Behavior* (New York: Macmillan, 1957).
16. L. Gomez-Mejia, H. Tosi, and T. Hinkin, "Managerial Control, Performance, and Executive Compensation," *Academy of Management Journal* 30 (1987): 51–70; M.C. Jensen and W.H. Meckling, "Theory of the Firm: Managerial Behavior, Agency Costs and Ownership Structure," *Journal of Financial Economics* 3 (1976): 305–360; D. Leech, "Ownership Concentration and the Theory of the Firm: A Sample Game Theoretical Approach," *Journal of Industrial Economics* 35 (1987): 225–240; W.A. McEachern, *Managerial Control and Performance* (Lexington, Mass.: Lexington Books, 1975); G.R. Salancik and J. Pfeffer, "The Effects of Ownership and Performance on Executive Tenure in U.S. Corporations," *Academy of Management Journal* 23 (1980): 653–664.
17. C.W. Hill and S.A. Snell, "Effects of Ownership Structure and Control on Corporate Productivity," *Academy of Management Journal* 32 (1989): 25–46; Leech, "Ownership Concentration"; Salancik and Pfeffer, "Effects of Ownership and Performance."
18. O.E. Williamson, *Economic Organization: Firms, Markets and Policy Control* (New York: New York University Press, 1986), pp. 6–27.
19. Gomez-Mejia, Tosi, and Hinkin, "Managerial Control, Performance"; McEachern, *Managerial Control and Performance.*
20. W.G. Lewellen and B. Huntsman, "Managerial Pay and Corporate Performance," *American Economic Review* 60 (1970): 710–720.
21. R.T. Masson, "Executive Motivations, Earnings, and Consequent Equity Performance," *Journal of Political Economy* 79 (1971): 1278–1292.
22. E.F. Fama, "Agency Problems and the Theory of the Firm," *Journal of Political Economy* 88 (1980): 288–307.
23. Y. Amihud, J.Y. Kamin, and J. Romen, "Managerialism, Ownerism, and Risk," *Journal of Banking and Finance* 7 (1983): 189–196.
24. Fama, "Agency Problems."
25. J. Child, *The Business Enterprise in Modern Industrial Society* (London: Collier-Macmillan, 1969).
26. D.R. James and M. Soref, "Profit Constraints on Managerial Autonomy: Managerial Theory and the Unmaking of the Corporation President," *American Sociological Review* 46 (1981): 1–18.
27. Ibid., p. 3.

28. Ibid.
29. S.A. Zahra and J.A. Pearce II, "Boards of Directors and Corporate Financial Performance: A Review and Integrative Model," *Journal of Management* 15 (1989): 292.
30. J. Bacon, *Corporate Directorship Practices: Membership and Committees of the Board* (New York: The Conference Board, 1973); J.C. Baker, *Directors and Their Functions* (Boston: Harvard University Press, 1945); Berle and Means, *Modern Corporation;* C.C. Brown and E.E. Smith, *The Director Looks at His Job* (New York: Columbia University Press, 1957); M.T. Copeland and A.R. Towl, *The Board of Directors and Business Management* (Boston: Harvard University Press, 1947); E.J. Epstein, *Who Owns the Corporation? Management vs. Shareholders* (New York: Priority Press, 1986); J.M. Juran and J.K. Louden, *The Corporate Director* (New York: American Management Association, 1966); H. Koontz, *The Board of Directors and Effective Management* (New York: McGraw-Hill, 1967); J.K. Louden, *The Director: A Professional's Guide to Effective Board Work* (New York: Amacom, 1982); M.L. Mace, *Directors: Myth and Reality* (Boston: Harvard University Press, 1971); O.E. Williamson, *The Economics of Discretionary Behavior: Managerial Objectives in a Theory of the Firm* (Englewood Cliffs, N.J.: Prentice-Hall, 1964); S.G. Winter, "Economic Natural Selection and the Theory of the Firm," *Yale Economic Essays* 4 (1964): 225–231.
31. A. Patton and J.C. Baker, "Why Won't Directors Rock the Boat?" *Harvard Business Review* 65, no. 6 (1987): 10–18.
32. L. Herzel, R.W. Shepro, and L. Katz, "Next-to-the-Last Word on Endangered Directors," *Harvard Business Review* 65, no. 1 (1987): 38.
33. Zahra and Pearce, "Boards of Directors," p. 295.
34. S.P. Sherman, "Pushing Corporate Boards to Be Better," *Fortune,* 18 July 1988, p. 60.
35. G.S. Crystal and F.T. Vincent, Jr., "Take the Mystery Out of CEO Pay," *Fortune,* 24 April 1989, p. 220.
36. M. Galen, "A Seat on the Board Is Getting Hotter," *Business Week,* 3 July 1989, p. 72; Sherman, "Pushing Corporate Boards," p. 62.
37. W.E. Green, "Directors' Insurance: How Good a Shield?" *The Wall Street Journal,* 14 August 1989.
38. B.D. Fromson, "The Big Owners Roar," *Fortune,* 30 July 1990, pp. 66–78.
39. J. Pfeffer, "Size, Composition, and Function of Hospital Boards of Directors: A Study of Organization-Environment Linkage," *Administrative Science Quarterly* 18 (1973): 349–364; J. Pfeffer and Salancik, *External Control of Organizations;* and K.G. Provan, "Board Power and Organizational Effectiveness Among Human Service Agencies," *Academy of Management Journal* 23 (1980): 221–236.
40. M.S. Mizruchi, "Who Controls Whom? An Examination of the Relation Between Management and Board of Directors in Large American Corporations," *Academy of Management Review* 8 (1983): 426–435.
41. Sherman, "Pushing Corporate Boards," p. 58.
42. Ibid., p. 60.
43. T.D. Schellhardt, "Managing," *The Wall Street Journal,* 19 October 1989.
44. T.B. Pickens, Jr., "Professions of a Short-termer," *Harvard Business Review* 64, no. 3 (1986): 75.
45. A. Smith, *An Inquiry into the Nature and Causes of the Wealth of Nations* (Chicago: Encyclopaedia Britannica, 1952); M. Friedman, "The Social Responsibility of Business Is to Increase Its Profits," *New York Times Magazine,* 13 September 1970, pp. 33, 122–125.

46. B. Bremner, A. Fine, and J. Weber, "Doing the Right Thing in South Africa?" *Business Week,* 27 April 1992, pp. 60, 64.
47. E.H. Bowman and M. Haire, "Strategic Posture Towards Corporate Social Responsibility," *California Management Review* 18 (Winter 1975): 49–58.
48. K. Labich, "The New Crisis in Business Ethics," *Fortune,* 20 April 1992, p. 172.
49. E.H. Bowman, "Corporate Social Responsibility and the Investor," *Journal of Contemporary Business* 2 (1973): 21–43.

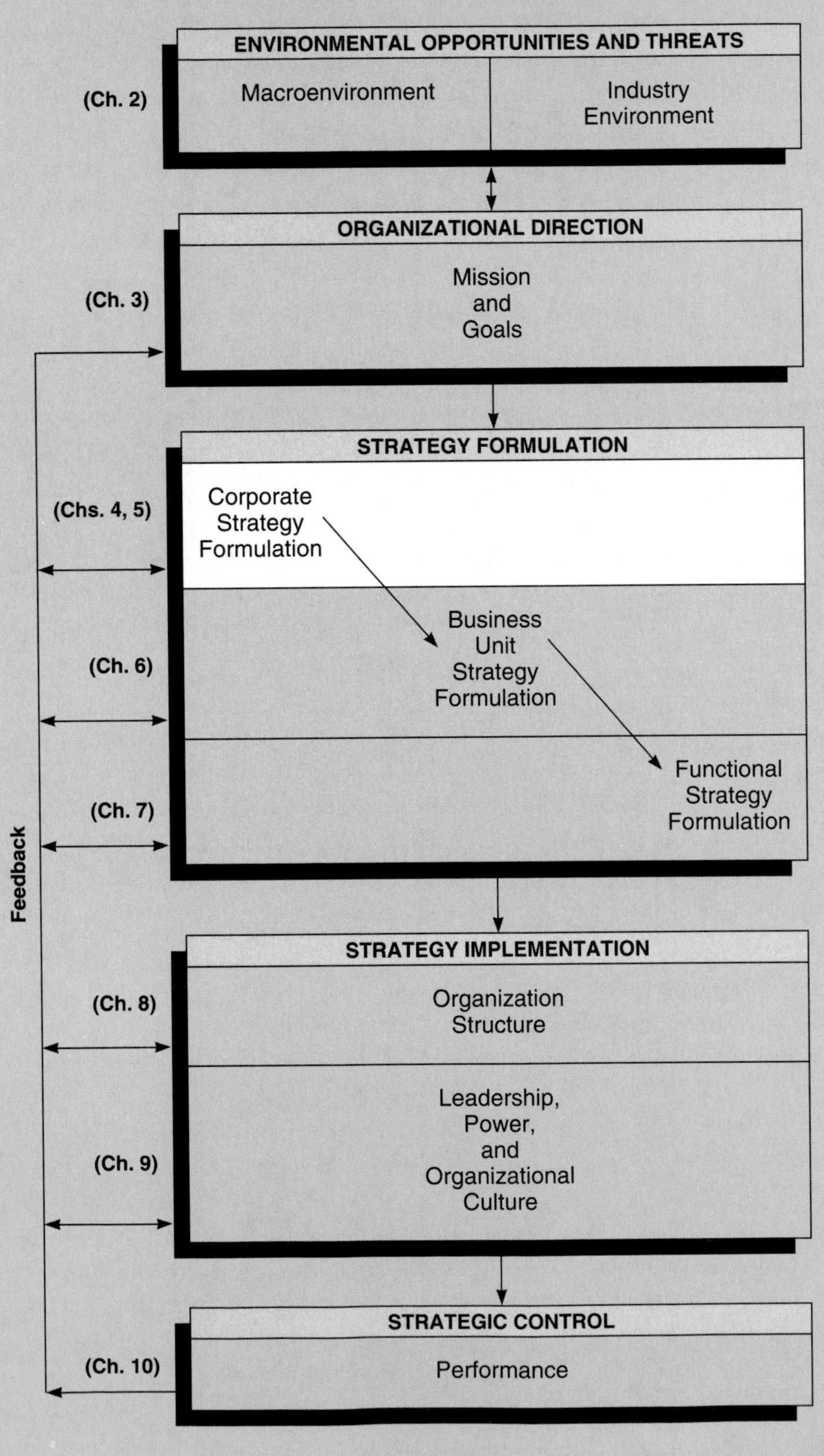
STRATEGIC MANAGEMENT MODEL
ENVIRONMENTAL OPPORTUNITIES AND THREATS
(Ch. 2)
Macroenvironment
Industry Environment
ORGANIZATIONAL DIRECTION
(Ch. 3)
Mission and Goals
STRATEGY FORMULATION
(Chs. 4, 5)
Corporate Strategy Formulation
(Ch. 6)
Business Unit Strategy Formulation
(Ch. 7)
Functional Strategy Formulation
Feedback
STRATEGY IMPLEMENTATION
(Ch. 8)
Organization Structure
(Ch. 9)
Leadership, Power, and Organizational Culture
STRATEGIC CONTROL
(Ch. 10)
Performance

Corporate-Level Strategies

Once the organization's mission, goals, and objectives are delineated, as was discussed in the preceding chapter, top management can formulate the firm's strategy. Strategies exist at three levels: the corporate level, the business unit level, and the functional level. The focus of this chapter and the one following it is **corporate-level strategy**—the strategy top management formulates for the overall company. The subsequent two chapters will discuss business unit and functional strategies. Although each of these chapters emphasizes strategy at a separate level, in reality, all three levels are closely intertwined.

At the corporate level, the basic strategic question facing top management is, In what particular businesses or industries should we be operating? The answer to this question depends upon the firm's particular strengths and weaknesses and the opportunities and threats posed by its environment. This chapter explores these topics.

STRATEGIC ALTERNATIVES

Before selecting a specific corporate-level strategy, top management must conduct an explicit analysis of the firm and its environment. This analysis helps management develop a particular corporate profile (to determine in which businesses and industries to operate). Given the corporate profile, management must decide whether the firm should pursue a strategy of growth, stability, retrenchment, or some combination of these alternatives. This section explores these vital issues.

■ S.W.O.T. Analysis

Underlying any successful selection of strategies is an analysis of the firm's internal strengths and weaknesses and the opportunities and threats that are posed by the external environment. This process of examining the firm and its environment is termed **S.W.O.T. analysis** (strengths, weaknesses, opportunities, and threats). The framework presented in Table 4.1 identifies many of the variables that management should analyze.

The point of the analysis is to enable the firm to position itself to take advantage of particular opportunities in the environment and to avoid or

Table 4.1 **Framework for S.W.O.T. Analysis**

Sources of Possible Environmental Opportunities and Threats			
Economic forces	Political-legal forces	Social forces	Technological forces
Industry forces			
Possible Organizational Strengths and Weaknesses			
Access to raw materials	Distribution	Management	Purchasing
Advertising	Economies of scale	Manufacturing and operations	Quality control
Board of directors	Environmental scanning	Market share	Research & development
Brand names	Financial resources	Organizational structure	Selling
Channel management	Forecasting	Physical facilities/ equipment	Strategic control
Company reputation	Government lobbying	Product/service differentiation	Strategy formulation
Computer information system	Human resources	Product/service quality	Strategy implementation
Control systems	Inventory management	Promotion	Technology
Costs	Labor relations	Public relations	
Customer loyalty	Leadership		
Decision making	Location		

minimize environmental threats. In doing so, the organization attempts to emphasize its strengths and moderate the impact of its weaknesses. The analysis is also useful for uncovering strengths that have not yet been fully utilized and in identifying weaknesses that can be corrected. Matching information about the environment with a knowledge of the organization's capabilities enables management to formulate realistic strategies for attaining its goals.

A firm's *resources* constitute its strengths and weaknesses.[1] They include human resources (the experience, capabilities, knowledge, skills, and judgment of all the firm's employees), organizational resources (the firm's systems and processes, including its strategies, structure, culture, purchasing/materials management, production/operations, financial base, research and development, marketing, information systems, and control systems), and physical resources (plant and equipment, geographic locations, access to raw materials, distribution network, and technology). In an optimal setting, all three types of resources work together to give a firm a **sustained competitive advantage,** as illustrated in Figure 4.1. Sustained competitive advantage refers to valuable strategies that cannot be fully duplicated by the firm's competitors and that result in high financial returns over a lengthy period of time.

Just as Chapter 2 explored environmental opportunities and threats, the following paragraphs will briefly examine each of the three types of resources that comprise a firm's strengths and/or weaknesses.

Human Resources

Because even the most superb organizational and physical resources are useless without a talented work force of managers and employees, we place most

Route to Sustained Competitive Advantage **Figure 4.1**

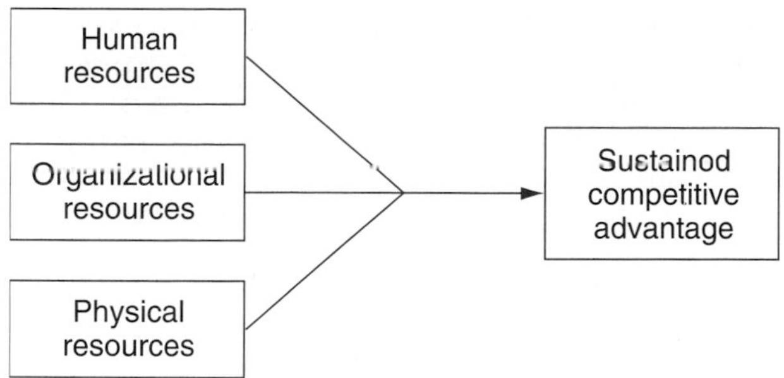

of our emphasis on a firm's human resources. These resources can be examined at three levels—the board of directors; top management; and middle management, supervisors, and employees.

Board of Directors. At the top of the human resource hierarchy sits the board of directors. Because board members are becoming increasingly involved in corporate affairs, they can materially influence the firm's effectiveness. In examining their strengths and weaknesses, the following questions may be asked.

- What contributions do the board members bring to the firm? Strong board members possess considerable experience, knowledge, and judgment, as well as valuable outside political connections.
- Are the members internal or external, and how widely do they represent the firm's stakeholders? Although it is common for several top managers to be board members, a disproportionate representation of them diminishes the identity of the board as a group apart from top management. And, ideally, board members should represent diverse stakeholders, including minorities, creditors, customers, and the local community. A diverse board membership can contribute to the health of the firm.
- Do the members own significant shares of the firm's securities? Significant stock ownership may increase the board's responsiveness to stockholders, while significant bond holdings may enhance its concern with the firm's creditworthiness.
- How long have the members served on the board? Long-term stability enables board members to gain knowledge about the firm, but some turnover is beneficial since new members often can bring a fresh perspective to strategic issues.

Top Management. The organization's top executives must establish and communicate a vision for the firm that encompasses the needs and desires of the firm's various stakeholders. Ideally, then, top managers should assume the role of "selfless stewards" concerned primarily with attaining stakeholders' goals.[2] Several questions might be asked in assessing the strengths and weaknesses of any firm's top management.

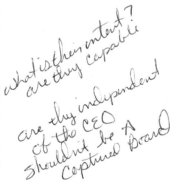

- Who are the key top managers, and what are their strengths and weaknesses in job experience, managerial style, decision-making capability, team-building, and understanding of the business? There are advantages, for instance, in having executives who have an intimate knowledge of the firm and its industry. On the other hand, managers from diverse backgrounds may generate innovative strategic ideas. And, of course, an organization's management needs may change as the firm grows and matures. For instance, start-up firms are often headed by entrepreneurs who are innovative but may be weak in administrative abilities. More mature firms need strong administration but must continue to be innovative.
- How long have the key top managers been with the firm? Lengthy tenure can mean consistent and stable strategy development and implementation, yet low turnover may breed conformity, complacency, and a failure to explore new opportunities.
- What are top management's strategic strengths and weaknesses? Some executives may excel in innovative strategy formulation, for instance, but may be weak in implementing strategy. Some may spend considerable time interacting with external constituents, while others concentrate on internal stakeholders and operations.

Middle Management, Supervisors, and Employees. A firm can have brilliant top managers and board members but if its work force is less than top-notch, even the most ingenious strategies cannot be implemented effectively. Each firm's human resources are unique. That uniqueness stems not only from the fact that every organization employs a different set of human beings, but also from the specific synergies that result from combining each firm's human resources with its particular organizational and physical resources. In this context, a firm's personnel and their knowledge, abilities, commitment, and performance tend to reflect the firm's human resource programs. These factors can be explored by asking several key questions about those programs to ascertain the strengths and weaknesses of the organization's managers and employees.

- Does the organization have a comprehensive human resource planning program? Developing such a program requires that the firm estimate its personnel needs, including types of positions and requisite qualifications, for the next several years based on its strategic plan. Many organizations do little planning in this area, and such short-term thinking rarely results in effective operations.
- How much emphasis does the organization place on training and development programs? Firms that ignore personnel training and development are virtually doomed to stagnation.
- What is the organization's personnel turnover rate compared to the rest of the industry? High turnover rates, compared to those of competitors, generally reflect personnel problems, such as poor management–employee relations, low compensation or benefits, weak personnel policies, or low job satisfaction due to other causes.
- How much emphasis does the firm place on performance appraisal? Effective programs provide accurate feedback to managers and employees, link rewards to actual performance, show managers and employees how to improve performance, and comply with all equal employment opportunity programs.

- How well does the organization manage a work force that increasingly reflects society's changing demographics? Most firms are only now beginning to evaluate and adjust practices that were designed for yesterday's more homogeneous work force. Those firms that lead the way have a decided advantage in attracting and retaining a highly qualified work force for tomorrow.

Organizational Resources

The assessment of organizational resources basically hinges on the question of whether the resources are properly aligned with the firm's strategies and whether they are sufficient for the strategies' implementation. While the issues are too numerous to cover completely here, some of the key questions are discussed.

- Are the corporate, business unit, and functional strategies consistent with the organization's mission and goals? The mission, goals, and strategies must be compatible and reflect a clear sense of identity and purpose.
- Are the organization's corporate, business unit, and functional strategies consistent with one another? These three levels of strategy must be closely intertwined and highly consistent. Hence, managers at the corporate, business unit, and functional level should be represented at each level of strategic planning. Recall that corporate strategies should influence business unit strategies, which, in turn, should influence functional strategies. But, at the same time, functional strategies affect business unit strategies, which then affect corporate strategies. So the influence is two-way.
- Is the organization's formal structure appropriate for implementing its strategy? The content of Chapter 8 is entirely devoted to this topic.
- Are the organization's decision-making processes effective in implementing its strategies? Issues of centralization versus decentralization are covered in the following chapter, and Chapter 9 includes an analysis of leadership team processes.
- Is the organization's culture consistent with its strategy? The latter part of Chapter 9 focuses on the role of culture in strategy formulation and implementation.
- How effective are the organization's strategic control processes? Chapter 10 examines this crucial issue.

Physical Resources

Although the types of physical resources possessed by firms differ considerably from one organization to another (consider, for example, the different physical plants required by an automobile maker versus a management consulting firm), some general questions assessing the strengths and weaknesses of physical resources might take the following form.

- Does the organization possess up-to-date technology? Although cutting-edge technology is no guarantee of success, competitors who have superior technology and know how to use it have a decided advantage in the marketplace.
- Does the organization possess adequate capacity? Although a continual backlog of orders indicates market acceptance of a firm's product, it may

conceal the lost business and declining customer goodwill that accompany insufficient capacity. On the other hand, numerous firms have restructured their operations in recent years to eliminate excess capacity that resulted from increased competition and/or economic recession.

- Is the organization's distribution network an efficient means of reaching customers? Note that distribution networks do not apply only to firms that manufacture products. American Airlines' domination of passenger gates at Dallas–Fort Worth Airport and United's similar control at O'Hare Field give both of these service companies a competitive advantage.
- Does the firm have reliable and cost-effective sources of supply? Suppliers who are unreliable, do not have effective quality control programs, or cannot control their costs well put the buying firm at a decided competitive disadvantage.
- Is the organization (and its branches) in an optimum geographic location? Appropriate location may depend on cost factors (land, building, and labor); the availability of skilled labor, natural resources, and sources of supply; customer convenience; and shipping costs.

What should be emphasized, according to resource-based theory, is the unique combination of human, organizational, and physical resources possessed by a firm. As the firm acquires additional resources, unique synergies occur between its new and existing resources. Because each firm already possesses a distinct combination of human, organizational, and physical resources, the particular types of synergies that occur will differ from one firm to another. For example, if the quality of a new resource in the external environment is represented by Z, once that resource is acquired by organization A the quality of the resource is transformed to ZA. If this resource were instead purchased by organization B, then Z's resultant quality would be transformed to ZB. ZB, of course, represents a qualitatively different value than ZA.

Corporate Profiles

S.W.O.T. analysis can help management determine in which business or businesses the firm should be operating. Broadly speaking, a firm may adopt any one of three corporate profiles: It can compete in one business or industry, in several related businesses or industries, or in several unrelated businesses or industries. Each profile has certain advantages and disadvantages.

By competing in only one industry, a firm benefits from the specialized knowledge that it derives from concentrating on a limited business arena. This knowledge can help firms offer better products or services and become more efficient in their operations. McDonald's, for instance, has been able to develop a steadily improved product line and maintain low per-unit cost of operations over the years by concentrating exclusively on the fast-food business. Wal-Mart has also benefited from operating only in the retailing industry. And Anheuser-Busch has limited its scope of operations largely to the brewing industry, from which it derives more than 80 percent of its sales and 90 percent of its profits.

Operating primarily in one industry, however, increases a firm's vulnerability to business cycles. Should industry attractiveness decline—through a decrease in consumer demand for the firm's products or an onslaught of severe competition from existing or new competitors—the firm's performance is likely to suffer.

Companies that compete in related businesses also face certain advantages and disadvantages. The primary advantage is that improvements in outputs and efficiencies in operations may be transferred from one business to another. For example, a number of operational and marketing strengths of Coca-Cola's soft-drink business have been applied to its Minute Maid fruit juice business. But firms operating in related areas may also face threats similar to those of single-business firms. A shrinkage in consumer demand or intensified price competition can adversely affect all of the firm's businesses.

This disadvantage can be overcome by operating in unrelated businesses. Rather than put all of its eggs in one basket or a few closely related baskets, the firm scatters its eggs around. So if one of the industries in which the company operates suffers a downturn, this decline in performance can be offset by increasing sales in the other unrelated industries in which the firm operates.

But operating in several unrelated industries is no panacea. Managing any large enterprise is a complicated endeavor, and that process becomes even more complex when it involves unrelated businesses. Well-known firms such as ITT, for example, have experienced performance problems in attempting to manage diverse and unrelated business units. In fact, ITT divested itself of a number of its unrelated business units to try to improve its performance.

As we have seen, each of the corporate profiles has its advantages and disadvantages. Deciding which profile is best suited for a particular company involves S.W.O.T. analysis. That is, comparing a company with its competitors by using the factors identified in Table 4.1 helps management develop the most appropriate profile. Note, however, that S.W.O.T. analysis is not a one-time occurrence. Systematic scanning of the environment and of the firm's strengths and weaknesses, vis-à-vis those of its competitors, helps management know when it is time to modify its corporate profile.

Once a particular profile has been adopted, over time it can be maintained or changed. In this context, top managers have four corporate-level strategies available to them. They may elect to pursue a strategy of growth, stability, retrenchment, or a combination of those. The available strategies are listed in Table 4.2.

S.W.O.T. analysis helps in determining which of these corporate strategies is most appropriate for a particular firm. In a broad sense, the firm's critical weaknesses or valuable strengths may be analyzed in the context of the abundant opportunities or critical threats posed by the macroenvironment and industry. This analysis is illustrated in Figure 4.2.

As shown in Figure 4.2, when a firm possesses valuable strengths and operates in an environment of abundant opportunities, a corporate growth strategy is appropriate. On the other hand, the corporate stability strategy is more suited for a firm that possesses moderate strengths in an environment of moderate opportunities. And a firm with critical weaknesses operating in a threatening environment will find a corporate retrenchment strategy most appropriate. Finally, a firm that operates several different businesses may require a combination of these strategies. One of its businesses, for instance, may need a growth strategy, another may be more suited for the stability strategy, and still another may require a retrenchment strategy. Each of these strategic alternatives is discussed in the following sections.

Table 4.2 **Corporate-Level Strategies**

1. Growth strategies
    a. Internal growth
    b. Mergers
    c. Acquisitions
        (1) Horizontal integration
        (2) Horizontal related acquisition
        (3) Horizontal unrelated (conglomerate) acquisition
        (4) Vertical related acquisition
        (5) Vertical unrelated acquisition
    d. Strategic alliances
2. Stability strategy
3. Retrenchment strategies
    a. Turnaround
    b. Divestment
    c. Liquidation
4. Combination strategies

Growth Strategies

Firms may select a **growth strategy** to increase their profits, sales, or market share. Growth may also be pursued to lower per-unit costs or to satisfy managerial motivations, as discussed in the following chapter. Regardless of the reason, growth may be attained in a variety of ways. The following subsections describe the key growth strategies firms can use.

Figure 4.2 **S.W.O.T. Analysis**

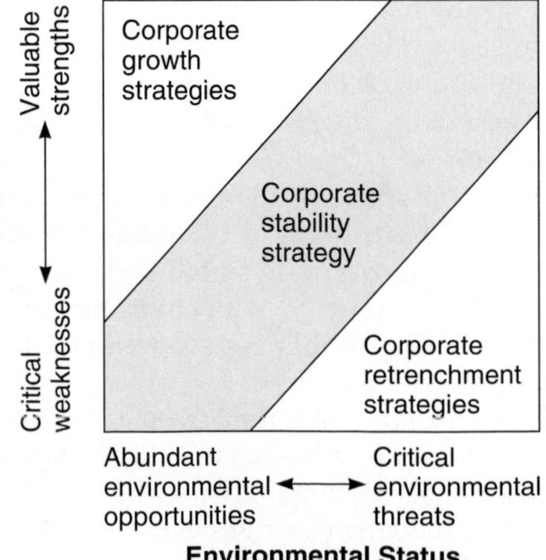

Internal Growth

Internal growth is achieved through increasing a firm's sales, production capacity, and work force. Some companies consciously pursue this route to growth rather than the alternative route of acquiring other firms. Their belief is that internal growth better preserves their organizational culture, efficiency, quality, and image. McDonald's, for instance, has never purchased other fast-food restaurant chains. To maintain its high standards for cleanliness, service, and product consistency, it has grown by granting franchises only to people who are willing to be trained in the McDonald's way.

Likewise, American Airlines prefers to grow internally. American was the only U.S.-based airline to expand its services to three continents (Europe, Asia, and South America) at once, and its chairman, Robert L. Crandall, was asked why American did not buy ailing Pan Am or TWA as a quick way to enter these overseas markets. He responded:

> We've always said we don't want to buy another airline. We don't want to acquire another airline's airplanes. We don't want another airline's people. . . .[3]

Internal growth not only includes growth of the same business, but it can also include the creation of new businesses, either in a horizontal or vertical direction. **Horizontal internal growth** involves creating new companies that operate in the same business as the original firm, in related businesses, or in unrelated businesses, as discussed later. **Vertical internal growth** refers to creating businesses within the firm's vertical channel of distribution and takes the form of supplier–customer relationships. For example, airlines normally purchase their in-flight meals from outside suppliers, such as Dobbs International, that prepare and deliver meals to the air carriers. However, United Airlines has created its own in-flight food service; hence, its food service business serves as a supplier to its in-house customer, the airline.

As already emphasized, internal growth helps preserve the organization's culture, efficiency, quality, and image. The chief disadvantage to internal growth, however, is the rising bureaucratic costs that generally accompany internal growth. United's in-flight food service, for example, requires its own management team, personnel procedures, accounting systems, and so on. Therefore, creating new businesses should only be undertaken when their benefits will exceed their costs.

Mergers

Many firms elect to grow through mergers. A **merger** occurs when two or more firms, usually of roughly similar sizes, combine into one through an exchange of stock. Mergers are undertaken to share resources and gain in competitive power. For example, Sperry and Burroughs merged to form Unisys several years ago in an attempt to compete more effectively against giant IBM in the computer industry.

Mergers are usually based on the core competencies of firms. **Core competencies** are the major strengths—present or potential—of organizations. Broadly speaking, core competencies can include operations excellence, superior technology, cutting edge research and development, effective marketing, and other strengths identified in Table 4.1. For example, two companies with **similar core competencies** in marketing may merge to strengthen their overall competitive position.

Alternatively, two firms may merge to combine **complementary core competencies.** A firm, for instance, that possesses a competency in its product distribution network but limited competence in research and development may merge with a firm that is a leader in research and development but weak in distribution. Each firm would obviously benefit from the merger.

The overall reason for a merger is to take advantage of the benefits of synergy. When the combination of two firms results in greater effectiveness and efficiency than the total yielded by them separately, then **synergy** has been attained. Synergy can result from either horizontal mergers, such as that between NCNB and C&S/Sovran (now named NationsBank), or from vertical mergers. The merger of Ocean Drilling and Exploration (an oil exploration and drilling firm) with Murphy Oil (a refiner) illustrates a vertical merger.

Either type of merger usually results in increased bureaucratic and coordination costs, so mergers should be undertaken only when the projected benefits exceed the merger's estimated costs.

Acquisitions

An **acquisition** takes place when one company acquires another company through a payment of cash or stock or some combination of the two. The acquiring firm may buy all or a percentage of the target company. Because acquisitions are both prevalent and controversial, they have been the focus of recent research.

In general, researchers have found that cash offers affect the acquiring firm's stock more favorably than do offers of common stock.[4] Additionally, the acquiring firm's stockholders are more likely to benefit if their firm makes an uncontested and unopposed bid for the target company.[5] An uncontested bid is one in which no other firms are seeking to acquire the target company. An uncontested bid is likely to cost the acquiring firm less because the lack of competitive bids keeps the acquisition price from rising. An unopposed bid is one in which neither the management nor the stockholders of the target company object to the acquisition. This situation is often referred to as a "friendly takeover." Unopposed bids are beneficial to the stockholders of the acquiring firm since they are usually less costly than "hostile takeovers" (acquisitions that are opposed by the target firm). Opposition to a takeover generally forces the acquiring company to "sweeten" the bid by offering to pay a higher price.

Acquisitions may be either horizontal or vertical. The following paragraphs discuss three kinds of horizontal takeovers and two types of vertical acquisitions.

Horizontal Integration. Many firms expand by acquiring other companies in their same line of business, a process called **horizontal integration.** ConAgra, for instance, acquired Banquet Foods in 1980, Armour Food in 1983, RJR Nabisco Frozen Foods (Morton, Patio, and Chun King) in 1986, Beatrice (Hunt's, Wesson, Swift, Eckrich, Butterball, and Orville Redenbacher's) in 1990, and Golden Valley Microwave Foods (Act II) in 1991.[6] There are several reasons for engaging in horizontal integration. One of the primary reasons is to increase market share. Along with increasing revenues, larger market share provides the company with greater leverage to deal with its suppliers and customers. Greater market share should also lower the firm's costs through scale economies. Increased size enables the firm to promote its products and

STRATEGIC INSIGHT

Horizontal Integration in the Paper Industry: Union Camp and Georgia-Pacific

The horizontal growth of one major firm in an industry is likely to affect all of its competitors. Consider the U.S. paper industry. For decades, the industry was characterized by nonantagonistic competition. Even when mergers occurred, they were considered friendly. Because competition was not cutthroat, firms like the $2.75 billion Union Camp Corporation were able to survive even during severe economic downturns.

Then in 1990, Union Camp's largest competitor, Georgia-Pacific, changed the rules of the game by acquiring Great Northern Nekoosa in a hostile takeover. The purchase gave Georgia-Pacific annual sales of more than $10 billion, placing it 34th on the 1990 Fortune 500. Overnight, Georgia-Pacific became the world's largest paper products producer. Its new size and synergistic fit with Great Northern Nekoosa gave it such economies of scale that Georgia-Pacific became the lowest-cost producer of several major lines of paper products.

Georgia-Pacific's low-cost position, combined with an economic recession, placed significant pressure on Union Camp and other companies in the industry to reduce their costs dramatically. As price pressures and discounting increased, these firms faced the unpleasant prospect of being underbid in the industry's price competition.

Union Camp, however, did enjoy some advantages. Its strong balance sheet enabled it to continue expanding aggressively, primarily through internal growth. Georgia-Pacific, on the other hand, found that its acquisition of Great Northern Nekoosa increased its annual interest expense from $63 million in 1989 to $163 million in 1990. To reduce its debt, it was forced to keep capital spending low and sell $1.5 billion in assets.

In 1992, Georgia-Pacific incurred a loss of $124 million on sales of $11.8 billion, while Union Camp showed a profit of $76 million on $3.1 billion of sales.

services more efficiently to a larger audience and may permit greater access to channels of distribution. Finally, horizontal integration can result in increased operational flexibility.

An example of horizontal integration is Chrysler's purchase of American Motors some years ago. The combination of these two firms is a greater competitive threat to other automobile manufacturers than were the two firms owned and operated separately. The combined firm is larger and financially stronger and can appeal to a broader group of customers through its more diverse product line.

Antitrust legislation, of course, restricts some forms of horizontal integration. The Chrysler purchase of American Motors was approved because Chrysler was far smaller and weaker than either General Motors or Ford and because American Motors was close to being forced out of business. But many mergers that would substantially lessen competition in an industry—such as a hypothetical one between GM and Ford—are usually prohibited by the U.S. Justice Department.

Horizontal Related Acquisition. When a corporation acquires a business that is in an industry outside of its present scope of operations but is related to the corporation's core competencies, the corporation has engaged in **horizontal**

related acquisition. Relatedness suggests that pertinent organizational competencies or strengths may be transferred or shared between the corporation and the acquired business. For instance, Coca-Cola's expertise in promoting consumer products could be transferred from its soft-drink business to the fruit juice business (Minute Maid) that it acquired. Also, Coca-Cola's sales force competency may be shared by these two units via a common sales force that simultaneously sells Coca-Cola and Minute Maid products. Examples of two other consumer products companies that have undertaken a number of horizontal related acquisitions are shown in Table 4.3.

Related acquisitions may revolve around similarities or complementarities in competencies. The acquiring and target firms may have similar core competencies (such as strong research and development capabilities), or they may have complementary core competencies (the acquiring firm may, for example, possess a strong research and development department, while the target firm has strong operations technology).

As is evident, the primary impetus for acquiring horizontally related businesses is to strengthen a firm's core competencies. By combining similar core competencies or adding complementary core competencies, a firm can benefit from the resultant synergy. Another important reason for acquiring related businesses is that external threats in the industry in which the firm operates may create the need for diversification into other related industries that hold promising opportunities.

Three major potential advantages are associated with horizontal related acquisitions: horizontal scope economies, horizontal scope innovations, and a combination of the two. Each of these possible advantages is discussed next.

Horizontal scope economies occur when a firm's multiple business units are able to transfer or share purchasing, research and development, marketing, or other functional activities at a lower total or per unit cost than would be available if the business units did not share. For instance, a firm that has several business units, each producing a type of major appliance, could reduce its total or per unit advertising expenses by spreading those costs over a broad

Table 4.3 **Examples of Corporations That Have Undertaken Horizontal Related Acquisitions**

Johnson & Johnson	***Gillette***
Dental products	Razors and blades
Oral contraceptives	Toiletries
Wound care products	Electrical shavers, curlers, toothbrushes, alarm clocks, coffeemakers
Prescription drugs	Stationery products and writing instruments
Hospital products	
Over-the-counter drugs	
Diapers	
Feminine hygiene products	
Infant products	

range of appliances. Similarly, a corporation may receive a quantity discount by purchasing common parts or supplies for several of its business units.

Horizontal scope innovations refer to improvements or innovations that can be transferred or shared across the corporation's business units. Consider Daimler Benz, for example. This producer of Mercedes-Benz vehicles has, over the past decade, acquired business units in defense electronics, aerospace, automation systems, appliances, and financial services. Together, Daimler Benz's business units share research and development innovations that help each of them offer superior, state-of-the-art products.

Daimler Benz also illustrates the **combination of horizontal scope economies and scope innovations.** By acquiring those business units, Daimler Benz not only benefits from technological and product innovations but also lowers its total research and development costs by spreading them among the business units.

Horizontal related acquisitions are often accompanied by two disadvantages: increased bureaucratic costs and greater costs of coordinating the activities of the multiple business units. As a result, such acquisitions should be preceded by a careful cost–benefit analysis.

Horizontal Unrelated Acquisition. When a corporation acquires a business in an unrelated industry, it has undertaken a **horizontal unrelated acquisition,**

STRATEGIC INSIGHT

Horizontal Related Acquisition at Daimler Benz

Sometimes acquisitions do not appear to be in related areas, but, upon more careful examination, common attributes become evident. Take, for example, Daimler Benz. One of the world's largest companies with $62 billion in annual sales, Daimler Benz conducts manufacturing and marketing operations around the world. Almost two-thirds of its sales stem from transactions outside of its home base of Germany.

This corporate giant operates four distinct business units: Mercedes-Benz cars and trucks, Deutsche Aerospace defense and military electronics, AEG nondefense electronics and consumer products, and Debis financial services. At first glance, washing machines, coffee makers, luxury cars, and military electronics seem to share few attributes. But closer inspection reveals that these businesses have a common technological core.

For instance, developments in technology at Deutsche Aerospace are helping engineers at the Mercedes-Benz car and truck division to design vehicles that can detect road hazards and improve the driver's vision. In fact, Daimler Benz has formed a centralized research and development center charged with creating innovations that can be transferred from one business unit to another. Daimler's CEO insists that every product line, from washing machines to jet fighters, incorporate innovations using microelectronics and new materials. The central R&D facility is responsible for helping transfer these new technologies from one product or service to another.

SOURCES: J. Templeman, D. Woodruff, and S. Reed, "Downshift at Daimler," *Business Week,* 16 November 1992, pp. 88–90; "The 'Stateless' World of Manufacturing," *Business Week,* 14 May 1990, p. 103; and J. Templeman, "Daimler's Drive to Become a High-Tech Speedster," *Business Week,* 12 February 1990, pp. 55–58.

or **conglomerate diversification.** Whereas horizontal related acquisitions are based on the premise of strategically managing and coordinating related businesses to create synergy and value, conglomerate diversification decisions are made primarily for financial investment reasons. The assumption, in the latter case, is that structuring a portfolio of businesses based on their potential financial benefits will create value.[7] Thus, while diversifying into related industries is strategically driven, diversifying into unrelated industries is largely financially driven.[8]

In one sense, conglomerate diversification is simpler than horizontal related acquisition because it is based on analyzing the financial potential of an enterprise and its industry without concern for the potential synergistic effects of combining core competencies. Also, since the acquired business units are unrelated to the firm's core business, the costs of coordination are relatively few. Bureaucratic costs, however, tend to increase with unrelated acquisitions. Again, firms are well advised to undertake a cost–benefit analysis before acquiring unrelated businesses.

USX provides an example of horizontal unrelated acquisition. Formerly known as U.S. Steel, this firm began to diversify out of the declining steel industry and into the more attractive energy industry by acquiring Marathon Oil. The firm hoped to increase its financial returns by entering an industry with greater opportunities.

A desire to reduce risk may lead to conglomerate diversification for firms operating in volatile industries that are subject to rapid technological change. However, financial economists argue that, from the perspective of the national economy, risk reduction should not drive acquisition strategies. Their point is that individual stockholders can reduce their financial risk more efficiently by diversifying their personal financial portfolios rather than by owning stock in diversified firms.

Earlier in the chapter, we referred to the problems involved in managing unrelated businesses. Some conglomerates, however, are managed quite effectively. TRW, for instance, has generally demonstrated successful financial performance. This firm, which began in Ohio as The Steel Products Company in 1916, now produces such diverse products and services as spacecraft, software and systems engineering support services, electronic systems, original and replacement automotive equipment, consumer and business credit information services, computer maintenance, pumps, valves, and energy services.

Vertical Related Acquisition. Acquiring a company with similar or complementary core competencies in the vertical distribution channel may be referred to as **vertical related acquisition,** or **vertical integration.** Here also, relatedness suggests that pertinent organizational competencies or strengths may be transferred or shared.

Vertical integration may be either backward or forward in the distribution channel. Backward vertical acquisition occurs when the companies acquired supply the firm with products or components. An example of backward vertical acquisition is Du Pont's purchase several years ago of Conoco. Conoco, an oil company, supplies petroleum products that Du Pont uses in manufacturing its chemicals. By buying its suppliers, a firm assures itself of a steady source of supply.

A firm engages in forward vertical acquisition when it acquires companies that purchase its products. The acquired companies are closer to the end user

STRATEGIC INSIGHT

Carlson Companies: From Conglomerate to Horizontal Related Acquisition

Until the late 1960s, Carlson Companies operated in a single business, trading stamps, as the Gold Bond Stamp Company. However, it followed the path of many other enterprises in the 1970s, diversifying into unrelated businesses. By the end of that decade, Carlson Companies had become a conglomerate involved in eleven different business lines. Carlson soon learned the lesson, however, that many other conglomerates did: It is difficult to manage divergent businesses profitably. Consequently, Carlson Companies sold most of its businesses to concentrate in only three related areas—travel, hospitality, and marketing services.

Today, Carlson is one of the nation's largest privately owned firms, with $8.1 billion in annual sales and 63,000 employees. Curtis L. Carlson serves as chairman of the board and CEO.

Management describes the firm as "synergistically diversified." Its individual business units complement, support, and create business for one another. For instance, its travel agents and tour companies book reservations in its hotels, resorts, motels, and inns. One of its hotel chains is Radisson Hotels. Radisson Hotels host conventions and meetings often arranged by one of Carlson's marketing services, such as the company that provides employee and sales motivation programs. Next door to the Radisson may be a TGI Fridays or Dalts, two of the restaurant chains owned by Carlson. Even more synergy should flow from Carlson's superluxury cruise ship, SSC *Radisson Diamond,* which was recently launched. Designed to serve the most upscale segment of the market, the huge ship has fully equipped meeting facilities.

Carlson Companies is extremely aggressive, expanding its operations almost constantly. To take advantage of the falling trade barriers in Europe in 1992, the firm bought a London-based marketing group in 1990. Carlson already provides twenty-eight different marketing services to businesses in the United States, Australia, and Japan. It is now expanding those services into France, Germany, Italy, and Spain.

The Radisson Hotel chain operates in the United States, Russia, Eastern Europe, Australia, India, Mexico, Switzerland, Spain, Thailand, Canada, and the Caribbean. It plans to add a new hotel every ten days through the end of this century. Currently, almost forty countries tie into Radisson's 800 number telephone line, and 45,000 travel agents worldwide access its reservation system. A recent advertising campaign claimed that "If there's not a Radisson Hotel where you're going, give us a few days."

and in some cases are retail organizations. When Exxon buys service stations from independent dealers, it is engaging in forward vertical acquisition. These actions enable a firm to gain greater control over the distribution, display, sale, and service of its products.

Vertical acquisition can range from partial to full integration. A shirt manufacturer, for instance, that acquires a chain of retail clothing stores exemplifies partial integration, whereas the same manufacturer acquiring cotton farms, textile producers, and retail clothing stores illustrates full integration.

Four principal advantages are associated with vertical related acquisitions. **Vertical chain economies** may result from eliminating production steps, reducing overhead costs, and coordinating distribution activities to attain greater synergy. **Vertical chain/horizontal scope economies** can occur when a corporation's horizontally related or unrelated business units purchase from one of the corporation's business units that serves as a supplier. If sufficiently large, such purchases can improve the supplier's economies of scale while reducing purchasing costs for the horizontal business units. Take, for example, a corporation with horizontal business units that produce hair dryers, industrial fans, cooling systems for electronic equipment, and electric pencil sharpeners. The electric motor parts for all these products are produced by another of the corporation's business units in its vertical chain. As a result of the large combined internal demand for these motor parts, the supplier business unit benefits from scale economies, which lower its per unit costs of operations. These lower costs are then passed along to the purchasing business units, which, in turn, can then sell their products at highly competitive prices.

Vertical chain innovations refer to improvements or innovations that may be transferred or shared among the corporation's business units in the distribution channel. For example, firms such as IBM, Ford, and Digital Equipment acquire suppliers that conduct research and development on promising technology.[9] Vertical chain innovations not only can promote the development of technologically superior outputs, but they can also help the firm differentiate its outputs through improved design, faster delivery, or better marketing practices.

A final advantage is a **combination of vertical chain economies and chain innovations.** As an example, consider Admiram Corporation. One of its business units produces electric switches and plugs, for which it purchases plastic fasteners from another of Admiram's business units. Several years ago, that same supplier produced steel fasteners for switches and plugs. As a result of extensive communication between the managers of the two business units, the fastener unit developed sturdy plastic fasteners to replace those made of steel. The business unit that produced the switches and plugs then redesigned its products around the new plastic fasteners. The shift from steel to plastic parts and the subsequent redesigned products resulted in substantial cost savings in supplies, production, and assembly. And customers benefited from redesigned products not only because of the improved design but also because of the product's lighter weight, which led to reduced transportation and handling costs.

Certain disadvantages are associated with vertical related acquisition. When market demand varies unpredictably over time, it becomes difficult to coordinate vertically integrated activities. A second disadvantage, but only in the short run, is that a technological innovation in the vertical channel may require all of the vertically linked businesses to modify their operations. Third, technological developments in the external environment present a challenge to integrated firms since their vertically linked businesses may be tied to outdated modes of operation, making change quite complex. Next, a firm that buys all of its needs internally may pay more if less expensive external sources of supply exist. Finally, the longer the chain, the greater will be the costs associated with increased coordination and bureaucracy. So, obviously, potential costs and benefits must be compared before engaging in vertical acquisition.

Vertical Unrelated Acquisition. While vertical related acquisition centers on transferring or sharing pertinent complementary or similar core competencies, **vertical unrelated acquisition** is undertaken with limited possibilities for transferring or sharing core competencies.[10] In some cases, however, vertical unrelated acquisitions can result in vertical chain/horizontal scope economies, vertical chain innovations, and combinations of chain economies and innovations.

The purchase by American Agronomics (a producer of citrus juices) of Precision Plastics (a manufacturer of plastic containers) is an example of vertical unrelated acquisition. Some juices, of course, can be marketed in plastic containers, but these containers also have multiple other uses. Also, the combination of a juice producer and a plastics company allows limited possibilities for transferring or sharing core competencies.

Managing vertically unrelated businesses can be associated with two major disadvantages: The more vertical businesses the firm owns, the higher the costs of bureaucracy, and perhaps coordination, are likely to be; and a firm that commits itself to buying all of its needs internally may pay higher costs by failing to seek competitive bids from outside suppliers.

Note that some acquisitions do not fall neatly into either a horizontal or a vertical category. For example, PepsiCo's purchase of KFC, Pizza Hut, and Taco Bell can be viewed as horizontal related acquisitions. Their common core would be the marketing of fast food and soft drinks within the restaurant industry. But these same purchases can also be viewed as forward vertical integration in that PepsiCo supplies soft drinks to KFC, Pizza Hut, and Taco Bell.

While growth strategies that consist of acquiring other companies—either in a horizontal or a vertical direction—involve taking partial or total ownership of those companies, growth may also be pursued through voluntary cooperation or alliances with other independent companies.

Strategic Alliances

Strategic alliances are partnerships in which two or more firms carry out a specific project or cooperate in a selected area of business. The firms comprising the alliance share the costs, risks, and benefits of exploring and undertaking new business opportunities.[11] Such arrangements include joint ventures, franchise/license agreements, joint research and development, joint operations, joint long-term supplier agreements, joint marketing agreements, and consortiums. Strategic alliances can be temporary, disbanding after the project is finished, or long term. Ownership of the firms, of course, remains unchanged.

Strategic alliances may be undertaken for a variety of reasons—political, economic, or technological. In certain countries, for instance, a foreign firm may be permitted to operate only if it enters into a strategic alliance with a local partner. In other cases, a particular project may be so large that it would strain a single company's resources. So that company may enter into a strategic alliance with another firm to gain the resources to accomplish the job. Other projects may require multidimensional technology that no one firm possesses. Hence, firms with different, but compatible, technologies may join together. Or in other cases, one firm may contribute its technological expertise while another contributes its managerial talent.

There are many examples of strategic alliances. IBM and Apple Computer recently agreed to exchange technology in an attempt to create a new computer

STRATEGIC INSIGHT

International Strategic Alliances

Strategic alliances between firms headquartered in different countries have become increasingly popular in recent years. Consider the following examples:

Nestlé and General Mills

Nestlé, the world's largest food company and headquartered in Switzerland, has joined with U.S.-based General Mills to form Cereal Partners Worldwide (CPW). Using Nestlé's powerful channels of distribution, General Mills is penetrating such markets as Europe, Asia, Africa, and Latin America with its Wheaties and Cheerios brands.

Polaroid and Minolta

Polaroid, headquartered in Massachusetts, has entered into a venture with Japan's Minolta to sell Polaroid's most expensive consumer instant camera. With sales of instant cameras stagnating, Polaroid wants to develop strategies to increase camera sales so that it can also sell more film, its most profitable product. Minolta, which does not have an instant-camera product, believes that the Polaroid, sold as the Minolta Instant Pro, will open new markets for the company.

General Motors and Raba

In the auto industry, General Motors entered a joint venture with Raba, a Hungarian truckmaker, to build engines and trucks for the recently opened East European market. Through the venture, GM gained quick access to the Hungarian market, and Raba acquired superior technology and management.

LSI Logic and Kawasaki Steel

California-based LSI Logic is the world's leading supplier of custom chips (CMOS application-specific integrated circuits) used in products such as disk drive controllers. It has combined its design skills with Kawasaki Steel's production capabilities to form a joint manufacturing venture. LSI Logic holds 55 percent of the joint venture, giving it the control it desires.

SOURCES: L. Therrien and C. Hoots, "Cafe au Lait, A Croissant—and Trix," *Business Week*, 24 August 1992, pp. 50–51; C. Knowlton, "Europe Cooks Up a Cereal Brawl," *Fortune*, 3 June 1991, pp. 175, 179; R. Suskind, "Minolta Puts Name on Polaroid," *The Wall Street Journal*, 23 June 1990; J.S. Lublin, "GM Pioneers Eastern Europe for Venture," *The Wall Street Journal*, 11 January 1990; and N. Gross, O. Port, and R. Brandt, "Making Deals—Without Giving Away the Store," *Business Week*, 17 June 1991, pp. 96–97.

operating system that would dominate the industry. The major U.S. automakers—GM, Ford, and Chrysler—are jointly conducting research, with the assistance of $120 million from the U.S. Department of Energy, to develop battery technology for electric cars. And GM, Lockheed, Southern California Edison, and Pacific Gas & Electric have formed a consortium to speed the development of electric vehicles and advanced mass transportation systems.

Strategic alliances have two major advantages. The first, due to the companies' remaining separate and independent, is little increase in bureaucratic and coordination costs. Second, each company can benefit from the alliance without bearing all the costs and risks of exploring new business opportunities on its own. On the other hand, the major disadvantage of forming a strategic alliance is that one partner may take more than it gives. That is, some partners in the alliance possess less knowledge and less advanced technology than other partners and may, in the future, use their newly acquired knowledge and technology to compete directly with their more progressive partners. Also, the profits from the alliance must be shared.

■ Stability Strategy

Rather than use a growth strategy, some firms or business units adopt a **stability strategy,** in which they attempt to maintain their size and current lines of business. These firms, then, do not attempt to grow either through increased sales or through the development of new products or markets.

Why might a firm adopt this strategy? In some cases, it may be forced to do so if it operates in a low-growth or no-growth industry. Second, it may find that the costs of expanding its market share or of entering new-product or new-market areas is higher than the benefits that are projected to come with that growth. Third, a firm that dominates its industry through its superior size and competitive advantage may pursue stability to reduce its chances of being prosecuted for engaging in monopolistic practices. And finally, smaller enterprises that concentrate on specialized products or services may choose stability because of their concern that growth will result in reduced quality and customer service.

As an example of the last reason, consider Peet's Coffee and Tea, a group of eight coffeehouses that employs 170 employees in the San Francisco Bay area. These establishments serve only the finest freshly roasted coffee to the accompaniment of piped-in classical music. Although the owner of Peet's, Gerald Baldwin, has received numerous lucrative offers to franchise his business nationwide, he has always refused. His concern is that with growth, quality may suffer. He fears, for instance, that some franchisees might serve coffee that was not freshly roasted in order to cut their costs and increase their profits.

■ Retrenchment Strategies

Growth strategies and the stability strategy are normally adopted by firms that are in satisfactory competitive positions. But when a firm's performance is disappointing or, at the extreme, when its survival is at stake, then **retrenchment strategies** may be appropriate. Retrenchment may take one of three forms: turnaround, divestment, or liquidation. Each strategy is described next.

Turnaround

The intent of a **turnaround** is to transform the organization into a leaner and more effective business. Turnaround includes such actions as eliminating unprofitable outputs, pruning assets, reducing the size of the work force, cutting costs of distribution, and rethinking the firm's product lines and target markets.

Take, as an example, what may be the most famous turnaround in American business history. Chrysler Corporation, by the late 1970s, was on the verge of bankruptcy. Its newly hired CEO, Lee Iacocca, implemented a dramatic turnaround strategy. Large numbers of blue- and white-collar employees were laid off, the remaining workers agreed to forgo part of their salaries and benefits, and twenty plants were either closed or consolidated. Iacocca also implemented a divestment strategy (discussed in the following section) by selling Chrysler's marine outboard motor division, its defense business, its air-conditioning division, and all of its automobile manufacturing plants located outside of the United States. These actions lowered the firm's break-even point from an annual sales level of 2.4 million cars and trucks to about 1.2 million. By 1982, Chrysler began to show a profit, after having lost $3.5 billion in the preceding four years.

Unfortunately, the turnaround failed to last. By 1991, Chrysler was losing over $2 million a day and had been replaced by Honda as the third-largest seller of cars in the United States. Chrysler once again began to cut costs energetically by closing plants and firing employees, sold its 50 percent share in its strategic alliance with Mitsubishi Motors, and modified its operating systems. For instance, Chrysler began assigning engineers to teams that design a single car, rather than continuing to place them in functional groups (such as engine design). This change cut product development time from 4 1/2 to 3 1/2 years. Chrysler also began implementing ways to cut the delivery time of cars to dealers. Although these measures helped, as Chrysler posted a 1992 profit of over $500 million, the firm's future largely hinged upon the success of its innovative LH series of midsize family sedans and the leadership ability of its new CEO.[12]

Divestment

When a corporation sells or "spins off" one of its business units, as Chrysler did, it is engaging in **divestment.** Divestment usually occurs when the business unit is performing poorly or when it no longer fits the corporation's strategic profile. The business unit may be sold to another company, to its managers and employees, or to an individual or group of investors. As companies reposition themselves in certain markets or product lines, such sales are fairly common. For instance, General Electric, Westinghouse, and Singer have all sold their computer businesses. Singer also sold its original core business unit that produced sewing machines and began to concentrate on high-technology electronics.

Divestment can also occur through a spin-off. In this case, shares of stock in the business unit that is to be spun off are distributed. The stock of the parent corporation and the spun-off business unit then begin to trade separately. For example, the Adolph Coors Company recently spun off business units that sell ceramic multilayer computer boards, packages for soaps and dog food, vitamins for animal feed, and automobile parts in order to concentrate more fully on the highly competitive beer industry.[13]

Liquidation

A strategy of last resort is liquidation. When neither a turnaround nor a divestment seems feasible, **liquidation** occurs through termination of the business unit's existence by sale of its assets. Most stakeholder groups suffer in liquidations. Stockholders and creditors often lose some or all of their funds, managers and employees lose their jobs, suppliers lose a customer, and the community suffers an increase in unemployment and a decrease in tax revenues.

Combination Strategies

In some cases, particularly in periods of rapid environmental change, **combination strategies,** utilizing two or more of the preceding strategies, may be required. As an example, consider Emerson Electric's competitive situation in the mid-1980s. For years, this firm maintained a reliable, high-quality image in its electric motor division. This division produced motors for power tools, industrial uses, and appliances. Emerson's strengths were not only reliability and quality but also continuous product improvements through research and development. Its weakness was high labor costs, since all of its operations were in the United States. The environmental opportunity for Emerson was the long economic recovery that started in the mid-1980s. This recovery provided increased demand for Emerson's products. Threats, however, appeared in the form of Japanese and Taiwanese firms with lower labor costs.

As the foreign firms began to invade the U.S. market with prices as much as 30 percent below Emerson's, Emerson was able to meet the threat effectively because of its understanding of its own strengths and weaknesses and of its environment. To reduce its costs, Emerson adopted a turnaround strategy by closing 49 of its 250 manufacturing plants and eliminating 3,000 high-cost jobs. Simultaneously, it integrated horizontally by acquiring overseas operations in such low-cost countries as Mexico and quickly expanded those operations. Because of its careful analysis and implementation, Emerson was able to meet this new competitive threat through a combination of strategies.

Companies that operate multiple business units often adopt a combination of strategies simultaneously. One business unit, for example, may grow internally while another grows by acquiring an independent firm and another is retrenching. These differences occur because the business units operate in varying markets, facing differing degrees of competition and dissimilar rates of environmental change.

Ideally, a firm should operate in business situations that allow a compatible strategic fit between the firm's strengths and the environment's opportunities, while minimizing the firm's weaknesses and avoiding environmental threats. The following chapter continues with this analytical framework by focusing on firms that manage more than one business, that is, that possess a portfolio of businesses.

SUMMARY

Prior to selecting a corporate-level strategy, top managers engage in S.W.O.T. analysis. By matching the organization's strengths and weaknesses with the environment's opportunities and threats, management is better able to formulate successful strategies for attaining its goals. A firm's strengths and weaknesses reside in its human resources, organizational resources, and physical resources. Ideally, all three work together to give the firm a sustained competitive advantage.

In choosing a strategy, top management may adopt any one of three general corporate profiles: They may compete in a single business, in several related businesses, or in several unrelated businesses. Given the corporate profile, top managers have four corporate-level strategies available: growth, stability, retrenchment, or a combination of the three.

Growth can be attained through internal growth of the same business or the creation of new businesses. New businesses can be created horizontally (in the same business as the original firm, in related businesses, or in unrelated businesses) or vertically (a supplier–customer relationship). Other avenues to growth are the merger (combining two or more firms into one through an exchange of stock) or acquisition (acquiring another company through a payment of cash or stock or some combination of the two). Acquisitions can be either horizontal or vertical. Horizontal acquisitions may take the form of horizontal integration (acquiring companies in the same line of business), horizontal related acquisition (acquiring a business that is in an industry outside of the firm's present scope of operations but is related to the firm's core competencies or major strengths—present or potential) or horizontal unrelated acquisition (acquiring a business in an unrelated industry). Vertical acquisitions may be related (acquisitions that allow the transferring or sharing of pertinent similar or complementary core competencies in the vertical distribution channel) or unrelated (a vertical acquisition with only limited possibilities for transferring or sharing core competencies). A final form of growth is the strategic alliance (a partnership in which two or more independent firms carry out a specific project or cooperate in a selected area of business).

Some firms adopt a stability strategy in which they attempt to maintain their size and current lines of business. Firms in less satisfactory competitive positions are forced to adopt a retrenchment strategy. Retrenchment may take one of three forms: turnaround (transforming the organization into a leaner and more effective business), divestment (selling or spinning off one or more business units), or liquidation (terminating a business unit's existence by sale of its assets).

In some cases, combination strategies, utilizing two or more of the preceding strategies, may be required. This is particularly true of firms that operate multiple business units.

KEY CONCEPTS

Acquisition A corporate-level growth strategy in which one company acquires another company through a payment of cash or stock or some combination of the two.

Combination of horizontal scope economies and scope innovations When a firm's multiple business units share or transfer competencies at a lower total cost than would be available if the business units did not share or transfer and, at the same time, they share or transfer improvements or innovations.

Combination of vertical chain economies and chain innovations When a firm, within its vertical distribution channel, is able to attain economies through its internal supplier–customer relationships while sharing or transferring improvements or innovations among its multiple vertical business units.

Combination strategies A corporate-level strategy involving some combination of the following strategies: internal growth, merger, horizontal integration, horizontal related acquisition, horizontal unrelated acquisition, vertical related acquisition, vertical unrelated acquisition, strategic alliance, stability, turnaround, divestment, or liquidation.

Complementary core competencies When one firm's core competency (such as strength in the R&D area) fits, in a complementary fashion, with another firm's core competency (such as strength in manufacturing).

Conglomerate diversification. See Horizontal unrelated acquisition.

Core competency A major strength of an organization—present or potential.

Corporate-level strategy The strategy that top management formulates for the overall company.

Divestment A corporate-level retrenchment strategy in which a firm sells one or more of its business units.

Growth strategy A corporate-level strategy designed to increase profits, sales, and/or market share.

Horizontal integration A form of acquisition in which a firm expands by acquiring other companies in its same line of business.

Horizontal internal growth A type of internal growth strategy in which a firm creates new companies that operate in the same business as the original firm, in related businesses, or in unrelated businesses.

Horizontal related acquisition A form of acquisition in which a firm expands by acquiring a business that is in an industry outside of its present scope of operations but is related to its core competencies.

Horizontal scope economies Economies of scale that occur when a firm's multiple business units are able to share functional activities at a lower total cost than would be available if they did not share.

Horizontal scope innovations Improvements or innovations that can be transferred or shared across a corporation's business units.

Horizontal unrelated acquisition A form of acquisition in which a firm expands by acquiring a business in an unrelated industry.

Internal growth A corporate-level growth strategy in which a firm expands by internally increasing its size and sales rather than by acquiring other companies.

Liquidation A corporate-level retrenchment strategy in which a firm terminates one or more of its business units.

Merger A corporate-level growth strategy in which a firm combines with another firm through an exchange of stock.

Retrenchment strategy A corporate-level strategy undertaken by a firm when its performance is disappointing or when its survival is at stake. A retrenchment strategy reduces the size of the firm.

Similar core competencies When one firm's core competency (such as strength in the R&D area) is the same as another firm's core competency.

Stability strategy A corporate-level strategy intended to maintain a firm's present size and current lines of business.

Strategic alliance A corporate-level growth strategy in which two or more firms form a partnership to carry out a specific project or cooperate in a selected area of business.

Sustained competitive advantage A firm's valuable strategies that cannot be fully duplicated by its competitors and that result in high financial returns over a lengthy period of time.

S.W.O.T. analysis A corporate-level analysis intended to match the firm's strengths and weaknesses (the *S* and *W* in the name) with the opportunities and threats (the *O* and *T*) posed by the environment.

Synergy A situation in which the combination of two or more business units results in greater effectiveness and efficiency than the total yielded by those businesses when they were operated separately.

Turnaround A corporate-level retrenchment strategy intended to transform the firm into a leaner and more effective business by reducing costs and rethinking the firm's product lines and target markets.

Vertical chain economies Scale economies in a firm's distribution channel that result from eliminating production steps, reducing overhead costs, and coordinating distribution activities to attain greater synergy.

Vertical chain innovations Improvements or innovations that may be transferred or shared among a firm's business units in the distribution channel.

Vertical chain/horizontal scope economies Scale economies that occur when a firm's horizontally related or unrelated business units purchase from one of the firm's business units that serves as a supplier in sufficiently large quantities to improve the supplier's economies of scale while reducing purchasing costs for the horizontal business units.

Vertical integration See Vertical related acquisition.

Vertical internal growth A type of internal growth strategy that generally takes the form of supplier–customer relationships within the firm's channel of distribution.

Vertical related acquisition A form of acquisition in which a firm expands by acquiring a company with similar or complementary core competencies in the distribution channel.

Vertical unrelated acquisition A form of acquisition in which a firm expands by acquiring a company that will provide limited synergy in its distribution channel.

DISCUSSION QUESTIONS

1. Explain the purpose of S.W.O.T. analysis. Why should it precede strategy selection?

2. Explain the distinction between horizontal and vertical internal growth.

3. What do you believe are the advantages that internal growth has over growth through mergers and acquisitions? What particular advantages might mergers and acquisitions have over internal growth?

4. Explain the distinction among horizontal integration, horizontal related acquisition, and horizontal unrelated acquisition.

5. Discuss the major advantages and disadvantages of horizontal related acquisition.

6. Explain the following statement: "While diversifying into related industries is strategically driven, diversifying into unrelated industries is largely financially driven."

7. Discuss the major advantages and disadvantages of vertical related acquisition.

8. Why would a firm prefer to engage in a strategic alliance over a more permanent arrangement?

9. Why would management adopt a stability strategy? Do you feel that such a strategy is viable over a lengthy period of time? Why or why not?

10. When is a retrenchment strategy appropriate? Identify some criteria that will help determine what particular retrenchment strategy should be used.

STRATEGIC MANAGEMENT EXERCISES

1. Select a well-known company for which there is a considerable amount of published information. Using Table 4.1 and the questions on human, organizational, and physical resources as your outline, conduct a S.W.O.T. analysis for this firm. (Note that you may be unable to address all of the issues covered in the chapter owing to a lack of information, and as you conduct your research, you may be able to identify factors not addressed in the chapter.)

   Now, using your S.W.O.T. analysis, recommend specific corporate-level strategies for this firm to adopt. Explain your rationale.

2. Using information in your library, identify three firms: one that is in a single business, one that is in two or more related businesses, and one

that is in unrelated businesses. Now, insofar as information permits, explain the advantages and disadvantages of the corporate profile that each company has selected.

3. Identify a particular type of business that you might wish to start, assuming that you have the necessary financial resources. Furthermore, assume that after some period of time during which the business is successful, you wish to adopt a growth strategy for your company. Explain how your firm might expand through each of the following strategies: internal growth, merger, horizontal integration, horizontal related acquisition, horizontal unrelated acquisition, and strategic alliance.

4. Identify a well-known company with which you are reasonably familiar. Explain how it might expand either through vertical related acquisition or vertical unrelated acquisition. What are the potential benefits and risks associated with the form of growth that you have selected for this particular company?

NOTES

1. J. Barney, "Firm Resources and Sustained Competitive Advantage," *Journal of Management* 17 (1991): 99–120; A. Lado, N. Boyd, and P. Wright, "A Competency-based Model of Sustainable Competitive Advantage: Toward a Conceptual Integration," *Journal of Management* 18 (1992): 77–91.

2. R. Jacob, "The Search for the Organization of Tomorrow," *Fortune,* 18 May 1992, p. 93.

3. B. O'Brian, "American Air Expands into Three Continents, Flexing Its U.S. Muscle," *The Wall Street Journal,* 8 June 1990.

4. See M. Fishman, "Preemptive Bidding and the Role of the Medium of Exchange in Acquisitions," *Journal of Finance* 44 (1989): 41–58; and S. Myers and N. Majluf, "Corporate Financing and Investment Decisions When Firms Have Information That Investors Do Not Have," *Journal of Financial Economics* 13 (1984): 187–221.

5. J. Franks, R. Harris, and S. Titman, "The Postmerger Share-Price Performance of Acquiring Firms," *Journal of Financial Economics* 29 (1991): 81–96.

6. L. Therrien, "ConAgra Turns Up the Heat in the Kitchen," *Business Week,* 2 September 1991, p. 59.

7. M.S. Salter and W.S. Weinhold, "Diversification Via Acquisition: Creating Value," *Harvard Business Review* 56, no. 4 (1978): 166–176.

8. M. Lubatkin, "Merger Strategies and Stockholder Value," *Strategic Management Journal* 8 (1987): 39–53; and J.B. Barney, "Returns to Bidding Firms in Mergers and Acquisitions: Reconsidering the Relatedness Hypothesis," *Strategic Management Journal* 9 (1988): 71–78.

9. K. Kelly, "Learning from Japan," *Business Week,* 27 January 1992, p. 53.

10. B.B. Pray, "Types of Vertical Acquisitions and Returns to Acquiring Firms," unpublished manuscript, Memphis State University, 1992.

11. A.A. Lado, "The Role of Strategic Intent in the Choice of Modes of Cross-Border Alliances: An Investigation of Select U.S. Multinational Companies," unpublished manuscript, Memphis State University, 1992.

12. W. Brown, "Chrysler's Driving Wheel Bids Farewell," *The Washington Post,* 27 December 1992; D. Woodruff, "Chrysler May Actually Be Turning the Corner," *Business Week,* 10 February 1992, p. 32; L. Reibstein and F. Washington, "Lee's Last Stand," *Newsweek,* 6 January 1992, pp. 30–32; and H. Collingwood, "Chrysler Hocks a Diamond," *Business Week,* 11 November 1991, p. 51.

13. R. Grover, "Coors Is Thinking Suds 'R' Us," *Business Week,* 8 June 1992, p. 34.

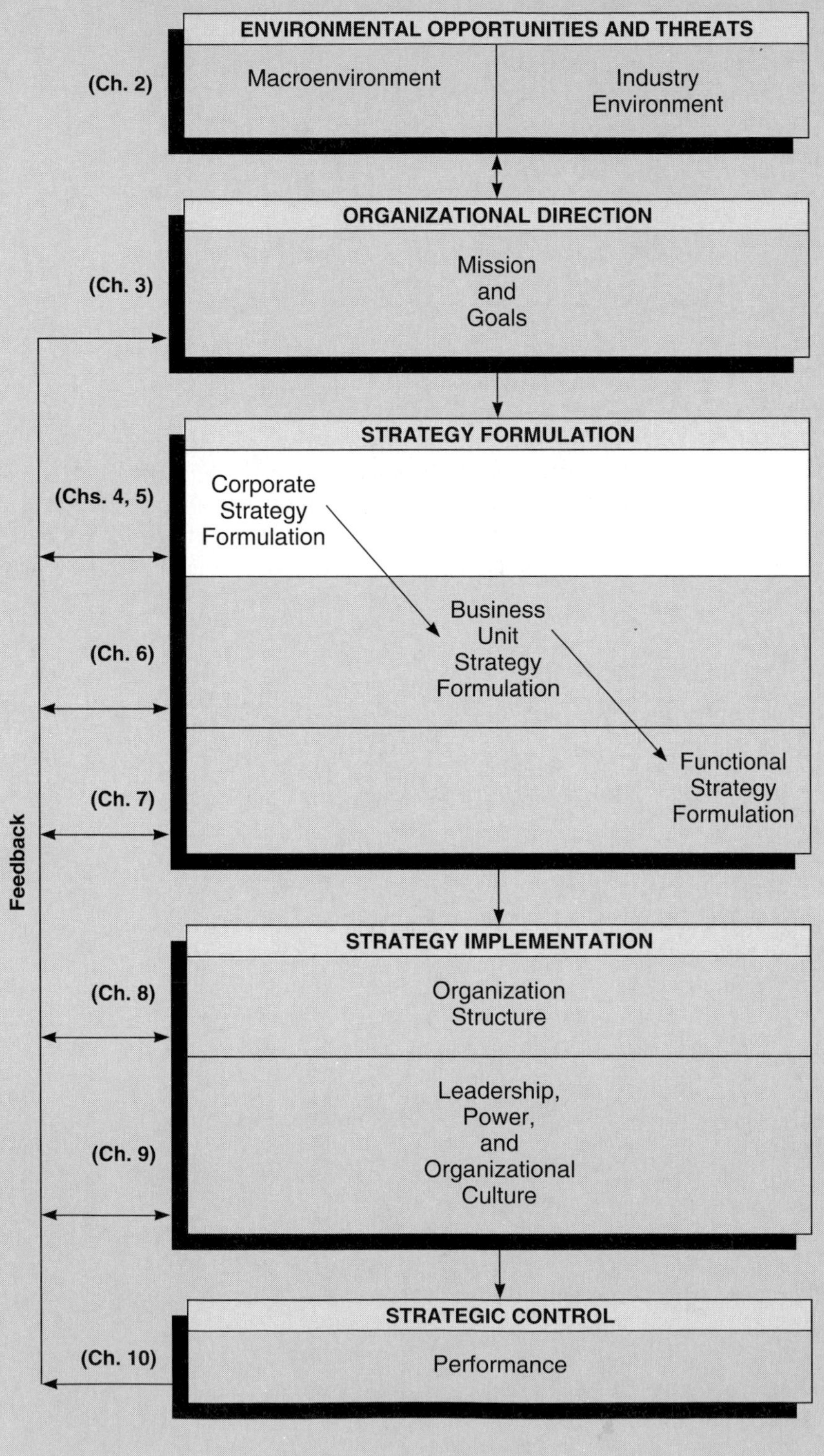
STRATEGIC MANAGEMENT MODEL
ENVIRONMENTAL OPPORTUNITIES AND THREATS
(Ch. 2)
Macroenvironment
Industry Environment
ORGANIZATIONAL DIRECTION
(Ch. 3)
Mission and Goals
STRATEGY FORMULATION
(Chs. 4, 5)
Corporate Strategy Formulation
(Ch. 6)
Business Unit Strategy Formulation
(Ch. 7)
Functional Strategy Formulation
Feedback
STRATEGY IMPLEMENTATION
(Ch. 8)
Organization Structure
(Ch. 9)
Leadership, Power, and Organizational Culture
STRATEGIC CONTROL
(Ch. 10)
Performance

5

Portfolio Management and Corporate-Level Strategy Issues

Many firms operate multiple business units in different environments and various situations. This chapter will examine, from a corporate strategy perspective, how these business units can be managed as a **portfolio.** Then discussion will focus on the financial returns associated with various corporate-level strategies and the role that top managers' motives may play in corporate acquisitions.

PORTFOLIO MANAGEMENT FRAMEWORKS

Traditionally, most commercial organizations start as a single business. Initially, the business follows a strategy of internal growth. Subsequent expansion may take the form of vertical acquisitions, followed by horizontal acquisitions. And, at various points along the way, the firm may use a stability or retrenchment strategy, as conditions require.

This traditional route is not necessarily the course that organizations should follow. The complexity and dynamism that characterize business environments provide a note of caution to any manager who believes that strategy can be shaped according to a formula. It is essential to understand, as the various portfolio frameworks are presented, that while each provides useful guidelines for the strategist, unique firm-specific conditions may require exceptions to the guidelines.

This section examines select analytical frameworks that can be used in portfolio management: our S.W.O.T. portfolio framework, the original and revised Boston Consulting Group frameworks, and the General Electric framework. Discussion then turns to the extent to which corporate-level top management may be involved in managing the firm's business units.

■ S.W.O.T. Portfolio Framework

Our **S.W.O.T. portfolio framework** is designed along two dimensions: the competitive status of the corporation and its business units (the corporate and business units' strengths and weaknesses relative to those of competitors, as discussed in Chapter 4), and the state of the environment (environmental opportunities and threats). By environment, we mean the macroenvironmental or industry factors discussed in Chapter 2. From this perspective, the corporation and its business units can be classified as having strong, average, or weak competitive status, and the environment of the corporation's business units can contain critical threats, moderate opportunities and threats, or abundant opportunities. The resultant matrix, showing the corporation and its business units' competitive status on the horizontal axis and the state of the environment on the vertical axis, is presented in Figure 5.1.

Recall that corporate, business unit, and functional strategies are intertwined. Hence, the strengths and weaknesses of each of these strategies can enhance or inhibit the organization's overall effectiveness. For instance, lower costs may be attained at the corporate level through scope economies, as discussed in the preceding chapter. Then the business unit level may further reduce costs by adopting its own low-cost strategy, discussed in the following chapter, and by adopting appropriate functional strategies (e.g., mass purchasing and mass production), as presented in Chapter 7. The strengths or weaknesses of strategies at any level, then, will affect the organization's overall performance. Thus, while the discussion that follows emphasizes the corporation's business units, it should be evident that the firm's strengths and weaknesses evolve collectively from corporate, business unit, and functional operations.

Understanding of the matrix in Figure 5.1 can be enhanced by looking at some examples. A corporation's business unit that operates in compartment A,

Figure 5.1 **S.W.O.T. Portfolio Framework**

State of the Environment	Competitive Status of the Corporation and Its Business Units: Strong	Average	Weak
Abundant environmental opportunities	**Compartment A** 1. Internal Growth 2. Vertical related acquisitions 3. Mergers 4. Horizontal integration	**Compartment D** 1. Mergers 2. Horizontal integration 3. Strategic alliances	**Compartment G** 1. Turnaround 2. Divestment
Moderate environmental opportunities and threats	**Compartment B** 1. Vertical related acquisitions 2. Horizontal related acquisitions	**Compartment E** 1. Stability 2. Mergers 3. Horizontal integration 4. Strategic alliances 5. Divestment	**Compartment H** 1. Turnaround 2. Divestment
Critical environmental threats	**Compartment C** 1. Horizontal related acquisitions 2. Horizontal unrelated acquisitions (conglomerate) 3. Vertical unrelated acquisitions 4. Divestment	**Compartment F** 1. Divestment 2. Horizontal related acquisitions 3. Horizontal unrelated acquisitions 4. Stability	**Compartment I** 1. Liquidation

for instance, has impressive competitive strengths with few weaknesses and competes in an environment with abundant opportunities and relatively few threats. On the other hand, a corporation's business unit operating in compartment F has average competitive strengths and weaknesses and operates in an environment full of critical threats and few opportunities. And a firm's business unit operating in compartment H possesses more weaknesses than strengths and does business in an environment with moderate opportunities and threats.

Our S.W.O.T. portfolio framework offers strategy guidelines for the corporation's business units that operate in any one of the framework's nine compartments. Each of these compartments will now be examined.

Compartment A

Compartment A is obviously a desirable category. The corporation's business units in this compartment possess impressive competitive strengths and few weaknesses and operate in an environment with abundant opportunities and few significant threats. In such a setting, a number of strategies may be appropriate. Internal growth can be an effective strategy if top management believes that it would best preserve the business unit's organizational culture, efficiency, quality, and image. Vertical related acquisition may be more suitable for business units that wish to assure themselves of predictable sources of supply or of outlets for their outputs. This strategy may also be appropriate if management feels that it will help reduce systemwide costs or improve output innovations. Mergers or horizontal integration may be appropriate, provided antitrust laws do not impede those strategies, if the business unit desires a larger market share and increased competitive clout.

Corporate growth need not always result in an expanding business unit. An alternative method is to divide the business unit into smaller, semiautonomous business units, with each concentrating on a growing, but narrower, market. For example, Johnson & Johnson (J&J) divides any of its business units that grow beyond what top management believes is optimal. As a result, J&J now has 166 highly decentralized businesses, each concentrating on a specific market for health and personal care products. Because the optimal size for a J&J business unit differs from one market to another, J&J's businesses range in size from $100,000 in annual sales to $1 billion.[1]

Compartment B

The corporation's business units that possess significant competitive strengths and operate in environments with moderate opportunities and threats may find that a vertical and/or horizontal related acquisition strategy is appropriate. Because the environment is only moderately promising, a compartment B business unit may enhance its success by diversifying into a related industry that has better prospects.

Consider PepsiCo as an example. The soft-drink industry presents only moderate opportunities. Although this industry has reasonable growth prospects, particularly outside of the United States, this opportunity is dampened by the immense competitive threat posed by Coca-Cola. By diversifying into a related industry, fast-food restaurants, PepsiCo has reduced its dependence on the soft-drink industry. Simultaneously, PepsiCo has used its core competence in marketing to expand its fast-food business units. This growth, in turn, helps protect an increasing amount of PepsiCo's soft-drink sales, because Taco Bell, KFC, and Pizza Hut serve only soft drinks produced by PepsiCo. (Recall that the preceding chapter suggested that PepsiCo's purchase of fast-food businesses can be considered both horizontal and vertical related acquisition.)

Compartment C

A business unit in compartment C has distinct competitive strengths but faces critical environmental threats. For some businesses, the appropriate strategy may be to diversify into more attractive related industries. Some tobacco firms, for instance, perceive that increasing social and political-legal threats reduce their opportunities for profit and growth. Philip Morris, as one example, has diversified into such related businesses as brewing (Miller) and consumer foods (Kraft General Foods). Such acquisitions have benefited from Philip Morris's core competence in consumer marketing.

In other cases, the desirable strategy could be to diversify horizontally or vertically into unrelated industries or to adopt a divestment strategy. Philip Morris's purchase of a packaging company for its tobacco and food products represents a vertical unrelated acquisition. On the other hand, Primerica at one time manufactured containers and packaging materials. Declining opportunities in those industries caused Primerica to diversify horizontally into such unrelated businesses as financial services and specialty retailing. Eventually, it divested itself entirely of its manufacturing businesses and became heavily involved in service industries.

Compartment D

In compartment D, abundant opportunities face a business unit that has moderate competitive strengths and weaknesses. In such a situation, management generally prefers to remain in the industry, because of its rich opportunities, but attempts to improve the business unit's competitive strength.

Moderate competitive strength can take either of two forms: The business unit may have only moderate core competencies, or its strengths may be offset by equivalent weaknesses. In either case, a firm can try to improve its competitive prospects by adopting strategies—merger, horizontal integration, and/or strategic alliance—that link the business unit to organizations that can provide synergistic core competencies. For example, both Nike and Reebok are considered to possess strengths in design and marketing but weaknesses in manufacturing. Consequently, both have forged strategic alliances with low-cost, high-quality manufacturers in Southeast Asia.[2]

Compartment E

Compartment E business units—those with average strengths and weaknesses and facing environments with moderate opportunities and threats—have several strategic alternatives available to them. If the business is reasonably profitable, it may elect a stability strategy. Alternatively, it may attempt to improve its competitive position through a strategy of merger, horizontal integration, or strategic alliance. Note that, should the business unit's competitive strength be enhanced as a result of any of these three strategies, it may eventually wish to diversify out of its present industry into a more promising environment in order to increase its potential opportunities. Should the business unit not become more competitive, the firm might consider divestment, which is also an option for firms that cannot find compatible partners for a merger, horizontal integration, or strategic alliance. Some leading corporations, such as General Electric, for example, divest any business unit that does not become one of the top two performers in its industry within a reasonable period of time.

STRATEGIC INSIGHT

Apple and IBM: Operating in Compartment E

The personal computer industry, once a market with abundant opportunities, has in the past several years become decidedly less attractive. A decade ago, the market for personal computers was expanding by 30 to 40 percent annually. That growth has now slowed to less than 7 percent, and the market has been flooded with competitors attempting to increase their market shares through drastic price cuts.

The two leading firms in the industry, IBM and Apple, now account for only slightly more than one-third of the $80-billion-a-year market. IBM's sales have stagnated because of a lack of product differentiation. Inexpensive IBM-clones use the same operating system, produced by Microsoft, as does IBM, significantly reducing IBM's competitive advantage. And Apple's distinctiveness has been reduced by Microsoft's release of Windows, software that allows IBM and IBM-clones to operate much like the Apple Macintosh.

In the face of this deteriorating situation, the two dominant firms have entered into a strategic alliance. Apple's Macintosh Software Architecture business unit (which develops operating systems and related software) and IBM's Personal Systems business unit (which produces personal computers, workstations, and related software) have created a joint venture known as Taligent. Its goal is to create a modular, easy-to-program, operating system for IBM and Apple personal computers and workstations. This "object-oriented" software will make it easier to customize computer software for specific applications, because the prefabricated chunks of software can be combined in whatever arrangement is desired.

The strategic alliance will involve extensive technology sharing between the two rival firms and should, ultimately, simplify linking Apple and IBM computers on networks. That should also help Apple make further inroads into large corporate accounts. IBM and Apple also hope that it will help them reduce Microsoft's dominant position as the primary provider of software to the computer industry. Immediately following the surprise announcement of the strategic alliance, IBM's stock price declined by $1, Apple's rose by $.875, and Microsoft's dropped by $4.125.

SOURCES: C. Arnst, "'This Is Not a Fun Business to Be in Right Now,'" *Business Week*, 6 July 1992, pp. 68–69; K. Rebello, "Apple's Daring Leap into the All-Digital Future," *Business Week*, 25 May 1992, pp. 120–122; E. Richards, "Apple Chairman Upbeat on Long-Term IBM Deal," *The Washington Post*, 2 August 1991; D.A. Depke, "IBM and Apple: Can Two Loners Learn to Say 'Teamwork'?" *Business Week*, 22 July 1991, p. 25; B. Powell and J. Stone, "'The Deal of the Decade,'" *Newsweek*, 15 July 1991, p. 40; G.P. Zachary and L. Hooper, "IBM and Apple Open New Front in PC Wars with Strategic Alliance," *The Wall Street Journal*, 5 July 1991; R.D. Hof, D.A. Depke, J.B. Levine, and E.I. Schwartz, "An Alliance Made in PC Heaven," *Business Week*, 24 June 1991, pp. 40–42.

Compartment F

Although a business unit in compartment F has moderate competitive strengths, it faces critical environmental threats. If the threats are anticipated to be relatively permanent, divestment may be an appropriate strategy for the firm because transforming a business unit into a top performer is extremely challenging in the face of critical threats. Alternatively, a firm may diversify out of the present industry into horizontally related or unrelated industries with more promising opportunities. If the environmental threats are deemed temporary, a stability strategy can be appropriate. For instance, some savings and loan firms chose stability in the latter 1980s and early 1990s because the environmental threats of economic recession and intense competition were expected to be relatively short-lived.

STRATEGIC INSIGHT

General Dynamics: Operating in Compartment F

With the demise of the Soviet Union and the cold war, analysts predicted that the United States could save billions of dollars in defense spending. Although that was good news for taxpayers, it was not so good for firms in the defense industry. One forecast predicted that a million jobs would be eliminated during the 1990s. By 1996, the United States planned to spend only 3.6 percent of its gross national product on defense, the lowest level since before World War II.

Companies in the defense industry reacted to the cutbacks in different ways. Some, such as General Electric and Boeing, were sufficiently diversified to absorb the impact. Others, such as Hughes Aircraft and Rockwell, attempted to diversify further through horizontal related acquisitions. General Dynamics, however, which sells 88 percent of its output to the U.S. government, elected to pursue a strategy of divestment. (The firm's unsuccessful attempt at diversification into telecommunications and other high-technology fields in the 1970s made it leery of pursuing further horizontal acquisitions.)

Although divestment would reduce General Dynamics' annual sales from $8.7 to $3.5 billion over four years, this manufacturer of M-1 tanks, Atlas rockets, and Trident submarines felt that it had no real choice but to downsize. Its strategy was to begin concentrating solely on three core businesses—nuclear submarines, armored vehicles, and space launch systems—and to bid only on new projects that would not require large, up-front investments and untested technologies.

To clear the path, General Dynamics placed a total of $3 billion in assets up for sale in 1991 and 1992 and quickly sold its missile business unit to Hughes Aircraft for $450 million. Within a year, one-quarter of its work force of 100,000 employees was gone—either through layoff or divestment—and its research and development budget was slashed by 50 percent.

SOURCES: N.J. Perry, "What's Next for the Defense Industry," *Fortune,* 22 February 1993, pp. 94–96; J. Cole, "General Dynamics Contemplates Selling Its Remaining Units," *The Wall Street Journal,* 3 November 1992; "General Dynamics Reports Lower Earnings," *The Washington Post,* 16 July 1992; B. Bremner, "General Dynamics Takes a Tomahawk to Itself," *Business Week,* 22 June 1992, p. 36; "How the Top Guns Are Faring," *Fortune,* 29 June 1992, p. 90; J. Barry, "The Coming Cutbacks in Military Money," *Newsweek,* 18 March 1991, pp. 42–43.

Compartment G

A turnaround strategy is particularly appropriate for business units in compartment G. They have few strengths and many weaknesses and operate in an environment with plentiful opportunities. The firm might spin off, eliminate, or outsource any activities in which it lacks competence. Simultaneously, management should attempt to cultivate the business unit's potential strengths. In some cases, granting the business unit significant autonomy from the corporate bureaucracy can unleash latent strengths.

For example, when Lexmark was a business unit of giant IBM, its needs were often neglected. Its printer and typewriter business was represented by IBM salespeople who were more interested in selling computers that brought higher sales commissions; typewriters and printer sales were no more than afterthoughts. Eventually, Lexmark was spun off by IBM. After eliminating 2,000 jobs, Lexmark's management divided the business into small, semi-autonomous units, with each concentrating on one product line such as printers, keyboards, printer supplies, or typewriters. Operating procedures were also modified. For instance, Lexmark's CEO, who had been the business unit's top manager when it was under IBM's centralized control, indicated that, while IBM had encouraged managers to acquire large budgets and then spend every cent of them, Lexmark would reward managers for coming in under budget.[3]

Divestment can also be an appropriate strategy for firms operating business units in compartment G. Because the environment's opportunities are ample, a business already in the industry can be attractive to other firms desiring to enter the industry on the belief that the business can be turned around. The proceeds from the divestment can be used to strengthen the corporation's remaining business units. Although other strategies—such as mergers, horizontal integration, and strategic alliance—are possible, they are unlikely choices. Other firms are rarely desirous of becoming partners with a business unit that has critical weaknesses.

Compartment H

A business unit in compartment H has critical competitive weaknesses and faces moderate environmental opportunities. In this case, the turnaround and divestment strategies seem most appropriate, although they are more challenging to implement than in compartment G, where opportunities are more prevalent. A turnaround would take more time and effort, and divestment would be more difficult because fewer potential buyers are interested in acquiring a business in a less-promising industry. Even if divestment were possible, the proceeds from the business's sale would be relatively small.

Compartment I

The worst case scenario exists for a business unit in compartment I, where the business's critical weaknesses are overwhelmed by extreme environmental threats. In such situations, liquidation is usually the most feasible strategy. Neither a turnaround nor a divestment strategy is practicable because the business's precarious position provides a poor foundation for either strengthening its operations or attracting outsiders.

Because liquidation is distasteful to virtually all of the firm's stakeholders, top management may delay in closing the business. Unfortunately, a delay can jeopardize the health of the entire corporation because the profits of some business units must be used to offset the losses of the business unit that should already have been liquidated. If overall losses exceed profits, the entire firm may have to declare bankruptcy. With some forms of bankruptcy, a firm can continue operating under the supervision of the courts in return for the settlement of the firm's financial obligations.

LTV Corporation is an example of such a firm. For years, its defense and aerospace business subsidized its unprofitable steel business. By 1986, its corporate operating loss amounted to $3 billion. In declaring bankruptcy, LTV's top management indicated that the corporation would liquidate its steel business to concentrate on its more attractive defense and aerospace business.[4]

The following three sections present other perspectives on portfolio management—two developed by the Boston Consulting Group and one by General Electric.

■ Original BCG Framework

The framework discussed in this section was developed in 1967 by the Boston Consulting Group (BCG), a firm that specializes in strategic planning. Originated by Alan J. Zakon of BCG and William W. Wommack of Mead Corporation, the framework has since been elaborated upon by Barry Hedley, a director of BCG.

The **original BCG portfolio framework** is illustrated by the matrix shown in Figure 5.2. The market's rate of growth is indicated on the vertical axis, and the firm's share of the market is indicated on the horizontal axis. Each of the circles represents a business unit. The size of the circle reflects the business unit's annual sales, the horizontal position of the circle indicates its market share, and its vertical position depicts the growth rate of the market in which it competes. For instance, the circle in the lower left corner of the matrix symbolizes a business unit with relatively large sales and a very high share of its market. Its market, however, is stagnant, exhibiting little growth. Using this framework, management can categorize each of its different businesses as stars, question marks, cash cows, or dogs, depending upon each business unit's relative market share and the growth rate of its market.[5]

A star is a business unit that has a large share of a high-growth market (one with an annual growth rate of 10 percent or more). Although stars are profitable businesses, they usually must consume considerable cash to continue their growth and fight off the numerous competitors that are attracted to fast-growing markets. Question marks are business units with low shares of rapidly growing markets. Many question marks are new businesses just entering the market. If they are able to grow and become market leaders, they evolve into stars; but if they are unable eventually to command a significant market share despite heavy financial support from corporate headquarters, they will usually be divested or liquidated.

Turning to the lower half of the matrix, a cash cow is a business unit that has a large share of a slow-growth market (one growing at an annual rate of less

The Original BCG Framework **Figure 5.2**

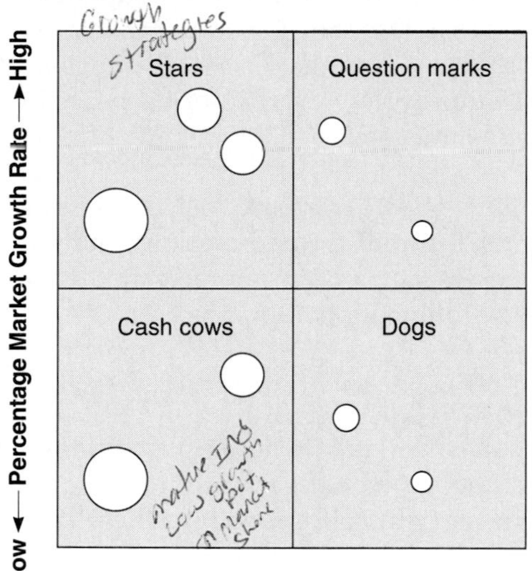

Source: Reprinted from *Long Range Planning*, Vol. 10, B. Hedley, "Strategy and the 'Business Portfolio,'" pp. 9–15, Copyright (1977), with permission from Pergamon Press Ltd., Headington Hill Hall, Oxford OX3 OBW, UK.

STRATEGIC INSIGHT

Neglecting a Cash Cow at Diamond International

From the perspective of the original BCG portfolio framework, U.S. Playing Card was a cash cow for its parent company, Diamond International. Although cash cows do not require vast expenditures for advertising or product promotions, they must still be managed carefully so that they will generate as much excess cash as possible to invest in stars and promising question marks. But Diamond International neglected its U.S. Playing Card subsidiary by allowing the number of highly paid unionized employees to grow without corresponding increases in productivity and by failing to maintain and replace aging machinery and equipment.

Over time, the cash cow became a dog and was divested by Diamond International. The business, however, continued to perform poorly until it was purchased in 1986 by Ronald Rule. Rule engaged in a successful turnaround through such actions as cutting labor costs by one-third, replacing the company's union labor with nonunion employees, and purchasing state-of-the-art machinery and equipment. Today, U.S. Playing Card produces 220,000 decks of cards daily and holds a 70 percent share of the U.S. market and a worldwide market share of 45 percent. Its annual sales amount to $83 million.

U.S. Playing Card is now owned by the Jesup Group of Stamford, Connecticut, although Rule remains its CEO. It accounts for over a quarter of Jesup's annual revenues and serves as a cash cow for some of Jesup's other product lines: laminated plastics, plastic materials and resins, adhesives and sealants, and synthetic rubber.

than 10 percent). Cash cows are highly profitable because they dominate a market that does not attract many new entrants. Because they are so well established, they need not spend vast resources for advertising, product promotions, or consumer rebates. The excess cash that they generate can be used by the corporation to support its stars and question marks. Finally, dogs are business units that have small market shares in slow-growth (or even declining) industries. Dogs are generally marginal businesses that incur either losses or small profits.

Ideally, a corporate portfolio should have mostly stars and cash cows, some question marks (because they represent the future of the corporation), and few, if any, dogs. To attain this ideal, corporate-level managers can use any of the four alternative strategies described in the following paragraphs.

Build Market Share

One of the portfolio strategies is to build market share. To accomplish this end, managers must identify promising business units that currently fall into the question mark category. Management then attempts to transform these businesses into stars. This process of increasing market share may involve significant price reductions, even if that means incurring losses or marginal profitability in the short run. The underlying assumption of this strategy is that once market share leadership is attained, profitability will follow.

Hold Market Share

Another strategy is to hold market share. In this situation, cash cows are managed so as to maintain their market shares, rather than to increase them. Holding a large market share generates more cash than building market share does. Hence, the cash contributed by the cash cows can be used to support stars and selected question marks.

Harvest

Harvesting means milking as much short-term cash from a business as possible, usually while allowing its market share to decline. The cash gained from this strategy is also used to support stars and selected question marks. The businesses harvested are usually dogs, question marks that show little promise of growth, and perhaps some weak cash cows.

Divest

Divesting refers to selling or liquidating a business unit. It usually provides some cash to the corporation (from the sale) and stems the cash outflow that would have been spent on the business in the future. As dogs and less promising question marks are divested, the cash provided is reallocated to stars and to question marks with the potential to become stars.

For example, one of Miller Brewing Company's few new-product failures was Matilda Bay wine coolers. Spending about $30 million to enter the market in 1987, Miller made Matilda Bay the number-four-selling wine cooler in the country by the end of 1988. However, its sales plunged 50 percent the next year, and it lost money for seven straight quarters. Discounts to retailers failed to revitalize the product. Miller attempted to sell Matilda Bay but was unable to find a buyer. So it liquidated its wine cooler business. Some analysts credited Miller with cutting its losses quickly. The funds that had been targeted for Matilda Bay were instead channeled into promising new products such as Miller's Genuine Draft beer.[6]

As is evident, the BCG portfolio framework heavily emphasizes the importance of market share leadership. Cash cows and stars are market share leaders. Some question marks are cultivated to become leaders as well, but less promising question marks and dogs are usually targeted either for harvesting or divestiture. This emphasis on market share has been heavily criticized, leading the Boston Consulting Group to reformulate its portfolio framework.

■ Revised BCG Framework

The **revised BCG framework** is illustrated in Figure 5.3. In place of the star, question mark, cash cow, and dog categories are volume, specialization, fragmented, and stalemate business units. Only the volume business is targeted for market share leadership. The volume business generates high profitability through large market share and its accompanying economies of scale. Business units denoted by specialization, however, are those able to yield high profits even though they have a low market share. Because they have selected a market niche in which to operate, they are able to distinguish themselves from their competitors in the market. The appropriate strategies for these two types of business units, according to BCG, are for the volume business unit to attempt to gain an even greater market share and for the specialization unit to maintain its low market share.

The next category is fragmented businesses. This term refers to business units operating in fragmented industries. A fragmented industry is one in which numerous firms, perhaps even thousands, exist. Examples include the motel, restaurant, and retail clothing industries. Fragmented industries are characterized by low barriers to entry. (By contrast, a consolidated industry, such as the U.S. automobile manufacturing industry, has high barriers to entry, and, therefore, contains only a few very large competitors.) Businesses in this category can be highly profitable—or unprofitable—regardless of their market share. A local motel or restaurant, for example, can be quite successful, as can Holiday Inn or McDonald's. So fragmented business units should be cultivated for profitability while the importance of market share is de-emphasized. The BCG recommends that profitable fragmented business units be maintained and supported and that unprofitable units be divested.

In the final category, a stalemate business is one that has low, or no, profitability because its industry offers poor prospects. Again, market share is not a consideration in this category. The recommendation for stalemate businesses is that they be divested.

These strategic recommendations are reflected in Figure 5.3. Business units shown on the left side of the figure should be maintained and supported, but those on the right side should be divested.

■ GE Framework

Another well-known portfolio framework was developed by General Electric with the help of McKinsey and Company, a consulting firm. As shown in Figure 5.4, the **GE framework** categorizes business units according to industry

Figure 5.3 **The Revised BCG Framework**

Maintain and Support	Divest
Volume (emphasize market share leadership)	Stalemate (regardless of relative market share)
Specialization (emphasize maintenance of low market share)	
Profitable fragmented (do not emphasize market share)	Unprofitable fragmented (regardless of relative market share)

attractiveness (low, medium, or high) and business unit strength (weak, average, or strong). The ideal business unit is one that is strong relative to its competitors and operates in an industry that is attractive. Some of the criteria used to determine industry attractiveness and business strength are shown in Table 5.1.

As shown in Figure 5.4, a corporation's most successful business units fall in the top left section of the diagram, and its least successful ones are in the bottom right section. Average business units fall in between. Strategically, the corporation should divest itself of the business units in the bottom right section while supporting those in the top left area. The average business units will receive less support than those in the upper left unless they are perceived as candidates that have the potential for becoming highly profitable operations.

The S.W.O.T., GE, and BCG portfolio frameworks may be used by corporate-level management to evaluate each of their business units, to make strategic

Figure 5.4 **The GE Framework**

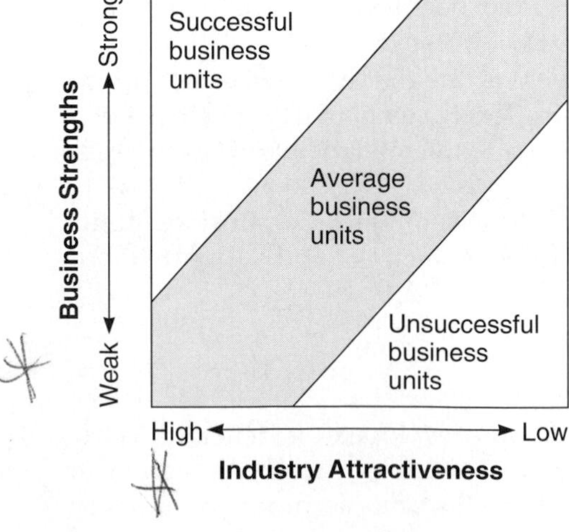

Table 5.1

Criteria for Determining Industry Attractiveness and Business Unit Strengths

Industry Attractiveness Criteria	*Business Unit Strength Criteria*
Annual industry growth rate	Market share
Cyclicality of the industry	Firm profitability
Historical profitability of the industry	Per-unit cost of operation
Macroenvironmental opportunities and constraints particularly relevant to the industry	Process R&D performance
Overall industry size	Product quality
Seasonality of the industry	Managerial and personnel talent
Intensity of competition	Market share growth
Industry predisposition to unionization	Operation capacity
Rate of innovation in the industry	Technological know-how
	Product R&D performance
	Brand reputation

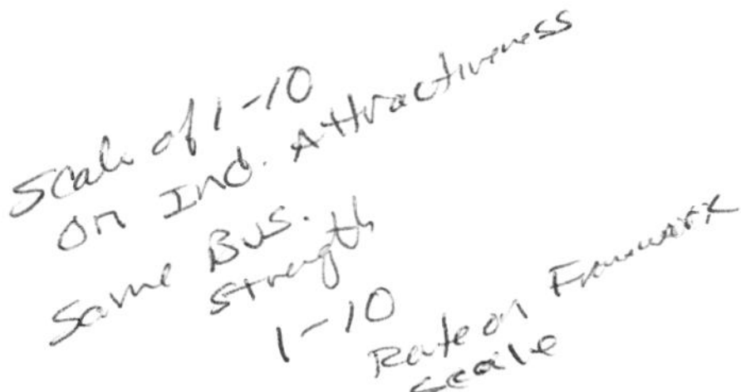

decisions, and to reallocate resources. Although our discussion has focused on large firms with multiple business units, some small, privately held companies are also active in a number of businesses. These frameworks may be used by their top managers to evaluate the strategies used by each of their businesses.

Corporate Involvement in Business Unit Operations

We have seen that corporations may have multiple business units in the same industry, in related industries, or in unrelated industries. How closely corporate-level managers become involved in the strategy formulation and operation of those business units varies from one firm to another. Historically, corporations that have diversified into unrelated businesses operate in a relatively decentralized fashion.[7] In **decentralization,** firms tend to employ small corporate staffs and allow the business unit managers to make most strategic and operating decisions. These decisions involve functional areas such as purchasing, inventory management, production, finance, research and development, and marketing. Examples of decentralized corporations are Paramount, Litton Industries, and Textron.

Alternatively, corporations whose business units are in the same industry or in related industries usually operate in a centralized fashion. Under **centralization,** most major decisions affecting the business units are made at corporate headquarters, so these companies have large corporate staffs. Examples include GE, Coca-Cola, and Sears, Roebuck.

Corporate involvement in business unit operations can be conceptualized as shown on the continuum below. Involvement can range from being highly centralized to being almost completely decentralized.

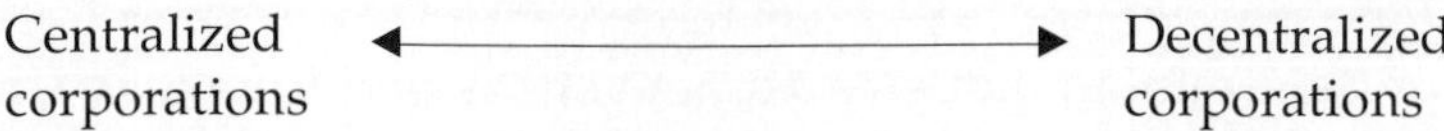

Corporations, of course, may be found at literally any point on this continuum. Decisions regarding centralization and decentralization are not of the either-or variety. Instead, a firm's decision-making processes are termed *relatively centralized* or *relatively decentralized.* Most companies, therefore, are not located at either of the extreme ends of the continuum.

Companies that are relatively centralized make many functional decisions—such as those in purchasing, marketing, finance, and production—at the corporate level. The more commonality in those functional activities across the firm's business units, the greater the tendency is to coordinate those activities at the corporate level. Such centralized decisions can result in efficiencies and consistencies across all business units.

For instance, quantity discounts are larger if the same products are purchased at the corporate level for all business units than if each business unit purchases them separately. As another example, a corporation can borrow more funds at a lower interest rate than separate business units can. And central coordination can encourage business units to buy components, if possible and economically feasible, from other business units within the same corporation instead of buying them from outside the company.

Centralization, however, also incurs costs. As the organization grows, larger and larger corporate staffs are required. As the staff increases, so does the distance between top corporate management and the business units. Top managers are forced to rely increasingly on their staff for information, and they communicate downward to the business units through their staff. These processes result in obvious problems in communication and coordination and in the proliferation of bureaucratic procedures.

Decentralized corporations are able to eliminate these problems since highly decentralized firms maintain only skeletal corporate staffs. But they are seldom able to benefit from coordinated activities across their business units, since each operates as at least a semi-independent entity. Therefore, synergy may be lower in a decentralized organization than in one that is centralized.

CORPORATE STRATEGIES AND RETURNS

In the preceding chapter, we discussed the advantages and disadvantages of various corporate growth strategies. Because most corporations adopt growth strategies of one or more types, considerable research has been conducted on the financial returns associated with these strategies. In this section, we examine the returns generated by corporate growth strategies that involve operating in more than one industry. The following chapter will look at the returns associated with businesses that confine their activities to a single industry.

Despite the volume of research on this topic, little consensus has been reached. Although numerous studies have concluded that the stockholders of target businesses (those being acquired) benefit financially from the takeover,[8] to what extent the acquiring firms' shareholders benefit is not clear. One reason for this lack of clarity is that researchers approach the topic from a variety of perspectives, as discussed next.

■ Acquisitions Are Not Beneficial

In microeconomics—as well as in one of its research streams, industrial organization—and in select financial theories, it is suggested that acquisitions do not benefit the shareholders of acquiring firms. According to the microeconomics perspective, markets are characterized by perfect competition (a perfectly competitive market contains a large number of firms, none of which can affect price or supply on its own; each firm has complete knowledge of the activities of all the other firms, including their profitability; there are many customers, none of whom can affect price on their own; all customers have complete knowledge of all products and prices; all of the industry's products are homogeneous; there are many identical potential acquiring firms, none of which on its own can affect the share price of target companies; all shareholders possess perfect information; and no shareholder alone can affect stock prices). If there were such a setting, all of the firms in a single industry would be identical in their attributes and strategies because, as soon as one attempted to differentiate its product or lower its price to attract more customers, the others would follow suit.

In such a setting, acquisitions could offer only above-average returns to the shareholders of the target companies. The acquiring firm's stockholders would receive only "normal returns" because, when the acquiring firm made a bid for another company, its competitors would also recognize the value of the target company and, hence, would engage in competitive bidding to drive up the price of the target company's stock until only normal returns could be realized. Within this context, firms should not make acquisitions because such takeovers will not benefit the shareholders of the acquiring firms. Scholars influenced by this perspective have generally found empirical support for their theories.[9] Furthermore, this view assumes that the major determinant of business strategy is the market or industry environment. The environment exerts pressures to which firms must react.[10] Those firms that successfully adapt to the external forces will prosper, while those that are unable to adapt will fail.

In industrial organization, a branch of microeconomics, it is similarly pointed out that the external environment determines the firm's strategy and returns. According to industrial organization, industry environments differ in their potential returns. Firms that operate business units in favorable industry environments will have higher returns than those operating in unfavorable industry environments.

Implicit in industrial organization is the premise that acquiring businesses in attractive industries is costly because of the higher returns afforded by those industries, so that acquisitions can yield no more than normal returns. Consequently, acquisitions should be avoided because they cannot benefit the shareholders of acquiring firms.

Select financial theories also emphasize the market environment rather than the firm. Since these theories assume that markets are competitive, acquiring attractive target companies would be costly. Therefore, the acquisition strategies of potential acquiring firms would be identical, and the market would set the price of any acquisition. Under such circumstances, these theories do not necessarily recommend acquisitions because they are not thought to be particularly beneficial to the acquiring firms' shareholders.

All of these streams of thought attribute importance to environmental factors (the vertical dimension in Figure 5.1) rather than to the relative strategic strengths and weaknesses of the corporation and its business units (the horizontal dimension in Figure 5.1). In summary, since acquisitions are viewed as identical strategies that yield only normal returns in competitive markets, scholars in these areas do not consider acquisitions to be advantageous to the shareholders of acquiring firms.

■ Acquisitions May Be Beneficial

Advocates of contingency theory and of resource-based theory suggest that acquisitions may benefit the acquiring firms' shareholders. Contingency theorists argue that returns are influenced not only by the environment but also by the strategic fit between the firm's business units and their environments. This school of thought more realistically views markets as imperfectly competitive (markets in which individual suppliers and/or customers can influence price or supply, where firms do not have complete information about other firms' activities nor do customers have complete knowledge of all products and prices, where products are differentiated, and where potential acquiring firms may benefit differentially from purchasing a target company so that they would submit dissimilar bids for the same company). Under this scenario, corporations may pursue different acquisition strategies and, hence, would earn different returns. Consequently, both environmental factors (the vertical dimension in Figure 5.1) and the strengths and weaknesses of the firm and its business units (the horizontal dimension in Figure 5.1) would be important in determining the firm's relative success.

Implicit in contingency theory is the assumption that related acquisitions may create shareholder value. Related acquisitions are those in which the acquiring and target firms are in related industries and have similar core competencies (such as both in research and development) or complementary core competencies (such as one in manufacturing and one in marketing). The results of research on acquisitions, relevant to this field of thought, are mixed. Some studies show that related acquisitions may be associated with relatively high returns to the acquiring firm's stockholders.[11] Other studies, however, have questioned the value of relatedness in acquisitions. Some have found no significant differences in the returns to the acquiring firm's shareholders whether the acquisition was related or unrelated.[12] Others have found that unrelated acquisitions are associated with higher returns to the acquiring firm's owners than are related acquisitions.[13]

According to advocates of resource-based theory, although the environmental opportunities and threats do matter, they are not the prime influences on an organization's performance, because they change so frequently. A more stable basis for developing strategy would be the firm's unique attributes or strengths. Resource-based theory, therefore, gives less emphasis to the externally imposed bounded opportunities for the firm than does the previously discussed contingency theory. Hence, from this perspective, the firm can behave in a highly proactive fashion. Similar to contingency theory, this school of thought also views markets as imperfectly competitive.

Implicit in resource-based theory is the assumption that related acquisitions create shareholder value, due to the synergies created by similar or complementary core competencies. Although few empirical investigations are based strictly on resource-based theory, the contention that synergies are possible due to similarities or complementarities in core competencies does have empirical support.[14]

So we have seen that, although the stockholders of target companies generally benefit from acquisitions, the evidence is mixed on the extent to which the shareholders of acquiring firms benefit. The question arises, therefore, as to why corporations continue to acquire other businesses in the face of this mixed evidence. Some researchers have argued that top managers may be motivated to acquire other companies because of certain benefits that may accrue to themselves, but not necessarily to the firm's owners.

MANAGERS' MOTIVES FOR ACQUISITIONS

Although, ideally, the interests of top management and the firm's owners should be congruent, they often are not.[15] In fact, according to numerous studies, the compensation of top-level managers appears unrelated to the financial success of their organizations.[16] Since their compensation often is not closely tied to bottom line results, top managers may select corporate strategies that could enrich them without necessarily benefiting their stockholders. This potential for conflict of interest is termed an **agency problem**—that is, a situation in which the owners' agents, the corporation's top managers, fail to act in the best interests of the owners.

Agency problems may be particularly prevalent in acquisition situations. Since an acquisition immediately increases the size of the acquiring firm and since higher compensation for top management is related to the size of the firm,[17] top managers may well be encouraged to acquire other companies. However, increased firm size is not always beneficial to shareholders. Acquisitions often involve taking on significant amounts of debt to finance the purchase, which can, at least for several years, depress profits. Depressed profits generally translate into lower stock prices and sometimes even reduced dividends.

Additionally, acquisitions of companies in other industries may also benefit the acquiring firm's top management but not its stockholders. Diversification may reduce the risk that top executives will lose their jobs[18] because it reduces the firm's overall risk by spreading risk across more than one industry. But, as suggested earlier, shareholders can better reduce their financial risk by diversifying their own investments (through buying stocks in companies in different industries or purchasing mutual funds) rather than having top management do it for them.

SUMMARY

Corporations with multiple business units often adopt a combination of strategies simultaneously. Because managing several businesses concurrently is quite complex, a number of portfolio frameworks are available to assist top managers. The S.W.O.T. portfolio framework helps corporate-level managers assess the strengths and weaknesses of each of their business units in light of the opportunities and threats presented by the business unit's environment.

Based upon the relative match between the environment and the business unit, this framework suggests which corporate-level strategy or strategies are appropriate for each of the firm's business units.

Other frameworks, by the Boston Consulting Group and by General Electric, assist corporate-level managers to evaluate the performance of each of their business units, to make strategic decisions for each unit, and to reallocate resources from one unit to another.

Corporate-level managers must decide on the extent to which they will be involved in strategic and operational decision making at the business unit level. Usually, corporations that have diversified into related businesses remain fairly centralized, while conglomerates operate in a relatively decentralized fashion.

Because of the prevalence of growth strategies, considerable research has been conducted on the financial returns associated with these strategies. To date, studies indicate that, in general, the stockholders of target businesses benefit financially from the takeover, but the extent to which shareholders of the acquiring firm benefit is not entirely clear. In some cases, acquisitions appear to yield no benefits, while in other cases, they do. Yet, even when takeovers do not benefit the acquiring firm's shareholders, top managers are often encouraged to acquire other firms because, by so doing, they can reduce the risk of losing their jobs while they increase their compensation.

KEY CONCEPTS

Agency problem A situation in which a corporation's top managers (who serve as the agents of the firm's owners, the stockholders) fail to act in the best interests of the owners.

BCG portfolio framework (original) A strategic-planning framework developed by the Boston Consulting Group that categorizes a firm's business units by the market share that they hold and the growth rate of their respective markets.

BCG portfolio framework (revised) The more recent framework developed by the Boston Consulting Group that categorizes a firm's business units as volume (generates high profitability through large market share), specialization (yields high profits by operating in a market niche), fragmented (operates in a fragmented industry in which market share is unrelated to profitability), and stalemate (incurs low or no profits because its industry offers poor prospects).

Centralization An organizational decision-making process in which most strategic and operating decisions are made by managers at the top of the organization structure (at corporate headquarters).

Decentralization An organizational decision-making process in which most strategic and operating decisions are made by managers at the business unit level.

GE framework A strategic-planning framework developed by General Electric Company that categorizes a corporation's business units according to industry attractiveness and business unit strength.

Portfolio management Managing multiple business units of a corporation.

S.W.O.T. portfolio framework Our strategic-planning framework that categorizes each of a corporation's business units according to its strengths and weaknesses and its environment's opportunities and threats. It goes on to provide guidelines as to which corporate strategies may be appropriate under particular situations.

DISCUSSION QUESTIONS

1. Explain the purpose of portfolio framework analysis.

2. Discuss how the S.W.O.T. portfolio framework can help corporate-level managers develop strategies for multiple business units.

3. Which corporate-level strategies are most viable for a business unit operating in compartment E in the S.W.O.T. portfolio framework? Under what circumstances might each of these strategies be appropriate?

4. Which corporate-level strategies are most viable for a business unit operating in compartment G in the S.W.O.T. portfolio framework? Under what circumstances might each of these strategies be appropriate?

5. Compare and contrast the S.W.O.T. portfolio framework with the original BCG portfolio framework.

6. What are the differences and similarities between the original and revised BCG frameworks?

7. Explain the differences and similarities between the original BCG framework and the GE framework.

8. What types of organizations are likely to operate in a relatively centralized (versus a relatively decentralized) fashion? Why?

9. When one firm acquires another, which group of stockholders—those of the acquiring firm or those of the target firm—is more likely to benefit financially? Why?

10. Even though the evidence is mixed on the extent to which the stockholders of acquiring firms benefit from acquisitions, the top managers of many firms continue to engage in acquisitions. Why?

STRATEGIC MANAGEMENT EXERCISES

1. Choose a real corporation that has multiple business units (either related or unrelated). Attempt to place each of the firm's business units into the appropriate compartment (A, B, C, etc.) in the S.W.O.T. portfolio framework.
2. Now place each business unit (Exercise 1) into the appropriate category in the original BCG portfolio framework (star, cash cow, question mark, or dog).

3. Place each of the business units (Exercise 1) into the appropriate category in the revised BCG portfolio framework (volume, specialization, fragmented, or stalemate).

4. Place each of the business units (Exercise 1) into the appropriate category in the GE portfolio framework (successful, average, or unsuccessful).

5. Now take one of these business units (Exercise 1) and compare the strategies that are recommended for it by the S.W.O.T. framework, the original BCG framework, the revised BCG framework, and the GE framework. Discuss why different frameworks have recommended different strategies for the same business unit (if they have).

NOTES

1. B. Dumaine, "Is Big Still Good?" *Fortune,* 20 April 1992, p. 51.
2. Ibid., p. 53.
3. P.B. Carroll, "Story of an IBM Unit That Split Off Shows Difficulties of Change," *The Wall Street Journal,* 23 July 1992; Dumaine, "Is Big Still Good?" p. 56.
4. M. Schroeder and A. Bernstein, "A Brawl with Labor Could Block LTV's Rebirth," *Business Week,* 16 March 1992, p. 40.
5. B. Hedley, "Strategy and the Business Portfolio," *Long Range Planning,* 10, no. 2 (1977): 9–14.
6. J.F. Siler, "How Miller Got Dunked in Matilda Bay," *Business Week,* 25 September 1989, p. 54.
7. D.K. Datta and J.H. Grant, "Relationships Between Type of Acquisition, the Autonomy Given to the Acquired Firm, and Acquisition Success: An Empirical Analysis," *Journal of Management* 16 (1990): 29–44.
8. D.K. Datta, G.E. Pinches, and V.K. Narayanan, "Factors Influencing Wealth Creation from Mergers and Acquisitions: A Meta-Analysis," *Strategic Management Journal* 13 (1992): 67–84; M.C. Jensen and R.S. Ruback, "The Market for Corporate Control: The Scientific Evidence," *Journal of Financial Economics* 11 (1983): 5–50.
9. Jensen and Ruback, "The Market for Corporate Control"; J.F. Weston, "Developments in Finance Theory," *Financial Management* 10 (1981): 15–22.
10. A.A. Lado, N.G. Boyd, and P. Wright, "A Competency-based Model of Sustainable Competitive Advantage: Toward a Conceptual Integration," *Journal of Management* 18 (1992): 77–91.
11. L. Everett, "Past Returns, Acquisition Strategies and Returns to Bidding Firms," unpublished manuscript, Memphis State University, 1992; R.P. Rumelt, *Strategy, Structure, and Economic Performance* (Boston: Division of Research, Graduate School of Business Administration, Harvard University Press, 1974); C.K. Prahalad and R.A. Bettis, "The Dominant Logic: A New Linkage Between Diversity and Performance," *Strategic Management Journal* 7 (1986): 485–501; R.M. Grant, "On Dominant Logic, Relatedness, and the Link Between Diversity and Performance," *Strategic Management Journal* 9 (1988): 639–642; C.K. Prahalad and G. Hamel, "The Core Competence of the Corporation," *Harvard Business Review* 68, no. 3 (1990): 79–91.
12. R.A. Bettis and W.K. Hall, "Diversification Strategy, Accounting Determined Risk, and Accounting Determined Return," *Academy of Management Journal* 25 (1982):

254–264; M. Lubatkin, "Merger Strategies and Stockholder Value," *Strategic Management Journal* 8 (1987): 39–53.

13. P.T. Elgers and J.J. Clark, "Merger Types and Stockholder Returns: Additional Evidence," *Financial Management* 9 (1980): 66–72; P. Dubofsky and P. Varadarajan, "Diversification and Measures of Performance: Additional Empirical Evidence," *Academy of Management Journal* 30 (1987): 597–608.
14. J.S. Harrison, M.A. Hitt, R.E. Hoskisson, and R.D. Ireland, "Synergies and Post-Acquisition Performance: Differences Versus Similarities in Resource Allocations," *Journal of Management* 17 (1991): 173–190; H. Singh and C.A. Montgomery, "Corporate Acquisition Strategies and Economic Performance," *Strategic Management Journal* 8 (1987): 377–386.
15. M. Kroll, P. Wright, and P. Theerathorn, "Whose Interests Do Hired Managers Pursue? An Examination of Select Mutual and Stock Life Insurers," *Journal of Business Research* 26 (1993): 133–148; G.P. Baker, M.C. Jensen, and K.J. Murphy, "Compensation and Incentives: Practice vs. Theory," *Journal of Finance* 43 (1988): 593–616; M.C. Jensen and K.J. Murphy, "CEO Incentives—It's Not How Much You Pay, But How," *Harvard Business Review* 14, no. 3 (1990): 138–153.
16. Jensen and Murphy, "CEO Incentives."
17. M. Firth, "Takeover, Shareholder Returns, and the Theory of the Firm," *Quarterly Journal of Economics* 94 (1980): 235–260; W.A. McEachern, *Managerial Control and Performance* (Lexington, Mass.: Lexington Books, 1975).
18. Y. Amihud and B. Lev, "Risk Reduction as a Managerial Motive for Conglomerate Mergers," *Bell Journal of Economics* 7 (Autumn 1981): 605–617.

STRATEGIC MANAGEMENT MODEL

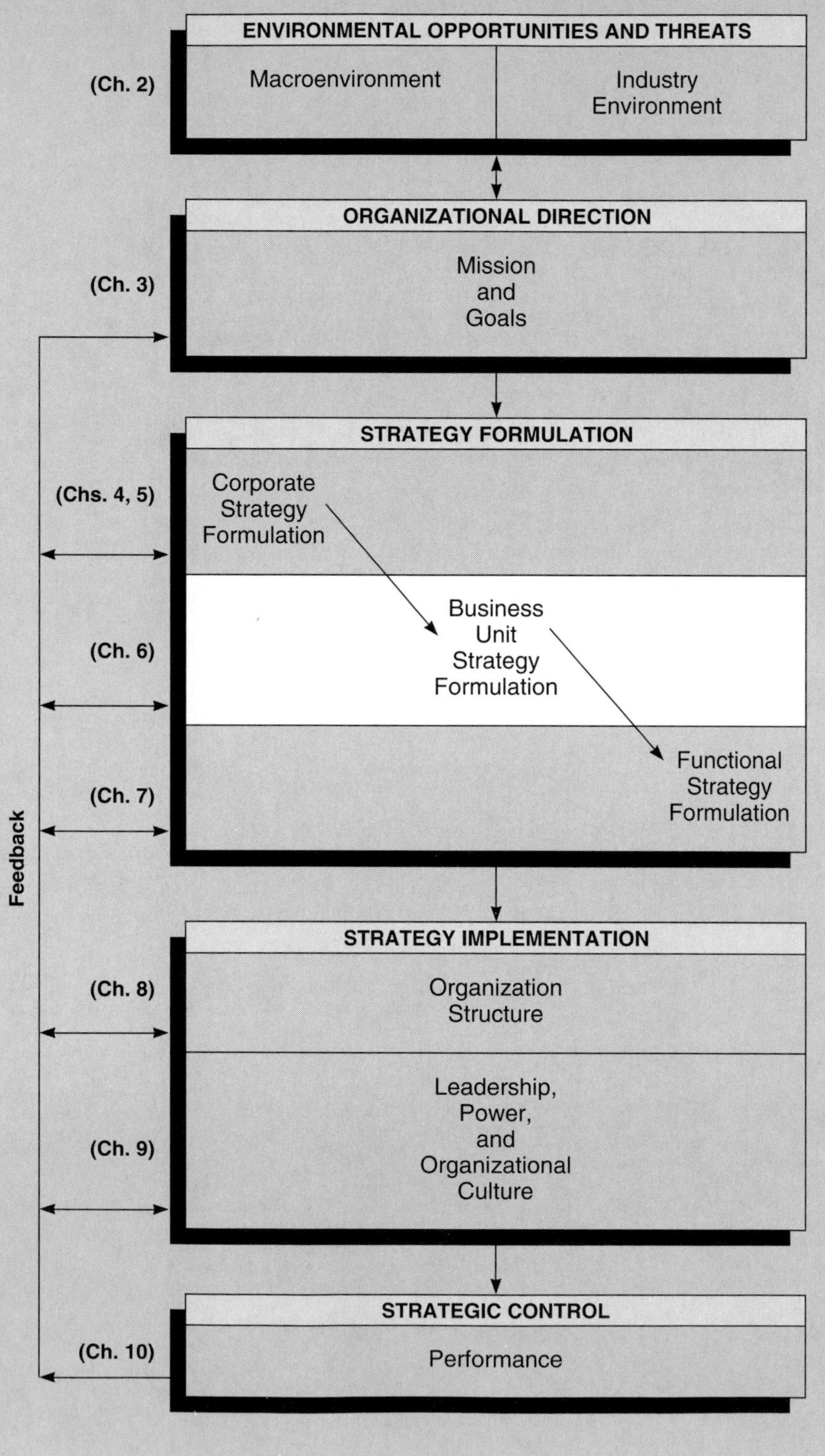

6

Business Unit Strategies

While the strategic question at the corporate level is, In what industries or businesses should we be operating? the appropriate question at the business unit level is, How should we compete in the chosen industry or business? A **business unit** is an organizational subsystem that has a market, a set of competitors, and a mission distinct from those of the other subsystems in the firm. The concept of the strategic business unit was pioneered by General Electric Company. At GE, for example, one business unit manufactures and markets major appliances such as ranges, refrigerators, dishwashers, and clothes washers and dryers. Another business unit is responsible for producing and selling jet engines to airplane manufacturers. In total, GE contains over two hundred strategic business units. Each of these business units adopts its own strategy consistent with the organization's corporate-level strategy. Because each business unit serves a different market and competes with different companies than do the firm's other business units, it must operate with its own mission, objectives, and strategy.

A single company that operates within only one industry is also considered a business unit. For instance, an independent company that builds and sells swimming pools is considered a business unit. In such an organization, corporate-level strategy and business unit strategy are the same. Hence, the focus of this chapter is on organizational entities that contain their own functional departments, such as production and sales, and operate within a single industry.

Managers of these business units can choose from a number of **generic strategies** to guide their organizations. These strategic alternatives are termed *generic* because they can be adopted by any type of business unit, whether it be a traditional manufacturing company, a high-technology firm, or a service organization. Of the seven strategies available and discussed in this chapter, three are most appropriate for small business units; the remaining four are used by large business units.

GENERIC STRATEGIES FOR SMALL BUSINESS UNITS

This section presents the generic strategies that are most appropriate for small business units: the niche-low cost, niche-differentiation, and niche–low-cost/differentiation strategies.

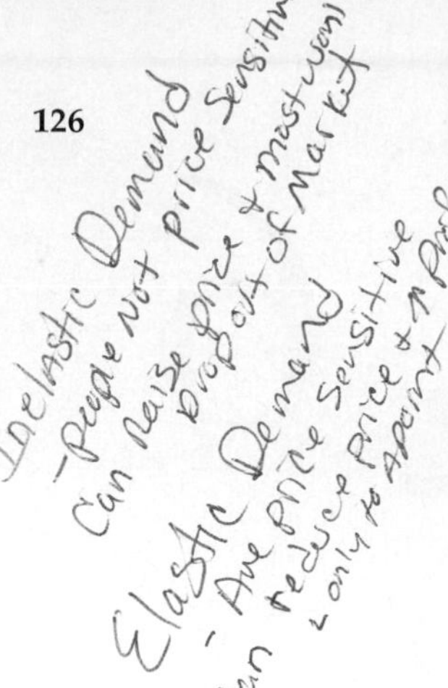

■ Niche–Low-Cost Strategy

The **niche–low-cost strategy** emphasizes keeping overall costs low while serving a narrow segment of the market. Business units that adopt this strategy produce no-frills products or services for price-sensitive customers in a market niche. The no-frills outputs of one business differ little from those of competing businesses, and market demand for these outputs is elastic.

Depending upon the prevailing industry forces, customers generally are willing to pay only low to average prices for no-frills products or services. Hence, it is essential that businesses using this strategy keep their overall costs as low as possible. Therefore, they emphasize keeping their initial investment low and holding operating costs down. For instance, these organizations will purchase from suppliers who offer the lowest prices, and they will emphasize the function of financial control. Research and development efforts will be directed at improving operational efficiency, and attempts will be made to enhance logistical and distribution efficiencies. Such businesses will de-emphasize the development of new or improved products or services that might raise costs, and advertising and promotional expenditures will be minimized.

Figure 6.1 portrays the strategic position of a business unit (Southwest Airlines) that competes with the niche–low-cost strategy. Its location on the chart reflects its strategy of low costs and minimal product/service differentiation. As Southwest executives say, "Southwest doesn't slap the big cats, . . . we just run between their legs."[1] By avoiding direct competition with the major airlines, Southwest has used its niche to build the industry's most successful profit record. Of course, if Southwest continues to expand its route system, it may eventually be following the low-cost strategy (discussed later) rather than the niche–low-cost strategy.

Ideally, the small business unit that adopts the niche–low-cost strategy competes only where it enjoys a cost advantage relative to large, low-cost

Figure 6.1 **A Business Competing with the Niche–Low-Cost Strategy**

STRATEGIC INSIGHT

Southwest Airlines' Niche–Low-Cost Strategy

Southwest Airlines, a Texas-based carrier with $1.3 billion in annual revenue, has used its niche–low-cost strategy so successfully that it has become one of the most profitable airlines in the United States. Beginning as a short-haul airline between the older in-town airports of Dallas and Houston in 1971, its no-frills, frequent-departure flights were instantly popular with price-sensitive and time-conscious travelers.

Even as it has expanded, the airline has maintained its policy of no assigned seating or first-class seats, it still serves no meals, does not transfer baggage to other carriers, and it has never belonged to a computer reservation system (which, in itself, saves the company $25 million annually). Its boarding passes are made of sturdy plastic so that they can be reused.

Yet even with its lack of frills, Southwest has a reputation for quality, as demonstrated by its youthful and fuel-efficient fleet of airplanes, excellent record for on-time flights, and few passenger complaints. Its secret of success in an industry where successes are few is its solid management. Southwest has been able to keep its operating costs low (e.g., a 43 percent cost advantage over giant American Airlines) while maintaining an ample supply of cash and a healthy balance sheet. Management places a heavy emphasis on high aircraft utilization and high employee productivity. And the airline only flies routes where it is the dominant carrier, so it is able to set passenger ticket prices.

By keeping its costs low, Southwest is price-competitive not only with other airlines but also with such alternative modes of transportation as personal automobiles and rental cars. For instance, at one time, competing airlines charged $62 for the flight from Dallas to San Antonio. Southwest charged $15 for the same flight. Obviously, this low price even beat the cost of making the 270-mile drive between the two cities.

competitors. For example, small short-line railroads are able to make a profit by serving shippers whose business is too insignificant for the large railroads. The small railroads do not have to hire union labor, so their wage rates are lower and they can use smaller crews than their larger rivals.[2]

Businesses that compete with the niche–low-cost strategy will deliberately avoid creating successively new outputs for fear of increasing their costs. Such businesses value technological stability in their organizations. Stable technologies enable them to produce no-frills outputs at low costs.

An important vulnerability of the niche–low-cost strategy is that intense price competition periodically occurs in markets with no-frills outputs. For instance, several years ago, Laker Airways used the niche–low-cost strategy very successfully by providing a first in the airline industry—no-frills, low-priced trans-Atlantic passenger service. However, the major airlines eventually responded by offering virtually identical service. The resulting price war drove Laker Airways out of business. The large competitors, because of their greater financial resources, were able to survive the shakeout even though many of them incurred financial losses.

Another important vulnerability of this strategy is technological obsolescence. Businesses that value technological stability, and consequently avoid responding to new product and market opportunities, may eventually find that their products have become obsolete and are no longer desired by their customers.

■ Niche-Differentiation Strategy

The **niche-differentiation strategy** is appropriate for business units that produce highly differentiated, need-fulfilling products or services for the specialized needs of a narrow range of customers or a market niche. Because these outputs are intended to fulfill a deeper set of customer needs than either no-frills goods or differentiated goods (discussed later under the differentiation strategy), and because the market demand for these outputs tends to be inelastic, these goods or services can command high prices. Hence, cost reduction efforts are not emphasized by businesses competing with the niche-differentiation strategy.

In fact, these businesses tend to be deliberately inefficient because they continuously attempt to create new product and market opportunities or respond to them. Both actions are costly. Therefore, they highly value technological fluidity in their organizations to create or keep pace with state-of-the-art developments in their industries.

Broadly speaking, high prices are acceptable to certain customers who need product performance, prestige, safety, or security. For instance, some customers may be willing to pay high prices for state-of-the-art stereo component systems that perform at wide-range frequencies and low sound distortions (performance needs). Another cluster of customers will pay very high prices for designer clothes (prestige needs). Yet another group of industrial buyers will pay significantly more to suppliers who continuously improve the reliability of the nuts and bolts they produce to fasten the wings of an airplane to its body (safety or security needs). Figure 6.2 shows the strategic position of a

Figure 6.2 **A Business Competing with the Niche-Differentiation Strategy**

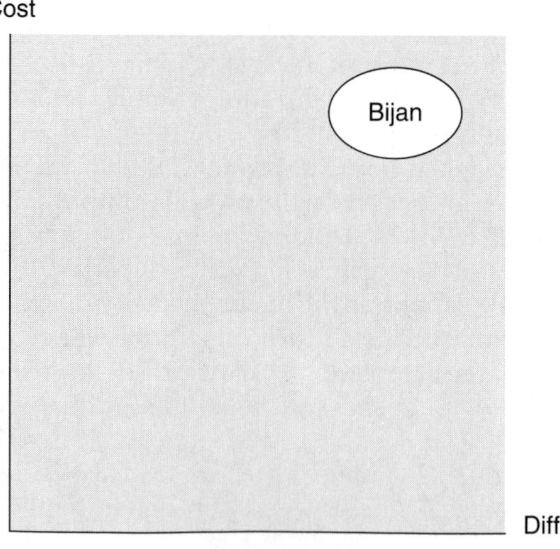

business unit (Bijan) that serves the specialized needs of select customers. Note that high costs and high product/service differentiation characterize the niche-differentiation strategy.

The exclusive Beverly Hills retailer Bijan demonstrates this strategy. Bijan buys specialized, quality products only for customized needs that tend to change frequently and carries one-of-a-kind costly merchandise. Shopping at Bijan is done only through personal appointment.

The chief vulnerability of this strategy is that competitors who emphasize cost control may be able to offer similar products at predatory prices. In fact, using niche-differentiation in conjunction with lower costs can be a particularly effective strategy for a number of small business units in select industries.

Niche–Low-Cost/Differentiation Strategy

Business units that compete with the **niche–low-cost/differentiation strategy** produce highly differentiated, need-fulfilling products or services for the specialized needs of a select group of customers or of a market niche while keeping their costs low. Figure 6.3 reflects the strategic position of a business unit (Porsche) that has adopted this strategy. Note that this business has low costs relative to Rolls-Royce, for instance, while offering a high degree of output differentiation.

How can a business simultaneously differentiate its products or services and lower its costs? The following discussion presents several ways these dual goals can be attained. These methods are listed in Table 6.1. (Note that although these routes are discussed in the context of small business units, they also pertain to large business units that adopt the low-cost–differentiation strategy, which is discussed later in this chapter.)

A Business (Porsche) Competing with the Niche–Low-Cost/Differentiation Strategy and Another Business (Rolls-Royce) Competing with the Niche-Differentiation Strategy **Figure 6.3**

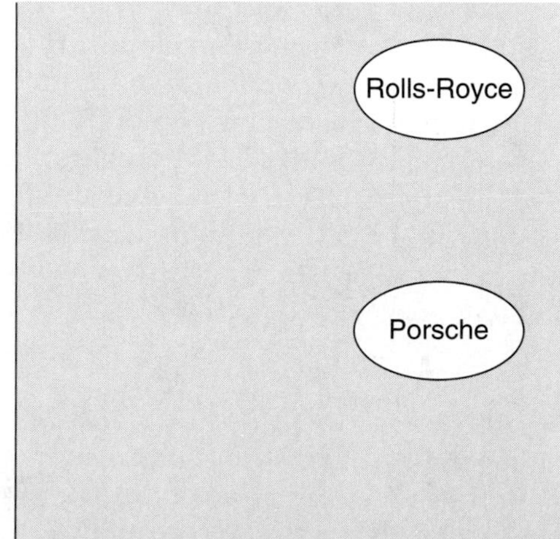

Table 6.1 **Ways Organizations Can Simultaneously Differentiate Their Products/ Services and Lower Their Costs**

Ways Organizations Can Simultaneously Differentiate Their Products/Services and Lower Their Costs
Dedication to quality
Process innovations
Product innovations
Systems innovations
Leverage through organizational expertise and image

Dedication to Quality

A consistent, continual dedication to quality throughout the business not only improves outputs but also reduces costs involved in scrap, warranty, and service after the sale. **Quality** is defined as "the totality of features and characteristics of a product or service that bear on its ability to satisfy stated or implied needs."[3] Hence, a high-quality product or service conforms to a predetermined set of specifications and satisfies the needs of its users. In this sense, quality is a measure of customer satisfaction with a product over its lifetime, relative to customer satisfaction with competitors' product offerings.[4] Note that the customer's perception of quality is the key criterion. While conformance to a predetermined set of specifications is necessary, perceived quality by the buyer provides the sufficient condition.

Quality consultant Philip B. Crosby states that building quality into a product does not cost a company more, because the costs of rework, scrap, and servicing the product after the sale are reduced, and the business benefits from increased customer satisfaction and repeat sales. If features are added to improve the product's fitness for use, fewer repairs are necessary and the customer is pleased. Even though adding a feature may require a manufacturer to charge a premium price, the cost of the product to the customer over the product's lifetime may actually be lower.[5]

Simultaneous emphasis on quality and low costs is feasible not only in manufacturing but also in service businesses.[6] For example, improved information systems allow banks to offer higher-quality services to their customers at lower costs.

In a broader sense, numerous companies in recent years have adopted **total quality management (TQM)** programs. Such approaches attempt to improve product and service quality and increase customer satisfaction by modifying a company's management practices. An essential attribute of TQM programs is that the customer is the final arbiter of quality. A U.S. General Accounting Office study of twenty companies that adopted TQM programs concluded that, in most cases, quality improved, costs fell, customer satisfaction increased, and market share and profitability grew.[7]

Process Innovations

Activities that increase the efficiency of operations and distribution are termed **process innovations.** Although these improvements are normally thought of as lowering costs, they can also enhance product or service differentiation.

> Recently, a computer manufacturer invested $20 million in a flexible assembly system. The investment made good operational sense because it paid for itself in less than a year. Strategically, the investment was even more attractive. Production time was cut by 80%, and product quality improved tenfold.[8]

In this case, costs were lowered, and the significant increase in product quality helped differentiate the product from those of the organization's competitors.

Product Innovations

Although it is common to think of **product innovations** in the context of enhancing differentiation, such improvements can also lower costs. For instance, over the years, Philip Morris developed a filter cigarette and then, later, cigarettes with low tar and nicotine levels. Although these innovations differentiated its product, they also helped lower its costs. The techniques used to produce these cigarettes (freeze drying and reconstituted tobacco sheets) allowed the company to use less tobacco per cigarette to produce a higher-quality product at a dramatic reduction in per-unit costs.[9]

Systems Innovations

Some of the most rewarding strategic advantages hinge not on new products or services but on a change in conventional systems for getting existing products or services to the market. As an example, Savin Business Machines employed **systems innovations** to differentiate its product and lower its costs through innovations at virtually every link of the business system. Savin purchased its components from outside suppliers that offered low prices. It developed a more efficient method of producing its office products systems. Then, it entered into contracts with office products dealers, rather than hire a costly sales force to parallel that of its rivals. The result was a higher-quality product that was produced at a lower cost.[10]

Leverage Through Organizational Expertise and Image

There are other innovative ways to lower costs and heighten differentiation. For instance, small manufacturers normally suffer from a disadvantage in purchasing relative to their larger competitors, since big firms can obtain quantity discounts and often receive substantial engineering support from their suppliers. However, Porsche, a relatively small manufacturer of sports cars, has overcome this problem.

> Even though Porsche purchases small quantities of goods for its operations, it gets competitive prices and significant technical support from its suppliers. The reason is that Porsche does quite a bit of outside engineering for giants such as General Motors, Ford, Volkswagen, etc. Suppliers wish to be a part of Porsche's outside engineering developments in order to have the inside track for future orders forthcoming from those larger companies. Hence, it is to the benefit of suppliers to keep Porsche a very satisfied customer.[11]

Porsche, then, is able to use its relative **organizational expertise**—a business's ability to do something particularly well in comparison with its competitors—in engineering to persuade its suppliers to discount their prices, which lowers Porsche's costs. At the same time, Porsche has obtained high-quality supplier support.

Porsche has also creatively lowered its costs and heightened its differentiation in the area of promotion. Rather than spend substantial sums on mass advertising, Porsche has concentrated its efforts on public relations. Knowing that automobile enthusiasts perceive a certain image or "mystique" associated with Porsche cars, the company has used this leverage to cultivate a close relationship with such magazines as *Road and Track, Motor Trend,* and *Car and Driver.* These magazines report extensively on Porsche cars, at no cost to Porsche.

GENERIC STRATEGIES FOR LARGE BUSINESS UNITS

This section presents the generic strategies that are most appropriate for large business units. These are the low-cost, differentiation, and low-cost–differentiation strategies. Finally, in some instances, large business units may employ some combination of generic strategies. This approach is termed multiple strategies.

■ Low-Cost Strategy

Large businesses that compete with a **low-cost strategy** produce no-frills products and services industrywide. That is, they address a mass market comprised of price-sensitive customers. The outputs of one business differ little from those of other businesses, and the market demand for the outputs is elastic. Consequently, companies using this strategy attempt to lower their costs in their functional areas. For instance, purchases are made from suppliers that offer quantity discounts and the lowest prices. Mass production is pursued whenever possible to lower production costs per unit. Finance plays an influential role since cost control is a high priority. Research and development efforts are directed at improving operational efficiency, and attempts are made to improve logistical and distribution efficiencies. Such businesses de-emphasize the development of new or improved products or services that may raise costs, and advertising and promotional costs are minimized. Figure 6.4 portrays the strategic position of a large business unit (Wal-Mart) that competes with the low-cost strategy. As may be seen, Wal-Mart offers low-differentiated services at low costs relative to Neiman-Marcus, for instance. Wal-Mart's purchasing costs are generally the lowest in the industry, and as in other discount department stores, its services are minimal.

Pursuing a low-cost strategy is consistent with acquiring a large share of the market. A large market share allows scale economies in such areas as purchasing (quantity discounts), manufacturing (mass production), financing (lower interest rates are usually available to large firms), and distribution (mass wholesaling and merchandising).

Small business units competing with the niche–low-cost strategy keep their costs down through a low initial investment and low operating expenses, but

A Business (Wal-Mart) Competing with the Low-Cost Strategy and Another Business (Neiman-Marcus) Competing with the Differentiation Strategy **Figure 6.4**

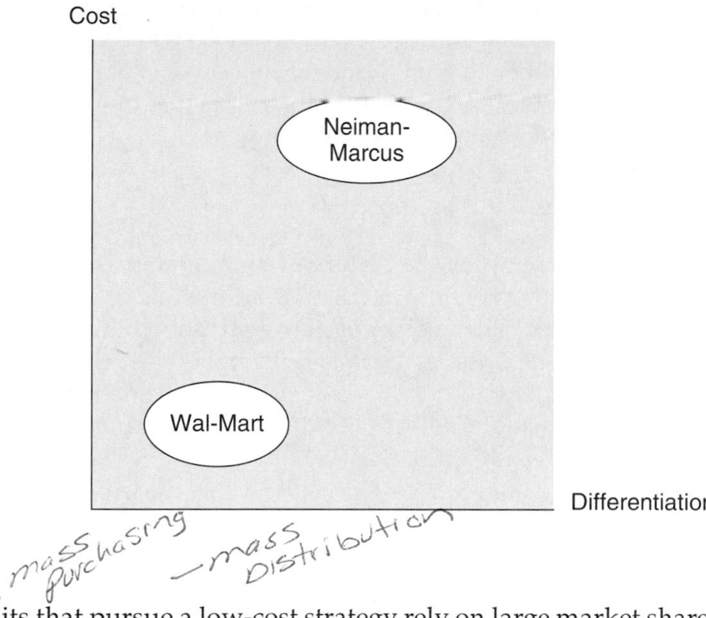

large business units that pursue a low-cost strategy rely on large market shares and scale economies. For example, a small bank offering no-frills services benefits from operating in a small, unpretentious building (low initial investment). Its fixed and variable costs are relatively low because it operates with few employees and limited assets relative to large banks with head offices, bank branches, and many employees. By contrast, a large bank offering no-frills services benefits from the economies of scale that can be gained through large-volume operations. So even though both the niche–low-cost strategy and the low-cost strategy rely on keeping costs down, the means of attaining this goal are different.

Examples of companies that compete with the low-cost strategy can be found in the commodities industries, which produce and sell no-frills products. A well-known historical example in the manufacturing arena is the Ford Motor Company, which used to compete with the low-cost strategy. The Model T, a no-frills automobile, was mass-produced and sold at a low price to a large and growing market.

Manufacturers that choose to use a low-cost strategy today, however, are particularly vulnerable to intense price competition, which drives profit margins down.[12] Under these circumstances, their ability to improve outputs, augment their products with superior services, or spend more on advertising and promotion is severely limited.[13] As they begin to lose customers to competitors with superior products, they will, in response, lower their prices, which puts even more pressure on their profit margins. The prospect of being caught in this vicious cycle keeps most manufacturers from adopting the low-cost strategy.

Another important vulnerability of this strategy is technological obsolescence. Manufacturers that value technological stability, and consequently avoid responding to new product and market opportunities, may eventually find that their products have become obsolete and are no longer desired by their customers.

Outside of manufacturing, however, there are successful businesses that compete through lower costs. Wal-Mart, for instance, purchases at rock-bottom prices because of its enormous volume and its well-known expertise and toughness in negotiations. Furthermore, it keeps inventory and transportation costs low through its well-designed, regionally located distribution centers. Nevertheless, Wal-Mart is potentially vulnerable to a repositioned Sears, Roebuck, Kmart, and other low-cost discounters.

Differentiation Strategy

Businesses that employ the **differentiation strategy** produce unique products or services industrywide. That is, they address large markets with a relatively inelastic demand. Their customers are generally willing to pay average to high prices for unique outputs. Because customers are relatively price-insensitive, businesses emphasize quality in each of their functional areas. For instance, purchases are made from suppliers that offer high-quality raw materials, parts, and components, even if the cost is relatively high. The production department emphasizes quality over cost considerations. Research and development activities focus on developing new or improved products and services, and the company's sales efforts are generously supported with advertising and promotion. Although the finance function is important, it does not dominate organizational decision making. If a business suddenly finds itself faced with a competitor's superior products, it may well borrow money immediately to improve its products, even if the prevailing interest rate is high.

Businesses that compete with the differentiation strategy attempt to create new product and market opportunities or respond to them.[14] These actions, of course, are costly. Therefore, such organizations value technological fluidity so that they may create or keep pace with new developments in their industries.[15]

Figure 6.5 portrays the strategic position of a business unit (Sony Engineering and Manufacturing, maker of televisions and video and audio hardware) that uses the differentiation strategy; note its high costs and high differentiation. Such a company requires a large market share so that it may establish a unique image throughout the industry. To attain this end, the business may either acquire patent protection or develop strong brands that create consumer loyalty. Sony is an example of a successful differentiator.

Others have not been as fortunate and have had to change their strategy. Xerox is an example of such a business. For years, Xerox copiers were made with costly, internally produced components, and they were heavily advertised and promoted. And for years, the company was able to pass along its high costs to its customers in the form of high prices.[16] However, Xerox, like other businesses using a differentiation strategy, found itself vulnerable to new competitors with similar products at lower costs and prices.[17] As Japanese competitors began to offer high-quality copiers that were produced more efficiently and priced significantly lower than Xerox products, Xerox saw its earnings and market share decline significantly. To rebound, it cut its manufacturing costs by 30 percent, reduced the time needed to develop new products by 50 percent, and greatly improved the quality of its copiers.[18] Xerox now follows the generic strategy, discussed next.

A Business Competing with the Differentiation Strategy **Figure 6.5**

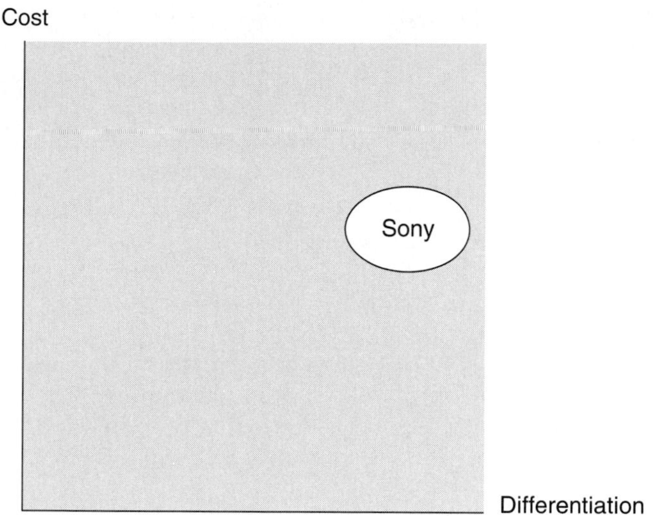

■ Low-Cost–Differentiation Strategy

Organizations that compete with a **low-cost–differentiation strategy** serve, for the most part, the same large, relatively price-insensitive markets for unique products or services that were already discussed. This strategy is illustrated in Figure 6.6. The business (Anheuser-Busch) shown in the figure maintains low costs while offering differentiation.

This particular strategy is relatively controversial. Some theorists believe that competing simultaneously with low costs and differentiation is inconsistent. That is, a business that emphasizes differentiation cannot also maintain low costs, and a business that keeps costs low cannot produce differentiated outputs.[19] However, a growing volume of theoretical and empirical work demonstrates that a dual emphasis on low costs and differentiation can result in high performance.

We believe that the low-cost–differentiation strategy is possible to attain and can be quite effective. This strategy begins with an organizational commitment to quality products or services. Thus, the organization is active technologically in order to improve output quality. By providing high-quality outputs, the business differentiates itself from its competitors. Because customers for particular products or services are drawn to high quality, the business unit that offers such quality will experience an increasing demand for its outputs. This increasing demand results in a larger market share, providing economies of scale that permit lower per-unit costs in purchasing, manufacturing, financing, research and development, and marketing. Such businesses as Anheuser-Busch and Coca-Cola and many of the large business units of General Electric differentiate their outputs through high quality while they simultaneously maintain low-per-unit-cost operations.

Figure 6.6 **A Business Competing with the Low-Cost–Differentiation Strategy**

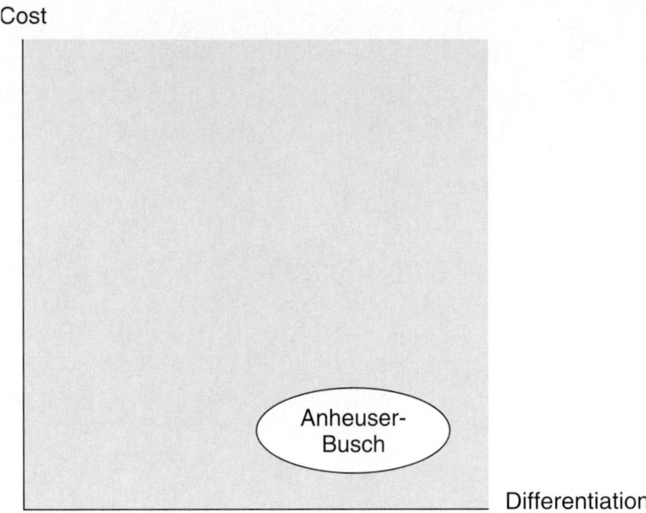

For instance, Anheuser-Busch is the largest producer of beer in the United States, with a market share of 42 percent. Because of its size, the company benefits from quantity discounts in purchasing and from other scale economies in its processing operations, its research and development activities, and its marketing functions. Even with its low costs, however, Anheuser-Busch differentiates itself through its taste and its advertising ("This Bud's for you" and "The night belongs to Michelob") and by emphasizing its high-quality raw materials ("choicest hops, rice and best barley") and its production process ("brewed by our original process"). Additionally, this business keeps pace with market developments and introduces new products periodically, with Bud Dry being a recent example.

In the service arena, Federal Express used the differentiation strategy to create the overnight delivery industry two decades ago. But, as competitors entered the industry and began to duplicate Federal Express's superb service, customers began shopping for companies with lower prices. By 1992, Federal Express was rapidly adopting the low-cost–differentiation strategy to stay competitive. It shut down most of its European operations, purchased more efficient aircraft, and developed new technology and productivity methods to lower its costs. Simultaneously, it differentiated its services by offering just-in-time shipments for customers' manufacturing and distribution processes and by installing computer terminals in large customers' offices so that they could track their own shipments.[20]

■ Multiple Strategies

In some cases, large business units employ **multiple strategies,** or more than one of the strategies identified in the preceding sections. For instance, a business that uses the differentiation strategy or the low-cost–differentiation strat-

STRATEGIC INSIGHT

The Low-Cost–Differentiation Strategy: A Giant Success at Giant Food

Perhaps no business has used the low-cost–differentiation strategy with any more success than the $3.3 billion Giant Food supermarket chain that dominates the Washington, D.C., area and is destined to grow nationally (it is already the 37th largest retailing company in the nation). The store has differentiated its services by being among the first to offer gourmet meals to go, fresh pizza made in-house, a half-price salad bar during the summer, and a "frequent-buyer" program that rewards customer loyalty with credits toward future shopping trips. Even further differentiation has taken the form of offering more Asian goods in areas with substantial Vietnamese and Thai populations and extensive lines of vegetarian foods in neighborhoods with large groups of Seventh-Day Adventists.

Yet at the same time, it has managed to keep its costs at rock bottom through such innovative ideas as manufacturing its own house brands, milk, soda, ice cream, ice cubes, and plastic packagings; developing the land and building many of the shopping centers in which its stores are located; producing its own television ads; and even doing its own exterminating. These operations make Giant one of the nation's more vertically integrated supermarket chains.

The chain, whose after-tax profit margins are triple the industry average, is highly competitive. When Safeway's restructuring raised its costs, Giant exploited that weakness by cutting its own prices further and increasing its coupon offerings. When threatened by no-frills stores, it has responded by offering its customers substantial coupon discounts.

No cost-savings potential is overlooked. When its shopping center construction crews are not building the chain's own centers, they are earning over $20 million annually from outside contracts.

SOURCES: K. Swisher, "Giant Plans 1st Expansion Outside Local Sales Region," *The Washington Post,* 28 January 1993; "The Service 500: The 50 Largest Retailing Companies," *Fortune,* 1 June 1992, p. 188; R.A. Pyatt, Jr., "Giant's Expansion Plans Made with Refreshing Optimism," *The Washington Post,* 29 November 1990; D. Foust, "Why Giant Foods Is a Gargantuan Success," *Business Week,* 4 December 1989, p. 80.

egy may also adopt one of the niche strategies used by small companies. Figure 6.7 portrays the strategies of two hotels: Hyatt uses both the differentiation strategy and the niche-differentiation strategy; Holiday Inn employs a combination of low-cost–differentiation and niche-differentiation strategies.

Large business units may compete with multiple strategies for either proactive reasons (attempting to modify some segment of their environment to enhance their effectiveness) or reactive reasons (reacting to environmental change to maintain their effectiveness). For example, Holiday Inn, a business unit of British brewing firm, Bass PLC, and one of the largest companies in the hotel/motel industry with 1,600 hotels worldwide, maintains its preeminent position by competing proactively with both low-cost–differentiation and niche-differentiation strategies.

Its low-cost–differentiation strategy is revealed through its use of scale economies in purchasing and financing and its nationwide reservation system, which keeps costs low, and its differentiation through its quality rooms and services. Additionally, the company heavily advertises and promotes its qual-

Figure 6.7 **Businesses Competing with Multiple Strategies: Hyatt Competes with Differentiation and Niche-Differentiation; Holiday Inn Competes with Low-Cost–Differentiation and Niche-Differentiation**

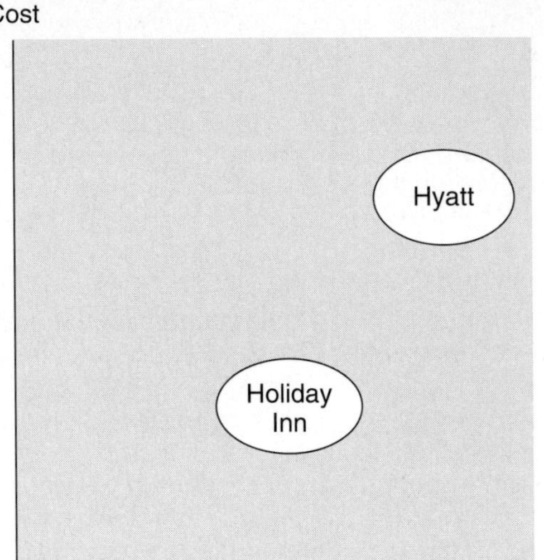

ity accommodations. But to appeal to more than one customer group, this business reserves a small section of some of its inns for the more discriminating customer. In these sections, spacious suites with plush furnishings, wet bars, refrigerators, and hair dryers are provided, along with complimentary food, newspapers, and beverages. As might be expected, the price that Holiday Inn charges for these suites is significantly higher than its price for ordinary rooms. This niche-differentiation strategy requires a higher initial investment per suite and higher operating costs. By using multiple strategies, Holiday Inn appeals to different groups of customers.

Likewise, Hyatt offers special suites in each of its hotels to elite customers. However, even its regular rooms are advertised to discriminating customers who are willing to pay higher-than-average prices for a hotel room.

R.J. Reynolds provides an example of a large business that reactively competes with multiple strategies. For years, Reynolds employed a low-cost–differentiation strategy for its cigarette brands. But as the Liggett Group and other smaller firms began to produce generic (no-brand) cigarettes in the early 1980s, Reynolds responded by also adopting a niche–low-cost strategy. The company positioned its otherwise lackluster-performing brand, Doral, against generic cigarettes by reducing its costs of production and its price.[21]

It is important to note several exceptions to the preceding discussion. First, a large business unit that uses a low-cost strategy is unlikely to employ multiple strategies. A combination of the low-cost strategy with a niche–low-cost strategy is redundant, since both strategies concentrate on no-frills outputs at low costs. Combining the low-cost strategy with either of the other niche strategies is probably unworkable because it is difficult for an organization to operate primarily on the foundation of a no-frills philosophy (and all that it implies) while simultaneously producing highly differentiated products.[22]

Second, a large business unit that competes with the differentiation strategy is unlikely to employ a niche–low-cost strategy or a niche–low-cost/differentiation strategy because low costs are not emphasized by its managers.

Third, large business units will not adopt as their sole strategy any of the three niche strategies identified earlier as being appropriate for small business units. A small market share with relatively low sales figures cannot justify sizable expenditures on research and development, operations, and marketing.[23] Of course, enlightened managers of small business units and entrepreneurs are well aware of these restrictions on the operations of large business units. Hence, small enterprises are often strategically buffered from head-to-head competition with large firms. The market that small companies have carefully chosen is simply too small to attract large organizations as major competitors.

The seven generic strategies that have been discussed in this chapter are summarized in Table 6.2. The emphasis of each strategy, its market coverage, the characteristics of its products and services, its market demand, and its pricing are all identified.

SELECTING A GENERIC STRATEGY

In theory, an industry progresses through certain stages during the course of its life cycle: embryonic, growth, shakeout, maturity, and decline. If so, then the

Generic Business Unit Strategies and Their Ramifications **Table 6.2**

Generic Business Unit Strategy	*Emphasis of Business Unit*	*Market Coverage*	*Characteristics of Products and Services*	*Market Demand*	*Pricing*
Niche–low-cost	Lower overall costs	Market niche	No-frills	Elastic	Depending on industry forces, low to average
Niche–differentiation	Specialized quality	Market niche	Highly differentiated	Inelastic	High
Niche–low-cost/differentiation	Specialized quality and low costs	Market niche	Highly differentiated	Inelastic	High
Low-cost	Lower overall costs	Marketwide	No-frills	Elastic	Depending on industry forces, low to average
Differentiation	Higher quality	Marketwide	Differentiated	Relatively inelastic	Depending on industry forces, average to high
Low-cost–differentiation	Higher quality and low cost	Marketwide	Differentiated	Relatively inelastic	Depending on industry forces, average to high
Multiple strategies	Mixed	Mixed	Mixed	Mixed	Mixed

STRATEGIC INSIGHT

A Change in Strategy at Compaq Computer

Founded in 1982 by three ex-employees of Texas Instruments, Compaq Computer quickly rose to prominence by adopting the niche-differentiation strategy. Its personal computers (PCs) were characterized by innovative technology, high quality, and premium prices. Compaq's corporate culture was one of "sparing no expense to launch only the very best PCs on the market."

But, by the late 1980s, Compaq's industry environment was changing. New low-cost clone producers such as Dell Computer and AST Research entered the market, driving prices down. At first, Compaq took little notice of these changes, continuing to operate in its customary fashion. But a 1990 loss of $324 million, a one-point decline in U.S. market share, and a fall in Compaq's stock price from the $60s to the $20s roused the company's board of directors. Co-founder and CEO Rod Canion was ousted and replaced by Eckhard Pfeiffer, the company's chief operating officer, who had been pressing for cost and price cuts.

Less than a year later, Compaq introduced a new line of desktop and laptop PCs to the market. Priced to compete directly with Dell and AST, these machines were to be marketed, not through the traditional network of Compaq dealers, but through mass merchandise outlets and computer superstores.

Supporting these new products was a massive cost-cutting program. Compaq eliminated 25 percent of its work force, forced suppliers to engage in competitive bidding, replaced some in-house production of components with outside contractors, reduced the quality of its packaging, shifted some production from Texas to lower-cost Singapore, and even abolished its tradition of offering free soft drinks to employees. At the same time, Compaq increased its U.S. advertising by 60 percent and set up a toll-free telephone number for its customers.

Despite cutting its manufacturing costs by 17 percent, Compaq remained a relatively high-cost producer. Its operating costs in 1992 were 26 percent of sales, compared to 21.2 percent at AST and 19 percent at Dell. It seemed that years of ignoring costs could not be erased overnight.

To add to its troubles, Compaq's dramatic price reductions triggered new price cuts from its competitors, placing the entire PC industry in a precarious financial position. But Compaq was determined not to back off. CEO Pfeiffer swore that Compaq would become "the low-cost provider."

SOURCES: D. Kirkpatrick, "The Revolution at Compaq Computer," *Fortune,* 14 December 1992, pp. 80–88; C. Arnst, S.A. Forest, K. Rebello, and J. Levine, "Compaq: How It Made Its Impressive Move Out of the Doldrums," *Business Week,* 2 November 1992, pp. 146–151; M. Allen, "Developing New Line of Low-Priced PCs Shakes Up Compaq," *The Wall Street Journal,* 15 June 1992 (source of first quotation); S.A. Forest and C. Arnst, "Compaq Declares War on the Clones," *Business Week,* 15 June 1992, p. 43 (source of second quotation).

appropriate generic strategy for a business unit would depend, at least to some extent, upon the particular stage of its industry's life cycle.

Of course, not all industries follow these exact stages. For instance, some industries, such as the laser disk industry, never advance beyond the embryonic stage. Others, following their decline, may be revitalized into new growth because of changes in the macroenvironment. For example, the bicycle industry fell into decline some years ago. It has now, however, been rejuvenated by society's interest in health and physical fitness.

The following paragraphs will demonstrate how generic strategies for business units are related to industry life cycle stages. This discussion is appropriate for those industries that follow the traditional life cycle, but it can also be useful for business units operating in industries that deviate from the traditional life cycle. First, we will examine the industry life cycle stages and then present a framework that integrates the business unit generic strategies with these life cycle stages.

Industry Life Cycle Stages

The traditional stages in an **industry's life cycle** are shown in Figure 6.8. A young industry that is beginning to form is considered to be in the *embryonic stage*. Consumer demand for the industry's outputs is low at this time because many consumers are not yet aware of these products or services. Virtually all purchasers are first-time buyers. At this stage in the industry's development, choice of technology is often not yet settled. For instance, at the beginning of the automobile industry, various small manufacturers experimented with electric, steam, and internal combustion technologies.

Normally, once the choice of technology is made and increasing numbers of consumers begin to desire the industry's outputs, the industry enters the *growth stage*. In the car industry, this stage began when the internal combustion engine became the accepted technology. Simultaneously, Henry Ford installed the assembly line to produce a single model car that many customers could afford. At this stage, most buyers are still first-time purchasers of the industry's outputs.

Over time, growth of the industry begins to slow as market demand approaches saturation. Fewer first-time buyers remain; most purchases are now for replacement purposes. As growth in demand begins to slow, some of the

Industry Life Cycle Stages

Figure 6.8

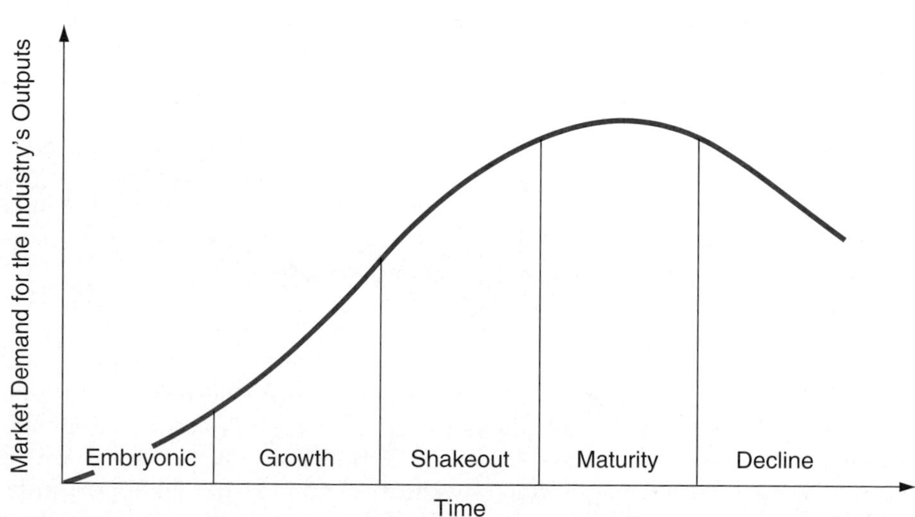

industry's weaker competitors may go out of business. This stage, therefore, is known as the *shakeout stage*. In the U.S. auto industry, the shakeout stage resulted in the demise of such independent car producers as Hudson, Packard, Studebaker, and American Motors, leaving General Motors, Ford, and Chrysler as survivors.

When the market demand for the industry's outputs is completely saturated, the *maturity* stage has been reached. Virtually all purchases are limited to replacement demand, and industry growth may be low, nonexistent, or even negative. The U.S. car industry is currently in the maturity stage.

Finally, market demand begins to fall steadily. This *decline* stage is often ushered in when consumers begin to turn to the products or services of substitute industries. These substitutes may have lower costs or greater convenience (such as mass transportation over car travel), they may be safer (such as chewing gum over tobacco products), or they may be technologically superior (such as the personal computer over the typewriter).

■ An Integrative Framework

How appropriate a generic strategy is for a given business unit depends upon the business's competitive status and the external forces in its industry life cycle stage. Recall that a business unit's competitive status is derived from the combined strengths and weaknesses of corporate-level, business unit, and functional-level strategies. For instance, a business unit's ability to differentiate its outputs may depend upon corporate scope innovations (discussed in Chapter 4) and functional strength in research and development (discussed in the following chapter).

Figure 6.9 presents general guidelines for choosing a generic strategy in light of a business unit's particular industry life cycle stage. The vertical axis represents the life cycle stage, while the size of the business unit is shown on the horizontal axis.

Cell 1

Virtually all businesses are small during an industry's embryonic stage since there has not yet been much opportunity for growth. In this situation, the niche-differentiation strategy is appropriate because businesses in cell 1 are attempting to create new product or market opportunities. Their costs tend to be high and the number of first-time buyers to whom their outputs appeal is limited. Such businesses value technological fluidity either to create or to keep pace with state-of-the-art developments in the new industry. Those customers who purchase the industry's outputs are willing to pay high prices because these products or services fulfill their particular needs.

Cells 2 and 6

As the industry grows, some businesses grow with it (those in cell 6) while others remain relatively small (those in cell 2). In cell 2, any of the generic strategies for smaller businesses may be appropriate, depending upon the particular business's strengths and weaknesses and the external opportunities and threats its management identifies. If a business can keep its costs down while serving price-sensitive customers, the niche–low-cost strategy can be

Generic Strategies in the Context of Industry Life Cycle and Size of Businesses **Figure 6.9**

Size of Businesses

Stage of Industry Life Cycle	Smaller Businesses	Larger Businesses
Decline	**Cell 5** Niche–low-cost Niche–low-cost/differentiation	**Cell 9** Low-cost Low-cost–differentiation Multiple
Maturity	**Cell 4** Niche–low-cost Niche–differentiation Niche–low-cost/differentiation	**Cell 8** Low-cost Differentiation Low-cost–differentiation Multiple
Shakeout	**Cell 3** Niche–low-cost Niche–differentiation Niche–low-cost/differentiation	**Cell 7** Low-cost Differentiation Low-cost–differentiation Multiple
Growth	**Cell 2** Niche–low-cost Niche–differentiation Niche–low-cost/differentiation	**Cell 6** Low-cost Differentiation Low-cost–differentiation Multiple
Embryonic	**Cell 1** Niche–differentiation	

appropriate. For instance, while the personal computer industry grew quickly during the 1980s, Kaypro remained small by serving the no-frills needs of certain price-sensitive customers.

Businesses that can produce highly differentiated, need-fulfilling outputs, however, may use the niche-differentiation strategy. For example, the industry for stereophonic products grew significantly during the 1960s and 1970s, but small companies such as Ampax thrived by producing exclusive, top-of-the-line products. Likewise, a small business that is able to control its costs while producing differentiated outputs may use the niche–low-cost/differentiation strategy.

Similarly, among those businesses that choose to grow along with the industry, any of the strategies available to larger businesses may be appropriate. A company can choose to grow at a rapid pace by emphasizing low costs and no-frills outputs, by differentiating its outputs to a large market, by simultaneously emphasizing low costs and differentiated outputs, or by employing multiple strategies.

Cells 3 and 7

The same strategies that were appropriate in the two preceding cells would also be suitable as the industry begins to "shake out" its less effective competitors. Although the growth in market demand is slowing, the industry is still expanding; and well-managed companies can thrive by following any of the generic strategies that best suit their strengths and weaknesses and their perception of the environment's opportunities and threats.

Cells 4 and 8

As the industry approaches zero or even negative growth, emphasis is placed on cutting costs and/or differentiating products/services to maintain sales levels. Without market expansion, competing successfully with high prices becomes increasingly difficult. Hence, the more viable smaller companies can normally be expected to adopt either the niche–low-cost or niche–low-cost/differentiation strategy in cell 4, and most viable larger businesses are likely to adopt either the low-cost or low-cost–differentiation strategies in cell 8. Some businesses with unique products or services may still be able to compete successfully with either the niche-differentiation or differentiation strategies, but there will be fewer of them than in cells 3 and 7.

Cells 5 and 9

As demand for the industry's outputs declines significantly, high-cost businesses find themselves unable to compete as companies slash prices to try to maintain their market shares. Virtually all surviving smaller business units will have adopted the niche–low-cost or niche–low-cost/differentiation strategies, while those larger companies that remain will be following the low-cost, low-cost–differentiation, or multiple strategies.

RELATIONSHIPS AMONG GENERIC STRATEGIES, BUSINESS UNIT SIZE, MARKET SHARE, AND PROFITABILITY

This section examines the relationship between generic strategy and business unit size, with a particular emphasis on midsized business units. Also discussed are the relationships among generic strategies, market share, and profitability.

▪ Generic Strategies and Business Unit Size

The preceding sections identified generic strategies appropriate for small and large business units. Midsized business units were not discussed because these organizations normally perform poorly in comparison with small or large competitors.[24] The reason is that midsized businesses do not possess the advantages of their smaller or larger counterparts. Whether the business unit is considered small, midsized, or large, of course, depends upon its size relative to the size of its competitors in the industry.

The competitive superiority that small businesses enjoy over midsized business units includes their flexibility in meeting specific market demands and their quicker reaction to environmental changes. Additionally, because of their lower investments, they can pursue small orders that would be unprofitable for midsized businesses. Finally, they can capitalize on their small market shares by creating an image of exclusivity. Customers who buy products for prestige purposes do so only if the market has relatively few of those products.[25] For instance, consumers who purchase Rolls-Royce automobiles would be alienated if they began to see a Rolls-Royce on every block, because the prestige of exclusivity is the primary reason for their purchase. Management at Rolls-Royce is satisfied with this situation, since nearly three months is required to build each car. The company's image is enhanced by the fact that 60 percent of the 115,000 cars it has produced can still be driven.[26]

The crucial advantage that a large business has over the midsized company lies in its ability to translate its economies of scale into lower costs per unit.

Therefore, since midsized business units do not have the advantages of either small or large firms, they have two strategic options to increase their effectiveness. First, they may, over time, expand their operations to take advantage of scale economies. Second, they may retrench in order to avail themselves of the advantages possessed by small companies. The feasibility of expansion or retrenchment depends upon various competitive and industry forces.[27]

■ Generic Strategies, Market Share, and Profitability

The discussion thus far suggests certain relationships among generic business strategies, market share, and profitability. Some of these possible relationships are shown in Figure 6.10. The vertical axis represents business unit profitability, and the horizontal axis reflects market share. The two U-shaped curves represent proposed relationships between market share and profitability.

Generic Strategies, Market Share, and Profitability **Figure 6.10**

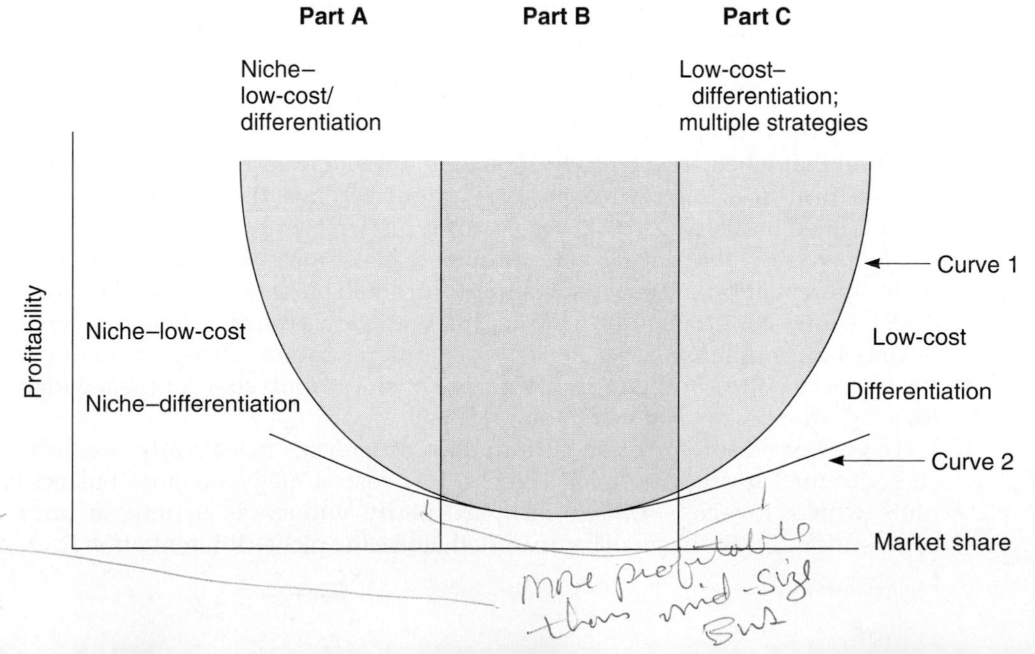

Part A of curve 1 represents business units that compete with the niche–low-cost/differentiation strategy. These are small businesses with small market shares, yet they are quite profitable because of their flexibility and their ability to produce outputs that fulfill customers' particular needs for prestige, performance, or safety.

Part C of curve 1 shows large business units that compete with the low-cost–differentiation strategy and those that compete with multiple strategies. These businesses have large market shares and are very profitable because of their scale economies and the unique nature of their outputs.

Part B of curve 1 portrays businesses with midsized market shares. Their profitability is lower than that of either of the other sets of business units because they do not have the flexibility of smaller businesses or their ability to produce outputs that fulfill customers' particular needs for prestige, performance, or safety. Nor can they achieve the scale economies of larger business units. To increase their profitability, these businesses may either retrench (and move up toward part A) or expand (to move up to part C).

On curve 2, part A shows business units that compete with the niche–low-cost strategy or the niche-differentiation strategy. These small businesses with small market shares are less profitable than those that adopt the niche–low-cost/differentiation strategy (on part A of curve 1).

Part C of curve 2 represents large business units competing with either the low-cost strategy or the differentiation strategy. Although they have large market shares, their profitability is less than that of businesses using the low-cost–differentiation strategy or multiple strategies (on part C of curve 1). Finally, part B of curve 2 converges into part B of curve 1 to portray midsized businesses with low profitability.

It is important to realize that these U-shaped relationships may not hold in all industries. For example, in retailing, recall that Wal-Mart has high profitability even though it employs the low-cost strategy. Also, the relationships will be distorted in fragmented industries containing numerous small companies of similar size. Examples are industries that produce adhesives and sealants, fasteners, and apparel. Alternatively, in consolidated industries with only a few businesses, the relationships may also not hold. For example, the aircraft manufacturing industry is comprised chiefly of Boeing, McDonnell Douglas, and Airbus. Since Airbus is owned by a consortium of European governments, Boeing devotes most of its resources to manufacturing commercial aircraft, and McDonnell Douglas has placed its emphasis on government contracts for military aircraft, this industry would not be accurately represented by the U-shaped curves.

Recall that when we refer to *large* or *small*, these terms are industry-specific. A large firm in a fragmented industry might be considered quite tiny in a consolidated industry.

We have seen that small business units that compete with the niche–low-cost/differentiation strategy may outperform small business units that employ a niche–low-cost strategy or a niche-differentiation strategy. Similarly, large business units that use either the low-cost–differentiation strategy or multiple strategies can often outperform those large business units that compete with a low-cost strategy or a differentiation strategy.

The major reason for these performance differences has already been discussed. Small businesses using a niche–low-cost strategy or large business units with a low-cost strategy are particularly vulnerable to intense price competition. Similarly, small companies that use the niche-differentiation strategy and large enterprises competing with a differentiation strategy eventually find themselves in competition with new entrants that are able to offer alternative products at lower prices. As we pointed out, however, we cannot conclude that these particular strategies are never effective. In fact, as we have seen, some businesses employ them most profitably. But the probability may be low that these strategies will be as effective as the niche–low-cost/differentiation, low-cost–differentiation, or multiple strategies.

VALUE ANALYSIS AND STRATEGIC GROUPS

This concluding section of the chapter analyzes how generic strategies are related to value and strategic groups. First, the generic strategies that are most likely to provide market value to consumers are discussed. Then the concept of strategic groups is examined.

■ Generic Strategies and Value Analysis

The marketplace rewards business units that are able to offer better **value,** which is the worth of a good or service in terms of its perceived usefulness or importance to consumers in relation to its price. Those businesses that compete with differentiation while maintaining low costs (niche–low-cost/differentiation, low-cost–differentiation, and multiple strategies) are usually better positioned to offer value than are business units that emphasize only differentiation (the strategies of niche-differentiation and differentiation) or low costs (the niche–low-cost and low-cost strategies).

The ultimate judge of value is the consumer. Consumers compare the price and quality of any one business unit's outputs with the price and quality of competitors' outputs. Business units that offer poor value to their customers in the form of relatively high prices and relatively low quality face negative prospects. If they hold to their price level, they will lose market share and profitability. Likewise, if they maintain their market share by discounting their prices, they will also suffer lower profits. In either case, they will be hard-pressed to generate the necessary funds to increase their product quality so that their value might be maintained or improved.

On the other hand, business units that offer good value (competitive prices and high quality) to their customers face bright prospects. If they increase their prices, they may be able to maintain their market share if consumers perceive that the new price–quality relationship is still fair relative to competitors' outputs. The worst that can happen is that they will lose market share but will be able to maintain or even increase their overall profits on the reduced sales through their higher prices. Alternatively, these businesses may reduce their prices, which will increase their market share and allow them to lower their costs through economies of scale. The result will be increased profitability.

Our discussion suggests that business units that compete with the niche–low-cost/differentiation strategy, the low-cost–differentiation strategy, or multiple strategies are usually better positioned to offer superior value to customers. Of course, better value is not confined to these strategies. Wal-Mart, for instance, offers superior value to its customers through its low-cost strategy. But the ability to offer high value is often enhanced by adopting one of these three strategies.

■ Generic Strategies and Strategic Groups

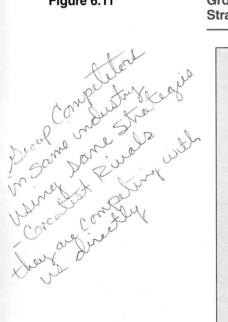

Most industries are comprised of a number of business units that compete more directly with certain businesses in the industry than with others. Groups of direct competitors are identified by the similarity of their strategic profiles, and each collection of direct competitors is termed a **strategic group.** As an example, assume that an industry contains many businesses, each of which employs one of the seven generic strategies that has been discussed. Such an industry can be portrayed as shown in Figure 6.11. All twenty business units in this industry compete with one another. But business units within each strategic group engage in more direct and intense competition with one another.

Businesses normally experience difficulty in moving from one strategic group to another. In fact, strategic groups are quite stable and remain distinct from one another because of this relative immobility. Group-specific mobility barriers arise because the businesses in each group make strategic decisions that cannot easily be duplicated by enterprises outside the group. Such decisions require "outsiders" to incur significant costs, elapsed time, and/or uncertainty about the outcome of their decisions.[28] Thus, businesses in a lower-performing strategic group find it difficult and costly to switch to a higher-performing strategic group.

Note should be taken that controversy exists over the strategic group concept. For instance, strategic groups have been identified in ways that differ

Figure 6.11 **Groups of Business Units in an Industry Competing with Different Generic Strategies**

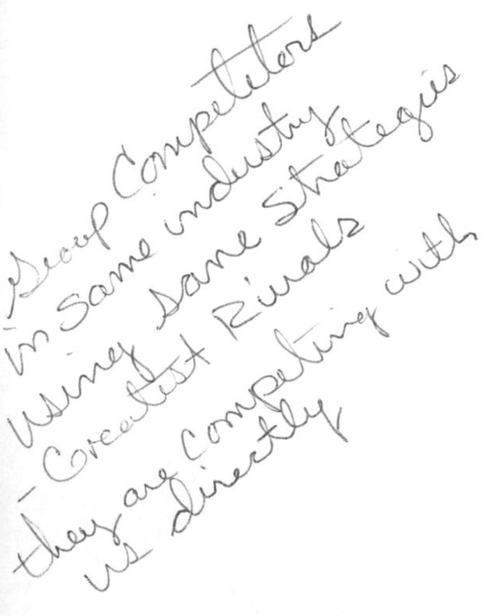

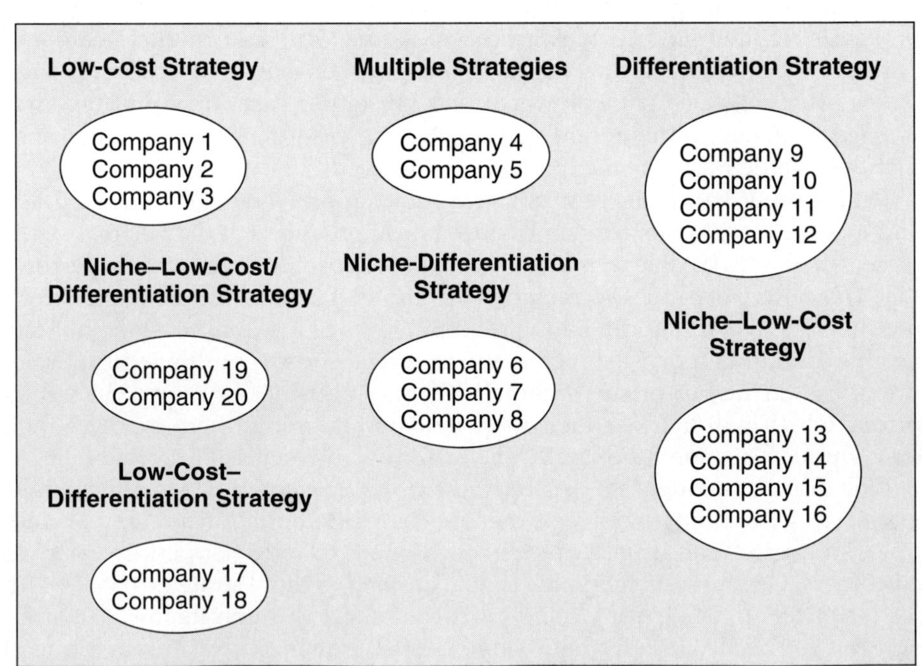

from our definition,[29] and some observers even question the existence of strategic groups.[30]

SUMMARY

While the strategic question at the corporate level is, In what industries or businesses should we be operating? the appropriate question at the business unit level is, How should we compete in the chosen industry or business? Three generic strategies are available for small business units: the niche–low-cost strategy, the niche-differentiation strategy, and the niche–low-cost/differentiation strategy. Large business units may choose from among the low-cost strategy, differentiation strategy, low-cost–differentiation strategy, or multiple strategies.

While the niche-differentiation strategy is most appropriate for businesses in the embryonic stage of an industry's life cycle, any of the three generic strategies for smaller businesses or any of the four generic strategies for larger businesses may be appropriate during the growth, shakeout, or maturity stages of the industry life cycle. The choice of a particular strategy depends upon the strengths and weaknesses of each company and the way in which its management perceives the environment's threats and opportunities. In the decline stage of the industry's life cycle, however, the industrywide emphasis on price competition renders the niche-differentiation and differentiation strategies ineffective.

Analysis of these strategies leads to the conclusion that either small or large business units are likely to be more effective than midsized business units. Small businesses have the advantages of flexibility and/or the ability to produce outputs that fulfill customers' particular needs for prestige, performance, or safety; and large companies possess the advantage of economies of scale. The evidence further suggests that for small businesses, the niche–low-cost/differentiation strategy is more likely to be successful in the long run than either of the other two strategies. For large business units, a choice of either the low-cost–differentiation strategy or multiple strategies is more likely to result in success than is the choice of either the low-cost or the differentiation strategy.

Within most industries, certain business units compete more directly with some businesses than with others. Businesses that engage in very direct and intense competition with one another are considered to be a strategic group. Most industries contain several strategic groups, each of which is composed of members possessing similar strategic profiles.

KEY CONCEPTS

Business unit An organizational subsystem that has a market, a set of competitors, and a mission distinct from those of the other subsystems in the firm.

Differentiation strategy A generic business unit strategy in which a business produces unique products or services industrywide for large markets with a relatively inelastic demand.

Generic strategy A strategy that can be adopted by any type of business unit, regardless of its industry or product/service line.

Industry life cycle The temporal stages (embryonic, growth, shakeout, maturity, and decline) through which many—but not all—industries pass.

Low-cost–differentiation strategy A generic business unit strategy in which a business maintains low costs while producing unique products or services industrywide for large markets with a relatively inelastic demand.

Low-cost strategy A generic business unit strategy in which a business produces, at the lowest cost possible, no-frills products and services industrywide for large markets with a relatively elastic demand.

Multiple strategies A strategic alternative for a business unit in which the organization simultaneously employs more than one of the generic business strategies.

Niche-differentiation strategy A generic business unit strategy in which a business produces highly differentiated, need-fulfilling products or services for the specialized needs of a narrow range of customers or a market niche. Since the business's outputs are intended to fulfill a deep set of customer needs, prices are high and demand for the outputs is relatively inelastic.

Niche–low-cost/differentiation strategy A generic business unit strategy in which a business produces highly differentiated, need-fulfilling products or services for the specialized needs of a select group of customers or a market niche while keeping its costs low.

Niche–low-cost strategy A generic business unit strategy in which a business keeps overall costs low while producing no-frills products or services for a market niche with elastic demand.

Organizational expertise An organization's ability to do something particularly well in comparison with its competitors.

Process innovations A business unit's activities that increase the efficiency of operations and distribution.

Product innovations A business unit's activities that enhance the differentiation of its products or services.

Quality The totality of features and characteristics of a product or service that bear on its ability to satisfy stated or implied needs.

Strategic group Within an industry, a select group of direct competitors who have similar strategic profiles.

Systems innovations A business unit's activities that increase the efficiency of any of its functional systems (e.g., purchasing, finance, marketing).

Total quality management (TQM) A broad-based program designed to improve product and service quality and increase customer satisfaction by modifying a company's management practices.

Value The worth of a good or service in terms of its perceived usefulness or importance to a consumer. Value is usually judged by comparing the price and quality of one business's outputs with those of its competitors.

DISCUSSION QUESTIONS

1. How does a business unit strategy differ from a corporate-level strategy?

2. Small business units have a choice of three generic strategies. Explain each of these strategies, and give an example of a business unit that competes with each strategy.

3. Large business units have a choice of four generic strategies. Explain each of these strategies, and give an example of a business unit that competes with each strategy.

4. Explain the difference between a niche–low-cost/differentiation strategy and a low-cost–differentiation strategy.

5. How is it possible for a business to differentiate its outputs and, simultaneously, lower its costs?

6. What strategy or strategies are most appropriate for business units in the embryonic stage of an industry's life cycle? Why? Now identify the strategies that are most effective in the decline stage of an industry's life cycle. Explain why.

7. Why might we expect the performance level of midsized business units to be lower than the performance level of either small or large business units?

8. Explain the relationship that we would expect to find between the generic strategy selected by a business unit and its market share and profitability.

9. Why might we hypothesize that business units that compete with the niche–low-cost/differentiation strategy, the low-cost–differentiation strategy, or multiple strategies are better positioned to offer superior value to customers than are business units that use other strategies?

10. What is a strategic group? Select an industry and identify, by name, some of the business units that comprise two of the strategic groups within that industry.

STRATEGIC MANAGEMENT EXERCISES

1. Assume that you have conducted market research that indicates the need for a bookstore close to your campus. Further assume that you believe that either of two generic strategies could be successful for the bookstore: the niche–low-cost strategy or the niche-differentiation strategy. Respond to the following questions for *each* of these two strategies. Note that your responses for the two strategies will be quite different.
   - What type of physical store should you create?
   - What kinds of books would you carry in your inventory?
   - What in-store services would you provide?
   - Would you generally charge low, average, or high prices?

Now, answer these same questions for a small business and a generic strategy of your own choosing.

2. Assume that you have the financial resources to own a national chain of video stores. Further assume that you believe that either of two generic strategies could be successful for this chain: the low-cost strategy or the low-cost–differentiation strategy. Describe the physical aspects of your stores, their services, their advertising programs, and so on, for *each* of these two strategies.

   Now, describe these same characteristics for a large business and a generic strategy of your own choosing.

3. Select an actual business and analyze its strategic profile (i.e., which generic strategy has it adopted?). What improvements might you suggest for this business?

NOTES

1. W. Zellner and E. Shine, "Striking Gold in the California Skies," *Business Week*, 30 March 1992, p. 48.
2. S.D. Atchison, "The Little Engineers That Could," *Business Week*, 27 July 1992, p. 77.
3. ANSI/ASQC, *Quality Systems Terminology, American National Standard* (1987), A3-1987.
4. D.A. Garvin, *Managing Quality* (New York: Free Press, 1988).
5. P. Crosby, *Quality Is Free* (New York: McGraw-Hill, 1979).
6. M. Helms, M. Ahmadi, and R. Driggans, "Quality and Quantity Goals in Service Industries: Compatible or Conflicting Strategies," *Journal of Business Strategies* 7 (1990): 120–133; S. Cappel, P. Wright, M. Kroll, and D. Wyld, "Competitive Strategies and Business Performance: An Empirical Study of Select Service Businesses," *International Journal of Management* 9 (1992): 1–11.
7. United States General Accounting Office, "Management Practices: U.S. Companies Improve Performance Through Quality Efforts," GAO/NSIAD-91-190, May 1991.
8. E.A. Haas, "Breakthrough Manufacturing," *Harvard Business Review* 65, no. 2 (1987): 76.
9. R.H. Miles, *Coffin Nails and Corporate Strategies* (Englewood Cliffs, N.J.: Prentice-Hall, 1982).
10. F.W. Gluck, "Strategic Choice and Resource Allocation," *The McKinsey Quarterly* 1 (1980): 22–23.
11. P. Wright, "Winning Strategies for Small Manufacturers," *Planning Review* 14 (1986): 20.
12. W.J. Abernathy and K. Wayne, "Limits of Learning Curve," in Harvard Business School, eds., *Survival Strategies for American Industry* (New York: Wiley, 1983), pp. 114–131; R. Luchs, "Successful Businesses Compete on Quality—Not Costs," *Long Range Planning* 19, no. 1 (1986):12–17.
13. R.D. Buzzell and B.T. Gale, *The PIMS Principles* (New York: Free Press, 1987).
14. P. Wright, "A Refinement of Porter's Strategies," *Strategic Management Journal* 8 (1987): 93–101.

15. P. Wright, M.J. Kroll, C.D. Pringle, and J.A. Johnson, "Organization Types, Conduct, Profitability, and Risk in the Semiconductor Industry," *Journal of Management Systems* 2 (1990): 33–48.
16. R. Buaron, "New Game Strategies," *The McKinsey Quarterly* 3 (1981): 24–40.
17. W.D. Vinson and D.F. Heany, "Is Quality Out of Control?" *Harvard Business Review* 55, no. 6 (1977): 114–122.
18. C. Willis, "Wall Street," *Money,* April 1992, p. 70.
19. M.E. Porter, *Competitive Advantage: Creating and Sustaining Superior Performance* (New York: Free Press, 1985).
20. C. Hawkins, "FedEx: Europe Nearly Killed the Messenger," *Business Week,* 25 May 1992, pp. 124–126.
21. Wright, "Refinement of Porter's Strategies."
22. P. Wright, "The Strategic Options of Least Cost, Differentiation and Niche," *Business Horizons* 22 (1986): 21–26.
23. Wright, "Refinement of Porter's Strategies."
24. S. Schoeffler, R. Buzzell, and D. Heany, "Impact of Strategic Planning on Profit Performance," *Harvard Business Review* 52 (1974): 137–145; M.E. Porter, *Competitive Strategy* (New York: Free Press, 1980); Wright, "Refinement of Porter's Strategies"; L. Feldman and J. Stephenson, "Stay Small or Get Huge—Lessons from Securities Trading," *Harvard Business Review* 66, no. 3 (1988): 116–123; M.T. Hannan and J. Freeman, "The Population Ecology of Organizations," *American Journal of Sociology* 82 (1977): 946–947.
25. P. Wright, "Systematic Approach in Finding Export Opportunities," in Harvard Business School, eds., *Managing Effectively in the World Marketplace* (New York: Wiley, 1983), pp. 331–342.
26. T. Aeppel, "Rolls-Royce Tries to Restore Luster as Car Sales Fade," *The Wall Street Journal,* 26 May 1992.
27. P. Chan and T. Sneyoski, "Environmental Change, Competitive Strategy, Structure, and Firm Performance: An Application of Data Development Analysis," *International Journal of Systems Science* 22 (1991): 1625–1636.
28. J. McGee and H. Thomas, "Strategic Groups: Theory, Research and Taxonomy," *Strategic Management Journal* 7 (1986): 141–160.
29. Ibid.
30. J.B. Barney and R.E. Hoskisson, "Strategic Groups: Untested Assertions and Research Proposals," *Managerial and Decision Economics* 11 (1990): 187–198.

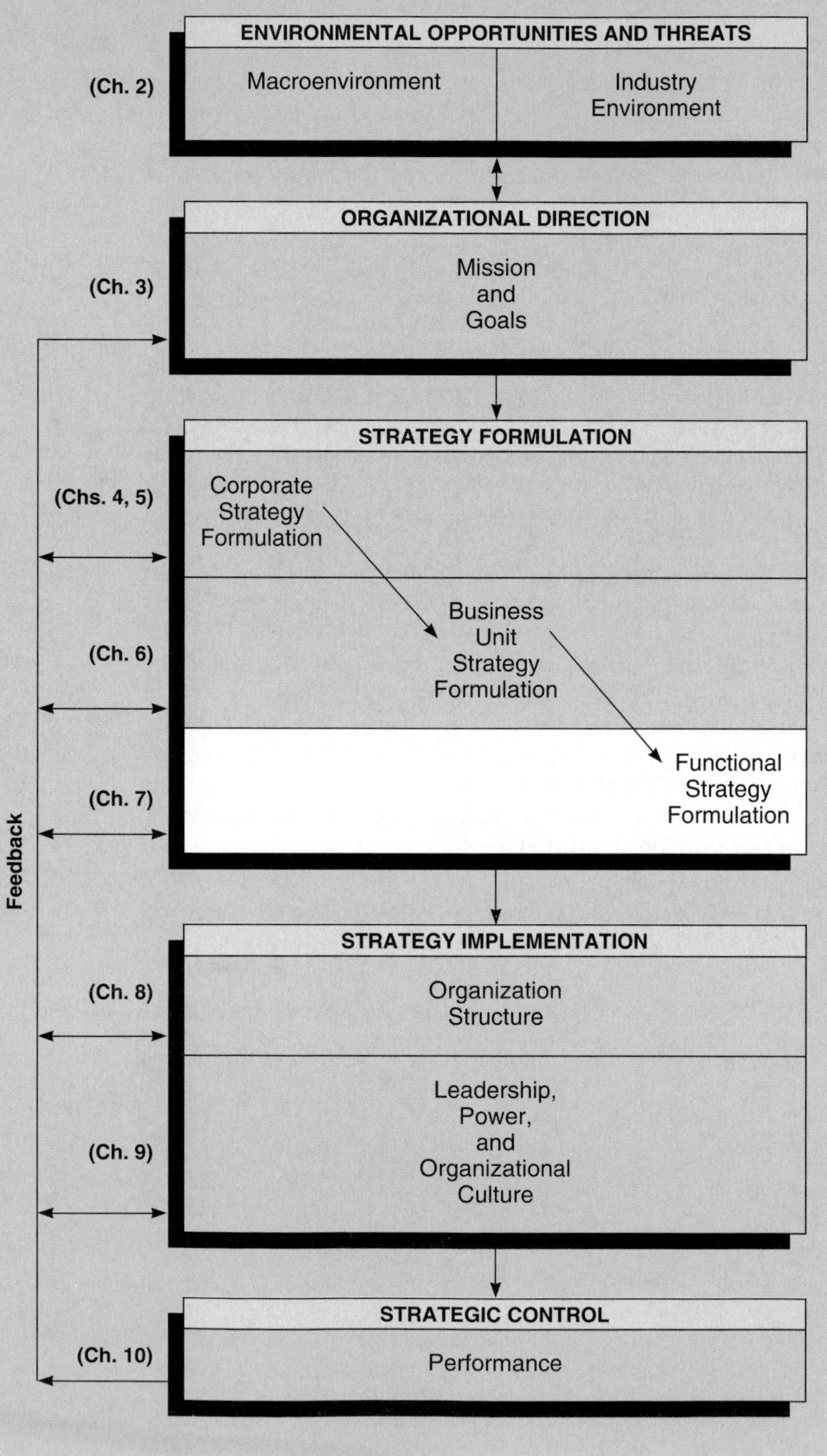

STRATEGIC MANAGEMENT MODEL
ENVIRONMENTAL OPPORTUNITIES AND THREATS
(Ch. 2)
Macroenvironment
Industry Environment
ORGANIZATIONAL DIRECTION
(Ch. 3)
Mission and Goals
STRATEGY FORMULATION
(Chs. 4, 5)
Corporate Strategy Formulation
(Ch. 6)
Business Unit Strategy Formulation
(Ch. 7)
Functional Strategy Formulation
Feedback
STRATEGY IMPLEMENTATION
(Ch. 8)
Organization Structure
(Ch. 9)
Leadership, Power, and Organizational Culture
STRATEGIC CONTROL
(Ch. 10)
Performance

7 Functional Strategies

We have seen in the preceding chapters that the corporation's mission, goals, and objectives establish the parameters within which the firm's individual business units operate. Each business unit, of course, develops its own goals and objectives within these parameters and then pursues those ends by implementing the generic strategy or strategies that appear most appropriate. Proper utilization of generic strategies requires that considerable attention be given to the business unit's functional areas. All organizations, regardless of their size, must perform certain functions—production, marketing, finance, research and development, and so on. No strategy can be successfully carried out without careful planning, execution, and coordination of these functional tasks.

In formulating **functional strategies**—the strategies pursued by the functional areas of a business unit—managers must be aware that these functions are interrelated. Each functional area, in attaining its purpose, must mesh its activities with the activities of the other functional departments, as shown in Figure 7.1. And a change in one department will invariably affect the way other departments operate. Hence, the strategy of one functional area cannot be viewed in isolation; rather, the extent to which all of the business unit's functional tasks mesh smoothly determines the effectiveness of the unit's generic strategy.

Many companies are learning this lesson. Boeing's unsettling experience, for instance, with discontinuities among its production, human resource, and marketing functions in the manufacture and delivery of its 747-400 airliner has resulted in significant changes. Its new 777 airplane will be designed and built by teams of marketing, engineering, manufacturing, finance, and service representatives so that each functional area will always know what the other is doing.[1]

This chapter examines functional strategies in the areas of purchasing and materials management, production/operations, finance, research and development, human resources, information systems, and marketing. Then the ways in which these functional strategies can be integrated are analyzed.

Figure 7.1 **Interrelationships Among Functional Departments**

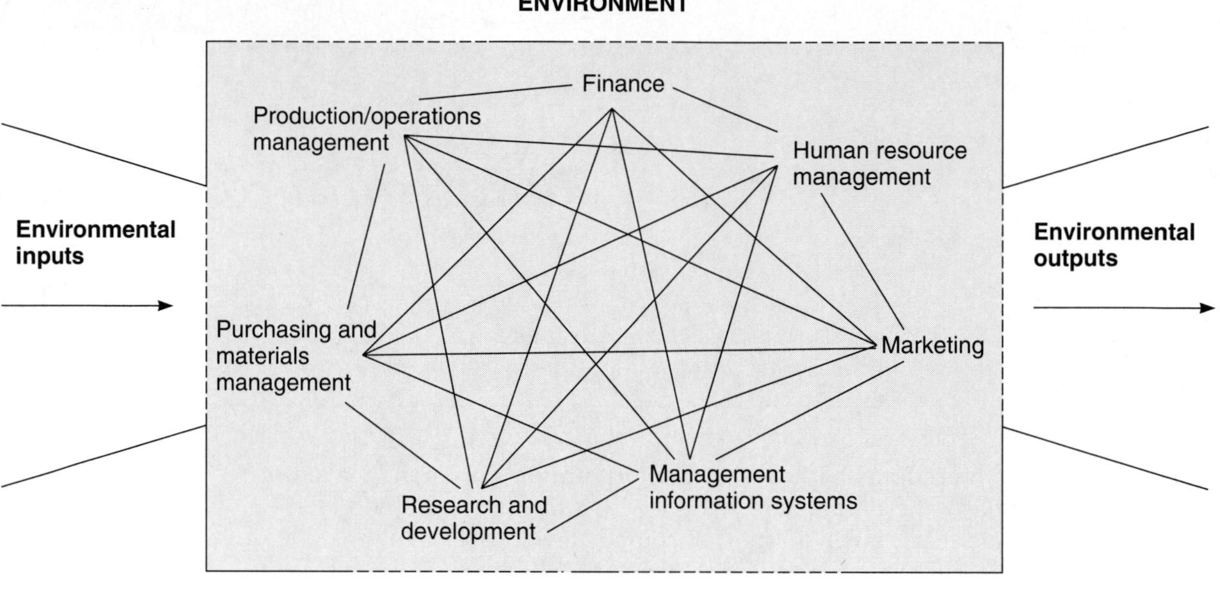

PURCHASING AND MATERIALS MANAGEMENT

All organizations have a purchasing function. For example, in manufacturing companies, the purchasing department buys raw materials and/or parts so that the production department may process them into a finished product for the marketing department to sell. In retailing organizations, individual buyers purchase clothing, toys, furniture, and other items from manufacturers for resale to the ultimate consumer.

Purchasing interacts extensively with the organization's environment, as illustrated in Figure 7.1. Its tasks are to identify potential suppliers, evaluate them, invite bids and price quotations, negotiate prices and terms of payment, place orders, follow up on those orders, inspect incoming shipments, and pay suppliers.

A business unit's purchasing strategy will differ, depending upon which generic strategy it adopts. Companies that use either the niche–low-cost strategy or the low-cost strategy emphasize purchasing at the lowest costs possible. Large organizations are able to purchase at low costs through their ability to demand quantity discounts. [The terms *large* and *small* are relative ones referring to an organization's size (usually measured in annual sales or total assets) in relation to the size of its competitors in the industry.] And buyers that are larger than their suppliers and whose purchases represent a significant percentage of their suppliers' sales also possess considerable negotiating clout.

Small companies, however, must attain low-cost purchasing in other ways. A recent purchasing trend for small businesses is to form industry networks—

that is, to band together with other small businesses in the same industry—to pool their purchasing requirements. Such a network is able to wield as much power as a single large business in demanding quantity discounts and exerting negotiating clout. Other small businesses may attempt to develop contacts with domestic and foreign suppliers that are able to offer limited supplies at low prices. In many cases, an extensive search can locate such suppliers.

We wish to emphasize that low costs are not the only consideration in purchasing activities. It is more accurate to state that businesses using niche–low-cost or low-cost generic strategies should seek out the "best cost." The best cost is as low as possible consistent with the quality of the purchased good or service. A low price is useless if the item breaks in the production process or fails to perform for the customer. On the other hand, excessive quality unnecessarily raises costs and prices.[2]

Organizations that use the generic strategy of niche-differentiation or differentiation emphasize the procurement of high-quality inputs, even if they cost more than alternative offerings. In these cases, the quality of the parts or products takes precedence over cost considerations.

When management pursues a niche–low-cost/differentiation or low-cost–differentiation generic strategy, however, emphasis is placed on buying high-quality inputs at low costs. As pointed out in the preceding chapter, even small businesses that adopt niche–low-cost/differentiation may be able to attain this purchasing goal through the development of organizational expertise, as Porsche has done.

Using multiple strategies, of course, requires a mixture of purchasing plans. At Holiday Inn, for instance, cost is a consideration in purchasing furnishings and accessories for the Inn's regular rooms. But the company buys higher-quality items—at higher costs—for its top-of-the-line suites. These suites feature more expensive linens, towels, soaps, shampoos, and beverages, which are provided free of charge.

The purchasing function is the first step in the materials management process. From the materials management perspective, purchasing, the operation of storage and warehouse facilities, and the control of inventory are interrelated functions;[3] consequently, they can only be efficiently and effectively conducted if they are viewed as parts of a single task.[4]

As an example of how these functions are interrelated, consider the **just-in-time inventory system (JIT).** This system of inventory management was popularized by Japanese manufacturers to reduce materials management costs. Using this technique, the purchasing manager asks suppliers to ship parts just at the time they are needed by the company to use in its production process. Such a system, of course, holds inventory, storage, and warehousing costs to a minimum.

Although American manufacturers are turning to this system in growing numbers, it is important to realize that just-in-time deliveries work particularly well in Japan because large Japanese manufacturers buy many of their inputs from small local companies. Hence, the giant buyers have considerable bargaining power over their much smaller suppliers. (In fact, some Japanese manufacturers own controlling interests in their suppliers, giving them even more power to control deliveries.) Such a system is likely to work well in the United States when the manufacturer has greater bargaining power than its suppliers. However, in the reverse situation, a just-in-time system is unlikely to evolve. Another hindrance to its use is that some suppliers, owing to the high demand for their products, are occasionally late in their deliveries by weeks or even months. However, most American-based suppliers are small concerns, with under $5 million in annual sales and fewer than thirty employees.[5] Hence, the just-in-time system may be applied for the majority of suppliers.

Another potential difficulty with the JIT system is the possibility that labor strikes can shut down a supplier. Recently, for example, one of the plants that supplies parts to GM's Saturn manufacturing operations shut down—fortunately, for a short time—due to a local labor dispute. Saturn, which uses the JIT system, suddenly found itself unable to produce cars—in a time of overwhelming consumer demand—because it had no inventory of the more than three hundred metal parts that it purchased exclusively from the supplier whose plant was struck.[6]

Most large U.S. manufacturers are currently reducing the number of suppliers that they use from a dozen or more to two or three to control delivery times and quality.[7] These companies then attempt to build strong and enduring relationships with their suppliers and provide them with detailed knowledge of their requirements and specifications. Buyer and supplier work together to improve the quality and lower the costs of the purchased items.

> This involves taking a *long* term view of the buyer/supplier relationship and also involves commitment to building an enduring cooperative relationship with individual suppliers where information is readily shared and both organizations work to meet shared goals.[8]

PRODUCTION/OPERATIONS MANAGEMENT

Production/operations management (POM) involves the process of transforming inputs, such as raw materials and parts, into outputs. Its basic goal is to ensure that the outputs produced have a value that exceeds the combined costs of the required inputs and the transformation process. Transformation process costs include labor, supplies, and physical plant and equipment.

Although POM is most often associated with manufacturing processes, managing operations is crucial to all types of organizations. Credit card companies, for instance, must satisfy customers' desires for timeliness, accuracy, and company responsiveness. Hospitals must diagnose medical problems and attempt to heal patients. Prisons must house prisoners and try to rehabilitate them. Insurance companies must meet their clients' demands for fast, responsible, thorough coverage. Each of these POM examples from service organizations requires a careful analysis of those organizations' operations. Hence, the transformation of inputs into outputs is not limited to manufacturers. The service organizations just described must transform a customer's credit purchase into a cash payment to the retailer, help sick patients become well, attempt to convert criminals into responsible citizens, and pay for restoring a damaged automobile or house to its original condition.

The following sections describe POM strategies for small and large business units and discuss the quality considerations emerging currently in POM.

■ POM Strategies for Small Business Units

POM strategies differ, of course, depending upon which generic strategy the business unit adopts. Small business units that compete with the niche–low-

STRATEGIC INSIGHT

Improving Supplier Quality Across Several Industries

Never before has there been such emphasis on the purchasing and materials management function. The primary impetus for this movement is the increasing intensity of foreign competition. The results to date have been a reduction in the number of suppliers used by most companies and growing pressure on those that remain to meet high-quality, cost, and delivery time standards.

As a buyer begins to pressure its suppliers, they, in turn, must convince their own suppliers to improve their quality. For example, Ford influenced its suppliers to improve their quality and cost levels. One of those suppliers, Motorola, has lowered its defect rate from 3,000 per million parts to less than 200 per million parts as a result. In fact, Motorola's emphasis on "doing it right the first time" has cut its waste, inspection time, and warranty costs by $250 million in two years. Now Motorola has urged its 3,000 suppliers (down from 10,000) to improve their quality by asking them to enter the competition for the Malcolm Baldrige National Quality Award (won by Motorola in 1988). Those that have chosen not to enter have been dropped as suppliers by Motorola.

Although more is being demanded from suppliers, the best ones become "partners" with their buyers. Their employees may receive training in new manufacturing and quality techniques from buyers, may become involved in the design of the buyers' new products, may receive free consulting assistance from their buyers, and may become privy to the strategic plans of the buyers. In some cases, such suppliers are even able to become the sole supplier of a particular part to a buyer. The result has been a significant decline in the number of suppliers from which an individual buyer will purchase. For instance, Xerox has gone from 5,000 suppliers to 425, and over the past decade, Ford pruned the number of its suppliers from 10,000 to less than 1,000.

These principles have been adopted by retail organizations as well as manufacturers. Dillard's, a fast-growing and highly profitable department chain in the South, Southwest, and Midwest, works closely with its vendors and is amazingly loyal to them. As one of its executives puts it:

> Sure, we might be tougher to sell to, but we're not going to go around switching vendors because someone can make something for us a little bit cheaper. We believe in building relationships, and that takes time.

SOURCES: J.R. Emshwiller, "Suppliers Struggle to Improve Quality As Big Firms Slash Their Vendor Rolls," *The Wall Street Journal,* 16 August 1991; A. Gabor, "The Front Lines of Quality," *U.S. News & World Report,* 27 November 1989, pp. 57–59; C. Skrzycki, "Suppliers Under Scrutiny," *The Washington Post,* 26 November 1989; S. Caminiti, "A Quiet Superstar Rises in Retailing," *Fortune,* 23 October 1989, pp. 167–174 (quote is from p. 169).

cost strategy emphasize low initial investments in their plants, equipment, and outlets to hold their fixed costs down, and they attempt to keep their variable operations costs as low as possible. Because of new technological innovations, some industries, such as steel manufacturing and film developing, can create small physical plants that are cost-competitive with much larger companies.

An example of this comparison is shown in Figure 7.2. The graph on the left depicts the per-unit production cost of a small business; the graph on the right shows the per-unit production cost of a large company. Note that the small business has achieved low per-unit costs similar to those of the larger organization because of its use of modern technology. Since the emphasis of business units that compete with the niche–low-cost generic strategy is on holding costs

Figure 7.2 **Per-Unit Cost of Production in a Small and in a Large Firm**

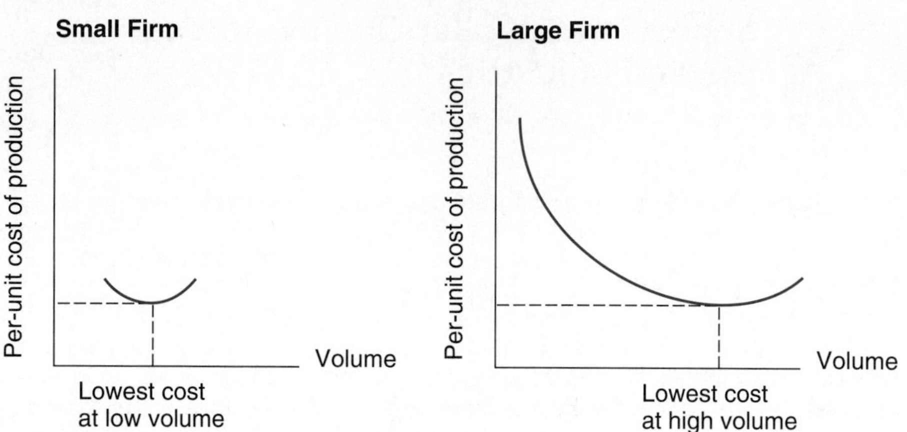

down, production/operations strategies are continuously scrutinized to make them more efficient. In some cases, production facilities may even be moved abroad to lower costs significantly.

Small business units that compete with the niche-differentiation strategy stress POM strategies that yield superior quality. In some instances, such strategies may involve hand-crafting processes versus the mass production operations of much larger businesses. Rolls-Royce, for example, stresses the hand crafting of many automobile components, and each component can be traced to the individual worker who took part in its creation. As is evident, low costs are not the primary concern of this niche-differentiation strategy.

Small business units competing with the niche–low-cost/differentiation strategy emphasize POM strategies that simultaneously lower costs and heighten differentiation. This strategy may initially involve higher costs, but over time, cost savings and quality improvements evolve. For instance, one American manufacturer of electronic products realized that moving its metal production processes overseas would result in a 15 percent cost reduction. But switching to plastics in place of metal would lower costs by 20 percent and could be accomplished in the United States. In addition, plastic materials would offer better value for electronic products because of their lighter weight. Elizabeth Haas, a consultant in manufacturing strategy and advanced technology, has documented businesses in a variety of industries that have managed both to lower costs and heighten differentiation.[9]

■ POM Strategies for Large Business Units

Large business units can take advantage of a number of factors that accompany their larger size. Each factor falls under the concept of the **experience curve:** the reduction in per-unit costs that occurs as an organization gains experience producing a product or service. The Boston Consulting Group has popularized this concept, noting that production/operations costs may be systematically reduced through larger sales volume.[10] That is, each time a company's output doubles, POM costs decline by a specific percentage, which varies from one industry to another. For instance, with a sales volume of 1 million units, per-unit costs may be $100 in a particular industry. With a doubling of volume to 2 million units, per-unit costs may decline by 30 percent. Another doubling of volume to 4 million units may lower per-unit costs another 30 percent. In other industries, however, each doubling of volume will reduce costs by other amounts. The experience curve has been observed in a wide range of industries, including automobiles, long-distance telephone calls, airlines, and life insurance. Note that both manufacturing and service industries are represented.

The experience curve concept is based on three underlying variables: learning, economies of scale, and capital-labor substitution possibilities. Learning refers to the idea that the more an employee performs a task, the more efficient he or she should become at the job. Increases in volume, therefore, permit the employee to perform the task more often, resulting in greater expertise. This reasoning holds for all jobs—line and staff, managerial and nonmanagerial—and at all levels—corporate, business unit, and functional. Learning does not occur automatically, however. For instance, as experience is gained with a particular product, production managers, operative employees, and design engineers have the opportunity to learn more about how to redesign the product for manufacturing and assembly. By taking advantage of this opportunity, a business is able to conserve material, gain greater efficiencies in the manufacturing process, and substitute less costly materials, while simultaneously improving the product's performance. Such techniques, for instance, allowed Ford Motor Company's business units to trim their manufacturing costs significantly. For instance, Ford plants can manufacture such midsize models as the Taurus and Mercury Sable in less than 17.2 hours, while such comparable models as the Chevrolet Lumina and Pontiac Grand Prix require 32.2 to 36.3 hours.[11]

Economies of scale at the business unit level refer to reductions in per-unit costs as volume increases. Capital-labor substitution means that as volume increases, an organization may be able to substitute labor for capital, or capital for labor, depending upon which combination produces lower costs and/or greater effectiveness. For example, a car manufacturer may operate highly automated factories in economically advanced nations because of the high cost of labor. But the same manufacturer may employ more labor and less automation in its factories located in developing nations, to take advantage of the lower cost of labor in those areas.

Putting all three of these variables together, Figure 7.3 portrays how the overall experience curve promotes lower unit costs as volume increases. Hence, as a business gains greater market share, its per-unit costs can decrease as it takes advantage of the experience curve. However, investing in greater plant capacity is not necessarily an automatic route to lower unit costs. As can be seen from the curve in Figure 7.3, the experience curve flattens at point *A* on the graph. Production beyond that point will not lower unit costs any further.

Although large business units benefit from the experience curve, the particular generic strategy adopted by a given business unit will have different ramifications for success. For instance, many (but not all) businesses that compete with the low-cost strategy tend to buy their way to lower costs. In other words, they sell their products or services at low prices, even if those prices are initially below their costs. The low prices increase their volume, thereby permitting them to lower their costs through use of the experience

Figure 7.3

Experience Curve

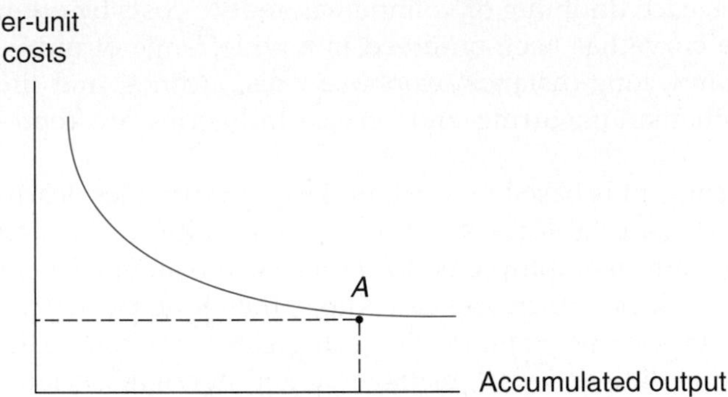

curve. These businesses, however, are particularly vulnerable to business units that are also able to attain low costs but offer better-quality products and services.[12]

A different approach is taken by business units that compete with the differentiation and low-cost–differentiation generic strategies. Instead of charging average or low prices, they charge average to high prices, seeking to gain market share by offering higher-quality outputs. The increase in sales also allows them to lower their costs. But the managers of the business units that adopt differentiation as their strategy do not actively capitalize on the opportunities presented by lower costs, whereas managers of businesses that compete with low-cost–differentiation do.[13] Hence, adopters of differentiation as a generic strategy are vulnerable to competitors that offer alternative products, but at lower, or even predatory, prices. The low-cost–differentiation adopter is less vulnerable than businesses using either of the preceding strategies, however, because this strategy emphasizes lower costs (as protection against low-cost companies) and high-quality outputs (to protect against differentiated businesses).

Regardless of the generic strategy adopted, large business units that use the experience curve take a significant risk. Increases in volume often involve substantial investments in plant and equipment and a commitment to the prevailing technology. The risk is that if technological innovations should make the plant's production processes obsolete, millions of dollars in capital equipment may have to be written off. How may this need to invest in plant and equipment be balanced against the risk that technology will change? History provides a partial answer.

Virtually any technology is improved upon over time. But at some point, further improvements become prohibitively expensive. At such times, emphasis should be placed on developing innovations, even at the risk of rendering obsolete the company's prevailing technology. A major vulnerability in using the experience curve is that managers become psychologically dependent upon the organization's technology both because they are familiar with it and because they have committed so many resources to it. Consequently, when a competitor develops a new technology, the company can quickly become technologically obsolete.

As an example, consider NCR, a business that once had the lowest costs (through the experience curve) in the mechanical cash register industry. When Burroughs and other competitors developed a fully integrated electronic cash register that was superior in performance, the market demand quickly shifted from the technologically obsolete mechanical cash register to the new product. As a result, NCR lost its competitive edge.

■ Quality Considerations

An issue of increasing importance in production/operations management in recent years is quality. This concept, introduced in Chapter 6, refers to the totality of features and characteristics of a product or service that bear on its ability to satisfy stated or implied needs. Historically, quality has been viewed largely as a controlling activity that takes place somewhere near the end of the production process, an after-the-fact measurement of production success. Over the years, however, more and more managers have come to realize that quality is not something that is measured at, or near, the end of the production process but, rather, is an essential ingredient of the product or service being provided. Consequently, quality is part of the overall approach to doing business and becomes the concern of all members of the organization. When quality comes to be viewed in this way, the following conditions prevail:

- Making a quality product decreases the quantity of defects, which causes yield to increase.
- Making a product right the first time reduces the number of rejects and time spent on rework.
- Making the operative employees responsible for quality eliminates the need for inspection.

These conditions also apply to service quality, whether the service is performed for the customer or for some other department in the same organization. The ultimate result is that quality is viewed as reducing, rather than increasing, costs.[14] As quality consultant Philip B. Crosby points out:

> Every penny you don't spend on doing things wrong, over, or instead of, becomes half a penny right on the bottom line. . . . If you concentrate on making quality certain, you can probably increase your profit by an amount equal to 5% to 10% of your sales.[15]

W. Edwards Deming, the world-renowned consultant, concurs by stating that improvement of quality converts the waste of employee hours and machine time into the manufacture of good product and better service. Management in some Japanese companies observed as early as the late 1940s that improvement of quality naturally and inevitably begets improvement of productivity.[16] This process is illustrated in Figure 7.4. As you can see, such a process is essential to businesses competing with the niche–low-cost/differentiation or low-cost–differentiation generic strategies. If below-average industry prices are charged, the business benefits because it may increase its market share and, subsequently, reduce its costs. If average or above-average industry prices are charged, the business benefits from greater profit margins. Even companies that adopt differentiation as their strategy can develop a

Figure 7.4 **The Deming Chain Reaction**

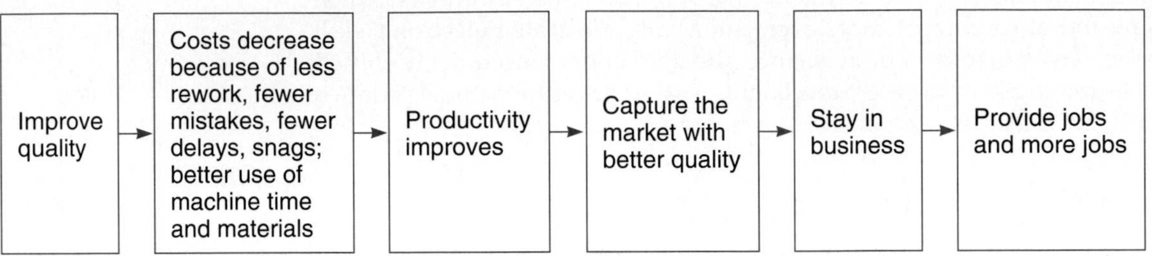

Source: Reprinted from *Out of the Crisis* by W. Edwards Deming by permission of MIT and W. Edwards Deming. Published by MIT, Center for Advanced Engineering Study, Cambridge, Mass. 02139. Copyright 1986 by W. Edwards Deming.

distinct competitive advantage by focusing on the quality of their products and services.

In fact, quality improvements in virtually any type of company seem to yield attractive results. A U.S. General Accounting Office study of twenty companies—including both large and small businesses in manufacturing and service industries—that had adopted total quality management programs concluded that quality improvements enhanced profitability, increased market share, decreased customer complaints, and improved customer satisfaction. These results occurred on an average of two and a half years after the TQM programs were adopted.[17] Although the exact form of each program differed from one company to another, these programs did contain the following common features:

- Corporate attention was focused on meeting customer requirements.
- Top management took the lead in emphasizing quality.
- All employees were trained, empowered, and involved in organizational efforts to improve quality and reduce costs.
- Systematic processes were integrated throughout the organization to foster continuous improvement.[18]

FINANCE

The finance function encompasses not only cash management but also the use of credit and decisions regarding capital investments. Ideally, each business would like to have a surplus of internally generated cash, beyond what is needed for expenditures, to allow it to reinvest the cash back into the business. In this way, the future viability of the enterprise is assured. However, a company resorts to borrowing funds when strategic decisions require cash beyond what can be generated from operations. Long-term capital investment decisions focus on the allocation of resources and, hence, are linked to corporate and business unit strategies in an obvious fashion.

Business units that compete with the niche–low-cost or low-cost generic strategies pursue financial strategies that are intended to lower their financial costs. Insofar as possible, they attempt to keep their costs within the limits of the funds they are able to generate from operations. If borrowing becomes necessary, they try to borrow during times when credit costs are relatively low. If they sell common stock to generate additional funds, they time the sale carefully to coincide with a bull market (a market in which stock prices, on the average, are rising). Their capital investment decisions center on plant and equipment, technology, and research and development efforts that can lower their cost positions even more. Furthermore, they attempt to time major equipment purchases from foreign producers when the dollar is strong relative to the foreign currency.

Business units that adopt the niche-differentiation or differentiation generic strategies pursue financial strategies that fund quality enhancements. To stay in step with their competitors' product improvements or innovations, they direct their financial efforts toward upgrading their present and future outputs. If internal funds are insufficient, then they will attempt to raise money either through selling common stock or borrowing funds. Stock may be sold even though stock prices in general are relatively low, and funds may be borrowed even if interests costs are relatively high. In other words, these business units place the highest strategic priority on quality maintenance and enhancement rather than on financial considerations.

Finally, those business units that compete with the niche–low-cost/differentiation, low-cost–differentiation, or multiple strategies use their financial function, on the one hand, to lower costs and, on the other hand, to promote quality enhancements. Because, as we saw earlier, such business units ordinarily perform well, they tend to have stronger financial positions than other business units, which allow them greater flexibility. These business units often have cash surpluses, can borrow funds at competitive rates, and are able to command high prices for new stock offerings. Hence, their investment strategies revolve around financial considerations that attempt to lower costs and heighten differentiation simultaneously. Further specifics on financial considerations are offered in Exhibit 1 of "Strategic Management Case Analysis."

RESEARCH AND DEVELOPMENT

Research and development (R&D) has two basic components: product/service R&D and process R&D. **Product/service R&D** refers to efforts that ultimately lead to improvements or innovations in the company's outputs. **Process R&D** aims at reducing the costs of operations and making them more efficient. The more dynamic the industry environment, the more important R&D efforts of both kinds become.

Business units that compete with the niche–low-cost and low-cost strategies emphasize process R&D to reduce their operations costs. However, those business units that use the niche-differentiation and differentiation strategies place more importance on product/service R&D to produce improved and new innovative outputs. Finally, adopters of the niche–low-cost/differentiation, low-cost–differentiation, and multiple strategies simultaneously stress both product/service R&D and process R&D efforts.

Organizations with effective R&D departments are, in essence, lowering their risks by making themselves more competitive. Product/service R&D

focuses on market competitiveness, and process R&D emphasizes cost competitiveness. But R&D efforts also involve risks of another kind.

Process innovations, for instance, may be too technologically sophisticated to be implemented effectively, or they may not even be used at all. For example, consider the United States Postal Service's experience with expensive, high-technology mail sorting machines. The use of these machines achieved only about a third of the expected productivity improvements. At 91 percent of the post office sites reviewed by the Postal Inspection Service, mail that was supposed to have been processed by the new machines was still being processed in the traditional way.[19]

Product/service innovations also involve risks. Once they are introduced, new products or services may find little market demand. RJR Nabisco, for example, spent millions of dollars to develop and produce its "smokeless" cigarette, Premier. Although introduced to the market with considerable fanfare, smokers refused to switch to the new product, and it was canceled within a few weeks of its introduction.

This example illustrates the problems inherent in **technology transfer,** the process whereby a company transforms its scientific discoveries into marketable products. Some companies accomplish this transfer exceedingly well. Hewlett-Packard, for example, estimates that about 60 percent of its research results in product applications. In fact, over 50 percent of its sales come from products developed within the past three years. This remarkable record results from a two-tier arrangement in which corporate R&D operations work on projects with three-to-seven-year time horizons, while each business unit has its own R&D function that concentrates on shorter-range product applications.[20] But no one method is best. General Electric, another highly innovative firm, operates through a corporate-level R&D department that then demonstrates its inventions to each of GE's business units. This system has resulted in some unexpected applications; for instance, a device that was invented to protect coal-spraying nozzles in a locomotive was subsequently used to create a new generation of energy-saving light bulbs. Likewise, a medical diagnostic instrument invented for human body imaging is now also used as a cost-saving tool for inspecting jet engines.[21]

Noted management consultant Peter Drucker emphasizes the importance of both process and product R&D. He stresses that Japanese companies "abandon" their new products as soon as they reach the market. This decision to minimize the life cycle of each new product forces the Japanese to develop new products immediately to replace the ones currently on the market. Such a swift cycle, they believe, gives them a considerable competitive advantage.[22] U.S. companies are responding by increasingly forming direct research links with their domestic competitors (GM, Ford, and Chrysler, for example, are jointly developing new battery technology for electric automobiles), asking their suppliers to participate in new-product design programs, and taking ownership positions in small startup companies that have promising technologies.[23]

HUMAN RESOURCE MANAGEMENT

The human resource management functions include such major activities as planning for future human resource needs, recruiting personnel, placing people in jobs, compensating them, evaluating their performance, developing them into more effective employees, and enhancing their work environment. Overall, the aim is to build a work force that enables the organization to achieve its goals.[24]

One of the major detriments to effective human resource management practices over the past decade was an unprecedented wave of mergers and acquisitions. This massive restructuring of American business resulted in widespread layoffs and disillusioned formerly loyal employees. Prior to this time, many workers assumed that as long as they performed well, they would have a job with their company for as many years as they wished. The past decade

STRATEGIC INSIGHT

Importance of Human Resources at Merck and Motorola

Merck, the New Jersey–based pharmaceutical company that has topped *Fortune*'s "Most Admired Corporations" list for several consecutive years, attributes its success to "attracting, developing, and keeping good people." And, indeed, companies in virtually every industry are becoming increasingly aware of the importance of their human resources.

Perhaps the biggest change in attitude has occurred in American factories. The unskilled, single-task job that typified factory work for most of this century is rapidly disappearing. Its replacement is a position on an empowered cross-functional team where each member must be a generalist who is able to participate in a variety of decisions. Many of these decisions are technical, involving computer-operated machinery and other manufacturing processes.

This need for technically sophisticated employees clashes with the public school system in the United States, where 27.8 percent of the students over the age of 15 drop out before finishing high school and students who have not yet mastered the skills in their current grade are routinely promoted. Examples of this conflict abound. For instance, several years ago, as Motorola was beginning to use empowered teams, management discovered that only half of its work force could solve the equation $4 + x = 10$. Programs to remediate this deficit cost Motorola $30 million over a five-year period—a cost, its management points out, that did not have to be borne by its major competitors in Japan and Sweden.

A National Association of Manufacturers poll revealed that 50 percent of the 360 companies surveyed reported serious deficiencies among their employees in fundamental math and reading skills. As *Business Week* concludes, "the issue is one of a growing gap between the skills people have and the skills that jobs demand."

Although the root of the problem may be in America's educational system, businesses—and American competitiveness—suffer from it. Consequently, many companies that are upgrading their technological processes or are moving to empowered cross-functional teams are investing sizable amounts of money in remedial math, reading, and writing programs. Observers report that employees tend to pay more attention to their teachers than they did in junior high or in high school because what they are learning is directly relevant to their continued employment.

SOURCES: C. Milloy, "Teaching Failure by Example," *The Washington Post,* 17 March 1993; F. Swoboda, "A New Breed on the Line," *The Washington Post,* 2 August 1992; T. Segal, K. Thurston, and L. Haessly, "When Johnny's Whole Family Can't Read," *Business Week,* 20 July 1992, pp. 68–70 (p. 68 is source of second quotation); K. Ballen, "America's Most Admired Corporations," *Fortune,* 10 February 1992, p. 43 (source of first quotation); J.D. Burge, "Motorola's Transition to a High Performance Workforce," an Executive Lecture at James Madison University, 20 February 1992.

not only ended that dream for those who were laid off but also created anxiety among those who survived the cutbacks. It is difficult for a company to eliminate as much as 20 percent of its work force and still retain a commitment among those who remain.

Hence, a priority in the 1990s for business units, regardless of their particular generic strategy, is to develop commitment among their employees to the organization and to the job. Companies that wish to foster that commitment and develop a strong, competitive work force must create—and maintain—certain working conditions for their employees. And progressive organizations consider human resources their most precious asset. Consequently, such companies give their employees' needs for customized benefits, child day care, parental leave, and flexible working hours equal consideration with such traditional needs as training and development, job enrichment, and promotional opportunities.

The work force of the 1990s is frequently characterized as "diverse." In rapidly increasing numbers, women, African-Americans, Hispanic-Americans, Asian-Americans, and disabled persons are transforming the traditional white, male image of many American corporations. As a result, managers must learn to help persons of diverse backgrounds and perceptions to work closely together. This necessity for teamwork, of course, is further impelled by the need for closer cooperation among the employees of the organization's functional areas. The success of such cooperative endeavors as cross-functional teams, quality circles, and just-in-time inventory systems requires a unity of action that can be achieved only through the mutual respect and understanding of others.

A spirit of togetherness is further fostered at some forward-looking organizations through reward systems that encourage teamwork and cooperation. Perhaps the most ambitious program in this regard is PepsiCo's "SharePower" system. Created in 1989, this stock option plan is offered to all 120,000 employees who average at least thirty hours of weekly work. (By contrast, traditional stock option plans usually are limited to top-level executives.) As D. Wayne Calloway, PepsiCo's chairman and CEO, puts it: "It's been part of our whole culture to say 'you are important' to every employee."[25] The intent of SharePower is to "make employees identify more with the company and their work, encourage them to stay longer, and increase productivity."[26] With this sort of innovative management, it is no accident that PepsiCo is widely recognized as one of the world's premier consumer products companies. Dozens of companies have followed PepsiCo's lead, developing stock option plans that help their "workers to think like owners."[27]

In a more narrow sense, a business unit's generic strategy also influences specific components of its human resource program. Take, for example, a company's reward system. Rewards—in the usual sense of recognition, pay raises, and promotions—should be tied to employee behavior that helps the business attain its goals. Hence, business units that follow a niche–low-cost strategy or a low-cost strategy must reward employees who help reduce operating costs. Businesses adopting the niche-differentiation or differentiation strategy should establish reward systems that encourage output improvements or innovations. Finally, those companies that use the niche–low-cost/differentiation strategy or a low-cost–differentiation strategy should have broad-based reward programs that foster activities that either lower costs or promote output improvements or innovations.

INFORMATION SYSTEMS MANAGEMENT

A well-designed information system can benefit all of a business unit's functional areas. A computer-based decision support system can permit each functional area to access the information it needs and to communicate electronically with the other functional departments to enhance interdepartmental coordination.

This advantage is not the only benefit of an effective information system, however. Such a system can cut internal costs (essential to business units pursuing the niche–low-cost, niche–low-cost/differentiation, low-cost, or low-cost–differentiation strategy) while promoting differentiation and quality through a faster response to the market's needs (vital to companies that follow the niche-differentiation, niche–low-cost/differentiation, differentiation, or low-cost–differentiation strategy). In fact, some businesses owe their high performance to their information systems. In the overnight package delivery industry, for example, the chairman and CEO of United Parcel Service (UPS), Kent Nelson, believes that "the leader in information management will be the leader in international package distribution—period."[28] Hence, UPS and such competitors as Federal Express use their core competencies in managing information to keep their costs low while giving their customers superb service (differentiation).

Leading retailers, such as The Limited, have also developed sophisticated information systems to manage their vertically integrated distribution channels. The Limited's system links its hundreds of retail stores throughout the United States to its Columbus, Ohio, headquarters and to its textile mills in Hong Kong. Sales information from each of the stores is gathered and analyzed in Columbus. Based on that analysis, within a few days, the Hong Kong textile mills are producing more fast-selling items and less slow-turnover goods.[29]

Because of the rapidity of change in information technology, some companies are increasingly *outsourcing*, or farming out, their information systems function. Kodak, for instance, has turned over to IBM its information processing through 1999. Kodak's management believed that it should concentrate on its core competencies and concluded that running computers was not one of those competencies. Enron, the Houston-based natural gas producer, likewise outsourced its information processing to EDS (the world's largest provider of information services) in order to focus on its goal to become the leading natural gas company in the nation. Says its chief financial officer, "Nothing in [our mission] says we want to be a provider of information systems."[30]

Although other functional areas—such as marketing, human resource management, or POM—are occasionally outsourced, farming out the information systems management function is more prevalent because many companies simply are unable to keep up with the frequent technological changes in this area. Additionally, outsourcing can lower a company's information costs, because such information systems providers as EDS, IBM, or Andersen Consulting can process data from several client companies through a single mainframe, thereby passing along the lower costs achieved through economies of scale.[31]

Whether it is conducted in-house or farmed out, an information system is effective, not because of its sophisticated nature, but because it helps the business carry out its strategy. Far too many companies emphasize the hardware and software components of their information system, rather than the system's ability to satisfy customer needs.[32] For that reason, some managers oppose outsourcing of information systems. Computer programmers, these managers maintain, are the key to creating software that can set a company apart from its competitors. They recommend that a business outsource only standard tasks, such as payroll processing or accounts receivables or payables, while retaining technologically creative information systems experts.[33]

MARKETING

Marketing consists of four strategic considerations: products/services, pricing, channels of distribution/location of outlets, and promotion. The particular generic strategy adopted by the business unit influences how these various marketing strategies are planned and executed.

As we saw in the preceding chapter, business units that compete with the niche–low-cost and low-cost generic strategies produce no-frills products/services. Although these outputs are undifferentiated or minimally differentiated with respect to those of their competitors, they are by no means unreliable or shoddy. For example, Motel 6 Inc. offers no-frills rooms. They are clean and contain comfortable, but low-priced, furniture and beds. Motel 6 offers few services; for instance, it has no restaurants or conference rooms. Its simple brand name, Motel 6, is intended to convey the impression of economy services.

Consistent with its no-frills outputs, Motel 6 normally charges low prices. In particular circumstances, it may be able to charge average prices, but only when competitors are either few or far removed. Because it is a service company, channels of distribution are not relevant, but geographic location is. Motel 6 has been successful in choosing locations, primarily near interstate highway exit ramps. Promotion efforts are undertaken at low costs and attempt to convey to the traveling public that Motel 6 offers satisfactory economy lodging.

Different marketing strategies are pursued by businesses that use the generic strategies of differentiation and low-cost–differentiation. Marketing unique, quality products and services that are distinguishable from the outputs of rivals requires approaches considerably at variance from those described in the preceding two paragraphs. For example, Holiday Inn offers larger rooms with better-quality furnishings than Motel 6. Holiday Inns also contain such features as restaurants, shops, swimming pools, and conference rooms. The brand name Holiday Inn is intended to give the impression of quality. Average to high prices are charged for Holiday Inn rooms, depending upon the competitive situation; and promotional efforts convey a unique, quality image.

Still other marketing strategies are followed by business units that adopt the niche-differentiation and niche–low-cost/differentiation generic strategies. These businesses tend to offer specialized, highest-quality products and services to meet the particular needs of a relatively small market. Holiday Inn Suites, featured in some Holiday Inns, offer spacious rooms, wet bars, hair dryers, and complimentary food, beverages, and newspapers. The brand name attempts to convey the impression that in addition to having access to Holiday Inns' restaurants, shops, swimming pools, and conference rooms, customers

STRATEGIC INSIGHT

The Importance of Distribution and Production Capacity at Colgate-Palmolive and Compaq Computer

The role of distribution is often overlooked amid the more glamorous marketing functions of advertising, selling, and designing products and packages. Although less visible, distribution is certainly as important as these other aspects of marketing.

Consider a company that has used distribution to its distinct advantage: Colgate-Palmolive. This multiunit company's most profitable business is not toothpaste or soap; it is, surprisingly, pet food. Part of the secret to the success of its Hill's Pet Products division is distribution. Unlike better-known and much larger competitors such as Ralston Purina, Hill's sells its pet food almost exclusively through veterinarians. Its premium-priced product (a single can of dog food costs about $2) comes in several formulations, ranging from diet food for overweight pets to low-sodium meals for animals with heart conditions. Although Ralston Purina and Iams have similar products, they face considerable difficulty breaking into Hill's long-established distribution channel.

On the other hand, a good product can be ruined by a lack of production capacity, so that the product cannot even reach the market. Compaq Computer, which lost touch with the personal computer market in the early 1990s, constructed its come-back strategy around a new computer line called ProLinea. This entry into the inexpensive, low-profit-margin market was enormously successful—at building consumer demand. Unfortunately, Compaq greatly underestimated demand, leading to widespread shortages of the much-desired ProLinea computer within a month of its introduction. Although Compaq hastily added manufacturing shifts at its three plants and tried to get suppliers to speed shipments of component parts, disappointed consumers turned to such competitors as Dell and Hyundai rather than wait weeks for ProLineas to arrive.

SOURCES: L. Hooper and K. Yamada, "IBM Signals Delay Affecting Low-Cost Line," *The Wall Street Journal,* 14 September 1992; K. Pope, "Compaq Can't Cope with Demand for ProLinea PCs," *The Wall Street Journal,* 10 July 1992; B. Hager, "The Pet Food That's Fattening Colgate's Kitty," *Business Week,* 7 May 1990, p. 116.

will be further pampered by these extra features. High prices are charged for these suites, and promotional campaigns address the relatively few potential customers who desire the suites' extra features.

A summary of our discussion to this point is shown in Table 7.1. The entries in the left column represent the generic strategy that a given business unit is following. The horizontal entries to the right indicate the particular strategy that should be used by each of the business unit's functional areas.

INTEGRATING THE FUNCTIONS

For a business unit's generic strategy to be successful, each functional area must do more than simply operate effectively. Overall strategic success requires that all functional activities be tightly integrated so that their operations mesh smoothly with one another. Those businesses that are best able to achieve functional integration are those most likely to attain the competitive advantages detailed in the following paragraphs.

Table 7.1 The Link Between Business Unit Strategies and Functional Strategies

Strategy	*Purchasing & Materials Management*	*Production/ Operations Management*	*Finance*	*Research & Development*	*Human Resource Management*	*Information Systems*	*Marketing*
Niche–low-cost	Purchase at low costs through networks and contacts with domestic and foreign suppliers. Operate storage and warehouse facilities and control of inventory efficiently.	Emphasize low initial investments in plants, equipment, and outlets. Emphasize low operation costs.	Lower financial costs by borrowing when credit costs are low, selling common stock during a bull market, etc.	Emphasize process R&D aimed at reducing costs of operations and distribution.	Emphasize reward systems that encourage lowering of costs.	Emphasize timely and pertinent information on costs of operations.	Emphasize low-cost distribution and low-cost advertising and promotion.
Niche-differentiation	Purchase high-quality inputs, even if they cost more. Conduct storage, warehouse, and inventory activities with utmost care, even if at higher costs (e.g., fine wine must be kept in high-cost storage with correct lighting and air-conditioned space).	Emphasize specialized quality in operations even at high cost, such as the handcrafting of products.	Emphasize obtaining resources and funding output improvements or innovations. Emphasize innovations even when financial costs may be high.	Emphasize product and service R&D aimed at enhancing the outputs of the business.	Emphasize reward systems that encourage output improvements or innovations.	Emphasize timely and pertinent information on the ongoing specialized processes that yield highly differentiated outputs.	Emphasize specialized distribution and targeted advertising and promotion.
Niche–low-cost/ differentiation	Purchase high-quality inputs, if possible, at low costs. This may be done through the development of organizational expertise, as Porsche has done. Conduct storage, warehouse, and inventory activities with utmost care, if possible, at low costs.	Emphasize specialized quality of operations, if possible, at low costs.	Emphasize obtaining resources and funding output improvements or innovations, if possible, at low costs.	Emphasize product and service R&D as well as process R&D.	Emphasize reward systems that encourage lowering of costs and output improvements or innovations.	Emphasize timely and pertinent information on costs of operations and on the ongoing specialized processes that yield highly differentiated outputs.	Emphasize specialized distribution and targeted advertising and promotion, if possible, at low cost, as Porsche has done.
Low-cost	Purchase at low costs through quantity discounts. Operate storage and warehouse facilities and control inventory efficiently.	Emphasize operation efficiencies through learning, economies of scale, and capital-labor substitution possibilities.	Lower financial costs by borrowing when credit costs are low, selling common stock during a bull market, etc.	Emphasize process R&D aimed at reducing costs of operations and distribution.	Emphasize reward systems that encourage lowering of costs.	Emphasize timely and pertinent information on costs of operations.	Emphasize low-cost distribution and low-cost advertising and promotion.

Differentiation	Purchase high-quality inputs, even if they cost more. Conduct storage, warehouse, and inventory activities with extensive care, even if at higher costs.	Emphasize quality in operations, even if at high cost.	Emphasize obtaining resources and funding output improvements or innovations. Emphasize innovations even when financial costs may be high.	Emphasize product and service R&D aimed at enhancing the outputs of the business.	Emphasize reward systems that encourage output improvements or innovations.	Emphasize timely and pertinent information on the ongoing processes that yield differentiated outputs.	Emphasize differentiated distribution and emphasize advertising and promotion on a broad scale.
Low-cost–differentiation	Purchase high-quality inputs, if possible, at low costs. Conduct storage, warehouse, and inventory activities with care, if possible, at low costs.	Emphasize quality in operations, if possible, at low costs.	Emphasize obtaining resources and funding output improvements or innovations, if possible, at low costs.	Emphasize product and service R&D as well as process R&D.	Emphasize reward systems that encourage output improvements or innovations and the lowering of costs.	Emphasize timely and pertinent information on costs of operations and on the ongoing improvement or innovation processes that are meant to yield differentiated outputs.	Emphasize differentiated distribution and emphasize advertising and promotion, on a broad scale, if possible, at low costs.
Multiple	Mixed	Mixed	Mixed	Mixed	Mixed	Mixed	Mixed

■ Superior Product Design

Although product design has been recognized as an important competitive dimension for years, only in the past few years has it received increased attention. Until recently, design was primarily associated with product appearance. But now, the concept is being broadened to include such features as designing a product for easy manufacturability so that fewer parts have to be purchased. Additionally, increased emphasis is being put on improving the product's functionality (its ability to perform its purpose) and quality. Overall, good design today addresses aesthetics as well as "the consumer's every concern—how a product works, how it feels in the hand, how easy it is to assemble and fix, and even, in this area of environmental concern, whether it can be recycled."[34]

Gaining a competitive advantage through superior product design involves all functional areas. Even in those companies where production/operations management has been the dominant function, the revised emphasis is on the interrelationships of all functional areas. For instance, when Caterpillar reorganized so that it could compete more effectively with heavy-equipment manufacturers from Japan, it first "intended to move only its design engineers to the plants to work more closely with the production people. . . . [Then the question became] why just the manufacturing and the engineering people . . . so marketing and pricing folks [also moved] into the plants."[35]

A well-designed product is attractive and easy to build, market, use, and maintain. Simplicity drives the best-designed products. But superior product design alone is not sufficient to gain a substantial competitive edge; design must be combined with superior service.

■ Superior Customer Service

Developing and maintaining the quality of customer service is often more challenging than improving product quality. The reason is that the consumer perceives service value primarily at the time the service is either rendered or not rendered. As one manager put it:

> You can tell me how awful someone's behavior was, but there is nothing for me to go back and look at. There aren't any artifacts, like broken gizmos I can go back and test.[36]

All functional areas must work together to provide the customer with product and service value. For example, a supermarket must fulfill several customer needs. First, it must offer value to customers in their shopping. Carrying the products that customers desire, at competitive prices, means that the purchasing, inventory, information systems, finance, and human resource management functions must communicate with one another and cooperate closely. Next, the store must make certain that its employees are able to respond to customer inquiries. This capability requires effective human resource management practices in hiring and training. Then, the supermarket must ensure that it stocks sufficient quantities of the items that it advertises. Meeting this objective requires interaction among the purchasing, inventory, information systems, and marketing functions. Finally, the store must provide the means for customers to check out their purchases accurately and quickly, requiring the close cooperation of information systems and human resource management.

STRATEGIC INSIGHT

Concurrent Engineering at Chrysler and Caterpillar

Impressive increases in manufacturing productivity in Japan and in Germany over the past twenty years and the deepening U.S. trade deficit have placed growing pressure on U.S. factories to become more efficient. Although there are a number of ways to increase industrial productivity, the process of concurrent engineering seems to hold particular promise.

During the 1980s, American manufacturers spent billions of dollars on factory automation, with no dramatic increase in productivity. Some experts believe the poor result was due to misplaced priority: The emphasis should have been on product design rather than on the production process. Even the most sophisticated automation equipment cannot compensate for a poorly designed product, in that design decisions "lock in" up to 90 percent of production costs long before the first item is ever produced. As a result, U.S. manufacturers are beginning to adopt concurrent engineering, a technique in which the product and its production processes are designed simultaneously.

Traditionally, an organization's R&D department came up with a new product idea. Then the idea went to design engineers who built a prototype, which was then turned over to the production department. Production had to develop a process for manufacturing the product, which usually meant that they had to give the blueprints back to design for revision. Further transfer of the blueprints back and forth between design and production could occur several times. Finally, purchasing would get copies of the finalized plans and ask for bids from suppliers. Then, eventually, actual production of the product would begin. If problems occurred during the production process, the product might have to be reworked in each of the preceding departments.

By contrast, concurrent engineering brings together personnel from R&D, design engineering, purchasing, production, and marketing, as well as from the company's suppliers, to work side by side and compare notes constantly from the very inception of the project. Using concurrent engineering, Chrysler was able to bring its powerful Dodge Viper to market in only three years—versus Chrysler's normal five-year development time. And adoption of concurrent engineering has helped Caterpillar cut its new product development time in half. One expert estimates that the use of concurrent engineering can save a company anywhere from 20 to 90 percent of its usual time to market, while its quality improves by 200 to 600 percent and its return on assets increases from 20 to 120 percent.

SOURCES: K. Kelly, A. Bernstein, and R. Neff, "Caterpillar's Don Fites: Why He Didn't Blink," *Business Week,* 10 August 1992, p. 57; D. Woodruff, "The Racy Viper Is Already a Winner for Chrysler," *Business Week,* 4 November 1991, p. 36; J. Main, "Manufacturing the Right Way," *Fortune,* 21 May 1990, pp. 54–64; O. Port, Z. Schiller, and R.W. King, "A Smarter Way to Manufacture," *Business Week,* 30 April 1990, pp. 110–117; "Making Big Gains from Small Steps," *Fortune,* 23 April 1990, pp. 119–122.

The importance of service cannot be overemphasized. In a recent survey, over one-third of the respondents indicated that they choose businesses that charge high prices but provide excellent service over companies that offer low prices but mediocre service.[37] As one observer points out:

> Despite all the talk these days about quality and customer satisfaction, most companies provide more lip service than customer service. Companies that really do provide service can command premium prices for their products. . . . [For example,] at Premier's [a business that provides hard-to-find fasteners and other

related items] . . . charges are typically between 10% and 15% more than competitors' prices—and sometimes as much as 200% higher.[38]

Personal attention is an important way that some businesses provide superior service. Personal attention involves paying heed to details, addressing customers' concerns, answering technical questions, and providing service after the sale. Such attention often plays an important psychological role as well. For example, the top managers of one industrial products supplier routinely visit plants to which the company has sold its products. In speaking of the psychological aspect of those visits, one manager indicated:

> We know our machine products are reliable and do not require visits. But when our clients see us physically inspecting their machines, sometimes merely dusting them off, they derive a sense of security and comfort that our products are in their plants, albeit at higher costs to them. When they are asked for a reference on suppliers, they usually suggest our firm.[39]

Recall that TQM not only involves producing a high-quality product, but it also implies quality in all of the services that accompany the product. In this regard, a TQM orientation means that a company must be willing to perceive the world from the customer's viewpoint and that the company can move quickly to satisfy the customer.[40] Consequently, we now examine the importance of superior speed.

■ Superior Speed

Speed in developing, making, and distributing products and services can give a business a significant competitive advantage. In fact, a survey of fifty major U.S.-based companies revealed that speed (alternatively referred to as "time-based strategy") was a top priority.[41] To illustrate the point, consider the comments of two managers:

> We can design, produce, and deliver before our big competitors get the paperwork done.
>
> We have a lock on our customers. You see, it may take some of our big buyers several weeks [to complete a purchase order], during which time their engineers request an order, their purchasing department receives the request and communicates it to the suppliers. We are in constant touch with the plant engineers, and normally we know what their next purchases are before their own purchasing departments. Consequently, we can normally deliver their needs overnight or within a few days.[42]

Some companies have taken these lessons to heart. Motorola, for instance, cut the time it takes to produce a cellular radio telephone, from 14 hours to 90 minutes. Concomitantly, the retail price of the phone dropped from $3,000 to $600 in three years.[43] Today, Coleman Company can produce and ship an order of camping stoves or lanterns in a week, versus two months just a few years ago. At the same time, it significantly reduced new product development time. Citibank estimates that Coleman's increased speed has enhanced the company's value by about $100 million.[44]

The importance of superior speed in serving customers should not be overlooked. For example, Premier, the fastener company mentioned earlier, received a call one day from one of its customers, Caterpillar. A $10 electrical relay had malfunctioned, bringing one of Caterpillar's assembly lines to a halt.

A Premier representative located a replacement part in a Los Angeles warehouse and had it placed immediately on a plane bound for St. Louis. When it arrived, a Premier employee picked the part up and delivered it to Caterpillar. As might be expected, Caterpillar and other firms are willing to pay significantly higher prices for Premier's products because of the superior service they receive.[45]

■ Superior Guarantee

Even in the best-managed businesses, problems occasionally arise that result in less-than-acceptable product or service quality. Hence, companies must take steps to guarantee an acceptable level of quality. Highly successful companies often go to great lengths to back their guarantees. For example, the famous retailer and mail-order house L.L. Bean accepts customer returns of its products for any reason, even after several years. A pair of hunting boots that was returned after ten years would be immediately replaced by a new pair with no questions asked.[46]

Many companies, however, ignore this competitive advantage. Often, guarantees lapse after a very short time period or contain too many exceptional conditions to be effective competitive weapons. For instance, some companies guarantee their electronic products for only ninety days; others are sufficiently confident of their product quality to offer one-year guarantees. Some airlines guarantee that their passengers will make connecting flights on time if no delays are caused by air traffic control problems or poor weather conditions. Unfortunately for the passengers, the majority of flight delays are due to these two factors.

Because of its intangible nature, a service guarantee is even more challenging to provide than a product guarantee. Christopher W.L. Hart, a business researcher and consultant, suggests that the following five desirable characteristics be included in service guarantees:[47]

- The guarantee should be unconditional, with no exceptions.
- It should be easily understood and written in simple language.
- The guarantee should be meaningful by guaranteeing what is important to the customer and making it worth the customer's time and effort to invoke the guarantee, should he or she be dissatisfied.
- The guarantee should be convenient to invoke and not require the customer to appeal to several layers of bureaucracy.
- The customer should be satisfied promptly, without a lengthy waiting period.

These characteristics, of course, should also be included in product guarantees.

SUMMARY

Once corporate-level and business unit generic strategies are developed, management must turn its attention to formulating and implementing strategies for each business unit's functional areas. Here, the manager should not view the strategy of one functional area in isolation, because it is the extent to which all of the functional tasks mesh smoothly that determines the effectiveness of the unit's generic strategy.

A business unit's purchasing strategy will differ depending upon which generic strategy it adopts. Companies that use the niche–low-cost strategy or the low-cost strategy emphasize purchasing at the lowest costs possible. Those that use niche-differentiation or differentiation stress the procurement of high-quality inputs, even if they cost more than alternative offerings. Organizations that pursue niche–low-cost/differentiation or low-cost–differentiation attempt to buy high-quality inputs at low costs, and those that employ multiple strategies use a mixture of purchasing plans. Purchasing is the first step in the materials management process, followed by storage and warehousing functions and inventory control. The latest trend in materials management, the just-in-time inventory system, ties these functions together.

The next functional strategic area is production/operations management (POM). Small business units that compete with the niche–low-cost strategy emphasize low initial investments in their plants, equipment, and outlets to hold their fixed costs down, and they attempt to keep their variable operations costs as low as possible. Small businesses competing with niche-differentiation stress POM strategies that yield superior quality, and those that use niche–low-cost/differentiation emphasize POM activities that simultaneously lower costs and heighten differentiation. Large business units, on the other hand, are able to take advantage of the experience curve by using learning, economies of scale, and capital-labor substitution possibilities to their advantage. To gain market share so that they may enjoy the experience curve, large business units that compete with the low-cost strategy may sell at low prices to increase volume. Large enterprises that use differentiation or low-cost–differentiation may attempt to gain market share by offering higher-quality outputs. But using the experience curve entails risks, such as becoming wed over time to an obsolete technology.

One of the primary considerations in any POM strategy is product or service quality. Businesses that build quality in, rather than attempt to inspect for quality after production has occurred, are able to enhance both productivity and profitability. Well-designed TQM programs, in particular, have yielded positive results.

In the finance function, business units that compete with the niche–low-cost and low-cost strategies pursue financial strategies intended to lower their financial costs. Companies that adopt niche-differentiation and differentiation strategies develop financial strategies that fund quality enhancements. And those that use niche–low-cost/differentiation, low-cost–differentiation, and multiple strategies use their financial function both to lower costs and to promote quality enhancements.

Research and development (R&D) has two basic components: product/service R&D and process R&D. Business units competing with the niche–low-cost and low-cost strategies emphasize process R&D to reduce their operations costs; those that use niche-differentiation or differentiation place greater importance on product/service R&D; and adopters of niche–low-cost/differentiation, low-cost–differentiation, and multiple strategies simultaneously stress both types of R&D.

In the 1990s, effective organizations will manage their human resource function so as to maintain a strong, competitive work force. This goal requires attention to personnel needs and the development of strategies that strengthen organizational and job performance commitment and teamwork across functional areas.

Tying all of these functions together is the organization's information system. Well-designed information systems are capable of cutting internal costs while they promote differentiation and quality through faster responses to the market's needs.

In marketing, the particular generic strategy adopted by a business unit influences the types of products or services the business offers, its prices for those products or services, the channels of distribution it uses, the location of its outlets, and its advertising and promotional policies. The key is to strive for consistency among these elements.

Finally, it is essential that the business's functional activities be tightly integrated. An organization that is able to mesh its functional strategies smoothly is more likely to gain a competitive advantage based on superior product design, customer service, speed, and/or guarantee.

KEY CONCEPTS

Experience curve The reduction in per-unit costs that occurs as an organization gains experience producing a product or service. The experience curve concept is based on three underlying variables: learning (the more an employee performs a task, the more efficient he or she should become at the job), economies of scale (the decline in per-unit costs of a product or service as the absolute volume of production increases per period of time), and capital-labor substitution possibilities (as volume increases, the organization may be able to substitute labor for capital, or capital for labor, depending upon which combination produces lower costs and/or greater effectiveness).

Functional strategy The strategy pursued by each functional area of a business unit. Functional areas are usually referred to as "departments" and include purchasing/materials management, production/operations, finance, research and development, marketing, human resources, and information systems. Their strategies may take various forms, depending upon which generic strategy the business unit adopts.

Just-in-time inventory system (JIT) An inventory system, popularized by the Japanese, in which suppliers deliver parts just at the time they are needed by the buying organization to use in its production process. Used properly, such a system holds inventory, storage, and warehousing costs to a minimum.

Process R&D Research and development activities that concentrate upon reducing the costs of operations and making them more efficient.

Product/service R&D Research and development activities that are intended to lead to improvements or innovations in the firm's products or services.

Technology transfer The process whereby a company transforms its scientific discoveries into marketable products.

DISCUSSION QUESTIONS

1. What is the relationship among corporate-level strategy, business unit strategies, and functional strategies?

2. Explain the linkage that a just-in-time inventory system provides between the purchasing and production functions. What are the implications for quality?

3. POM concepts are equally applicable to manufacturing and service organizations. Explain the POM process at a university.

4. What are some of the more important relationships among the POM, finance, and R&D functions?

5. What sorts of POM strategies might a small business unit adopt to compete effectively with a large business unit?

6. Relate the concept of the experience curve to the production operations of an automobile assembly plant.

7. Explain the relationship between quality and productivity.

8. What is the linkage between long-term capital investment decisions and the organization's corporate and business unit strategies?

9. Give, and explain, an example of (a) a business that emphasizes product/service R&D, and (b) another business that emphasizes process R&D.

10. What are some of the major relationships among marketing, information systems, and human resources management?

STRATEGIC MANAGEMENT EXERCISES

1. Assume that two groups of investors are each planning to start a restaurant in the same city. The first group wishes to appeal to family meal needs, and the second wants to appeal to the needs of people who prefer gourmet food in particularly nice surroundings on special occasions. As is evident, different functional strategies will need to be adopted by the two restaurants. How would you suggest that each restaurant plan and implement its functional strategies? Be specific in your suggestions. If you need further information, either conduct relevant research or make reasonable assumptions.

2. Assume that you are asked to consult for a top-of-the-line restaurant in New York City that competes with the niche-differentiation strategy. While attending management's strategic-planning session, you learn that the managers would like to broaden their appeal in the New York City market. One way of doing that, they believe, is to reduce their prices. To attain that end, they must cut costs. Therefore, one manager suggests that to reduce costs, they should make some of their purchases locally instead of purchasing from the highest-quality suppliers worldwide. (Currently, the restaurant flies in certain foods from for-

eign countries at considerable cost.) Another manager believes that the restaurant should use less expensive tablecloths and napkins. Finally, another wishes to cancel the restaurant's live musical entertainment to save money. Through these cost-cutting measures, the managers believe that they can reduce their prices and become more competitive.

What advice would you give these managers regarding their functional strategies?

3. Contrast the functional strategies that are followed by two automobile manufacturers: (a) Ford, which, as one of the world's largest producers, competes with the low-cost–differentiation strategy; and (b) Rolls-Royce, a relatively small company, which uses the niche-differentiation strategy. Specifically, how might you expect these two companies to differ in carrying out each of the following functional strategies: purchasing/materials management, production/operations, finance, research and development, marketing, human resources, and information systems?

4. Select a specific company on which you will be able to obtain information.

   a. Determine which generic business unit strategy this company has adopted.
   b. Analyze the company's functional strategies in purchasing/materials management, production/operations, finance, research and development, marketing, human resources, and information systems.
   c. Analyze the extent to which these functional strategies mesh smoothly with one another and with the business's generic strategy.
   d. Make suggestions for improvements in the company's functional strategies.

NOTES

1. J. Cole, "Boeing's Dominance of Aircraft Industry Runs into Bumpiness," *The Wall Street Journal,* 10 July 1992; D.J. Yang, M. Oneal, S. Toy, M. Maremont, and R. Neff, "How Boeing Does It," *Business Week,* 9 July 1990, pp. 46–50.
2. E.E. Scheuing, *Purchasing Management* (Englewood Cliffs, N.J.: Prentice-Hall, 1989), p. 4.
3. T.H. Hendrick and F.G. Moore, *Production/Operations Management,* 9th ed. (Homewood, Ill.: Irwin, 1985), p. 336.
4. J.G. Miller and P. Gilmour, "Materials Managers: Who Needs Them?" *Harvard Business Review* 57, no. 4 (1979): 145.
5. S.P. Galante, "Distributors Bow to Demands of 'Just-in-Time' Delivery," *The Wall Street Journal,* 30 June 1986.
6. F. Swoboda, "GM's Saturn Plant Closed by Strike," *The Washington Post,* 28 August 1992.
7. J. Dreyfuss, "Shaping Up Your Suppliers," *Fortune,* 10 April 1989, p. 116.

8. J. Browne, J. Harhen, and J. Shivnan, *Production Management Systems: A CIM Perspective* (Workingham, England: Addison-Wesley, 1988), pp. 158–159.
9. E.A. Haas, "Breakthrough Manufacturing," *Harvard Business Review* 65, no. 2 (1987): 75–81.
10. See Boston Consulting Group, *Perspectives on Experience* (Boston: The Boston Consulting Group, 1976); G. Hall and S. Howell, "The Experience Curve from an Economist's Perspective," *Strategic Management Journal* 6 (1985): 197–212.
11. A. Taylor III, "Can GM Remodel Itself?" *Fortune,* 13 January 1992, p. 33.
12. T. Peters and N. Austin, *A Passion for Excellence* (New York: Random House, 1985), p. 53.
13. R.D. Buzzell and B.T. Gale, *The PIMS Principles* (New York: Free Press, 1987), Chap. 6.
14. R. Johnson, W.O. Winchell, and P.B. DuBose, *Strategy and Quality* (Milwaukee: American Society for Quality Control, 1989).
15. P. Crosby, *Quality Is Free* (New York: McGraw-Hill, 1979), p. 1.
16. W.E. Deming, *Out of the Crisis* (Cambridge, Mass.: Massachusetts Institute of Technology, Center for Advanced Engineering Study, 1986).
17. United States General Accounting Office, "Management Practices: U.S. Companies Improve Performance Through Quality Efforts," GAO/NSIAD-91-190, May 1991.
18. Ibid., p. 4.
19. M. Lewyn, "The Post Office Wants Everyone to Pay for Its Mistakes," *Business Week,* 5 March 1990, p. 28.
20. G. Bylinsky, "Turning R&D into Real Products," *Fortune,* 2 July 1990, pp. 72–73.
21. A.K. Naj, "GE's Latest Invention: A Way to Move Ideas from Lab to Market," *The Wall Street Journal,* 14 June 1990.
22. P.F. Drucker, "Japan: New Strategies for a New Reality," *The Wall Street Journal,* 2 October 1991.
23. K. Kelly, O. Port, J. Treece, G. DeGeorge, and Z. Schiller, "Learning from Japan," *Business Week,* 27 January 1992, p. 53.
24. P.M. Wright and G.C. McMahan, "Theoretical Perspectives for Strategic Human Resource Management," *Journal of Management* 18 (1992): 298.
25. J. Solomon, "Pepsi Offers Stock Options to All, Not Just Honchos," *The Wall Street Journal,* 28 June 1989.
26. Ibid.
27. J. Weber, "Offering Employees Stock Options They Can't Refuse," *Business Week,* 7 October 1991, p. 34.
28. P. Coy, "The New Realism in Office Systems," *Business Week,* 15 June 1992, p. 128.
29. R.B. Chase and D.A. Garvin, "The Service Factory," *Harvard Business Review* 67, no. 4 (1989): 67.
30. D. Kirkpatrick, "Why Not Farm Out Your Computing?" *Fortune,* 23 September 1991, p. 104.
31. Ibid.
32. P. Coy and C. Hawkins, "UPS: Up from the Stone Age," *Business Week,* 15 June 1992, p. 132; Coy, "The New Realism in Office Systems," pp. 129–130.
33. Kirkpatrick, "Why Not Farm Out Your Computing?" p. 112.
34. B. Dumaine, "Design That Sells and Sells and . . . ," *Fortune,* 11 March 1991, p. 86.
35. J. Main, "Manufacturing the Right Way," *Fortune,* 21 May 1990, p. 54.
36. A. Bennett, "Making the Grade with the Customer," *The Wall Street Journal,* 12 November 1990.

37. A. Bennett, "Many Consumers Expect Better Service and Say They Are Willing to Pay for It," *The Wall Street Journal,* 12 November 1990.
38. D. Milbank, "Service Enables Nuts-and-Bolts Supplier to Be More Than Sum of Its Parts," *The Wall Street Journal,* 16 November 1990.
39. P. Wright, "Competitive Strategies for Small Businesses," in A.A. Thompson, Jr., A.J. Strickland III, and W.E. Fulmer, eds., *Readings in Strategic Management* (Plano, Tex.: Business Publications, 1984), p. 90.
40. F. Rose, "New Quality Means Service Too," *Fortune,* 22 April 1991, pp. 97, 100.
41. B. Dumaine, "How Managers Can Succeed Through Speed," *Fortune,* 13 February 1989, p. 54.
42. Wright, "Competitive Strategies," p. 89.
43. J.D. Burge, "Motorola's Transition to a High Performance Workforce," an Executive Lecture at James Madison University, 20 February 1992.
44. B. Dumaine, "Earning More by Moving Faster," *Fortune,* 7 October 1991, pp. 89, 94.
45. S. Phillips, A. Dunkin, J. Treece, and K. Hammonds, "King Customer," *Business Week,* 12 March 1990, p. 88.
46. B. Uttal, "Companies That Serve You Best," *Fortune,* 7 December 1987, p. 98.
47. C.W.L. Hart, "The Power of Unconditional Service Guarantees," *The McKinsey Quarterly,* Summer 1989, pp. 75–76.

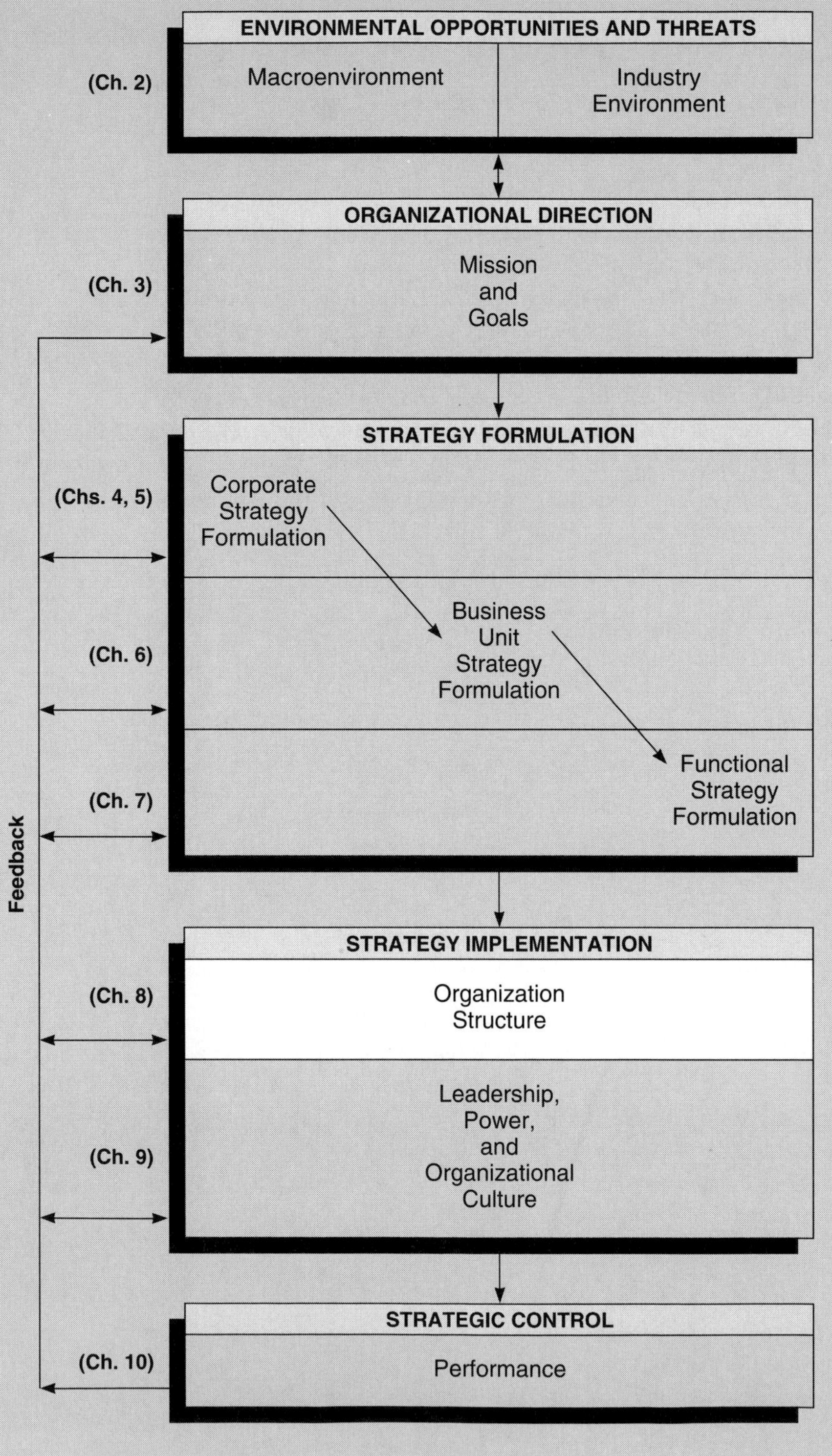
STRATEGIC MANAGEMENT MODEL
ENVIRONMENTAL OPPORTUNITIES AND THREATS
(Ch. 2)
Macroenvironment
Industry Environment
ORGANIZATIONAL DIRECTION
(Ch. 3)
Mission and Goals
STRATEGY FORMULATION
(Chs. 4, 5)
Corporate Strategy Formulation
(Ch. 6)
Business Unit Strategy Formulation
(Ch. 7)
Functional Strategy Formulation
Feedback
STRATEGY IMPLEMENTATION
(Ch. 8)
Organization Structure
(Ch. 9)
Leadership, Power, and Organizational Culture
STRATEGIC CONTROL
(Ch. 10)
Performance

8

Strategy Implementation: Organizational Structure

The four preceding chapters dealt with strategy formulation at the corporate, business unit, and functional levels. This chapter and the following one address the implementation of these strategies. Successful strategies not only must be well formulated to match environmental opportunities and constraints or threats but also must be carried out effectively.

Effective strategy implementation requires managers to consider a number of key issues. Chief among them are how the organization should be structured to put its strategy into effect and how such variables as leadership, power, and organizational culture should be managed to enable the organization's employees to work together in carrying out the firm's strategic plans. This chapter deals with the first of these key issues—structuring the organization. Leadership, power, and organizational culture will be addressed in the following chapter.

ORGANIZATIONAL GROWTH

Organizational structure refers to the ways that tasks and responsibilities are allocated to individuals and the ways that individuals are grouped together into offices, departments, and divisions. The structure, which is reflected in an organization chart, designates formal reporting relationships and defines the number of levels in the hierarchy.[1]

Normally, when small businesses are started, they consist of an owner-manager and a few employees. Neither an organization chart nor formal assignment of responsibilities is necessary at this stage. Structure is fluid, with each employee often knowing how to perform more than one task and with the owner-manager involved in all aspects of the business. If the organization survives those crucial first years and becomes successful, it is because of the increased demand that it has created for its products or services. To meet this increased demand, the business must grow. With growth, the organization of the business begins to evolve from fluidity to a status of more permanent division of labor. The owner-manager, who once was involved in all functions of the enterprise on a hands-on basis, now finds that his or her role is becoming more managerial and less operational. As new employees are recruited, each is assigned to perform a specialized function.

As Figure 8.1 illustrates, growth expands the organization's structure, both vertically and horizontally. In this figure, the owner-manager's hands-on activities have been taken over by managers who specialize, respectively, in manufacturing and marketing. Each of them manages employees who work only in one specialized functional area. The organization has now added one vertical level—a managerial one—and has expanded horizontally into two separate departments. The following sections discuss these two types of organizational growth.

■ Vertical Growth

Vertical growth refers to an increase in the length of the organization's hierarchical chain of command. The **hierarchical chain of command** represents the company's authority-accountability relationships between managers and employees. Authority flows down the hierarchy from the highest levels in the organization to those at the bottom, and accountability flows upward from bottom to top. In Figure 8.1, the organization on the right has three levels in its hierarchy. Employees at each level report to the manager who is in charge of their specific operations. The number of employees reporting to each manager represents that manager's **span of control.**

Figure 8.2 illustrates two extremes in organizational configuration. At the left is a **tall organization,** comprised of many hierarchical levels and narrow spans of control. The other structure is a **flat organization,** which has few levels in its hierarchy and a wide span of control from top to bottom. It is important to note that each of these configurations represents an extreme. Rather than being at either extreme, many organizations fall somewhere in between. Hence, we speak of organizations as being "relatively tall" or "relatively flat."

According to John Child, a management researcher, the average number of hierarchical levels for an organization with 3,000 employees is seven.[2] Consequently, we might consider an organization with about 3,000 employees and

Figure 8.1 **Organization of the Enterprise at Start-up and with Growth**

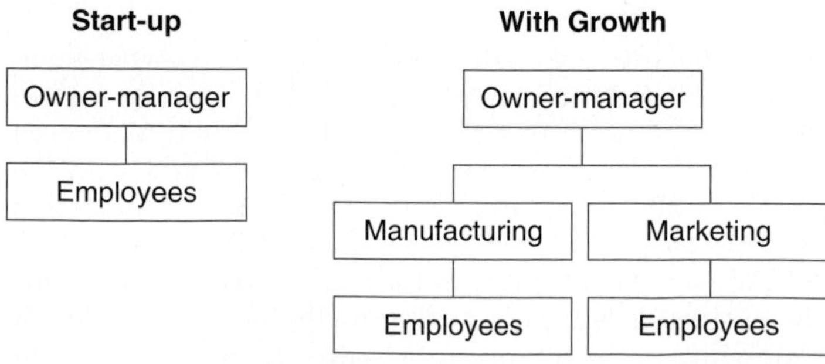

Tall and Flat Organizational Structures **Figure 8.2**

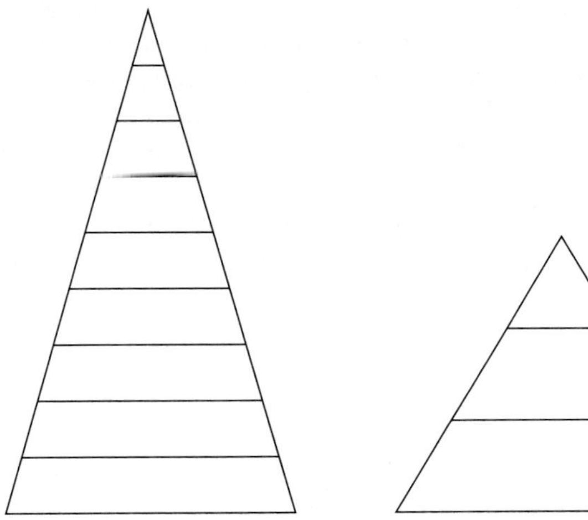

Tall organization, with 9 levels   Flat organization, with 3 levels

four hierarchical levels to be relatively flat, but another of similar size with nine levels to be relatively tall.

Because relatively tall organizations have a narrow span of control, the managers in such organizations have a relatively high degree of control over their subordinates. The opposite, of course, is true in relatively flat structures. Both managers and operative employees in tall organizations also tend to have jobs that are more narrowly specialized than those in relatively flat structures. Because managers in tall organizations have more control readily available to them and because almost everyone in the company is a specialist, authority in tall organizations is usually centralized at the top of the hierarchy. Only at that level are there individuals who deal with and understand all parts of the organization's operations.

Conversely, authority is more decentralized in relatively flat structures, because a manager with a broad span of control must grant more authority to his or her employees; the manager is unable to keep up sufficiently with all developments to make the best decisions. Decisions are more likely to be made by the employee who is on the scene and is most familiar with the situation. As might be expected, employees in flat organizations are less specialized than those in taller ones.

Strategically speaking, both organizational types have certain advantages.[3] The relatively tall, centralized organization allows for better communication of the business's mission, goals, and objectives to all employees. It also enhances coordination of functional areas to ensure that each area works closely with the other functions and that all work together to attain the business's goals and objectives. Finally, in these organizations, planning and its execution are relatively easy to accomplish since all employees are centrally directed. Tall organizational structures are well suited for environments that are relatively stable and predictable.

Relatively flat structures also have their advantages. Administrative costs are usually less than those in taller organizations, because fewer hierarchical levels require fewer managers, which, in turn, means fewer secretaries, offices, and fringe benefits. A second advantage is that decentralized decision making allows managers at various levels to have more authority, which may increase their motivation to assume responsibility for their areas' performance. Third, because of the greater freedom in decision making, innovations are encouraged. Flat structures, therefore, are appropriate for more dynamic environments.

For example, Alcoa, the world's largest producer of aluminum, recently flattened its structure in an attempt to lower costs and speed up decision making in its increasingly competitive environment. The company eliminated two levels of top management—including the offices of president and three group vice presidents, and twenty-four staff positions—and granted considerable autonomy to its twenty-five business unit managers. Each business unit manager, for instance, now has authority to spend up to $5 million without higher-level approval, an increase of 400 percent over the previous spending limit, and reports directly to the CEO rather than to a group vice president.[4]

■ Horizontal Growth

Returning to our earlier illustration of a small business with an owner-manager, recall that success necessitates growth. This growth is not only vertical, as just discussed, but also horizontal. **Horizontal growth** refers to an increase in the breadth of an organization's structure. In Figure 8.1, the small business segmented itself horizontally into two departments—manufacturing and marketing. If the company continues to grow, it will eventually need specialists in such areas as personnel, accounting, and finance. Right now, the owner-manager is carrying out those functions; but with growth, his or her expertise will be increasingly needed for strategic management. Individuals will need to be hired to manage the personnel, accounting, and finance activities. Thus, with growth, the structure of an organization is broadened to accommodate the development of more specialized functions.

As an example, consider the comments of T.J. Rodgers, founder of Cypress Semiconductor Corporation. Using a niche-differentiation strategy, this enterprise grew to a $135 million company in five years by developing superfast memory chips. With such rapid growth, however, Rodgers quickly found himself overextended.

> At about $50 million in revenues, I felt I could run it. . . . I could name everybody in the company. But as it grew larger, I found myself stretched. One Friday night at 11 P.M., I realized that if there wasn't a change, I'd have to stop sleeping within six months to keep up the pace.[5]

In other words, a new business may originally have its owner-manager and its few employees performing multiple functions on a daily basis. With growth, however, each function expands so that ultimately no one individual can be intimately involved—either physically or intellectually—in all of the company's functions. This is the point at which various key functional areas are formally set apart as departments and existing employees and new hires are each assigned to one of these newly formed functional units.

This functional structure, elaborated upon in the following section, is the way small businesses typically organize as they experience growth. This structure, of course, is not the only form available to management. After the functional structure is discussed, other forms are also presented. But, in all cases, growth involves both vertical and horizontal elaboration. It is the strategic direction of the firm that determines the specific type of structure that is most appropriate.

ORGANIZATIONAL STRUCTURE

As an enterprise grows to become an established business, it will adopt one of a number of different organizational structures to implement its strategy. Over time, as its situation changes, the enterprise may shift to another structure. Many large, well-known companies change structures several times in a decade in order to carry out their strategy more effectively. This section discusses six major types of structures that are available to organizations: functional, product divisional, geographic divisional, multidivisional, strategic business unit, and matrix.

Functional Structure

As suggested in the preceding section, the initial growth of an enterprise often requires it to organize by functional areas. The **functional structure** is characterized by the simultaneous combination of similar activities and the separation of dissimilar activities on the basis of function. This structure is by no means limited to small businesses. Companies of any size that have a single product line or a few similar product lines are well suited to the functional

A Functional Structure with Vertical and Horizontal Growth **Figure 8.3**

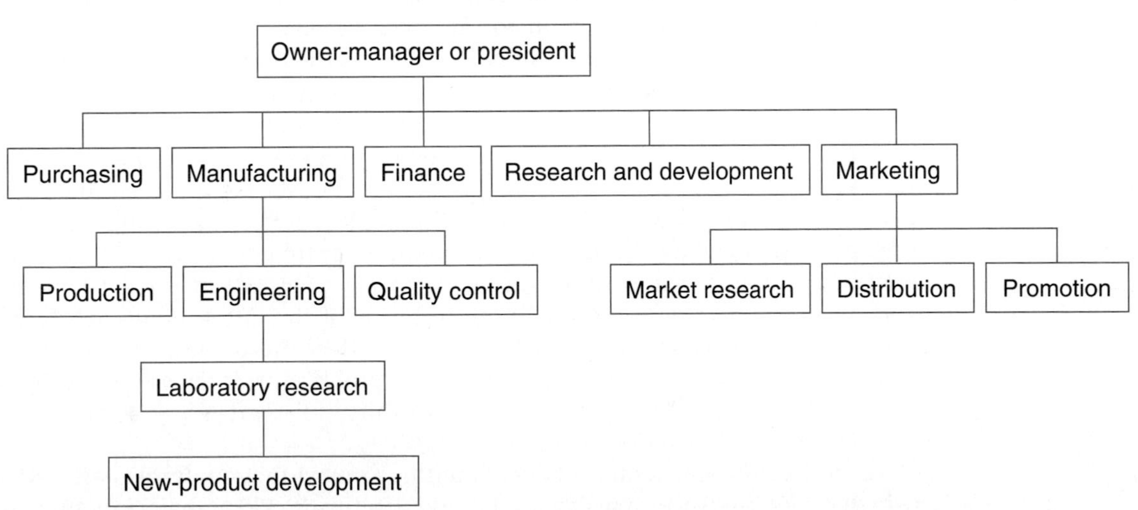

organizational structure. Small businesses, however, are likely to have only a few functional departments; larger organizations may be quite differentiated, both horizontally and vertically. Figure 8.3 shows a large business that has experienced both vertical and horizontal growth.

Comparing this business with the one shown in Figure 8.1, we can see that growth brings about more extensive horizontal expansion. Rather than simply dividing its employees into manufacturing and marketing functions, this organization has grown so that it also needs specialists in purchasing, finance, and research and development. Furthermore, its growth has also resulted in vertical extensions. Manufacturing has become so complex that it has had to segment itself into the functions of production, engineering, and quality control. Engineering contains two additional levels—laboratory research and new-product development. Likewise, marketing has been divided into market research, distribution, and promotion functions.

A functional structure has certain strategic advantages and disadvantages. On the plus side, this structure emphasizes the functions that the organization must carry out. Specialization by function is encouraged, with the resulting benefits that specialization brings. For instance, when functional specialists interact frequently, they may realize synergies that increase their department's efficiency and effectiveness. Furthermore, their interaction can result in improvements and innovations for their functional area that may not have occurred had there not been a critical mass of specialists organized within the same unit. On the psychological side, working closely on a daily basis with others who share one's functional interests is likely to increase job satisfaction and, hence, contribute to lower turnover.

In addition, the functional organization facilitates the processes of planning, organizing, motivating, and controlling groups of personnel. Translating the organization's mission, goals, and objectives into action is easier when each functional area is activated to plan, organize, motivate, and control within its own boundaries. Finally, the training and development of personnel is often more efficient than in other structures because the training centers on standard types of functional skills.

This structure, however, is accompanied by some disadvantages. Because the business is organized around functions, rather than around products or geographic regions, it is difficult to pinpoint the responsibility for profits or losses. If an organization's sales have declined, is the problem due to purchasing, research and development, manufacturing, or marketing? In a functional structure, such problem analysis can be quite ambiguous.

Along these same lines, a functional structure often creates a narrow perspective of the organization among its members. Marketing personnel, for instance, are likely to view the organization totally from a marketing perspective, because they have little experience with other functional areas. The same is true for employees in manufacturing, finance, and other functions. Problems and opportunities are perceived more in terms of the interests of each functional area rather than in the way that they affect the overall organization. Consequently, different solutions to the same problem or different strategies to take advantage of an environmental opportunity are advanced as desirable by the various functional departments.

Finally, communication and coordination across functional areas are often difficult. For instance, employees in manufacturing view their function as central to organizational success and attribute operational problems to other functional areas. Marketing, meanwhile, views increased sales as primarily attributable to its efforts but sees slow sales as manufacturing's fault. It should be clear that as functional departments begin to proliferate, coordination becomes increasingly difficult. Functional differentiation presents management with the challenging task of coordinating disparate activities so that a unified, logical whole may be attained.

Whenever an organization begins to expand its product lines significantly, grow geographically, or acquire other businesses, the functional structure begins to lose its strategic usefulness. Management then faces the issue of changing its organization's structure to one more appropriate to its strategy.

■ Product Divisional Structure

The product divisional structure is well suited for businesses with several product lines. Rather than organizing the firm around functions, the **product**

STRATEGIC INSIGHT

Removing the Blinders at Ford

One of the potential weaknesses in a functional structure is that it can encourage employees to take a narrow perspective of their organization. It is easy for functional managers and operative employees to look at problems from the standpoint of marketing or production or some other functional specialty rather than see them from the viewpoint of the company as a whole.

Ford Motor Company, America's third-largest corporation with over $100 billion in sales, has devised a program to reduce this problem. In a 5½-day session for middle managers, the managers are first grouped by their functional specialties. Then they are asked to "think about how their function works within the company, how others perceive it, and how it ought to work."

As they discuss their thoughts with managers from other functional areas, they begin to realize how narrow their perspective is. That is, they tend to view Ford primarily as a manufacturing company or a finance company or a company that specializes in personnel. As a result of the session, they learn to take a broader view of the organization, realizing that their particular function is only one of many interrelated activities that must be accomplished for Ford to attain its goals. Ford terms this process "chimney-breaking."

In a broader sense, Ford's strategic alliance with Mazda to develop jointly several cars and sport-utility vehicles has helped Ford engineers expand their perspective. From working with Mazda, Ford has learned to emphasize quality over price in purchasing parts, to design more exacting tolerances for its parts, to construct stamping operations at each assembly plant (rather than continue to use centralized stamping plants), and to improve its employee suggestion program.

Mazda, incidentally, has benefited from the joint venture as well. From Ford, it has learned how to control engine emissions better, measure noise and vibration more accurately, gather and use consumer survey information more effectively, and improve its marketing.

SOURCES: "The Fortune 500 Largest U.S. Industrial Corporations," *Fortune,* 19 April 1993, p. 184; J.B. Treece, K.L. Miller, and R.A. Melcher, "The Partners," *Business Week,* 10 February 1992, pp. 102–107; J.B. Treece, "How Ford and Mazda Shared the Driver's Seat," *Business Week,* 26 March 1990, pp. 94–95; W. Kiechel III, "The Organization That Learns," *Fortune,* 12 March 1990, pp. 133–136 (source of quotation).

divisional structure focuses on the company's product categories. Figure 8.4 illustrates this structure for a firm that manufactures and sells home appliances. Its activities and personnel are grouped into three product divisions: refrigerators and ranges, washers and dryers, and small appliances. Each product division will contain its own functional areas. The small-appliances division, for instance, may have its own manufacturing and marketing departments because the products that it makes and sells may require different manufacturing methods and channels of distribution than those of the other two divisions. Other functions, however, such as finance, may be centralized at the top of the organization because they benefit the organization as a whole and because economies of scale can be realized. For example, the corporation as a whole can obtain more favorable interest rates when borrowing money than could the small-appliances division alone.

This structure is also widely used in nonmanufacturing organizations. For instance, supermarkets typically have a number of product managers (e.g., produce manager, meat manager, dairy manager, and bakery manager) who report to the store manager; and department stores are divided into product areas such as women's sportswear, men's shoes, children's wear, furniture, and appliances. Universities, being service organizations, are also usually organized by "product" divisions: history, mathematics, computer sciences, marketing, art, and so on.

The advantages of the product divisional structure are several. Rather than emphasize the functions that the organization performs, the structure emphasizes product lines. The result is a clear focus upon each individual product category and a greater orientation toward customer service. Also, the ability to pinpoint the responsibility for profits or losses is greatly enhanced, since each product division becomes a profit center to which profits or losses can be directly attributed. A **profit center** is an organizational unit charged with a well-defined mission and is headed by a manager accountable for the center's revenues and expenditures. So it is clear to upper management which divisions are operating profitably and which are incurring losses. Furthermore, the product divisional structure is ideal for training and developing managers, since each product manager is, in effect, running his or her "own business." Hence, product managers develop general management skills—an end that can be

Figure 8.4 **Product Divisional Structure**

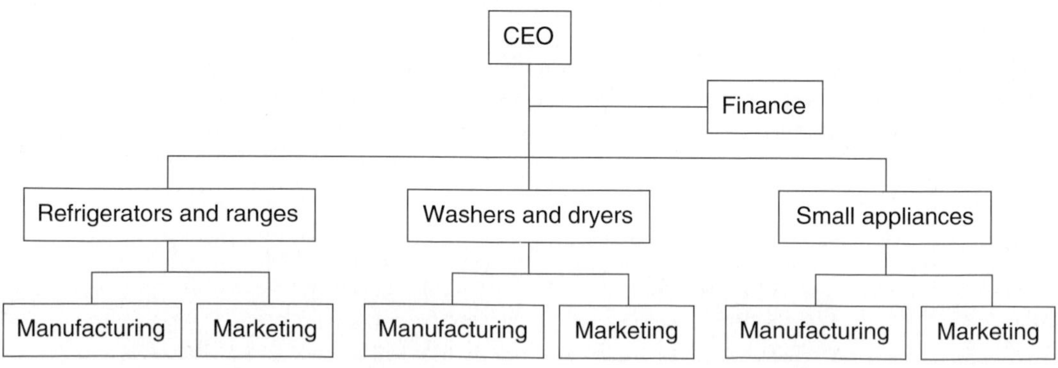

accomplished in a functional structure only by rotating managers from one functional area to another.

Even relatively small companies can use a product divisional structure. Stryker Corporation, with annual revenues of $281 million, recently converted from a functional structure to one with several semiautonomous product divisions. Now, Stryker employs a highly trained sales force for each division to market a specialized product—such as hospital beds, hip implants, medical video cameras, or surgical power tools—rather than use one companywide sales force to sell all of these products. As its president says, "It's achieving focus through decentralization."[6]

Of course, the product divisional structure also has its disadvantages. In some ways, it can be more expensive to operate than a functional structure, because more functional personnel may be required. In Figure 8.4, for example, because the firm has three manufacturing departments rather than only one, the total personnel expense for manufacturing is likely to be higher than if only one department were necessary. Such extra expenses raise the firm's break-even point. Obviously, this disadvantage is offset to some extent by the ability of each manufacturing department to focus upon producing only its own outputs. Second, the coordination of activities at headquarters becomes more difficult. Top management finds it harder to ensure that all of the firm's marketing personnel, for instance, are following the same policies and procedures when serving customers. This problem can become fairly significant when an organization has forty or fifty product divisions, which is fairly common among large firms. In addition, the customer can be confused by being called on by different sales representatives from the same firm. Third, since each product manager emphasizes his or her own product area, what may be in the best interests of the firm may be overlooked as product managers compete for resources such as money, physical space, and personnel.

In fact, disadvantages like these led Nestlé's U.S.-based subsidiary to convert its product divisional structure to a functional structure in 1991. By consolidating such product lines as Carnation, Stouffer Foods, Quik, and Taster's Choice under one manager, Nestlé saved at least $30 million in overhead and administrative expenses. It also allowed the business unit to benefit from increased scope and scale economies.[7]

■ Geographic Divisional Structure

When a firm operates in various geographical areas, an appropriate structure may be the **geographic divisional structure,** in which activities and personnel are grouped by specific geographic locations. This structure may be used on a local basis (a city may be divided into sales regions), on a national basis (northeast region, mid-Atlantic region, southeast region, midwest region), or on an international basis (North American region, Latin American region, Western European region, Middle Eastern region). Figure 8.5 illustrates a national company (at the top) and an international company (at the bottom) organized by geographic divisions.

There are a number of advantages to organizing geographically. First, products and services may be better tailored to the climatic needs of specific areas. For example, retailers may stock heavier clothing for their outlets in northern states and lighter clothes in southern stores. Second, a geographic divisional structure allows a firm to respond to the technical needs of different interna-

Figure 8.5 **Geographic Divisional Structures**

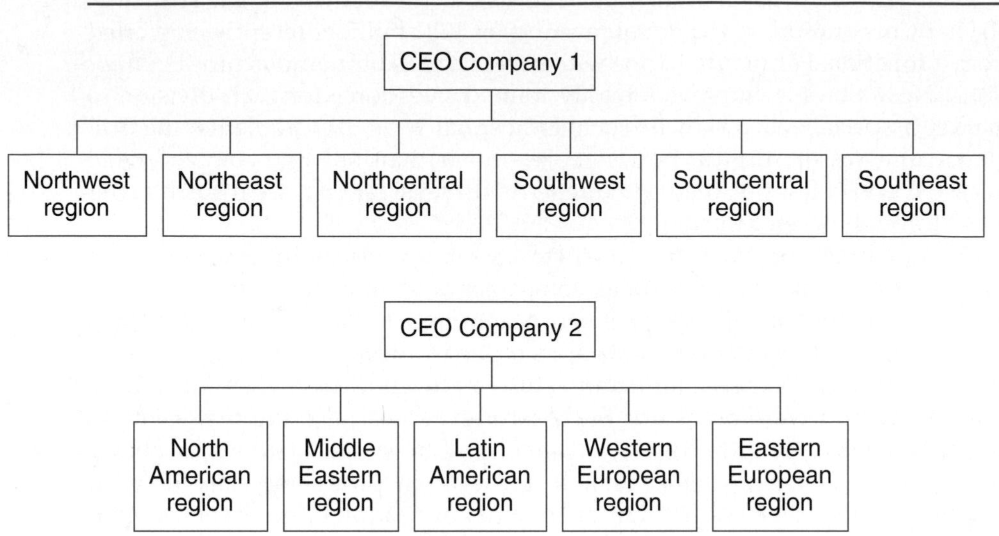

tional areas. For instance, in many parts of the world, the electrical system is different from that in the United States; the geographic structure allows firms to accommodate these geographic differences. Third, producing or distributing products in different national or global locations may give the organization a competitive advantage. Many firms, for example, produce components in countries that either have a labor cost advantage or are located close to essential raw materials. The final product may then be assembled in still another location that is more appropriate for the advanced technology required or that is closer to the final consumer. Fourth, a geographic organization may better serve the consumer needs of various nations. For instance, the need for hair-grooming products differs from one society to another, and the geographic structure allows firms to respond to these differing needs. Fifth, organizing along geographic lines enables a company to adapt to varying legal systems. Automobile insurance companies within the United States, for example, often have a geographic division for each state, because no two states have the same insurance regulations. Finally, geographic divisions allow firms to pinpoint the responsibility for profits or losses, because each division is a profit center.

The disadvantages of a geographic divisional structure are similar to those identified earlier for the product divisional structure. Often, more functional personnel are required than would be the case for a functional structure, because each region has its own functional departments. Coordination of companywide functions is more difficult than in a strictly functional organization, and regional managers may emphasize their own geographic areas to the exclusion of a companywide viewpoint.

■ Multidivisional Structure

As a firm continues to expand by adding more and more product lines, it may outgrow all of the preceding structures. At this stage, firms with multiple product lines may adopt the **multidivisional structure,** in which the company is partitioned into several divisions, with each division responsible for one or more product lines.

Consider Maytag as an example. At one time in its history, this appliance firm had a fairly simple structure with three product divisions—gas range products, laundry products, and electric range products. But it continued to expand its product lines by acquiring Magic Chef (a producer of air conditioners, refrigerators, and furnaces), Toastmaster (a manufacturer of small appliances), and Hoover (a maker of vacuum cleaners and European major appliances). Maytag's current structure is depicted in Figure 8.6. As you can see, the multidivisional structure encompasses several divisions, with each division comprised of one or more product lines.

The multidivisional structure has several advantages. First, continued growth is facilitated. As new product lines are created or acquired, those lines may be integrated into an existing division or may serve as the foundation for a newly developed division. Second, since each division has its own top-level strategic managers, the work load of the CEO's headquarters staff is lightened. This gives the CEO more time to analyze each division's operations and to decide on resource allocations on the basis of the portfolio analysis techniques discussed in Chapter 5. Third, authority is delegated downward to each division and, within each division, to each product line. This decentralization allows for a better alignment of each division and product line with its unique external environment. Fourth, accountability for performance can be logically evaluated at the product line level as well as at the divisional level.

As is true with each structure discussed, however, the multidivisional structure has certain disadvantages. First, the distribution of corporate overhead costs across the divisions is difficult and relatively subjective. Inevitably, the

Multidivisional Structure of Maytag **Figure 8.6**

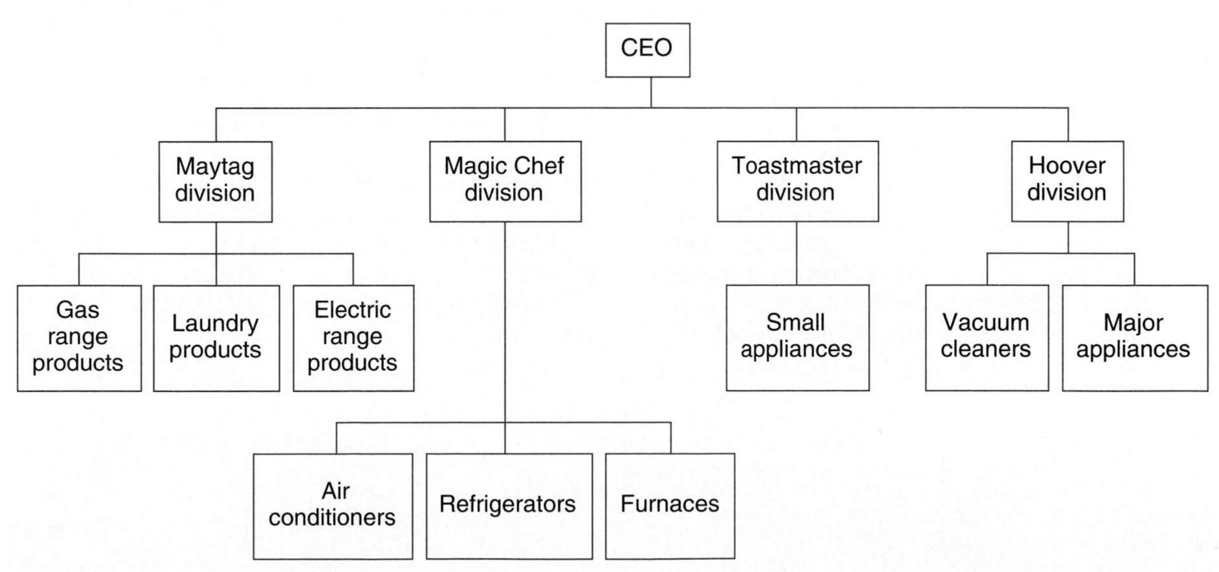

distribution results in some divisional managers feeling that their divisions have received too heavy an allocation. Second, dysfunctional divisional rivalries often emerge as each division attempts to secure a greater share of the firm's resources. Third, when one division makes components or products that another division needs, conflicts can arise in setting transfer prices. *Transfer pricing* refers to the price that one division charges another division for its products or parts. The selling division normally prefers to charge a relatively high transfer price to increase its profits, but the purchasing division prefers to pay a relatively low transfer price to lower its costs.

■ Strategic Business Unit Structure

Organizational growth may ultimately require that related product lines be grouped into divisions and that the divisions themselves then be grouped into

STRATEGIC INSIGHT

ITW's Multidivisional Structure

Illinois Tool Works (ITW), headquartered in a Chicago suburb, is a low-profile manufacturer of almost 100,000 products, including nails, screws, bolts, strapping, wrapping, valves, capacitors, filters, adhesives, tools and machines, plastic buckles, plastic loops that hold six-packs together, Zip-Pak resealable food packages, and Kiwi-Lok nylon fasteners. ITW ranked 168th on *Fortune's* 1992 list of the 500 largest industrial corporations in the United States, with sales of $2.8 billion and 15,700 employees. Its primary markets are the construction, automotive and truck, electronics, agricultural, and telecommunications industries. Nearly half of its revenue comes from foreign sales.

The company searches for market niches and often dominates those in which it operates. At the corporate level, the firm follows a growth strategy, with most of its business units pursuing a niche–low-cost or niche–low-cost/differentiation strategy.

In addition to focusing on internal growth, ITW pursues a strategy of horizontal integration and related diversification by regularly acquiring smaller firms that complement ITW's core businesses. Its ninety product lines are grouped into nine divisions. Most of the product lines are relatively small, with about $30 million in annual revenue. Each product line manager controls manufacturing, marketing, and research and development. When a new product with commercial possibilities is developed, it is often split off to form a new business unit.

ITW seeks to keep costs as low as possible. Its largest division, the construction products group, generates $420 million a year but has only three headquarters employees: a president, a controller, and a shared secretary.

Its carefully formulated strategy and appropriate structure have helped ITW to rank consistently toward the top in the metal products industry in Fortune's annual survey of "Most Admired Corporations."

SOURCES: C. Willis, "Wall Street," *Money,* April 1992, pp. 69–70; "The Fortune 500 Largest U.S. Industrial Corporations," *Fortune,* 19 April 1993, p.190; "How Companies Rank in 32 Industries," *Fortune,* 11 February 1991, p. 72; *Moody's Handbook of Common Stocks* (New York: Moody's Investors Service, Spring, 1991); *Wards' Business Directory of U.S. Private and Public Companies,* Vol. 1 (Detroit: Gale Research, 1991); R. Henkoff, "The Ultimate Nuts & Bolts Co.," *Fortune,* 16 July 1990, pp. 70–73.

strategic business units. This **strategic business unit structure** is particularly well suited to very large, diversified firms. An example of such a firm is illustrated in Figure 8.7.

The major advantage of the strategic business unit structure is that it reduces corporate headquarters' span of control. Rather than managers at the corporate level having to control many divisions, they need control only relatively few strategic business units. This reduction in span of control also lessens the chance that headquarters will experience information overload as the various organizational units report on their operations. A final advantage is that this structure permits better coordination between divisions with similar missions, products, markets, or technologies.

The strategic business unit structure, however, has a number of disadvantages. First, corporate headquarters becomes more distant from the division and product levels with the addition of another vertical layer of management. Second, rivalry between the strategic business unit managers for greater shares of corporate resources can become dysfunctional and can negatively affect the corporation's overall performance. Third, this structure complicates portfolio analysis. For instance, a strategic business unit may be considered a poor performer overall, but some of its divisions may be stars.

Note that it is important not to confuse the concept *strategic business unit* with that of *strategic business unit structure.* When we are discussing strategy formulation, the term *strategic business unit* may be used in more than one way.[8] A single company that operates within a single industry (e.g., a business that builds swimming pools) is a strategic business unit. But a product division or geographic division of a large multidivisional firm is also a strategic business unit. *Strategic business unit* may even be used to refer to the large firm's multidivisional level that combines several product divisions or geographic divisions. More specifically, a strategic business unit is an organization or a division, product line, or profit center of an organization that produces a set of products/services for well-defined markets or customers in competition with identifiable competitors.

Strategic Business Unit Structure **Figure 8.7**

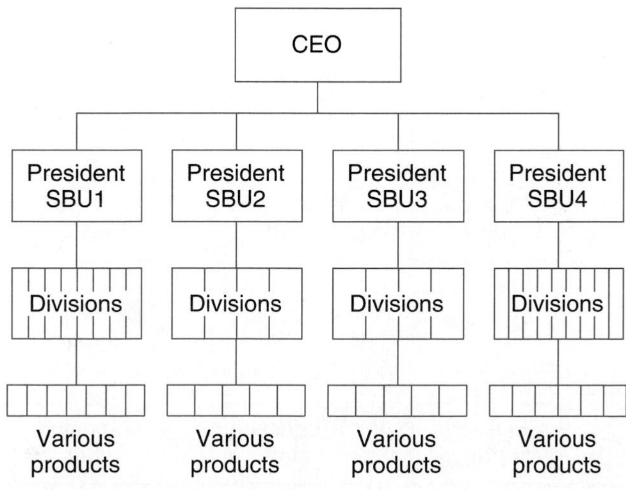

When our reference point is strategy implementation, however, the term *strategic business unit structure* is used to identify the organizational structure type discussed in this section of the chapter. That is, a strategic business unit structure is one in which related product lines are grouped into divisions and those divisions are then grouped into larger entities referred to as strategic business units, as shown in Figure 8.7.[9]

■ Matrix Structure

Up until this point, each of the organizational structures discussed has possessed a single chain of command. That is, each employee in those structures reports to only one manager. The structure discussed in this section, however, is unique in that it possesses a dual chain of command. The **matrix structure** is one in which both functional and project managers exercise authority over organizational activities. Hence, personnel within the matrix have two supervisors—a project manager and the manager of their functional department.

The matrix structure is most commonly used in organizations that operate in industries where the rate of technological change is very fast. For example, firms such as TRW, Lockheed, and Boeing all use a matrix structure. As shown in Figure 8.8, a matrix structure contains literally two organizations—a functional organization (shown horizontally across the top) and a project organization (shown vertically at the left of the chart). In project A, for example, the project manager has brought together some members of the organization's functional departments to work on a specific project. In a construction company, for instance, that project might be the building of a refinery in Thailand. When it is completed, the personnel in project A will return to their functional departments. As another example, in the computer industry, project A might

Figure 8.8 **Matrix Structure**

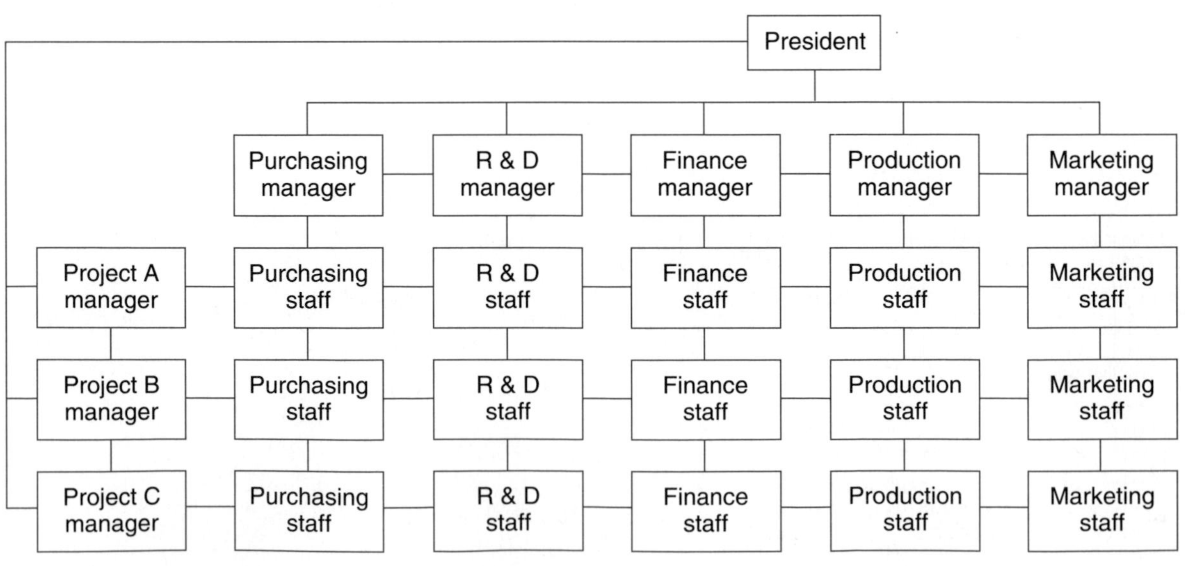

be the development of a new, more powerful personal computer. During the time they are assigned to the project, the employees are accountable not only to the project manager but also to the manager of the functional department from which they came.

Some companies use a matrix even though the rate of technological change in their industry is not particularly fast. For example, Toyota used the matrix structure to develop the Lexus, its entry into the top-of-the-line luxury-car market. A number of engineering, marketing, R&D, and finance personnel were brought together to work on developing an automobile that would compare favorably with the best offered by the German, British, and U.S. automakers.[10]

A variation to the traditional project form of the matrix structure is reflected in Procter & Gamble's (P&G) use of this system. Although many people associate the matrix structure most closely with high-technology enterprises, P&G actually pioneered this form of organization in 1927. At P&G, rather than a project manager being in charge of a temporary project, each of P&G's individual products has a brand manager. The brand manager pulls various specialists, as they are needed, from their functional departments. For instance, if a detergent, such as Tide, is experiencing slowing sales, the brand manager for Tide might call together members of the R&D department to develop a new additive, members of the advertising staff to create ads for "new, improved Tide," members of the packaging department to design a new container for the detergent, and so on. Each brand manager reports to one of twenty-six category managers, an individual who is in charge of all related products in a single category (e.g., detergents such as Tide, Cheer, and Ivory Flakes). It is this manager's responsibility to coordinate the advertising and sales of related products so that competition among the products is minimized.[11] As we can see, then, P&G uses a mixture of a matrix structure and a multidivisional (category) structure.

In whatever form it is used, the matrix structure offers certain advantages. First, by combining both the functional structure and the project (or product) structure, a firm can enjoy the advantages of both forms. Second, the matrix is a cost-efficient structure because project managers pay only for the services of functional personnel when they need them. The remainder of the time, these functional employees are working in their own departments and are not on the payroll of any particular project. By contrast, in a strictly project form of organization, the functional employees are employed full-time within a single project or product division.

Third, a matrix organization has considerable flexibility. Employees may be transferred with ease between projects, a flexibility that is greatly reduced in a more permanent form of structure. Fourth, a matrix permits lower-level functional employees to become intimately involved in a project. They are responsible for making and implementing many of the decisions at the project level. Hence, their motivation may be enhanced, and their job satisfaction is also likely to be relatively high.

Fifth, the matrix structure is an excellent vehicle for training and developing general managers. Each project manager, in a sense, is running his or her "own business." The skills developed at this level are essential skills for higher-level positions in the organization. Finally, top management in a matrix is freed from day-to-day involvement in the operations of the enterprise and is, therefore, able to concentrate on strategic problems and opportunities.

Although the matrix has numerous advantages, it is also accompanied by some significant disadvantages. First is the greater administrative cost associated with its operation. Because coordination across functional areas and across projects is so important, matrix personnel spend considerable time in meetings exchanging information. Although this communication is essential, it consumes valuable time that could otherwise be spent on actual project implementation. Second, matrix structures are characterized by considerable conflict, which takes two forms. One is conflict between project and functional managers over budgets and personnel. The other is conflict among the project managers themselves over similar resource allocation issues.

Finally, working in a matrix can be a source of considerable stress for some functional employees. Reporting to two managers can create significant amounts of role ambiguity and role conflict for an individual. As might be expected, some organizations, such as PepsiCo and Digital Equipment, have found managing a matrix to be so complicated that they have reverted to more traditional structures.

ASSESSMENT OF ORGANIZATIONAL STRUCTURE

The key issue in this chapter is how an organization can implement its strategy by designing its structure appropriately. In this section, we wish to examine how managers can assess the effectiveness of their organization's current structure in that regard. There are, unfortunately, no hard-and-fast rules for evaluating the appropriateness of an organization's structure. However, the extent to which a structure is—and will continue to be—effective in helping the organization implement its strategy can be at least partially assessed by answering the following questions. These questions are highlighted in Table 8.1.

- *Is the structure compatible with the corporate profile and the corporate strategy?* Recall that at the corporate level, a firm may be in one business, several related businesses, or several unrelated businesses. Although the one-business company may effectively adopt the functional structure, that

Table 8.1 **Checklist for Determining the Appropriateness of Organizational Structure**

1. Is the structure compatible with the corporate profile and the corporate strategy?
2. At the corporate level, is the structure compatible with the outputs of the firm's business units?
3. Are there too few or too many hierarchical levels at either the corporate or business unit level of analysis?
4. Does the structure promote coordination among its parts?
5. Does the structure allow for appropriate centralization or decentralization of authority?
6. Does the structure permit the appropriate grouping of activities?

option may be less viable for organizations that are in several related or unrelated businesses. The reason is that the functional structure promotes specialization of functional activities. This form of specialization is beneficial for a business that primarily produces and markets a single-product line such as home furniture or semiconductors, but it may be inappropriate for one in multiple businesses. In such cases, a product divisional or multidivisional structure can more appropriately emphasize the company's products and services rather than its functions. Hence, an organization's structure should be compatible with its corporate profile.

Its structure should also be compatible with its corporate-level strategy. For instance, if the corporation intends to grow continuously, it may find its growth eventually stymied by a product divisional or geographic divisional structure. The reason is that horizontal expansion places an ever-increasing burden on corporate-level management owing to the widening span of control. At some point, it is not humanly possible to keep up with the activities of all of the firm's product or geographic divisions. Hence, continued growth may eventually require adopting the multidivisional or strategic business unit structure.

- *At the corporate level, is the structure compatible with the outputs of the firm's business units?* A product divisional structure, for instance, may be more appropriate than a geographic divisional structure for a corporation with business units that produce fasteners, cutting tools, and hand tools. The reason is that the demand for these products is based on their technical specifications and perceived quality. Each product division can, therefore, concentrate on producing and marketing its own product line. However, a geographic divisional structure may be better suited to a corporation with business units that sell retail clothing and shoes. These items are sold together, and demand for them will differ from one geographic region to another depending on climate, culture, and tradition. Hence, they can be marketed more effectively through specialization based on geographic location.
- *Are there too few or too many hierarchical levels at either the corporate or business unit level of analysis?* It is important that an organization's structure match the nature of the environment in which it operates. Flat organizations, with relatively few hierarchical levels and wide spans of control, are better suited for dynamic, fast-changing environments than tall structures are. Conversely, tall organizations, with relatively numerous hierarchical levels and narrow spans of control, operate more effectively in stable, predictable environments than flat ones do.

  Corporate-level managers must also realize that the firm's business units need not necessarily have the same structures. Some business units may operate in relatively dynamic environments, and others may compete in relatively stable environments, necessitating differences in their structures.

  Overall, in answering this particular question, a manager may find it helpful to compare the configuration of his or her organization with those of its competitors.
- *Does the structure promote coordination among its parts?* Varying degrees of coordination among an organization's parts may be necessary, depending upon the particular situation. For instance, firms with multiple unrelated business units that operate fairly autonomously may find that relatively little coordination among the business units' operations is required. However, within each business unit, management may find it essential to coordinate closely the activities of functional departments. Firms with

multiple related businesses usually require greater coordination of their business units' activities, and companies that operate in only one business generally concentrate on coordinating their functional processes.

As a rule, the more complex an organization, the more difficult coordination is to achieve. This problem is especially evident in organizations with related businesses. Very complex businesses may have to establish special, permanent coordinating units that integrate, for example, the activities of R&D, production, and sales.

- *Does the structure allow for appropriate centralization or decentralization of authority?* The extent to which decision making should be systematically delegated downward in an organization depends upon a number of factors. One, obviously, is organizational size. In general, very large organizations tend to be more decentralized than very small ones, simply because it is difficult for the CEO of a very large company to keep up with all of the organization's operations.

  Another factor is the number and type of businesses a firm is in. Firms with large numbers of unrelated businesses tend to be relatively decentralized, allowing the heads of the diverse business units to make most of the decisions affecting those units. In such cases, corporate-level management's primary responsibility is to determine the overall corporation's mission, goals, and strategy and leave the actual operating decisions to those on the scene. By contrast, organizations in only one business can more easily be managed in a centralized fashion.

  The type of environment affects the need for decentralization. Organizations in rapidly changing environments must be relatively decentralized so that decisions can be made quickly by those who are closest to the situation. At the other end of the spectrum, organizations in relatively stable environments can be managed effectively through centralized decision making, since change is relatively slow and fairly predictable. In such cases, the majority of decisions follow a routine pattern, and procedures can be established in advance for many decision-making situations.

  Finally, the degree of decentralization must be compatible with the organization's structure. Decentralization is far easier to attain in product divisional, geographic divisional, multidivisional, strategic business unit, and matrix structures, because each division, strategic business unit, or project can be operated as a relatively autonomous profit center. Functional structures, however, do not easily lend themselves to decentralization. It is difficult for an organization to be effective when personnel, finance, production, marketing, and R&D operate independently of one another.
- *Does the structure permit the appropriate grouping of activities?* The extent to which organizational activities are appropriately grouped affects how well strategy is implemented. For instance, related product lines should be grouped together. Customers are confused when they are called on by one sales representative for personal computers but have to contact another sales representative from the same company to purchase a printer for the computer. Likewise, some department stores insist on selling men's suits in one department, but ties and dress shirts are in another department down the aisle. As another type of example, it is difficult to hold a product divisional manager fully responsible for sales of a product when he or she had no control over either the development or the production of the product. A true profit center concept requires that one individual be in charge of all of the functions affecting a product's sale.

TRENDS IN RESTRUCTURING ORGANIZATIONS

As a result of increasingly intense competition over the past decade, extensive corporate restructurings have become quite common. Although the specifics differ from one firm to another, most restructurings involve two primary and closely related processes.

The first is reducing operating costs by removing one or more hierarchical levels from the organization's structure. Most frequently, the levels eliminated are those staffed by vice presidents or other middle managers, although headquarters staff positions are also common targets. The primary objective of these moves is not only to cut costs (and thereby improve the corporation's ability to compete) but also to abolish some of the bureaucratic maze and red tape that invariably accompany multiple organizational layers.

This first change must necessarily be accompanied by the second: a pushing of decision making downward in the organization. As we have seen, organizational flexibility is required to operate successfully in a dynamic environment. By removing one or more hierarchical levels, an organization reduces the number of individuals in the chain of command who must approve decisions. Hence, decision-making speed increases. More importantly, since fewer levels result in a broader span of control for upper-level executives, more decisions must be made by lower-level personnel. Otherwise, continuing to refer most decisions upward would quickly overload top management.

To ensure that the desired decentralization occurs, many large firms are restructuring in such a way that each product or service area becomes a separate division. Hence, corporations are increasingly adopting the product divisional structure, multidivisional structure, or strategic business unit structure. Each of these structures can be combined with elements of the matrix structure for added flexibility.

Each product or service division is operated as a semiautonomous business, with its managers responsible for results. The idea is to give the division's employees the feeling of running their own business and to allow them—the people on the scene—to make their own operating decisions without having to seek approval from multiple layers of higher management.

Some companies, such as 3M and Johnson & Johnson, even form a division for each promising new product idea they devise. Appropriate personnel are assigned full time to the new division so that the budding idea gets undivided attention, without the usual distractions that accompany day-to-day operations. Although this system is similar to a small entrepreneurial venture, it possesses the additional advantage of being supported by the corporate parent's considerable financial resources.

A LOOK AT THE FUTURE

Some knowledgeable observers believe that the wave of the future will be a structure variously termed the "modular corporation," the "virtual corporation," or the "network pattern."[12] In this configuration, an organization "outsources," or contracts with other companies for all of its functions except for its core competencies. For instance, a company might concentrate on designing and marketing a product while letting other companies manufacture the prod-

STRATEGIC INSIGHT

A Structural Revolution at IBM

One of the world's largest and most successful firms of the past fifty years found itself floundering as it entered the 1990s. In 1991, IBM's sales dropped 6.1 percent, to $64.8 billion, its first decline in revenue since 1946. And, for the first time in its history, IBM incurred a loss—$2.8 billion. And that loss grew to $5 billion in 1992.

Its problem? IBM was operating as it always had, but its environment had changed dramatically. The computer industry today is one of continually accelerating change. For instance, the life cycle of a notebook computer may be as short as three months. Many of IBM's competitors, moreover, are aggressive, flexible, and extremely quick, garnering the rewards that accrue to those who are first to the market with new technology.

At the center of this dynamic environment stood huge, bureaucratic, centralized IBM—a company still dominated by its mainframe computer division. As it always had, IBM required that all major decisions be made at corporate headquarters at Armonk, N.Y. Those decisions were guided by policies that virtually forbade any internal competition with the mainframe division, subjected new product plans to endless discussion, and kept IBM divisions from competing unfettered with their more nimble competitors. As a result, IBM introduced its personal computer four years after Apple did, entered the PC-compatible laptop market five years behind Toshiba, and followed Digital Equipment into the minicomputer market only after an eleven-year lag.

To turn the corporation around, top management unveiled an extensive structural reorganization. Some of the major changes being implemented are:

- The creation of fourteen semiautonomous business units, with each able to make its own product development, manufacturing, and pricing decisions. Ten of those units are businesses that develop and manufacture products—such as mainframes, personal computers, minicomputers, software, printers, and chips—while the remaining four are geographical marketing divisions—North America, Latin America, Asia/Pacific, and Europe/Middle East/Africa.
- Profit and loss responsibility for each business unit. Every business unit manager must sign an annual contract with corporate management agreeing to objectives in such areas as growth, profit, return on assets, quality, and customer satisfaction. Each business unit decides for itself how it will meet those objectives.
- A drastic reduction in work force. Overall, employment at IBM fell by about 150,000 employees between 1986 and 1993. Miraculously, most of this reduction was accomplished through voluntary buyout and early retirement programs. By design, the percentage of managerial and staff employees dropped significantly, while the percentage of employed individuals who manufacture, sell, or service products grew from 43 to 57 percent.

Several obstacles to effective implementation of the restructuring remain. One is the need to change IBM's culture, which, historically, has not encouraged autonomy. Another is the issue of how to sell a diverse product line. Initially, IBM's management decided to maintain its traditional corporatewide sales force rather than allow each business unit to sell its own products. The business units, however, feared that the sales force would continue to emphasize mainframe sales. The personal computer unit quickly circumvented this obstacle by marketing its product line through independent retailers—such as Sears and computer stores—and its own 800 telephone number. Eventually, it was even given its own sales force.

SOURCES: L. Hooper, "IBM Will Raise Number of Jobs It Plans to Trim," *The Wall Street Journal,* 11 February 1993; J. Schwartz, "Available: One Impossible Job," *Newsweek,* 8 February 1993, pp. 44–51; J. Burgess, "IBM to Cut More Jobs, Trim Size of Plants," *The Washington Post,* 30 September 1992; C. Arnst, "Big Blue's New Baby," *Business Week,* 14 September 1992, p. 32; C. Arnst and M. Lewyn, "Stand Back, Big Blue—and Wish Me Luck," *Business Week,* 17 August 1992, pp. 99–102; D. Kirkpatrick, "Breaking Up IBM," *Fortune,* 27 July 1992, pp. 44–58; "The Fortune 500: Largest U.S. Industrial Corporations," *Fortune,* 20 April 1992, p. 220.

uct, deliver it, and bill customers for their purchases. Such a system allows a company to concentrate on those functions in which it possesses a particular competence, without having to divert its resources to other activities. The amount of capital investment is obviously much lower than it would be if the company itself handled all of the functions, and this lowered-investment level means that the company has considerable flexibility to change with its environment.

For instance, neither Reebok nor Dell Computer owns a manufacturing plant. Both outsource all manufacturing functions to contractors. This system, of course, is not new. Construction companies and publishing houses have been structured in this fashion for decades. But it is clear that organizations in other industries are increasingly interested in shedding fixed assets and gaining flexibility by adopting elements of a modular structure.

SUMMARY

Implementing strategy requires management to consider how the organization should be structured. In new, small companies, structure is fluid, with each employee often knowing how to perform more than one task and the owner-manager being involved in all aspects of the business. Success leads to growth, however—both vertical and horizontal. With growth comes a more permanent division of labor.

Vertical growth refers to an increase in the length of the organization's hierarchical chain of command. Organizations in stable, predictable environments often become relatively tall, with many hierarchical levels and narrow spans of control. Conversely, companies in dynamic, rapidly changing environments usually adopt flat structures with few hierarchical levels and wide spans of control.

Horizontal growth refers to the segmentation of the organization into departments or divisions. The first formal structure usually adopted by a growing business is the functional structure, an organizational type that forms departments along functional lines—manufacturing, marketing, finance, research and development, personnel, and so on. Its strengths are that it emphasizes the functions that the organization must carry out, which results in a number of advantages; it facilitates the processes of planning, organizing, motivating, and controlling; and it is an efficient structure for the training and development of personnel. Its weaknesses, however, are that it makes pinpointing the responsibility for profits or losses difficult, it creates a narrow perspective of the organization among its members, and it inhibits communication across functional areas and coordination of their disparate activities. Whenever an organization begins to expand its product lines significantly or grow geographically, the functional structure begins to lose its strategic usefulness.

The product divisional structure is well suited for a business with several product lines because the firm is structured around its product categories. This structure's strengths are that it emphasizes the firm's product lines, it makes coordination of functions easier because each product division has its own functions, it allows responsibility for profits or losses to be pinpointed since each product division is a responsibility center, and it encourages development of general managers. Its weaknesses are that it may be more expensive to operate than a functional structure because more functional personnel are required, it inhibits coordination of functions at the corporate level, and it creates dysfunctional competition among division managers for corporate resources.

The geographic divisional structure is used by firms that operate in various geographic areas. Structuring around location provides such advantages as tailoring products/services to climatic needs of specific areas, responding to the technical needs of different international locations, gaining a competitive advantage by producing or distributing products in different locations, serving the consumer needs of various nations better, adapting to varying legal systems, and pinpointing the responsibility for profits or losses. The disadvantages of this structure are the same as those for the product divisional structure.

As a firm adds more product lines, it may eventually adopt the multidivisional structure, in which similar product lines are organized into divisions. This structure facilitates continued growth, frees corporate management for strategic planning, decentralizes authority to individual divisions and product lines so that decision making is quicker, and enables management to pinpoint responsibility for profits and losses. Its unique weaknesses are that distribution of corporate overhead costs is subjective and difficult to make, dysfunctional divisional rivalries often occur, and transfer pricing from one division to another can become a source of contention.

Further growth may lead an organization to adopt the strategic business unit structure. In this case, divisions with similar missions, products, markets, or technologies are combined under a strategic business unit. This restructuring further reduces corporate headquarters' span of control and permits better coordination. However, it also distances corporate headquarters from the product level, can create dysfunctional rivalries between strategic business units, and complicates portfolio analysis.

A final organizational form is the matrix structure, which is a combination of the functional structure and the product/project structure. The matrix enjoys the advantages of both structural types, it is cost-efficient for each individual project or product, it is flexible, it permits lower-level employees to become highly involved in projects, it helps train and develop general managers, and it frees top-level management for planning. But the matrix also is associated with greater administrative costs, greater conflict, and higher stress.

To determine whether an organization's structure is appropriate for implementing the organization's strategy, a manager must analyze how compatible the structure is with such features as the organization's corporate profile, corporate strategy, business unit strategy, need for coordination, number of hierarchical levels, degree of decentralization, and grouping of activities.

In recent years, organizations have restructured with increasing frequency. Most restructurings involve two closely related processes: reducing operating costs by removing one or more hierarchical levels from the organization's structure, and pushing decision making downward in the organization.

KEY CONCEPTS

Flat organization An organization characterized by relatively few hierarchical levels and a wide span of control.

Functional structure A form of organizational structure in which jobs and activities are grouped on the basis of function—for example, sales, manufacturing, and finance.

Geographic divisional structure A form of organizational structure in which jobs and activities are grouped on the basis of geographic location—for example, northeast region, midwest region, and far west region.

Hierarchical chain of command The authority and accountability chain that links managers and employees in an organization.

Horizontal growth An increase in the breadth of an organization's structure.

Matrix structure A form of organizational structure that combines a functional structure with some form of divisional structure (usually product or project divisions). It contains a dual chain of command in which the functional manager and the project/product manager exercise authority over the same employees.

Multidivisional structure A form of organizational structure that contains several divisions, with each division comprised of one or more product lines.

Organizational structure The formal ways that tasks and responsibilities are allocated to individuals and the ways that individuals are formally grouped together into offices, departments, and divisions.

Product divisional structure A form of organizational structure whereby jobs and activities are grouped on the basis of types of products or services—for example, automobiles, computer services, and electronics.

Profit center An organizational unit charged with a well-defined mission and headed by a manager who is accountable for the unit's revenues and expenditures.

Span of control The number of employees reporting directly to a given manager.

Strategic business unit structure A form of organizational structure in which related product lines are grouped into divisions and those divisions are then grouped into larger entities referred to as strategic business units.

Tall organization An organization characterized by relatively many hierarchical levels and a narrow span of control.

Vertical growth An increase in the length of the organization's hierarchical chain of command.

DISCUSSION QUESTIONS

1. Why does organizational growth require greater formalization of roles within the organization?

2. Why does organizational growth require both vertical and horizontal expansion?

3. Explain why a relatively tall organizational structure is not appropriate for a dynamic, rapidly changing environment.

4. Why is a functional structure often appropriate for small businesses?

5. As an organization that is structured functionally begins to add new products to its original product offerings, it often changes its structure to a product divisional form. Explain why.

6. What is the rationale underlying the geographic divisional structure?

7. Explain the difference between a multidivisional structure and a strategic business unit structure.

8. A matrix structure is a combination of which two forms of organizational structure? Explain.

9. Of all of the forms of organizational structure discussed—functional, product divisional, geographic divisional, multidivisional, strategic business unit, and matrix—which is the most flexible? Explain why.

10. Most restructurings involve a flattening of the organization's structure and a move toward decentralized decision making. What is top management attempting to accomplish with these two changes?

STRATEGIC MANAGEMENT EXERCISES

1. Assume that you have started a pizza restaurant in your town. Furthermore, assume that your restaurant has become very successful and that you eventually expand on a national basis. Draw an organization chart that portrays your business at the very beginning. Then, draw two more organization charts that show the vertical growth and the horizontal growth of your company as it grows to become a nationwide business.
2. Assume that you own a business that produces casual furniture. Draw a functional organization chart for your business. Now, assume that your business expands into furniture retailing. Draw a product divisional structure that encompasses your manufacturing and retailing operations.
3. Choose a company and examine its latest annual report. Sometimes, an explicit organization chart is contained in the report. Other times, a summary chart is provided. In still other cases, there may be no structure depicted, but there is sufficient information for you to draw a rough sketch of the structure. Once you have determined the organization's structure, identify what type it is (functional, product divisional, geographic divisional, multidivisional, strategic business unit, matrix or a combination of two or more of these). Explain your reasoning.
4. Select a business that has existed for at least ten years. Detail how its organizational structure has evolved over time. Explain why it

changed from one structure to another at certain junctures. Or if it has maintained the same structure during its life, explain why. Can you offer suggestions for improving its present structure?

5. From library research, identify an organization that is using a corporate growth strategy (discussed in Chapter 4). Analyze how this organization's strategy has influenced its structure. Is its current structure the optimal structure for this enterprise? If not, what structure might be more appropriate?

6. From library research, identify an organization that is using a corporate retrenchment strategy (Chapter 4). Analyze how this organization's strategy has influenced its structure. Is its current structure the optimal structure for this enterprise? If not, what structure might be more appropriate?

NOTES

1. J. Child, *Organization: A Guide for Managers and Administrators* (New York: Harper & Row, 1977), p. 10.
2. Ibid., pp. 50–70.
3. P.R. Lawrence and J.W. Lorsch, *Organization and Environment: Managing Differentiation and Integration* (Homewood, Ill.: Irwin, 1969); R. Duncan, "What Is the Right Organizational Structure?" *Organizational Dynamics* 7 (Winter 1979): 59–80.
4. M. Schroeder, "The Recasting of Alcoa," *Business Week,* 9 September 1991, pp. 62–64.
5. J.A. Byrne, "Is Your Company Too Big?" *Business Week,* 27 March 1989, p. 90.
6. Z. Sawaya, "Focus Through decentralization," *Forbes,* 11 November 1991, pp. 242–244 (quotation from p. 244).
7. Z. Schiller and L. Therrien, "Nestlé's Crunch in the U.S.," *Business Week,* 24 December 1990, pp. 24–25.
8. See C.W. Hoffer, "Toward a Contingency Theory of Business Strategy," *Academy of Management Journal* 18 (1975): 784–810.
9. R.P. Rumelt, *Strategy, Structure, and Economic Performance* (Boston: Harvard University Press, 1974).
10. A. Taylor, "Here Comes Japan's New Luxury Cars," *Fortune,* 14 August 1989, pp. 62–66.
11. B. Dumaine, "P&G Rewrites the Marketing Rules," *Fortune,* 6 November 1989, pp. 34–48; A. Swasy, "In a Fast-Paced World, Procter & Gamble Sets Its Store in Old Values," *The Wall Street Journal,* 21 September 1989; Z. Schiller, "No More Mr. Nice Guy at P&G—Not by a Long Shot," *Business Week,* 3 February 1992, pp. 54–56.
12. S. Tully, "The Modular Corporation," *Fortune,* 8 February 1993, pp. 106–116; J.A. Byrne, R. Brandt, and O. Port, "The Virtual Corporation," *Business Week,* 8 February 1993, pp. 98–103; J. Wilson and J. Dobrzynski, "And Now The Post-Industrial Corporation," *Business Week,* 3 March 1986, pp. 64–71; and M. Piore and C. Sabel, *The Second Industrial Divide* (New York: McGraw-Hill, 1984).

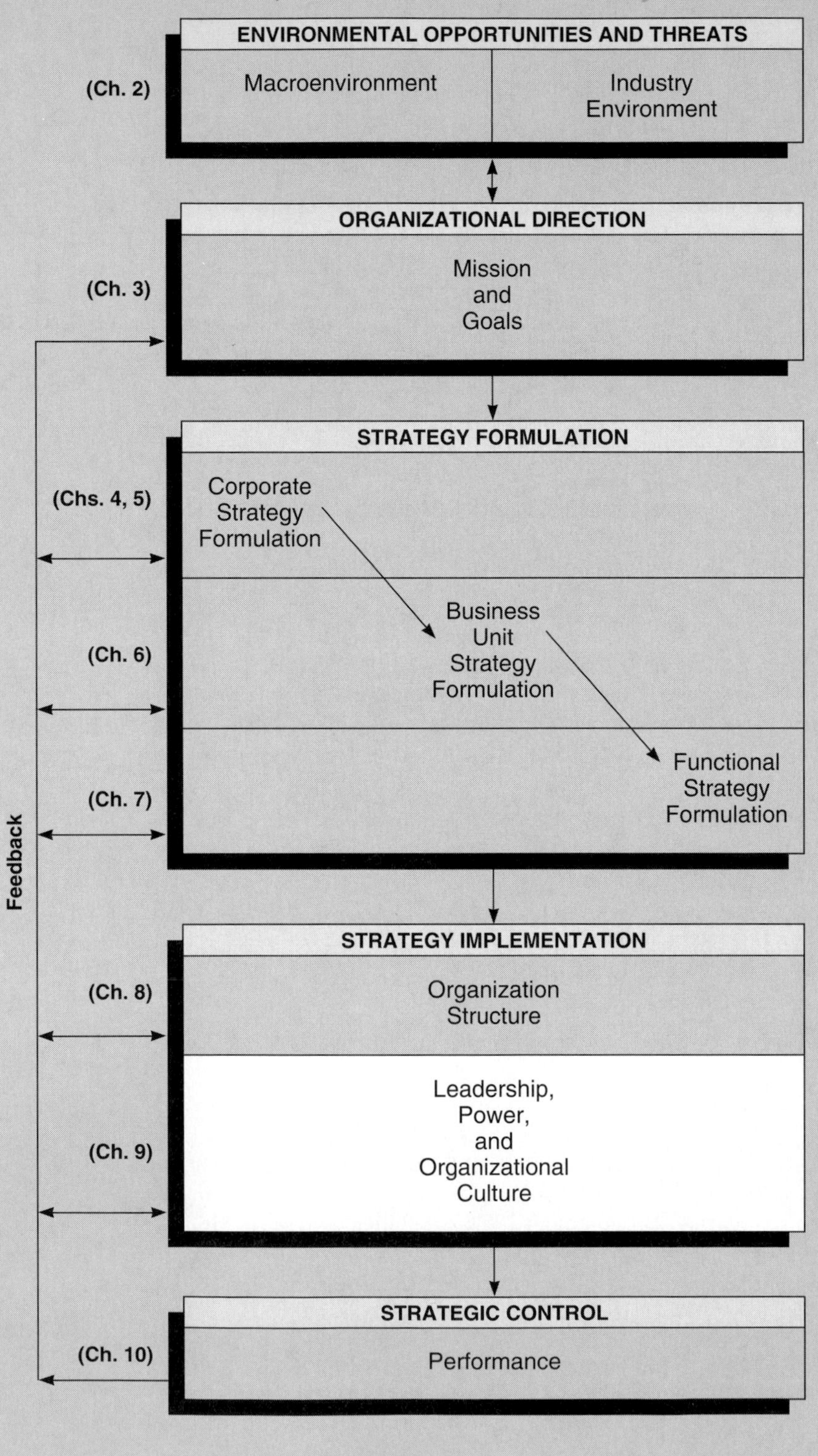

STRATEGIC MANAGEMENT MODEL
ENVIRONMENTAL OPPORTUNITIES AND THREATS
(Ch. 2)
Macroenvironment
Industry Environment
ORGANIZATIONAL DIRECTION
(Ch. 3)
Mission and Goals
STRATEGY FORMULATION
(Chs. 4, 5)
Corporate Strategy Formulation
(Ch. 6)
Business Unit Strategy Formulation
(Ch. 7)
Functional Strategy Formulation
Feedback
STRATEGY IMPLEMENTATION
(Ch. 8)
Organization Structure
(Ch. 9)
Leadership, Power, and Organizational Culture
STRATEGIC CONTROL
(Ch. 10)
Performance

Strategy Implementation: Leadership, Power, and Organizational Culture

Any strategy, no matter how well conceived, is doomed to failure unless it is effectively implemented. The preceding chapter examined how an organization should be structured to carry out its strategy. This chapter analyzes implementation from another perspective. Our interest here is in how an organization's chief executive officer (CEO) as well as other top managers can use their office and influence to ensure that the organization's members are implementing strategies effectively.

The top management team has at least two means at its disposal to encourage managers and other employees to put their full efforts into strategy implementation. The first resource is leadership. The CEO is recognized as the organization's principal leader, one who sets the tone for the members of the firm. By influencing the behavior of others through formal and informal means, the CEO and other top managers attempt to ensure that organizational members channel their efforts into appropriate directions. The second resource is organizational culture. All organizations have a culture; the key for the CEO and other top managers is to understand and manage the culture in such a way that it facilitates—rather than hinders—the firm's strategic actions.

LEADERSHIP

Although some people equate *leadership* with *management*, the two concepts are not synonymous. For example, over time, a manager plays many roles. Several of them are not directly related to leadership. For instance, as a *resource allocator*, the manager determines the distribution of organizational resources such as money, time, and equipment. As a *monitor*, he or she receives information and analyses related to internal operations and external events. And as a *disseminator*, the manager transmits information received from the external environment to members of the organization. All of these roles are part of the manager's job. Another role is that of *leader*.[1] A manager exhibits **leadership** when he or she secures the cooperation of others in accomplishing an objective.

Hence, it is evident that the term *manager* is considerably broader than the term *leader.*

Although this chapter emphasizes the role of the CEO as the organization's leader, it is important not to overlook the fact that leadership is required at all organizational levels and in all functional areas. Strategies cannot be implemented through the CEO's efforts alone.

The need for organizational leadership has never been more important. As John P. Kotter, a management researcher, points out, in the relatively stable and prosperous 1950s and 1960s, the saying "If it ain't broke, don't fix it" prevailed. Under this axiom, it was clear that too much leadership "could actually create problems by disrupting efficient routines."[2] But as has been emphasized throughout this book, today's world is too dynamic and turbulent for an organization to compete effectively by simply continuing—no matter how efficiently—to do what it did in past years.

Our concern in this chapter is with strategic leadership, which differs from leadership at the middle-management and supervisory levels in a number of ways. **Strategic leadership** is concerned with both the external environment and with the firm's internal operations (rather than primarily with the latter); the process is characterized by greater ambiguity, complexity, and information overload; it involves the complicated task of integrating multiple functional areas rather than managing only one or a few functions; and it requires managing through others rather than directly supervising operations.[3] The job of strategic leadership is to establish the firm's direction—by developing and communicating a vision of the future—and to motivate and inspire organization members to move in that direction.[4] Not surprisingly, a recent review of leadership research concludes that top-level managers have a substantial impact on organizational performance.[5]

Just as strategic leadership is more important now than in past decades, it most surely will become even more essential in the coming years. Frequent environmental change and the growing complexity of organizations are trends that are likely to accelerate. Figure 9.1 portrays how external environmental changes and internal organizational complexity increase the importance of competent leadership.

It is important to remember throughout this chapter that good leadership is a necessary, but not sufficient, condition for organizational effectiveness. Although research demonstrates that leadership is an important determinant of organizational performance, it is clear that organizational effectiveness also depends on factors beyond the leader's control.[6] As we saw in Chapter 2, such factors as economic conditions, industry structure, international developments, governmental policies, and technological innovations influence organizational results.

This section examines the concept of leadership. First, the formal role, or office, of the strategic leader is explored. Then the focus turns to the leader's style of leadership—the way the leader behaves in exercising authority and making decisions. Finally, how the leader works with other managers as a member of the top management team is analyzed.

■ The Office of the Leader

Anyone who occupies the office of chief executive officer has the right to influence the behavior of the organization's members. In the case of a corpora-

The Changing Business Scene and Its Consequences for the Leadership Factor **Figure 9.1**

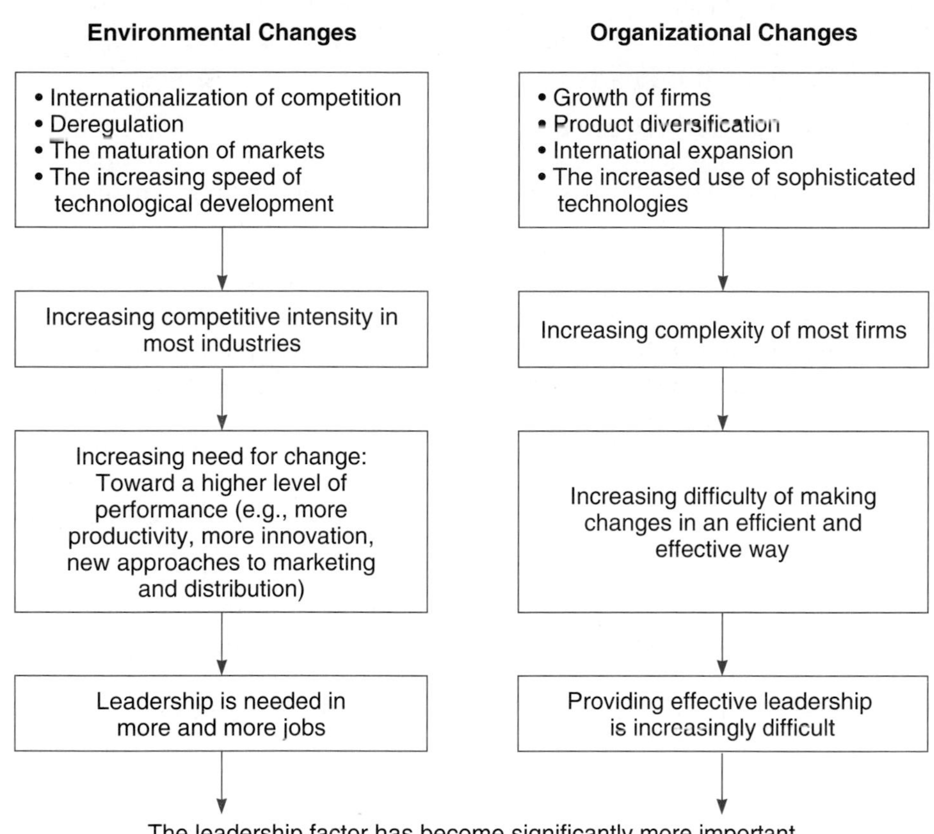

Source: Reprinted with permission of The Free Press, A Division of Macmillan, Inc., from *The Leadership Factor* by John P. Kotter. Copyright © 1988 by John P. Kotter, Inc.

tion, the CEO has been granted **formal authority** by the board of directors to influence specific aspects of employees' behavior. In a small entrepreneurial company, the CEO's authority may stem from ownership of the firm.

Why do employees follow the direction of the CEO? Their motivation may be "an internalized value, such as obedience to authority figures, loyalty to the organization, respect for law, reverence for tradition, or merely the recognition that submission to authority is a necessary condition for membership in the organization."[7]

In any case, the chief mechanism for wielding formal authority is through the CEO's control over resources and rewards. These elements can cover a broad spectrum, including pay and bonuses, career progress, budgets, delegation of authority and responsibility, formal recognition of accomplishments, and status symbols.[8] The effective leader ensures that the organization's reward systems are consistent with its strategic direction. For instance, a company that wants to emphasize product innovation must allocate sufficient budget resources to R&D personnel, reward risk-taking behaviors, and not reward actions that are designed to maintain the status quo. For example, at 3M, pay raises and promotions are tied to innovative results. Managers and employees are simply not rewarded for standing still.

■ The Style of the Leader

Every leader has a distinctive **leadership style**—the characteristic pattern of behavior that a leader exhibits in the process of exercising authority and making decisions. Some leaders are flamboyant; others are quiet and contemplative. Some seek broad-based participation when making decisions; others arrive at decisions primarily on their own with little input from others. Whatever the style, an organization's leader sets the tone for the firm's members. His or her style is a matter of considerable interest to employees at virtually all levels, and it is an important variable in determining how committed the employees are to the firm's mission and objectives and how much effort they will put into implementing the company's strategies.

The most appropriate leadership style is a matter of some controversy and, in any case, is partially constrained by the personality of the leader. Because the bulk of research in this area focuses upon the styles of leaders of relatively small groups, the usefulness of that research for our purposes is limited. Here, our concern is with leaders of entire organizations or business units. As we have already emphasized, upper-level leadership is qualitatively different from leadership at lower levels.[9] From this perspective, the most pertinent body of knowledge available is the recent work on transformational and transactional leadership styles.[10] These styles and how they are used in practice are discussed in the paragraphs that follow.

Transformational and Transactional Leadership Styles

With **transactional leadership,** managers use the authority of their office, much as we just described, to exchange rewards such as pay and status for employees' work efforts. By contrast, with **transformational leadership,** managers inspire involvement in a mission, giving followers a "dream" or "vision" of a higher order than the followers' present reality. In effect, the transformational leader motivates followers to do more than they originally expected to do by stretching their abilities and increasing their self-confidence. Organizational members are "transformed" by becoming more aware of the importance of their tasks and by being helped to transcend their own self-interest for the sake of the organization's mission.[11]

Steven Jobs, the founder of Apple Computer, serves as an example of a transformational leader. In the company's early days, he was able to inspire his employees with his vision of making computing power accessible to a wide range of customers. Without his employees' willingness, and even enthusiasm, to put in long hours of work and to generate innovative ideas, Apple would never have been able to revolutionize the computer industry. By contrast, transactional leaders are less interested in inspiring followers than in ensuring that their organizations operate effectively and efficiently. The typical transac-

STRATEGIC INSIGHT

Leadership Style at Southwest Airlines

Herb Kelleher has built Southwest Airlines into one of the most profitable and fast-growing airlines in the country through fastidious implementation of a niche–low-cost strategy. In doing so, he has managed to win the trust and respect of his employees.

Now the nation's seventh-largest airline, Southwest has grown from a local carrier in Texas that specialized in no-frills flights between Dallas and Houston to one that offers service to both the Midwest and the West Coast. As it continues to grow, Southwest's strategy will evolve from niche–low-cost to low-cost. It has expanded profitably even though it offers no on-board meals, no assigned seating, no interairline baggage transfers, and no listings on computer reservation systems. In some areas, standby tickets can be purchased through automated teller machines in convenience stores.

The market for this bare-bones service is short-haul passengers who value price and frequent departures. To serve these passengers efficiently, Southwest's planes are able to arrive at an airport gate, unload baggage and passengers, load new baggage and passengers, and leave within ten minutes. How? By having employees who are considerably more productive than those in the rest of the airline industry. High productivity, combined with the airline's lack of frills, gives Southwest a 43 percent cost advantage over huge American Airlines.

Why are employees this dedicated? One pilot says that "it's not a Mary Kay-type atmosphere where we're all starry-eyed. It's mutual respect." This respect starts at the top with CEO Kelleher. He has established excellent rapport with his employees and seems to be able to work out amenable agreements with which both sides are happy, unlike the bitter negotiations that have characterized labor contracts at several other airlines. Through profit-sharing plans, cross-utilization of workers, and Kelleher's concern for employees, the company has managed to forge an atmosphere of trust and loyalty.

Kelleher, for instance, is highly visible. He often takes Southwest flights and frequently visits the service areas where the planes are maintained. The visits are invariably upbeat and optimistic, with Kelleher dressing in a casual fashion (often in a Southwest Airlines shirt) and kidding with the crew. He knows individuals' names and sends birthday and Valentine's Day cards to each employee.

Most of all, though, he seems to care. As he puts it: "If you don't treat your own people well, they won't treat other people well." His actions support his words. He and all the other top managers of Southwest Airlines work at least once every three months as baggage handlers, ticket agents, and flight attendants. The point is to create an understanding of what each employee encounters on his or her job. As Kelleher explains, "When you're actually dealing with customers, and you've done the job yourself, you're in a better position to appraise the effect of some new program or policy."

His words are reinforced by the head of Southwest's mechanics and cleaners union: "How many CEOs do you know who come into the cleaners break room at 3 A.M. on a Sunday passing out doughnuts or putting on a pair of overalls to clean a plane?"

SOURCES: B. O'Brian, "Southwest Airlines Is A Rare Air Carrier: It Still Makes Money," *The Wall Street Journal,* 26 October 1992 (source of fourth quotation); R.S. Teitelbaum, "Southwest Airlines: Where Service Flies Right," *Fortune,* 24 August 1992, p. 116 (source of second quotation); W. Zellner, A. Rothman, and E. Schine, "The Airline Mess," *Business Week,* 6 July 1992, p. 53; A. Farnham, "The Trust Gap," *Fortune,* 4 December 1989, pp. 56–78 (source of third quotation, p. 78); S. Loeffelholz, "The Love Line," *Financial World,* 21 March 1989, pp. 26–28; "Patchy Applause for Cash Machines," *Fortune,* 5 December 1988, p. 16; F. Gibney, Jr., "Southwest's Friendly Skies," *Newsweek,* 30 May 1988, p. 49 (source of first quotation).

tional leader is often concerned with increasing sales, market share, and profits incrementally rather than with "transforming" the organization.

Management researcher Bernard M. Bass proposes that most leaders exhibit both transactional and transformational styles, although they do so in different amounts.[12] Ultimately, the distinction between the two leadership styles is that leaders who are largely transactional continue to move their organizations in line with historical tradition, resulting in incremental improvements. Transformational leaders, however, lead their organizations toward a future that may result in significantly different processes and levels of performance.[13] This proposed difference is illustrated in Figure 9.2.

Note that transactional leadership is hypothesized to enhance an organization's performance steadily, but not dramatically. The proponents of transformational leadership, on the other hand, suggest that it can make significant changes in organizational performance. Also note that we propose that an organization's performance declines somewhat shortly after the transformational leadership process begins. Dramatic changes in the way an organization operates often result in short-term declines in performance, because organizational members may initially resist changing from the status quo and may experience difficulty in rising to the new expectations.

Both transactional and transformational leaders can exhibit all of the leadership styles identified in the well-known leadership theories. These include such commonly studied styles as task-oriented leadership (emphasizing task effectiveness) or relationship-oriented leadership (emphasizing the building of relationships with employees), as well as those styles that emphasize directing employees, encouraging employee participation in decision making, or setting goals. But even as these two types of leaders engage in the same style, their intent may be quite different. For instance, the transactional leader may delegate responsibility to an employee as a reward for fulfilling an agreement, but a transformational leader may delegate for the purpose of developing employee skills.[14]

Figure 9.2 **Hypothesized Results of Transactional and Transformational Leadership Styles**

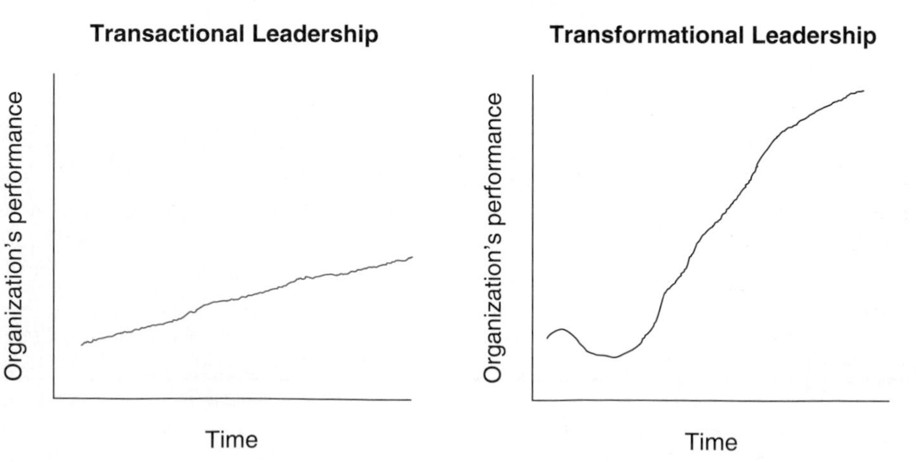

STRATEGIC INSIGHT

Henry Ford: Transactional and Transformational Leadership

Henry Ford (1863–1947) illustrates a leader who combined both transactional and transformational leadership styles:

> In 1914, he made a deal that workers found hard to resist. He offered them the unusually high wage for that time of $5 a day in exchange for their accepting rigid control of their behavior both inside and outside the plant. No idle time was to be tolerated. Internal spies were employed to enforce disciplinary rules. Yet, it was this same Henry Ford who revolutionized the automobile industry, making possible the mass production of the cheap, affordable automobile for the mass market.

How did Henry Ford transform the automobile industry? The transformation began with an argument between Ford and his partner Alexander Y. Malcolmson in 1905. Ford wanted to produce a simple, inexpensive car, but Malcolmson favored a more expensive and exclusive line. Malcolmson lost the argument and subsequently sold his interest in the company, leaving Ford to concentrate on the Model T—a sturdy, black automobile with a four-cylinder, 20-horsepower engine. Introduced in 1908, the car sold for $825.

The Model T clearly met the needs and the financial resources of American consumers. Over ten thousand cars were sold the first year. Within five years, annual unit sales reached about a half-million. When production of the car ceased in 1927, 15 million Model Ts had been sold by Ford Motor Company.

By concentrating on one type of affordable automobile, Henry Ford created a mass market for the Model T. In turn, the huge demand for the car gave rise to the use of assembly line production with standardized parts. The volume enabled Ford to reduce the price of the car without decreasing profits. By 1913, the car's selling price had dropped to $500. It fell to $390 two years later and sold for $260 in 1925. Meanwhile, the time required to produce the car declined from 12½ worker-hours in 1912 to 1½ worker-hours in 1914.

This single car literally transformed not only the automobile industry but also the lifestyle and work habits of an entire nation. The impact of Henry Ford's transformational leadership continues to this day.

SOURCES: Arthur M. Johnson, "Henry Ford," in *The Encyclopedia Americana, International Edition,* Vol. 11 (Danbury, Conn.: Grolier, 1990), pp. 566–567; Robert Sobel, "Henry Ford," in *The World Book Encyclopedia,* Vol. 7 (Chicago: World Book, 1990), p. 380; B.M. Bass, *Leadership and Performance Beyond Expectations* (New York: Free Press, 1985), p. 27 (source of quotation).

Leadership Style in Practice

When is a transactional style needed, and when might a transformational style be required? As we have already seen, most leaders will exhibit both behaviors, although one may predominate. In general, we can propose that organizations that are meeting or exceeding their objectives and that do not foresee significant changes in their environment can be well led through a transactional style. Increasingly, however, because of the intensity of domestic and foreign competition and dramatic environmental changes, many organizations require transformational leadership. Even casual perusal of such publications as *The Wall Street Journal, Business Week,* and *Fortune* will illustrate the strategic difficulties that many firms are facing.

Consider, for instance, the different strategic directions taken by IBM and Canon when they entered the copier business in the 1970s. Pursuing a transactional style, IBM's top management concentrated on developing products that were similar to those of the market leader—Xerox—and they imitated Xerox's service, pricing, and distribution. IBM's efforts were such a failure that it withdrew from the copier market. By contrast, Canon's top management used a transformational approach. Rather than duplicating Xerox's strategy, Canon concentrated on smaller copiers and taught its sales force to make presentations directly to department managers and secretaries who desired decentralized copying facilities, rather than a centralized copy center. This approach contrasted dramatically with the traditional route of selling to the head of the duplicating department. Today, Canon is a major player in the copier industry.

Because transformational leadership is of considerable importance and is likely to take on even more significance, we will examine that process in detail at this point. Researchers Tichy and Devanna, who studied twelve CEOs, propose a three-stage process of transformational leadership.[15] Each stage is described below.

Recognize the Need for Change. First, the transformational leader must recognize the need for change and be able to persuade key managers in the organization of that need. This task may be difficult when changes in the environment are gradual and the organization is still meeting its objectives. As Peter F. Drucker, a management theorist and consultant, emphasizes, the best time to cast off the past is when the organization is successful—not when it is in trouble. When an organization is successful, its resources are allocated "to the things that *did* produce, to the goals that *did* challenge, to the needs that *were* unfulfilled."[16]

To overcome this tendency, Tichy and Devanna suggest that leaders measure the performance of their organizations against that of their competitors and not just against last year's performance. Additionally, measures of organizational performance must include more than the typical economic indicators, such as earnings per share, market share, and return on investment or assets. They should also include such measures as customer satisfaction, product quality as compared with competitors', new-product innovations, and other similar indicators.

Managers of troubled organizations more readily recognize the need for change. Increasingly, such firms are replacing their CEOs with managers from other corporations. For example, in recent years, Hughes Aircraft hired its CEO away from IBM, the CEO of Gulfstream Aerospace came from Xerox, and Campbell Soup's CEO was recruited from Gerber Products. An outsider can sometimes make the hard decisions, such as to initiate mass layoffs, that an insider might be reluctant to make. And outsiders, of course, bring a fresh perspective to the firm and its problems. On the other hand, outsiders may have to spend months just learning the business and industry and trying to develop a network of contacts before they are able to take any decisive actions. Furthermore, hiring an outsider generally sends a message to the firm's vice presidents and other top managers that they were not considered worthy of promotion. For that reason, the act of hiring an outsider is often followed by an exodus of some of the company's top managerial talent.[17]

Create a Shared Vision. Once the need for change is recognized, the leader must inspire organizational members with a "vision" of what the organization can become. In entrepreneurial ventures, this vision may be developed by the leader; but in large corporations, the vision is more likely to evolve through a participative process involving the CEO and key managers in the firm.[18] But Andrall E. Pearson, former CEO of PepsiCo, makes it clear that it is the leader's role to "spearhead" this effort, not just preside over it.[19] He also emphasizes that no strategic vision is permanent: "Lasting competitive edges are hard to generate."[20] Therefore, the transformational process is ongoing and not a one-time event.

An important part of the vision is high performance standards. From observation, it is clear that transformational leaders "stretch" their followers' abilities. High-performing organizations rarely pursue moderate goals or performance standards. Pearson observes, "This doesn't mean arbitrary, unrealistic goals that are bound to be missed and motivate no one, but rather goals that won't allow anyone to forget how tough the competitive arena is."[21] In such cases, the CEO must provide a role model for the organization's members. Transformational CEOs must "set a personal example in terms of the long hours they work, their obvious commitment to success, and the consistent quality of their efforts."[22] Furthermore, their public behavior should reflect their own excitement and energy, and the more contact they have with employees at all levels, the more contagious their excitement is likely to be.[23]

Besides serving as role models, transformational leaders must communicate their vision clearly and completely to all members of the organization. Management researchers Warren G. Bennis and Burt Nanus reinforce the importance of this suggestion by stating that the lack of a clear vision is a major reason for the declining effectiveness of many organizations in recent years. Clear communication of a vision creates a focus for the employees' efforts, and it is important that this vision be repeated over and over and not be allowed to fade away.[24] Few suggestions are more timely. The consulting firm Booz, Allen & Hamilton reported in 1990 that only 37 percent of senior managers think that other key managers completely understand new organizational goals, and only 4 percent of the senior managers believe that middle managers totally understand those goals.[25]

The common conception of the transformational leader as a dynamic, charismatic personality is only occasionally true. Many CEOs have effectively led their organizations through major transformations without being charismatic figures. Undoubtedly, charisma helps a leader influence others, but it is hardly a requirement for a transformational leader.

Institutionalize the Change. Finally, the transformational leader must institutionalize the changes that have been created. The CEO must first ensure that the change is proceeding as planned. As David A. Nadler, a management researcher, points out, all too many CEOs have learned, to their chagrin, that the changes they ordered never occurred. The reason is usually a lack of feedback mechanisms. Those mechanisms that were effective during stable periods often break down during turbulent change periods. In such situations, top management must develop multiple and highly sensitive feedback devices.[26] Feedback through multiple channels is essential, because change programs, even though successful, often have side effects such as the creation of new problems.

The CEO must also realize that the institutionalization of significant change (i.e., making the new ways of behaving a regular and normal part of organizational life) takes time. Encouraging organizational members to work and interact in different ways requires a new reward system. Since people are likely to behave in ways that lead to the rewards they desire, rewards such as pay increases and promotions should be linked to the types of behavior that are required to make the organization change effective. Management researcher Aaron J. Nurick recommends that if the organization benefits financially from the change program, then its members should share in the gains. The connection between organizational improvement and the employees' well-being thus becomes clear. Without such rewards, employees are unlikely to see involvement as worthy of their efforts.[27]

At all three of these stages identified by Tichy and Devanna, it is essential that the CEO have clear, accurate, and timely information. Bennis makes a number of suggestions, based on his own experience and research, for ensuring that such information reaches the CEO.[28] These suggestions include that the CEO not rely exclusively on his or her assistants and intimate associates for information. Thus, the CEO should be accessible to the members of the organization and to its customers and should read more than staff summaries for information on the environment. Second, he proposes that CEOs rotate their key assistants every two years to ensure continuing openness. He also recommends that these assistants be in contact with the organization's constituent groups so that they will understand their obligations and the limits of their power. Finally, he believes that CEOs should actively encourage their advisers to act as devil's advocates so that "groupthink" (the situation that results when group members emphasize the importance of solidarity over critical thinking) does not prevail.

■ The Leadership Team

Although this chapter focuses primarily upon the CEO, no single individual can possibly lead a complex organization alone. Therefore, most CEOs spend considerable amounts of time and effort developing a team of top-level managers. Typically, the **top management team** is headed by the CEO and is comprised of executives immediately below the CEO's level on the organization chart. However, such teams may also include middle managers, depending upon the desires of the CEO and the situation facing the particular company. A group of compatible managers who work well together and complement one another's abilities can provide a very powerful sense of direction for a company.

Why are many organizations today emphasizing team building at the top management level? There are a number of excellent reasons:[29]

- The CEO has a complex integrative task and cannot possibly be effective at that task without working closely with the individuals who are in charge of the organization's major activities (functions, products, regions, etc.).
- Subordinate managers usually possess greater expertise about the operating components of the organization and their own fields than the CEO does.

- The outcomes of a team's deliberations—versus the decisions of a single manager—are more likely to be innovative, because they come from a group of individuals possessing different skills, perspectives, and information.
- Team members, and their divisions or departments, should be more understanding and supportive of organizational decisions because they have a voice in shaping those decisions.
- Communication among top managers is enhanced because of their regular, frequent meetings.
- The lower-level managers on the team receive valuable developmental experience.

Furthermore, a recent study of top management teams in 460 midwestern banks revealed that technical and administrative innovations were more likely to occur when the team members represented diverse functional areas. Cross-functional communication was considered essential to organizational innovation.[30]

One well-known firm that has used its top management team advantageously is UAL Corporation. Chairman and CEO Stephen M. Wolf works closely on a daily basis with the executives in charge of such areas as finance, marketing, employee relations, public relations, and the legal department. The successful turnaround that UAL has achieved since Wolf took over in 1987 is partially attributed to his ability to assemble a talented top management team.[31]

Some corporations have gone even further, replacing their chief operating officer (COO) with an executive team—or committee—that reports directly to the CEO. For example, Xerox has a six-person executive team, Nordstrom (the Seattle-based department store) is run by four "co-presidents," and Microsoft's three-person "office of the president" reports directly to Chairman William Gates III. Such arrangements, of course, can sometimes prove unwieldy. Their success often depends upon the interpersonal compatibility of the executives and the extent to which each is willing to be a "team player."[32]

POWER

To influence the behavior of others, a leader must possess power. This section examines the need to acquire power and then explores the ways a leader can use power to implement strategy

■ The Role of Power

Although the popular conception of a CEO is of an individual who wields great amounts of power, this perception is far from correct. In fact, each time a manager climbs to a higher rung on the hierarchical ladder within an organization, he or she becomes more, not less, dependent upon other people.[33] In some sense, the CEO is the most dependent of the managers in an organization, because how well or how poorly the CEO (and, consequently, the organization) performs depends upon the performance of all of the organization's members. This is not to say that a CEO does not have formal authority to influence the behavior of employees, because he or she does. But we do wish to emphasize that trying to control the behavior of others solely through formal authority has its limitations.

The first of these limitations is that CEOs soon find out that not everyone in today's organizations passively accepts and enthusiastically carries out a constant stream of orders from above. Subordinates may resist orders, subtly ignore them, blatantly question them, or even quit. As Robert H. Miles, a management researcher, points out: "The raw use of power doesn't have the acceptance it did 25 years ago. People aren't willing to put up with it."[34]

Second, CEOs are always dependent upon some individuals over whom they have no formal authority.[35] Common examples include members of the board of directors, customers, and influential members of government regulatory agencies.

Hence, effective implementation of strategy requires the CEO to influence the behavior of others in ways that rely upon formal authority but also in ways that do not. In the latter sense, the CEO must acquire power over those individuals upon whom he or she is dependent. By **power,** we refer to the ability—apart from formal authority or control over resources and rewards—to influence the behavior of other people. The following section explains how top managers can use power to implement strategies.

▪ Techniques of Using Power

Top managers can wield power in a number of ways, as illustrated in Figure 9.3. This section discusses these common techniques that CEOs and other top-level managers employ to implement organizational strategies.

Expertise

A major source of power for many top managers is expertise.[36] Managers generally establish this power base through visible achievement. The greater the achievement, the more power the manager is able to accumulate.[37]

Figure 9.3 **Techniques of Using Power**

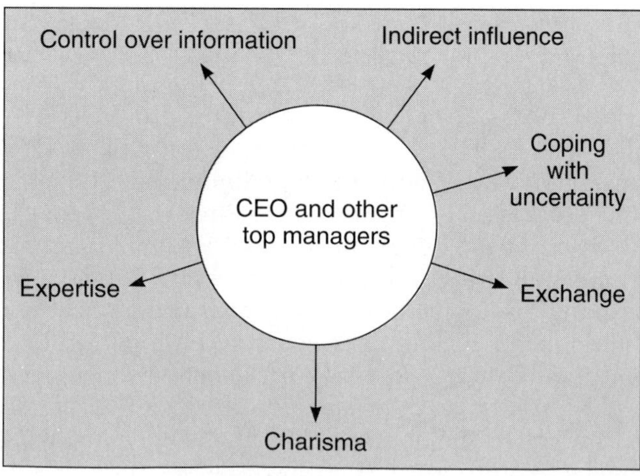

Expertise refers to a manager's ability to influence the behavior of others because these individuals believe that their manager is more knowledgeable about a problem, an opportunity, or an issue than they are. Managers who reach the CEO's office by rising through the firm's ranks will often be viewed as experts because it is clear to the organization's members that their CEO mastered a variety of jobs on the way to the top and, hence, is familiar with the employees' tasks. An executive who is hired from outside the firm to become its CEO may or may not enter that job with expert power, however. If the individual is from a company in the same industry, though, he or she is more likely to be viewed as an expert.

For example, Lee Iacocca was probably perceived as an expert by Chrysler's employees when he was hired as that firm's CEO, because he had spent most of his career prior to that time at Ford, where he had successfully held a variety of jobs. On the other hand, when John Sculley became CEO of Apple Computer, his expertise was as a marketing whiz at PepsiCo. Although much of his marketing experience could be transferred to the personal-computer business, one could have predicted that his expert power would be constrained by his limited knowledge of computers. To overcome this constraint, Sculley attempted to learn all that he could about computers after being hired at Apple.

Management researcher Gary A. Yukl suggests that leaders who possess expert power must take care in how they communicate that expertise to others. He cautions such leaders to avoid acting superior to others who possess less expertise and not to speak in an arrogant, condescending manner. As he points out, sometimes expert leaders who are trying to sell their proposals to others "fire a steady stream of arguments, rudely interrupt any attempted replies, and dismiss any objections or concerns without serious consideration."[38]

Control over Information

Control over information refers to a manager's access to important information and control over its distribution to others.[39] Henry Mintzberg's research indicates that the CEO is normally the single best-informed member of an organization. He or she is formally linked to all of the organization's key managers. Since each of these managers is a specialist relative to the CEO, the CEO is the person who best sees the totality of the organization and is most knowledgeable about its internal activities. He or she also has a number of external contacts—in other companies, in regulatory agencies, and so on—which provide excellent sources of information. Although the CEO may not know everything, he or she usually knows more than anyone else.[40]

Since the CEO has more information than anyone else, he or she is able to interpret information in order to influence the perceptions and attitudes of others.[41] If the leader's information is more complete than that of any other individual, no one will be able to question his or her decisions effectively. Even the board of directors may prove impotent, because its power based on legal standing can be overcome by the CEO's power of information and knowledge.[42]

Exchange

The use of exchange as a power base is very common. In **exchange,** a leader does something for someone else and can then expect that person to feel a sense of obligation toward the leader. Hence, when the leader makes a special request of that person later, the person will usually feel obligated to carry out that request. CEOs may even develop friendships with others in terms of exchange, knowing that friendship carries with it certain obligations.

For instance, a top manager's relationship with the corporation's CEO or board of directors can add to—or detract from—the manager's power. As an extreme example, take the case of one COO who supported higher pay for his chairman; insisted that the chairman's country club dues be paid by the firm; deferred in public to the CEO, invariably addressing him as "Mr. Chairman"; and even donated $250,000 in company funds to a university to honor the chairman. This manager, not surprisingly, was later named CEO by the chairman.[43]

Quite often, building reciprocal relationships with organizational members requires the ability to submerge one's ego. Those who set aside their status and power are more likely to be viewed favorably by those who are either above or below them in the organization's hierarchy. Such managers, of course, are more able to secure the enthusiastic cooperation of others.[44]

Indirect Influence

Top managers can often get others to implement the organization's strategies through **indirect influence**—that is, by modifying the situation in which individuals work. One variation of this technique involves making permanent changes in the organization's formal reward systems. In such cases, only those individuals who correctly carry out the organization's strategy will receive bonuses, pay raises, or promotions. For example, each of the six persons on the executive team that runs Xerox has a specific area of responsibility. However, to encourage the executives to work closely together, Xerox's board of directors has developed a compensation system for the executive team members that rewards overall company results—not simply the results of each person's own area.[45] Carrying this concept further, a manager can modify the organization's structure or even the physical layout of offices and departments to weaken groups or individuals who oppose certain aspects of the strategy.

Opposition to an organization's strategy is not unusual. Strategic change often reduces the status and power of some individuals while enhancing that of others. Those who believe that their status will be diminished often oppose the new strategy, if not openly, then through delaying tactics and other quiet forms of noncompliance.

In another type of indirect influence, the CEO may place only those individuals who are supporters in responsible positions. A loyal supporter, for instance, can be placed in charge of an important task force or committee to ensure that the group's recommendation coincides with the strategic direction set by the manager. Obviously, this technique must be used with care. If the CEO is surrounded only by loyal supporters, strategic decisions can become characterized by groupthink, and questions and objections that should be voiced may never arise.

Charisma

Another highly effective power base for influencing the behavior of others is charisma. **Charisma** refers to a leader's ability to influence others through his or her personal magnetism, enthusiasm, and strongly held convictions. Often, leaders are able to communicate these convictions and their vision for the future through a dramatic, persuasive manner of speaking.[46] As Yukl points out, charismatic leaders attempt to create an image of competence and success. Their aura of success and personal magnetism make them role models for their employees. The more that followers admire their leaders and identify with them, the more likely they are to accept the leaders' values and beliefs. This acceptance enables charismatic leaders to exert considerable influence over their followers' behaviors.[47]

The more success the charismatic leader has, the more powerful he or she becomes. This combination of charisma and expertise can be extremely potent in influencing the behavior of others. Hence, charismatic leaders who set high standards of performance that are realistic are likely to have highly motivated and committed organization members.

As some researchers have pointed out, charismatic leaders are most likely to be effective during periods of organizational crisis or transition.[48] Times of stress are more likely to encourage employees to respond to a leader who appears to have the answer to the problems that the organization is facing. If the leader's strategy results in early successes and if organizational performance begins to improve, the leader's power base will increase dramatically.

Coping with Uncertainty

Every organization faces environmental contingencies; these may consist of various trends or developments, such as competition, governmental regulations or laws, cost pressures, new technologies, and so on. The relative importance of these many contingencies will vary from one organization and industry to another. But when a development or trend has an important implication for any particular organization at a specific time, it can be termed a **critical contingency.**[49]

For example, in the highly competitive and rapidly changing financial services industry, the critical contingency is developing new financial products. Those companies that are most effective at anticipating and meeting the market's needs are more likely to be profitable. Thus managers in those companies who create popular new financial products are able to amass significant amounts of power to influence organizational decisions. Likewise, in an industry whose critical contingency is efficiency/cost control—such as in the airline industry—managers who lower their organization's cost structure can gain considerable amounts of power.[50]

Relating these ideas to the business unit strategies presented earlier in Chapter 6, we can surmise that, in industries in which the critical contingency is external product/market trends or events, companies that adopt either the niche-differentiation strategy or the differentiation strategy are more likely to be profitable. In those companies, most of the power therefore will likely be held by managers in marketing, advertising, and/or product R&D. Similarly, in environments in which the efficiencies of processing or delivering products/services comprise the critical contingency, those businesses that adopt the niche–low-cost strategy or the low-cost strategy will be most effective. Hence, their operating decisions are most likely to be influenced by managers in accounting, production/operations, or process R&D. Finally, in environments in which both operating efficiencies and product/service differentiation are the critical contingencies, executives in any—or all—of these areas are likely to wield power.

ORGANIZATIONAL CULTURE

Organizational culture refers to the values and patterns of belief and behavior that are accepted and practiced by the members of a particular organization.[51] Because each organization develops its own unique culture, even organizations within the same industry and city will exhibit distinctly different ways of operating. The following sections discuss the evolution of organizational culture, the impact of culture on an organization's strategy, and the methods leaders use to shape organizational culture.

■ The Evolution of Culture

The purpose of organizational culture is to enable a firm to adapt to environmental changes and to coordinate and integrate its internal operations.[52] But how do appropriate values, behaviors, and beliefs develop to enable the organization to accomplish these ends?

For many organizations, the first—and major—influence upon their culture is their founder. His or her assumptions about success form the foundation of the firm's culture.[53] For instance, the primary influence upon McDonald's culture was the fast-food company's founder, Ray A. Kroc, who died in 1984. His philosophy of fast service, assembly line food preparation, wholesome image, and devotion to the hamburger are still reflected in McDonald's operations today. Kroc's influence is the primary reason why McDonald's did not diversify outside the fast-food industry, did not specialize in made-to-order hamburgers, prohibited franchisees from being absentee owners, encouraged franchisees to experiment with new products, targeted advertisements and sales promotions to both adults and children, and opened Ronald McDonald Houses near major medical centers to provide low-cost housing to families of sick children.

As Yukl points out, the set of beliefs about the distinctive competence of the organization (i.e., what differentiates it from other organizations) is one of the most important elements of culture in new organizations. These beliefs directly affect organizational strategies and operations. For example, a company that owes its success to developing innovative products is likely to respond to a decline in sales with new-product introductions; a company that offers a common product at a low price would respond with attempts to lower costs even further.[54]

However, as time passes, Yukl notes, "segments of the culture that were initially functional may become dysfunctional, preventing the organization from adapting successfully to a changing environment."[55] McDonald's, for instance, has departed from some of Kroc's precepts in order to continue its success under changing conditions. As customers have become more interested in a diversified menu, McDonald's has expanded from hamburgers to fish and chicken sandwiches and even pizza. Increasing societal emphasis on healthy diets has led to new products such as salads, cereal, and low-fat hamburgers and yogurt, as well as to modifications in the food preparation process. The company even made its first departure from fast food to take advantage of its strong brand name by licensing Sears, Roebuck & Company to sell children's clothing with the McDonald's name emblazoned on it.[56]

So, in general, we can say that the foundation of an organization's culture reflects the values and beliefs of its founder. But the culture is modified over time as the environment changes. Environmental change renders some of the firm's culture obsolete and even dysfunctional. New elements of the culture must be added as the old are discarded in order for the organization to maintain its success. But as Figure 9.4 illustrates, a given organization's culture may also change to reflect the powerful influence of a transformational leader other than the founder.

For example, in recent years, the culture of Walt Disney Company has changed significantly. The founder's influence on the conservative family entertainment company was such that for years after his death, executives would wonder "What would Walt have done?" before making decisions. As the company lost ground to its competitors by releasing an outdated line of family movies, its newly hired CEO, Michael Eisner, brought in a new team of managers who had never known Disney. By freeing its top management of the elements of the past, which had become dysfunctional, Eisner was able to begin producing the types of movies that are popular with today's moviegoers.[57]

■ Impact of Culture on Strategy

Organizational culture can facilitate or hinder the firm's strategic actions. A recent study showed that firms with "strategically appropriate cultures"—such as PepsiCo, Wal-Mart, and Shell—outperformed selected other corporations with less appropriate cultures over an eleven-year period. The successful firms experienced an average revenue increase of 682 percent (versus 166 percent for the other organizations), their stock prices rose by 901 percent (versus 74 percent), and growth in their net income outpaced the other firms by 756 percent to 1 percent. These successful firms had developed cultures that

Evolution of Organizational Culture **Figure 9.4**

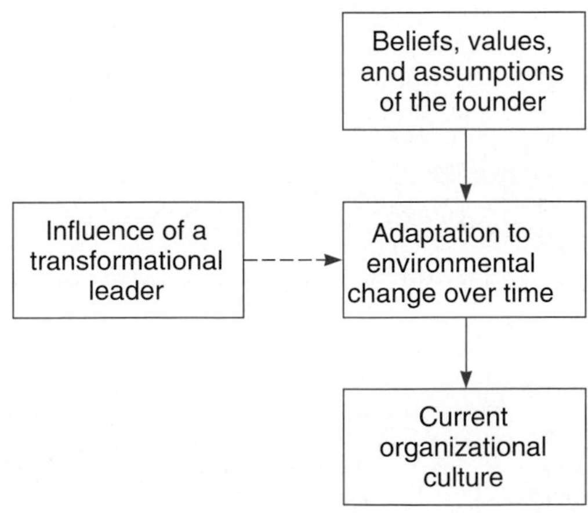

STRATEGIC INSIGHT

Leadership and Organizational Culture at Wal-Mart

Wal-Mart's culture cannot be separated from the beliefs of its founder, Sam Walton, who died in 1992. During his career, "Mr. Sam" provided the guiding vision that took his company from a single store in Arkansas in 1962 to the position of world's largest retailer by 1990. This meteoric growth was not due simply to low prices or store location. Many retailers that offered low prices, such as Korvette's or Woolco, no longer exist; and, if location were the primary key to success, Sears and Macy's would be highly profitable. Rather, to a great extent, the biggest difference between Wal-Mart and other retailers was Sam Walton himself.

From the beginning, Walton realized that retailing begins with the customer. The concepts of customer service and customer satisfaction are ingrained into every one of Wal-Mart's 400,000 "associates" (the firm's term for employees). Each week, Wal-Mart's regional vice presidents follow in Walton's footsteps by spending three or four days visiting stores in their region, talking to customers and associates, and comparing Wal-Mart's prices and merchandise with those of such competitors as Kmart. And, each Saturday, all of Wal-Mart's top managers meet to compare findings and decide what changes are needed in their stores during the coming week. Some even say that the first lesson Walton instilled in his associates was a "bias for action," so that change in the stores is constant.

As the company grew, Walton realized that empowering associates was the most efficient way of keeping in touch with the customer. Hence, associates are kept informed weekly about their store's—and even their own department's—performance. From the department manager up, all associates know their cost, their markup, their overhead, and their profit. Walton believed that the more associates understand about their business, the more interested they'll be in serving their customers. Each department manager acts as an entrepreneur, running his or her own business, and each is encouraged to experiment. Those whose experiments are successful are invited to the Saturday meeting at company headquarters in Bentonville, Arkansas, to explain their ideas to top management.

Finally, Sam Walton realized that giving motivational speeches and leading associates in the "Wal-Mart cheer" ("Give me a W! Give me an A! Give me an L! Give me a squiggly! . . .") could only go so far in helping them identify with the organization. So, early on, he decided to make associates a real part of the company by making every associate who has been with Wal-Mart for at least a year eligible for profit-sharing. Wal-Mart contributes about 6 percent of each associate's salary to the plan, and associates can take their share in cash or in Wal-Mart stock whenever they leave the company. As a typical example, one Wal-Mart truck driver related that, after driving for another company for thirteen years, he received only $700 when he resigned. But, in his nineteen years with Wal-Mart, he had already accumulated $707,000 in profit sharing. As a result of these and other programs, CEO David Glass believes that there is no other company where 400,000 people work so closely together as true partners.

SOURCES: B. Saporito, "A Week Aboard the Wal-Mart Express," *Fortune,* 24 August 1992, pp. 77–84; W. Zellner, "Mr. Sam's Experiment Is Alive and Well," *Business Week,* 20 April 1992, p. 39; S. Walton and J. Huey, *Sam Walton: Made in America* (New York: Doubleday, 1992); J. Huey, "America's Most Successful Merchant," *Fortune,* 23 September 1991, pp. 46–59.

emphasized three key groups of stakeholders—customers, stockholders, and employees. Note that the point is *not* that these corporations have strong cultures, for many less successful firms—such as Sears, General Motors, and Citicorp—possess strong cultures. The point, rather, is that the culture of a successful firm must be appropriate to—and supportive of—that firm's strategy. Furthermore, the culture must contain values that can help the firm adapt to environmental change.[58]

Because culture reflects the past, periods of environmental change often require significant modification of the organization's culture. It is essential that changes in strategy be accompanied by corresponding alterations in organizational culture; otherwise, the strategy is likely to fail. Conservative organizations do not become aggressive, entrepreneurial firms simply because they have formulated new goals and plans.[59]

Management researcher Edgar H. Schein points out that a firm caught in changing environmental conditions may devise a new strategy that will make sense from a financial, product, or marketing point of view. Yet the strategy will not be implemented because it requires "assumptions, values, and ways of working" that are at variance with the organization's culture.[60] An organization can change its strategy and its structure and yet will find its employees reverting to their prior ways of operating if it does not confront the assumptions underlying its culture.[61]

As an example of a company modifying both its culture and its strategy, consider EDS.[62] Founded in the early 1960s by H. Ross Perot, EDS exemplified a powerful "can-do, anything-is-possible" entrepreneurial spirit. Strongly non-union, the company had an extremely stringent hiring process followed by a grueling trial and training period. Those who survived displayed unusually high morale and a devotion for doing whatever was required to accomplish the task. By the early 1980s, EDS possessed a culture that could be described as "macho" and "gung ho."

But, in the mid-1980s, EDS was acquired by General Motors, and Perot left the company within two years. In a brief period of time, EDS found itself without its strong leader, without its independence, and with a work force that had expanded almost overnight from several thousand to 60,000 employees. To compound its identity crisis, EDS failed to win an important contract with Kodak, leading its top management to reassess both its strategy and its culture.

EDS is now undergoing some material changes under chairman and CEO Les Alberthal. His vision for EDS is that it be recognized "as the premier provider of information technology services based on its contributions to the success of its customers."[63] Toward that end, Alberthal emphasizes that EDS must help its customers succeed by understanding their needs. To accomplish that goal, EDS's structure is being transformed from that of a big company to an organization of many smaller companies (multiple business units with decentralized decision-making authority). Since each business unit focuses upon a specific segment of the market, this move puts EDS employees in closer contact with customers and their needs. At the same time, EDS is transforming its historical "trust us" type of customer service to one that is more characterized by listening and cooperation.

To support this strategy/structure transformation, EDS's culture is being modified. Employees are to be viewed as "volunteers" who may, if their needs are not fulfilled, leave EDS for other employment. Managers will be evaluated not only on revenue and profit figures but also on the extent to which they motivate and empower their employees. Managerial training programs are being altered to help managers become more involved with their employees and to learn to serve as mentors to them. Overall, the manager's role is changing from that of "taskmaster" to one of "servant" to the employee. These shifts

STRATEGIC INSIGHT

PepsiCo's Distinctive Culture

Surely one of the most distinctive U.S. corporate cultures is PepsiCo's. New managers are put through a rigorous training program likened to Marine Corps boot camp, with those who can't meet the standards washing out. Once through the program, each manager is given considerable freedom. Risk taking is encouraged, and second guessing is rare. After PepsiCo lost $16 million on its ill-fated Grandma's Cookies venture, the executive who designed the project was made the head of KFC because the cookie undertaking "made sense" at the time.

An important value is winning. "Employees know they must win merely to stay in place—and must devastate the competition to get ahead." Not surprisingly, the typical managerial work week is sixty hours. In fact, when an internal survey revealed that some employees at headquarters were disturbed that they didn't have sufficient time to do their laundry at home, the company installed dry cleaning equipment rather than reduce the work week.

PepsiCo may take management development more seriously than almost any other corporation. CEO Wayne Calloway spends about half of his time reviewing the performance of the firm's top 600 managers. He also personally interviews all applicants for positions at the vice-presidential level and up. He expects those below him to spend about 40 percent of their time on personnel development and performance evaluation.

The managers who survive the intense atmosphere are rewarded with first-class air travel, stock options, bonuses that can reach 90 percent of salary, fast promotions, and fully loaded company cars. Those who don't meet the firm's expectations are out.

These values are consistent with PepsiCo's strategic direction. Managers are given considerable autonomy and are encouraged to "love change" and move quickly to take advantage of opportunities. These quick reflexes are of paramount importance in marketing consumer products and have made PepsiCo one of the premier marketing firms in the world.

SOURCES: A. Rothman, "Can Wayne Calloway Handle the Pepsi Challenge?" *Business Week,* 27 January 1992, pp. 90–98; M.J. McCarthy, "Pepsi Is Going Better with Its Fast Foods and Frito-Lay Snacks," *The Wall Street Journal,* 13 June 1991; P. Sellers, "Pepsi Keeps on Going After No. 1," *Fortune,* 11 March 1991, pp. 62–70; B. Dumaine, "Those High-Flying PepsiCo Managers," *Fortune,* 10 April 1989, pp. 78–86; A. Dunkin, "Pepsi's Marketing Magic: Why Nobody Does It Better," *Business Week,* 10 February 1986, pp. 52–57; "Corporate Culture: The Hard-to-Change Values That Spell Success or Failure," *Business Week,* 27 October 1980, pp. 148–154 (quotation from p. 148).

are viewed as essential to attracting talented employees in an increasingly diverse work force.

▪ How Leaders Shape Culture

CEOs, other than the founder, can be influential in shaping the organization's culture so that it becomes more appropriate for its present or anticipated environment. Transactional leaders are less likely to modify the firm's culture than transformational leaders. As Bass points out: "The transactional leader works within the organizational culture as it exists; the transformational leader changes the organizational culture."[64]

How can a leader change the organization's culture? Schein advocates five "primary embedding mechanisms" for altering culture.[65] The first mechanism is systematically paying attention to certain areas of the business. This objective may be accomplished through formally measuring and controlling the activities of those areas or, less formally, through the CEO's comments or questions at meetings. For instance, a top manager can direct the attention of organizational members toward controlling costs or to serving customers effectively. By contrast, those areas that the leader does not react to will be considered less important by employees.

The second mechanism involves the leader's reactions to critical incidents and organizational crises. The way a CEO deals with a crisis—such as declining sales, new governmental regulation, or technological obsolescence—can emphasize norms, values, and working procedures—or even create new ones. For instance, some companies have reacted to declining profits by cutting compensation across the board; all employees, including top management, take the pay cut. This action emphasizes a belief that "we are a family who will take care of one another." Other firms, by contrast, lay off operative employees and middle managers, while maintaining (or even increasing) the salaries of top management. Nonadaptive cultures frequently reflect top management's values of arrogance and insularity. Self-interest takes precedence over concerns about customers, stockholders, or employees.[66]

The third mechanism is to serve as a deliberate role model, teacher, or coach. As we have seen earlier in the chapter, the visible behavior of the leader communicates assumptions and values to subordinates.

The way top management allocates rewards and status is a fourth mechanism for influencing culture. Leaders can quickly communicate their priorities by consistently linking pay raises, promotions, and the lack of pay increases and promotions to particular behaviors. For instance, General Foods found that the changing environment of the 1980s rendered its historical emphasis on cost control and earnings less effective. To redirect the efforts of managers toward diversification and sales growth, top management revised the compensation system to link bonuses to sales volume rather than only to increased earnings and began rewarding new-product development more generously.[67]

The fifth mechanism identified by Schein involves the procedures through which an organization recruits, selects, and promotes employees and the ways it dismisses them. An organization's culture can be perpetuated by hiring and promoting individuals whose values are similar to the firm's. By contrast, an organization attempting to alter its culture can accelerate that change by hiring employees whose beliefs and behaviors more closely fit the organization's changing value system.

In addition to these five primary embedding mechanisms, Schein also identifies several "secondary reinforcement mechanisms."[68] These include the organization's structure, its operating systems and procedures, the design of its physical space, various stories or legends that are perpetuated about important events and people, and formal statements of organizational philosophy. These mechanisms are labeled *secondary* because they work only if they are consistent with the five primary mechanisms. The primary embedding mechanisms and secondary reinforcement mechanisms are summarized in Table 9.1.

As an example of the secondary mechanisms, the belief that open communication and close working relationships are important is reflected in the open designs of the headquarters of companies such as Levi Strauss in California and Nike in Oregon.[69] As another example, Food Lion—a rapidly growing supermarket chain in the southeastern United States that emphasizes low

Table 9.1 **Mechanisms for Embedding and Reinforcing Organizational Culture**

Primary Embedding Mechanisms

1. What leaders pay attention to, measure, and control
2. Leader reactions to critical incidents and organizational crises
3. Deliberate role modeling, teaching, and coaching
4. Criteria for allocation of rewards and status
5. Criteria for recruitment, selection, promotion, retirement, and excommunication

Secondary Articulation and Reinforcement Mechanisms

1. Organization design and structure
2. Organizational systems and procedures
3. Design of physical space, facades, buildings
4. Stories about important events and people
5. Formal statements of organizational philosophy, creeds, charters

Source: E.H. Schein, *Organizational Culture and Leadership* (San Francisco: Jossey-Bass, 1985), Chap. 10.

prices in no-frills stores and a constant awareness of costs—illustrates the use of stories about important people. One tale reveals how obsessed with numbers the chain's founder, Ralph Ketner, is. While waiting for freight trains at railroad crossings, he even adds the numbers on the cars, delivering the total as the caboose passes by. His numerical obsession is conveyed to Food Lion employees, who quickly learn to focus their attention on figures such as individual product prices, costs, sales volume, and linear shelf space.[70]

Schein emphasizes the critical linkage between leadership and organizational culture by stating that "the unique and essential function of leadership is the manipulation of culture."[71] Culture is created by the actions of leaders; it is institutionalized by leaders; and when it becomes dysfunctional, leadership is required to change it. What a CEO needs most, according to Schein, is an understanding of how culture can help or hinder the organization in attaining its mission and the skills to make the appropriate changes.[72]

SUMMARY

Top-level managers have two tools to encourage organizational members to put their full efforts into strategy implementation: strategic leadership and organizational culture. In today's dynamic and turbulent world, the importance of strategic leadership cannot be overemphasized. The firm's leaders must articulate the organization's mission and objectives and then inspire, motivate, and support the firm's members as they work together to implement the organization's strategies.

The CEO, simply by virtue of the office, possesses the potential to influence the behavior of the organization's employees. This source of influence is termed *formal authority.* Through it, the CEO can control resources and rewards. Additionally, each CEO has a distinctive leadership style that sets the tone for the firm's members. Some leaders use a transactional style, exchanging rewards for employees' work efforts. This style can be effective in firms that are already performing well and do not anticipate significant environmental change, because it encourages employees to continue to engage in high performance.

In companies that are experiencing competitive difficulties or are undergoing environmental change, a transformational leadership style is preferable. A transformational leader inspires involvement in a mission, giving followers a "vision" of a higher order and motivating them to stretch their abilities. Such leadership is thought to make significant changes in organizational performance.

Because no single CEO, regardless of how talented he or she may be, can lead a complex organization single-handedly, most companies emphasize top management teams. Led by the CEO, such teams of executives are able to enhance the organization's coordinative activities, creativity, information flows, and strategy implementation.

In influencing the behavior of others, CEOs and other top managers have available, in addition to their formal authority and leadership style, various other techniques for wielding power. For instance, managers who are perceived as experts in their field often have significant influence over the behavior of others. They can also use their access to important information and control over its distribution to affect behavior. Leaders often use exchange as a power base, doing something for others to create a sense of obligation. Also, a manager can indirectly influence others by modifying the organization's structure, physical layout, or reward system. And a manager who possesses charisma can have a powerful impact upon followers. Finally, managers who deal successfully with critical environmental contingencies can acquire significant power.

Organizational culture refers to the values and patterns of belief and behavior that are accepted and practiced by the members of an organization. A given organization's culture reflects the influence of its founder, its experiences after the departure of its founder, and, at times, the powerful influence of a transformational leader other than the founder.

An organization's culture can facilitate or hinder the firm's strategic actions. Successful strategy implementation requires a "strategically appropriate culture"—one that is appropriate to, and supportive of, the firm's strategy. Moreover, that culture must contain values that can help the firm adapt to environmental change.

A leader can change the organization's culture through such mechanisms as paying systematic attention to certain areas of the business, serving as a deliberate role model, and allocating rewards and status. Leaders can also set an example for the firm's members through the way in which they react to organizational crises and through the processes the organization uses to attract, hire, and promote employees.

KEY CONCEPTS

Charisma A leader's ability to influence the behavior of others through his or her personal magnetism, enthusiasm, strongly held beliefs, and charm.

Control over information A situation in which a manager has access to important information and controls its distribution to others to influence their behavior.

Critical contingency An environmental trend or development that has important implications for an organization. Managers who cope successfully with such contingencies acquire significant amounts of power.

Exchange A situation in which a leader does a favor for someone so that he or she will feel a sense of obligation toward the leader.

Expertise A manager's ability to influence the behavior of others because they believe that the manager possesses greater expertise or is more knowledgeable about a situation than they are.

Formal authority The official, institutionalized right of a manager to make decisions affecting the behavior of subordinates.

Indirect influence The influence on the behavior of others brought about by modifying the situation in which they work.

Leadership The capacity to secure the cooperation of others in accomplishing an objective.

Leadership style The characteristic pattern of behavior that a leader exhibits in the process of exercising authority and making decisions.

Organizational culture The values and patterns of belief and behavior that are accepted and practiced by the members of a particular organization.

Power The ability, apart from functional authority or control over resources or rewards, to influence the behavior of others.

Strategic leadership The process of establishing the firm's direction—by developing and communicating a vision of the future—and motivating and inspiring organization members to move in that direction.

Top management team A team of top-level executives, headed by the CEO.

Transactional leadership The capacity to motivate followers by exchanging rewards for performance.

Transformational leadership The capacity to motivate followers by inspiring involvement and participation in a mission.

DISCUSSION QUESTIONS

1. Explain the difference between leadership and management. Give examples of each concept.

2. Delineate the relationship between an organization's reward system and its strategic decisions.

3. Explain transactional leadership, and give examples. Identify the conditions under which it is likely to be effective.

4. Explain transformational leadership, and give examples. Identify the conditions under which it is likely to be effective.

5. What is the role of clear, accurate, and timely information in each of the three stages of the transformational process?

6. Explain the concept of managerial dependency and why it requires the CEO to develop sources of power other than formal authority.

7. Give examples of leaders you have known who wielded power through expertise; through control over information; through exchange; through indirect influence; and through charisma.

8. Think of an organization with which you are quite familiar. Describe its culture. Explain how its culture may have evolved.

9. Give an example of an organization whose culture is appropriate for its strategy. Now, give an example of a firm whose culture has hindered its strategy.

10. Relate a story about an important event or a person that reflects elements of a particular organization's culture.

STRATEGIC MANAGEMENT EXERCISES

1. Assume that you are the CEO of a commercial airline that competes with the low-cost strategy. Describe an appropriate organizational culture for your company.
2. Assume that your airline (Exercise 1) has now changed its strategy from low-cost to low-cost–differentiation. As CEO, what changes might you consider implementing in style of leadership, exercise of power, and organizational culture?
3. Find, in your library, an example of transformational leadership. Explain the situation fully: Who is the leader? What is the organization? Why was transformational leadership necessary? What characteristics and/or behaviors made the manager a transformational leader? What were the results of his or her attempts to transform the organization? (Particularly good sources for this exercise are *The Wall Street Journal, Business Week,* and *Fortune.*)
4. Strategies involving mergers and acquisitions are particularly vulnerable to cultural problems. Mergers between two organizations often are easier to accomplish on paper than in reality. Reality may reveal that the cultures of the organization fail to mesh as easily as corporate assets. From library research, identify two companies that are currently merging or have engaged in a merger within the past few years. Learn as much as you can about each company's organizational culture. What problems are the two businesses having in combining their cultures? From your research, what other problems can you predict will occur in the future?

NOTES

1. H. Mintzberg, *The Nature of Managerial Work* (New York: Harper & Row, 1973), Chap. 4.
2. J.P. Kotter, *The Leadership Factor* (New York: Free Press, 1988), p. 11.
3. D.C. Hambrick, "Guest Editor's Introduction: Putting Top Managers Back in the Strategy Picture," *Strategic Management Journal* 10 (1989): 6.
4. J.P. Kotter, *A Force for Change: How Leadership Differs from Management* (New York: The Free Press, 1990), p. 5.
5. D.V. Day and R.G. Lord, "Executive Leadership and Organizational Performance: Suggestions for a New Theory and Methodology," *Journal of Management* 14 (1988): 453–464.
6. G.A. Yukl, *Leadership in Organizations,* 2nd ed. (Englewood Cliffs, N.J.: Prentice-Hall, 1989), pp. 263–266; J. Pfeffer, "The Ambiguity of Leadership," *Academy of Management Review* 2 (1977): 104–112.
7. Yukl, *Leadership in Organizations,* p. 15.
8. Ibid., pp. 17–18.
9. Day and Lord, "Executive Leadership," p. 459.
10. This distinction was first made by J.M. Burns, *Leadership* (New York: Harper & Row, 1978).
11. B.M. Bass, *Leadership and Performance Beyond Expectations* (New York: Free Press, 1985).
12. Ibid., p. 22.
13. B.M. Bass, "Leadership: Good, Better, Best," *Organizational Dynamics* 13 (Winter 1985): 26–40; N.M. Tichy and D.O. Ulrich, "SMR Forum: The Leadership Challenge—A Call for the Transformational Leader," *Sloan Management Review* 26 (Fall 1984): 59–68.
14. Bass, *Leadership and Performance,* p. 29.
15. N.M. Tichy and M.A. Devanna, *The Transformational Leader* (New York: Wiley, 1986).
16. P.F. Drucker, *Managing in Turbulent Times* (New York: Harper & Row, 1980), p. 44.
17. J.S. Lublin, "More Companies Tap Industry Outsiders for Top Posts to Gain Fresh Perspectives," *The Wall Street Journal,* 21 February 1992; J. Cole and P.B. Carroll, "GM's Hughes Division Hires Armstrong from IBM to Become Chairman, Chief," *The Wall Street Journal,* 20 February 1992; B. Hager, L. Driscoll, J. Weber, and G. McWilliams, "CEO Wanted. No Insiders, Please," *Business Week,* 12 August 1991, pp. 44–45.
18. Tichy and Devanna, *Transformational Leader.*
19. A.E. Pearson, "Six Basics for General Managers," *Harvard Business Review* 67, no. 4 (July–August 1989): 96.
20. Ibid., p. 97. Reprinted by permission of the *Harvard Business Review.* Excerpt from "Six Basics for General Managers" by Andrall E. Pearson (July–August 1989). Copyright © 1989 by the President and Fellows of Harvard College; all rights reserved.
21. Ibid., p. 95. Reprinted by permission of the *Harvard Business Review.* Excerpt from "Six Basics for General Managers" by Andrall E. Pearson (July–August 1989). Copyright © 1989 by the President and Fellows of Harvard College; all rights reserved.

22. Ibid. Reprinted by permission of the *Harvard Business Review.* Excerpt from "Six Basics for General Managers" by Andrall E. Pearson (July–August 1989). Copyright © 1989 by the President and Fellows of Harvard College; all rights reserved.
23. A.M. Mohrman, Jr., S.A. Mohrman, G.E. Ledford, Jr., T.G. Cummings, E.E. Lawler III, and Associates, *Large-Scale Organizational Change* (San Francisco: Jossey-Bass, 1989), p. 106.
24. W. Bennis and B. Nanus, *Leaders: The Strategies for Taking Charge* (New York: Harper & Row, 1985), pp. 27–33, 87–109.
25. S. Feinstein, "Labor Letter," *The Wall Street Journal,* 1 May 1990.
26. D.A. Nadler, "Managing Organizational Change: An Integrative Perspective," *Journal of Applied Behavioral Science* 17 (1981): 294.
27. A.J. Nurick, "The Paradox of Participation: Lessons from the Tennessee Valley Authority," *Human Resource Management* 24 (Fall 1985): 354–355.
28. W. Bennis, *Why Leaders Can't Lead: The Unconscious Conspiracy Continues* (San Francisco: Jossey-Bass, 1989), pp. 140–141.
29. The first two reasons are based on Hambrick, "Guest Editor's Introduction," p. 6. The remaining reasons are based on R.A. Eisenstat and S.G. Cohen, "Summary: Top Management Groups," in J.R. Hackman, ed., *Groups That Work (and Those That Don't): Creating Conditions for Effective Teamwork* (San Francisco: Jossey-Bass, 1990), pp. 78–79. See also D.C. Hambrick and P.A. Mason, "Upper Echelons: The Organization as a Reflection of Its Top Managers," *Academy of Management Review* 9 (1984): 193–206.
30. K.A. Bantel and S.E. Jackson, "Top Management and Innovations in Banking: Does the Composition of the Top Team Make a Difference?" *Strategic Management Journal* 10 (1989): 111.
31. K. Kelly, "United Wants the Whole World in Its Hands," *Business Week,* 27 April 1992, pp. 64–68; K. Kelly, "He Gets By with a Lot of Help from His Friends," *Business Week,* 27 April 1992, p. 68.
32. D.J. Yang, "Nordstrom's Gang of Four," *Business Week,* 15 June 1992, pp. 122–123; A. Bennett, "Firms Run by Executive Teams Can Reap Rewards, Incur Risks," *The Wall Street Journal,* 5 February 1992.
33. J.P. Kotter, "Power, Dependence, and Effective Management," *Harvard Business Review* 55, no. 4 (July–August 1977): 125–136.
34. T.A. Stewart, "New Ways to Exercise Power," *Fortune,* 6 November 1989, p. 53.
35. Kotter, "Power, Dependence," p. 128.
36. J.R.P. French, Jr., and B. Raven, "The Bases of Social Power," in D. Cartwright, ed., *Studies in Social Power* (Ann Arbor, Mich.: University of Michigan Press, 1959), pp. 150–167.
37. Kotter, "Power, Dependence," p. 130.
38. Yukl, *Leadership in Organizations,* p. 47.
39. A. Pettigrew, "Information Control as a Power Resource," *Sociology* 6 (1972): 187–204.
40. H. Mintzberg, *Power in and Around Organizations* (Englewood Cliffs, N.J.: Prentice-Hall, 1983), pp. 121–122.
41. A. Kuhn, *The Study of Society: A Unified Approach* (Homewood, Ill.: Irwin, 1963).
42. Mintzberg, *Power in and Around,* p. 122.
43. J. Pfeffer, *Managing with Power: Politics and Influence in Organizations* (Boston: Harvard Business School Press, 1992), p. 107.
44. Ibid., pp. 182–185.

45. Bennett, "Firms Run by Executive Teams."

46. D.E. Berlew, "Leadership and Organizational Excitement," in D.A. Kolb, I.M. Rubin, and J.M. McIntyre, eds., *Organizational Psychology: A Book of Readings,* 2nd ed. (Englewood Cliffs, N.J.: Prentice-Hall, 1974); R.J. House, "A 1976 Theory of Charismatic Leadership," in J.G. Hunt and L.L. Larson, eds., *Leadership: The Cutting Edge* (Carbondale, Ill.: Southern Illinois Press, 1977).

47. Yukl, *Leadership in Organizations,* p. 206.

48. Bass, *Leadership and Performance,* pp. 37–39; J.A. Conger and R. Kanungo, "Toward a Behavioral Theory of Charismatic Leadership in Organizational Settings," *Academy of Management Review* 12 (1987): 637–647.

49. D.J. Hickson, C.R. Hinings, C.A. Lee, R.E. Schneck, and J.M. Pennings, "A Strategic Contingencies Theory of Intraorganizational Power," *Administrative Science Quarterly* 16 (1971): 216–229.

50. G.R. Salancik and J. Pfeffer, "Who Gets Power—And How They Hold on to It: A Strategic-Contingency Model of Power," *Organizational Dynamics* 5 (Winter 1977): 5; D.C. Hambrick, "Environment, Strategy, and Power Within Top Management Teams," *Administrative Science Quarterly* 26 (1981): 253–276.

51. C.D. Pringle, D.F. Jennings, and J.G. Longenecker, *Managing Organizations: Functions and Behaviors* (Columbus, Ohio: Merrill, 1988), p. 594.

52. E.H. Schein, *Organizational Culture and Leadership* (San Francisco: Jossey-Bass, 1985), p. 9.

53. E.H. Schein, "The Role of the Founder in Creating Organizational Culture," *Organizational Dynamics* 12 (Summer 1983): 14.

54. Yukl, *Leadership in Organizations,* pp. 215–216.

55. Ibid., p. 216.

56. For articles on McDonald's culture, see R. Henkoff, "Big Mac Attacks with Pizza," *Fortune,* 26 February 1990, pp. 87–89; R. Gibson and R. Johnson, "Big Mac, Cooling Off, Loses Its Sizzle," *The Wall Street Journal,* 29 September 1989; and P. Moser, "The McDonald's Mystique," *Fortune,* 4 July 1988, pp. 112–116.

57. K. Kerwin and A.N. Fins, "Disney Is Looking Just a Little Fragilistic," *Business Week,* 25 June 1990, pp. 52–54; B. Dumaine, "Creating a New Company Culture," *Fortune,* 15 January 1990, p. 128.

58. J.P. Kotter and J.L. Heskett, *Corporate Culture and Performance* (New York: The Free Press, 1992).

59. Pringle et al., *Managing Organizations,* p. 309.

60. Schein, *Organizational Culture,* p. 30.

61. Ibid., p. 33.

62. This account is largely based on "The Transformation of EDS' Culture," *Open Line EDS* 11 (Spring 1990): 2–6; "Interview," *Open Line EDS* 11 (Spring 1990): 7–9; and, to a lesser extent, on Pringle et al., *Managing Organizations,* p. 310.

63. "The Transformation of EDS' Culture," p. 2.

64. Bass, *Leadership and Performance,* p. 24.

65. This discussion is based on Schein, *Organizational Culture,* pp. 224–237.

66. Kotter and Heskett, *Corporate Culture and Performance,* p. 142.

67. "Changing the Culture at General Foods," *Business Week,* 10 February 1986, pp. 52–57.

68. Schein, *Organizational Culture,* pp. 237–242.

69. M. Alpert, "Office Buildings for the 1990s," *Fortune,* 18 November 1991, pp. 141–142; T.R.V. Davis, "The Influence of the Physical Environment in Offices," *Academy of Management Review* 9 (1984): 273.
70. W.E. Sheeline, "Making Them Rich Down Home," *Fortune,* 15 August 1988, pp. 50–55.
71. Schein, *Organizational Culture,* p. 317.
72. Ibid., pp. 316 317, 320.

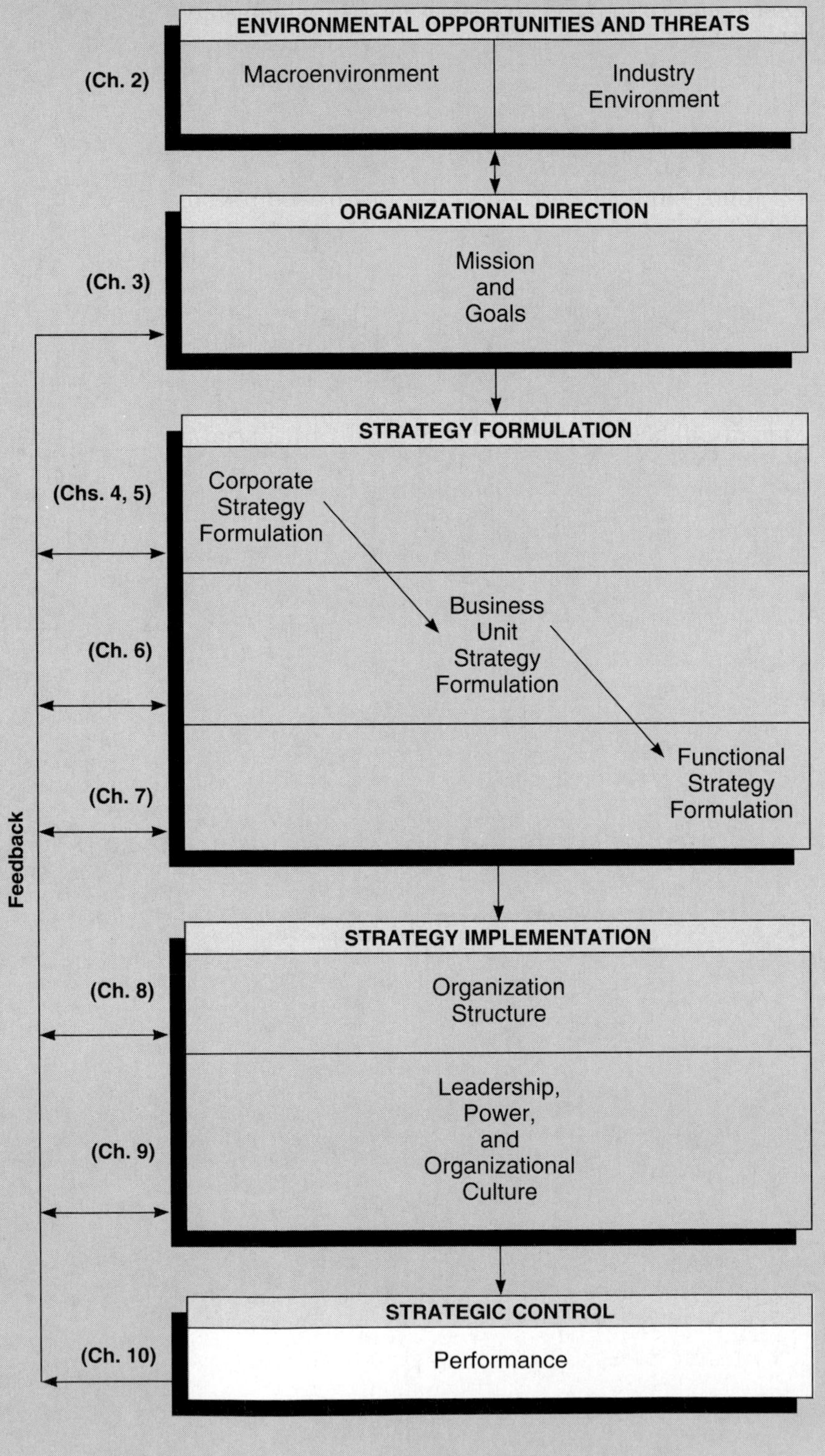
STRATEGIC MANAGEMENT MODEL
ENVIRONMENTAL OPPORTUNITIES AND THREATS
(Ch. 2)
Macroenvironment
Industry Environment
ORGANIZATIONAL DIRECTION
(Ch. 3)
Mission and Goals
STRATEGY FORMULATION
(Chs. 4, 5)
Corporate Strategy Formulation
(Ch. 6)
Business Unit Strategy Formulation
(Ch. 7)
Functional Strategy Formulation
Feedback
STRATEGY IMPLEMENTATION
(Ch. 8)
Organization Structure
(Ch. 9)
Leadership, Power, and Organizational Culture
STRATEGIC CONTROL
(Ch. 10)
Performance

10

Strategic Control

The activities of planning, implementing, and controlling are closely linked. Chapters 3, 4, 5, 6, and 7 focused on planning—establishing the organization's mission and goals and developing its corporate-level, business unit, and functional strategies. Then, implementing those strategies was discussed in Chapters 8 and 9. We now turn to the task of control.

Strategic control consists of determining the extent to which the organization's strategies are successful in attaining its goals and objectives. If the goals and objectives are not being reached as planned, then the intent of control is to modify the organization's strategies and/or implementation so that the organization's ability to accomplish its goals will be improved.

Control, in the business administration sense, is most often discussed in the context of budgeting. It is important to understand that strategic control is much broader than this traditional usage of the term. In the control of budgeted expenditures, the focus is usually for a time span of a year or less; quantitative measurements are used to determine whether actual expenditures are exceeding planned spending; the emphasis is on internal operations; and corrective action is often taken after the budget period has elapsed. But in strategic control, the focal time period usually ranges anywhere from a few years to over a decade; qualitative and quantitative measurements are taken; management assesses both internal operations and the external environment; and the process is ongoing, because top management cannot wait for several years to evaluate results. By then, it may be too late. These differences are summarized in Table 10.1.

OVERVIEW OF THE STRATEGIC CONTROL PROCESS

The strategic control process consists of several steps. First, top management must decide what elements of the environment and of the organization need to be monitored, evaluated, and controlled. Then, standards must be established with which the actual performance of the organization can be compared. These first two steps will be strongly influenced by the organization's mission, goals, and objectives, which direct management's attention to certain organizational and environmental elements and to the relative importance of particular standards.

Table 10.1 **Differences Between Strategic Control and Budgetary Control**

Strategic Control	*Budgetary Control*
Time period is lengthy—ranging from a few years to over ten years.	Time period is usually one year or less.
Measurements are quantitative and qualitative.	Measurements are quantitative.
Concentration is internal and external.	Concentration is internal.
Corrective action is ongoing.	Corrective action may be taken after budget period has elapsed.

Next, management must evaluate the company's actual performance. These evaluations will generally be both quantitative and qualitative. The performance evaluations will then be compared with the previously established standards. If performance is in line with the standards or exceeds them, then no corrective action is necessary. (When performance exceeds standards, management should consider whether the standards are appropriate and whether they should be raised.) However, if performance falls below the standards, then management must take remedial action. These steps are delineated in Figure 10.1.

FOCUS OF STRATEGIC CONTROL

The focus of strategic control is both internal and external. Neither element can be examined in isolation, because it is top management's role to align advantageously the internal operations of the enterprise with its external environ-

Figure 10.1 **Steps Involved in Strategic Control**

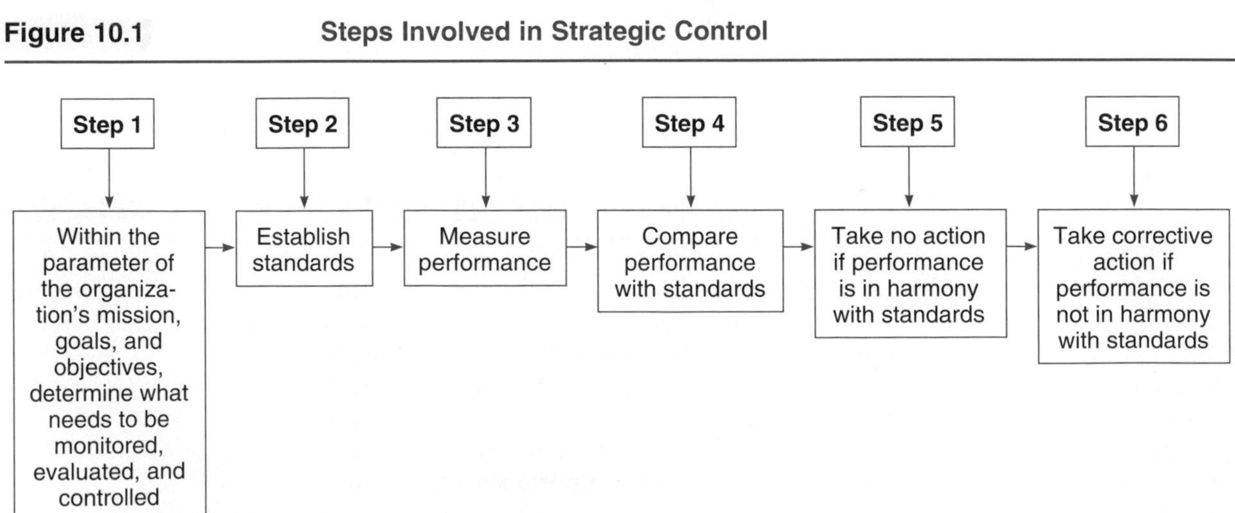

ment. In fact, strategic control can be visualized as "mediating" the ongoing interactions between environmental variables and the company's internal dimensions. Relying upon quantitative and qualitative performance measures, top management uses strategic control to keep the firm's internal dimensions aligned with its external environment. The role of strategic control as a mediator is portrayed diagrammatically in Figure 10.2.

The following sections discuss three key areas that must be monitored and evaluated in the process of strategic control: the macroenvironment, the industry environment, and internal operations.

■ Macroenvironment

The first focus of the strategic control process is usually the organization's macroenvironment. Although individual businesses normally exert little, if any, influence over the forces in the macroenvironment, these forces must be continuously monitored. Changes or shifts in the macroenvironment have strategic ramifications for the company. Consequently, strategic control involves continuously examining the fit between the company and its changing external environment.

In this context, strategic control consists of modifying the company's operations to defend itself better against external threats that may arise and to capitalize on new external opportunities. For instance, during the economic downturn of the early 1990s, several discerning companies prospered by taking advantage of recession-induced opportunities. Campbell Soup, for example, reacted to the trend toward less expensive cook-at-home products by

Strategic Control as a Mediator **Figure 10.2**

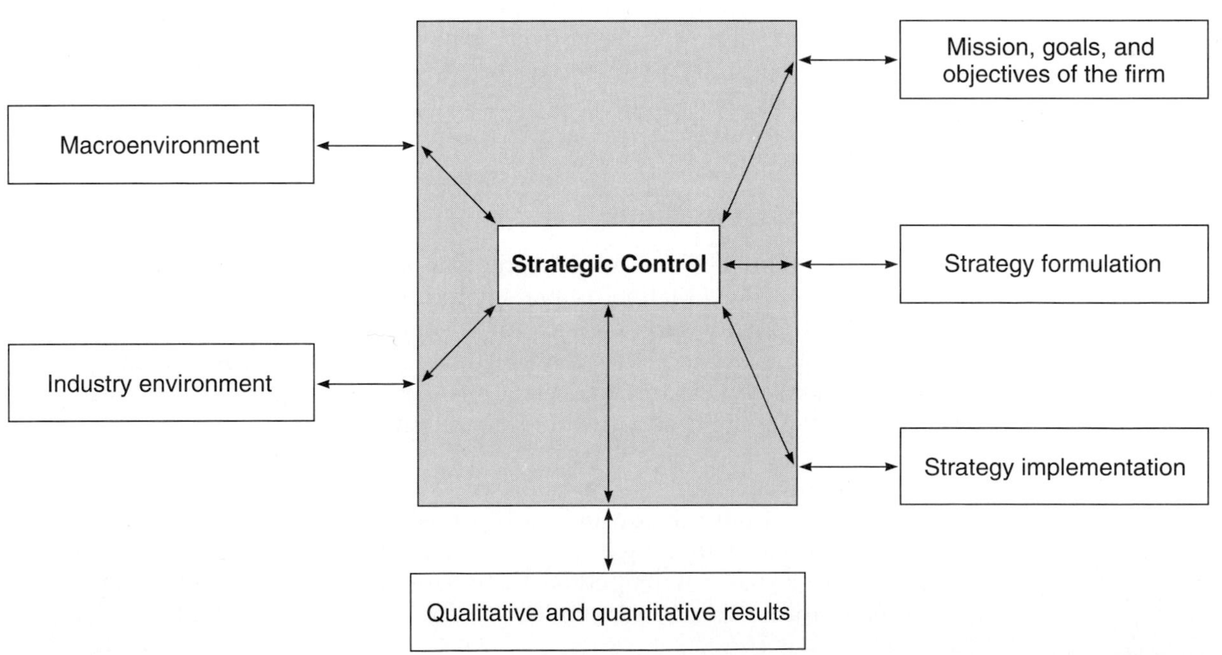

repackaging its high-end Gold Label cream of broccoli soup into the red-and-white can and marketing it as a base for meals that could be prepared at home. In slightly more than a year, consumers bought 55 million cans, making it one of Campbell's best-sellers ever.[1]

Another company that prospered during the economic rough times was Electronic Transaction Corporation. This relatively small business, which verifies checks written by customers, attracted 115 new clients in 1991, among them such retailing giants as Wal-Mart and Kmart.[2]

■ Industry Environment

Strategic control also involves monitoring the industry environment. Again, the purpose is to modify the company's operations so that it can better defend itself against threats and better capitalize on opportunities. It is important to remember in this regard that environmental analysis—both at the macroenvironment and at the industry levels—is not confined to the past or present; top management also needs to estimate future environmental trends.

Take, for instance, the response of one car producer to escalating costs in the automobile industry. BMW, in expanding its manufacturing operations, decided to escape Germany's average 1992 hourly labor cost per car of $24.36 by locating its new plant in South Carolina. (U.S. average hourly labor costs per car were only $15.39; additionally, the average U.S. autoworker received twenty-three annual vacation days and holidays compared to forty-two days in Germany.) BMW hoped that this lowering of production costs would enable it to price its cars more competitively vis-à-vis such Japanese products as Lexus and Infiniti.

Through this decision, BMW is using strategic control to look toward the future. Its U.S. and Japanese competitors are becoming increasingly cost-efficient while, at the same time, continuing to improve product quality. As Nissan, Toyota, and Honda open manufacturing plants in Europe, and GM Europe continues to enjoy considerable success, BMW finds itself surrounded on all sides. Hence, it wants to become more globally competitive by producing cars in the United States—the world's largest auto market. By reducing its manufacturing and shipping costs, BMW hopes to reverse its recent sales decline in the United States by 1995.[3]

■ Internal Operations

Strategic control also involves the internal operations of the business through monitoring and evaluating its strategy formulation and implementation. Corrective action may then be necessary. Monitoring and evaluating the company's operations involve viewing its present and future strategic posture relative to its past posture and that of its rivals. The bases for monitoring and evaluating are the qualitative and quantitative standards established by top management.

Qualitatively, the broad question asked is: How effective is our strategy in accomplishing our mission and goals? Consider the goal of product leadership, for instance. In evaluating its product leadership, an organization compares its products with those of competitors and determines the extent to which it pioneers in the introduction of basic products and product improvements.

But pioneering is not enough. A company must also follow through. Xerox, for instance, introduced the first commercial fax machine in 1964, but today, its machines account for only 7 percent of U.S. fax sales. Likewise, Raytheon was the first company to market a microwave oven—in 1947—but today, 75 percent of all microwave ovens in U.S. homes are made in the Far East.[4]

In the broad quantitative sense, management will ask: How effective is our strategy in attaining our objectives? (Recall that objectives are specific, quantifiable versions of goals, which, in turn, are desired general ends toward which organizational efforts are directed.) For instance, management can compare the firm's 11.2 percent rate of return on investment over the past year with its stated objective of 10 percent and conclude that its strategy has been effective in that particular respect.

Whether evaluating a strategy's effectiveness is undertaken relative to the company's rivals or relative only to itself, the point of strategic control is to take corrective action if negative gaps exist between intended and actual strategic results. Viewed in this fashion, strategic control has provided the impetus for the development of portfolio frameworks, presented in Chapter 5, and it underlies the PIMS program discussed in the following section.

STRATEGIC CONTROL STANDARDS

Evaluating an enterprise's performance may be accomplished in a number of ways. Management, for instance, often compares current operating results with those from the preceding year. A qualitative judgment may be made about whether the business's products or services are superior to, inferior to, or about the same as last year's. Several quantitative measures may also be used, including return on investment (ROI), return on assets (ROA), return on sales (ROS), and return on equity (ROE).

Confining control standards only to comparisons of current performance versus past performance, however, can be myopic, because it ignores important external variables. For example, assume that a business's ROI has increased from 8 to 10 percent over the past year. Management might consider that a significant improvement. But the meaning of this measure depends upon the industry in which the company operates. In a depressed industry, an ROI of 10 percent may be outstanding, but that same return in a growth industry will be disappointing, since the leading firms may earn 15 to 20 percent. An improvement in a company's ROI is less encouraging, then, if its past performance has been significantly behind that of its major competitors.

Increasingly, strategic control standards are based on the practice of **competitive benchmarking**—the process of measuring a firm's performance against that of the top performers in its industry. After determining the appropriate benchmarks, a firm's managers then set goals to meet or exceed the performance of the firm's top competitors. Taken to its logical conclusion, competitive benchmarking—if practiced by all of the firms in an industry—would result in increased industrywide performance.

This section examines a variety of competitive benchmarking standards that can be used for strategic control. These standards can be based on data derived from the PIMS program, published information that is publicly available,

STRATEGIC INSIGHT

Competitive Benchmarking at Xerox and Ford

Competitive benchmarking is the process by which one organization learns how other firms perform specific activities more efficiently. The first major adopter of this technique was Xerox, a firm that was shocked in 1979 when Japanese competitor Canon introduced a mid-sized copier for a retail price that was below Xerox's *production costs*. At first, Xerox managers thought that Canon was selling its copier below cost to capture market share, but investigation revealed that Canon was simply far more efficient than Xerox.

As a response, Xerox began a successful turnaround by not only studying how Canon achieved its cost efficiencies, but by investigating how other firms performed certain functions. In one case, for instance, it observed the product shipping process at L.L. Bean (an outdoor clothing manufacturer and catalog retailer). Bean's order-filling system was similar to Xerox's in that both required employees to handle products that varied in shape and size, but Bean could fill orders three times as fast as Xerox. As a result of imitation, Xerox reduced its order-filling costs by 10 percent.

More recently, Ford learned that its strategic alliance partner, Mazda, was processing accounts payable with fewer than ten employees. Ford, which had 500 accounts payable processing workers, studied Mazda's system carefully and, by 1993, had reduced its staff by 75 percent.

Experts on competitive benchmarking emphasize that an organization must first understand its own processes in detail before studying those of other firms. And it is imperative that the individuals sent to observe those processes in other firms are the people who actually must implement the changes within their own organization. But they are cautioned that any changes they introduce into their own department or division are likely to affect processes in other parts of the organization.

SOURCES: O. Port and G. Smith, "Beg, Borrow—And Benchmark," *Business Week*, 30 November 1992, pp. 74–75; and J. Main, "How to Steal the Best Ideas Around," *Fortune*, 19 October 1992, pp. 102–106.

ratings of product/service quality, innovation rates, and relative market share standings. Viewed broadly, these standards include both quantitative and qualitative information.

■ PIMS Program

Clearly, then, a thorough evaluation of a business's performance must take into account the performance of its competitors. For that reason, the PIMS program was developed; the **PIMS (profit impact of market strategy) program** is a data base that contains quantitative and qualitative information on the performance of more than three thousand business units. It helps management of participating companies evaluate the performance of their companies relative to the performance of other businesses in the same industry. When a company's results compare unfavorably with others in the same industry, strategic control is required.

PIMS was developed as a result of General Electric's efforts to evaluate systematically the performance of its business units in the 1960s.[5] Using a program developed by Professor Sidney Schoeffler of Harvard University, GE's

STRATEGIC INSIGHT

Broadening a Myopic Perspective at GM

Three decades ago, General Motors developed a quantitative standard for measuring the quality of the automobiles it was manufacturing. On its scale, a score of 100 was perfect; each defect a new car contained lowered its score by one point. So a car with a score of 80 contained 20 defects. GM's management established a score of 60 as "passing."

But when too many cars failed to attain a passing grade, rather than take corrective action and improve the quality of its outputs, management decided to modify the standard. The new standard for perfection was raised from 100 to 145. As a result, a car with 41 defects that would have "failed" under the old standard now had a passing score of 104.

GM and the other U.S. automakers, however, became increasingly serious about product quality as pressure from foreign competition steadily increased during the 1970s. But even by 1980, the quality of American-made cars was still suspect. A Detroit consulting firm, Harbour & Associates, reported that GM's 1980 cars averaged 7.4 defects per car, Chrysler's averaged 8.1, and Ford's averaged 6.7. Meanwhile, Japanese-made autos averaged only 2.0 defects.

American manufacturers continued to stress quality improvements throughout the 1980s and into the present decade, however. By 1992, a GM factory in Oklahoma City produced the most defect-free cars (Buick Centuries and Oldsmobile Cutlass Cierras) of any plant in North America—.71 defect per car. Second was a Toyota plant in Ontario.

GM increasingly began to realize the role that customer service played in quality considerations. When 1,836 of its new Saturn sedans were recalled because they left the factory with improperly mixed antifreeze that would create holes in the cooling systems, GM took a large step forward in customer service. Rather than recall the cars for free repairs, the usual approach of automakers, GM offered to exchange each car with the defective coolant for a new Saturn.

This service-oriented approach, combined with Saturn's superb quality (it now has the same low defect rate as Honda), resulted in Saturn dealers' selling an average of 115 cars per month—twice the sales/dealer rate of second-place Toyota.

SOURCES: D. Woodruff, J.B. Treece, S.W. Bhargava, and K.L. Miller, "Saturn," *Business Week,* 17 August 1992, p. 86; K. Kerwin, J.B. Treece, T. Peterson, L. Armstrong, and K.L. Miller, "Detroit's Big Chance," *Business Week,* 29 June 1992, p. 89; J.B. Treece, "Getting Mileage from a Recall," *Business Week,* 27 May 1991, pp. 38–39; P. Ingrassia, "Auto Industry in U.S. Is Sliding Relentlessly into Japanese Hands," *The Wall Street Journal,* 16 February 1990; A. Taylor III, "Why U.S. Carmakers Are Losing Ground," *Fortune,* 23 October 1989, p. 100; M. Keller, *Rude Awakening: The Rise, Fall, and Struggle for Recovery of General Motors* (New York: Morrow, 1989), pp. 29–30.

top managers and corporate staff began to assess business unit performance in a formal, systematic fashion. Subsequently, other companies were invited to join the project, and in 1975, Professor Schoeffler founded the Strategic Planning Institute to conduct PIMS research. The program now consists of more than three thousand business organizations.

Each of the participating businesses provides quantitative and qualitative information to the program. Included are data on variables such as relative market share, product/service quality (relative to leading competitors), new products and services introduced as a percentage of sales, relative prices of products and services, marketing expenses as a percentage of sales, value of plant and equipment relative to sales, and research and development expenses as a percentage of sales. Two profitability measures are used: net operating profit before taxes as a percentage of sales (ROS), and net income before taxes as a percentage of total investment (ROI) or of total assets (ROA).

Each of these variables may be used for strategic control purposes. For instance, if a business's product quality is consistently judged to be below average in its industry, then this information can be used to improve quality. Below-average profitability signals management that changes in strategy formulation or implementation may be necessary.

To take full advantage of PIMS, a business needs to be a participating member of the PIMS program. However, all businesses may improve their strategic control by comparing their situations with some of the PIMS principles.[6] PIMS, of course, is not the only source of strategic control data. A number of other information bases are discussed in the following section.

■ Published Information for Strategic Control

Fortune annually publishes the most- and least-admired U.S. corporations with annual sales of at least $500 million in such diverse industries as electronics, pharmaceuticals, retailing, transportation, banking, insurance, metals, food, motor vehicles, and utilities. Corporate dimensions are evaluated along the following eight lines:

- Quality of products/services
- Quality of management
- Innovativeness
- Long-term investment value
- Financial soundness
- Community and environmental responsibility
- Use of corporate assets
- Ability to attract, develop, and keep talented people

The most-admired companies are those that rank high on these variables, and, interestingly enough, they are also businesses that exhibit relatively high profitability.

Although *Fortune*'s list consists of very large, publicly traded companies, the information in the listing may nevertheless provide valuable guidelines for the strategic control of smaller businesses in similar industries. In addition to *Fortune*, publications such as *Forbes*, *Industry Week*, *Business Week*, and *Dun's Business Month* also evaluate the performance of companies in various industries.

Which particular measures of comparison to use, of course, must be determined by top management. But a number of competitive benchmarking variables are considered important for strategic control because they significantly affect performance. They are discussed in the following sections.

■ Product/Service Quality

Interestingly, over the years, there has been a positive relationship between the quality of products and services that companies produce and the profitability of those firms. This relationship is illustrated by the *Fortune* listing just described. Recall that quality has two key aspects—the conformance of a product or service to the internal standards of the firm and the ultimate consumer's perception of the quality of that product or service. It is important to distinguish between these two aspects of quality, because a number of products that have conformed to internal standards have not sold well. So although conformance to standards is a necessary condition for a product's or service's success, it is not sufficient. Ultimately, a firm's outputs must be perceived as superior by the marketplace.[7]

To evaluate product quality, *Fortune* asks some eight thousand executives, outside directors, and financial analysts to judge the outputs of the largest firms in the United States. About four thousand responses are usually received.[8] According to the results, those firms whose outputs are perceived to possess high quality are also the higher-performing companies.

Taking a different approach, the PIMS program assesses quality through judgments made by both managers and customers.[9] A meeting is held by a team of managers in each of the PIMS participating businesses. These managers identify product/service attributes that they believe influence customer purchases. They then assign a weight to each attribute. Finally, they rate the quality of each attribute of their company's outputs relative to those of the products/services produced by the leading competitors in their industry. These ratings are augmented by survey results from customers who also rate the quality of the products produced by businesses in the industry. The results of the PIMS program suggest a strong positive correlation between product quality and business performance.

One publication, *Consumer Reports,* may be used by executives as a means for strategic control of output quality. Literally hundreds of products are evaluated by this publication annually. Since the evaluation by *Consumer Reports* is unbiased (it does not accept advertising), it is an excellent source of product quality information for competing businesses. Even if the products of a particular business are not evaluated by this publication, that company can still gain insight on its competitors' product quality.

Specific published information may also exist for select industries. Perhaps the best known is the "Customer Satisfaction Index" released annually by J.D. Power for the automobile industry. A questionnaire survey of seventy thousand new-car owners each year examines such variables as satisfaction with eighty-one aspects of vehicle performance; problems reported during the first ninety days of ownership; ratings of dealer service quality; and ratings of the sales, delivery, and condition of new vehicles.[10]

Certainly, it is imperative that an enterprise, regardless of its size, engage in some means of assessing the relative quality of its products and services. If the quality of its outputs compares favorably with that of the competition, then no direct action may be necessary, although emphasizing high quality in future advertising might prove to be advantageous. If the company's outputs do not compare favorably with the competition's, then corrective action is essential.

■ Innovation

Innovation may be conceptualized, measured, and controlled in different ways. Many researchers have approached this subject by focusing on expenditures for product research and development (R&D) and process R&D.[11] These studies conclude that the more money spent on developing new or improved products and processes, the higher the level of innovation is likely to be. This same approach is taken in the PIMS program.

Some firms plan and control their programs for innovation very carefully. 3M, for instance, has established a standard that 25 percent of each business unit's sales should come from products introduced to the market within the past five years. The standard is taken quite seriously by 3M managers, since "meeting the 25% test is a crucial yardstick at bonus time."[12] Currently, almost a third of 3M's sales come from products introduced within a five-year period. Not surprisingly, 3M invests between 6 and 7 percent of its sales revenue in R&D, a figure that is double the average of U.S. industry.[13]

Some observers have suggested that the strategic control of innovation must emphasize incremental improvements in products and services rather than sweeping, fundamental innovations. Several attribute the Japanese superiority over U.S. business performance in some industries to the Japanese emphasis on incremental innovations. A continuous series of incremental innovations means that each year, the company's outputs improve as a result of small, but numerous and cumulative, innovations.[14]

■ Relative Market Share

A business's size and market share, relative to its largest rivals in the industry, are important in formulating and implementing strategy and in controlling the company's strategic direction. Recall from Chapter 6 that both small and large market shares can lead to high performance. In large, leading companies, relative market share and growth in relative market share play important roles in managerial performance evaluations.[15] Managers at all levels in the organization are partially evaluated on their contributions to the company's gains in relative market share. Such gains, of course, also depend upon other strategic variables, such as product quality, innovation, pricing, and industry forces. Thus, changes in relative market share may serve as a strategic control gauge for both internal and external variables.

For instance, several years ago, Johnson & Johnson chose to extend its product line of baby shampoo, baby powder, and baby oil to mail-order educational toys. But after a decade, its annual toy sales had still not exceeded $25 million, a very small share of the gigantic toy market. In 1989, newly appointed chairman and CEO Ralph S. Larsen made the strategic decision to divest the toy business. As he stated, "If a business doesn't have a reasonable prospect of achieving leadership, we have a responsibility to exit it."[16]

For successful smaller businesses, relative market share serves as a strategic control barometer in another way. The discussion in Chapter 6 suggested that some businesses may strategically plan to maintain a low market share. In this event, the strategic control of market share may emphasize variables that do not promote market share growth. Such variables may include policies that encourage high prices and discourage sales events and price discounts. Empirical research has concluded that for certain companies in particular industries, emphasizing increases in relative market share is counterproductive.[17]

Strategic control actions for maintaining a small market share may include limiting the number of product/markets in which the company will compete. A small market share combined with operations in limited product/markets "enables a company to compete in ways that are unavailable to its larger rivals."[18]

EXERTING STRATEGIC CONTROL

Strategic control may be exerted in a number of different ways to ensure that the organization is performing in accordance with its mission, goals, and objectives. Some of the more important ways are presented in this section.

■ Control Through Multilevel Performance Criteria

Strategic control through **multilevel performance criteria** involves setting performance standards for individuals, functions, products, divisions, and strategic business units. In the first instance, controlling individual performance depends upon what the individual employee does. An office worker's performance might be monitored by measuring the number of orders processed per day; a factory worker's daily production could be evaluated; and a sales representative's monthly sales figures could be appraised. Some jobs, of course, are less subject to quantitative measurement. Examples include a research and development scientist, whose work might not show results for months or years; a corporate planner; and individuals who work in teams.

Control at the functional level may include controlling for the volume of production and defect rates incurred in the manufacturing function. In marketing, performance control might include evaluating sales volume and measuring the level of customer satisfaction through interviews or questionnaire surveys.

At the product, divisional, and strategic business unit levels, strategic control of performance may include evaluating productivity improvements, sales growth, and changes in market share. In a qualitative sense, performance control can also include judging how product, divisional, and strategic business unit executives cooperate with one another to attain synergy for the overall organization.

At all levels, from the individual to the strategic business unit, corrective action should be taken if actual performance is less than the standard that has been established. On the other hand, should performance in some area—such as a function, division, or strategic business unit—be far above the standard, management should attempt to ascertain the reasons for the excellent performance. In some cases, the methods that one unit is using to achieve above-standard performance can be transferred to other organizational units, thereby improving their performance as well.

■ Control Through Performance

Control through performance can take place by monitoring the company's return on investment (ROI), return on equity (ROE), or other measures of profitability that were mentioned earlier. These evaluations take the form of comparisons vis-à-vis the performance of competitors in the marketplace. The PIMS program, of course, evaluates profitability in this manner. Growth in relative market share may also be evaluated for strategic control.

In addition to monitoring and evaluating the key areas discussed earlier in the chapter, top management monitors the price of the company's stock. Price fluctuations suggest how investors value the performance of the firm. Management is always very concerned over sharp price changes in the firm's stock. A sudden drop in price will make the firm a more attractive takeover target. Sharp increases often mean that an investor or group of investors is accumulating large blocks of stock to engineer a takeover or a change in top management. Hence, managers continuously monitor price changes in their firm's stock.

Control Through Organizational Variables

A final way that strategic control can be exerted is through organizational variables. Control can be effected directly through the formal organization or indirectly through the informal organization.

The Formal Organization

The **formal organization**—the management-specified structure of relationships and procedures used to manage organizational activity—can facilitate or impede the accomplishment of the enterprise's mission, goals, and objectives. As we have already seen, the formal organization determines who reports to whom, how jobs are grouped, and what rules and policies will guide the actions and decisions of employees. Chapter 8 illustrated, for instance, how an organization's structure can become outmoded and no longer appropriate for its mission. At such times, strategic control will dictate a change from, say, a functional structure to a product divisional structure. That change will have to be accompanied by appropriate modifications in organizational reward systems so that the new forms of required behavior will be rewarded and older, less appropriate behaviors will not be.

For example, some organizations that have changed from functional or product divisional structures to matrix structures have experienced considerable difficulty. Such a dramatic change cannot be accomplished overnight, yet some top managers have evidently believed that by drawing a new organization chart and explaining it to their employees, new appropriate behaviors would naturally follow. But they do not. Employees must understand the compelling reasons underlying the change to a matrix structure to divorce them from their old ways of behaving, and they must then be trained extensively in the new types of behaviors that will be required. After this groundwork is laid, the change to the matrix structure must be accompanied by a new organizational reward system that encourages teamwork, frequent reassignment of personnel, greater participation, and open communication. Concomitantly, it should discourage loyalty to a functional area and to one supervisor.

The importance of clearly communicating the organization's values to all employees and establishing a reward system that reinforces those values cannot be overemphasized. When management overlooks the key role that values and rewards play, or when the relationship among values, communication, and rewards is inconsistent, then informal organizational patterns develop to counterbalance the flaws and inconsistencies.

The Informal Organization

The **informal organization** refers to the interpersonal interactions that naturally evolve when individuals and groups come into contact with one another.

STRATEGIC INSIGHT

Downsizing as Strategic Control

One of the most common corrections in strategic control made by corporations over the past decade has been "downsizing"—shrinking an organization's work force, permanently, to cut costs and make the firm more competitive. But two studies by consulting firms show that these results are not often attained.

Wyatt Company surveyed 1,005 firms, the majority of which had downsized during the preceding five years. Following the downsizing, only 46 percent of the firms achieved their goals of reducing expenses, only 32 percent increased profits as they had hoped, only 22 percent met their increased productivity goals, only 19 percent improved their competitive advantage as much as they desired, only 13 percent attained their sales goals, and only 9 percent reached their product quality goals.

A Mitchell & Company study of sixteen large firms in various industries revealed that, two years after downsizing, the stock prices of twelve of these sixteen corporations were trading in a range that was 5 to 45 percent below the stocks of comparable firms in their industries.

What's wrong? Although the reasons vary from one corporation to another, one common problem seems to be that the changes in the formal organization created by downsizing result in dysfunctional consequences in the informal organization. As one downsizing consultant puts it:

> The numbers might be right, the forecasts might be right and the stock analysts might approve wholeheartedly, but if the human aspects aren't managed well, the effort can go into the tank.

All too often, unfortunately, the human aspects aren't managed well. For instance, those employees who survive the cuts are often left stunned and wondering whether they'll be next. (And they often are next, according to an American Management Association study that shows that companies that downsize once are more likely to downsize again in the future.) Obviously, such emotions are not usually associated with highly motivated, committed employees.

Work force reductions are made in various ways. Some firms simply cut, say, 10 or 15 percent of their employees, "across the board." In such cases, efficient departments lose employees just as do inefficient departments. Other firms attempt to minimize morale problems by offering early retirement to employees who have been with the firm for a certain number of years. Although this technique sounds more rational, these firms are often shocked to find that "a lot of training, experience, and skills [are] going out the door. . . ."

Although workers realize that their firms must reduce expenses during tough economic times, they resent cost-cutting programs that invariably affect employees first. They recognize that there are many reasons for high costs, and employees are only one of them. Yet, they often seem to be the most expendable. But layoffs are no substitute for solving an organization's fundamental problems.

Not all companies operate this way, of course. Some attempt to retain their human resources during recessionary periods through such practices as implementing hiring freezes, retraining and redeploying workers, reducing pay temporarily, shortening the workweek, or simply never overstaffing in the first place during those earlier, more profitable years.

SOURCES: E. Lesly and L. Light, "When Layoffs Alone Don't Turn the Tide," *Business Week,* 7 December 1992, pp. 100–101; E. Faltermayer, "Is This Layoff Necessary?" *Fortune,* 1 June 1992, pp. 71–86 (source of second quotation, p. 72); A. Knox, "The Downside and Dangers of Downsizing," *The Washington Post,* 15 March 1992 (source of first quotation); A. Bennett, "Downsizing Doesn't Necessarily Bring an Upswing in Corporate Profitability," *The Wall Street Journal,* 6 June 1991.

These informal relationships can play destructive or constructive roles in helping the organization pursue its mission, goals, and objectives.

When it is obvious to everyone that what is valued by the organization is also what is actually rewarded, then the informal organization tends to promote the attainment of the organization's desired purposes. But when the organization's value system is ambiguous, or when inconsistencies exist between what is valued and what is rewarded, then the informal organization develops its own set of consistent values and rewards. For example, most organizations claim to reward high job performance. If, in fact, employees discern that most of the major promotions and pay raises actually go to individuals who have the greatest seniority, regardless of their level of performance, then this "informal value" is communicated throughout the organization. Managers' exhortations to perform better will be largely ignored by employees, because they realize that the formally touted value of high performance is vacuous.

The informal organization cannot be directly controlled by management. It can, however, be influenced indirectly by ensuring that the formal organization is consistent in the sense that it clearly communicates its values and then rewards behaviors that are compatible with those values. It may also be influenced through the informal behavior of managers.

For instance, when managers interact with employees during the workday or off-hours, employees learn quickly whether their ideas are solicited, respected, and taken seriously. Informal bonds of mutual trust and respect are translated into loyalty to the organization and to the supervisor.

Managers may also communicate informally simply through their behavior. One manager commented on his CEO's work schedule as follows:

> He was the first one in the office. His car was in the lot by 7:00 every morning, and he never left before 6 p.m. That told people a lot about what he expected from us.[19]

In another case, the owner-manager of an amusement park asks different employees to walk with him through the park during their breaks. As they walk, the manager smiles and greets customers. If there is litter on the grounds, he picks the trash up and deposits it into receptacles. If customers ask questions or appear to need directions, he assists them. The message is very clear. The owner-manager values a clean amusement park and a friendly, courteous, customer-oriented staff.

SUMMARY

Strategic control consists of determining the extent to which the company's strategies are successful in attaining its goals and objectives. If the goals and objectives are not being reached as planned, then the intent of control is to modify the enterprise's strategies and/or implementation so that the organization's ability to accomplish its goals will be improved. In strategic control, the focal time period usually ranges from a few years to over a decade; qualitative and quantitative measurements are taken; management assesses both internal operations and the external environment; and the process is continuous and ongoing.

On the basis of the organization's mission, goals, and objectives, top management selects what elements of the environment and of the organization need to be monitored, evaluated, and controlled. Then, standards are established to which the actual performance of the business will be compared. Next, management measures the company's actual performance—both quantitatively and qualitatively. If performance is in line with the standards or exceeds them, then no corrective action is necessary. However, if performance falls below the standards, then management must take remedial action.

The focus of strategic control is both internal and external. Top management's role is to align advantageously the internal operations of the business with its external environment. Hence, strategic control can be visualized as "mediating" the interactions between environmental variables (in both the macroenvironment and the industry environment) and the organization's internal operations.

Evaluating a company's performance may be accomplished in a number of ways. For instance, current operating results can be compared with results from the prior year, both quantitatively and qualitatively. However, management must also evaluate important external variables such as the performance of competitors. Several competitive benchmarks can be used, but chief among them are the focal company's relative product/service quality, its innovative ability to develop new products and services and improve its production and customer service delivery processes relative to those of its competitors, and its relative market share.

Strategic control can be exerted by top management in a number of different ways. First, management can control performance at several different levels—individual, functional, product, divisional, and strategic business unit. Control can also focus on performance through monitoring key financial ratios and changes in the firm's stock price. Finally, strategic control can be exerted directly through the formal organization by clear communication of the organization's values and a determination that the company's reward system is consistent with those values; and it can be exerted indirectly through the informal organization by appropriate managerial behavior.

KEY CONCEPTS

Competitive benchmarking The process of measuring a firm's performance against that of the top performers in its industry.

Formal organization The management-specified structure of relationships and procedures used to manage organizational activity.

Informal organization Interpersonal relationships and interactions that naturally evolve when individuals and groups come into contact with one another.

Multilevel performance criteria Performance standards that are established for each of the following levels: individual employee, function, product line, division, strategic business unit, and organization.

PIMS program A data base, termed the profit impact of marketing strategy (PIMS), that contains quantitative and qualitative information on the performance of more than three thousand business units.

Strategic control Determining the extent to which an organization's strategies are successful in attaining its goals and objectives.

DISCUSSION QUESTIONS

1. Although strategic control and control in the more traditional budgetary sense are similar in some respects, they also differ significantly. Explain their similarities and differences.

2. What roles do the organization's mission, goals, and objectives play in strategic control?

3. Explain how strategic control mediates the interactions between the business's internal dimensions and its external environment.

4. In strategic control, management might compare the organization's performance this year with its performance in previous years. What are the strengths and weaknesses of this one comparison?

5. Explain how competitive benchmarking is used in strategic control. What are some commonly used competitive benchmarks?

6. What is the PIMS program? How can it aid in strategic control?

7. "If a business unit's performance is below standard, corrective action should be taken. If its performance is above standard, no managerial action is necessary." True or false? Why?

8. What is the relationship between strategic control and changes in the firm's stock price?

9. How are organizational values and rewards related to strategic control?

10. Give an example from your own experience of a manager who communicated organizational values through his or her informal behavior.

STRATEGIC MANAGEMENT EXERCISES

1. On the basis of your own perceptions as a consumer, compare the relative quality of two competing products (other than automobiles) or services that you have purchased. How might your perceptions be used by the manufacturers or sellers of these products and services in strategic control?
2. Over the past decade, the U.S.-based automobile companies have attempted to improve the quality of their cars relative to those of Japanese manufacturers. One way U.S. executives can exert strategic control is through comparing the quality of their cars with the quality of Japanese automobiles. Assume that you are a top-level manager with one of the U.S.-based car companies. Refer to a recent *Consumer Reports* issue that evaluates cars. Determine how the quality of the American company's car(s) compares with that of its Japanese rival(s). From your strategic control assessment, would you say that the American car company should take corrective action? Justify your answer.
3. Select a company of your choice. From library research, what source or sources of information can you obtain that may assist the man-

agement of that company in making strategic control decisions? Describe the source(s), the information contained, and how the information might be used by management for strategic control.

4. Select an airline company. Conduct library research on your chosen company so that you can elaborate on how strategic control has affected the direction of the company. Recall that strategic control consists of modifying a company's operations to maintain a compatible fit between the company and the changing environment.

NOTES

1. J. Weber, W. Zellner, and Z. Schiller, "Seizing the Dark Day," *Business Week*, 13 January 1992, p. 27.
2. D.J. Yang and G. Smith, "Where Gloom and Doom Equal Boom," *Business Week*, 13 January 1992, p. 28.
3. W. Brown, "BMW to Build Car Assembly Plant in U.S.," *The Washington Post*, 24 June 1992; P. Ingrassia and T. Aeppel, "Worried by Japanese, Thriving GM Europe Vows to Get Leaner," *The Wall Street Journal*, 27 July 1992.
4. T.A. Stewart, "Lessons from U.S. Business Blunders," *Fortune*, 23 April 1990, p. 128.
5. C.H. Springer, "Strategic Management in General Electric," *Operations Research* 21 (1973): 1177–1182.
6. R.D. Buzzell and B.T. Gale, *The PIMS Principles* (New York: Free Press, 1987).
7. J.M. Groocock, *The Chain of Quality* (New York: Wiley, 1986).
8. P. Wright, D. Hotard, J. Tanner, and M. Kroll, "Relationships of Select Variables with Business Performance of Diversified Corporations," *American Business Review* 6, no. 1 (January 1988): 71–77.
9. Buzzell and Gale, *The PIMS Principles*, Chap. 6.
10. A. Taylor, III, "More Power to J.D. Power," *Fortune*, 18 May 1992, pp. 103–106.
11. Buzzell and Gale, *The PIMS Principles*, Chap. 6; P. Wright, M. Kroll, C. Pringle, and J. Johnson, "Organization Types, Conduct, Profitability, and Risk in the Semiconductor Industry," *Journal of Management Systems* 2, No. 2 (1990): 33–48.
12. R. Mitchell, "Masters of Innovation: How 3M Keeps Its New Products Coming," *Business Week*, 10 April 1989, p. 61.
13. K. Kelly, "3M Run Scared? Forget About It," *Business Week*, 16 September 1991, p. 59.
14. O. Port, "Back to Basics," *Business Week*, Special 1989 Bonus Issue, pp. 14–18.
15. Buzzell and Gale, *The PIMS Principles*, Chap. 5.
16. J. Weber and J. Carey, "No Band-Aids for Ralph Larsen," *Business Week*, 28 May 1990, p. 86.
17. W.E. Fruhan, Jr., "Pyrrhic Victories in Fights for Market Share," and R.G. Hamermesh, M.J. Anderson, and J.E. Harris, "Strategies for Low Market-share Businesses," in R.G. Hamermesh, ed., *Strategic Management* (New York: Wiley, 1983), pp. 112–125; 126–138.
18. Hamermesh, Anderson, and Harris, "Strategies for Low Market-share Businesses," p. 135.
19. J. Gabarro, "Socialization at the Top—How CEOs and Subordinates Evolve Interpersonal Contacts," *Organizational Dynamics* 7 (Winter 1979): 14.

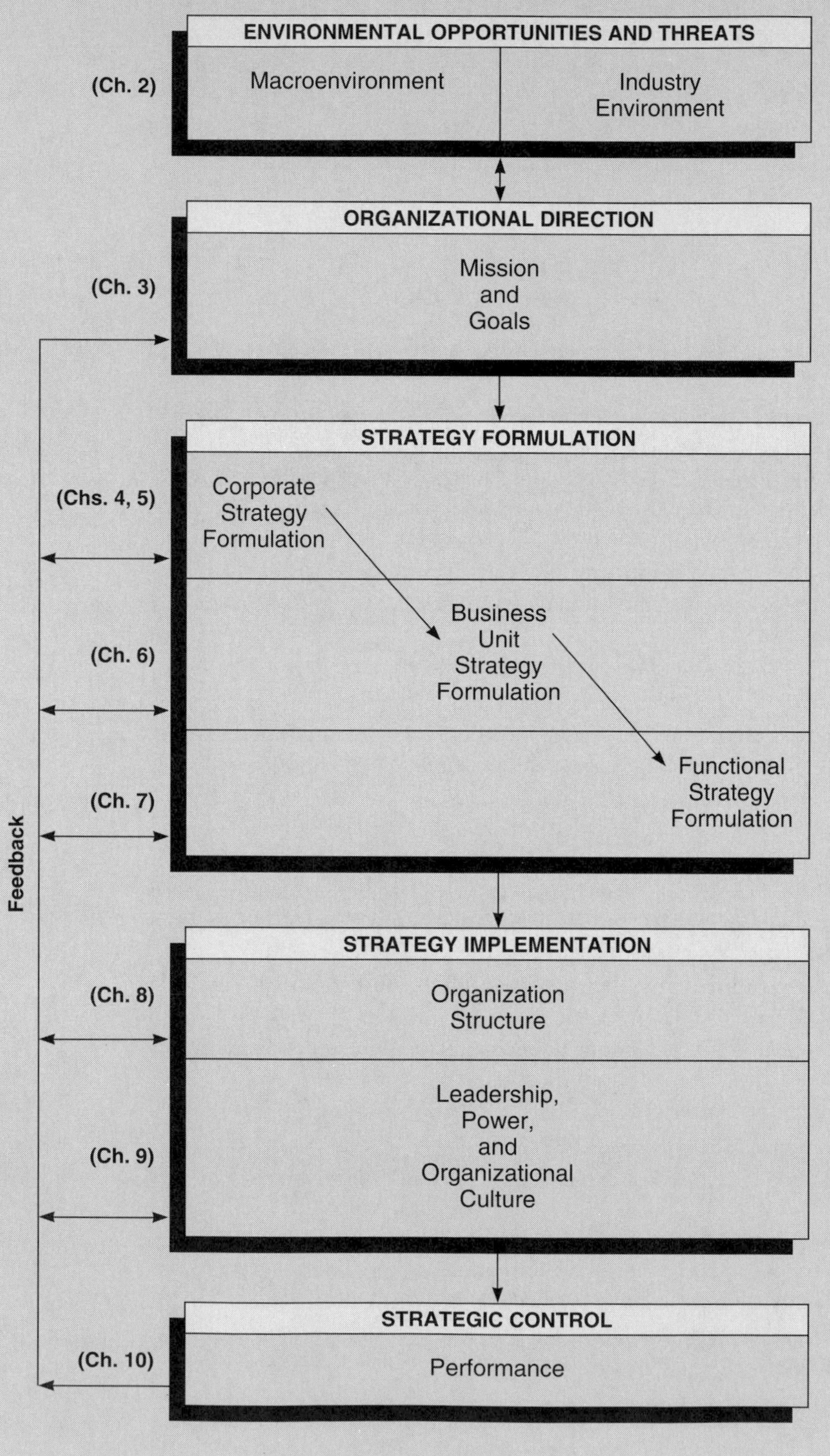

STRATEGIC MANAGEMENT MODEL
ENVIRONMENTAL OPPORTUNITIES AND THREATS
(Ch. 2)
Macroenvironment
Industry Environment
ORGANIZATIONAL DIRECTION
(Ch. 3)
Mission and Goals
STRATEGY FORMULATION
(Chs. 4, 5)
Corporate Strategy Formulation
(Ch. 6)
Business Unit Strategy Formulation
(Ch. 7)
Functional Strategy Formulation
Feedback
STRATEGY IMPLEMENTATION
(Ch. 8)
Organization Structure
(Ch. 9)
Leadership, Power, and Organizational Culture
STRATEGIC CONTROL
(Ch. 10)
Performance

11

Strategic Management and the World Marketplace

Few businesses based in the United States can escape the impact of foreign competition. Besides widely publicized international competition in such industries as automobiles, motorcycles, steel, tires, and watches, American-made goods also compete head to head in their home markets with foreign firms in product lines such as fans, luggage, outerwear, jewelry, musical instruments, dolls, hand tools, consumer electronics, sporting goods, zinc, blouses, suits, semiconductors, and shoes. Among the home bases of the 500 largest industrial corporations in the world, 34 countries are represented, including Zambia and Panama. U.S.-based corporations still dominate the list with 157 companies, followed by Japan with 119 and Britain with 43.[1] In select areas, the United States is no longer at the top. In banking, for instance, the United States places only 4 banks in the world's top 50; Japan accounts for 20, Germany has 8, and 6 are based in France.[2]

Even though a company may choose to operate only within a confined local area, that choice does not exempt the business from foreign competition. Foreign firms conduct business in virtually every industry represented in the United States. Some American-based businesses, of course, choose to operate in other countries through one or more of the ways that this chapter discusses. But in any case, virtually every top manager must have an understanding of the issues involved in international strategic management.

OVERVIEW OF INTERNATIONAL OPERATIONS

This chapter focuses primarily on businesses that choose to operate internationally. This involvement may range from limited activities such as purchasing from foreign sources or exporting to a foreign market to operating throughout the world as if there were no national boundaries. To give you some idea of the magnitude of international trade, we list some selected statistics on U.S. exports and imports in Table 11.1.

Table 11.1 **U.S. Exports, Imports, and Balance of Trade (in billions of dollars)**

Year	*Exports*	*Imports*	*U.S. Balance of Trade*
1970	42.7	40.0	+ 2.7
1975	107.7	98.5	+ 9.2
1980	220.6	244.9	- 24.3
1985	213.1	345.3	-132.2
1990	393.6	495.3	-101.7
1991	421.9	488.1	- 66.2

Source: Statistical Abstract of the United States, 1992 (U.S. Department of Commerce, Bureau of the Census), p. 796.

Ordinarily, international operations evolve gradually. Most enterprises begin their involvement with foreign countries through importing or exporting products. If particular sites overseas possess attractive resources or markets, a business may become further involved through licensing select organizations in those countries to use its technology, production processes, or brand name. Alternatively, the enterprise may enter into partnerships or joint ventures with foreign companies as a means of penetrating certain markets. Gradually, the company may become more deeply involved by initiating direct investments in select countries. Such investments may include the company's starting its own operations abroad or buying portions or all of the ownership of foreign-based organizations. U.S. and foreign direct investments are shown in Table 11.2.

In this chapter, business operations will be considered on three levels: international, multinational, and global. **International businesses** are those that are minimally or moderately involved in foreign operations. They may purchase from foreign companies, export to other nations, enter into licensing agree-

Table 11.2 **U.S. and Foreign Direct Investment (in millions of dollars)**

Year	*U.S. Direct Investment Abroad*	*Foreign Direct Investment in the United States*	*Largest Targets of U.S. Direct Investments (1990)*		*Largest Foreign Direct Investors in the United States (1990)*	
1970	75.5	13.3	1. Canada	68.4	1. United Kingdom	108.1
1975	124.1	27.7	2. United Kingdom	65.0	2. Japan	83.5
1980	215.4	83.0	3. West Germany	27.7	3. Netherlands	64.3
1985	230.3	184.6	4. Switzerland	23.7	4. West Germany	27.8
1990	421.5	403.7	5. Netherlands	22.8	5. Canada	27.7

Source: Statistical Abstract of the United States, 1992 (U.S. Department of Commerce, Bureau of the Census), pp. 786 and 789; *Statistical Abstract of the United States, 1990,* pp. 704 and 707; *Statistical Abstract of the United States, 1981,* p. 834.

Direct investment refers to investors in one country owning at least 10 percent of a private enterprise in another country.

ments with foreign-based organizations, or conduct strategic alliances with foreign firms. **Multinational organizations** are companies that are heavily involved in overseas operations through direct investments abroad. They function on a country-by-country basis, with their subsidiaries operating independently of each other. **Global firms** are also heavily involved in foreign business and have made direct investments overseas, but their subsidiaries operate interdependently. These distinctions are summarized in Table 11.3. Further elaborations on these differing levels of involvement are made in many of the following sections of this chapter. We begin with an examination of the international macroenvironment.

MACROENVIRONMENT

As an organization's environment expands from domestic to international, management faces not only a larger number of environmental elements but also far greater environmental complexity. Chapter 2 suggested how certain macroenvironmental forces have strategic implications for top management. This section follows that same format but concentrates upon international forces in the macroenvironment: political-legal forces, economic forces, technological forces, and social forces.

■ Political-Legal Forces

All nations have their own particular laws and regulations that affect business activities. Some countries, for example, have rigid guidelines for hiring and

Varying Levels of International Operations **Table 11.3**

Organization	*Level of International Involvement*
Domestic organization	Chooses to operate totally within the confines of the United States.
International organization	Elects minimal or moderate international involvement. May purchase from foreign sources, export to other countries, license operations to foreign firms, or enter into strategic alliances with foreign-based companies.
Multinational organization	Chooses heavy international involvement. Makes direct investments abroad through starting its own operations in other countries or buying part or all of the ownership of foreign-based firms. Subsidiaries operate independently of one another on a country-by-country basis.
Global organization	Elects heavy international involvement. Makes direct investments abroad through starting its own operations in other countries or buying part or all of the ownership of foreign-based firms. Subsidiaries operate interdependently as a single, coordinated system.

firing employees; some require that a certain percentage of those employed by a foreign-owned business be citizens of the country in which the business operates; and some require that a portion of what is produced within their boundaries be exported in order to earn foreign exchange. These laws and regulations that are particular to each nation offer opportunities or pose threats to the business interested in operating across national boundaries. At times, the degree of opportunity or threat is influenced by major world political-legal trends.

The years between the end of World War II and the early 1980s can be characterized as a period during which the predominant political-legal trend was for the governments of industrialized countries to exert more influence over business operations. This trend was exhibited by governments in such countries as Great Britain, France, West Germany, Italy, Canada, and Japan. In some cases, governments even owned major manufacturers. For instance, Great Britain owned Jaguar and British Leyland, and West Germany owned Lufthansa. In France, the socialist government of Prime Minister François Mitterrand nationalized some major firms such as ITT-France and Honeywell-Bull in 1981. And Canadian legislation was passed requiring that energy companies operating within the borders of Canada be owned by Canadians.

This same trend also characterized the operations of businesses in less industrialized parts of the world. Communist governments, of course, permitted little, if any, free enterprise, preferring to run their economies through centralized state planning. In developing nations, key industries such as utilities, communications, steel, and raw materials extraction were generally owned by the government.

A second political-legal trend during this time period involved increased trade protection. Many countries increased the protection of their domestic industries through tariffs, import duties, and import restrictions. For example, in Latin American countries, import duties on a variety of products ranged from under 40 percent to more than 100 percent.[3] European and Southeast Asian nations also imposed heavy duties on imports. Even the United States imposed import fees on a variety of products, including food, steel, and cars. Furthermore, the United States convinced Japanese manufacturers to restrict "voluntarily" their exporting of cars to the United States. Likewise, European countries instituted import quotas on selected products such as Japanese stereos and watches.

Protectionist measures not only involved the protection of home industries from foreign imports, but restrictions were also placed on exporting advanced technology to other countries. The United States, for instance, banned the export of certain electronic, nuclear, and defense-related products to many nations.

There were, of course, countervailing trends. To offset the impact of some of the protectionist measures, twenty-three countries entered into the cooperative General Agreement on Tariffs and Trade (GATT) in 1947. GATT has assisted in eradicating or relaxing quota and import license requirements, introducing fairer customs evaluation methods, opposing discriminatory internal taxes, and serving as a mediator between governments on trade issues. GATT membership has now reached ninety-five nations.

By the middle 1980s to the early 1990s, however, trends toward the reversal of trade protectionism and strong governmental influence in business opera-

STRATEGIC INSIGHT

Entering the Japanese Auto Market

Much has been made of the barriers erected by the Japanese government to prevent foreign-made automobiles from being sold in Japan. And, in truth, many barriers exist. But aggressive automakers seem to find ways to compete on Japanese soil.

BMW, for example, viewed Japan as a growth market as early as a decade ago. It was able to penetrate the market by adapting its models to Japanese regulations and consumer needs, offering extended warranties, investing heavily in service facilities and parts inventories, conducting its own training for Japanese mechanics, and supervising its operations closely. Its commitment was unwavering; analysts estimated that BMW paid almost half a billion dollars alone for choice real estate on which to build showrooms in Tokyo. By 1992, BMW had over 125 outlets in Japan and sold over 33,000 cars there.

Other German companies, such as Volkswagen, Mercedes, and Audi, were following suit. The result? In 1991, about two-thirds of the foreign-made cars registered in Japan were built in Germany. Mercedes and BMW each sold twice as many cars as GM, Ford, and Chrysler combined. Not coincidentally, both German automakers sold through their own dealers, while all three American companies continued to rely heavily on importers to sell their cars. And it wasn't until late 1992 that some American products began arriving in Japan with steering wheels on the right, as the Japanese prefer.

The Germans' aggressive move into Japan could pay off for years to come. Japan is the world's second-largest automobile market, and Japanese car buyers have exhibited extreme brand loyalty. In fact, some analysts estimate that almost 70 percent of them buy from the same company—and often even from the same salesperson—every time they purchase a new car.

SOURCES: "Foreign Car Sales in Japan," *Parade,* 22 March 1992, p. 16; P. Ingrassia, "Detroit's Big Three Are Trying to Conquer a New Market: Japan," *The Wall Street Journal,* 19 November 1991; K.L. Miller, "What's This? American Cars Gaining in Japan?" *Business Week,* 22 July 1991, pp. 82–83; T.R. Reid, "U.S. Automakers Grind Gears in Japan," *The Washington Post,* 23 September 1990; C. Rapoport, "You Can Make Money in Japan," *Fortune,* 12 February 1990, p. 92; B. Yates, "The Road to Mediocrity," *The Washington Post Magazine,* 17 December 1989, p. 35; M. Berger, "How Germany Sells Cars Where Detroit Can't," *Business Week,* 9 September 1985, p. 45.

tions were becoming evident. In the United States, new economic policies reduced, on the whole, governmental influence in business operations by deregulating certain industries, lowering corporate taxes, granting more generous depreciation allowances, and relaxing rules against mergers and acquisitions. A similar trend was evident in Great Britain. Jaguar, for instance, was sold to individual investors (and later purchased by Ford Motor Company), as was British Telecom. As the trend spread, France's insurance industry and previously nationalized banks and manufacturing businesses were sold to investors.

Furthermore, the countries of Europe banded together to develop a trade-free European Community. Today, Europe is moving gradually, but steadily, toward a single market of 340 million consumers. The European Economic Area, as it is called, is the largest trading bloc on earth, accounting for over 40 percent of the world's gross domestic product (GDP).[4] Meanwhile, across the

Atlantic, the United States, Canada, and Mexico proposed a North American Free Trade Agreement to create a $6 trillion tariff-free market within a decade.

This trend toward less regulation even extended to communist countries. As the countries of Eastern Europe overturned their governments, they began to permit free-enterprise operations and to invite foreign investment in their economies. As a result of these developments, numerous firms worldwide have found a more receptive political-legal climate throughout much of the globe.

■ Economic Forces

Common economic indicators such as gross national product (GNP) can suggest opportunities for businesses when an economy is expanding or, conversely, can warn of threats when the economy is contracting. But the most challenging international economic variables for strategic planners are interest rates, inflation rates, and currency exchange rates.

For example, the cost of borrowing is very high in a number of Latin American countries, with annual interest rates sometimes exceeding 100 percent. These high interest rates are often accompanied by excessive rates of inflation. In small nations, like Bolivia, annual inflation has been as high as 26,000 percent![5] But even larger and more industrialized countries, like Brazil, have experienced annual inflation rates of 2,700 percent.[6] Such common decisions as pricing products or estimating costs become almost impossible to make under such conditions. Furthermore, high inflation rates cause the prices of goods and services to rise and, hence, become less competitive in international trade.

Currency exchange rates present challenges because of their dramatic changes over time. For instance, the Mexican peso was devalued by about 75 percent relative to the world's major currencies during the 1980s. Since U.S. firms operating in Mexico received pesos for their products and services, their pesos would buy far fewer dollars than before the devaluation. The devaluation, therefore, reduced their profits considerably. By the early 1990s, wild fluctuations in exchange rates had moderated and the rate of inflation had declined in many nations of the world.

■ Technological Forces

Technology has a major impact on international business operations. For years, manufacturing firms in technologically advanced societies have sought plant location sites in countries with low labor or raw materials costs. Developing nations have generally welcomed such entrants. With them come an influx of financial resources, the opportunity for work force training, and the chance to acquire new technologies. In many cases, this interaction has benefited the developing country. Furthermore, some observers have even predicted that production technologies will be transferred from more advanced countries to such newly industrializing nations as Mexico, Brazil, Spain, Taiwan, Hong Kong, Singapore, and South Korea.[7] (In this chapter, the term **technologically advanced nations** is used to refer to the United States, Canada, Japan, Australia, New Zealand, and the major industrial powers of Europe. The term **newly industrializing nations** refers to developing nations that have experienced rapid industrial growth over the past two decades. They were identified earlier in this paragraph. **Developing nations** is the term employed to refer to countries that have not yet experienced significant industrial development and includes any country not grouped under the two other categories.)

However, the experiences of other developing nations have been quite disappointing. Although the firm's decision to operate in a foreign country is made for economic reasons, the host country often expects—but does not necessarily get—specific economic and social help in the form of assistance to local entrepreneurs, the establishment of research and development facilities, and the introduction of products relevant to its home market.[8] Such relationships do provide on-the-job training and improve the local economy, but the overall long-term contribution to the host country is questionable in the minds of some leaders of developing nations.[9]

Among the disappointments have been the results of technology transfer from the foreign firm to the host country:

> For example, firms such as Leyland Motors, General Electric, and Daimler Benz have structured plants in various [developing nations]. The basic problem has continued to be the almost total dependence of the host countries on the multinationals for the provision of parts, motors, and product innovations.[10]

However, technology transfer is not the only source of disappointment for host countries. Their leaders also point to discontent with extractive industries:

> Whatever the raw material, it is argued, the nature of extractive industry constitutes a systematic depletion of the valuable national assets of the host country, while leaving little of enduring value. . . . All the training and technological transfer of this kind are highly specific to the nature of the industry. When bauxite, coal, and other ores are exhausted, the local people's gained knowledge can rarely be transferred to other national undertakings.[11]

Within this context, some of the leaders of developing nations have acquired negative attitudes toward foreign firms. Nevertheless, these countries will continue to need the expertise of the technologically advanced nations. The key is for each party—the company and the host country—to develop an understanding of the wants and needs of the other. In an economic and technological sense, both parties need each other, and both can benefit significantly from a successful relationship.

■ Social Forces

Each of the world's countries has its own distinctive **culture**—that is, its generally accepted values, traditions, and patterns of behavior. Not surprisingly, these cultural differences interfere with the efforts of managers to understand and communicate with those in other societies. The unconscious reference to one's own cultural values—the **self-reference criterion**—has been suggested as the cause of most international business problems. Individuals become so accustomed to their own ways of looking at the world that they believe that any deviation from their perspective is not only wrong but also, perhaps, incomprehensible. But companies that can adjust to the culture of a host country will usually have the competitive edge. For instance, by adapting to local tastes rather than rigidly adhering to those of its U.S. customers, Domino's has found profitable business overseas through selling tuna and sweet corn pizzas in Japan and prawn and pineapple pizzas to Australians.[12]

Culture strongly influences the values that individuals hold. In turn, values influence the goals that individuals and organizations in a particular society set for themselves. The goals of managers in firms from technologically advanced countries, therefore, are likely to clash with the goals of the leaders of developing nations:

> On a macro-level, incongruencies in values have resulted in a major controversy over whether business unit goals should be influenced by market forces or by political priorities. The leaders of the multinationals have argued for market conditions influencing business decisions, whereas the developing nations have primarily sought corporate undertakings which benefit long-term social programs as well as business decisions which boost local employment.[13]

On a micro level, managers of firms from technologically advanced nations often hold goals that are based on valuing mass production and efficient operations. However, mass production assumes certain worker–machine ratios, and efficient operations require particular worker–machine interfaces. Thus, these managers may demand behavior from local personnel that gives priority to productivity. The local employees, however, may resist these demands because they believe, on the basis of their own values, that business decisions should be secondary to social and religious norms. For instance, in some countries, it is customary to take a nap after lunch. In others, religious requirements call for taking several breaks during the workday to pray.[14]

It is clear that cross-cultural differences in norms and values require modifications in managerial behaviors:

> Doing business abroad often requires a great deal of patience and perseverance. In America, "getting down to business" and being efficient in pursuing and attempting to close sales agreements are considered desirable. . . . The U.S. businessperson is seen as displaying perseverance by quickly moving on to the next potential customer rather than by patiently pursuing an uninterested prospect. . . . Perseverance takes on a different connotation overseas. Whereas the American persists in certain large markets to make sales, successful foreign businesspersons are tenacious with select customers within those markets.[15]

In some countries, making the first business deal may take months or even years. The reason is that until personal friendships and trust develop between the potential buyer and seller, the people of those countries are unwilling to commit themselves to major business transactions.[16] After the first breakthrough, however, business transactions may become routine.

Social norms that are not well understood by outsiders often constrain business transactions. For instance, Japanese business executives expect their clients or suppliers to interact socially with them after working hours. These interactions can consume up to three or four hours an evening, several times a week. Westerners who decline to attend such social gatherings regularly are seriously handicapped in transacting business, because these social settings are requirements for serious business relationships.

Finally, managers of U.S.-based corporations operating abroad should remember that their firms have exceptionally high visibility because of their American origins. Hence, citizens of countries whose culture encourages strong political activism may disrupt the business operations of American corporations to send a political "message" to the U.S. government. For exam-

STRATEGIC INSIGHT

Tips for Doing Business in Asia

- Realize that the Japanese rarely express negative emotions to foreigners. Hence, you can misread their intentions because they may smile even when angry.
- Exchange business cards with your hosts. Bilingual cards are especially appreciated. Show respect by carefully reading each card you receive.
- Control your physical gestures: Don't backslap, pat heads, or cross your legs. Even using your hands may make Japanese executives uncomfortable.
- Avoid jokes and conversation about politics.
- Always eat a bit of whatever food is offered; but never completely clean your plate, or you will be perceived as still being hungry.
- In Hong Kong, to signal your waiter to bring the check, pantomime a writing motion, using both hands. Never curl your index finger at anyone. That gesture is reserved for animals.
- Avoid giving flowers, since the wrong color or type can insult the recipient.
- Do not call on a company without an introduction. In Japan, particularly, meetings are taken very seriously.
- Don't employ the typical American "let's-get-to-the-point" negotiating style. The Japanese, in particular, want to get to know the people they are dealing with before doing business with them.
- Never bring your company's lawyer to a meeting before a deal is closed. Business relationships should be built on trust.
- Never brag—not even about your family. The Japanese, for instance, tend to be humble, even about their children's accomplishments.
- If you receive a compliment from a Chinese executive, deny it politely. Although the Chinese offer frequent compliments, they consider a "thank you" in response to be impolite.
- Never address South Koreans by their given names; that practice is thought to be rude.

SOURCES: J.T. Yenckel, "Fearless Traveler: Sorting Through the Chaos of Culture," *The Washington Post,* 20 October 1991; A.B. Stoddard, "Learning the Cultural Tricks of Foreign Trade," *Washington Business,* 18 June 1990, p. 11; F.H. Katayama, "How to Act Once You Get There," *Fortune, Special Issue: Asia in the 1990s,* Fall 1989, pp. 87–88; T. Holden and S. Woolley, "The Delicate Art of Doing Business in Japan," *Business Week,* 2 October 1989, p. 120.

ple, only two months after Euro Disneyland opened in France, hundreds of French farmers blocked its entrances with their tractors. The farmers wished to convey their displeasure with cuts in European Community farm subsidies that had been encouraged by the United States.[17]

INDUSTRY ENVIRONMENT

The nature of industry competition in the international arena differs from one country to the next. In some nations, competing successfully may not necessarily depend on such familiar American concepts as bargaining power, the threat of new entrants, or substitute products. Rather, engaging in competition may be possible only if the company is willing to barter by trading the firm's products and services for goods from the host country. A number of Japanese companies, as an example, trade their products for oil in some markets of the Organization of Petroleum Exporting Countries (OPEC).

The industry environment is complicated by the potential for linkages between domestic and international competitive forces. For instance, when a strong overseas competitor enters the domestic market of a firm, the firm's most effective response may be to counter its foreign competitor's move by entering its domestic market:

> Effective counter-competition has a destabilizing impact on the foreign company's cash flows, product-related competitiveness, and decision making about integration. Direct market penetration can drain vital cash flows from the foreign company's domestic operations. This drain can result in lost opportunities, reduced income, and limited production, impairing the competitor's ability to make overseas thrusts.[18]

From a global perspective, industry analysis can be quite challenging. A firm, for instance, may produce its parts in one nation, assemble them in other countries, and sell the final product to another group of nations. As an example, RCA has located its business units in such diverse countries as Taiwan, Japan, Mexico, and Canada. The operations of these business units are coordinated with those of other RCA units located in the United States. Each business unit performs complementary manufacturing or support functions. Hence, one unit may manufacture components; others may perform subassembly work, warehousing, or distribution. Each business unit is an integral link in the overall strategy of RCA's world operations.[19] As might be expected, such industry forces as market position, bargaining power of suppliers and customers, and the threat of new entrants or substitute products have different ramifications for each of RCA's business units, even though, in unison, these units produce television sets.

The world's constantly improving communication networks have, in a sense, "shrunk" some global industries to the extent that a few corporations are able to use one television advertisement to promote their products or services. Cable News Network (CNN), for instance, is beamed into 78 million households in more than a hundred countries, and MTV Network reaches twenty-eight nations. Taking advantage of this "homogeneity," Levi Strauss, for example, produces one advertisement worldwide. It promotes its jeans through ads featuring American rock music and nonspeaking actors. As the director of MTV Europe states: "Eighteen-year-olds in Paris have more in common with 18-year-olds in New York than with their own parents. . . . They buy the same products, go to the same movies, listen to the same music, sip the same colas."[20] However, most firms must still customize the advertisements for their products along particular national or regional boundary lines.

MISSION, GOALS, AND OBJECTIVES

An organization's mission, the reason for its existence, may be closely intertwined with international operations in several ways. For instance, a firm may have the need for inputs from abroad. Wrigley, the chewing gum manufacturer, would be unable to produce its products without the gum base derived from trees in Southeast Asia. Virtually all of Japan's industries would come to a standstill if imports of raw materials from other nations were halted, since Japan's natural resources are quite limited.

Organizational mission and international involvement are also connected through the economic concept of **comparative advantage.** This concept refers to the idea that certain parts and products may be produced more cheaply or with higher quality in particular countries owing to advantages in labor costs or technology. Also, certain raw materials and natural resources may be extracted more economically in particular locales. For instance, the cost of drilling for oil is significantly lower and its availability is significantly greater in Saudi Arabia than in Europe. Since oil is the basic raw material for producing many chemical products, European chemical firms have sought joint ventures with oil companies in Saudi Arabia. For this reason, Japanese chemical companies are not major world competitors. Japan has no oil, and Japanese chemical firms have, to date, been unsuccessful in arranging joint ventures with firms in oil-producing countries.

Finally, some firms' missions require international connections for prestige reasons. The attempt to surround a perfume product, for instance, with a certain "mystique" seems to necessitate New York, London, and Paris connections. You may have noticed that the more prestigious brands of cosmetics and perfumes often have "New York, London, and Paris" conspicuously inscribed on their packages.

A firm's goals and objectives may also require global involvement. To reduce costs, for example, a firm may seek production sites in foreign countries. Or for political-legal reasons, organizations may need to locate manufacturing facilities abroad. For instance, establishing production facilities in selected countries can avoid problems with protectionist trade legislation. Finally, making products in other countries helps management understand the needs of foreign customers. Ford, for example, has twenty plants in Western Europe. Manufacturing there helped Ford engineers design windshield wipers for cars engaged in high-speed driving on the German autobahns.[21]

CORPORATE-LEVEL STRATEGIES

In Chapters 4 and 5, we saw that firms have available to them several corporate-level strategies: growth, stability, retrenchment, or a combination of these. Using growth strategies, many firms attempt to gain market share to reduce their unit costs of operations. Large increases in sales are sometimes available only through global expansion. Coca-Cola and PepsiCo realized many years ago that significant increases in sales were more likely to be achieved overseas rather than in the already saturated U.S. marketplace.

Likewise, Caterpillar has become one of the world's leading construction equipment makers because of its global involvement.[22]

> Two-thirds of the total product cost of construction equipment is in heavy components—engines, axles, transmissions, and hydraulics—whose manufacturing costs are capital intensive and highly sensitive to economies of scale. Caterpillar turned its network of sales in different countries into a cost advantage by designing product lines that use identical components and investing heavily in a few large-scale, state-of-the-art component manufacturing facilities to fill worldwide demand.[23]

Corporate growth strategies may include strategic alliances, license agreements, or direct investments. **International strategic alliances** are partnerships of two or more firms from different nations that join together to accomplish specific projects or to cooperate in select areas of business. One of the best-known examples of an international strategic alliance is the automobile production facility in California that is owned jointly by General Motors and Toyota.

An **international license agreement** is the granting of permission by a firm in one country to a company in another nation to use its technology, brand name, production processes, or other operations. A fee is paid to the granting firm by the company being licensed. For example, pharmaceutical firms such as Merck and Upjohn have licensed organizations in other parts of the world to produce and sell their brands of drugs.

International franchising is a special type of licensing in which a local franchisee pays the franchisor, headquartered in another country, for the right to use the franchisor's brand names, promotion, materials, and procedures.[24] Examples may be found in hotels (Hilton), soft-drink bottling (Coca-Cola), and fast food restaurants (McDonald's).

Direct investments may take place in one of two ways. A firm may engage in internal growth by establishing physical facilities and operations in another country. Many well-known companies, such as IBM and Citicorp, pursue this route. Alternatively, a company may grow externally by merging with or by acquiring all or part of the ownership of a foreign firm. For example, Electrolux of Sweden purchased U.S.-based Poulan/Weedeater.

Stability is a corporate strategy that a firm adopts when its goal is to maintain its current size and scope of operations in the world. Such a strategy obviously would not include engaging in new strategic alliances, license agreements, or direct investments.

When a firm's performance is disappointing, a corporate retrenchment strategy may be necessary. Retrenchment may involve revising products/markets in particular nations, pruning assets and work forces in other locations, selling or spinning off parts of world operations, selling the entire business, or—in the worst-case scenario—liquidating it. Firestone, for instance, attempted to reverse its poor performance in the early 1980s by selling its operations in five foreign countries and reducing its ownership to a minority position in other foreign subsidiaries. Eventually, however, Firestone was sold to Bridgestone, a Japanese-based competitor.[25]

The following subsection examines how management can analyze the organization's strengths and weaknesses and the environment's opportunities and threats on an international scale. Then we look at the extent to which individual organizations can become involved in overseas business.

International S.W.O.T. Analysis

In determining corporate-level strategies, top management must evaluate the firm's strengths and weaknesses and the international environment's opportunities and threats. In the first part of the S.W.O.T analysis, management can use the following questions as guidelines in evaluating the company's strengths and weaknesses:

- Does the firm have a strong market position in the countries in which it operates?

STRATEGIC INSIGHT

Strategic Alliances: A Popular Way to Enter Foreign Markets

Increasingly, American companies are looking to strategic alliances as efficient ways to enter foreign markets. In the past decade, for instance, U.S.-based firms formed over 2,400 strategic alliances with European companies. And such companies as Occidental Petroleum, Atlantic Richfield, Texaco, Xerox, and Coca-Cola have engaged in strategic alliances with firms in China since the mid-1980s.

Why the popularity of strategic alliances? Both partners often hope to achieve several ends: lower the costs (and the risks) of high-technology product development, increase sales so that greater economies of scale may be attained, broaden a firm's product line by joining with a company that makes complementary products, and gain a lookout post so that other competitors' moves may be more easily tracked.

Sony's Venture with Apple Computer

A few years ago, the giant Japanese consumer electronics manufacturer, Sony, grew interested in the personal computer (PC) industry. During this same time, U.S.-based Apple Computer felt the need to expand its product line to include a small laptop computer. But Apple didn't have the required miniaturization skills. Because the PC industry is characterized by frequent product introductions and brief product life cycles, Apple's management believed that the company couldn't wait to develop internally the skills that were needed.

So Apple asked Sony to manufacture the laptop for them. The result was the Macintosh PowerBook 100, which quickly became a best-seller.

The two companies were an ideal match. For some years, Sony had produced some of the floppy disk drives, monitors, and power supplies used in Apple's larger Macintosh computers. And Apple CEO John Sculley pointed out another important similarity: "[Our] common ground is an insatiable excitement over building great products that define new markets."

Chrysler's AMC Venture with Beijing Automotive Works

Of course, some strategic alliances end in failure. After four years of on-again and off-again negotiations, American Motors Corporation (AMC), now a subsidiary of Chrysler, and the Chinese-owned Beijing Automotive Works jointly agreed to produce Jeeps. China offered not only a huge market but also low labor costs and an excellent location for exporting to all of Asia. AMC investors responded to news of the strategic alliance by pushing AMC's stock price up by 40 percent in two weeks.

But problems arose quickly. Most fundamentally, the two partners could never agree on the nature of the Jeep to be produced. And AMC learned too late that it did not have the right to convert its Chinese earnings into dollars—meaning that the venture often did not have enough hard currency to buy parts from Detroit, because most of its output was sold inside China. As the shaky partnership continued, American managers learned that Beijing Automotive Works was hoarding proceeds from Chinese sales at about the same time that China announced a hefty increase in duties on parts kits imported from Detroit. Shortly thereafter, in June 1989, the Chinese government's repression of the Tiananmen Square demonstrators convinced AMC officials to depart from the country, leaving the Chinese to run the assembly line on their own.

SOURCES: B.R. Schlender, "Apple's Japanese Ally," *Fortune,* 4 November 1991, pp. 151–152 (quotation is from p. 151); K. Rebello, "Apple Gets a Little More Help from Its Friends," *Business Week,* 28 October 1991, p. 132; P.A. Langan, "The New Look of Globalization," *Fortune,* 23 April 1990, p. 18; "Top American Joint Venture Investments in China," *The Washington Post,* 28 May 1989; L. Kraar, "Your Rivals Can Be Your Allies," *Fortune,* 27 March 1989, pp. 66–76; J. Mann, *Beijing Jeep* (New York: Simon & Schuster, 1990).

- Does the firm's product/service quality compare favorably with that of its world competitors?
- Does the firm have a technological advantage in the world regions where it operates its major businesses?
- Does the firm have a strong brand reputation in the countries in which it sells its products/services?
- Are the firm's managers and employees more talented than those of its major world competitors?
- Does the firm's financial profile compare favorably with the industry's?
- Is the firm consistently more profitable than its world rivals?
- Are the firm's product and process R&D efforts likely to produce better results than its competitors'?
- Are the firm's various world operations subject to unionization?

Answers to these questions may serve as a basis for evaluating the firm's strengths and weaknesses relative to those of its competitors.

The following questions can guide management's thinking about the second part of the S.W.O.T. analysis, the opportunities and threats that exist in the firm's external environment:

- What threats and opportunities do political-legal forces present?
- What threats and opportunities are presented by economic forces?
- What threats and opportunities do technological forces present?
- What threats and opportunities are presented by social forces?
- What is the size of the industry?
- What are the growth rate and growth potential of the industry?
- Is the industry cyclical? If so, can the cyclicality be smoothed out across different world markets?
- Is the industry subject to fluctuations in demand because of seasonal factors? If so, can these seasonal factors be smoothed out across different world markets?
- How intense is world competition in the industry?
- What is the median industry profitability? What is its potential profitability?
- Is the industry susceptible to unionization?
- What is the rate of innovation in the industry?

■ Level of Operations and Market Share

As we saw earlier in this chapter, a business may be involved only in its domestic market or it may compete overseas at one of three levels: international, multinational, or global. Within the domestic, international, or multinational context, an enterprise may compete successfully with a high or low market share. However, firms that choose to compete at the global level usually operate effectively only through maintaining a high market share. The relationship between level of operations and market share is illustrated in Figure 11.1.

Some businesses may be involved only in their domestic market. In certain cases, they may not yet be subject to foreign competitive pressures. Some realty companies that compete only in local towns serve as examples. On a national basis, these companies operate with very small market shares. Other competi-

Competing Domestically, Internationally, Multinationally, Globally, and Market Share Goals **Figure 11.1**

LEVEL OF OPERATIONS

MARKET SHARE GOALS	Domestic Organizations	International Organizations	Multinational Organizations	Global Organizations
High	Domestic, high share	International, high share	Multinational, high share	Global, high share
Low	Domestic, low share	International, low share	Multinational, low share	

tors, such as Century 21, sell real estate nationwide and have large market shares.

Moving outside the domestic market, some companies choose to be involved on an international basis. They operate in various countries but limit their involvement to importing, exporting, licensing, or strategic alliances. The act of exporting alone can significantly benefit even a small company. For instance, Vita-Mix Corporation, a small Ohio business ($15 million in annual sales), recently began exporting its blenders to such countries as Norway and Venezuela. Since that move, Vita-Mix has more than doubled its work force by hiring sixty-three new employees even though it is located in an economically depressed area and its overall market share is tiny.[26]

Still other companies are involved multinationally. They have direct investments in other countries, and their subsidiaries operate independently of one another. As an example, Colgate-Palmolive has attained a large worldwide market share through its decentralized operations in a number of foreign markets.

Finally, some firms are globally involved. They have direct investments abroad and operate their subsidiaries interdependently. Caterpillar is an example of such a firm. Some of its various world subsidiaries produce components in different countries, other subsidiaries assemble these components, and still other units sell the finished products. Caterpillar has achieved its low-cost position by producing its own heavy components for its large global market. If its various subsidiaries operated independently and only produced for their individual regional markets, Caterpillar would be unable to realize economies of scale.

Global firms must attempt to gain a high market share. Coordinating an interdependent global system is extremely complex, and this complexity—and

STRATEGIC INSIGHT

Coca-Cola: A Multinational Firm

Almost half of all the soft drinks consumed in the world are made by Coca-Cola. (Its nearest competitor, PepsiCo, has less than one-fourth of the world market.) And its overseas business is quite profitable. About 68 percent of Coca-Cola's sales and 80 percent of its profits come from 170 countries outside the United States.

What's the secret behind Coke's international success? There may be several.

First, the firm's brand name has been well known across the globe since World War II. Second, Coke's management is patient. It spent several million dollars in China and waited fifteen years to make a profit. Third, the firm pays attention to the details. Coke considers no retail outlet too small to sell its products. In Japan, for instance, Coca-Cola has held seminars for owners of mom-and-pop stores on how to compete with larger outlets. Not surprisingly, Coca-Cola–Japan is Coca-Cola's largest profit center, even larger than Coke–U.S.

Fourth, Coca-Cola is consistent, unless the situation requires flexibility. In much of the world, Coke's package, logo, taste, and advertising are the same. But in countries that are unfamiliar with soft drinks, Coke has modified the flavor of its products to conform more closely to local tastes.

Fifth, it enters new markets intelligently. For instance, to cut through red tape and speed up the entry process, Coke often offers bottling franchises to the nation's most powerful companies. Then to control the bottlers, it sometimes buys part of the firm. In the last decade alone, Coke invested more than $1 billion in bottling strategic alliances.

And the future looks bright indeed. Although annual sales growth in the United States averages only 2 or 3 percent, yearly sales increases in such large markets as Mexico and Brazil are about 25 percent. And the best news is that people outside the United States currently consume only 14 percent as much soda as Americans. The company predicts that its sales in the year 2000 will be double those of 1990. Its biggest challenge during this decade, says Chairman Roberto Guizueta, will be keeping up with demand.

SOURCES: D. Moreau, "When Coke & Pepsi Battle, More Than Cola Is at Stake," *Kiplinger's Personal Finance Magazine*, February 1992, p. 32; D. Shinsato, "Cola Wars in the Japanese Theater," *The Wall Street Journal*, 8 July 1991; W. Konrad, "The Real Thing is Getting Real Aggressive," *Business Week*, 26 November 1990, pp. 94–104; P. Sellers, "Coke Gets Off Its Can in Europe," *Fortune*, 13 August 1990, pp. 68–73; M.J. McCarthy, "As a Global Marketer, Coke Excels by Being Tough and Consistent," *The Wall Street Journal*, 19 December 1989.

expense—can be justified only when a high market share is attainable and it is feasible to coordinate the operations of multiple subsidiaries.

BUSINESS UNIT AND FUNCTIONAL STRATEGIES

Business units may adopt any one of a number of generic strategies, as discussed in Chapter 6. If low market share is the business unit's goal, then management may choose from among the strategies of niche–low-cost, niche-differentiation, or niche–low-cost/differentiation. These strategies are appropriate for domestic, international, and multinational enterprises. For instance, Rolls-Royce, an international company, uses the niche-differentiation strategy.

It maintains a small market share internationally by selling its cars only to very wealthy buyers in particular nations.

On the other hand, if the goal of a business unit is to attain a large market share, it has available the low-cost, differentiation, low-cost–differentiation, or multiple strategies. These strategies may be adopted by domestic, international, multinational, and global companies. An example of a domestic business that uses the low-cost strategy successfully is Wal-Mart. McDonald's is an international company that has experienced success with the low-cost–differentiation strategy. Colgate-Palmolive serves as an illustration of a multinational firm that has successfully employed the low-cost–differentiation strategy. And Caterpillar operates with success as a global firm using low-cost–differentiation.

No generic strategy can be successfully implemented without careful planning, execution, and coordination of each business unit's functional departments. In formulating functional strategies, managers must be aware that functions are interrelated. Each functional area, in attaining its purpose, must mesh its activities with the activities of the other functional departments. The extent to which all of the business unit's functional tasks mesh smoothly determines the effectiveness of the unit's generic strategy.

For domestic, international, and multinational companies, the coordination of functional strategies is undertaken independently within each business unit. Hence, international and multinational companies generally coordinate functional strategies on a country-by-country basis. Global firms, however, coordinate functional strategies across the firm's business units located in various countries, since their units' actions are interdependent.

STRATEGY IMPLEMENTATION

Earlier, in Chapters 8 and 9, we learned that structure and behavior are key aspects of strategy implementation. Whatever organizational structure is adopted by a business that operates in two or more countries, the relationship between its headquarters and its subsidiaries may be either bilateral or multilateral.[27] International and multinational firms generally have bilateral, independent relationships between their headquarters and subsidiaries. This type of relationship, in which the headquarters interacts independently with each subsidiary, is depicted in Figure 11.2.

There are advantages to bilateral relationships. Take, for instance, the case of Bausch & Lomb, the maker of such optical products as Ray-Ban sunglasses and contact lenses. Headquarters sets the firm's overall strategic direction and then allows local management to make all other decisions. As a result of recently permitting managers on the scene to determine the design for sunglasses—so that the designs for the European and Asian markets are now quite different—Bausch & Lomb's international sales have increased from 25 to 46 percent of its total revenue and the firm now controls 40 percent of the world market for sunglasses.[28]

Global firms, on the other hand, usually maintain multilateral, interdependent relationships between their headquarters and subsidiaries. Figure 11.3 portrays this situation in which the operations of the subsidiaries are interdependent.

Figure 11.2 **Bilateral Relationships Between Headquarters and Subsidiaries of International or Multinational Organizations**

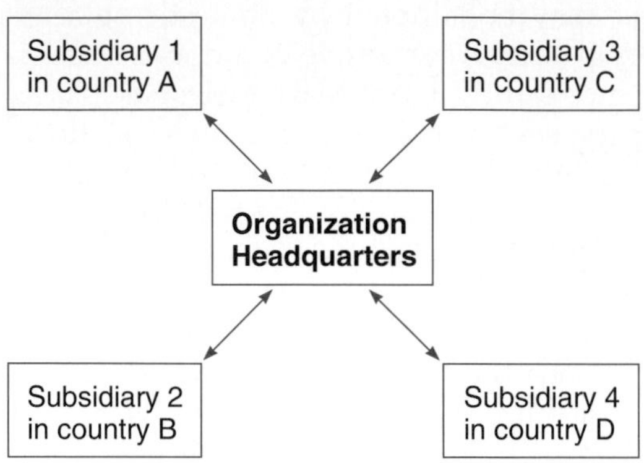

Certainly, operating outside one's own country offers special challenges in areas such as leadership and maintaining a strong organizational culture. Some countries, for instance, resist innovation and radical new approaches to conducting business. Others, however, welcome such change. Swedish companies, for instance, have led the way in employing autonomous work groups that manage themselves.

Recall the dangers of the self-reference criterion. All too often managers believe that the leadership styles and organizational culture that worked in their home country should work elsewhere. But as we have seen, each nation has its own unique culture, norms, traditions, values, and beliefs. Hence, it should be obvious—but often is not—that leadership styles, motivation pro-

Figure 11.3 **Multilateral Relationships Between Headquarters and Subsidiaries of a Global Organization**

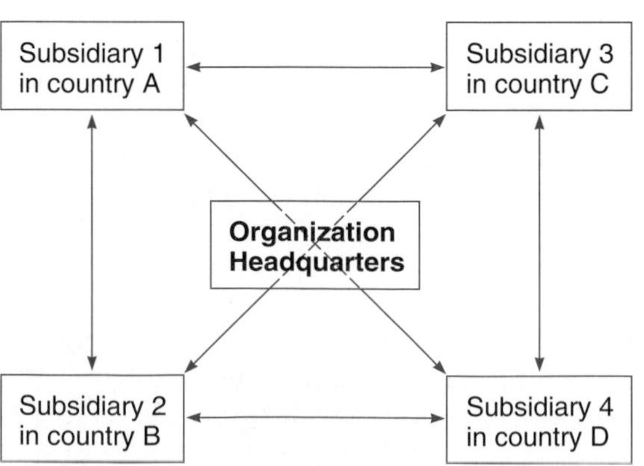

grams, and organizational values and norms must be tailored to fit the unique culture of each country in which the organization operates.

SUMMARY

This chapter focuses on businesses that choose to operate internationally. Ordinarily, international operations evolve gradually. Most companies begin their involvement with foreign countries through importing or exporting products. They may become further involved through licensing select organizations in other countries to use their technology, production processes, or brand names. Or they may enter into partnerships or strategic alliances with foreign companies as a means of penetrating certain markets. Still deeper involvement may be achieved by initiating direct investments in particular countries.

There are three levels of foreign business operations: international, in which a domestic company is minimally or moderately involved in foreign operations through importing, exporting, licensing, or conducting strategic alliances; multinational, in which the enterprise makes direct investments abroad and operates each of its foreign subsidiaries independently on a country-by-country basis; and global, in which the firm also makes direct investments abroad but operates its subsidiaries in an interdependent fashion.

Much as a domestic company does, the organization that chooses to engage in international commerce must analyze its macroenvironment and industry environment. The difference, of course, is that as an organization's environment expands from domestic to international, management faces not only a larger number of environmental elements but also far greater environmental complexity.

Within the organization, mission, goals, and objectives may be closely intertwined with international operations in several ways. Likewise, corporate-level strategies must take into account unique international considerations.

Enterprises that operate at the international or multinational level may compete successfully with either a high or a low market share, depending upon their particular mission and goals. Global firms, however, must usually maintain a high market share for effective operations.

At the business unit level, the generic strategies of niche–low-cost, niche-differentiation, and niche–low-cost/differentiation are appropriate for international and multinational businesses that desire to maintain a low market share. On the other hand, if the business unit's goal is to attain a high market share, it has available the low-cost, differentiation, low-cost–differentiation, and multiple strategies. These strategies may be adopted by international, multinational, and global companies.

In determining functional strategies, international and multinational businesses coordinate their functional activities on a country-by-country basis. Global firms, however, coordinate functional strategies across the firm's business units located in various countries, since their units' actions are interdependent.

As management implements its strategies, it must take into account the unique culture of each country in which its business operates. The leadership styles, motivation programs, and organizational culture that worked in the United States may need to be tailored to each individual international setting.

KEY CONCEPTS

Comparative advantage The concept that products or parts can be produced less expensively or with higher quality or that natural resources can be extracted more economically in particular geographic locations owing to advantages in labor costs, technology, or availability of such natural resources as minerals and timber.

Culture The generally accepted values, traditions, and patterns of behavior of a societal group.

Developing nation A country that has not yet experienced significant industrial development.

Direct investment When investors in one country own at least 10 percent of a private enterprise in another country.

Global organization A firm, heavily involved in foreign trade through direct investments, that operates its subsidiaries in an interdependent fashion.

International franchising A special type of licensing in which a local franchisee pays the franchisor, headquartered in another country, for the right to use the franchisor's brand names, promotion, materials, and procedures.

International license agreement The granting of permission by an organization in one country to a company in another nation to use its technology, brand name, production processes, or other operations. A fee is paid to the granting organization by the company being licensed.

International organization A business that is minimally or moderately involved in foreign operations. It may import or export goods, enter into licensing agreements with foreign-based organizations, or conduct strategic alliances with foreign companies.

International strategic alliance A partnership of two or more organizations from different nations that join together to accomplish specific projects or to cooperate in selected areas of business.

Multinational organization An organization, heavily involved in overseas operations through direct investments, that functions on a country-by-country basis, with its subsidiaries operating independently of one another.

Newly industrializing nation A developing nation that has experienced rapid industrial growth over the past two decades. This category includes Mexico, Brazil, Spain, Taiwan, Hong Kong, Singapore, and South Korea.

Self-reference criterion The unconscious reference to one's own cultural values.

Technologically advanced nation A nation that is grouped among the major industrial powers of the world. This category includes the United States, Canada, Japan, Australia, New Zealand, and the industrialized nations of Europe.

DISCUSSION QUESTIONS

1. Identify as many types of businesses as you can that are not directly affected by foreign competition.

2. Get the latest listing of the world's largest industrial corporations. How many U.S.-based firms are on the list? How does this figure compare with a listing from 1960 or 1970?

3. Explain how a domestic company, over time, expands to become a global firm. What are the normal stages in this process?

4. Discuss fully the differences between a multinational enterprise and a global firm.

5. What is the major distinction between an international enterprise and a multinational organization?

6. Forecast what future world political-legal trends might affect international business.

7. How do the objectives of a multinational or global organization differ from those of the host country? Why do they differ?

8. Explain how the self-reference criterion can lead to problems for U.S. managers operating abroad.

9. Why might an organization's mission influence management to engage in international operations?

10. Explain the relationship between a business's level of operations and its market share goals.

STRATEGIC MANAGEMENT EXERCISES

1. Select a well-known energy company. From your recollection of current events, what global opportunities and threats does the macroenvironment pose for this company? Identify several specific opportunities and threats for each of the following forces: political-legal, economic, technological, and social.
2. Identify a particular company in a well-defined industry, such as automobiles or computers. From your recollection of current events, analyze that company's industry environment from an international perspective. You may wish to use relevant sections of the "Industry Analysis Worksheet" from Exercise 2 in Chapter 2 to guide your analysis.
3. Acquire the annual report of a business that operates in more than two countries. Does its annual report specifically identify its mission and goals in international terms? What suggestions would you make to improve this company's mission and goal statements?

4. Using a global firm of your choice, determine what corporate-level and business unit–level strategies it has adopted. Give evidence to support your answers.

5. Assume that you are a member of the top management team of a food-processing company that follows a corporate growth strategy. Your company has decided to expand into both the western and eastern regions of the European continent. Specifically, which countries would you suggest as appropriate for licensing agreements? Why? In which would you prefer to make direct investments? Why?

NOTES

1. "The Global 500 by Country," *Fortune,* 27 July 1992, pp. 218–228.
2. "International Bank Scoreboard," *Business Week,* 6 July 1992, p. 63.
3. *International Financial Statistics Yearbook* (Washington, D.C.: International Monetary Fund, 1989).
4. C. Rapoport, "Europe Looks Ahead to Hard Choices," *Fortune,* 14 December 1992, p. 145.
5. *International Financial Statistics Yearbook.*
6. C.S. Manegold and M. Kepp, "Elegant Armed Robbery," *Newsweek,* 2 April 1990, p. 30.
7. R.B. Reich, *The Next American Frontier* (New York: Times Books, 1983).
8. A.R. Negandhi, "Multinational Corporations and Host Governments' Relationships: Comparative Study of Conflict and Conflicting Issues," *Human Relations* 33 (1980): 534–535.
9. P. Wright, D. Townsend, J. Kinard, and J. Iverstine, "The Developing World to 1990: Trends and Implications for Multinational Business," *Long Range Planning* 15, no. 4 (July–August 1982): 116–125.
10. Ibid., p. 119. Reprinted from *Long Range Planning,* Vol. 15, P. Wright et al., "The Developing World to 1990: Trends and Implications for Multinational Business," pp. 116–125, Copyright (1982), with permission from Pergamon Press Ltd, Headington Hill Hall, Oxford OX3 OBW, UK.
11. Ibid., p. 119. Reprinted from *Long Range Planning,* Vol. 15, P. Wright et al., "The Developing World to 1990: Trends and Implications for Multinational Business," pp. 116–125, Copyright (1982), with permission from Pergamon Press Ltd, Headington Hill Hall, Oxford OX3 OBW, UK.
12. M.J. Williams, "Rewriting the Export Rules," *Fortune,* 23 April 1990, p. 89.
13. P. Wright, "MNC—Third World Business Unit Performance: Application of Strategic Elements," *Strategic Management Journal* 5 (1984): 232.
14. P. Wright, "Doing Business in Islamic Markets," *Harvard Business Review* 59, no. 1 (January–February 1981): 34–40.
15. P. Wright, "Systematic Approach to Finding Export Opportunities," in D.N. Dickson, ed., *Managing Effectively in the World Marketplace* (New York: Wiley, 1983), pp. 338–339.
16. P. Wright, "Organizational Behavior in Islamic Firms," *Management International Review* 21, no. 2 (1981): 86–94.

17. "No Fun: Tourists Stranded As Farmers Cut Off 'Euro Disneyland' Site," *Harrisonburg (Va.) Daily News-Record,* 27 June 1992.

18. C.M. Watson, "Counter-Competition Abroad to Protect Home Markets," in D.N. Dickson, ed., *Managing Effectively in the World Marketplace* (New York: Wiley, 1983), p. 359.

19. P. Wright, "The Strategic Options of Least-Cost, Differentiation, and Niche," *Business Horizons* 29, no. 2 (March–April 1986): 22.

20. K. Wells, "Global Ad Campaigns, After Many Missteps, Finally Pay Dividends," *The Wall Street Journal,* 27 August 1992.

21. T. Eiben, "U.S. Exporters on a Global Roll," *Fortune,* 29 June 1992, p. 94.

22. T. Hout, M. Porter, and E. Rudder, "How Global Companies Win Out," in D.N. Dickson, ed., *Managing Effectively in the World Marketplace* (New York: Wiley, 1983), pp. 188–191.

23. Ibid., p. 189.

24. P. Chan and R. Justis, "Franchise Management in East Asia," *Academy of Management Executive* 4 (1990): 75–85.

25. Z. Schiller, "Can Bridgestone Make the Climb?" *Business Week,* 27 February 1989, pp. 78–79; "Survival in the Basic Industries: How Four Companies Hope to Avoid Disaster," *Business Week,* 26 April 1982, pp. 74–76.

26. W.J. Holstein and K. Kelly, "Little Companies, Big Exports," *Business Week,* 13 April 1992, p. 70.

27. Wright, "MNC—Third World Business Unit Performance," pp. 231–240.

28. R. Jacob, "Trust the Locals, Win Worldwide," *Fortune,* 4 May 1992, pp. 76–77.

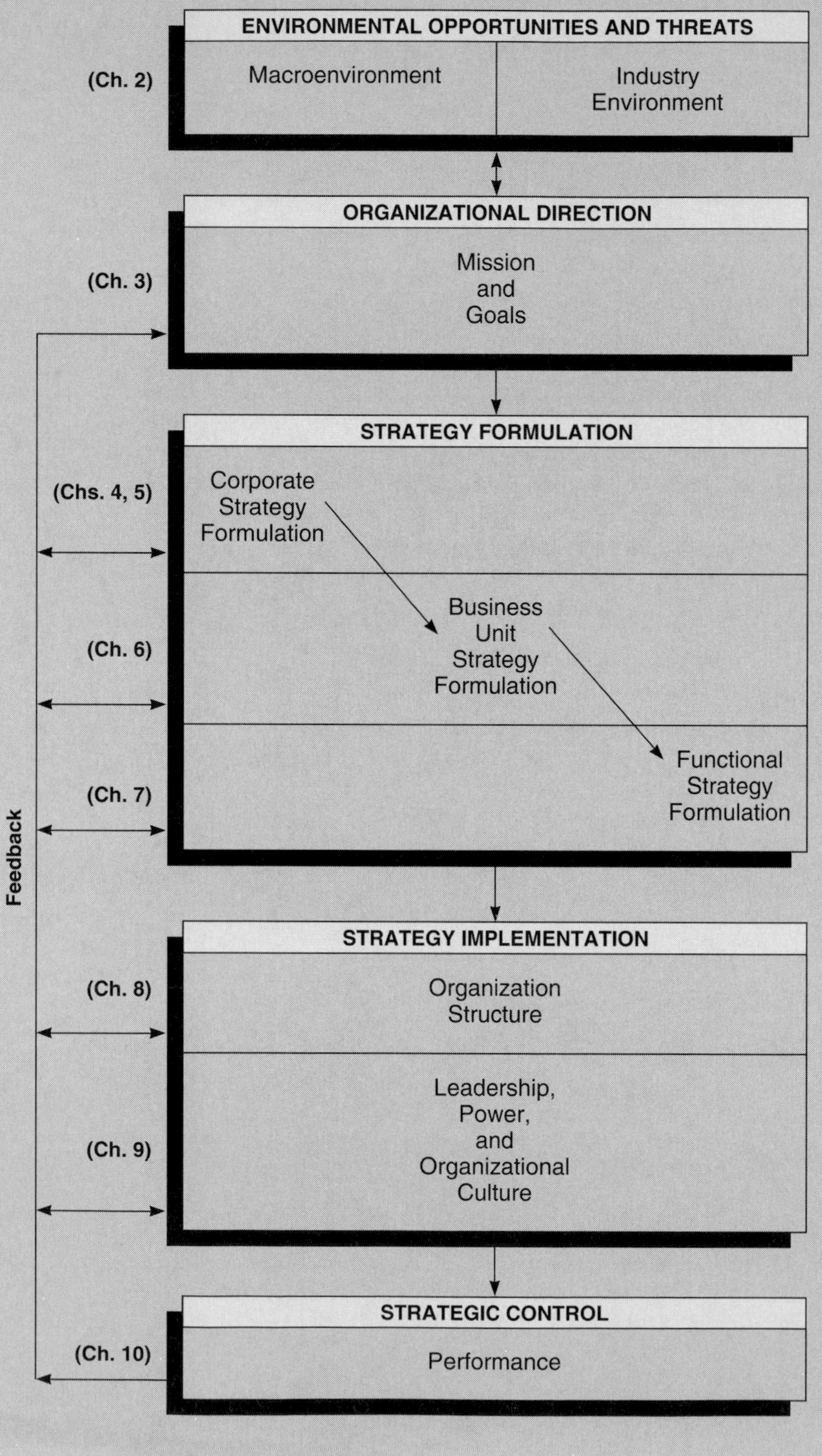

STRATEGIC MANAGEMENT MODEL
ENVIRONMENTAL OPPORTUNITIES AND THREATS
(Ch. 2)
Macroenvironment
Industry Environment
ORGANIZATIONAL DIRECTION
(Ch. 3)
Mission and Goals
STRATEGY FORMULATION
(Chs. 4, 5)
Corporate Strategy Formulation
(Ch. 6)
Business Unit Strategy Formulation
(Ch. 7)
Functional Strategy Formulation
Feedback
STRATEGY IMPLEMENTATION
(Ch. 8)
Organization Structure
(Ch. 9)
Leadership, Power, and Organizational Culture
STRATEGIC CONTROL
(Ch. 10)
Performance

12

Strategic Management in Not-for-Profit Organizations

The basic principles of strategic management presented in this book are equally applicable to profit and not-for-profit organizations. It is important, for instance, that all organizations analyze their environment; formulate a mission, goals, and objectives; develop appropriate strategies; implement those strategies; and control their strategic direction. However, in a more specific sense, there are some distinct differences between profit and not-for-profit organizations that have significant strategic implications. This chapter examines those differences.

TYPES OF NOT-FOR-PROFIT ORGANIZATIONS

Although not-for-profit organizations can be categorized in a number of ways, a basic classification consists of two groups: private not-for-profit organizations (which we will refer to as nonprofit organizations) and public not-for-profit organizations (which we will term public organizations). Some significant differences between business organizations and these two types of not-for-profit organizations are illustrated in Table 12.1.

Nonprofit organizations are entities that attempt to contribute to the good of society and are supported by private funds. Examples of such organizations include the following:

- Private educational institutions (e.g., Harvard University, the University of Chicago).
- Charities (e.g., Easter Seal Society, March of Dimes).
- Social service organizations (e.g., Alcoholics Anonymous, Girl Scouts of the U.S.A.).
- Health service organizations (e.g., Houston's Methodist Hospital, Johns Hopkins Health System).
- Foundations (e.g., Ford Foundation, Rockefeller Foundation).
- Cultural organizations (e.g., Los Angeles Philharmonic Orchestra, Chicago's Field Museum of Natural History).

Table 12.1 **Some Differences Between Profit and Not-for-Profit Organizations**

	Business Organization	*Nonprofit Organization*	*Public Organization*
Ownership	Private	Private	Public
Funding	Sales of products and services	Membership dues, contributions from private and/or public sources, sale of products and services	Taxes and user fees
Types	Single proprietorship, partnership, corporation	Educational, charitable, social service, health service, foundation, cultural, religious	Federal government, state government, local government

- Religious institutions (e.g., St. Patrick's Cathedral, Memphis's Bellevue Baptist Church).

Public organizations are those created, funded, and regulated by the public sector. They are largely synonymous with what we commonly term *government* and include agencies at all levels of government, such as the following:

- Federal government agencies (e.g., Internal Revenue Service, United States Navy, Environmental Protection Agency).
- State government agencies (e.g., University of Kentucky, Texas Department of Corrections, Pennsylvania Turnpike Authority).
- Local government agencies (e.g., Dallas Public Library, Dade County Sheriff's Department, New York City Transit Authority).

In the United States, almost 18.5 million people are employed in public organizations, more than the number employed in manufacturing jobs.[1]

Both nonprofit and public organizations are indispensable to maintaining a civilized society. Many of society's essential needs cannot be provided by for-profit organizations. For instance, most individuals could not afford to pay for private police protection; and each major city has one or more "charity" hospitals where the indigent can receive medical care.

The products and services of businesses can be obtained only by those who pay for them, but the outputs of public organizations and those of many nonprofit organizations are available to virtually all members of society. For instance, anyone—even a tourist—can receive the protection of a city's police force; anyone can travel along a toll-free interstate highway; and any child with birth defects is eligible for help from the March of Dimes. Some nonprofit organizations, of course, restrict their goods or services only to those who pay for the cost of providing the outputs. Examples are private universities (which exist to provide the public an alternative to secular or mass education) and some cultural organizations (which must sell tickets to cover their costs but also usually offer some special annual events that are free to the public at large).

STRATEGIC ISSUES FOR NONPROFIT AND PUBLIC ORGANIZATIONS

This section examines some key strategic management issues in nonprofit and public organizations. First, we look at how environmental analysis is conducted by these organizations. Then, we determine how they develop their mission, goals, and objectives. We analyze next how they formulate, implement, and control their strategies. Finally, we suggest some ways that not-for-profit organizations can increase their strategic management effectiveness.

■ Environmental Analysis

As the environment of not-for-profit organizations becomes increasingly dynamic, strategic management becomes more and more important. For example, nonprofit organizations have recently experienced reductions in federal aid and changes in tax laws that have reduced the incentive for corporations and individuals to make contributions. Simultaneously, competition for financial donations among nonprofits has increased with the rise of organizations dedicated to combating AIDS, Alzheimer's disease, child abuse, and drunk driving.[2]

Likewise, public organizations that once had a near monopoly in certain services, such as the U.S. Postal Service, are experiencing rapid change. Over the past few years, the Postal Service has felt increasing competitive pressure in express mail and the parcel business from such rivals as United Parcel Service and Federal Express. Additionally, in first-class mail, the Postal Service is losing business to a product substitute—the business-owned facsimile (fax) machine. Under such conditions, the necessity of planning well and operating effectively and efficiently becomes clear.

Two of the primary ways in which the environment of not-for-profit organizations differs from the environment of business organizations are in their sources of revenue and in the composition and concerns of their stakeholder groups. The following subsections explore these differences.

Sources of Revenue

Although there are a number of differences between businesses and not-for-profit organizations, perhaps the chief distinction is the source of the organization's revenues. Business income is derived almost exclusively from a single source—the sale of its products and services to individuals or organizations. Not-for-profit organizations, however, may receive revenue from a number of sources: taxes, dues, contributions, and in some instances, sale of their products or services. These differences are illustrated in Figure 12.1.

Some of the contributors of revenue to certain organizations may never use, at least in a direct sense, the organizations' outputs. For instance, consider a family violence center. The center's purpose is to provide a haven for women and their children from abusive spouses, but the center must rely on others, who may never use the center, for financial support. Another example is the local public school system. Public schools have been asked to shoulder increasing responsibilities as society has changed. They are being looked to as sources of prevention training for drug abuse and teenage pregnancy, as locations for after-school care for latchkey children, and as institutions that must increase

Figure 12.1 **Sources of Income for Profit and Not-for-Profit Organizations**

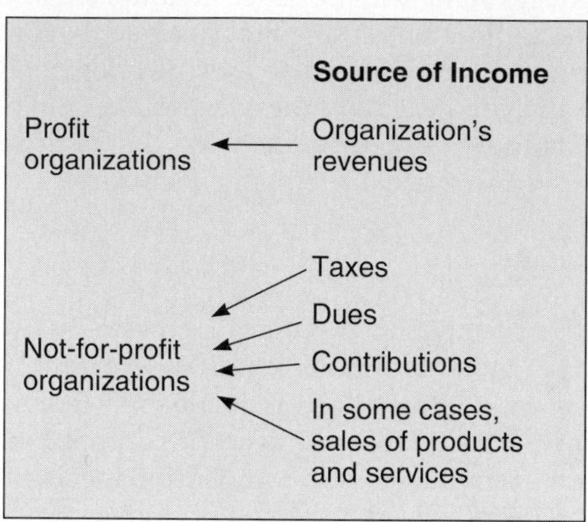

the quality of education for their children. The financial support for pursuing these goals must come from all of the school district's taxpayers—not just the parents of the students who attend the schools. Consequently, some taxpayers may be reluctant to support higher taxes for the public schools.[3]

Successful businesses know their customers and their needs. They recognize that satisfying their customers' needs is the sole reason for their existence. But not-for-profit organizations have a less direct relationship with their "customers." Those they serve are not necessarily those who contribute financially to their operations. Hence, their strategic planning must be twofold: planning for serving their clients or customers, and planning for securing the financial funding to provide those services.

The first type of planning—to serve customers—may sometimes have to be done with little or no input from the customers. For instance, agencies that handle the problems of the mentally ill or those that safeguard children can hardly survey their clients to ascertain their needs. In such cases, agencies often plan their services on the basis of discussions with professionals who have expertise in that particular field and of what similar agencies in other locales have done. The second type of planning—to acquire financial funding—may become quite political. A government agency, for instance, must compete against other agencies for the limited funds available; and those that are most successful are often the ones that acquiesce to demands made of them by those who control the funds. Defense Department appropriations, for instance, often depend upon the department's compliance with congressional wishes.

External Constituencies and Stakeholders

Strategic planning in business, as we have seen, involves taking into account the varying goals of the organization's stakeholders (e.g., its owners, employees, customers, creditors). The same is true for not-for-profit organizations, but the stakeholder groups and concerns are significantly different. This difference can best be seen in public organizations.

Although the managers of a government entity may engage in rational strategic planning, these plans may be ignored by political leaders who must respond to public pressure to win reelection. What may be rational in an economic sense may be politically unwise.

> Political leaders have learned that government often works only when a consensus forms to deal with a perceived crisis. The solutions may not conform with any plan, and governmental actions may be taken without regard to rational priorities. Nevertheless, the most important consideration may be that the actions are acceptable to the various constituency groups that are able to affect the decision. Since this occurs at all levels of government on a regular basis, it will be frustrating to managers who want government to function in an orderly manner. Government is not an orderly procedure because there are too many people with a variety of perspectives who are involved in reaching decisions.[4]

This greater number and diversity of stakeholders may result in less managerial autonomy for public agency managers than for managers in business. Because government agencies are "owned" by all citizens, their activities may often be more closely monitored by their constituents. This greater visibility means that managers' decisions are more public.

For example, Los Angeles County's Transportation Commission, a public agency, recently solicited bids from engineering firms to build high-tech electronic trolley cars. Only two builders responded—Idaho-based Morrison Knudsen Corporation and Sumitomo Corporation, headquartered in Tokyo. When word leaked out that the Transportation Commission's construction unit would recommend awarding the contract to Sumitomo, the chairman of Morrison Knudsen, William Agee, attempted to get the decision reversed. Joining with him were various members of the public who strongly argued for a "Made in America" decision, politicians from both California and Los Angeles, and numerous lobbyists, lawyers, and political activists. As a result of the furor, the Transportation Commission reopened the bidding.[5]

In addition to being subject to public visibility, managerial actions are also scrutinized carefully by oversight agencies such as legislative bodies, courts, and executive groups. Hence, although managers of public organizations may not need to concern themselves with such business threats as hostile takeovers, foreign competition, or bankruptcy, they have a complicated environment in which to operate. They must serve customers or clients who may be separate from the organization's sources of funding. But the organization's operations must satisfy both the customers and the funding sources, as well as a number of other constituents and oversight agencies. This complexity is illustrated in Figure 12.2.

■ Mission, Goals, and Objectives

Not-for-profit organizations need clearly-defined missions, goals, and objectives. This section explores this need and examines some reasons why clarity in organizational direction is often lacking.

Mission

Certainly, having a well-focused mission and clear goals and objectives is as important to not-for-profit organizations as it is to businesses. Management

Figure 12.2 **Stakeholder Constraints on Public Organizations**

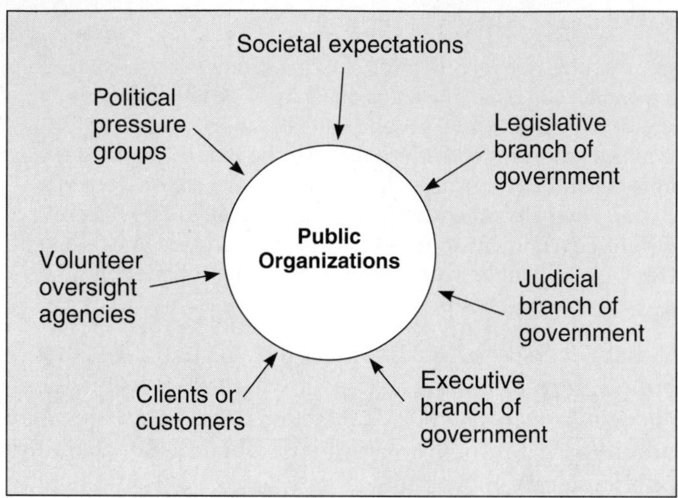

researcher and consultant Peter F. Drucker points out that "the best nonprofits devote a great deal of thought to defining their organizations' missions."[6]

As an example, consider the Girl Scouts of the U.S.A.[7] In 1976, Frances Hesselbein became national executive director of the organization, which was experiencing several problems. In a diverse society, it was comprised mostly of white, middle-class girls; scout leaders were becoming increasingly difficult to recruit as women entered the work force in growing numbers; the Boy Scouts of America were considering extending membership to girls; and membership in the Girl Scouts had declined steadily for eight years.

Hesselbein's first step was to examine the mission of the Girl Scouts. The organization's management considered these questions: "What is our business?" "Who is the customer?" "What does the customer consider as value?" They decided that the Scouts existed for one major reason: to help girls reach their highest potential. As Hesselbein explained:

> More than any one thing, that made the difference. Because when you are clear about your mission, corporate goals and operating objectives flow from it.[8]

This strong self-identity helped the Scouts reject pressures from women's rights activists to support their causes and from charities to act as door-to-door canvassers. Today, although Hesselbein is no longer president, the organization numbers 2.3 million girls (15 percent of them are from racial minorities); conducts market research to determine the needs of modern girls; awards the most popular proficiency badges for math and computer expertise instead of for good grooming and hosting a party; sports uniforms designed by Halston and Bill Blass; and publishes monographs on such issues as teen pregnancy, drug use, and child abuse.

In the public arena, as Congress attempts to reduce the federal deficit, efforts are being directed toward clarifying the respective missions of the Navy, Army, Air Force, and Marine Corps. For instance, critics have charged for decades

STRATEGIC INSIGHT

A Nonprofit Organization's Mission: Howard Hughes Medical Institute

An important—but little known—nonprofit organization is the Howard Hughes Medical Institute. Founded in 1953 by billionaire aviator-industrialist Howard R. Hughes, the Institute states its mission as follows:

> The primary purpose and objective of the Howard Hughes Medical Institute shall be the promotion of human knowledge within the field of the basic sciences (principally the field of medical research and medical education) and the effective application thereof for the benefit of mankind.

The Institute is a scientific and philanthropic organization with the principal purpose of conducting biomedical research in five broad areas: genetics, immunology, neuroscience, structural biology, and cell biology and regulation. It accomplishes its scientific mission by funding research through laboratories located in some of the most prestigious academic medical centers, hospitals, universities, and other research institutions in the United States, Canada, Mexico, Australia, and New Zealand. Its philanthropic goals are attained by financially supporting various aspects of science education, from elementary school through postgraduate training.

At the beginning of 1992, the Institute had total assets of about $6.9 billion, including $6.3 billion invested in equities, private partnerships, and nonequity securities. Earnings from this investment portfolio support the Institute's operations. In 1991, the Institute funded $214 million in medical research and support services and spent an additional $46 million on science education.

How effective are these expenditures? In the past few years, Hughes investigators at various locations have made scientific discoveries that will help in the fight against colon cancer, cystic fibrosis, atherosclerosis, HIV-1 virus, immune deficiencies, hypertension, and an inherited form of blindness.

SOURCE: *The Annual Report of the Howard Hughes Medical Institute 1991* (Bethesda, Md.: Howard Hughes Medical Institute).

that the United States has the only military with four air forces (all four branches of the service have their own airplanes and helicopters). Furthermore, both the Air Force and the Navy have bomber aircraft. As the defense budget shrinks, much thought is being given to reducing this expensive overlap by defining clearly just what the mission of each military branch should be.[9]

Goals and Objectives

Although having a clearly defined mission and goals is essential to an organization's success, many not-for-profit organizations fail in this regard. Businesses, for instance, can easily measure sales, market share, profits, return on investment, and so on. But not-for-profit organizations do not usually have such clear goals.

One of the reasons for this lack of clarity is that many of the goals are value-laden. Some states, for example, held fierce debates over mandatory seat belt laws. Was the goal to protect the lives of automobile drivers and passengers, or was it to protect the rights of those individuals to choose—or not to choose—to buckle up? Is the goal of a prison system rehabilitation of prisoners or punishment?

Second, not-for-profit goals often involve important trade-offs. This situation can be illustrated by the debate surrounding the potential closing of any military base. Its closing will reduce the federal deficit, but it will also harm the economy of the local area. Which is the more important consideration? During the 1992 presidential campaign, economist Herbert Stein emphasized the trade-off dilemma that any president faces: "He has to choose between assisting Russia, assisting urban ghettos in the U.S. and promoting aggregate growth in the American economy."[10] There is simply not sufficient funding available to accomplish all three goals.

Third, goals may often be deliberately vague, broad, and general, such as "protect our environment" or "help the homeless." Broad, general goals are more likely to secure the support of diverse stakeholders and provide inspiration for organization members. Also, vague goals are less likely to invite close scrutiny and debate than specific goals are and, hence, may avoid alienating potential supporters. Universities, for instance, often publicize their goal of offering a high-quality education. Few could argue with such a goal, and it helps skirt such issues as whether research or teaching is more important, how selective the university's admissions policies should be, and how much emphasis will be given to sports programs. Debates on any of these issues are almost certain to alienate some stakeholders, thereby reducing the flow of funds to the university.

Goals in public organizations are often vague because leadership is subject to frequent turnover. Changes in direction, for instance, can occur in a state where a Democrat replaces a Republican governor. Four years later, election results can alter the state's direction yet again. Vague goals, such as "operate the state for the benefit of all of its citizens," therefore, are likely to have more permanency and lend more of an aura of stability than very specific goals will.

Goals may sometimes not reflect the needs of the organization's "customers" as much as they reflect the wishes of the organization's financial donors. Church-affiliated universities, for instance, may make decisions that anger their students but conform to the wishes of the denomination that accounts for much of their financial backing. Some nonprofit organizations, in fact, may be reluctant to turn down substantial funding, even if the donor insists that the funds be used for a purpose outside the basic mission of the organization. Again, vague goals may appear more appropriate in such situations.

The question, of course, is whether these reasons for establishing vague goals are valid. We do not believe they are. Although formulating goals and objectives is more challenging in not-for-profit organizations than in businesses, having clarity in direction is essential if organizations are to operate effectively. Perhaps the major reason for our belief is that without clear goals, an organization has no way to measure its progress or its effectiveness.

Both nonprofit and public organizations must bring together their various stakeholders to hammer out a set of specific, measurable goals. The process will often not be smooth, since each stakeholder group may have its own agenda. Even so, without this process, these organizations will be unable to measure their performance.

Virtually every organization can define specific, if not quantifiable, objectives. Ways of determining cost–benefit ratios and standards are essential. For instance, the family violence center mentioned earlier could formulate a means

STRATEGIC INSIGHT

Strategies for Churches

Internal Growth Strategy

One of the nation's largest churches is Houston's Second Baptist Church. With a Sunday morning attendance of twelve thousand, the church complex covers 32 acres. In 1984, however, the church was simply a conventional church on a large plot of land. Its incoming pastor, H. Edwin Young, was familiar with the demographics of the area: thousands of young families and single people new to Houston. He sold his vision of a growing church to his congregation and persuaded them to pledge over $17 million needed for new physical facilities while the church borrowed over $26 million for additional construction costs.

Pastor Young dispatched church members to study office management techniques at Xerox and IBM and parking and people skills at Disney World. He varied religious services to fit particular needs. In addition to the traditional Sunday morning service, a Sunday evening service caters to a mostly singles crowd; and on Wednesday nights, separate services are offered, one traditional and one with religious rock music.

Today, computers regulate mood lighting during church services; shuttle buses bring latecomers in from outlying parking decks; parking attendants empty the church's numerous parking lots every Sunday in half an hour; billboards and television ads invite people to visit this "Fellowship of Excitement"; an information desk is staffed with cheerful attendants; aerobics classes are held daily beginning at 6:00 A.M.; and a restaurant offers two types of menus: "saints," for those who prefer a low-calorie meal, and "sinners," for those who desire richer food.

Turnaround Strategy

The U.S. Catholic Church, like many organizations, is trying to overcome stagnant revenues and steadily rising costs. Taking the lead in this fight is the Archdiocese of Chicago, which has taken the following steps:

- Sold assets of $6.2 million
- Restructured archdiocesan offices and laid off fifty employees to save $1.5 million
- Required all parishes to submit three-year budgets and quarterly financial reports
- Had each parish establish a local advisory council of business leaders
- Devised repayment plans for loans made to the parishes and began charging interest on these loans
- Increased tuition at parish schools
- Raised the assessment each parish pays the archdiocese from 6.5 to 10 percent of its annual revenues
- Consolidated parishes and schools in the archdiocese
- Encouraged church members to increase their giving
- Began marketing the services of the church to new groups, such as young adults

Although some of the changes have met with resistance, Joseph Cardinal Bernardin maintains that there is little choice. He emphasizes that to "fulfill our mission, we have to have the resources."

SOURCES: K. Kelly, "Chicago's Catholic Church: Putting Its House in Order," *Business Week,* 10 June 1991, pp. 60–65 (quotation is from p. 65); R.G. Niebuhr, "Megachurches Strive to Be All Things to All Parishioners," *The Wall Street Journal,* 13 May 1991.

of measuring how effectively it is able to prevent its clients from suffering further abuse and how well it enhances its clients' self-esteem. However, it also needs to define such performance ratios as expenditures per client per day. Since such organizations typically cannot begin to help all of those who need their help, the more tightly they can control their costs, the more clients they can serve. Broad measures of costs per month or per year cannot help control costs as effectively as more specific ratios. Such standards act as a surrogate performance measure when profit figures are not applicable.[11]

■ Strategy Formulation, Implementation, and Control

The processes of implementing and controlling strategy are often more complicated in not-for-profit organizations than in businesses. This section examines some of those complications.

Strategy Formulation and Implementation

Corporate and business unit strategies are usually the same ones used in not-for-profit organizations. In general, we can say that most of these organizations attempt to satisfy specific societal needs. For instance, the American Red Cross rushes to aid victims of natural disasters; the Salvation Army ministers to the physical and religious needs of homeless persons. The U.S. Navy keeps the sea lanes of the world open; the Army concentrates on ground defense. Within a state, some universities serve as major research and graduate institutions; others concentrate on teaching undergraduates.

Often, one of the features that distinguishes not-for-profit organizations from businesses is the presence of greater political constraints upon the strategic choices of not-for-profits. In public organizations, for instance, many decisions are subject to the approval of oversight agencies and the legislative and executive branches of government. These strategic decisions become even more politicized by their public visibility in the press. Several years ago, for example, the National Academy of Public Administration complained about the complexity of the controls and rules over managerial decisions in the federal government.[12]

Even if strategy could be formulated unfettered by political considerations, implementation of the strategy can be a problem. Public managers have weaker authority over their subordinates than business managers do. Such decisions as pay, promotion, termination, and disciplinary action are often subject to rules rather than to managerial discretion. And employees who enthusiastically carry out the strategy of the organization may receive the same rewards as those who ignore the strategy to pursue their own ends. In one of the most flagrant examples of restrictive work rules, New York City public school custodians are required to sweep school floors only every other day and to mop them only three times a year. Furthermore, cafeteria floors need be mopped only once a week. The average annual salary for such work in 1992 was $57,000.[13] In a similar case, *The Wall Street Journal* reported that restrictive work rules at Philadelphia's International Airport required three employees to change one lightbulb: a building mechanic to remove the light panel, an electrician to insert the new bulb, and a janitor to clean up the area.[14]

Many functional strategies are also greatly constrained by rules governing such areas as purchasing and personnel. For instance, a recent General Accounting Office survey of federal government employees revealed that 5.7 percent of those surveyed were "poor performers." Although some of these employees improved their performance, voluntarily quit, or were removed from their jobs, almost 40 percent never improved and were not asked to leave. That group received over $1 billion in annual salaries.[15] Finally, the frequent turnover of leadership, discussed earlier, may discourage employees from channeling much effort into strategy implementation, since they know that the current strategy may be short-lived.

Because our political system is designed to ensure frequent turnover through regularly scheduled elections and through limitations on how long individuals can hold some offices, government leaders are encouraged to take a short-range approach to strategic management. Voters in the next election may be more likely to reelect officials who have benefited them during the past several months than those who have an excellent long-range plan but have demonstrated little in the way of immediate results.

Although nonprofit organizations may operate under fewer constraints than public organizations do, implementation of strategy can be constrained by those who oppose the strategy. For instance, public abortion clinics may be picketed by right-to-life advocates. More important, however, may be the constraints imposed by the nature of the work force in many nonprofit organizations. Often, the bulk of the workers are volunteers who receive no pay for their services. As long as the direction of the organization is consistent with their values and beliefs, they will cooperate in implementing strategic decisions. But should the agency's direction deviate from their values, they may quit the organization and even actively oppose its operations.

In fact, many nonprofit organizations develop their organizational culture around a cause. Often, the founder of the organization and the members exhibit the attitudes and behaviors of "true believers" who are willing to work long hours at little or no pay to further their particular beliefs and values. Many environmental groups as well as pro- and antiabortion organizations possess such powerful cultures. Few businesses are able to develop their culture around such powerful and emotional goals.

Another consideration is that businesses often have more attractive financial compensation packages than not-for-profit organizations do. Individuals who are motivated by such considerations, therefore, will often seek employment in business organizations. This choice reduces the pool of talented workers from which public and nonprofit organizations can choose. In addition, the trend toward two-income families has certainly diminished the number of volunteers available to nonprofit organizations.

Not-for-profit organizations may also implement their strategies in a more centralized fashion than businesses.[16] As we saw in an earlier chapter, many businesses have responded to increasing environmental change by decentralizing their decision making. Although environments in many cases are equally dynamic for public and nonprofit agencies, the same trend has not occurred there. Because so many differing stakeholder groups must be considered when management implements strategy, often only the top managers are fully aware of how stakeholders' attitudes are changing.[17] For this reason, implementation decisions are made at the top levels of the organization. In addition, under the civil service system in public organizations, which primarily rewards seniority rather than merit, few employees are able to perceive a connection between their job performance and their compensation. Since incentives are not used to channel their behavior into the appropriate areas of strategy implementation, their behavior is instead controlled through an extensive network of rules and procedures, resulting in a bureaucratic configuration in which decision-making authority is centralized.

A further difficulty with implementation of strategy in some not-for-profit organizations is that these institutions are staffed largely by professional people who see themselves as committed to the profession rather than to the particular organization for which they currently work. For instance, physicians are said to be engaged in the practice of medicine (a profession) rather than working for a particular hospital. College professors are often referred to (and view themselves) as professors of physics or history rather than as employees of a specific university. In such cases, they "will probably publish more, spend less time on college committees, devote less time to teaching and students, attend more professional meetings, and be more willing to leave the college"[18] than the individual who identifies more with the organization than the profession. The problem that this perspective poses from the organization's viewpoint is that such persons may have primary loyalty to their profession rather than to the organization that employs them.[19] Therefore, strategic managers may need to persuade middle- and lower-level managers to emphasize their responsibilities to the organization as well as those to their profession.

Strategic Control

Without clearly stated goals and objectives, strategic control becomes very difficult to achieve. For instance, the quality of education in public schools might be measured in several ways. One way is to determine how well students can solve problems and communicate those solutions, with the measurement taken once at the beginning of a period of time and again at the end of that time period. If the results are less than the school district has set as its goal, then corrective action must be taken. Likewise, a church that did not increase its membership as much as it desired during a particular year would have to take some corrective action, as would a police department that failed to meet its goal of solving 80 percent of the crimes committed during a twelve-month period.

Control is more difficult, obviously, when goals are not clear or when an organization has conflicting goals. Recall the example of the family violence center used earlier. The particular community in which it operates feels that it has been successful because its services are well publicized and fully used. However, it has very nearly gone bankrupt trying to help all who need its services, and its director feels that the center has just begun to scratch the surface!

In some cases, nonprofit organizations have literally had no goals in certain key areas. The prestigious University of Chicago hospital, for instance, had no budgeting system to track its costs until 1989.[20] Without standards, the hospital's management could not determine the cost of a procedure, such as an appendectomy. Lack of both cost goals and cost information made the control of costs virtually impossible.

Even under conditions in which the corrective actions that should be taken are clear, control may still not occur. For instance, in business, when a project or program is no longer contributing to a firm's profits, decisions are made either to rejuvenate the program, if appropriate and possible, or to terminate it. Hence, profit serves as a readily acceptable yardstick to help management determine the amount of resources that various programs should receive.[21]

This means of control is not available to not-for-profit organizations. In fact, only rarely are programs terminated, particularly in government. This fact can be demonstrated quickly by virtually any debate on how to reduce the federal deficit. Few individuals want their taxes raised, but any proposal to terminate a program (and, hence, lower expenditures) quickly brings an outcry from those stakeholders who will be adversely affected by the program's demise. As a result, governments at all levels continue to add programs that are needed but rarely end any of their ongoing programs. But strategic control requires that a manager make choices, because it is simply not possible to do everything well.[22] Even when a lack of funding makes it imperative to cut programs, the programs cut are not necessarily the ones least needed; often, the programs eliminated are the ones that are less likely to create a highly vocal protest from their constituents.

STRATEGIC INSIGHT

Strategic Control at the Post Office

The U.S. Postal Service faces increasing competition from air express companies, facsimile machines, long-distance telephone companies, electronic mail, and interactive cable television. While its revenue growth (about $47 billion a year) stagnates, its operating expenses continue to escalate. A 1992 General Accounting Office report revealed that, even though considerable automation of post office operations had occurred, operating expenses were $295 million more than expected. In fact, while the volume of mail delivered declined, the number of work hours increased.

As a result, major attempts at strategic control are under way. The first try, however, failed. Postmaster General Anthony Frank's request for a one-cent increase in first-class postage—which would have raised $800 million annually—was denied by the Postal Service Board of Governors. Although the vote was 6 to 3 in favor of the increase, a unanimous vote is required. Frank responded: "I'm the only CEO of a major corporation in America who doesn't have control over his own prices." Before leaving office, however, he managed to cap labor costs (which amount to 83 percent of operating expenses) and give management more flexibility in hiring temporary workers. He also announced an early-retirement plan designed to trim payrolls, hired a polling company to measure customer satisfaction, and extended window hours.

Frank was succeeded by Marvin Runyon, who continued the strategic control measures by eliminating—through early retirement—25 percent of the Postal Service's managerial positions. (Prior to the reductions, the Postal Service had one manager for each six employees.) He also restructured the organization, replacing its 73 regional divisions with two functional divisions: one for processing and distributing mail and one for customer services.

SOURCES: W.R. Cummings, "Reinventing the Post Office," *The Wall Street Journal*, 11 January 1993; R. Davis, "Postal Chief Wants Service That Delivers," *USA Today*, 10 August 1992; S. Rudavsky, "Postal Service Plans Sweeping Overhaul," *The Washington Post*, 7 August 1992; "That Was Then, This Is Now," *The Washington Post Magazine*, 14 June 1992, p. 11; M. Lewyn, "Pushing the Envelope at the Post Office," *Business Week*, 25 November 1991, pp. 56–57 (quotation is from p. 56).

Even charitable, nonprofit organizations may behave in similar ways. For instance, sometimes, the mission of an agency is actually accomplished or its environment changes so that its mission becomes unnecessary. As an example, consider the Mothers' March of Dimes organization, which was originally established to support research that would lead to a cure for polio. With the widespread distribution of the Salk vaccine in the 1950s, polio ceased to be the threat it once was. But the March of Dimes did not go out of existence. Instead, it adopted a new cause—birth defects—in order to sustain itself.

■ Improving Strategic Management

Although some of the difficulties in implementing strategic management concepts in not-for-profit organizations are unlikely to disappear (e.g., the desire of elected officials to be reelected minimizes an emphasis on long-range planning), other problems can be overcome. The concepts of effective strategic management presented in this book are not limited to business institutions. Both nonprofit and public organizations can benefit significantly by analyzing their environmental opportunities and constraints and by formulating a mission and goals that allow them to fulfill the needs of some segment of society. They must then develop a strategy that relates their strengths and weaknesses appropriately to their environment and allows them to create a distinctive competence in their operating arena. An organization structure must be fashioned that enables the agency to deal effectively with its environmental demands; and a culture should be established that enhances—rather than interferes with—its operational effectiveness.

Some not-for-profit organizations are highly effective, of course. But for those that are not, these basic principles of strategic management can be most useful in increasing their ability to carry out their mission. In some of these situations, the culture may be such that improvement is virtually impossible without a major change. Strong transformational leadership may be required, along with a significant modification in policies, so that employees' attitudes and practices can be unfrozen and changed. Top management's commitment to the concept of change must be complete and highly visible. Concurrently, reward systems must be altered to encourage creativity, new ways of doing old things, and service to the agency's clients or customers.

Certainly, such change cannot occur overnight. One authority suggests that top management start gradually to chip away at detrimental cultural aspects and look for special opportunities to implement strategic management principles in narrow, well-defined areas. In this way, management can devote the resources and time that are required for success.[23]

Finally, we would be negligent if we did not emphasize the need for managerial training. In some nonprofit organizations, the top-level managers may be individuals who were sensitive to a particular need in our society and created an organization to serve that need. But even the best of intentions cannot serve society as effectively as good intentions combined with managerial skills. The most socially oriented of programs must, in the long run, use each of its dollars and the time of its employees as effectively and efficiently as it possibly can. Otherwise, all of those who are in need of its services may never receive them or may receive only partial care.

STRATEGIC INSIGHT

Strategic Alliances for Public Organizations

An increasing number of public organizations are finding that strategic alliances with private industry can improve their operating effectiveness. In some cases, for instance, "privatizing" government functions can reduce costs and improve revenue flows.

Take, for example, Chicago's parking enforcement program. During the 1980s, $420 million of parking ticket fines went unpaid. That's because, after a ticket was written, it took an average of two years for the ticket to be recorded. But, in 1990, Chicago turned the recording process over to Dallas-based Electronic Data Systems (EDS). Now the 14,000 parking tickets written by police officers each day are electronically imaged and stored on optical disks by EDS personnel the very same day. Other parking tickets, written by "meter maids," are entered by the ticket writer directly into hand-held computers and are electronically transferred into EDS's computer. The city is now saving about $5 million a year in administrative expenses, ticket revenues are increasing substantially, and parking meter revenues are significantly higher.

In other developments, such states as California and New York are experimenting with contracting out some welfare functions to private companies. For instance, in New York, a welfare mother costs the state about $23,000 annually. But, in its contract with America Works (a private company), New York pays only $5,300. America Works and other similar firms, such as MAXIMUS and Lockheed IMS, can cut expenses by superior use of computer technology, a lack of restrictive work rules, and little bureaucracy. America Works is not only less expensive for the taxpayers, but it also succeeds at getting almost 70 percent of its clients off of the welfare rolls.

Meanwhile, Baltimore has turned over the management of nine inner-city schools to a Minneapolis-based company—Education Alternatives. This company hopes to save money while reducing the student–teacher ratio and increasing the use of technology in these schools. Its profit will come from part of the savings.

Some government agencies are even forming strategic alliances with nonprofit organizations. Florida's prison system, for instance, paroles some of its first offenders into the custody of the Salvation Army. About two-thirds of these parolees become "permanently rehabilitated" (they are not indicted for another crime for at least six years).

As budget deficits mount at the federal, state, and local levels, government officials continue to search for creative ways to lower costs. Strategic alliances with private industry and nonprofit organizations show considerable promise in helping officials attain this goal.

SOURCES: J. Huey, "Finding New Heroes For a New Era," *Fortune,* 25 January 1993, p. 65; J. Mathews, "Taking Welfare Private," *Newsweek,* 29 June 1992, p. 44; A. Kotlowitz, "For-Profit Firm to Manage Public Schools in Baltimore," *The Wall Street Journal,* 11 June 1992; P.F. Drucker, "It Profits Us to Strengthen Nonprofits," *The Wall Street Journal,* 19 December 1991; R. Henkoff, "Some Hope for Troubled Cities," *Fortune,* 9 September 1991, p. 126.

SUMMARY

Strategic management principles apply equally to businesses and not-for-profit organizations. But these two types of institutions differ in some important ways that have strategic implications.

Perhaps the chief distinction is their source of revenue. Businesses generate income in the form of sales revenue; not-for-profit firms may receive revenue from such diverse sources as taxes, dues, contributions, or even sales. But a business's revenue is derived directly from its customers—those who purchase its products or services. However, a not-for-profit's revenue often comes from individuals who may never even use the outputs of that organization. For instance, a public organization may provide welfare payments to families below the poverty level. However, the sources of those funds are taxes paid by income earners with relatively higher salaries. Similarly, a nonprofit organization such as a privately owned museum may allow the public to view its exhibits for no admission fee. But its revenues may be generated by the interest from an endowment created by a family many decades ago. Therefore, not-for-profit organizations must engage in two types of strategic planning—how to serve their clients or customers, and how to secure the necessary financial funding to provide those services.

A second distinction between businesses and nonprofits is that planning in some not-for-profit firms, particularly public organizations, may be complicated by political considerations, which are not relevant to businesses. The large number and diversity of stakeholders in a government agency means that its managers' decisions are more public than they are in other types of organizations. These decisions must be responsive to the wishes of varying constituencies, requiring management to engage in a difficult balancing act.

Although having a clear mission and goals is essential to an organization's success, many not-for-profit organizations fail in this area. Several reasons account for this shortcoming: Goals tend to be value-laden; they often involve important trade-offs; they may be deliberately vague, broad, and general; leadership is subject to frequent turnover, particularly in public organizations; and the goals may not reflect the needs of the organization's customers as much as they reflect the wishes of the organization's financial supporters. The problem, of course, is that vague goals cannot help management measure an organization's progress or its effectiveness.

Strategy implementation in not-for-profit organizations, particularly public agencies, is often highly visible and political. But even if strategies could be implemented in a rational fashion, public managers would still operate under another unique constraint. They have weaker authority in such areas as pay, promotion, termination, and disciplinary action than business managers have. By the same token, managers in private nonprofit firms must often supervise a work force comprised largely of volunteers, which poses a different set of constraints. Other distinctions exist as well. For instance, research shows that not-for-profit organizations implement their strategies in a more centralized fashion than businesses do, and they are sometimes staffed by professional people who may be more committed to their profession than to the organization for which they currently work.

Strategic control, of course, is difficult to achieve when goals are not clearly defined and measurable. It is made even more difficult by the fact that not-for-profit organizations, unlike businesses, cannot usually terminate programs even if they have outlived their usefulness. Just the threat of program termination quickly brings an outcry from those stakeholders who will be adversely affected by the program's demise, and they often wield sufficient political power to forestall termination indefinitely.

However, both nonprofit and public organizations can benefit significantly by following the principles presented in this book. They, as well as businesses, should analyze their environmental opportunities and constraints and formulate mission and goals that allow them to fulfill the needs of some segment of society. They should then develop a strategy that relates their strengths and weaknesses appropriately to their environment and allows them to create a distinctive competence in their operating arena. To implement their strategy, they must fashion an organization structure that enables them to deal with their environmental demands and a culture that enhances their organizational effectiveness. Cultures and reward systems that are too constraining must be altered to improve the organizations' operating efficiency and their long-term effectiveness.

KEY CONCEPTS

Nonprofit organization A form of not-for-profit organization that is supported by private funds and exists to contribute to the good of society.

Public organization A form of not-for-profit organization that is created, funded, and regulated by the public sector.

DISCUSSION QUESTIONS

1. Your text states that "nonprofit and public organizations are indispensable to maintaining a civilized society." Explain why.

2. Explain how not-for-profit organizations differ from businesses in the way that they derive their revenue. What are the implications of these differences for strategic management?

3. We have seen that the top managers of public organizations probably have less autonomy than do business CEOs because of the greater number and diversity of stakeholders in public organizations. Explain how multiple stakeholder interests can reduce managerial autonomy.

4. Why do not-for-profit organizations often have vague, general goals rather than clear, specific ones?

5. What are the disadvantages of vague, general goals?

6. Select a not-for-profit organization and describe the specific societal needs that it attempts to satisfy. Does it have any competitors? If so, who are they?

7. How does the implementation of strategy in not-for-profit organizations differ from that in businesses?

8. Why is strategy implementation more centralized in not-for-profit organizations than in businesses?

9. From a strategic perspective, what are the difficulties of managing professional employees? Volunteer employees?

10. Why do public organizations have more difficulty terminating programs than businesses have?

STRATEGIC MANAGEMENT EXERCISES

1. Assume that you have the resources and backing to found a university. Formulate a mission statement for your university. Now, develop a set of goals for the university. How would you ensure that the needs of your university's "customers" are met through the goals that you have devised? (Note that customers would include employers of the university's graduates, graduate schools that accept your graduates, students, parents who pay tuition, etc.)
2. Use your own university to answer the following questions: What is your university's mission? What are its major goals? Base your answers on written documents, if they exist; otherwise, you will need to derive your answers from interviews and observation. After gathering information on your university, determine how it might formulate and implement appropriate strategies to serve its constituents and stakeholders better. Give specific examples.
3. The United Way of America is supposed to provide financial support for a wide variety of charitable causes. But in the early 1990s, news reports revealed that much abuse and fraud had taken place in its headquarters' organization. From library research of this scandal, suggest how the use of strategic control techniques might have prevented these problems from ever occurring at the United Way of America.

NOTES

1. B. Vobejda, "In Job Strength, Manufacturing Eclipsed by Public Sector," *The Washington Post*, 18 August 1992.
2. J.A. Byrne, "Profiting from the Nonprofits," *Business Week*, 26 March 1990, p. 67.
3. W.H. Newman and H.W. Wallender, "Managing Not-for-Profit Enterprises," *Academy of Management Review* 3 (1978): 24–31.
4. Reprinted from W.H. Eldridge, "Why Angels Fear to Tread: A Practitioner's Observations and Solutions on Introducing Strategic Management to a Government Culture," in J. Rabin, G.J. Miller, and W.B. Hildreth, eds., *Handbook of Strategic Management* (New York: Dekker, 1989), p. 329, by courtesy of Marcel Dekker Inc.
5. F. Rose, "How a U.S. Company Used Anti-Japan Mood to Help Reverse a Loss," *The Wall Street Journal*, 22 April 1992.
6. P.F. Drucker, "What Business Can Learn from Nonprofits," *Harvard Business Review* 67, no. 4 (1989): 89.
7. Bryne, "Profiting from the Nonprofits," pp. 67, 70–74.
8. Ibid., p. 72.
9. J. Lancaster, "Hill Takes Aim on Duplication in Military Services," *The Washington Post*, 8 August 1992.
10. H. Stein, "Risky Business—A Non-Politician as President," *The Wall Street Journal*, 9 July 1992.

11. P.D. Harvey and J.D. Snyder, "Charities Need a Bottom Line Too," *Harvard Business Review* 65, no. 1 (1987): 14–22.
12. National Academy of Public Administration, *Revitalizing Federal Management* (Washington, D.C.: National Academy of Public Administration, 1986).
13. R. Flick, "How Unions Stole the Big Apple," *Reader's Digest*, January 1992, pp. 39–40.
14. "Philly Thinks Private," *The Wall Street Journal*, 30 June 1992.
15. D. Priest, "Study Ties Job Success to Bosses," *The Washington Post*, 9 October 1990.
16. P.C. Nutt, "A Strategic Planning Network for Non-Profit Organizations," *Strategic Management Journal* 5 (1984): 58.
17. J. Ruffat, "Strategic Management of Public and Non-Market Corporations," *Long Range Planning* 16, no. 4 (1983): 75.
18. W.G. Bennis, N. Berkowitz, M. Affinito, and M. Malone, "Reference Groups and Loyalties in the Out-Patient Department," *Administrative Science Quarterly* 2 (1958): 484.
19. Newman and Wallender, "Managing Not-for-Profit Enterprises," pp. 24–31.
20. J.F. Siler and T. Peterson, "Hospital, Heal Thyself," *Business Week*, 27 August 1990, p. 68.
21. Eldridge, "Why Angels Fear to Tread, p. 329.
22. Ibid., p. 330.
23. Ibid., p. 335.

II

Cases in Strategic Management

Strategic Management Case Analysis

Most of you are majoring in some aspect of business administration and are already familiar with case analysis. A case portrays a real organizational situation and requires you to analyze that situation and then develop recommendations for future action. The difference between the cases in strategic management and those in previous courses is that the cases here assume a broader perspective. Cases in finance have a financial orientation, and those in organizational behavior usually focus on individual or group behavior; but the cases in this book reflect a broad, companywide perspective. Each case presents a real business organization, and businesses in a wide variety of industries and operating situations are represented.

You have probably already taken a series of courses that specialize in various functional areas, such as marketing, accounting, finance, and production/operations management. This knowledge can prove very useful to you when you begin working as a functional specialist (e.g., accountant, financial analyst, or sales representative). However, most successful business executives eventually move above the functional level into general management positions. As this upward movement occurs, they typically encounter a very different set of problems from those that they dealt with as functional specialists. Unfortunately, their functional expertise is of limited assistance to them in either diagnosing or resolving these general management problems. Success in such activities requires the integration of knowledge in a wide variety of areas, both theoretical and functional. Hence, the goal of this textbook—and the course it accompanies—is to help you develop a general management capability by exposing you to a number of situations that require the integration of knowledge from different functional areas. The contents of this book provide the fundamental framework needed to bring together and integrate what you have learned in other courses so that you will be able to analyze these cases from a company-wide perspective.

This introduction should help you to analyze the cases contained in this textbook and assist you in organizing and presenting your thoughts in written form.

READING THE CASE

Case analysis requires you to read the case carefully and to read it more than once. Some students read the case quickly to get an overview of the situation presented and then reread it slowly, taking notes on the important issues and problems. Subsequently, they begin to organize and analyze the case information. However, each person must develop his or her own approach to case analysis. No single technique works well for everyone.

Since cases reflect reality, it should not be surprising that some of the information is not well organized, that irrelevant information is presented, and that relevant information may be dispersed throughout the case. Information rarely comes to us in neatly tied packages. One of your first tasks, therefore, is to organize the information in the case. An outline that can help you organize the material is discussed in the following section, or your professor may provide you with his or her own guidelines for organizing the issues in the case.

Students often have questions about the time frame of a particular case. We have found it most efficient to assume that you are analyzing the case in the year(s) that the case covers. For instance, if the last year covered in the case is 1992, then you should not ordinarily analyze the case with information gathered since that date. In some instances, however, your professor may ask you to update the case, particularly if, at the case's end, significant pending problems and issues are still unresolved.

WRITING THE CASE ANALYSIS

The guidelines presented in the following subsections for the written analysis of cases are offered to help you organize and present your thoughts. (If your professor gives you a set of guidelines, by all means, use those.) As you read the case carefully, you may organize and analyze the information in the case under each of the headings used for the following subsections.

■ Macroenvironment

The macroenvironment, the broadest of all the sections in your analysis, is intended to help you decipher the macroenvironmental information you extract from the case and organize it selectively under such headings as "Political-Legal," "Economic," "Technological," and "Social," as shown in Chapter 2. You should read the case for both explicit and implicit information in these categories. Outside research may be necessary to increase the information available in one or more of these areas. Then within each category, your task is to determine what opportunities and threats are presented to the firm featured in the case by the macroenvironmental force.

One way of accomplishing this end is to use headings and, under each heading, discuss how the external forces may act as opportunities or threats to management. Another way is to use brief, descriptive sentences for each heading's topic. For example, if the case is on General Motors, the following "Economic" heading may be used with a brief sentence:

Economic

(Opportunity) The relatively low recent value of the dollar (compared with its value in the early 1980s) versus foreign currencies has helped GM become more price-competitive.

A threat or constraint may be noted as follows:

Political-Legal

(Threat) The U.S. government is demanding higher and higher fuel efficiency standards from U.S. automakers.

A number of different factors may be listed under each of the macroenvironmental headings, depending upon the range of information provided in the case and the extent of your research outside what's given in the case. Some cases may have many relevant factors under, for instance, the heading "Political-Legal" but few under "Technological."

■ Industry Environment

The industry environment section requires you to extract information from the case and from any other available source through your own research and then organize and analyze it under the five industry forces discussed in Chapter 2: "Threat of Entry," "Intensity of Rivalry Among Existing Competitors," "Pressure from Substitute Products," "Bargaining Power of Buyers," and "Bargaining Power of Suppliers." You should use these headings to help you organize your analysis.

For example, assume that the case you are analyzing is on General Motors' automobile business units. Under the heading, "Threat of Entry," you might mention that economies of scale act as a barrier to domestic companies that may seek to enter the U.S. automobile industry. However, more and more vehicle producers from abroad have entered the American market over the past several years. Thus, although the threat of new entry from U.S. sources is limited, the threat of foreign automakers' exporting their products to America and even building manufacturing facilities in the United States is certainly present.

Under "Bargaining Power of Suppliers," you might mention that most suppliers of automobile parts do not have strong positions relative to GM. For instance, the major U.S. steel companies are not working at full capacity and, hence, would be anxious to sell to GM.

This is not to say that suppliers generally have weak bargaining power. In certain industries, some suppliers possess relatively strong bargaining power relative to buyers. For instance, Monsanto's NutraSweet unit had a strong bargaining position as a supplier to the soft-drink producers until its patent for aspartame expired in 1992.

The point of analyzing the macroenvironment and industry environment, of course, is to relate the opportunities and threats in these two areas to the firm featured in the case. A review of Chapter 2 should help you in this analysis.

■ Mission, Goals, Objectives, Social Responsibility, and Ethics

Parts or all of the heading "Mission, Goals, Objectives, Social Responsibility, and Ethics" may be used for your analysis. Sometimes, information is explicitly provided on these topics; other times, it is implicit, forcing you to read between the lines. One question that you might consider posing and analyzing is the following:

1. Is there an explicit or an implicit statement of the firm's mission? Does it accurately portray the direction in which the firm is going, or are the firm's operations incompatible with its mission?

You may recall that in Chapter 3, the mission of General Motors (to continue our example) is stated in the following way:

> The fundamental purpose of General Motors is to provide products and services of such quality that our customers will receive superior value, our employees and business partners will share in our success, and our stockholders will receive a sustained, superior return on their investment.

Unfortunately for GM, there has been a gap between its mission and its actual operating results. Surveys of car owners indicate that GM is not perceived as offering superior value to its customers.[1] In fact, a car produced by Toyota and sold under the GM brand (Geo Prism) has sales far below those of its "twin" product, Corolla, which is produced and marketed by Toyota.[2] Furthermore, GM has laid off large numbers of employees, and its stock has not been a top performer.

Another question you might consider:

2. Are the expressed or implied goals and objectives of the firm consistent with one another? Is there evidence that these goals and objectives are being attained?

In Chapter 3, we indicated that the goals of various stakeholders often differ. And Chapter 9 pointed out that compromise may be important in helping resolve these differences. Sometimes, however, compromise is not attainable, and the effectiveness of the firm suffers as a result. For example, in the middle to late 1980s, H. Ross Perot—head of Electronic Data Systems, a subsidiary of GM; a member of the GM board of directors; and a major stockholder in GM—desired a course of action for GM that differed significantly from the course favored by GM's top management. Because compromise was unattainable, GM's management purchased Perot's stock holdings for about $750 million, at a time when GM had just incurred a large quarterly loss.

Here is another question you might consider for your analysis.

3. Is the firm operating in a socially responsible manner? Are the decisions and actions of its managers ethical?

As we emphasized in Chapter 3, analysis in the areas of social responsibility and ethics can be difficult because the guidelines are not always clear-cut. If the case contains these issues, you may have to formulate your own answer to dilemmas such as whether it is socially responsible to lay off employees to enhance a firm's competitiveness or whether social responsibility can be better served by keeping the employees on the payroll, even at the expense of the firm's profits and, perhaps, survival.

■ Corporate-Level Strategies

As we pointed out in Chapter 4, the basic question facing top management at the corporate level is, In what particular businesses or industries should we be operating? The answer to this question depends upon the firm's particular strengths and weaknesses and the opportunities and threats in the environment. As Chapter 4 emphasizes, a firm's strengths and weaknesses reside in its resources. Hence, you may wish to use the questions listed in Chapter 4 regarding the firm's human, organizational, and physical resources to determine the corporation's particular strengths and weaknesses.

The next step is to answer the following questions: Which specific strategies has the firm adopted—growth, stability, retrenchment, or a combination of these? How effective have these strategies been? Some corporations have effectively adopted growth strategies, but others have been less successful. Some companies have grown by developing or acquiring businesses with a common core. General Electric, for example, has attained success through involvement in businesses that share a common technological core. As another instance, Philip Morris has been one of the world's most successful consumer products firms, particularly with its tobacco and food businesses. However, Philip Morris was unable to transfer its expertise in consumer products to its marketing of 7-Up, which it eventually divested.

Some corporations or business units have effectively adopted the stability strategy. For instance, some enterprises have decided not to expand, because they are concerned that growth may reduce their product or service quality. In some industries, the cost of growth may be greater than its projected benefits. And some large firms may elect stability to avoid being prosecuted for engaging in monopolistic practices.

A strategy of retrenchment may be appropriate in certain situations. For instance, Tambrands diversified in the 1980s from a single-product company into such unrelated businesses as home diagnostics and cosmetics. These acquisitions, however, provided "little more than a stream of operating losses and management distraction that has hurt its basic tampon business."[3] In its retrenchment strategy, Tambrands sold both the diagnostics and cosmetics businesses at a loss. However, since pruning those operations, it has performed well by concentrating solely on its tampon business.

■ Portfolio Management and Corporate-Level Strategy Issues

Many firms operate multiple business units in various industries, as we saw in Chapter 5. At the corporate level of such enterprises, the task is to use S.W.O.T. analysis to analyze each business unit within a portfolio framework context. For example, a very weak business unit that faces critical external threats would be placed in compartment I of our proposed S.W.O.T. framework. (Alternatively, this same business would be classified as a "dog" in the original BCG framework, would be placed in the "divest" compartment of the revised BCG framework, and would be considered an "unsuccessful business unit" in the GE framework.) Once the business unit is placed in the appropriate category in the portfolio framework, then the guidelines associated with its placement may be used to recommend corporate growth, stability, or retrenchment strategies. In the example we are using, the guideline in our S.W.O.T. framework is to liquidate the business. (The original BCG, revised BCG, and GE frameworks recommend either liquidating or divesting the business.)

You may also wish to determine how involved corporate-level top management should get in formulating and implementing business unit strategies.

Recall from Chapter 5 that centralized decision making may be appropriate for corporations with related businesses, while decentralization may be more effective for firms operating unrelated businesses. Finally, you may wish to explore such issues in the case as corporate returns and top management's motives for engaging in acquisitions.

■ Business Unit Strategies and Functional Strategies

If the case is about a corporation with individual business units, then the units may have adopted different generic business unit strategies. If the firm is in a single business, such as McDonald's or Tambrands, then its business unit and corporate-level strategies are the same. In either case, your task is to identify which business unit strategy the firm has adopted and to evaluate how appropriate that strategy is. Is it compatible with the firm's corporate strategies and with its objectives for market share? Does it enable the company to compete effectively? Here you will wish to refer to Chapter 6 and review the seven generic strategies available to business units.

As discussed in Chapter 7, business unit strategies influence functional strategies; and conversely, the extent to which functional strategies are effectively formulated helps determine the success of the business strategies. In this section of your analysis, you will want to explore the consistency of the business unit strategies and the supporting functional strategies.

For example, if the corporation emphasizes scope economies and if the business unit has adopted a low-cost strategy, then it would be inconsistent for the business unit to formulate a marketing strategy with costly advertising and promotion. However, expensive promotional campaigns would be consistent with corporate scope innovations and the adoption of the differentiation strategy.

Your analysis may extend to other considerations as well. For instance, a firm that produces a high-priced luxury product with the niche-differentiation strategy should not pursue a goal of substantially increasing its production/operations capacity and market share. Consumers who purchase luxury products or services do so only as long as the items are perceived as exclusive.

■ Strategy Implementation

The actual implementation of corporate, business unit, and functional strategies is considered in this part of your analysis. Reference to Chapter 8 will help you in evaluating the relationship of the firm's organizational structure to its strategies. Is this structure suitable for a firm with these strategies? Or has the firm outgrown the need for this structure?

Chapter 9 should assist you in determining whether the CEO's leadership style and use of power are appropriate for the firm's strategies. Also consider whether the organization's culture is supportive of the strategies that it is attempting to implement.

Note that some cases will give you considerable information on strategy implementation, organizational charts, organizational culture, and the CEO. Others will provide little data on these matters. If your professor encourages outside research, you can usually collect at least some information on these issues if the firm is a large, publicly held corporation.

■ Strategic Control

Although strategic control was discussed in Chapter 10, the actual process involves every aspect of strategic management. That is, strategic control is a process that must occur in the analysis of the following aspects of the firm:

- Macroenvironment
- Industry environment
- Mission, goals, and objectives
- Strategy formulation
- Strategy implementation

In this section of your analysis, you will want to determine which aspects of the case are in particular need of strategic control scrutiny and, if possible, attempt to bring them together to draw overall conclusions. It is helpful, as Chapter 10 points out, to compare this year's results with those of the firm in previous years. Alternatively, strategic control may be examined by comparing the firm's qualitative and quantitative results with those of its rivals. If you have access to the PIMS program, you may wish to use it for these comparisons.

Besides PIMS, there are other sources of data available for assessing strategic control. They include Dun & Bradstreet's *Industry Norms and Key Business Ratios* and various publications by Value Line, Standard and Poor's, Moody's, and Robert Morris Associates. Additional information can be gleaned from annual reports and 10-K reports of the firm's chief competitors. Recall that strategic control involves not only quantitative data but also qualitative information. Annual reports and industry analyses, such as those by Standard and Poor's and Moody's, are particularly rich in qualitative information.

Financial ratios are central to your quantitative analysis. The idea is to discern trends by calculating certain key ratios and then comparing them with (1) the median ratios in the industry, (2) the ratios of the firm's major competitors, and (3) the firm's ratios in prior years. Exhibit 1 lists many of the most important ratios, shows how to calculate them, and indicates what they mean.

A less common ratio, market to book value, should also be calculated. Simply divide the firm's latest stock price by its book value per share; the result helps indicate whether investors view the firm's future positively. If the ratio is greater than 1, then investors forecast that the company's return on equity is expected to be greater than its required rate of return. If it is less than 1, then the firm's forecasted return on equity is less than its required rate of return. This ratio allows you to assess how favorably the stock market views the strategic direction of the firm.

■ Your Recommendations for Future Action

In the preceding sections of your analysis, you have probably identified issues, problems, and inconsistencies that need to be addressed. At this point, you should make recommendations in those areas. That is, what should the company do next? In some cases, modifications may need to be made in the firm's corporate-level or business unit strategies; in others, only one or several of the

Exhibit 1 **Financial Ratios**

Ratio	*Formula*	*What the Ratios Represent*
Liquidity Ratios		
Current ratio	$\frac{\text{Current assets}}{\text{Current liabilities}}$	Indicates how much of the current liabilities the current assets can cover; ordinarily, a ratio of 2 to 1 or better is desirable
Quick ratio or acid-test ratio	$\frac{\text{Current assets} - \text{inventory}}{\text{Current liabilities}}$	Indicates how much of the current liabilities the current assets can immediately cover, excluding the inventory (since inventories may not be subject to immediate sale or may have a lower market value than book value)
Inventory-to-net working capital ratio	$\frac{\text{Inventory}}{\text{Current assets} - \text{current liabilities}}$	Indicates to what extent net working capital may be threatened by inventory buildup
Activity Ratios		
Inventory turnover	$\frac{\text{Net sales}}{\text{Inventory}}$	Indicates how many times average inventory of finished goods is sold per year
Days of inventory	$\frac{\text{Inventory}}{\text{Cost of goods sold} \div 365}$	Indicates the number of one day's inventory the firm has at a given time
Net working capital	$\frac{\text{Net sales}}{\text{Net working capital}}$	Measures how efficiently net working capital is used to produce net sales
Asset turnover	$\frac{\text{Sales}}{\text{Total assets}}$	Measures how efficiently the company's total assets are used to produce sales
Fixed-asset turnover	$\frac{\text{Sales}}{\text{Fixed assets}}$	Measures how efficiently fixed assets (plant, equipment, buildings, etc.) produce sales
Average collection period	$\frac{\text{Accounts receivable}}{\text{Sales for year} \div 365}$	Measures the number of days it takes to convert accounts receivable into cash
Accounts receivable turnover	$\frac{\text{Annual credit sales}}{\text{Accounts receivable}}$	Measures the number of times accounts receivable is turned over in a year
Accounts payable period	$\frac{\text{Accounts payable}}{\text{Purchases for year} \div 365}$	Indicates the number of times accounts payable is turned over in a year
Days of cash	$\frac{\text{Cash}}{\text{Net sales for year} \div 365}$	Measures the number of days of cash on hand within the context of recent revenue levels
Leverage Ratios		
Debt-to-asset ratio	$\frac{\text{Total debt}}{\text{Total assets}}$	Indicates the percentage that borrowed funds are utilized to finance the assets of the firm
Debt-to-equity ratio	$\frac{\text{Total debt}}{\text{Stockholders' equity}}$	Indicates the ratio of funds provided by creditors as compared with owners
Long-term debt-to-equity ratio	$\frac{\text{Long-term debt}}{\text{Stockholders' equity}}$	Indicates the percentage of funds provided by long-term creditors as compared with owners
Times interest earned	$\frac{\text{Profit before taxes} + \text{interest charges}}{\text{Interest charges}}$	Measures the capability of the firm to make good on its yearly interest costs
Profitability Ratios		
Return on investment	$\frac{\text{Net income before taxes}}{\text{Total assets}}$	Measures rate of return on total assets employed
Return on equity	$\frac{\text{Net profit after taxes}}{\text{Stockholders' equity}}$	Measures the rate of return on the book value of total stockholders' equity
Return on sales	$\frac{\text{Net operating profit before taxes}}{\text{Net sales}}$	Indicates ratio of return on net sales

functional strategies (e.g., financial strategy or marketing strategy) may need improvement. Alternatively, changes may need to be made in the way the strategies are implemented.

The recommendations should be addressed to the firm's top management and should be well organized and well thought through. Also, they should be feasible in terms of human, organizational, and physical resources. Here, your ability to convince your instructor and classmates of the accuracy of your analysis and the power of your recommendations is of utmost importance.

In the final part of this section, you may want to deal with a synthesis of your proposals as they affect the entire organization. Remember that a change that you recommend in one aspect of the organization's strategies or operations may affect several other parts of the company.

We must emphasize that not all cases provide comprehensive information on all of the topics discussed in this chapter. Some may focus only on specific areas, such as ethics or new-product development. The framework presented here encompasses the total organization within its environment. Consequently, you may or may not be able to use this entire set of topics in analyzing any particular case. However, in any case analysis, you may find the information in Exhibit 2 useful. This table relates each section of your analysis to the corresponding chapter in this textbook. Prior to beginning your analysis, it may help you to scan or reread the discussion in the text regarding a particular issue.

COURSEWORK SUGGESTIONS

We would like to conclude by offering you some suggestions on how to perform well in the strategic management course.

Cross-Reference Information for Case Analyses **Exhibit 2**

Section of Analysis	*Textbook Chapter*
Macroenvironment	Chapter 2, "Environmental Opportunities and Threats"
Industry environment	Chapter 2, "Environmental Opportunities and Threats"
Mission, goals, objectives, social responsibility, and ethics	Chapter 3, "Organizational Direction: Mission and Goals"
Corporate-level strategies	Chapter 4, "Corporate-Level Strategies"
Portfolio management and corporate-level strategy issues	Chapter 5, "Portfolio Management and Corporate-Level Strategy Issues"
Business unit strategies and functional strategies	Chapter 6, "Business Unit Strategies"; Chapter 7, "Functional Strategies"
Strategy implementation	Chapter 8, "Strategy Implementation: Organizational Structure"; Chapter 9, "Strategy Implementation: Leadership, Power, and Organizational Culture"
Strategic control	Chapter 10, "Strategic Control"

1. Be actively involved in the course. At a minimum, you should attend all classes and participate fully in the class discussions. Participation involves asking questions, expressing your views, providing relevant examples from your own experience or outside reading, and helping extend the discussion to other related issues. Of course, case discussions can be exciting only when you have prepared for each class by knowing the facts and understanding the issues in the case. Thorough preparation will enable you to convey your knowledge and understanding to others clearly and persuasively. These skills are of considerable importance to a practicing manager.

2. As you participate, remember that this is a broad-based course in strategic management. Regardless of your particular academic major, attempt to view the issues in the case more broadly than you ordinarily might from the more limited perspective of a marketing major or a finance major, for instance. Remember that the goal is an integrated set of recommendations to top management.

3. Do not approach class discussions with a closed mind. A good discussion can bring out many different facets in a case—probably more than you can generate through an individual analysis. Listen to the other members of the class and evaluate their contributions carefully.

4. Do not let yourself be intimidated by a bad experience. Eventually, everyone in class may make an inane comment, may panic and lose the train of thought in midsentence, or may realize as he or she is speaking that what is being said is incorrect. Do not let these experiences affect your willingness to participate in the future. Participation in case analysis is an excellent training ground for future business presentations and committee meetings.

5. Do not suggest the use of a consultant. You are the consultant and should have specific, detailed recommendations for top management.

6. Learn to work well within a group. Many professors form teams of students in the strategic management course. Teamwork adds realism to the study of cases since, in reality, groups of key executives deal with strategic planning in business organizations. Working in a group, however, presents a particular set of challenges. Hence, we offer these suggestions:

- If you are allowed to select your group members, ensure that they have similar objectives for their grade in the course (if you are aiming for an A, do not join a group of students who wish to just squeak by, even if they are your best friends) and that you all have compatible schedules that permit you to meet outside of class.
- Try to form a group of individuals with different academic majors. Synergy is more likely to occur when the group has students who are majoring in different fields, such as finance, accounting, information systems, human resource management, and production/operations management.
- Do not divide the case into parts and assign an individual to each part. This technique will result in a fragmented, piecemeal, and disjointed analysis. Even if the primary responsibility for various parts of the case is assigned to specific individuals, every member of the group should be involved in all parts of the case analysis.

- Cooperate closely with one another. Through cooperation and a free exchange of ideas, the team should be able to devise innovative solutions to case problems. But the only way to accomplish this is for every member to participate fully during the team meetings. Ideally, only one person should talk at a time, while the others listen. One member should record all of the ideas expressed. If one person is particularly shy, others should encourage that person to talk by using such techniques as asking "What is your opinion on that issue?"
- Divide the work equitably. If one member is not doing his or her fair share, you must diplomatically, but quickly, inform that person that more is expected.
- Prepare thoroughly for the oral presentation. It is essential that you rehearse, as a group, several times. Ensure that each member knows his or her cue for speaking. Do not bring extensive notes and read from them. On the other hand, do not memorize your part word for word. Rather, prepare an outline of your part, and then let the key points on the outline guide your presentation.
- Be sure that your oral presentation fits neatly into the time allotted by your professor. It is not uncommon to see case presentations that either do not fully utilize the time allotted or run out of time before alternatives and recommendations can be thoroughly addressed. It is your responsibility to know the time allotment, provide detailed analysis, and set priorities so that key issues can be covered without rushing at the end.
- Get accustomed to speaking before people. Such presentations are routine in most aspects of the business world, so this course gives you an excellent opportunity to overcome your hesitancy to talk before a large group. If you have prepared well and have rehearsed several times, your presentation will be well received by your audience, even though you personally may feel a bit uncomfortable.

SUMMARY

The remainder of this book contains cases. A case portrays a real organizational situation and requires you to analyze that situation and then develop recommendations for future action. To accomplish these ends, you will need to take a broad, companywide perspective.

After reading the case carefully several times, you will want to take notes to organize your analysis and presentation. We suggest that you analyze the case by using the following outline:

- Macroenvironment
- Industry environment
- Mission, goals, objectives, social responsibility, and ethics
- Corporate-level strategies
- Portfolio management and corporate-level strategy issues
- Business unit strategies and functional strategies
- Strategy implementation
- Strategic control
- Your recommendations for future action

Finally, we offer several suggestions for enhancing your performance in the strategic management course and for working within a group.

NOTES

1. P. Ingrassia and J.B. White, "With Its Market Share Sliding, GM Scrambles to Avoid a Calamity," *The Wall Street Journal*, 14 December 1989; K. Kerwin, J.B. Treece, T. Peterson, L. Armstrong, and K.L. Miller, "Detroit's Big Chance," *Business Week*, 29 June 1992, pp. 82–90.
2. J.B. Treece, "Will Detroit Cut Itself Loose from Captive Imports?" *Business Week*, 4 September 1989, p. 34.
3. A. Dunkin, "They're More Single-Minded at Tambrands," *Business Week*, 28 August 1989, p. 28.

CASE 1

Nike, Inc.

Randall K. White, University of Auburn at Montgomery

INTRODUCTION

In his letter to shareholders in the 1991 annual report, Philip H. Knight, Chairman and CEO, projected his outlook for the company:

> Around the world, people of all cultures are increasing their participation in fitness activities. All are motivated by the common desire for athletic and personal excellence.
>
> Nike—a simple sneaker company to many newspaper readers—is transforming into an international consumer products company. Companies attacking international markets generally will take one of two approaches: (1) lay a solid infrastructure and build off of it forever, or (2) cream it without regard to the long term. Obviously, we have chosen the first approach.
>
> Specifically, over the past decade, we have built an international management team of more than 1500 people. In Western Europe, we own the distribution rights over 90% of our sales. Nike has hired more than 1000 people in the last 12 months, mostly dictated by our desire to service and support our international growth.
>
> Shortly after the middle of the decade, Nike will be a bigger company outside the United States than inside. Given the speed and power of global communications, there will no longer be a different brand leading the market in each hemisphere. There will be one world leader in sports and fitness. You can easily guess which brand gets my vote.
>
> The payoff from overcoming all these challenges can be seen in our 1991 international growth of 80% to $862 million in revenues. We are at last, after many sometimes comical fits and starts, after 10 years of hard work, a serious threat not only in Europe, but in Asia as well.

Reflecting Knight's comments, Nike experienced continued growth in net income, from $167 million in 1989 to $243 million in 1990 to over $287 million

---

This case is intended for classroom discussion only, not to depict effective or ineffective handling of administrative situations. All rights reserved to the author.

in 1991, an increase of over 71% since 1989. This impressive growth was in sharp contrast to the reported income of $36 million in 1987. The company reported that the decline in 1987 was due to three factors: the "decrease in volume of Air Jordan basketball products, the elimination in 1987 revenues from the company's unprofitable Japanese subsidiary which was sold, and increased competition. . . " [1]. However, profits rebounded to over $101 million in 1988,

> . . . partly because of a swing in buyer's tastes. After years of preferring stylish Reeboks, the trendsetters are now clamoring for "performance" shoes such as Nike's. [4]

Sales followed a relatively similar pattern. From 1989 to 1990, revenues climbed from over $1.7 billion to about $2.2 billion, a 29% increase. The following year, 1991, revenues exceeded $3 billion, a 34% increase.

The company's inventory position increased from $309 million in 1990 to about $586 million in 1991, a $277 million increase. Approximately $157 million of this increase was in domestic footwear, while international inventories increased $102 million to handle the increased demand.

Nevertheless, as it faced stiff challenges in its various market segments, the question remained whether Nike could respond fast enough to remain a top athletic shoe manufacturer. Other strategic questions were facing the company. (a) Nike was a low-cost producer with overseas manufacturing facilities in Asia—notably South Korea, Thailand, and Taiwan where 51%, 15%, and 13%, respectively, of shoes were produced. About 43% of the company's apparel production was also located in Asia and in South America. Could the potential political risks, increasing costs, and a declining U.S. dollar compel the company to retrench and make other sourcing arrangements? (b) Did it have the financial muscle and customer franchise to counter such strong competitors as Reebok, L.A. Gear, and others? (c) Would the intense competition in the industry compel the company to sell its high-quality athletic footwear as private-branded products for major retailing chains? Or, should it position itself as the premier athletic shoe company?

BRIEF HISTORY

Incorporated in 1968 in Oregon, Nike began years earlier "when Knight, a former college miler, sold running shoes from the back of his station wagon at track meets" [2]. A native of Oregon and born in 1938, Knight graduated from the University of Oregon in 1959 with a BBA and later received his MBA from Stanford in 1962. His interests in running shoes remained strong during this period after visiting Japan, which he felt would become a major player in the athletic shoe market. Knight joined Coopers & Lybrand as an accountant from 1963 to 1964 and then moved to Price Waterhouse from 1964 to 1967. He later became an assistant professor in business administration at Portland State University from 1967 to 1969. Both *Fortune* and *Business Week* magazines provided interesting personal glimpses of Knight:

> He is no match for Bo Jackson, the pro football and baseball player who displays a stunning athletic versatility in the ubiquitous TV ads for Nike shoes. But for a middle-aged CEO who gently complains about "old bones," Phil Knight, 51, does all right. He runs 18 to 30 miles a week, lifts weights, plays tennis. [4]

> Philip H. Knight, shy? In private, yes. A foot twitches nervously while the blond, bearded chief executive officer of Nike Inc. talks about himself. But watch the former college runner in competition, and "shy" is not a word anyone would dare hang on Phil Knight. He is emotional about Nike, even prone to watery eyes during his employee pep talks. And when a guy like that gets beat, he usually gets even. [4]

Knight and his track coach, William Bowerman of the University of Oregon, formed Blue Ribbon Sports on an initial investment of $500 each and began importing Tiger brand shoes from Japan. The venture enjoyed considerable success as sales surged from its modest beginning of $3 million in 1972 to fiscal year-end 1988, when sales exceeded $1 billion. However, disputes with the company's large supplier led the company to design and market its own shoes, which the founders named Nike, after the Greek goddess of victory.

Highly regarded within the company as the driving entrepreneurial force that ultimately transformed Nike into a world-class athletic footwear manufacturer, Knight visualized the company focusing on three core areas: shoes, related clothing, and accessories. At the same time, he viewed timely acquisitions as a way to strengthen the company's position in the highly competitive athletic footwear market. Moreover, Knight envisioned the company primarily as a producer of performance-oriented shoes, not a fashion shoe company.

ORGANIZATION

Nike's organizational structure is shown in Exhibit 1. Although generally regarded as a company with a deliberately lean structure intended to foster autonomy and an entrepreneurial climate, Nike has a formalized management structure that defines accountability and responsibility. This presumably freed Knight to deal with long-term strategic issues.

The company's experienced executive officers and the board of directors are listed in Exhibit 2. Outsiders accounted for one-half of the board membership; in addition, six of its officers, including Knight, are CPAs.

Nike's basic mission is the design, development, and worldwide merchandising of high-quality footwear and apparel products for a wide range of sport, athletic, and leisure activities. Nike does not see itself as a manufacturer but more a market-driven company. Consequently, it does a number of things very well—for example, maintaining and nurturing the ability to pinpoint future trends in the industry, continuing to strengthen its R&D capability for new and technologically superior athletic footwear, and cultivating its existing and potential relationships with its various domestic and international contract manufacturers in order to ensure product quality.

In effect, Nike, as well as many other U.S. companies, has essentially become a marketer for foreign producers; that is, a company such as Nike, which designs, develops, and markets products worldwide, does not manufacture anything! In contrast to traditional manufacturers, these firms are labeled "hollow corporations" [14, p. 57]. As many U.S. firms move to low-cost overseas producers (e.g., Taiwan, South Korea, and others), this continued outsourcing could bring about a decline in U.S. manufacturing capability. Some see these "hollow corporations" as "network companies"—that is, companies that depend on other firms for manufacturing and other functional support.

Exhibit 1 **Nike Management Organization Chart**

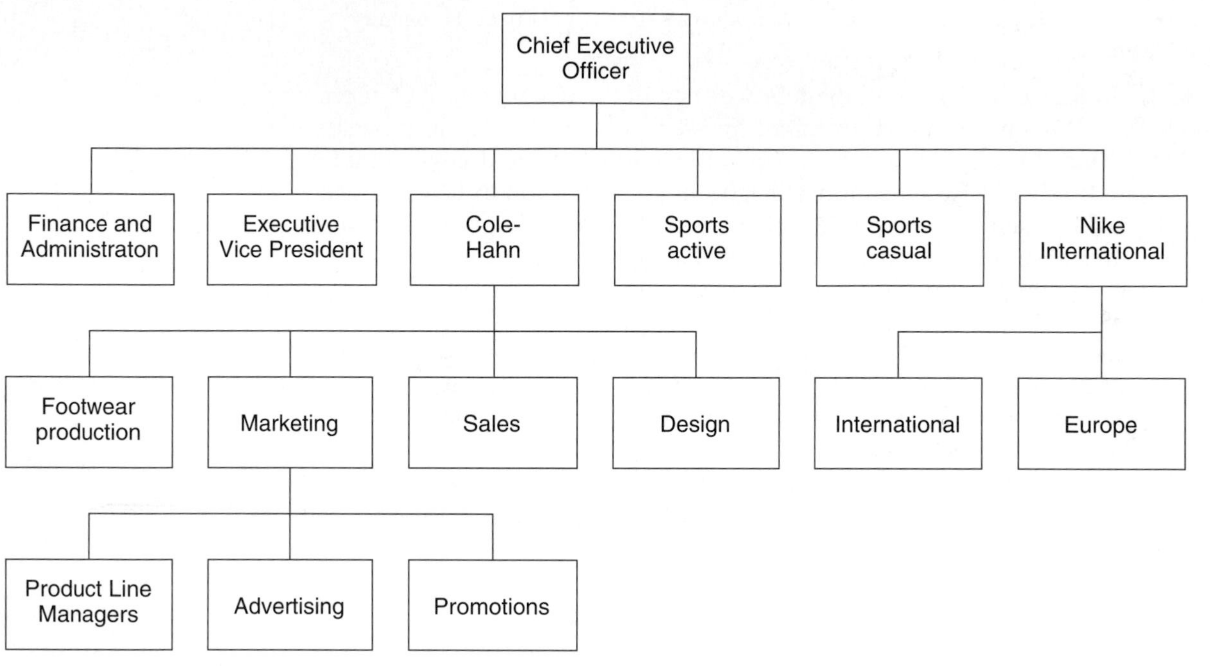

MARKETING

■ Product

Although the company's footwear products are targeted for athletic use, many buyers tend to wear them also for casual and leisure purposes. To complement its footwear merchandise and round out its athletic image, Nike produces a variety of accessory and apparel items such as athletic bags, hats, socks, jackets, warm-up suits, shorts, T-shirts, and tank tops. The company also introduced the Nike Monitor, an electronic monitoring training aid.

Jones [2] reported that Nike may need to diversify to stay ahead in the highly competitive and mature running shoe market, and perhaps, "to change its image from a running shoe company to a total-fitness-oriented operation." However, it was unlikely it would abandon the running shoe market—a unique Nike strength.

To protect its market share from fast-growing fashion-oriented competitors such as Reebok and L.A. Gear, Nike introduced, in late 1988, a new line called Side One,

> . . . a nontechnical shoe for teenager girls who buy athletic, or athletic-looking shoes, to make a fashion statement. Those customers are the core of Keds' and L.A. Gear's business. [7]

The company missed the shift in consumer preferences toward fashion and sport-styled shoes, and consumer desire to stay fit through a variety of such

Nike, Inc. Officers and Directors

Exhibit 2

Name	***Age***	***Position with Nike, Principal Occupation, and Business Experience***
Philip H. Knight*,**(1) Chairman and CEO	50	Co-founder of the company and has served as its Chairman of the Board and, except for the period June 1983 through September 1984, as its President since its organization in 1968.
Richard K. Donahue*,**(1) President and Chief Operating Officer	n/a	Partner, Donahue & Donahue, Attorneys, Lowell, Massachusetts
William J. Bowerman*,**(2) Deputy Chairman of the Board of Directors and Senior Vice President	77	Co-founder of the company, has served as Sr. Vice President and a Director since 1968 and was elected Senior Vice President and Deputy Chairman of the Board in 1980.
Delbert J. Hayes*,**(4) Executive Vice President	53	Joined the company as Treasurer and Executive and became a Director in 1975. He thereafter served as Treasurer and in a number of executive positions, primarily in manufacturing, until his election as Executive Vice President in 1980. He is a certified public accountant.
Thomas E. Clarke* General Manager and Vice President	n/a	n/a
Harry C. Carsh* Vice President	49	Joined the company in 1977 and was elected Vice President in June 1984. Mr. Carsh has held executive positions in accounting, manufacturing, and European marketing. He has served as Vice President in charge of the International Division and is currently Vice President in charge of merchandising operations. Prior to joining the company, he served for four years as Vice President of Finance for Laneet Medical Industries. He is a certified public accountant.
Nicholas Kartalis* Vice President	n/a	n/a
Ronald E. Nelson* Vice President	45	Has been employed by the company since 1976, with primary responsibilities in finance, marketing, and production. He is currently Vice President in charge of the company's footwear production operations. He was elected Vice President in 1983. He is a certified public accountant.
Mark G. Parker*	n/a	n/a

Continued

Exhibit 2

Nike, Inc. Officers and Directors (continued)

Name	*Age*	*Position with Nike, Principal Occupation, and Business Experience*
George E. Porter* Vice President—Finance	57	Joined the company as Vice President in 1982 and has held executive positions in administration, research and development, and footwear. He became Vice President—Finance in February 1985. Prior to joining the company, he was employed for nine years by Evans Products Company, Portland, Oregon, as Vice President and Controller. He is a certified public accountant.
David B. Taylor* Vice President	n/a	n/a
John E. Jaqua*,**(3)(5) Secretary	67	Has been Secretary and a Director of the company since 1968. He has been a principal in the law firm of Jaqua, Wheatley, Gallagher and Holland, P.C., Eugene, Oregon since 1962.
Lindsay D. Stewart* Vice President & Corporate Counsel	n/a	n/a
Thomas Niebergall* Assistant Secretary	n/a	n/a
Jill K. Conway**(2)	n/a	Visiting Scholar, Massachusetts Institute of Technology, Boston, Massachusetts.
Robert T. Davis**(2)	n/a	Professor of Marketing, Stanford University, Palo Alto, California.
Robert D. DeNuncio** (3)(4)(5)	n/a	n/a
Douglas G. Houser**(2)	n/a	Assistant Secretary, Nike, Inc.; Partner—Bullivant, Houser, Bailey, Pendergrass & Hoffman, Attorneys, Portland, Oregon.
Thomas O. Paine**(3)(5)	n/a	Chairman, Thomas Paine Associates, Los Angeles, California.
Charles W. Robinson**(4)	n/a	Chairman, Energy Transition Corporation, Santa Fe, New Mexico.
John R. Thompson, Jr.**(3)	n/a	Head Basketball Coach, Georgetown University.

*Officers, annual report.
**Directors
(1) Member—Executive Committee
(2) Member—Audit Committee
(3) Member—Personnel Committee
(4) Member—Finance Committee
(5) Member—Stock Option Committee

activities as running, weightlifting, aerobics, tennis, and other sports activities [3]. To meet this need, Nike developed the cross-training shoe, which was a natural product evolution for the company, whose prime attention was directed toward specialized products. The company pinpointed the product's marketing message toward the shoe's economy and the convenience of buying, wearing, and carrying only one pair of shoes for diverse fitness activities. The shoe was a result of the company's commitment to thorough research of the foot's biomechanical movements. To convey the cross-trainer's technical qualities, Nike contracted with 100 of the top U.S. fitness instructors and provided them with samples of the product to influence their students as well as to take part in trade shows and other sales activities [15].

To further expand its product lines, Nike acquired, in May 1988, Cole-Hahn Holdings, Inc., "a leading designer and marketer of high quality casual and dress shoes." Nike paid for the acquisition with $89.2 million in cash and the issuance of 243,713 shares of Nike stock, which had a market value of $5.8 million, for the remainder [1]. Knight estimated the company's efforts to broaden its lines would increase sales by $150 million and would position Nike with the "most prestigious brands at both ends of the footwear spectrum" [8]. Knight added that about "69% of the company's shoe sales come from models costing between $44 and $73 a pair" [8].

■ Promotion

Advertising and promotion expenditures steadily increased, from $135 million in 1989 to $190 million in 1990 (a 40% increase), then doubled from 1989 to 1991, to $286 million. Promotional activities include brochures, print and TV advertising, as well as point-of-purchase displays. Posters are used to depict new footwear models promoted by the company.

Other promotional efforts have included publication of the book *Walk On*, which was co-authored by the former sports research laboratory director and a senior editor of *American Health Magazine*. Containing extensive information on walking—a potentially large growth area for the company—the book provided relevant consumer and product information. Back-to-school campaigns broadened the children's line of such new products as the Air Jordan, Air Max, and the Air Trainer; these were competitively promoted in the "fifty-dollar" range. Other new children's shoes were designed exclusively for children's activities such as skateboarding and biking. In addition, a licensing arrangement with Major League Baseball allowed the company to market specially designed baseball apparel; this unique opportunity would enable Nike to transfer its favorable sports image to both on and off the field.

Nike has also developed a co-op advertising program whereby a retailer can accumulate a 1% to 3% credit allowance based on its total footwear purchases. For example, assuming a 1% allowance on $100,000 of footwear purchases, the retailer could build up $1,000 of credit with Nike whereby it could use this "credit" to buy certain promotional items such as watches, sunglasses, and ankle weights. The applicable percentage for the retailer is based on population and buying power data.

To a large extent, Nike relies heavily on endorsements by prominent athletes from a variety of sports such as running, walking, track, tennis, basketball, football, baseball, and racquetball, and from such general fitness activities as aerobics. Hence, the high performance of Nike is consistently advertised by these top athletes. The company's Air Ace tennis shoe achieved a milestone when it received the first endorsement of a U.S.-based shoe manufacturer by a Soviet sports federation; this allowed the company to introduce its products into the Soviet Union. The company has also promoted the higher-priced cross-training shoe, the Air Trainer, as one-shoe for all purposes! To further develop this concept, the company signed Bo Jackson, the versatile NFL (Los Angeles Raiders) and Major League Baseball (Chicago White Sox) superstar to endorse the cross-training line [6].

The company achieved a milestone in 1985, when it signed Chicago Bulls basketball star Michael Jordan to a contract. Jordan, who had just completed an outstanding rookie year in the National Basketball Association, was hired to introduce the new Air Jordan leather basketball shoe [9]. This shoe, which had a special gas pocket in its sole, provided extra spring and better protection from serious injuries usually encountered by the professional basketball athlete to the foot, leg, and back. The Air Jordan was cited as one of several "new products" for the year by *Fortune* magazine [10]. Nike also signed Charles Barkley of the Phoenix Suns [9].

■ Distribution

Domestic

The company's approximately 17,000 retail accounts racked up over $2 billion in sales in 1991, about 71% of total revenues. Retailers included department, footwear, and sporting goods stores as well as tennis and golf shops and other specialty retailers. The three largest retail customers accounted for about 30% of domestic sales; military sales were handled in-house.

Independent regional sales representatives are assigned several associate representatives and specific accounts within their jurisdictions. These associate representatives, who work solely on commission, are especially careful to ensure that retailer orders are handled promptly and within monthly deadlines. To establish and maintain a solid loyal dealer network as well as control the demands placed on the company's transportation and delivery system, Nike set up its innovative Futures ordering program whereby retailers could place their orders five to six months in advance and Nike would guarantee that 90% of their orders would be delivered on a set date at a fixed price. The Futures program has had some success in controlling inventory; for example, 81% of domestic footwear shipments in 1991 (excluding Cole-Hahn) were made under this program compared to 82% and 79% in 1990 and 1989, respectively [1]. As ocean and air carriers are used to transport products produced overseas into the United States, Nike exerts much effort to work closely with U.S. Customs Service to avoid the inspections and seizures other importers face. This working relationship also helps the company to detect counterfeiters of athletic footwear, apparel, and sports bags [16]. Additionally, imported products are subject to duties collected by the Customs Service.

Another innovation is Nike's next-day guarantee shipment for certain "team accounts" such as colleges and universities. According to one source, if the university faces an emergency when a few athletes require a certain size or type of shoe, the institution can contact Nike's Promotion Division for a special shipment of this equipment. The shoes are shipped via Federal Express. The program is reported to be very successful because of the high degree of loyalty these accounts provide Nike. Team accounts also have access to Nike's Futures program; for example, orders placed in December will be delivered by June or July of the following year. Regional distribution centers for footwear are located in Wilsonville and Beaverton, Oregon; Memphis, Tennessee; Greenland, New Hampshire; and Yarmouth, Maine. Apparel goods are shipped exclusively from Memphis.

The company also has 40 wholly owned retail outlets. *Chain Store Age Executives,* a trade publication, described one of Nike's innovative retail outlets. It cited the store's attractive display of styles and colors for footwear and clothing, which are geared toward a variety of sports. Knowledgeable sales personnel staff the store; they know the product, can explain it, and use it themselves. Shoes are turned upside down to show their soles, thus differentiating the various types of athletic footwear. Apparently, Nike capitalized on the simple idea that customers prefer to buy from salespeople who really know what they sell [17].

Twenty-two outlets sell primarily "B grade" and closeout merchandise. "B grade" merchandise has "cosmetic" defects such as discoloration, poor stitching, and so on and is therefore not first quality. As this merchandise is not first line, these products are sold in plain white boxes marked "blemished."

Foreign

Nike markets its products through independent distributors, licensees, subsidiaries, and branch offices located in about 66 countries outside the United States. Foreign sales accounted for 29% of revenues in 1991, compared to 21% and 20% for 1990 and 1989, respectively. Branch offices are located in Canada, Brazil, Belgium, Denmark, France, Great Britain, Hong Kong, Italy, Norway, South Korea, Spain, Sweden, Taiwan, West Germany, the Netherlands, Indonesia, Malaysia, Singapore, and Thailand. Since 1972, the Japanese trading company Nissho Iwai American Corporation (NIAC) has provided Nike with substantial financing and export–import services, enabling Nike to buy through NIAC almost all of its athletic footwear and apparel for U.S. and European sales. Nike also bought goods for other foreign sales through NIAC. In 1991, the largest single foreign supplier outside the United States accounted for about 7% of total production.

RESEARCH AND DEVELOPMENT

The company takes an aggressive stance in designing and marketing innovative footwear products based on such customer benefits as performance, reliability, quality, and reduction or prevention of injury—factors that appeal to both the professional and nonprofessional athlete. In-house specialists come from a variety of such backgrounds as "biomechanics, exercise physiology, engineering, industrial design and related fields" [1, p. 2]. The company set up advisory boards and research committees to review designs, materials, and product concepts; these groups included a broad range of experts such as athletes, coaches, trainers, equipment managers, orthopedists, podiatrists, and other professionals. R&D expenditures averaged over $8.4 million from 1989 to 1991.

Its Sports Research Lab, reputedly one of the most sophisticated among shoe manufacturers, is equipped to do biomechanical and anatomical checks on footwear "using the latest traction-testing devices and high-speed video cameras." Through careful testing procedures, Nike evaluates shoes in diverse locations under varying climatic conditions. Over a 90-day period, testers log reports of "total miles and terrain traversed, reporting every 2 weeks on cushioning, flexibility, perception of weight, and durability" [18]. The company's advanced product engineers, regarded as the cornerstone of their R&D efforts, "devised the multisport cross-trainer shoe and conceived what became the aqua sock," now used widely by swimmers. Compounds and molds for footwear are also tested in a rubber laboratory; the molds for soles are constructed in a model shop, after which samples are manufactured by a small-scale shoe factory. A physical testing lab also evaluates shoe tension and adhesion.

Nike has an exclusive worldwide license to manufacture and sell footwear using its technology to deliver the ultimate cushioning agent: compressed air. According to *Science Digest*, Nike Air shoes feature

> gas-filled mattresses encapsulated in polyurethane. The walls of the mattress's inflated plastic tubes are supposed to be virtually leak-proof. The gas never breaks down, and it returns to the foot much of the energy of additional impact, acting somewhat like a trampoline. [19, p. 80]

Additional stability for the shoe is provided by using denser polyurethane, which collars the heel, plus a wider sole "along the inside of the foot near the arch." This feature helps to prevent the "foot's natural tendency to roll inward after landing," a tendency called pronation. E.C. Frederick, Nike's former director of the Sports Research Lab, called pronation the "'herpes' of the running crowd" [20]. This Air Revolution, as Nike called it, helped to introduce twelve new Nike-Air models. The research lab also pioneered other new materials such as durathane, a synthetic, and washable leather.

To protect itself from patent infringement, the company registered its Nike trademark and the well-known "Swoosh" design in over 70 countries. The company felt that these distinctive marks were important in marketing its products as well as distinguishing them from competitors' goods.

MANUFACTURING

In fiscal 1991, about 47% of Nike's apparel production was manufactured in the United States, by independent contract manufacturers located primarily in the southern states. The balance was manufactured by independent contractors in Asia and in South America, mainly in Hong Kong, Malaysia, Singapore, Taiwan, Thailand, Chile, and Peru. Almost all of its footwear is produced by Asian contractors in Taiwan, Indonesia, South Korea, and Thailand. Management contracts also exist with independent factories in Brazil, Hungary, Italy, Mexico, and the United States. Nike also has a management contract with the People's Republic of China (PRC) and has experienced no stoppages at these plants. The Chinese produce about 11% of its shoes [8, 1].

As mentioned earlier, South Korean, Thai, and Taiwanese contractors account for 51%, 15%, and 13%, respectively, of the company's total footwear production. Considering the magnitude of the company's dependence on Korean manufacturers, Nike's financial condition could be seriously affected by any disruptions in delivery of their products. However, the company has indicated that it has the ability to develop over a period of time alternative sources of supply for its products. Moreover, Nike claims that at the present time, it is not materially affected by this risk. Still another risk Nike faces with certain Asian manufacturers is increasing labor costs.

Management contracts are a critical part of Nike's overall strategy to provide its 17,000 retail accounts with a reliable delivery system. Moreover, these contracts allow the company to solidify its Futures program and enable Nike to guarantee retailers' orders by a set date and a fixed price. Additionally, the company is better able to refine its sales forecasts and, equally important, control inventory build-up and the subsequent costs. These independent domestic and foreign contractors provide Nike with two advantages: greater flexibility to take advantage of low-cost foreign labor and less capital requirements. Yet, foreign sourcing could cause the company a number of problems such as political instability, currency fluctuations, and the inability to repatriate profits.

Because of the volume of overseas production, Nike maintains a keen interest regarding any legislation passed by Congress that would impose quotas on certain countries that have been cited as having unfair trading practices. For example, Japan has been cited as having restrictive trade barriers that deny U.S. firms access to the Japanese market. Hence, the U.S. could assess an increase in duty rates on certain Japanese products imported into the United States. In addition, legislation has been introduced that could revoke the "most favored nation" status of the PRC and, consequently, result in a significant increase in tariffs on goods imported from China.

Raw materials such as canvas, rubber, nylon, and leather used in Nike's footwear products are purchased in bulk and are generally available in the countries where these products are manufactured. The company also acquired Tetra Plastics, Inc., in 1991, its only supplier for the air-sole cushioning components used in footwear. Hence, Nike encounters little difficulty in meeting its raw materials requirements. Moreover, to assure uniform product quality, Nike provides its contractors with exacting product guidelines, which, according to one source, are closely monitored through on-site expatriate quality control personnel. It should be noted that there is an industry trend to move from relatively high labor cost countries such as Taiwan and South Korea to other low-cost Asian countries.

THE COMPETITION

Several firms can be identified as competitors in the U.S. athletic shoe market (see Exhibits 3 and 4). This $5.8 billion wholesale market in 1991 was characterized as one with a shoe for any occasion. According to *Marketing and Media Decisions*, about 80% of the athletic shoes purchased are not used for the activity they are designed for; hence, the shoes' look counts. Moreover, basketball shoes are the largest segment, with a 28% share of the market, claimed the Sporting Goods Manufacturers Association [21]. Exhibits 5 through 9 show the financial picture for Nike, followed by Exhibits 10 through 13, which detail the financial picture for its competitors.

Exhibit 3

Athletic Footwear World Market Share, 1991

Nike*	20.72%
Reebok*	16.18
Adidas	9.89
L.A. Gear*	5.23
ASICS (Tiger)	4.95
Aritmos (includes Etonic, Puma)	3.51
Keds*	3.14
Converse*	3.09
Others (includes licenses)	33.29

*U.S.-based company.

Source: Sporting Goods Intelligence, as cited in *The Wall Street Journal,* July 11, 1992, p. 417.

Exhibit 4

Financial Data, 1989–1991 (in millions)

	1989	***1990***	***1991***
Net Sales			
Nike	$1710.8	$2235.2	$3003.6
Reebok	1822.1	2159.2	2734.5
L.A. Gear	617.1	902.2	618.1
Net Income			
Nike	167.1	243.0	287.1
Reebok	175.0	176.6	234.7
L.A. Gear	55.1	31.3	d45.0
Net Profit Margin			
Nike	9.8%	10.9%	9.6%
Reebok	9.6%	8.2%	8.6%
L.A. Gear	8.9%	3.5%	NMF
% Earned Net Worth			
Nike	29.7%	31.0%	27.8%
Reebok	20.7%	17.7%	28.5%
L.A. Gear	32.7%	15.2%	NMF

Source: Value Line.

Nike Revenues by Product Categories for the Fiscal Years Ended May 31, 1991, 1990, 1989 **Exhibit 5**

	1991	*Percent Change*	*1990 (in thousands)*	*Percent Change*	*1989*	*Percent Change*
Domestic footwear	$1,676,400	22	$1,368,900	29	$1,058,400	40
Domestic apparel	325,700	22	266,100	28	208,200	46
Other brands	139,400	16	120,500	26	95,500	—
Total United States	2,141,500	22	1,755,500	29	1,362,100	51
International						
Europe	664,700	99	334,300	38	241,400	3
Canada	98,100	7	92,100	76	52,200	66
Other	99,300	86	53,300	(3)	55,100	45
Total International	862,100	80	479,700	38	348,700	15
Total Nike	$3,003,600	34	$2,235,200	31	$1,710,800	42

Source: 1991 annual report.

■ Reebok International, Ltd.

A closely held firm (about 60%) and a major competitor of Nike, Reebok was founded in 1979 when it acquired exclusive use of the name in North America—it bought the original English Reebok firm later, in mid-1985. The company was incorporated in Massachusetts to design, develop, and market athletic shoes and related accessories. It was initially a successful marketer of women's fashion aerobic shoes; however, in order to grow, the company needed to expand into men's performance athletic footwear such as basketball and tennis shoes. Exhibits 10 and 11 provide financial and operating data.

According to Steve Race, its general manager of athletic footwear, a shoe could have fashion and performance; moreover, fashion is "a very important function of our performance shoes. And in fashion shoes, performance in terms of comfort is a very important element" [21]. To stress performance, the company contracted with such professional athletes as Dominique Wilkins of the NBA's Atlanta Hawks and PGA professional Greg Norman. The company also added children's shoes to its product lines.

Reebok acquired the Rockport Company, a major walking and leisure shoe manufacturer, for about $119 million cash in late 1986 and followed with another major acquisition, for about $180 million in early 1987, of Avia Group International, a premium-priced athletic footwear and hiking shoes producer. Other acquisitions included the North American operations of the Italian Ellesses International for about $60 million; Ellesses manufactures premium-priced tennis shoes and ski fashions. Other acquisitions were the John A. Frye Company, a boot and loafer manufacturer, and Boston Whaler, a power boat firm [11, 12].

Six plants are located in Massachusetts and one in Oregon, the home state of Nike. The company sources over 70% of its footwear with contract manufacturers in South Korea, in addition to other plants located in Taiwan and the Philippines.

Exhibit 6

Nike, Inc. Consolidated Balance Sheet As of Fiscal Years May 31, 1991, 1990 (in thousands)

	1991	1990
Assets		
Current Assets		
Cash and equivalents	$ 119,804	$ 90,449
Accounts receivable, less allowance for doubtful accounts of $14,288 and $10,624	521,588	400,877
Inventories	586,594	309,476
Deferred income taxes	25,536	17,029
Prepaid expenses	26,738	19,851
Total current assets	1,280,260	837,682
Property, plant and equipment	397,601	238,461
Less accumulated depreciation	105,138	78,797
	292,463	159,664
Goodwill	114,710	81,021
Other assets	20,997	16,185
	$1,708,430	$1,094,552
Liabilities and Shareholders' Equity		
Current Liabilities		
Current portion of long-term debt	$ 580	$ 8,792
Notes payable	300,364	31,102
Accounts payable	165,912	107,423
Accrued liabilities	115,824	94,939
Income taxes payable	45,792	30,905
Total current liabilities	628,472	273,161
Long-term debt	29,992	25,941
Non-current deferred income taxes and purchased tax benefits	16,877	10,931
Commitments and contingencies	—	—
Redeemable preferred stock	300	300
Shareholders' equity		
Common Stock at stated value:		
Class A convertible—27,438 and 28,102 shares outstanding	164	168
Class B—47,858 and 46,870 shares outstanding	2,712	2,706
Capital in excess of stated value	84,681	78,582
Foreign currency translation adjustment	(4,428)	1,035
Retained earnings	949,660	701,728
	1,032,789	784,219
	$1,708,430	$1,094,552

Source: 1991 Annual Report.

Nike, Inc. Consolidated Statement of Income Fiscal Years Ended May 31, 1989, 1990, and 1991 (in thousands, except per share data)

Exhibit 7

	1991	*1990*	*1989*
Revenues	$3,003,610	$2,235,244	$1,710,803
Costs and expenses:			
Cost of sales	1,850,530	1,384,172	1,074,831
Selling and administrative	664,061	454,521	354,825
Interest	27,316	10,457	13,949
Other (income) expense	(43)	(7,264)	(3,449)
	2,541,864	1,841,886	1,440,156
Income before income taxes	461,746	393,358	270,647
Income taxes	174,700	150,400	103,600
Net income	$ 287,046	$ 242,958	$ 167,047
Net income per common share	$ 3.77	$ 3.21	$ 2.22
Average number of common and common equivalent shares	76,067	75,668	75,144

Source: 1991 annual report.

Nike, Inc. Selected Financial Data Year Ended May 31, 1987 through 1991 (in thousands, except per share data)

Exhibit 8

	1991	*1990*	*1989*	*1988*	*1987*
Revenues	$3,003,610	$2,235,244	$1,710,803	$1,203,440	$877,357
Net income	287,046	242,958	167,047	101,695	35,879
Net income per common share	3.77	3.21	2.22	1.35	.46
Cash dividends declared per common share	.52	.38	.27	.20	.20
Working capital	$ 651,788	$ 564,521	$ 422,478	$ 298,816	$325,200
Total assets	1,708,430	1,094,552	825,410	709,095	511,843
Long-term debt	29,992	25,941	34,051	30,306	35,202
Redeemable preferred stock	300	300	300	300	300
Common shareholders' equity	1,032,789	784,219	561,804	411,774	338,017

Source: 1991 annual report.

Note: All per common share amounts have been adjusted to reflect the 2-for-1 stock split paid October 5, 1990. The company's class B common stock is listed on the New York and the Pacific Stock Exchanges and trades under the symbol NKE. At May 31, 1991, there were approximately 4,500 shareholders of record.

Exhibit 9

Nike, Inc. Operations by Geographic Areas Fiscal Years Ended May 31, 1991, 1990, and 1989 (in thousands)

	1991	*1990*	*1989*
Revenues from unrelated entities			
United States	$2,141,461	$1,755,496	$1,362,148
Europe	664,747	334,275	241,380
Other international	197,402	145,473	107,275
	$3,003,610	$2,235,244	$1,710,803
Intergeographic revenues			
United States	$ 9,111	$ 4,765	$ 1,757
Europe	—	—	—
Other international	11,892	5,628	4,323
	$21,003	$ 10,393	$ 6,080
Total revenues			
United States	$2,150,572	$1,760,261	$1,363,905
Europe	664,747	334,275	241,380
Other international	209,294	151,101	111,598
Less intergeographic revenues	(21,003)	(10,393)	(6,080)
	$3,003,610	$2,235,244	$1,710,803
Operating income			
United States	$ 325,257	$ 315,246	$ 230,156
Europe	134,069	55,098	35,376
Other international	51,745	42,880	30,173
Less corporate, interest, and other income (expense) and eliminations	(49,325)	(19,866)	(25,058)
	$ 461,746	$ 393,358	$ 270,647
Assets			
United States	$1,156,091	$ 786,775	$ 600,629
Europe	370,104	162,383	102,744
Other international	94,212	74,329	50,756
Total identifiable assets	1,620,407	1,023,487	754,129
Corporate cash and eliminations	88,023	71,065	71,281
	$1,708,430	$1,094,552	$ 825,410

Source: 1991 annual report.

Reebok International, Ltd. Consolidated Balance Sheet As of December 31, 1990 ($000)

Exhibit 10

	1990	*1989*
Assets		
Cash & cash equivalents	227,140	171,424
Accounts receivable, net	391,288[a]	289,363[a]
Inventory	367,233	276,911
Deferred income taxes	31,673	34,845
Prepaid expenses	12,328	11,735
Total current assets	1,029,662	784,278
Gross property & equipment	160,132	136,776
Less: Accumulated depreciation & amortization	49,017	30,542
Property & equipment, net	111,115	106,234
Intangibles, net of amortization	255,051	261,398
Other noncurrent assets	7,397	14,457
Total noncurrent assets	373,563	382,089
Total assets	1,403,225	1,166,367
Liabilities		
Notes payable to banks	8,855	1,651
Commercial paper	59,805	—
Current maturity of long-term debt	1,411	598
Accounts payable & accrued expenses	166,061	148,360
Income taxes payable	49,071	43,834
Dividends payable	8,576	8,538
Total current liabilities	293,779	202,981
Long-term debt, net current maturity	105,752	110,302
Deferred income taxes	6,975	7,788
Common stock	1,144[b]	1,139[b]
Additional paid-in capital	281,478	275,336
Retained earnings	707,336	564,987
Unearned compensation	dr 191	dr 524
Foreign currency translation adjusted	cr 6,962	cr 3,358
Stockholders' equity	996,729	844,296
Total liability and stockholders' equity	1,403,225	1,166,367
Net current assets	735,883	581,297
Book value	$6.48	$5.12

[a]Allowance for doubtful accounts: 1990, $33,730,000; 1989, $28,704,000.

[b]Par value $.01; Auth shs: 1990, 250,000,000; 1989, 250,000,000.

Source: Reebok Annual Reports.

Exhibit 11

Reebok International, Ltd. Consolidated Income Account
Years Ended December 31, 1990, 1989, 1988 ($000)

	1990	*1989*	*1988*[a]
Net sales	2,159,243	1,822,092	1,785,935
Other income (exp)	dr 893	11,377	dr 1,351
Gross operating revenues	2,158,350	1,833,469	1,784,584
Cost of sales	1,288,314	1,071,751	1,122,226
Selling expenses	353,983	278,939	260,891
General & administrative expenses	202,352	174,972	149,195
Amortization of intangibles	15,646	14,427	14,216
Interest expense	18,857	15,554	14,129
Interest income	15,637	12,953	6,633
Total costs & expenses	1,863,515	1,542,690	1,554,024
Income before income taxes	294,835	290,779	230,560
Income taxes	118,229	115,781	93,558
Net income	176,606	174,998	137,002
Previous retained earnings	564,987	424,002	320,886
Dividends declared	34,257	34,013	33,886
Retained earnings	707,336	564,987	424,002
Earnings per common share	$1.54	$1.53	$1.20
Common shares (000):			
Year end	114,428	113,856	112,951
Average	114,654	114,176	113,767
Depreciation & amortization	20,156	13,512	8,850

[a]Reclassified to conform to current presentation.
Source: Reebok Annual Reports.

Sales grew steadily, from over $1.7 billion in 1988 to about $1.8 billion in 1989, then exceeded to $2.1 billion in 1990. Net income increased from $137 million in 1988 to over $174 million in 1989, a 20% increase; this was followed by another increase of over 18% from 1989 to 1990.

■ L.A. Gear, Inc. [13]

Robert Y. Greenberg, CEO and owner of 25% of the company's stock, founded L.A. Gear in 1985. L.A. Gear carved its niche as a developer, designer, and marketer of stylish, high-quality, and youthful shoes for aerobics, athletics, and leisure. The line was later expanded to include a variety of other footwear, such as walking, tennis, and overall fitness shoes, for children and men. Sales surged from over $223 million in 1988 to $902 million in 1990, a threefold increase. Although net income rose 15%, from $22 million in 1988 to over $55 million in 1989, it then declined 43% from 1989 to 1990. Exhibits 12 and 13 provide financial and operating data.

Exhibit 12

L.A. Gear, Inc. Consolidated Balance Sheet As of November 30, 1990, 1989 (in thousands of dollars)

	1990	*1989*
Assets		
Cash	$ 3,291	$ 353
Accounts receivable, net	156,391	100,290
Inventory	160,668	139,516
Prepaid expenses & other current assets	16,912	12,466
Deferred tax charges	1,097	4,589
Total current assets	338,359	257,214
Gross property & equipment	28,599	9,888
Accumulated depreciation	4,975	1,809
Property & equipment, net	23,624	8,079
Other assets	1,972	1,265
Total assets	363,955	266,558
Liabilities		
Line of credit	94,000	37,400
Accounts payable	22,056	25,619
Accrued expenses & other current liability	39,672	17,627
Accrued compensation	2,350	16,906
Income taxes payable	—	783
Total current liabilities	158,078	98,335
Common stock	91,179[a]	84,363[a]
Retained earnings	114,698	83,360
Total shareholders' equity	205,877	168,223
Total liabilities & stock equity	363,955	266,558
Net current assets	180,281	158,879
Book value	$10.61	$8.80

[a]No par value; Auth shs: 1990, 80,000,000; 1989, 80,000,000.

Source: L.A. Gear Annual Reports

The company moved into the highly competitive "60% chunk of the $4.2 billion U.S. athletic-shoe market" in basketball and running, a market dominated by Nike and Reebok. Skeptics were doubtful about the success of L.A. Gear's shoes for the male-dominated basketball segment, as males typically paid less attention to style and leaned more toward the inner structure of the shoe supporting the feet. Commented a competitor, technology was the fashion. However, to promote its acceptance in this market, the company signed

Exhibit 13

L.A. Gear Inc. Consolidated Income Statement Years Ended November 30, 1990, 1989, 1988 (in thousands of dollars)

	1990	*1989*	*1988*
Net sales	902,225	617,080	223,713
Cost of sales	591,740	358,482	129,103
Gross profit	310,485	258,598	94,610
Sell, general & administrative expenses	240,596	154,449	53,168
Interest expense, net	18,515	12,304	4,102
Earned income before taxes	51,374	91,845	37,340
Income tax expense	20,036	36,786	15,310
Net earnings	31,338	55,059	22,030
Previous retained earnings	83,360	28,301	6,271
Retained earnings	114,698	83,360	28,301
Earnings per common share	$1.56	$3.01[a]	$1.29[b]
Common shares (000):			
Year-end	19,395	19,109[a]	16,374[b]
Average	20,041	18,308[a]	17,110[b]

[a]2-for-1 stock split, 9/25/89.

[b]Reclassified to conform to 1989 presentation.

Source: L.A. Gear Annual Reports

42-year-old Kareem Abdul-Jabbar, the retired superstar of the Los Angeles Lakers. As one analyst remarked, this was a move to the "geriatric crowd." Later, other notable basketball athletes were signed to contracts—Akeem Alajuwan of the Houston Rockets and Karl Malone of the Utah Jazz. Michael Jackson was also contracted to design shoes and apparel [21].

The company's footwear is sold principally in department, shoe, sporting goods, and athletic footwear stores, while its apparel is distributed through department, specialty, and sporting goods stores. Products are also distributed through independent distributors in 20 countries, primarily in Japan, Canada, and West Germany. Manufacturing is done by 13 suppliers in South Korea and 2 in Taiwan; both countries also manufacture Nike footwear. The company maintains offices in both countries.

To further expand its product offerings, L.A. Gear has ventured into the jeans and watch markets where, presumably, its brand name and distribution network will enhance its market position.

THE INDUSTRY

Exhibit 14 depicts a growing sales trend for the shoe industry from 1989 to 1992. Other data in the exhibit show varying performances for this same period.

Generally regarding athletic footwear as discretionary items, consumers would be likely to limit their spending for these products during an economic downturn. Moreover, with rising consumer debt and decreasing personal savings, buyers' confidence could be seriously affected. At the same time, buyers

Selected Industry Composite Indicators, 1989–1992

Exhibit 14

	1989	*1990*	*1991**	*1992**
Sales ($ Mil)	7762.8	8905.2	10365.0	11250.0
Operating margin (%)	12.7	12.1	10.5	11.0
Net profit margin (%)	6.7	6.2	5.9	6.5
Return on net worth (%)	20.9	19.1	20.5	21.0

*Estimated.

would prefer footwear that is not only durable but also suitable for a variety of activities.

The long-term prospects for the industry appear promising. The trend toward physical fitness should accelerate as it becomes a pastime for increasing numbers of buyers. Also, certain demographic changes favor continued industry growth; for example, Census Bureau projections for adults in the 25–44 age segment—major buyers for sporting and athletic equipment—are estimated to approximate 82 million people by 1992, about one-third of the total population. Moreover, this age group is forecasted to grow at twice the rate for the total population. Another important buyer segment is the 45–54 age group, projected to increase annually by 3.6% between 1987 and 1992 in contrast to a 1% growth for the total population.

Other key growth indicators include the increasing participation of women in sports, not only to improve their physical fitness, but also for recreation and competition. According to a National Sporting Goods Associations study, women were the major participants in 10 of 45 activities it surveyed; these activities include aerobic exercise, gymnastics, and exercise walking. Additionally, the increasing presence of women in the work force and decisions to delay childbearing and have fewer children, should bring about higher household incomes, thus allowing for more discretionary spending and more leisure time available for recreation. In essence, greater emphasis may be directed toward fitness-related products.

As mentioned earlier in the case, there is a continuing movement by U.S. manufacturers to produce overseas through manufacturing contracts. However, as these newly industrialized countries become more developed—which exerts upward pressure on production costs—manufacturers will be compelled to seek other low-cost producer countries.

THE FUTURE

Nike management faces a number of challenges for the future. Can Nike move fast enough in a rapidly changing market with strong competitors such as Reebok, L.A. Gear, and others to remain the premier athletic shoe manufacturer? Given Nike's low-cost production in Taiwan, South Korea, and the People's Republic of China, will recent political demonstrations in the latter two countries compel Nike to seek other low-cost Asian producers or increase its U.S. domestic manufacturing? Should Nike consider manufacturing private-branded products for major retailing chains?

REFERENCES

1. Annual Reports, various years, and Forms 10–K.
2. Lynn Strongin Dodds, "Heading Back on the Fast Track," *Financial World,* August 21–September 3, 1985, p. 90. See also *Who's Who in Finance & Industry,* 1983–84, p. 431.
3. Sheryl Franklin, "The Other Side," *Bank Marketing,* August 1987, p. 62.
4. Barbara Buell, "Nike Catches Up with the Trendy Frontrunner," *Business Week,* October 24, 1988. p. 88. See also "Walking on Air at Nike," *Fortune,* January 1, 1990, p. 72.
5. See reference 11.
6. Marcy Magiera, and Pat Sloan, "Sneaker Attack", *Advertising Age,* June 20, 1988, p. 3.
7. Marcy Magiera, ". . . . As Nike Flexes Its Fashion Sense", *Advertising Age,* January 30, 1989, p. 76.
8. James P. Miller, "Nike Chairman Concurs with Estimates of Net Rise for Year of as Much as 65%", *The Wall Street Journal,* July 7, 1989, p. A5A. See also "Increase in Sales Expected by Nike", *The New York Times,* February 11, 1989, p. 37; Dori Jones Yang, "Setting Up Shop in China: Three Paths to Success," *Business Week,* October 19, 1987, p. 74.
9. "Nike Pairs Michael Jordan with a Down-to-Earth Guy", *The New York Times,* February 14, 1989, p. D7.
10. Carri Gottlieb, "Products of the Year", *Fortune,* December 9, 1985, p. 112. See also Jon Wiener, "Exploitation and the Revolution", *Advertising Age,* June 29, 1987, p. 18.
11. Douglas C. McGill, "Reebok's New Models, Fully Loaded", *The New York Times,* February 14, 1989, pp. D1–D2.
12. Christopher Chipello, "Reebok to Buy CML Unit for $42 Million, Signalling Expansion of Product Line", *The Wall Street Journal,* August 8, 1989, p. A4.
13. Kathleen Kerwin, "L.A. Gear Is Going Where the Boys Are", *Business Week,* June 19, 1989, p. 54. See also "The Best of 1989 so Far", *Business Week,* June 26, 1989, p. 112.
14. "The Hollow Corporation", *Business Week,* March 3, 1986, pp. 57–85.
15. Sheryl Franklin, "'Word of Foot' Helps Nike Stay One Step Ahead," *Bank Marketing,* August 1987, p. 62.
16. "Nike Outdoes Competition in Delivery to Customers," *Global Trade,* March 1988, p. 8. See also *U.S. Industrial Outlook,* 1988, pp. 49–9.
17. "The Nike Store Breaks New Ground," *Chain Store Age Executive,* July 1990, pp. 90–91.
18. Dori Jones Yang, "Step by Step with Nike," *Business Week,* August 13, 1990, pp. 116–117. See also "When Your Feet Are Spending the Day Underwater," *Business Week,* February 27, 1989, p. 136.
19. Tom Yulsman, "Anatomy of the High-Tech Running Shoe," *Science Digest,* April 1985, pp. 46, 80, 83. See also Jean Sherman, "No Pain, No Gain," *Working Woman,* May 1987, p. 82.
20. *Ibid.*
21. Brian Bagot, "Shoeboom!", *Marketing and Median Decisions,* June 1990, pp. 61–65.

CASE 2

L.A. Gear, Inc.

Brentt Eads, Loyola Marymount University

During his seven-year tenure at L.A. Gear, Sandy Saemann, executive vice president and the second highest in command at L.A. Gear, saw his company jump from fifteenth in the industry to third in sales because of its successful penetration into women's athletic footwear. As he flipped through the channels on his TV, he came across an ad for Side 1, a brand of Nike shoes designed to appeal to fashion-oriented women. It was obvious that Nike, the largest shoe manufacturer in the country, was trying to increase its presence in the women's fashion market—the core of L.A. Gear's business. (Where Nike was recognized as the leader in athletic performance footwear, L.A. Gear was looked upon as the industry leader in athletic fashion footwear.) Now this position was under attack. Saemann thought how much more worried he would be if his company was dependent only on women's shoes and had not diversified into other lines of apparel.

L.A. Gear entered the athletic shoe market in 1985 with brightly colored designs, including palm trees and ocean waves, imprinted on its shoes. Emphasizing the fun and glamour of the Southern California lifestyle, the shoe company, based in the beach city of Marina-del-Rey, California, immediately became a success with first-year sales topping $10 million and approaching $1 billion only five years later.

Saemann also witnessed the down side of the volatile athletic shoe business as L.A. Gear began facing its first major problems. In June 1990, even as record sales were announced for the 2nd quarter, L.A. Gear revealed that profits had declined 36% because of an increase in the sale of lower-profit, promotionally priced items in an effort to achieve greater market share. Nike filed suit, alleging patent and design infringements. Also, analysts believed the rapid growth in the industry would decline as evidenced by a growth slowdown of 14% from 1988 to 1989. Saemann knew that his company, like others in the

---

This case is intended for classroom discussion only, not to depict effective or ineffective handling of administrative situations. All rights reserved to authors and the North American Case Research Association.

industry, had to continue producing innovative products and marketing strategies to maintain its profit share in the footwear market.

HISTORY

The beginnings of L.A. Gear can be traced to one man, founder, chairman, and president Robert Greenberg. The son of a Boston produce distributor, Greenberg grew up reading business magazines and dreamed of building a name for himself in women's fashion. In the 1960s, Greenberg sold wigs to beauty shops in Boston, and in the 1970s sold imported jeans to department stores. He started a chain of roller skate stores in Los Angeles in 1979, and in 1982 made a quick profit ($3 million grossed in three months) licensing the movie character E.T. on children's shoelaces.

The next year Greenberg opened a 6500-square foot retail store on fashionable Melrose Avenue in Los Angeles. The store, called L.A. Gear, sold its own line of apparel and casual wear in addition to name brands. By 1984, L.A. Gear had evolved into a full-fledged marketer of casual footwear and had grown to the point where Greenberg could bring Saemann, his key marketing man since 1979, on board as executive vice-president. (Previously, Saemann had been president of Pacific Strand, the advertising firm in charge of the L.A. Gear account.) After he had joined the company, all marketing functions were directed by the executive vice president who, along with directing the marketing functions, served as copywriter, creative director for ads, and director for TV commercials. Shortly thereafter, the company introduced the women's canvas shoe "The Workout," which boosted monthly sales from $200,000 to $1.8 million by mid-year, 1985.

In 1986, the company went public and sales reached $30 million (see Exhibit 1; for further financial data see Appendix 3). Trouble loomed, however, in the 4th quarter of 1990 when a loss of $7.1 million was incurred—the first loss since the firm had gone public. Greenberg believed that L.A. Gear was suffering because of a recession and because of unavoidable growing pains after a four-year period in which it was rated the most profitable company among nearly 1,200 major U.S. firms surveyed by *Forbes* magazine.

Exhibit 1 **Financial Highlights (in 000, except per share data)**

	For the Years Ended November 30				
	1990	*1989*	*1988*	*1987*	*1986*
Net sales	$902,225	$617,080	$223,713	$70,575	$36,299
Net earnings	31,338	55,059	22,030	4,371	1,745
Net earnings per common share	1.56	3.01	1.29	27	14
Working capital	180,281	158,879	37,180	20,482	17,028
Total assets	363,955	266,558	128,833	36,794	28,741
Total liabilities	158,078	98,335	87,524	14,675	10,993
Shareholders' equity	205,877	168,223	41,309	22,119	17,748
Net book value per common share	10.61	8.80	2.53	1.37	1.10

Greenberg and Saemann were compensated over $5 million each in 1989 because of bonuses tied to pre-tax profits. Both figures dropped in 1990 to $3.47 million and $2.54 million, respectively, because of 4th quarter losses that continued through the first quarter of 1991. Greenberg, the largest shareholder with 20% of the company's stock, vowed that he would begin working without pay until the company turned a quarterly profit again.

INDUSTRY

Sneakers have come a long way from the canvas tops and heavy rubber soles of the past. Athletic shoes today incorporate fashion and performance with such high-tech features as "air-cylinder suspension" and "energy return systems." Customers can buy specialized shoes for running, walking, aerobics, wrestling, and even cheerleading. The ranges and names of a company's sports shoes change so rapidly that it is difficult for consumers to keep up with them. Shoes are now updated twice a year. In 1990, Reebok planned 250 new designs; it already had 175 models in 450 colors (an average of $2\frac{1}{2}$ color variations per style). Nike offered 300 models with 900 styles for twenty-four different sports, while L.A. Gear and Adidas both produced around 500 styles.

The global market for athletic shoes in 1990 approached $10 billion in retail sales, up over 15% from 1988. Americans alone buy 200 million pairs of brand-name sneakers a year. Four brand names account for nearly all sport shoe sales—Nike, Reebok, L.A. Gear, and Converse (Exhibit 2). Adidas and Converse were two of the market share leaders in the 1970s, but each lost around 25% of the market when new competitors such as L.A. Gear and Nike were able to more effectively follow buyers' trends.

According to *Footwear News*, more than 80% of all athletic shoes purchased are used for casual wear and not for sports. While Nike, Converse, Adidas, and

U.S. Athletic Shoe Industry: Market Share for Top Five Companies, 1990 **Exhibit 2**

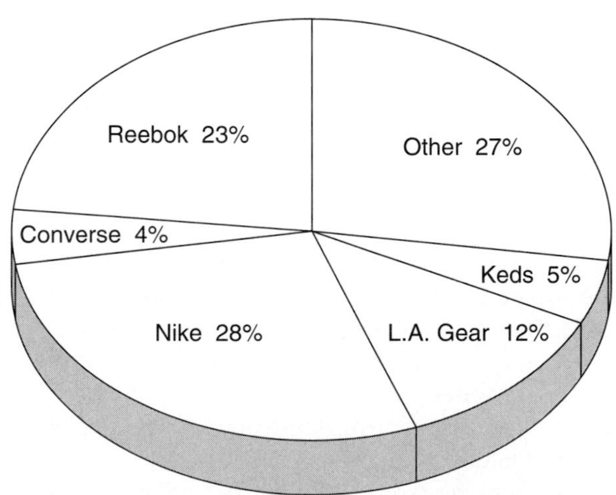

Source: Sporting Goods Intelligence; company reports.

Avia, a subsidiary of Reebok, have built a reputation based on performance, Reebok and L.A. Gear have promoted a fashion image, thereby capturing a large share of the women's athletic shoe market. Brand status has become extremely important within the last ten years and has allowed a $15–$20 pair of shoes to be priced upwards of $100 and more.

TARGET MARKETS

> L.A. Gear has really hit on a formula no one else has. They take a shoe that's not a real technical shoe, so not expensive to produce, put some spangles and some colored trim on it, and put their money into marketing and advertising.—John Horan, publisher of *Sports Management News*

In addition, new niche markets have emerged during the past twenty years in athletic footwear. These include the tennis craze in the mid-seventies, running and jogging in the late seventies and early eighties, and aerobics in the mid-eighties. Because of continuously changing markets, it has been critical for shoe companies to monitor and foresee fashions and trends of consumer behavior, particularly fashion-sensitive Reebok and L.A. Gear.

The most significant key to L.A. Gear's success was Greenberg's keen sense of what consumers wanted in athletic shoes. In 1986, while dropping his daughter off at her junior high school in the San Fernando Valley, he observed young girls wearing boys hightop basketball shoes. Within a few months his company was producing female hightops in white, pink, turquoise, and silver. Over 1.5 million pairs of this model were eventually sold. Greenberg continued to stay close to his customers by posing as a salesclerk for several hours each Saturday. He claimed he was a "malloholic" and would "get the shakes" if he could not visit a mall at least twice a week.

The work atmosphere has been credited as another factor in the shoe company's quick responses to new trends and ideas. Employees describe the work environment as creative and unregulated, and claim to share the "entrepreneurial spirit" of Greenberg and Saemann. An open door policy has allowed management and workers to share creative ideas. Marketing research has included product testing, focus groups, store and consumer interviews, and surveys as well as trend forecasters who attend fashion and art shows to monitor new trends and salespeople who file monthly reports detailing new fashion and sales patterns.

With 70% of its customers being girls and women between 12 and 35, L.A. Gear found a very profitable segment to target. Greenberg believed girls and younger women were more interested in style than function, and made his company a trendy fashion-setter by using fluorescent or pastel trim, tassels, rhinestones, and buckles. One top seller was the Street Brat ($60), which had marbleized leather and tongues that stood straight up. Another $60 style had a western flavor with imitation-silver buckles. The pink and white hightop sneaker at $45–$55 was also a strong seller.

Despite the enormous success with the young teen market, others in the industry knew that what is hot in fashion one week is often not the next. John Gills, a spokesman for Reebok, underscored the volatility of the market when he said, "We think that kids are finished wearing funky, trendy fashions and are moving toward plainer clothes." L.A. Gear believed the sun and sand image might take them only so far and began to diversify their fashion image to appeal to everyone (for demographic data see Appendix 2).

To be competitive with frontrunners Nike and Reebok, company officials also believed they would have to enter into the men's market, which, although cutthroat and less fashion oriented, was more stable and lucrative. The majority of sport shoe sales (60%) were from men's basketball and running sneakers. Men typically have paid less attention to style, instead concentrating on how well the inner structure supports the foot. The target for the performance shoe has generally been the hard-core athlete, 18 and older. Nike, a performance leader, sold roughly 70% of its shoes to men, while L.A. Gear, a fashion leader, sold only 29% of its shoes to men.

Whereas Nike has allocated 5% or more of sales to research and development and makes the R&D department a high-visibility area, L.A. Gear has used a less-structured, less-expensive approach. The company has waited for a trend to develop before designing a product. With L.A. Gear spending a fraction of what competitors have on research and development, industry leaders were skeptical that the shoe manufacturer could be a technical leader. Nevertheless, Robert Greenberg predicted men's shoe sales could increase to as much as $400 million in 1990, compared to the $20 million sold in 1988. Analysts believed the shoe maker would need to reach $500 million to be a legitimate player in the men's segment.

Initial performance shoe results were less than expected. One of the earliest models, the Kareem Abdul-Jabbar line, was used by several college basketball teams but occasionally would tear apart at the sole. Company officials felt tighter quality control and increased knowledge of the stress and pounding affecting the shoes would eliminate most of the problems. In February 1991, the most advanced of the performance line, the Catapult, with its air cushions, impact absorption, and anti-fatigue systems, was unveiled to compete with the top-of-the-line performance shoes of competitors. L.A. Gear leaders believed they could bring out equal or better technology while selling a lower-priced item, and the Catapult typified this approach.

ADVERTISING

Athletic shoe sales have traditionally been very dependent on marketing and advertising, which have become more sophisticated and competitive. All the top manufacturers have hired celebrities, especially such athletes as Michael Jordan, Magic Johnson, Bo Jackson, and Joe Montana, to push their products. Entertainers such as Michael Jackson and Paula Abdul have signed on to represent a stylish look. The race for famous spokespersons has created intense battles, greatly increasing advertising budgets. In 1989, the top three producers (Nike, Reebok, and L.A. Gear) accounted for 87% of the top five's $93.7 million total in ad expenditures (see Exhibit 3).

By 1990, expenses for advertising and promotional activities were over $71 million (8% of net sales) and included participation in national and regional shows for sporting goods and shoes that introduced spring and fall lines. Much of the increase was due to L.A. Gear's efforts to penetrate the men's market. In February 1990, quarterback Joe Montana signed a three year contract estimated at $3–$5 million, to be a spokesman for the company and

Exhibit 3 **Athletic Footwear Media Expenditures (000), 1989**

	Media Total	*BAR Network Television*	*BAR Spot Television*	*BAR Cable Television*	*BAR Syndicate T.V.*	*RER Spot Radio*	*LNA Magazines*	*MR Newspapers*	*LNA Outdoor*
Nike	$33,331	$12,437	$1,023	$2,289	$3,428	$465,670	$13,191	$225	$262
Reebok	33,025	16,370	6,723	1,938	2,327	—	5,663	—	4
L.A. Gear	15,371	2,163	8,220	1,179	1,290	253,718	2,127	—	140
Converse	4,307	427	110	385	444	650,752	1,944	32	315
Avia	7,929	—	2,823	492	—	—	4,094	—	520

Sources: Arbitron's Broadcast Advertisers Report (BAR); Radio Expenditure Reports (RER); Leading National Advertisers (LNA); Media Records (MR).

endorse a line of cross-training shoes. L.A. Gear hoped the football celebrity would bolster the training line, which trailed those of Nike and Reebok. In line with the company's "Unstoppable" campaign, Montana was featured in 15- and 30-second commercials. Other athletes brought in to represent the company included basketball players Kareem Abdul-Jabbar, Hakeem Olajuwon, and Karl Malone.

In a countermove to maintain the company's fashion image, singer Michael Jackson was signed for an estimated $20 million in August 1990 to help design shoes and other apparel and to represent an $80 pair of black athletic shoes called the "MJ." Company officials hoped the "MJ" line would be introduced at the same time as the singer's newest video and greatest hits album, but both projects were delayed. At the time the shoes were released, shoe industry experts were optimistic that the new item would be successful.

To many observers' surprise, the "MJ" line did not sell well domestically. Retailers reported few sales during the back-to-school period, which should have been one of their biggest periods. Some felt the design of the shoe, covered with buckles, was rejected by parents who didn't like a possible gang-associated image. Although disappointed with domestic sales, L.A. Gear executives knew the shoes would sell much better in Japan and Europe, where Jackson's music and concerts were very popular. Many West Coast retailers reported large numbers of sales to Japanese and European tourists.

AD AGENCY

Since its inception, L.A. Gear had always maintained control of advertising through an in-house agency, L.A. Ad, which had become one of the nation's largest in-house agencies. The company was the only one of the top three to create all of its own advertising, which saved 15% in costs. Saemann explained why all advertising and promotional campaigns were done by the company: "By keeping this function in-house, we maintain complete control over advertising material. As a result, we can respond quickly and accurately to changing market conditions." A media-buying expert and a creative director were hired to bolster advertising, which critics said was not aggressive enough and had a low quality look.

Despite the criticisms, the shoe maker believed its ads were successful. One company official said, "A lot of people in the advertising industry have criticized L.A. Gear advertising from a creative perspective. The point is that the advertising worked. It created sales. It created an image in the mind of consumers that they wanted to be associated with." Several industry experts agreed, saying L.A. Gear ads were more effective than those placed by higher budget firms. L.A. Gear leaders also pointed to the fact that in 1985 L.A. Gear was the first of the athletic shoe companies to advertise on TV.

Company officials, however, believed that business would soon overwhelm the firm's ability to handle advertising and decided to sign an outside agency to manage the $68 million account. Although the large account was attractive to outside agencies, many were hesitant to try for it because of L.A. Gear's reputation for controlling all aspects of creative matters. One agency chairman stated what many believed when he said L.A. Gear executives "had made it clear [in the past] that they do not hold agencies in high regard."

Finally, the agency BBDO of Los Angeles was hired, but resigned the account after only two months because of creative differences. Agency executives claimed L.A. Gear representatives would not accept their advice, would insist on controlling all aspects of advertising, and would keep top agency officials waiting for hours before seeing them.

A controversial television spot for the Catapult shoe also caused problems between L.A. Gear and BBDO. The commercial was rejected by the TV networks NBC and CBS because of its theme line, "Everything else is just hot air." BBDO was equally unhappy that the theme was used, saying, "We thought the commercial was a cheap shot." NBC officials later reversed their position and the ad was shown for the first time during the Super Bowl telecast.

PRODUCT MIX

> We have continued to add to our product line. We began with women's athletic footwear and subsequently added men's shoes and shoes for infants and children. . . . All of these products are designed for our primary customers—fashion-conscious consumers of all ages and athletic abilities. —Robert Greenberg, President of L.A. Gear

In 1987, almost three-quarters of L.A. Gear's total revenues were from women's domestic fashion footwear. Only two years later, that percentage had dropped to less than 50% as Robert Greenberg and his company expanded into such varied lines as men's and women's footwear, including basketball, court, cross-training, fitness, and casual shoe lines, athletic and casual apparel, jeanswear, and watches (see Appendix 1).

L.A. Gear's product mix strategy was to diversify away from its core strength of women's fashion/athletic shoe lines. Examples of the strategy included the introduction of the Catapult performance shoe, the Kareem Abdul-Jabbar model, the "Fire" basketball line, the "Street-Hiker" line, and the Michael Jackson fashion-oriented shoe.

Domestic footwear sales continued to be the shoe maker's strength, comprising over 85% of revenues. The men's shoe market grew from 22% of domestic sales in 1989 to 29% in 1990. New products included the Star Player and Muscle lines of cross-training shoes. Winter streetwear with an outdoor look was introduced for men and women. L.A. Gear's footwear for children included downsized versions from the most popular of the men's and women's lines and represented 27% of total footwear sales in 1990.

The company expanded its line of activewear from t-shirts and other products designed primarily to promote the name "L.A. Gear" and enhance footwear sales to a line of sweat tops, pants, shirts, and jackets. A new line of women's fashion shoes and apparel was created to be promoted by singer Paula Abdul. The jeanswear group, formed in late 1988, also expanded its line of products, including the "Flame" jean, which bore the same name and look as a line of footwear. The line of accessories included sports bags, hats, and moderately priced watches introduced in 1988.

MANUFACTURING AND DISTRIBUTION

L.A. Gear footwear products are manufactured to specification by offshore independent producers, primarily in South Korea and Taiwan. Factories have also been used in Italy, Thailand, and Indonesia. It generally takes three months to develop an idea, manufacture the shoes, and ship the final product to the United States where inventory is stored in three California distribution facilities. The process takes half the time compared to competitors who place a specific order with their manufacturers based on a customer purchase order.

The firm's overall distribution strategy differs from those of competitors in that it is more oriented toward department stores and traditional shoe stores where the fashion appeal is emphasized. L.A. Gear was the first large athletic shoe maker to distribute through department stores when J.C. Penney accepted its account. Currently, approximately 20,000 department stores, sporting goods stores, and specialty retail stores throughout the United States sell L.A. Gear items. In a typical department store, the company's products can be found in several departments including men's, women's, junior's, children's, and toddlers'. "Department stores and traditional shoe stores have a solid and continuing customer base. They have historically accounted for a higher percentage of sales for L.A. Gear than for other significant companies in our industry. As these retail sections continue to increase their commitment to athletic footwear, L.A. Gear should benefit enormously from the successful relationships we already have in place with them," says Chairman Robert Greenberg.

The distribution strategy places a high priority on customer service. Retail outlets may order as few as four pairs of shoes in any size, color, or style. L.A. Gear fills most orders from its own substantial inventory in a system known as "open stock" which enables it to respond to customer orders in a timely fashion. By quickly replenishing sizes of a particular style that has sold out, a retailer is encouraged to continue to devote shelf space to that style. The system is also advantageous in that shoes can be supplied and sold while a particular fashion or trend is popular, as opposed to supplying a shoe weeks or months after it has been ordered and running the risk that it could be out of style.

The major disadvantage to the system is having excess inventory that becomes expensive to warehouse, hard to sell, and movable only through a discount on the merchandise. Retailers have worried that the shoe's image could become damaged because the shoe would be sold at discount stores, swap meets, and even from the back of trucks. This blanket of distribution, retailers fear, would give customers the impression that they were being overcharged in the retailers' stores. As a consequence, many store owners have been reluctant to give the new L.A. Gear shoes shelf space. L.A. Gear officials claimed much of the discounting was done by unauthorized merchants, who, like other shoe manufacturers facing the same problem, had little or no control over the situation. Greenberg admitted that sometimes it was necessary to sell off the inventory aggressively, which would include discounting.

In 1990, net earnings dropped because, as *Sporting Goods Intelligence* claimed, "They overestimated what the market would bear in L.A. Gear shoes this year." The company shipped much of its product into the market, which was then discounted when unsold. One industry expert predicted that the shoe company would achieve its billion dollar sales goal by sacrificing profit for volume.

INTERNATIONAL SALES AND DISTRIBUTION

Internationally, L.A. Gear has established relationships with distributors serving approximately 100 countries, principally Japan, Canada, and Germany. Sales abroad accounted for 9% of total sales in 1988 and 1989, reaching almost $53 million. By 1990, international sales had reached $162 million, a 206% increase. In 1990, the total volume of footwear sold worldwide increased 38%, with increases in all categories, namely, women's, men's, and children's (see Exhibit 4). Orders from international customers (as well as from large domestic customers) are placed by L.A. Gear directly with the manufacturer and are shipped directly to the customer rather than through the normal allocation and distribution facilities. In 1989, L.A. Gear appointed ASICS, the largest athletic shoe company in Japan, as a key distributor. Robert Greenberg stated, "Their (ASICS') resources and selling experience, coupled with our innovative products and creative marketing skills, should help us become a major force in the Japanese market." Until the agreement, Japan contributed only 10% to the company's international revenues.

European and Japanese markets are predicted to have great potential for U.S. shoe manufacturers. Athletic shoe sales outside of the American market total $3.5 billion; however, the total combined market share abroad for the top three U.S. companies is only 22% of the total international market.

Exhibit 4

Volume of Footwear Sold (in number of pairs): Percentage Increases for 1990 over 1989

	Domestic	*International*	*Total*
Women's	1.4%	168.2%	15.8%
Men's	65.8%	111.0%	78.3%
Children's	35.3%	247.4%	48.0%
Total percentage increase	22.7%	148.8%	38.2%

THE DILEMMA

L.A. Gear ran the risk of blurring its image as a women's trendsetter by positioning itself as a serious performance shoe, or as one competitor put it, L.A. Gear was in danger of "cannibalizing its cachet." Many industry analysts doubted men would buy shoes associated with teenage girls when they were more interested in a shoe's technical features. As one expert said, "Technology has been the fashion." One jogger/analyst remarked, "I enjoy looking at their ads, but I'm not going to spend $60 or $70 for their shoes."

FUTURE DECISIONS

Sandy Saemann walked through the design department and looked at the hundreds of prototype shoes in all colors and styles lining the walls. Most of the models would never reach the manufacturing stage, but nevertheless exhibited the interest of the company in designing whatever might appeal to current or future markets. With the promotion of Nike's Side 1 campaign, Saemann knew there would be added pressure to maintain L.A. Gear's market of fashion footwear. But, he wondered, how much should his company invest in maintaining its present position in comparison to its efforts to penetrate further into the men's market and expand into other lines? Saemann knew it could be a challenge to reposition L.A. Gear as a leader in men's performance shoes while maintaining the fashion image, just as Nike was trying to establish a foothold in the casual market while maintaining a performance edge. Additionally, the executive vice president knew that whatever decisions were made had to show quick results. The losses of the two previous quarters had put the company into technical default on its bank loans, and under the newest bank agreement, L.A. Gear was required to return to profitability in the current quarter.

APPENDIX 1: L.A. GEAR PRODUCT INFORMATION

L.A. Gear Product Mix **Exhibit 5**

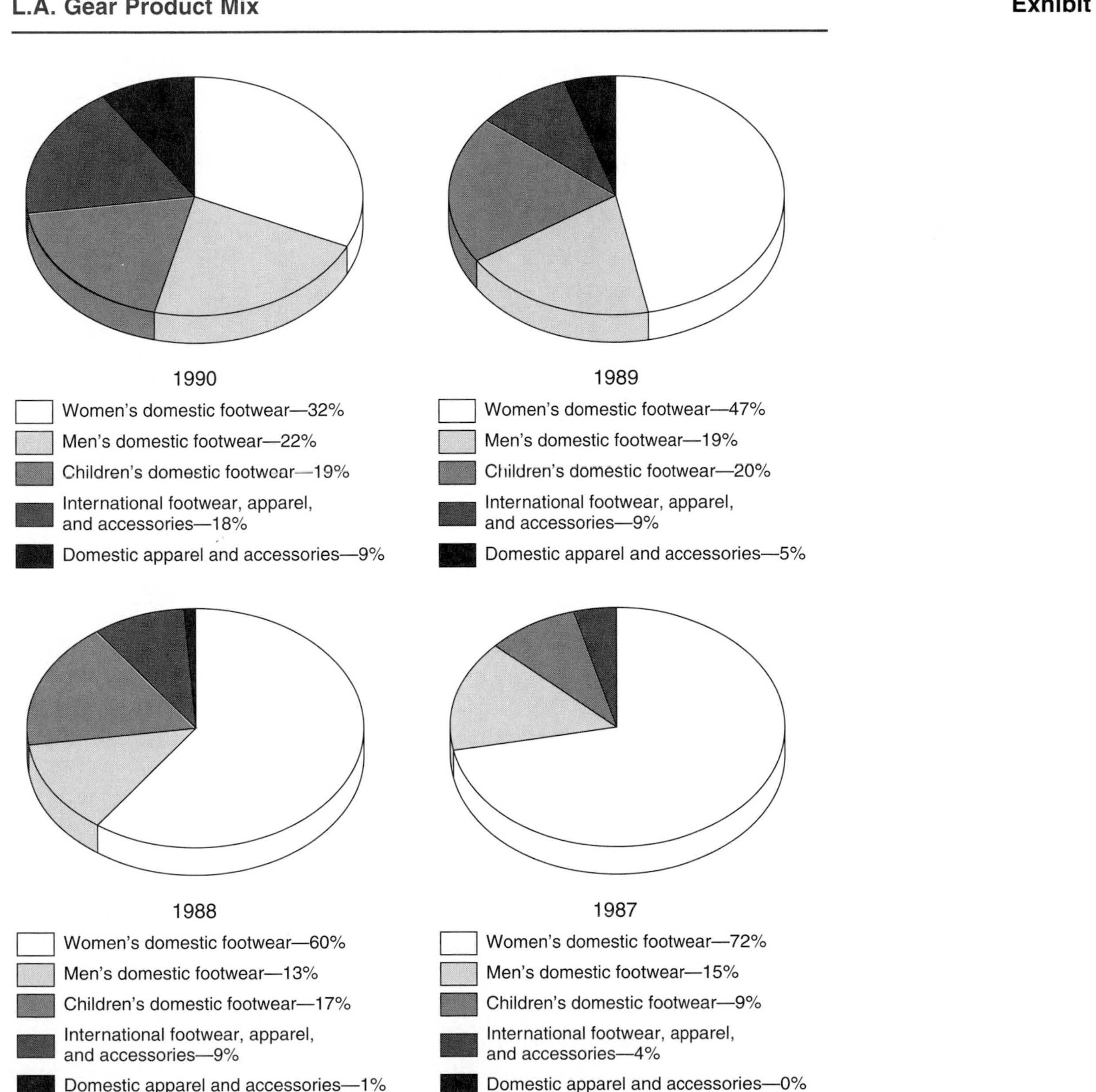

Source: L.A. Gear Annual Report, 1990.

APPENDIX 2: U.S. POPULATION DATA

Exhibit 6

Total U.S. Population, by Sex, Race, and Age: 1989 (in thousands)

Age	*Total*	*Male*	*Female*	*White*	*Black*
Under 5 yrs.	18,753	9,598	9,155	15,050	2,890
5–9 yrs. old	18,212	9,321	8,891	14,628	2,802
10–14 yrs. old	16,949	8,689	8,260	13,574	2,679
15–19 yrs. old	17,848	9,123	8,725	14,367	2,767
20–24 yrs. old	18,885	9,529	9,356	15,490	2,695
25–29 yrs. old	21,830	10,979	10,851	18,192	2,861
30–34 yrs. old	22,219	11,151	11,068	18,622	2,767
35–39 yrs. old	19,676	9,782	9,894	16,664	2,273
40–44 yrs. old	16,908	8,319	8,589	14,571	1,731
45–49 yrs. old	13,529	6,608	6,921	11,678	1,396
50–54 yrs. old	11,377	5,511	5,866	9,790	1,223
55–59 yrs. old	10,726	5,121	5,605	9,310	1,116
60–64 yrs. old	10,867	5,079	5,788	9,569	1,035
65–69 yrs .old	10,169	4,631	5,538	9,029	916
70–74 yrs. old	8,013	3,464	4,549	7,193	661
75–79 yrs. old	6,033	2,385	3,648	5,430	486
80–84 yrs. old	3,728	1,306	2,422	3,409	256
85–89 yrs. old	1,962	588	1,374	1,791	142
90–94 yrs. old	789	195	594	719	61
95–99 yrs. old	229	53	176	200	25
100 yrs. old and over	61	13	48	50	9
Median age	32.7	31.5	33.8	33.6	27.7
Total	**248,763**	**121,445**	**127,318**	**209,326**	**30,791**

Projections of the Total U.S. Population by Age and Sex: 1995 to 2010 **Exhibit 7**

	Population (1000)				*Percent Distribution*		*Percent Change*	
Age and Sex	*1995*	*2000*	*2005*	*2010*	*2000*	*2010*	*1990–2000*	*2000–2010*
Total	**260,138**	**268,267**	**275,603**	**282,574**	**100.0**	**100.0**	**7.1**	**5.3**
Under 5	17,799	16,898	16,611	16,899	6.3	6.0	–8.2	.01
5–17	48,374	48,815	47,471	45,747	18.2	16.2	7.0	–6.3
18–24	24,281	25,231	26,918	27,155	9.4	9.6	–3.5	7.6
25–34	40,962	37,149	35,997	37,572	13.8	13.3	–15.4	1.1
35–44	42,336	43,911	40,951	37,202	16.4	13.2	15.9	–15.3
45–54	31,297	37,223	41,619	43,207	13.9	15.3	46.0	16.1
55–64	21,325	24,158	29,762	35,430	9.0	12.5	13.1	46.7
65–74	18,930	18,243	18,410	21,039	6.8	7.4	–.7	15.3
75 yrs. old and over	14,834	16,639	17,864	18,323	6.2	6.5	26.2	10.1
16 yrs. old and over	201,018	210,134	219,301	227,390	78.3	80.5	8.9	8.2
Male, total	**127,121**	**131,192**	**134,858**	**138,334**	**100.0**	**100.0**	**7.3**	**5.4**
Under 5	9,118	8,661	8,517	8,668	6.6	6.3	–8.1	.1
5–17	24,787	25,027	24,350	23,473	19.1	17.0	7.1	–6.2
18–24	12,290	12,770	13,628	13,752	9.7	9.9	–3.4	7.7
25–34	20,579	18,662	18,091	18,878	14.2	13.6	–15.5	1.2
35–44	21,104	21,945	20,458	18,586	16.7	13.4	16.8	–15.3
45–54	15,292	18,296	20,585	21,432	13.9	15.5	47.5	17.1
55–64	10,149	11,557	14,321	17,173	8.8	12.4	14.4	48.6
65–74	8,476	8,242	8,407	9,691	6.3	7.0	.9	17.6
75 yrs. old and over	5,326	6,032	6,501	6,681	4.6	4.8	28.9	10.8
16 yrs. old and over	96,834	101,392	105,984	110,024	77.3	79.5	9.2	8.5
Female, total	**133,017**	**137,075**	**140,747**	**144,239**	**100.0**	**100.0**	**7.0**	**5.2**
Under 5	8,681	8,237	8,094	8,231	6.0	5.7	–8.3	–.1
5–17	23,587	23,788	23,121	22,274	17.4	15.4	6.9	–6.4
18–24	11,991	12,461	13,290	13,402	9.1	9.3	–3.6	7.6
25–34	20,384	18,487	17,906	18,694	13.5	13.0	–15.4	1.1
35–44	21,233	21,966	20,493	18,616	16.0	12.9	14.9	–15.3
45–54	16,005	18,927	21,034	21,775	13.8	15.1	44.7	15.0
55–64	11,175	12,601	15,441	18,257	9.2	12.7	11.9	44.9
65–74	10,454	10,001	10,004	11,348	7.3	7.9	–2.0	13.5
75 yrs. old and over	9,507	10,607	11,364	11,642	7.7	8.1	24.7	9.8
16 yrs. old and over	104,184	108,742	113,317	117,366	79.3	81.4	8.6	7.9

APPENDIX 3: L.A. GEAR FINANCIAL STATEMENTS

Exhibit 8 **L.A. Gear, Inc., and Subsidiaries: Consolidated Balance Sheets**

	November 30,		
	1990	*1989*	*1988*
Assets			
Current assets			
Cash—$3,000,000 restricted at Nov. 30, 1988	$ 3,291,000	$ 353,000	$ 4,205,000
Accounts receivable, net of allowance for doubtful accounts and merchandise returns	156,391,000	100,290,000	49,526,000
Inventory	160,668,000	139,516,000	66,556,000
Prepaid expenses and other current assets	16,912,000	12,466,000	3,383,000
Deferred tax charges	1,097,000	4,589,000	1,034,000
Total current assets	338,359,000	257,214,000	124,704,000
Property and equipment, at cost, net of accumulated depreciation and amortization of $4,975,000, $1,809,000, and $610,000 in 1990, 1989, and 1988, respectively	23,624,000	8,079,000	3,110,000
Other assets	1,972,000	1,265,000	1,019,000
	$363,955,000	**$266,558,000**	**$128,833,000**
Liabilities and Shareholders' Equity			
Current liabilities			
Line of credit	$ 94,000,000	$ 37,400,000	$ 57,230,000
Accounts payable	22,056,000	25,619,000	7,748,000
Accrued expenses and other current liabilities	39,672,000	17,627,000	12,402,000
Accrued compensation	2,350,000	16,906,000	5,927,000
Income taxes payable	—	783,000	4,217,000
Total current liabilities	**158,078,000**	**98,335,000**	**87,524,000**
Shareholders' equity			
Common stock, no par value. Authorized 80,000,000 shares; issued and outstanding 19,395,170 shares at November 30, 1990, 19,108,753 shares at November 30, 1989, and 16,373,788 shares at November 30, 1988	91,179,000	84,863,000	13,008,000
Preferred stock, no stated value. Authorized 3,000,000 shares; no shares issued	—	—	—
Retained earnings	114,698,000	83,360,000	28,301,000
Total shareholders' equity	205,877,000	168,223,000	41,309,000
Commitments and contingencies	—		—
	$363,955,000	**$266,558,000**	**$128,833,000**

L.A. Gear, Inc., and Subsidiaries: Consolidated Statements of Cash Flows (years ended November 30, 1990, 1989, and 1988)

Exhibit 9

	1990	*1989*	*1988*
Cash flow from operating activities			
Net earnings	$31,338,000	$55,059,000	$22,030,000
Adjustments to reconcile net cash used in operating activities			
Depreciation and amortization	3,394,000	1,199,000	446,000
Issuance of stock to employees as compensation	—	558,000	—
(Increase) decrease in			
Accounts receivable	(56,101,000)	(50,764,000)	(34,378,000)
Inventory	(21,152,000)	(72,960,000)	(50,743,000)
Prepaids and other current assets	(4,446,000)	(9,083,000)	(2,432,000)
Deferred taxes payable	3,492,000	(3,555,000)	(1,020,000)
Increase (decrease) in			
Accounts payable	(3,563,000)	17,871,000	7,197,000
Accrued expenses, accrued compensation and other current liabilities	7,489,000	16,204,000	8,319,000
Income taxes payable	(783,000)	(3,434,000)	3,894,000
Net cash used in operating activities	(40,332,000)	(48,905,000)	(46,687,000)
Cash flows from investing activities			
Capital expenditures	(18,939,000)	(6,168,000)	(2,546,000)
Other assets	(707,000)	(246,000)	(406,000)
Net cash used in investing activities	(19,646,000)	(6,414,000)	(2,952,000)
Cash flows from financing activities			
Exercise of stock options and warrants	908,000	1,309,000	495,000
Tax benefits arising from the exercise of incentive stock options	5,408,000	1,372,000	—
Proceeds from issuance of common stock	—	68,616,000	—
Borrowings under credit agreements	56,600,000	(19,830,000)	50,104,000
Net cash provided by financing activities	62,916,000	51,467,000	50,599,000
Net cash flow	2,938,000	(3,852,000)	960,000
Cash at beginning of year	353,000	4,205,000	3,245,000
Cash at end of year	**$3,291,000**	**$353,000**	**$4,205,000**

CASE 3

Dell Computer Corporation

John K. Ross III, Michael J. Keefe, Bill J. Middlebrook, Southwest Texas State University

Treat the Customer like he is the ONLY one you Have!
Anonymous sign on
Dell's Sales/Support area wall

"Customer satisfaction" and "customer service" are two of the most repeated buzz words in major corporations, especially from the producer rather than the consumer side of the equation. Michael Dell does not want service and satisfaction to simply be repeated by his corporate employees and support staffs; he requires them to practice what he preaches. For example, the preamble to the 1990 annual report states:

> This report is about a personal relationship. One that does not exist between traditional computer manufacturers and the people that ultimately use their products. This report is about Dell Computer Corporation and the personal partnership we share with our customers.
>
> . . . No other computer manufacturer is so completely dedicated to serving its customers one-to-one. Ours is a direct link between the people who use computers and the people who make them. This partnership is what sets Dell Computer Corporation apart.

Dell's commitment to this concept of customer satisfaction and service can be shown through the policies of the corporation. First, there is an unconditional, 30-day money-back guarantee for all of Dell's computer systems and a "no questions asked" return policy. Second, Dell's toll-free technical support organization is available from 7:00 A.M. to 7:00 P.M., coast to coast (including Mexico). These technicians solve 95 percent of customer problems in less than six minutes. Additionally, a TechFax system is available 24 hours a day, seven days a week. Customers can request technical information through a fax cata-

---

This case is intended for classroom discussion only, not to depict effective or ineffective handling of administrative situations. All rights reserved to the authors and the North American Case Research Association.

logue, and problem solving instructions are returned by fax. A third-party network of on-site service representatives can be dispatched, when problems are not solved over the phone. If necessary, unresolved problems are expedited to the design engineers to ensure complete customer satisfaction. Dell users can also access an on-line technical support group via CompuServe. Finally, Michael Dell openly invites customers to write or call him with comments about the quality of Dell's products and the level of support received from service and support personnel.

This emphasis on quality and service has won accolades from customers and industry analysts. From October 1988 to February 1990, Dell was voted "tops in customer satisfaction" by *PC Week* magazine over all other computer manufacturers (see Exhibit 1). Datapro, an industry market research firm, stated in 1989 that Dell ranked first in customer satisfaction in the United Kingdom, ahead of IBM and Compaq. Dell has consistently been recognized as the best in customer support and satisfaction, ahead of all other computer manufacturers. J.D. Power and Associates, known for their auto rankings, recently rated Dell number one in customer satisfaction in its first end-user survey for the computer industry.

HISTORY OF DELL COMPUTER CORPORATION

The most publicized story of a company start-up in the computer industry is that of Steven Jobs and Stephen Wozniak's designing and marketing of Apple computers. These young entrepreneurs took a concept from a garage manufacturing arena and evolved Apple into a multi-million-dollar organization. The story of Michael Dell and the development of the Dell Computer Corporation rivals that of Jobs and Wozniak.

In 1983, Michael Dell, then a freshman pre-med student at the University of Texas, decided to earn additional money by selling disk drive kits and random access memory (RAM) chips at computer-user meetings in Austin, Texas. Within a few months, he had sufficient funds to acquire excess personal computers at reasonable prices from IBM dealers having difficulties meeting their sales quotas. He modified these machines and began selling them through contacts in the local area and was reported to be grossing approximately

Exhibit 1 **Customer Satisfaction**

Dell System 316	No. 1	February 12, 1990
Dell System 325	No. 1	February 5, 1990
Dell System 200	No. 1	April 17, 1989
Dell System 310	No. 1	April 10, 1989
Dell System 386/16	No. 1	October 24, 1988
Dell System 200	No. 1	October 17, 1988

Source: PC Week.

$80,000 per month by April 1984. In May 1984, Michael formed a corporation named Dell Computer Corporation to sell "PC's Limited" brand computers and conducted operations out of his dormitory room at the University of Texas. After dropping out of school (against the wishes of his parents), he began attending computer trade fairs where he sold these IBM PC-compatible computers, one of the first custom "clones" on the market.

The results of Michael's endeavors were immediate. During the first year of business, sales were approximately $6 million and grew to $257 million within the next four years. In 1988, the brand name was changed to "Dell," and for the fiscal 1990 year, the organization sold $546 million in PC-compatibles and peripheral equipment.

In 1987, Dell established its first international subsidiary in the United Kingdom to enter the growing European computer market. European countries had a lower PC saturation rate than the United States, and there were no large PC manufacturers in Europe. From 1988 to 1991, the organization developed wholly owned subsidiaries in Canada, France, Italy, Sweden, Germany, Finland, and the Netherlands and is in the process of launching other subsidiaries in Finland, the Netherlands, and Spain. An Irish manufacturing facility opened in 1991 to provide systems for the European market. In addition, a support center was located in Amsterdam to provide technical support throughout Europe. Dell reports that fourth quarter 1991 international sales are up 109 percent over the same quarter in 1990. Currently, 40 percent of sales are derived from international subsidiaries, after only five years of operations.

Dell Computer Corporation is headquartered in Austin, Texas, with approximately 1,685 employees (2,269 worldwide). Michael Dell had the foresight to surround himself with people having expertise in computer engineering and marketing and serves as both chief executive officer and chairman of the board of directors (see Exhibit 2 for corporate officers and members of the board of directors). The company still operates on the principles espoused by Michael Dell during its inception: customer service and a personal relationship with Dell system users.

PERSONAL COMPUTER INDUSTRY OVERVIEW

The short history of the personal computer industry is one of "booms" and "slumps." The stellar performance of the industry during the early to mid-1980s was followed by a consolidation of existing companies and a slowdown in sales during the 1986–1987 period. Industry sales have increased through 1990, and projections show that corporate capital-equipment spending should grow at a 7 to 8 percent annual rate into the early 1990s. Some analysts contend that the growth rate of the PC industry is uncertain, as the growth rate of the economy slows. For example, Volpe & Covington, a San Francisco–based PC investment consulting firm, believes that a 15 percent long-term growth in revenues for high-end PCs and a 12 percent compound growth rate for the industry is a reasonable assumption. Other analysts contend that PC sales will grow at only 5 to 7 percent in 1991, less than half as fast as sales grew in the late 1980s. Currently, the PC market is a $35 to $40 billion dollar industry with several emerging market segments.

Exhibit 2

Dell Computer Corporation

Officers		
Dell, Michael S.	25	Chairman of the Board, CEO
Henry, G. Glenn	47	Subsidiary Officer
Harris, Andrew R.	34	Senior Vice President
Kocher, Joel J.	33	Subsidiary Officer
Ammel, M. Peter	39	Managing Director
Collis, Donald D.	44	Vice President, CFO
Ferrales, Savino R.	39	Vice President
Hindmarch, James R.	46	Vice President
Germani, Americo	57	Vice President
Register, David S.	34	Vice President
Roberts, B. Kent	50	Vice President
Salwen, Richard E.	47	Vice President, Legal Counsel, Secretary
Sinclair, D. Bruce	39	Division President
Slagter, Martin R.	33	Managing Director
Spilker, Stephen C.	38	Vice President
Welling, Gary M.	47	Vice President
Directors		
Dell, Michael S.	25	Chairman of the Board, CEO Nominee
Hirschbiel, Paul, Jr.	37	Nominee
Inman, Bobby R.	59	Nominee
Kozmetsky, Georg	72	Nominee

■ PC Industry Strategies

Two macro industry strategies for competing in the PC industry can be combined with two macro segments of the PC market to assess competitors and competitive approaches. First, PC manufacturers can approach the market as either innovators or imitators. IBM is the accepted innovation leader, as both computer manufacturers and customers watch IBM's product development and base their production and purchase decisions on current IBM products. Other computer manufacturers approach the market as innovators by developing hardware and software to satisfy specific market segments.

Most firms approach the market by building clone PCs. These firms (sometimes called value-added remarketers) use the base MS-DOS technology of innovators and attempt to improve on the system configuration and/or differentiate their product on some basis such as marketing channel used, service and support, product reliability, and/or price. Essentially, value-added remarketers buy components and software from various vendors to configure systems sold under their own brand labels. The success of the imitative approaches is evidenced by the performance of companies such as Compaq,

Prime Computer, CompuAdd, and Dell. Many "clone" firms believe that to be successful in the PC industry, they must be concerned with market pressures to reduce price and, thus, must constantly monitor costs and search for ways to reduce those costs.

▪ PC Markets

Macro segments in the PC industry are usually defined as business, home, government, or education users. Business users want high performance, reliability, and value in a system for their computing needs. State-of-the-art technology, the ability to network and communicate with other systems, customer service and support, and cost are primary purchase determinants for the business user. One of the fastest growing segments in the business market is the portables market, which is expected to grow at an annual rate of 20 percent for the next few years.

Home market demand was initially from the innovator and early adopter segments of the market. This group began the personal computer's diffusion through the innovation cycle. Most home users are price conscious, planning to spend less than $1,200 for a system. Value, ease of operation and service, and support from the manufacturer are major concerns. A 1985 survey of consumers found that more than 75 percent of shoppers could not justify the purchase of a home computer system, and this high percentage is expected to continue into the 1990s. This market will not be as lucrative as it was in the early to mid-1980s, but replacement sales (sales to previous PC owners) and sales to those still intending to buy a home PC should make this market moderately attractive. (For a list of competitors by market share, see Exhibits 3 and 4.)

Government and education users comprise the remaining macro segments of the PC market. Both of these segments represent large, important segments, yet they typically yield lower margins than either the business or home markets. Typical purchase decisions are based on a bidding system, with the contract going to the lowest qualified bidder. The education market was considered important, for its supposed ability to generate long-term brand loyalty among early users (students). Apple was one of the earliest entrants into this segment and currently holds 66 percent of the education market. It is questionable, however, if the anticipated brand loyalty of early users is actually realized.

In 1985, total PC sales to the U.S. federal government were $2 billion; in 1986, $2.2 billion; $3.1 billion in 1987, with growth expected throughout the 1990s. This segment, like the business segment, is interested in integrated systems designed to perform to the buyer's specific needs. Increased competition for this market had led to increased downward pressure on prices.

▪ Competitors

Major competitors of Dell include most traditional PC manufacturers, such as IBM, Compaq, Zenith, and Tandy. These firms rely on selling through a professional sales force or through retail outlets. Competitors of Dell that use a direct marketing and/or retailing approach (primarily value-added remarketers) include CompuAdd, which offers a full line of 286- and 386-based machines; Northgate, which offers machines similar to Dell's at savings of up to $2,000 over Dell equipment; and Everex, which offers machines similar to Dell's

Exhibit 3

Market Share of 286-Based PCs: 1988 Unit Shipments of U.S. Based Vendors

Vendor	*U.S. Shipments (000)*	*Market Share (%)*	*International Shipments (000)*	*Market Share (%)*	*Worldwide Shipments (000)*	*Market Share (%)*
IBM	895	24	545	42	1440	28.3
Zenith	283	7.6	45.8	3.4	328.8	6.5
Compaq	179	4.8	97	7.2	276	5.4
Tandy	139	3.7	31	2.3	170	3.3
Everex	120.1	3.2	2.5	0.2	122.6	2.4
HP	113	3	125	9.2	238	4.7
AST	109.179	2.9	36.39	2.7	145.569	2.9
WYSE	104	2.8	33	2.4	137	2.7
NEC	75	2	0	0	75	1.5
EPSON	75	2	0	0	75	1.5
Dell	69.8	1.9	10.2	0.8	80	1.6
Packard Bell	62	1.7	6	0.4	68	1.3
CompuAdd	61.4	1.6	0	0	61.4	1.2
Acer	52	1.4	0	0	52	1

Exhibit 4

Market Share of 386-Based PCs: 1988 Unit Shipments of U.S.-Based Vendors

Vendor	*U.S. Shipments (000)*	*Market Share (%)*	*International Shipments (000)*	*Market Share (%)*	*Worldwide Shipments (000)*	*Market Share (%)*
Compaq	175	20	85	22.6	260	20.8
IBM	140	16	80	21.3	220	17.6
NEC	35.8	4.1	0	0	35.8	2.9
Intel	25	2.9	25	6.7	50	4
Zenith	24.8	2.8	5.6	1.5	30.4	2.4
Everex	23.25	2.7	0.55	0.1	23.8	1.9
Tandy	20.5	2.3	4.5	1.2	25	2
ALR	20	2.3	5	1.3	25	2
Acer	17.4	2	0	0	17.4	1.4
WYSE	17	1.9	5.5	1.5	22.5	1.8
Dell	15.2	1.7	3.8	1	19	1.5
Toshiba	15	1.7	0	0	15	1.2
AT&T	15	1.7	1	0.3	16	1.3
HP	12	1.4	14.5	3.9	26.5	2.1

but claims that they are faster than Dell PCs. (None of these firms have the service and satisfaction reputation of Dell Computer.) CompuAdd is located in Austin, Texas; Northgate in Plymouth, Minnesota; and Everex in Freemont, California.

Changes in the industry will be driven by four factors as the market matures. First, the Gartner Group, a market research firm, estimates that the number of customers replacing their outdated systems is expected to outnumber first-time purchasers by 1995. (In 1990, over 72 percent of Dell customers were replacement purchasers, up from 67 percent in 1989.) Second, an investment report on the PC distribution industry shows that PC saturation rates are relatively low. (Only about 33 percent of white-collar workers use PCs on the job, and only 17 percent of all domestic households have a PC.) This becomes more important when one considers that the largest growth opportunities are in small to medium-size accounts (businesses with fewer than 500 employees), which employ more than 70 percent of white-collar workers. Third, the ratio of price to performance for equivalent functions continues to improve by approximately 20 to 25 percent per year, making the purchase of state-of-the-art machines more attractive to many segments. Fourth, competition should intensify. Value-added remarketers more than doubled during the 1988–1989 period, with the number of firms increasing from 350 to more than 1,000. With increased demand by business users, improved software and networking capabilities, and increased competition through differentiation and focus-oriented marketing strategies, industry analysts forecast additional changes in both market approaches used by major competitors and further segmentation of the market. The 1990s should be a period of change for the industry, rivaling changes that occurred during the 1980s.

DELL COMPUTER OPERATIONS

Dell's success can be attributed to its commitment to customer service and satisfaction and the marketing of state-of-the-art systems to business users through direct marketing strategies.

■ Product Line

Dell Computer Corporation offers a wide range of microcomputer systems, from printers and disk drive systems to the Dell system 433TE, a stand-alone system based on Intel's 486 microprocessor. Dell has also entered the battery-powered portable market with the 320 LT and the 316LT laptops and the 212N and 312N notebooks based on 286 and 386SX chips and VGA display technology. (For a list of Dell products, see Exhibit 5.)

Each machine segment of the Dell product line showed positive growth in fiscal 1990 over 1989. Sales of the 386-based machines tripled, and the 386SX machine is experiencing strong demand in the marketplace. Sales breakdown by product line are as follows: 9–10 percent of sales from 286-based machines, 69 percent from 386- and 486-based machines, and 21 percent from accessories and other equipment. The laptop and the 486 machine are relative newcomers to the market, but they are expected to show strong growth in the near future.

Exhibit 5 **The Dell Product Families**

Portables			
Dell System	320N 20 MHz	386SX	Notebook
Dell System	212N 12 MHz	286	Notebook
Dell System	320LT 20 MHz	386SX	Laptop
Dell System	316LT 16 MHz	386SX	Laptop
Low-Profile Systems			
Dell System	433P 33 MHz	i486	Desktop
Dell System	333P 33 MHz	386	Desktop
Dell System	325P 25 MHz	386	Desktop
Dell System	320SX 20 MHz	386SX	Desktop
Dell System	316SX 16 MHz	386SX	Desktop
Dell System	210 12.5 MHz	286	Desktop
Mid-Sized Systems			
Dell System	333D 33 MHz	386	Desktop
Dell System	325D 25 MHz	386	Desktop
Dell System	433DE 33 MHz	i486	Desktop
Dell System	420DE 20 MHz	i486SX	Desktop
Servers			
Dell System	433TE 33 MHz	i486	Floorstanding
Dell System	425TE 25 MHz	i486	Floorstanding

■ Manufacturing

Dell's computers for the domestic market are manufactured in facilities located in Austin, Texas. The purchase of a 126,000 square foot manufacturing facility in 1989 doubled Dell's manufacturing capability. A 135,000 square foot facility located in Limerick, Ireland, is expected to satisfy the growing international demand for Dell systems. Dell utilizes a total quality approach, whereby enthusiastic workers compete in product quality competitions for bonuses and recognition. During the last quarter of fiscal 1989, Dell overestimated demand and had considerable surplus inventories of finished goods. Dell attacked this problem and reduced inventories by $36 million in fiscal 1990. Inventory levels for the third and fourth quarters of 1991 were between 8.6 and 10.3 weeks of sales, respectively, below industry averages.

The manufacturing strategy utilized at Dell is one of building each computer system to the buyer's specifications. Buyers can add options to customize a system for their own needs. The order is then assembled and shipped with peripherals and upgrades requested by the customer. Manufacturing at Dell actually consists of the assembly and testing of vendor procured parts, assemblies, and subassemblies. The assembly line is not automated at present, and Dell has not indicated plans to do so.

■ Marketing

One factor leading to Dell's success is the marketing approach used by the organization. Dell approached the market from a service and customer satisfaction standpoint, combined with lower prices than comparable brands. Sales leads are generated through several sources, the primary source being advertising in PC and business publications. An outside sales force located in major markets addresses the needs of large corporate customers. Dell's sales force is channelized according to the market it serves: small/medium business and home users, corporate buyers, and government/education/medical. Each of these sales channels is supported by its own marketing, customer service, and technical support organization. This organizational structure ensures high accountability for the satisfaction of each customer, as well as feedback from daily direct contact with the customer. PC makers dealing through the retail channel do not have this advantage and are not able to respond as quickly to market and service demands as the direct channel. Additional face-to-face exposure occurs at industry shows.

Dell's entire product line, from 286- to 486-based machines and peripherals, is sold by telephone sales representatives who answer more than 4,000 incoming calls per day. In addition to answering customer-initiated calls, the Austin-based sales force responds to sales leads and supports the efforts of its team members in the field.

Sales orders are downloaded to the manufacturing facility several times each day, and all systems are custom-configured according to customer specifications. Trucks load up at Dell's manufacturing facility throughout the day, and overnight services are utilized for expedited orders. Lead times on systems vary from three to seven days.

Internationally, Dell is similar in marketing approach and culture to its domestic operation. Dell's wholly owned subsidiaries give it access to over 70 percent of the available worldwide market for PCs.

Currently, over 50 percent of revenues are received from major accounts, with sales to small and medium-sized businesses accounting for about 48 percent. Dell sells to major buyers through a small (25-person) sales force located in major metropolitan areas throughout the United States and services those accounts with management teams consisting of sales, customer service, and technical support representatives. Sales to government and education increased to approximately 40 percent of worldwide revenues, up from 30 percent in 1989. Dell believes that the small to medium-sized business represents the greatest growth potential for PC-based systems.

■ The CompUSA Connection

In 1990, Dell contracted with CompUSA, Inc., a Dallas-based chain of 20 superstores, to sell Dell products through 1993. CompUSA is a computer version of Toys 'R Us with approximately 21,000 square feet of retail space per store, a service center with a "fast service pickup" for corporate clients, and over 5,000 items at discount prices. Nathan Morton, a former senior executive with Home Depot and Target Stores, is CEO and expects sales to top $1 billion in 1991, after only two years of operations. CompUSA is adding new stores in major metropolitan areas and sells Dell systems for the same prices as Dell's direct sales. Dell added Staples Office Supply Superstores to its mass merchandising channel in mid-1991 as well. Staples markets to a less sophisticated computer user than does CompUSA. Although Dell systems are sold through this superstore channel, Dell maintains its same level of customer support to these buyers. Users who purchase Dell systems through CompUSA and Staples are entered into Dell's customer data base, as if they had ordered directly through Dell.

Dell's mass merchandising move may provide a serendipitous opportunity for the company, even though computer retailing is seen by some industry analysts as poised for a shakeout. Dataquest, Inc. believes that traditional retailers will see their share of PC sales shrink through 1994. Analysts state that, to be successful, marketers will have to move toward the ends of the retail spectrum, either concentrating on high-volume, low-price selling or specializing in market niches or other customized services that mass marketers neglect. Already, smaller operations that emphasize service along with price are showing the greatest gains. Superstores may be one retail format that not only survives the shakeout, but prospers. (For a forecast of PC sales by channels, see Exhibit 6.)

Dell has also arranged to sell its systems through integrators like Electronic Data Systems (EDS) and Anderson Consulting, increasing their sales potential. This move from traditional channels was prompted by the fact that the mail order market is only 16 percent of a $35 to $40 billion market, less than

Exhibit 6 **Retail PC Sales by Channel**

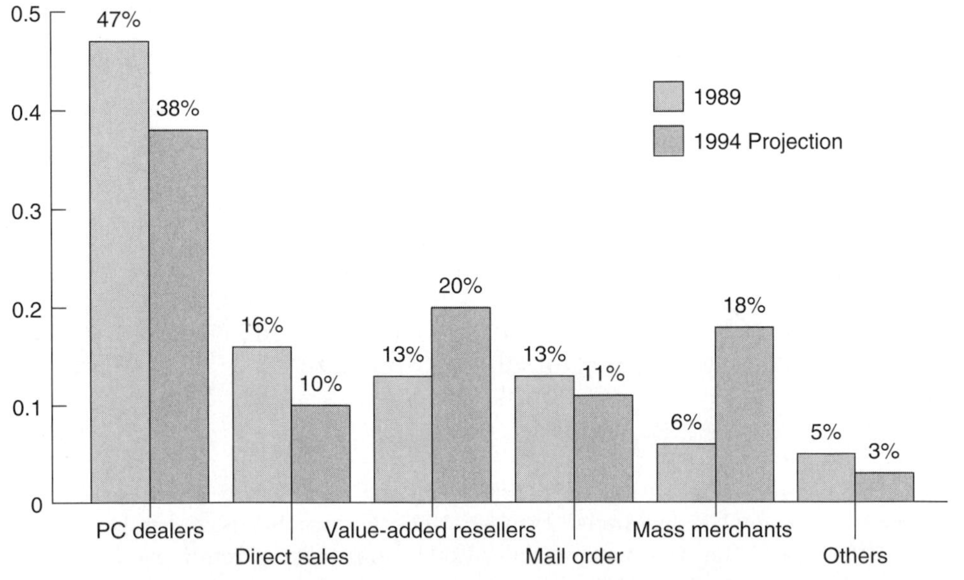

Source: "All Keyed Up for Change," *Austin American-Statesman*, March 10, 1991, p. D2.

one-fifth the size of sales of computer stores. (Dell currently has 25 percent of the mail order market.)

■ Research and Development

During the last few years, Dell's revenue growth has allowed the organization to devote considerable resources to building a first-class technological capability. Research and development spending in fiscal 1989 increased 29 percent over the previous year, doubled in fiscal 1990, and is estimated to be in excess of $18 million in 1991. Dell's efforts are enhanced, since Intel added Dell to its preferred purchaser list in 1989. Dell uses the standard MS-DOS, MS-OS/2, and UNIX operating systems on its 286-, 386-, and 486-based machines.

During fiscal 1990, the first products to utilize the Dell proprietary integrated circuit chip were shipped to customers. Dell is no longer restricted to standard vendor technologies when customizing its machines for specific usages. In 1990, Dell filed 45 patent applications to protect Dell-developed technologies and designs. It has currently been awarded six patents.

■ Finance

The financial summary of Dell Computer Corporation is presented in Exhibits 7 and 8. The organization does not pay dividends to investors; instead, it relies on appreciation of stock prices. Dell has experienced good sales and profit growth, especially after instituting tighter inventory controls following the overstock of 1989. (The 1989 inventory problem caused the stock price to drop 42 percent, from a high of $12 to $7 per share.) Dell is currently searching for ways to reduce costs without sacrificing customer service and technological performance of its systems.

Dell has managed to reduce its short-term debt from $27.1 million in 1989 to $0 at the end of fiscal 1991. (Dell's fiscal year is from February 1 to January 31.) Dell has a $40 million revolving line of credit to finance working capital. This line of credit is from strong domestic and foreign banks, headed by Security Pacific National Bank with 9.7 percent, which expires at the end of May 1993. Dell has obligations to pay $44 million in lease payments until 1991 for facilities in Austin, regardless of the firm's performance.

ISSUES AND CONCERNS

The most pressing concern of investors, regarding Dell operations, is Michael Dell. Michael Dell has been very successful in building his organization with an entrepreneurial style of management, but former employees have some concerns. For example, some former executives of Dell say that Michael Dell is not a patient person and has a one-man management style. They contend that Michael Dell should listen more to his people and place less reliance on intuition. Michael Dell contends that he is not an analysis person, preferring to be a mover rather than an analyst. Although Michael Dell was cited as Entrepreneur of the Year by *Inc. Magazine,* critics of Dell wonder whether he is capable of making the transition of moving Dell Computer Corporation from a stage I entrepreneurial mode to a stage II professionally managed company.

Exhibit 7 **Dell Computer Corporation Consolidated Statement of Income (in thousands)**

	February 2, 1992	February 3, 1991	February 2, 1990	January 27, 1989
Net sales	$889,939	$546,235	$388,558	$257,810
Cost of sales	607,768	364,183	278,972	176,693
Gross profit	$282,171	$182,052	$109,586	$ 81,117
Operating expenses				
Marketing and sales	$141,139	$ 87,806	$ 62,211	$ 38,742
General and administrative	39,223	26,354	17,380	12,456
Research and development	33,140	22,444	17,069	7,097
Total operating expenses	$213,502	$136,604	$ 96,660	$ 58,295
Operating income	$ 68,669	$ 45,448	$ 12,926	$ 22,822
Financing and other income (Expenses)	$ 4,746	$ (1,876)	$ (4,656)	$ (1,659)
Income before income taxes	$ 73,415	$ 43,572	$ 8,270	$ 21,163
Provision for income taxes	22,504	16,340	3,156	6,735
Net Income	$ 50,911	$ 27,232	$ 5,114	$ 14,428

Exhibit 8 **Dell Computer Corporation Condensed Consolidated Balance Sheet (in thousands)**

	February 2, 1992	February 3, 1991	February 2, 1990	January 27, 1989
Assets				
Current assets				
Cash	$ 55,460	$ 36,627	$ –0–	$ 2,631
Marketable securities	99,392	–0–	–0–	–0–
Accounts receivable, net	164,960	89,699	60,042	36,360
Inventories	126,554	88,462	68,246	103,999
Other current assets	65,814	21,480	14,228	6,439
Total current assets	$512,180	$236,268	$142,534	$149,429
Property and equipment, net	$ 44,661	$ 26,483	$ 26,170	$ 14,854
Other assets	2,722	1,471	3,088	2,749
Total assets	$559,563	$264,222	$171,792	$167,032
Liabilities and stockholders' equity				
Current liabilities				
Accounts payable	$ 97,389	$ 77,911	$ 51,475	$ 33,550
Notes payable	–0–	–0–	6,500	27,139
Accrued liabilities	114,816	70,099	27,997	25,614
Income taxes	17,329	–0–	–0–	–0–
Total current liabilities	$229,534	$148,010	$ 85,972	$ 86,303
Long-term debt	$ 41,450	–0–	–0–	–0–
Obligations under capital leases	14,399	4,207	6,041	5,472
Stockholders' equity	274,180	112,005	79,779	75,257
Total liabilities & equity	$559,563	$264,222	$171,792	$167,032

Dell Computer Corporation and Michael Dell have also been the target of several negative newspaper stories and suffer from some public misconceptions. These stories, primarily originating in Austin, have made some customers wary of establishing a long-term relationship with the organization.

Another concern is Dell's current move to include retail sales in addition to its traditional strength of telemarketing. This move is designated to broaden Dell's appeal to small business and the home PC user, but retailers historically have not shown loyalty to any particular brand of machine and may stock several different brands in their stores. Additionally, Dell's emphasis on telemarketing is a double-edged sword. Telemarketing does reduce the need for a field sales force and does eliminate channel markups, but Dell is considered by some to be little more than a dim, dusty warehouse that sells cheap, undistinguished PCs.

Lastly, the question also arises whether Dell can continue to grow as quickly as it would like and still have the same emphasis on service, performance, and satisfaction. There is also the situation of more intense competition as the industry matures and growth slows. Dell is still one of the infants in an industry populated by giants and must be aware of potential entry into its market niche by these financial and technological colossuses.

Total U.S. Microsystems Market Units Sales by Manufacturer (units in thousands) **Exhibit 9**

Vendors	*1988*[a]	*Percent Market Share*	*1991*	*Percent Market Share*	*1992*	*Percent Market Share*
Apple Computer	NA	NA	1305	11.1	1578	11.7
Compaq	354	12.2	419	3.6	429	3.2
Dell	85	2.9	270	2.3	455	3.4
Epson	75[b]	2.7	293	2.5	318	2.4
Gateway 2000	NA	NA	250	2.1	396	2.9
Hewlett-Packard	125	4.3	189	1.6	426	3.2
IBM	1035	35.8	1471	12.4	1265	9.4
NEC	111	3.8	298	2.5	301	2.2
Packard Bell	62[b]	2.1	472	4.0	510	3.8
Tandy	160	5.5	472	4.0	548	4.1
Toshiba	15[c]	0.5	264	2.2	299	2.2
Other vendors	872	30.2	6113	51.7	6915	51.5
Total	2894	100.0	11,816	100.0	13,440	100.0

[a]These are based on 286 and 386 PCs and were assumed to be the total market.
[b]These are based on 286 PCs.
[c]These are based on 386 PCs.

Exhibit 10 **Total U.S. Microsystems Market Units Sales by Manufacturer (units in thousands)**

Vendors 286 PCs	***1988***	***Percent Market Share***	***1991****	***Percent Market Share****	***1992****	***Percent Market Share****
Compaq	179	4.8	212	2.2	217	2.0
Dell	70	1.9	222	2.3	374	3.4
Hewlett-Packard	113	3.0	171	1.8	385	3.5
IBM	895	24.0	1272	13.3	1094	10.1
NEC	75	2.0	202	2.2	204	1.9
Tandy	139	3.7	411	4.3	478	4.4
Other vendors	2262	60.6	7067	73.9	8107	74.7
Total	3733	100.0	9456	100.0	10,859	100.0
Vendors 386 PCs						
Compaq	175	20.0	207	9.1	212	8.2
Dell	15	1.7	48	2.1	81	3.2
Hewlett-Packard	12	1.4	18	0.8	41	1.6
IBM	140	16.0	199	8.8	171	6.6
NEC	36	4.1	96	4.2	97	3.8
Tandy	21	2.3	61	2.7	70	2.7
Other vendors	477	54.5	1641	72.3	1909	73.9
Total	876	100.0	2270	100.0	2581	100.0

*These are based on 1988 % market shares of total 1988 data for 286 and 386 based PCs.

CASE 4

Cincinnati Milacron

Joseph Wolfe, University of Tulsa

The decade of the 1980s was supposed to have been one of high earnings recovery and the realization of new growth and market plans for Cincinnati Milacron (CM). Industry analysts and "the Mill's" top management team believed it had all the requisites for success. It was the largest machine tool company in the United States, and it could afford to develop and market the new manufacturing technologies needed for the factories of the future. CM had a diversified customer base and was not dependent on the capital investment swings and fortunes of just one industry. It also had a strong reputation in plastics molding equipment, and plastics were rapidly replacing metals in many applications. Most important, the company had especially bright prospects for its newly developed "cutting edge" line of robots and computer-controlled manufacturing systems.

The period's realities were much more harsh. Instead of obtaining high earnings, Cincinnati Milacron operated in the red over the years of 1981–1991 and lost as much as $80 million in 1987. After starting the decade as America's largest machine tool company, it ended it as merely "one of America's largest" after turning its top managers over in 1988 and eliminating the jobs of almost half of its employees. Moreover, Milacron found itself outclassed and outmaneuvered in its high-tech diversifications into robots, lasers, and semiconductor wafers, which were supposed to protect it from the fearsome competitive strength of Japan's machine tool companies. The robotics industry, which was expected to amount to $4.0 billion in American sales by 1990, never took off, and the company's profits and market responsiveness were hampered by production inefficiencies, rigid assembly techniques, and a slow, cumbersome management system. After suffering high losses on the robotics line, it was sold in April 1990 to the Swedish-Swiss manufacturer Asea Brown Boveri, after failing to find a manufacturing partner for its excellently designed equipment.

This case is intended for classroom discussion only, not to depict effective or ineffective handling of administrative situations. All rights reserved to the authors.

As 1992 begins, Cincinnati Milacron's new strategy is to return to its core business of standard machine tools. While this strategy pits the firm squarely against the mainly Japanese competition it attempted to avoid in the first place, Daniel J. Meyer, the company's chief executive officer, says it is the correct path to follow because "we have more confidence in machine tools." More important, for the company's long-term fortunes, "we have a 107-year reputation in manufacturing, and the opportunity for success is still there, based on the history we have. We're not going to lose."

MACHINE TOOLS AND THE MACHINE TOOL INDUSTRY

The machine tool industry (SIC 3541) consists of metal-cutting and metal-forming power machinery. It is the business of making the machines that make the machines of industry, as almost all manufacturing processes require these tools. A nation's manufacturing capabilities are highly dependent on the quantity and quality of its machine tools. Accordingly, this industry is of strategic importance to a country's ability to compete internationally. The major users of machine tools are the auto industry (roughly 20.0% to 40.0% of annual sales orders), the oil and gas industry, and the makers of farm and industrial machinery, appliances, aircraft, and electronic equipment. Exhibit 1 describes the various machine tools manufactured by this industry as well as cites America's major machine tool suppliers. Exhibit 2 displays the value of domestic and foreign machine tool shipments by major category.

While firms using metals and plastics as part of their manufacturing processes are the consumers of machine tools, the basic demand for them is derived from a number of production-related factors. Machine tools can alter a factory's production levels, are capital-intensive, and affect the skill levels and number of machinists needed to operate them. Therefore, the demand for machine tools is dependent on (1) the sales expectations for the products the tools support and (2) the supply and cost of skilled labor. The role of sales expectations and projected factory utilization rates can be seen in Exhibit 3. When capacity utilization rates begin to rise above the 85.0% mark, the demand for machine tools tends to rise. This relationship is somewhat delayed, however, depending on the complexity of the machinery being produced and labor/capital substitution considerations. The historical lag between orders and shipments graphed in Exhibit 4, shows it ranges from five to six business quarters. When Detroit's car manufacturers planned for the production of their redesigned transmissions and engines for the 1991 and 1992 model years, the machine tools for them were ordered in late 1987 and nearly all of 1988. The lag between orders and shipments, however, is much shorter for standard, commodity-like machine tools. These are sold "off-the-shelf" from inventories with no customizing and little manufacturer's service or support.

In the short term, weakened labor unions or an ample supply of machinists may cause manufacturers to delay purchasing labor-saving machine tools. Weak labor unions have difficulty protesting the labor replacement and skill-lowering aspects of programmed machine tools, while an ample supply of skilled machinists tends to dampen the workers' demands for higher wages. Moreover, in the long term, labor is a variable cost and can be adjusted to

Major Categories and Manufacturers of Metal-Working Machinery and Tools

Exhibit 1

Machine Tools

As a general class, machine tools are power-driven, metal-working devices that shape or form metal by using cutting, sawing, pressing, pounding, or electrical discharges.

Within this general class, there are two types of machine tools classified by their operating method—metal-cutting and metal-forming machines. Metal-cutting machines shape metal by cutting away the material not wanted in the final product. This carving can be accomplished by any of the following methods alone or in combination:

1. Turnings—Machines turn or spin the object being shaped against a cutting edge. Examples of these types of machines are lathes, automatic bar machines, and screw machines.
2. Boring—Machines cut circles or cylindrical shapes into metal from either a horizontal or vertical plane.
3. Planing and shaping—Machines shear metal in continuous strokes.
4. Drilling—Smaller-diameter holes are pierced through the metal by a continuous rotating action.
5. Grinding and honing—Metal is shaped through the use of abrasives.

Metal-forming machines operate through the actions of forging, shearing, hammering, extruding (stretching), bending, die casting, or pressing. The automobile industry is the largest market for these types of machines. As plastics, ceramics, and exotic materials have begun to be used more frequently in cars and other products, these tools have been modified or applied to those applications. America's largest manufacturers of machine tools are Cross & Trecker, Cincinnati Milacron, Giddings & Lewis, Industrial Automation Systems (Litton Industries), and Ingersoll Milling Machine.

Automatic, Numerically Controlled Machine Tools

Numerically controlled (NC) machine tools use some type of medium to control the tool being used. This degree of automation eliminates human mistakes, lowers labor costs, and allows the machine to easily switch jobs. Three kinds of NC tools are currently available:

1. Conventional NC systems—Also known as hard-wired NC tools, the functions of these machines are precoded into a fixed and unalterable routine or activity sequence.
2. Computerized numerical control (CNC) systems—Also known as soft-wired NCs, a small computer is used to control the machine tool's functions. A set of programs controlling those functions are stored in the computer's memory, and these programs can be called upon by the machine's operator when desired. While conventional NC systems are still the major sellers in this market, CNCs have been rapidly increasing their market shares through the availability of low-cost, freestanding minicomputers in the late 1960s.
3. Direct numerical control (DNC) system—In this system, a main computer simultaneously controls the actions and functions of a number of machine tools. Rather than using punched cards, paper, or magnetic tape to control the machine's actions, jobs and routines are called and corrected through the use of a display screen.

The principal manufacturers of these types of machines are General Electric, Allen-Bradley (Rockwell International), and Fanuc of Japan. Cincinnati Milacron, Cross & Trecker, Monarch Machine Tool, Giddings & Lewis, and Ex-Cell-O Corporation (Textron, Inc.) are also major players in this industry's segment.

(Continued)

Exhibit 1

Major Categories and Manufacturers of Metal-Working Machinery and Tools (continued)

Expendables and Accessories

These are products or supplies employed during the metal-working process. These are taps, dies, twist drills, chucks, gauges, reamers, and jigs. Because these products wear out in proportion to their use, the demand for them is closely tied to industry's level of activity. National Twist Drill, Acme-Cleveland, and Vermont American are the largest manufacturers of twist drills, while the major manufacturers of taps, dies, and gauges are United- Greenfield, TRW Geometric Tools (TRW, Inc.), and Ex-Cell-O Corporation.

Hand Tools and Mechanics' Precision Tools

Hand tools can employ either human or electrical/mechanical energy to accomplish their task. Hand tools are pliers, hammers, screw drivers, tool boxes, and interchangeable socket wrenches. These are primarily manufactured by Snap-On Tools, Stanley Works, McDonough Co., and Triangle Corporation. Power-driven hand tools are of two power types—portable pneumatic tools and portable electric tools. The pneumatic, air-driven tools, which include drills, screw drivers, nut setters, ratchet wrenches, hoists, grinders, sanders, polishers, and shipping and riveting hammers, are usually made to customer specifications and are sold to mass production assemblers. America's largest manufacturer of these types of tools is Chicago Pneumatic Tools followed by Ingersoll-Rand and Thor Power Tool (Stewart-Warner).

Portable electric tools are used for both metal and woodworking and for home maintenance purposes. Professional electric tools include electric drills, saws, sanders, polishers, hammers, lawn and garden tools, and chain saws. Black & Decker is the largest producer of these type of tools. Other manufacturers are Rockwell International, McGraw-Edison (Cooper Industries), and Ingersoll-Rand.

When accomplishing their tasks, mechanics employ various measuring devices. These hand-operated devices include micrometers, steel rules, combination squares, calipers, verniers, and protractors. Among many manufacturers in the United States, the largest are Brown & Sharpe, L.S. Starrett, and the Triangle Corporation.

Sources: "Machinery Outlook," *Standard & Poor's Industry Surveys: Steel and Heavy Machinery,* Vol. 158, No. 30, Sect. 1 (August 9, 1990), p. 28; and various *Value Line* Machine Tool Industry overviews, 1980 to 1991.

Exhibit 2

Shipments of Complete Machine Tools ($000,000)

Tool Type	*1979*	*1980*	*1981*	*1982*	*1983*	*1984*	*1985*	*1986*	*1987*	*1988*	*1989*
Metal-cutting											
Domestic	2,606	3,206	3,550	2,599	1,200	1,484	1,538	1,685	1,499	1,400	2,059
Foreign	324	475	551	296	172	123	194	206	178	174	299
Total	2,930	3,681	4,101	2,895	1,372	1,607	1,732	1,891	1,677	1,574	2,358
Metal-forming											
Domestic	860	878	824	600	430	608	744	621	538	702	704
Foreign	87	133	167	110	43	71	60	67	109	122	133
Total	947	1011	991	710	473	679	804	688	647	824	837

Source: Adapted from *The Economic Handbook of the Machine Tool Industry,* National Machine Tool Builders' Association (the Association for Manufacturing Technology), various years.

Machine Tool Shipments and Net Orders **Exhibit 3**

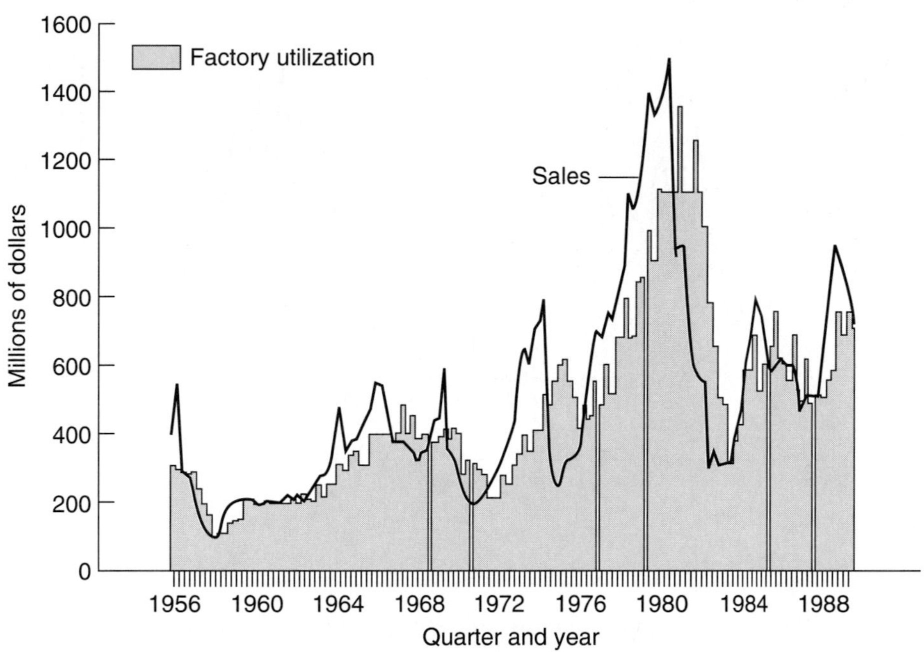

different plant production levels. Once new machine tools are purchased, they become fixed expenses that must be covered regardless of the factory's utilization rate. Producers are reluctant to commit to these fixed obligations unless there is a guarantee these expenses can be recovered in a reasonable amount of time. If in doubt, many will wait regarding fixed expenses until the future is more certain.

CHANGING INDUSTRY STRUCTURE

America's machine tool industry has traditionally been fractionalized and craft-related. Companies were often founded on a single, good idea. One such idea by one firm and one man led to the wire electrical discharge machine segment, which currently has sales of $700.0 million per year. Victor Harding's job during World War II was to remove broken bits of metal left in the grooves of newly threaded pieces. By rigging a spark-producing copper electrode to his machine, he found the sparks eroded the metal, thereby loosening waste material. Because his employer was not interested in his innovation, Harding started his own company, and by the mid-1960s, his Elox Corporation was selling an entire line of "electron drills."

Product and entrepreneurial patterns such as this resulted in an industry comprised of a large number of small firms producing a few particular machine tools. It was a highly segmented industry and its manufacturers had

Exhibit 4 **Machine Tool Orders versus Factory Operating Rates**

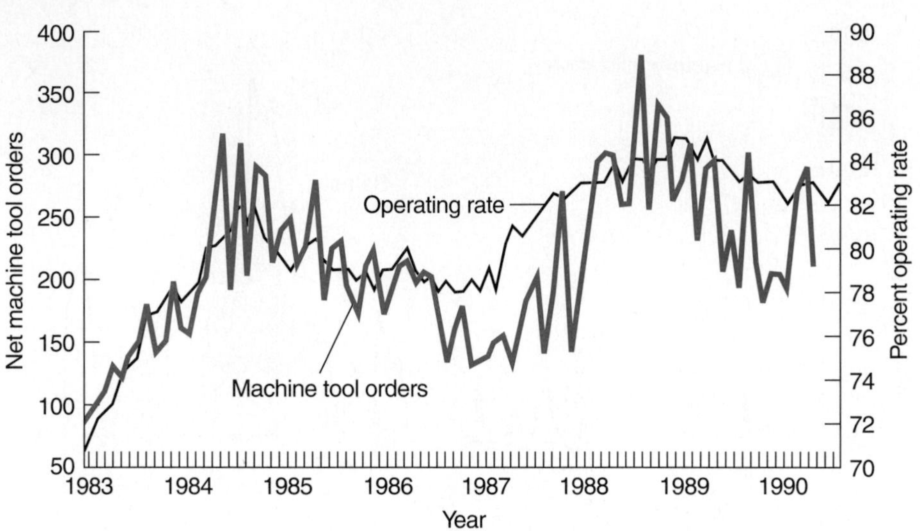

limited economies of scale. Despite this fractionalized nature, America's producers were the world's leaders as they possessed the most advanced technology and almost one-third of the world's sales.

In the late 1970s, however, the introduction of NC and CNC machine tools began to change the industry's economics. The new technologies of electronics and computers were added to the machine tool manufacturer's production matrix. Higher capital investments, new skills, and plant retooling expenses had to be financed, and those operating on a small scale were unable to do so. Also coming into play were learning curve effects associated with high technology electronics. Being basically small, single-line producers, many firms could not upgrade or acquire these skills or capture these learning curve effects. To stay in business, many gravitated toward the market's lower and technologically simpler end comprised of standard machine tool products.

For many American companies, this was a disastrous strategy. Japan's machine tool firms had just come on the domestic scene and they were pursuing the same market niche. Many U.S. firms were quickly overwhelmed by that country's superior, lower-priced products. By the mid-1980s, Japan had captured 80.0% of new sales in the American NC lathe and machining center market after only having entered it in 1976. The fate of Victor Harding's Elox Corporation is an example in miniature. It is now a small-time player in the segment it created as over 80.0% percent of America's market in wire electrical discharge machines has been captured by the Japanese firms of Mitsubishi, Fujitsu Fanuc, Sodick, and Hitachi.

On the international scene, America's machine tool firms experienced similar problems during this period. Japan's share of world exports of machine tools grew from 3.5% in 1970 to 15.0% in 1983, while America's share fell from 11.7% to 4.8%.

JAPAN'S MACHINE TOOL INDUSTRY POLICY

How did this sweep of the American machine tool industry come about? What did the Japanese do to overwhelm an industry that had the United States as its leading participant?

As part of its economic revival in the 1950s, the Japanese government's policies have been guided by "developmental capitalism." Under this system, the state works hand in hand with private enterprise to further the nation's economic development. Through its Ministry of International Trade and Industry (MITI), various "vision" statements are intermittently authored. These statements generally specify the strategies and the industries to be targeted for special emphasis. As early as 1956, MITI recognized the strategic value of the machine tool indusry by passing the Extraordinary Measures Law for the Promotion of Specified Machinery Industries.

Teeth were soon put into MITI's vision for Japan's machine tool industry. To obtain rationalization and economic efficiency within the domestic industry itself, it recommended the following:

1. Japanese domestic firms would stop manufacturing any product line whose Japanese market share was less than 5.0%; or
2. Firms would stop manufacturing any product line that was less than 20.0% of the firm's total production. Once rationalization was achieved within the industry, then
3. All machine tool firms would concentrate on NC tools. This machine tool type should account for over 50.0% of the industry's total output by 1980.

After having accomplished rationalization within its own industry by the early 1970s, new policies were adopted to promote overseas sales with the United States being a prime target. Exhibit 5 summarizes these policies and actions, while Exhibit 6 summarizes the competitive strategies employed by Japan's machine tool companies.

As the Japanese have succeeded in the United States via the relatively safe strategy of exporting their machines into the country, they are now establishing deeper roots and greater equity commitments on American soil. These roots and commitments have taken the following form:

- Joint ventures—Fujitsu Fanuc Ltd.–General Motors; Okuma Machinery Works Ltd.–DeVlieg; Toyota–Bendix; Toshiba–Cross & Trecker; Yokogawa Electric Manufacturing–Gould; Dijet Industrial–Kennametal
- United States subsidiary operations—U.S. Mazak, a subsidiary of Yamazaki; Mori Seiki, OSG Manufacturing; Sonoike Manufacturing, Hitachi
- Acquisitions—Makino acquisition of LeBlond

These strategies and commitments have been so effective that about 30.0% of America's machine tool capacity is now provided by the Japanese firms of Mazak Corp., LeBlond Makino Machine Tool Co., and Okuma Machinery Works, Ltd. This presence will be even greater in the early 1990s. In July 1990, Mitsubishi Heavy Industries America Inc. opened a plant in Hopkinsville, Kentucky, to make horizontal and vertical machining centers and NC lathes. Mazak completed a $55.0 million expansion of its Florence, Kentucky, plant in

Exhibit 5 **MITI's Policies and Maneuvers for the Machine Tool Industry**

Policy	*Maneuvers*
Industry structure	Rationalization of the machine tool industry through forced or encouraged mergers, the divestment of extraneous or nonstrategic product lines, and the achievement of economies of scale.
Product line	Concentration on NC machine tools. This type to be at least 50.0% of all output by 1980. Certain companies would specialize in particular products. Export cartels created to facilitate joint export activities. Government research funds and tax credits provided for joint research in earmarked technologies. All activities coordinated by a machine tool industry association.
Customer financing	Small businesses receive loans and special depreciation allowances made to firms purchasing machine tools. Leasing of Japanese-made robots subsidized by Japan Robot Leasing Authority.
Exports	Export cartel set floor prices on NC lathes and machining centers exported to the United States, Canada, and the EEC. Expenses shared regarding exporting, market research, and international marketing information.

Source: Adapted from Ravi Sarathy, "The Interplay of Industrial Policy and International Strategy: Japan's Machine Tool Industry," *California Management Review* (Spring 1989), pp. 138–141.

March 1990, and this raises its monthly capacity from 80–85 units to 100–120 units.

CURRENT INDUSTRY CONDITIONS

The composite results for a number of benchmark American machine tool companies indicates the difficulties they experienced in the 1980s. Exhibit 7 shows combined losses in 1987–1988 and 1990 for Acme-Cleveland, Brown & Sharpe, Cincinnati Milacron, Cross & Trecker, Gleason Works, and the Monarch Machine Tool Company. Future profits are expected to be relatively low. The health of today's firms appears to be partially related to their past strategies. As described in Exhibit 8, some companies attempted to diversify away from the extremely competitive machine tool industry while others tried to apply their core strengths to exotic applications. During the past decade, about half of America's machine tool companies went out of business and a large number of consolidations occurred. Despite the resulting greater industry concentration, the average U.S. tool firm has less than $3.0 million in annual sales and fewer than 25 employees. It can be expected that more casualties will be experienced in the 1990s.

Industry observers have cited two sets of factors that could improve the industry's prospects. The first set of factors are historical and demographic in nature. A historically weakening dollar has made American goods more price

Japanese Machine Tool Competitive Strategy

Exhibit 6

Strategy	***Implementation***
Company cost structure	Lower the company's manufacturing cost structure through high volume production of standardized products in capital-intensive factories. From 1975 to 1986, Japan's major machine tool manufacturers reduced their labor expenses from 25.0% to 12.2% and general overhead from 16.2% to 14.2% of sales. This was accomplished by heavy capital investment per employee. Capital stock increased from ¥2.15 million in 1975 to ¥6.19 million by 1986, resulting in greater productivity. Sales per employee were ¥9.83 million in 1975 and they increased to ¥34.76 million by 1986.
Product/market niches	Sell standardized, off-the-shelf machine tools to small- and medium-sized firms. Designed small, cheaper, and lower-performance CNC lathes for Japan's own medium- and smaller-sized firms. These standard products were subsequently widely distributed in the U.S. through independent dealers rather than through company-controlled sales engineers who were only needed for custom-fitted machine tool applications.
R&D	Efforts aimed at simplifying the product and making it easier to manufacture and be produced in large volumes via assembly-line techniques.
Pricing	Sell the product for less. By 1982, Japan's prices were lower by 19.0% on 25 hp horizontal spindles, 39.0% for 50 hp horizontal spindles, 32.0% for vertical spindle lathes, and 44.0% for horizontal spindles with a y-axis of over 40.0 inches. Machining centers were 30.0% to 41.0% lower in price.
Delivery and distribution	Standardized, off-the-shelf products easier to warehouse and deliver during boom times. Import penetration tends to increase when domestic order backlogs exceed 9.5 months. Japan's products were immediately available from stockpiled warehouses, and they made large inroads. Heavy use of distributors rather than direct customer sales.
Foreign direct investment	Obtain an American manufacturing presence through either transplants, acquisitions, or joint ventures. The American firm LeBlond was acquired by Makino, allowing it to manufacture machining centers in the U.S. with Japanese parts. Mori Seiki, OSG Manufacturing, Sonoike Manufacturing, and Hitachi have created American subsidiaries. Joint ventures have been established between General Motors and Fanuc, Okuma with DeVlieg, Toyota and Bendix, Toshiba and Cross & Trecker, Gould and Yokogawa Electric Manufacturing, and Dijet Industrial with Kennametal.

Source: Adapted from Ravi Sarathy, "The Interplay of Industrial Policy and International Strategy: Japan's Machine Tool Industry," *California Management Review* (Spring 1989), pp. 149–153.

competitive with foreign goods. This could generally give American manufacturers an incentive to increase their capacity; and for the machine tool manufacturers themselves, it means American-built machine tools will continue to be price competitive with those built overseas. Regarding demographics, America's aging population and declining birth rate translates into a shortage of industrial skilled labor. This shortage of skilled labor can be compensated for by "smarter" machine tools which also have the advantage of being depreciated.

Exhibit 7

Composite Machine Tool Industry Revenues ($000,000)

	1987	*1988*	*1989*	*1990*	*1991**	*1992**	*1994–1996**
Sales	1882.8	1944.2	1945.5	1933.4	2003.0	2083.1	2703.5
Operating profit	90.4	108.9	118.7	97.7	100.2	104.2	135.2
Deprecitation	80.5	71.9	58.7	59.1	60.0	65.0	90.0
Net profit	–111.2	–26.2	–6.3	–34.5	13.9	46.3	117.9

Sources: Theresa Brophy, "Machine Tool Industry," *Value Line Industrial Survey* (May 17, 1991), p. 1336; David Altany, "Going, Going, Gone," *Industry Week* (January 7, 1991), pp. 54–57.

Note: Composite companies are Acme-Cleveland, Brown & Sharpe, Cincinnati Milacron, Cross & Trecker, Gleason Works, and Monarch Machine Tool Company.

*Estimate.

The second set of factors are competitive in nature. American firms are under continuing pressure to lower costs and raise quality. Efficient and accurate machine tools are at least a partial solution. Much of America's manufacturing equipment is more than twenty years old and needs replacement. Due to inefficiencies in the face of foreign competition, these factories must retool to survive. Improvements in computer and manufacturing technology are also occurring more rapidly and these could force the industry's remaining firms to use these technologies as competitive weapons. Computer prices have fallen drastically, thus lowering the costs of various CNC and DNC units. This means factories can adopt "cutting edge" technology at a lower cost.

Many U.S. companies are finally realizing they must modernize if they are to succeed. Caterpillar, Inc. will have spent about $3.4 billion from 1986 to 1992 to build its new automated "Plant with a Future." When completed, it will produce more heavy duty equipment than ever but with 3.0 million square feet less manufacturing space. Pressures for modernization should also increase when Europe completes its unification plans in 1992 and Japan completes its current capital improvement program. Additional markets will be opening with the emergence of Eastern and Central Europe as invigorated customers. In June 1990, the Coordinating Committee on Multilateral Export Controls, of which the United States is a major partner, agreed to ease its 41-year-old embargo on the sale of machine tools to the Eastern bloc countries.

Because America's automobile manufacturers are the machine tool industry's single largest customer, trends and expectations in that industry are extremely important. Japan's superiority in engine design and transmissions may force Detroit to retool its plants even though the Motor City's sales prospects and capacity utilization rates for the mid-1990s are not that bright. Japan has taken the lead in producing multi-valve engines and electronically controlled transmissions. The engines boost performance without increasing pollution or diminishing fuel economy, and electronically controlled five-speed automatic transmissions provide better fuel economy and smoother gearshifts. Regardless of what the Japanese do, the U.S. government is redefining its automobile emission standards, and Detroit will probably want to invest in new drive train programs for the 1993 and 1994 models.

Company Profiles

Exhibit 8

Cross & Trecker—In the 1980s, Cross & Trecker emphasized the machine tool market's more specialized end. This did not work out well. Companies pursuing this strategy take all the risks of designing customized tools, but this does not guarantee their ultimate sale. This strategy has the attendant problems of estimating expenses and therefore many contracts are underpriced and unprofitable. Cross & Trecker had to suspend its first dividend in 1986, and in 1987 took a large charge against earnings to consolidate operations and write down old equipment and inventories. Dislocations caused by its corporate restructuring hampered sales in 1989 and it has been struggling for a number of years. Giddings & Lewis will finalize its acquisition of this company in fall 1991.

Giddings & Lewis—The AMCA International Corporation acquired this company in 1982. After losing $6.1 and $138.1 million in 1986 and 1987, it was sold off in July 1989. Giddings & Lewis quickly earned a profit of $17.1 million in 1989 after increasing its revenues 38.0% in one year. By August 1990, the company had no long-term debt and it generated cash in excess of capital spending and normal needs. Giddings has been very successful with large, yet flexible, integrated manufacturing systems selling for up to $30.0 million each. Chairman William J. Fife, Jr., vows, "We're not going into competition with the Japanese. [They] move low-end machine tools by the truckload. We're going to stay away from truckload sales." As one of America's most profitable machine tool companies, it will be the industry's largest firm after it completes its acquisition of Cross & Trecker.

Gleason Works—In the mid-1980s, Gleason attempted to capitalize on its dominance of the bevel gear grinding industry. It soon lost money marketing a complex differential for sports cars. It has subsequently retrenched to its gear-making specialty. As of May 1991, its new line of simplified computer- controlled gear production machinery is generating relatively healthy company earnings. Gleason has also begun to reduce design and manufacturing costs by using standardized parts. The company is basically a niche manufacturer as it dominates the worldwide market for bevel gear making machinery. Its sales are concentrated in the automobile industry.

Monarch Machine Tool—This venerable company was established in Sidney, Ohio, in 1909. It produces highly computerized, yet standardized, lathes and machining centers in antiquated plants in Sidney and Cortland, New York. Monarch was very profitable in the early 1980s when it earned as much as $19.0 million on sales of $139.0 million in 1981. Losses occurred shortly thereafter. To save money, management stopped all "unnecessary" spending including dividends, research and development, and new shop floor machinery. Only old, used equipment was purchased, which pushed further back Monarch's already outdated manufacturing operations. The company has relatively little exposure to the auto industry and CEO Robert Siewert says they will focus on customer service. "We haven't done business that way in the past. It was forced upon us by the Japanese. It was our way of staying in this business."

Newell Company and Stanley Works—Along with Vermont American, these companies cater to the relatively healthy do-it-yourself and equipment maintenance markets. In late 1991, the Newell Company announced its intentions of buying up to 15.0% of Stanley Works' common stock with the later aim of making a complete acquisition.

Norton—This company is a high-tech materials and grinding wheel manufacturer. It began to benefit from a cost reduction program it launched in 1986. In the late 1980s, Norton restructured itself and it has been carried by profits from its non-machine tool operations.

Detroit's automobile manufacturers currently have excess capacity, so they will probably not build new plants, but instead attempt to make given capacity more efficient. Ford has indicated it has about 20.0% more capacity than it needs. Instead, it will spend about $600.0 million to retool and "prep" its Van Dyke plant in Sterling Heights, Michigan, to produce four- and five-speed automatic front-wheel-drive transmissions for cars and light trucks.

While many are hoping for a rosy future for the machine-tool industry, a number of unsettling factors remain. The dollar must remain weak if mere price competitiveness is to be employed by the American machine tool manufacturers. Moreover, neither the weak dollar nor the trade restrictions the American government has placed on foreign machine tool manufacturers have kept the Japanese manufacturers from making serious inroads into the U.S. machine tool market. Regarding the capital/labor substitution effects associated with the installation of labor-saving machine tools, there are other less expensive and more flexible ways to increase a factory's efficiency. Quality circles and just-in-time methods can increase efficiency and these methods can be quickly turned on or off depending upon the company's needs for efficiency.

Closer to home within the American automobile industry itself, the Japanese have begun to produce and assemble their cars in transplants. When this is done, the tendency has been to employ their own country's machine tool equipment in their factories rather than purchasing American machine tools. The Japanese nameplates of Honda, Toyota, Nissan, Mazda, Mitsubishi, and others garnered a 31.0% share of America's 1991 automobile sales, and this was an 11.0% increase over their 1990 share. To circumvent the import restrictions that have been placed on them, more and more of these cars are being manufactured in the United States. While an opportunity exists for American machine tools to be used in Japan's transplants, sales to them have been difficult. Most Japanese manufacturers are part owners of the machine tool companies they use. They find it financially and culturally beneficial to continue these relationships regardless of the comparative quality or cost of the tools themselves.

Strategies for handling the foreign competition, especially the Japanese with the most efficient manufacturing facilities in the world, are varied. Some companies emphasize the "Made in America" label, while others emphasize service, which may be a disguised method of taking advantage of foreign producer's unfamiliarity with American customs, values, and decision making methods. The standardized products segment, where service is not of great importance, has all but surrendered to the Japanese. American companies have tended to concentrate on the highly sophisticated CNC machines priced from $300,000 to $2.0 million. As noted by Henry Mamlok, President of Jacobson Tool & Manufacturing Corp., "The Japanese are awfully hard to beat in the commodity end of the business. We focus on customized tools made to fill a special need with prices up to $500,000 or so."

Some companies have emphasized a niching strategy. Harvey Rohmiller of the Lodge and Shipley division of Manuflex Corporation says,

> To be successful, American companies—even the small ones—have to get better at defining their markets more narrowly and deciding what products will fit that market. Twenty years ago, a company like ours was manufacturing driven. We'd produce a new tool with the confidence it would soon have wide appeal. With so much more engineering and technology in the industry today, the stakes are higher and we've all had to become market-driven.

Then there is the last group of companies. They feel their fortunes are tied to the degree to which they can capitalize on whatever eventualities occur with their product's major users. Accordingly, they are attempting to hold on and keep their options open.

CINCINNATI MILACRON

Within the machine tool industry, Cincinnati Milacron currently manufactures and sells industrial process equipment and systems. These products are gathered into three groups with independent profit accountability:

- Machine Tool Group—Machine tools, composites processing equipment, advanced manufacturing systems, and electronic controls. The machine tool product lines include vertical and horizontal machining centers, turning centers, aerospace profilers and routers, bridge and portal mills, die- and mold-making machines, horizontal boring machines, grinding machines, and special machines.
- Plastics Machinery Group—Reaction injection molding machines, systems for extrusion, blow molding and blown film, auxiliary equipment, and contract services.
- Industrial Products Group—*Cimcool* metal-working fluids, precision grinding wheels, and LK measurement and inspection systems.

This product array is far different, however, from the one pursued just ten years before and came about after much soul searching and upheaval. In late February 1991, Milacron's management explained the rationale for their newest strategy.

> For several decades in the post-World War II era, Milacron's strategy was diversification and we brought to market new manufacturing technologies in many fields: electronics, plastics, robotics, laser, and flexible manufacturing systems, to name only a few. Certain new product lines, such as plastics machinery, were highly successful. However, the widely predicted large markets for other technologies never evolved. So, for the 1990s, we have honed a new strategy. We are channeling and focusing all Milacron's creativity, innovation, and entrepreneurial spirit directly into our core businesses, which are products and services for the metal-working and the plastics processing industries.
>
> Today, global markets for machine tools and plastics machinery are large and growing steadily. Annual worldwide sales of machine tools have doubled since the mid-1980s and now exceed $40.0 billion. The world market for plastics processing machinery, although smaller, is growing even faster. It is currently approaching $8.0 billion, with a real growth rate higher than the GNP. These are the primary markets Milacron is targeting in the 1990s.
>
> In the late 1970s and early 1980s, facing record-high demand for capital equipment, fierce foreign competition, and the over-valued dollar, Milacron and other U.S. machine tool builders moved away from producing *standard* machine tool products, i.e., basic machining centers and turning centers. Instead, we concentrated on highly engineered and custom-designed machines and systems for automotive, aerospace, and other important industries. The standard machine business, however, offers excellent economies of scale in manufacturing and the benefits of a broad marketing network. So now, Milacron is going back after the standard machine tool market, not only in the U.S. but throughout the world. And we're doing it by building cost-competitive, all-metric machines with world-class quality and features.

In pursuing its original diversification strategy, the company jettisoned its original stodgy name of the Cincinnati Milling Machine Company and became the space-age-sounding company called Cincinnati Milacron. Donald Shively, who would later be passed over for the company's top spot because he was too much a machine tool man, recalled, "The board decided we were beating a dead horse with machine tools, so the decision was made to more or less abdicate the standard line." Exhibit 9 lists the various diversifications and acquisitions the company made as it implemented this strategy. The exhibit also lists the ultimate deposition of many of those activities.

As the 1980s proceeded, management took solace that it often did not perform as badly as other firms in the machine tool industry. In 1981, Milacron's orders did not fall as much as the industry's because of its strong position in the less cyclical special machine tool market rather than in commodity-type tools. Additionally, the company was able to offer attractive credit terms to its customers through its financial subsidiary and it also benefitted from close ties to its customers through its direct marketing channels. A year later, management stated, "Although our operating results were down for the year, it should be kept in mind that Milacron performed better than many capital goods companies, and while the size of our markets declined, we gained share in our major product lines." In 1990, the company observed that orders for the American machine tool industry had declined 27.0% while its

Exhibit 9 **Diversifications, Acquisitions, and Divestitures**

Diversifications	*Acquisitions*	*Divestitures, Plant Closings, and Liquidations*
Pre-1976—Small business systems	1983—Purchased a line of injection molding machines from Emhart Corporation's Farrel Rochester Division.	1978—Liquidated its German machine tool manufacturing subsidiary at a loss of $3.6 million.
1976—Computer-controlled industrial robots	1984—Purchased LK Tool Company, Ltd., of England, a manufacturer of coordinate measuring machines.	1982—$10.0 million write-down on the closing of a British machine tool plant.
1978—Silicon wafers and circuit board composite material	1986—Purchased Laser Machines Corporation of Indianapolis, Indiana.	1988—Sold metals fabrication division to Cast-Fab Technologies, Inc.
1986—Plastic packaging film	1986—Purchased Sano Design and Machine Co., Inc., a manufacturer of plastic packaging films.	1989—Semiconductor materials business sold to a subsidiary of Japan's Osaka Titanium Co., Ltd.
1987—Expert Systems software and PC-based shop floor management software	1988—Purchased Chesapeake Laser Systems, Inc., as a compliment to the LK Tool Company.	1990—Sold all laser operations to The 600 Group, PLC, for a $4.5 million loss.
	1989—Acquired a line of plastics extrusion blow molding machines from the Bemis Company's Hayssen Manufacturing Co.	1990—Sold entire robot line to Asea Brown Boveri for a $1.7 million loss.
	1990—Bought SL Abrasives, Inc., a grinding wheel manufacturer.	1990—Closed Vlaardingen, Holland machine tool plant.
	1990—Acquired from Pratt & Whitney its die and mold product line.	

Net Profits for Cincinnati Milacron versus Benchmark Machine Tool Companies

Exhibit 10

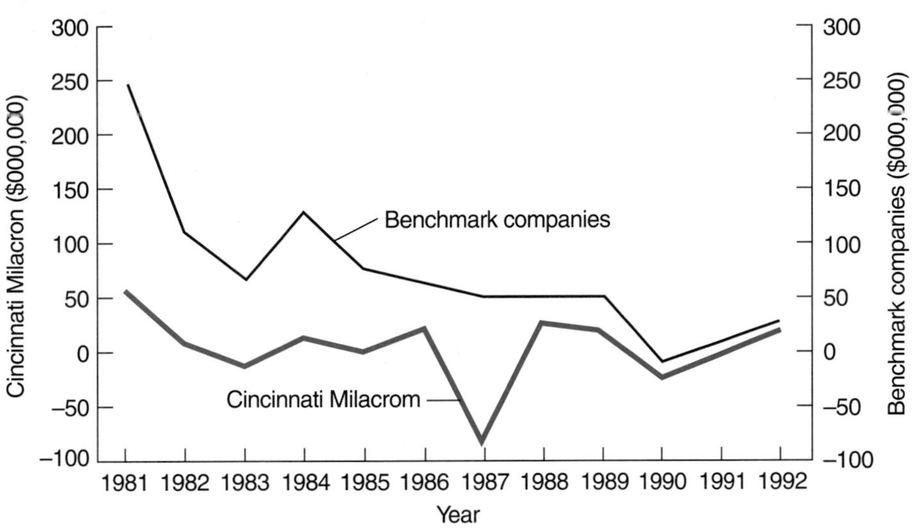

own orders declined only 14.0%. Exhibit 10 plots Cincinnati Milacron's net profits versus those obtained by its major competitors for the years 1981 to 1992. Exhibit 11 reports the company's overall profits and expenses for the same period.

To provide better guidance, top management enunciated various goals and predictions for the firm during the mid-1980s. In 1985, James A.D. Geier, then-chairman and CEO, forecast Milacron's sales would surpass $1.0 billion before 1990 and that plastics machinery revenues would be more than $300.0 million by that year. To provide a level of financial comfort, management's goal for 1989 was to produce a debt-to-total capital ratio in the low- to mid-30s. In December 1986, this ratio was 43.0% and it was deemed inappropriate.

Cincinnati Milacron Sales, Expenses and Earnings ($000,000)

Exhibit 11

	1981	*1982*	*1983*	*1984*	*1985*	*1986*	*1987*	*1988*	*1989*	*1990*	*1991**	*1992**
Sales	934.4	759.7	559.0	660.5	732.2	850.0	828.0	877.8	850.6	837.7	850.0	985.0
Cost of goods sold	691.5	569.8	458.4	535.0	549.2	595.0	612.7	657.3	625.3	647.5	646.0	712.3
Gross profit	242.9	189.9	100.6	125.5	183.0	255.0	215.3	220.5	225.3	190.2	204.0	272.7
General administration	142.4	121.6	57.6	48.4	115.3	163.5	229.7	135.3	152.5	156.4	154.5	158.2
R&D	22.4	35.7	30.2	36.3	36.6	40.0	35.6	35.2	31.5	34.3	31.5	32.7
Depreciation	17.3	20.4	23.1	26.0	29.6	28.3	30.0	25.0	22.9	23.7	23.0	24.0
Profit before taxes	60.8	12.2	−10.3	14.8	1.5	23.3	−80.0	25.0	18.5	−24.3	− 5.0	57.8
Taxes	25.4	6.5	0.0	4.1	0.0	6.9	0.0	10.7	8.8	−11.6	0.0	36.8
Profit after taxes	35.4	5.7	−10.3	10.7	1.5	16.4	−80.0	14.3	9.7	−12.7	− 5.0	21.0

Source: Adapted from annual August *Value Line* reports.

*Estimated from *Value Line* data.

Exhibit 12 **Actual and Target Percent of Assets Employed by Product Division**

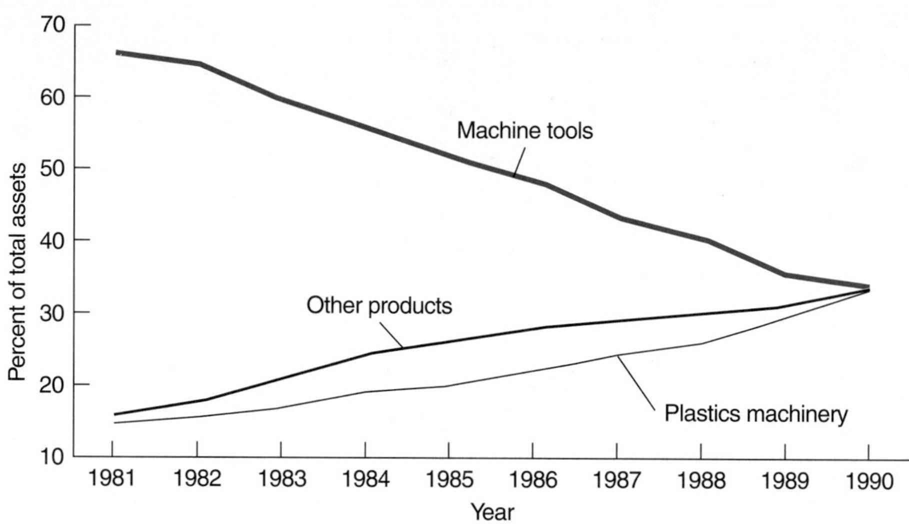

More important, asset usage was to be realigned according to the schedule shown in Exhibit 12. Between 1980 and 1985, the company closed five plants and reduced its machine tool work force by 46.0%. In 1981, 65.7% of its assets were dedicated to machine tools and this had been cut back 21.0% by 1985. Still, there was too much capacity in this money-losing line. In 1986, operations were discontinued in one of its Cincinnati plants, in the robot plant in Greenville, South Carolina, and at its turning center in Wilmington, Ohio. Overall, over 200 pieces of equipment were taken out of production that year. Exhibits 13 and 14, respectively, show Milacron's capital expenses and asset maneuvers from 1985 to 1991 and the recent operating results of its two latest divestitures.

In carrying out its reallocations, Cincinnati Milacron established the following new investment or new product criteria in 1985:

1. The investment or product had to provide now, or provide by 1990, at least $100.0 million in revenues and good profits.
2. They exist in a product area where Milicron already has a leadership position.
3. They be sold on the basis of technology and service rather than on price alone.

Accordingly, the product areas to be emphasized would be process plastics, flexible manufacturing cells and systems, special machinery for advanced applications, automation for advanced composites, metrology and inspection systems, and silicon epitaxial wafers.

With a firmer grasp on the products to be pursued, the company turned next to rationalizing its production facilities. This was spelled out in its most ambitious and comprehensive reorganization plan approved by the Board on February 16, 1988. A number of "focus factories" were created. These factories were to operate as independent business units with full profit and loss respon-

Asset Changes and R&D Activities ($000,000) — Exhibit 13

	*1991**	*1990*	*1989*	*1988*	*1987*	*1986*	*1985*
Capital expenditures							
Machine tools	15.0	16.1	17.0	9.9	8.0	11.8	9.2
Plastics machinery	12.0	14.0	14.0	4.7	3.4	10.6	11.6
Industrial products	3.0	4.0	2.6	6.9	4.3	6.9	23.6
Total	30.0	34.1	33.6	21.5	15.7	29.3	44.4
Write-downs, reorganization charges, and liquidation losses							
Machine tools	90.0	34.0			54.0		46.3
Plastics machinery							
Industrial products			4.5		24.0		
Headquarters					5.0		27.2
Total	90.0	34.0	4.5		83.0		73.5
Research and development	37.0	34.4	31.4	35.3	35.6	39.6	36.8

*Projected by management.

Operating Performance of Industrial Robots and Laser Machines ($000) — Exhibit 14

	1990	*1989*	*1988*
Sales			
Industrial robots	$31,182	$30,527	$38,697
Laser machines	—	3,180	7,036
	31,182	33,707	45,733
Net loss from operations			
Industrial robots	- 441	- 588	- 911
Laser machines	—	−2,313	−1,459
	- 441	−2,901	−2,370
Net loss on sales of assets	−1,700	−4,474	—

Source: 1990 company 10-K.

sibility. Each was dedicated to manufacturing and marketing similar or complementary product lines. This reorganization's goal was a reduction of the company's burdensome and overcentralized bureaucracy and faster responses to the marketplace. The following "focus factories" were created at this time, and they were to be fully operational by mid-1989:

1. Robots—Factory in Greenwood, South Carolina, with support functions being moved from Cincinnati to Greenwood. Liaison with the American automobile industry would be continued through its technical center in Detroit.
2. Aerospace and special-purpose machines—Cincinnati, Ohio.

3. Turning centers—Wilmington, Ohio.
4. Machining centers—Fountain Inn, South Carolina, and Birmingham, England.
5. Grinding machines—Worcester, Massachusetts.
6. Service parts—Cincinnati, Ohio.
7. Plastics machinery—most products produced in Afton, Ohio, with the systems for extrusion, reheat blow molding, and thermoforming moved to a plant in Cincinnati, Ohio.

In early 1990, Milacron had created a specific process for developing new products. Initially called "team engineering" but now termed Wolfpack Projects, the idea is to create world-class products designed simultaneously for marketability and "manufacturability." The anticipated outcomes from creating new product development teams were a shortened product development cycle, lower product manufacturing costs, improved machine tool performance and quality, and increased market share. Top management also spelled out the process for creating a Wolfpack Project.

1. Create a team of personnel relevant to the production, sale, and service of a product. The team members would typically come from the departments of design engineering, production, marketing, purchasing, cost analysis, manufacturing engineering, assembly, and inventory control.
2. Analyze and conduct market research on all competitive products. The features, design, materials, electronics, and performance of all products are studied and the reasons why the competitive products are succeeding or failing are cited.
3. Apply the principles of "simultaneous" or "concurrent" engineering to work with potential customers and suppliers. To be approved for commercialization, a Wolfpack Project's product must demonstrate that it can (a) capture significant new market share in existing or new markets, and (b) provide at least a 30.0% manufacturing cost savings over the product it would replace in the line. Through concurrent engineering, the company will create products that fill a place in the market and are easier and less costly to manufacture.

As of February 1991, the Wolfpack Program had slashed Milacron's manufacturing costs on standard machine tools by as much as 40.0%. About 20.0% of its standard tools can match the foreign competition's prices and quality. Overall manufacturing costs have been reduced about 30.0% by using fewer and standard, off-the-shelf parts in the product's assembly. The typical, newly designed tool has about two-thirds of its parts outsourced, where before it was less than half. The results are also lower warranty and installation costs.

Management has already introduced a new line of simplified plastics injection-molding machines, and Milacron is the country's lowest-cost producer of these tools. The *Vista* line has been very successful and additional products have made it the broadest line available from an American manufacturer. In 1988, the plastics operation was increased by 100,000 square feet with a capital inclusion of $4.7 million; in 1989, an additional $14.5 million was budgeted with about 70.0% of that amount going into a 78,000-square-foot expansion of its Mt. Orab, Ohio, plastics parts plant. While management is pleased with the results it has obtained through Wolfpack programs, it does not believe their outcomes will be fully realized until the mid-1990s. On this basis, top management is optimistic about the company's future.

Management also believes problems caused by its past reorganization efforts and production "bugs" are over. In 1985, sales of $17.8 million were lost on machine tools alone. The tools scheduled for shipment used new designs, innovative software, and higher precision and performance standards, resulting in longer-than-anticipated production times. Sales for that year had to be delayed until early 1986. The company also experienced serious bottlenecks in making grinding machine shipments in November 1989. These bottlenecks caused lost sales through cancellations. It also did not allow the company to obtain part of the $45.0 million per year savings it had projected from its most recent reorganization effort. Additional bottlenecks occurred in February 1990 as production and equipment was shifted between plants to create its numerous "focus factories."

1992 AND BEYOND

As part of its new strategy to make competitively priced $100,000 standard machine tools, Cincinnati Milacron points with pride to its Cincinnati-based "incubator" demonstration plant. The factory makes the company's *Talon* computer-controlled turning centers and uses the most efficient production and management techniques available. The *Talons* employ just-in-time parts deliveries, use only 16 outside vendors, and need 60.0% fewer parts. More important, they can be made for 40.0% less. C. William Murray, Milacron's Division Manager for standard machine tools, says, however, that it might take five years for the techniques used in this 19-person plant to spread to the company's other plants and employees. Others are more pessimistic about this and other company actions.

Manufacturers in the Cincinnati area have noticed that Milacron is losing key people and that morale has sagged badly in recent months. Based on the number of resumes and job inquiries, many of the "Mill's" middle managers fear they may lose their jobs in another reorganization move or they may be pushed onto the shop floor. Cincinnati Milacron's recently retired chief technical officer, Richard C. Messinger, says, "They've got the basic technology and capability, but they have had a problem in that it's very difficult to change the culture and direction of that kind of organization."

It has also been noted that of its 27 current Wolfpack Projects, several are actually imported products and many of its "American-made" tools use almost 50.0% foreign parts. To Jack Addy, an independent Detroit machine tool distributor, this makes Milacron's "Made in the U.S.A." label a fraud. He says the company is "importing just like the Japanese, and what they're importing are not good machines."

The quality of the company's new products may also suffer in the long term. To save money, Milacron has not increased its engineering staff, which would be needed to implement future plant efficiencies like those found in the "incubator" plant, and it is spending only 4.1% of sales on research and development. Leading firms such as Giddings & Lewis spend about 10.0% on similar efforts. As an additional money-saving move, the company has retreated from its promise to its distributors to spend $250.0 million on machine tools over the next five years.

Given that plastics machinery has been a highlight of the company's operations, it takes pride in noting that it has helped lower Japan's market share in plastics machinery. That country's sales have fallen 20.0% since 1987 to about 50.0% of the American market. By cutting prices on the *Vista* line, Milacron was able to win back the business of General Motors and the Toyota Motor Corporation of America. Financial analysts, however, are pessimistic about Cincinnati Milacron's near-term and long-term prospects. Both Moody's Investors Service and Standard & Poor's downgraded Milacron's debt in early October 1991. In making its judgment on the firm's financial security, Standard & Poor's particularly noted the company's debt level of 55.0% to 60.0% of total capital and they questioned the wisdom of the new strategy being pursued by the company. As observed by David Sutliff, a S.G. Warburg & Company analyst, "I give them credit for giving it the old college try, but I don't think it's too smart. They're going into the most competitive sector again, where the Japanese sell tools like cookies."

ADDITIONAL READINGS

Murphy, H. Lee, "Machine Tool Marketers Emerge from 'Drought,'" *Business Marketing,* November 1988, pp. 36–38.

Sarathy, Ravi, "The Interplay of Industrial Policy and International Strategy: Japan's Machine Tool Industry," *California Management Review* (Spring 1989), pp. 132–160.

Sciberras, E., and J. Payne, *Machine Tool Industry: Technical Change and International Competitiveness.* Essex: Longman, 1985.

Slutsker, Gary (Ed.), "Struggling Against the Tide," *Forbes* (November 12, 1990), pp. 312–320.

Yoffie, David B., "Protecting World Markets," in Tom McCraw (Ed.), *America Versus Japan: A Comparative Study in Business Government Relations.* Boston: Harvard Business School Press, 1986.

Yoffie, David B., and Helen V. Milner, "An Alternative to Free Trade or Protectionism: Why Corporations Seek Strategic Trade Policy," *California Management Review* (Summer 1989), pp. 111–131.

APPENDIX 1: PRODUCT AND FINANCIAL INFORMATION

Operating Margins by Product Group

Exhibit 15

Product Group	*1981*	*1982*	*1983*	*1984*	*1985*	*1986*	*1987*	*1988*	*1989*	*1990*	*1991*
Machine tools	83.1	42.8	−14.5	− 8.1	−30.0	11.0	−47.9	20.2	− 7.6	4.3	− 2.2
Plastics machines	11.5	− 8.6	0.0	20.8	17.7	26.3	25.5	30.9	35.0	18.0	8.3
Industrial products	9.5	− 5.1	− 7.4	4.0	5.0	26.3	−12.0	19.1	18.7	16.7	13.0
Total	104.1	29.1	−21.9	16.7	− 7.3	63.6	−34.4	70.2	46.1	39.0	19.1

Cincinnati Milacron: Quarterly Income Statements ($000)

Exhibit 16

	6/15/91	*3/23/91*	*10/6/90*	*6/16/90*
Net sales	173,069	181,054	233,959	204,804
Cost of goods	136,571	143,840	177,702	159,233
Gross profit	36,498	37,214	56,257	45,571
R&D expenditures	n.a.	n.a.	n.a.	n.a.
Selling, general and administration	36,946	37,465	48,430	36,643
Income before depreciation and amortization	−448	−251	7,827	8,928
Depreciation and amortization	n.a.	n.a.	n.a.	n.a.
Nonoperating income	853	− 131	1,217	810
Interest expense	4,389	4,452	5,830	4,916
Income before taxes	−3,984	−4,834	3,214	4,822
Provision for income taxes	541	1,078	1,155	1,708
Net income before extra items	−4,525	−5,912	2,059	3,114
Extra items and discontinued operations	n.a.	n.a.	−515	n.a.
Net income	−4,525	−5,912	1,544	3,114

Source: Company 10-K.

Exhibit 17

Cincinnati Milacron: Quarterly Balance Sheets ($000)

	6/15/91	*3/23/91*	*10/6/90*	*6/16/90*
Assets				
Cash	15,031	15,780	22,607	16,810
Receivables	171,124	181,347	185,377	191,752
Raw materials	9,394	9,401	8,737	8,750
Work in progress	173,406	169,708	229,594	215,516
Finished goods	46,274	52,173	54,170	45,192
Other current assets	11,638	14,183	16,028	12,918
Total current assets	426,867	442,592	516,513	490,938
Property, plant, & equipment	428,397	440,688	435,087	422,567
Accumulated depreciation	282,010	283,069	283,041	273,047
Net property & equipment	146,387	157,619	152,046	149,520
Deposits and other assets	43,758	44,285	44,494	43,486
Total assets	617,012	644,496	713,053	683,944
Liabilities				
Notes payable	8,255	9,452	12,972	36,446
Accounts payable	42,139	54,479	57,987	55,126
Accrued expenses	95,644	90,778	85,013	101,796
Income taxes	7,177	10,713	8,826	n.a.
Other current liabilities	45,496	41,607	48,083	46,996
Total current liabilities	198,711	207,029	212,881	240,364
Deferred charges	7,852	8,408	13,214	13,329
Long-term debt	156,960	157,148	162,297	162,169
Other long-term liabilities	38,901	40,887	41,116	41,969
Total liabilities	402,424	413,472	429,508	457,831
Preferred stock	n.a.	n.a.	n.a.	n.a.
Common stock net	173,654	173,642	n.a.	n.a.
Capital surplus	n.a.	n.a.	173,174	121,892
Retained earnings	48,436	57,945	105,271	108,444
Other liabilities	–7,502	–563	5,100	–4,223
Shareholder equity	214,588	231,024	283,545	226,113
Total liabilities and net worth	617,012	644,496	713,053	683,944

Source: Company 10-K.

Cincinnati Milacron: Balance Sheets, Fiscal Years Ending in December ($000) **Exhibit 18**

	1990	*1989*	*1988*
Assets			
Cash	45,100	32,894	17,868
Receivables	196,953	198,512	235,823
Inventories	233,396	249,642	254,070
Other current assets	14,139	18,160	20,155
Total current assets	489,676	499,208	527,916
Net property & equipment	159,234	146,478	152,683
Deposits and other assets	44,072	40,484	40,881
Total assets	692,982	686,170	721,480
Liabilities			
Notes payable	10,753	13,604	15,902
Accounts payable	72,764	65,385	80,723
Current long-term debt due	1,408	16,080	4,386
Accrued expenses	99,168	93,546	106,459
Income taxes	9,741	13,580	15,837
Other current liabilities	42,317	37,956	35,224
Total current liabilities	236,151	240,151	258,531
Deferred charges	8,799	11,461	11,365
Long-term debt	157,273	165,831	42,171
Other long-term liabilities	43,089	42,148	182,122
Total liabilities	445,312	459,591	494,189
Preferred stock	6,000	6,000	6,000
Common stock net	27,303	24,327	24,202
Capital surplus	139,430	90,360	88,968
Retained earnings	68,842	111,991	112,375
Other liabilities	6,095	–6,099	–4,254
Shareholder equity	247,670	226,579	227,291
Total liabilities and net worth	692,982	686,170	721,480

Source: Company 10-K.

Exhibit 19

Cincinnati Milacron: Income Statements, Fiscal Years Ending in December ($000)

	1990	1989	1988
Net sales	837,689	820,087	850,794
Cost of goods	647,759	625,403	637,324
Gross profit	189,930	194,684	213,470
R&D expenditures	n.a.	n.a.	n.a.
Selling, general, and administration	157,185	143,426	149,396
Income before depreciation and amortization	32,745	51,258	64,074
Depreciation and amortization	n.a.	n.a.	n.a.
Nonoperating income	–30,807	7,372	4,003
Interest expense	19,734	22,460	22,048
Income before taxes	–17,796	36,170	46,029
Provision for income taxes	4,351	17,139	19,595
Net income before extra items	–22,147	19,031	26,434
Extra items and discontinued operations	–2,141	–1,663	10,655
Net income	–24,288	17,368	37,089

Source: Company 10-K.

CASE 5

Systematics, Inc.

Joseph Wolfe, University of Tulsa

After experiencing dramatic growth by providing financial services to both American and foreign banks since its formation in Little Rock, Arkansas, in 1968, Systematics Incorporated now faces many internally and externally generated problems and opportunities. Since it was acquired by ALLTEL Corporation in May 1990 for $528.0 million in stock, Systematics has suddenly obtained access to a vast amount of capital that it can use to pursue additional growth avenues. For its part, ALLTEL expects its average annual five-year growth rate of 10.0% to be greatly enhanced by Systematics' 21.1% rate while simultaneously capturing various operating and technological synergies.

In the face of this pressure for profits and growth, John Steuri, president and chief executive officer of Systematics, must deal with several violent changes occurring in the banking industry. Some describe a general sickliness associated with America's banking institutions. In recent years profit performance has been low or negative, much of the banking public has lost confidence in the system's strength and integrity, and massive consolidations and mergers have been completed in attempts to seek either safety in size or to obtain various operating economies or portfolio diversifications. These problems have affected Systematics, which is a major supplier of software and other financial services to over 800 banks in forty-five states and nearly twenty countries.

How Systematics should respond to these pressures has divided its management team. Many feel the company should stick to the banking industry, which has been the source of its past successes. Other executives feel they must capitalize on ALLTEL's strengths as a telephone holding company that has diversified into cellular telephone and other communications services.

This case was based on a graduate student research project conducted by Robert Knapp. This case is intended for classroom discussion only, not to depict effective or ineffective handling of administrative situations. All rights reserved to the authors and the North American Case Research Association.

THE BANK FINANCIAL SERVICES INDUSTRY

In 1980, the *ABA Banking Journal* sensed the development of a new trend in bank operations management. Given that an average-sized bank devotes about 8.0% of its expense to data processing (DP), various economies could be realized by a bank if this work could be "farmed out" to a more efficient data processor. Five forces seem to be driving this development:

1. The scarcity and high price of technical talent—Many banks find it difficult to attract and hold DP personnel. Rather than create their own programs, many banks must buy off-the-shelf software or contract outside technical labor.
2. Pressure for more sophisticated applications—As technological capabilities increase, banks, as well as their customers, wish to realize the advantages of cost and convenience these technologies can bring to an operation.
3. Greater competition from bank saturation or industry deregulation—Competition is fierce between the savings and loan banks versus commercial banks and credit unions. Small banks are attempting to match the services provided by the larger banks while the larger banks are attempting to prevail by providing the best services available.
4. Pressure for profits—As various markets converge and prevent growth from increased revenues, banks must find profit sources through operating efficiencies.
5. Changes in the capabilities of those offering financial services to the banking industry—Computer service companies have grown in size and in financial stability; thus, they have become dependable suppliers of DP skills and applications. Many service organizations have created software and possess technical talent that can only be duplicated by individual banks at a very high cost.

It has been estimated that by 1994 this trend will result in the doubling of the industry to one with sales of over $2.6 billion, or an annual growth rate of over 17.0% per year. This growth has occurred mainly amongst the smaller institutions, although various industry experts feel the trend may spread to the larger banks once they succumb to the natural pressures building within the industry.

A bank's data processing system helps in the delivery of many bank services:

1. Basic operations—This entails keeping track of teller operations, handling demand and time-deposit accounting, and processing installment and mortgage loan applications and payments.
2. Trust services—Manages the various investments contained in customers' trust portfolios.
3. Financial analysis—Poses "what if" questions to aid in the selection and balancing of investment portfolios owned by either bank customers or the bank itself.
4. Automated customer services—Handles the accounting and electronic operation of the bank's automated teller machines.
5. Specialized services—These services vary from bank to bank based on the clientele it wishes to cultivate and special needs associated with that clientele. Once this audience is identified, the operations associated with this group are automated through computer support.

Banks have historically attempted to solve their data processing needs three ways. Some have done all the work themselves from programming to computer operations with in-house personnel. This has been difficult to do even by the largest banks. Most banks use what is called a double approach. They employ outside services for their routine DP work while using in-house personnel to handle their unique or critical needs. A third approach has been to completely rely upon third-party consulting firms to perform all DP work. These firms range from general accounting firms to specialized DP management consulting companies.

Just as competition within the banking industry has increased, competition between those servicing the industry has also increased. More than 640 vendors supply the industry, and these vendors differ regarding their product strategies. Some can satisfy all of a bank's data processing needs while others offer a more limited variety of products or services. Those products and services are the following:

1. Software packages—These are preprogrammed computer programs purchased by the bank rather than having the bank create its own programs with in-house personnel. The DP servicer's range of participation can vary from merely selling the software off-the-shelf to installing and customizing the product (within its own preprogrammed limitations) to meet the bank's specific needs.
2. Remote computing services—These are mainframe computer time-sharing operations in which banks use on-line computing through an off-site computer via office terminals in a real time mode.
3. Remote batch processing—This is a slower data processing method that involves the bank entering data on-site and sending it to a central computer that will process the data overnight and redistribute the information the following day.
4. Turnkey purchase—This method does not entail the direct purchase of equipment or software by the bank, but instead has the vendor select the equipment, program it, get it up and running, and provide on-going maintenance once the bank itself has taken custody of the operation.
5. Facilities management—This is the most comprehensive set of services a vendor can provide. In this method, the vendor assumes full responsibility for hiring and training operators, installing and running the computer, programming all bank computer applications, and delivering results according to the basic contract in force between the bank and the facilities management supplier.

Exhibit 1 outlines the products and services offered by several firms in the information technology industry while Exhibit 2 outlines the characteristics of some of the industry's major competitors. Among the top ten suppliers, seven sell application software, nine offer data processing services of some kind, and three offer facilities management. In 1990, the aggregate revenues for these firms were $3.7 billion. This was a 32.0% increase over the prior year, although this increase was less than the 50.0% increment that occurred between 1987 and 1988.

Given the banking industry's rather bleak profit situation, a strong cost control trend has exerted itself. As observed by Frank Martire, chairman of Citicorp Information Resources, a devilish dilemma exists within the industry:

> What we hear—and we talk regularly to a couple of hundred bankers across the country—is cost control, and it's not different by the size of bank or location—it's across the country. If banks can delay investments, they're going to do it, but

Exhibit 1 Products and Services Offered by Selected Bank Vendors

Vendor	*1989 Revenue (in millions)*	*Products and Services*
Electronic Data Systems, Plano, TX	$900.0 (68 million accounts)	Applications software Turnkey systems Local batch processing Remote noninteractive processing Interactive processing Facilities management Custom programming Consulting Education/training
First Financial Management, Atlanta, GA	$741.0 (10.1 million accounts)	Applications software Turnkey systems Local batch processing Remote noninteractive processing Interactive processing Custom programming Consulting Education/training
Systematics, Little Rock, AR	$224.7 (30.1 million accounts)	Applications software Remote noninteractive processing Interactive processing Turnkey systems Facilities management Custom programming Consulting
Mellon Information Services, Pittsburgh, PA	$170.9	Applications software Interactive processing
NCR, Dayton, OH	$168.1 (14.5 million accounts)	Applications software Interactive processing Custom programming Consulting Education/training
SunGard Data Systems, Wayne, PA	$125.0	Applications software Interactive processing
Citicorp Information Resources, Stamford, CT	$104.0 (16 million accounts)	Turnkey systems Interactive processing Facilities management Custom programming
Unisys, Detroit, MI	$99.9	Applications software Consulting
BISYS, Houston, TX	$54.2	Facilities management Custom programming Consulting
The Kirchman Corporation, Orlando, FL	$54.0	Applications software Local batch processing Education/training
National Computer Systems, Eden Prairie, MN	$38.4	Turnkey systems
Financial Information Trust, West Des Moines, IA	$31.1 (4.5 million accounts)	Interactive processing

Sources: Adapted from "America's Top Fifty Banking Software Products," *Banking Software Review,* Autumn 1990, pp. 28–31; and *Savings Institutions,* Savings Institutions Data Processing Survey (Annual), August 1989, p. 56.

Company Sketches **Exhibit 2**

Electronic Data Systems (EDS)—This company has been providing services in general for more than 25 years to all 50 states and 27 countries. It attempts to create solutions through its 2,000 employees that best accomplish the individual financial institution's goals while still maintaining EDS's unique corporate personality. EDS offers an almost complete line of services including systems integration and communications facilities management. Because of its size, it can process more than 3.0 billion instructions per second, 24 hours a day, 365 days a year. It can transmit voice, data, and video around the world using terrestrial, satellite, microwave, and fiber optic technology.

IBM Corp.—IBM brings its image of reliability plus its dominance of the mainframe computer to the financial services industry. It is a prime contractor in many banks, but daily operations are subcontracted to a third-party vendor. IBM's marketing strategy involves tailoring each contract to the customer's individual requirements; it refuses to use the term "facilities management", as it implies an off-the-shelf approach that they reject.

Software Alliance—Software Alliance markets its UNIX-based Total Banking Solution to small- to medium-sized banks while it markets its Marshall & Isley Integrated Banking System to larger banks. The company's software interfaces with all IBM compatible computers. Rather than developing its own applications, Software Alliance obtains the marketing rights from successful software developers. After obtaining these rights, it targets banks with up to $750.0 million in assets and a second group of those with assets ranging from $2.0 to $200.0 billion.

Newtrend Miser2—Founded in 1977, this company's software consists of over 40 deposit, loan, customer service, financial control, management support, and EFT/ATM applications, all operating on Unisys hardware. Newtrend's components are not sold individually. Customers purchase an integrated core system to which modules are added as needed. The company is well known for individually customizing its integrated system, which is available through in-house use, a service bureau, or facilities management.

The Kirchman Corporation—Kirchman claims over 6,000 clients and it allocates approximately 20.0% of its gross revenues to research and development. The company operates solely on IBM machines designed for single or multibank environments. Their newest product is called Dimension Software, which is an integrated system for small- to medium-sized banks.

> intelligent banks with real foresight are not going to try to control costs so much that it harms service to the customer. They still want to position the right product or right service for a recovery, which will come in 1993 or 1994.

Accordingly, banks have begun to look more intensely at the financial service industry's offerings. Extreme concentration has been placed on maximizing short-term efficiency along with major, long-term technological improvements. Many feel this will lead to an increase in banking's search for alliances and technology partners to aid in sharing the costs and risks of technological advancement during a period of severe cost control.

SYSTEMATICS, INC.

Systematics, Inc., was founded by Walter Smiley after having been a systems engineer for IBM and an eight-year data processing manager for the First National Bank of Fayetteville, Arkansas. By 1977, its sales had grown to $13.3

million after having begun as an eight-person company just nine years before. In 1980, the company began to market software packages to banks other than the one it was servicing in Fayetteville, and by 1981, its sales had reached $36 million. Shortly after that, Systematics began to service international customers and Smiley began to voluntarily take on a less-dominant role within the company.

In August 1988, John Steuri took over Smiley's position as Systematics' CEO. Steuri was himself a 24-year IBM veteran beginning as a sales representative in Topeka, Kansas, and ultimately headed an IBM marketing force of 9,000 people doing more than $6.0 billion worth of business a year. Systematics was an attractive opportunity for him when he left IBM at the age of 49 with an attractive early-out package.

> The qualities I admired in IBM were evident in Systematics. It was a well-run, focused, growth-oriented company with a commitment to customer service. Systematics also was still small enough that I felt I had a chance to be a part of a real entrepreneurial enterprise.

Sales have continued to grow, and many expect, as shown in Exhibit 3, that its revenue prospects are very bright. Exhibit 4 displays the income from operations obtained by Systematics. Industry experts feel the firm's strengths lie in the integrated, IBM-based COBOL software it possesses as well as in its reputation for quality service. The software addresses a wide range of applications, including deposits, loans, profitability analysis, branch automation, electronic funds transfer, and marketing. Its newest product is entitled Extended Application Architecture (EAA), which allows banks to migrate to new technologies, such as regional databases, in an orderly manner when it becomes cost effective. Systematics has also begun to offer an Advanced Loan System which was created with the EAA. This is a comprehensive loan servicing system that allows users to introduce new loan products with little programming support. It also offers many debt management features not offered by other systems.

Systematics delivers its products three ways depending on the size of the bank being serviced. First, it provides facilities management and data process-

Exhibit 3

Systematics, Inc.: Actual and Forecasted Revenues (in millions of dollars)

Year	*Revenues*
1985	$ 95.9
1986	122.6
1987	141.6
1988	179.5
1989	206.8
1990	254.8
1991	305.5
1992	365.0
1993	440.0

Source: 10-K reports; and the Yankee Group, 1991.

Note: Revenues after 1991 are Yankee Group estimates.

Systematics, Inc.: Operating Income (in millions of dollars) **Exhibit 4**

Year	*Operating Income*
1985	$11.5
1986	14.2
1987	16.4
1988	22.5
1989	28.5
1990	34.0

Source: Company stockholder reports.

ing services for 390 American and foreign bank clients. Second, it sells its applications software to financial institutions for their in-house use. Third, they sell turnkey operations consisting of mid-range systems and applications software through an IBM remarketing agreement.

Approximately 75.0% of its revenues are derived from facilities management. In December 1990, Systematics, Inc., signed a 10-year service contract valued at between $350.0 and $500.0 million with the City National Bank of Beverly Hills, California, and another contract to operate First New Hampshire Bank's data processing center was announced in February 1991. As of January 1991, Systematics had over 80 on-site financial management agreements. Exhibit 5 presents a summary of the company's past and forecasted activity in the area of facilities management.

To some degree, the banking industry's generally poor financial condition and the closing or consolidation of smaller banks, which are an important target group for Systematics, Inc., have had an effect on the company's thinking. Steuri, however, saw a silver lining in this cloud.

> Everyone knows there is a general malaise in the financial sector. Granted, that hurts our software sales, which accounted for only 10% to 12% of our business last year. There is another side, though. If they can turn their data processing over

Actual and Forecasted Facilities Management Contracts **Exhibit 5**

Activity	*1984*	*1985*	*1986*	*1987*	*1988*	*1989*	*1990*	*1991*	*1992*	*1993*
New contracts added	4	6	6	12	16	13	12	14	15	16
Contract expirations due to										
Client mergers and consolidations	1	2	4	6	2	4	2	3	4	6
In-house conversions with Systematics software	0	0	0	1	1	0	0	1	1	2
Year-end contracts in effect	39	43	45	50	63	72	82	92	102	110
Contracts renewed	6	8	10	5	5	7	8	6	8	12

Sources: Systematics Inc.; and the Yankee Group, 1991.

Notes: Activities are for fiscal years ending May 31. Data after 1990 are Yankee Group estimates.

> to us, we can help them. We can reduce their costs at least 10% to 15% and put money on their bottom line real fast.

Despite the industry's doldrums, Systematics met its 12-month goal for facilities management contracts within the first nine months of the 1990 fiscal year. In fact, Steuri has said, "There have been occasions when our sales reps have been sent home for a week or two so we would not sign more contracts than we could service."

ALLTEL ENTERS THE PICTURE

With the acquisition of Systematics, Inc., another Little Rock, Arkansas, company, ALLTEL, became a $1.57 billion operation with diversified interests in cellular telephone systems, natural gas service, air traffic control voice switching and control systems, signal data converters, encrypted voice communication systems, and high-resolution color graphic display systems. Exhibit 6 shows that Systematics would garner about 16.0% of ALLTEL's total sales but would contribute more than that percentage to its operating income. Accordingly, Joe Ford, ALLTEL's president and CEO, called this acquisition "one of the most significant of our strategic moves." Various industry observers are more skeptical about the acquisition and its long-term benefits to either company. James Stork, a security analyst for Duff & Phelps Inc., stated:

> There are really no strategic reasons or synergies [here]. We do not view this as a strategic acquisition. Although data processing and telecommunications may be converging, it is difficult to see how the combination of these two companies will result much in the way of synergy over the next five years. We get the impression that ALLTEL acquired Systematics simply because it became available, and ALLTEL felt it could increase its consolidated growth potential for a reasonable price.

Both John Steuri and Joe Ford have begun to rise to the occasion. Steuri says, "We foresee some potential synergies as the communications and computer industries continue to converge." Because there are about 1,300 telephone companies currently competing in the United States, he felt they could be approached by the same sales pitch used when they recruited banks and savings and loan institutions. "Let us do your data processing for you. We can do it cheaper and more effectively than you can do it in-house."

Exhibit 6 **ALLTEL 1990 Sales and Operating Income by Business Segment ($000)**

Business Segment	*Sales*	*Operating Income*
Telephone	$818,150	$290,032
Systematics	254,806	34,159
Product distribution	331,565	22,507
Cellular systems	42,272	2,227
Other	126,992	14,965

Source: 10-K report.

Note: Fiscal year ending December 31, 1990.

In this quest for synergies between the two companies, Systematics completed a deal in March 1991 to acquire C-TEC Corporation's cellular telephone billing and information system, and ALLTEL turned its cellular data processing operation over to Systematics. ALLTEL has also begun to sell off various operations not related to telecommunications and information processing. It sold its natural gas distribution systems in Nevada and California to Southwest Gas Corporation for $16.0 million in June 1991 and it is attempting to sell off its Ocean Technology, Inc., subsidiary as well as its alternative energy investments.

Although moves are being made to make this a successful acquisition for ALLTEL, and John Steuri feels pressure is being placed on him to help his new parent corporation realize its own growth goals, he thinks numerous diverse factors need to be considered. Admittedly, the banking industry is in a state of turmoil, but Systematics' business strengths lie within the industry. What path or paths should Systematics pursue? Should the company attempt to ride out the banking industry's storm while possibly incurring the wrath of ALLTEL's management for failing to move ahead with applications in the telecommunications industry? Could Systematics attempt to fill other product/service niches in the banking industry despite the awesome size of its major competitors? Does Systematics have any other options?

APPENDIX 1: FINANCIALS

Exhibit 7

Systematics, Inc.: Balance Sheets, 1987–1989 ($000)

	1989	*1988*	*1987*
Cash	2,858	4,931	879
Marketable securities	32,477	22,013	37,704
Receivables	26,569	20,536	20,083
Other current assets	3,941	1,123	1,156
Total current assets	65,845	48,603	59,822
Property, land, and equipment	108,313	95,855	80,078
Accumulated depreciation	51,788	44,683	34,243
Net property and equipment	56,525	51,172	45,835
Other noncurrent assets	5,635	5,635	-0-
Deposits and other assets	4,768	1,658	1,848
Total assets	132,773	107,068	107,505
Notes payable	1,456	9,366	1,010
Accounts payable	15,272	8,812	4,003
Accrued expenses	12,052	10,237	7,035
Income taxes	1,446	910	2,296
Other current liabilities	12,427	5,407	5,015
Total current liabilities	42,653	34,732	19,359
Deferred charges	7,109	6,443	8,936
Long-term debt	5,626	2,911	3,777
Other long-term liabilities	-0-	-0-	5,631
Total liabilities	55,388	44,086	37,703
Net common stock	278	276	272
Capital surplus	28,876	26,655	24,917
Retained earnings	44,602	34,703	43,570
Treasury stock	3,629	1,348	1,043
Shareholder equity	77,385	62,982	69,802
Total liabilities and net worth	132,773	107,068	107,505

Source: 10-K reports.

Note: Fiscal year ends May 31.

Systematics, Inc.: Income Statements, 1987–1989 ($000)

Exhibit 8

	1989	*1988*	*1987*
Net sales	206,786	179,474	141,577
Cost of goods sold	153,223	133,262	105,053
Gross profit	53,563	46,212	30,524
R&D expenditures	9,476	9,064	7,741
Selling and general administration expenses	15,056	14,070	11,895
Interest expense	517	621	514
Operating income	28,514	22,457	16,374
Nonoperating income	1,702	2,425	3,164
Pretax income	30,216	24,882	19,538
Taxes	11,352	9,458	9,376
Net income	18,864	15,424	10,162

Source: 10-K reports.

Note: Fiscal year ends May 31.

CASE 6

American Ref-Fuel: A Joint Venture in Waste Management

James W. Clinton, University of Northern Colorado

INTRODUCTION

Browning-Ferris Industries (BFI), of Houston, Texas (the number two refuse disposal company in the United States) and Air Products and Chemicals (APC) of Allentown, Pennsylvania (principal supplier of hydrogen to the U.S. government's space program) in 1986 formed a joint venture, American Ref-Fuel, to design, build, own, and operate facilities that burn unprocessed solid waste and recover energy and other materials. APC, primarily a gas and chemical company, provided expertise in plant equipment operations and energy sales, and BFI offered knowledge and experience related to solid waste handling.

After obtaining a contract to construct their first resource recovery (incinerated waste is converted into energy) plant at Hempstead, Long Island, the joint venture partners formed an affiliate, American Ref-Fuel of Hempstead. The plant was constructed by the affiliate, which also owns and operates the Hempstead facility. American Ref-Fuel of Hempstead is a general partnership whose ownership is equally divided between BFI and APC. (See Exhibit 1 for the organization of American Ref-Fuel.)

The collaboration between a public entity, the town of Hempstead, and a private company (in this case, American Ref-Fuel) to combine resources and resolve the local government's waste disposal problem is not unusual. Over 160 resource recovery plants, according to Edward L. Overtree, general counsel of American Ref-Fuel, presently are operating in the United States and almost all are privately owned and operated on behalf of a municipality.

This case is intended for classroom discussion only, not to depict effective or ineffective handling of administrative situations. All rights reserved to the author and the Midwest Society for Case Research.

Exhibit 1 **American Ref-Fuel Company Organizational Structure**

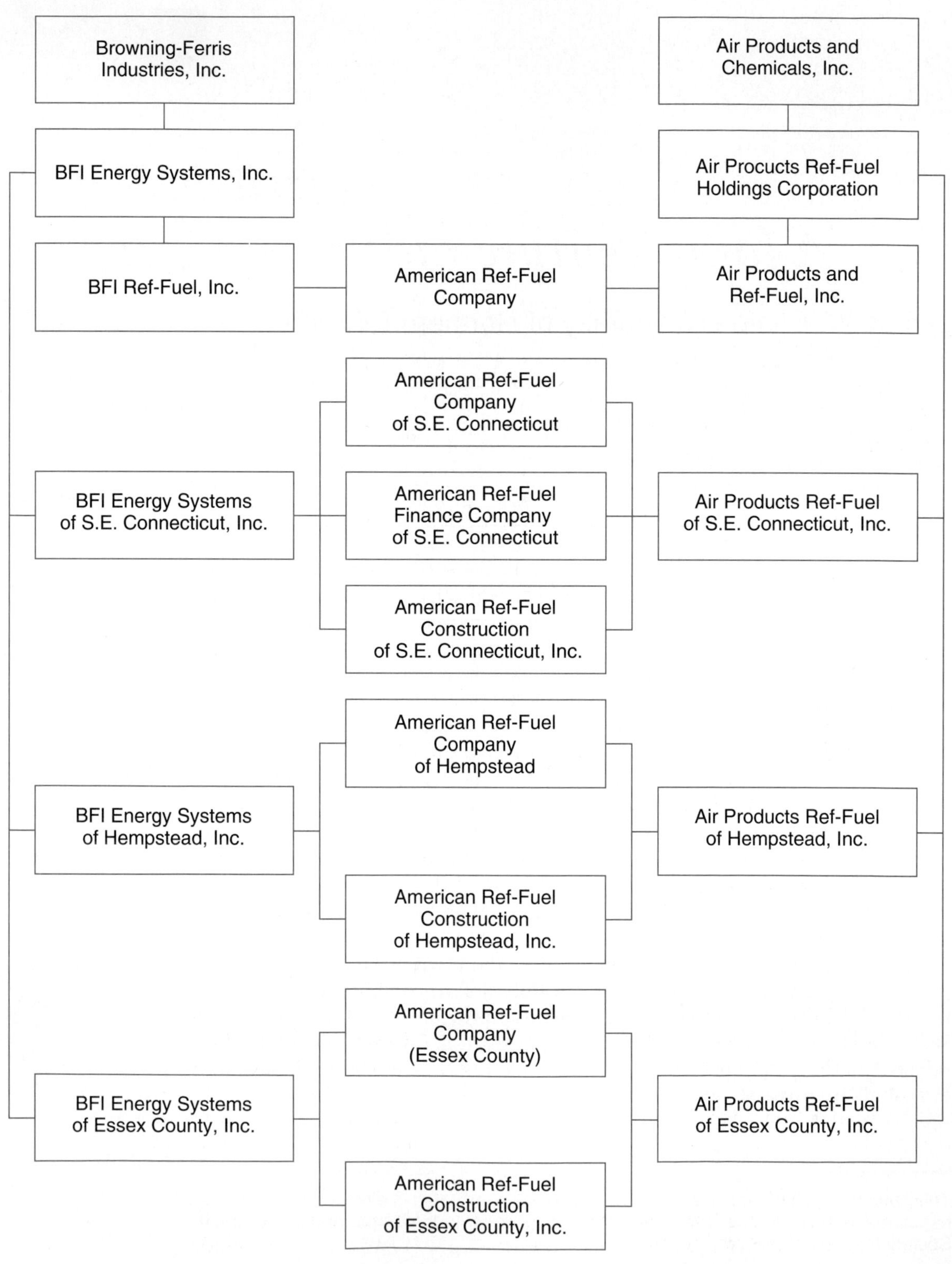

American Ref-Fuel of Hempstead, through service contracts, obtains a variety of technical assistance and support from American Ref-Fuel, such as financial management, environmental compliance services, engineering troubleshooting, and legal representation. American Ref-Fuel of Hempstead, according to Overtree, is known as a "project company." American Ref-Fuel designed the plant, obtained the necessary authorization permits from governmental bodies, and participated in raising money to pay for construction of the plant.

American Ref-Fuel is constructing similar facilities in Essex County, New Jersey, and Preston, Connecticut, through separate partnerships (see Exhibit 1) established by a subsidiary company. The Essex County facility began operations on November 3, 1990. As in Hempstead, the facility in Preston is designed to incinerate municipal solid waste and generate electricity.

American Ref-Fuel, embarking on an ambitious expansion program, has been selected for or is in contract negotiations to construct facilities at or near (1) New Haven, Connecticut; (2) Wilmington, Delaware; (3) Boston, Massachusetts; (4) Albany, New York; and (5) Oyster Bay, New York. (A plant scheduled for construction in Bergen County, New Jersey, was canceled, and most of the trash expected to be incinerated at that plant presently is being processed at American Ref-Fuel's facility in Essex County, New Jersey.) Each completed facility will process up to 1,000 to 1,650 tons per day, using technologies similar to those used at the Hempstead plant. Costs of construction will range from $150 million to $250 million per project.

STRATEGIC ISSUES FACING AMERICAN REF-FUEL

Issues of major concern to American Ref-Fuel as well as joint venture parents, BFI and APC, are: (1) how many waste to energy plants should it contract for construction and over what period of time, (2) how many facilities can be efficiently and effectively managed at one time, (3) to what extent is it both feasible and advisable to extend American Ref-Fuel's area of operations outside of the Northeastern United States, (4) to what extent will competing waste disposal mechanisms reduce present profit margins, and (5) are alternative economic and environmental cost–benefit rationales necessary to effectively market the joint venture's resource recovery technology to a broader range of potential customers?

FINANCE

The joint venture companies, APC and BFI, each contributed $55 million (a total of $110 million) toward construction of the Hempstead plant. (See Exhibits 2 and 3 for selected financial data pertaining to APC and BFI.) APC capital expenditures for the period 1986–1989 totaled $1.9 billion. APC expects to spend an additional $550–$600 million on capital expenditures in 1990. BFI spent $2.8 billion on capital expenditures between 1985 and 1989 and expects to spend an additional $4.7 billion on capital expenditures over the next five years.

The town of Hempstead's Industrial Development Agency loaned an additional $288 million from the 1986 sale of tax-exempt industrial revenue bonds

Exhibit 2

Selected Financial Data, APC, 1986–1989

	1989	*1988*	*1987*	*1986*
Sales	$2,642	$2,432	$2,132	$1,942
Net income	222	214	156	5
Plant and equipment (net)	2,218	2,062	n/a	n/a
Total assets	3,366	3,000	2,705	2,661
Stockholders' equity	1,445	1,272	1,147	1,100
Long-term debt	854	668	616	707
Cash flow from operations	445	472	460	444
Earnings per common share	$4.04	$3.90	$2.76	$0.08
Market price per share	49–37	55–29	54–33	42–26
Book value per common share	$26.23	$23.19	$20.66	$19.21

Source: Form 10-K, APC, September 30, 1989.

Exhibit 3

Selected Financial Data, BFI, 1986–1989

	1989	*1988*	*1987*	*1986*
Sales	$2,551	$2,067	$1,657	$1,328
Net income	263	227	172	137
Plant and equipment (net)	1,909	1,429	1,193	793
Total assets	3,017	2,258	1,938	1,227
Stockholders' equity	1,242	1,043	874	747
Long-term debt	945	630	591	101
Cash flow from operations	512	462	343	264
Earnings per common share	$1.74	$1.51	$1.15	$0.95
Market price per share	25–41	17–34	17–36*	15–24*
Book value per common share	$8.22	$6.94	$5.85	$5.11*

**Value Line Investment Survey,* 9/17/91.

Source: Form 10-K, BFI, September 30, 1989.

for the facility's design, construction, and acceptance testing. Interest and principal on these bonds are to be paid by APC and BFI as the bonds mature between 1990 and 2010. American Ref-Fuel of Hempstead is estimated to earn as much as $6 million in 1990 from the plant's operations, and may earn annual profits of up to $15 million by 1995 (*The Wall Street Journal*, May 31, 1990). (No other financial data pertaining to the joint venture was available in either BFI or APC public reports.)

American Ref-Fuel (ARF) attempts, wherever possible, to develop a private–public partnership for construction of waste to energy plants. ARF's Newark facility, for example, is financed by APC and BFI (the joint venture partners), together with a $200 million loan from the Port Authority of New York and New Jersey and state and local grants of $20 million.

According to Edward L. Overtree, General Counsel for American Ref-fuel:

> Communities do not add additional debt when they authorize construction of a privately owned resource recovery facility such as Hempstead. Indeed, private ownership greatly reduces communities' financial exposure, since they pay the private owner/operator only when they deliver trash and in proportion to the amount of service they use. Communities have no liability whatsoever to repay debt on a private facility, only the private owner/operator does.
>
> Thus, a public-private partnership in public works projects actually solves the problem of declining creditworthiness in the public sector. Private credit defers and "stretches out" scarce public financial resources. For that reason, I believe the public–private partnership for public service projects is the most exciting and intriguing aspect of our industry.

These combined sources of capital determine whether plant construction is feasible. ARF of Hempstead, for example, derives one-half of its income from the sale of electrical power to Lilco (Long Island Lighting Company, a public utility). With respect to operating costs and revenues, American Ref-Fuel's Waffenschmidt noted that:

> Three basic elements influence how a financial deal affecting a resource recovery facility is assembled. One, is the cost to bring refuse into the facility. Two, is what can be sold, primarily electricity, occasionally steam, and a minor amount of ferrous material salvaged from ash residue. If a variety of waste processing techniques are utilized, other products may be available for sale. Three, is the ash. Those three items determine what revenue streams go to the vendor and what costs are assumed by the host municipality.

THE HEMPSTEAD RESOURCE RECOVERY PLANT

The town of Hempstead, Long Island, typifies those municipalities that discover that they are unable to solve their waste disposal problem and must seek outside help.

All landfills on Long Island (a body of land adjoining and including sections of New York City) are required, according to a New York state law, to close by December 18, 1990, forcing Long Island municipalities to arrange alternative methods of trash disposal. One of the Long Island municipalities directly affected by this law is the town of Hempstead, the nation's largest town, with a population of about 750,000 and located about thirty miles east of New York City.

Hempstead ceased to bury waste, including agricultural waste, construction debris, and compost, in one of the town's two landfills in 1984. The second landfill closed in 1986. Subsequently, the town contracted to have its trash carted by truck, 97 miles away, to a landfill in the town of Goshen in upstate New York. According to Anthony J. Santino, press secretary for Hempstead, New York, the cost to transport the town's waste, approximately 1,800 tons of garbage a day to Goshen, was estimated at over $75 million a year.

Fortunately for Hempstead's residents and commercial businesses, the town's political leadership also decided in 1984 that a long-term solution to its waste disposal problem, which combined resource recovery and recycling, must be found.

■ History of the Hempstead Facility

In 1979, Hempstead completed construction of a facility to receive, process, and incinerate garbage for the town. Garbage received was saturated with water and processed through a series of machines designed to produce electric power while burning the garbage. The incineration, however, produced considerable odors. Some violations of Occupational Safety and Health Administration (OSHA) regulations within the plant occurred, and emissions from the plant's smokestack were thought to contain dioxin. (The U.S. Environmental Protection Agency later admitted there were no dioxin emissions.) The plant's cooling system also created occasional icing hazards on an adjacent parkway. Several times, labor disputes led to closure of the plant.

The plant was permanently closed in 1981, two years after opening and after operating a total of only 18 months. The closure of the plant was a turning point. The town's presiding supervisor, Thomas Gulotta [now Nassau County (New York) supervisor], decided that the town must find a lower-cost method of garbage disposal. The town wished also to be more certain of future waste disposal costs and wanted an assured method of disposal. The costs of transporting its garbage elsewhere were not within the town's control, since nearby communities also were experiencing the same problem, thus enhancing the negotiating position of trash haulers and remote landfill operators at the expense of users. In the worst case, alternative landfills might, due to unanticipated changes in state and federal environmental regulation or even opposition by communities in which such landfills were located, be withdrawn for use by the town.

The town requested bids, through a request for proposal, from contractors to build a new plant with the proviso that some of the existing plant be salvaged. American Ref-Fuel was awarded the contract to construct the waste-to-energy plant at the existing site. Included in the contract was a renewable provision in which the contractor agreed to dispose of the town's burnable waste for 20 years. Plant construction began in December 1986. All of the existing plant was leveled, with the exception of the tipping hall area, where incoming refuse is temporarily stored before incineration, and the administration building. Completed in April 1989, the plant became fully operational in the fall of 1989, processing all of Hempstead's combustible waste.

■ Plant Operations

The Hempstead plant operates 24 hours a day, seven days a week. By maintaining continuous operations, the amount of fuels consumed in running the plant is minimized, since startup and shutdown of the plant increase the potential for increased pollution emissions. Continuous operation also makes more steam available to produce electricity.

Hempstead's waste stream declines during the winter months. Peak efficiency, however, is achieved when the plant operates at full capacity. Consequently, American Ref-Fuel also contracts for delivery to the plant of privately collected trash on a short-term or spot basis to compensate for shortfalls in Hempstead's waste stream. American Ref-Fuel currently receives up to $67 a ton for such garbage.

Each of Hempstead's three-quarter million residents generates about a ton of waste per year–a total of 750,000 tons. Plant capacity is presently rated at slightly over 900,000 tons per year.

■ Trash Collection

Customers serviced by the town's waste disposal system are residential, commercial, and—to a limited extent—manufacturing. Customers are primarily households. In addition to household waste, the plant accepts nonhazardous commercial and nonhazardous industrial waste. The bulk of the waste is from Hempstead; some originates from outside of Hempstead. All trash generated in Hempstead is processed through the plant with the exception of recyclable materials. About 13% of the town's waste stream, including glass, newspaper, and metal cans and containers, are recycled. Separation of waste occurs at residences, businesses, and the town's two transfer stations, located at what used to be the town's landfills.

Waste collection in Hempstead is somewhat complex. A variety of governmental entities and municipal employees pick up the trash. Several municipalities are located within the town's geographical boundaries. Bulk pickup is offered so that bulky materials (bed springs, white goods such as refrigerators and stoves, etc.) are not taken to the plant, but handled separately and recycled elsewhere.

All recycled materials collected from households are sold to the Empire Returns Corporation (ERC) of Utica, New York. ERC is presently constructing a permanent transfer station with a target processing capacity of 200 tons of recyclable materials per shift. (It is estimated by American Ref-Fuel that every noncombustible ton of waste that is recycled saves Hempstead $63.)

Newspaper, according to a news release of Hempstead (April 26, 1988), is either sold to domestic paper mills or exported. Glass is sorted, crushed, cleaned, and sold to glass manufacturers in the United States. Tin and steel are also recycled.

Waste collection and delivery to the waste-to-energy plant (distance between pickup and delivery averages five miles) is accomplished by two different types of vehicles: packer trucks and transfer trailers. Packer trucks (3–6 ton capacity) pick garbage up from residences. Most packer trucks deliver their loads to the town's two transfer stations. Transfer trailers, which handle about 20 tons, take the garbage to the plant. About three hundred trucks of various sizes—both public and private—unload their garbage at the plant each day.

■ Waste Disposal Costs and Charges

The town of Hempstead guarantees to deliver a minimum of 540,000 tons of garbage to the plant per year. Similarly, American Ref-Fuel guarantees the town a very favorable rate to trucks delivering garbage to the plant (called a tipping fee). The town thus can budget and predict waste disposal costs.

Hempstead's tipping fees are low because all revenues derived from the electricity generated by the plant's operation are retained by American Ref-Fuel. The plant has a 72-megawatt generator and presently sells 64 megawatts (equal to the power needs of about 50,000 homes, or more than 25% of the population of Hempstead) to the public utility, Lilco.

Significantly, the town's tipping fees were directly influenced by a decline in interest rates from 11% to 7% between 1985 and 1986 (when the plant was being designed and its permit for construction was obtained), which lowered the cost of borrowing to finance the plant's construction. American Ref-Fuel agreed to pass along the interest rate savings to Hempstead at the time the contract was initially negotiated. Consequently, an initial tipping fee proposal of $32.00 per ton to the town has since been reduced—on a permanent basis—by $14.00. Because the contract also accounts for inflation (termed an allowance for escalation), which as of the spring of 1991 amounted to $6.00, the town's tipping rate is approximately $24.00 per ton.

Tipping fees vary appreciably throughout the country and are a function of population density, land area available for landfill, methods of waste disposal, prices charged by competitors, volume and composition of waste accepted for disposal, companion recycling programs, etc. Yankton, South Dakota, a sparsely populated community, for example, utilizes a recycling program in conjunction with a waste disposal system that converts most of the waste collected into fuel pellets. Yankton pays a tipping fee of $7.50 a ton to a private contractor operating the city's energy conversion plant. Minneapolis, Minnesota, tipping fees range from $75 to $80 a ton.

The town is responsible for disposing of ash, a significant expense, since ash represents approximately 10% of the volume (but 25% of the weight) of the refuse entering the plant for disposal. The town has contracted with Browning-Ferris Industries to haul ash residue to a landfill at Charles City, Virginia, at a cost of $140 a ton.

Overall, total waste disposal costs (transfer fees, tipping fees, ash disposal, and administrative costs) to the town are about $60–$70 per ton of incoming waste—$24.00 for incineration, $30.00 for ash removal, and $8.00 in administrative costs—a total of $62.00 vs. the approximate $160 per ton it cost to haul the town's waste to upstate New York in the period after the town's landfills were closed and before the plant began operation. Municipalities within Hempstead which truck refuse to the plant pay the town $79 per ton of refuse delivered to the plant. Municipalities presently transporting their garbage from Long Island to distant locations are paying $100–$130 a ton to dispose of their garbage.

Ash disposal costs approximate $18.9 million annually (25% of the town's guarantee of 540,000 tons, i.e., 135,000 tons times $140). New York State is conducting field pilot studies that will examine the feasibility of converting incinerator ash into construction blocks, road bed materials, etc., which, if practical, would alleviate a major expense in the disposal of incinerator ash residue.

"Garbage disposal systems," according to John Waffenschmidt, regional environmental engineer for American Ref-Fuel, "are money-losing operations. Municipalities do not make money selling their garbage; municipalities incur costs to get rid of garbage."

▪ Plant Technology

The mass burn technology employed in the Hempstead plant makes possible the daily disposal of several thousand tons of combustible waste previously destined for a landfill. American Ref-Fuel facilities use the solid waste mass-burning technology of Deutsche Babcock Anlagen, a West German company. American Ref-Fuel is the exclusive licensee for this technology under a licensing agreement that expires in 2000 but which may be renewed. The roller grate technology has been in use in Europe and elsewhere for over 25 years.

Although more than 60 incineration units worldwide presently use the same roller grate technology used by ARF-Hempstead, the Hempstead plant represents the first time this technology has been used in the United States.

A computerized combustion control maximizes burning efficiency and minimizes unwanted emissions. Air quality is also protected by an acid-gas scrubber and a fabric-filter bag house which captures particulates (see Exhibit 4 for definitions). Plant design prevents the escape of unwanted emissions from the plant and confines the flow of air needed for combustion within the plant, thus eliminating odors. Plant management believes that the level of pollution controls at this plant, which solves multiple environmental needs and concerns, is appropriate not only for the refuse industry, but also for other industries.

■ Public Relations

American Ref-Fuel of Hempstead maintains multiple channels of communication with Hempstead residents that include direct mail, availability of plant managers for meetings with community groups to answer questions and concerns about quality of life issues, a telephone hot line for inquiries, provision for access to plant records pertaining to plant emissions, and numerous guided tours of the plant. These modes of access and openness have created a very favorable impression of the plant within the community. Since the plant opened there has been no objection to the plant's operations by any consumer group.

After two years of operation, the plant appears to have satisfied the objectives of the town's political leadership and residential inquiries and complaints concerning the plant have been minimal. The plant, as a result, is perceived as a good neighbor by residents of the surrounding community. ARF is in full compliance with the terms of the contract, and the plant operates with minimal downtime. The town, according to Hempstead's press secretary, Anthony San-

Definitions Used in Technology at ARF — Exhibit 4

Acid-gas scrubber. Sprays lime solution on combustion gases to remove acid gases, which are pollutants.

Compost. A mixture of decaying organic materials usually made from yard waste. Because compost has no nutrient value, it is useful only for its texture.

Fossil fuels. Created by organisms, such as coal, centuries ago.

Hazardous materials. Discarded waste, such as explosives, caustic liquids, pesticides, and solvents, that are harmful to the environment and those who inhabit it.

Mass-burn technology. A combination of procedure and equipment in which all waste materials received are burned as received in the combustion chamber.

Particulates. Very small traces of combustion residue.

Recyclable. Solid waste capable of conversion into usable raw materials or products.

Resource recovery. A technology that converts waste into energy.

Stack emissions. Vapor or gases exiting the plant's smokestack.

Waste stream. Generally refers to the flow of waste materials discarded by residents and all other facilities through a collection and/or recycling system in which waste not recycled is either incinerated or buried in landfills.

tino, is very pleased with the plant and its operation and anticipates that the facility will accommodate the trash disposal needs of Hempstead indefinitely.

■ Government Regulation

The federal Environmental Protection Agency (EPA) and New York State's Department of Environmental Conservation (DEC) currently monitor the plant's operations. DEC determined that emissions from the plant's smokestack were acceptable and that the contents of the ash residue represented no danger to the environment. DEC, as a result, recommended that the plant be certified for operation. The EPA, satisfied that the state's oversight is sufficient, has deferred to DEC. Operation of the plant is consistent with the EPA's present emphasis on reduction of waste volumes and recycling of waste rather than the use of landfill. The plant was issued a permit to operate by the state of New York. The plant recently completed its second series of formal emissions testing for the state. The company reports that the latest results were among the lowest recorded anywhere in the world for such a plant, and management anticipates emissions may be even lower when next tested.

■ Operational Concerns

1. *Plant capacity.* The Hempstead waste-to-energy plant capacity is sufficient to process waste presently generated by existing householders and businesses. Population growth and an increase in commercial establishments may at some time in the future stress the capacity of the plant. On the other hand, if recycling efforts are exceptionally successful and household and commercial growth levels off, the town's annual payment to American Ref-Fuel will remain constant, although the fee paid per ton may vary.

2. *Accident or natural disaster.* The plant is an irreplaceable resource to Hempstead. The possibility (although admittedly low) of a natural disaster, such as an earthquake, lightning strike, or the very remote possibility of a major accident within the plant, would have serious repercussions for the town, even though an extensive insurance program covers the financial burden of such natural disasters. American Ref-Fuel of Hempstead operating procedures and policies, moreover, reflect significant concern for safety and security for all phases of the plant's operations.

3. In May 1990, the town recycled 13% of its waste. An anticipated change in federal regulations that would have required the town to double its present rate of recycling did not occur. In December 1990, the Environmental Protection Agency chose not to levy more stringent recycling requirements. Some groups associated with environmental issues, such as the Natural Resources Defense Council, oppose the lower standard and may be expected to press for higher levels of recycling. Seattle, Washington, presently recycles 24% of residential waste; New York City set a recycling target of 25% for 1994, a target date (August 1991), which subsequently was extended by New York's Mayor Dinkins until 2000.

If the town's population stabilizes, an increase in recycling will reduce the volume of Hempstead garbage processed by the plant, perhaps below that necessary for efficient and economical operation. ARF of Hempstead, consequently, would then become somewhat dependent upon an alternative waste stream generated outside of the town because of the plant's need to develop assured sources of garbage.

Related to the possibility of recycling is yard waste, which presently is being collected and hauled to the resource recovery plant. Some communities are collecting yard waste and creating very large compost piles, which are subsequently used as fertilizer in community projects. Opinion is divided as to what is the best use of yard waste or if communities should require residents to utilize lawn care equipment that reduces the generation of grass clippings. This and other issues related to the total system of the environment in which waste is created and disposed of will receive increasing study by both the town of Hempstead and the American Ref-Fuel Company.

4. *Disposal of ash.* The Hempstead plant must continue to have access to a landfill outside the municipality that will accept the town's ash residue.

WASTE MANAGEMENT CONCERNS

According to a Form 10-K issued by BFI in December 1989:

> All of the Company's principal business activities are regulated by federal, state and local laws and regulations pertaining to public health and the environment. . . . The economic viability of waste incineration facilities may be adversely affected by (i) the availability of commercially reasonable energy purchase contracts; (ii) the scarcity of available landfills for the disposal of ash residue, bypass and non-processible waste; (iii) possible new federal standards applicable to the disposal of ash residue that will limit the sites that might otherwise be available for such disposal; (iv) increased air emission standards applicable to such plants; and (v) the cost of other alternatives for waste disposal.
>
> . . . There is diminishing disposal capacity in the Northeastern United States, and many Eastern and Midwestern states are taking action to ban or otherwise restrict the importation of wastes for disposal, imposing discriminatory fees on imported wastes, limiting the volumes that may be disposed of at existing disposal facilities and exploring ways to regulate the prices that may be charged for waste disposal.

BFI, which at one time stored, treated, or disposed of hazardous wastes, closed all of its hazardous waste facilities on April 13, 1990.

The number of landfills in the United States has declined significantly in the last decade and may continue to do so, exerting upward pressure on fees charged for use of the remaining landfills. More stringent federal or state regulations, or both, if enacted, will raise the cost of plant operations and perhaps test the limits of processing and disposal technology.

TOUGH DECISIONS

Although BFI and APC possess the financial resources that would enable them to accelerate the rate of construction of new resource recovery plants and although American Ref-Fuel's future prospects appear favorable, BFI and APC are understandably cautious about the dimension and rate of future contract commitments (typically for a period of 20 years) undertaken by American Ref-Fuel, for the following reasons (some of which have already been mentioned):

a. Availability of present and future waste disposal sites is uncertain.

b. Competitors may develop technology that offers cost advantages over American Ref-Fuel's present technology.

c. Regulators at all levels of government may impose environmental regulations and constraints that may significantly lower profit margins.

d. BFI and APC are engaged in various activities in which resource recovery plays a minor part (see Exhibits 5 and 6). What is the best use of company funds?

e. Residents of some communities object to facilities such as the Hempstead plant because of mistaken perceptions with regard to health hazards, based on earlier facilities constructed before today's regulatory climate; such residents prefer other waste disposal alternatives, even if more costly, and less environmentally benign.

f. The supply of engineers and staff qualified to operate plants such as at Hempstead is limited and places a cap on any expansion plan.

g. Some municipalities in less-populated areas of the country prefer to use landfills that presently are cheaper (for them) than resource recovery facilities.

h. Many municipalities are burdened with debt and unable to assume additional debt needed to co-finance plant construction, even though such

Exhibit 5

Percentage of Revenues by Business Segment, APC, 1987–1989

	1989	*1988*	*1987*
Industrial gases	57%	58%	59%
Chemicals	37	34	31
Equipment and technology	6	8	10
Totals	100	100	100

Source: Form 10-K, APC, September 30, 1989.

Exhibit 6

Percentage of Revenues by Business Segment, BFI, 1987–1989

	1989	*1988*	*1987*
Solid waste collection services	74%	75%	79%
Solid waste processing and disposal	16	15	13
Special services	8	6	3
Chemical waste services	2	4	5
Totals	100	100	100

Source: Form 10-K, BFI, September 30, 1989.

plants would improve waste disposal management and be economically feasible over the life of the contract.

These issues are difficult to quantify and ultimately may be resolved only through management's best judgment. Other factors, not presently known or even under consideration, may also influence BFI and APC's (through American Ref-Fuel) decision of how many plants, where, at what rate, and under what terms they should be constructed.

CASE 7

Sun Microsystems

William C. House, University of Arkansas at Fayetteville;
Walter E. Greene, University of Texas–Pan American

INTRODUCTION

In 1982, four 27-year-old individuals combined forces to found Sun Microsystems, with the objective of producing and marketing computer workstations to scientists and engineers. Two of the four were Stanford MBA graduates—Michigan-born Scott McNealy and Vinod Khosla, a native of India. They were joined by Andreas Bechtolsheim, a Stanford engineering graduate who had constructed a computer workstation with spare parts in order to perform numerical analysis, and UNIX Software expert William Joy from the Berkeley campus. Sun's founders believed there was a demand for a desktop computer workstation costing between $10,000 and $20,000 in a market niche ignored by such microcomputer makers as IBM, Data General, DEC, and Hewlett-Packard.

Sun Microsystems is the market leader in the fast-growing workstation industry, with expected sales revenue growth of 30% annually during the next five years, compared to 5% to 10% for the personal computer industry. Workstations can be used in a stand-alone fashion or as part of a network configuration. The product lines range from low-priced diskless units to higher-powered graphics-oriented stations at the top of the line.

In contrast to personal computers, workstations are characterized by a 32-bit, instead of 16-bit, microprocessors. There is a strong tendency to use the UNIX operating system, instead of MS/DOS, because of the more sophisticated software and graphics capabilities, larger storage capacities, faster processing speeds, and the ability to function effectively in a networking environment. The

---

This case is intended for classroom discussion only, not to depict effective or ineffective handling of administrative situations. All rights reserved to authors and the North American Case Research Association.

principal users of workstations have been engineers and scientists. However, price reductions and technological improvements have broadened the appeal of workstations so that they are finding use in financial trading, desktop publishing, animation, mapping, and medical imaging applications.

Sun, the fastest-growing company in the computer hardware industry, has revenues that are increasing at a five-year compounded rate of 85% and income increasing at a 67% rate from 1985 to 1990 (3). For fiscal year 1991, Sun's revenues were $3.2 billion and net income was $190 million (13). The company's rapid growth rate has severely drained its cash resources.

CHAIRMAN AND CEO OF SUN MICROSYSTEMS

Scott McNealy, the current chairman of Sun, is a native of Detroit and grew up on the fringes of the U.S. automobile industry. Originally rejected by both Harvard and Stanford Business Schools, he graduated from Harvard with a major in economics. In between his Harvard and Stanford academic careers, he accepted a job as a foreman at Rockwell's International truck plant. After two months of hectic workplace activity, he was hospitalized with hepatitis. He entered Stanford University in 1978, on his third try.

In 1981, at the age of 26, McNealy became manufacturing director at Onyx systems, a small minicomputer maker. The company was faced with serious quality problems. In two months, the operation showed drastic improvements as McNealy probed work rules and production bottlenecks, encouraging workers to identify problems and overcome obstacles on the way toward improving workplace efficiency.

In 1982, former Stanford classmates Andy Bechtolsheim and Vinod Khosla asked him to join them as director of operations in a new company called Sun Microsystems. Two years later, McNealy was chosen by the board of directors to be CEO, over Paul Ely, now executive vice-president of Unisys. During the first month after he became CEO, one of the three co-founders resigned; the company lost $500,000 on $2 million in sales, and two-thirds of its computers did not work.

A workaholic, McNealy works from daylight to dark, seven days a week, rarely finding time for recreational activities. The frantic pace at Sun, engendered by McNealy, is sometimes referred to as "Sunburn." There is a tendency for Sun executives to take on too many projects at once, thereby creating tremendous internal pressure and organizational chaos.

McNealy's philosophy can be capsuled in these company sayings (9):

1. On decision making—Consensus if possible, but participation for sure.
2. On management cooperation—Agree and commit, disagree and commit, or just get out of the way.
3. On market response—The right answer is the best answer. The wrong answer is second best. No answer is the worst.
4. On individual initiative—To ask permission is to seek denial.

He has stated that the company is trying to achieve four goals—significant increases in revenue and in book value, improved product acceptance, and higher profit margins.

CHIEF COMPUTER DESIGNER

Andreas Bechtolsheim, chief computer designer, was one of Sun's co-founders. At age 35, he has the title of vice president of technology. A native of West Germany, Bechtolsheim designed his first computer in 1980, while still a graduate student at Stanford University. It was a workstation designed for scientists and engineers. However, he was unable to sell the idea to any computer company then in existence. Shortly thereafter, he joined Joy, Khosla, and McNealy in founding Sun Microsystems. The company's first product was based on his machine.

Initially, Bechtolsheim persuaded Sun to use off-the-shelf products to develop its workstations, instead of following the usual industry practice of utilizing proprietary components. This meant company products would be easy for competitors to copy, but it also allowed quick entry into the marketplace. As nonproprietary open systems came to be more widely accepted, competitors such as Apollo, DEC, and IBM encountered problems in keeping pace with product lines that lacked the flexibility and performance of Sun's products. When Steve Jobs formed Next, Inc. and announced the development of a desktop workstation, Bechtolsheim urged Sun officials to build a true desktop computer. There was considerable resistance to the project, and he almost left the company at that point.

Almost at once, he began working on the new computer on his own. He spent $200,000 of his own funds on the project, without any official company backing. He also formed a small company called Unisun to provide the vehicle for marketing his new computer and persuaded Khosla, a member of Sun's board of directors, to become president of Unisun. Khosla offered Sun the right to invest in or purchase the smaller company outright. Sun seriously considered both possibilities, but McNealy was fearful that the new venture might be considered a competitor of Sun.

In view of the possible negatives of a smaller company selling an identical clone of Sun, the larger company finally agreed to build the new computer and call it Sparcstation I. Initially, restrictions were placed on the project, and only engineers who said they would resign otherwise were allowed to join the project. Because the company has had a culture based on building bigger boxes, Sparcstation was widely criticized within the company as being too small. However, Bechtolsheim stubbornly refused to change the specifications and eventually prevailed.

FIELD OPERATIONS DIRECTOR

Carol Bartz, national sales director and the number two executive at Sun Microsystems, has about half of the company's 12,000 employees reporting to her. Although many outsiders feel she will soon be named chief operating officer, she abruptly dismisses the idea, observing that she does not believe the company needs a COO. At 42, the hard driving and aggressive executive seems to be reaching new heights in her career.

Bartz attended the University of Wisconsin, receiving a bachelor of computer science degree in 1971. After that, she spent seven years with Digital

Equipment Corporation. Since joining Sun in 1983, she has become intimately involved in marketing operations, including supervising field support activities and a subdivision that sells to federal government agencies. Bartz has indicated that her relationship with McNealy permits her to tell him what he is doing wrong, as well as what he is doing right. According to Bob Herwick, an investment analyst, Bartz is a very effective problem solver, turning around a sluggish service organization and ensuring that the company fully exploits the market potential in the government market (5).

TEAM AND CONSENSUS MANAGEMENT AT SUN

McNealy, current Sun chairman, attended Cranbrook, a North Detroit prep school. While there, he excelled in a variety of activities, including music, tennis, golf, and ice hockey. According to Alan de Clerk, a high school classmate, McNealy developed a strong self-image and competitive spirit as a result of participating in sports and competing with two brothers and a sister. Through the years, he has approached all activities as if they were team sports. McNealy has a strong commitment to a consensus management style. His brother, William, believes it may be a reaction to the type of environment in which they were raised, for their father ruled his household with an iron hand (2).

McNealy's efforts to build a consensus among executives before a decision is made have become famous throughout the company. As he has stated, "Give me a draw, and I will make the decision, but I will not issue an edict if a large majority is in favor of an alternative proposal" (9). A frequently quoted example occurred in 1988, when he stubbornly resisted changing prices, at a time when rapidly increasing memory costs were reducing profit margins. With a consensus arrayed against him, he finally agreed to some product price increases that were enacted without reducing sales. In fact, he has a hard time saying no to any project pushed by one or more company groups. He demands complete loyalty within his concept of teamwork and becomes very angry if he believes that individuals or teams have let him down. (9).

PRODUCT LINE FOCUS

The Sparcstation I was introduced in April 1989 at a stripped-down price of $9,000. A lower-priced version was introduced in May 1990, costing $5,000. The machine processes data at 12 mips and runs about twice as fast as personal computers. Sun expects the lower price to facilitate sales to large companies that base computer purchases on quantity discounts. However, the low-end Sparcstation does not have disk drives, color monitors, or add-in slots. Therefore, it must be networked and cannot be used as a stand-alone unit.

An improved version of Sparc I was introduced in the summer of 1990, with an improved graphical interface, a color monitor, and sales price of $10,000. Sun has asserted that a personal computer with the same characteristics as the new machine would cost $15,000 to $20,000 and would have only about one-third the processing power of this workstation model. The Sparcstation is now

Sun's top seller among all its product lines, and Sparcstation products produce 80–90% of total company revenues.

Exhibit 1 shows prices and specmarks (a measure of processing power and speed) for two Sun models, as well as for the latest Hewlett-Packard and IBM workstation models. From this table, the relative performance of the Sun computers, in terms of computing power per dollar, can be compared with that of its major competitors.

COMPANY STRATEGY

Early on, Sun executives believed they only had a short time to focus on growing demand for computer workstations from scientists and engineers, before large companies such as IBM, DEC, and Hewlett-Packard would aggressively move into that market niche. Therefore, Sun's strategy was designed to emphasize gaining market share, concentrating on all-out sales growth, no matter what the cost. At one point, the organization was adding more than 300 employees and a new sales office each month. Company engineers developed a steady stream of innovative but sometimes impractical prototypes. Products were sold largely by word of mouth, with virtually no formal sales promotion programs.

As part of the market share focus in the mid-1980s, the company began creating autonomous divisions to develop and market its products. This policy allowed rapid movements into such market areas as sales to government agencies, universities, and financial institutions. A special team was created in 1986 to successfully counter the threat posed by Apollo. Sun can win market share battles in such cases, noted F.H. Moss, formerly vice-president for software development at Apollo, because it has no strong preconceptions about what can or cannot be done (2). The autonomous groups did create unnecessary duplications and contributed to development costs that were almost twice the industry average. When attempts were made to consolidate functions, fierce turf battles resulted and top executives were forced to step in and referee the conflicts.

The market share/sales growth emphasis created many unexpected problems. Needed investments in customer service and data processing activities had to be postponed. The existence of independent, autonomous divisions caused numerous difficulties for both sales and manufacturing activities. At

A Comparison of Performance Measures for Major Workstation Makers **Exhibit 1**

	Price	*Specmarks*	*Price per Specmark*
Hewlett-Packard 9000	$11,990	55.5	$216.00
Sun Sparcstation ELC	4,995	20.1	248.50
IBM RS/6000	13,992	32.8	426.50
Sun Sparcstation IPX	13,495	24.2	557.60

Source: J.A. Savage, "Price Takes Backseat with Users," *Computerworld,* September 2, 1991, p. 4.

one point, the company had more than 10,000 computer and option combinations to keep track of. Three different product lines, based on three different microprocessors—Sparc, Motorola 68000, and Intel 386—required excessive investment and extensive coordination to ensure that they all worked on the same network. Overlaps and duplications in marketing and finance made forecasting all but impossible. At its current size, the company can no longer scramble madly to meet shipping deadlines at the last minute.

By the summer of 1989, the company was experiencing projection bottlenecks, as discounted sales of older products mushroomed. Demand for newer products also increased faster than expected. Large backlogs of sales orders were not being entered in the inventory control system, preventing the company from knowing how many or what kinds of products it needed to produce.

In the last quarter of 1989, Sun experienced a $20 million loss, due to misjudging consumer demand for its new Sparcstation and incurring parts shortages. A new management information system produced inaccurate parts forecasts, which contributed to order snafus and lower earnings. However, it posted a $5 million profit in the first quarter of 1990. Sun produced revenues of $2.5 billion in fiscal 1990 and is expected to achieve revenues of $3.3 billion in 1991 (8). Sun is now changing its approach to place more emphasis on profitability and less on growth, expanding customer service and hiring fewer employees. Sun president McNealy has recently tied executive pay to before tax return on investment. In the 1989 annual report, he stated that he desired performances to be judged on the basis of significant increases in revenues, acceptance of new products, improvements in profit margins, and increases in book value.

McNealy was one of the early pioneers pushing open systems which would allow computers of many different manufacturers to be linked together in networks. In fact, Sun has actually encouraged competition with itself, through its focus on open systems development, and invited the industry to build Sparc-based clones in order to expand the position of the workstation industry. As the percentage of total Sparc-based computers sold by Sun has begun to decline, Sun appears to be changing its position on clones. Recently, it told its own dealers they would incur Sun's displeasure if they sold Sun clones along with Sun workstations. Many of these dealers are angry at what they perceive to be Sun's arrogance.

Sun has consistently maintained a narrow product line focus. It has gradually phased out all microprocessors, expect Sparc, and has concentrated on low-end workstations with the greatest market share growth possibilities. It has avoided entering markets for higher-priced lines and the personal computer segment with emphasis on low price and compactness. However, recently Sun announced plans to move into high-end workstation markets where processing speed and power requirements necessitate linking a series of microprocessors and using sophisticated software. Sun may encounter problems in this market similar to those it experienced in product upgrades of its lower-level models, since it does not have a good record in managing product introductions.

As workstations become more powerful and less expensive, workstation manufacturers face a serious challenge in maintaining profit margins. Current models now combine high functionality with high volume, in contrast to an earlier focus on producing highly functional units in small quantities. Extensive use of application-specific integrated circuits with fewer components reduces system size, increases reliability, and lowers product costs. Sun and other companies increasingly follow the practice of involving manufacturing representatives in the design process as early as possible in order to minimize manufacturing problems. Increased attention is also being paid to maintaining product quality and improved product testing before systems are shipped.

In past years, Sun's strategies have included focusing on lower prices, well-developed marketing programs, and third-party software development. From 1,500 to 2,000 applications are available for the Sun Sparcstation, compared to approximately 1,000 for the Hewlett-Packard and DEC products. The company is licensing its Sparc chip to third-party clone companies with the desire of expanding the installed computer base using this chip. The overall company goal is to deliver a complete processing solution, including graphics, input–output, software, and networking.

DISTRIBUTION CHANNELS AND CUSTOMER SERVICE

Workstation makers have traditionally sold their units using manufacturers' sales forces and specialized hardware resellers who repackage specialized software with other companies' workstations. Sun has about 300 VARs (i.e., value added resellers), compared to more than 500 for Hewlett-Packard, with Digital and IBM falling somewhere in between. Some authorities think the majority of VARs are not capable of selling workstations (11). Sun is now considering the possibility of selling some of its models through retailers such as Microage, in a manner similar to personal computer sales now made by IBM, Compaq, and Apple. Such a move would reduce selling and inventory costs, but is meeting initial resistance from dealers unaccustomed to handling complex workstation models.

Sun still sells a large number of workstations through its 1,000-person sales force. In July 1990, Sun selected 200 dealers from three retail chains and gave them training in selling workstations. The company expects to sell $30 million worth of workstations through retail dealers in fiscal 1990, but a full-fledged dealer network may require several years to develop. Because of the higher average selling prices and greater product differentiation and uniqueness of workstations compared to personal computers, many PC vendors are expressing interest in handling workstations, in spite of the small volumes generated.

One area of concern has been Sun's field service organization, which has not been very effective in supporting customer software. Bartz has stated that the company wants to improve on customer service, without making large monetary expenditures or building a dinosaur service group (2). In line with this, Sun has announced plans to start using company-trained, third-party service personnel who can be dispatched to customer locations on demand.

CUSTOMER CATEGORIES

The workstation market for engineers and scientists is rapidly becoming saturated. About one-third of Sun's customers now come from the commercial side, up from only 10% several years ago. The company is now concentrating more of its efforts on airlines, banks, insurance, and finance companies, trying to persuade users to utilize Sun workstations to solve new problems. Sun vice-president Eric Schmidt says that Sun tends to sell to early adopters of new technology (7). Often, by starting with a pilot program that proves successful, workstations can be expanded to other areas in a customer's operations. Eastman Kodak began using Sun workstations in engineering design and soon expanded their use to marketing data bases and mailroom operations.

Sun machines are being used by Wall Street firms Merrill Lynch, Shearson/Lehman/Hutton, and Bear/Sterns on the trading floor. Northwest Airlines uses 500 workstations in Minneapolis to monitor ticket usage, check the correctness of air fare charges, and assess the impact of flight delays or cancellations on revenues and profits. To increase customer satisfaction, Sun has had to change product designs, making its machines easier to install, and improving understandability of product manuals. As Sun has discovered, commercial customers need more help than engineers.

Dataquest says that by 1994, 29.1% of workstation sales will be made to commercial users, as opposed to scientific/engineering users, in a market that is expected to reach $22 billion (16). Workstation makers are moving into the personal computer area by offering UNIX versions that will run on both workstations and personal computers. Workstations provide much greater computing power at a lower cost than would be required to enhance a personal computer so that it possesses the equivalent capability of a typical workstation. Workstations seem to be making their biggest inroads into central processing unit–intensive applications, formerly done on mainframes (e.g., stock transactions, airline reservations).

Sun's first major TV advertising effort occurred in April 1991, taking the form of a 30-second commercial seen on CNN, ESPN, and the three major TV networks. The commercial was not directed specifically at a consumer audience, but instead, was an attempt to get broad exposure for a new message beamed at the business market. Sun expected the advertisement to reach 59% of U.S. households and 42% of the target market of senior-level corporate and computer executives. The campaign also included an eight-page insert in the *Wall Street Journal.*

Sun's advertising budget of approximately $4.6 million in 1990 was spent on computer and general interest business publications. Sun's advertising budget is only about 0.25% of sales revenues, compared to 1.0% to 1.5% spent by its major competitors. Some observers have questioned the cost-effectiveness of a high-priced TV advertisement by a company that sells high-priced computers to a limited group of customers.

SOFTWARE DEVELOPMENTS

Availability of software still remains a major problem in expanding sales of workstations. Only about 5% to 10% of UNIX-based software is designed for business and commercial applications. Sun is trying to convince software developers to produce UNIX-based versions of many common personal computer products. It now has UNIX-based versions of such popular PC software as Lotus 1-2-3 and DBASE IV. It hopes the increased availability of software, plus the narrowing cost gap between low-end workstations and high-end personal computers, will help it penetrate the personal computer market. However, it must sell users on the benefit–cost performance of workstations, compared to personal computers, and also needs to expand its existing base of software developers.

The type of software to be run is often the determining factor in deciding between a personal computer or a workstation. For productivity and business applications, PCs can be more cost-efficient. For technical and graphics applications, workstations are more appropriate. Differences in costs are no longer a differentiating factor.

An entrenched personal computer MS/DOS operating system base and lack of commercial workstation software has hampered the switch from high-end personal computers to workstations. MS/DOS-based computers appear adequate for a majority of user needs, especially with the advent of the WINDOWS operating environment. PC users are more likely to change if complex applications such as multimedia, integrated data base, or windowing become desirable, rather than on the basis of price alone. Workstations may become less attractive if personal computers based on Intel's 80846 chip, with considerably more computing power than today's systems, become more widely available.

Product/price performance is no longer as important a differentiating factor as it used to be. Software availability and usability is increasing in importance. In recognition of this, Sun has formed two software subsidiaries—one for application software and the other to concentrate on improvements in the UNIX operating system. The Open Look Graphical Interface has been added to make Sun products more user friendly. The key to maintaining market position seems to be improving systems software and selling software developers and users on the benefits of workstations over other hardware options.

Sun has announced that it will release a new version of its operating system designed to run on Intel-based personal computers. Some analysts say that Sun will face a stiff test in competing with Microsoft's DOS/Windows combination and that it is a defensive move, made in realization that Sun no longer can generate enough revenue from its own machines to meet its growth goals. McNealy denies that the Sun announcement is defensive, saying that high-powered PC owners will move to Sun's operating systems to take advantage of advanced capabilities (e.g., running multiple programs simultaneously), which is something that has been vaguely promised by Microsoft's Windows new NT versions (13). McNealy has sharply criticized Windows NT version, referring to it as illusionary or not there.

Sun's Solaris operating system will not be available until mid-1991; it runs on both Intel's X86 series and Sun's Sparc processors. The new operating system will make it easier for Sun's customers to link Sun workstations with other computers in a network and increase the number of Sun users. Sun hopes that this will encourage independent software houses to write new programs for Sun OS. So far, approximately 3,500 application programs are available for Sun OS, compared with more than 20,000 for IBM-compatible personal computers (12).

COMPETITION IN THE MARKETPLACE

Although still the market leader, Sun is facing increasing competition from much larger computer companies. Sun shipped 146,000 workstations in 1990 (39% of the market) out of a total of 376,000 and is expected to ship 200,000 in 1991 (4). Having fully absorbed Apollo into its organization, Hewlett-Packard with about 20% of the market, is selling about two-thirds as many workstations as Sun. DEC, which has completely reworked its product lines, has about 17% of the workstation market. Hewlett-Packard has also introduced a new workstation model comparable in price to the Sparcstation, but it runs about twice as fast as Sun's current model. Exhibit 2 shows the 1989 and 1990 market shares for the major firms in the workstation market.

IBM has made a significant comeback in the workstation market with the RS/6000, after its first workstation model proved to be a slow seller. In 1990, IBM shipped more than 25,000 workstations, producing revenue of $1 billion and attaining a market share of 6.6%, more than doubling its 1989 market share (4). In 1991, some analysts estimate that IBM will sell between $2 and $3 billion worth of workstations. IBM has a stated goal of overtaking Sun by 1993 by achieving a 30% market share, although some experts predict it is more likely to achieve a 15% market share by that date (14).

With the workstation market expected to exceed $20 billion by the mid-1990s, competition is expected to be fierce. IBM's late entry, entrenched positions of competitors in the market, lack of a low-priced entry-level model, and the use of nonstandard operating and graphics environments are likely to hamper its efforts to achieve a market share much above 15% (6). IBM's service and sales reputation, its large reseller base, and strong position in commercial markets should give the company leverage to enter the fast-growing markets for network servers and small or branch office multiuser systems. However, if IBM focuses its efforts on penetrating these markets with its RS/6000, it runs a serious risk of undercutting sales of its own AS/400 unit.

Exhibit 2 **Computer Workstation Market Shares**

Company	*1989*	*1990*
Sun Microsystems	30.4%	38.8%
Hewlett-Packard	26.1	20.1
Digital Equipment	26.6	17.0
Intergraph	7.0	3.8
IBM	1.2	4.5
Silicon Graphics	5.1	2.6
Sony	—	3.3
Next	—	2.6
Other	3.6	7.0
Total	100.0	100.0

Cost no longer seems to be the primary factor in decisions to acquire workstations. Workers must become more accustomed to graphics, as opposed to character-based systems, before adoption by current PC users becomes more widespread. Some companies feel that workstations have yet to demonstrate significant productivity advantages over personal computers. The biggest shortcomings of workstations are their lack of application software and integration difficulties.

FINANCIAL ANALYSIS

Exhibit 3 shows revenues, expenses, and income for the five-year period 1986 to 1990. Revenues have increased at a more rapid rate than net income during the period being considered. Return on sales has declined significantly, to 4.5% from the peak of almost 7% in 1987, with revenue per shipment also declining in 1990 compared to 1989 and 1988. Book value per share and unit shipments have increased significantly during the five years.

Exhibit 4 indicates that Sun's sales, income, and asset growth were higher than the industry average in 1989 and 1990, with market value/equity also above the industry average. However, net income/sales was below the industry average in 1989 and slightly above the industry average in 1990. As Exhibit 5 indicates, Sun appears to be very close to the industry average, in terms of two common productivity measures, sales/assets and sales/employee. In reviewing the common leverage measures, Sun is well above the industry average for R&D expenses/revenues and R&D expenses/employee.

Revenues, Expenses, and Income for Five Years (millions of $) **Exhibit 3**

	1990	*1989*	*1988*	*1987*	*1986*
Net revenue	2,466	1,765	1,052	538	210
Cost of sales	1,399	1,010	550	273	102
Gross profit	1,067	755	502	265	108
R&D outlays	302	234	140	70	31
Selling, administrative, & general expenses	588	433	250	127	57
Total	890	667	390	197	88
Operating income	177	88	112	68	20
Interest income	(23)	(10)		834	369
Income taxes	43	17	44	33	9
Net income	111	61	68	869	380
Net income/sales	4.5%	3.4%	6.3%	6.8%	5.3%
Net income/share	1.21	0.76	0.89	0.55	0.21
Book value/share	9.82	7.77	4.75	3.57	2.04
Unit shipments (000s)	118.3	80.7	48.4	24.6	9.9
Revenue/unit shipped (000s)	20.8	21.9	21.7	21.8	21.2

Source: Adapted from 1990 annual report.

Exhibit 4 Computer Industry Data for Years 1989 and 1990

	Sales Growth		Income Growth		Asset Growth		Net Income/ Sales		Mkt Value/ Equity	
Company	*1990*	*1989*	*1990*	*1989*	*1990*	*1989*	*1990*	*1989*	*1990*	*1989*
Apple	1.07	1.21	1.14	1.05	1.12	1.24	8.7	8.2	4.81	3.21
Compaq	1.25	1.39	1.36	1.31	1.30	1.31	12.6	11.6	3.26	3.31
DEC	1.01	1.05	0.00	0.72	1.03	1.10	–.72	6.8	1.21	1.13
Hewlett-Packard	1.10	1.20	0.95	0.97	1.09	1.31	5.7	6.6	1.83	1.98
Intergraph	1.21	1.07	0.79	0.80	1.06	0.97	6.0	9.2	1.79	1.73
IBM	1.10	1.05	1.60	0.68	1.30	1.06	8.7	6.0	1.75	1.62
NCR	1.06	0.99	0.90	0.94	1.01	0.95	5.9	6.9	3.54	3.40
Silicon Graphics	1.41	1.73	1.97	1.94	1.37	0.94	8.3	5.9	3.57	4.30
Sun mcrs	1.34	1.41	318.	0.40	1.49	1.50	5.5	1.8	2.72	1.41
Wang	0.87	0.9	0.00	0.00	0.72	0.87	–6.7	–13.9	1.27	0.87
Average	1.14	1.20	32.7	0.88	1.15	1.12	5.4	4.9	2.58	2.37

Source: Business Week 1000 Companies, 1991, 1990.

Exhibit 5 Computer Industry Data for Years 1989 and 1988

	Sales/ Assets		Sales/ Employee		Adv. Exps./ Sales		R&D Exps./ Sales		R&D Exps./ Employee	
Company	*1990*	*1989*	*1990*	*1989*	*1990*	*1989*	*1990*	*1989*	*1990*	*1989*
Apple	1.82	1.91	364	377	7.34	8.30	8.0	6.7	28937	25233
Compaq	1.32	1.38	303	289	1.75	2.87	4.6	3.6	13945	10849
DEC	1.13	1.15	101	94	1.38	1.01	12.0	11.4	12123	10753
Hewlett-Packard	1.22	1.21	125	113	2.69	2.35	10.7	10.4	13358	11713
Intergraph	1.20	1.07	105	110	1.00	1.00	10.6	11.1	11157	12216
IBM	0.79	0.81	164	154	1.17	0.44	8.3	7.4	13572	11415
NCR	1.38	1.32	106	100	1.06	0.53	7.5	7.0	7964	6940
Silicon Graphics	1.22	1.19	180	105	1.00	1.00	11.9	15.8	21150	21908
Sun mcrs	1.27	1.41	172	148	1.00	0.74	13.3	13.3	22934	19733
Wang	1.35	1.12	109	97	1.00	1.02	9.8	8.7	10543	8510
Average	1.27	1.26	173	159	2.64	1.93	9.7	9.5	15568	14027

Source: Business Week 1000, 1990, 1991; Innovation in America, Business Week Issues, 1990, 1988.

REFERENCES

1. Susan E. Fisher, "Vendors Court Reseller Partners as Workstations Go Mainstream," *PC Week*, July 30, 1990.
2. Jonathan B. Levine, "High Noon for Sun," *Business Week*, July 24, 1989, pp. 71, 74.
3. John Markoff, "The Smart Alecs at Sun Are Regrouping," *New York Times*, April 28, 1991.
4. Andrew Ould, "IBM Challenges Sun in Workstation Market," *PC Week*, February 28, 1991.
5. Andrew Ould, "Carol Bartz: Star Is Still Rising for Hard Driving Executive," *PC Week*, September 3, 1990.
6. Andrew Ould, "What's Behind Lower Workstation Prices," *UNIX World*, July 1990.
7. Julie Pitta, "The Trojan Horse Approach," *Forbes*, April 15, 1991.
8. Kathy Rebello, "Sun Microsystems on the Rise Again," *USA Today*, April 20, 1990.
9. "Sun Microsystems Turn on the Afterburners," *Business Week*, July 18, 1988.
10. G. Paschal Zachary, "Sparc-station's Success Is Doubly Sweet for Sun Microsystem's Bechtolsheim," *Wall Street Journal*, May 29, 1990.
11. Susan E. Fisher, "Vendors Court Resellers as Workstations Go Mainstream," *PC Week*, July 30, 1990.
12. Robert D. Hof, "Why Sun Can't Afford to Shine Alone," *Business Week*, September 9, 1991.
13. G. Paschal Zachary, "Sun Challenges Microsoft's Hold Over Software," *Wall Street Journal*, September 4, 1991.
14. Bob Francis, "Big Blue's Red Hot Workstation," *Datamation*, October 15, 1990.
15. Lawrence Curran, "HP Speeds Up Workstation Race," *Electronics*, April 1991.
16. "Getting Down to Business," *Information Week*, January 14, 1991.

BIBLIOGRAPHY

Lawrence Abbott, "Good Buys Abound in RISC Workstations," *Datamation*, April 15, 1991.

Michael Alexander, "PC Workstation Firms Prepare for Price War," *Computerworld*, September 20, 1989.

William Brandell, "Managers Find RISC Not Worth Gamble," *Computerworld*, March 5, 1990.

Laura Brennan, "Resilient Sun Is on the Rise in PC's Turf," *PC Week*, September 3, 1990.

William L. Bulkeley, "DEC's New Workstations May Shake Up Hot Market," *Wall Street Journal*, January 11, 1989; "Digital Unveils New Work Stations; Cuts Some Prices," *Wall Street Journal*, April 4, 1990.

Paul Bush, "Dangerous Liaisons," *Prepared Foods*, August 1990.

Peter B. Carroll, "New Workstation Line Aims for Credibility," *Wall Street Journal*, February 12, 1990.

Peter Coffee, "RISC Software Has Turned the Corner," *PC Week*, S-18, 20; "Price, Support, and Integration Are Key in Evaluating Software," S-25; *PC Week*, April 2, 1990.

Peter Coffee, "Desktop Sizzlers," and "Japan Eyes Workstation Market," *Computerworld*, December 25–January 1, 1990.

James Daly, "Can Sun Ride Out Stormy Weather," *Computerworld*, July 24, 1989; "Workstation Market Leaving PC's Far Behind," *Computerworld*, February 5, 1990, and "Sun Users Staying Loyal for Now," *Computerworld*, March 5, 1990.

Susan E. Fisher, "Vendors Court Reseller Partners As Workstations Go Mainstream," *PC Week*, July 30, 1990.

Mary Jo Foley, "Microcomputers: High-End PC's vs. Workstations," *Systems Integration*, April 1990.

Barbara Francett, "Workstations Dust Off After Rough Year's Ride," *Computerworld*, September 25, 1989.

Bob Francis, "Big Blue's Red Hot Workstation," *Datamation*, October 15, 1990, and "Sun Compatibles: Who's Putting the Sizzle in Sparc," *Datamation*, May 1, 1991.

Richard Freiburn and Ronald E. Roades, "The Workstation Revolution," *Information Executive*, Winter 1991.

John Gantz, "PC vs. Workstation Dominance Looms Near," *Infoworld*, May 14, 1990.

"Get It While It's Hot: Slicing up the Worldwide Workstation Market," *PC Week*, January 29, 1990.

Neal Gross, "Why Sun Is Losing Its Heat in the East," *Business Week*, September 10, 1989.

John Hilkirk, "Workstations, PCs Gain Popularity," *USA Today*, April 26, 1989.

Kathleen Hurley and Carl Flock, "PCs vs. Workstations: The Battle Revisited," *Computer Graphics Review*, June 1990.

Robert D. Hof, "Will Sun Also Rise in the Office Market," *Business Week*, May 21, 1990; and "Where Sun Means to be a Bigger Fireball," *Business Week*, April 15, 1991.

Thomas Kucharvy, "Can IBM Catch Up with the Workstation Market," *Computer Graphics Review*, June 1990.

Michael R. Leibowitz, "UNIX Workstations Arrive," *Datamation*, June 1, 1990.

Peter H. Lewis, "With Both Feet, IBM Jumps into Workstations," *New York Times*, February 18, 1990; and "Can Old Processing Technology Beat Back New Challenge," *New York Times*, February 25, 1990.

Jonathan B. Levine, "Hewlett Packard's Screeching Turn Toward Desktops," *Business Week*, September 11, 1989; "Can Sun Stand the Heat in the PC Market," *Business Week*, April 24, 1989; and "High Noon for Sun," *Business Week*, July 24, 1989.

Gerald Lubernow, "An Upstart's Rite of Passage," *Business Month*, May 1990.

John Markoff, "The Niche That IBM Can't Ignore," *New York Times*, April 25, 1989; "A Prescription for Troubled IBM," *New York Times*, December 10, 1989; and "The Smart Alecs At Sun Are Regrouping," *New York Times*, April 28, 1991.

Melanie McCrossen, "Workstations: A Market Niche Raises Eyebrows," *Standard and Poor's Industry Surveys*, April 1990, C81–82.

Andrew Ould, "Sun's Color Workstation Bridges UNIX, High End PC's," *PC Week*, July 30, 1990; "IBM Challenges Sun in Workstation Market," *PC Week*, February 28, 1991; "Carol Bartz: Star Is Still Rising for Hard Driving Executive," *PC Week*, September 3, 1990.

Andrew Ould, "What's Behind Lower Workstation Prices," *UNIX World*, July 1990.

Julie Pitta, "The Trojan Horse Approach," *Forbes*, April 15, 1991.

Gary McWilliams, "DEC Is Changing with the Times—A Little Late," *Business Week*, April 9, 1990.

Dave Methvin, "RISC-Based Systems Find Strength in Simplicity," *PC Week*, April 2, 1990.

Kathy Rebello, "Sun Microsystems on the Rise Again," *USA Today*, April 20, 1990; "Workstation Makers Try to Reboot Sales," and "Sun to Market Workstation with PC Price," *USA Today*, May 14, 1990; "Sun Targets PCs with Workstation,"

USA Today, July 26, 1990; "H-P to Rattle Workstation Market," *USA Today,* March 18, 1991.

J.A. Savage, "HP/Apollo Duet Not Yet in Tune," *Computerworld,* April 16, 1990; "PCs Repel Workstation Wave," *Computerworld,* September 17, 1990; and "Price Takes Back Seat with Users," *Computerworld,* September 2, 1991.

Tara Sexton, "IBM Raises the Ante in High Stakes RISC Arena," *PC Week,* April 2, 1990, S-8, S-9.

Laura Speigelman, "RISC Buyers Turn Eyes Toward IBM," and "Sun Focuses on SPARC to Fend Off Growing Competition," *PC Week,* March 19, 1990.

John Schneidawaind, "DEC Launches Workstation Attack," *USA Today,* April 12, 1990; and "Sun Expected to Win Place in Fortune 1000," *PC Week,* October 8, 1990.

"Sun Microsystems Turn on the Afterburners," *Business Week,* July 18, 1988.

"The Versatility of the New Workstations," *I/S Analyzer,* January 1989.

"Trends: Technical Workstations," *Computerworld,* February 26, 1990.

John W. Verity, "IBM Is Finally Saying in UNIX We Trust," *Business Week,* February 12, 1990.

Therese R. Welton, "Workstations: Prophecies Coming to Pass," *Industry Week,* January 2, 1989.

Jethro Wright, "What Is A Workstation?" *MIS Week,* February 15, 1990.

Stephan K. Yoder et al., "Workstation Options Expanding," *Wall Street Journal,* May 9, 1990; and "Rivals Take Aim at IBM's Workstations," *Wall Street Journal,* February 15, 1990.

G. Paschal Zachary and Stephan K. Yoder, "A Line Dividing Workstations and PC's Blurs," *Wall Street Journal,* March 20, 1990.

G. Paschal Zachary, "Sun Microsystems's Slump Has Endurance," *Wall Street Journal,* August 11, 1989; "Sparcstation's Success is Doubly Sweet for Sun Microsystem's Bechtolsheim," *Wall Street Journal,* May 29, 1990; and "Sun Introduces Its PC Priced Workstation," *Wall Street Journal,* May 16, 1990.

CASE 8

Bosworth Steel

Jennings Marshall, Fred Hendon, Samford University

In late September 1990, Tom Bosworth, CEO of Bosworth Steel, became concerned about his company's future. A large Chicago-based company had acquired local production facilities and installed state-of-the-art mills that would put it in direct competition with Bosworth in its southwest geographical base of operations.

Actually, when Tom considered his firm's position at the time, he was not surprised by the added competition. Bosworth Steel's primary business was the production of carbon steel mechanical and structural piping and tubing made from sheet steel stock purchased from basic steel producers. Over the last few years, company sales and profits have grown very rapidly. Annual tonnage shipped grew from about 20,000 in 1977 to over 100,000 in 1990, roughly a 14% annual growth rate. By 1980, Bosworth had an estimated 20% share of the market in its geographical market area. As a result of this rapid growth, present production facilities were operated close to capacity, and the company's success obviously attracted the attention of competitors. Bosworth Steel had also become very profitable during this period of growth. Recent financial results are provided in Exhibit 1.

The growth in sales and profits convinced Bosworth executives to seriously consider acquiring or building a plant in another geographical region contiguous to its present geographical market in the Southwest.

Tom Bosworth realized that although the firm's management group and salespeople had a very good intuitive feel for their present customers and their needs, they were uncertain of the dimensions of the overall market and had very little knowledge of the details in the surrounding regional markets where expansion was being considered. These circumstances led Bosworth to seek the help of a consulting team.

This case is intended for classroom discussion only, not to depict effective or ineffective handling of administrative situations. All rights reserved to the authors and the North American Case Research Association.

Exhibit 1

Condensed Financial Statements Bosworth Steel
December 31, 1990 Balance Sheet

Assets		
Cash		$ 10,600,000
Accounts receivable		$ 5,460,000
Inventory		$ 18,800,000
Plant, property, & equipment	$31,750,000	
Less accumulated depreciation	$15,380,000	
		$ 16,370,000
		$ 51,230,000

Liabilities	
Accounts payable	$ 15,620,000
Bank loans	4,600,000
Equity	$ 31,010,000
	$ 51,230,000

Income Statement	
Sales	$110,820,000
Cost of sales	$ 89,918,000
	$ 20,902,000
Operating expenses	8,105,000
Net income	$ 12,797,000

BACKGROUND OF BOSWORTH STEEL

Bosworth Steel began operations in 1948 in Houston, Texas. The company's founder was Erick Bosworth, Tom's grandfather. Initially, the company produced flat-rolled steel products, but over the years, it expanded into carbon steel mechanical and structural piping and tubing, as well as into a line of painted steel sheet products. In the early years, these products were sold mainly to service centers rather than to the specific end users. Service centers (in effect steel product wholesalers) break down large lots and sell smaller amounts to end users in construction and various steel fabrication markets.

In more recent years, the composition of Bosworth's customer base had changed considerably. Sales to service centers rose in absolute dollar terms, but declined as a percentage of total sales. On the other hand, sales to original equipment manufacturers (OEMs) increased dramatically in both absolute and relative terms. As part of the changing customer base, Bosworth found that it was selling to fewer but larger customers.

The change in customer composition also increased the company's knowledge of the end uses to which its products were put. Sales to service centers were essentially in small lots of a wide variety of sizes and shapes of piping, tubing, and other products. As a result, Bosworth had no real idea of who the final users were or the specific uses for the products. However, as sales to OEMs increased, the end uses of the products became much more certain. Important customers were acquired in the farm implement, automotive, metal furniture, and athletic equipment industries. More recently, a potentially important export market had opened up in Latin America with the growth of automobile assembly in that area (the auto industry buys tubing for alternators and starters).

Bosworth's management believed that its OEM customers purchased piping and tubing based on four criteria. In descending order of importance, they are:

1. price,
2. availability (speed of delivery),
3. personal relations with sales force, and
4. quality.

Quality is considered to be an important criterion, but it is difficult to define in all cases.

Bosworth's production facilities are located in Pasadena, Texas, a suburb of Houston and Beaumont, 80 miles northeast on the ship canal. The plants collectively have four Yoder high-frequency electric metal tube mills that are capable of producing a range of sizes of tubing from $\frac{1}{2}$" square by 16 gauge, to 6" by 6" by $\frac{3}{8}$" with comparable rectangular sizes. Bosworth produces two types of tubing: electric welded and seamless. Structural tubing, a type of electric welded tubing, is used mainly as strength-bearing members in agricultural, oil, and construction equipment; in material-handling systems; and in general industrial applications. A second type of electric welded tubing is drawn-over-mandrel tubing, which is used for numerous purposes. In the automotive industry, it is used in front-wheel drive components, drive shafts, transmission shafts, and suspension system components. Seamless tubing is used mainly in the production of bushings, bearings, shafts, and in other mechanical applications that require heavy wall thicknesses and alloy grade steels. It is available in carbon grades as well.

The principal raw material used in the manufacture of electric welded and seamless tubing consists of flat-rolled steel. The flat-rolled steel is shaped into a tube by one of Bosworth's four Yoder high-frequency electric metal tube mills. Flat-rolled steel of various thicknesses (gauge) is shaped into a cylinder that is welded, thus forming a tube. These round tubes have many applications, and they can also be shaped into rectangles and squares for other applications. Bosworth's mills are capable of producing tubes as small as $\frac{1}{2}$" square by 16 gauge, to 6" by 6" square with a thickness of $\frac{3}{9}$". The tubes are cut to suit the customer's length requirements. At present, however, Bosworth lacks the mill capability of producing sizes as large as 12" by 12" with a thickness of $\frac{3}{8}$", which are produced by other companies.

The new competition in the area has the capability of producing the larger sizes. This fact, Bosworth feels, constitutes a real threat, as customers tend to prefer to do business with suppliers who can meet all of their needs.

Bosworth's management feels that its major competitive market advantage is quality service, and also that it has been the only producer of the product line in that part of Texas for some time. Bosworth owns a trucking subsidiary

(Boshaul), which is located on the production premises in Pasadena. Having its own trucks allows Bosworth to guarantee next-day delivery to its customers within a 300-mile radius of the plant. Boshaul, thus, is able to offer its customers something approaching just-in-time delivery services. However, it is difficult to compete beyond 300 miles because of mounting transportation costs. The effective market range could be extended beyond 300 miles, if Bosworth were willing to absorb the added freight cost.

On many occasions, management has reminded itself that the company's main product is quality service. In fact, a survey of Bosworth's customers revealed that they strongly support this notion. Tom Bosworth is confident that the company's almost personal attention to service and customer needs is the major reason it has prospered in recent years.

THE NEED FOR MARKET RESEARCH

The entry of a new competitor in the Bosworth market area raised serious questions regarding the nature and direction of the proposed expansion. Rapid sales and profit growth had certainly created a motive and the financial means for expansion. Initially, management had only thought in terms of expanding into one of the market areas more or less contiguous to its present location. Four cities outside the present market area are considered to be good potential production and distribution sites: Birmingham, Alabama; Charleston, South Carolina; Cincinnati, Ohio; and Kansas City, Missouri. The form of expansion considered was to be either the construction of a new plant or the acquisition of an established producer and its facilities.

A competitor had installed efficient, modern mills in the Houston location, thus eliminating Bosworth's location advantage. (See Appendix 1, Exhibit 2 for competitor details.) With the modern facilities, it was likely to have relatively low costs of production. Bosworth's facilities, on the other hand, are somewhat dated, perhaps placing it at a cost disadvantage relative to the competitor. As a result, Bosworth's management had to also consider the need for modernizing the Pasadena facilities. Modernization would create still another problem, however. The plant would be closed during the process, resulting in lost sales. Thus, another possibility considered was to build a new, efficient, up-to-date plant in Bosworth's present market area, perhaps in Dallas, then later, refurbish the Houston mill. This strategy (building a new mill and revamping the old) ran the risk of creating excess capacity in Bosworth's market area.

In summary, Bosworth's management faced a dilemma. On the one hand, growth and profits seemed to call for and justify expansion outside the present market area. On the other hand, the new local competitor created some anxiety concerning the ability to compete in the home market base. It seemed logical to consider the possibility of trying to duplicate the company's success in the Southwest by expanding into another, relatively close geographical area. To determine the feasibility of doing so, Bosworth's management realized that it needed to obtain a better feel for the market potential centered on alternative expansion sites. Bosworth's management felt that in order to consider its situation rationally, the company first needed to get some feel for the potential of its market. As a result, management decided to call in a consulting team. The consultants, after visiting with Bosworth's management, determined that an analysis of the pipe and tube market must accomplish the following:

1. Determine the long-term trends in the national market for the two product categories (mechanical and structural piping and tubing),
2. Determine how sales of the two product groups respond to the business cycle fluctuations over short-run periods,
3. Determine the amounts consumed annually by the major end-user industries for the two product groups.
4. Estimate the market potential for each product type by end user in each of the five market regions, including the home market (see Exhibit 14 for a list of the states that make up each market region).

In late January 1991, the consultants presented their findings to Bosworth management. The first part of the study concerns itself with broad national trends, cycle relationships, and identification of important end-use industries (see Appendix 2). The second part deals with regional market potential centered on alternative expansion sites. Data used by the consultants to make regional market tonnage estimates are also included in Appendix 2.

CONCLUSIONS

Questions facing Tom and the management of Bosworth are: Should the firm expand production capacity? If so, where should the expansion take place? Finally, how can these questions be answered, given the new competitive threat in the home market?

REFERENCES

Economic Indicators, prepared for the Joint Economic Committee by the Council of Economic Advisers, 1973–1991.

Current Industrial Reports, Steel Mill Products MH33B, U.S. Bureau of the Census 1973–1991.

Steel Pipe and Tube (Industry 3317), Census of Manufacturers, 1982.

Annual Statistical Report, American Iron and Steel Institute, 1973–1991.

Metal Statistics, Purchasing Guide of the Metal Industries, American Metal Management, 1973–1991.

Blast Furnaces, Steelworks, and Rolling and Finishing Mills (Industries 3312, 3313, 3315, 3316, and 3317), Census of Manufacturers, 1987.

Steel Mill Products, Current Industrial Reports, U.S. Department of Commerce, 1987, 1990.

Current Industrial Reports, U.S. Department of Commerce, 1982.

Current Industrial Reports, U.S. Department of Commerce, 1972.

APPENDIX I: ELECTRICWELD CORPORATION: BOSWORTH STEEL'S HOME MARKET COMPETITOR

Electricweld Corporation is a manufacturer of welded and seamless steel tubing and bimetallic rod, wire and strand. It was organized in 1919 as an Illinois corporation, and on June 7, 1986, became a Delaware corporation pursuant to a merger agreement. The corporation functions as a holding company, and as a result, engages in business only indirectly, but derives its operating income from subsidiaries. Through its subsidiaries, two principal types of products are produced: tubing and bimetallic products.

Electricweld Tubing Company, an Illinois subsidiary of Electricweld Corporation, produces a full range of electric welded and seamless tubing products. Electricweld Tubing Company has three facilities, as follows:

Name of Plant	*Location*	*Status*
Chicago Steel Tube	Chicago, Il.	Owned
Buckeye Tube Division	Dayton, Ohio	Owned
Houston Tube Division	Houston, Tx.	Leased

(a) The plant in Chicago has floor space of approximately 850,000 square feet. The principal equipment consists of a piercing and sizing mill, an Assel mill, and three electric weld tube mills. This facility has an annual production capacity of approximately 50,000 tons of seamless tubing and approximately 153,000 tons of welded tubing. Capacity utilization has been approximately 68%.

(b) The plant at Dayton has floor space of approximately 450,000 square feet. The principal equipment consists of two electric weld tube mills and a $\frac{5}{8}$"-capacity slitting line. The facility has an annual production capacity of approximately 180,000 tons of structural tubing. Capacity utilization has been approximately 70%.

(c) The Houston Tube Division is a newly formed division of Electricweld. The plant at Houston has a floor space of approximately 230,000 square feet. The principal equipment includes one electric weld tube mill and a $\frac{1}{2}$"-capacity slitting line. The corporation intends to install a second smaller electric weld tube mill in 1990. The facility will have an annual production capacity of approximately 120,000 tons of structural tubing upon installation and startup.

Electricweld's net sales for the year ended December 31, 1990, were relatively unchanged from the prior year. Net sales for 1989, on the other hand, were 35% above 1988's. Sales in tubing were down by 4.3%, however; this drop was offset by a 16% increase in sales of bimetallic products. A condensed financial statement for Electricweld is presented in Exhibit 2.

Condensed Financial Statements Electricweld Corporation December 31, 1990 Balance Sheet **Exhibit 2**

Assets		
Cash		$ 34,705,961
Accounts receivable		$ 34,873,216
Inventory		$ 37,898,894
Plant, property, & equipment	$227,970,000	
Less accumulated depreciation	$102,104,380	$125,865,620
		$233,343,691
Liabilities		
Accounts payable		$ 66,875,490
Long-term debt		46,462,471
Equity		$120,005,730
		$233,343,691
Income Statement		
Sales		$327,478,940
Cost of sales		$263,704,830
		$ 63,774,110
Operating expenses		37,894,000
Net income		$ 25,880,110

APPENDIX 2: MARKET SURVEY

PURPOSE

The purpose of this market survey was twofold: first, to identify the long-term trends and short-term cyclical relationships between the general economy and the market for carbon steel mechanical and structural piping and tubing, and to determine the most important industry end-user industries for the two product categories; second, to focus on the market for both products in a seventeen-state region (roughly the southeastern United States).[1] The overall purpose is to estimate the market potential for the region and to determine the most important submarket districts within the region. As a result, we can identify both the strongest submarkets and the largest end-user industry types in those submarkets.

THE ANALYSIS

■ National Economic Relationships

The steel industry has been a shrinking part of the total economy over the last twenty years, during which time, industry production has been very volatile, relative to real GNP over the business cycle. In the period 1973 through 1990, the value of steel products consumed as a percentage of GNP declined rather steadily, from 2% in 1973 to 1% in 1990. Steel production was also very sensitive to general economic changes over the short-run business cycle.

Exhibit 3 plots the percentage change in steel production against the percentage change in real GNP from 1973 through 1990. The vertical bars in Exhibit 3 mark off recession periods. Note that steel production fluctuated, in percentage terms, more than the level of economic activity, as measured by percentage change in real GNP. Statistically over the period, each 1% change in real GNP coincided with a 4.3% change in steel production. Steel production was, thus, approximately four times as volatile as the total economy.

---

[1]The seventeen states were Alabama, Georgia, Mississippi, Florida, Louisiana, Texas, Arkansas, Oklahoma, Kansas, Missouri, Tennessee, North Carolina, South Carolina, Kentucky, Ohio, West Virginia, and Indiana.

Steel Production and Real GNP Percentage Change

Exhibit 3

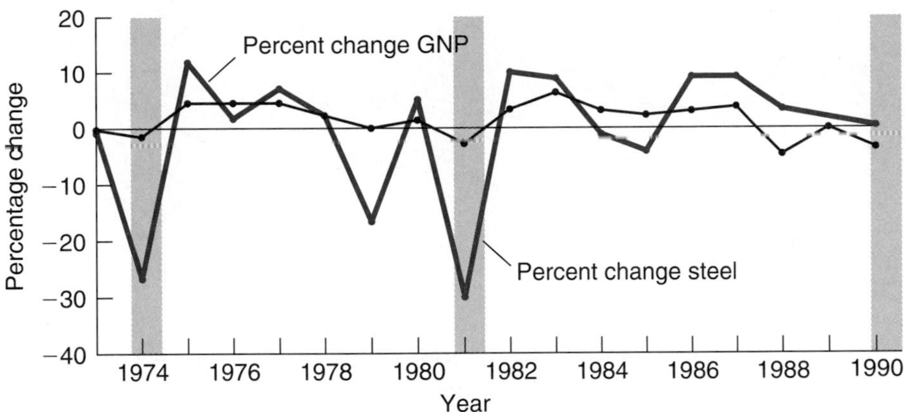

Source: Economic Indicators, Council of Economic Advisers, 1973–1991.

The relationship between the total steel market and the economy, just discussed, was also paralleled in the submarket for mechanical and structural piping and tubing. The two pipe and tube markets followed the total steel market generally with regard to trend and closely with cyclical movements.

Exhibit 4 illustrates the consumption pattern for total steel and mechanical pipe and tube. Care should be taken in reading the graph, since tonnages of both products are not to scale on the vertical axis. They were plotted closely together to highlight the cyclic relationship. In fact, mechanical tonnage was slightly less than 2% of total steel tonnage. However, it is clear that the trend and cyclic movement of mechanical tonnage shipped followed that of total steel shipped. Since steel production had been declining as a percentage of the total economy, the same was true for mechanical piping and tubing. Average

Consumption Pattern: Total Steel and Mechanical Piping and Tubing

Exhibit 4

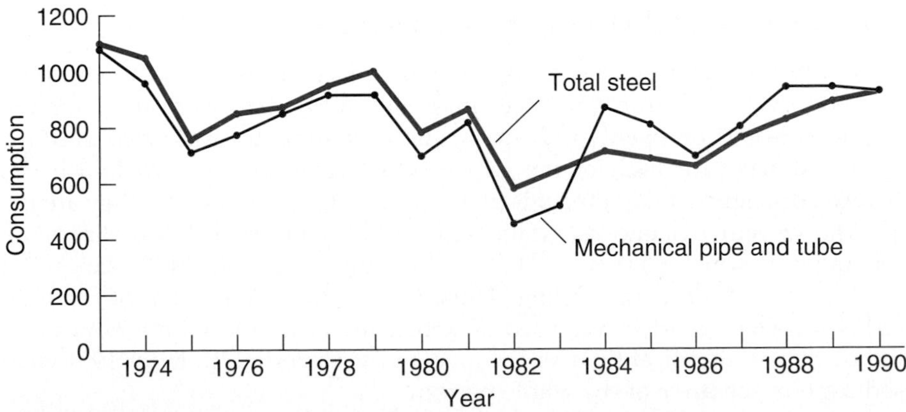

Source: Current Industrial Reports, Steel Mill Products, MH33B. U.S. Bureau of the Census, 1973–1990.

Note: Not to scale; mechanical is less than 2% of total steel production.

Exhibit 5 **Consumption Pattern: Total Structural Piping and Tubing**

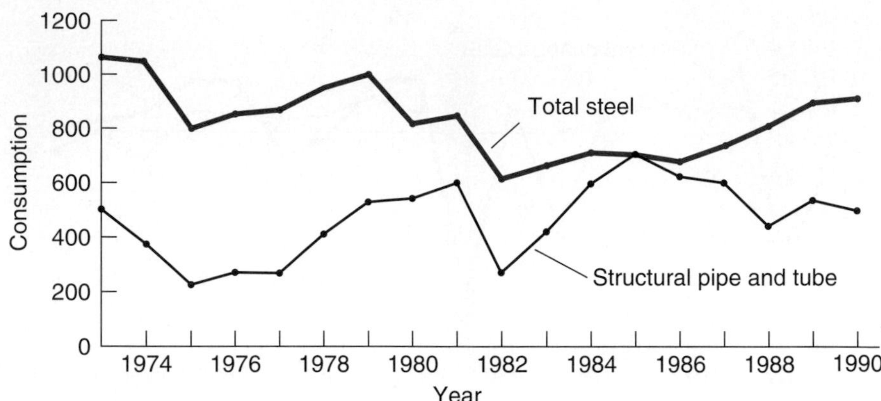

Source: Current Industrial Reports, Steel Mill Products, MH33B. U.S. Bureau of the Census 1973–1990.

Note: Not to scale; structural is less than 1% of total steel production.

tonnage shipped of mechanical fell 1.5% per year over the 1973–1990 period. The consumption of mechanical also exhibits approximately the same variability over the business cycle as total steel—this is the same 1 to 4 relationship that existed between the percentage changes in real GNP and demand for mechanical piping and tubing.

Structural pipe and tube tonnage showed a slightly different relationship to steel consumption over the 1973–1990 period. Nationwide structural tonnage was less than 1% of total steel tonnage or roughly half that of the mechanical tonnage. Exhibit 5 shows the relationship between total steel and structural consumption for the seventeen-year period. Although the two series generally fluctuated together (except for the short period 1986–1988), the trends were different. The trend for structural tonnage rose, on average, about 3.5% per year from 1973 to 1988 (see Exhibit 6 for industry production data).

■ Nationwide End-User Industry Demand

To identify the major end-user industries for mechanical and structural pipe and tube, American Iron and Steel Institute (AISI) data were used for the period 1973–1991 on twenty industries, and each industry was rated in terms of total tonnage for each of the two product categories. A problem exists because AISI figures do not include all tonnage shipped. However, they are the only known source of end-user data. Since AISI data represent over 30% of all pipe and tube tonnage, it is felt that it constitutes a representative sample of the market for piping and tubing. Thus, each industry's percent of the total market tonnage reported was used as a measure of industry importance and did not change significantly over the nineteen-year period. Data for 1991 were used as representative of the whole period.

Exhibit 7 shows the important end-user industries for mechanical piping and tubing for 1990. (See Exhibit 8 for end-user data.) Of the twenty industries reported, three stood out as the most important. In descending order of importance, they are machinery, with 31% of tonnage; service centers, with 22% of total tonnage; and the auto industry, with 17% of total tonnage. These three industries together made up 70% of the total mechanical tube market. Nonclassified was a catch-all for many types of small end-user industries.

Exhibit 9 shows the important end-user industries for structural piping and tubing. Of the twenty-one different industries examined, three made up the major share of the market in 1988. (See Exhibit 10 for end-user data.) Again in descending order of importance, they are service centers, with 57% of tonnage; electrical equipment, with 13% of tonnage; and construction with 12% of tonnage. Eighty-two percent of the demand for structural piping and tubing was accounted for by these three industries.

■ Seventeen-State Region

Next, the mechanical and structural market in a seventeen-state region of interest to Bosworth was examined. The purpose was to establish the importance of the region, relative to the nation, in each product category and to note any differences between demand patterns in the region and the nation as a whole. For the region, only data for the years 1986, 1988, and 1990 were available. Nevertheless, we believe this gives an accurate picture of the region during the 1980s.

Exhibit 11 shows the regions of the national market for both mechanical and structural for 1986, 1988, and 1990. The region's share has averaged 55% to 56% of the national market for the two product categories in the 1980s. In 1990, the region's share was almost 60%. However, we lack enough data to determine whether this was a trend of increasing share for the region.

Exhibit 12 shows the actual tonnage figures for the nation and region for 1986, 1988, and 1990 for mechanical pipe and tube. In 1986, nationwide consumption of mechanical was 1,997,428 tons. For the region in the same year, consumption of mechanical was 957,450 tons. In 1988, mechanical consumption was 1,751,900 tons for the nation. For the region, it was 846,500 tons in the same year. For 1990, national tonnage for mechanical was not available, so we compare the 1989 tonnage nationwide with the regional for 1990. The 1989 national tonnage was 2,087,359 compared with 1,163,200 tons for the region. Over the 1980s, the national and regional trend appears relatively flat, with the region slightly less than 50% of the national market for mechanical.

Exhibit 13 shows the national and regional tonnage for structural for the same years. In 1986, nationwide, 639,982 tons were consumed, with 523,400 tons of that consumed in the region. In 1988, the national and regional totals were 793,645 and 581,100 tons, respectively. Finally, for 1990, comparing 1989 national and 1990 regional data, we have 764,682 and 527,000 tons, respectively. Note, that in the seventeen-state region, structural was a far larger percentage of the national market than mechanical. Exhibit 11 shows that for both categories of piping and tubing, the region was about 55–56% of the national market in the 1980s. However, this figure hides the fact that regional consumption of structural was a far larger percentage of the national (73%) than mechanical. Note, the long-term trend for structural tonnage appears to be rising at about 3.5%, while the mechanical trend was slightly negative (-1.5%). Therefore, the structural market was expanding compared to the mechanical market and also was relatively strong in the region compared to the nation (see Exhibit 14).

Exhibit 6

National Steel Production Data in Tons

Year	U.S. Steel Mill Produc. Total Shipments	U.S. Raw Steel Produc. Net Tons	U.S. Capacity Utilization	AISI Carbon Mechan. Produc.	AISI Carbon Struct. Produc.
1973	111,430	150,799	*	1,092,843	543,642
1974	109,472	145,720	*	1,005,053	409,921
1975	79,957	116,642	76.20	755,530	258,003
1976	89,447	128,000	80.90	813,331	297,434
1977	91,147	125,333	78.40	889,769	289,707
1978	97,935	137,031	86.80	964,425	421,284
1979	100,262	136,341	87.80	965,812	539,778
1980	83,853	111,835	72.80	740,117	568,389
1981	88,450	120,828	78.30	848,183	596,038
1982	61,567	74,577	48.40	483,080	299,057
1983	67,584	84,615	56.20	489,457	236,949
1984	73,739	92,526	68.40	601,992	269,587
1985	73,043	88,259	66.10	529,554	218,515
1986	70,263	81,606	63.80	492,331	169,741
1987	76,654	89,151	79.50	513,996	180,198
1988	83,840	99,924	89.20	563,196	177,960
1989	92,320	97,868	107.20	513,946	120,619
1990	93,793	95,858	105.90	571,174	137,111
1991	*	*	101.90	478,725	150,835

Sources: Steel Mill Products, MH33B, U.S. Bureau of Census, 1973–1991; Annual Statistical Reports, American Iron and Steel Institute (AISI), 1973–1991; Economic Indicators, Prepared for the Joint Economic Committee by the Council of Economic Advisors, 1973–1991.

*Date not available.

AISI Imports Carbon and Alloy Mech.	*AISI Imports Carbon and Alloy Struct.*	*Census Bureau Carbon Struct. Pipe & Tube*	*Census Bureau Carbon Mech. Pipe & Tube*
*	*	*	*
*	*	*	*
*	*	*	*
*	*	*	*
*	*	*	*
*	*	*	*
*	*	7	*
*	*	814,069	1,821,521
*	*	860,028	1,958,927
49,424	*	525,357	1,485,260
40,124	186,621	541,119	1,702,329
283,248	320,691	639,982	1,977,482
328,251	502,112	669,125	1,754,440
237,247	479,768	793,643	1,751,900
283,619	428,758	764,682	2,087,359
381,682	278,870	*	*
281,059	323,921	828,507	2,414,320
186,243	275,435	917,665	2,399,401
169,833	209,826	*	*

End-Use Industries: Mechanical Piping and Tubing 
Exhibit 7

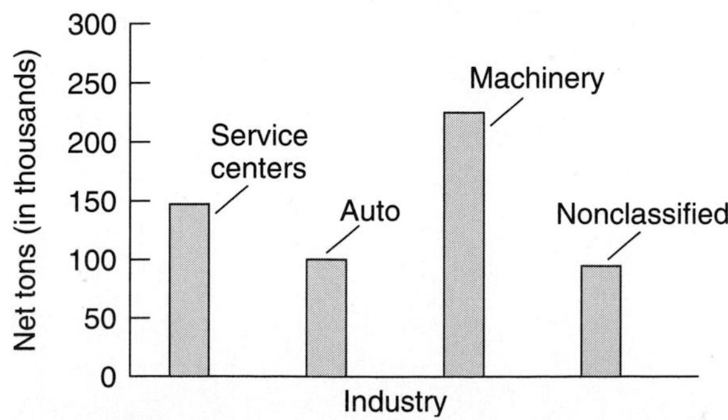

Source: Annual Statistical Report, American Iron and Steel Institute, 1991.

Exhibit 8 **Shipments of Steel Mill Products by Market Classification, Mechanical Piping and Tubing (in tons)**

Year	*Steel for Convert. Process*	*Steel Service Centers Dist.*	*Const. & Maint.*	*Con-tractors Product*	*Auto-motive*	*Rail Trans.*	*Aircraft & Aero-space*	*Oil & Gas*	*Mining Quarry & Lum-bering*	*Agri-culture*
1973	7,425	275,836	50,900	28,940	278,964	3,155	1,591	26,139	2,979	25,611
1974	12,253	294,218	67,510	27,849	223,462	4,085	1,458	30,605	3,492	22,382
1975	10,956	249,771	1,373	34,772	177,853	2,099	1,580	43,899	5,180	19,935
1976	9,199	194,651	15,510	19,057	232,617	12,562	1,796	34,956	3,991	25,013
1977	12,352	239,176	3,784	30,377	253,911	2,333	1,652	49,660	2,793	23,824
1978	4,758	276,188	4,807	35,811	252,935	2,892	2,024	64,110	4,378	24,636
1979	6,706	319,044	6,557	6,557	203,927	6,659	2,111	62,531	4,016	31,915
1980	4,369	221,104	6,779	42,039	106,183	2,014	2,664	73,867	4,534	22,108
1981	9,364	303,100	9,533	49,185	124,818	934	1,623	126,974	3,895	18,149
1982	2,396	133,427	6,862	9,185	88,948	317	1,695	72,115	2,379	10,525
1983	4,901	139,096	4,768	5,597	120,402	280	1,173	14,088	1,076	9,202
1984	5,933	211,474	6,533	15,344	126,676	811	1,052	31,068	1,280	9,371
1985	3,894	205,647	6,033	12,840	127,385	761	1,102	35,181	796	11,560
1986	4,241	146,266	9,858	4,713	134,427	541	1,330	16,559	1,041	11,235
1987	12,590	178,281	8,081	4,055	130,360	574	1,326	8,373	1,648	18,993
1988	17,785	195,403	16,319	5,952	151,093	679	1,251	25,437	1,887	13,899
1989	14,263	148,671	13,073	9,385	141,616	720	920	28,503	467	11,187
1990	27,713	165,890	12,929	4,201	137,030	424	959	52,538	555	15,542
1991	25,710	140,701	8,987	3,330	122,050	252	996	32,797	353	13,095

Source: Annual Statistical Reports, American Iron and Steel Institute (AISI), 1973–1991.

*Data not available.

Machine Industr. Equipt. Tools	Elect. Equip.	Appli-ances Utensils & Cutlery	Other Domestic & Commerc. Equipt.	Con-tainer Pack. & Ship. Mater.	Ord-nance & Other Military	Export	Non-Classi-fied	Total Carbon & Alloy	Total Only Carbon
412,310	34,272	8,665	18,342	435	3,547	14,034	391,627	1,585,078	1,092,843
418,088	5,022	6,730	15,608	1,151	4,239	17,836	346,652	1,503,110	1,005,053
349,615	3,702	6,880	7,917	6,908	4,233	12,716	262,832	1,202,427	755,530
354,176	5,384	6,398	12,115	4,047	3,184	10,502	314,300	1,259,891	813,331
372,433	4,910	7,609	16,693	141	3,241	12,124	324,596	1,361,692	889,769
405,614	6,418	4,920	16,133	144	2,304	15,688	356,052	1,479,951	964,425
423,451	5,365	4,764	16,215	620	2,796	25,476	353,245	1,506,810	965,812
333,266	3,886	4,941	15,181	1,379	2,417	23,028	289,446	1,159,404	740,117
330,934	3,583	5,645	18,552	5,660	2,111	23,495	310,168	1,347,820	848,183
166,026	2,713	4,033	13,554	2,452	1,945	17,360	226,248	762,256	483,080
190,821	3,433	4,757	16,260	2	2,257	14,676	214,491	*	*
262,629	3,126	5,220	14,999	1,655	1,653	20,309	218,537	940,186	601,992
183,995	4,302	5,546	14,941	1,457	2,196	19,590	174,010	811,615	529,554
201,680	4,324	8,432	15,259	0	4,445	17,398	166,601	748,439	492,331
219,965	3,659	8,122	19,593	64	6,483	10,092	134,486	766,987	513,996
280,397	2,681	9,617	14,892	66	4,765	15,524	143,414	901,272	563,196
244,594	1,542	9,567	20,055	0	4,561	19,771	140,433	806,301	513,996
229,512	3,240	6,800	18,915	0	5,990	19,814	164,631	862,773	571,174
199,526	2,354	4,818	21,157	0	1,222	15,345	153,498	743,924	478,725

End-User Industries: Structural Piping and Tubing — Exhibit 9

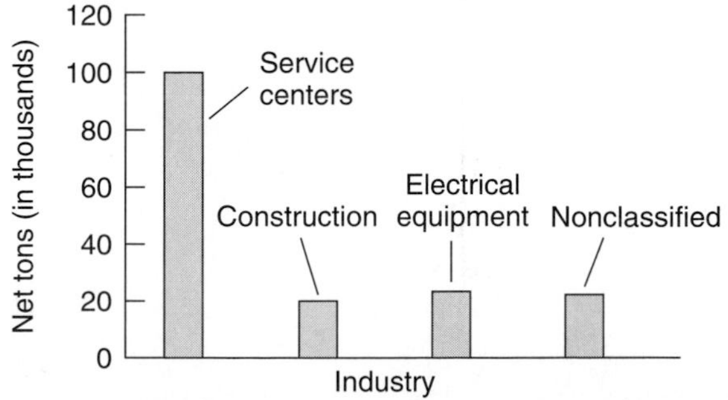

Source: Annual Statistical Report, American Iron and Steel Institute, 1991.

Exhibit 10 **Shipments of Steel Mill Products by Market Classification, Structural Pipe and Tube Markets**

Year	Steel for Convert. Process	Steel Service Centers Dist.	Const. Inc. Mainten.	Con-tractor Product	Auto-motive	Rail Trans.	Ship-building	Aircraft & Aero-space	Oil & Gas	Mining Quarry & Lum-bering
1973	1,908	338,001	118,488	17,130	596	95	191	*	10,657	536
1974	14,202	228,881	99,268	16,365	301	303	112	*	6,239	152
1975	627	175,258	25,769	14,227	339	184	149	*	3,020	690
1976	1,110	143,437	29,355	8,457	526	157	66	*	61,507	*
1977	469	147,856	23,666	8,417	503	164	*	*	58,906	13
1978	12,864	196,814	17,838	8,449	552	283	80	*	92,528	213
1979	2,968	268,776	21,386	8,466	1,836	775	*	*	143,261	316
1980	1,195	239,552	33,555	3,994	1,148	1,706	127	22	196,924	*
1981	1,005	276,107	46,942	3,278	704	493	401	21	184,867	*
1982	1,899	153,317	10,438	2,016	450	1,320	435	*	58,782	*
1983	1,695	141,976	24,816	833	1,690	65	12,508	*	27,899	49
1984	1,720	118,725	35,895	199	1,439	217	509	*	53,260	*
1985	1,299	80,130	44,610	186	628	96	*	*	53,738	*
1986	159	85,996	41,687	174	28	21	*	*	7,700	*
1987	809	61,781	64,746	875	*	*	*	*	6,746	*
1988	127	100,715	20,905	717	*	*	*	*	1,439	*
1989	204	79,154	22,507	1,235	2	*	*	*	1,230	*
1990	*	75,536	21,364	3,063	69	*	*	*	15,648	*
1991	89	123,844	*	2,528	*	*	*	*	15,204	*

Source: Annual Statistical Reports, American Iron and Steel Institute (AISI), 1973–1991.

*Data not available.

Agri-culture	Machin. Industr. Equipt. Tools	Elect. Equip.	Appli-ances Utensils & Cutlery	Other Domestic & Commer. Equipt.	Con-tainer Pack. & Shipp. Mater.	Ord-nance & Other Military	Export	Non-classi-fied	Total Carbon & Alloy	Total Only Carbon
13,993	1,122	2,719	*	2,214	*	*	9,562	30,488	547,700	*
12,572	490	2,673	*	541	1,232	*	4,187	23,472	410,990	*
15,026	1,380	1,313	21	844	*	*	490	18,880	258,217	*
18,908	1,516	1,768	*	1,043	*	*	2,470	27,849	298,169	*
18,876	1,451	1,792	*	490	*	*	1,466	25,967	290,036	*
19,279	1,690	20,790	*	965	1,051	*	3,100	46,229	422,725	*
17,503	2,204	24,920	7	1,951	745	*	2,168	43,702	540,984	*
12,422	1,446	25,561	*	591	811	*	729	49,657	569,440	*
8,560	1,071	31,878	*	281	2,465	*	305	39,323	597,701	*
3,956	463	20,957	*	247	1,733	*	*	45,036	301,049	*
3,715	525	10,932	*	468	*	*	9	10,278	*	*
7,442	3,630	3,013	*	87	698	*	5	42,380	270,119	*
7,948	11,702	15,296	*	475	*	*	64	2,688	218,860	*
2,503	5,650	31,582	*	114	*	*	*	1,954	177,568	*
74	4	31,779	*	3,383	*	*	*	10,001	180,198	*
1,649	7,497	23,231	*	218	*	*	196	21,266	177,960	*
2,503	1,922	432	*	102	*	*	250	11,166	120,619	*
4,118	3,240	466	*	209	*	*	333	13,060	137,111	*
4,691	3,428	485	*	128	*	*	481	0	150,835	*

Exhibit 11

17-State Region Share of Total Market

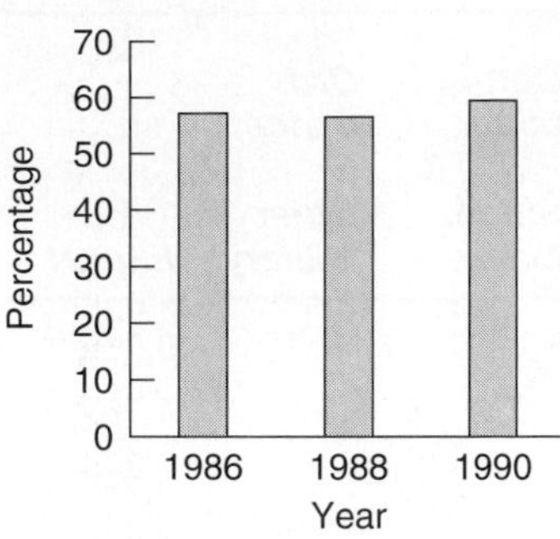

Source: Marshall, Hendon, Minter & Associates, Inc. 1991.

Exhibit 12

Mechanical Piping and Tubing

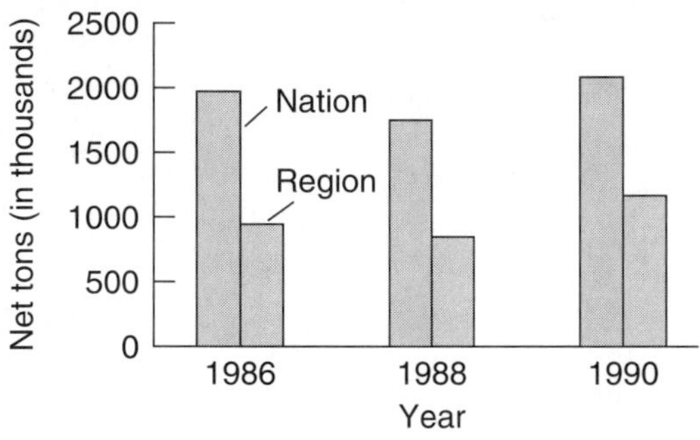

Source: Marshall, Hendon, Minter & Associates, Inc. 1991.

Exhibit 13

Structural Piping and Tubing

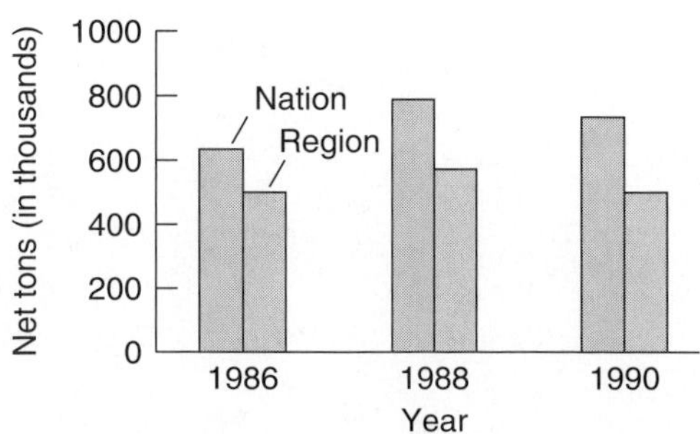

Source: Marshall, Hendon, Minter & Associates, Inc. 1991.

Exhibit 14

Tons of Structural and Mechanical Piping and Tubing Shipped and the Amount as a Percentage of Total Shipments

	Total 1986	*Percent of 1986 Total*	*Total 1988*	*Percent of 1988 Total*	*Total 1990*	*Percent of 1990 Total*
Northern District						
West Virginia						
Structural	19,300	1.30	21,800	1.53	20,100	1.19
Mechanical	39,500	2.67	33,000	2.31	44,800	2.65
Total	58,800	3.97	54,800	3.84	64,900	3.84
Indiana						
Structural	80,300	5.42	89,800	6.29	86,200	5.10
Mechanical	266,800	18.02	238,600	16.71	323,600	19.15
Total	347,100	23.44	328,400	23.00	409,800	24.25
Ohio						
Structural	34,100	2.30	39,000	2.73	36,000	2.13
Mechanical	104,700	7.07	94,500	6.62	131,000	7.75
Total	138,800	9.37	133,500	9.35	167,000	9.88
Kentucky						
Structural	8,300	0.56	9,400	0.66	8,600	0.51
Mechanical	10,650	0.72	9,500	0.67	13,000	0.77
Total	18,950	1.28	18,900	1.33	21,600	1.28
District total	563,650	38.06	535,600	37.52	663,300	39.25
Southwest District						
Texas						
Structural	89,000	5.94	83,700	6.12	68,000	4.08
Mechanical	115,500	7.80	102,200	7.16	142,400	8.43
Total	204,500	13.74	185,900	13.28	210,400	12.51
Oklahoma						
Structural	19,300	1.30	20,500	1.44	17,500	1.04
Mechanical	17,100	1.15	14,500	1.02	19,400	1.15
Total	36,400	2.45	35,000	2.46	36,900	2.19
Louisiana						
Structural	18,200	1.23	19,300	1.35	17,800	1.05
Mechanical	25,600	1.73	23,300	1.63	32,400	1.92
Total	43,800	2.96	42,600	2.98	50,200	2.97
Arkansas						
Structural	12,500	0.84	14,200	0.99	13,800	0.78
Mechanical	22,300	1.45	19,100	1.27	24,600	1.46
Total	34,800	2.29	33,300	2.26	38,400	2.24
District total	319,500	21.44	296,800	20.98	335,900	19.91

Continued

Exhibit 14

Tons of Structural and Mechanical Piping and Tubing Shipped and the Amount as a Percentage of Total Shipments (continued)

	Total 1986	*Percent of 1986 Total*	*Total 1988*	*Percent of 1988 Total*	*Total 1990*	*Percent of 1990 Total*
Northwest District						
Missouri						
Structural	30,800	2.08	37,400	2.62	34,500	2.04
Mechanical	63,000	4.25	51,600	3.61	73,800	4.37
Total	93,800	6.33	89,000	6.23	108,300	6.41
Kansas						
Structural	15,200	1.03	17,200	1.20	15,800	0.93
Mechanical	21,800	1.47	19,500	1.37	26,400	1.56
Total	37,000	2.50	36,700	2.57	42,200	2.49
District total	130,800	8.83	125,700	8.80	150,500	8.59
Southeastern District						
South Carolina						
Structural	22,000	1.49	24,800	1.77	23,300	1.38
Mechanical	17,900	1.14	15,200	1.06	20,700	1.22
Total	39,900	2.63	40,000	2.83	44,000	2.60
North Carolina						
Structural	32,300	2.18	36,700	2.57	33,800	2.00
Mechanical	37,900	2.56	34,200	2.40	46,900	2.77
Total	70,200	4.74	70,900	4.97	80,700	4.77
Georgia						
Structural	28,600	1.93	34,000	2.38	32,000	1.89
Mechanical	65,200	4.40	58,600	4.10	81,500	4.82
Total	93,800	6.33	92,600	6.48	113,500	6.71
Florida						
Structural	50,400	3.40	59,200	4.01	55,600	3.11
Mechanical	50,200	3.39	42,800	3.00	59,300	3.45
Total	100,600	6.79	102,000	7.01	114,900	6.56
District total	304,500	20.49	305,500	21.29	353,100	20.64

Continued

Tons of Structural and Mechanical Piping and Tubing Shipped and the Amount as a Percentage of Total Shipments (continued) **Exhibit 14**

	Total 1986	*Percent of 1986 Total*	*Total 1988*	*Percent of 1988 Total*	*Total 1990*	*Percent of 1990 Total*
Southcentral District						
Mississippi						
Structural	27,800	1.88	31,200	2.19	29,100	1.72
Mechanical	50,200	3.39	42,000	2.94	57,000	3.37
Total	78,000	5.27	73,200	5.13	86,100	5.09
Tennessee						
Structural	13,800	0.93	15,600	1.09	14,400	0.85
Mechanical	11,700	0.79	11,300	0.79	15,600	0.92
Total	25,500	1.72	26,900	1.88	30,000	1.77
Alabama						
Structural	22,500	1.52	25,200	1.77	23,200	1.37
Mechanical	39,300	2.65	37,600	2.63	51,800	3.06
Total	61,800	4.17	62,800	4.40	75,000	4.43
District total	165,300	10.71	162,900	11.41	191,100	11.29

Source: Marshall, Hendon, Minter & Associates, Inc., 1991.

CASE 9

Del Rio Foods, Inc.

Hooshang Kuklan, Cecil Chacon, North Carolina Central University

BACKGROUND

Del Rio Foods, Inc., is a farm and processed foods company established in 1933 (Exhibits 1, 2, 3). Del Rio is the result of a marriage of two California land holders, Maria Sanchez and Bob Gilly, in 1932. Maria Sanchez is descended from the old-time Spanish settlers. Her family owned about two thousand acres of farm land. She had, since the death of her father, managed the ranch and farms singlehandedly. Maria is the sole surviving heir of the Sanchez family.

Bob Gilly's family also owned large agricultural holdings in the central valley of California on the San Joaquin River. Bob is of Irish origin. His father had started with only a hundred-acre farm, but had expanded into a three-thousand-acre agricultural enterprise. Bob grew up working in the fields. In 1931, he graduated from the University of California at Davis with a degree in agricultural sciences.

Soon after Bob and Maria were married, Bob's father was forced to relinquish the entire operation to Bob because of his rapidly deteriorating health. Late in 1933, Bob's father died. Subsequently, Bob and Maria incorporated the two businesses under the name of Del Rio Foods, Inc.

The 1930s were difficult times because of a worldwide depression. Bob and Maria worked long and hard hours to keep the farm solvent. Many farmers could not meet their financial obligations. Del Rio, however, managed to survive and even experience small growth during this time. They had many long-time loyal employees, and Bob's balanced agricultural background, which had come from both formal training and practical experience, proved to be a real asset during this period.

This case is intended for classroom discussion only, not to depict effective or ineffective handling of administrative situations. All rights reserved to the authors.

Exhibit 1

Del Rio Foods, Inc.: Consolidated Balance Sheets (in thousands of dollars)

	1989	*1990*
Assets		
Current assets		
Cash	276	203
Accounts receivable	1,383	1,721
Inventories		
Raw materials	779	803
Work in process	112	145
Finished goods	523	601
Total	3,073	3,473
Property, plant, and equipment		
Land	5,473	5,603
Buildings	789	821
Equipment	2,424	2,615
Total	8,686	9,039
Other assets		
Notes and interest receivable	104	153
Total assets	11,863	12,665
Liabilities and Stockholders' Equity		
Current liabilities		
Notes payable	793	621
Accounts payable	1,872	2,002
Taxes, including income taxes	1,363	1,484
Total	4,028	4,107
Stockholders' equity		
Common stock	2,795	3,121
Retained earnings	5,040	5,437
Total	7,835	8,558
Total liabilities and shareholders' equity	11,863	12,665

One day in the summer of 1940, Bob and Maria went to San Francisco to visit Antonio Carla, Bob's former agricultural business instructor. Bob and Antonio have long been friends. Antonio is a third generation Californian whose family also held extensive agricultural holdings. Antonio told the Gillys how his family had integrated their wine business to include, not only the growing of grapes, but also wine making, bottling, and marketing the final product. Antonio told Bob that the business researchers at Stanford felt that California would soon be the agricultural center of North America. Antonio urged the Gillys to consider diversifying into the food processing business and perhaps even consider marketing their products on a national basis.

On the return trip home, Bob and Maria's conversation crackled with excitement about the possibility of diversifying. It was 1940 and the economy was rapidly improving. They both agreed the time was right. Del Rio had for years sold produce to a cannery in El Rio. Bob had previously talked to the owner

Del Rio Foods, Inc.: Condensed Income Statement (in thousands of dollars) **Exhibit 2**

	1987	*1988*	*1989*	*1990*
Sales	19,264	19,470	21,065	21,706
Less cost to produce	9,613	10,082	11,016	11,156
Gross margin	9,651	9,388	10,049	10,550
Total operating expenses	7,394	6,956	7,460	7,872
Net operating income	2,257	2,432	2,589	2,678
Income taxes				
Federal	1,012	1,150	1,185	1,225
State and local	306	273	336	344
Net Income	939	1,009	1,068	1,109

about selling. The owner was old and in poor health. Bob was familiar with the plant and knew it to be clean and well maintained.

During the following month, Bob inspected the cannery in El Rio three times and hired several consultants to give advice. After three months of negotiation, Del Rio mortgaged 2,500 acres of farm land and closed the deal. The acquisition assured Del Rio of the continued availability of canning capacity.

In 1941, Bob was able to win a contract to produce canned food products for the U.S. military. World War II was a blessing in disguise for Del Rio Foods, Inc. During the war, thousands of people migrated into California. The demand for agricultural produce was at an all time high. The demand for canned products was also at its highest point in history. In 1944, the Del Rio cannery was expanded and another cannery in Pasa Robles was built. The new facility was ultra modern and highly efficient.

Maria gradually became less active in the management of Del Rio Foods as the company grew and as Bob hired more experts. In 1954, Maria gave birth to their only child, whom they named Alvarez.

The fifties and sixties were growth years for the U.S. economy, and Del Rio shared in this growth. The company purchased another food processing facility. Bob still ran the company even though he had many experts on the staff. Bob looked forward to the day when his son Alvarez would share the management role.

Their son never really developed the work ethic Bob and Maria had in the 1930s. Bob and Maria had made him work on the farm in the summer when he was young, but after becoming a teenager he was primarily interested in expensive cars, clothes, and parties. Bob hoped though that he would someday realize where his future was and become devoted to Del Rio.

In 1978, Alvarez graduated from a small California college with a business degree. Alvarez had not been a good student in college and had been dismissed from Cal Davis and UCLA. Alvarez joined Del Rio Foods, Inc., in 1979 after a six-month graduation vacation in which he toured several countries. He worked primarily in the financial planning unit under the vice president for administration and finance (Exhibit 3). As time went on, he began to take on more responsibility and grow in maturity.

Exhibit 3 **Del Rio Foods, Inc.**

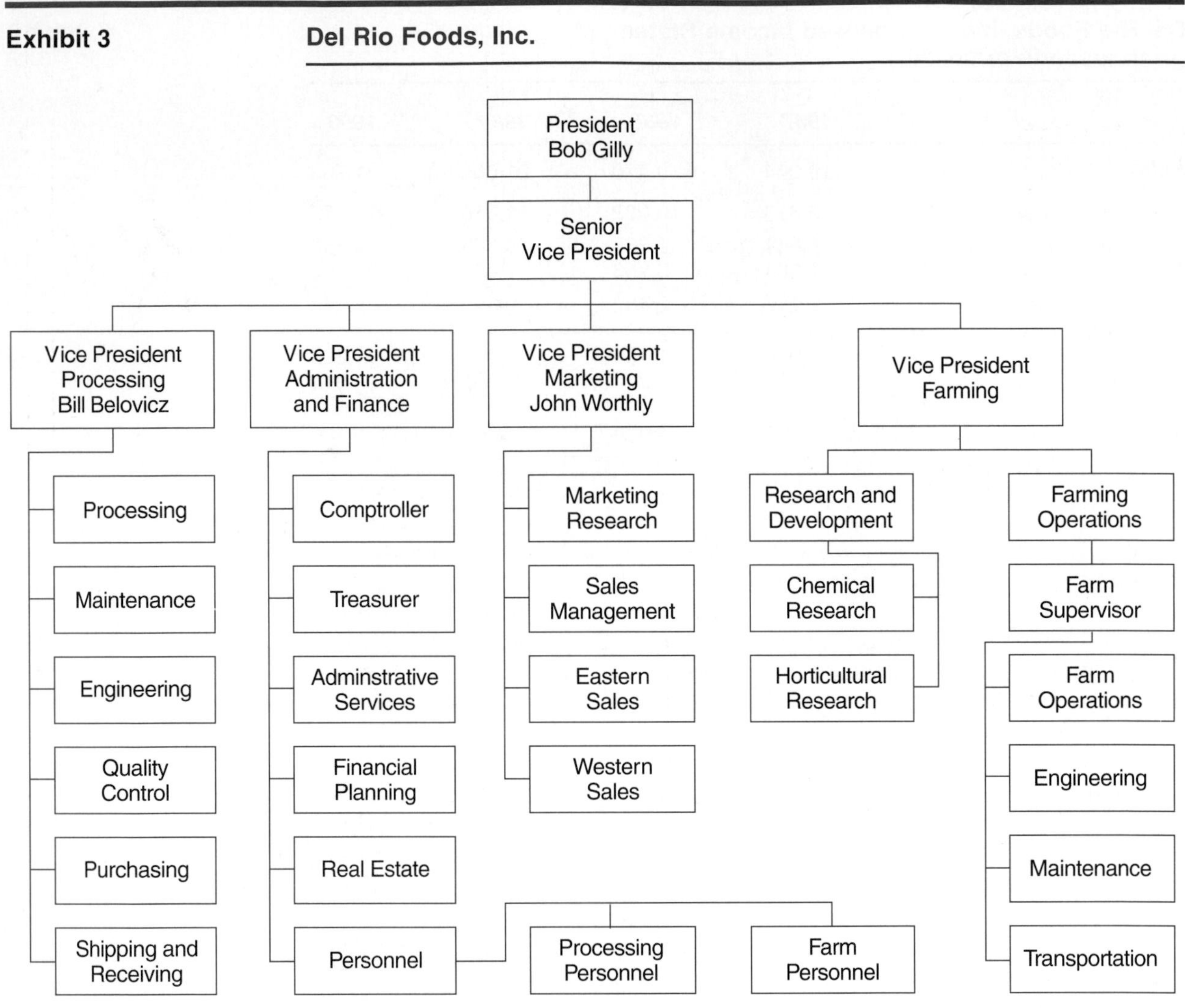

EAST COAST EXPANSION

On a trip to Atlanta in 1977, Bob had signed an exclusive distributorship agreement with a large retail grocery chain in the Southeast. Prior to this, Del Rio had only dealt with wholesalers in the East. The new venture turned out well and Bob was very interested in gaining greater access to the eastern market. High transportation cost and quality control of such a distant market was a concern. Bob had discussed with some of his top managers and Maria the possibility of purchasing some processing capacity in the Southeast. They all agreed that it was well worth exploring.

In 1991, a member of the management team returned from a trip to the East with a list of several processing plants that could be purchased. One was located in Richmond, Virginia, one in Columbia, South Carolina, and one in Wilmington, North Carolina. Bob called together a meeting of the top managers in processing for a discussion of the locations. The group sent the two managers in charge of planning and real estate to visit the locations and study the possibilities. The following week, the two managers returned with the recommendation that Del Rio either build or buy in Wilmington, a rapidly growing area, the home of a university and a deep-water port. Owning a processing plant in Wilmington would mitigate transportation cost to ocean terminals. The managers talked with the owner of Cape Fear Processing and Canning Co. in Wilmington, and he informed them the plant was for sale. The asking price was $2,000,000.

Bob had never given Alvarez any direct responsibility in decision making on any major project. The intended expansion into the Southeast seemed to be an ideal project to break Alvarez into the high-level decision-making area. Bob envisioned opening a large operation in the East just as he had done in California years before. He remembered how exciting it had been for him and Maria, and he hoped that Alvarez would become just as excited about the Wilmington operation. That night over dinner Bob revealed his plans for Alvarez to Maria. He told her that he wished to gain a large market share in the Southeast by opening a processing plant there. He informed her that he wished to capture a large segment of the processing facilities and then perhaps to expand into agricultural production in the future. He planned to eventually make Alvarez the manager of the entire eastern operations. He felt that this would perhaps prepare him for the top job at Del Rio someday.

The next day, Bob informed Alvarez of his plans. Alvarez had indeed matured and was anxious to assume more responsibility. Alvarez was to go to Wilmington and inspect every aspect of the processing plant. Bob told him to pay special attention to the following:

1. The community, parks, recreation facilities, and schools.
2. The local economy, and the availability and cost of energy.
3. The local labor situation, wages, unions, and educational levels.
4. The local and state of North Carolina tax situation.
5. The agricultural situation and practices.
6. Every single aspect of the Cape Fear plant, both historical and future projections.

Bob told Alvarez to use any resources that Del Rio had available to reach a sound decision on whether or not to buy the Cape Fear plant.

CAPE FEAR PROCESSING AND CANNING COMPANY

The Cape Fear Processing and Canning Company in Wilmington, North Carolina, had been started in 1945 and was solely owned by Bob Jones. Bob Jones had been serving as the president of the company since its inception with four vice presidents reporting to him: a VP of administration, overseeing financial management and personnel; a VP of engineering, in charge of the technical aspects of the plant; a VP of marketing; and a VP of operations, supervising manufacturing, quality control, purchasing, and shipping and receiving (Exhibit 4). Bob Jones was 64 years old and wished to enjoy the rest of his years with his ailing wife, without the worry of business decisions. The plant employed 91 people and had been doing fairly well during most of its years since 1945 (Exhibits 5 and 6).

Exhibit 4 Cape Fear Processing and Canning Company

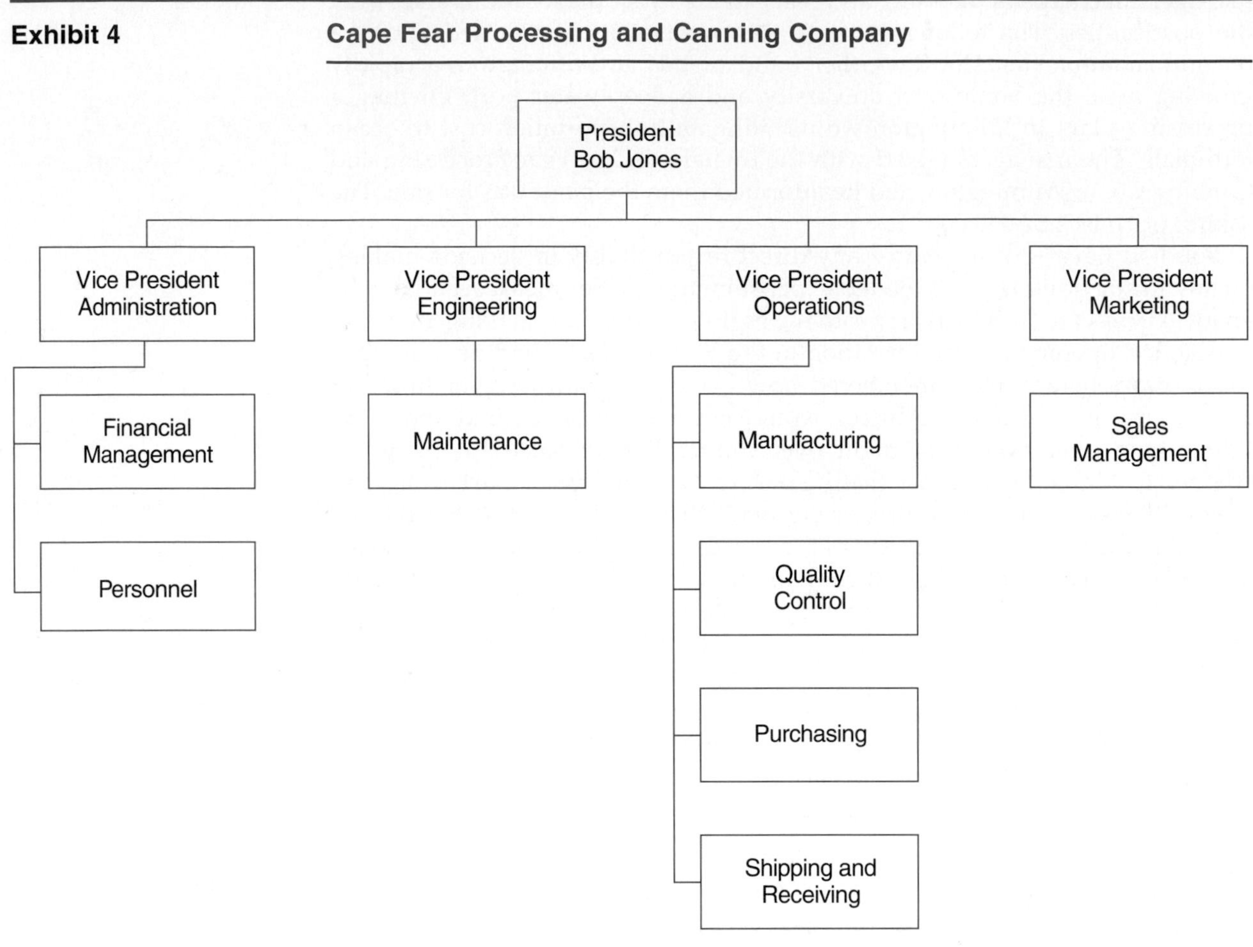

Alvarez flew to Wilmington to investigate the plant for possible purchase. He took with him two young Del Rio officers. One was an accountant from the comptroller's office and the other a finance specialist from the financial planning unit (Exhibit 3). The trio spent two weeks looking over the situation at the Cape Fear processing and canning facility. All three agreed that a good evaluation and projection could be made by using the past and present financial data. Besides visiting the plant, the party managed to take in the sights and sounds of the local beaches. Alvarez visited the nuclear power plant at Southport, a few miles south of Wilmington, and the port facilities in downtown Wilmington. He was very favorably impressed by these and also by all the greenery of the area, which was so different from the hills of California.

After several days of study, the three young executives came to the conclusion that they had a good grasp of the financial situation of Cape Fear and that it seemed to be a good deal. They noticed that the plant did not seem as clean or as well maintained as the California plants they had visited, but they concluded that the positive aspects outweighed the negative. They had taken two extensive tours of the facilities, once with the marketing manager and again with Bob Jones' attractive young secretary. Bob Jones was very helpful

Cape Fear Processing and Canning Company: Consolidated Balance Sheets (in thousands of dollars) **Exhibit 5**

	1989	*1990*
Assets		
Current assets		
Cash	55	48
Accounts receivable	291	310
Inventories		
Raw materials	105	110
Work in process	62	65
Finished goods	131	142
Total	644	675
Property, plant, equipment		
Land	102	111
Buildings	185	192
Equipment	284	276
Total	571	579
Total assets	1,215	1,254
Liabilities		
Current liabilities		
Notes payable	68	72
Accounts payable	253	261
Total	321	333
Owner's equity		
Robert Jones, capital	894	921
Total liabilities and owner's equity	1,215	1,254

and gave them a free hand to inspect any pertinent records or visit any part of the operation. Alvarez called in a statistician from the marketing research department of the Del Rio home office to do a statistical analysis of trends and projections. The statistician suggested that Alvarez call in someone from the agricultural department and an industrial engineer, but Alvarez had heard that a company from New York was planning on visiting the plant in a week to make an inspection for possible purchase. He was afraid that, if he did not act quickly, Del Rio might get into a bidding war with the New York firm. All of the group agreed that the plant seemed to be worth the asking price.

The next day, the group returned to California. Bob asked Alvarez to address a meeting of the top level managers and present his findings and proposals. The following day Alvarez was sitting in his office and pondering over the presentation that he had to make in a few minutes to the Del Rio board of managers regarding the purchase of the Cape Fear plant. For a moment, he felt a troubling sense of uneasiness. His mind wondered about the gravity of the recommendation that he was just about to make. It dawned upon him that this was his very first major decision. What if the Cape Fear plant was not really a good addition for Del Rio? He reviewed in his mind what led him to believe

Exhibit 6

Cape Fear Processing and Canning Company: Condensed Income Statement (in thousands of dollars)

	1987	*1988*	*1989*	*1990*
Sales	2,115	2,121	2,168	2,213
Less cost of goods sold	801	809	812	820
Gross margin	1,314	1,312	1,356	1,393
Operating expenses				
Wages	785	792	811	817
Salaries	198	201	209	214
Maintenance	112	120	126	135
Other	68	61	71	74
Total operating expenses	1,163	1,174	1,217	1,240
Net income	151	138	139	153

that the acquisition of the Cape Fear plant was a good expansion for Del Rio. The financial picture at Cape Fear looked quite good. The plant was successfully in operation for about forty years. Wilmington was a very favorable location in the East. The time was of particular essence. Any delay in making the final decision might give the New York-based firm a chance to purchase the Cape Fear plant. Alvarez was convinced that though the plant did not look up to par from a technical point of view, some face-lifting and renovation could remedy the situation. Alvarez felt that sooner or later he had to begin making important decisions at Del Rio. He wanted to show other Del Rio executives that he had what it took to make major decisions.

Alvarez lifted his head and his eyes caught the time on the clock on the wall in front of him. It was time for him to go to the board meeting. Alvarez shook his head, stood up, took a deep breath, picked up the Cape Fear folder which was sitting on his desk, and marched toward the conference room.

In the meeting, Bob immediately turned the floor over to Alvarez and looked on proudly. Alvarez said:

> As you all know, I have just come back from a visit to Wilmington, North Carolina, where we examined Cape Fear Processing and Canning Company for possible purchase. In this visit, I headed a team of four Del Rio personnel. I would like to briefly share with you now some of the findings and observations of the team and also our recommendation.
>
> From a financial point of view, the purchase will yield a return on investment of about 8 to 10 percent based on the performance of the Cape Fear plant in 1991 and depending on the final selling price which will be agreed upon. There is the possibility of some owner financing at 8 percent for up to 20 percent of the purchase price. This would be in the form of a five-year balloon payment including both the principal and the interest. Considering the present high interest rate, this certainly is a positive point. During the past four years, Cape Fear's rate of return on sales has been approximately 7 percent. Despite the rather low returns on investment and sales, and the fact that there has been no appreciable increase in their sales and net income from 1988 to 1991, we believe that with Del Rio's management, experience, and expertise, we should be able to improve sales and the profit margin steadily.

> In our judgment, the Cape Fear plant enjoys a sound current and long-run financial position. The working capital has been about $323,000 and $343,000 for 1990 and 1991, respectively. The firm seems to have adequate financial strength to meet its short-term obligations. Their current ratio for 1990 and 1991 has remained basically the same at the comfortable level of about two. The acid test ratio for both of these years has been at the satisfactory level of slightly over one.
>
> From a long-run point of view, the debt/asset and equity/asset ratios for 1990 and 1991 show that only slightly over one-fourth of assets has been financed by debt leaving an equity of about 75 percent. We also note that the debt/equity ratio is about 36 percent. These are all indications that the firm is in a sound long-run financial position.
>
> The team's overall recommendation is to continue our negotiations with Bob Jones, the owner of the Cape Fear Company, to finalize the purchase price and other terms of the agreement. He has agreed to stay on at the Cape Fear plant during the transition.

Alvarez stopped and looked around the table to see if there were any questions or comments. Some executives had reservations about expanding into the Southeast and several had reservations about Alvarez's inexperience. But they were all impressed with his positive presentation and remained silent. Each executive knew that Bob Gilly was grooming Alvarez for the top job someday. They were reluctant to voice opposition toward their future boss. Many of these men had been with the company for over twenty years and they had come to respect Bob Gilly's business instincts.

After a short pause, Bill Belovicz, vice president in charge of processing, asked quietly:

> Al, what is your evaluation of the Cape Fear plant from a technical point of view? Their processing facilities, quality control practices, and maintenance procedures? How do you think they compare with our system?

Alvarez replied:

> The Cape Fear plant does not seem to have any significant technical problem. The production and processing facilities appear to need some cleanup and renovation if we decide to bring them up to Del Rio's standards.

Bill Belovicz continued looking in the direction of Alvarez for a few seconds expecting to hear more. As Alvarez offered no more comments, Bill turned his head toward John Worthly, vice president for marketing, who was sitting next to him, and whispered, "Is this the extent of their inspection of the plant? If it is good enough for Bob Gilly, I do not see why we should come between the father and the son and interfere." John looked at Bill, smiled briefly, gave a nod of confirmation, and said in a low voice: "I also had questions for him, but with answers such as the one he gave you, I guess, we can do without."

As no one else asked any questions, Alvarez continued with his financial review of the Cape Fear plant for a few more minutes. When he was finished, Bob Gilly stated that he would keep the managers informed as they continued their negotiations with Bob Jones. He then adjourned the meeting.

That evening, Bob flew Maria into Los Angeles for a movie premiere. On the way back, Maria questioned Bob on the Cape Fear deal. Bob told her that he was impressed with Alvarez's report and that although it contained perhaps too much technical financial analysis, he generally liked the prospects. He told Maria that he and a couple of more experienced executives were going to fly to Wilmington to double check the validity of the information. Maria said:

> Bob, I'm not as active in the business as I once was, but I feel that we should let this be totally Alvarez's decision and not look over his shoulder. From what I've heard, the plant is well priced, and meets many of our needs for market expansion.

The conversation continued for a while and Bob eventually agreed with Maria but with some reluctance.

The next morning Bob informed Alvarez that he was going to act solely on the recommendations from his visit and that he and his mother trusted his opinion entirely. Bob told Alvarez that he would be the new president of the Cape Fear plant, but to count heavily on the expertise of Bob Jones. Alvarez was instructed to spend as much time as possible in Wilmington, North Carolina, but to also keep close touch with the California operations.

Alvarez felt confident that the Cape Fear plant was going to do well. He had thoroughly inspected the financial records. The price seemed to be right. The location was excellent. The Cape Fear plant was going to be Del Rio's long awaited foothold on the East Coast. Three days later, the final deal was consummated with Cape Fear Processing and Canning at a price of $1.85 million. Del Rio became the new owner in December of 1991.

NEW OWNERSHIP

Alvarez immediately assumed the position of president of Cape Fear. Alvarez seemed to have things in control. Cape Fear continued to purchase okra, corn, lima beans, tomatoes, and several other vegetables that were processed, canned and sold to wholesale distributors.

During the first quarter, things generally went well for the new venture. There were no major surprises. Alvarez was very anxious to see the results for the second quarter of 1992, but the news was not good. Net income before taxes dropped by 30 percent. Bob Jones informed Alvarez that this was typical for post-winter months. Alvarez began to become aware of how much he needed to learn about managing a processing plant especially under such new conditions.

The next day, Alvarez flew to California to discuss matters with Bob Gilly. Bob told Alvarez that the Cape Fear plant obviously had some problems that they had overlooked in the investigation. He stated that based on the information provided to him the plant was in trouble and needed an injection of capital. Bob and Alvarez decided to hire a consulting firm from Raleigh, North Carolina, to see exactly what the problems were. Bob told Alvarez to get all of the managers together and try to determine the problems and to propose short-range and long-range solutions.

Alvarez returned to Wilmington and immediately began to institute his father's suggestions. He contracted with a consulting firm, and a team of consultants consisting of five experts in finance, accounting, maintenance, quality control, and industrial engineering arrived in three days. The team was to remain in Wilmington and present their findings and recommendations in two weeks.

Alvarez began the first of a series of regular meetings with the managers. He wanted to establish open and candid communication with the managers and get as much information from them as he could before hearing from the consultants. He was not prepared for what he was about to hear. The maintenance manager was the first to speak. After a brief introduction, he stated that he thought the problem was one of lack of maintenance over the last few years. He went on that the machinery was old and needed constant repair and that he was not being given sufficient resources to do the job. The industrial engineer agreed that this was a major problem. Bob Jones questioned the maintenance manager why he had not brought this to his attention previously. The maintenance manager said that he did not want anyone to think that he was incapable of doing his job.

The agricultural purchasing agent stated that much of the problem was due to a sharp increase in the price of raw materials. He added that the price of fresh produce had been higher this past year in North Carolina due to a decrease in supply caused by a drought. Alvarez asked why farmers did not irrigate. The purchasing agent explained that the majority of farms in the South were small. He stated that most of the larger farms grew tobacco and that the smaller farmers from which they relied on for their supply of fresh produce could not afford the expensive irrigation equipment and had to rely on the weather. Alvarez was unaware of this problem. The agricultural practices of California were very different.

The personnel manager offered that it was hard to motivate the workers to do good work and that some of them wanted to organize a union. He added that part of the problem was the low wages that Cape Fear paid. He said:

> Most applicants have not even finished high school. Absenteeism is very high, especially on Mondays. The pay of regular plant workers is not much higher than the minimum wage. About 50 percent of workers are paid an average of four dollars an hour, 40 percent an average of five dollars an hour, and only 10 percent are paid about five dollars fifty cents per hour.

Alvarez interrupted the personnel director and said quickly:

> I should inform you that my father, as the founder and president of Del Rio, is particularly proud of his employee relations. I can assure you that something will be done quickly about the whole matter. No labor union will ever usurp authority from Del Rio management. Del Rio has always been a wage leader in both canning and farming in California.

The sales manager attributed the sales drop in the last few months to a decrease in quality. He added that an entire load of canned goods was returned recently for poor quality and that Cape Fear might have lost this particular wholesaler permanently. With this statement, all eyes turned to the quality control manager. He confirmed the drop in quality. He said:

> The reasons are many, some of which were mentioned here today. Others include the fact that the plant is not clean and my department is understaffed. We have the same number of inspectors as we did 15 years ago, yet production has doubled during that same time.

He went on to remind the group of how the plant had barely passed the last health department inspection and that there seemed to be a general state of apathy on the processing lines concerning quality. Alvarez seemed baffled. He was gradually realizing the depth and scope of the problems. Del Rio never had any of these problems that he knew of. Bob Jones asked to speak to the group. He told the managers that he was unaware of the intensity of the problems. He apologized for allowing the situation to get so bad, but he reminded the managers that they had not previously brought these problems to his attention. Turning to Alvarez, Bob Jones said in a low voice:

> I admit that I recently did not take as much interest in the business as I did in the past. My wife has been battling with a terminal disease and I knew I was going to sell the plant soon.

CONSULTANTS' PRELIMINARY REPORT

Two weeks later, the consultants met with Alvarez to present the highlights of the preliminary report. In this meeting, Jack Brown, the senior consultant, started the presentation. He said:

> Mr. Gilly, as you know the purpose of this meeting is to keep you informed about what our views and observations are at this time. I will briefly review the highlights of our preliminary report. First, I will name some of the problems that we have identified in various parts of the plant. Then, the options now available will be briefly reviewed. Next, I will share with you some of our preliminary recommendations.
>
> **Financial Outlook**
>
> During the past six years, net income has had no real growth. The overall income has in fact dropped during this period. Real sales have also dropped. The modest increase in sales can account for only one-third of the average inflation rate for this period (Exhibit 5). During the second quarter of this year, net income before taxes decreased by about 30 percent. We believe that under existing conditions the drop in sales and net income will continue.
>
> **Production and Quality Control**
>
> We have found the output and also the input quality control inadequate and ineffective. During the last twelve months, there have been thirty-two cases of complaints about the quality of various products from wholesale and retail customers. According to eye witnesses, substandard raw materials have been accepted from suppliers on fourteen occasions during the same period. We have also discovered that raw materials have repeatedly gone bad while in storage. On four occasions during the last year alone, inadequate supply of some items has either stopped or slowed down production. It should also be noted that the morale among production workers is found to be very low.
>
> **Machinery and Equipment**
>
> The production facilities are too old. About 60 percent of the machinery is semi-obsolete. Further, the facilities are maintained at a substandard level. We have also noticed that the maintenance budget has not increased in proportion to the age of the machinery. It is also important to note that during the last five years, there has practically been no renovation of the production process.
>
> At this time, the critical questions are: What can be done? What are the options? And what is the best way out of this crisis? We believe that there are three basic options: selling the plant as is, repairing it to sell, or repairing and renovating it to keep. Let me briefly review some of the characteristics of these options, the way we see them.
>
> **Sell as Is**
>
> If you decide to sell the plant as is, we estimate the loss to range between 5 to 40 percent of your original purchase price. Moreover, should Del Rio decide to buy

an existing plant or build a new one to replace Cape Fear, the new subsidiary will have to compete with Cape Fear under its new ownership. In addition to the economic loss, selling the plant as is would be an admission of an outright failure and, as such, psychologically damaging particularly to those who were instrumental in putting the deal together.

Repair to Sell

If the intention is to sell the Cape Fear plant, it seems advisable to repair it first. By doing so, the salability of the plant will increase and the estimated loss will be reduced to about 15 to 30 percent of the purchase price. It should be noted that in this case too, the Cape Fear plant under new owners will be a potential source of competition for Del Rio's new operations in the East. Whether the plant is sold as is or it is repaired before it is sold, the loss is irreversible. If the plant is repaired to keep, the cost would be viewed as an expense potentially recoverable in the future.

Repair to Keep

If Del Rio decides to repair, renovate, and keep the plant, the cost is estimated to be approximately $750,000. As I pointed out before, though this amount is considerably higher than the cost under option two, this route has some potential advantages: The cost is not an irreversible loss. Such a major renovation of the plant would bring it up to Del Rio's considerably high standards and minimize future risks. According to our estimate, the cost of building a new plant comparable to a renovated version of Cape Fear will be in the neighborhood of $3 million. Keeping Cape Fear has other advantages such as having established customers, suppliers, and marketing channels. Further, the Cape Fear plant will not become a new source of competition. The employees at Cape Fear have survived under very unfavorable working conditions. Improving the conditions similar to those at Del Rio's plants in California will improve the morale of workers because they can compare the new conditions with the immediate past and appreciate the change.

Which option to adopt depends on whether or not Del Rio still pursues the objective of geographic expansion to the east. If the answer is negative, then the goals should obviously be to sell the Cape Fear plant. If so, we recommend option two. If Del Rio intends to continue its presence in North Carolina, we believe that option three needs to be considered very carefully. Though expensive and troublesome, it offers some advantages which should not be overlooked.

In addition to these observations and suggestions, we also have a few general recommendations. If the decision is to keep the Cape Fear plant we suggest:

- Purchasing the adjacent land which is now for sale for possible future expansion of the Cape Fear plant. This will facilitate Del Rio's long-term objective of expanding its operations to the entire East.
- Purchasing farm lands to grow all or part of the produce needed. This will reduce Cape Fear's dependence on smaller farms which have proven not to be dependable suppliers, and is also quite compatible with Del Rio's practice in California.
- Because of the apparent inadequacies of the process which led to the purchase of the Cape Fear plant, we also recommend developing and installing a systematic, comprehensive, and balanced policy and procedure for acquisition decisions. This would systematize the acquisition process and offer assurances that all pertinent factors are duly considered before future acquisition decisions are made.

During the entire presentation, Alvarez listened very attentively. As Jack Brown completed his presentation and looked at Alvarez for his comments and reactions, Alvarez said quietly: "There will be a general meeting of the managers tomorrow at ten. I would like you to attend this meeting and present your preliminary report."

At a general meeting of Cape Fear, managers held to hear the consultants' report Alvarez was suddenly interrupted to take an emergency telephone call from his mother. She informed Alvarez that, while vacationing in Santa Monica, his father had developed severe chest pains. She explained that the doctors had decided that he had some blockages and may need heart surgery. They had prescribed complete bed rest.

Alvarez turned to the managers and the consultants and offered an apology. He explained about his father's illness. He asked the consultants to continue with their briefing, but before they had a chance to start, the telephone rang again. This time it was the assistant plant manager. Alvarez turned pale as he listened to the message. He slowly hung the phone up and looked mournfully at the group. He said: "A catwalk has collapsed in building two. Four workers have been very seriously injured by the fall and are enroute to New Hanover Memorial Hospital." Alvarez buried his face in his hands and said aloud, "What next?" As he looked up at the group, he paused for a few seconds and then continued in a low voice:

> Due to these tragic developments, I adjourn this meeting until tomorrow at the same time. After hearing our consultants' report, all of you will report to me in a week as to what you believe our options are now and how we can best combat the crises at hand. I have to leave for California today.

THE AFTERMATH

Alvarez returned to California to visit his father. The weight of the decisions affecting the Wilmington plant seemed overbearing. He was pleased to learn that the men injured in the fall were expected to recover. Bob's condition turned out to be not as bad as had been initially thought. Still, doctors advised him to take some time off and temporarily relinquish his duties as CEO of Del Rio.

In two weeks, Bob was out of the hospital and feeling much better. He was anxious to get back into harness. Maria persuaded Bob to take the doctor's advice and vacation for a few months. Bob thought that he could combine business and recovery by moving to the beach near Wilmington, North Carolina. By so doing, he could be available to advise Alvarez as needed, but yet not be involved directly with the stress of day-to-day business decisions. Bob appointed his long-time friend and senior vice president Joseph Funez to chair his position for six months. Del Rio purchased a large beach home on Shell Island (six miles from Wilmington) to be used to entertain visitors. Bob and Maria moved into this house as their temporary residence in the East.

Because of his health, Bob was not yet informed about the seriousness of the problems at the Cape Fear plant. One week after they were settled in the new home, Alvarez decided that it was time to bring his father up-to-date about the situation in Wilmington. One day Alvarez very gradually informed Bob of all the things that were wrong with the Cape Fear plant. As expected, Bob was quite displeased with what Alvarez had to say. That night Bob and Maria walked along the beach and discussed the Wilmington situation and the options that the consultants had suggested. Bob confided in Maria that he was disappointed in Alvarez for not having adequately researched the situation in Wilmington. Maria and Bob agreed that all of the reasons that existed for their expansion into the East Coast were unchanged. Maria knew that if they abandoned their previous decision to expand, then Alvarez's self-confidence would be seriously jeopardized. Bob also hated to just quit something. The next morning, he called Alvarez and told him that they were going to keep the Wilmington plant and remodel it to become a very modern production facility.

Bob wanted to make the plant immaculate. He instructed his son to feel free to call in any expert from California or to hire consultants where necessary. He also told Alvarez to simultaneously explore the possibility of purchasing farm land in North and South Carolina. Bob felt that the recent attacks on smoking would cause a reduction in value of tobacco farm land. Many of the local small farmers were in financial difficulty. Alvarez was instructed to assemble a committee to explore the possibility of further expansion into the Southeast. Bob thought that initially it would be smart to establish a distribution center and later another production facility. Bob also expressed concern over the employee relations in Wilmington. He instructed Alvarez to call in Fred Velarde from the California home office to immediately start work on improving employee relations. Bob's main concern was to get the Wilmington plant repaired and in full production as soon as possible. He knew that Del Rio presently had an edge on any potential competitor. He wanted to maintain this edge and to achieve inroads into the southeastern market without delay.

Within days, Alvarez had the wheels in motion. He was determined to carry out his appointed task with maximum efficiency. Technical experts were being brought in from California and hired locally. Contracts were signed for the purchase of the new equipment and for the renovation of existing structures.

Alvarez spent most of his time in the plant and reported to his father almost daily on the work progress. Bob was very pleased because the engineers had planned the project so that the old plant could operate at approximately 70 percent of capacity during repairs. Within three months, 40 percent of the repair project was completed. Operations were going much better than anyone had expected. Bob Gilly was extremely pleased and began to look forward to greater things for Del Rio.

As Bob's health improved, he began to make frequent trips to California to keep in touch with West Coast operations. During one such trip, he called Alvarez with some disturbing news. Before Bob could deliver the message, however, Alvarez told him that they were well over halfway complete. He informed his father they they should be completely finished in two months. Bob said:

> That's great, son, but we need to start reexamining some of our East Coast plans. Starr Foods of Oxnard, California, has recently been acquired by a major tobacco, brewing, and food processing concern. Starr has announced plans to build ultramodern processing facilities in Georgia, North Carolina, and Alabama. Like Del Rio, Starr has had much experience and deep roots in agriculture. They are planning to buy several large farms near each of the processing operations. Further, they intend to be operational within one year to eighteen months. I know all of this because I have met with the president of Starr on two different occasions after they expressed sincere interest in purchasing the Wilmington plant from Del Rio. Starr has offered two million dollars for the Wilmington plant as is.

After a long pause Bob continued:

I think we have four options:

1. Sell the plant to Starr or someone else as is:
2. Complete the plant and then sell;
3. Complete the plant and keep the facility, but expand very cautiously; or
4. Complete the plant and proceed with plans to expand aggressively in the southeastern markets.

Assemble and inform all the top level managers in Wilmington immediately. All the West Coast vice presidents will be in Wilmington in two days. You and your management team should be prepared to either present and defend one of these four options or develop and defend another alternative.

CASE 10

Lockheed Corporation

Robert N. McGrath, Franz Lohrke, Gary J. Castrogiovanni,
Louisiana State University

By 1990, the Lockheed Corporation was a national institution and had been one for many decades. Its pioneering efforts in the fields of aviation and space were legendary. In fact, Lockheed's contributions during times of both war and peace suggest that it was an instrument of national security as well as a profit-seeking enterprise.

It is a business, however, and like other aerospace companies, it has experienced dramatic boom-to-bust cycles due primarily to shifts in government expenditures. The U.S. government and principally the Department of Defense (DoD) are the corporation's major customers by far. Their political and military strategies are the principle determinants of Lockheed's corporate strategy.

At the end of the 1980s, Lockheed found itself in a crisis of uncertainty. It had survived the post-Vietnam cutbacks, several contracting scandals, a disastrous attempt to get back into the civilian sector, and the changing tides of defense policy. It had then healed and profited through the initiatives of the Reagan Administration. Headquartered in Calabasis, California, having its airplane-related component in Burbank, California, and its space-related component a few hundred miles north in Sunnyvale, California, Lockheed prospered in the graces of a California president devoted to matching global military threats. Sales doubled from 1983 to 1988. At the close of the decade, however, world events seemed to conspire against its business once again—the Soviet hegemony was crumbling in metaphor as the Berlin wall crumbled in fact. The Defense Department, based on Secretary of Defense Cheney's voluntary proposal in 1989, was poised to cut spending by about $180B and reduce the overall size of the armed forces by 25% in just a few years. Naturally, these events caused a severe political and military reassessment of programs under development, and companies like Lockheed suddenly found themselves poised to become big losers.

This case is intended for classroom discussion only, not to depict effective or ineffective handling of administrative situations. All rights reserved to the authors.

The Lockheed posture was not a slave to the situation, though. Dan Tellep, corporate veteran for over three decades and a renaissance-man, became CEO at the end of 1988. He dotes on innovation and encourages nontraditional thinking. His proudest achievement has been to garner sales of $1 billion in space station and Star Wars contracts. For four years, he ran the Lockheed Missiles and Space Company and was the driving force behind the D-5 missile program, which the House Armed Services Committee chairman dubbed as the "best-managed program I've seen." Though Tellep admits to knowing nothing about airplanes (perhaps the proudest part of the Lockheed legacy), corporatewide changes in strategy certainly seem imminent.

A LIVING HISTORY

From the corporation's initiation to World War II, Lockheed's technical accomplishments are impressive, but the business aspect sometimes stumbled. The Lockheed founders are Allan and Malcolm Loughhead who, in 1912, built one airplane as part of a business that lasted only one year. Later, the Loughhead Aircraft Manufacturing Company surfaced in Santa Barbara, California, from 1916 to 1921, and resurfaced in 1926 as the Lockheed Aircraft Company. In 1929, Lockheed became a division of the Detroit Aircraft Corporation. When that firm went bankrupt in 1931, Lockheed went into receivership. It resurrected itself in 1932 and has since operated continuously.

Though business results are cyclical, contributions to history are steady and significant. The Vega line of aircraft boasted endurance and speed accomplishments in aviation's halcyon era. Wiley Post's "Winnie Mae" was a Vega. Charles Lindbergh broke records in a Vega. It was in 1933 that a young engineer named Clarence "Kelly" Johnson contributed to the design of a series to be known as Electra. Amelia Earheart flew an Electra. Howard Hughes set his round-the-world record in an Electra. Neville Chamberlain flew to meet Hitler in an Electra. A follow-on series called Orion was the mainstay airliners of the day, and Lodestar, Ventura, and Harpoon models were almost as common. Despite the depression, Lockheed did a steady civilian business and assets grew to $3M in 1936. (See Exhibit 1.)

With World War II things changed. A bomber derivative of the Electra named the Hudson was ordered and was the largest order ever placed with an aircraft company—$25 million. Kelly Johnson designed the P-38 Lightning, one of the greatest fighters ever and feared as the "forked tailed devil" by the Japanese. More than 10,000 were produced, which is more than any other craft ever produced by Lockheed. Employment in 1939 was at 7,300, a fifteenfold increase in well under a decade. By 1941, employment was at 50,000, a hundredfold leap. At the time Pearl Harbor was bombed, Lockheed was the biggest aircraft company in the country. During the war, it produced 19,297 airplanes, and employment peaked at 93,000. From 1939 to 1943, sales went from $35.3 million to $697.4 million, net income from $442,111 to $8.2 million. Clearly, government business was smart business.

Contributing quietly during the war years was the advent of the Lockheed "Skunk Works." In 1944, Kelly Johnson assembled a 128-man team and produced one of the first jet aircraft, *from scratch*, in 139 days! That incredible accomplishment coined the term Skunk Works (because of the odor of a revo-

Exhibit 1

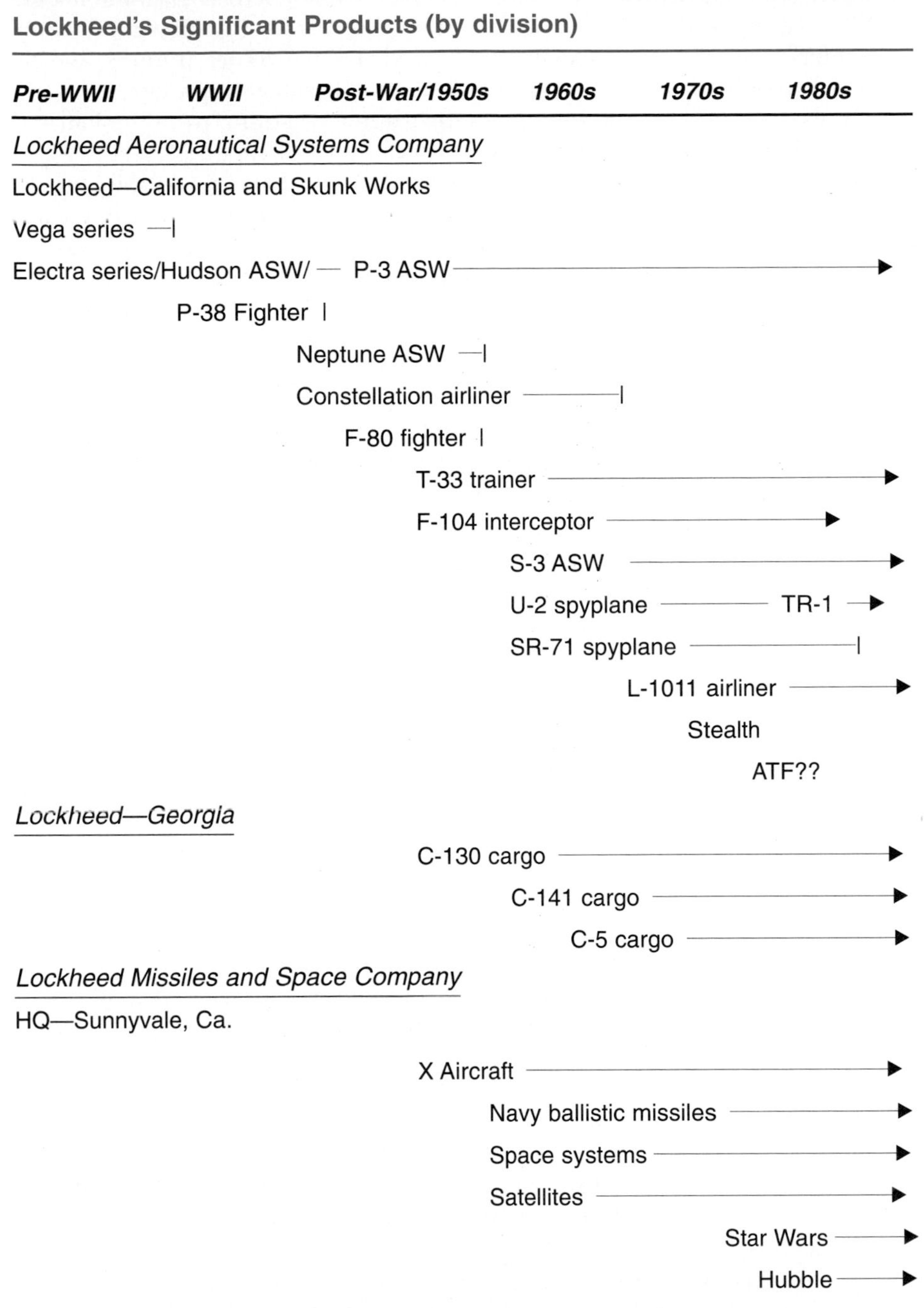

Note: Lines represent approximate operational life of product.

lutionary epoxy) and started a string of innovations and management miracles that never stopped.

With war's end, hard lessons were learned. The air force canceled 600 Lockheed contracts and 42,000 purchase orders, worth over $1 billion. By September 1945, employment was at 35,000, and by 1947, 14,000. Sales in 1946 were $112.7 million, down 87% from 1943. Net income fell to a $2.5 million loss. Fortunately, the company survived by selling 5,691 F-80s (the first production jet fighter) over the next sixteen years, and 5,691 T-33 jet trainers, which became a worldwide mainstay for decades. Also of critical importance was the sale of 856 Constellation airliners, modified into everything from the PanAm and TWA flagships to Air Force One.

During this era, Lockheed also established a firm foothold in the narrow area of maritime patrol aircraft and anti-submarine warfare (ASW) technology. Between 1946 and 1962, 1,052 Neptune aircraft were built for many countries, giving Lockheed unrivaled expertise in the maritime patrol niche. Then, building on the Electra design, the new Orion was produced, eventually becoming the standard maritime patrol aircraft through at least the end of the century. Lockheed's prowess in ASW also produced the ungainly Viking, a carrier-based aircraft that took the ASW mission to new levels of aviation technology. Though a narrow business, ASW technology provided a steady cash flow source that was to be instrumental in saving the corporation during hard times ahead.

In 1954, Lockheed again demonstrated its technological prowess by introducing the F-104 Starfighter, the first Mach-2 aircraft known as the "missile with a man in it." Over 2,500 were sold to many air forces. Another of Kelly Johnson's masterpieces, in 1958 it set an altitude record the same day it won the prestigious Collier Trophy for the year's greatest achievement in aviation. It was so "hot" that even NASA bought versions to train astronauts and do exotic performance tests.

It is difficult to underestimate the importance of the Skunk Works during this period, and especially of Kelly Johnson up to his retirement in 1975. His leadership, born of technical genius, may be the most significant single contribution to aviation ever. In addition to the projects mentioned, the Skunk Works produced the U-2 spy plane, famed not only because of its use in Cold War crises but also because of its technical capabilities. It was eventually replaced by the TR-1, so remarkably similar that it stood as testimony to the original design. Perhaps the most mysterious project, though, was the Mach-3 (and up) SR-71 Blackbird. This spyplane, with a theoretically unlimited (and never divulged) top speed, holds all speed records. Every detail of the airplane had to be invented to withstand high-speed/high-altitude rigors, such as oil that gets so hot it is solid until the plane warms up, and titanium skin that expands so much from the heat at those speeds that it is porous at ground conditions. Its advanced state was still unmatched even at its retirement after almost thirty years. (Only arrays of satellites could do more in terms of surveillance.) The SR-71 became *the* symbol of Lockheed excellence. Additionally, the Skunk Works produced the F-117 Stealth Fighter, secretly operational for the better part of a decade before the Northrop Stealth Bomber even flew as prototype. It is hard to imagine what would have happened to Lockheed without the Skunk Works and Kelly Johnson.

While technological limits were pushed, Lockheed was strong in other areas of aviation as well. In 1951, a simple contract to take the B-29 Bomber production line out of mothballs for the Korean War effort evolved into one of the strongest businesses Lockheed ever had. At a plant in Georgia, the air force subsequently contracted Lockheed to build a new, rugged cargo aircraft. This was to be the C-130 Hercules, which was designed so well that over 30 distinct derivatives were sold for at least as many purposes in over 45 countries.

Production was almost continuously sold out for at least 40 years. This established a tradition of heavy aircraft, for next came the C-141 Starlifter, the air force's workhorse airlifter. The next step was to build the C-5 Galaxy, which was for years to be the largest airplane in the world, holding outsize and gross-weight cargo records for many years.

Ironically, the C-5 program almost crippled the company. Although the air force agreed to buy the plane, the rival Boeing 747 was successfully marketed commercially, killing hopes for volume efficiencies. Also, the technical problems of building a plane so big and yet so versatile were costly. Overruns inspired the Pentagon to cancel 31 of the 115 originally ordered. Corporate losses in 1970 were $187.8 million, the worst in Lockheed's history. The value of common stock dropped almost in half. In the end, $250 million was written off. Eventually, though, the C-5A established a good technical reputation such that 50 follow-on C-5B versions were ordered, worth $6.6 billion.

Confident in its success with big airplanes, Lockheed decided to re-enter the civilian sector in the late sixties. It had not produced an airliner since the mid-forties, the Constellation. Nevertheless, Lockheed saw an unmistakable market for at least three hundred 250-passenger airliners, and invested over $1 billion in the development of the L-1011 TriStar. Unfortunately, McDonnell-Douglas saw the same opportunity, and eventually the L-1011 split the market with the DC-10. Nevertheless, Lockheed continued. Part of its strategy was to contract Rolls Royce as its engine manufacturer, hoping for inroads to subsequent European markets. Rolls Royce went bankrupt in the meantime, though, and efforts to save the engine manufacturer for the sake of the TriStar almost destroyed Lockheed financially. Because of Lockheed's importance for national defense, Congress saw fit to guarantee a $250 million line of credit. Though the government eventually profited by $30 million from that guarantee agreement, negative publicity gave Lockheed a scandalous reputation. After the L-1011 write-off in 1981, net income began to increase again. From $207.3 million in 1982 it tripled in three years to $401 million, while sales increased from $5.6 billion to $9.5 billion. Predictably, TriStar demonstrated technical superiority, establishing records in the civilian aviation industry and admiration for Lockheed.

Of equal technical excellence, Lockheed established itself as a leader in the missiles and space segment of the aerospace industry. In the fifties, Kelly Johnson again proved his genius by participating in the development of a series of "X" (for eXperimental) aircraft which were the pioneers into ranges of air and near-space necessary for further exploration. From this experience, Lockheed was to produce the Polaris, Poseidon, and Trident missiles, which in concert constituted the entire U.S. navy submarine-launched ballistic missile capability. These programs in themselves were models of managerial acumen, achieving results ahead of schedule and pioneering organizational techniques. Involvement with the national space programs developed into steady, understated, but vital business as well.

PRESENT BUSINESS ENVIRONMENT

As mentioned, the Reagan Administration brought in a new era for defense contractors, raising real spending 55% during the first five years. Reagan's advocacy of the Stealth Bomber, the "Star Wars" concept of nuclear deterrence, and a 600-ship navy, are examples of the expansion. Defense spending peaked in 1985, though, and from that point until the end of the decade the defense outlook eroded at an increasing rate. It is predicted that by 1995 defense spending will fall by 13.6% to $261 billion, and to $225 billion by 2000. Military aerospace and missiles are expected to drop at least 10% a year, mostly by canceling new programs. By 1990, up to 1,000,000 defense-related jobs might be lost. Lockheed is extremely vulnerable to these forces.

By the mid-1980s, public opinion and burgeoning defense budgets had influenced a fairly strict policy of "fixed price." This term is almost self-explanatory. A contract stipulates (in voluminous detail) a product to be delivered and one price to be paid for it. Again, almost all front-end risk has been shifted to the contractor, for major contracts always need some level of engineering development and R&D. A strategy of winning business by bidding low became popular, though it is frequently financially ruinous to do so. In concept, "fixed price" might be good free-market economics, but in practice it threatens to undermine national security by driving out important players, reducing incentives for innovation, and discouraging participation in defense contracting itself.

The hostility of this environment is made worse by other issues. A policy of separating development and production awards, with no guarantee that a production contract will be awarded, aggravates the risks of development. Further, the loser of a contract competition often wins second-source contracts. In other words, in the interest of national security, the government frequently contracts a second company for a major product as a back-up source. This player, usually the runner-up in the original competition, is frequently *given* the results of developmental work expensively performed by the "winner." Runners-up are winners in their own way, deterring unique technological risk.

Additionally, the DoD adopted policies of (a) requiring contractors to pay for tooling and test equipment, (b) demanding long-term warranties, (c) establishing strict guidelines for calculating allowable profits, and (d) making progress payments more frugal. Finally, a policy of criminal liability took effect. Periodic accusations of fraud and abuse induced a trend of pursuing criminal action against not only contractors, but their employees. Many veteran players simply opted out of this environment. Risks are just too severe.

The geopolitical scene and the Cheney reduction plan also make the industry consider major restructuring. A 25% reduction in force, massive base closings, the crumbling Soviet bloc, and a serious domestic agenda make prospects for enormously expensive new systems increasingly speculative. Obviously, the major companies will be pursuing fewer programs. Even within existing (already fielded) systems, costly technological upgrades will be competing for scarce resources. On the other hand, an equally likely possibility will be for the DoD to pursue upgrades as a cheaper alternative to buying new systems. It is impossible to predict which will be sacrificed to finance what. The Advanced Tactical Fighter program, for example, undergoing fierce competition between a Lockheed-led team and a Northrop-led team and still in R&D, might be scrapped in favor of upgrading existing fleets of F-15 and/or F-16 Fighters, or producing enhanced derivatives. Or, a limited number of Advanced Fighters might be bought as a short-term budget compromise, destroying economies of scale. Any acquisition combination is possible, and no one can make an accurate prediction.

In the industry, long-range marketing and operating strategies began to emerge. Principally, industry wisdom emphasizes reorganizing production/operations, securing subcontracting work, upgrading existing programs, and diversifying into stronger growth areas in order to maintain a business base on which to compete for future programs. However, most past efforts to diversify out of this industry have been catastrophic. After Vietnam, Grumman had tried its hand at subway cars. McDonnell had forayed into computer services. Hundreds of millions were lost. There are some success stories, but horror stories are the rule. One explanation is that defense contractors build up huge bureaucracies in order to serve the Pentagon, while commercial companies must stay flexible. It is not uncommon for a defense contract to take five times as long as a civilian program. Also, defense contractors build to specifications with minimal risk. Technical prowess is valued over cost control. Fixed price concepts, common in the civilian sector, wreaked havoc in the defense sector.

However, the lure of the civilian aviation sector is powerful. Operating profits in that industry in 1988 alone were $2.5–$3.0 billion. The demands there are huge and long-term. World traffic is expected to grow at a rate of 5.4% through 2005. Generally favorable economic conditions and airline deregulation, favorable tourism policies, and a favorable investment climate sustain a buying spree augmented by concerns of airlines over aging fleets and a trend toward larger aircraft. The key elements for market share are affordable equipment and low operating and maintenance costs. As such, major steps toward advanced technology or all-new aircraft programs are avoided. Long-range market prospects are for $516 billion in aircraft sales by 2005. There is little doubt that civilian aviation has a bright future in almost every segment.

In strategic defense, the environment is somewhat different again. Arms limitation talks notwithstanding, there is little or no evidence that Soviet economic troubles are impacting their growth in strategic capability: missiles, submarines, military adventurism in space, and the like. To balance the threat, American strategic funding has grown faster in real terms than that for conventional forces, absorbing about 15% of the defense budget. Despite the need for balance, the administration is forced by economics to take a gradualist approach to new systems and modernizations. Three major modernization programs are expected to consume the lion's share of the strategic budget—the navy's Trident 2 D-5 missile (a Lockheed product), Rockwell's B-2 Bomber, and a replacement for the aging Intercontinental Ballistic Missile force, all many years into development. Despite its cost of $35 billion, the Trident missile seems to be the most politically secure. The Northrop B-2 Stealth Bomber, in the prototype stage, is in the severest doubt. The future of the Strategic Defense Initiative (Star Wars) is almost totally unpredictable.

LOCKHEED'S POSITION

■ Organization

By the end of the 1980s, Lockheed was organized into five major business groups. The largest was the Aeronautical Systems Company (LASC), with about half of the corporation's employment of over 90,000 people, and headquartered in Burbank, California. Most of the remainder of LASC employees were located in Marietta, Georgia, just outside Atlanta. (See Exhibit 2.)

LASC activities in California included production of the P-3 Orion antisubmarine aircraft and the TR-1 reconnaissance aircraft. Production of these air-

Exhibit 2 **Organizational Chart (case-simplified)**

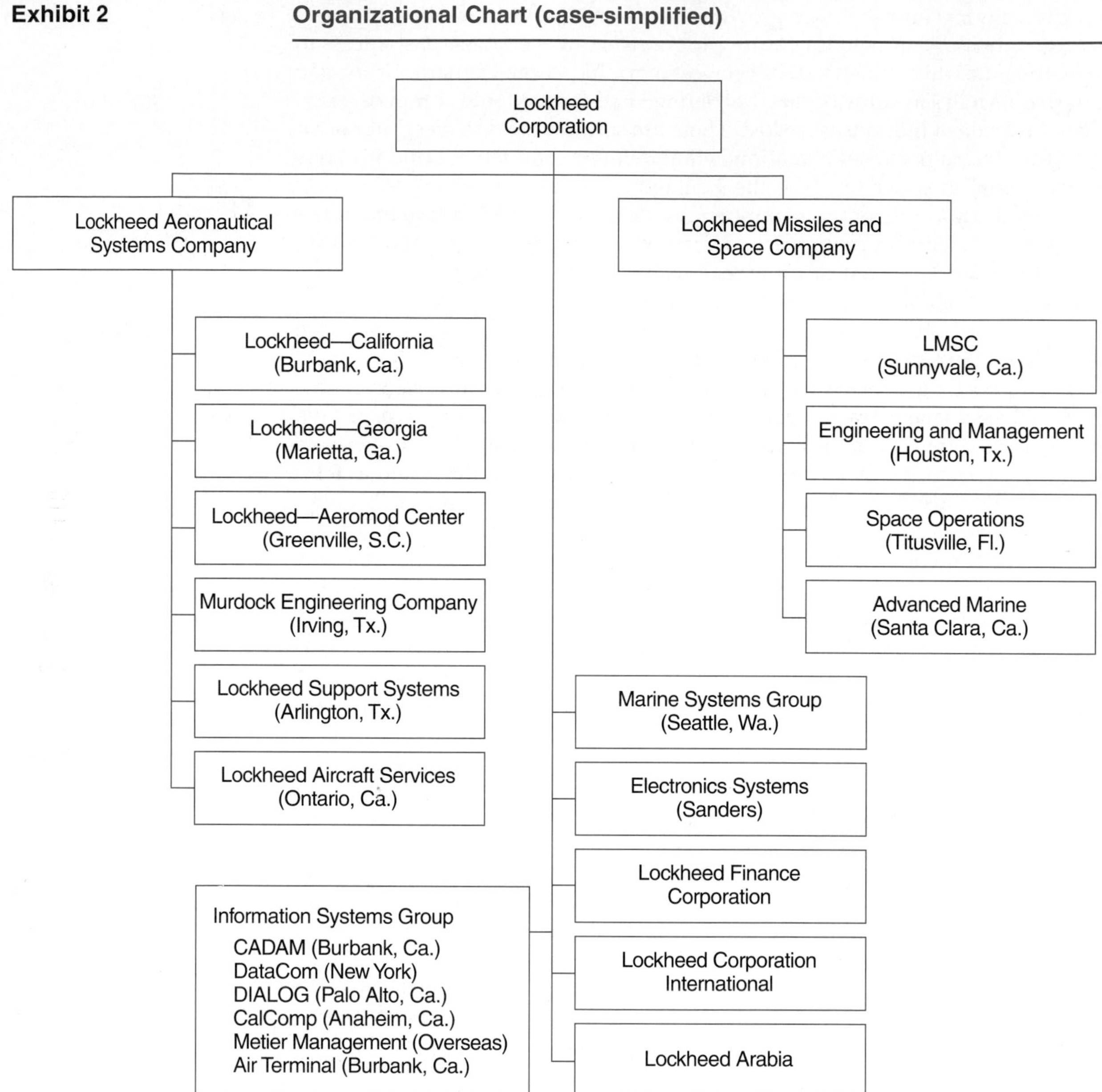

craft would be completed soon. There was a good deal of service/support business related to the S-3 Viking carrier-based ASW aircraft and the L-1011 TriStar. The Advanced Development Projects (Skunk Works) office was also part of this organization, having recently delivered the last of about 50 F-117 Stealth Fighters. The Skunk Works was also currently developing the F-22 advanced tactical fighter (ATF).

In Georgia, ongoing activities included the production of the last C-5Bs under contract, steady but modest production of the venerable C-130 transport, and almost continuous modernization/support projects for existing fleets of C-141, C-130, and C-5 transports.

Niche and service-oriented components of LASC included the Lockheed Aeromod Center in Greenville, South Carolina; the Murdock Engineering Company in Irving, Texas; Lockheed Support Systems in Arlington, Texas; and Lockheed Aircraft Services in Ontario, California.

While LASC was essentially half the corporation, the other half was essentially the Lockheed Missiles and Space Company (LMSC). Headquartered in Sunnyvale, California, its principle activities included the development and production of all U.S. Navy fleet ballistic missiles, and development/production of spacecraft and space systems for NASA and the U.S. Air Force. The list of projects was long, and included the D-5 Trident Missile, advanced observation satellites, information retrieval systems, advanced materials (e.g., space shuttle exterior silica tiles and lithium batteries), physical sciences research (e.g., atomic and molecular physics, astronomy, nuclear physics, nuclear weapons effects, plasma physics, and reentry physics), ground vehicles, ocean systems (deep-diving vehicles), ocean mining (and vehicles), advanced tactical systems (radiometric area correlation guidance, airfield destruction, offensive suppression systems), extensive Star Wars R&D (accredited with "major" breakthroughs), remotely piloted vehicles, and the pride-and-joy Hubble Telescope. (With resolution up to ten times better than any earth-based telescope, it would allow a view into 350 times more of the universe than ever seen before and revolutionize our understandings through an array of sensors unprecedented in technological capacity.) Futuristic possibilities included a rejuvenated idea for a supersonic transport, a role in the hypersonic national aerospace plane, and liquid hydrogen aircraft fuel.

Components of LMSC included the Engineering and Management Service Company in Houston, Texas; the Space Operations Company in Titusville, Florida; and Advanced Marine Systems in Santa Clara, California.

Lockheed's Information Systems Group (the corporation's smallest division) included CADAM (Computer-Aided Design and Manufacturing) in Burbank, California; DataCom Systems of New York City; DIALOG Information Services of Palo Alto, California; CalComp of Anaheim, California; Metier Management Systems (five computer companies with offices in the Far East and Europe); and Lockheed Air Terminal, established in 1941 to manage the company-owned Burbank Airport. (The airport was eventually sold but Lockheed stayed in the airport management business.)

The Marine Systems Group, headquartered in Seattle, Washington, concerned itself with ship designs, engineering, construction, overhaul, repair, and logistical support. It employed about 1 percent of Lockheed's work force.

The Electronics Systems Group was formed in 1986 with the acquisition of Sanders Associates, Inc. It developed and manufactured advanced electronic systems for both military and civilian applications.

Unassigned to company groups were the Lockheed Finance Corporation, formed to help customers finance business with Lockheed; Lockheed Corporation International, which provided marketing and support services for all of Lockheed worldwide; and Lockheed-Arabia, a joint venture concerned with a broad spectrum of basic aviation needs.

■ Posturing for the 1990s

At the end of the 1980s, Lockheed found itself on a knife's edge. The Pentagon supplied 77% of its business. Though the corporation had its highest earnings ever in 1988 ($624 million), this was due to a beneficent receivables schedule and is not completely representative of the immediate realities. Earnings in 1989 were $2 million on $9.9 billion in sales. Some of the reasons for this situation strike right at the heart of the Lockheed identity.

One is the paucity of new business in LASC. Except for the F-117 Stealth Fighter, no new aircraft types have been introduced since 1972. All business is either ongoing or derivative (Skunk Works rumors aside). This stands in stark contrast to the decades before, when on average one new type was introduced every year.

The legacy of Lockheed's "heavies" has been broken. The contract for the next generation of cargo aircraft, the C-17, was awarded to McDonnell-Douglas. (To add insult to injury, Lockheed's poor performance as a subcontractor for C-17 wing parts caused that business to be canceled, about $1 billion in revenue.) Delivery of the last C-5Bs occurred in 1989. Production of the C-5B had accounted for 20% of corporate sales of $11.2 billion in 1986. In 1987 it accounted for $2 billion, $1.2 billion in 1988, and $.2 billion in 1989. Production of the C-130 is steady but short-term, averaging production of 36 aircraft a year. Solid revenues are expected for modifications of all types of transports for years, but no new models are on the horizon.

Though the last delivery of the P-3 Orion ASW aircraft was also imminent, that business was expected to continue with the development of its replacement, the P-7. However, in 1989 Lockheed suddenly announced that the P-7 program was $300 million over budget, virtually wiping out the profit made elsewhere in the corporation (mostly in LMSC). Because of technical insufficiencies, schedule delays, eroding performance promises, and the world and budget scenes, the navy poised itself to cancel the $5 billion program outright. If it did so, it would be the largest cancellation ever in DoD history.

Not much else was left in LASC beside the possibility of the Advanced Tactical Fighter. About $1 billion was being invested in the R&D stage to chase about $100 billion in future contracts, spread over the life of the system and across the winning consortium of companies. Within a year, Lockheed's ATF was scheduled to fly as prototype and would compete with the Northrop competitor for the entire procurement package. Analysts were undecided as to which was more likely to win, and strategic reassessments and budget constraints were threatening major portions (if not all) of the eventual buy.

On the other hand, in LMSC Lockheed was on contract for $5.3 billion worth of 52 D-1 missiles and an extrapolated forecasted demand for $20 billion more in the 1990s. Star Wars projects were generating about $300 million a year in revenue, but politics made that business unpredictable.

On balance, stockholders were not happy. Despite a booming stock market, their average total return in the last three years had fallen 1.9%. The collective market value of the seven purest defense contractors had fallen 23% in three years. The tradition of underbidding early to get business, save jobs, keep the production lines rolling, and position for the next big program was serving employees but not investors.

Lockheed became a takeover target. Dallas investor and turnaround artist Harold Simmons owned 19% of common stock and was not happy with his paper losses of about $100 million. Though he had never taken over an aerospace firm before, his record was outstanding. It seemed that he wanted to take over Lockheed, boost profits, and help raise stockholders' value. He openly vowed to invest heavily in the aerospace and defense segments and sell other assets. He embarked on a proxy fight to elect his own cadre of 15 directors.

CEO Tellep had entirely different ideas. In late 1988, he set up a division in Washington, D.C., to stay close to emerging defense computer and electronics demands. The idea was to replace the shrinking aircraft business by growing electronics from the present 40% of total volume to 60%. Not only would Lockheed chase modest programs like fire-control systems for tactical weapons, but giant contracts as well. He planned to transfer Lockheed's experience with computer-controlled weapons and space systems to a potential $1.5 billion contract to network air force computer systems, and a similar $2 billion project for the Treasury Department. Facing competition from IBM, Honeywell, EDS, Computer Sciences and other veterans, he hired a former vice-president of Computer Sciences Corp. and the former assistant defense secretary for the Pentagon's "Command, Control, Communications and Intelligence" strategy. Though the Sanders acquisition in 1986 had produced disappointing results so far, it was expected to be a key player in efforts like this.

In April 1989, a major restructuring plan was inaugurated. It was intended to focus on Lockheed's core business of aircraft, missiles, space and electronics, while growing in markets like government services and antisubmarine warfare (ASW). Some details of the plan included:

- The phasing out of the Information Systems Group and the sale of CalComp, CADAM, Metier, and Lockheed DataPlan, which had combined revenues in 1988 of $589 million.
- Establishment of a technology services group to capitalize on modernization and maintenance needs.
- Formation of an ASW office in Washington, headed by a retired navy vice-admiral.
- Pursuit of a role as a subcontractor for the final assembly of McDonnell Douglas's new airliner, the MD-11, to offset the vacuum left by the C-5B program completion. As well, Fokker (of Germany) was approached for similar subcontracting work.
- Establishment of an employment stock ownership plan with 17% total corporate ownership.
- Acceleration of a general LASC migration from Burbank to sites in Palmdale, California, Rye Canyon, California, and the move of the Skunk Works to Palmdale.
- Rumors of massive layoffs.

The aggressive lobbying of employees by Harold Simmons, however, grew as Wall Street's opinion of Lockheed continued to deteriorate. Tellep was forced to all but abandon his restructuring plan.

REFERENCES

Anderson, R. A., *A Look At Lockheed,* Princeton University Press, USA, 1983.

Aviation Week and Space Technology, "Aircraft Upgrades Will Be Critical to Maintaining Tactical Defenses," March 14, 1988, pp. 38–41.

Aviation Week and Space Technology, "Budget Realities Forcing Tough Strategic Choices," March 20, 1989, pp. 49–51.

Aviation Week and Space Technology, "Commercial Airframe Makers Take Conservative Approach," March 20, 1989, pp. 197–198.

Aviation Week and Space Technology, "Congress Saddled with Years of Tough Defense Positions," March 14, 1988, pp. 63–67.

Aviation Week and Space Technology, "Contractors Must Adapt to Survive Under New U.S. Acquisitions Policies," March 20, 1989, pp. 76–79.

Aviation Week and Space Technology, "Declining Military Aircraft Sales Weather Aerospace Market Forecast," March 14, 1988, pp. 75–76.

Aviation Week and Space Technology, "Defense Acquisition Policies Hinder Contractors' Ability to Innovate," March 14, 1988, pp. 69–71.

Aviation Week and Space Technology, "Defense Budget Actions Delayed by Administration's Slow Start," March 20, 1989, p. 65.

Aviation Week and Space Technology, "Defense Cuts Will Trim Aerospace Firms' Earnings, Despite Civil Gains," March 20, 1989, pp. 82–83.

Aviation Week and Space Technology, "Defense Firms Re-Order Programs, Operations to Survive Lean Years," May 30, 1988, pp. 59–64.

Aviation Week and Space Technology, "Growth Trends: Air Transport, 1979–1991," March 20, 1989, p. 193.

Aviation Week and Space Technology, "Growth Trends: U.S. Aerospace Industry," March 20, 1989, pp. 38–39.

Aviation Week and Space Technology, "Growth Trends: U.S. Military Aircraft, 1979–1991," March 20, 1989, p. 45.

Aviation Week and Space Technology, "Growth Trends: U.S. Space Sales, 1979–1991," March 20, 1989, p. 105.

Aviation Week and Space Technology, "Lockheed Implements Restructuring to Focus on Primary Business," April 10, 1989, p. 31.

Aviation Week and Space Technology, "Market Focus," March 14, 1988, p. 243.

Aviation Week and Space Technology, "Tactical Aircraft Producers Face Diminishing Returns," February 22, 1989, p. 34.

Aviation Week and Space Technology, "U.S. Armed Forces Vary Means of Coping with Tight Budgets," March 20, 1989, pp. 52–53.

Business Week, "Defenseless Against Cutbacks," January 14, 1991, p. 69.

Business Week, "Harold Simmons Is Playing a Crafty War Game," March 12, 1990, p. 40.

Business Week, "If Simmons Boards Lockheed, Can He Fly It?" April 2, 1990, pp. 77–78.

Business Week, "Lockheed Dons New Armour to Keep the Raiders at Bay," April 17, 1989, pp. 20–21.

Business Week, "Lockheed's Lesson: It's Open Season On Yes-Man Boards," April 16, 1990, p. 25.

Business Week, "Lockheed's New Top Gun Comes Out Blazing," September 5, 1988, pp. 75, 88.

Business Week, "Oh, What a Difference a Year Makes," February 25, 1991, p. 37.

Business Week, "The $75 Billion Question: Whose Fighter Will Win?" April 8, 1991, pp. 64–65.

Business Week, "Who Pays for Peace?" July 2, 1990, pp. 64–70.

Fortune, "The Arms Makers' Next Battle," August 27, 1990, pp. 84–88.

Moody's Industrial Manual, Lockheed, 1991.

Standard and Poor's Industrial Manual, Lockheed, 1991.

Yenne, W., *Lockheed,* Crown Publishers, Inc., USA, 1987.

APPENDIX 1: FINANCIALS AND COMPANY-RELATED INFORMATION

Lockheed's Balance Sheet (millions)

Exhibit 3

	1990	*1989*
Assets		
Cash and equivalent	372	86
Accounts receivable	1,880	1,786
Inventories	1,187	1,266
Other current assets	139	260
Total current assets	3,578	3,398
Prop, plt & equip at cost	4,064	4,053
Less accum depr & amort.	2,205	2,150
Net property	1,859	1,903
Excess of purc price over fair asset val.	858	895
Other noncurrent assets	565	596
Total assets	6,860	6,792
Liabilities		
Short-term borrows	40	19
Accounts payable	778	732
Salaries and wages	317	326
Inc tax, primarily defer	230	728
Customers' advs in excess of rel. costs	439	228
Curr portion of long-term debt	25	22
Other current liabilities	793	840
Total current liabilities	2,622	2,895
Long-term debt	1,929	1,835
Common stock	70	70
Additional cap	707	707
Retained earnings	2,332	2,103
Treasury shares, at cost	(328)	(328)
Guartantee of ESOP obligs	(472)	(490)
Total shareholders' equity	2,309	2,062
Total liabilities & shareholders' equity	6,860	6,792
Net current assets	956	503
Book value	$22.98	$18.47

Source: Annual Report of Lockheed Corp.

Exhibit 4

Business Segment Sales and Profits (000)

	12/31/90	*12/31/89*
Sales		
Missiles and space	5,116,000	4,780,000
Aeronautical systems	2,329,000	2,572,000
Technical services	1,550,000	1,432,000
Electronics	963,000	1,107,000
Total	9,958,000	9,891,000
Costs and expenses	9,397,000	9,838,000
Profits		
Missiles and space	379,000	368,000
Aeronautical systems	96,000	(377,000)
Technical services	58,000	36,000
Electronics	28,000	26,000
Total	561,000	53,000

Source: Annual Report of Lockheed Corp.

Exhibit 5

The Top Ten Defense Suppliers: Projected 1990 Revenues and Percent of Sales

Company and Products	*1990 Est. Rev. from Govt. Sales ($B)*	*% of Total Sales*
McDonnell-Douglas: airplanes, missiles, helicopters, electronics, space	10.2	67
Lockheed: airplanes, missiles, electronics, space	9.0	91
General Dynamics: airplanes, submarines, tanks, missiles, space, electronics	8.6	87
General Electric: engines, electronics	8.2	18
Boeing: airplines, helicopters, missiles, space	5.6	20
Martin Marietta: missiles, electronics, space	5.4	90
Rockwell International: electronics	5.3	44
General Motors (Hughes): electronics, space, missiles	5.2	4
United Technologies: engines, helicopters	5.2	24
Northrop: airplanes, missiles, electronics	4.6	88

Sources: Perry, Nancy J. (Aug. 27, 1990), "The arms makers' next battle," *Fortune,* 84–88; company reports; United States Department of Defense.

U.S. Aerospace Industry Market Forecast: Estimated Sales (in billions of current dollars)

Exhibit 6

	1988	*1989*	*1990*	*1991*
Grand total—aerospace	126	140	155	170
Military aircraft	38	40	41	44
Missiles	14	15	16	17
Space	27	28	32	37
Commercial air transport	23	31	37	42
Business flying	2	2	3	3
Avionics	37	39	43	47
Military computers	22	25	30	34
Engines/parts—Military	7	8	9	9
Engines/parts—Civil	6	7	9	11
Flight simulators/trainers	1	2	2	3

Sources: Aviation Week & Space Technology (March 20, 1989), "Defense Cuts Will Trim Aerospace Firm's Earnings Despite Civil Gains," pp. 80–83; Aerospace Industries Association.

Employment Effects of Pentagon Cutbacks

Exhibit 7

	Est. Number of Workers Employed		
Professions Hit Hardest	*1988*	*1991*	*1994*
Communications equipment	349,600	261,400	213,400
Guided missiles	134,900	122,600	105,100
Shipbuilding/repair	102,300	79,400	61,700

Source: Based on *Business Week,* July 2, 1990.

CASE 11

Chem-Trol, Inc.

Leslie A. Toombs, Mark J. Kroll, Robert B. Welch, Larry D. White,
University of Texas at Tyler

Clinton R. Ross looked out from his executive suite offices in downtown Houston at the city's skyline. The working day had ended some hours before for most of the offices. Ross, however, was deeply involved in thoughts about the future of the corporation he had been named to lead only thirty days ago. His 10-year-old daughter had just come into the office, accompanied by his wife. The little girl smiled up at Ross as she sat down and began to spin around in his plush leather chair. "The big cheese," she said with a grin.

"Right," Ross thought, as he smiled in return. He was indeed the "big cheese." With this prestigious title, however, had come some formidable challenges. As newly installed CEO of Chem-Trol Corporation, he was faced with a great number of critical decisions. Over the next six months, these decisions would shape his future, as well as that of his company and its 1,800 employees, for years to come.

It is late 1990. Chem-Trol, Inc. is a diversified firm with global operations and annual net revenue of approximately $300 million. Clinton Ross's experience with Chem-Trol began in 1973 as general manager of the company's specialty plastics division. Since joining the company, he had seen Chem-Trol's total net sales increase by almost $50 million. His own division had been a significant contributor. Ross held both a bachelor's and master's degree in chemical engineering and had over ten years of related industry experience before joining Chem-Trol, Inc.

He is concerned about his company's current performance and its prospects for the future. The company is heavily dependent on the sale of specialty chemical products to the struggling petroleum industry.

This case is intended for classroom discussion only, not to depict effective or ineffective handling of administrative situations. All rights reserved to the authors.

COMPANY HISTORY

Chem-Trol, Inc. is primarily a manufacturer and supplier of oil field and industrial specialty chemicals. It is a publicly held corporation, with shares traded on the NASDAQ. In spite of this official public status, over 54% of the outstanding common stock is held by a family trust, controlled by the heirs of the company's founder. The current chairman of the board is a family member who is recognized as being responsible for the interests of the trust. Excluding Ross, who is now CEO, other members of Chem-Trol's thirteen-person board are traditionally assigned on the basis of their personal relationship to the chairman and other family members.

Corporate planning and day-to-day direction of the company's operations has historically been left up to professional management. The chairman's direct involvement is limited only to insistence on "reasonable" growth and return on investment. Actual targets are established by management and agreed upon by the board on an annual basis. The one "nonnegotiable" item regarding company performance is payment of stable or increasing quarterly dividends on outstanding common shares.

Chem-Trol, Inc. began its 52-year history as a manufacturer and supplier of oil field chemical products. Since that time, operations have been diversified into four major areas: the original oil field specialty chemicals, industrial specialty chemicals, process equipment/monitoring instruments, and specialty plastic production. Management views specialty chemicals as the company's core operation. The other ventures are considered natural extensions of this activity. Chem-Trol's 1990 operating group revenue is shown in Exhibit 1.

The company's chemical products are used in all areas of industrial and oil field fluid treatments. Applications include corrosion control, demulsification, and other production and process requirements. Chem-Trol has remained focused largely on oil field production chemical markets. The industrial chemical manufacturing and sales effort were added in 1982. The products involved in this sector primarily accomplish the same function as the oil field products. Sales efforts, however, are directed at industrial firms using various processes requiring water treatment.

The equipment and instrument business segment, like the majority of the specialty chemicals business, is focused primarily on the needs of the oil

Exhibit 1 **Chem-Trol Operating Group Revenue, 1990 (revenue in 000s)**

Source	*Revenue*
Specialty chemicals	
Oil field	$213,137
Industrial	20,559
Total chemicals	$233,696
Equipment/instruments	16,891
Special plastics	40,262
Total revenue	$290,849

production industry. Products include process vessels and electronic monitoring equipment for oil/water separation and clean-up.

The specialty plastic business has been a part of Chem-Trol for approximately 27 years. It involves the manufacture and sale of special waxes and plastic foam products used for packaging. The company does not actually mold the products into their final form for the end user, but transforms raw petroleum–based materials into an intermediate bulk form.

THE FOUR CHEM-TROL OPERATING UNITS

The products produced by Chem-Trol and its direct competitors can be considered "niche" offerings in the chemical manufacturing industry. The company does not compete with large commodity suppliers such as Dow, Celanese, and Du Pont. These companies are actually suppliers of the raw materials necessary for Chem-Trol's special products.

Because of Chem-Trol's heavy involvement in oil field–related products, its performance has historically fluctuated with this highly volatile industry (see Exhibit 2). Its Oil Field Chemicals and Equipment/Instruments business segments are directly tied to oil and other gas production. The Industrial Chemicals and Specialty Plastics segments are affected by oil, largely because petroleum is the key source of necessary raw materials.

■ Market Conditions and Outlook

The current market for Chem-Trol's oil field specialty chemicals is considered to be in a recovery phase stemming from the oil price collapse of 1986. During this crisis, the most stable segments of Chem-Trol's business portfolio were the Specialty Plastics and Industrial Chemicals segments.

The specialty plastics industry is viewed as a stable and growing business. This optimism is due in part to the increasing use of wax and plastic products for packaging purposes.

Crude Oil Prices and Net Earnings, Chem-Trol Corporation **Exhibit 2**

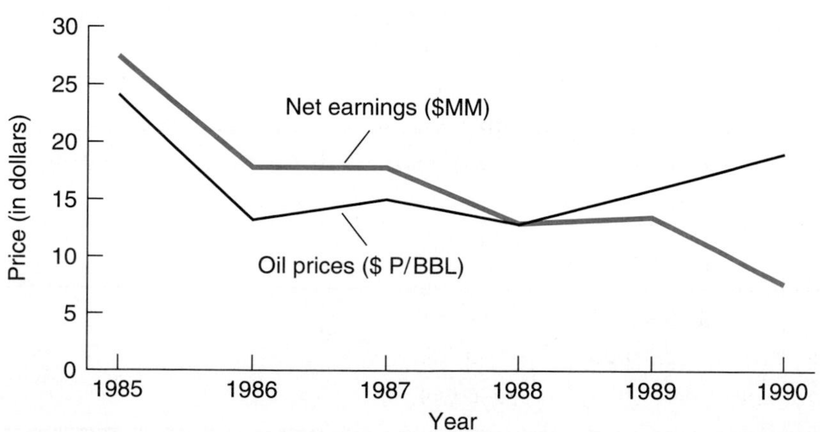

The industrial specialty chemical business, because of its relation to industrial output, is closely tied to the fortunes of the general economy. This market has enjoyed sustained but limited growth for most of the 1980s. However, within the company and industry, it is hoped that industrialization of Third World and East European nations will lead to expanded opportunities. This is Chem-Trol's most promising venture, outside the energy industry.

THE COMPETITION

■ Oil Field Chemicals

Chem-Trol has three primary competitors in the area of specialty chemical sales to the oil industry: Nalco, Betz, and Celanese. The total domestic market value is estimated to be $520 million. In 1990, Chem-Trol estimated that its share was approximately 32% of this domestic total. The next largest competitor commanded approximately 24%, with the remaining market shared by the other two companies and a number of smaller independents. Chem-Trol's 1990 international sales in oil field specialty chemicals totaled $47 million, out of a market valued at approximately $500 million. Although Chem-Trol is the market leader, the industry is quite fragmented. Competition in this arena comes from essentially the same companies as the domestic market.

■ Industrial Chemicals

Industrial chemical sales efforts, while still a specialty niche, brought the company into direct competition with much larger and well-established firms. The estimated total domestic market in 1990 was approximately $5 billion. In 1990, Chem-Trol posted sales of approximately $20 million in this market. Well-known competitors, such as Nalco Industrial Chemicals, Betz, and Celanese, hold the majority of the market (see Exhibit 3). In overseas markets, these same companies, as well as others, are also present.

■ Equipment/Instruments

The Equipment/Instruments segment enjoys very limited competition in its market niche, but it also has limited potential for growth in the market it presently serves. The primary "competition" for its products does not come from newly manufactured equipment, but from the worldwide surplus of

Exhibit 3 **Chem-Trol Industrial Competitors: Net Revenues for Global Operations, 1990 (dollars in 000s)**

Company	*Net 1990 Revenue*
Nalco	$ 682,000
Betz	320,000
Celanese	3,050,000

equipment resulting from the downturn in oil exploration. Much of this surplus is from Chem-Trol's own past production. Chem-Trol estimates that it has approximately 47% of the market share for these products. The total market was valued at $36 million in 1990.

■ Specialty Plastics

The Specialty Plastics segment holds a significant market share in what is deemed a high-growth industry. While heavily resource-dependent on petroleum production, this segment of the company supplies intermediate materials for packaging of consumer goods. The estimated market size in 1990 was approximately $125 million, over $40 million of which was captured by Chem-Trol (see Exhibit 4). It is estimated that this product market will continue to grow with overall consumer spending.

Unfortunately, in terms of financial performance, Chem-Trol has not kept pace with its key competitors. Exhibit 5 provides comparative ratios. Apparently, Chem-Trol's performance, in terms of return on equity and investment, has fallen far behind that of the competition.

ORGANIZATION PLANNING AND STRUCTURE

In spite of its past success, Chem-Trol now finds itself struggling with a rapidly changing environment and marketplace. It will be Clinton Ross's challenge to take the company from its present position and assure continued growth into the next decade and beyond.

Ross recently replaced Chem-Trol's former CEO, who had risen from the ranks of the research and development department. This occurred when the chairman of the board became frustrated with the company's reaction to the dramatic downturn in the petroleum business (for a comparison of oil prices and Chem-Trol earnings, see Exhibit 2). Ross was given a free hand to do

Chem-Trol Relative Global Market Share by Operating Group, 1990 (dollars in 000s) **Exhibit 4**

Source	*Chem-Trol Revenue*	*Total Market*	*Market Share*
Specialty chemicals			
Oil field			
Domestic	$165,873	$ 520,000	32%
Foreign	47,264	449,000	11
Industrial			
Domestic	18,550	5,000,000	0.4
Foreign	2,009	7,000,000	N/A
Total chemicals	$233,696		
Equipment/instruments	16,891	36,000	47
Special plastics	40,262	125,000	32
Total	$290,849		

Exhibit 5 **1990 Comparative Ratio Analysis**

	Betz	*Nalco*	*Baker Hughes*	*Chem-Trol*	*Industry*
Current ratio	2.3	2.3	2.1	2.5	1.3
Accounts receivable turnover	6.9	6.4	4.7	5.1	3.8
Days sales in A/R	52.7	57.5	77.0	65.0	95.7
Inventory turnover	5.6	7.1	2.8	7.6	n/a
Days sales in inventory	65.4	51.2	132.5	74.6	n/a
Gross profit margin as a % of revenue	64.1%	51.5%	37.4%	35.8%	n/a
Operating expenses as a % of revenue	17.4%	17.4%	9.9%	3.2%	n/a
Pretax earnings as a % of revenue	18.0%	17.1%	6.9%	3.5%	10.2%
Return on investment	15.3%	12.6%	5.1%	4.0%	10.4%
Return on equity	29.7%	28.8%	10.0%	4.0%	10.3%

"whatever it took" to improve performance. The only guidelines he was given were (1) stable or growing common stock prices and dividends and (2) progress toward the chairman's vision of a "billion-dollar company" by the year 2000.

■ The Billion-Dollar Plan

Company projections call for approximately 90% of the growth from present revenue levels of $300 million to come from the two specialty chemicals groups. The remaining 10% is to come from Specialty Plastics and Equipment/Instruments. It is expected that market share gains and increasing demand will provide much of this growth. However, it is also recognized that key acquisitions and/or additional diversification will be necessary to reach the final goal.

Industrial Chemicals, it is believed, should supply approximately 70% of the growth required from specialty chemical sales because of the size of the vast domestic market, as well as potential growth in overseas markets. The Oil Field group should provide the remaining 30% growth in chemical operations. As mentioned, the Specialty Plastics and Equipment/Instruments businesses are to provide the balance of the total targeted growth.

■ Clinton Ross's Agreement

Clinton Ross feels that Chem-Trol's "billion-dollar" plan for the year 2000 is ambitious, given its current focus and markets. He is, however, certain the company has several significant strengths, which, if properly exploited, can make the plan a reality. At the corporate level, Chem-Trol is burdened with very little debt. Cash flows have been declining, but have remained positive (see Exhibit 6). Because of its somewhat unique ownership situation, the com-

Exhibit 6

Chem-Trol Corporation Consolidated Cash Flow for Years 1988–1990 (dollars in thousands)

	1990	*1989*	*1988*
Cash Flows from Operating Activities			
Net earnings	$ 7,127	$ 13,016	$ 11,879
Adjustments to reconcile net earnings to net cash provided by operations			
Depreciation	$ 14,662	$ 14,591	$ 14,838
Reorganization Equipment/Instruments	2,944	0	0
Gain on sale of assets	(559)	(253)	(450)
Write-off on investment in affiliate	0	0	2,567
Changes in assets and liabilities			
Marketable securities	2,693	1,416	195
Accounts receivable	2,388	4,172	(3,792)
Inventories	2,019	(563)	(5,742)
Other current assets	(2,575)	(530)	409
Pre-paid pension contributions	(931)	(624)	(3,378)
Accounts payable and accrued liabilities	(677)	(6,092)	4,517
Deferred income tax	(1,197)	933	1,570
Others	69	(439)	233
Net cash provided by operations	$ 25,963	$ 25,627	$ 22,846
Cash Flows from Investing Activities			
Capital expenditures, net of minor disposals	$(18,404)	$(20,433)	$(16,615)
Acquisition of subsidiary	0	0	(4,039)
Net cash used in investing activities	$(18,404)	$(20,433)	$(20,654)
Cash Flow from Financing Activities			
Short-term borrowing, net	$ 6,907	$ 633	$ 1,968
Additional long-term debt	0	1,350	2,560
Repayment of long-term debt	(1,953)	0	(5,000)
Dividend paid	(12,695)	(12,695)	(12,846)
Proceeds from stock issued as options	0	0	987
Purchase of treasury stock	0	(3,332)	0
Net cash used in financing activities	$(7,741)	$(14,044)	$(12,331)
Net increase (decrease) in cash and equivalents	$ (182)	$(8,850)	$(10,139)
Cash and equivalents at beginning of year	7,182	16,032	26,171
Cash and equivalents at end of year	$ 7,000	$ 7,182	$ 16,032

pany is relatively immune from takeover, assuming, of course, that the family trust, and current chairman, remains in control and is disinclined to sell out.

The company has a very strong commitment to research and development and boasts a multimillion dollar laboratory facility to support its efforts. Chem-Trol employs over 50 research chemists and support personnel who collectively register approximately 200 patents per year pertaining to special chemical processes. Unfortunately, a limited number have been introduced as commercial products, but several show significant potential in applications ranging from industrial, agricultural, energy, and pharmaceuticals. The former CEO planned to utilize the research capabilities to position the company for a number of proposed joint ventures outside the company's current operations.

Ross believes Chem-Trol can reach its objectives if he correctly focuses the company's strengths. Acquisitions will be necessary, as well as continued growth in existing businesses. Choosing the correct types of acquisitions will be the key.

■ The Corporate Structure

Ross feels his first priority should be to address the company's current management structure. Additionally, he is convinced the company lacks a well-defined sense of mission or purpose. The former CEO attempted to move the company away from its traditional divisional structure toward a matrix design. Because of difficulties with an entrenched corporate culture and the recent poor business climate, little progress has actually been made (see Exhibits 7 and 8 for financial/asset data).

The original four divisions—Oil Field, Industrial Chemicals, Specialty Plastics, and Equipment/Instruments—were redesignated as "groups." The research and development department is an independent entity and is allowed to establish its own objectives with the approval of the CEO. Support functions, such as distribution, personnel, and accounting, once duplicated for all groups, were combined. Manufacturing and marketing are the exceptions. Marketing remains part of each individual group and usually is assigned as a part of the sales effort. Manufacturing is a common function for the two specialty chemicals groups, but Equipment/Instruments and Plastics are necessarily separate (see Exhibit 9).

The intent in moving toward a matrix structure had been to increase the synergies among the former operating divisions. What emerged was a process in which corporate, and even business-level decision making, is now done on a consensus basis, with all group general managers involved. The former CEO had positioned himself in the role of arbitrator, settling any disputes among the respective group managers. Regardless of intent, the result is paralysis concerning key decisions as to what Chem-Trol's strategic and operational objectives are to be.

ROSS'S ASSESSMENT OF THE SITUATION

Ross realizes that he has limited experience in most of the operating groups, with the exception of Specialty Plastics. He believes that in addition to problems related to management structure, individual group performance may need closer scrutiny. Ross also realizes that he will have to make a number of assumptions about each group's projected future contributions to the corporation.

■ The Manufacturing Function

The Oil Field Chemicals and Industrial Chemicals groups share worldwide manufacturing capacity. The company maintains facilities capable of produc-

Chem-Trol Corporation Selected Financial Data for Years 1985–1990 (dollars in thousands, except per share data) **Exhibit 7**

	1990	*1989*	*1988*	*1987*	*1986*	*1985*
Summary of Operations						
Net revenues	$ 290,849	$ 301,269	$ 278,642	$ 279,953	$ 308,298	$ 294,068
Gross profit	104,183	113,774	109,247	114,673	119,425	122,299
Earnings from operations	9,164	16,792	21,527	24,047	28,952	38,487
Interest expense	1,736	1,260	892	453	2,406	1,191
Nonrecurring (charge) credit	0	820	(5,217)	0	0	0
Earnings before income taxes	7,428	16,352	15,418	23,594	26,546	37,296
Income taxes	2,154	5,070	5,717	9,013	11,139	14,814
Net earnings	5,274	11,282	9,701	14,581	15,407	22,482
Percent of revenues	1.8	3.7	3.5	5.2	5.0	7.6
Return on average stockholders' equity	3.3	6.7	5.6	8.9	9.2	14.3
Year End Financial Position						
Working capital	$ 71,043	$ 76,329	$ 82,014	$ 86,905	$ 100,614	$ 99,796
Current ratio	2.46:1	2.71:1	2.53:1	2.96:1	3.51:1	3.18:1
Total properties:						
Gross	233,317	234,826	222,484	206,868	186,042	164,745
Net	99,262	105,698	102,983	94,061	83,186	72,235
Total assets	231,113	237,335	248,171	231,404	227,961	221,514
Long-term debt	1,800	2,700	2,560	5,000	6,250	7,500
Stockholders' equity	160,688	168,925	172,005	164,554	167,663	156,943
Per Share Data						
Net earnings*	$ 0.47	$ 0.99	$ 0.85	$ 1.26	$ 1.32	$ 1.90
Dividends	1.12	1.12	1.12	1.12	1.12	1.03
Stockholders' equity	14.18	14.90	14.98	14.37	14.31	13.40
General, For the Year						
Dividends	$ 12,695	$ 12,695	$ 12,846	$ 12,974	$ 13,120	$ 12,189
Capital expenditures, net	11,737	16,530	18,965	25,321	23,627	11,323
Depreciation	14,640	14,576	14,838	14,029	13,447	13,218
Research	12,029	12,284	12,031	12,131	12,402	12,065
Average number of shares outstanding	11,334,873	11,349,850	11,466,683	11,572,817	11,714,648	11,834,648
Number of shares outstanding	11,334,873	11,334,873	11,484,573	11,451,248	11,714,648	11,714,648

*Earnings per share based on weighted average number of shares outstanding during each year.

ing its entire product line (3,000+ products) worldwide. This consists of two plants in the continental United States, one in Houston, the other in California, as well as plants in West Germany, Brazil, and Mexico.

Due to the dependence on oil field sales, 1990 capacity utilization in the two U.S. facilities was less than 60%. West Germany, which supplies the growing

Exhibit 8

Chem-Trol Corporation Consolidated Balance Sheets for Years 1988–1990 (dollars in thousands)

	1990	*1989*	*1988*
Assets			
Current assets:			
Cash and equivalents	$ 7,000	$ 7,182	$ 16,032
Marketable securities	13,443	16,136	17,552
Accounts receivable	51,389	51,720	56,004
Inventories	38,136	38,578	38,115
Other current assets	9,216	7,681	7,886
Total current assets	$119,184	$121,297	$135,589
Investment in affiliated companies	$ 4,373	$ 4,691	$ 4,050
Other assets	$ 6,112	$ 6,125	$ 5,549
Properties			
Buildings	$ 50,087	$ 50,299	$ 48,247
Machinery and equipment	177,231	169,520	165,565
Construction in progress	12,137	13,889	3,544
Accumulated depreciation	(134,138)	(129,203)	(119,501)
	$105,317	$104,505	$ 97,855
Land	$ 4,869	$ 5,163	$ 5,128
Total assets	$239,855	$241,781	$248,171
Liabilities and Stockholders' Equity			
Current liabilities:			
Short-term borrowing	$ 20,504	$ 13,597	$ 12,964
Accounts payable	24,689	25,741	27,898
Income tax payable	1,481	1,887	4,983
Accrued vacation pay	3,694	3,691	3,566
Other current liabilities	6,922	3,200	4,164
Total current liabilities	$ 57,290	$ 48,116	$ 53,575
Other liabilities			
Long-term debt	1,800	3,800	2,560
Other liabilities	2,597	2,263	2,395
Total other liabilities	$ 4,397	$ 6,063	$ 4,955
Deferred Income Taxes, net	$ 17,480	$ 18,677	$ 17,636
Stockholders' Equity			
Capital stock without par value			
Authorized 35,000,000 shares			
Issued 12,177,097 shares	$ 8,200	$ 8,200	$ 8,200
Reinvested earnings	173,461	179,029	178,708
Cumulative translation adjustment	(3,324)	(655)	(586)
Total	$178,337	$186,574	$186,322
Less Treasury stock	($ 17,649)	($ 17,649)	($ 14,317)
Total	$160,688	$168,925	$172,005
Total liabilities and stockholders' equity	$239,855	$241,781	$248,171

Organization Chart: Chem-Trol **Exhibit 9**

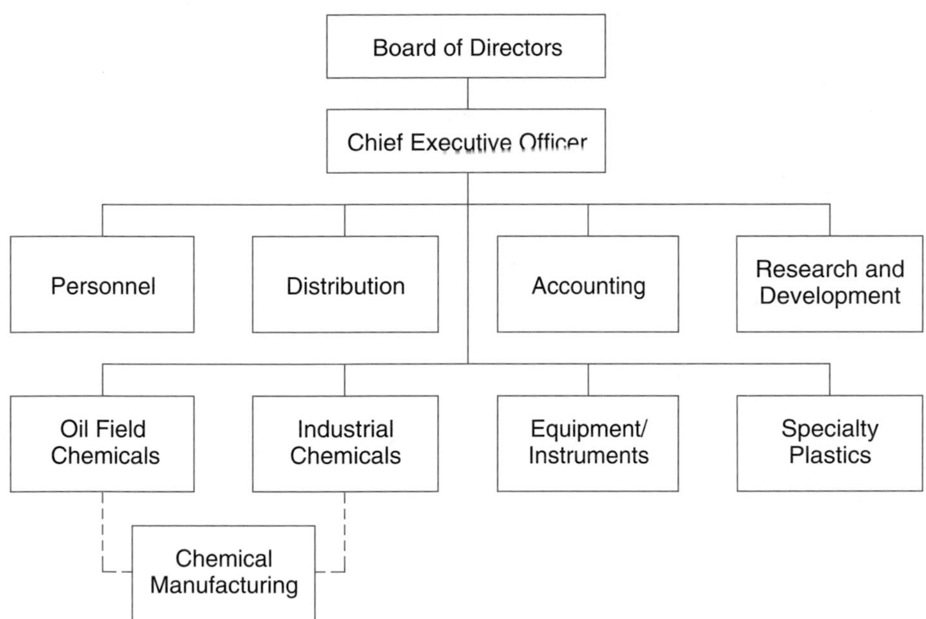

oil field markets in the Middle East, as well as European industrial markets, was at 90% of capacity. Both the Brazilian plant and the Mexican operation were severely underutilized at approximately 20% and 50%, respectively (see Exhibit 10).

■ The Oil Field Group

Present Operations

The Oil Field Group has historically led its segment of the specialty chemical industry in percentage share of the available oil field market. This business is the foundation from which Chem-Trol was built. Early in its history, Chem-Trol pioneered many of the products used in the industry. Consequently, many of its products have become synonymous with their functions, much as "Coke" has become synonymous with soft drinks. Since the products are considered specialty, rather than commodity items, the company has been able to command premium prices.

The group consists of over 700 employees composing a seasoned, stable work force, with average experience of over 15 years. The group is represented in every major oil field in the world through a network of employees, agents, and distributors.

Ross sees some potential internal problems for the group, stemming from the small number of qualified new employees coming on board and sporadic training efforts. He also is not satisfied with the application of new chemical technology. While research and development produce a number of new products each year, very few are ever introduced commercially.

Exhibit 10 **Chem-Trol Plant Utilization, 1990**

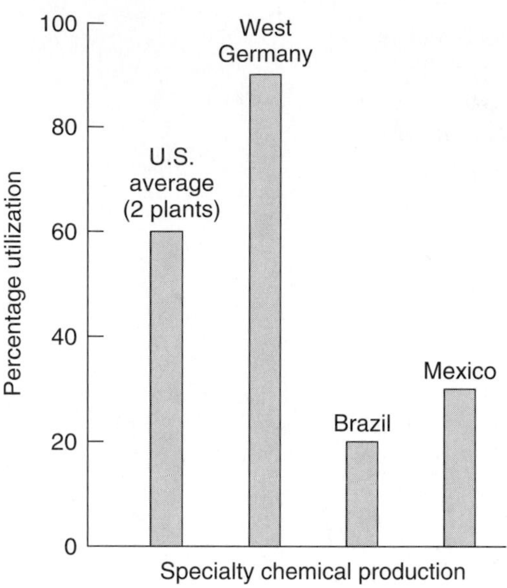

Chem-Trol provides products that are applicable in both crude oil and natural gas production. This offers some market fluctuation protection, since these are often seen as substitute energy sources. Ross sees opportunity in both areas, as the energy industry as a whole is projected to continue its current modest rate of recovery. International sales hold particular promise.

Threats to the Oil Field Group include future potential fluctuations in the petroleum business due to price instability. This threat of demand instability is coupled with increased price competition from a growing number of small firms, jeopardizing Chem-Trol's historic profit margins. Also, some major new potential competitors, such as Procter & Gamble and Pfizer, are beginning to show an interest in oil field specialty chemicals. Another future consideration, Ross realizes, is the uncertain effect of the growing environmental movement.

Finally, an irony in this segment of the business is raw material prices. In spite of falling crude oil prices, most of the raw petroleum derivatives from which Chem-Trol's products are manufactured have actually become more expensive. This is in response to efforts by the vertically integrated major energy companies to maintain their profits on the downstream side of the industry.

The Future

The management of the Oil Field Group is lobbying heavily for the acquisition of some of their smaller competitors. The current downturn in demand is seen as temporary and is viewed as an opportunity to purchase competitive market share at discounted prices. The initial cost, it is believed, will be rapidly recovered, as the fortunes of the oil industry continue to improve. Because of this group's historic contributions, their arguments are compelling. Ross knows that he has to be particularly cautious in dealing with this group, since Robert Nixon, the general manager, is a particular favorite of the chairman of the board. Only Nixon's limited educational background excluded him from serious consideration for the job Ross now occupies. Nixon has never been employed anywhere but Chem-Trol, having risen from delivery driver to group general manager during his career.

■ The Industrial Chemicals Group

Present Operations

Ross feels that the Industrial Chemicals Group is the future of the company. He is especially impressed with the new general manager's commitment to the marketing function. Howard Ciglione joined Chem-Trol only four months before Ross was promoted to CEO. Ciglione has considerable industry experience from his tenure with a major competitor, where he served as marketing director. Ross feels that given direction and time, Ciglione will put this group on the path to success.

The challenges, however, are many. Ciglione has to overcome the perception of Chem-Trol as primarily an oil field company. The costs of market penetration are high, and efforts thus far have met with limited success. The group currently has only a 50-person sales force worldwide. The former CEO wanted to "see the group stand on its own," before committing additional resources to marketing.

The Future

Provided the challenges can be met, the opportunities for industrial chemicals are excellent. The large market in industrial water treatment offers tremendous growth possibilities for this group. Worldwide plant capacity utilization for all manufacturers of industrial water treatment chemicals is approaching 100% (see Exhibit 11). There are also additional opportunities in other areas such as specialty fuel additives.

However, the potential market projections for the Industrial Chemicals Group also indicate some potential problems. Forecasts call for a decline in U.S. industrial activity in the coming decade. This will force the group to consider focusing on the possibilities in difficult foreign markets. A number of especially large and formidable European competitors can make expansion into these markets difficult. Finally, the problems with environmental issues and increasing government regulation are significant considerations.

■ The Equipment/Instruments Group

Present Operations

Ross recognizes that the strengths of this group are based largely on the success of the oil field chemicals operation. Many of the Equipment/Instruments Group's products are natural "follow-ons" to chemical sales. Problems of management conflict, however, pose difficulties in coordinating the two group's activities. There is little, if any, cross communication.

Exhibit 11 **Global Plant Utilization, 1985–1990: Industrial Water Treatment Chemicals**

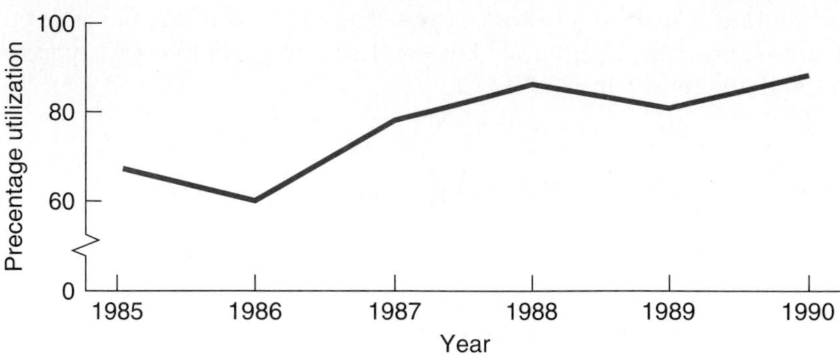

The Future

Much of the Equipment/Instruments Group's potential, based on current capabilities, is found in foreign locations such as the Pacific Rim and Asia, where even the Oil Field Group's representation is limited, and the group has limited marketing and customer support capacity in these markets. Ross feels that if Equipment/Instruments has a future, it lies in the increasing demand for improved industrial water quality and the need to measure that quality through accurate monitoring technology.

The group is not specifically positioned to take advantage of this opportunity, however. This would involve what has been presented to Ross as "significant" capital expenditures to retool manufacturing facilities. Ross asked the general manager to prepare more specific projections regarding these possibilities.

■ The Specialty Plastics Group

Present Operations

Since Ross served as general manager of this group prior to being elevated to CEO, he has an excellent understanding of the group's operations and potential. He has confidence in the manager he named as his replacement. There are, however, both internal and external trouble spots. Internally, the Specialty Plastics Group is the only area of the company that has a unionized manufacturing operation. Demands for increasing wages and benefits constantly jeopardize the group's operating margins.

Externally, Ross sees the group's greatest threat as a shortage of raw material. The wax and plastic intermediates manufactured by the Specialty Plastics Group depend on a stable supply of high-paraffin-content crude oil. This is a product that was historically plentiful and relatively inexpensive. Its primary source, however, is stripper oil production in the southwestern United States. This is precisely the type of crude oil production that has suddenly become uneconomical to produce, due to falling oil prices.

The Future

Ross feels that one of the most exciting opportunities for the Specialty Plastics Group is the increasing demand for plastic foams used in the manufacture of packaging. The group is also developing special intermediate raw materials for use in the cosmetics industry. Largely because of this, Ross feels the projected growth for Specialty Plastics is conservative.

SUMMARY

Chem-Trol Corporation has, in the past, enjoyed a number of years of sustained growth, primarily due to the rapid expansion of the markets it served. The corporation's success has been largely the result of taking advantage of opportunities as they arose. By 1990, however, an extremely turbulent operating environment, and the increasing complexity of global competition, precluded continuation of "business as usual." Clinton Ross, charged with the task of managing Chem-Trol, is proud of his company, but he has many concerns.

The greatest of these concerns is the lack of defined strategic plans. Ross is convinced that Chem-Trol has the resources, both human and material, to achieve the "billion-dollar plan." To do so, however, these resources need to be utilized in an organized fashion. He also recognizes that the company will need to define contingency plans to allow for rational reactions to uncertain, shifting markets. Additionally, Ross is uncomfortable with the lack of involvement by the chairman and the board of directors. He feels they should at least be actively reviewing the direction the corporation takes toward its goals.

Questions exist concerning the corporation's management structure. Ross wants the group managers to operate as a team, but also to accept responsibility for their groups' performance and to act accordingly. Ross will be dependent upon the group managers of the four operating units to provide him with realistic assessments of current and future business conditions. Past information often resulted in the classic "hockey stick" projections and rosy forecasts. In addition, the absence of an integrated strategic information system hampered planning at all levels in the company. Ross is particularly dismayed at the perceived lack of importance of the marketing function. It is his opinion that this is a central issue in defining an organization's direction.

Ross realizes that he will need to make critical decisions regarding the corporate business portfolio. He is not convinced the mix is correct for Chem-Trol's environment. He realizes that reaching the objectives defined by the chairman's vision will require significant growth. It will also most certainly require acquisitions. Ross has to be sure that these both complement the company's present strengths and position it to take advantage of future opportunities.

Despite the challenges, Clinton Ross remains optimistic. His company has enjoyed a long history of success. He has the resources and expertise represented by this legacy to support his efforts in positioning Chem-Trol for the future. Ross believes that with proper planning and allocation, the future will be assured.

CASE 12

United States Gypsum Corporation

A.J. Almaney, DePaul University

INTRODUCTION

U.S. Gypsum, as its name indicates, produces and markets gypsum-based products used in construction, as well as other related building products. Gypsum is a mineral that is found in mines and quarries around the world. Known as the "mineral with memory," gypsum can be melted down and processed into a host of forms with many uses. Legend has it that thousands of years ago, a Chinese shepherd built his campfire on some white rock (which was gypsum). The fire removed the water from the gypsum (gypsum is 28% water by weight) and left a white powder. The next morning the shepherd dumped water on the embers of the campfire. The water mixed with the white powder to form a fluid that later hardened into rock (gypsum). At that time, the shepherd thought he had witnessed a miracle; however, what he observed is essentially the process used today to change gypsum into plaster. Historical evidence indicates that gypsum was used 5,000 years ago to build the pyramids in Egypt. Artists, such as Leonardo da Vinci, created works on gypsum plaster in palaces. In the late 1700s, Lavoisier, a French chemist, worked with gypsum (also referred to as plaster of paris) to determine its secrets.[1]

In the United States, the first very large-scale use of gypsum in buildings was at the 1893 World's Columbian Exposition in Chicago, where several model buildings were completely structured with gypsum. In the early 1900s, gypsum board was used for partitions in New York City's buildings.[2] Gypsum's near fireproof quality made it a prime candidate for building construction.

The author wishes to express his appreciation to graduate students J. Jenkins, K. Landauer, R. Pekosh, and D. Schacht for assisting him in the preparation of this case.

This case is intended for classroom discussion only, not to depict effective or ineffective handling of administrative situations. All rights reserved to the author and the Midwest Society for Case Research.

United States Gypsum Corporation, a Fortune 200 company, is composed of six units: United States Gypsum Company, USG Interiors Company, L&W Supply Company, DAP Inc., Canadian Gypsum Co., Inc. (CGC), and USG International Ltd.

Producing gypsum and gypsum-related products is the major function of the United States Gypsum, L&W, and CGC subsidiaries. In this arena, the major competitors in North America are National Gypsum Company, Domtar, Inc., Georgia Pacific Corporation, and the Celotex Corporation. In 1989, United States Gypsum Company had a U.S. market share of 34% and was labeled the leading gypsum producer in the world, supported by L&W Supply and Canada-based CGC.[3] Gypsum accounted for 57% of USG's 1990 sales and 75% of its profits.[4]

USG Corporation's subsidiary, USG Interiors, and a portion of CGC, Inc. are responsible for producing building interiors. CGC is the leading gypsum board producer in Eastern Canada. In 1989, USG Interiors was cited for the success of its ceiling tile sales to Europe, a market that is expected to grow 20% over the next few years. DAP's primary responsibility is the manufacture of materials for remodeling and repair purposes. DAP boasts several leading competitive brands. For the interiors market, the major competitors are Celotex Corporation, National Rolling Mills, Armstrong World Industries, and the Chicago Metallic Corporation. These non-gypsum-producing entities are responsible for approximately 40% of USG's total sales and were growing by approximately 10% in 1990, due to USG's presence in Europe and the Far East.[5] USG International, Ltd. is responsible for the corporation's global operations.

The primary products generated by the gypsum-producing unit, the company's core business, include wallboard, sheathing, baseboard, mobile home board, lay-in panels, soffit board, lawn and garden gypsum, agricultural gypsum, plaster, industrial gypsum cements and fillers, spray textured finish, textured panels, cement board, and joint compound.[6]

Unfortunately, the past few years have been relatively unkind to USG Corporation. It has faced numerous lawsuits for asbestos-related illnesses, price-fixing, and violation of employees' rights. In the mid-1980s, USG's stock price began to fall, and one of USG's stockholders, Desert Partners Ltd., threatened to take over the company. USG's board of directors and management opposed the hostile bid and decided to fight back through recapitalization.

In the third and fourth quarters of 1990, USG experienced an $11 million loss. This resulted from the slump in new-home and building construction that has been going on for the past four years[7] and is expected to continue for the next decade, particularly in large cities.[8] In the meantime, USG's inventories are accumulating, forcing its plants to operate only six days a week rather than the usual seven. What can USG do in response? Can USG resolve its dilemma by divesting some of the company's assets? Or is filing for bankruptcy the only possible alternative?

HISTORY OF UNITED STATES GYPSUM CORPORATION

To understand USG's present situation, one must understand the evolution of the company. USG was founded in 1902 by a group of small gypsum suppliers. It was incorporated in Illinois in 1920 as United States Gypsum Company.

USG's original mission at the time of its founding in 1902 was to "develop and produce gypsum products of such consistent quality and performance that they would become the industry standard of excellence."[9]

In 1906, USG's president, Sewell Avery, was largely responsible for recruiting a competent staff and implementing modern manufacturing and marketing policies needed to develop USG. USG hired geologists to search for gypsum deposits, skilled engineers to mine the mineral, and researchers to experiment to find its best uses. In the early years, USG prided itself on its efficient production processes and a concern for employee safety that was uncommon in the early 1900s.[10]

The year 1915 marked the beginning of USG's product line expansion. It began producing lime and sheetrock gypsum wallboard. Sheetrock paved the way for development of gypsum sheathing, drywall, and panels. Two of gypsum's biggest assets are its ease and speed in construction and near fireproof quality. These features led the U.S. government to contract with USG during both world wars. In World War II, USG supplied over one billion square feet of wallboard for military facilities.[11]

Through the years, USG continued to expand product lines through innovation and diversification. The company began producing acoustical wood fiber, metal insulation, roofing, and water-resistant gypsum core. Today, gypsum wallboard has replaced plaster in almost all new office buildings and homes.[12] In its diversification efforts, USG has acquired a myriad of companies and resold several of them, including BPB Industries, Ltd., London, England; United Cement Company of Alabama; Warren Paint and Color Company in Nashville; Kinkhead Aluminum Industries; Float-Away Door Company; Chicago Mastic Company; and Hollytex Carpet Mills of California.[13]

THE BOARD OF DIRECTORS

The board of directors is composed of five USG officers and nine outside directors. The board also has a representative from BPB Industries, a London-based construction company. Board functions are performed by six committees: executive, compensation, audit, public affairs, finance, and director nomination. The board meets on a regular basis to review company operations and counsel the chief executive officer concerning the corporation's future direction.

MANAGEMENT

Eugene B. Connolly, the chief executive officer of USG, was born in 1932 in New York. He received a bachelor's degree in management in 1954 and an MBA degree in marketing in 1964, both from Hofstra University. From 1955 to 1958, Connolly served as an officer in the U.S. Navy.

Connolly joined United States Gypsum Company in May 1958. He has served in a variety of management positions, including president and chief executive officer of USG Corporation, executive vice president of USG Corporation, president and chief executive officer of USG Interiors, Inc., president and chief executive officer of DAP Inc., and president and chief operating officer of U.S. Gypsum Company.[14]

Connolly follows a participative decision-making style. He often meets with various managers and seeks the advice of members of the board before making a decision.

USG's executive officers are all between the ages of 45 and 65; some have both a legal and a business background. All have held senior positions in various areas of the corporation for five or more years. Some also serve on boards of other corporations.

CORPORATE CULTURE

USG's corporate culture is built around the notion of providing customers with high-quality products and consistent, reliable service. The essence of the culture is captured in what the company executives refer to as "The USG Franchise."

Four ingredients make up the USG Franchise. First is safety, which has been firmly ingrained in every employee. Considered the most important part of every manufacturing job, safety extends from the plant to the construction site. Second is USG's customer service orientation. Customers are treated in a way that guarantees repeat business and encourages loyalty to USG products. Third, USG emphasizes high ethical standards. These standards apply to every aspect of the corporation's business. The fourth ingredient of the corporate culture is USG's commitment to technological innovation. Being on the forefront of technology has enabled USG to increase productivity, lower operating costs, reduce lead time, and increase market share.

Supporting the USG Franchise is a philosophy that permeates the organization—namely, the corporation is committed to maintaining and expanding its leadership position in its core businesses. This goal is accomplished by using expertise in product and process development, a comprehensive sales and distribution network, low-cost manufacturing facilities, and the ability to deliver consistently high-quality building products at low prices.

USG UNITS

United States Gypsum Company is the largest manufacturer of gypsum in North America. The company holds a 34% market share of total gypsum board sales in the United States. This makes the company a leading player in the industry, followed by National Gypsum with 25%, Georgia Pacific with 12%, Domtar with 11%, and Celotex with 7%. The remaining 11% is shared by several smaller companies.

In 1990, net sales and profits of USG declined. The primary reason for the decline was an 8% lower selling price for gypsum wallboard, which management attributed to growing industry overcapacity. During 1990, about 14%, or 3.5 billion square feet, of gypsum wallboard manufacturing capacity in the industry remained unused, compared to about 2% during the peak year of 1986.[15]

USG Interiors, Inc. manufactures and markets a diverse product line of ceiling, wall, and floor systems. Specifically, it produces ceiling tile and suspension systems for commercial and residential applications, access floors, and relocatable wall systems. Since 1987, USG Interiors' operating profit has risen 28%, but profits from nonresidential business have declined by over 7%.

During 1990, USG Interiors implemented an operational improvement effort, known as the Quality Way, among its hourly and salaried employees. Quality improvement teams (QITs) were established at every USG Interiors office and plant location. Under the direction of its QIT, each location controls its own training, problem solving, and employee participation. According to management, the program resulted in noticeable improvement in product quality.[16]

L&W Supply Corporation is the nation's largest distributor of gypsum board and other building materials. It operates 128 distribution centers in 33 states and supplies about 9% of all gypsum board sold in the United States. In 1990, both net sales and operating profit of L&W were lower than those of 1989.

In 1991, L&W will continue to be adversely affected by declining housing starts, lower gypsum board prices, and overcapacity in distribution.

Canadian Gypsum Co., Inc. (CGC Inc.) is 76% owned by USG Corporation and is the leading gypsum board producer in eastern Canada. CGC had 1990 total sales of $173 million in U.S. dollars, which compared with $208 million for 1989. Operating profit in 1990 totaled $27 million in U.S. dollars, compared with $49 million in 1989. The decline in operating profit was due primarily to sharply lower volume and selling prices for wallboard. An extended commercial construction trade strike in Ontario also contributed to the earnings decline.

CGC and two of its competitors began a cooperative program in 1990 to accept scrap wallboard from new construction for recycling. With landfills rapidly reaching capacity levels, Toronto banned the dumping of wallboard scrap in landfills. Under the new program, CGC's Hagersville, Ontario, plant is expected to receive between 20,000 and 30,000 tons of wallboard scrap per year for recycling.

USG expects the current Canadian economic recession to continue throughout 1991. High interest rates, a new value-added tax, and a depressed economy have contributed to extremely soft housing and nonresidential construction activity.

DAP Inc. is the nation's leading manufacturer of caulks and sealants and holds strong market positions in a variety of products for the new–remodel segments of the construction industry. DAP products also include adhesives, wood preservatives, paints and coatings, grouts and mortars, glazing and spackling compounds, and other specialty products. In 1990, poor economic conditions and a slowdown in growth of personal disposable income led to a drop in the company's sales and operating profits.

In May 1991, USG put DAP Inc. on the market in order to raise the funds necessary to cover interest charges.

In 1990, USG Corporation formed a separate operating unit called USG International, Ltd. to manage the corporation's international business. The new unit was charged with the responsibility of formulating and implementing the corporation's strategy of becoming a global leader in the development, manufacturing, and marketing of building systems.

USG International combines into one operation the previous international marketing and manufacturing operations of USG Interiors, the export functions of United States Gypsum Company, and its investment in Thai Gypsum.

The global market is viewed by USG as offering a substantial opportunity. To capitalize on this market, the corporation established an acoustical ceiling tile plant in Aubang, Belgium, in addition to its facilities in Australia, Mexico, New Zealand, and Malaysia.[17]

As a result, sales outside of the United States and Canada grew to $184 million, or 10% of total sales in 1990. Including Canada, total international sales in 1990 accounted for 18.6% of total net sales. The corporation's long-term goal is not only to sell products in the international market, but also to market its business expertise and technology. For data on sales and profits of USG units, see Exhibit 1.

HOSTILE TAKEOVER BID

In October 1987, one of USG's common shareholders, Desert Partners, Ltd., indicated that it had purchased 9.8% of USG common shares and proposed a leveraged buyout, which USG rejected. In February 1988, Desert Partners offered to purchase 21.5 million shares of common stock at $42 per share. The tender offer was later amended to increase the amount of common stock subject to purchase to 39 million shares. The USG board refused the offer and searched for ways to make the hostile buyout difficult to carry out. Toward that end, USG developed a recapitalization plan in May of 1988 that offered each shareholder $37 per share in cash, $5 pay-in-kind securities, and one new share of common stock in the new company for each old share. Although the deal was valued at $49 per share, compared to $42 per share from Desert Partners, this promise to shareholders caused USG to take on $2.6 billion in debt.[18]

USG sought to finance this debt by acquiring $1.6 billion from foreign and domestic banks, by divesting some divisions, and by strictly managing cash flow. In 1988, the company sold its Masonite division for $400 million, the Kinkead Division for $58 million, and the Marlite division for $18 million. The company also sold its corporate headquarters to Manufacturers Life Insurance

Exhibit 1 **Sales and Profits of USG Units (in millions)**

	Sales		*Profits*	
	1990	*1989*	*1990*	*1989*
USG	$928	$1,032	$115	$173
USG Interiors	564	549	na	na
L&W	478	485	4	7
CGC	173	208	27	49
DAP	181	186	10	12
USG International	184	na	na	na

Co. of Toronto for $60 million and received $6.4 million for the sale of its corporate jet.[19] Cash proceeds from these divestitures and sales were used to repay its loan debt.

Further cutbacks included:

- DAP's closure of two plants in California and Georgia.
- L&W Supply's closure or consolidation of 18 distribution centers and a new policy of leasing rather than buying cars and trucks for transport.
- CGC's consolidation of ceiling and acoustical tile into one division called CGC Interiors.[20]

In addition, more than 550 salaried positions were eliminated during 1990, bringing the total number of employee reductions since mid-1987 to nearly 1,600 (excluding eliminations resulting from asset sales). These reductions eliminated one in four salaried positions, resulting in an annual overhead reduction of about $65 million. Despite these efforts, USG was still left with total debt of $2.4 billion.

Some financial analysts questioned USG's recapitalization decision. First, the company based its decision on expectations of steady housing starts, growth from remodeling, and increased nonresidential construction. USG's ten-year forecast failed to include a contingency plan to address the possibility of a recession. Second, the company expected to receive more money from the sale of its three businesses than it actually did. Analysts believe that one positive aspect of the recapitalization is that employees now own a much larger share of the company, which may protect USG from another hostile takeover threat.[21]

As of October 30, 1990, USG's common stock was selling for less than $2 per share, which is largely due to the company's current financial condition. USG's bond prices have also dropped, as a result of National Gypsum's and Celotex's recent filings for Chapter 11. Additionally, USG is paying high interest expenses for the loans used to recapitalize the company. Recent articles report that USG suffered an $11 million net loss during the current quarter and will be forced to further restructure its organization and implement even tighter cash flow solutions.[22] (See Exhibits 2–4.)

MARKETING

USG maintains a long-standing policy of producing high-quality products along with a total commitment to excellence in providing consistently reliable customer service before and after a sale. USG's products, however, are seasonal. Sales are generally greater from the middle of spring through the middle of autumn than during the remaining part of the year. The business is also affected by the cyclical behavior of the new-residential and nonresidential construction markets.

The company's gypsum board product is distributed by L&W Supply Corporation, a USG subsidiary that operates 128 distributorships strategically located throughout the United States. The specific distribution channels L&W relies upon include mass merchandising, building material dealers, contractors, and industrial and agricultural users. A computer-generated distribution program introduced at U.S. Gypsum enabled the company to refine product distribution. This program resulted in lower distribution costs, without affect-

Exhibit 2

USG Corporation Consolidated Statement of Earnings (all dollar amounts in millions except per-share figures)

	Year ended December 31		
	1991	*1990*	*1989*
Net sales	$1,712	$1,915	$2,007
Cost of products sold	1,385	1,499	1,506
Gross profit	$ 327	$ 416	$ 501
Selling and administrative expenses	194	203	209
Restructuring expenses	–	18	–
Operating profit	$ 133	$ 195	$ 292
Interest expense	333	292	297
Interest income	(11)	(8)	(10)
Other expense, net	5	5	15
Nonrecurring gains	–	(34)	(33)
Earnings/(loss) from continuing operations before taxes on income	$ (194)	$ (60)	$ 23
Taxes on income/(income tax benefit)	(53)	(6)	3
Earnings/(loss) from continuing operations	$ (141)	$ (54)	$ 20
Discontinued operations			
Operating earnings, net of taxes	–	5	6
Reserve for DAP divestiture and gains on other divestitures, net of taxes	(20)	(41)	2
Net earnings/(loss)	$ (161)	$ (90)	$ 28
Earnings/(loss) per common share			
Continuing operations	$ (2.53)	$ (.99)	$ .37
Discontinued operations	(.38)	(.66)	.14
Net earnings/(loss) per common share	$ (2.91)	$ (1.65)	$ .51

Source: USG Corp., 10-K Form, 1991, p. 23.

ing customer service and delivery schedules. During the first year of full operation, the program increased wallboard profitability by more than $10 million.

As was noted earlier, Gypsum product prices have declined steadily since 1987. This price decline has been due in part to both greater industrywide production and recent depressed construction activity levels.

PRODUCTION

Gypsum is the corporation's major raw material and is obtained from the corporation's mines and quarries throughout North America. USG's mines and quarries provide the essential raw material for manufacturing gypsum wallboard.

Proven reserves contain about 249 million tons, of which about 69% are located in the United States and 31% in Canada. The corporation's total average annual production of crude gypsum in the United States and Canada

USG Corporation Consolidated Statement of Cash Flows

Exhibit 3

	Year ended December 31		
	1991	*1990*	*1989*
Cash Flows from Operating Activities			
Earnings/(loss) from continuing operations	$ (141)	$ (54)	$ 20
Reserve for DAP divestiture, net of taxes	(20)	(41)	–
Adjustments to reconcile earnings/(loss) from continuing operations to net cash:			
Depreciation, depletion and amortization	68	76	79
Interest expense on pay-in-kind debentures	63	54	46
Deferred income taxes	(13)	2	8
Net gain on asset dispositions	(3)	(37)	(22)
(Increase)/decrease in working capital:			
Receivables	(16)	(7)	(20)
Inventories	(7)	6	1
Payables	(14)	(23)	(27)
Accrued expenses	132	20	(14)
(Increase)/decrease in other assets	(9)	3	14
Increase/(decrease) in minority interest	(2)	(1)	(6)
Other, net	(9)	–	2
Net cash flows (to)/from operating activities	$ 29	$ (2)	$ 81
Cash Flows from Investing Activities			
Capital expenditures	$ (49)	$ (64)	$ (76)
Net proceeds from asset dispositions	5	65	53
Net proceeds from divestitures of discontinued operations	80	–	20
Net cash flows (to)/from investing activities	$ 36	$ 1	$ (3)
Cash Flows from Financing Activities			
Issuance of debt	$ 65	$ 60	$ 4
Repayment of debt	(68)	(82)	(266)
Deposit of restricted cash	(84)	–	–
Revolving credit facility, net	–	140	–
Net cash flows (to)/from financing activities	$ (87)	$ 118	$ (262)
Net Cash Flows (to)/from Discontinued Operations	$ 2	$ (9)	$ (2)
Net Increase/(Decrease) in Cash and Cash Equivalents	$ (20)	$ 108	$ (186)
Cash and cash equivalents as of January 1	$ 175	$ 67	$ 253
Cash and cash equivalents as of December 31	$ 155	$ 175	$ 67
Supplemental Cash Flow Disclosures			
Interest paid	$ 154	$ 275	$ 284
Income taxes paid	$ 15	$ 27	$ 49

Source: USG Corp., 10-K Form, 1991, p. 25.

Exhibit 4 **USG Corporation Comparative Five-Year Summary (unaudited) (dollar amounts in millions except per-share figures)**

	1991	*1990*	*1989*	*1988*	*1987*
*Operating Items**					
For years ended December 31:					
Net sales	$ 1,712	$ 1,915	$ 2,007	$ 2,070	$ 2,165
Cost of products sold	1,385	1,499	1,506	1,536	1,530
Gross profit	327	416	501	534	635
Selling and administrative expenses	194	203	209	223	253
Recapitalization and restructuring expenses	–	18	–	20	53
Operating profit	133	195	292	291	329
Interest expense	333	292	297	178	69
Interest income	(11)	(8)	(10)	(13)	(5)
Other expense, net	5	5	15	16	16
Nonrecurring gains	–	(34)	(33)	–	(50)
Taxes on income/(income tax benefit)	(53)	(6)	3	43	129
% actual income tax/(benefit) rate	(27.5)	(9.8)	14.3	39.4	43.1
Earnings/(loss) from continuing operations	(141)	(54)	20	67	170
Net earnings/(loss)	(161)	(90)	28	125	204
% to average total capital employed	5.3%	6.5%	18.2%	15.7%	15.5%
Per common share:					
Earnings/(loss) from continuing operations	(2.53)	(.99)	.37	1.26	3.31
Net earnings/(loss)	(2.91)	(1.65)	.51	2.38	3.96
Cash dividends	–	–	–	.56	1.12
Capital expenditures	49	64	76	81	143
*Financial Items**					
As of December 31:					
Working capital/(deficit)	$(2,372)	$(2,198)	$ 51	$ 102	$ 561
Current ratio	.21	.24	1.09	1.15	2.39
Property, plant, and equipment, net	$ 819	$ 825	$ 837	$ 859	$ 862
Total assets	$ 1,626	$ 1,675	$ 1,585	$ 1,806	$ 1,940
Total debt	$ 2,660	$ 2,600	$ 2,428	$ 2,643	$ 795
Total stockholders' equity/(deficit)	$(1,680)	$(1,518)	$(1,438)	$(1,471)	$ 610
Market value per common share	$ 1.63	$ .81	$ 4.50	$ 5.63	$ 29.13**
Average number of employees	11,800	12,700	13,400	14,400	15,200

Source: USG Corp., 10-K Form, 1991, p. 47.

*Results reflect DAP (sold in 1991), the Marlite Division of USG Interiors (sold in 1989), Wiss, Janney, Elstner Associates, Inc. (sold in 1989), Masonite Corporation (sold in 1988), the Kinkead Division (sold in 1988) and A.P. Green Industries, Inc. (spun-off in 1988), as discontinued operations. A.P. Green's 1987 results of operations were included in a divestiture reserve and therefore are not reflected in 1987 consolidated net earnings. Financial items reflect the distribution of A.P. Green common stock as though it had occurred as of December 31, 1987.

between 1985 and 1990 was 9.4 million tons. For the locations of USG's production facilities, see Exhibit 5.[23]

The corporation maintains an active program of finding and developing new reserves, with corporate geologists estimating that recoverable reserves of gypsum are sufficient for more than 30 years of operation based on recent average annual production.

Locations of USG's Production Facilities **Exhibit 5**

United States	
Baltimore, Maryland	Norfolk, Virginia
Boston (Charlestown), Massachusetts	Oakfield, N.Y.
Detroit (River Rouge), Michigan	Plaster City, California
East Chicago, Indiana	Plasterco (Saltville), Virginia
Empire (Gerlach), Nevada	Santa Fe Springs, California
Fort Dodge, Iowa	Shoals, Indiana
Fremont, California	Sigurd, Utah
Galena Park, Texas	Southard, Oklahoma
Gypsum, Ohio	Sperry, Iowa
Jacksonville, Florida	Stony Point, N.Y.
New Orleans, Louisiana	Sweetwater, Texas

Canada	*Mexico*
Hagersville, Ontario	Puebla, Puebla
Montreal, Quebec	(two locations)
St. Jerome, Quebec	

The other major component of drywall is paper for outer coating; this material is produced from waste paper, which is in abundant supply. The waste paper and other raw materials used in this industry are purchased from numerous local and national firms.

USG's gypsum and other plants are substantial users of thermal energy. The company uses primarily six major fuel types in the following order: natural gas 74%, electricity 10%, coal 6%, oil 5%, coke (coal by-product) 4%, and steam 1%. These fuels come from various suppliers, and USG feels that there will be sufficient supplies for the foreseeable future.[24] No shortages of raw materials used by the corporation are expected for the foreseeable future.

The company's North Kansas City, Missouri, paper plant was recognized for initiating and promoting sound waste management practices and was awarded the Missouri Waste Control Coalition's Outstanding Achievement Award in the recycling and resource recovery category. The Shoals, Indiana, mine received the mining industry's top safety award in the underground nonmetal category for the sixth time. Two other U.S. Gypsum mines, in Oakfield, N.Y., and Sperry, Iowa, placed second and third, respectively.

Expenditures for plant modernization increased to $46 million for 1989, even though total corporate capital spending was down by 7%, from $84 million in 1988 to $78 million in 1989. The emphasis on plant modernization was prompted by the company's desire to enhance quality control and to maintain its reputation of providing high-quality products. The plants, however, remained underutilized due to weak demand. As a result, production has been reduced to six days per week.

The company is now studying the possibility of using computer models of the gypsum wallboard manufacturing process. The purpose of such models is to assist in pinpointing trouble spots and fine-tuning the manufacturing process.

RESEARCH AND DEVELOPMENT

USG owns three research facilities: one in Libertyville, Illinois, which focuses on product development; one in Avon, Ohio, which focuses on interior products; and one in Dayton, Ohio, which concentrates on sealant products. Due to to USG's recapitalization and the recent weakened gypsum market, research expenditures were reduced from $24 million in 1987 to $19 million in 1989.

Despite the cut in R&D budget, USG introduced, in 1990, DUROCK underlayment, a water-resistant tile substrate created especially for floors and countertops. The new product is $\frac{2}{10}$ inch thinner than standard DUROCK interior panels and is designed to compete with traditional lightweight, wood-based underlayments.[25]

The company also introduced SHEETROCK lightweight setting-type joint compounds, a line of chemically setting powder compounds for drywall interiors and exteriors. Unlike conventional setting-type compounds, this product sands easily and allows for same-day joint finishing with next-day decoration, thereby speeding job completion and saving time and money. Also introduced were TUF-TEX wall and ceiling spray texture and tinted PLUS 3 joint compound.

HUMAN RESOURCES

USG employed 12,700 people in 1990, down from 13,400 in 1989. The decline resulted from the company's efforts to streamline operations and pay off debt. Employee layoffs eliminated one in four salaried positions, resulting in an annual overhead reduction of about $65 million. One positive aspect of the hostile takeover bid was the company's effort to provide financial incentives to employees to purchase the company's outstanding common stock. As a result, employees became the company's largest group of shareholders—26%.

Employee ownership, in turn, resulted in improved corporate communication. Said Eugene B. Connolly, the company CEO, "We had to expand communications with our employees to directly share the good and the disappointing news, the challenges, strategies, and goals we need to attain."[26] The company developed five ways to keep employees informed, including *USG Bulletin,* a daily publication of urgent messages; *Looking Ahead,* a bimonthly publication that deals with company's debt; *USG Today,* an 800 telephone number for updated information on USG; *USG Employee Communications Guide,* a tool that USG officers and managers use to make presentations to employees; and *Video News,* a financial reference for USG.

Prior to these efforts, the company's communication program left much to be desired. During the restructuring phase, for example, USG came under severe criticism from employees for not keeping them abreast of what was going on. Employees were forced to find out, through rumors and the press, where cuts were being made and whose jobs were affected.[27]

The new, improved communication, however, proved inadequate in mollifying employees' ire over a company policy ordering the employees of USG's Acoustical Products unit to stop smoking on the job and at home, or they would lose their jobs. This policy was inspired by the fact that USG was named in numerous asbestos-related lawsuits. The company chose this route as one of the measures to protect itself against future lawsuits from workers who might develop lung cancer. The policy was based on information obtained from the World Health Organization that indicated that smokers who worked in an asbestos-laden environment were more likely than nonsmokers to get lung cancer. Because the affected workers did not have a union, they could be forced to accept the policy at work, which was stated to them formally, in writing, and in person. However, many employees and activist groups felt that trying to enforce nonsmoking at home would not only be impossible but would infringe on people's rights, so USG backed down on that policy.[28]

LEGAL PROBLEMS

In 1975, USG, together with National Gypsum and Georgia Pacific, was accused by the U.S. Justice Department of price-fixing. The charges were dropped in 1980, in exchange for a $2.9 million tax settlement that USG paid to the Internal Revenue Service.[29]

One of the corporation's subsidiaries, United States Gypsum, is among numerous defendants in lawsuits that seek to recover compensatory and, in many cases, punitive damages for costs associated with maintenance or removal and replacement of products containing asbestos that were installed in buildings more than a decade ago, when U.S. Gypsum ceased manufacturing such products.

The lawsuits have been brought by a variety of plaintiffs, including school districts, state and local governments, colleges and universities, hospitals, and private property owners. Two of these cases have been certified as class actions, and others request such certification. U.S. Gypsum has settled property damage claims of about 140 plaintiffs, including three cases involving 83 school district plaintiffs. Of the nineteen cases tried in the courts, twelve were won by U.S. Gypsum and seven were lost. In the cases lost, compensatory damage awards totaled $3.5 million. Punitive damages totaling $1.5 million were entered against U.S. Gypsum in three trials, which the company has appealed. As of December 31, 1990, 124 damage cases were pending against U.S. Gypsum.

FINANCE

As of December 31, 1990, total current liabilities exceeded total current assets by $2.2 billion, and the ratio of current assets to current liabilities was 0.24 to 1, compared to 1.09 to 1 as of December 31, 1989, when current assets exceeded current liabilities by $51 million. Current liabilities in 1990 increased significantly due to the reclassification of the outstanding balance of the term loan, as well as most other long-term debt issues, to current liabilities.

In February 1991, USG defaulted on about $40 million in interest payments. Skipping a payment could, in theory, have prompted lenders to force USG into involuntary bankruptcy. Or it could have triggered a Chapter 11 bankruptcy filing by the company if it wanted to seek protection from creditors. USG, however, expected creditors to provide it with a grace period and did not plan on filing for bankruptcy. In the meantime, and according to Sheryl Van Winkle, a Merrill Lynch analyst, the company continues to be, "in a very, very horrible position."[30] For financial data, see Appendix.

INDUSTRY

The gypsum industry is dependent on new residential and nonresidential markets, as well as the repair and remodel market. These markets are tied to the economy, interest rates, inflation, and availability of credit. Thus, the building materials industry is cyclical. It slacks off when the economy is poor and picks up when the economy improves. Also, "sales of gypsum products are seasonal to the extent that sales are generally greater from middle of spring through the middle of autumn than during the remaining part of the year."[31]

The outlook for the building materials industry for 1991 looks bleak. *Value Line Investment Survey* states:

> Improvements in the building materials industry doesn't look to be at hand. Weak demand in the new housing market, coupled with economic weakness in many parts of the country and stricter lending standards, is likely to prevent any gains in the residential and commercial construction sectors of the economy.[32]

Value line goes on to state that even though unemployment "has been fairly stable and at a relatively low level for some time now, we sense a certain uneasiness among potential home buyers about the course of the economy. This skittishness will likely keep the new residential construction market in a slump into 1991."[33]

Iraq's invasion of Kuwait in August 1990 exacerbated the situation. The invasion caused the price of crude oil to more than double in just two and a half months. The invasion created more uneasiness among potential home buyers about the future of the economy. In fact, new-home construction "slumped for an eighth straight month in September," creating "the longest slide since statistics were first kept in 1959, and activity slowed nationally to a recession-era pace."[34]

Another event that hurt the building material industry has been the savings and loan crisis. "The home building industry, which drives the building materials segment, relies on massive amounts of credit to buy land and purchase materials for building houses. The S&L crisis, however, has spawned new regulations that prevent S&Ls from lending large amounts to any one creditor in the real estate industry."[35]

Overall, the industry in which USG competes is headed for hard times in the future. The Iraqi invasion, the S&L crisis, legal problems, and predictions of an economic recession may all combine to reduce the size of the market in which USG operates.

COMPETITORS

■ National Gypsum

National Gypsum is an integrated, diversified manufacturer and supplier of products and services for the building, construction, and shelter markets.[36] The company has three business segments. The first is the Gold Bond Building Products Division, which produces gypsum wallboard and related products. Second, the Austin Company provides design, engineering, and construction services. The third segment encompasses specialty items including a limestone quarry and plant, two vinyl manufacturing plants, and a metal products plant. The company is estimated to have 25% of the U.S. gypsum products market.[37]

The company has gypsum manufacturing plants in Arizona, California, Georgia, Illinois, Indiana, Iowa, Louisiana, Maryland, Michigan, New Hampshire, New Jersey, New York, North Carolina, Ohio, and Texas. National Gypsum owns several mines in the United States, one in Mexico, and one in Nova Scotia. It has enough estimated recoverable gypsum to last approximately sixty-seven years, based on 1988 production. It also owns three mills that manufacture paper used in the production of wallboard. The company estimates that it operates at a 96% annual utilization of its optimum production capacity.[38]

Exhibit 6 presents data on the sales and net income of National Gypsum Co.

■ Georgia-Pacific

Georgia-Pacific is an integrated manufacturer and distributor of a wide range of building products and pulp and paper products. It sells these products through 144 distribution centers located in the United States. Gypsum products are sold by the corporation's distribution centers to building supply retailers ranging from traditional lumber yards to consumer-oriented home centers. These distribution centers enable Georgia-Pacific's manufacturing plants to operate at efficient rates of output by providing outlets for the plants' full production.[39]

Georgia-Pacific ranks third in the manufacture of gypsum products in the United States, accounting for approximately 12% of the total domestic production. The company owns gypsum mines, quarries, and deposits in Iowa, Kansas, Michigan, Nevada, Texas, Utah, Wyoming, and Nova Scotia. It owns ten gypsum board plants located adjacent to these deposits or on ports served from the Nova Scotia quarry ocean vessels. The gypsum plants are running at approximately 78% of capacity. The company estimates that its current reserves are sufficient for a 45-year supply. Gypsum research is based in Decatur, Georgia. Laboratories at universities and other institutions are also utilized in the development of new products.[40]

The company employs approximately 44,000 people. The majority of the hourly workers are members of unions. The company considers its relationship with employees to be good.[41]

Sales and Net Income of National Gypsum ($ in millions) **Exhibit 6**

	1991	*1990*	*1989*
Sales	1,136	1,332	1,364
Net income	–95	–529	–58

Source: National Gypsum Co., *10-K Form, 1991.*

Georgia-Pacific has had a long-standing concern for environmental quality. The company's operations are subject to extensive regulation by federal, state, and local agencies for environmental compliance. In the past, Georgia-Pacific has made significant capital expenditures to comply with such regulations and expects to make significant expenditures in the future to maintain compliance. Capital expenditures for pollution control facilities were approximately $39 million in 1989 (0.4 of 1% of net sales) and budgeted for $66 million in 1990.[42]

Exhibit 7 provides data on the sales and net income of Georgia-Pacific Corp.[43]

■ Domtar

Domtar Inc. is a Canadian-based company that manufactures and markets a wide range of products through four operating groups: pulp & paper products, packaging, chemicals, and construction materials. It has 16,000 employees and operates 61 facilities in Canada and 14 in the United States. Operations are supported by a network of warehouses and sales offices across Canada and in certain areas of the United States, as well as by representatives abroad. Twenty-nine percent of consolidated sales comes from the construction materials group, with gypsum products as the largest component.[44]

The company holds approximately 11% of the U.S. gypsum market and 35% of the Canadian market. It produces gypsum board at five plants in Canada and eight plants in the United States. Eight of the plants are integrated with their own rock supply. Domtar estimates that its current reserves of gypsum are ample for 25 years, at current and anticipated production levels.[45] Domtar's sales and net income are presented in Exhibit 8.

■ Celotex

The Celotex Corporation is a subsidiary of Jim Walter Corporation, which in turn is owned by Hillsborough Holdings Corporation. Jim Walter Corporation is a diversified company that started in the business of selling, constructing, and financing shell-type and partially finished homes. It has expanded into the manufacture and distribution of a wide range of building materials for residential, commercial, and renovation/remodeling uses, products for industrial uses, products for water and waste transmission, and the development of natural resources, including coal, marble, granite, limestone, oil, gas, and gypsum. The company's other businesses include production of industrial chemicals, distribution of a full line of fine printing papers, retail and wholesale credit jewelry operations, and insurance services.[46]

Exhibit 7 **Sales and Net Income of Georgia-Pacific Corp. ($ in millions)**

	1991	*1990*	*1989*
Sales	$11,524	$12,665	$10,171
Net income	142	365	661

Source: Georgia Pacific Corp., *10-K Form, 1991.*

Sales and Net Income of Domtar, Inc. ($ in millions) **Exhibit 8**

	1991	*1990*	*1989*
Sales	$1,804	$2,314	$2,515
Net income	−148	−294	33

Source: Domtar, Inc., *Ontario Securities Commission Filings,* December 31, 1991.

The Celotex Building Products Division manufactures foam insulation, gypsum board, mineral ceiling tiles, lay-in panels, and fiberboard sheathing. It markets its products primarily to building materials dealers and wholesalers, distributors, and specialized applicators. The company employs 16,750 people.

Celotex's policy is to own its plants and facilities and mineral deposits. Its gypsum reserves are located at three gypsum plants estimated to be sufficient for more than 50 years, at present and projected annual rates of consumption.[47] Data of sales and income for Celotex are not available.

CUSTOMERS

USG's customers vary from large to small. Products are distributed through different channels to mass merchandisers, building material dealers, contractors, distributors, and industrial and agricultural users. USG's export sales to foreign unaffiliated customers represented less than 10% of consolidated net sales. Also, no single customer accounted for more than 4% of consolidated net sales.[48]

GOVERNMENT REGULATORS

As a generator of hazardous substances, the industry in which USG operates is highly regulated. Owners of sites containing hazardous waste are subject to claims brought by state and federal regulatory agencies pursuant to statutory authority. Since 1981, the EPA has sought compensation and remedial action from waste generators, site owners and operators, and others under the Comprehensive Environmental Response, Compensation, and Liability Act of 1980 (CERCLA or Superfund), which authorizes such action by the EPA regardless of fault or the legality of the original disposal.[49]

DEMOGRAPHICS

Based on U.S. Census Bureau statistics, housing starts are expected to decline in the 1990s. The housing industry contributed nearly $220 billion to the Gross National Product (GNP) of the United States in 1988. However, a decrease of 100,000 housing starts will result in a drop of $12.5 billion in the GNP. The number of new housing units started dropped from 1.8 million in 1986 to 1.4

million in 1989. This drop reflects about a $50 billion drop in the GNP in the last four years. Economists expect that trend to continue with an estimated 1.2 million housing starts in 1990 and 1.0 million in 1991.[50] The dramatic decline in housing starts is attributed to the fact that fewer young people will be demanding homes. Americans from 25 to 34 years old make up the age group most likely to be first-time home buyers. In the United States, this age group is expected to decline from 43.3 million in 1987 to 36.2 million in the year 2000.[51]

Other factors that decrease the demand for housing include the trends of Americans' marrying at a later age, divorcing less frequently, and staying in their parents' homes longer. Also, the Bureau of Labor Statistics calculates that inflation-adjusted investment in residential construction will increase just 0.4% annually during the 1990s, compared to 3.9% in the 1970s and 1.2% in the 1980s.[52] Canadian sales volumes of gypsum board products have been hurt by a drop in housing starts more severe than in the United States.[53]

ECONOMY

The gypsum industry is cyclical as well as seasonal. Recently, demand for gypsum products has declined, due to the lackluster new residential construction market. The reduced demand, in turn, led to a reduction in price. One manufacturer, for example, lowered its price from $89.93 per thousand square feet in 1988 to $87.36 in 1989. The price peaked at $127.50 per thousand square feet in the fourth quarter of 1985 and hit the previous cyclical bottom of $74.73 in 1982. The 1989 prices were below the 1982 price level when adjusted for inflation.[54]

Another contributing factor to the soft demand for gypsum is the weak office building market, evidenced by a 17% vacancy rate nationwide. Cities such as Chicago, Cleveland, Washington, D.C., and New York are particularly overbuilt. The demand for gypsum products in the repair and remodeling market, which tends not to be cyclical, has been strong, but not strong enough to make up for the weakness in the residential and nonresidential/commercial markets. The repair and remodeling market continues to grow and command a larger share of the total demand annually.[55]

Economic forecasts that the economy is likely to slide into a severe recession do not bode well for USG or the industry.

TECHNOLOGY

New sources of gypsum have been found as a result of companies' efforts to control acid rain, which came to be viewed as a serious environmental threat in the United States as well as in Canada. Efforts to reduce the amount of sulphur emissions from coal-burning power stations have resulted in a new supply of gypsum. One desirable by-product from the process of scrubbing sulphur that is sent up the power station chimneys is gypsum. The desulphurization process removes at least 90% of the sulphur dioxide, while it produces gypsum that is 95% pure, which makes it suitable for commercial use.[56]

Northern Indiana Public Services Company (NIPSCO), prompted by impending federal acid rain legislation and U.S. Energy Department monetary contributions, is installing what could become the prototype scrubber for other urban area electric generators in the 1990s. The NIPSCO scrubber is scheduled to open in mid-1992 and will produce 150,000 tons of gypsum annually—enough gypsum for 150 million square feet of wallboard, which is enough for 18,750 single-family homes. USG is negotiating to purchase NIPSCO's gypsum, a move that could save USG the 900-mile rail transportation costs from its nearest gypsum mine, in addition to mining costs.[57]

The scrubber, however, may have a limited application. First, gypsum is abundant in most parts of the United States, a fact that is reflected in the dirt-cheap price of $2.00 a ton. Second, gypsum is a heavy mineral, and transportation is the most expensive component of the cost in the gypsum wallboard industry. Thus, potential power plants that could economically use scrubbers need to be near large metropolitan areas that use large quantities of wallboard. Currently, only three of five electric generators that produce gypsum can sell their output. The other two either produce inferior-quality gypsum or cannot find buyers. The U.S. Environmental Protection Agency has identified 115 power plants that will fail to comply with recent federal acid rain legislation. Some utilities will likely switch to low-sulphur coal, and others will shut down. Experts predict that an average of 10 new scrubbers a year will open, either on existing plants or incorporated into new plants, in the 1990s.[58]

European efforts to curtail acid rain are ahead of those in the United States. The Central Electricity Generating Board (CEGB) in Britain has one desulphurization plant that produces 1.1 million tons of gypsum annually. BPB Industries controls 96% of the British gypsum market and mines 3 million tons of gypsum a year. If the CEGB includes similar plants at other power stations, it will have the capacity to produce as much gypsum as BPB mines annually. In West Germany, the power stations produce so much gypsum that they pay plaster board manufacturers to take the gypsum off their hands.[59]

USG has recently developed a new wallboard product called fiber gypsum board. Fiber gypsum board does not need the two sheets of paper liner used on typical gypsum board, which represent about 30% of the cost of making wallboard. Instead, it uses wood fiber within the board, which should give the board greater strength, better soundproofing, and more enhanced fire-retardant properties than typical wallboards. Also, the new technology reduces energy costs per unit of production.[60] The new technology should give USG a significant cost advantage over its next largest competitor, National Gypsum.

SUMMARY

Up until 1987, USG was one of the most profitable and respected corporations in the United States. In that year, however, the company's "good times" came to an end when one of its shareholders, Desert Partners, Ltd., purchased 9.8% of its common stock and made an offer to acquire the company through a leveraged buyout.

USG's top management and the board of directors rejected the offer and began exploring ways to thwart the hostile buyout. As a result, the company developed a recapitalization plan in 1988 that offered each shareholder $49 per share, compared to $42 per share from Desert Partners. This strategy caused USG to take on $2.6 billion in debt.

USG sought to finance the debt by divesting some of its divisions, selling assets, and laying off salaried employees. The company also based its recapitalization plan on a continued growth in the economy and a steady increase in residential and nonresidential construction. USG's forecast of the future did not pan out, however; instead of the hoped-for growth, the economy began to sink into a severe recession, causing its common stock to fall to less than $2 per share. The company is now hemorrhaging red ink, and unless something is done to assuage the creditors, USG could very well file for bankruptcy.

ENDNOTES

1. "Products and Processes," *USG Corporation Training Manual* (Chicago: USG Corporation, 1990), pp. 5–9.
2. Ibid., p. 8.
3. United States Gypsum Corporation, *1989 Annual Report,* p. 10.
4. Stuart J. Benway, "Building Materials," *Value Line Survey* 45 (1990), part 3, p. 877.
5. Ibid.
6. United States Gypsum Corporation, *1989 10-K Report,* p. 5.
7. "11 Million Net Loss Prompts USG Layoffs," *Chicago Tribune,* 24 October 1990, Section 3, p. 1.
8. "Chicago's Office Glut Could Outlast Decade," *Crain's Chicago Business,* 26 October 1990, p. 56.
9. Ibid., p. 5.
10. Ibid.
11. Ibid., p. 7.
12. "Wall to Wall," *Forbes,* 2 July 1984, p. 45.
13. *Moody's Industrial Manual, 1990,* pp. 6400–6401.
14. *Standard and Poor's Register of Corporate Directors* (New York: Standard and Poor's, 1990), p. 286; USG Corporation, *Biography of Eugene B. Connolly,* June 1991.
15. United States Gypsum Corporation, *1990 Annual Report,* p. 7.
16. Ibid., p. 9.
17. *1990 USG Annual Report,* op cit., p. 5.
18. *Chicago Tribune,* op. cit.
19. *1989 USG Annual Report,* op. cit., p. 4.
20. Ibid.
21. "A Vote for Readers," *Financial World,* 27 December 1988, pp. 10–11.
22. "National Gypsum and Parent Seek Chapter 11 Status," *The Wall Street Journal,* 30 October 1990, p. B8.
23. *1990 USG Annual Report,* op. cit., p. 7.
24. *1989 USG 10-K Report,* op. cit, pp. 5, 8.
25. Ibid., p. 8.
26. *1989 USG Annual Report,* op. cit., p. 2.
27. "Lending an Ear to Employee Relations," *Chicago Tribune,* 29 June 1989, Section 3, p. 4.
28. "Hup 2-3-4! No Smoking," *Industry Week,* 9 February 1987, pp. 24–25.
29. *Moody's Industrial Manual,* op. cit., 1990, p. 6400.

30. David Greising, "USG's Remodeling May Mean Gutting the House," *Business Week,* 21 January 1991, pp. 54–55.
31. *1989 USG 10-K Report,* op. cit., p. 5.
32. Stuart J. Benway, op. cit.
33. Ibid.
34. *1989 USG 10-K Report,* op. cit., p. 5.
35. "Midwest Bucks Housing Slide," *Chicago Tribune,* 18 October 1990, Section 3, pp. 1 and 5.
36. Stuart J. Benway, op. cit., p. 851.
37. *Moody's Industrial Manual, 1990,* p. 314.
38. *1988 USG 10-K Report,* pp. 2–5.
39. Ibid.
40. *Moody's Industrial Manual,* 1990, op. cit., p. 314.
41. National Gypsum Co., *1988 10-K Report,* p. 4.
42. Ibid.
43. Ibid.
44. Domtar, *1989 10-K Report,* p. 4.
45. Ibid., p. 16.
46. Jim Walter Corporation, *1987 10-K Report,* p. 2.
47. Ibid., p. 7.
48. *1989 USG Annual Report,* op. cit., p. 30.
49. *1988 USG 10-K Report,* op. cit., p. 30.
50. *Construction Review,* July/August 1990, p. 9.
51. "What's Pulling the Rug Out from Under Housing," *Business Week,* 23 January 1989, pp. 104–105.
52. Ibid.
53. Stuart J. Benway, op. cit., p. 877.
54. "Gypsum Also in the Doldrums," *Industry Surveys—Building and Forest Products,* 14 December 1989, p. B87.
55. Ibid.
56. "Utility to Generate Walls as Well as Watts," *Chicago Tribune,* 22 April 1990, Section 7, pp. 1–2.
57. Ibid.
58. Ibid.
59. "Gypsum: Acid Cloud, Silver Lining," *Economist,* 15 October 1988, pp. 73–74.
60. Ibid.

APPENDIX 1: USG CORPORATION'S FINANCIAL STATEMENTS, 1991, 1990, 1989, 1988, AND 1987

Exhibit 9

USG Corporation's Consolidated Balance Sheet, as of December 31

	1991
Assets	
Current assets	
Cash and cash equivalents (primarily time deposits)	$ 155,000
Receivables (net of reserves, 1991—$9; 1990—$8)	298,000
Inventories	110,000
Net assets of discontinued operations	–
Restricted cash	84,000
Total current assets	$ 647,000
Property, plant, and equipment, net	819,000
Purchased goodwill, net	73,000
Other assets	87,000
Total assets	$ 1,626,000
Liabilities and Stockholders' Equity	
Current liabilities	
Accounts payable	$ 95,000
Accrued expenses:	
Interest	178,000
Restructuring	6,000
Reserve for DAP divestiture	–
Other	156,000
Notes payable	8,000
Revolving credit facility	140,000
Long-term debt maturing within one year	427,000
Long-term debt classified as current	2,009,000
Taxes on income	–
Total current liabilities	$ 3,019,000
Long-term debt	$ 76,000
Deferred income taxes	200,000
Minority interest in CGC	11,000
Stockholders' equity/(deficit):	
Preferred stock—$1 par value; authorized 36,000,000 shares; $1.80 convertible preferred stock (initial series); outstanding as of December 31, 1991—none	–
Common stock—$0.10 par value; authorized 300,000,000 shares; outstanding as of December 31, 1991—55,770,981 shares (after deducting 354,822 shares held in treasury)	5,000
Capital received in excess of par value	24,000
Deferred currency translation	–
Reinvested earnings/(deficit)	(1,709,000)
Total stockholders' equity/(deficit)	$(1,680,000)
Total liabilities and stockholders' equity	$ 1,626,000

Source: USG Corp., 1991 10-K Form, p. 24.

All dollar amounts in thousands except per-share figures.

USG Corporation's Consolidated Balance Sheet, as of December 31

Exhibit 10

	1990
Assets	
Current assets	
Cash and cash equivalents (primarily time deposits)	$ 175,000
Receivables (net of reserves, 1990—$8; 1989—$11)	282,000
Inventories	103,000
Net assets of discontinued operations	137,000
Total current assets	$ 697,000
Property, plant, and equipment, net	825,000
Purchased goodwill, net	75,000
Other assets	78,000
Total assets	$ 1,675,000
Liabilities and Stockholders' Equity	
Current liabilities	
Accounts payable	$ 104,000
Commercial paper and notes payable	–
Accrued expenses	
Interest	60,000
Payrolls	12,000
Taxes other than taxes on income	12,000
Recapitalization and restructuring	18,000
Reserve for Dap Inc. planned divestiture	43,000
Other	113,000
Notes payable	156,000
Long-term debt maturing within one year	268,000
Long-term debt and debentures classified as current	2,104,000
Taxes on income	5,000
Dividends payable	–
Total current liabilities	$ 2,895,000
Long-term debt	72,000
Deferred income taxes	213,000
Minority interest in subsidiaries	13,000
Stockholders' equity/(deficit):	
Preferred stock—$1 par value; authorized 36,000,000 shares $1.80 convertible preferred stock (initial series)—outstanding at December 31, 1990	
Common Stock—$0.10 par value: authorized 300,000,000 shares; outstanding at December 31, 1990—55,097,676 shares	5,000
Capital received in excess of par value	23,000
Deferred currency translation	–
Reinvested earnings/(deficit)	(1,546,000)
Total stockholders' equity/(deficit)	$(1,518,000)
Total liabilities and stockholders' equity	$ 1,675,000

Source: United States Gypsum Corporation, *1990 Annual Report,* p. 18.

All dollar amounts in thousands except per-share figures.

Exhibit 11 **USG Corporation's Consolidated Balance Sheet, as of December 31**

	1989
Assets	
Current assets	
Cash and cash equivalents (primarily time deposits)	$ 67,000
Receivables (net of reserves, 1990—$8; 1989—$11)	275,000
Inventories	109,000
Net assets of discontinued operations	139,000
Total current assets	$ 590,000
Property, plant, and equipment, net	837,000
Purchased goodwill, net	75,000
Other assets	81,000
Total assets	$ 1,583,000
Liabilities and Stockholders' Equity	
Current liabilities	
Accounts payable	$ 123,000
Commercial paper and notes payable	–
Accrued expenses	
Interest	70,000
Payrolls	21,000
Taxes other than taxes on income	14,000
Recapitalization and restructuring	12,000
Reserve for Dap Inc. planned divestiture	–
Other	121,000
Notes payable	1,000
Long-term debt maturing within one year	168,000
Long-term debt and debentures classified as current	–
Taxes on income	9,000
Total current liabilities	$ 539,000
Long-term debt	$ 2,259,000
Deferred income taxes	211,000
Minority interest in subsidiaries	14,000
Stockholders' equity/(deficit):	
Preferred stock—$1 par value; authorized 36,000,000 shares $1.80 convertible preferred stock (initial series) outstanding at December 31, 1989—none	–
Common stock—$0.10 par value: authorized 300,000,000 shares; outstanding at December 31, 1989—54,155,686 shares (after deducting 422,043 and 102,467 shares, respectively, held in treasury)	5,000
Capital received in excess of par value	15,000
Deferred currency translation	(5,000)
Reinvested earnings/(deficit)	(1,455,000)
Total stockholders' equity/(deficit)	$(1,438,000)
Total liabilities and stockholders' equity	$ 1,583,000

Source: United States Gypsum Corporation, *1990 Annual Report,* p. 18.

All dollar amounts in thousands except per-share figures.

USG Corporation's Consolidated Balance Sheet, as of December 31

Exhibit 12

	1988
Assets	
Current assets	
Cash and cash equivalents (primarily time deposits)	$ 250,045
Receivables (net of reserves, 1990—$8; 1989—$11)	278,288
Inventories	124,608
Net assets of discontinued operations	20,412
Total current assets	$ 673,353
Property, plant, and equipment, net	906,382
Purchased goodwill, net	146,469
Other assets	94,974
Total assets	$ 1,821,178
Liabilities and Stockholders' Equity	
Current liabilities	
Accounts payable	$ 125,411
Commercial paper and notes payable	1,308
Accrued expenses	
Interest	72,672
Payrolls	25,879
Taxes other than taxes on income	16,140
Recapitalization and restructuring	30,112
Other	112,089
Long-term debt maturing within one year	259,314
Taxes on income	23,027
Dividends payable	15,657
Total current liabilities	$ 681,609
Long-term debt	$ 2,384,326
Deferred income taxes	206,200
Minority interest in subsidiaries	19,988
Stockholders' equity/(deficit):	
Preferred stock—$1 par value; authorized 36,000,000 shares $1.80 convertible preferred stock (initial series) outstanding at December 31, 1988—none	–
Common stock—$0.10 par value: authorized 300,000,000 shares; outstanding at December 31, 1988 (after deducting 11,810 shares held in treasury)	5,397
Capital received in excess of par value	12,183
Deferred currency translation	(5,830)
Reinvested earnings/(deficit)	(1,482,695)
Total stockholders' equity/(deficit)	$(1,470,945)
Total liabilities and stockholders' equity	$ 1,821,178

Source: United States Gypsum Corporation, *1988 Annual Report,* p. 20.

All dollar amounts in thousands except per-share figures.

Exhibit 13

USG Corporation's Consolidated Balance Sheet, as of December 31

	1987
Assets	
Current assets	
Cash and cash equivalents (primarily time deposits)	$ 31,309
Receivables (net of reserves, 1990—$8; 1989—$11)	274,051
Inventories	144,107
Net assets of discontinued operations	415,100
Total current assets	$ 864,567
Property, plant, and equipment, net	909,078
Purchased goodwill, net	148,896
Other assets	34,980
Total assets	$ 1,957,521
Liabilities and Stockholders' Equity	
Current liabilities	
Accounts payable	$ 141,553
Commercial paper and notes payable	38,830
Accrued expenses	
Interest	12,550
Payrolls	25,509
Taxes other than taxes on income	18,429
Recapitalization and restructuring	47,681
Reserve for Dap Inc. planned divestiture	–
Other	84,008
Long-term debt maturing within one year	33,043
Taxes on income	14,761
Dividends payable	–
Total current liabilities	$ 416,364
Long-term debt	$ 724,938
Deferred income taxes	193,600
Minority interest in subsidiaries	12,786
Stockholders' equity/(deficit):	
Preferred stock—$1 par value; authorized 36,000,000 shares $1.80 convertible preferred stock (initial series) outstanding at December 31, 1987	68
Common stock—$0.10 par value: authorized 300,000,000 shares; outstanding at December 31, 1987—51,632,623 shares (after deducting 15,993,754 shares held in treasury)	206,530
Capital received in excess of par value	5,410
Deferred currency translation	(9,083)
Reinvested earnings/(deficit)	406,908
Total stockholders' equity/(deficit)	$ 609,833
Total liabilities and stockholders' equity	$ 1,957,521

Source: United States Gypsum Corporation, *1988 Annual Report,* p. 20.

All dollar amounts in thousands except per-share figures.

CASE 13

Hasbro, Inc.

Stephanie Newport, Creighton University; S. Regena Farnsworth, Texas A&M University

CASE OBJECTIVES AND USE

A major objective of this case is to enable the student to analyze and understand the threat to corporate culture that stems from the loss of a key individual whose leadership was critical to the success of the growth strategy of the firm, both in acquisitions and in product development. Second, the student has the opportunity to examine the financial and managerial consequences of related diversification through acquisition. Finally, the student is challenged to develop strategic alternatives for the established leader in a fragmented, faddish, and increasingly global industry.

CASE SYNOPSIS

Hasbro, Inc. is the number one toy manufacturer in the United States, producing such familiar toys as G.I. Joe, Monopoly, and Mr. Potato Head. The toy industry is highly fragmented and extremely faddish. The only major competitive challenger to Hasbro's dominance is Mattel, Inc. Hasbro's primary concern is to avoid the complacency that frequently undermines industry leaders and to devise a strategy that will sustain its growth in the 1990s. The death of Stephen Hassenfeld in July 1989 left the company under the sole direction of his brother, Alan. The loss of Stephen's visionary leadership in marketing, finance, and product development will certainly challenge Alan, whose expertise has been primarily in the area of operations. Hasbro's 1991 acquisition of debt-laden Tonka Toys is congruent with the company's history of acquisition

---

This case is intended for classroom discussion only, not to depict effective or ineffective handling of administrative situations. All rights reserved to the authors and the North American Case Research Association.

strategies, but the $486 million deal could frustrate Hasbro's plans for growth because of the company's heavy debt load. Key questions involve Alan's ability to incorporate Tonka with the same finesse displayed by Stephen during prior acquisitions and the effect, both in the short and long term, of Tonka's troubled financial condition on Hasbro's historically impeccable balance sheet. Will the Tonka product lineup contribute to future growth and international expansion, or will Tonka's debt erode Hasbro's financial base?

INTRODUCTION

On July 25, 1989, Stephen Hassenfeld, chairman of the board and chief executive officer of Hasbro Toy Company, died of complications of pneumonia at the age of 46. Stephen, elder of the third generation of Hassenfeld brothers to run the company, was said to be one of the few innovators in the toy industry. He had been instrumental in strengthening the company's management team, diversifying its product lines, and turning it into the largest American toy company in an industry that is extremely competitive, highly fragmented, seasonal, and faddish. Hasbro's strategic goal is to "continue our record of profitable growth, further improve our control of costs, strengthen our core franchises, and seek out attractive growth opportunities inside and outside the company, both domestically and internationally." Hasbro is acknowledged as the industry leader, but it faces the 1990s with the challenge of maintaining the company's dominance in the industry, without Stephen's leadership.

THE TOY INDUSTRY

Although toy manufacturers number nearly 800 nationwide, most of these firms are quite small, often employing fewer than 100 workers. The industry is dominated by a handful of giant companies, the largest of which is Hasbro, followed by Mattel and Fisher Price. The 1980s were characterized by consolidation and restructuring within the industry. Worlds of Wonder, maker of Teddy Ruxpin, and Coleco, producer of Cabbage Patch Kids, filed for bankruptcy. The largest toy makers became even larger through acquisitions. Hasbro alone bought such recognizable companies as Playskool, Milton Bradley, and Coleco, among others.

Acquisitions, besides reducing competition, allow companies to (1) enter new domestic and international market segments; (2) exploit economies of scale in manufacturing, distribution, research and development, and advertising; and (3) diversify product lines with well-known trademarks, often under the direction of expert managers retained from the acquired companies.

Toys are a labor-intensive enterprise, and the hand painting and assembly requirements, while not technically complicated, demand some talent, patience, and attention to detail. Asia provides an enormous, inexpensive labor pool. A large percentage of U.S. toy manufacturers have production facilities or import agreements in Asia, specifically in China, Korea, Taiwan, and Hong Kong. The reliance on offshore manufacturing and importation has grown dramatically over the last four decades.

Raw materials involved in toy production are varied and include paint, paper, plastic, and textiles. Ordinarily, supplies are plentiful and easily procured. Ethylene, a petroleum product, is the primary ingredient in the plastics essential to toy production. The severe fluctuation in petroleum prices in the last two decades has forced manufacturers attempting to keep prices stable to absorb excess costs. Hasbro suspended production of the $11\frac{1}{2}$" G.I. Joe from 1973 to 1982 because production costs virtually eliminated its profit margin.

Manufacturers of toys commonly categorize their products as "staple" or "promotional." Staple toys include a myriad of basic play items like building blocks, toy trucks, and baby dolls. Their consistent demand requires almost no advertising, and their prices and profit margins are low and stable. Lincoln Logs and Erector sets have been on the market for over 50 years. Promotional toys are introduced to the market amid massive advertising campaigns, the expense of which is a gamble a company undertakes to win the attention and dollars of toy buyers. Hasbro's Transformers, plastic cars that can be twisted about to become robots, were featured in television commercials and a half-hour-long action cartoon series. Tonka's Pound Puppies, plush stuffed animals that are "adopted" like Cabbage Patch Kids, starred in multiple television and print advertisements. The life span of most toys averages five years, but promotional toys can move into and out of fashion in a matter of months. High initial pricing of "hit" or "blockbuster" toys is intended to offset effects of their rapid decline.

Manufacturers recognize that their survival depends on their continuous search for the next "hit" toy and their ability to convert promotional toys into staple products. Hasbro spends over 5% of revenues on research and development, an amount that is 50% more than Mattel's expenditures and much more than that of any other toy company. Many products originate in the workshops of individual investors, and toy companies monitor these product sources regularly. Some toys are produced under licensing agreements such as Hasbro's Disney, Sesame Street, and Muppet characters.

Toy products must, admittedly, appeal to children. They must, however, also appeal to adults who control discretionary income. Demographic shifts in the last twenty years have had both positive and negative effects on the industry. When women's concentration on careers postpones childbearing, both spouses tend to be older, better educated, and employed outside the home. Although firstborn children outnumber sibling births, and parents and grandparents tend to spend more money on firstborns, the overall U.S. birthrate from the end of the post–World War II baby boom until recently was relatively flat. Increases in toy purchases can be attributed to dual-income families and to blended families with multiple grandparents who are living longer. Increases in the number of single-parent families and in the number of families receiving welfare support, on the other hand, dim sales prospects for more expensive toy products.

At the retail level, toy superstores like Toys 'R' Us offer millions of square feet for toy and game display. International expansion by Toys 'R' Us aids such expansion by their suppliers. The formation of the European Common Market will create a global toy market from the multiple small markets that now exist. Privatization of television broadcasting in Europe will afford toy companies the chance to export their highly effective advertising techniques. Competition in these markets should not be underestimated. European toys, despite their higher prices, also have global appeal and offer specialty stores a means of distinguishing themselves from their larger competitors. Asian competition has forced price cuts on baby dolls and their accessories.

Retail buyers require fast response from manufacturers to aid in minimizing stockouts and slow-moving items. Predicting demand is extremely difficult, and retailers, ordering Christmas stock often two years in advance, order conservatively to avoid being stuck with suddenly passe inventory. Manufacturers usually include generous return clauses in purchase contracts or concede discounts on subsequent product lines and extend credit terms through the holiday season.

The toy industry, according to Mattel Vice President Robert Sansone, is characterized by unpredictable demand, short-term, rapid changes in consumer preferences, international supply lines, currency fluctuations, intense competition, and extremely poor logistics. This is the domain in which Hasbro has chosen to compete.

HASBRO COMPANY HISTORY

The Hasbro Toy Company began in 1923 as a small textile by-product company. The Hassenfeld brothers, Henry and Hillel, immigrants from Poland, eventually discovered that the textile remnants brought a higher price when used to line pencil boxes and hats. Eventually, they began making and selling pencils. During World War II, they began making toys, since the buyers and outlets were often the same for toys and school supplies.

The second generation of Hassenfeld brothers operated the toy and pencil companies as separate entities. Merrill, with sons Stephen and Alan, ran the toy company from Rhode Island. The pencil company was located in Shelbyville, Tennessee, under the direction of Harold. When co-founder Henry Hassenfeld passed away in 1960, a serious rift developed between the brothers Merrill and Harold. There was continual disagreement over long-term goals, financing, and operational details. What once were routine management decisions on advertising budgets or inventory control became complicated negotiations. Stephen was appointed president in 1974 by his father, Merrill. When Merrill died in 1979, Harold refused to recognize Stephen as chief executive officer. Stephen had made some major errors in his first few years at the head of the toy company, but by 1979, he had become an effective manager. His track record of profitability in 1979 and 1980 provided shareholders with enough confidence to vote for a total separation of the two companies in 1980.

Stephen's first actions as an independent CEO involved cutting product offerings from 180 to 120. He justified his streamlining by saying, "In this business, more people die of indigestion than starvation." He also refined product development by polling opinions of parents, children, and industry experts earlier in the development process and preshowing more toys. These actions increased the success rate of new offerings and allowed more money per product to be spent on advertising. At the end of 1983, following a series of shrewd acquisitions, Hasbro was the sixth largest U.S. toy company, with sales of $225.4 million.

In 1984, Hasbro's friendly takeover of Milton Bradley Company and its Playskool subsidiary absorbed $360 million of internal funds, generated principally from sales of G.I. Joe products. This acquisition gave Hasbro a broader product base, complementary product lines, and a global presence through Milton Bradley's numerous international product sources and marketing outlets. In 1985, Hasbro moved ahead of Mattel to become the largest U.S. toy company.

In 1987, Stephen once again cleaned house, eliminating products that were moving too slowly, closing a plant in West Germany, and reorganizing the research and development area. In 1988, Hasbro acquired Coleco's riding toy and outdoor furniture divisions. These products accounted for about $15 million in sales for Coleco. Following Coleco's bankruptcy in 1989, the rights to produce and market the once phenomenally profitable Cabbage Patch Kids were also acquired. In 1990, Hasbro's expertise in revitalizing older products had once again led from a dismal 1988 sales figure of under $50 million to predictions of $100 million in sales for the Cabbage Patch Kids line.

Exhibit 1 provides a list of significant events in the company history.

Hasbro, Incorporated: Chronology of Important Events **Exhibit 1**

Date	*Event*
1923	Began business, Mound Metalcraft, Inc.
1926	Incorporated company in Rhode Island
1960	Henry Hassenfeld, founder, passed away
1968	Acquired Mallard Pen and Pencil Company
1969	Formed Hasbro Industries, Inc. Acquired Romper Room, Inc. Acquired Claster Enterprises, Inc. Acquired Ace Plastic Industries, Inc.
1972	Formed Hasbro Industries, Ltd. (Canada) Discontinued Nursery School Operations
1976	Discontinued Hasbro House Products, Inc.
1977	Acquired toy division of Aviva Enterprise, Inc.
1979	Merrill Hassenfeld passed away
1980	Stephen Hassenfeld named CEO
1983	Acquired Knickerbocker Toy Company Acquired Glenco Infant Items, Inc. Sold 39% Interest in company to Warner Communications
1984	Acquired Milton Bradley Company
1985	Overtook Mattel as the largest U.S. toy company
1989	Acquired Coleco Industries, Inc. Stephen Hassenfeld passed away
1991	Acquired Tonka Corporation

Sources: D. Bottorf, "War of Dollars Overshadows Fun and Games," *New England Business* 11 (March 1989):17–18. "Hasbro Names Chairman," *The New York Times,* 7 July 1989, p. D11(L). Hasbro, Inc., *1989 Form 10-Q Second Quarter Report.* Hasbro, Inc., *1987 Annual Report.* Hasbro, Inc., *Standard and Poor's Corporate Record* (New York: Standard and Poor's, 1988), pp. 3951–3953. *Moody's Industrial Manual, 1988, 1*(AI), pp. 2936–2937.

COMPANY STRUCTURE AND CULTURE

In 1964, Stephen Hassenfeld, a 22-year-old senior at Johns Hopkins University majoring in political science, left school to join his father's company. He served in various capacities in the company over the next ten years, being groomed to run the company and advancing to executive vice president in 1973 and president in 1974. His father gave him full authority of that office. His first experiments were adding day care centers and a line of housewares to Hasbro's product lines, but both were failures. He then championed a monster toy called Terron the Terrible, which resulted in a net loss for the company in 1978. His attempt to develop a return-on-investment analysis for toys was also discarded. Stephen, however, learned from his mistakes and began to rely on "gut feeling" in running the company, and he was well known for listening to ideas, regardless of their source, and approaching arguments with an open mind. It was his phenomenal intuition that was credited with moving Hasbro to number one in the toy industry and that earned him the title "mastermind of Hasbro."

Alan Hassenfeld graduated from the University of Pennsylvania in 1970 with a degree in English and creative writing. He joined the company that year and spent the next eight years setting up the international division. His major responsibilities included locating suppliers and production contractors and overseeing the licensing of Hasbro products. In 1978, he moved to marketing and sales, and in 1984, he was named president and chief operating officer of the company.

The second level of key officers includes Alfred J. Verrecchia, Barry Alperin, and George R. Ditomassi, Jr. Each of these individuals was promoted from within and took on his current position during 1990. Verrecchia is the chief operating officer, Domestic Toy Operations. Prior to holding that position, he held several others, including control of Hasbro's financial and administrative functions. Barry Alperin is the company's vice chairman, having held a number of other key positions in the organization, including co-chief operating officer, executive vice president, and president. Ditomassi was promoted to chief operating officer, Games and International, from group vice president of the Milton Bradley division.

Hasbro traditionally has been successful in recruiting key toy industry executives away from their companies and into the Hasbro lineup. Roy Wagner, a past president of Mattel, is currently a consultant to Hasbro. Bernard Loomis, a former executive at Kenner-Parker and creator of Strawberry Shortcake and Care Bears, is participating in a joint venture with Hasbro.

COMPANY CULTURE AND PHILOSOPHY

Hasbro is well known for its "family" work atmosphere, a quality that has always been important to the Hassenfelds. The relationship between Stephen and Alan was exceptional. It was based on mutual respect and was never, not even in childhood, weakened by sibling rivalry or competition. They worked together for 19 years, each making his own unique contribution to the company. Stephen's specialties encompass finance, marketing, and product development. Alan's expertise includes domestic and international operations. He serves as Hasbro's "point man" in the toy industry. Although they did not see each other much during the workday, the bachelor brothers Stephen and Alan shared living quarters and often discussed the day's events over a quiet dinner. Each generation of Hassenfelds believed in being good people, not just good businessmen, in all of their relationships—with toy inventors, customers, and employees. The earliest Hasbro employees were treated as extended family, and it was believed that if everyone in the company could feel good about himself or herself and one another, productivity would take care of itself.

Although some of the "family" atmosphere can be lost as a company grows, Stephen Hassenfeld believed in good communication and in attracting and keeping good people. The fraternal, informal, and productive atmosphere at Hasbro is a key element in employees' effectiveness and creativity. The Hasbro management team is known to listen to subordinates and outside contractors and to always be open to new ideas. Therefore, many inventors prefer to deal with Hasbro because they know their ideas will get a quick and fair hearing. Hasbro currently has over 7,000 employees, almost half of whom are represented by unions. Increasing pressure to move manufacturing offshore for labor cost advantages would suggest vigilance on the part of unions to protect existing jobs. The company, however, believes its relationship with the union is satisfactory. Employees enjoy a wide variety of benefits, including stock options and warrant plans and postretirement paid health insurance.

When Hasbro acquired Milton Bradley, many of the Bradley employees were skeptical about the merger, having heard rumors of layoffs and factory closings. Instead, the company's size actually increased by about 33%, adding $11 million to payroll expense. Stephen remarked, "There is no point to corporate marriage without an affectionate embrace." Many people, often two and three steps below senior management, attended gatherings at one another's plants and really got to know one another. The unique Hasbro culture made the smooth transition possible.

Another manifestation of the Hasbro commitment to caring for people is the Hasbro Children's Foundation, instituted in 1984. The foundation helps with health care for homeless children; contributes to AIDS education programs for children; and provides support for hearing-impaired and disabled children, sickle cell disease research, and literacy programs.

PRODUCT DEVELOPMENT

At Hasbro, many new product ideas originate internally with design, development, and marketing teams. A good portion of research and development costs cover a corporate staff that includes almost 700 designers, artists, and engineers. Additionally, thousands of free-lance inventors submit their new product ideas each year for Hasbro's review. An example of one such successful product is the Milton Bradley game "A Question of Scruples." The game was invented and originally sold by a former English lecturer from Winnepeg, Canada. Hasbro purchased the rights to market the game worldwide, except for Canada. Royalties are usually paid to such inventors in exchange for the exclusive rights to the design or idea. Hasbro also develops products that are licensed, such as characters from popular television shows, movies, or comic strips.

Taking the product from the concept stage to final form is a detailed process at Hasbro. Consumer research is conducted among children, parents, and trade members to determine reaction to the product and to learn what modifications, if any, would improve it. Then, if the product concept is still viable, a prototype is constructed so that production costs can be projected accurately. Then, the new product goes through packaging design, marketing, and advertising planning stages.

Hasbro does not always rely on market research when choosing products. Managers' intuition is also trusted. Market research indicated that My Little Pony would not be a popular toy, but management introduced it anyway, to a very receptive market.

Products usually take from a few months to a couple of years to develop, and each year's new product line is introduced at an annual toy fair in February. At any point in the product development process, a product may be "killed," no matter how much money or time has been invested. The termination of the development of NEMO, an interactive video entertainment system, serves as an example. After spending $15 million and two and a half years on its development, NEMO was canceled in late 1988. The projected retail price of between $250 and $300 was far above competitors' prices, and Toys 'R' Us declined to stock the toy.

NEMO was Hasbro's first venture into high-tech toys. When electronic game sales hit $3 billion in 1983, Hasbro was labeled "Has-Been Toys" for not having an electronic product to offer. Avoiding electronic toys had been a conscious choice, and a sound one, since this market quickly became overloaded with hundreds of hopeful competitors. No leader ever emerged from the confusion, and when the market collapsed in 1985, sales had plummeted to $100 million. Wholesalers and retailers were left with overwhelming inventories of unwanted games and cartridges.

PRODUCT LINES

Prior to its recent acquisition of Tonka, Hasbro had three major product divisions: Milton Bradley Games, Hasbro Toys, and Playskool Toys and Infant Items. Hasbro will integrate products from the Tonka line to Hasbro and Playskool; the Kenner and Parker Brothers product lines will remain separate divisions. Hasbro feels that this move may be more costly in the short run than full integration but that it will allow a stronger market position in the long run. Exhibits 2 and 3 provide examples of products sold by each of these divisions.

The Milton Bradley division uses a combination of tradition and innovation in product design to maintain strong representation in several areas. It is now the company's largest division, with a leading position in both the domestic and the international game and puzzle segment. Some of the best sellers and long-time favorites include A Question of Scruples, Battleship, Chutes and Ladders, Lite Brite, Yahtzee, and Password.

The Hasbro Toy division offers products ranging from fashion dolls and adventure toys to dress-up kits and plush toys. The division includes a higher percentage of promotional toys than the Milton Bradley or Playskool lines. As such, they are riskier, but offer a higher payoff. The 90 items in the G.I. Joe line

Hasbro Product Divisions

Exhibit 2

Hasbro	*Milton Bradley*	*Playskool*
G.I. Joe	Game of Life	Playskool Baby
Transformers	Bingo	Preschool Basics
My Little Pony	Head of the Class	Ride-Ons
Maxi	Candyland	Wooden Classics
Pogo Ball	Bed Bugs	Construction Toys
Love-A-Bye Baby	Hungry Hippo	Mighty Mos
Fairy Tails	Scruples	Fun'n Functional
B.A.B.Y.	Win, Lose, Draw	Food Fun
Now You're Cooking	Lite Brite	Preschool Dolls
Fazz	Tuba Ruba	Potato Head
Body Rap	Puzzles	Definitely Dinosaurs
Squarbles	Headache	Elect. Play'n Learn
Army Ants	Mousetrap	Puzzles
Road Hogs	Crossfire	Sports Starters
Visionaries	Yahtzee	Plush
Cops		

Adapted from Toy Survey, *Drexel Burnham Lambert,* December 1988.

Tonka Product Divisions

Exhibit 3

Tonka	*Kenner*	*Parker Brothers*
Truck & Vehicles	Ghostbusters	Nerf
Pound Puppies	Starting Lineup	Monopoly
Splash Darts	Playdoh	Risk
Spiral Zone	Always Sisters	Clue
Willow	Skyball	Boggle
Mapletown	Wish World Kids	Puzzles
Pet Store Pals	Mask	Card Games
Hollywoods	Furrever Friends	
Keypers	Silver Hawks	
Dress & Dazzle	Fashion Star Fillies	
	Bone Age	
	Special Blessings	
	Kenner Classics	
	Sky Commanders	
	Shimmers	

Source: Adaped from L. Maladowitz and D.R. Lee, "Toy Industry Year-End Review," *Drexel Burnham Lambert,* February 1989, pp. 1–18.

accounted for 15% of 1987 net revenues; the 100 versions of Transformers contributed 8%. Other items targeted at boys include Army Ants, COPS action figures, and Road Hogs. Popular items targeted at girls include My Little Pony, Maxie, and Fazz costume jewelry.

The Playskool division has strong brand awareness and a reputation for value and quality in infant and preschool products. Established toys include Tinkertoys, Lincoln Logs, Mr. Potato Head, and Raggedy Ann and Andy. Other items marketed more for the parents of infants include Baby Guards safety items and Nursa disposable bottles.

Of the Tonka divisions, the best known may be Tonka, for its toy trucks and other vehicles. However, the Kenner division also has some very successful products, such as the Starting Lineup Professional Sports figures, the Real Ghostbusters action figures, Pound Puppies, and Playdoh. The Parker Brothers division sells the ever-popular Monopoly and Clue, as well as other card games and puzzles. Additionally, Tonka distributes the Sega Video system through a joint venture with a Japanese firm. Sega runs a close second to Nintendo and offers Hasbro a strong and much needed entry into electronic toys.

Consistent with the overall product diversification strategy of Hasbro, no product is expected or desired to produce too high a percentage of overall revenue. Revitalizing older, basic toys that appeal to the nostalgia of parent-purchasers, introducing new offerings in planned stages, and stabilizing long-term sales across product lines are factors that characterize Hasbro's conservative product management style.

MARKETING

■ Advertising and Promotion

Hasbro's "marketing prowess" in supporting its new products and in regenerating its older ones is an important determinant in the company's success. New products can account for as much as 30% of Hasbro's sales each year. Second editions of popular games and accessories for toys are strong marketing tools. The Game of Life has been revised many times since its invention by Milton Bradley in 1860; the current edition is 28 years old. A second edition of A Question of Scruples was offered in 1988. G.I. Joe was reintroduced in 1982, as a 4-inch action figure, and has nearly a hundred accessories that can be purchased over a long period of time.

The company often takes an experimental approach to advertising. For example, in 1987, a live model was used to promote the Maxie doll through public appearances and television ads. Maxie's formidable competition is Mattel's Barbie. Mattel has always avoided linking Barbie with a living person, believing that her "personna" should remain a creation of children's imaginations. Tie-in promotions with food companies have been tried, such as the joint project with Wendy's Hamburgers to sell Bristle Blocs. A similar arrangement was made with McDonald's for selling Holiday Huggable Muppet Babies. In a cross-industry promotion with Kraft foods, rebates on toys were offered for food purchases, and newspaper inserts and in-store displays were used.

A significant amount of advertising expenditures go to commercial television and for the production of children's television programs based on Hasbro dolls and action figures. My Little Pony, G.I. Joe, and Transformers have each starred in a television show. Consumer groups, such as Action for Children's Television (ACT), have been active in lobbying for tougher regulations governing the commercialization of children's programming. ACT has posted guidelines for advertisers and is particularly opposed to TV shows based on toys. ACT questions the ethics of what it considers "dressed up half hour commercials" targeted at children. Hasbro executives do not see such consumer activism as a significant problem, since Hasbro has its own code of ethics, which the company believes is more stringent than those posed by outside groups.

Hasbro's guidelines include:

1. Do not talk down to children, because they are much smarter and more in tune than adults think they are.
2. Do make ads that entertain children.
3. Do make ads that explain the product.
4. Do not use comparative advertising. There is nothing to be gained. Be more product-specific in children's advertising than in adult advertising.
5. Do not make promises that cannot be fulfilled.

■ Distribution

Hasbro's products are sold nationally and internationally to toy wholesalers; large retailers; chain, department, and discount stores; and mail order houses. Hasbro maintains a sales force of 348 and uses 76 outside manufacturers' representative organizations. Of net sales, 96% were made through this sales force. Hasbro has six showrooms in the United States, and 11 in foreign countries.

Hasbro serves more than 2,500 commercial customers in the United States and Canada and more than 22,000 in other countries. Toys 'R' Us represents 12% of net revenues. Most of the finished products sold in the United States are manufactured in domestic plants. Similarly, almost all of the finished goods manufactured in foreign plants are sold in the region of manufacture. Only 39% of 1988 sales involved finished goods imported from Korea, Taiwan, or Hong Kong. All of Hasbro's imports arrive at the port of Seattle. Products are packaged there and can reach most U.S. destinations in three to four days. In a survey in which retailers rated toy items, Hasbro earned high ratings, compared to its competitors, for providing good profit margins, good cooperative and consumer advertising support, and on-time delivery.

FINANCIAL STRUCTURE

Hasbro's balance sheet has been considered impeccable by industry analysts, and its financial position was one of the strongest in the industry in 1990. Hasbro has the highest gross margin of all publicly owned toy companies, a full 5% above Mattel's.

Hasbro's financial position provides the staying power and means to exploit attractive acquisition opportunities. Between 1983 and 1990, most acquisitions were funded internally. Hasbro's debt-to-equity ratio has been steadily declining in recent years. As the company entered the 1990s, it had the lowest debt and interest payment in the industry.

The Hassenfeld family currently owns 18% of the outstanding shares of Hasbro. Stock splits are not uncommon, some as high as 3 for 2 and 5 for 2. Stock prices ranged from a low of $7.59 to $11.93 in 1982, and from $15.25 to $40.88 in 1991. Earnings per share have fluctuated over the years. In 1980, they were $1.02; in 1987, $.87, in 1988, $1.24, and in 1991, $.94. Recent financial statements are included in Exhibits 4–6.

KEY ISSUES FOR THE FUTURE

■ International Considerations

There are important international issues Hasbro must consider in the years ahead. First, there is a growing market in Europe. With the changes in the European Economic Community in 1992, and the democratization of the Eastern Bloc, there exist huge potential markets. The expansion of specialty toy retail shops and toy superstores overseas would favor increasing foreign op-

Exhibit 4

Hasbro, Inc. Financial Statements Consolidated Statements of Earnings (thousands of dollars except share data)

	Year Ending December		
	1991	*1990*	*1989*
Net revenues	$ 2,141,096	$ 1,520,032	$ 1,409,678
Cost of sales	967,359	697,817	662,486
Gross profit	$ 1,173,737	$ 822,215	$ 747,192
Expenses			
Research and product development	$ 78,983	$ 62,277	$ 58,876
Royalties	113,468	69,030	57,572
Advertising	325,282	208,342	191,785
Selling, distribution, and administrative	418,631	322,274	268,880
Total expenses	$ 936,364	$ 661,923	$ 577,113
Operating profit	$ 237,373	$ 160,292	$ 170,079
Nonoperating (income) expense			
Interest expense	$ 42,597	$ 16,523	$ 24,288
Restructuring charge	59,000	–	–
Other (income), net	(9,775)	(8,679)	(11,002)
Total nonoperating expense	$ 91,822	$ 7,844	$ 13,286
Earnings before income taxes	$ 145,551	$ 152,448	$ 156,793
Income taxes	63,897	63,266	64,599
Net earnings	$ 81,654	$ 89,182	$ 92,194
Per common share			
Earnings	$ .94	$ 1.02	$ 1.04
Cash dividends declared	$ .16	$ .13	$ .11

Source: Hasbro Annual Reports.

Hasbro, Inc. Financial Statements Consolidated Balance Sheets (thousands of dollars except share data)

Exhibit 5

	Year Ending December 29,	
	1991	*1990*
Assets		
Current assets		
Cash and cash equivalents	$ 120,614	$ 289,297
Accounts receivable, less allowance for doubtful accounts of $60,500 in 1991 and $43,100 in 1990	551,385	352,955
Inventories	208,443	137,362
Prepaid expenses and other current assets	144,807	81,956
Total current assets	$1,025,249	$ 861,570
Property, plant and equipment, net	$ 225,192	$ 169,189
Other assets		
Cost in excess of acquired net assets, less accumulated amortization of $41,400 in 1991 and $29,768 in 1990	$ 496,120	$ 153,665
Other intangibles, less accumulated amortization of $59,179 in 1991 and $44,426 in 1990	156,102	82,092
Other	47,464	18,249
Total other assets	$ 699,686	$ 254,006
Total assets	$1,950,127	$1,284,765
Liabilities and Shareholders' Equity		
Current liabilities		
Short-term borrowings	$ 36,084	$ 29,004
Trade payables	152,429	84,559
Accrued liabilities	324,391	183,935
Income taxes	80,904	60,071
Total current liabilities	$ 593,808	$ 357,569
Long-term debt, excluding current installments	$ 380,304	$ 56,912
Deferred liabilities	20,746	2,457
Total liabilities	$ 994,858	$ 416,938
Shareholders' equity		
Preference stock of $2.50 par value. Authorized 5,000,000 shares; none issued	—	—
Common stock of $.50 par value. Authorized 150,000,000 shares; issued 86,793,061 shares in 1991 and 57,862,041 shares in 1990	$ 43,397	$ 28,931
Additional paid-in capital	276,725	286,433
Retained earnings	580,211	512,291
Cumulative translation adjustments	60,297	58,233
Treasury stock, at cost, 608,784 shares in 1991 and 1,366,400 shares in 1990	(5,361)	(18,061)
Total shareholders' equity	$ 955,269	$ 867,827
Commitments and contingencies	—	—
Total liabilities and shareholders' equity	$1,950,127	$1,284,765

Source: Hasbro Annual Reports.

Exhibit 6 **Five-Year Summary, Selected Financial Information (thousands of dollars except share data)**

	1991[a]	*1990*	*1989*	*1988*	*1987*
Operating information					
Net revenues	$2,141,096	$1,520,032	$1,409,678	$1,357,895	$1,345,089
Cost of sales	967,359	697,817	662,486	638,835	647,342
Research and product development	78,983	62,277	58,876	62,439	69,472
Royalties	113,468	69,030	57,572	52,544	43,137
Advertising	325,282	208,342	191,785	189,974	213,684
Selling, distribution, and administrative	418,631	322,274	268,880	260,044	238,969
Restructuring expense	59,000	–	–	–	–
Other nonoperating expense	32,822	7,844	13,286	22,624	32,850
Earnings before income taxes	145,551	152,448	156,793	131,435	99,635
Net earnings	81,654	89,182	92,194	72,421	48,223
Common share data[b]					
Price at year end	$ $25\frac{5}{8}$	$ $10\frac{1}{4}$	$ $12\frac{1}{2}$	$ 10	$ $8\frac{1}{4}$
Earnings per share	$ .94	$ 1.02	$ 1.04	$ .83	$ .54
Book value per share	$ 11.08	$ 10.24	$ 9.11	$ 8.42	$ 7.67
Price/earnings ratio	27.26	10.05	12.02	12.05	15.28
Price/book value ratio	2.31	1.00	1.37	1.19	1.08
Statistics and ratios					
Gross profit margin	54.8%	54.1%	53.0%	53.0%	51.9%
Operating profit margin	11.1%	10.5%	12.1%	11.3%	9.8%
Net profit margin	3.8%	5.9%	6.5%	5.3%	3.6%
Effective tax rate	43.9%	41.5%	41.2%	44.9%	51.6%
Long-term debt to capitalization	39.8%	6.6%	7.2%	18.0%	19.8%
Return on average assets	4.7%	7.2%	7.8%	6.3%	4.3%
Ratio of earnings to fixed charges[c]	3.76	7.58	6.09	4.63	3.63
Supplementary data					
Capital expenditures	$ 56,004	$ 36,168	$ 42,268	$ 54,434	$ 62,692
Depreciation and amortization	$ 52,524	$ 39,734	$ 42,856	$ 50,963	$ 52,077
Property, plant, and equipment, net	$ 225,192	$ 169,189	$ 169,870	$ 164,981	$ 176,253
Cash dividends declared	$ 13,734	$ 11,447	$ 10,474	$ 9,177	$ 7,573
Number of employees	10,500	7,700	8,200	8,200	8,300

Source: Hasbro Annual Report.

[a]Includes the operations of Tonka Corporation since May 7, 1991, which accounted for $486,000 of net revenues.

[b]Adjusted to reflect the three-for-two stock split declared on February 18, 1992, for payment on March 16, 1992.

[c]For purposes of calculating the ratio of earnings to fixed charges, fixed charges include interest, amortization of debt expense, and one-third of rentals; earnings available for fixed charges represent earnings before fixed charges and income taxes.

erations, but decisions will have to be made about the scope of such an expansion.

Second, after years of court battles, the recent ruling by the U.S. Court of Appeals that classifies G.I. Joe as a doll, not a toy soldier, is a costly defeat for Hasbro. The doll designation means that Hasbro will be required to pay the 12% tariff on imports of G.I. Joe from manufacturing subcontractors in Hong Kong. Additionally, a new international classification system, the Harmonized

Commodity Description and Coding System, also places G.I. Joe in the doll category. This ruling will have significant effects on a number of Hasbro products manufactured in and imported from foreign countries.

■ Growing Pains

Although Hasbro earns, with regularity, the praise of industry analysts for its ability to revitalize older product lines, the company has not performed well in the area of new product development. Despite sizable expenditures in R&D and success overseas, the U.S. sales performance of "Record Breakers," miniature cars that can reach speeds of 30 mph, has been disappointing. Industry analysts stated that there has not been a blockbuster toy to hit the market in years and that it is not likely to happen before the mid-1990s. Hasbro must determine how much of the new product difficulty is self-inflicted and how much is an industry phenomenon.

Since the $85 million acquisition of Coleco's major assets, Hasbro has updated and reintroduced the Cabbage Patch Kids. The dolls grossed nearly $600 million in sales in 1985, then plummeted to less than $50 million in 1988. In 1990, Hasbro expects the line, supported by $12 million in TV ad campaigns and broader distribution, to produce $100 million in sales.

In 1991, Alan Hassenfeld spearheaded the $486 million acquisition of financially troubled Tonka with its classics Monopoly, Clue, Playdoh, and Tonka Trucks. Tonka had been the third largest company in the industry since 1987, following the friendly takeover of Kenner Parker for $555 million. The deal promised cash flow benefits, production and marketing synergies, and a more diverse product line. In June 1990, Tonka still owed $412 million and was staggering under the debt service requirements. The acquisition gives Hasbro a sizable lead over Mattel, since it automatically adds scores of new products to Hasbro's toy and game lineup. Although profits are expected to be increased by $40 million as a result of the purchase, Hasbro will have paid $59 million in consolidation expense.

From the time of its founding in 1932 until the end of December 1988, Hasbro operated with a functional organizational structure. The "family" corporate culture seemed to permeate all employment levels. The company decided to adopt a more decentralized, product-oriented structure with the intent to increase managerial focus and accountability on product lines, rather than on managerial services. At that time, the company reorganized into three operating divisions: the Hasbro Toy Division, the Playskool Division, and the Hasbro Manufacturing and Service Division. With the acquisition of the Tonka assets, two additional divisions will be added: Kenner and Parker Brothers. Reorganizations require adjustment periods, but within three years, Hasbro has undergone two major changes in organizational structure and suffered the loss of Stephen Hassenfeld. There can be little doubt that the old structure worked. It would not surprise industry analysts if the company's performance shows the strain of these major adjustments.

■ Executive Succession

Finally, the death of Stephen Hassenfeld could still have repercussions in the future. Will Alan be able to handle the company effectively without Stephen's visionary and supportive partnership? During the ten years that Stephen headed the company, revenues increased tenfold and investors earned a 51% average annual return. In 1990, profits were off slightly and stock prices dropped $5 a share. Although analysts attribute these events to industrywide problems stemming from video game competition, it is hardly a strong start for Alan's first year at the helm. In 1991 there were suggestions that the Hassenfeld family may decide to sell out altogether. Some possible buyers may include Nintendo, Time-Warner (already a shareholder owning 18% of Hasbro), and Walt Disney.

■ An Interview with Alfred Verrecchia

Recently, Alfred Verrecchia, formerly executive in charge of the financial and administrative functions of Hasbro and currently chief executive officer, Domestic Toy Operations, was kind enough to allow an informal interview. Mr. Verrecchia offered some candid observations about the nature of video game competition, shared concerns about international production and imports, and provided insights into the challenges facing the company in the near term. The text of this interview follows.

Question: In everything that we've read, Steve was very critical to Hasbro's success. How would you describe him?

Answer: Stephen was a very creative person who paid a great deal of attention to detail and always looked to the future—what the company would look like in five years. He had an excellent grasp of operations, but was smart enough to surround himself with people who handled operations so he could concentrate on the creative side of the business. He had little use for formalized, five-year plans and disliked doing them. He valued strategic planning, but had an informal approach to it.

Question: What kind of trends do you see for the sale of video toys through the next five years or so? What will Hasbro's strategy be in this segment?

Answer: Certainly, Nintendo is very strong. GameBoy is doing very well. There may be some "softness" beginning in the software market. There are lots of games coming out—very high number—maybe 25% are successful, the rest are mediocre to poor. Prices are going to come down eventually. Hardware is a different story—it should remain strong. Upgrading is unlikely (from 8-bit to 16-bit unit, for example), unless some real payoff is out there. Hasbro will certainly watch the market for something that is fresh and really different. Other companies took a bath with video, when Hasbro avoided the market. Atari and Colecovision were very hot and very strong in their day; then they hit the wall. This can happen overnight in the toy business. Companies with a hot item will make a big commitment to inventory, and if the toy dies, it is very expensive. It can pull a company under. With video games, microchip orders must be made six to nine months in advance. This is a very long lead time. If the toy dies while you are in production, you could be stuck with a lot of inventory you can't sell.

Question: How attractive are Hong Kong, South Korea, and Singapore as alternative production sites, relative to China?

Answer: If China were to lose its "most favored nation" status, that would be a major problem. South Korea was once very big in toy manufacturing. Most of that business is shut down now, and most of them moved to China and Singapore. It would not be easy to move back to Korea, but it could be done. Another possibility is that they could move to Taiwan, Thailand,

Malaysia, Indonesia. Indonesia and Thailand are the most attractive right now. If import duty rises to 70%, we would all be in very big trouble.

Question: Is there any concern about possible takeovers following Stephen's death? Has Time-Warner increased their holding beyond 20%?

Answer: Time-Warner doesn't own quite 20% any more. They have 10 million shares out of 58 million. We have a repurchase agreement with them, as well as a standstill that is still in effect. We're not concerned any more than we ever were about a takeover. As long as we keep the company well run and keep shareholder value up, we shouldn't have a problem. Unfriendly takeovers in the toy industry are not common.

Question: Can you share any of Hasbro's intentions regarding the Cabbage Patch Kids?

Answer: Maintain the original concept and continue to market them as before with the adoption papers. We have worked very closely with Xavier Roberts and have introduced some new, fresh ideas within the line.

Question: If you had to guess, how many inventors contact Hasbro about new products ideas each year?

Answer: Hasbro looks at 2000 to 3000 different products in a year. Very few of them will eventually be adopted, but we keep development people available. There is an "inventor community" out there that is a primary source of ideas.

CASE 14

American Airlines in a Deregulated Environment

Hooshang Kuklan,* North Carolina Central University

COMPANY HISTORY

A number of small airline companies were consolidated in 1929 into Aviation Corporation.[1] This conglomeration was incorporated in 1930 into American Airways and underwent another reorganization in 1934 and became American Airlines.

■ The Early Years

Soon after its formation in 1934, American Airlines developed an airways traffic control system that was later adopted by other airlines and administered by the U.S. government. In 1936, American inaugurated commercial flights between Chicago and New York with the DC-3, which was built to American's specifications and became one of the most famous commercial airplanes in history. By the end of the 1930s, American was the nation's number one domestic air carrier.

■ The Forties

American entered the airline catering business in 1942 with a subsidiary called Sky Chefs. Development of new commercial airplanes, which had stopped dur-

*The author wishes to extend his sincere appreciation to the management of American Airlines for sharing with us their deregulation strategies. Special thanks go to Brad Jensen, Managing Director of Schedules Planning. This case relies on the generous supply of data provided to the author by American Airlines.

This case is intended for classroom discussion only, not to depict effective or ineffective handling of administrative situations. All rights reserved to the authors.

ing World War II, resumed after the war, and American became the first airline to retire its DC-3s. By 1949, American had become the only airline in the United States with a completely post-war fleet of pressurized passenger airplanes.

▪ The Fifties

In the early 1950s, American developed a new electronic reservation system, and in 1962, it installed SABRE, a highly sophisticated airline reservation system. SABRE was expanded in 1972 and again in 1975.

In 1953, American pioneered nonstop transcontinental service in both directions across the United States with the DC-7. In 1957, the company became the first airline to establish a special facility for flight attendant training called the American Airlines Stewardess College. It was later renamed the Flight Service College and subsequently the Learning Center. The size of the facility more than doubled from 1957 to 1986, and training activities widened to include instruction of other American Airlines personnel. In 1959, the company began the first cross-country jet service using the new Boeing 707.

▪ The Sixties

The Boeing 727 was added to the fleet in 1964. In 1968, American was the first to order the McDonnell Douglas DC-10, a big, versatile, quiet tri-jet that made its first scheduled flight in August 1971.

▪ The Seventies

American gained its first Caribbean routes through a merger with Trans Caribbean Airways in 1970, introduced one-stop automated check-in in 1974, completed the final phase of a plan to consolidate its eleven U.S. mainland reservation offices into four regional centers in 1977, and invented Super Saver fares to stimulate discretionary travel in 1977.

In October 1978, Congress passed the Airline Deregulation Act, which amended the Federal Aviation Act of 1958 and ended an era of far-reaching federal control over the operations of airlines. The law intended to encourage price competition, eliminate restrictions on fares, routes, and frequency of flight changes, remove several barriers of mergers and acquisitions, and, in brief, make the airline industry more competitive. The 1978 deregulation was the most significant development in the history of U.S. civil aviation.

In the summer of 1979, American moved its headquarters from the New York metropolitan area to the Dallas/Fort Worth region. Robert L. Crandall became president of American Airlines in 1980.

AMERICAN AIRLINES IN A DEREGULATED ENVIRONMENT

An executive of American Airlines characterized the impact of the legislation on American as follows:

> Deregulation, as anticipated, opened the industry to intense competition and made it highly cost-conscious. Only the low cost airlines had a chance to succeed. American Airlines just could not compete with such new low-cost carriers as

> People Express, New York Air, Northeast, and later the reborn Continental Airlines. The cost structure at low-cost airlines was up to 22 to 35 percent lower than ours. American had to get its cost down to the new market-place levels.
>
> In brief, American was confronted with a number of most challenging tasks. To survive in a highly competitive deregulated environment, American had to find ways of changing its fleet and route structure, expanding its ground facilities, lowering its cost to competitive levels, and changing the nature and scope of its operations.[2]

American Airlines responded to the deregulation of 1978 with four major strategies in order to improve its competitive posture:

1. Improve the aircraft mix and increase the seating density of the fleet.
2. Minimize labor costs.
3. Restructure and strengthen the route system.
4. Maximize revenue by expanding the use of American's computer reservation system, developing new frequent flyer programs, establishing a system of feeder service to American's major hub cities, and initiating structural readjustments.

Improving Fleet Mix

One of the biggest deregulation tasks confronting American was to replace the inefficient portion of its fleet with fuel-efficient aircraft. At the 1989 price level, a fuel price increase of one cent would raise American's monthly fuel costs by $1,750,000.

Twenty-six of the 707s, a fuel-inefficient aircraft, were removed from service in January 1981, and the remaining 36 aircraft (including nine 707s freighters) were retired by the summer of the same year.

In anticipation of the retirement of 707s, American placed an order in November of 1978 to buy 30 transcontinental twin-engine 767s. The 767 accommodates 204 passengers in a mixed first class and coach arrangement and performs the same mission as the 707 but does so providing greater comfort and fuel efficiency. In November 1982, American introduced into service the first of 30 Boeing 767 jetliners.

In 1983, American further expanded its fuel-efficient fleet with the acquisition of 20 Super 80 aircraft from McDonnell Douglas Company. Later, 13 more Super 80s were acquired. On February 29, 1984, American announced the largest airplane buy in commercial aviation history up to that point when it placed an order for 67 Super 80s and acquired options to purchase an additional 100 planes.

In 1987, the company announced that it would acquire two new types of long-range wide-body jets (25 A300-600ERs from Airbus and 15 Boeing 767-ERS) for its international routes. And in 1988, American ordered 50 757-200 aircraft with an option for 50 more.

From 1978 to 1985, the percentage of American's fuel-efficient fleet increased from 15 to 44, and the percent of seats in the fuel efficient portion of the fleet jumped from 29 to 53 during the same seven-year period following deregulation. The fuel-efficient portion of American's fleet and also of its seating capacity were anticipated to increase to 64 and 69 percent, respectively, by 1991.

The restructuring of the fleet mix resulted in a drop in fuel cost from about 30 percent of the airline's total operating expenses in 1978 to 14.4 percent by the end of 1990.

■ Programs to Minimize Labor Costs

Labor costs constitute a significant part of total operating expenses in the airline industry. As part of its deregulation strategies, American had to find a way to lower its labor costs. An American Airlines executive characterized the situation as follows:

> Regarding the labor cost, we had two ways to go about getting the cost down. One way was to cut down the pay of existing employees, which, we all agree, is a very painful and hard thing to do. Continental did it successfully. They filed for bankruptcy and took the position that they could not survive with their existing contractual obligations including their labor contracts. The Continental situation could never happen again the same way it happened for Continental. The strategy that the senior officers of American adopted was to seek a negotiated solution to the problem. American negotiated with the unions to protect current employees at their existing salaries, but hire new employees at market rates. We succeeded in convincing our labor unions that this was the only way we could survive in the deregulated environment.[3]

The collective bargaining agreement signed by American and the Transport Workers Union and the Pilot and Flight Attendant Unions in 1983 was the first airline agreement to include the so-called "two tier," "new hire," or "market rate" wage scale. Under this system, historical rates of pay for existing employees were preserved while providing that new employees be hired at market rates. In return for the union agreement to the two-tier scheme, American promised internal growth rather than growth through mergers and acquisitions. Labor costs rose by only 1.5 percent in 1984 (the lowest increase in more than 15 years), the first full year that American had the benefit of the new system. In September 1985, the Transport Workers Union agreed to a continuation of the market rate scales as approved in 1983, and in 1987, the Association of Flight Attendants approved the same plan for newly hired flight attendants. In 1989, the two-tier pay scale was the standard compensation scheme in the airline industry.

The two-tier pay scale gave American a strong incentive to adopt the growth strategy, the systematic reduction of labor cost through growth. By the end of 1985, the proportion of American's market-rate employees had increased to 36 percent of its nearly 44,000 work force. American expects 50 percent of its employees to belong to the market rate pay scale before 1995.

In November 1986, American revealed plans to buy the ACI, the parent company of AirCal in an attempt to strengthen its market position on the West Coast. The decision was defended as a tactical move in response to the strong consolidation forces present in the industry but not a departure from the company's commitment to internal growth.

■ Strengthening and Restructuring of Route System

Air travel can be either point-to-point or through a hub-and-spokes system supported by smaller feeder airlines. In the point-to-point market, the airplane flies from point A to point B and so do all the passengers on the airplane. In a more complex and post-regulation system, passengers are taken from point A to an intermediate point, a hub, where they can connect to any of the many points on the other side of the hub. The hub system creates connections, making it less desirable than the nonstop service, but it serves many more markets. As part of its response to the 1978 deregulation and the growth strategy, American Airlines adopted the strategy of evolving from mostly a point-to-point system to primarily a hub-and-spokes system of operations. By the end of 1989, American had seven hubs.

Dallas/Fort Worth

American has invested close to $500 million on the development and expansion of its Dallas/Fort Worth mega-hub. Since its opening in 1981, the number of terminals has more than doubled, from 23 to 47. American offers nonstop passenger service to over 100 domestic and 14 international cities with a total of 406 departures daily from this hub location.

Chicago

American's second largest hub, located at O'Hare International, has continued to grow since its opening in 1982. Chicago now offers 38 gates, serving 82 cities nonstop and 11 international routes for a total of 316 daily flights.

Nashville

In 1986, the Nashville hub was established to provide greater north/south coverage for American. In 1987, the Nashville operations were moved into an all new 25-gate terminal complex and, soon after, construction began to develop new runways at Nashville's Metropolitan Airport. In 1988, Nashville began to offer its first international flight to Toronto, Canada. In 1989, Nashville served 29 cities nonstop with 86 daily departures.

Raleigh/Durham

In June of 1987, American opened its hub at Raleigh/Durham airport. This hub was to further expand American's north/south route coverage. Six months after its opening, American was offering 96 daily flights to 36 cities. Since then, six more cities nonstop and 21 more daily flights have been added. To further its commitment toward growth and development of its north/south expansion, American opened a $30 million reservation facility close to Raleigh/Durham. The facility is to serve the reservation needs of a nine-state region from Pennsylvania to Florida.

San Juan

In late 1986, American began operations of its hub facility at Luis Munor Marin International Airport. The opening of this hub was designed to provide same day services for customers flying to the Caribbean. By the end of 1989, San Juan served 23 cities nonstop, including 50 departures and nine international routes. This hub is expected to play an increasing role in American's presence in the Caribbean market. In anticipation of the growth potential of this hub, American began construction of an $8.2 million reservations office in this area.

San Jose

As a result of the acquisition of AirCal, American, desiring to increase its West Coast coverage, began hub operations at San Jose. Since its opening in 1988, San Jose has increased its daily flights from 69 to 72 with nonstop service to 16 cities. American hopes that this expansion will also aid in the West Coast/Caribbean route expansion.

Miami

American's newest hub, located in Miami, opened in September 1989. This hub provides nonstop service to 17 domestic and 7 Caribbean and Central American cities. American plans to expand services at this hub to 20 more cities in 15 Latin American countries as well as to Madrid, London, and Toronto.

■ Programs to Maximize Revenue

American's efforts to maximize profit in the deregulated environment focused primarily on its computer reservation system, frequent flyer program, American Eagle commuter airline, and programs of internal diversification and consolidation.

SABRE (Semi-Automated Business Research Environment)

SABRE is American's computer reservation system (CRS) and the largest in the industry. United's APOLLO ranks second. SABRE is powered by seven massive IBM mainframes in an underground concrete bunker outside Tulsa. It was conceived in 1959 as an internal link between the airline's offices and ticket counters to help track reservations. In 1962, it was installed as American's computer reservation system. In 1975, talks between travel agents and the major carriers aimed at developing an industrywide reservation system broke down and American began marketing SABRE to outsiders.

Deregulation opened up pricing competition and as a result, U.S. and foreign carriers continually adjust fares to match rival companies. Nearly 1.5 million new industry fares are loaded into SABRE every day. In January 1990, it had over 14,000 subscribers and more than 58,000 terminals in use at travel agencies in 47 countries, accounting for more than 40 percent of all terminals installed in the industry. The system calculates flight plans for about 2,300 American flights each day, handles all aircraft and crew scheduling, and controls all baggage routing and freight tracking. It also provides fares and schedules for 665 airlines, as well as information on prices and availability for more than 20,000 hotels and 52 rental car companies. Further, SABRE maintains inventory control on nearly one billion spare parts distributed among American's maintenance centers.

In its increasing efforts to maximize revenues, SABRE continues to push to expand its services into the European markets. In 1989, SABRE signed ticketing agreements with Swiss Air, KLM, Sabena, and Austrian Airlines. This agreement is thought to be the beginning of a new expansion era for SABRE.

In 1989, American and Delta agreed to merge their computer reservation services (SABRE and DATAS II) to form an independently operated travel information network. Under this agreement, Delta would pay American $650 million. This merger was thought to enhance the ability of both American and Delta to compete in the international CRS market. Plans for this merger, however, were abandoned due to the opposition of the Department of Justice.

SABRE is a source of significant revenue for AMR, the parent company of American Airlines. Aviation analysts comment that American earns a higher return on investment by booking tickets than it does by flying planes.[4]

Frequent Flyer and Super Saver Programs

Following deregulation, the low-cost airlines began promoting several forms of systemwide deep discount fares. Instead of offering such across-the-board discount fares, in 1981 American pioneered a focused discount program intended to reward loyal and frequent customers. The program was called "AAdvantage," which had 11 million members by 1989.

American Eagle

The year 1984 was marked by the formation of American Eagle, a network of commuter regional airlines integrated into the American Airlines domestic route system. American Eagle provides franchise feeder service into American's hub cities and also serves markets not economically feasible for service with American's aircraft. American Eagle schedules are integrated into American's timetable. Eagle in-flight personnel are trained by American. Eagle reservations are handled through American's SABRE terminals. By December 1989, American Eagle fleet included 201 aircraft offering 1435 flights a day to 161 cities in 27 states, the District of Columbia, and 15 Caribbean/Bahamian islands.

Internal Diversification and Consolidation

In its efforts to boost revenues and to strive toward growth, American has experienced several structural changes since deregulation.

AMR Corporation. On May 19, 1982, American Airlines' stockholders voted to approve a plan of reorganization under which a new holding company, AMR Corporation, was formed and became the parent company of American Airlines. The holding company was established to provide increased flexibility for financing and investment.

AMR Service Corporation. This company began operations in 1984 to provide ground handling services for other airlines on a contractual basis. The company performs a variety of aircraft service functions including loading and unloading, baggage handling, cabin cleaning, de-icing, freight warehousing, passenger processing, building cleaning, security and ground transportation, fueling services, flight information, and weather services.

American Airlines Direct Marketing Corporation. Established in 1984, AADMC contracts with other firms to perform telemarketing services from its telephone centers in Dallas/Fort Worth and Honolulu. By 1986, this unit had grown to become one of the largest fully automated telemarketing operations in the world, employing 1,100 employees and generating $40.1 million in revenues. In addition to telemarketing operations, it also publishes the "American Traveler," an in-flight merchandise catalog, and directs several other direct mail programs.

AMR Information Services. This organization was formed in 1986 to maximize the utilization of the skills developed by American in the area of computer reservation systems, the SABRE. This subsidiary was organized along six operating units to market new data processing applications and information services: AMR Airline Automation Services, which sells automation support to other airlines; AMR Technical Training, which develops programs to teach skills to aid in the utilization of automation; AMR Travel Services, which provides marketing automation services to other segments of the travel industry including car rental companies and hotels; AMR Cable services, which provides automation for cable television franchise operations; Video Financial Services, offering home banking and telephone bill paying services to financial institutions; and Caribbean Data Services, which performs data entry services for other companies.

AMR Investment Services. This organization was established in 1987 to provide cash and pension fund management services to small and medium-sized companies and institutionalized investors. By the end of 1989, the company was managing a large share of AMR's investments and pension funds, as well as managing over $4.3 billion in assets for outside customers.

In 1986, American Airlines Training Corporation, AMR Energy Corporation, and Sky Chefs (providing food service for American and other airlines) were all sold so that efforts could be concentrated on those areas that AMR felt had the greatest potential for future growth.

By 1986, AMR's subsidiaries accounted for 3 percent of the parent's revenues and a considerably greater percentage of its profits. American expects the revenues from the subsidiaries to reach 15 percent of the revenues of the company by the mid-1990s.

OPERATIONS, WORK FORCE, AND LEADERSHIP

■ Operations

As of the end of 1985, American's total fleet consisted of 291 aircraft. By the end of 1989, the fleet size had grown to 500 aircraft, an increase of 72 percent. In terms of scheduled services, in 1989, American had over 811,000 departures with a daily average of 2,224—more than double the performance in 1984. During 1989, approximately 72 million passengers boarded American flights. The daily average was about 198,000 passengers. Comparable numbers for 1984 were 34 million and 93,000, respectively. The available passenger seat miles (total seats available multiplied by miles flown) rose from 49,485 million in 1979 to 115,222 million in 1989, an increase of over 130 percent. Revenue passenger seat miles (one revenue passenger mile equals one paying passenger flown one mile) increased from 33,364 million in 1979 to 73,503 million in 1989. The passenger load factor (percentage of seats filled) stayed around 64 percent during most of the 1980s. In 1989, the revenue yield per passenger mile was at its highest (12.03 cents) since 1981.

The revenue ton miles (one revenue ton mile equals one ton of cargo or mail transported one mile) went up from 4,151 million in 1979 to 8,239 million in 1989 (Exhibits 1 and 2).

In February 1990, American served 104 points on the U.S. mainland and 44 points outside the U.S. mainland.

International Services

American was primarily a domestic airline during the 1930s. It began service to Toronto in 1941 and to Mexico in 1942. For a period of about five years—1945 to 1950—American operated a transatlantic division, American Overseas Airline, which served a number of European countries. That division was sold to Pan American in September 1950.

American became an international airline again in August 1970, when flights were started from the U.S. mainland to Hawaii, American Samoa, the Fiji Islands, New Zealand, and Australia. Service to all these points except Hawaii was suspended in March 1974 because of government-imposed route restrictions and limited profitability. In June 1975, American conducted a route exchange agreement with Pan Am under which American traded its Pacific routes (except Boston/St. Louis–Honolulu) for Pan Am's U.S.–Bermuda, New York–Santo Domingo, and New York–Barbados authority. In 1978, American suspended its nonstop flight between Boston/St. Louis and Honolulu. In 1982, American's route system included a single daily flight to Europe and a small number of flights to Canada, the Caribbean, and Mexico. However, by January 1990, American flew to 48 destinations outside the United States. Its international routes, which represent about 14 percent of its total system, now spread throughout Europe, deeper into the Caribbean, to Tokyo, and to the South Pacific.

American plans to continue growing in Europe and to expand its air services into Central and South America, the Soviet Union, Eastern Europe, and the Pacific beyond its single Dallas/Fort Worth–Tokyo route.

Freight Services

In 1986, American managed to fly 489 million freight ton-kilometers (FTKs), up 11.8 percent from 1985. In 1987, FTKs rose 17.2 percent to 533 million. Again, in 1988, FTKs showed a 24.6 percent increase to 720 million FTKs. The growth

Exhibit 1

U.S. Major Carriers—System Traffic: 1984–1990

Airline	Passengers (000)	RPKs (000)	FTKs (000)	Load Factor
		1990		
American	73,253	123,829,517	1,193,928	62.3
Continental	36,204	64,833,469	789,720	60.9
Delta	65,789	94,995,574	837,222	59.1
Eastern	21,505	26,950,048	117,164	60.3
Northwest	41,046	83,977,853	2,062,024	66.8
Pan Am	17,930	50,826,928	1,007,435	65.5
TWA	24,416	55,735,948	682,953	62.3
United	57,612	122,503,295	1,552,291	66.2
US Air	60,250	57,522,369	166,744	59.9
		1989		
American	72,383	118,266,053	931,413	63.8
Continental	35,660	63,599,963	759,362	62.0
Delta	68,258	95,554,426	757,439	63.4
Eastern[1]	14,569	18,709,048	99,749	60.7
Northwest	38,860	75,862,865	2,441,053	66.3
Pan Am	17,383	47,720,798	1,062,370	61.3
TWA	25,346	56,571,705	720,609	61.2
United	54,951	112,048,681	1,438,296	66.6
US Air[2]	61,345	54,547,055	143,990	60.7
		1988		
American	64,310	104,215,524	719,409	63.5
Continental	37,861	66,077,068	717,594	66.6
Delta	60,010	83,265,911	695,588	58.3
Eastern	35,712	46,453,788	240,154	61.6
Northwest	35,952	65,727,816	2,168,281	65.9
Pan Am	16,969	47,273,237	1,058,310	63.3
Piedmont	27,123	21,009,757	109,729	59.1
TWA	25,198	55,998,336	652,659	61.8
United	56,372	111,184,091	1,375,562	67.9
US Air[3]	35,052	29,719,306	35,304	60.9
		1987		
American[4]	56,949	92,448,390	577,322	63.9
Continental[5]	40,294	64,124,531	598,295	61.9
Delta[6]	58,958	74,673,357	576,447	56.0
Eastern	44,713	58,143,698	349,439	64.4
Northwest[7]	37,305	64,019,774	1,808,406	64.5
Pan Am	14,986	42,428,321	886,881	63.1
Piedmont	25,355	18,340,269	56,330	60.4
TWA[8]	24,722	53,119,502	599,742	63.4
United	55,180	106,503,620	1,336,852	65.2
US Air	24,985	21,392,463	22,442	65.5

(Continued)

U.S. Major Carriers (continued)

Exhibit 1

Airline	Passengers (000)	RPKs (000)	FTKs (000)	Load Factor
		1986		
American	46,076	78,508,482	488,788	65.5
Continental	20,409	33,707,485	378,671	63.2
Delta	41,062	50,479,762	351,696	57.7
Eastern	42,687	56,188,077	461,861	60.2
Northwest[7]	35,401	60,088,473	1,552,519	60.2
Pan Am	12,448	34,844,375	807,968	53.0
Piedmont	22,813	16,481,883	34,145	58.7
TWA[8]	24,636	48,100,035	539,727	57.9
United	59,690	96,569,393	1,028,180	64.8
US Air	21,951	18,332,318	21,491	61.7
Western	12,234	17,661,769	154,630	58.2
		1985		
American	41,232	71,017,593	431,824	64.6
Continental	16,150	26,407,254	271,336	64.8
Delta	39,829	48,410,921	364,301	56.5
Eastern	41,825	53,321,943	446,442	60.3
Northwest	14,706	36,995,473	1,304,907	60.8
Pan Am	13,183	43,977,471	806,865	63.0
Piedmont	18,074	13,168,270	30,749	55.9
Republic	17,465	17,275,703	69,267	58.8
TWA	20,876	51,570,917	585,844	65.2
United	38,169	66,998,507	593,531	63.0
US Air	19,514	16,060,658	22,212	59.6
Western	11,921	16,799,577	146,172	59.8
		1984		
American	34,132	59,033,747	680,038	63.3
Continental	11,123	17,581,394	215,177	63.5
Delta	37,363	43,535,001	352,322	54.5
Eastern	38,127	47,566,408	391,616	58.3
Northwest	13,333	32,395,335	1,415,300	61.4
Pan Am	14,175	45,714,627	933,358	63.9
Piedmont	14,288	10,067,485	25,287	54.1
Republic	15,200	13,831,628	87,791	54.1
TWA	18,491	45,557,347	616,783	63.3
United	41,308	75,110,434	827,798	61.4
US Air	17,269	13,564,749	20,029	59.0
Western	10,653	15,148,401	164,980	58.6

Source: U.S. DOT and *Air Transport World*, June 1991.

Note: RPKs = Revenue passenger kilometers; FTKs = Freight ton kilometers; Load factor = percentage of plane filled by revenue passengers.

[1]Eastern on strike.
[2]US Air and Piedmont merged in August 1989.
[3]Includes PSA.
[4]Includes AirCal.
[5]Includes New York Air, People Express, and Frontier.
[6]Includes Western.
[7]Includes Republic.
[8]Includes Ozark.

Exhibit 2 **American Airlines, Inc.—Eleven-Year Comparative Summary**

	1990	*1989*	*1988*	*1987*
Operating Results (in millions)				
Revenues				
Passenger	$ 9,742.8	$8,839.2	$7,555.1	$6,150.9
Cargo	428.9	361.7	287.8	260.9
Other	837.0	760.0	707.7	712.7
Total operating revenues	11,008.7	9,960.9	8,550.6	7,124.5
Expenses				
Wages, salaries and benefits	3,608.7	3,233.6	2,820.8	2,399.8
Aircraft fuel	1,898.8	1,367.1	1,094.1	1,008.5
Other	5,433.2	4,629.4	3,834.7	3,243.0
Total operating expenses	10,940.7	9,230.1	7,749.6	6,651.3
Operating income (loss)	$ 68.0	$ 730.8	$ 801.0	$ 473.2
Operating statistics				
Revenue yield per passenger mile	12.64¢	12.03¢	11.66¢	10.83¢
Revenue yield per ton mile	125.67¢	120.91¢	119.64¢	114.35¢
Operating expenses per available passenger seat mile	8.84¢	8.01¢	7.59¢	7.50¢
Operating expenses per available ton mile	66.28¢	60.20¢	57.26¢	56.75¢
Operating expenses per revenue ton mile	124.89¢	112.03¢	108.43¢	106.75¢
Available passenger seat miles (in millions)	123,773	115,222	102,045	88,743
Revenue passenger miles (in millions)	77,085	73,503	64,770	56,794
Passenger load factor	62.3%	63.8%	63.5%	64.0%
Breakeven passenger load factor	61.8%	57.9%	56.0%	58.5%
Available ton miles (in millions)	16,506	15,332	13,535	11,720
Revenue ton miles (in millions)	8,760	8,239	7,147	6,231
Cargo revenue ton miles (in thousands)	1,051,605	888,226	669,902	551,142
Freight revenue ton miles (in thousands)	767,096	637,955	489,748	394,333
Mail revenue ton miles (in thousands)	284,509	250,271	180,154	156,809
Number of operating aircraft at year-end	552	500	468	410

Source: AMR Annual Report.

of American cargo service continued in 1989 when FTKs grew 28 percent to 931 million.

■ The Work Force

In 1979, American's work force consisted of approximately 47,000 employees. In 1986, the total number of American Airlines employees topped 50,000 for the first time. In January 1990, American had a total work force of 78,445 employees. This work force consisted of 11,262 (14.3 percent) management/specialists, 8,119 (10.3 percent) pilot/flight engineers, 14,388 (18.3 percent) flight attendants, 25,302 (32.3 percent) ground service personnel, 18,820 (24.0 percent) agent/clerical staff, and 604 (1 percent) persons working in various other jobs. Labor unions represented about 62 percent of American's employees.

1986	1985	1984	1983	1982	1981	1980
$4,960.5	$4,985.5	$4,335.8	$3,885.3	$3,414.2	$3,377.0	$3,154.4
220.4	235.3	315.0	299.3	302.8	329.8	316.0
675.6	638.5	436.6	347.8	260.8	216.8	235.7
5,856.5	5,859.3	5,087.4	4,532.4	3,977.8	3,923.6	3,706.1
2,053.3	1,951.9	1,748.7	1,601.2	1,472.9	1,417.4	1,372.7
837.3	1,141.8	1,091.8	1,038.6	1,070.2	1,115.7	1,114.8
2,573.8	2,259.1	1,907.8	1,643.1	1,452.9	1,346.5	1,329.7
5,464.4	5,352.8	4,748.3	4,282.9	3,996.0	3,879.6	3,817.2
$ 392.1	$ 506.5	$ 339.1	$ 249.5	$ (18.2)	$ 44.0	$ (111.1)
10.17¢	11.30¢	11.81¢	11.39¢	11.04¢	12.13¢	11.12¢
109.94¢	122.65¢	117.75¢	110.70¢	106.54¢	112.76¢	104.83¢
7.28¢	7.83¢	8.09¢	8.17¢	8.19¢	8.57¢	8.19¢
54.93¢	58.82¢	58.45¢	58.67¢	58.36¢	59.41¢	55.41¢
102.58¢	112.05¢	109.90¢	104.61¢	107.03¢	111.50¢	107.97¢
75,087	68,336	58,667	52,447	48,792	45,264	46,634
48,792	44,138	36,702	34,099	30,900	27,798	28,178
65.0%	64.6%	62.6%	65.0%	63.3%	61.4%	60.4%
59.3%	57.3%	57.1%	60.4%	63.7%	60.5%	62.8%
9,948	9,100	8,123	7,300	6,847	6,531	6,889
5,327	4,777	4,321	4,094	3,734	3,480	3,535
447,588	363,518	650,049	674,375	641,884	692,790	686,953
334,788	295,770	471,278	514,061	493,392	552,064	538,461
112,800	67,748	178,771	160,314	148,492	140,726	148,492
330	291	260	244	231	232	242

■ Leadership

In January 1990, the upper management structure of AMR included a chairman and president, two executive vice presidents, seven senior vice presidents, thirty vice presidents, and five subsidiary corporation presidents. Robert L. Crandall was chairman, president, and chief executive officer.

Crandall was the head of the computer programming division of Hallmark Cards in 1966 when he joined TWA as assistant treasurer. In 1973, he left TWA and accepted the position of the chief financial officer at American Airlines. In July 1980, he was named the president and became the chairman of the board of AMR in 1985. Crandall has led American through the post-regulation era. He is known as the architect of American's deregulation strategies. Under

Crandall, American become the most profitable U.S. major carrier and the second largest airline in the world after Aeroflot.[5]

Crandall is credited for his forward-thinking vision of the industry, aggressiveness, creative leadership, and relentless work habits. He is reported to be notoriously hard-driving and highly demanding of his executives.[6] In a commentary on airline managers, *Air Transport World* characterizes Crandall as follows:

> "Crandall may not have started a business from scratch. . . , but he and his managers have, in important ways, shaped the modern (airline) industry."[7] "Crandall . . . knows how to communicate. . . . His quest for information is extraordinary. . . . He prefers consensus and confers constantly, always seeking more input. . . . He spends hours in employee forums answering questions. . . . There is no large airline besides Delta where morale is higher in the ranks. . . ."[8]

Exhibit 3 shows an aviation analyst's assessment of airline managements. American Airlines management receives the highest marks among all U.S. major carriers.

Despite all the achievements, the senior management of American has also been criticized for some of its strategic moves. The decisions in 1950 and 1974 to pull out of international routes are believed to have been a strategic misjudgment. By early 1990, American was scrambling to recapture and rebuild its international routes. Crandall concedes that they blundered badly in the 1980s when they failed to buy Pan Am's Asian Division when it was for sale.[9] The soundness of the decision to open the dual north/south hubs in Nashville and Raleigh/Durham is yet to be supported by long-term operational results at these two hub sites.

Exhibit 3 **One Analyst's Assessment of Airline Managements**

Key Elements	*AMR*	*CO*	*DAL*	*EA*	*NWA*	*PN*	*TWA*	*UAL*	*U*
Strong management team	A	B+	A	B+	B	B	B	A	B
Control of a computer res. system	A	A	C	A	B–	NG	B–	A	B–
Strong EPS momentum	A	C	C	C	B	C	B	B	B
Flex. capital spending program	A	A	A	A	A	A	B+	A	A
Strong balance sheet	B	C–	A	C–	A	D	C	C	B
Low cost of capital	A	C	A	D	A	D	C	B–	B–
Fuel-efficient fleet	A	C–	A	C	C	D	D	C	B
Positive cash flow	C	C–	B	D	B	D	B	C	B
Labor peace	A	A	B	D	C	D	C	B–	B
Slow cost increases	B	B	B	C–	C	D	C	C	C
Strong revenue growth outlook	A	B+	B	C	B	D	C	B	B

Source: Helane Becker, Shearson Lehman Hutton; *Air Transport World,* June 1989, p. 62.

Note: Key to letter grades: A = excellent, B = okay, C = fair, D = poor, NG = no grade. These airlines don't own a system, which is negative, but since they cohost in other systems, some credit should be given. Key to companies: AMR = AMR Corp., CO = Continental, DAL = Delta Air Lines, EA = Eastern, NWA = NWA Inc., PN = Pan Am, TWA = Trans World Airlines, UAL = UAL Corp., U = USAir Group (incl. Piedmont).

THE FINANCIAL OUTLOOK

In 1988, AMR Corporation surpassed number one U.S. carrier United Airlines and set a new record in profitability, posting an operating income of $801.0 million and a net of $476.8 million.

During the eleven years (1979–1989) after deregulation, American's total operating revenues rose from $3,252.5 million in 1979 to $9,960.9 million in 1989. The total operating expenses for the same period grew from $3,247.6 million to $9,231.0 million with an operating income increase of $725.9 million. From 1979 to 1989, American's passenger revenues grew from 85 percent to 89 percent of the total operating revenues. During the same time, while American's cargo revenues dropped by 5 percent, its revenues from other sources experienced a 2 percent increase.

In 1989, AMR Corporation's total operating revenues, total operating expenses, operating income, and net earning (in millions) were $10,479.6, $9,735.6, $744.0, and $454.8, respectively. In the same year, American Airlines accounted for 95 percent of AMR Corporation's total operating revenues (Exhibits 2, 4, and 5).

THE AIRLINE INDUSTRY

In 1984, there were twelve U.S. major passenger carriers: American, Continental, Delta, Eastern, Northwest, Pan Am, Piedmont, Republic, TWA, United, U.S. Air, and Western. Through a number of consolidation measures, Republic, Western, and Piedmont left the pack, and by January 1990, the number of U.S. majors was reduced to nine. In December 1989, U.S. major airlines accounted for 36.4 percent of world passengers, 36.6 percent of world revenue passenger kilometers, and 21.9 percent of world freight ton kilometers.[10] From 1984 to the end of 1989, total number of passengers carried by the U.S. majors grew from 265.7 to 389.0 million. During the same six-year period, total revenue passenger kilometers and freight ton kilometers for the U.S. major airlines increased by 53 and 48 percent, respectively. Further, from 1984 to 1989, the cumulative operating revenue of the U.S. majors increased by 72 percent and their net income rose by 84 percent (Exhibits 1 and 4). Discounted fares also grew significantly along with the increase in the volume of air travel. From 1981 to 1988, the discount traffic as a percent of total traffic rose from 70.6 percent to 90.5 percent and the average discount jumped from 46.2 to 66.5 percent (Exhibit 6). It is estimated that during the first decade of deregulation, air travel discounts have saved airline customers over $100 billion.[11]

Exhibit 7 shows the world's top 25 airlines in 1989 ranked by total passengers carried, passengers-kilometers flown, total air freight, number of employees, fleet size, operating revenue, and operating profit. With the exception of air freight and operating profit, all U.S. majors were among the world's top 25 airlines and ranked very high in the above categories.

In 1985, the total international revenue passenger miles of all U.S. majors amounted to 61.7 billion miles. This total was increased to 100.4 billion miles in 1989. Among the U.S. majors, only Eastern and TWA experienced a slight decrease in their international revenue passenger miles for this period (Exhibit 8).

Exhibit 4 **U.S. Major Carriers—Financial Performance: 1984–1990**

Airline	*Total Operating Revenue (000)*	*Total Operating Expenses (000)*	*Operating Profit/ Loss (000)*	*Net Income/ Loss (000)*
		1990		
American	$11,008,677	$10,940,704	$ 67,973	$ (76,777)
American West	1,321,642	1,353,273	(31,631)	(74,671)
Continental	5,202,234	5,444,049	(241,815)	(1,236,387)
Delta	8,746,083	8,981,211	(235,128)	(154,033)
Eastern[1]	2,181,796	2,715,150	(533,354)	(1,125,908)
Northwest	7,257,110	7,398,776	(141,666)	(10,412)
Pan Am	na	na	na	na
Southwest	1,186,831	1,105,215	81,616	47,083
TWA	4,606,082	4,768,288	(162,206)	(237,564)
United	10,956,059	11,010,310	(54,252)	95,755
US Air	6,084,704	6,627,939	(543,235)	(410,749)
		1989		
American	$ 9,960,947	$ 9,230,151	$ 730,798	$ 423,100
Continental	4,044,223	4,788,009	156,217	3,059
Delta	8,648,315	7,971,765	676,550	473,174
Eastern[1]	1,551,678	2,416,400	(864,721)	(852,316)
Northwest	6,553,827	6,263,766	290,061	355,247
Pan Am	3,611,853	3,930,672	(318,819)	(414,730)
TWA	4,507,348	4,482,971	24,378	(296,547)
United	9,641,888	9,185,032	456,855	358,088
US Air[2]	6,251,000	6,230,000	21,000	(63,000)
		1988		
American	8,550,586	$ 7,749,591	800,995	449,445
Continental	4,553,349	4,469,887	83,462	(315,520)
Delta	7,393,275	6,868,638	524,637	344,523
Eastern	3,888,131	4,097,557	(209,426)	(335,351)
Northwest	5,587,783	5,392,145	195,638	162,789
Pan Am	3,592,617	3,697,903	(105,286)	(274,595)
Piedmont	2,363,178	2,085,818	277,362	159,441
TWA	4,364,332	4,104,912	259,420	249,743
United	8,796,352	8,127,785	668,567	477,672
US Air[3]	2,980,363	2,840,196	140,167	57,711
		1987		
American[4]	7,124,481	6,651,297	473,184	213,828
Continental[5]	3,973,213	3,946,702	26,511	(258,085)
Delta[6]	6,093,331	5,659,088	434,243	233,297
Eastern	4,529,208	4,470,310	58,896	(130,761)
Northwest[7]	5,073,726	4,868,611	205,115	140,716
Pan Am	2,912,251	3,025,544	(113,293)	(274,595)
Piedmont	1,963,706	1,803,467	160,239	98,550
TWA[8]	4,056,435	3,815,999	240,435	106,200
United	7,862,795	7,711,577	151,217	33,338
US Air	2,070,311	1,806,855	263,456	164,113

(Continued)

U.S. Major Carriers (continued)

Exhibit 4

Airline	Total Operating Revenue (000)	Total Operating Expenses (000)	Operating Profit/ Loss (000)	Net Income/ Loss (000)
		1986		
American	$5,856,546	$5,464,484	$ 392,062	$ 249,254
Continental	2,052,095	1,908,881	143,214	17,947
Delta	4,496,044	4,271,041	225,003	193,706
Eastern	4,522,144	4,457,130	65,014	(130,161)
Northwest[7]	3,589,174	3,422,529	166,645	76,941
Pan Am	2,580,392	2,922,545	(342,153)	(484,931)
Piedmont	1,656,910	1,506,995	149,915	72,363
TWA[8]	3,181,464	3,257,185	(75,721)	(106,328)
United	6,688,120	6,698,127	(10,007)	(80,634)
US Air	1,786,958	1,622,825	164,133	89,162
Western	1,234,781	1,227,512	7,269	6,825
		1985		
American	5,859,334	5,352,850	506,484	322,640
Continental	1,731,055	1,575,585	155,468	64,280
Delta	4,738,168	4,506,961	231,207	156,775
Eastern	4,815,069	4,593,454	221,615	6,310
Northwest	2,650,008	2,573,755	76,253	72,961
Pan Am	3,090,324	3,288,000	(197,676)	51,750
Piedmont	1,366,641	1,259,166	107,475	66,710
Republic	1,734,397	1,568,067	166,330	177,006
TWA	3,860,696	3,924,275	(63,579)	(193,092)
United	4,920,132	5,248,136	(328,004)	(88,223)
US Air	1,749,126	1,582,204	166,922	109,850
Western	1,306,546	1,230,042	76,504	67,134
		1984		
American	5,194,445	4,749,645	339,065	208,606
Continental	1,186,467	1,089,618	107,545	53,669
Delta	4,495,417	4,208,180	287,344	258,641
Eastern	4,365,430	4,175,867	189,631	(37,927)
Northwest	2,462,833	2,365,584	96,842	50,101
Pan Am	3,305,159	3,410,788	(107,382)	(206,836)
Piedmont	1,135,084	1,009,756	125,750	58,175
Republic	1,547,187	1,447,892	100,002	29,511
TWA	3,645,605	3,570,769	75,150	29,885
United	6,096,818	5,547,712	550,005	252,416
US Air	1,630,127	1,437,061	192,724	118,331
Western	1,182,395	1,170,354	11,412	(29,115)

Source: U.S. DOT and *Air Transport World,* June 1991.

[1]Eastern on strike.
[2]US Air and Piedmont merged in August 1989.
[3]Includes PSA.
[4]Includes AirCal.
[5]Includes New York Air, People Express, and Frontier.
[6]Includes Western.
[7]Includes Republic.
[8]Includes Ozark.

Exhibit 5 **AMR Corporation—Eleven-Year Comparative Summary (in millions, except share and per share amounts)**

	1990	1989	1988	1987
Total operating revenues	$ 11,719.6	10,479.6	8,824.3	7,198.0
Total operating expenses	$ 11,595.6	9,735.6	8,017.8	6,736.9
Operating income (loss)	$ 124.0	744.0	806.5	461.1
Earnings (loss) from continuing operations before extraordinary items	$ (39.6)	454.8	476.8	198.4
Net earnings (loss)	$ (39.6)	454.8	476.8	198.4
Earnings (loss) from continuing operations before extraordinary items per common share				
Primary	$ (0.64)	7.16	7.92	3.28
Fully diluted	$ (0.64)	7.15	7.66	3.28
Net earnings (loss) per common share				
Primary	$ (0.64)	7.16	7.92	3.28
Fully diluted	$ (0.64)	7.15	7.66	3.28
Total assets	$ 13,353.6	10,877.4	9,792.2	8,423.3
Long-term debt	$ 1,674.2	808.9	1,206.5	1,235.2
Obligations under capital leases	$ 1,597.7	1,496.9	1,543.0	1,546.9
Redeemable preferred stock	$ –	–	–	–
Non-redeemable preferred stock	$ –	–	150.0	150.0
Common stock and other stockholders' equity	$ 3,727.4	3,765.8	3,148.0	2,681.1
Dividends paid per common share	$ –	–	–	–
Common shares outstanding at year end (in thousands)	62,311	62,244	58,841	58,816
Book value per common share	$ 59.82	60.50	53.50	45.58
Preferred shares outstanding at year end				
Redeemable preferred stock	–	–	–	–
Non-redeemable preferred stock	–	–	300	300

By mid-1990, while aviation analysts talked of the demise of three of the U.S. majors (Pan Am, TWA, and Eastern), American Airlines—with AMR's 1989 net earnings of $454.8 million, total revenues of $10.5 billion, and 17 percent of the $72 billion domestic industry—was characterized as the strongest U.S. major airline.[12]

ENDNOTES

1. Colonial Airways, Embry-Riddle, Interstate Airlines, Southern Air Transport, and Universal Airlines System.
2. Brad Jensen, Managing Director of Schedules Planning.
3. Brad Jensen, Managing Director of Schedules Planning.
4. *Business Week,* June 22, 1987, p. 116.
5. *New York Times Magazine,* 9/23/90, p. 25.
6. *Fortune,* 9/24/90, p. 44.

1986	1985	1984	1983	1982	1981	1980
6,018.2	6,131.0	5,353.7	4,763.3	4,177.0	4,108.7	3,821.0
5,607.3	5,594.4	4,085.2	4,481.8	4,167.9	4,036.5	3,907.2
410.9	536.6	368.5	281.5	9.1	72.2	(86.2)
279.1	345.8	233.9	227.9	(19.6)	16.8	(151.7)
279.1	345.8	233.9	227.9	(19.6)	47.4	(75.8)
4.63	5.94	4.37	4.79	(1.00)	.16	(5.70)
4.63	5.88	4.16	4.48	(1.00)	.26	(5.70)
4.63	5.94	4.37	4.79	(1.00)	1.21	(3.06)
4.63	5.88	4.16	4.48	(1.00)	1.16	(3.06)
7,528.0	6,421.1	5,260.9	4,728.2	3,896.8	3,738.2	3,277.9
1,228.7	920.5	774.8	726.6	751.8	717.9	669.4
1,183.3	910.2	766.6	785.0	764.8	798.6	601.7
24.0	88.6	126.8	105.4	110.6	109.5	108.4
–	–	125.0	125.0	–	–	–
2,484.9	2,180.9	1,513.4	1,299.6	836.2	731.2	695.1
–	–	–	–	–	–	.1
58,747	58,681	48,453	48,374	37,241	28,766	28,698
42.30	37.00	30.98	26.59	22.07	24.88	23.64
960	2,970,742	4,602,460	4,749,000	5,000,000	5,000,000	5,000,000
–	–	5,000,000	5,000,000	–	–	–

(Continued on next page)

7. *Air Transport World*, 1/89, p. 61.
8. *Air Transport World*, 1/89, p. 67.
9. *Fortune*, 9/24/1990, p. 24.
10. *Air Transport World*, 9/90.
11. *AMR 1989 Annual Report*, p. 16.
12. *New York Times Magazine*, 9/23/90, p. 46.

Exhibit 5 **(Continued)**

Consolidated Balance Sheet	***December 31*** 1990	1989
Assets		
Current assets		
Cash	$ 113.5	$ 120.3
Short-term investments	835.8	480.9
Receivables, less allowances for uncollectible accounts (1990–$13.4; 1989–$14.9)	951.4	886.1
Inventories, less allowances for obsolescence (1990–$109.2; 1989–$97.4)	608.5	490.4
Other current assets	148.6	113.5
Total current assets	2,657.8	2,091.2
Equipment and property		
Flight equipment, at cost	6,234.0	5,971.0
Less accumulated depreciation	2,025.1	2,068.2
	4,208.9	3,902.8
Purchase deposits for flight equipment	1,385.9	946.4
	5,594.8	4,849.2
Other equipment and property, at cost	3,569.9	2,785.4
Less accumulated depreciation	1,312.1	1,057.5
	2,257.8	1,727.9
	7,852.6	6,577.1
Equipment and property under capital leases		
Flight equipment	1,641.1	1,516.8
Other equipment and property	288.0	269.5
	1,929.1	1,786.3
Less accumulated amortization	634.1	543.8
	1,295.0	1,242.5
Other assets		
Route acquisition costs	402.5	36.7
Funds held by bond trustees	103.6	136.6
Other	1,042.1	793.3
	1,548.2	966.6
	$13,353.6	$10,877.4

(Continued) **Exhibit 5**

	December 31	
	1990	*1989*
Liabilities and Stockholders' Equity		
Current liabilities		
Accounts payable	$ 966.3	$ 929.3
Accrued salaries and wages	416.7	423.9
Other accrued liabilities	1,005.1	823.5
Air traffic liability	1,117.5	869.4
Short-term borrowings	1,209.7	162.9
Current maturities of long-term debt	50.3	210.1
Current obligations under capital leases	59.1	60.0
Total current liabilities	4,824.7	3,479.1
Long-term debt, less current maturities	1,674.2	808.9
Obligations under capital leases, less current obligations	1,597.7	1,496.9
Other liabilities		
Deferred federal income tax	650.4	802.4
Deferred gains	531.0	231.8
Other liabilities and deferred credits	348.2	292.5
	1,529.6	1,326.7
Commitments, leases, and contingencies		
Stockholders' equity		
Common stock—$1 par value; 100.0 shares authorized, shares issued and outstanding: 1990—62.3; 1989—62.2	62.3	62.2
Additional paid-in capital	1,242.9	1,238.5
Retained earnings	2,422.2	2,465.1
	3,727.4	3,765.8
	$13,353.6	$10,877.4

(Continued)

Exhibit 5 **(Continued)**

Consolidated Income Statement	Year Ended December 31, 1990	1989	1988
Revenues			
Passenger	$10,113.1	$ 9,107.3	$7,677.0
Cargo	429.7	362.3	288.2
Other	1,176.8	1,010.0	859.1
Total operating revenues	11,719.6	10,479.6	8,824.3
Expenses			
Wages, salaries and benefits	3,883.1	3,446.2	2,937.1
Aircraft fuel	1,939.4	1,392.3	1,102.3
Commissions to agents	996.6	867.9	737.1
Rentals and landing fees	987.7	796.5	582.7
Depreciation and amortization	723.1	612.7	552.8
Maintenance materials and repairs	631.9	513.8	405.6
Other operating expenses	2,433.8	2,106.2	1,700.2
Total operating expenses	11,595.6	9,735.6	8,017.8
Operating income	124.0	744.0	806.5
Other income (expense)			
Interest income	84.0	109.9	112.6
Interest expense	(337.4)	(238.7)	(233.4)
Interest capitalized	116.2	65.0	24.3
Miscellaneous—net	(20.1)	38.2	30.7
	(157.3)	(25.6)	(65.8)
Earnings (loss) before income taxes	(33.3)	718.4	740.7
Provision for income taxes	6.3	263.6	263.9
Net earnings (loss)	$ (39.6)	$ 454.8	476.8
Earnings (loss) per common share			
Primary	$ (0.64)	$ 7.16	$ 7.92
Fully diluted	$ (0.64)	$ 7.15	$ 7.66

Source: AMR Annual Report.

Exhibit 6 **Analysis of U.S. Airline Fares, 1981–1988**

	Revenues per Revenue Passenger Mile (yield)					
	Total Yield ¢	*Discount Yield ¢*	*Full Fare Yield ¢*	*Discount Fare Yield as Pct. of Full Fare*	*Discount Traffic as Pct. of Total*	*Average Discount*
1981	12.85	10.26	19.10	53.8%	70.6%	46.2%
1982	12.06	10.15	18.87	53.8	77.7	46.2
1983	12.14	10.31	19.98	51.6	81.5	48.4
1984	13.25	11.00	22.70	48.5	80.7	51.5
1985	12.48	10.51	23.83	44.1	85.3	55.9
1986	11.32	9.78	25.27	38.7	90.1	61.3
1987	11.66	10.21	26.77	38.1	91.3	61.9
1988	12.45	10.78	29.29	36.8	91.0	63.2
1989 Oct.	12.85	10.91	31.30	34.9	90.5	66.5

Source: Salomon Brothers. Air Transport Association data; *Air Transport World,* March 1990, p. 148.

The World's Top 25 Airlines in 1990 — Exhibit 7

In Passengers / *In RPKs* / *In FTKs*

Rank	Airline	No. of Pass. (000)	Rank	Airline	No. of RPKs (000,000)	Rank	Airline	No. of FTKs (000,000)
1	Aeroflot	137,742	1	Aeroflot	243,847	1	Federal Express	6,309
2	American	73,251	2	American	123,891	2	Lufthansa	4,104
3	Delta	65,789	3	United	122,528	3	Japan Airlines	3,477
4	US Air	60,059	4	Delta	94,996	4	Air France	3,440
5	United	57,612	5	Northwest	83,978	5	Aeroflot	2,675
6	Northwest	41,046	6	British Airways	65,906	6	Korean	2,526
7	Continental	35,496	7	Continental	63,030	7	UPS	2,397
8	All Nippon	33,048	8	US Air	57,202	8	KLM	2,138
9	British Airways	25,172	9	TWA	55,744	9	Northwest	2,062
10	TWA	24,416	10	Japan Airlines	55,195	10	Singapore	1,697
11	Japan Airlines	23,464	11	Pan Am	50,827	11	United	1,552
12	Lufthansa	22,400	12	Lufthansa	41,503	12	El Al	1,543
13	Eastern	21,505	13	Air France	36,778	13	Cathay Pacific	1,448
14	Southwest	19,831	14	All Nippon	33,007	14	Cargolux	1,186
15	Alitalia	18,203	15	Singapore	31,270	15	Alitalia	1,168
16	Pan Am	17,930	16	Qantas	27,754	16	Qantas	1,123
17	Air Inter	16,163	17	Eastern	26,950	17	American	1,117
18	Air France	15,731	18	KLM	26,739	18	China	1,116
19	America West	15,624	19	Air Canada	26,672	19	Rosenbalm	1,041
20	Iberia	15,500	20	Cathay Pacific	24,461	20	Pan Am	1,007
21	SAS	14,955	21	Canadian	23,434	21	Air Canada	942
22	Japan Air System	13,437	22	Alitalia	22,754	22	Swissair	927
23	Korean	12,259	23	Iberia	22,100	23	Varig	924
24	Air Canada	11,800	24	Thai Int'l	19,869	24	Thai Int'l	867
25	Saudia	10,311	25	Korean	19,277	25	Delta	837

In Employees / *In Fleet Size*

Rank	Airline	No. of Employees	Rank	Airline	No. of Aircraft
1	Aeroflot	400,000	1	Aeroflot	1,379
2	American	82,655	2	American	552
3	United	75,025	3	United	462
4	Delta	55,000	4	US Air	452
5	US Air	52,000	5	Delta	444
6	British Airways	50,658	6	Continental	339
7	Lufthansa	47,619	7	Northwest	332
8	Northwest	40,000	8	Federal Express	259
9	Air France	39,000	9	British Airways	227
10	Continental	33,000	10	TWA	210
11	Eastern	30,000	11	Lufthansa	177
12	TWA	29,815	12	Pan Am	162
13	Alitalia	29,641	13	Eastern	142
14	Iberia	28,000	14	UPS	135
15	Varig	25,654	15	Alitalia	133
16	KLM	25,195	16	SAS	128
17	Pan Am	24,600	17	Metro Airlines	115
18	Saudia	23,787	18	Air France	113
19	Air Canada	23,109	19	Air Canada	106
20	SAS	22,179	19	All Nippon	106
21	Singapore	21,355	19	Southwest	106
22	Swissair	20,655	20	America West	104
23	Japan Airlines	20,498	20	WestAir	104
24	India	20,177	21	Japan Airlines	98
25	Pakistan	19,950	22	Iberia	97
			23	Canadian	89
			24	Saudia	85
			25	Varig	80

(Continued on next page)

Exhibit 7

The World's Top 25 Airlines (continued)

In Operating Revenue			*In Operating Profit*		
Rank	*Airline*	*Op. Revenue (000,000)*	*Rank*	*Airline*	*Op. Profit (000,000)*
1	American	11,009	1	Singapore	775
2	United	10,956	2	Japan Airlines	468
3	Delta	8,746	3	Cathay Pacific	464
4	Federal	7,613	4	Federal Express	424
5	Northwest	7,257	5	Thai Int'l	268
6	Japan Airlines	6,711	6	SAS	264
7	US Air	6,085	7	Swissair	240
8	Air France	5,800	8	Korean	144
9	Continental	5,202	9	Southwest	82
10	TWA	4,606	10	ABX Air	69
11	Alitalia	4,488	11	American	68
12	SAS	3,616	12	Philippine	67
13	Swissair	3,581	13	Braanens	60
14	Air Canada	3,419	14	Malaysia	55
15	Singapore	2,917	15	Britannia	47
16	Qantas	2,552	16	Avisco	46
17	Cathay Pacific	2,540	17	Atlantic Southeast	40
18	Canadian (PWA)	2,383	18	TAT	31
19	Korean	2,344	19	Air India	31
20	Eastern	2,182	20	Martinair	24
21	Varig	1,985	21	Evergreen	23
22	Thai Int'l	1,929	22	Aviogenex	19
23	Air Inter	1,817	23	Southern Air	
24	China	1,400		Transport	19
24	UTA	1,400	24	World	18
25	American West	1,322	25	Alaska	17

Source: Direct airline reports; *Air Transport World,* 1991; DOT.

Exhibit 8

American Abroad: International Revenue Passenger Miles (in billions of miles)

	1985	*1986*	*1987*	*1988*	*1989*	*1990*
American	4.1	4.9	7.2	8.9	10.7	13.7
Continental	2.7	3.5	6.4	9.1	10.4	11.2
Delta	2.2	2.4	4.1	5.8	6.9	8.1
Eastern	2.8	3.1	3.3	3.4	2.0	1.3
Northwest	11.2	12.0	13.8	15.8	18.7	22.6
Pan Am	22.0	17.6	20.8	22.7	22.3	24.2
TWA	15.4	9.7	12.1	13.7	14.1	14.3
United	1.3	7.6*	10.3	12.5	15.1	21.1
US Air	—	—	—	—	.2	1.0

Source: Adapted from the *New York Times Magazine*, September 23, 1990, p. 25. *Air Transport World*, 6/91, p. 184.

*In 1986 United acquired Pan Am's lucrative Pacific routes for $715 million.

CASE 15

Delta Air Lines, Inc.: Taking the Family Global

Paul M. Swiercz, Georgia State University

In the post-deregulation era of air travel, Delta Air Lines has continued its transformation from a regional domestic air carrier into a powerful international competitor. In 1978, Delta ranked number five in the industry, transporting 3.3 million passengers on total revenues of $2.05 billion. By 1990, it moved up to number three, transporting 67.2 million passengers and generating total revenues of $8.58 billion.

Delta's success—it has been the most consistently profitable airline in the United States—can be attributed to many factors, but CEO Ron Allen does not hesitate when asked for an explanation: "We simply have the best work force in the industry and we are committed to maintaining our reputation as a great place to work."

Delta's strategy, as revealed over its sixty-year history, is distinguished from those of other major corporations by both its apparent simplicity and unyielding consistency. C.E. Woolman, its first CEO and still its guiding spirit, set the course. He created a firm with a simple mission—to be the best air carrier in the business. All of its principal leaders have been men nurtured within the Delta family, dedicated to Woolman's vision of the firm as an outstanding passenger airline (Exhibit 1 provides a brief profile of Delta CEOs).

But until deregulation, Delta was viewed as a regional carrier, confining most of its operations to the southeast and building its reputation as a premier carrier with an excellent reputation for service. From its Atlanta headquarters, its leaders focused on finding better ways to serve its passengers the large doses of southern hospitality for which Delta had become famous. Delta's primary objective was to create the "Delta family feeling," principally within the firm, but also between the company and its passengers.

This case is intended for classroom discussion only, not to depict effective or ineffective handling of administrative situations. All rights reserved to the authors and the North American Case Research Association.

Exhibit 1 **Delta Chief Executives**

C. E. Woolman	Graduated from the University of Illinois in 1912 with a bachelor's degree in agriculture. In 1925, he joined Huff Deland Dusters, Inc., following a brief career as an agricultural extension agent. In 1934, he became "general manager" of Delta and reigned as the company's most powerful executive until his death on September 11, 1966.
Charles H. Dolson	Began his airline career as a pilot for American Airlines. He joined Delta in 1934 and helped organize Chapter 44 of the Airline Pilots Association two years later. After a steady series of promotions, he became chief executive officer following Woolman's death. He introduced team management at Delta and retired in 1972.
W. T. Beebe	A veteran personnel officer who joined Chicago & Southern in 1947. He entered Delta with the merger in 1953 and quickly rose to the rank of senior vice- president for administration. In November 1971, he became chairman of the board and chief executive officer.
David C. Garret, Jr.	A Delta employee since 1946, he played a key role in helping the airline enter the jet age. With Dolson's promotion to president in 1965, he became vice-president of operations. In 1972, he was appointed president and in 1978 chief executive officer.
Ron Allen	Graduated from Georgia Tech in 1963 and immediately began working for Delta. As a protege of Tom Beebe, he quickly moved up the organization. In 1967, he was appointed assistant v.p. for administration. From 1970 to 1979, he served as senior v.p. for personnel. He was appointed president and chief operating officer in 1983 and chairman and CEO in 1987.

Ron Allen joined the firm in 1963 fresh out of the industrial engineering program at Georgia Tech. In 1987, at age 45, he left his position as president and chief operating officer to follow in the footsteps of his mentor Tom Beebe as chairman and chief executive officer. Allen had little time to adjust to transition; changes were moving too quickly and he soon announced that Delta intended to become the "most respected airline in the world."

By the end of 1990, much had been accomplished. The company had successfully made the transition from a large regional to global carrier. Nonetheless, the international competitive arena was still far from settled, and the final demise of its long-term competitor, Eastern, signaled new challenges in the domestic market.

As Allen reflected on his tenure, three events stood out in his mind. The first was the result of the National Transportation Safety Board's investigation in the August 1988 crash of Flight 1114 in Dallas–Fort Worth. The crash took the lives of twelve passengers and two crew members. The board accused Delta of lax training procedures, and a headline in the industry's major trade publication read "Probe Finds Fault with Captain's Approach to Cockpit Discipline."[1]

The second arose out of recent contract negotiations with the pilots. A contract had been signed and the pilots retained their position as the highest paid in the industry. But the twenty months of negotiations had been difficult, more rancorous than any in the company's modern history.[2]

The third occurred on August 10, 1990, when president and chief operating officer Hollis L. Harris announced he was leaving Delta to become CEO of Continental Airlines Holdings Inc. At age 58, Harris had spent his entire 36-year career at Delta. He was the highest ranking executive in the company's history to jump ship and was described by industry insiders as the "quintessential Delta man."

These difficulties, in the larger scheme, seemed modest. Delta, while strongly disagreeing with the Safety Board's conclusion, moved to tighten training procedures. The labor contract was settled and both parties were satisfied with the terms of the agreement. And the departure of Harris was moderated by the depth of managerial talent from which to draw his replacement.

Nonetheless, as Allen reflected upon these events and the competitive battles ahead, a simple question demanding a complex answer drew his attention: "How can we maintain the family spirit and competitive vigor of a regional carrier and simultaneously compete in a deregulated global market?" He decided to take this question to the executive committee.

COMPANY HISTORY

Delta was formed in 1928 in Monroe, La., by C.E. Woolman and a group of investors from the assets of Huff Deland Dusters, Inc. Like numerous others, they were caught in the enthusiasm for air travel flowing from Charles Lindbergh's transatlantic flight in April of the previous year. Organized under the name Delta Air Services Inc., the company set its sights on the passenger air market.

Over the next two years, Woolman and his associates scrambled to prepare the company for its future. In 1930, they reorganized again, this time changing the name to the Delta Air Corporation and making application for the all important air mail contract. Optimism was running high because the company was well capitalized and had the latest equipment and some of the best pilots in the business. Most important, however, they had done their homework. They pioneered Route 24 running from Charleston to Fort Worth via Columbia, Augusta, Atlanta, Birmingham, Meridian, Jackson, Monroe, Shreveport, and Dallas. All that could be done had been done and all that remained was receipt of the air mail contract from the Post Office.

[1] *Aviation Week and Space Technology*, April 2, 1990, pp. 62–65. The investigatory report stated in part, "In light of this discussion the safety board finds the slow implementation of procedural modifications by Delta Air Line was a contributory factor in this accident" (p. 63).

[2] Delta signed a contract on September 4, 1990. It called for a weighted average wage increase over its 54-month life span of 10.3 percent. The contract was made retroactive to March 1989.

In January, the celebration they had planned was turned into a wake by the vagaries of a corrupted post office contracting system. The company was forced to sell many of its assets and return to its crop-dusting roots just as the Great Depression tightened its stranglehold on the national economy. Prospects were poor as the company struggled to remain solvent.

Fortuitously, congressional action by aggressive New Deal legislators intervened, and in 1934, the company was awarded the life-giving air mail contract. The first passengers boarded the new Delta on August 5, 1934, for a flight from Atlanta to Dallas.

In 1941, the company moved its base of operations to Atlanta. Brash, boisterous, and committed to growth, the city provided not only facilities at the Atlanta Airport but also business travelers with their generous travel budgets. In 1953, it merged with struggling Chicago and Southern Airways, simultaneously opening up access to the prosperous industrial Midwest and converting itself into the sixth ranking domestic carrier. In 1972, Northeastern joined the family, bringing with it routes along the heavily traveled eastern shore corridor.

Delta enjoyed steady growth right up until deregulation traumatized the industry in 1978. Delta, a vocal opponent of deregulation, struggled to adjust to the new world of competitive air travel. New low-cost carriers entered the industry on what seemed like a daily basis. The 1981–1982 recession hit the weakened industry hard, and Delta reported its first money-losing year in four decades. Belt tightening and an overall improvement in the economy returned the company to profitability in 1983.

Delta's conservative business practices, its highly dedicated and well-paid work force, and its strong market position combined to make it a stand-out performer throughout the following seven years of economic prosperity. In 1986, it purchased Western Airlines, acquiring important hubs in Los Angeles and Salt Lake City. Delta now has four major hubs and four minor hubs (Exhibit 2). It has 2,446 daily departures to 150 domestic and 27 international cities. In addition, Delta's four commuter partners offer another 1,800 daily

Exhibit 2

A Summary of Delta's Hubs

Hub	***Departures***	***Share %/Position***	***Gates***
Atlanta	430	70/1	62
Cincinnati	145	85/1	25
Dallas/Ft. Worth	254	29/2	31
Salt Lake City	159	84/1	33
Orlando	70	34/1	24
Los Angeles	106	17/1	17
Boston	54	20/1	13
Portland	30	30/1	9

Source: Adapted from H. Becker, "Delta Airlines Inc.," Shearson Lehman, Hutton, N.Y., October 10, 1991. CIRR, SLBC-91 (90-1883)F.

departures. The four partners, Atlantic Southeast, Comair, Business Express, and Skywest, are all 20 percent owned by Delta.

DELTA'S STRATEGY 1934–1990

Passenger airlines compete in one of the most intricate industries born of the modern industrial revolution. The flying public witnesses only the most superficial elements in this system. An air carrier's strategy for success in this demanding environment can therefore be no less multifaceted and subtle than the industry itself. Nonetheless, certain elements stand out to distinguish Delta from its competitors (Exhibit 3). These elements include the following:

Independence. For many years, observers of the airline industry have described it as an "oligopoly." In economics, an oligopoly is a market condition in which sellers are so few that the actions of any one of them will naturally affect price and hence have a measurable impact upon competitors.

Oligarchy in the airline industry has been a fact of life for most of its history. At different times, it has either directly been encouraged or at least tolerated by those charged with providing consumers with the benefits of free market competition. The largest carriers long ago developed sophisticated informal mechanisms for controlling competition in the industry. Delta is unique among the major carriers because it has always sought to position itself an arm's length away from its fellow carriers.

Part of this reluctance to join the inner circle dates back to C.E. Woolman's experience with the cost of collusion in the firm's formative years. In 1930, Woolman attended, but did not participate in, the infamous "spoils conference"—where Eastern and the other major carriers received valuable route

Delta's Strategy 1934–1990 **Exhibit 3**

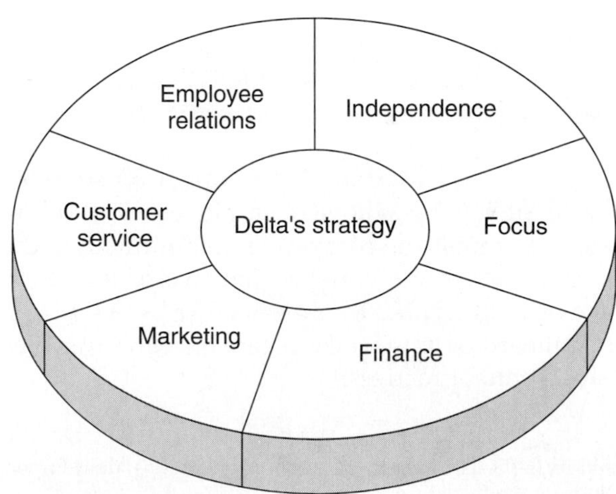

Exhibit 4

Personnel Expenses per Employee

Company	*Expenses per Employee*
Delta	$56,077
Northwest	50,880
United	47,192
TWA	46,346
American	46,174
Pan Am	45,536
US Air	44,240
Southwest	42,844
Continental	36,424
America West	28,738

Source: Adapted from Helane Becker, "Pan Am," Shearson Lehman Brothers, October 11, 1990.

concessions. This meeting raised a storm of controversy and led to President Roosevelt's six-month nationalization of air mail delivery. In order to ensure that the company would not be tainted by the experience when the contracts were again opened for competitive bidding, Woolman, on May 22, 1934, stepped down as an officer and director to assume the role of general manager.

Employee Relations. Delta's reputation for being a model employer is legendary with the business community. Legends by definition contain elements of romanticism, and for many years critics charged that Delta's reputation was more myth than reality. These doubters were silenced in 1982 when Delta employees presented management with the gift of a new $30 million Boeing 767, christened "The Spirit of Delta."

The extraordinary level of employee commitment at Delta is in no small part the direct consequence of conscious planning on the part of top management. All of the executive staff routinely call public attention to the accomplishments and contributions of Delta employees.

Good words and an egalitarian culture are, however, not the only elements in Delta's human resource strategy. Delta, despite the almost total absence of unions,[3] has a high profile personnel department and it pays the highest wages in the industry (Exhibit 4).

From its earliest days, the company worked toward providing rock solid job security. Its promote-from-within policy has allowed employees to explore wide ranging job opportunities. So strong is the company's commitment to the recognition of personnel as a critical strategic variable that two of its CEOs, W.T. Beebe and Ron Allen, have been promoted to the top office directly from the personnel office, a practice unheard of in most corporate boardrooms. (See Exhibit 5 for a summary of its personnel practices.)

[3]Only its pilots, members of ALPA, and its flight dispatchers, members of the independent Professional Airline Flight Control Association, are unionized.

Personnel Practices at Delta **Exhibit 5**

Compensation	Consistently a market leader in both direct and indirect compensation. Executive compensation is modest relative to firms of similar size. Free air travel is an important benefit.
Recruitment & selection	Each day, Delta receives between 1000–2000 unsolicited applications. The vast majority of employees enter through one of four entry level jobs. Individuals without previous industry experience are preferred. There is just one employment office staffed by a dozen personnel representatives.
Promotions & transfers	The personnel office posts all approved openings on bulletin boards with job titles, salaries, locations, and descriptions. Anyone in the company may apply. Employees are expected to actively seek out opportunities.
Problem solving	There is an official "open-door policy." Anyone with a problem who cannot resolve it through the normal chain of command can go see anyone in the hierarchy without worrying about it reflecting badly on them.
Training	Regulations require that certain employee groups—pilots, mechanics, & flight attendants—receive continuous training. Delta's open transfer and promotion policies dictate that a large portion of the non-regulated work force is also continuously trained.
Job security	The company is committed to full employment. In this cyclical industry, other carriers have frequently resorted to work force reductions in order to lower payroll costs. No early retirement programs have been offered. Delta voluntarily extended job offers to all non-officer, full-time, permanent Western employees.
Culture	Informal. Managers encourage employees to address them on a first name basis. "Customer service" is a central theme. Loyalty to the company is expected. Economy is preached daily; executive offices are spartan and paper clips are used until they wear out.
Communication	Management goes to great lengths to keep in touch with employees. Small groups of workers meet at least every 18 months with the senior management of their department.

Customer Service. Delta has consistently sought a competitive service advantage. That is, a market presence that clearly differentiates one company from another in the customer's perception of the quality of service rendered. Elements of quality in the airline industry include: in-flight service amenities (wider seats, better meals, free beverage service), convenient flight times and greater flight frequency, fewer delays and flight cancellations, superior baggage handling, better safety records, and more frequent-flyer bonus points. Delta's personal touch to customer service is reflected in its routine ranking of number one in the industry for fewest customer complaints.

Focus. In its early years, Delta was a true two-product company. For the first eight years of its existence, the crop dusting division subsidized the passenger services division. It was not until 1938 that the passenger division showed its first surplus. This single-minded devotion to passenger air service has been a hallmark of the company ever since. In contrast with many of its competitors, Delta has never experimented with diversification. For the past sixty years, Delta executives have concentrated solely on the problem of moving passengers from point A to B in the safest, most cost efficient manner possible. Ron

Allen has stated the company's objective clearly, "We're not striving to be the biggest in the world, just the most profitable."[4]

Finance. Profitability is a cherished concept at Delta. Throughout its history as a public corporation, Delta has routinely rewarded its investors with a steady stream of profitable reports.

Delta's financial strategies have been consistently restrained and devoid of experimentation. On the surface, it appears as though Delta's financial planners have failed to enter the modern age of finance capitalism; their conservative tendencies seem better suited to the era of prop-drive crop dusters rather than high-thrust jumbo jets. And that is exactly the image Delta executives like to portray.

Delta financial strategies, in truth, are neither backward nor dated. For example, Delta has a history of timing its major financial decisions out of synch with the industry. In the early 1950s, when getting to the market first was viewed as all important, Delta held back. Eastern, its main competitor, purchased a fleet of MD DC-6 propeller planes. Delta decided to wait and purchase the first generation of jets. Delta did the same in the 1970s, when it chose once again to forgo route expansion and instead purchase new, more fuel efficient planes. When deregulation and volatile fuel prices arrived, Delta had the youngest, most fuel efficient fleet in the industry. Delta executives cling to the notion that market share comes second to operational efficiency and people skills.

Conservatism is also observed in a number of other financial areas. In accounting, the company depreciates its equipment over a 10-year period vs. the 15-year period typical of other airlines. It also amortizes investment tax credits over the tax life of the property rather than deducting it the year the equipment is put into service.

Marketing. Delta's primary marketing thrust has been word-of-mouth advertising, supported by a focused effort to nurture customer loyalty. Delta has used the same advertising agency, BBDP, for the past forty years. In that period, it has launched a series of advertising campaigns designed to promote its service image. Its current campaign—the airline that "LOVES TO FLY AND IT SHOWS"—is consistent with this long-term strategy.

Deregulation in 1978 had its most significant impact on Delta's marketing efforts. In the volatile world of deregulated air travel, customer loyalty was severely tested by the enticements of lower fares. Delta's competitors, especially Eastern, decided to compete on the basis of price rather than service. As part of this strategy, they directed their marketing efforts at a new target. Braniff, Air Florida, People Express, and Continental were drawing crowds of nontraditional flyers with inexpensive no-frill flights. These aggressive upstart companies decided to compete with cars, buses, and trains for passenger traffic rather than other carriers.

Initially, Delta hoped to stay above the battle. Its customer base had always been business travelers. Delta expected that some might be lost temporarily, but that they would eventually return once the blood-letting price wars ended.

This wait-and-see strategy was plausible, but it failed to take into consideration two critically important marketing innovations. In 1981, American Air-

[4]"If Delta's Going to Make a Move, 'It's Now or Never,'" *Business Week,* June 3, 1991, p. 95.

lines introduced the first frequent-flyer program. Other carriers followed in rapid succession. These programs soon became recognized as a big hit with business travelers.

The other innovation of importance was the emergence of the travel agent in the marketing channel. The development of large networked computer systems made it possible for independent agents to perform duties previously reserved for the airline's customer service representative. United was the first company to recognize the importance of this change and launch a nationwide computerized reservation system. United and American owe much of their current success to these sophisticated information systems.

THE FUTURE

Delta's current plans call for it to continue along the course of disciplined expansion, especially into the international market. It has filed applications for an additional fourteen international destinations (Exhibit 6). Right now, 13 percent of available seat miles are international, but by 1994, this percentage is expected to increase to 20 percent.

Managers are currently planning for a 6 percent annual growth in capacity through the remainder of the 1990s. To meet this goal, plans call for the expenditure of $21.8 billion for the acquisition of new equipment and terminals. Total employment is expected to grow by 5 percent. Delta currently employs 63,439 people, of which 56,907 are domestic permanent employees, 5,107 are temporary, and 1,423 are in the international division (see Exhibit 5).

Overall growth is expected to take place along two distinct paths. First, the company is prepared to make acquisitions from troubled carriers as they become available. Pan Am, TWA, Continental, and Midway are all operating under bankruptcy protection, and each has assets that could complement Delta's route system.

The second path involves further use of strategic global alliances. Delta, Singapore Airlines, and Swissair are collaborating on a range of activities—from simple marketing agreements to complex operations exchanges—that will have far-reaching consequences for the industry and individual firm profitability. Thus far, they have agreed that the goal of the alliance is profit, rather than market share or growth for growth's sake.

International Route Applications **Exhibit 6**

Atlantic		***Pacific***	
Atlanta to	Manchester	Portland to Hong Kong	
	Moscow	Los Angeles to	Tokyo
	Leningrad		Seoul
	Tbilsi (Soviet Georgia)		Nagoya
	Rome/Milan		Taipei
	Barcelona		Bangkok
	Madrid		
	Berlin		

POTENTIAL THREATS

■ Reregulation

Public concern over the negative effects of deregulation has expressed itself in a profusion of regulatory plans despite Transportation Department insistence that competition is working.[5] A count prepared by the House Public Works and Transportation Committee discovered 94 airline related bills pending in the 101st Congress. High among the lawmaker concerns is continuing concentration in the industry. A 1990 study by the Transportation Department revealed that nine of the 29 carriers flying large aircraft provide 90 percent of all revenue passenger miles. At six of the largest hubs—those handling four million or more passengers annually—three-fourths or more of all departures were made by a single carrier. In Atlanta, for example, Delta now controls 82.6 percent of the market.[6]

Legislators are concerned that the already powerful carriers will move to stifle competition even further by coupling their power over scarce airport gates and landing slots with such marketing tools as computerized reservation systems,[7] frequent-flyer bonus programs, and inducements to travel agents. America West Chairman, Edward R. Beauvais, is among those calling for a reexamination of public policy. His company has prospered in the new environment, but he claims that restrictive access to airports and abuse of computerized reservation systems, among other things, have been major impediments to continued expansion by carriers like America West.[8]

Gate and landing slot access at major airports has been a problem for years. To control congestion, in 1969 the FAA allocated takeoff and landing slots at four high-density airports: Chicago's O'Hare, Washington National, and New York's LaGuardia and JFK. In 1986, it initiated a rule permitting carriers with those slots, to sell them to other bidders. Because of their extraordinary value, most carriers have chosen to retain ownership and lease them to noncompeting carriers. The result is that no independent carrier has been able to establish new service at these airports since 1986. At 55 airports, including 15 of the 27 largest, incumbent carriers can exercise veto control over the construction of new gates. Delta exercises such control at Atlanta; Chattanooga, Tennessee; Cincinnati; and Lexington.

■ Internationalization

The battle for competitive advantage in international air markets is well underway. Spurred by the consolidation of the European Community's air markets, the collapse of regimes in Eastern Europe, and the growing importance

[5]James Ott, "Competition Study Identifies Few Problems in U.S. System," February 19, 1990, *Aviation Week and Space Technology*, pp. 74–75.

[6]"Airlines Gradually Filling Eastern's Void," *Atlanta Journal Constitution*, May 18, 1991, p. B3.

[7]Paul Desmond, "Justice Department Probes Legality of Airline Network," *Network World*, 7(29) (July 16, 1990), pp. 13–14.

[8]Michael Mecham, "Regulation Bills Prompt Carriers to Counterattack," *Aviation Week and Space Technology*, 131(20) (November 13, 1989), pp. 70–71.

of Asian and Latin American economies, the international air transportation community is in turmoil.

The battle for new international air route authorities is pitched, as carriers struggle to secure footholds in the key North American, Asian, and European markets. The North American market now accounts for 40 percent of world air traffic, and it is expected to grow at about 6 percent through the end of the century. The Far Eastern market, driven by the fast economic growth of the region's four tigers—Japan, Korea, Taiwan, and Singapore—is expected to grow at more than 9 percent through the end of the century.

Carriers such as British Airways, Air France, Lufthansa, and JAL are entrenched leaders in the international travel market, a role that is in part due to their legacy as government-owned flag carriers and the preferential treatment they enjoyed as a consequence. The U.S. has never had a designated flag carrier, although for many years, Pan Am unofficially played this role. As late as 1978, Pan Am and the U.S.'s other international pioneer, Transworld Airlines, together controlled 64.2 percent of the U.S. international passenger traffic. Both have been in financial difficulty for years and together they now control less than one-third of their former market share.

The best positioned U.S. carrier for a dominant international presence is American. Like its competitors, it seeks to balance fluctuations in its higher-cost, lower-yield domestic traffic by expanding international operations.

Despite its promising lead, American's domestic competitors are not about to abandon efforts to tap into the rich international market. On the European front, marketing agreements have been made by USAir and Alitalia, Swissair and Delta, Pan American and Aeroflot, and United Airlines and British Airways.[9]

In the Pacific, United and Northwest already dominate transpacific traffic from the United States, sharing the market with Asian carriers. And in 1989, Delta, Swissair, SAS, and Singapore Airlines completed a network of joint operating and marketing agreements that enable each airline to book its passengers on worldwide flights.

Aspiring United States carriers face intense competition from three sources: (1) the strong former flag ship airlines—Lufthansa, British Air, JAL; (2) healthy domestic rivals such as United and Delta; and (3) a host of very strong niche carriers from around the world—Air Canada, Hong Kong Air, and All Nippon Airways.

■ Transportation Alternatives

Major airports around the world are becoming overburdened by increases in air traffic. In the United States, twenty-two airports currently face serious traffic delays, and that number is expected to double by the end of the 1990s. Research indicates that the situation is similar in Europe and even worse in Asia.[10]

Two airport options are attracting increasing attention. Satellite airports, usually neglected older airports, are continuing to receive attention with the

[9]James Ott, "North Atlantic Traffic to Hit Record with New Services," *Aviation Week and Space Technology*, 132(25), January 18, 1990, pp. 90–91.

[10]Robert J. Hannan, "Airport Work Takes Wing," *ENR*, Vol. 225(10) (September 6, 1990), pp. 76–77.

proven success by Midway in Chicago and Continental at Newark. Southwest has established a foothold in the North at the almost forgotten Detroit City Airport, which is twice as close to General Motors and Chrysler headquarters as the main airport. In California, United Airlines has bolstered its flight offerings to and from satellite airports at Ontario and Oakland.[11]

A second option is the development of new airports designed specifically to accommodate short take-off and landing aircraft (STOL). Aircraft designed to take full advantage of these airports (vertiports), such as the Bell/Boeing V-22 tilt-rotor, are not yet in production, but technology appears promising. The British have moved ahead with a more conventional airport design. In 1987, London opened the first STOL port in Europe.[12] The airport's objective is to tap the city's business traveler market by offering a fast and easy route to Europe that will get passengers to Paris in less time than it takes them to get to the regional airport at Heathrow.

In Atlanta, municipal airports northeast and west of Hartsfield have been economically significant due to their ability to accommodate corporate aircraft.

Trains, until the emergence of jet engines in the 1950s, were strong airline competitors. New technologies hold out the promise of reviving this competition once again. High-speed ground transportation (HSGT) has already proved itself in Japan and Europe and it may appear in the United States in the near future.

HSGT is potentially superior to both airplanes and automobiles for trips between 100 and 600 miles.[13] A trip from Paris to Geneva, for example, takes $3\frac{1}{2}$ hours by train vs. 65 minutes by plane. The one-way, first-class train ticket costs $89; a one-way unrestricted plane ticket sells for $277. By train, it takes four hours to travel from Milan to Rome, 65 minutes by plane. A first-class, one-way train ticket is priced at $70; one-way plane fare is $153.

No high-speed rail systems currently operate in the United States, but a number of promising schemes are in progress. Recently, a Texas consortium announced plans for a route connecting Dallas, Houston, and San Antonio scheduled to begin operation in 1998.

CONCLUDING COMMENT

Delta's emergence as a winner in the post-deregulation era was due in large part to the policies and practices it developed in the four decades preceding deregulation. In retrospect, its dependence, paternalistic style of employee relations, commitment to personalized customer service, focus on a single business, conservative financial strategies, and follow-the-leader marketing efforts weathered the storms of change in the U.S. market exceptionally well. But it remains an open question, as to whether the same will hold true for change in the international market.

As the leaders of Delta consider their efforts to maintain the family spirit and competitive vigor of a regional carrier and yet simultaneously compete in

[11]Jim Ellis, "When a 'Satellite' Airport May Be Just the Ticket," *Business Week* (Industrial/Technology Edition), July 16, 1991, pp. 170–171.

[12]Marion Cotter, "Where the Sky's the Limit for Profits," *Marketing* (October 22, 1987), pp. 27–28.

[13]Richard A. Uher, "Levitating Trains: Hope for Gridlocked Transportation," *Futurist* 24(5) (September–October 1990), pp. 28–32.

a deregulated global market, they must carefully reassess their competitive strategy. This reconsideration must not merely address each component independently, but it must also consider the interrelationship between each of the six key elements. A change in financial policy, for example, could exert a major impact on employee relations, particularly with respect to the compensation system. A willingness to enter into cooperative agreements with competitors could not only challenge Delta's effort to remain independent, it could also have a significant impact on the definition of customer service. Delta is changing as part of its effort to find a niche in the global market, but will the new Delta continue to resemble the old Delta?

APPENDIX 1: FINANCIALS

Delta Air Lines, Inc.: Five-Year Summary — **Exhibit 7**

Date	Sales ($000)	Net Income	EPS
1990	8,582,231	302,783	5.28
1989	8,089,484	460,918	9.37
1988	6,915,377	306,826	6.30
1987	5,318,172	263,729	5.90
1986	4,460,062	47,286	1.18
Growth rate	17.7	59.0	45.4
Operating expenses: FY 1990, $ Mil			
Salaries and related		3,426.0	
Aircraft fuel*		1,232.6	
Aircraft maintenance and repairs		241.0	
Aircraft rent		325.8	
Other rent		219.7	
Landing fees		137.3	
Passenger service		367.4	
Passenger commissions		813.8	
Other cash costs		939.9	
Depreciation and amortization		459.2	
Total operating expenses		8,162.7	

*Delta uses two billion gallons of jet fuel annually. A one-cent change equals $20 million, pretax.

Exhibit 8 **Delta Air Lines, Inc.: Consolidated Balance Sheets (June 30, 1991 and 1990)**

Assets (in thousands)	*1991*	*1990*
Current assets		
Cash and cash equivalents	$ 763,702	$ 68,457
Accounts receivable, net of allowance for uncollectible accounts of $59,257 at June 30, 1991, and $18,835 at June 30, 1990	772,550	726,105
Refundable income taxes	60,254	—
Maintenance and operating supplies, at average cost	70,327	68,344
Prepaid expenses and other	225,494	155,127
Total current assets	1,892,327	1,018,033
Property and equipment		
Flight equipment owned	6,831,503	6,399,117
Less: Accumulated depreciation	2,873,249	2,568,655
	3,958,254	3,830,462
Flight equipment under capital leases	173,284	173,284
Less: Accumulated amortization	91,699	71,356
	81,585	101,928
Ground property and equipment	1,890,384	1,617,786
Less: Accumulated depreciation	854,192	707,242
	1,036,192	910,544
Advance payments for new equipment	564,636	556,006
	5,640,667	5,398,940
Other assets		
Marketable equity securities	244,707	244,092
Investments in associated companies	173,792	167,402
Cost in excess of net assets acquired, net of accumulated amortization of $40,391 at June 30, 1991, and $31,896 at June 30, 1990	300,863	309,358
Leasehold and operating rights, net of accumulated amortization of $665 at June 30, 1991	51,220	—
Other	107,103	89,177
	877,685	810,029
	$8,410,679	$7,227,002

(Continued) **Exhibit 8**

Liabilities and Stockholders' Equity (in thousands, except share amounts)	*1991*	*1990*
Current Liabilities		
Current maturities of long-term debt	$ 9,079	$ 27,593
Current obligations under capital leases	13,950	12,495
Short-term borrowings	56,020	65,351
Accounts payable and miscellaneous accrued liabilities	698,345	583,273
Air traffic liability	969,047	748,477
Accrued vacation pay	163,207	145,209
Accrued rent	156,285	134,792
Transportation tax payable	72,759	78,668
Accrued income taxes	16,789	47,783
Total current liabilities	2,155,481	1,832,641
Noncurrent Liabilities		
Long-term debt	1,938,112	1,180,909
Capital leases	120,483	134,290
Accrued rent	236,674	153,555
Other	94,116	55,229
	2,389,385	1,523,983
Deferred Credits		
Deferred gain on sale and leaseback transactions	865,030	596,653
Deferred income taxes	378,246	505,972
Manufacturers credits	100,603	119,681
Unamortized investment tax credits	13,409	26,572
Other	2,409	3,298
	1,359,697	1,252,176
Commitments and Contingencies		
Employee Stock Ownershyip Plan Preferred Stock:		
Series B ESOP Convertible Preferred Stock, $1.00 par value, $72.00 stated and liquidation value; issued and outstanding, 6,941,593 shares at June 30, 1991, and 6,944,450 shares at June 30, 1990	499,795	500,000
Less: Unearned compensation under employee stock ownership plan	450,664	477,367
	49,131	22,633
Common Stockholders' Equity:		
Common stock, $3.00 par value; authorized, 100,000,000 shares; issued, 54,389,941 shares at June 30, 1991, and 54,346,572 shares at June 30, 1990	163,155	163,040
Additional paid-in capital	883,888	879,660
Reinvested earnings	1,761,103	2,157,919
Less: Net unrealized loss on noncurrent marketable equity securities	13,514	13,896
Treasury stock at cost, 4,983,162 shares at June 30, 1991, and 8,260,462 shares at June 30, 1990	337,647	591,154
	2,456,985	2,595,569
	$8,410,679	$7,227,002

Source: Annual Report, 1992.

Exhibit 9

Delta Air Lines, Inc.: Consolidated Statements of Income (for the years ended June 30, 1991, 1990, and 1989, in thousands, except for per share amounts)

	1991	*1990*	*1989*
Operating revenues			
Passenger	$8,566,676	$8,042,496	$7,579,716
Cargo	475,547	416,168	393,662
Other, net	128,390	123,567	116,106
Total operating revenues	9,170,613	8,582,231	8,089,484
Operating expenses			
Salaries and related costs	3,752,398	3,425,865	3,122,279
Aircraft fuel	1,599,165	1,232,561	988,734
Aircraft maintenance materials and repairs	326,218	241,024	224,500
Aircraft rent	413,106	325,781	329,763
Facilities and other rent	255,742	219,761	206,429
Landing fees	168,307	137,278	119,850
Passenger service	409,420	367,504	341,296
Passenger commissions	923,122	768,140	747,269
Depreciation and amortization	521,457	459,162	393,095
Other	1,251,660	985,643	937,944
Total operating expenses	9,620,595	8,162,719	7,411,159
Operating income (loss)	(449,982)	419,512	678,325
Other income (expense)			
Interest expenses	(162,828)	(83,937)	(70,647)
Less: Interest capitalized	65,287	57,226	31,778
	(97,541)	(26,711)	(38,869)
Gain on disposition of flight equipment	16,843	17,906	16,562
Miscellaneous income, net	30,496	57,205	55,200
	(50,202)	48,400	32,893
Income (loss) before income taxes	(500,184)	467,912	711,218
Income taxes credited (provided)	162,646	(186,722)	(279,214)
Amortization of investment tax credits	13,158	21,593	28,914
Net income (loss)	(324,380)	302,783	460,918
Preferred stock dividends, net of tax benefits	(18,592)	(18,144)	—
Net income (loss) available to common stockholders	$ (342,972)	$ 284,639	$ 460,918
Net income (loss) per share			
Primary	$(7.73)	$5.79	$9.37
Fully diluted	$(7.73)	$5.28	$9.37

CASE 16

Mesa Airlines, Inc.

Roy A. Cook, Jeremy J. Coleman, Fort Lewis College

INTRODUCTION:

Mesa Airlines is a regional carrier, headquartered in Farmington, New Mexico, pro- viding local passenger service to the Rocky Mountain, southwestern, and midwestern regions of the United States. Regularly scheduled flights feed passengers into the company's primary hubs of Denver, Albuquerque, Phoenix, and Milwaukee. Exhibit 1 shows the system route maps of the cities and towns served by Mesa Airlines and its subsidiaries from their respective hub cities. The company's routes to and from these hubs are served on scheduled flights under three separate names: Mesa Airlines, United Express, and Skyway Airlines.

Founder, president, and CEO Larry L. Risley has shepherded Mesa's meteoric growth from one aircraft serving two cities to a fleet of 42 aircraft serving 61 cities in the ten years between 1980 and 1990. In fact, during the past five years, Mesa's revenues have grown at an average annual rate of over 46%, with growth in net earnings equaling or exceeding these increases. Mesa's growth has been fueled by a dual strategy consisting of internal expansions and acquisitions. "Mesa operates as a low cost, low fare, high frequency carrier offering one-class seating, advanced ticketing, and courtesy baggage handling, with emphasis on customer service."[1] These growth figures are especially impressive when compared to those of major and many regional carriers that have, at best, experienced only single-digit growth percentages.[2,3]

BACKGROUND

According to Larry L. Risley, "Mesa Airlines is absolutely a product of a deregulated environment."[4] Although the concept for regional airlines such as

---

This case is intended for classroom discussion only, not to depict effective or ineffective handling of administrative situations. All rights reserved to the authors and the Midwest Society for Case Research.

Exhibit 1 Mesa Airlines, Inc. Route Systems

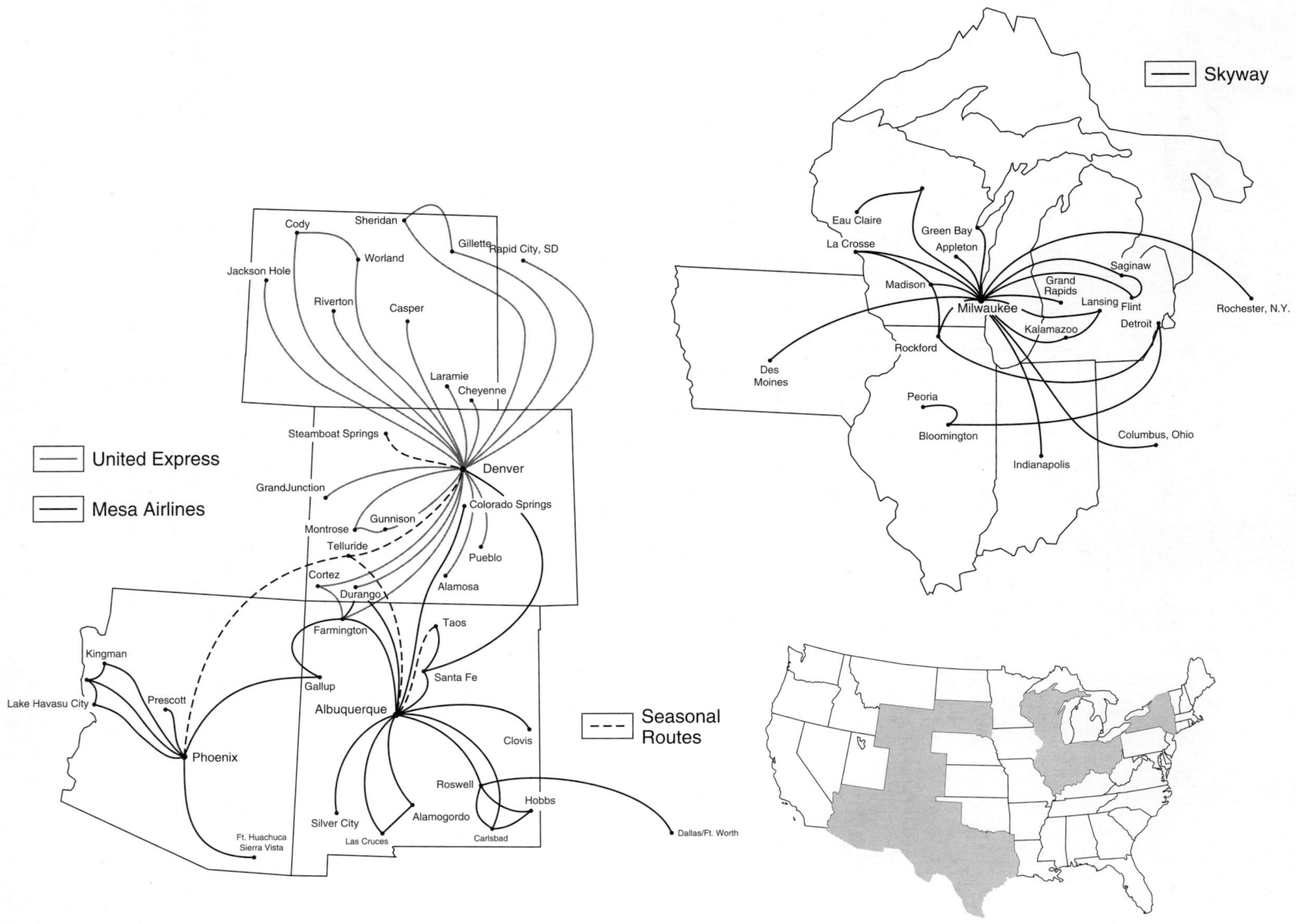

Mesa was originated in 1967, with inaugural short-haul flights and smaller craft by US Air, it was not until the Airline Deregulation Act of 1978 that the commuter airline industry began to flourish. "'Regional carriers' revenue passenger miles grew to 7.61 billion in 1990 from 2.09 billion in 1981. But even so, the entire regional industry represents just 2% of the total 457.9 billion scheduled passenger miles flown by U.S. airlines in 1990."[5]

The Airline Deregulation Act of 1978 was designed to create a competitive environment where market forces could freely operate to provide an efficient and effective air transportation system. Through this act, air routes were openly available to all providers, and new carriers were encouraged to provide a variety of low-priced services and schedules. "Deregulation was supposed to open the door to new airlines. Faced with huge fixed costs and cyclical demands, most startups were overwhelmed by the established carriers."[6] The act specifically resulted in the following changes:

1. Prior to 1978, air carriers had little, if any, pricing freedom. The simple fare structure was based on a three-tier pricing structure: economy, coach, and first class. Since deregulation, the fare structure has become incredibly complex, with literally thousands of published fares.
2. Prior to 1978, airlines planning to begin services to one or more new cities had to apply to the Civil Aeronautics Board (CAB) for approval. In the current environment, there is little to prevent a carrier from entering a new market, other than the capacity of the airport in that market to handle the increased traffic safely.
3. Prior to deregulation, airlines wishing to discontinue services to a city had to apply for and obtain formal approval from the CAB, 90 days in advance. The CAB, in turn, could require the airline to continue service until an alternate carrier was found for that city.
4. As part of the deregulation of the airline industry, the Essential Air Service Program, designed to provide guaranteed levels of service to specified cities, was placed under the administration of the U.S. Department of Transportation (DOT). Under this program, the DOT may authorize subsidies to compensate designated carriers for providing service to unprofitable markets.

Competition has intensified and resulted in industry consolidation as operators have adjusted to the realities of a deregulated environment. In fact, the number of regional carriers has decreased from a record 246 in 1981 to only 150 by the end of 1990.[7]

In the wake of deregulation, the air transportation system in the United States has been developed around the hub-and-spoke concept, with major carriers dominating key hub cities and the regional airlines feeding into these hubs. The hub-and-spoke system allows passengers to fly with the same airline from point of origin to destination. As the hub system has evolved, the major carriers have structured their scheduling so that regional airlines can feed passengers into hub cities under a code-sharing system. Code-sharing agreements with dominant carriers in key hub cities are so important that "the success or failure of any regional carrier . . . is tied to the performance of the major carrier to which it is aligned."[8]

> Most major carriers have established affiliations with regional airlines to provide air service between the major carriers' hubs and medium-sized and smaller communities. These affiliations benefit both the major carriers by enabling them

> to market air service from their hubs to medium-sized and smaller cities, some of which cannot support large jet air service, and the regional airlines by enabling them to publish their flights under the major carriers' two-letter designator codes in computer reservations systems. These arrangements provide the airline with a competitive advantage in booking passengers who make connections at hub airports served by the affiliated major carrier.[9]

Code-sharing allows a passenger to purchase, through one airline, a single ticket for all segments of one's flight. The regional airlines share not only common reservation systems, but also company logos and other identifying service marks of their code-sharing major airline partners such as US Air, United, Continental, TWA, and American. Although Mesa Airlines has encountered some marketing turbulence in this deregulated environment, it has been able to overcome these rough spots by capitalizing on new opportunities.

HISTORY

In 1979 when Larry and Janie Risley moved to Farmington, New Mexico, to begin running a fixed-base operation (FBO), starting scheduled airline service was not a part of their long-range plans. Fixed-base operators serve such needs of private aircraft owners and renters as refueling, tiedown, and hanger services. In addition, they provide flight instruction and charter services. Due to the early lack of success in this business, the Risleys began to search for additional ways to generate revenues and utilize their aircraft.

Based on suggestions from friends, in October 1980, Risley began his "scheduled operation," using a single-engine Piper Saratoga. This was a four-times-a-day, fair-weather shuttle between Farmington, a city of 25,000 in northwestern New Mexico, and Albuquerque, 200 miles to the southeast. According to Risley, "In those early days, if the weather got bad, I didn't fly and I don't know what the passengers did because I didn't ask them."[10] Thus, as a part of a fixed-base operation, the Mesa Air Shuttle was born. Although Risley served as president of the company, he had no ownership position at this time. He was merely operating the company for his brother-in-law, whose primary interests were in the oil and gas business.[11]

August 1982 marked a milestone in the history of the present company. At that time, fixed-base operations were eliminated, and the primary business of Mesa became passenger service. In addition, the original partners, who had financed the fixed-base operations, decided that the financial returns for the passenger service business were too marginal for the risk involved. Faced with a loss of his financial backing, Risley was forced to search for sufficient capital to continue operations. He found it by mortgaging the Risley home and car. This mortgage provided enough capital to purchase the aircraft and the right to use the name Mesa Air Shuttle.[12]

During the first year of operation under Risley's control, Mesa Air Shuttle carried 10,000 passengers between Farmington and Albuquerque. In comparison, just nine years later, Mesa was serving 61 cities and was carrying approximately 650,000 passengers per year. Operations expanded rapidly, due to the origination, in April 1989, of the Milwaukee, Wisconsin–based Skyway operations and the code-sharing agreement reached with United Airlines, in April 1990, to operate United Express into Denver. These two additions to Mesa's operating system doubled the number of passengers carried. As a consequence of its success, Mesa Airlines has quadrupled in size over the past five years and it has successfully driven its largest competitor, Air Midwest, out of the New Mexico market.[13,14]

Mesa's growth has not been without mistakes. One of the more turbulent periods in its growth occurred in 1987. During 1987, Mesa purchased the routes of Centennial Airline, a regional carrier serving Riverton, Wyoming. This was the first time Mesa had operated in a competitive environment containing code-sharing carriers. Mesa, operating as an independent carrier, found itself to be noncompetitive with its code-sharing rival, Continental Express. Mesa was unable to generate sufficient volume to achieve profitability on the newly acquired Centennial routes. Since 85% of all reservations were made on the first screen of computerized reservation systems, and as an independent, its flights were listed on the third screen of the system, Mesa found itself at a competitive disadvantage. Even though Mesa offered better fares and connections than its on-line rival, the traveling public was unaware of these services due to the peculiarities of airline reservation systems. "That's where we learned not to compete with a code-sharing carrier unless you have the same power to deal with him."[15]

In all, 1987 proved to be an eventful year for Mesa Airlines. In addition to the ill-fated acquisition of the Centennial Airline routes, Mesa also went public and changed its name from Mesa Air Shuttle to Mesa Airlines, Inc. The year 1989 proved to be another action-packed period, with Mesa fighting off a takeover attempt by States West Airlines and launching an initial attempt to acquire Wichita, Kansas–based Air Midwest.[16] The attempted acquisition of Air Midwest was aborted when an amicable solution to the details of the takeover agreement could not be reached. This is in keeping with Risley's stated policy of avoiding engagements in hostile takeovers.

MARKETING

When Mesa Air Shuttle began serving the Farmington and Albuquerque markets, it was in direct competition with four other commuter airlines serving the market with a total of 23 flights a day. The initially intense competition between these carriers resulted in fares dropping to as low as $25 one-way. In the face of this competition, the fare on Mesa flights was lowered to $24. By comparison, a comparable fare today is quoted at $69.00 one-way. According to Risley:

> That's where I found I had a competitive edge over the competition and that I had a business that just happened to be an airline.[17]

By focusing on a strategy of developing a low-cost business, rather than on that of developing a typical high-cost operation, Mesa was able to offer these $24 fares on a profitable basis. Mesa's low-cost strategy, consisting of low fares/high volume, cross-utilization of employees, high frequency of service, and sizing aircraft to the market, allowed it to survive in a very competitive marketplace serving many small, widely dispersed cities. Shortly after these fare wars began, competitors began to raise their prices, while Mesa retained its lower prices, thus allowing it to increase its market share and eventually drive all of its competitors out of the Farmington–Albuquerque market.[18] Mesa's low-cost strategy has allowed it to attain the lowest cost structure of any publicly held commuter airlines in the Unites States.

These early battles for survival and market share have helped shape Mesa's competitive posture. "Where Mesa faces competition, it will compete aggressively by lowering fares, increasing frequency, and scheduling competitive aircraft for flights that occur at the same time as those of the competitors."[19] Although Mesa has proven its ability to compete successfully in crowded markets, it also has a stated strategy, "to provide service between medium-sized and small cities that do not have other scheduled airline service or where the company believes other service [is] insufficient."[20]

The operating strategy used by Mesa, as it enters new markets, is to first test these markets by inaugurating scheduled service with smaller aircraft. Then, based on the level of demand, larger aircraft and/or more frequent services may be added on these new routes. At the same time, if demand decreases or does not materialize, a similar reverse strategy is utilized, thus conserving resources.

Although Mesa's preference is to operate as an independent carrier under its YV (Yankee Victor) code in the computer reservation system, it realizes the importance to a regional carrier of name recognition in primary hub cities, afforded by code-sharing arrangements. Through code-sharing agreements, regional carriers are listed in the computer reservation systems under the primary carrier's code. Mesa was initially precluded from entering code-sharing agreements with any of the major carriers in its geographic service areas because these major carriers already had existing contracts with feeder airline partners.

In 1989, an opportunity presented itself to purchase the routes of Aspen Airways, a United Express code-sharing carrier in the Denver market. Mesa entered into the purchase agreement for Aspen's routes, realizing that United Airlines was not obligated to extend the use of its computer reservation code to Mesa. To convince United Airlines to code-share, Mesa first had to demonstrate how it could improve United Airlines's Denver market share. Mesa was able to accomplish this task by providing a consistent and dependable level of service and by acquiring four 30-passenger Brasilia aircraft from Air Midwest to serve this market. Based on its demonstrated levels of performance, Mesa was able to eventually enter into a five-year code-sharing agreement with United Airlines to serve as a feeder into its Denver hub.[21]

Mesa, like most other scheduled airlines, depends heavily on an effective hub-and-spoke system, reservations generated through travel agencies, and the steady repeat patronage of business travelers. Much of Mesa's marketing success can be attributed to focusing on these three key areas. Management has estimated that approximately 60% of its passengers make interline connections in Albuquerque, Denver, or Phoenix; 55% of its business is generated through travel agencies; and 80% of its passengers are business travelers.[22,23]

OPERATIONS

According to Risley:

> Mesa Airlines only hires people, [it] does not hire pilots, ticket agents, [or] presidents. While [an employees's] primary job might be to fly an airplane or

> work on an airplane, they are there to perform whatever service is needed to accommodate the passenger.[24]

Based on this concept, Mesa has been able to gain a competitive advantage because its employees can be cross-utilized in all operational positions. "Cross-utilization of employees, a tradition dating back to the days when Larry and Janie did everything, helps keep costs down."[25]

Management of Mesa Airlines can be typified as being hands-on. In fact, Risley himself is a qualified mechanic and still serves as maintenance director. The hierarchical management layers between the president/CEO and operating ground crews are limited. Decision making is centralized at the top level of the company, with very limited latitude in decision making at the lower levels of the organization.

Even in the face of its rapid expansion, Mesa has retained a very lean management staff, but it is beginning to show the strains of its explosive growth. According to Risley:

WEAKNESS:
Management lacks the depth necessary to meet rapid growth.

> We do not have the depth of experience we need. We doubled our fleet and our pilots and maintenance staff, but the management and administrative staff increased only 13%.[26]

Jonathan Ornstein, Mesa's vice president, Planning and Scheduling, echoes this sentiment by noting that "[w]e're all entrepreneurial and everyone in management hates to give up any responsibilities."[27]

Mesa Airlines prides itself on its relationships with aircraft manufacturers and its ability to perform its own maintenance work. During 1989, the level of training of its mechanics was enhanced, and additional equipment expenditures were made so that maintenance service on its fleet could be retained in-house. In-house maintenance, combined with a limited variety of aircraft in its fleet, has also contributed to the company's ability to achieve its low-cost strategy. The configuration of Mesa's current fleet, which is the most modern in the industry, can be seen in Exhibit 2.

STRENGTH:
Aircraft maintenance is performed in-house.

STRENGTH:
Mesa has a new and efficient fleet of aircraft.

The driving force behind Mesa's spectacular growth is the 46-year-old president, chief executive officer, and chairman of the board of directors—Larry L. Risley. Prior to the incorporation of the company in 1983, Risley served as president of Mesa Aviation Services Incorporated, the predecessor fixed-base operator of the present company. Risley and his wife, Janie, who serves as executive vice president and also sits on the board of directors, together control over 27% of Mesa's outstanding common stock.

Mesa Airlines, Inc., Flight Equipment* (as of August 1990) **Exhibit 2**

Type of Aircraft	*Passenger Capacity*	*Number in Fleet*
Beechcraft 1900	19	19†
Beechcraft 1300	13	10
Cessna Caravan	9	2
Embraer Brasilia	30	2

*Approximate average age of fleet less than two years.

†Represents oldest aircraft in fleet, ranging from one to five years.

FINANCE

STRENGTH:
Mesa is in a strong financial position.

The need for additional capital to fuel its rapid growth caused Mesa to enter the public financial markets in 1987. Prior to this time, growth had been fueled through internally generated and privately borrowed funds. The strong demand for initial public offerings during 1987 prompted Mesa to tap this funding source. According to Risley, going public encompassed the good, the bad, and the ugly:

> The good side is [that we] have a lot of money. The bad side is [that you] hang all your laundry out for everybody to look at and the competition knows exactly the condition of the airline. The ugly [is that you] have stockholders. [We now] have basically 400 owners of Mesa Airlines. About 396 of those are great people. The other four are a pain.[28]

Mesa once again tapped the financial markets, in December 1990, completing a secondary public offering consisting of 862,500 shares of new common stock selling at $7.25 per share, yielding $5,400,000. Consolidated balance sheets and statements of income for Mesa Airlines, Inc. are presented in Exhibits 3 and 4.

GROWTH THROUGH ACQUISITIONS

The Airline Deregulation Act has resulted in a free-entry market and, according to Risley, "We're here to provide a level of service to those communities that can't justify the type of service from larger scheduled aircraft that they feel they need. Mesa Airlines built its business on sizing aircraft to market. We're dedicated to providing whatever service a community can prove it can support."[29] Regional air carriers have continued to grow at a faster pace than the major airlines by focusing on routes that average less than 200 miles in length; regionals posted a 12.4% increase in revenue passenger miles compared to a 5.7% increase in revenue passenger miles for the entire airline industry during 1990.[30] Mesa Airlines has been able to grow and prosper in an environment that has proven to be hostile to many startup airlines such as World Airways, Midway Airlines, People Express, Air Florida, and Metro Airlines.

As Larry Risley charts the future for Mesa Airlines, he seeks growth through acquisitions. In a renewed bid to execute this strategy, on January 24, 1991, Mesa once again attempted to expand its service areas by launching a friendly offer for Wichita, Kansas–based Air Midwest. The offer included a package of cash and stocks valued at approximately $27 million. This is the equivalent of $8 per share for all of Air Midwest's outstanding common stock.[31] At the time of the offer, the 52-week trading range for Air Midwest stock ranged from a low of $$3\frac{3}{8}$ to a high of $$6\frac{1}{4}$. On the date of the offer, Air Midwest stock closed at $6 per share.

The offering price of $8 a share for all outstanding Air Midwest common stock is structured to yield $1 per share in cash and between .63 and .82 shares of newly issued Mesa common stock. The exact distribution of common stock is to be based on the average closing bid/ask price of Air Midwest stock on the five trading days prior to the close of the transaction. If Air Midwest is trading

Mesa Airlines, Inc., Consolidated Balance Sheets (000 omitted) **Exhibit 3**

	Fiscal Year Ending		
	9/30/1990	*9/30/1989*	*9/30/1988*
Assets			
Current assets			
Cash and marketable securities	$ 4,143	$ 4,606	$ 2,361
Receivables	5,487	2,186	1,556
Inventory	1,123	922	573
Other current assets	398	253	156
Total current assets	$11,151	$ 7,967	$ 4,646
Fixed assets			
Property, plant, and equipment	16,433	15,686	17,982
Other assets	5,502	1,467	1,673
Total assets	$33,086	$25,120	$24,301
Liabilities and Stockholders' Equity			
Accounts payable	$ 1,789	$ 1,100	$ 784
Current long-term debt	921	1,043	1,175
Accrued expenses	1,333	362	326
Income taxes	511	43	—
Other current liabilities	1,358	575	381
Total current liabilities	$ 5,912	$ 3,123	$ 2,666
Long-term debt	9,608	11,921	13,875
Deferred charges	5,377	1,560	335
Total liabilities	$20,897	$16,604	$16,876
Stockholders' equity	12,189	8,516	7,425
Total liabilities and stockholders' equity	$33,086	$25,120	$24,301

at below $\$8\frac{1}{2}$, then .82 shares will be issued. On the other hand, if Air Midwest is trading at or above $\$11\frac{1}{8}$, then .63 shares will be issued. If the closing price falls between these two quotes, then the number of shares issued will be factored based on the actual closing price. The proposed Air Midwest acquisition provides Mesa with many opportunities and threats in an expanded market area.

BACKGROUND INFORMATION ON AIR MIDWEST

In May 1990, Air Midwest celebrated its 25th anniversary of operations. As can be seen from the consolidated balance sheets and statements of income presented in Exhibits 5 and 6, 1989 was a year of extreme turmoil resulting from the $1,200,000 loss in passenger revenue, due to the bankruptcy of its code-sharing partner in the Kansas City market, Braniff Inc. In addition, "the com-

Exhibit 4

Mesa Airlines, Inc., Consolidated Statements of Income (000 omitted)

	Fiscal Year Ending		
	9/30/1990	*9/30/1989*	*9/30/1988*
Net sales	$45,954	$22,508	$17,509
Cost of goods	22,740	9,583	6,749
Gross profit	$23,214	$12,925	$10,760
Selling, general, and administrative expenses	15,435	7,887	6,366
Income from operations	$ 7,779	$ 5,038	$ 4,394
Depreciation and amortization	1,854	3,138	2,421
Nonoperating income	385	1,467	232
Interest expense	1,119	1,690	1,564
Income before taxes	$ 5,191	$ 1,677	$ 641
Income taxes	2,018	636	238
Net income before extraordinary items	$ 3,173	$ 1,041	$ 403
Extraordinary items	455	0	0
Net income	$ 3,628	$ 1,041	$ 403
Outstanding shares	1,675,065	1,669,140	1,654,765

pany faced operating seven 30-passenger aircraft and thirteen 17-passenger aircraft in the Kansas City–based market where connecting traffic had disappeared."[32] Subsequently, the company was able to downsize its fleet to the current configuration shown in Exhibit 7. Regularly scheduled flights for Air Midwest feed passengers into its primary hubs of Kansas City and St. Louis, Missouri.

Exhibit 8 shows the system route maps of the cities and towns served from these two hub cities.

LOOKING INTO THE FUTURE

As Mesa enters 1991, many questions about its future growth and success remain. (Exhibit 9 provides traffic data as well as a profile of Mesa's aircraft fleet.) Can the rapid growth rate in sales and markets served be maintained? Will the acquisition strategy continue to be effective? What role will changes in aircraft technology play in the future of the company? How far should Mesa Airlines expand its operations outside of its current market areas? Can the company continue to maintain its low-cost strategy in light of its anticipated growth? What changes, if any, will need to be made in the company's management structure and administrative policies and procedures? These and many more questions face management as decisions are made to prepare Mesa Airlines to face the turbulent twenty-first century.

Air Midwest, Inc., Consolidated Balance Sheets (000 omitted)

Exhibit 5

	Fiscal Year Ending		
	12/31/1989	*12/31/1988*	*12/31/1987*
Assets			
Current assets			
Cash and marketable securities	$ 2,101	$ 2,096	$ 2,642
Receivables	4,533	2,166	2,959
Inventories	7,195	8,228	6,698
Other current assets	478	684	515
Total current assets	$14,307	$13,174	$12,814
Net property, plant, and equipment	38,882	49,782	58,120
Other assets	5,472	4,340	4,128
Total assets	$58,661	$67,296	$75,062
Liabilities and Stockholders' Equity			
Current liabilities			
Payables	$ 9,912	$10,370	$10,783
LTD (current)	1,021	2,184	2,453
Leases (current)	2,557	3,228	2,841
Accrued expenses	1,857	1,502	1,695
Income taxes	0	0	0
Other current liabilities	2,205	1,066	1,274
Total current liabilities	$17,552	$18,350	$19,046
Debt			
Long-term debt	5,814	10,368	12,552
Deferrals	1,502	506	210
Capital leases/other liabilities	18,646	20,614	24,434
Total liabilities	$43,514	$49,838	$56,242
Stockholders' equity	15,147	17,458	18,820
Total liabilities and stockholders' equity	$58,661	$67,296	$75,062

Exhibit 6

Air Midwest, Inc., Consolidated Statements of Income (000 omitted)

	Fiscal Year Ending		
	12/31/1989	*12/31/1988*	*12/31/1987*
Net sales	$81,100	$74,099	$83,314
Cost of goods	51,031	62,997	69,225
Gross profit	$30,069	$11,102	$14,089
Selling, general, and administrative expenses	24,644	2,740	3,968
Income from operations	$ 5,425	$ 8,362	$10,121
Depreciation and amortization	4,227	5,016	6,139
Nonoperating income	420	552	531
Interest expense	4,012	5,281	5,731
Income before taxes	$ (2,394)	$ (1,383)	$ (1,218)
Income taxes	0	0	0
Net income before extraordinary items	$ (2,394)	$ (1,383)	$ (1,218)
Extraordinary items	0	0	0
Net income	$ (2,394)	$ (1,383)	$ (1,218)
Outstanding shares	3,913,509	3,891,541	3,837,298

Exhibit 7

Air Midwest, Inc., Flight Equipment* (as of December 1989)

Type of Aircraft	*Passenger Capacity*	*Number in Fleet*
Fairchild Metro II	17	19†
Fairchild Metro II-A	17–19	2†
Jetstream Super 31	19	5
Saab Fairchild 340	30	5
Embraer Brasilia	30	8

*Approximate average age of fleet greater than six years.

†Represents oldest aircraft in fleet, averaging ten or more years.

Air Midwest Route System

Exhibit 8

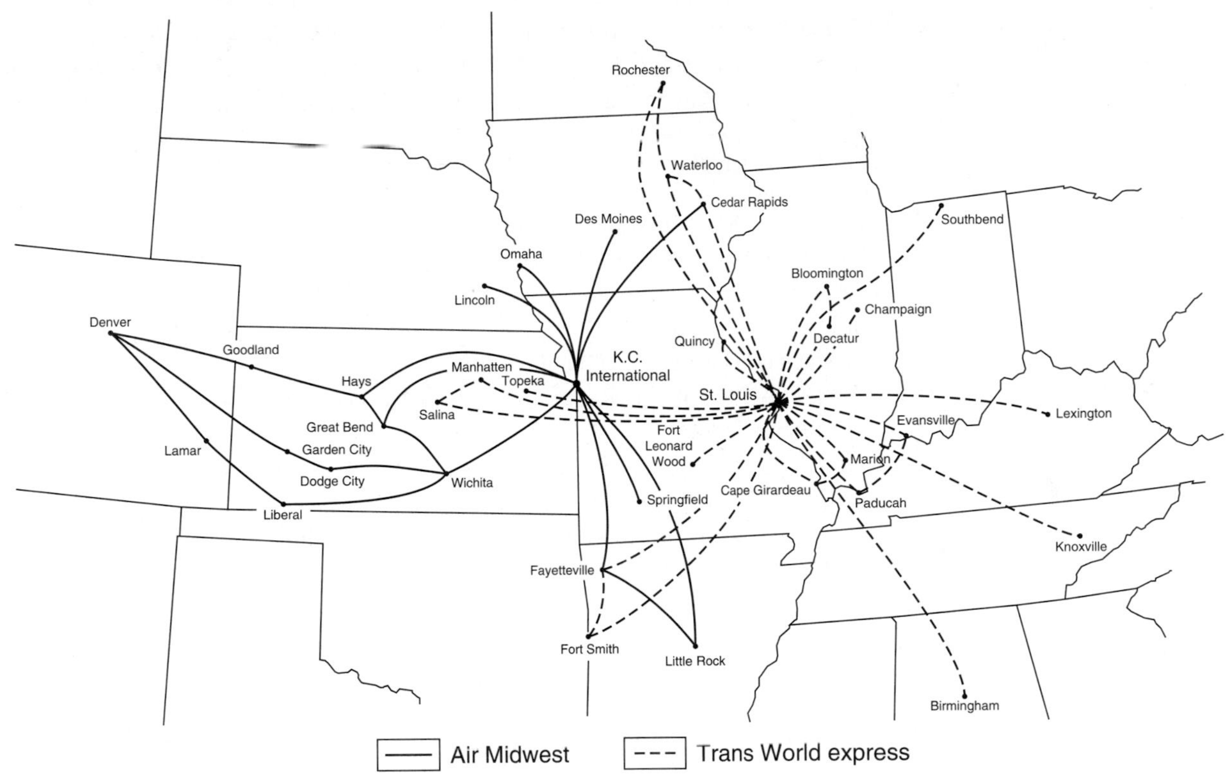

Mesa Airlines, Inc., Flight Equipment as of September 1991 and Traffic Statistics for the First Five Months of 1991

Exhibit 9

Type of Aircraft	*Passenger Capacity*	*Number in Fleet*
Beechcraft 1900	17	46
Embraer Brasilia	30	4
Fairchild Metro II	17	4

Traffic Statistics Through May (thousands)	*1991*	*1990*
Total passengers	430	316
Revenue passenger miles	75,491	48,143
Available seat miles	176,941	104,029
Load factor	42.7%	46.3%

ENDNOTES

1. Mesa Airlines, Inc., Form 10-K., 1989, p. 2.
2. "Flying Fortresses," *The Economist* 314, 10 March 1990, pp. 72–74.
3. Joseph Conlin, "Puddle Jumpers," *Successful Meetings,* December 1990, pp. 89–95.
4. Presentation by Larry L. Risley, CEO, Mesa Airlines, Executive Speaker Series: Fort Lewis College, Durango, Colorado, 1990.
5. Farrell Kramer, "Small Airlines Hit Turbulence But Stay Aloft," *Investor's Daily,* 5 April 1991, p. 34.
6. Eric Schain, Mark Maremont, and James E. Ellis, "Can These Startup Airlines Handle the Heavy Weather?" *Business Week,* 1 October, 1990, pp. 122–123.
7. Kramer, 1991.
8. Ibid.
9. Air Midwest, Inc., Form 10-K, 1989, p. 6.
10. Presentation by Larry L. Risley, CEO, Mesa Airlines, 1990.
11. Ibid.
12. Ibid.
13. Mesa Airlines, Inc., 1990 Annual Report, p. 5.
14. Danna K. Henderson, "Mesa Airlines Embraces Code Sharing," *Air Transport World* 27 September 1990, pp. 178–185.
15. Presentation by Larry L. Risley, CEO, Mesa Airlines, 1990.
16. Henderson, 1990.
17. Presentation by Larry L. Risley, CEO, Mesa Airlines, 1990.
18. Ibid.
19. Mesa Airlines Inc., Form 10-K, 1989, p. 7.
20. Ibid.
21. Presentation by Larry L. Risley, CEO, Mesa Airlines, 1990.
22. Ibid.
23. Mesa Airlines Inc., Form 10-K, 1989, p. 2.
24. Presentation by Larry L. Risley, CEO, Mesa Airlines, 1990.
25. Henderson, 1990, p. 180.
26. Ibid.
27. Ibid.
28. Presentation by Larry L. Risley, CEO, Mesa Airlines, 1990.
29. Ibid.
30. Kramer, 1991.
31. "Mesa Airlines Launches Offer for Air Midwest," *Denver Post,* 25 January 1991, p. C1.
32. *Annual Report,* Air Midwest, 1989, p. 1.

CASE 17

Federal Express: The Road to Globalization

Howard S. Tu, Sherry E. Sullivan, Memphis State University

It is January 1990. Thomas R. Oliver, senior vice president of international operations, is on his way to meet with the members of his "Tigerclaws" committee. The operational merger of Flying Tigers with Federal Express was supposed to be concluded last August. Yet, anticipated and unanticipated problems keep surfacing. International operations are draining financial resources, and there are problems that must be resolved immediately. Oliver met with Frederick Smith several days ago and was given the job of heading a special task force to direct the Flying Tigers merger efforts and resolve the resulting problems. Oliver requested and got representatives of senior executives from every department of the company, to form what he now named the "Tigerclaws Committee" (see Exhibit 1). This committee has the power to cut across departmental bureaucratic lines. It has the resources of all the departments behind it to reach fast-track solutions to any problems that exist. Even with such commitments, Oliver realizes what a formidable task he and his committee are facing. One of the major differences to be considered by the committee is the services in which each firm has specialized. Federal Express has focused on time-sensitive, express delivery, whereas Flying Tigers has focused on the delivery of heavy freight.

The authors thank Federal Express Corporation and its employees for their efforts in assisting with the research and review of this case. This study was funded in part by a grant from the SHRM Foundation. The interpretations, conclusions, and recommendations, however, are those of the authors, and do not necessarily represent those of the foundation.

This case is intended for classroom discussion only, not to depict effective or ineffective handling of administrative situations. All rights reserved to the authors.

Exhibit 1 **Departments Represented on the Tigerclaws Committee**

Memphis SuperHub	Hub Operations
Business Application	Personnel Services
Airfreight Systems	International Operations
Q.A. Audits	Central Support Services
Planning and Administration	Customer Support
International Clearance	COSMOS/Pulsar System Division
Communications	COO/Quality Improvement
Ramp Plans/Program	

EXPRESS AND FREIGHT FORWARDING INDUSTRIES

STRENGTH:
Federal Express has a strong domestic reputation.

THREAT:
Competition (e.g., United Parcel Service) is stiff in the industry.

Sending documents or packages by priority mail is now viewed as a necessary convenience rather than a luxury. The domestic market is led by Federal Express Corporation with 53% of the market followed by United Parcel Service (UPS) at 19%. The U.S. Postal Service has 3%–4% of the market (Curry, 1989). The overnight letter business is characterized by slow growth because of the increased use of facsimile machines.

The increasing competition between express delivery services and the traditional air freight industry is changing the face of international cargo transportation. Many independent freight carriers complain that big couriers and integrated carriers are poaching on their market niches. Others ignore the competition, believing that the personalized relationships that traditional air freight companies provide will keep clients coming back. Still, companies such as Federal Express are having a big effect on the air freight industry. Express couriers are building their nondocument business by 25% to 30% a year. Proprietary consolidation and expedited treatment at Customs have been the major factors influencing this growth rate. In an effort to move deeper into the cargo sector, some express companies are marketing themselves as providers of third-party logistics services (Strugatch, 1990). These services go above and beyond the shipment of parcels and include customs assistance, trafficking, and various forms of consultation.

■ Express Service in the United States

Federal Express, UPS, Airborne Express, and the U.S. Postal Service are quickly introducing services that promise to translate the fundamentals of speed and information into a powerful competitive edge. They are stressing good service at lower costs. Major carriers also are introducing "next-generation services." For example, Federal Express is introducing a time-sensitive business through its new Business Logistics Services division. This business allows customers to select the level of service desired, including overnight delivery with either morning or afternoon delivery. UPS has started offering discounts to its bigger customers and shippers that send over 250 pieces weekly. In addition, UPS is building an $80 million computer and telecommunications center to provide support for all operations worldwide. Airborne's chief advantage is that it operates its own airport and has begun operating a "commerce park" around its hub in Wilmington, Ohio.

■ Europe

The international document and parcel express delivery business is one of the fastest growing sectors in Europe. Its scope should grow even faster when most European customs barriers are removed in 1992. Although the express business will become more important in the single European market, none of the four principal players is European: DHL, Federal Express, and UPS are U.S. companies, and TNT is Australian. Europe is not expected to produce a challenger; because the "big four" are buying smaller rivals at such a fast pace, the odds seem to be heavily against a comparable competitor emerging (Arthur, 1989).

■ Pacific Rim

The Asia-Pacific air express market is expanding by 20%–30% annually, and the world's major air express and air freight companies have launched massive infrastructure buildups to take advantage of this growth. Industry leader DHL recently strengthened its access to air service by agreeing to eventually sell 57.5% of the equity of its international operation to Japan Air Line, Lufthansa, and Nissho Iwai trading company. TNT Skypak's strength lies in providing niche services and in its ability to tap into the emerging Asian–East European route with its European air hub. Two new U.S. entrants, Federal Express and UPS, are engaged in an undeclared price war. Willing to lose millions of dollars annually in order to carve out a greater market share, Federal Express has already captured about 10% of Pacific express business and 15% of freight. UPS's strategy is to control costs and to offer no-frills service at low rates. All four companies are seeking to expand the proportion of parcels, which can yield about twice the profits of express documents business (Guyot, 1990).

■ Major Airlines

Since the common adaptation of wide-body jets, major international airlines have cargo space in their planes. Japan Airlines and Lufthansa are two of the worldwide players, with most national airlines providing regional services.

Airlines are expanding and automating their cargo services to meet the challenges presented by fast-growing integrated carriers. Two strategies are being employed: (1) the development of new products to fill the gap between the demand for next-day service and traditional air cargo service and (2) computerization of internal passenger and cargo operations (McKenna, 1989b).

FEDERAL EXPRESS CORPORATION

Frederick W. Smith, founder of Federal Express Corporation, went to Yale University, where he was awarded a now-infamous C on an economics paper that outlined his idea for an overnight delivery service (Foust, 1989). After college and military service, Smith began selling corporate jets in Little Rock, Arkansas. In 1973, he tapped his $4 million inheritance, rounded up $70 million in venture capital, and launched Federal Express, testing his college paper's thesis. The company turned profitable after three years. It became a $4.6 billion-a-year juggernaut in 1991. In 1991, Federal Express handled more than a million packages a day, flew 380 planes, operated 31,000 delivery vans, and employed 95,000 people (Pearl, 1991).

STRENGTH:
Fred Smith provides strong leadership.

STRENGTH:
Federal Express has a strong employee base; employees brag about their salaries and benefits.

THREAT:
The high wages paid to employees may reduce Federal Express's ability to remain price competitive.

Federal Express has always taken pride in its people-oriented approach and its emphasis on service to its customers. Smith believes that in the service industry, it is the employees that make their business (Smith, 1991). The philosophy of Smith and his managing staff is stated in the company motto: People, Service, Profit. This philosophy is manifested in many ways, including (1) extensive orientation programs, (2) training and communications programs, (3) promotion of employees from within, and (4) a tuition reimbursement program. Federal Express's Open Door Policy for the expression of employee concerns also illustrates the commitment of top management to resolve problems (Trunick, 1989).

As to services, Federal Express stresses the importance of on-time delivery and has established a 100% on-time delivery goal. The company has achieved a record of 95% on-time delivery. In 1990, Federal Express was one of the five U.S. firms to win the Malcolm Baldridge National Quality Award. This award is given by the U.S. government to promote quality awareness, recognize the quality achievements of U.S. companies, and publicize successful quality strategies.

Frederick W. Smith has a vision for the overnight express delivery business. Although Federal Express is the number one express firm in the United States, Smith firmly believes that globalization is the future for the express business (*Journal of Business Strategy*, 1988). From 1986 to 1988, Federal Express struggled to become a major player in international deliveries (see Exhibit 2). The company has run head on into entrenched overseas rivals, such as DHL, and onerous foreign regulations (Foust, 1989).

OPPORTUNITY:
Federal Express can seek to acquire additional firms in the global arena.

OPPORTUNITY:
With the Flying Tiger merger, Federal Express can continue to develop internationally.

Frustrated with the legal processes in negotiating for landing rights that are restricted by bilateral aviation treaties (*Journal of Business Strategy*, 1988), Mr. Smith reversed his promise to build only from within and started on a series of acquisitions. From 1987 to 1988, Federal Express purchased 15 minor delivery companies, mostly in Europe (see Exhibits 3, 4, and 5). In December 1988, Smith announced the merger with Tiger International, Inc., best known for its Flying Tigers airfreight service. On paper, the merger of Federal Express and Tiger International, Inc. seemed to be a marriage made in heaven. As one Federal Express executive pointed out, "If we lay a route map of Flying Tigers over that of Federal Express, there is almost a perfect match. There are only one or two minor overlaps. The Flying Tiger routes are all over the world, with highest concentration in the Pacific rim countries while the Federal Express routes are mostly in domestic U.S.A." As a result of the merger, Federal Express's world routes are completed. For example, the acquisition of Flying

The Global Routes of Federal Express **Exhibit 2**

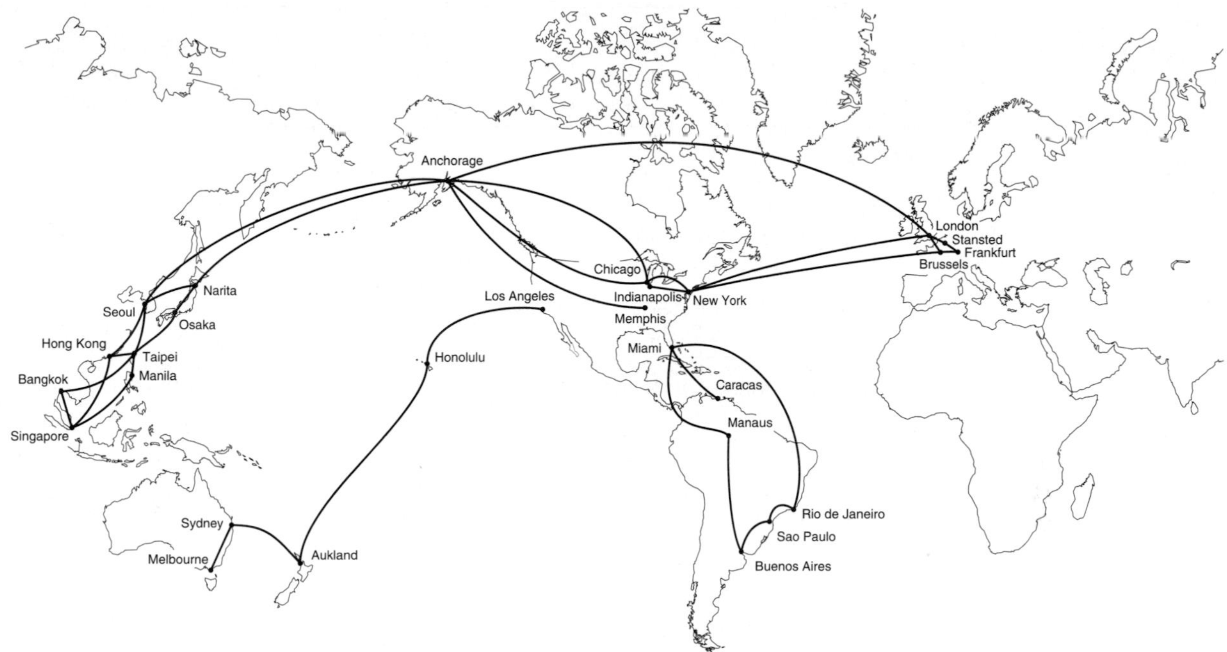

Source: Federal Express, August 1989.

Tigers brought with it the unrestricted cargo landing rights at three Japanese airports that Federal Express had been unsuccessful in acquiring for three years (Calonius, 1990).

■ Tiger International, Inc.

Tiger International, Inc., better known for the Flying Tigers Line, Inc. freight service or Flying Tigers, was founded 40 years ago by Robert Prescott. Over the years, the company became modestly profitable. But in 1977, Smith won his crusade for air cargo deregulation over the strident objection of Flying Tigers' founder, the late Robert Prescott. Heightened competition, troubled acquisitions, and steep labor costs led to big losses at Tigers. In 1986, Stephen M. Wolf, the former chairman of Republic Airline, Inc., came on board at Tigers and managed to get all employees, including those represented by unions, to accept wage cuts. As Tigers rebounded financially, it was ripe to be taken over by one of the major delivery service companies (see Exhibits 6 and 7). In 1988, Federal Express announced the acquisition of Tigers to the pleasure of some and the dismay of others. At the announcement, some Tigers employees shouted "TGIF"—Thank God It's Federal. Robert Sigafoos, who wrote a corporate history of Federal Express, commented that "Prescott must be turning over in his grave" (Foust, 1989).

Flying Tigers always had a distinctive culture, one that partly developed from the military image of its founder. Tigers' employees stressed "Tiger

Exhibit 3

Federal Express Corporation and Subsidiaries, Consolidated Balance Sheets (in thousands)

	May 31,	
	1987	*1988*
Assets		
Current assets		
Cash, including short-term investments of $35,200 and $15,000	$ 21,685	$ 54,945
Receivables, less allowance for doubtful accounts of $17,100 and $16,230	399,333	491,324
Spare parts, supplies, and fuel	39,933	48,798
Prepaid expenses and others	46,529	34,938
	507,480	630,005
Property and equipment, at cost		
Flight equipment	1,138,875	1,301,978
Package handling and ground support equipment	587,430	755,585
Computer and electronic equipment	321,651	438,527
Other	664,096	853,019
	2,712,052	3,349,109
Less accumulated depreciation and amortization	850,620	1,117,234
Net property and equipment	1,861,432	2,231,875
Other assets	130,599	146,669
	$2,499,511	$3,008,549
Liabilities and Stockholders' Investment		
Current liabilities		
Current portion of long-term debt	$ 60,393	$ 69,138
Accounts payable	192,877	199,328
Accrued expenses	250,455	303,586
Total current liabilities	503,725	572,052
Long-term debt, less current portion	744,914	838,730
Deferred income taxes and other commitments and contingencies	171,952	267,088
Common stockholders' investment		
Common stock, $.10 par value; 1,000,000,000 shares authorized, 52,862,124 and 51,630,316 shares issued	5,163	5,286
Additional paid-in capital	571,071	623,057
Retained earnings	536,386	726,036
	1,112,620	1,354,379
Less deferred compensation related to stock plan	33,700	23,700
Total common stockholders' investment	1,078,920	1,330,679
	$2,499,511	$3,008,549

Source: Federal Express Corporation 1988 Annual Report.

Federal Express Corporation and Subsidiaries, Consolidated Statements of Changes in Financial Position (in thousands) **Exhibit 4**

	May 31,		
	1986	*1987*	*1988*
Funds Provided By			
Income from continuing operations	$ 192,671	$ 166,952	$ 187,716
Charges to income not requiring working capital:			
Depreciation and amortization	193,544	239,291	289,578
Deferred income taxes and other	44,046	69,018	40,769
Working capital provided from continuing operations	430,261	475,261	518,063
Increase in long-term debt	284,387	299,911	251,265
Disposition of property and equipment:			
Sale-leaseback transactions	251,533	2,852	117,848
Other	5,012	3,899	6,956
Proceeds from issuance of common stock	191,257	39,521	52,109
Decrease in other assets	17,256	–	–
Other	(3,996)	2,635	37,206
Total funds provided	$1,175,710	$ 824,079	$ 983,447
Funds Used For			
Acquisition of property and equipment	$ 674,771	$ 722,369	$ 784,713
Reduction of long-term debt	323,137	116,713	157,449
Increase in other assets	–	26,302	19,371
Increase in deferred compensation related to stock plan	50,000	–	–
Discontinued operations	52,688	136,320	(32,284)
Total funds used	1,100,596	1,001,704	929,249
Increase (decrease) in working capital	$ 75,114	$ (177,625)	$ 54,198
Increase (Decrease) in Working Capital by Component			
Cash	$ 172,847	$ (163,351)	$ 33,260
Receivables	54,213	52,323	91,991
Spare parts, supplies, and fuel	(7,195)	(9,409)	8,865
Prepaid expenses and other	(29,719)	14,627	(11,591)
Current portion of long-term debt	(28,249)	12,586	(8,745)
Accounts payable	(56,813)	(8,343)	(6,451)
Accrued expenses	(29,970)	(76,058)	(53,131)
Increase (decrease) in working capital	$ 75,114	$ (177,625)	$ 54,198

Source: Federal Express Corporation 1988 Annual Report.

Spirit" or team work. Since Wolf took over as the chairman and CEO at an extremely difficult time, the general orientation of Flying Tigers was to keep the company flying.

In October 1980, Flying Tigers purchased Seaboard World Line. The Seaboard merger was characterized by layoffs, lack of compensation, and many other problems. The net result of the merger and the continued cost cutting required for Tigers' turnaround left some survivors of the Seaboard merger

Exhibit 5

Federal Express Corporation and Subsidiaries, Selected Consolidated Financial Data (in thousands, except per share amount)

	Year Ended May 31		
	1988	*1987*	*1986*
Operating Results			
Revenues	$3,882,817	$3,178,308	$2,573,229
Operating expenses	3,503,365	2,813,565	2,229,208
Operating income	379,452	364,743	344,021
Other income (expense)	(77,124)	(52,858)	(38,936)
Income before income taxes	302,328	311,885	305,085
Income taxes	114,612	144,933	112,414
Income from continuing operations	187,716	166,952	192,671
Loss from discontinued operations	—	(232,523)	(60,832)
Net income (loss)	$ 187,716	$ (65,571)	$ 131,839
Earning Per Share			
Earning (loss) per share			
Continuing operations	$ 3.56	$ 3.22	$ 3.87
Discontinued operations	—	(4.48)	(1.22)
Net earnings (loss) per share	$ 3.56	$ 1.26	$ 2.65
Average shares outstanding	52,670	51,905	49,840
Financial Position			
Current assets	$ 630,005	$ 507,480	$ 613,290
Property and equipment, net	2,231,875	1,861,432	1,551,845
Total assets	3,008,549	2,499,511	2,276,362
Current liabilities	572,052	503,725	431,910
Long-term debt	838,730	744,914	561,716
Common stockholders' investment	1,330,679	1,078,920	1,091,714
Other Operating Data			
Average daily package volume	877,543	704,392	550,306
Average pounds per package	5.3	5.1	5.3
Average revenue per pound	$ 3.10	$ 3.33	$ 3.40
Average revenue per package	16.32	16.97	17.92
Average number of employees	48,556	41,047	31,582
Aircraft fleet at end of year			
McDonnell Douglas DC10-10s	8	8	6
McDonnell Douglas DC10-30s	13	11	9
Boeing 737-200s	—	—	—
Boeing 727-100s	47	39	35
Boeing 727-200s	21	21	18
Cessna 208s	109	66	34
Fokker F-27-500	5	—	—
Dassault Falcons	—	—	—
Vehicle fleet at end of year	21,000	18,700	14,500

Source: Federal Express Corporation 1988 Annual Report.

(Continued) **Exhibit 5**

Year Ended May 31						
1985	*1984*	*1983*	*1982*	*1981*	*1980*	*1979*
Operating Results						
$2,015,920	$1,436,305	$1,008,087	$803,915	$589,493	$415,379	$258,482
1,757,303	1,247,553	857,350	684,449	489,758	348,378	218,370
258,617	188,752	150,737	119,466	99,735	67,001	40,112
(46,345)	(11,948)	(521)	(11,614)	(1,691)	(7,628)	(6,329)
212,272	176,804	150,216	107,852	98,044	59,373	33,783
73,532	51,373	61,283	52,695	39,908	21,644	13,400
138,740	125,431	88,933	55,157	58,136	37,729	20,383
(62,663)	(10,001)	—	—	—	—	—
$ 76,077	$ 115,430	$ 88,933	$ 55,157	$ 58,136	$ 37,729	$ 20,383
Earning per Share						
$ 2.95	$ 2.76	$ 2.05	$ 1.32	$ 1.45	$ 1.03	$ .62
(1.33)	(.22)	—	—	—	—	—
1.62	$ 2.54	$ 2.05	$ 1.32	$ 1.45	$ 1.03	$ .62
46,970	45,448	43,316	41,788	40,222	36,564	32,732
Financial Position						
$ 423,144	$ 328,136	$ 265,171	$194,265	$166,952	$ 85,454	$ 48,975
1,346,023	1,112,639	596,392	457,572	373,250	277,702	123,844
1,899,506	1,525,806	991,717	730,291	570,112	395,030	179,823
316,878	255,910	175,293	114,596	113,846	64,351	43,681
607,508	435,158	247,424	223,856	162,705	142,465	45,729
812,267	717,721	503,794	350,319	270,875	168,745	74,946
Other Operating Data						
406,049	263,385	166,428	125,881	87,191	68,022	45,833
5.6	5.5	5.8	6.5	8.4	9.8	10.7
$ 3.45	$ 3.80	$ 4.02	$ 3.81	$ 3.15	$ 2.43	$ 2.03
19.19	21.03	23.42	24.79	26.29	23.81	21.72
26,495	18,368	12,507	10,092	8,080	6,806	4,883
6	6	6	4	4	2	—
5	4	—	—	—	—	—
—	—	—	—	1	5	—
35	35	38	31	25	17	12
18	12	—	—	—	—	—
9	—	—	—	—	—	—
—	—	—	—	—	—	—
—	—	32	32	32	32	32
12,300	9,000	5,000	4,000	2,500	2,200	1,700

Exhibit 6 **Flying Tiger Line, Inc. and Subsidiaries, Consolidated Balance Sheets (in thousands)**

	December 31, 1987	December 31, 1988
Assets		
Current assets		
Cash, including certificates of deposit	$ 47,699	$ 59,178
Short-term interest-bearing investments at cost, which approximates market value	200,315	186,581
Cash and short-term interest-bearing investments	248,014	245,759
Receivables, net	142,740	150,307
Inventories	16,974	19,612
Prepaid expenses and others	19,323	21,035
Total current assets	427,051	436,713
Property and equipment		
Equipment used in flight operations	813,282	863,929
Buildings and leasehold improvements	45,356	46,410
Other equipment	78,262	82,487
Equipment and facilities acquisition in process	186	11,239
	937,086	1,004,065
Less accumulated depreciation and amortization	486,664	548,586
	450,422	455,479
Other assets		
Deposits, deferred charges, and investments	47,709	38,268
Cost in excess of fair value of net assets of an acquired business, net	41,181	39,455
	88,890	77,723
Total Assets	$966,363	$969,915
Liabilities and Stockholders' Equity		
Current liabilities		
Current portion of long-term debt obligations	$ 33,719	$ 30,481
Accounts payable and accrued liabilities	184,771	186,628
Total current liabilities	218,490	217,109
Long-term obligations		
Notes payable and equipment obligations	255,393	220,181
Capital lease obligations	217,806	207,839
	473,199	428,020
Deferred credits		
Deferred income tax	3,707	24,611
Overhead liabilities—leased flight equipment	29,589	24,142
Other	34,826	39,212
Total deferred credits	68,122	87,965
Commitments and contingencies		
Stockholders' equity		
Common stock, $1 par value		
Authorized—30,000,000 shares; Outstanding—18,189,504 shares	18,189	18,189
Additional paid-in capital	213,025	174,438
Retained earnings	50,284	44,194
	281,498	236,821
Amounts due from parent and affiliates, net	74,946	—
Total stockholders' equity less amounts due from parent and affiliates	206,552	236,821
Total liabilities and stockholders' equity	$966,363	$969,915

Source: Flying Tiger Inc. 1988 Annual Report.

Exhibit 7

Flying Tiger Line, Inc. and Subsidiaries, Consolidated Statements of Cash Flows (in thousands)

Increase (Decrease) in Cash and Short-Term Interest-Bearing Investments For the Year Ended December 31,

	1986	*1987*	*1988*
Cash Flows from Operating Activities			
Net income (loss)	$ (18,645)	$ 81,710	$ 74,406
Adjustment to reconcile net income (loss) to net cash provided by operating activities:			
Depreciation and amortization	56,509	55,557	58,533
Overhead provision, net of payments	13,865	5,527	1,230
Provision for doubtful accounts and revenue adjustments	27,756	21,820	11,167
Loss on yen denominated debt	27,491	—	—
Increase in deferred income taxes	—	2,716	21,200
Increase in current assets other than cash and short-term interest-bearing investments	(8,271)	(42,245)	(23,084)
Increase (decrease) in accounts payable and accrued liabilities	(6,956)	18,305	14,830
Decrease in accrued interest	(4,653)	(2,793)	(1,989)
Increase (decrease) in income taxes payable	—	17,184	(10,984)
Others, net	6,501	20,204	13,514
Net cash provided by operating activities	93,597	177,985	158,823
Cash Flows from Investment Activities			
Capital expenditures	(8,437)	(8,466)	(55,093)
Retirements of property and equipment	786	1,868	103
Others, net	(2,351)	(10,181)	(3,358)
Net cash used in investing activities	(10,002)	(16,779)	(58,348)
Cash Flows from Financing Activities			
Proceeds from debt financing	389	140,000	102,041
Payments on debt and capital lease obligations	(64,113)	(196,335)	(145,627)
Cash dividends paid	—	—	(58,963)
Call of public warrants and others, net	—	—	(181)
Net cash used in financing activities	(63,724)	(56,335)	(102,730)
Net Increase (Decrease) in cash and short-term Interest-bearing Investments	19,871	104,851	(2,255)
Cash and Short-term Interest-bearing Investments at Beginning of Year	123,288	143,159	248,014
Cash and Short-term Interest-bearing Investments at End of Year	$143,159	$248,010	$245,759
Supplemental Disclosures of Cash Flow Information			
Cash paid during the year for:			
Interest	$ 61,281	$ 62,305	$ 51,462
Income taxes	—	$ 5,000	$ 32,784

Source: Flying Tiger Inc. 1988 Annual Report.

bitter. With the effects of the Seaboard merger fresh in their minds, some Tigers employees were quite nervous about their new merger with Federal Express.

▪ The Merger

Federal Express announced the acquisition of Flying Tigers in December 1988. However, because of government regulations, the actual operational merging of the two companies did not occur until August 1989. Although the two companies are supposed to now become one, problems from the merger keep surfacing. Some of these problems were to be anticipated with the merger of two companies of these sizes. However, many problems, as detailed in the following sections, were not anticipated and have become very costly to the company.

Exhibit 8 summarizes some of the differences between Federal Express and Flying Tiger Line, Inc.

Human Resource Management Problems

THREAT: Unionization remains a possibility.

Unions. Federal Express has traditionally been a nonunion shop, whereas the Flying Tigers employees were predominantly unionized. During the merger, the National Mediation Board could not determine a majority among the pilots

Exhibit 8

A Comparison of Federal Express and Flying Tiger

Dynamic	***Federal Express***	***Flying Tiger***
Type of business	Time-sensitive, express	Heavy freight
Quality goals	100%	95–96%
1988 revenues	$3.9 billion	$1.4 billion
1988 fleet	24 DC-10s, 68 727s, 133 Cessna 208s, 5 Fokker F-27s	22 747s, 11 727s, 6 DC-8s
Work force	Primarily part time, young	Primarily full time, older, long-tenured
Conflict resolution	Guaranteed Fair Treatment, Survey Feedback	Grievance procedure for union employees, no method for nonunion
Procedures	Highly formalized, strict appearance codes	Flexible, no uniforms
Supervisor authority	Within framework of policies and procedures	High—boss able to bend rules
Locus of power	Fred Smith, CEO	"Tiger Spirit" or team work
General orientation	People Oriented	Keep Flying Tigers flying
Heroes	Fred Smith, founder	Robert W. Prescott, founder
Myths	Inception of firm based on Yale assignment for which Smith received a C	Exploits and mystique of Flying Tiger pilots
Symbols	Awards (e.g., Bravo Zulu)	Lean and mean Tiger

at Federal Express and Flying Tigers. The board requires that a majority decide the union status at any firm. Because a majority could not be determined, the Mediation Board decided to allow the temporary mixed union and nonunion employees until the fall of 1989, when elections would determine whether there would be union representation. The ruling has created ambiguities in employee status and raised some important financial and legal issues for Federal Express, unions, and employees (Ott, 1989).

Different Cultures. The employees of Federal Express believe that it is a great place to work mainly because of its people-oriented policies. Because of this belief, most of the managers thought that the Flying Tigers employees would "welcome the merger with open arms." They failed to recognize that many Flying Tigers employees were mourning the death of their beloved organization. Flying Tigers had a strong organizational culture and a rich and long history. Tigers employees pride themselves on their team spirit and their willingness to take pay cuts for the good of the Flying Tigers Line, Inc. during the lean years. Many people were upset over the loss of the Tigers name during the merger (*World Wide*, 1989). As a consequence, a certain degree of "we–they" mentality has resulted.

Job Assignments. During the announcement of the merger, Smith made a job offer to all the employees of Flying Tigers. Approximately 80% of the 6,600 former Tigers employees accepted the offer. In a two-week period, from July 15 to 31, over 4,000 new jobs were to be created, and Flying Tigers employees transferred to these jobs. Many employees had to be relocated because the old Tigers' hub in Columbus, Ohio, was phased out, and primarily only freight and maintenance personnel were kept at the hub in Los Angeles. During the haste, there were quite a number of mismatches of jobs and employees.

Unrealistic Expectations. To help former Flying Tigers employees determine whether to accept Federal Express's job offers, Federal Express provided the employees with detailed information about the company. Videotapes introducing Federal Express and explaining the benefits of working for the company were mailed to the homes of Tiger employees. Additionally, many Tigers employees were flown into Federal Express's headquarters in Memphis and given the "grand tour." "Express Teams," groups of four to five employees, visited Flying Tigers locations and gave them previews of what it was like to work for Federal Express. Such promotional efforts may have caused high expectations for some Flying Tigers employees that were not met later.

Operational Management Problems

Operational Procedures. Although Flying Tigers had operational policies and procedures for handling international freight, they were not being used after the official date of the operational merger. Because Federal Express was not in the traditional cargo business, it did not have such a manual. Coupled with the inexperience of most Federal Express managers at the ports of entry, many international cargo shipments were being moved before going through U.S. Customs. Because of the lack of operational procedures, top managers could not hold anyone responsible for these mistakes.

Computer Systems. Federal Express developed the Cosmos II Positive Tracking System. The system, one of the most famous examples of strategic information systems, was honored as the 1990 Computerworld Smithsonian Award winner in the transportation category. The key component of the system is SuperTracker, a hand-held computer. It can accept data from key entry, barcode scanning, or electronic coupling and can withstand rough treatment in warehouses and trucks. The system is designed to track and handle high-quantity movement of small packages (Margolis, 1990).

Flying Tigers used the KIAC system. This system was designed to handle large-volume cargoes with limited consignments. Unfortunately, these two systems are not 100% compatible, and currently Federal Express is using both systems, with limited communication between the two.

Maintenance of Tiger Fleet. Federal Express discovered after the merger that most of Flying Tigers' planes had been poorly maintained and would require considerable maintenance upgrading or retirement. This extra expenditure and the problems it created were not anticipated before the merger.

Marketing Problems

Products. Federal Express moves pieces of 150 pounds or less, primarily with smaller transports. Flying Tigers' forte was heavy cargo and used primarily Boeing 747 freighter aircraft (McKenna, 1989a).

Customer Relations. Many of Flying Tigers' customers, including UPS, are competitors of Federal Express. Previously, they paid Flying Tigers to carry packages to countries where they had no landing rights. Freight forwarders, companies that transport cargo to and from airports, made up a good portion of Flying Tigers' customer base. Because Federal Express handled local logistics for its operations, international freight forwarders complained that Federal Express would take away their business. In response to these complaints, Federal Express has compromised by guaranteeing that it will use its own couriers and custom-clearing services for pieces weighing less than 150 pounds. Forwarders will get the business for pieces heavier than 150 pounds. However, freight forwarders are still suspicious, and Federal Express has been losing heavy-freight business since the merger (Calonius, 1990).

Financial Problems

In March 1991, Federal Express reported a nine-month loss of $200 million from overseas operations. The poor showing caused Federal Express to report its first-ever quarterly operating loss since 1976. Since then Federal Express's stock has slipped 16%. With $2.4 billion in debt and heated competition at home from United Parcel Service of America, Inc. and Airborne Freight Corp., Federal Express cannot continue to hemorrhage overseas without damaging its domestic operation. As a result, Standard & Poor's and Moody's have lowered Federal Express's long-term debt rating. The international business "doesn't have a lot of time to return to profitability," warned David C. Anderson, Federal Express's chief financial officer (Pearl, 1991). Exhibit 9 provides updated information on Federal Express's financial situation.

Exhibit 9

Federal Express Corporation and Subsidiaries, Selected Consolidated Financial Data (in thousands, except per share amount)

	Year Ended May 31		
	1991	*1990*	*1989*
Operating Results			
Revenues	$7,688,296	$7,015,069	$5,166,967
Operating expenses	7,408,503	6,601,490	4,742,532
Operating income	279,793	413,579	424,435
Other income (expense)	(238,851)	(195,156)	(126,103)
Income before income taxes	40,942	218,423	298,332
Income taxes	35,044	102,659	131,881
Income from continuing operations	5,898	115,764	166,451
Credit for accounting change	—	—	18,100
Net income (loss)	$ 5,898	$ 115,764	$ 184,551
Earning per Share			
Earning (loss) per share			
Continuing operations	$ .11	$ 2.18	$ 3.18
Discontinued operations	—	—	—
Net earnings (loss) per share	$ .11	$ 2.18	$ 3.53
Average shares outstanding	53,350	53,161	52,272
Financial Position			
Current assets	$1,282,847	$1,315,403	$1,100,080
Property and equipment, net	3,624,026	3,566,321	3,431,814
Total assets	5,672,461	5,675,073	5,293,422
Current liabilities	1,493,722	1,240,214	1,089,096
Long-term debt	1,826,781	2,148,142	2,138,940
Common stockholders' investment	1,668,620	1,649,187	1,493,524
Other Operating Data			
Average daily package volume	1,309,973	1,233,628	1,059,882
Average pounds per package	5.5	5.3	5.4
Average revenue per pound	$ 3.11	$ 3.14	$ 3.04
Average revenue per package	17.08	16.53	16.28
Average number of employees	81,711	75,102	58,136
Aircraft fleet at end of year			
McDonnell Douglas DC-8s	—	6	6
McDonnell Douglas DC10-10s	11	10	8
McDonnell Douglas DC10-30s	16	16	16
McDonnell Douglas MD-11s	1	—	—
Boeing 727s	18	19	21
Boeing 737-200s	—	—	—
Boeing 727-100s	92	89	80
Boeing 727-200s	57	41	26
Cessna 208s	194	184	147
Fokker F-27-500	26	19	7
Dassault Falcons	—	—	—
Vehicle fleet at end of year	32,800	31,000	28,900

Source: Federal Express Corporation Annual Report, 1991.

SUMMARY

Since 1985, Federal Express's international business has lost approximately $74 million and given company executives a lifetime supply of headaches (Foust, 1989). To improve Federal Express's competitive position with its overseas rivals and overcome the foreign regulations regarding landing rights, Frederick Smith announced, in December 1988, the acquisition of Tiger International, Inc. Although the combined companies will have a debt of $2.1 billion, Flying Tigers is expected to provide Federal Express with desperately needed international delivery routes. The Tiger acquisition will allow Federal Express to use its own planes for overseas package delivery where Federal Express used to contract other carriers. In addition, Tigers' sizable long-range fleet can be used to achieve dominance in the international heavy-freight business that Federal Express has yet to crack.

Suppose you were in Thomas Oliver's shoes and were the head of the Tigerclaws committee. What are the major problems and opportunities facing Federal Express? What should be the priorities of the Tigerclaws committee? How will you solve or reduce the problems and exploit the opportunities?

REFERENCES

Arthur, Charles. 1989. "The War in the Air." *Business [UK]*, November, pp. 60–66.

Calonius, Erik. 1990. "Federal Express Battle Overseas." *Fortune*, 3 December, pp. 137–140.

Curry, Gloria M. 1989. "Package Delivery Service: The Options Are Plentiful." *Office*, August, pp. 60–62.

Foust, Dean. 1989. "Mr. Smith Goes Global." *Business Week*, February 13, pp. 66–72.

Guyot, Erik. 1990. "Air Courier Fight for Pacific Business." *Asian Finance [Hong Kong]*, 15 July, pp. 22–23.

Journal of Business Strategy. 1988. "Federal Express Spreads Its Wings" 9, no. 4, July/August: 15–20.

McKenna, James T. 1989a. "Federal Express/Tiger Merger Would Reshape Cargo Industry." *Aviation Week & Space Technology*, January 2, p. 106.

McKenna, James T. 1989b. "Airline Boosts International Cargo Services to Protect Market Shares." *Aviation Week & Sports Technology*, November 20, pp. 124–125.

Margolis, Neil. 1990. "High Tech Gets It There on Time." *Computer World*, July 2, p. 77.

Ott, James. 1989. "Board Decision Muddle Rules on Union Role After Merger." *Aviation Week & Space Technology*, 28 August, p. 68.

Pearl, Daniel. 1991, "Innocents Abroad: Federal Express Finds Its Pioneering Formula Falls Flat Overseas." *Wall Street Journal*, 15 April, p. A1, col. 6.

Smith, Frederick W. 1991. "Empowering Employee." *Small Business Reports*, January, pp. 15–20.

Strugatch, Warren. 1990. "Air Cargo Report: Reliability Is the Buzzword." *Global Trade*, April, pp. 48–51.

Trunick, Perry A. 1989. "Leadership and People Distinguish Federal Express." *Transportation & Distribution*, December, pp. 18–22.

World Wide. 1989. "A Tiger's Eye View," vol. 1, no. 5.

CASE 18

HEALTHSOUTH Rehabilitation Corporation

W. Jack Duncan, Peter M. Ginter, University of Alabama at Birmingham; Michael D. Martin, HEALTHSOUTH Rehabilitation Corporation

STRENGTH: HRC has a proven track record and is in a very solid financial position.

HEALTHSOUTH Rehabilitation Corporation is by all measures one of the most successful business ventures in modern health care. Its growth has been nothing less than phenomenal. Yet, growth involves its own challenge. As Richard M. Scrushy, chairman, CEO, and president of HEALTHSOUTH Rehabilitation Corporation (HRC), read the first quarter 1991 earnings release (Exhibit 1) and reflected on the company's first seven years of growth, he wondered about HRC's future.

With 19 consecutive quarters of earnings growth, HEALTHSOUTH had been the darling of Wall Street. The Medical Rehabilitation niche within the health care industry has been as successful as originally believed. The company had achieved and exceeded all of the objectives of its original business plan.

Scrushy realized that in order to sustain growth, continued hard work was even more necessary than during the start-up period. He also knew that some key strategic decisions would have to be made: (1) Should the company continue to focus on the rehabilitation business? (2) Should the company concentrate more on one business segment? (3) Should the company diversify further into the acute care hospital business? (4) What pitfalls lie ahead? (5) Can success continue? (6) Where should we go from here?

BEGINNING OF SUCCESS

The company was organized in 1983 as AMCARE, Inc., but in 1985 changed its name to HEALTHSOUTH Rehabilitation Corporation. HEALTHSOUTH was

---

This case is intended for classroom discussion only, not to depict effective or ineffective handling of administrative situations. All rights reserved to the authors and the North American Case Research Association.

Exhibit 1

News Release

For Immediate Release
April 16, 1991

HEALTHSOUTH's Net Income for First Quarter up 64%

Birmingham, Ala.—HEALTHSOUTH Rehabilitation Corporation (NYSE: HRC) reported today that it generated a net income of $4,230,000 on net revenues of $50,574,000 for the quarter ended March 31, 1991. This represents a 64% increase as compared to the net income generated in the first quarter, 1990. Net revenues were 17% greater in this quarter than those experienced in the same period prior year. Primary earnings per share for the quarter were 31 cents, an increase of 29% as compared to last year. On a fully diluted basis, earnings per share for this quarter were 28 cents, a seven cent increase as compared to the 1990 quarter.

"During the first quarter," said Richard M. Scrushy, Chairman of the Board, President and CEO, "we opened four new outpatient centers, bringing the total number of operating locations to 55. The construction of our Kingsport, Tenn. rehabilitation hospital is on schedule and is expected to contribute to our operating results in the third quarter."

HEALTHSOUTH Rehabilitation Corporation, a leading provider of comprehensive medical rehabilitation services in the United States, currently operates 55 locations in 22 states.

Summary of Operating Results
(unaudited, in thousands except per-share data)

	Three Months Ended March 31,	
	1991	*1990*
Net Revenues	$50,574	$43,308
Net Income	4,230	2,573
Weighted average common and common equivalent shares outstanding	13,709	10,826
Earnings per share		
Primary	$.31	$.24
Fully diluted	$.28	$.21

founded by a group of health care professionals, led by Scrushy, who were formerly with LifeMark Corporation, a large publicly held, for-profit health care services chain that was acquired by American Medical International (AMI) in 1984.

In 1982, Richard Scrushy indicated how he first recognized the potential for rehabilitation services, in the following statement.

> I saw the Tax Equity and Fiscal Responsibility Act (TEFRA) guidelines and the upcoming implementation of Medicare's Prospective Payment System (PPS) as

> creating a need for outpatient rehabilitation services. It was rather clear that lengths of stay in general hospitals would decrease and that patients would be discharged more quickly than in the past. It became obvious to me that these changes would create a need for a transition between the hospital and the patient's home.

Medicare provided financial incentives for outpatient rehabilitation services by giving Comprehensive Outpatient Rehabilitation Facilities (CORFs) an exemption from prospective payment systems and allowing the services of these facilities to continue to be reimbursed on a retrospective, cost-based basis.

Mr. Scrushy anticipated the impact of the upcoming reimbursement changes.

> I also saw that LifeMark, my current employer, would suffer significant reductions in profitability as the use of the then lucrative ancillary inpatient services was discouraged under the new reimbursement guidelines. I discussed my concerns about the upcoming changes in Medicare with LifeMark management and proposed that we develop a chain of outpatient rehabilitation centers.
>
> I saw that the centers I proposed were LifeMark's chance to preserve its profitability under PPS, and when they rejected my proposal, I saw cutbacks and a low rate of advancement in the future.

Mr. Scrushy repeated his proposal for AMI's management when it acquired LifeMark, but AMI could not implement the program immediately after a major acquisition. Scrushy resigned his position to move to Birmingham, Alabama, a city with an international reputation in health care, and there founded HEALTHSOUTH Rehabilitation Corporation in conjunction with three colleagues from LifeMark.

■ Early Development

Initially organized as an Alabama corporation and subsequently reorganized as a Delaware corporation, HRC began operations in January 1984. Its initial focus was on the establishment of a national network of outpatient rehabilitation facilities and a rehabilitation equipment business. In September 1984, HRC opened its first outpatient rehabilitation facility at Little Rock, Arkansas, followed by another one at Birmingham, Alabama, in December 1984. Within five years, HRC was operating 29 outpatient facilities located in 17 states throughout the Southeastern United States. In the first nine months of 1990, it opened eight more outpatient facilities and its business was booming as illustrated in Exhibit 2.

In June 1985, HRC started providing inpatient rehabilitation services with the acquisition of an 88-bed facility in Florence, South Carolina. During the next five years, the company established 11 more inpatient facilities in 9 states, with a twelfth under development. While the rehabilitation equipment business portion of the corporation had grown rapidly, in August 1989 most of it was sold to National Orthopedic and Rehabilitation Services, Inc., in order to concentrate resources on HRC's core business. As of April 1991, HRC was a publicly traded for-profit health care services company that operated 43 outpatient and 11 inpatient facilities in 24 states. Its stock was listed on the New York Stock Exchange.

Exhibit 2

Healthsouth Rehabilitation Corporation: Quarterly Number of Outpatient Visits and Inpatient Days

		Outpatient		
		Facilities	*Visits (000s)*	*Visits/ Facility*
1986	Q1	7	17.5	2,500
	Q2	8	27.5	3,438
	Q3	8	32.8	4,100
	Q4	9	35.0	3,889
	Total	8	112.8	13,927
1987	Q1	11	38.0	3,455
	Q2	12	48.0	4,000
	Q3	12	53.6	4,467
	Q4	13	60.0	4,615
	Total	12	199.6	16,537
1988	Q1	16	69.0	4,313
	Q2	17	78.0	4,588
	Q3	20	85.5	4,275
	Q4	21	86.7	4,129
	Total	19	319.2	17,305
1989	Q1	22	92.2	4,191
	Q2	23	104.2	4,530
	Q3	28	111.7	3,989
	Q4	30	123.0	4,100
	Total	26	431.1	16,810
1990	Q1	31	124.5	4,017
	Q2	33	140.7	4,265
	Q3	35	150.9	4,310
	Q4	37	168.1	4,490
	Total	34	584.2	17,082
1991	Total	45	800.0	17,778

Source: Company information and Alex. Brown & Sons estimates.

[a]Does not include HEALTHSOUTH Medical Center.

[b]Calculated as average daily census divided by available beds. Available beds at some facilities differs from licensed beds.

■ South Highlands Hospital

A key development in HRC's growth strategy was the acquisition in December 1989 of the 219-bed South Highlands Hospital in Birmingham, Alabama. Now renamed HEALTHSOUTH Medical Center (HMC), this hospital is being developed into a flagship facility.

South Highlands was a marginally profitable facility, but due to an inability to obtain financing, it was unable to meet the needs of its physicians, particu-

Inpatient[a]				
Licensed Beds	Available Beds	Inpatient Days	Avg. Daily Census	Occupancy[b]
88	83	2,747	30	36.4%
88	83	3,164	35	41.9%
268	261	7,525	83	31.7%
358	351	17,129	188	53.6%
201	195	30,565	84	43.1%
358	351	20,543	226	64.3%
358	351	19,334	212	60.5%
618	457	20,722	228	49.8%
618	457	23,201	255	55.8%
488	404	83,800	230	57.0%
678	497	26,100	287	57.7%
830	597	28,578	314	52.6%
856	623	28,720	316	50.7%
856	623	30,511	335	53.8%
805	585	113,909	313	53.5%
960	707	35,617	391	55.4%
960	707	38,533	423	59.9%
960	707	39,214	431	61.0%
960	727	42,928	472	64.9%
960	712	156,292	429	60.3%
960	727	44,135	485	66.7%
1,020	787	45,500	500	63.5%
1,020	787	46,865	515	65.4%
1,020	787	48,230	530	67.3%
1,005	772	184,730	508	65.8%
1,140	907	219,000	600	66.2%

larly Drs. James Andrews and William Clancy, both world-renowned orthopedic surgeons. As Mr. Scrushy noted:

> My immediate concern was to maintain the referral base that Drs. Andrews and Clancy provided. HRC had benefitted from the rehabilitation referrals stemming from the extensive orthopedic surgery performed at South Highlands. The surgeons needed a major expansion at South Highlands to practice at maximum effectiveness and Drs. Andrews and Clancy would seek the facilities they needed elsewhere if something wasn't done. On the surface our acquisition of South Highlands was defensive.

The purchase of South Highlands Hospital for approximately $27 million was far from a defensive move. HRC immediately began construction of a new $30 million addition to the hospital. Even during construction, referrals continued to flow from HMC to other HRC facilities. The construction created interest in the medical community, which in turn, created business. The emergency facility at HMC eliminated the necessity of delaying evaluation and treatment of athletic injuries that could be quickly transferred to the facility through HRC's extensive linkages with 396 high school and college athletic programs. A brief overview of selected events in HRC's history is shown in Exhibit 3.

INDUSTRY OVERVIEW

Medical rehabilitation involves the treatment of physical limitations through which therapists seek to improve their patients' functional independence,

Exhibit 3 **Key Events in HEALTHSOUTH's History**

1984	Company started by Richard Scrushy and others Raised $1 million in venture CitiBank Venture Capital Opened two outpatient centers
1985	Acquired first inpatient facility Opened four new outpatient facilities
1986	Initial public offering raised $15 million Acquired two inpatient facilities Opened three outpatient centers
1987	Secondary stock offering raised $24 million Acquired two inpatient centers Opened four outpatient centers
1988	Developed and acquired three inpatient facilities Opened eight outpatient centers
1989	Issued $52 million of subordinated convertible debentures Listed stock on New York Stock Exchange Developed two inpatient facilities Acquired South Highland Hospital (HEALTHSOUTH Medical Center) Opened eight outpatient facilities Listed as the 11th fastest growing company by *Inc. Magazine* Listed as the 41st largest percentage gainer on the New York Stock Exchange by *Fortune Magazine* Divested equipment businesses
1990	Developed one inpatient facility Opened ten outpatient facilities Listed as the 35th largest percentage gainer on the New York Stock Exchange by *Fortune* Secondary stock offering raised $49 million

relieve pain, and ameliorate any permanent disabilities. Patients using medical rehabilitation services include the handicapped and those recovering from automobile, sports, and other accidents, strokes, neurological injuries, surgery, fractures, and/or disabilities associated with diseases, and conditions such as multiple sclerosis, cerebral palsy, arthritis, and heart disease.

■ Rehabilitation Services

Medical rehabilitation provider services include inpatient rehabilitation in dedicated freestanding hospitals and in distinct units of acute care hospitals, comprehensive outpatient rehabilitation facilities (CORF), specialty rehabilitation programs, such as traumatic brain injury and spinal cord injury, pediatric and occupational and industrial rehabilitation, and rehabilitation agencies. For a summary of types of providers, see Exhibit 4.

The availability of comprehensive rehabilitation services is limited in the United States. Provision of rehabilitation services by outpatient departments of acute-care hospitals is fragmented because services are provided through

Rehabilitation Industry Segments, 1989 (estimated) **Exhibit 4**

	Capacity		*Revenues*		*Pay or Mix*		
Industry Segment	*Facilities*	*Beds*	*$ Billions*	*Per Day or Visit*	*Private*[1]	*Medicare*	*Medicaid & Other Govt.*
Acute-care hospitals							
Inpatient units	625	15,000	$2.4	$700–900	30%	55%	15%
Outpatient departments	2,270	NA	$1.1	$85–110	60%	25%	15%
Freestanding rehabilitation hospitals	120	13,200	$2.3	$550–750	40%	45%	10%
Traumatic brain injury programs[2]	450	12,000	$3.0	$115–1,300	40%	NM	60%[3]
Outpatient rehabilitation							
CORFs[4]	170	NA	$0.2	$85–110	40%	40%	20%
Other facility-based	100	NA	$0.1	$85–110	40%	40%	20%
Other[5]	1,000++	NA	$0.5	$75–100	25%	60%	15%
			$9.6				

Sources: American Hospital Association of Rehabilitation Facilities; National Head Injury Foundation.

[1]Includes workers' compensation, self-pay, Blue Cross/Blue Shield, commercial insurers, managed care.
[2]Includes acute and extended rehabilitation as well as transitional living programs.
[3]Contracted rates between provider and government programs, typically 10–15% discount from charges.
[4]Medicare-certified Comprehensive Outpatient Rehabilitation Facilties.
[5]Highly fragmented market including 1,000 Medicare certified agencies and private practitioners.

several departments, and private practice therapists rarely provide a full range of comprehensive rehabilitation services. Often, patients requiring multidisciplinary services will be treated by different therapists in different locations, which can result in uncoordinated care.

Comprehensive inpatient rehabilitation services are provided by free-standing rehabilitation hospitals, distinct units in acute-care hospitals, and skilled nursing facilities. As of September 1990, there were 136 dedicated rehabilitation hospitals and 625 distinct inpatient rehabilitation units in acute-care hospitals as shown in Exhibit 4.

According to analysts with Goldman Sachs, the rehabilitation services segment of the health care industry in the United States will grow at a rate of 15–20 percent through 1993. Major factors influencing this growth include:

- *Increasing need for services.* The incidence of major disability increases with age. Improvements in medical care have enabled more people with severe disabilities to live longer. Data compiled by the National Center for Health Statistics show that in 1989, there were 35 million people in the United States (one out of every seven people) with some form of disability. The National Association of Insurance Commissioners points out that seven out of ten workers will suffer a long-term disability between the ages of 35 and 65.

- *Economic benefits of services.* Purchasers and providers of health care services, such as insurance companies, health maintenance organizations, businesses, and industry are seeking economical, high quality alternatives to traditional health care services. Rehabilitation services, whether outpatient or inpatient, represent such an alternative. Often, early participation in a disabled person's rehabilitation may prevent a short-term problem from becoming a long-term disability. Moreover, by returning the individual to the work force, the number of disability benefit payments is reduced, thus decreasing long-term disability costs. Independent studies by companies such as Northwestern Life have shown that of every dollar spent on rehabilitation, a savings of $30 occurs in disability payments. Also, early rehabilitation may prevent a short-term disability from becoming long-term.

- *Favorable payment policies for services.* Inpatient rehabilitation services are organized as either dedicated rehabilitation hospitals or distinct units and, as noted previously, are currently eligible for exemptions from Medicare's prospective payment system. Outpatient rehabilitation services that are organized as comprehensive outpatient rehabilitation facilities (CORF) or rehabilitation agencies are eligible to participate in the Medicare program under cost-based reimbursement programs. Inpatient and outpatient rehabilitation services are typically covered for payment by the major medical portion of commercial health insurance policies.

■ Competition

HRC's operating units are located in 36 primary markets in 24 states (see Exhibit 5). The competition faced in each of these markets is similar, with uniqueness arising from the number of health care providers in specific metropolitan areas. The primary competitive factors in the rehabilitation services

HEALTHSOUTH's National Network **Exhibit 5**

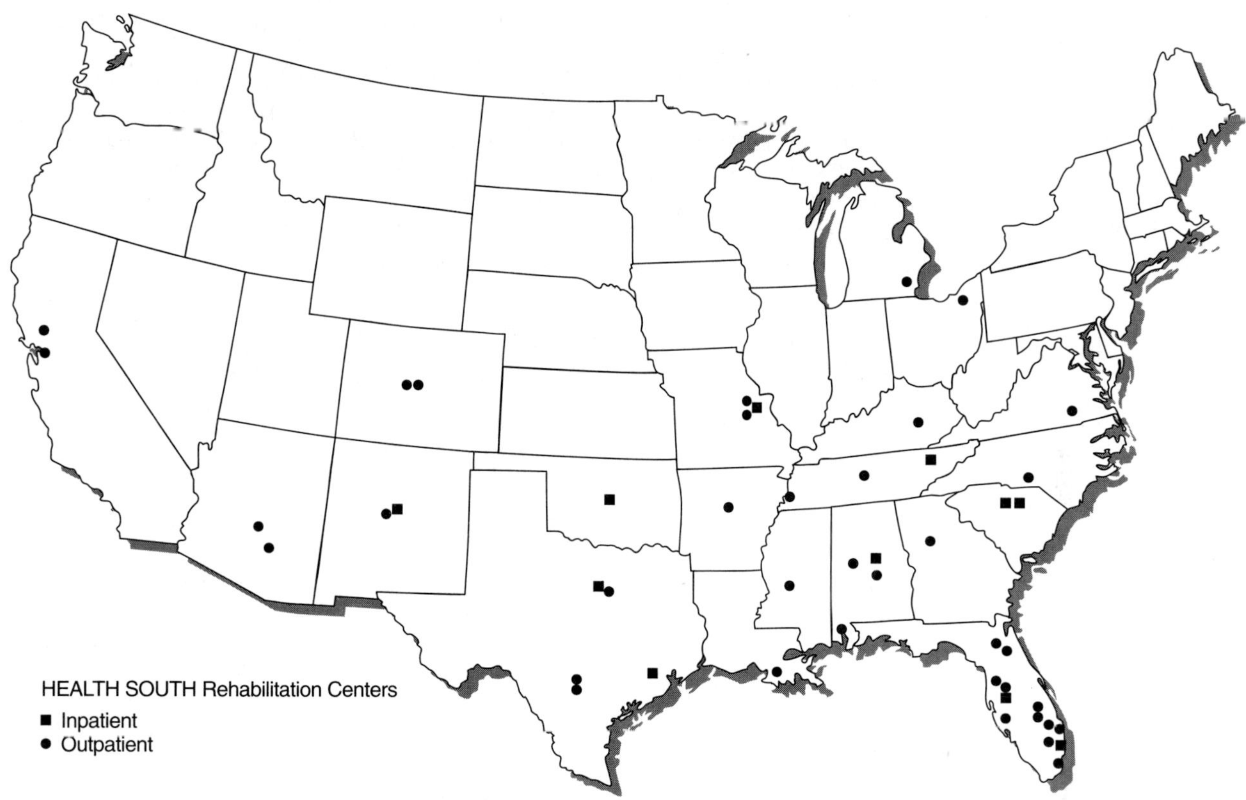

Source: Annual Report.

business are quality of services, projected patient outcomes, responsiveness to the needs of the patients, community and physicians, ability to tailor programs and services to meet specific needs, and the charges for services.

HEALTHSOUTH faces competition every time it initiates a Certificate of Need (CON) project or seeks to acquire an existing facility or CON. This competition may arise from competing companies (national or regional) or from local hospitals filing competing applications that oppose the proposed CON project. Although the number of states requiring CON or similar approval is decreasing, HRC continues to face this requirement in several states. The necessity for these approvals, which is somewhat unique to the health care industry in that states having CON requirements demand that organizations wanting to open new facilities or purchase expensive and specialized equipment convince a regulatory or planning agency that such facilities or equipment are really needed and will not merely move patients from one provider to another, serves as an important barrier to entry and has the potential to limit competition by creating a franchise to provide services to a given area.

According to industry analysts with Donaldson, Lufin, and Jenrett:

Medical rehabilitation represents less than 2 percent of the health care industry. Relatively few providers of significant size exist. Therefore, competition is fragmented. Major rehabilitation providers include four public companies (Continental Medical Systems, Greenery Rehabilitation Group, HEALTHSOUTH Rehabilitation Corp., and Nova Care, Inc.), National Medical Enterprises' Rehab Hospital Services Corp. (a subsidiary of NME), and New MediCo (a privately held trauma rehabilitation provider). Of a total of $8.2 billion in estimated 1988 revenues, these six largest providers represented less than 20 percent of total rehabilitation provider revenues. Consolidation is likely to occur around the stronger entities because of their access to capital, strong clinical programs, and sophisticated management systems. However, presently major companies in this industry tend not to compete directly with each other because they generally target different market niches and/or different geographic markets.

■ Reimbursement

Reimbursement for services provided by HRC can be divided into two distinct categories: private pay and Medicare. The percentage of each varies with business segment and facility. Private pay represents 90 percent of all outpatient business and 50 percent of all inpatient business, or 62 percent of total revenues.

Private Pay

Approximately 80 percent of the population under age 65 has medical insurance coverage. The extent of the coverage varies by location. Generally, charges for inpatient rehabilitation are reimbursed 100 percent under general hospitalization benefits, and outpatient rehabilitation is reimbursed 100 percent like all other outpatient services. Insurers prefer established programs that can demonstrate functional outcomes. The private-pay segment includes general medical insurance, workers' compensation, health maintenance organizations, preferred provider organizations, and other managed care plans.

Medicare

Industry sources estimate that Medicare spent approximately $1.9 billion on inpatient medical rehabilitation during 1988. These sources also estimate that Medicare represents 45 percent of freestanding general rehabilitation inpatient stays and revenues, 55 percent of acute care hospital rehabilitation unit stays and revenues, and 40 percent of CORF revenues.

Since 1983, the federal government has employed a prospective payment system (PPS) as a means of controlling general acute-care hospital costs for the Medicare program. In the past, the Medicare program provided reimbursement for the reasonable direct and indirect costs of the services furnished by hospitals to beneficiaries, plus an allowed return on equity for proprietary hospitals. As a result of the Social Security Act Amendments of 1983, Congress adopted a prospective payment system to cover the routine and ancillary operating costs of most Medicare inpatient hospital services.

Under PPS, the Secretary of Health and Human Services established fixed payment amounts per discharge based on diagnosis-related groups (DRGs).

With limited exceptions, a hospital's payment for Medicare inpatients is limited to the DRG rate, regardless of the number of services provided to the patients or the length of the patients' hospital stay. Under PPS, a hospital may retain the difference, if any, between its DRG rate and its operating costs incurred in furnishing inpatient services, and it is at risk for any operating costs that exceed its DRG rate. HMC is generally subject to PPS with respect to medicare inpatient services.

At this time, Medicare pays certain distinct units, freestanding rehabilitation facilities, and certified outpatient units on the basis of "reasonable costs" incurred during a base year (the year prior to being excluded from Medicare's prospective payment system—PPS—or the first year of operation) adjusted by a market basket index. However, many rehabilitation providers have faced an increase in rates that is less than that of their actual costs. In addition, many Medicare intermediaries have an incomplete understanding of rehabilitation services and therefore may deny claims inappropriately; further education is necessary.

■ Regulation

The health care industry is subject to regulation by federal, state, and local governments. The various levels of regulatory activity affect business activities by controlling its growth, requiring licensure or certification of its facilities, regulating the use of its properties, and controlling the reimbursement for services provided. In some states, regulations control the growth of health care facilities.

Capital expenditures for the construction of new facilities, addition of beds, or acquisition of existing facilities may be reviewable by state regulators under a statutory scheme that is sometimes referred to as a CON program. States with CON programs place limits on the construction and acquisition of healthcare facilities and the expansion of existing facilities and services.

Licensure and certification are separate, but related, regulatory activities. The former is usually a state or local requirement and the latter is a federal requirement. In almost all instances, licensure and certification will follow specific standards and requirements set forth in readily available public documents. Compliance with the requirements is monitored by annual on-site inspections by representatives of various government agencies.

In order to receive Medicare reimbursement, each facility must meet the applicable conditions of participation set forth by the U.S. Department of Health and Human Services relating to the type of facility, its equipment, its personnel, and its standards of medical care, as well as compliance with all state and local laws and regulations. In addition, Medicare regulations generally require entry into such facilities through physician referral.

HEALTHSOUTH TODAY

When patients are referred to one of HEALTHSOUTH's rehabilitation facilities, they undergo an initial evaluation and assessment process that results in the development of a rehabilitation care plan designed specifically for that patient. Depending upon the patient's disability, this evaluation process may involve the services of a single discipline, such as physical therapy for a knee injury, or of several disciplines, as in the case of a complicated stroke patient. HRC has developed numerous rehabilitation programs, which include stroke, head injury, spinal cord injury, neuromuscular, sports, and work injury, that combine certain services to address the needs of patients with similar disabilities. When a patient enters one of these programs, the professional staff tailors the program to meet the specified needs of the patient. In this way, all of the facility's patients, regardless of the severity and complexity of their disabilities, can receive the level and intensity of those services necessary for them to be restored to as productive, active, and independent a lifestyle as possible.

The professional staff at each facility consists of licensed or credentialed healthcare practitioners. The staff, together with the patient, the family, and the referring physician, form the "team" that assists the patient in attaining his or her rehabilitation goals. This interdisciplinary team approach permits the delivery of coordinated, integrated patient care services.

■ Outpatient Rehabilitation Services

HEALTHSOUTH operates the largest group of affiliated proprietary CORFs in the United States. Comprehensive outpatient rehabilitation facilities play an important role in the health care industry by offering quality care at a reasonable price. The continuing emphasis on reducing health care costs, as evidenced by PPS, reduces the length of stay for patients in acute-care facilities. Some even suggest patients do not receive the intensity of services that may be necessary for them to achieve a full recovery from their diseases, disorders, or traumatic conditions. CORFs satisfy the increasing needs for outpatient services because of their ability to provide hospital-level services at the intensity and frequency needed.

HEALTHSOUTH has much to offer when compared to most small therapy centers. It possesses state-of-the-art equipment that can cost $100,000 for an individual item. HEALTHSOUTH's experience in operating its many outpatient centers offers:

- an efficient design that aids in the delivery of rehabilitation services in terms of quality and cost;
- efficient management of the business office function—accounting, billing, managing, staffing, etc.;
- the ability to provide a full spectrum of comprehensive rehabilitation services;
- the ability to draw referrals from a large mass of sources due to its lack of affiliation with one specific group.

■ Inpatient Services

HEALTHSOUTH is one of the largest independent providers of inpatient rehabilitation services in the United States. HRC's inpatient rehabilitation facilities provide high quality comprehensive services to patients who require intensive institutional rehabilitation care. These patients are typically experiencing physical disabilities due to various conditions, such as head injury, spinal cord injury, stroke, certain orthopedic problems, and neuromuscular disease. Except for the St. Louis, Missouri, facility, which exclusively provides head injury rehabilitation services, these inpatient facilities provide the same professional healthcare services as the company's outpatient facilities but on a more intensive level. In addition, such facilities provide therapeutic recreation and 24-hour nursing care. An interdisciplinary team approach, similar to that used in the outpatient facilities, is employed with each patient to address individual rehabilitation needs.

■ HEALTHSOUTH Medical Center

HMC is a world class orthopedic surgery and sports medicine complex. It is an acute care hospital and therefore is reimbursed under the prospective payment system. The key to the hospital's success is the affiliation with a group of renowned orthopedic surgeons. These surgeons have treated famous patients such as Bo Jackson, the King and the Prince of Saudi Arabia, golfers Jack Nicklaus and Greg Norman, Charles Barkley of the Philadelphia Seventy-Sixers, and Troy Aikman of the Dallas Cowboys. The prestige and publicity of these patients enhances the demand for local services, HEALTHSOUTH's main business. One patient's father stated, "If HEALTHSOUTH was good enough for Charles Barkley then it's good enough for my son" (a high school football player who suffered a knee injury). The group of surgeons has 8 to 10 fellows or physicians who spend a year studying under the group before returning to their practices. This provides a network for future business and additional outpatient and inpatient development for HEALTHSOUTH. Since acquiring HMC in 1989, the prominence of the affiliation has led to several new acquisitions and many more opportunities.

■ Rehabilitation Management

HEALTHSOUTH Rehabilitation Corporation provides, as an extension of its outpatient and inpatient rehabilitation services, one or more of its clinical services to clients other than its own facilities on a contractual basis. These contract opportunities represent a limited investment and capital risk and are only a small portion of the company's total revenues.

FUNCTIONAL CONSIDERATIONS

HRC's management is comprised of a group of young, energetic professionals. The average age is 38 years. See HRC's organization chart in Exhibit 6.

The corporate climate is characterized by a sense of urgency and is instilled in all of HEALTHSOUTH's employees directed by the chairman, chief executive officer, and president. Scrushy founded HEALTHSOUTH at the age of 32.

Exhibit 6 HEALTHSOUTH's Organization Chart

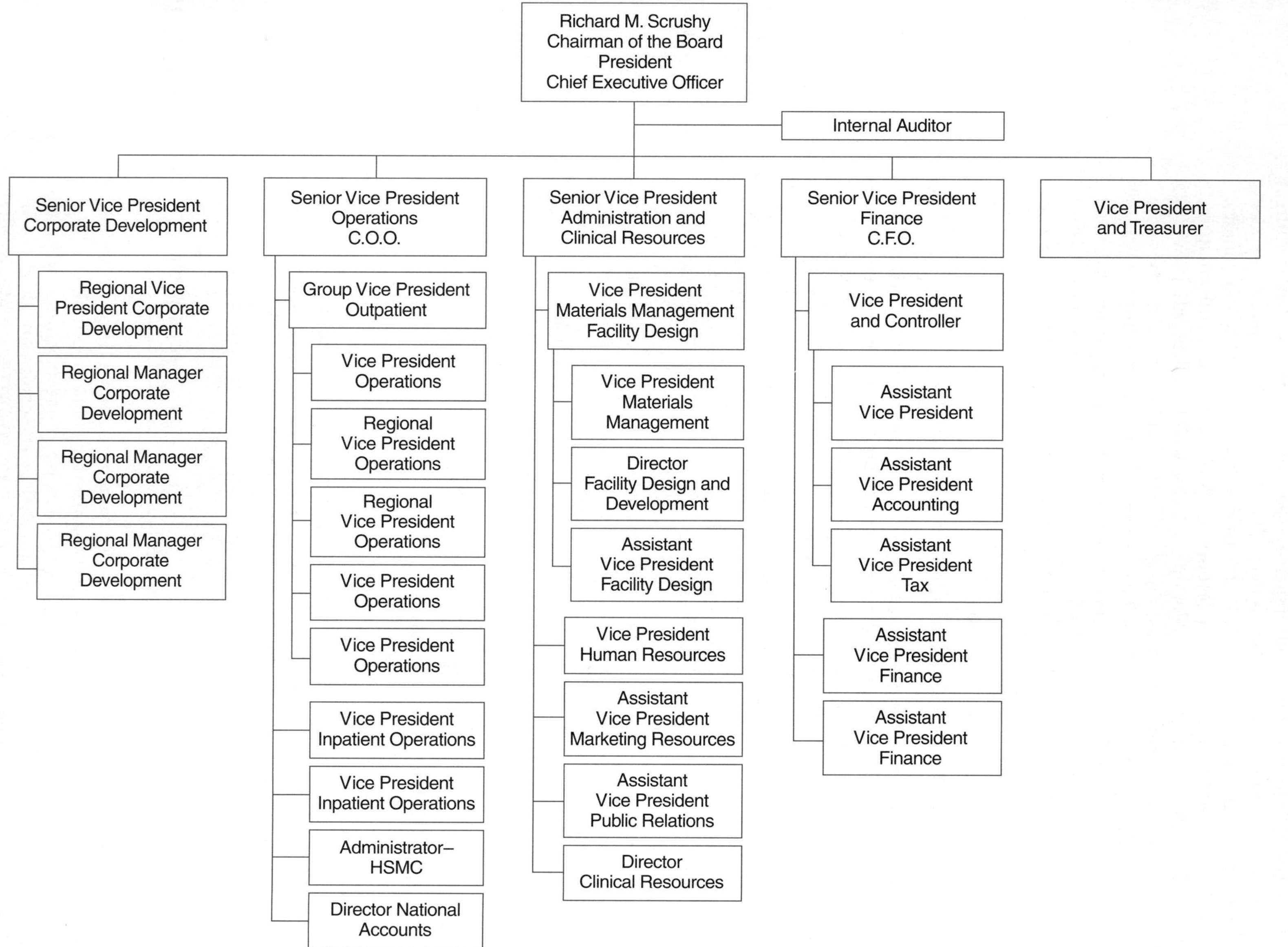

Like many entrepreneurs, he is a visionary but has the ability to make things happen. He worked virtually 365 days a year, 16 to 20 hours a day for the first 5 years, waiting until 1989 before taking his first vacation. His pace remains furious, working over 75 hours a week.

As a result of Scrushy's "hands-on" style, HRC is run; it does not drift. One of the Company's most effective tools is a weekly statistical report that is compiled every Thursday and distributed on Friday. The report includes weekly statistics and trends such as payor mix, census, and revenue. It is reviewed over the weekend, and if there is a negative trend, it is corrected. Thus, any problem is short-lived. In this manner, the management team is focused on real and developing problems.

Another tool is effective communications. Every Monday morning at 7:00 there is a meeting of the company's officers that includes personnel from operations, development, finance, and administration. In this meeting, each employee makes a presentation detailing what he or she accomplished in the previous week and plans to accomplish in the current week. Questions are answered and problems are resolved. One additional benefit is that each employee is held accountable for his or her actions. While this could be perceived to be overkill, it is believed to be necessary and helpful to the participants. At one time, the meetings were stopped for about six weeks. After the company experienced a slight dip in performances and coordination, the meetings were immediately reinstated.

■ Staffing and Compensation

Unlike many other health care companies, HEALTHSOUTH has not experienced staffing shortages. Clinicians are in short supply, but HRC has been able to recruit and maintain excellent personnel. The ability to offer a challenging environment has been a key factor. A HEALTHSOUTH inpatient facility in a metropolitan location typically competes favorably against other hospitals and nursing homes for the skills of new therapists. HEALTHSOUTH's outpatient facilities offer an attractive alternative to the clinician by offering 8-hour workdays with weekends and holidays off.

All of the company's employees are competitively compensated. One compensation tool used is employee incentive stock options offered to key corporate and clinical personnel. The options require a vesting period of four years with 25 percent of the amount being vested annually. Employees who leave for another job loose their options. With the tremendous success of the company, the stock options have created "golden hand cuffs." Many employees have options that can be exercised at prices under $10 a share. In August 1991, the stock was trading for $30 per share. Additionally, during August the company created an employee stock ownership plan whereby eligible employees received HRC stock at a rate of about 100 shares per $20,000 of compensation.

■ Development

A key element of HEALTHSOUTH's growth has been its ability to develop and acquire new facilities. The company has a development team led by three individuals who have been with the HRC since its beginning. Each is responsible for the development of facilities in a particular business segment. Before seeking to develop or acquire an inpatient or outpatient facility, a number of factors must be considered including population, number of orthopedic surgeons and physical therapists, industry concentrations, reimbursement, competition, and availability of staff. HEALTHSOUTH has a stated goal to develop or acquire two new inpatient facilities and eight to ten outpatient centers per year. The acquisition of another acute care hospital specializing in orthopedic surgery, like HEALTHSOUTH Medical Center, is a possibility but is not a part of the stated plan.

Outpatient Development

HEALTHSOUTH's outpatient units are usually acquired. The company buys existing centers that are seeing 50 or more patients per day. New centers are set up as limited partnerships, typically with the former owners (physicians and therapists) maintaining a limited partnership interest and providing an incentive to continue referring patients to the center. The limited partners share in the cash flow of the center. Additionally, HEALTHSOUTH brings in other physicians and groups as partners and may give up 40 percent ownership in the facility. Interestingly, on the average, only 40 percent of the visits come from referrals of partners.

The cost of acquiring and opening a center ranges from $300,000 to $800,000. This includes equipment and buildings of $200,000–$350,000 and acquisition costs of $100,000–$450,000. All centers are leased except one, allowing for lower capital requirements. The company is evaluating all of its leases and could possibly move toward acquiring buildings where existing facilities are proven and meet financial requirements.

Inpatient Development

Inpatient facilities are usually developed. They are customarily located in regulated environments requiring a CON. The Company has targeted a number of markets for rehabilitation hospitals. HEALTHSOUTH's competition is usually seeking the same markets.

HEALTHSOUTH has never lost a CON battle because of two reasons: (1) the quality of care provided by existing HEALTHSOUTH facilities, and (2) the lower cost of the facility, which creates lower healthcare costs.

HEALTHSOUTH's inpatient facilities are typically located on or near the campus of an acute care hospital that serves as a trauma center. This provides a steady stream of patients when trauma victims are discharged from the hospital. Additionally, physical therapy can be conducted by HEALTHSOUTH for the hospital on an inpatient and outpatient basis. Typically, HEALTHSOUTH's inpatient facilities cost from $6 to $10 million compared to its competitors' cost of $10–$12 million.

The development of additional acute care hospitals stressing orthopedics like HMC is a future possibility. A potential acute care hospital acquisition must possess an orthopedic concentration. The cost of an acute care hospital meeting HEALTHSOUTH's criteria ranges from $20 to $50 million depending on its size and types of equipment.

■ Marketing

The company's marketing efforts are similar for each business segment. The demand is controlled by physicians, workers' compensation managers, insurance companies, and other intermediaries. Administrators and clinicians are involved in the marketing effort. The company has hired, with great success, a number of individuals who were formerly case managers with local intermediaries.

HRC recently entered into contracts to be the exclusive provider for rehabilitation services directly to industry. Firms like General Motors are excellent targets since they have many employees in various markets that HEALTHSOUTH serves. In such cases, significant new business can be generated, and in return HEALTHSOUTH could discount its charges.

HEALTHSOUTH has established a national marketing effort with training programs, national account managers, case managers, and a carefully developed plan. The objective is to put into place a consistent sales methodology throughout HEALTHSOUTH and to take advantage of its national system of rehabilitation facilities. This national coverage enables HEALTHSOUTH to provide services for national as well as regional companies.

HEALTHSOUTH's pricing is usually lower than its competition's. The company's daily inpatient charges are sometimes as much as $100–$400 per day less than those of its competition due to its lower cost of capital and business. HEALTHSOUTH *focuses mainly on quality of services and outcomes as the best marketing tool.*

■ Financial Structure

HEALTHSOUTH's growth has been funded through a mix of equity and debt. The company raised $13 million of venture capital before going public in 1986. Because of the company's startup nature in its early years, commercial banks were reluctant to lend significant funds for development. After the company's initial public offering, commercial bankers were more responsive to financing growth plans. HRC continues to use a conservative mix of equity and debt and believes its cost of capital is the lowest in the health care industry. A decision to give up ownership was an easy one. The founders understood that a smaller percentage ownership of a larger company would be worth more and would not carry as much risk.

Earnings growth has been significant with compounded earnings growth of 416 percent from 1986 to 1990. About 75 percent of HRC's revenues are generated primarily through inpatient services. Typically, a mature inpatient facility generates $10–$15 million annually in revenues while an outpatient center generates $2–$3.5 million annually and an acute care facility generates $40–$60 million. The operating margin on inpatient business ranges from 15 to 25 percent while outpatient margins are 20–30 percent. The return on assets of a given facility ranges from 10 to 30 percent with an average of 17 percent for all

Exhibit 7

HEALTHSOUTH Rehabilitation Corporation and Subsidiaries: Consolidated Balance Sheets, December 31, 1989, and 1990 (in thousands)

	1989	*1990*
Assets		
Current assets		
Cash and marketable securities	$ 31,830	$ 71,201
Accounts receivable, net of allowance for doubtful accounts and contractual adjustments of $13,020,000 in 1989 and $20,093,000 in 1990	47,771	48,988
Inventories, prepaid expenses and other current assets	7,213	7,626
Total current assets	86,814	127,815
Other assets	8,613	9,848
Property, plant and equipment—net	94,081	126,732
Intangible assets—net	29,622	36,785
Total assets	$219,130	$301,180
Liabilities and Stockholders' Equity		
Current liabilities		
Accounts payable	$ 5,866	$ 7,342
Salaries and wages payable	3,414	3,972
Accrued interest payable and other liabilities	3,978	4,522
Current portion of long-term debt and leases	1,637	1,394
Total current liabilities	14,895	17,230
Long-term debt and leases	132,748	149,801
Other long-term liabilities	3,870	5,172
Minority interests—limited partnerships	1,742	1,076
Stockholders' equity		
Preferred stock, $.10 par value—1,500,000 shares authorized; issued and outstanding—none	—	—
Common stock, $.01 par value—25,000,000 shares authorized; 10,290,000 and 12,713,000 shares issued at December 31, 1989 and 1990, respectively	103	127
Additional paid-in capital	49,777	100,443
Retained earnings	15,995	27,331
Total stockholders' equity	65,875	127,901
Total liabilities and stockholders' equity	$219,130	$301,180

HEALTHSOUTH Rehabilitation Corporation and Subsidiaries: Consolidated Statements of Income, Years Ended December 31, 1988, 1989, and 1990 (in thousands, except per share amount)

Exhibit 8

	1988	*1989*	*1990*
Net revenues	$77,493	$118,862	$180,482
Operating expenses	59,312	90,068	135,822
Provision for doubtful accounts	1,415	2,512	5,120
Depreciation and amortization	4,088	7,110	11,056
Interest expense	3,822	8,121	11,547
Interest income	(942)	(1,954)	(4,136)
	67,695	105,857	159,409
Income before minority interests and income taxes	9,798	13,005	21,073
Minority interests	857	495	924
	8,941	12,510	20,149
Provision for income taxes	3,208	4,363	7,226
Net income	$ 5,733	$ 8,147	$ 12,923
Weighted average common and common equivalent shares outstanding	10,392	10,707	12,139
Net income per common and common equivalent share	$ .55	$ .76	$ 1.06
Net income per common share— assuming full dilution	$ .55	$ .73	$ .96

facilities. HRC financial statements are provided in Exhibits 7–10. Revenue summaries are shown in Exhibits 11 and 12.

WHERE DOES HEALTHSOUTH GO FROM HERE?

Richard Scrushy was reviewing company projections for continued success of HEALTHSOUTH Rehabilitation Corporation. Money managers continued to reward the company for its historical and expected performance with the stock trading at a price earnings ratio of 30:1.

Craig Dickson, an analyst with Rauscher, Pierce, Refsnes, asked Scrushy if HEALTHSOUTH can continue the trend; Scrushy paused, reflected on all the questions he asked himself earlier, and wondered to himself if the trend would continue. What will I need to do to make it happen? Are there things we should be doing differently? How can I ensure that HEALTHSOUTH does not out-

Exhibit 9 **HEALTHSOUTH Rehabilitation Corporation and Subsidiaries: Consolidated Statements of Stockholders' Equity, Years Ended December 31, 1988, 1989, and 1990 (in thousands)**

	Common Stock	*Additional Paid-In Capital*	*Retained Earnings*	*Treasury Stock*	*Total Stockholders' Equity*
Balance at January 1, 1988	$100.2	$ 48,400.0	$ 2,783.8	$ (.3)	$ 51,283.7
Proceeds from issuance of 16,969 common shares	.2	279.8	—	—	280.0
Proceeds from exercise of options	.6	176.2	—	—	176.8
Purchase of limited partnership units	—	—	(191.4)	—	(191.4)
Purchase of treasury stock (1,550 shares)	—	—	—	(.1)	(.1)
Net income	—	—	5,733.4	—	5,733.4
Balance at December 31, 1988	101.0	48,856.0	8,325.8	(.4)	57,282.4
Proceeds from exercise of options	2.0	953.1	—	—	955.1
Purchase of treasury stock (1,250 shares)	—	—	—	(15.3)	(15.3)
Treasury stock used in the exercise of options	(.1)	(9.5)	—	9.6	—
Common stock exchanged in the exercise of options	—	(22.7)	—	—	(22.7)
Sale of treasury stock	—	—	—	6.1	6.1
Purchase of limited partnership units	—	—	(477.8)	—	(477.8)
Net income	—	—	8,147.3	—	8,147.3
Balance at December 31, 1989	102.9	49,776.9	15,995.3	—	65,875.1
Proceeds from issuance of 48,196 common shares	.5	1,096.0	—	—	1,096.5
Proceeds from issuance of 2,221,182 common shares	22.2	48,476.6	—	—	48,498.8
Proceeds from exercise of options	1.5	1,115.8	—	—	1,117.3
Common stock exchanged in the exercise of options	—	(22.6)	—	—	(22.6)
Purchase of limited partnership units	—	—	(1,587.3)	—	(1,587.3)
Net income	—	—	12,923.2	—	12,923.2
Balance at December 31, 1990	$127.1	$100,442.7	$27,331.2	$ —	$127,901.0

grow its resources (capital and management)? Does the market provide ample opportunity to grow at 20–30 percent per year? What external factors do we face? What should we do to ensure that medical rehabilitation continues to be favorably reimbursed? What is the real number of facilities needed and how many acquisition targets are there?

Specifically, there are a number of strategic options facing HEALTHSOUTH that demand consideration. A few of the most obvious are:

1. Further related diversification into areas like acute care hospitals. If this is considered a viable option, what geographical areas are the best alternative for this type of expansion?

HEALTHSOUTH Rehabilitation Corporation and Subsidiaries: Consolidated Statements of Cash Flows, Years Ended December 31, 1988, 1989, and 1990 (in thousands)

Exhibit 10

	1988	*1989*	*1990*
Operating Activities			
Net income	$ 5,733	$ 8,147	$12,923
Adjustments to reconcile net income to net cash (used) provided by operating activities			
Depreciation and amortization	4,088	7,110	11,056
Income applicable to minority interests of limited partnerships	857	495	924
Provision for deferred income taxes	1,410	606	1,788
Provision for deferred revenue from contractual agencies	597	(101)	(230)
Changes in operating assets and liabilities, net of effects of acquisitions			
Increase in accounts receivable	(11,906)	(15,806)	(183)
Increase in inventories, prepaid expenses and other current assets	(2,295)	(738)	(390)
Increase in accounts payable and accrued expenses	198	3,854	2,255
Net cash (used) provided by operating activities	(1,318)	3,567	28,143
Investing Activities			
Purchase of property, plant and equipment	(16,934)	(19,992)	(37,548)
Additions to intangible assets, net of effects of acquisitions	(7,323)	(8,908)	(9,051)
Assets obtained through acquisition, net of liabilities assumed	(5,592)	(30,110)	(5,239)
Additions to notes receivable	(116)	(586)	(1,553)
Reduction in notes receivable	—	144	394
Proceeds received on maturity of long-term marketable securities	2,124	1,849	1,659
Investment in long-term marketable securities	(1,864)	(3,239)	(7,522)
Deposits placed in escrow related to acquisitions	(288)	288	—
Net cash used by investing activities	(29,993)	(60,554)	(58,860)
Financing Activities			
Proceeds from borrowings	$41,460	$104,246	$57,243
Principal payments on debt and leases	(15,129)	(34,169)	(40,531)
Proceeds from exercise of options	177	923	1,095
Common stock issued on acquisition	—	—	1,096
Proceeds from issuance of common stock	—	—	48,499
Purchase of Treasury stock	—	(15)	—
Sale or transfer of Treasury stock	—	16	—
Proceeds from investment by minority interests	423	998	247
Purchase of limited partnership interests	(365)	(733)	(1,460)
Payment of cash distributions to limited partners	(1,370)	(1,547)	(1,964)
Net cash provided by financing activities	25,196	69,719	64,225
(Decrease) Increase in cash and cash equivalents	(6,115)	12,732	33,508
Cash and cash equivalents at beginning of year	21,959	15,844	28,576
Cash and cash equivalents at end of year	$15,844	$28,576	$62,084
Supplemental Disclosures of Cash Flow Information			
Cash paid during the year for			
Interest	$ 4,589	$ 7,657	$13,062
Income taxes	2,375	3,617	5,008

Noncash investing and financing activities

Common stock was issued in 1988 for satisfaction of $280,000 due on a purchase agreement.

Assets related to three of the company's rehabilitation equipment businesses, having a net book value of $5,783,000, were sold during 1989. The consideration for the assets consisted of a note receivable, an interest in the purchaser's company and the assumption of certain liabilities.

Exhibit 11 **HEALTHSOUTH Rehabilitation Corporation: Quarterly Revenues (in millions)**

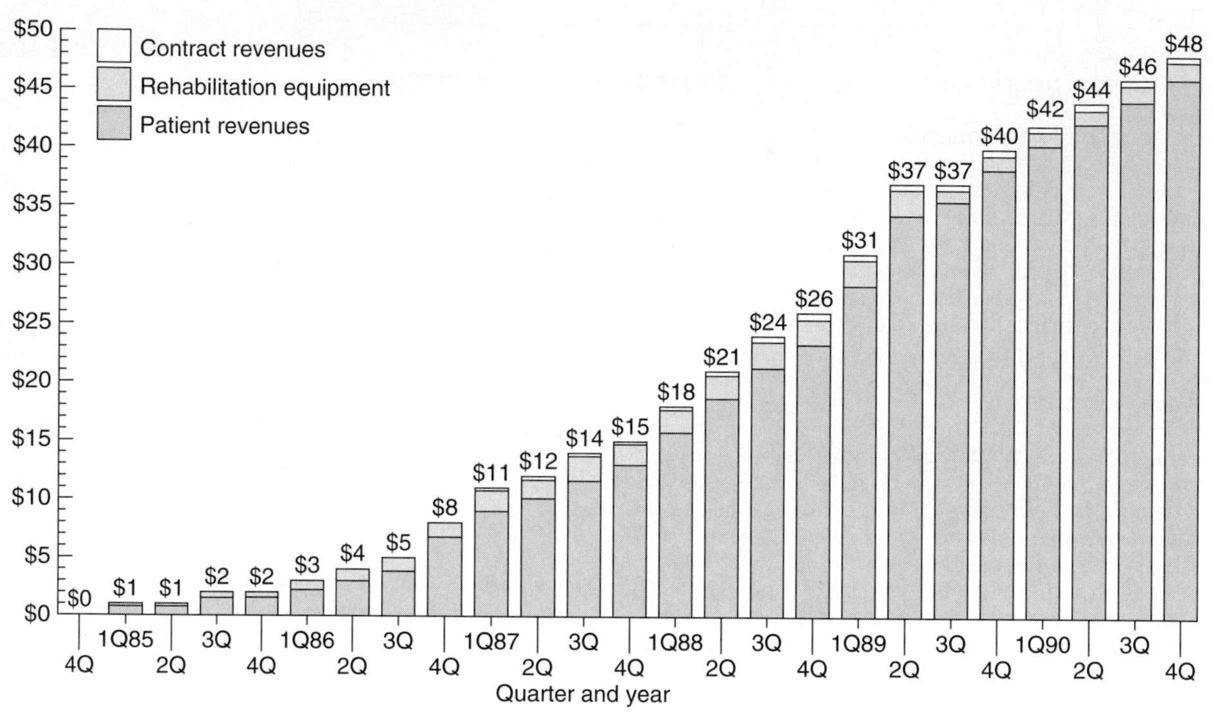

2. Should HEALTHSOUTH revisit the issue of vertical integration as it once did with the rehabilitation equipment business? Perhaps other forms of vertical integration should be examined like nursing homes and hospices.
3. Is unrelated diversification into areas like parking decks and hotels a promising option?
4. Is additional market share building an advisable strategy? If so, in what areas is HEALTHSOUTH likely to experience its best likelihood of success?
5. With the rising cost of health care, the serious problems with worker injuries and workers' compensation costs, long-term disabilities, and an aging work force, rehabilitation as an industry will grow tremendously and be the most attractive choice of treatment for patients with short-term and long-term disabilities. Should HEALTHSOUTH simply concentrate on this type of business that it knows so well? If so, how should such concentration be accomplished?

Scrushy focused on answering the questions. He knew that he could formulate a plan to ensure HEALTHSOUTH's success. In fact, in a probing interview in *Rehabilitation Today* (May 1991), Mr. Scrushy was careful to state that he would consider any acquisition where he believed "value could be added" and dismissed the possibility that the company's "regional name" implied that his aspirations were regional. Clearly, he was willing to go anywhere, anytime he believed there were opportunities to be exploited.

HEALTHSOUTH Rehabilitation Corporation: Quarterly Gross Patient Revenues (in millions) **Exhibit 12**

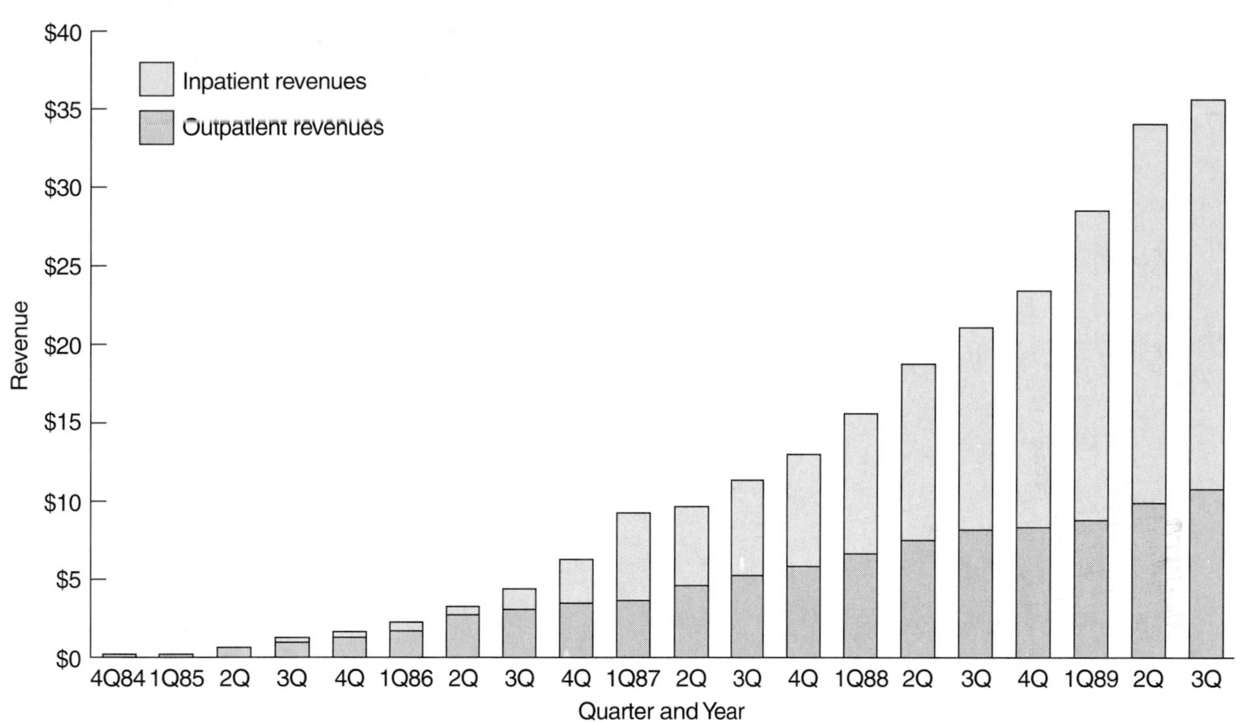

Source: HEALTHSOUTH Rehabilitation Corporation.

SOURCES

Brown, Alex & Sons, Inc. *Research Report*. Health Care Group. October 23, 1991. Baltimore, MD.

Smith, Barney. *Research Report*. September 20, 1991.

Wilder, Marvin. "The Powerhouse behind HEALTHSOUTH," *Rehabilitation Today*, May 1991, 22–31.

CASE 19

Wisconsin Central Ltd.

Paul R. Reed, Sam Houston State University; Otto P. Dobnick, Southeastern Wisconsin Regional Planning Commission

INDUSTRIAL BACKGROUND

In the 125-year history of railroading in the United States, the industry has traveled through some its most profound changes during the most recent two decades. The combination of deregulation in the transportation arena, basic changes in the nature and output of American heavy industry, the loss of local business, and the dramatic increase in long-distance coal movement for power generation have caused the railroads of today to be far different from the traditional railroads of yesterday. Railroads were once responsible for hauling almost everything and everybody into and out of every city and village and accounted for 75% of all United States intercity freight ton-miles in 1929.[1] The volume of freight handled by today's railroads is more than double that of 1929, although the railroad industry's share of freight has been eaten away by trucks, river carriers, and pipelines. In 1990, railroads handled 37% of all freight ton-miles.[2] Thus, railroads have evolved from general freight carriers to specialized freight carriers primarily handling large-volume bulk commodities, oversized or bulky loads, and general products and merchandise when combined into container or truck trailer–sized lots.

The Interstate Commerce Commission (ICC) classifies all of the common carrier railroads operating within the United States into one of three categories based primarily on annual operating revenue. The major rail freight carriers are defined as Class I railroads and must meet an adjustable revenue threshold for a period of three continuous years. In 1989, this threshold was $93.5 million. Regional railroads are those carriers that operate at least 350 miles of track

This case is intended for classroom discussion only, not to depict effective or ineffective handling of administrative situations. All rights reserved to the authors and the North American Case Research Association.

and/or earn revenue between $40 million and the Class I threshold. The Wisconsin Central Ltd. (WCL) was classified as a regional railroad, the largest of 31 such mid-sized carriers in the the United States. Local railroads are all those that fall below the regional railroad criteria and include switching and terminal railroads. A comparison of these three types of railroads is shown in Exhibit 1.

■ Antecedents of the the Wisconsin Central Ltd.

The Soo Line was one of the mid-level players of the seven railroads that competed for the Chicago–Minneapolis–St. Paul corridor traffic. It was considered a conservative, well-managed firm that returned a tidy profit to its principal owner, the Canadian Pacific Railroad. The route system was directed north and northwest from Chicago, and its many rail lines served Wisconsin, the Upper Peninsula of Michigan, Minnesota, the Dakotas, and Montana. It had a fairly strong on-line traffic base, plus a healthy interchange with parent Canadian Pacific, of goods moving to and from Chicago and other midwestern destinations.

The mid-1970s saw many rail lines, including several of Soo Lines competitors, suffering heavy losses and either in or facing bankruptcy. This general malaise, coupled with new legislation and more flexible regulatory agencies, contributed to a massive industry restructuring. Many lines merged, severely downsized, or disappeared with bits and pieces purchased by former competitors or entrepreneurs. The Soo Line saw three of its Chicago–Twin Cities competitors disappear. During the same period, it and the other remaining three competitors were busily getting their houses in order.

The Soo Line recognized that a portion of its traffic base had been lost to trucks and the decline in midwestern heavy industry. To ensure its future, it would have to expand its traffic mix and look for new gateways.[3] The Milwaukee Road was chosen as the likely candidate to satisfy both of these requirements. Although it competed with the Soo Line for Chicago–Twin City traffic, its route was much shorter and enjoyed flatter grades. In addition, it added new routes from both the Twin Cities and Chicago to Kansas City.

The Soo Line successfully bid against two competitors and acquired the Milwaukee in February 1985. The Soo Line did not obtain enough additional

Exhibit 1

Types of Railroads in the United States: 1989

Type of Railroad	*Number*	*Miles Operated*	*Employees*	*Annual Revenue*
Class I	13	137,504	221,704	$27,059
Regional	31	18,554	12,361	1,290
Local	464	21,216	14,402	1,237
Totals	508	177,274	248,467	$29,586

Source: Association of American Railroads, *Railroad Facts: 1990,* p. 3.

Note: Annual revenue shown in millions of dollars.

traffic from this purchase to justify full operation of the two roughly parallel main lines from Chicago to the Twin Cities. As a result, most of the through traffic was consolidated on the more direct main of the former Milwaukee Road. Soon, Soo Line's former main became a lightly trafficked branch line, and it, along with other important Soo Line trackage, became secondary feeders on the "new" enlarged Soo.

By 1986, the Soo Line began to face serious financial difficulties. The heavy debt burden connected with the Milwaukee Road purchase, plus large expenditures associated with needed track maintenance, that had been too long deferred by its former owners, was beginning to prove too much. After casting about for possible solutions, the Soo Line finally decided that its fiscal viability would be best assured by selling off its former Chicago–Twin Cities Main plus its connecting secondary and branch line network.

▪ Wisconsin Central Transportation Corporation (WCTC)

Several parties showed keen interest in Soo Line's early January 1987 sale offering. The ultimate winners were a five-man entrepreneurial team headed by Ed Burkhardt and Tom Power, both seasoned railroad executives. The sale price of $122 million, largely debt financed, purchased 2,134 miles of track or trackage rights plus associated buildings and adjoining property. Notably absent were locomotives and freight cars, some of which, however, were purchased from the Soo Line in a separate transaction.[4]

The principals organized their operations as a holding company, Wisconsin Central Transportation Corporation (WCTC), doing business through three wholly owned and consolidated subsidiaries: Wisconsin Central Ltd. (WCL), WCL Railcars, Inc. (Railcars), and Sault Saint Marie Bridge Company (Bridges). WCL was to be the railroad portion of the operations that leased a majority of its locomotives and freight cars from Railcars and utilized Bridges' series of bridges and trestles across the St. Mary's River separating Sault Ste. Marie, Michigan, from its Canadian counterpart. The holding company's revenues would be derived solely from WCL's operations.[5]

▪ Wisconsin Central Ltd.—The Beginnings

Although both parties reached agreement by early April 1987, it would be over six months before the actual transfer took place. The Soo Line had to phase down operations and move large amounts of materials, supplies, and equipment that were not included in the sale. WCL's tasks were much more complex. First, financing had to be obtained. The five founders, together with Berkshire Partners, an organization that arranges leveraged buyouts for companies, provided $15 million in equity. A syndicate of seven banks furnished $100 million in long-term loans and another $10 million line of revolving credit. In addition, $20 million in subordinate debt was purchased by New York Life. The $145 million was used to pay Soo Line ($122 million), provide working capital ($13 million), and cover start-up and future expenses ($10 million).[6]

With financing in hand, the acquisition of needed locomotives, freight cars, and maintenance equipment began. WCL stayed away from new equipment purchases because of high costs, particularly for locomotives, and focused instead on the large available supply of used freight cars and maintenance equipment. The supply of used locomotives had tightened somewhat due to an economic upturn in 1987. Nevertheless, WCL managed to purchase or lease sufficient numbers of locomotives and cars to begin operations.

Recruiting a trained work force was a major item on the agenda. WCL was not bound by Soo Line's union labor agreements and was therefore not required to have a union work force. Beginning salaries were pegged anywhere between 28% and 33% below comparable jobs on unionized railroads, but were well above the average Wisconsin wage earner's income. Work rules were designed to permit far more flexibility than was the case on the Soo Line.[7]

WCL's hiring announcements were met by a deluge of responses. Applicants outnumbered job openings by almost three to one. Initial priority was given to Soo Line employees because of their experience and familiarity with the lines purchased. Some 400 accepted WCL's offer. Most were maintenance, shop, and mechanical employees. Very few operating (engineers, conductors, and brakemen) or clerical employees joined the WCL, choosing instead to retain their seniority with Soo Line.[8] This forced WCL to hire from outside of the immediate region, and, eventually, these types of jobs were filled by people from 42 states. The majority of these new employees had been laid off as a result of the downsizing of major (Class I) railroads.

WCL's startup was the epitome of Murphy's Law. A surprise ICC decision to issue a stay order so that it could restudy its earlier approval of the sale, put a halt to all planning. Hiring was put on hold, and leased locomotives were sent out on short-term subleases, in an effort to reduce expenses. After four agonizing weeks, the ICC lifted the stay and informed both Soo Line and WCL that the transfer could take place three days later, on October 11, 1987.

As soon as operations began, WCL was hit with another shock. Someone, probably a disgruntled clerk departing from Soo Line, scrambled the computer data concerning waybill information on 2,700 cars that were on line at the time of transfer.[9] In effect, WCL did not know the contents of each car, its current location, or its intended destination. This, coupled with a large number of new employees and a short-term shortage of locomotives, caused chaos across the system.

This chain of catastrophic events seemed to bond management and workers together, and by almost a superhuman effort, they began to untangle the railroad. "Lost" cars were found and sent on their way, while at the same time, the flow of day-to-day traffic began to reach normalcy. Slowly, concerned customers and connecting railroads began to gain confidence in WCL. The four-week delay, coupled with the disappearing waybills, cost the railroad at least $8 million in unbudgeted expenses.

DESCRIPTION OF THE WCL RAILROAD

The WCL owned and operated track in Wisconsin, the Upper Peninsula of Michigan, eastern Minnesota, and northeastern Illinois. WCL main lines extended from Chicago through Fond du Lac to Stevens Point, and then on to Minneapolis–St. Paul and Duluth-Superior, as shown on Exhibit 2. A main line also extended from Neenah-Menasha north to Gladstone and Sault Ste. Marie.

WCL Track System **Exhibit 2**

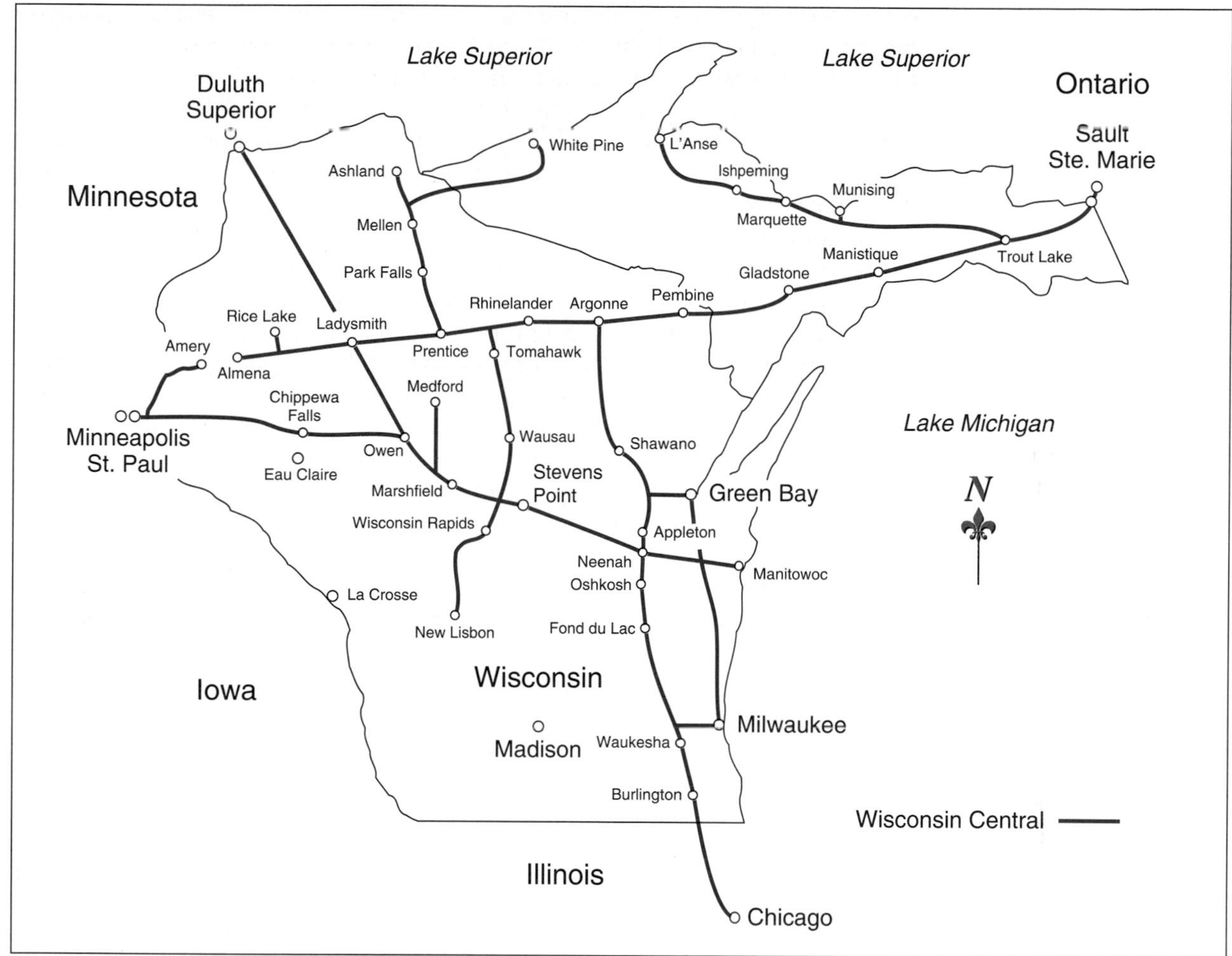

The majority of the main line permitted freight train speeds of 40 to 50 mph, which was comparable with many Class I railroads and better than most regional railroads. The main line between Chicago and Owen was equipped with a centralized traffic control (CTC) system, which enabled sidings, junctions, and signals to be controlled by a dispatcher in Stevens Point. A system of secondary and branch lines were located throughout eastern, central, and northern Wisconsin, and northern Michigan. Most of these permitted freight train speeds of 25 mph, typical of such lines on all sizes of railroads.[10]

Freight cars were sorted and blocked at two major hubs—the classification yards at Fond du Lac and Stevens Point—and at two minor hubs—the classification yards at Neenah and Gladstone. WCL's principal gateways were at Chicago, Minneapolis, Superior, and Sault Ste. Marie, where direct interchange was made with all major connecting rail carriers. Access to most of its gateways and other interchanges was normally via trackage rights on other railroads. The company owned and operated car and locomotive repair shops at

Fond du Lac, Stevens Point, and Gladstone for its own equipment and offered repair service to other railroads and clients.[11]

The railroad's fleet of rolling stock included 115 diesel-electric locomotives, and 5,183 freight cars for revenue service. The locomotives and a majority of the cars were acquired through the used equipment market, a typical procedure for newly formed railroads. The company placed a heavy emphasis on maintenance. Over one-half of the active locomotives had been rebuilt or had received a major overhaul since 1987. About one-third of the freight car fleet was rebuilt, received a major overhaul, or was acquired new since 1987. The availability rate for locomotives was between 83% and 88% and for the freight cars, at least 92%.

About 60% of the railroad's traffic was paper industry related, much of it consisting of inbound raw and partially processed materials and supplies destined for the numerous on-line pulp and paper mills. A variety of commodities made up paper industry carloadings. Inbound shipments to the mills included pulpwood logs, wood chips, wood pulp, clay, chemicals, coal, machinery, and waste paper. Outbound shipments included wood pulp, light and heavy papers, paperboard, boxboard, corrugated stock, and some by-products such as lignin. Many of the paper industry's big names were represented on WCL sidings, including Mead Corporation, Consolidated Papers Inc., Georgia-Pacific Corporation (formerly Great Northern Nekossa), Kimberly-Clark Corporation, Procter & Gamble Company, and Weyerhaeuser Company. Of the ten shippers that accounted for over 50% of the railroad's gross revenues in both 1989 and 1990, seven were paper and pulp mills.

Much of the remaining traffic came from various, shifting markets, depending on the demand and prices for raw materials and products worldwide. The railroad had made a habit of tracking those shifting markets for additional business. For example, WCL had handled large volumes of taconite (a form of iron ore) moving from Minnesota's Mesabi iron range to steel mills during the winter season, when the ore could not move by boat on the Great Lakes. Also, large volumes of large-diameter pipe for a major pipeline project had been handled between Chicago and Northern Michigan.

■ Mission

In the words of President Ed Burkhardt, WCL's mission is "to offer superior transportation consisting of more frequent, dependable train service, at competitive prices, with proper equipment, accomplished by customer-minded employees."[12]

■ Management

Exhibit 3 sets forth information about each person who served as one of the company's directors or executive officers.

Ed Burkhardt has served as a director, president, and chief executive officer of the company since its formation in 1987. He also serves as the president and chief executive officer and a director of WCL, Railcars, and Bridges. From 1967 to 1987, Burkhardt was employed by the Chicago and North Western Transportation Company, based in Chicago, most recently as vice president, transportation. He has 30 years of railroad management experience.

Key Management **Exhibit 3**

Name	*Age as of May 1, 1991*	*Title*
Edward A. Burkhardt	52	President, Chief Executive Officer, and Director
Thomas F. Power, Jr.	50	Executive Vice President, Chief Financial Officer, and Director
Walter C. Kelly	47	Vice President Finance
Glenn J. Kerbs	50	Vice President, Engineering, WCL
William R. Schauer	46	Vice President, Marketing, WCL
John L. Bradshaw	39	Vice President, Operations, WCL
Robert F. Nadrowski	44	Vice President, Mechanical, WCL
Ronald G. Russ	36	Treasurer
Robert H. Wheeler	45	Director
Donald J. McLachlan	54	Director
Roland V. McPherson	57	Director
Carl Ferenbach	49	Director
Richard K. Lubin	44	Director

Source: Wisconsin Central Transportation Corporation, 1991, *Prospectus*, pp. 40–42.

Thomas Power has served as a director, executive vice president, and chief financial officer of the company since its formation in 1987. He also serves as the executive vice president and a director of WCL, Railcars, and Bridges. From 1985 to 1987, Power was a private consultant. From 1970 to 1985, he was employed by the Chicago, Milwaukee, St. Paul and Pacific Railroad Company, Chicago, Illinois, most recently as chief financial officer. Thomas Power has 25 years of railroad management experience.

Walter Kelly has served as vice president, finance, of the company since September 1988. Prior to joining the company, he served as corporate controller for Spiegel, Inc. (a catalog retailer) from 1987 to 1988, as an independent consultant during 1986, and as vice president, finance for Wilton Enterprises, Inc. (a distributor of housewares) during 1985. From 1969 to 1985, he held various positions with Arthur Andersen & Co., United Stationers, Inc. (a wholesaler of office products), and McKesson Corporation (a supplier of pharmaceuticals and health-care products).

Glenn Kerbs has served as vice president, engineering, of WCL since its acquisition. From 1974 until 1987, he was employed by the Chicago and North Western Transportation Company, most recently as director of maintenance operations.

William Schauer has served as vice president, marketing, of WCL since October 1988, and as assistant vice president, marketing, of WCL since its acquisition. From 1986 until 1987, he was employed by Chicago and North Western Transportation Company as general marketing manager. From 1963 to 1985, Schauer was employed by the Chicago, Milwaukee, St. Paul and Pacific

Railroad Company in various positions, most recently as director of marketing and pricing.

John Bradshaw has been employed as vice president, operations, and general manager of WCL since its acquisition. From 1969 until 1987, he was employed by Chicago and North Western Transportation Company, most recently as assistant vice president and division manager, Northern Division.

Robert Nadrowski has been employed as vice president, mechanical, of WCL since its acquisition. From 1985 until 1987, he was involved in the ownership and operation of a marina and a motel in Wisconsin. From 1966 to 1985, he was employed by the Chicago, Milwaukee, St. Paul and Pacific Railroad Company, most recently as assistant vice president and chief mechanical officer.

Ronald Russ has been employed as treasurer of the company since its acquisition. From 1986 until 1987, he was a private consultant. From 1985 until 1986, he was employed by Soo as manager for financial planning. Prior to that, he held various positions with the Chicago, Milwaukee, St. Paul and Pacific Railroad Company, most recently as manager, financial planning.

Robert Wheeler is a member of the law firm of Oppenheimer Wolff & Donnelly and has served as general counsel to the company, a nonexecutive office, since its formation. He also serves as a director of the company, WCL, Railcars, and Bridges, since their formation in 1987. Prior to December 1987, Wheeler was a member of the law firm of Isham, Lincoln & Beale, Chicago, Illinois, which acted as counsel to the company in connection with its formation and the acquisition.

Donald McLachlan is a member of the law firm of McLachlan, Rissman & Doll and has served as secretary to the company, a nonexecutive office, since its formation. He has also served as a director of the company, WCL, Railcars, and Bridges since their formation in 1987. Prior to 1986, McLachlan was a member of Isham, Lincoln & Beale, and from January 1, 1987, until December 1, 1987, was employed by Isham, Lincoln & Beale in a professional capacity. McLachlan was appointed as chairman of the board in June 1991.

Roland McPherson has served as a director of the company and WCL since the acquisition. Since 1989, he has been employed as the chairman and chief executive officer of Sullivan Industries, Inc., Claremont, New Hampshire (a manufacturer of air compressors). From 1988 until 1989, McPherson was self-employed. From 1974 until 1988, he was employed as chairman and chief executive officer of Armstrong Containers, Inc., Chicago, (a manufacturer of metal containers).

Carl Ferenbach has served as a director of the company and WCL since the acquisition. Since 1986, he has been a member of Berkshire Partners, Boston, Massachusetts, a private partnership sponsoring and investing in private company acquisitions and recapitalizations. Prior to forming Berkshire Partners, Ferenbach was a managing director of the Thomas H. Lee Company, a sponsor and investor in private companies, which he joined in 1983. He has also served as a director of Inter-American Packaging, Inc., the Loveshaw Corporation, Community Capital Bank, and Marson Corporation.

Richard Lubin has served as a director of the company and WCL since the acquisition. Since 1986, he has been a member of Berkshire Partners, Boston, Massachusetts. Prior to forming Berkshire Partners, he was a managing director of the Thomas H. Lee Company, which he joined in 1982. Mr. Lubin also served as a director of Fresh Start Foods, L.P., Lechmere, Inc., and Shepard Clothing Company, Inc.

All directors of the company are elected annually. The executive officers are elected annually by and serve at the discretion of the company's board of directors. The members of the board of directors who are not full-time employees of the company are compensated at the rate of $10,000 per year, plus $500 for each meeting attended, including meetings of the boards of the company's subsidiaries. Members of the committees of the board of directors are compensated at the rate of $250 per meeting, including committees of subsidiaries' boards. Members are compensated for only one meeting, if meetings of the board of directors of the company and a subsidiary are held on the same day.

Ownership of Stock

The principal owners of the company's common stock are as listed in Exhibit 4.

Corporate Philosophy

WCL officers made a long-term commitment to provide rail freight service and not diversify into nonrail areas. At the start-up in 1987, the business plan relied primarily on originating, terminating, and local traffic, and not on overhead traffic, as a base for revenues. Overhead traffic is through traffic received from one railroad and delivered to another. It is susceptible to diversion over other railroads, making it very competitive and usually having small profit margins. In 1990, originating traffic accounted for 21% of total carloads, terminating accounted for 38%, overhead traffic for 21%, and local traffic for 20%. Once a

Principal Owners **Exhibit 4**

Name	*Shares Beneficially Owned*	*Percent of Outstanding Shares*
The Berkshire Funds[1]	1,068,499	16.7
New York Life Insurance Company[2]	773,510	12.1
Edward A. Burkhardt	583,956	9.1
Donald J. McLachlan	484,063	7.5
Roland V. McPherson	189,796	3.0
Thomas F. Power, Jr.	164,406	2.6
Robert H. Wheeler	124,448	1.9
Carl Ferenbach	15,821	0.2
Richard K. Lubin	15,821	0.2
Directors and officers as a group (16 persons)	1,760,735	27.4%

Source: Wisconsin Central Transportation Corporation, 1991, *Prospectus,* p. 48.

[1]The Berkshire Funds were comprised of two Ltd. partnerships, the First Berkshire Fund, which held 791,090 shares, and the Berkshire Fund, which held 277,409 shares.

[2]Of these shares, 386,755 were owned by New York Life Insurance and Annuity Corporation, a wholly owned subsidiary of New York Life Insurance Company.

stable base of originating, terminating, and local traffic was assured, the company would consider going after certain overhead traffic markets where the conditions were favorable for WCL.

Overall, WCL believed in strengthening its position as a rail freight carrier in the upper Midwest by making its existing system more efficient and better serving its present territory. Accordingly, WCL increased its carloadings and revenues by enlarging its market share of freight shipped by existing customers, by regaining customers that had shifted to trucking when the railroad was operated by previous owners, and by serving new shippers in its territory. The railroad continued to employ a strategy of strengthening its existing traffic base and increasing its market share within the territory it served, rather than expanding much beyond Wisconsin and Michigan. By proceeding in this direction, it was attempting to utilize the investment in fixed plant and equipment already in place.

To this end, WCL has aggressively gone after traffic from both large and small shippers. Much of this traffic had been diverted from rail to trucks years ago.[13] WCL has made multiyear long-term agreements or contracts with major shippers such as the Mead Corporation (one of its largest shippers, located near Gladstone, Michigan) to help stabilize its traffic base. The railroad continues to look at ways to streamline operations and facilities through improving track layouts that cause bottlenecks, sharing facilities with other railroads so that duplicative track can be removed, or adding or rescheduling local switch crews to better serve customers. WCL has also acquired the operations of smaller connecting links to serve nearby customers directly, such as a Kimberly-Clark paper mill at Munising, Michigan, and the Pfizer Specialty Minerals quarry at Gulliver, Michigan.

■ Human Resources

The WCL, unlike a majority of its railroad competitors, stresses the importance of the human factor in its operations. Again, President Ed Burkhardt states, "When we formed this railroad, we decided on a three-point program for dealing with our employees: stress good communications, reduce layoff fears, and treat everyone as if they were a part of management."[14]

Good Communications

Burkhardt formally schedules employee meetings four times a year at the railroad's four major locations. In addition, he holds many informal gatherings during his many visits across the system. His open communications philosophy has percolated down through the chain of command, and, now, manager and corporate staff visits out on the line have become the rule rather than the exception. For example, Jim Chestnutt, a director in the Human Resources Department, spent time working alongside the maintenance of way crews and helped train brakemen to perform their car switching tasks. Jim Chestnutt was honored by the train brakemen when they presented him with his own switch padlock key. This face-to-face interchange is supplemented by a quarterly newsletter, the *Waybill,* which keeps employees informed as to the current status of operations. One innovation was the installation of an 800 number that allows any WCL employee to personally talk with Ed Burkhardt or, in his absence, leave a message. Employee feedback seems quite positive. Those who have called, or knew of someone who had, seem both proud and pleased that they have talked with "Ed." Train engineer Carl Winkelman may have best expressed it when he commented, "You know—these people (management) really listen."[15]

Reduced Layoff Fears

WCL places great emphasis on creating a stable work force. Judicious hiring to meet actual or forecast increases in traffic demand minimizes subsequent layoffs during slack periods. Also, being nonunion permits the company to assign employees where they are needed rather than where work rules permit. An active cross-training program was implemented to permit this desired flexibility. The end result has been that furloughs have become a rarity. Exhibit 5 shows the general increase in average employment during the first three years of operations.

Pay and Benefits

The company admitted from the beginning that it would be unable, at least in the short run, to match the pay of its unionized competitors. Pay ranged from 15% to 30% below comparable jobs, and the work week often ran several hours longer. To partially offset this disparity, the WCL placed all employees on salary and instituted a profit-sharing plan. There would also be pay raises if conditions warranted. Hours worked beyond 40 are covered by compensatory time. Compensation increases, since start-up, are provided in Exhibit 6.

The WCL has emphasized to employees that during the same time period union workers received none of the above-mentioned increases. The benefit package offered WCL employees exceeds that provided by the unionized rail lines. Exhibit 7 gives a sample comparison.

Training

The WCL training program serves several purposes. First, it enables many employees to prepare themselves for better-paying jobs. For example, those

Average Number of Employees **Exhibit 5**

	Year Ended December 31,		
Employees	*1990*	*1989*	*1988*
General and administrative	86	80	84
Marketing	26	26	20
Engineering (maintenance of way)	289	256	245
Mechanical (maintenance of equipment)	215	163	138
Transportation (engineers, conductors, brakemen)	360	349	364
Totals	976	874	851

Source: Wisconsin Central Transportation Corporation, 1991, *Prospectus,* p. 28.

Exhibit 6

Compensation Increases

Year	*Special Bonus*	*Percent Profit Sharing*	*Percentage Pay Raise*
1988	$100	—	—
1989	$200	3.1	4.0
1990	—	3.3	4.5
1991	—	—	4.5

Exhibit 7

Sample Benefit Comparison

Benefit	*WCL*	*Unionized National Railroad Plan*
Life insurance	Annual salary	$10,000
Accidental D&D	Annual salary	8,000
Supplemental sick leave	80% of salary up to 6 months	Not provided
401 (K)	Yes	Not provided
Profit sharing	Yes	Not provided
Maximum medical	$1 million	$500,000
Deductible	$100—individual $200—family	$100 each individual
Maximum out-of-pocket	$500—individual $1,000—family	$2,000 each person covered

Source: WCL Benefit Plan Comparison Brochure, September 1990.

interested in the transportation area can apply to attend the one-week train conductors' program or the eight-week train engineers' course held in Stevens Point. These programs, coupled with seniority and increased business, permit temporary work as extra train crews and possible later movement to full-time transportation status. In the interim, such employees continue to work in their original jobs.

As mentioned earlier, cross-training permits employees to perform multiple tasks, thus increasing their productivity and offering job protection. This latter point is particularly evident in the case of maintenance of way personnel who used their newly acquired mechanical skills in the repair shops during the winter. Management and staff also participate in this cross training. In a pinch, several could be called upon to operate an engine, throw a switch, or drive a spike.

Work Rules

The lack of restrictive work rules is a second major factor in increased employee productivity. Unionized railroads are normally required to have a train crew of four to five persons—two or three of whom often perform no useful function. Similar train runs on the WCL are normally handled by an engineer and a conductor. On occasion, a brakeman is added when complicated car switching is required.

Crew pay on the WCL is based upon hours worked, rather than distance traveled. Yard switching crews normally work an eight- to a ten-hour day, while road crews work an average ten to twelve hours. If required, crews can perform both switching and over-the-road duties in the same day. On unionized roads, the 108-mile workday (often performed in three to four hours), coupled with ubiquitous work restrictions, severely limits flexibility.

Union

Although the WCL's initial work force was comprised almost totally of former rail union members, there was little sentiment for unionization. Many employees partially blamed the unions for their loss of former jobs with the major Class I carriers. Some had grown tired of continual union–management confrontations. Others were just satisfied to be back in their profession. The majority liked what they heard about WCL's innovative approach to operating the railroad and were pleased with an operation that went after new traffic and markets.

Initial union reaction to the WCL was muted. The United Transportation Union seemed to express some interest in early 1988, but never made a concerted effort to begin organizing efforts. The only serious attempt was made by the Brotherhood of Locomotive Engineers (BLE), who initiated a soft-sell campaign to organize the engineers and, separately, by the trainmen (conductors and brakemen). By early spring 1990, the BLE had obtained the necessary 35% authorization cards, and the National Mediation Board called for elections to commence on September 24. The WCL immediately began its own counter-campaign, and in the end, the union failed when only 21% of locomotive engineers and 15% of trainmen voted to be represented by the BLE.

Looking back, Ed Burkhardt faulted some of his management team for a portion of the union's early success.[16]

> Many of our managers were brought up on the Class I railroads, in a military style organization, with adversarial relationships with unions and employees. Some of our managers still have problems with our entirely new way of managing. We are trying to work with them to bring about necessary change. If I had it to do over, I would have had human relations training required in the early stages of our start-up.

SERVICE AND MARKETING

The marketing of services is guided by WCL's goals of providing frequent and dependable freight service at competitive prices by customer-minded employees. To accomplish this, all regular freight trains are scheduled so that they connect in an efficient manner with one another, as well as with other carriers' trains. Regardless of the number of freight cars ready to move, WCL trains adhere to their schedules, allowing for a high degree of schedule predictability for individual cars, fast transit times, and reliable arrival estimates for shippers.

This is in contrast to much of the railroad industry operations, wherein trains operate as unscheduled extras that depart only after certain tonnage requirements are filled. Keeping the cars moving and not waiting at intermediate yards also helps minimize car-hire expenses, typically a large operating expense on any railroad. The WCL applies a standard that all cars received by the railroad are to be delivered within 24 to 36 hours. Accordingly, shipments on the WCL have typically become one to two days faster than under the previous owners or on-rail competitors. The strict scheduling of trains also improved car utilization. For example, some cars that used to make three or four round trips per month on the previous carrier now make eight on the WCL.[17]

Constant communication between the railroad and its 450-plus customers is emphasized. The WCL has no sales department personnel as such. On-line customer contact is handled by operations managers and local train crews who have the authority to make service adjustments without waiting for approval from higher officials. In fact, customer service functions are actually part of the operating department. The railroad's Customer Service Center (CSC), which coordinates day-to-day contact with customers, is centrally located with the railroad operating center at Stevens Point. These two functions, unlike those of other railroads, are purposely kept close together to keep the operations of the railroad tuned to the needs of shippers. The marketing department, located in the corporate headquarters in Rosemont, Illinois, is organized by industry type instead of territory, and does pricing, car ordering, and other tasks by customer. In many cases, WCL has gotten rate quotations back to customers in hours, instead of the more typical days.

An important tool is a state-of-the-art system of integrated computer programs known as the Transportation Control System (TCS), which covers train and terminal operations, car scheduling, data exchange with other carriers, waybill and billing functions, car accounting and distribution, equipment maintenance, marketing data, and operations status reports. The railroad expanded its electronic data interchange (EDI) capabilities to allow customers to do their own billing and car tracing functions. To keep customers informed of railroad activities and progress, a professionally produced bimonthly newsletter is widely distributed.

■ Summary of Financial Performance 1987–1991

As previously mentioned, the WCL has continued to improve its financial condition since start-up in 1987. The railroad generated $93.7 million in operating revenues in 1988, while traffic volume was 144,800 carloads. Operating revenues for 1989 were $101.3 million, and traffic volume 159,100 carloads, an 8.1% increase in revenues and a 9.9% rise in traffic volume. In 1990, WCL had $113.3 million in operating revenue with 181,900 carloads, an increase of 11.8% and 14.3%, respectively, over comparable 1989 levels. During the first six months of 1991, operating revenues were $57.8 million compared to $56.7 million for the same period in 1990, a 2% increase. At the same time, carloadings rose to 93,100 from 91,600, an improvement of 1.7%. Net income during the first three years of operation increased from $2.9 in 1988 to $7.5 million in 1990.[18] Net income during the first six months of 1991 declined $37,000 due to higher fuel and labor expenses.[19] Undoubtedly, the greatest indicator of success was expressed in May 1991 by the investors who oversubscribed the company's 2.1 million share initial public offering. Supporting data plus other comparisons can be found in Exhibit 8 (condensed consolidated statements of income) and Exhibit 9 (operating data comparisons).

Revenues

Traffic volume during the period increased in 12 of the 14 commodity groups, with an overall increase of 25.6%. The largest percentage increases were in wood pulp, wood fibers, intermodal, sand, stone, and minerals. There were decreases in lumber (due to the housing slump) and steel (due to a decline in demand for drilling pipe). Increases were due mainly to higher production levels at the paper mills and diversion of traffic from trucks. Exhibit 10 compares WCL's 1988–1990 traffic volume and gross and average revenues for carload by commodity group. Increases in gross revenues were due primarily to the increases in carloads and, in part, from automatic price increases included in WCL's transportation contracts. In some cases, price increases were less than authorized in order to meet competition. In addition, selective price changes were made on an individual basis for certain commodities or customers.

Wisconsin Central Transportation Corporation and Subsidiaries, Condensed Consolidated Statements of Income ($ in thousands, except per share data) **Exhibit 8**

	Six Months Ended June 30,		*Year Ended December 31,*			*Inception to December 31,*
	1991	*1990*	*1990*	*1989*	*1988*	*1987*
	(Unaudited)			(Audited)		
Income statement data						
Operating revenues	$57,803	$56,689	$113,289	$101,264	$93,670	$17,610
Operating expenses	(47,432)	(45,284)	(89,592)	(77,935)	(74,424)	(16,319
Income from operations	10,371	11,405	23,697	23,329	19,246	1,291
Gains on sales of excess assets	—	—	3,805	2,767	1,174	—
Rental income	—	—	1,167	1,397	1,693	698
Other income (expense), net	54	(869)	(2,228)	(2,407)	(2,765)	(595
Interest expense	(5,217)	(6,104)	(14,744)	(16,157)	(15,814)	(3,257
Income (loss) before income taxes and extraordinary items	5,208	4,432	11,697	8,929	3,534	(1,863
Provision for income taxes	(2,008)	(1,536)	(4,151)	(3,167)	(1,261)	—
Income (loss) before extraordinary items	3,200	2,896	7,546	5,762	2,273	(1,863
Extraordinary item—tax benefit of net operating loss carryforward	—	—	—	—	772	—
Extraordinary item—early extinguishment of debt, net of income taxes	(341)	0	—	(358)	—	—
Net income (loss)	$ 2,859	$ 2,896	$ 7,546	$ 5,404	$ 3,045	$ (1,863
Net income (loss) per share (dollars)	$ 0.64	$ 0.72	$ 1.89	$ 1.35	$ 0.75	$ (0.46

Sources: Wisconsin Central Transportation Corporation, 1991, *Prospectus,* p.12; Wisconsin Central Transportation Corporation, 1991, *2nd Quarter Form 10-Q,* p. 3.

Exhibit 9 **Operating Data Comparisons ($ in thousands, except per share data)**

	Quarter Ended March 31,		*Year Ended December 31,*		*Inception to December 31,*	
	1991	*1990*	*1990*	*1989*	*1988*	*1987*
Revenue ton miles of freight traffic (millions)[1]	820	843	3,321	2,854	2,573	579
Revenue per ton-mile[2]	3.4¢	3.3¢	3.3¢	3.4¢	3.5¢	2.9¢
Operating ratio[3]	86.2%	81.2%	79.1%	77.0%	79.5%	92.7%
Gross ton-miles per freight train hour (thousands)[4]	52.91	61.14	58.02	51.58	48.74	42.51
Gross ton-miles per locomotive in service (millions)[4]	16.21	18.79	66.63	58.40	55.92	25.51
Fuel consumption (thousand gallons)	3,225	3,620	12,347	11,365	10,914	1,767
Fuel cost per gallon (average)	81¢	65¢	70¢	61¢	50¢	64¢
Gross ton-miles per gallon of fuel[4]	525.53	509.92	566.72	519.39	492.86	496.31
Total carloads	47,432	47,045	181,980	159,121	144,838	27,823
Carloads from originating, terminating and local traffic	81.1%	72.3%	79.1%	81.1%	82.5%	83.5%
Gross revenues from originating, terminating and local traffic	84.1%	79.8%	84.0%	82.1%	83.0%	84.0%
Workdays lost due to employee injury	72	142	456	1,125	1,266	185
Net freight loss and damage as a percent of gross freight revenues[5]	0.68%	0.35%	0.47%	0.50%	0.37%	0.39%

Sources: Wisconsin Central Transportation Corporation, 1991, *Prospectus,* p. 13.

[1]A revenue ton-mile equals the product of weight in tons of freight carried for hire and the distance in miles between origin and destination.

[2]Revenue per ton-mile equals net freight revenue divided by revenue ton-miles of freight traffic.

[3]Operating ratio equals operating expenses divided by operating revenues.

[4]A gross ton-mile equals the product of train weight in tons (excluding locomotive weight but including weight of freight cars and freight carried) and miles traveled by the train.

[5]Net freight loss and damage was the cost to the company of damaged and destroyed customer freight, net of salvage and insurance recoveries.

Operating Expenses

Expenses were $89.5 million in 1990, as compared to $77.9 million in 1989 and $74.4 million in 1988. Exhibit 11 sets forth comparison of WCL's expenses during 1990, 1989, and 1988: Labor expenses increased some $7 million during the period. These increases were due to increased traffic volume, pay raises of 4.3% (1989) and 4.5% (1990), a 25% increase in fringe benefit costs, and $2.7 million in profit sharing.

Diesel fuel expenses rose as increased traffic volume raised consumption by 14.7% and the per-gallon cost increased 20 cents. Materials expense rose as increased business levels required additional locomotives, freight cars, and track material. Equipment rents moved up slightly due to leases of 400 covered hopper cars. Joint facilities costs rose, due mainly to higher rent charges for movement of traffic over another railroad's trackage. Additions to the value of

Carload and Gross Revenue Comparison by Commodity Group, 1989–1990

Exhibit 10

Commodity Group	*Carloads*			*Gross Revenues ($ in thousands, except per carload)*			*Revenue per Carload*		
	1990	*1989*	*1988*	*1990*	*1989*	*1988*	*1990*	*1989*	*1988*
Paper	20,911	20,803	20,704	$ 19,788	$ 18,119	$ 16,400	$946	$871	$792
Wood pulp	21,080	19,176	16,777	20,924	18,977	15,804	993	990	942
Pulpboard	18,074	17,605	17,699	9,778	9,506	9,132	541	540	516
Lumber products	6,206	6,614	7,017	4,076	4,162	4,617	657	629	658
Wood fibers	14,734	12,926	11,239	7,470	6,662	6,034	507	515	537
Chemical and petroleum products	14,965	14,234	12,650	13,305	12,802	12,246	889	899	968
Intermodal	20,654	12,252	10,580	3,810	2,559	2,314	184	209	219
Sand, stone, and minerals	17,239	9,962	4,291	7,162	4,499	2,803	415	452	653
Clay products and granules	14,275	12,426	10,954	13,570	11,813	9,817	951	951	896
Coal	12,878	12,845	12,503	7,168	7,950	7,224	557	619	578
Food and grain	10,952	9,656	10,194	7,549	6,859	8,336	689	710	818
Waste and scrap	7,231	7,068	6,271	4,945	4,681	3,950	684	662	630
Steel	1,068	2,276	2,456	1,261	2,567	2,900	1,181	1,128	1,181
Miscellaneous	1,713	1,278	1,503	1,283	1,142	1,054	749	894	701
Totals	181,980	159,121	144,838	$122,089	$112,298	$102,631	$ 671	$ 706	$ 709

Source: Wisconsin Central Transportation Corporation, 1991, *Prospectus*, pp. 17–21.

Operating Expense Comparisons, 1988–1990

Exhibit 11

	1990	*1989*	*1988*
Labor expense (including payroll taxes and fringe benefits	$35,692	$31,972	$28,682
Diesel fuel	8,386	6,810	5,463
Materials	7,595	6,780	6,732
Equipment rents, net	13,193	12,584	12,891
Joint facilities, net	3,366	2,268	2,080
Depreciation	5,486	5,220	4,895
Casualties and insurance	4,649	2,737	3,182
Property taxes	2,037	2,309	1,701
Other	9,188	7,255	8,798
Operating expenses	$89,592	$77,935	$74,424

Source: Wisconsin Central Transportation Corporation, 1991, *Prospectus*, pp. 19–22.

roadway, structures, and equipment caused depreciation charges to increase. Casualties and insurance varied with derailment costs and claims experience. Property tax evaluation changes caused the rise and fall of these expenses. Other expenses increased as a result of higher legal costs, travel and business expenses, and lease costs for the WCL's headquarters.

Liquidity and Capital Resources

Cash generated from operations have historically been WCL's primary source of liquidity and is used principally for debt service, to cover capital expenditures, and to meet working capital requirements. As of December 31, 1990, some $31.3 million of the WCL's original $100 million long-term loan had been retired through scheduled debt payments. The company's initial public stock offering in May 1991 generated $36.2 million in net proceeds and was used to retire an additional $36.2 million of the term loan. Resultant interest payments will be reduced approximately $1.9 million for 1991 and some $3.3 million for 1992. (See Exhibit 12.) Through December 1990, the WCL had funded $47.6 million in capital expenditures. Over $11.9 million had been used to purchase locomotives, railcars, and other transportation equipment. The remaining $35.7 million was expended on roadway and structure improvements as indicated in Exhibit 13.

By early August, the WCL had finished approximately half of its 1991 roadway improvement program. Work completed included installation of 64.3 thousand ties, resurfacing of 347 miles of track, application of 104.2 thousand tons of ballast, and laying of 2.6 miles of continuous welded rail.[20]

The WCL believes that its cash flow from operations, plus cash on hand and a $19.5 million line of credit, will allow it to meet its liquidity and capital expenditure requirements for the foreseeable future.

ECONOMY

■ National

The economy in the United States during WCL's first four years of existence could be described as one of slow, steady decline. Gross National Product (GNP) growth peaked at a 4.2% annualized rate in the fourth quarter of 1988, then plunged below 2% in 1989, and continued its fall to -2.6% by the end of March 1991. Railcar loadings lagged the GNP slide by some two years. Ton-miles showed a gradual increase from 1988, until late 1990, when volume began to fall. By the end of March 1991, carloadings had dropped 5.5% from the previous March. Almost every commodity group was down, with motor vehicles declining 18.2%, lumber 21.3%, and grain 10.7%. Even intermodal was off .8%. The only major commodity to show an increase was paper, some .5%. The economy in the upper Midwest generally paralleled that of the rest of the nation, with manufacturing down particularly in heavy industry. A bright spot in Wisconsin and northern Michigan was paper and related products. High production levels were maintained even during moderate economic downturns, since the marginal cost of paper was usually well below its selling price.[21]

Wisconsin Central Transportation Corporation and Subsidiaries, Consolidated Balance Sheets ($ in thousands) **Exhibit 12**

	June 30,	December 31,	
	1991	1990	1989
Assets	(Unaudited)	(Audited)	
Current assets			
Cash and cash equivalents	$ 5,390	$ 15,601	$ 2,708
Receivables, net	24,573	27,052	23,451
Materials and supplies	8,107	7,747	6,487
Other current assets	990	1,065	705
Total current assets	39,060	51,465	33,351
Properties			
Roadway and structures	161,268	156,111	143,660
Equipment	22,938	20,342	23,232
Total and properties	184,206	176,453	166,892
Less accumulated depreciation	(17,747)	(15,579)	(12,401)
Net properties	166,459	160,874	154,491
Other assets			
Financing and organization costs, net	5,598	7,240	9,436
Total assets	$211,117	$219,579	$197,278
Liabilities and Stockholders' Equity			
Current liabilities			
Long-term debt due within one year	$ 3,650	$ 9,985	$ 12,336
Accounts payable	16,195	20,524	15,890
Accrued expenses	23,074	22,674	17,393
Amount due under asset purchase agreement	—	—	5,384
Interest payable	1,368	1,449	1,409
Affiliated interest payable	8	1,308	7
Total current liabilities	44,295	55,940	52,419
Long-term debt			
Affiliated	20,500	20,500	20,650
Other	61,703	98,508	97,387
Total long-term debt	82,203	119,008	118,037
Other liabilities	7,849	8,379	1,600
Deferred income taxes	8,297	7,109	3,625
Total liabilities	142,644	190,436	175,681
Stockholders' equity			
Preferred stock par value $1.00; authorized 1,000,000 shares; issued and outstanding none in 1991 and 1990	—	—	—
Common stock, par value $0.01; authorized, 10,000,000 shares; and 4,000,000 shares at December 31, 1990	64	40	40
Paid in capital	51,468	15,021	15,021
Retained earnings	16,941	14,082	6,536
Total stockholders' equity	68,473	29,143	21,597
Total liabilities and stockholders' equity	$211,117	$219,579	$197,278

Sources: Wisconsin Central Transportation Corporation, 1991, *Prospectus,* pp. F4–5; Wisconsin Central Transportation Corporation, 1991, *2nd Quarter Form 10-Q,* p. 2.

Exhibit 13

Roadway and Structure Improvements

	Year Ended December 31,			*Inception to December 31,*
	1990	*1989*	*1988*	*1987*
Track miles surfaced[1]	559	427	368	30
Track miles of rail laid	14.7	13.9	12.9	2.2
Tons of ballast applied (thousands)	258.1	147.3	127.5	5.4
Ties installed	167,826	98,189	68,436	1,192

Source: Wisconsin Central Transportation Corporation, 1991, *Prospectus*, p. 25.

[1]Surfacing was the process by which track was aligned and cross-leveled in conjunction with the application of ballast and the installation of ties.

■ Regional

The state of Wisconsin was characterized by a variety of diversified and productive manufacturers, supported by a highly educated labor force with a strong work ethic. According to a recent study on the state's economy by the University of Wisconsin School of Business, the state was particularly strong in durable goods production, especially industrial machinery, primary and fabricated metals, lumber, and instrumentation.[22]

The paper industry was of prime importance to Wisconsin, employing about 50,000 people, or 9% of the state manufacturing employment. Wisconsin ranked first among all states in paper industry employment and in paper production. In 1988, the state produced over 4.5 million tons of paper, or 12% of the nation's total output. Pulp and paper mills are located throughout central and northern Wisconsin, but heavy concentrations are found along the Wisconsin River Valley between Wisconsin Rapids, Stevens Point, Wausau, and Tomahawk; and along the Fox River Valley between Neenah-Menasha, Appleton, and Green Bay. Of the 52 active pulp and paper mills in the state in 1990, 25, most of them large-capacity, were directly served by WCL. Two more large mills are located on a local, short-line railroad whose only interchange is with the WCL. The railroad also serves four of the seven mills in Michigan's Upper Peninsula, plus one in Sault Ste. Marie, Ontario.

Large capital expenditures for expansion and modernization at these mills during the 1980s and continuing into the 1990s are expected to help them maintain Wisconsin's dominant position as a papermaker. These investments are not only going toward expansion, but also to increase the plants' ability to utilize wastepaper and to meet tighter environmental standards. Wisconsin forest resources are plentiful. Although the harvesting of timber has been increasing, only about 60% of forest growth has been cut in recent years. Eight major paper converting mills are also located on WCL in Wisconsin.

Printing and publishing are also a big business in Wisconsin. One of the state's largest—Quad/Graphics—has three plants located on-line, all of which were designed to receive printing paper by rail. Other major manufacturing concerns served by WCL include firms that produce food products, lumber and wood products, chemicals, fabricated metals, electrical machinery, and plastics.

Mining is expected to remain a relatively small industry in Wisconsin, mostly engaged in the extraction of sand, gravel, and stone.[23] No metallic minerals are mined in the state, but copper, zinc, and related metal deposits have been found both in northwestern Wisconsin near Ladysmith and in northeastern Wisconsin near Crandon. Mining concerns have begun the application process, but environmental and market factors have not allowed these projects to proceed to date. In Michigan, the White Pine Copper Mine near Ironwood and two taconite mines near Marquette are in operation.

COMPETITION

WCL's operations are subject to competition from other railroads, trucks, and lake vessels.

■ Rail

Competition comes principally from the Chicago and NorthWestern (CNW), the Green Bay and Western (GBW), and the Fox River Valley (FRVR). The CNW competes for Canadian National Railroad interchange traffic between Duluth/Superior and Chicago. In addition, the CNW's iron ore haul from Ishpeming, Michigan, to Green Bay, Wisconsin, is much shorter than WCL's circuitous route via Trout Lake, Michigan, and Argonne, Wisconsin.

The GBW competes directly for paper mill traffic between Green Bay and Wisconsin Rapids. Its western connection with the Burlington Northern (BN) near East Winona, Wisconsin, is being upgraded to permit intermodal service between East Central Wisconsin and major western U.S. markets (see Exhibit 14). The GBW moved about 32,000 cars in 1990.

The FRVR was formerly a part of the CNW and served as a bridge route connecting CNW's truncated northern iron ore lines with its Chicago–Milwaukee–Twin Cities main route. The FRVR also competes with WCL for local and through traffic at Green Bay (see Exhibit 14). The FRVR moved about 42,000 cars in 1991.

■ Trucking

Trucking dominates the transportation market area of WCL. In the all-important paper industry, the WCL handled the majority of inbound raw materials, chemicals, coal, and clay. Outbound paper products transported by the WCL consisted of printing paper, kraft (brown) paper, and pulpboard. The WCL seems to have won back some sheet paper, consumer, and sanitary products business, but the majority of this traffic remained with trucks due to relatively low product weight and off-line delivery requirements.

WCL's biggest success in this continuing struggle has been in the intermodal area. The opening or improvement of intermodal loading facilities in Green bay, Neenah, and Stevens Point, coupled with the bankruptcies of several

Exhibit 14 **Green Bay and Western Rail System**

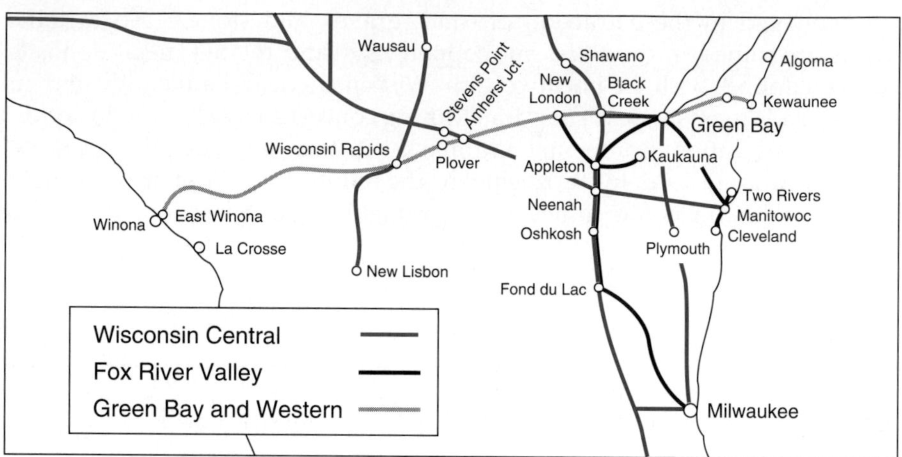

competing truck lines, caused intermodal volume to increase by 69.9% and gross revenue by 81% for the first six months of 1991, compared to the same period in 1990.

■ Lake Vessels

WCL competes with lake vessels for coal deliveries to a copper smelter in White Pine, Michigan, and the seasonal movement of iron ore from the Mesabi Range in Minnesota and steel mills in Indiana and Pennsylvania. Favorable weather conditions, permitting earlier lake vessel shipment, are a continuing threat in these operations.

LEGAL/POLITICAL

WCL operations are subject to various federal, state, and local laws and regulations relating in various degrees to almost every phase of its operations.

■ Environmental

The Environmental Protection Agency and similar bodies govern the management of hazardous wastes, discharge of pollutants, and disposal of certain substances. Two areas of possible concern to WCL are the release of these materials due to train mishap or improper handling of diesel fuel. As of mid-1991, the WCL had not been involved in any proceedings with a governmental agency, with respect to environmental clean-up. The railroad has held discussions with both Michigan and Wisconsin concerning oil spills at three or four locations. Costs of possible clean-up are thought to be minor.

■ Engineer Certification

A series of nationwide rail accidents involving locomotive engineer operating errors or substance abuse caused the Federal Railroad Administration to institute a host of strict regulations and penalties. Effective November 1, 1991, all engineers must be certified, tested a minimum of twice a year, and retrained and recertified every three years. WCL's 130 full-time locomotive engineers received automatic certification, and one-third will receive training and recertification each year. Part-time engineers are also required to receive this training and certification. In the long run, WCL hopes to certify all trainmen (conductors and brakemen) as part of its job skill enhancement program.[24]

■ Staggers Rail Act

The greater competitive freedoms afforded the railroads by this legislation are continually under attack by nonrail competitors and certain shipper groups. Additionally, certain U.S. representatives and senators have expressed interest in supporting legislation that would seriously curtail this new found rail flexibility.

■ Longer Trucks

The trucking industry continues its efforts to induce state and federal legislatures to authorize longer and/or more trailers and greater weight limits. By early 1991, thirteen states permitted the use of double or triple trailers, subject to certain restrictions. Two of the four states served by the WCL permitted the use of such vehicles on their highways.

■ Railroad Labor Review Panel

In mid-July 1991, a special labor review board authorized by Congress and named by President Bush confirmed an earlier presidential emergency board's recommendation that unionized railroads shed many work rule restrictions. The decision ordered a substantial increase in mileage that train crews must travel to earn a day's pay. It also set in motion events that would result in cuts in train crew size. In some instances, through-freight crews would be reduced from four to two members. It is estimated that when fully implemented, railroad labor costs will be lowered by more than $1 billion.

■ State and Local Activities

State and local government interaction with the railroad industry has traditionally centered on a few issues such as safety, grade crossings, branchline abandonments, and freight service preservation. To a large degree, this is due to the fact that railroads are for-profit concerns that own and operate over their own rights-of-way, unlike trucks and barges, which operate over publicly owned and maintained rights-of-way. During the 1970s and 1980s, the state of

Wisconsin's rail programs and policies—like those of most states—focused on preservation of certain light-density branch lines and service provided by major railroads facing bankruptcy. Thus, Wisconsin's rail policies and programs were able to address preservation of endangered rail line segments, track rehabilitation assistance on light density lines, and mitigation of abandonment impacts on rail using businesses.

WCL participated in several of these kinds of programs. For example, in 1990, the railroad completed rehabilitation of the 46-mile-long Manitowoc branch, using a $1.25 million grant and a $750,000 low-interest loan from the state. Also in 1989, the state of Michigan approved a $300,000 loan to WCL to upgrade 19 miles of mainline track.

More recently, Wisconsin officials recommended that the state's rail freight policies and programs be modified to change their focus from that of service preservation to economic development. In a recent draft Freight Rail Policy Plan,[25] the Wisconsin Department of Transportation suggested a series of actions designed to facilitate this evolution. Among these were several legislative actions, including revising the state constitution's "internal improvements" clause to allow the state to directly make rail improvements allowing the state to have the ability to directly manage the use of state owned rail lines, and expanding the requirements in the track rehabilitation program to include a broader range of eligible rail lines. The last item might offer the greatest opportunity for additional assistance to WCL. Other recommended actions included additional legislative items dealing with grade crossings and right-of-way fencing, as well as administrative and study recommendations. State officials believe that such a revised policy, when acted on together with the private sector and local government, will serve the public interest by providing technical and financial assistance and by ensuring that state regulations do not constrain rail freight viability.

On June 11, 1991, the Wisconsin Senate approved a state constitutional amendment to allow the use of state bond sale proceeds for rail projects and included railroads as part of the state transportation system. The amendment will require voter approval. In an opposite move, Governor Thompson signed a bill that removed rail carriers' exemption from state corporate income tax. In 1990, WCL paid Wisconsin some $1.8 million in ad valorem taxes. This new tax increased the effective overall tax rate from 33 to 39% of pretax income.[26]

A FUTURE: A NEW STRATEGY?

On May 21, 1991, President Burkhardt announced an agreement with the Chicago and North Western to purchase their line from Cameron into the Duluth-Superior gateway. On July 3, he informed the press that a parallel Soo Line route from Ladysmith into the two cities would also be acquired. (See Exhibit 15.) Both purchases would be subject to ICC approval and would together cost the WCL $21.75 million. These purchases would give the WCL access to the 110,000 cars per year that Canadian National (CN) then interchanged with the CNW, Soo and Burlington Northern (BN). WCL's new Duluth–Chicago route would be 461 miles in length versus up to 591 miles for the three other competitors.

Superior Line Purchases **Exhibit 15**

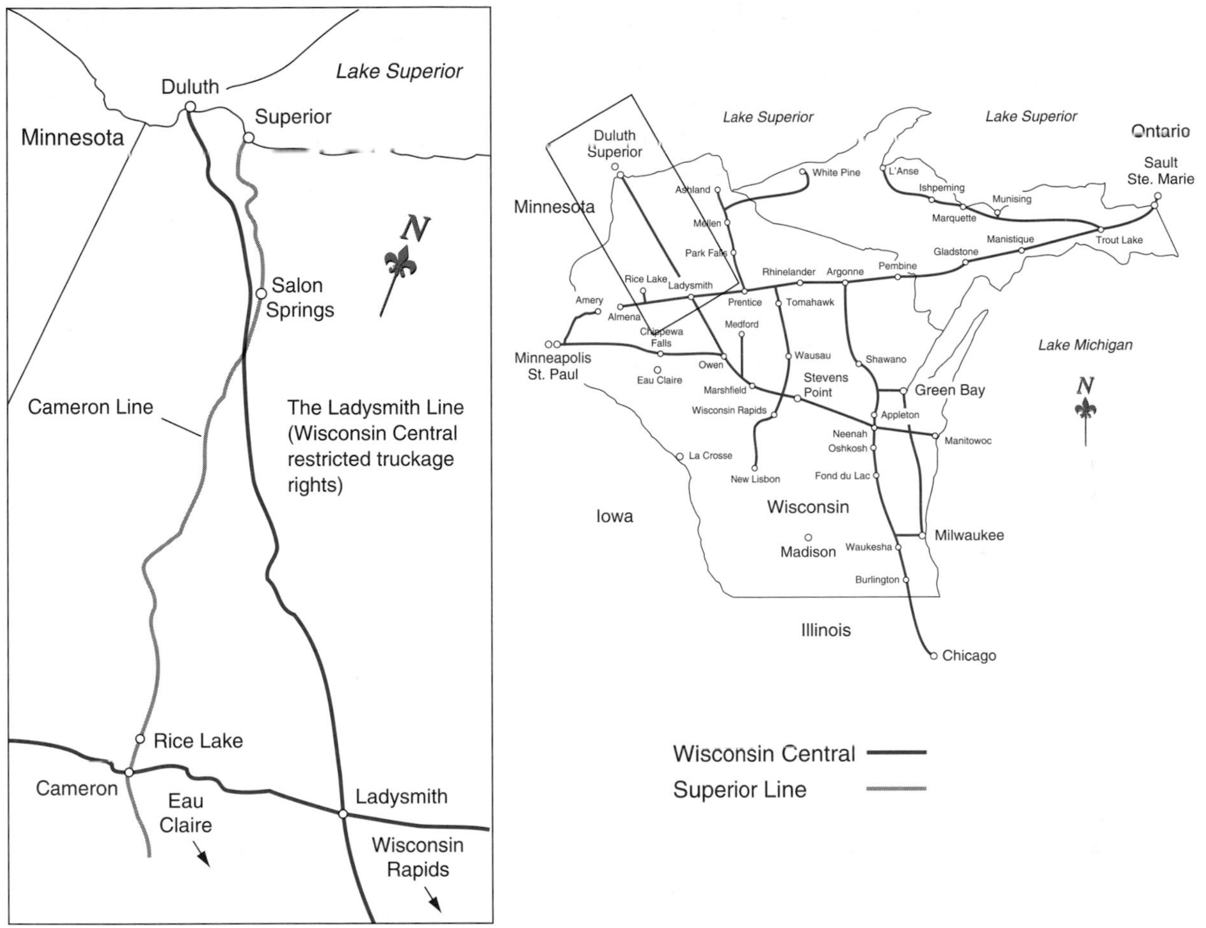

Even with ICC approval, the movement into the Duluth–Superior gateway is not without challenges. While both cities will provide some originating traffic, WCL's success will be dependent on garnering overhead traffic to and from Canada. The three older lines, particularly the powerful BN, will not take lightly to WCL's entry onto the scene. President Burkhardt and staff will have to find answers to such questions as: What changes to the marketing mix will be necessary to acquire overhead traffic and to retain and increase present traffic? What will be the impact on such functional areas as finance, HRM, operations, and MIS? In brief, will the WCL have the wherewithal to support a multiple corporate strategy?

EPILOGUE

The ICC did approve WCL's purchase of the parallel lines into Duluth–Superior. WCL immediately began petitioning for line abandonments of CNW,

Cameron to Solon Springs and Soo, Solon Springs–Superior (see Exhibit 15). The CN began playing BN, CNW, Soo, and WCL one against the other to attain the lowest rates possible. No interchange agreements had been reached as of April 1, 1992. WCL did open traffic offices in western Canada and was garnering increased interchange business. Interchange with CP had not increased appreciably.

In late February 1992, WCL and Itel Corporation announced agreement of the sale of both GBW and FRVR to WCL for $61.2 million. The sale is subject to ICC approval, which may take as long as one year.

GLOSSARY

Bridge route. A railroad that serves as a connection that joins two or more noncontiguous rail lines.

Car hire. The renting of freight cars from another railroad. Charges are computed on a daily basis.

Gateway. A rail center where freight cars from connecting railroads are interchanged.

Intermodal. Freight that is moved by differing modes of transportation enroute to its destination.

Local traffic. Freight that originates and terminates on the trackage of the same railroad.

Originating traffic. Freight that originates on one railroad but is interchanged with another in order to reach its final destination.

Overhead traffic. Freight received from one railroad for delivery to a second railroad.

Terminating traffic. Freight that is received from another railroad for delivery to its final destination.

Trackage rights. A right to use the tracks of another railroad. A rights fee is normally charged.

Waybill. A document, prepared by the carrier of freight, that contains details of the shipment, route, and charges.

ENDNOTES

1. Association of American Railroads, *Railroad Facts: 1990 Edition,* Economics and Finance Department, Washington, D.C.
2. Luther S. Miller, "Putting Railroads in Their Place," *Railway Age,* September 1991, p. 4.
3. Otto P. Dobnick, "The Wisconsin Central Story, Part 1: Acting Like a Class I, But Not Always Thinking Like One," *Trains,* September 1990, pp. 32–47.
4. Ibid, p. 35.
5. Wisconsin Central Transportation Corporation, 1991, *Prospectus.*
6. Dobnick, "Part 1," p. 36.
7. "Another Route to Railroading," *The Chicago Tribune,* 25 January 1988, Sec. 4, p. 7.
8. Dobnick, "Part 1," p. 36.
9. Ibid, p. 37.
10. Otto P. Dobnick, "The Wisconsin Central Story, Part 2: A Hub-and-Spoke System for Trains," *Trains,* October 1990, pp. 40–53.
11. Dobnick, "Part 1," pp. 32–47.

12. Interviews with President Edward A. Burkhardt, Wisconsin Central Transportation Corporation, 16–19 July 1991.
13. William R. Schauer, "Wisconsin Central Marketing: Plan, Pledge, Performance," *Progressive Railroading,* October 1990, p. 27.
14. Burkhardt, Interviews, 16–17 July 1991.
15. Interviews with Engineer Carl Winkelman, Wisconsin Central Railroad Ltd., 20 July, 1991.
16. Burkhardt, Interviews, 16–19 July 1991.
17. Dobnick, "Part 1," pp. 32–47.
18. *Prospectus*, p. 5.
19. Wisconsin Central Transportation Corporation, 1991, Form 10-Q, 2nd Quarter, pp. 9–10.
20. Wisconsin Central Ltd., *Waybill,* 4 October 1991, p. 4.
21. *Prospectus*, p. 31.
22. John P. Klus and William A. Strang, *Wisconsin's Economy in the Year 2000* (Madison: University of Wisconsin Press, 1991), pp. 58–85.
23. Ibid. pp. 58–85.
24. *Waybill*, p. 3.
25. Wisconsin Department of Transportation, Division of Planning and Budget, *Freight Rail Policy Plan: Draft for Public Review* (Madison, 1991), pp. 3–7, 41–57.
26. "Tax Bites: Wisconsin Lines Face New Levy," *Rails,* 9 August 1991, pp. 1–3.

CASE 20

Qwik Paint & Body Centers, Inc.

Clifford E. Darden, Pepperdine University

During the winter of 1991, Philemon Cordova, president of Qwik Paint & Body Centers, met with an external consultant to discuss how to improve the overall performance of the company, particularly the 28 operating centers that are the heart of the business. Recently issued 1990 financial statements showed a decline in sales, gross margins, and net profits of 7.5%, 11.6%, and 49.2%, respectively (see Exhibit 1).

As Cordova saw it, 1990 operating results were not primarily a consequence of a series of recent corporate reorganizations, or even of the economic downturn that began in the fourth quarter of 1990. Rather, he suspected that the decline reflected more fundamental problems—problems that perhaps had been masked by years of prosperous growth. Since the basic approach to running the business had not changed appreciably in more than a decade, Cordova believed that the starting point for making sense of the recent operating performance was a close examination of Qwik Paint's management processes and structure, hence, the requested organizational analysis.

"Time is of the essence," he explained, as he concluded the meeting. "The chairman is quite upset, both with 1990 operating results and with the loss of seven of our best center managers over the course of the last year. I'm concerned that he may soon simply start taking unilateral actions, well conceived or not."

OVERVIEW OF COMPANY HISTORY

In May 1972, 33-year-old Ricardo de la Monte, a regional manager for Karl Schwab Paint Shops, Inc., decided to approach his superiors to request a 5%

This case is intended for classroom discussion only, not to depict effective or ineffective handling of administrative situations. All rights reserved to the author and the North American Case Research Association.

Exhibit 1

Qwik Paint & Body Centers, Inc., Comparative Income Statements for Fiscal Years 1986–1990 (all financial data rounded to 000s)

	1986	*1987*	*1988*	*1989*	*1990*
Sales					
Wholesale	$ 7,323	$ 7,338	$ 8,919	$ 9,669	$ 9,211
Retail	10,168	12,842	19,851	19,631	17,879
Total sales	$17,491	$20,180	$28,770	$29,300	$27,090
Cost of sales	9,195	10,313	14,443	15,476	14,870
Gross margin	$ 8,296	$ 9,867	$14,327	$13,824	$12,220
Center overhead	1,210	1,528	2,273	2,315	2,167
Corporate overhead	2,755	3,612	5,466	5,714	5,851
Selling expenses	1,867	2,038	2,935	3,018	2,790
Profit before tax	$ 2,464	$ 2,689	$ 3,653	$ 2,777	$ 1,412
Number of centers	20	20	27	27	27
Number of employees	427	427	579	564	545

Notes: Sales: Margins on retail sales were 35%–50% higher than wholesale margins. The above figures include parts and sublet revenues, but not the approximately $1.25–$1.5 million in annual sales of Regal Paint & Body Boutique, the company's sole custom paint shop, which operated under different performance standards than did the other 27 locations.

Gross Margin: On center manager P&L statements, gross margin was stated as a percentage, not in actual dollars. Regional and center managers were not held responsible for any P&L items below the gross margin line, and financial data below the gross margin line were not shared with them.

raise. Having reasoned that as one of Karl Schwab's top performing managers a raise was "very much in order," de la Monte was both disappointed and angered by the response. "They turned me down flat," he recalled. "No raise was possible, I was told."

Little did the top management of Karl Schwab suspect that the rejection of de la Monte's request would lead to the launching of what would become one of their strongest regional competitors. Within six months of the rejection, de la Monte had borrowed sufficient capital from relatives and friends to open the first Qwik Paint & Body Center. From this initial, one-booth operation, Qwik Paint expanded to its present total of 28 centers, located mainly in Los Angeles and Orange counties, but also in San Diego, San Bernadino, Sacramento, and Las Vegas.

The company's growth occurred in "periodic spurts," according to Jake Upshaw, the former Schwab regional manager who joined Qwik Paint during its second year of operation and became vice president of operations in 1987. "Ricardo or I would be driving along some street and see what looked like a good location. Or, maybe we'd hear from a paint supplier that so-and-so's shop was up for sale. And we'd say, 'Hey, let's go for it!' " Of the 12 centers that the company had in operation in its tenth year of existence, approximately half had been developed internally and half were acquired. By the close of 1987, the company operated out of 20 locations—with the majority of the eight new locations, added between 1982 and 1987, having been internally developed. Of the eight centers added since 1987, all but three were acquisitions of existing businesses.

Along with his old friend Upshaw, de la Monte initially played a key role in the running of the business—for example, supervising the central staff and directing the acquisition and development of new centers. However, in late 1989, having lost confidence in Jake Upshaw's ability to run operations effectively, he initiated the first of a series of significant managerial changes aimed at improving the company's performance. Upshaw was moved to the newly created position of vice president of quality control, a change that afforded de la Monte himself direct control of operations. Additionally, one of the three regional managers was dismissed, while the remaining two, Emilio Bravo and Victor Lazulli, were made corporate vice presidents in charge of wholesale (e.g., automobile dealerships) and retail accounts, respectively.

Although intended to promote better coordination of wholesale and retail business strategies, this new structure (see Exhibit 2) soon precipitated a financial and managerial crisis, the origins of which (according to Clayton Luneson, vice president of finance) could be traced to Bravo and Lazulli's unhappiness with de la Monte's 1987 choice of Upshaw as the first vice president of operations. "All along, they [Lazulli and Bravo] both coveted Upshaw's job," asserted Luneson, who joined the company in 1980. When de la Monte himself became "interim" head of operations in 1989, Lazulli and Bravo each sought to position himself to assume the post when de la Monte stepped aside. Luneson continued:

> So, instead of cooperating, they went after each other with a vengeance. You'd have Lazulli walking into a shop one day, telling the manager to forget about his wholesale business—to just concentrate on the retail side. The next day Bravo would get wind of it, and call the same manager and tell him to put all his effort into wholesale accounts. It got so bad that the managers started taking sides, and morale and profits took a real nosedive. When Ricardo finally saw what was happening, he was *furious* and demoted both of them.

Thus, in early 1990, de la Monte restored the previous structure in which the regional managers have both retail and wholesale responsibilities within assigned territories. By April, however, the pressures inherent in his "high-involvement" approach to managing operations, as well as the ongoing Bravo-Lazulli feud, precipitated a nervous breakdown. To facilitate continued direction of the company, an "office of the president"—comprised of four of de la Monte's long-term advisers—was established in April 1990. De la Monte's chief financial adviser, Jacob Axelman, CPA, served as de facto chairman of the office and assumed the largest degree of responsibility for executive decision making during the six-month period of de la Monte's incapacity.

This arrangement allowed the company to continue functioning, but was marginally effective in stemming the decline in operating results that had begun in mid-1989. Further, the regional managers—particularly, Bravo and Lazulli—chafed greatly under what they considered to be both the absence of unified direction and Axelman's "dictatorial actions." Describing this interim structure as "one of the dumbest things the company ever did," Bravo vividly recalled the "total chaos" that prevailed in operations when Axelman—with limited knowledge of the business, but much convinced of Bravo and Lazulli's culpability for de la Monte's illness—began bypassing regional management and issuing instructions directly to managers in the centers.

During the tenure of the office of the president, Jim Vernon, a 37-year-old former entrepreneur with no previous experience in the paint and body busi-

Exhibit 2 **Qwik Paint & Body Centers, Inc.: Organizational Structure as of Late 1989**

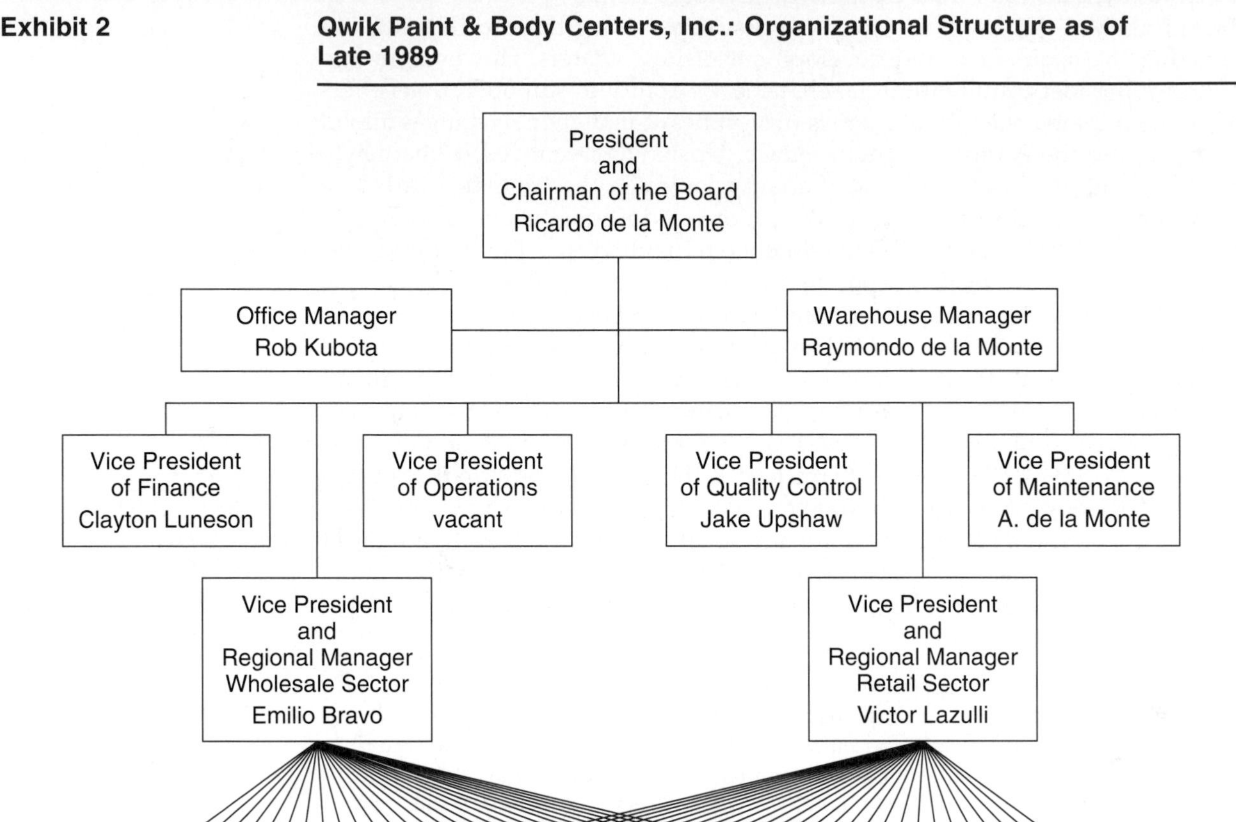

Center Managers of all twenty eight locations

Note: Only the "key" managerial and executive positions are depicted on the above chart.

ness, was hired (August 1990) to fill the new position of director of marketing. Soon thereafter (October 1990), de la Monte resumed executive control and disbanded the office of the president. Six weeks later, he announced (to the surprise of the board and senior management) that he had hired a "professional manager," Philemon Cordova, to whom he would relinquish his duties as president and chief operating officer while retaining the responsibilities of chief executive officer (see Exhibit 3).

A 1979 graduate of the Harvard Business School, 39-year-old Cordova brought both marketing expertise and several years of line experience as vice president of international operations for a large U.S. consumer goods manufacturer. While his lack of experience in the paint and body business was a continuing source of skepticism among several senior executives, Cordova was confident that he possessed the managerial skills to revitalize the company's performance. (See Exhibit 4 for a list of the principal Qwik Paint executives.)

Qwik Paint & Body Centers, Inc.: Organizational Structure as of Late 1990 **Exhibit 3**

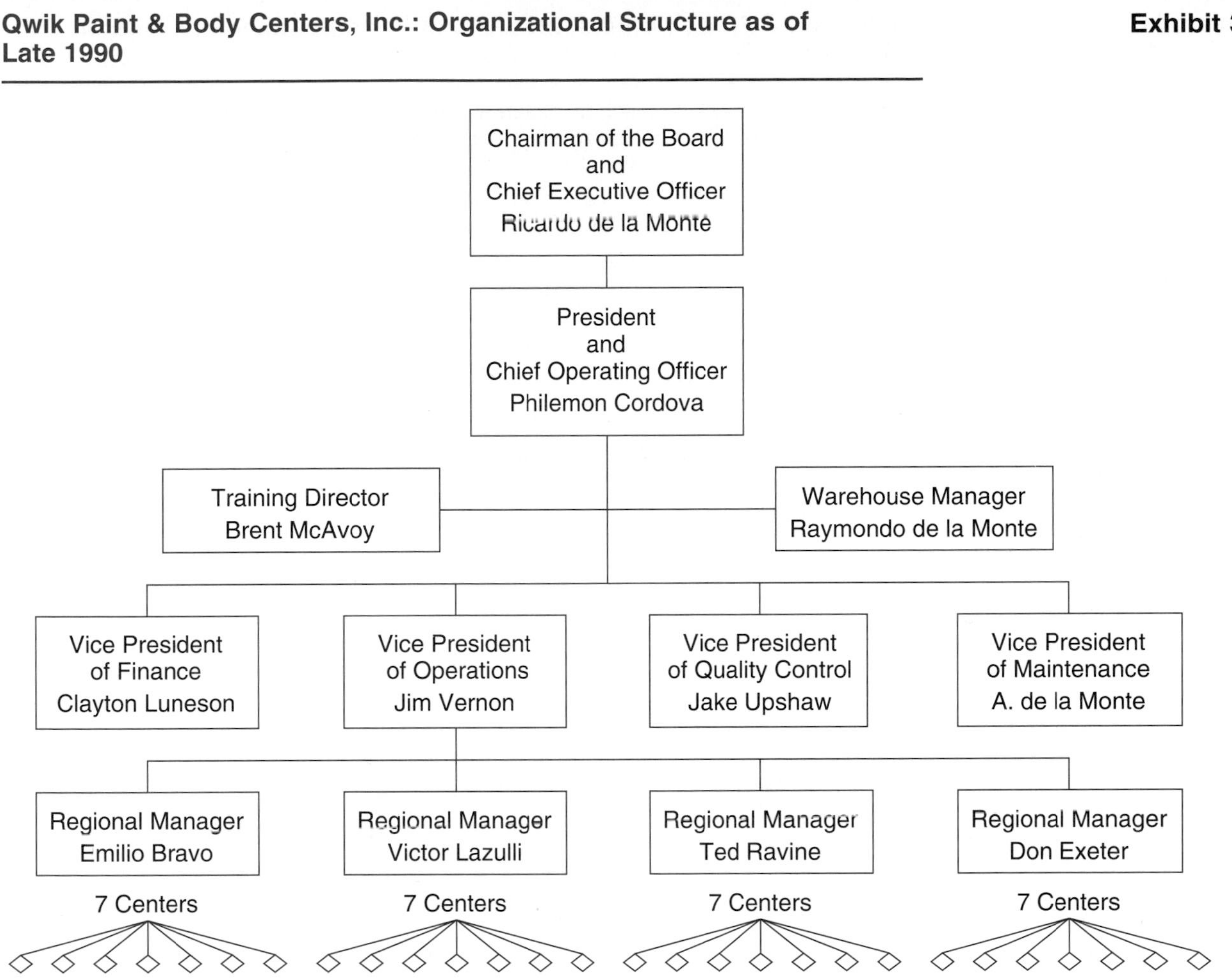

Note: Only the "key" managerial and executive positions are depicted on the above chart.

COMPETITIVE DYNAMICS OF THE BUSINESS

The eight-county southern California region constituted one of the nation's largest markets for paint and body services. Of the estimated 9.8 million passenger cars in the region, approximately 17% required bodywork and/or painting each year. Furthermore, both new passenger car registrations (increasing at an average annual rate of approximately 4.1% during the late 1980s) and the average age of the region's fleet (estimated at 3.8 years in 1990) indicated an expanding market for paint and body services.

■ The Competition

With minimal barriers to entry, this growing market has traditionally been served by hundreds of small, owner-managed shops. In recent years, however, several large companies, including two national chains, have emerged as ma-

Exhibit 4 **Qwik Paint & Body Centers, Inc.: List of Principal Executives as of Early 1991**

Chairman/CEO:	**Ricardo de la Monte,** 53, high school diploma (Texas). Formerly, a regional manager with Schwab Paint Shops. [Founded company in 1972; he and his wife and children own all its stock.]
President/COO:	**Philemon Cordova,** 39, M.B.A. (Marketing), Harvard. Previously, VP—International Operations for large U.S. consumer goods manufacturer. [Hired in November 1990.]
VP—Operations:	**Jim Vernon,** 37, B.A. (Economics), UCLA. Previously founder/manager of small novelty products company (tee-shirt silkscreening). [Hired as marketing director in August 1990. Promoted to vice president in September 1990.]
VP—Finance:	**Clayton Luneson,** 62, B.B.A. (Accounting) Iowa State College. Previous experience as staff accountant in public accounting firms and as owner of small accounting firm. Avid Civil War history buff and collector of hand-guns. [Hired as chief accountant in 1980, and awarded title of vice president in 1982.]
VP—Quality:	**Jake Upshaw,** 58, high school diploma (Chicago). Previously, a regional manager ("super salesman") with Schwab Paint Shops. [Joined company in mid-1973. Made operations VP in 1987. Reassigned as VP—Quality, October 1989.]
"Vice President"/ Regional Manager:	**Emilio Bravo,** 50, high school diploma (Los Angeles). Prior to joining company: maître d' at local restaurant. [Hired as regional manager in 1975. Made VP—Wholesale, October 1989. Back to regional manager, February 1990.]
"Vice President"/ Regional Manager:	**Victor Lazulli,** 55, high school diploma (Brooklyn, N.Y.). Previously, regional manager with Schwab Paint Shops. [Hired as regional manager in 1976. Promoted to VP—Retail, October 1989. Back to regional manager, February 1990.]
Regional Managers: (two relatively recent appointees)	**Ted Ravine,** 43, high school diploma (Georgia). Previously, nearly two decades as master sergeant in U.S. Army. [Hired as center manager, June 1987. Promoted to regional manager, February 1990.] **Don Exeter,** 41, A.A. (Business Management) Orange Coast College. [Hired as center manager, March 1988. Promoted to regional manager, February 1990.]

jor forces. Foremost among these are Day-Glo Paint & Body Shops (a franchise company that is especially strong in southern California), Karl Schwab Paint Shops (a publicly traded company with a chain of company-owned shops), and two smaller chains—Come 'n Go Paint Boutiques and Jiffy Paint & Body Shops.

Although its 225 locations nationwide make Karl Schwab Paint Shops the largest company in the business, Qwik Paint management has not traditionally viewed Schwab as their most serious competitive threat. "First of all," explained Jake Upshaw, "Schwab, with their $99 paint jobs, goes after the *bluest* of the blue-collar workers, while we attract a more upscale clientele—people wanting a quality paint job, without paying a custom paint shop price." Pointing out that because Qwik Paint's usage of superior materials produced a "visibly superior" paint job, Upshaw confided that the average Qwik Paint Center produced about three times the sales volume of the typical Karl Schwab shop.

The other relatively large paint and body companies—Day-Glo, Come 'n Go, and Jiffy—are a more consistent menace in Qwik Paint's southern California stronghold, as they tend to target the same market niche. Indeed, several Qwik Paint executives expressed the belief that these firms' aggressive expansion strategies were aggravating Qwik Paint's turnover problem by "siphoning off" its management. Asserting that Qwik Paint was "widely known for having the best-trained managers in the business," Upshaw stated that competitor "raids" have become such a serious concern that de la Monte, angry over the loss of a couple of good managers, had recently written to one competitor and threatened a lawsuit.

■ The Production Task

The mechanics of transforming a vehicle, with a dented body and a faded or peeling paint cover into a finished product of enhanced value to the customer varies little from one paint and body shop to another. The process begins with the removal of dents and the restoration of the vehicle's metal frame to its original shape. The vehicle is then sanded, after which paint primers are applied and the car is sanded again. It is then masked (with chemically inert paper and tape) and driven into a paint booth where it receives one or two coats of paint, depending on the specific paint job. Before applying the second coat of paint (if any), a few firms apply a coat of sealer paint, which significantly increases the prospects of a trouble-free and lasting paint job. Finally, to prevent the accumulation of atmospheric debris on the freshly painted vehicle, most shops bake the painted automobile in a forced-air "oven" for a predetermined period of time. The vehicle is then "detailed" (i.e., masking materials are removed), vehicle emblems are reinstalled, the painted surface is buffed to remove any imperfections, and areas of paint overspray are corrected. The vehicle is then ready for customer pickup.

■ Qwik Paint Competitive Strategy

According to knowledgeable observers, the automotive services industry has suffered over the years from a tarnished public image, as a result of customer dissatisfaction with shoddy workmanship and/or overcharging. As Jake Upshaw put it, "Everyone knows someone who has dealt with a paint shop, repair shop, or whatever—and got thoroughly ripped off." It has been against this background of an industry with a somewhat spotty reputation that Qwik Paint's competitive strategy had been devised.

As de la Monte surmised in 1972, the universality of the "production" process essentially confined the bases for competitive advantage to locational convenience, quality workmanship, customer service, and price. With both the low- and high-price ends of the market facing strong competition from "pure production" and custom paint shops, de la Monte sought competitive advantage via a strategy of offering the "best value at a fair, competitive price." Thus, a Qwik Paint center's long-term viability depends on the utilization of its resources in such a manner that a reputation for quality workmanship and customer service, at a "fair" price, can be established and maintained.

Qwik Paint executives feel that the company's rise to dominance in the southern California market is evidence of the potency of this strategy, as are findings of a 1990 market research study which indicated that 40% of the company's walk-in business was generated by word-of-mouth advertising from satisfied customers. "We preach that customer satisfaction is *not* a by-product of painting cars," de la Monte explained. "It *is* the product."

Furthermore, while Qwik Paint seeks to generate volume, via a $1 million-a-year, multi-media advertising campaign, executives emphasize that over the long run, advertising is effective only if the centers consistently deliver the quality and service that customers expect. "In our market, no amount of advertising will save you if the word gets out that you do lousy paint jobs," Upshaw averred.

■ Key Operational Tasks

With direct labor and materials consuming approximately 45% of each sales dollar (see Exhibit 5), the preparation of accurate job estimates and the close control of labor and materials constitute key aspects of the center manager's job. Job estimating requires skillful diagnosis of vehicles and realistic estimates of the resources required to transform existing paint jobs into ones of acceptably high quality to the customer.

Inaccurate estimates negatively impact a center's financial performance. With company prices already "somewhat higher than the industry average," overestimates tend to diminish the prospects of a given sale, thereby depressing both revenues and profits. Underestimates have an equally adverse impact, of either an immediate or delayed nature. If the underestimated job is performed at the quality level desired by the customer, future sales (from word-of-mouth advertising from a satisfied customer) would be obtained at the expense of the desired profit margin on the first job. On the other hand, preservation of the desired margin might be attained at the sacrifice of future profits, if the quality of work performed resulted in a dissatisfied customer.

Intentional underestimates also negatively impact profit margins. A fairly widespread practice during the December–February slow season, such "margin shaving" is usually motivated by the desire to obtain sufficient volume to keep intact at least a core production group. Hence, the estimating task frequently involves a "trade-off" between gross margin preservation and crew retention. Center financial performance greatly depends on the effectiveness of those involved in making these "real-time" trade-off analyses—the "mental programs" that are complex and tax the mental agility of all involved in the estimating task.

Qwik Paint executives generally frown on the practice of intentionally underbidding jobs, because of a potentially adverse impact on customer satisfaction. "If, for example," explained Jim Vernon, who became vice president of operations in September 1990, "the bodymen perceive a big discrepancy between the time required to do the bodywork and the amount of gain from their [percentage] commission, they will do a rushed job—and you will have a highly upset customer on your hands." For this reason, center managers are advised to start and stick with a realistic estimate.

ORGANIZATION AND MANAGEMENT OF OPERATIONS

■ Structure

After the 1990 reorganization, the 28 centers were grouped into four regions, supervised by four regional managers who are responsible for assisting the centers in achieving financial targets, in staffing the key center managerial jobs, and in ensuring compliance with company policies. As top management wishes to achieve the "right chemistry" between center and regional manag-

Qwik Paint & Body Centers, Inc.: Qwik Paint Center #19, Statement of Income and Expense: January 1, 1990–June 30, 1990

Exhibit 5

	Month of June		*Year to Date*	
Sales				
Auto painting	$142,959		$636,420	
Body repairing	42,823		186,127	
Materials	8,806		36,110	
Parts & sublet	17,565		70,206	
Total sales		$212,153		$928,863
Cost of sales				
Cost of materials				
Beginning inventory	$ 12,702		$ 12,702	
+ Purchases				
Paint	20,521		68,930	
Supplies	20,186		84,665	
– Ending inventory	12,702		12,702	
Cost of materials	$ 40,707		$153,595	
Direct labor costs				
Painting labor	$ 32,286		$146,148	
Bodywork labor	15,764		72,406	
Cost of direct labor	$ 48,050		$218,554	
Center Overhead				
Payroll taxes	$ 3,176		$ 21,287	
Parts expenses	6,974		27,102	
Sublet expenses	3,892		20,643	
Shop repairs/maintenance	1,919		5,805	
Laundry	256		1,429	
Equipment rental	108		384	
Utilities	1,727		12,262	
Telephone	885		4,367	
Shop damage	404		2,710	
Vacation payroll	2,212		9,474	
Total center overhead	$ 21,553		$105,463	
Total Cost of Sales		–110,310		–477,612
Gross Margin		$101,843		$451,251
Selling Expenses				
Management salaries	$ 20,658		$ 91,850	
Payroll taxes	2,066		9,185	
Total selling expenses		– 22,724		–101,035
Selling Margin		$ 79,119		$350,216

Notes: (i) "Car Cost" consists of cost of materials plus direct labor for painting only. Bodywork labor was not included in "Car Cost" because bodymen worked on a 40% commission.
(ii) Inventory figures were purposely set at identical amounts, and physical inventories were taken only once each year.

ers, the regions are not formed along strictly geographical lines. That is, centers in close proximity to one another are often assigned to different regions, and most centers rotate through the supervision of each of the regional managers.

In early 1991, there were seven classes of centers, based primarily on annual sales volume (see Exhibit 6). With classification determining the permissible number and type of personnel, a center's management team consists of anywhere from two to five persons. For example, class 1 centers, the smallest shops, are permitted only a manager and an outside salesperson, who is responsible for wholesale accounts. Thus, class 1 center managers (with periodic assistance from the outside salesperson) not only supervise production operations, but also write work estimates, perform various recordkeeping tasks, and answer telephone calls. By contrast, class 7 centers, the largest shops, are staffed by a manager, an outside salesperson, a production manager, a counterperson, and a secretary. In these centers, the production manager supervises the production crew, the counterperson assists the manager with work estimates, and the secretary handles administrative chores.

Exhibit 6 **Qwik Paint & Body Centers, Inc.: Center Classification Scheme with Associated Staffing and Salary Levels**

Classes of Centers	*Bonus % and Salary*	*Secretary* < = >		*3rd Assistant* < = >	*2nd Assistant* < = >	*1st Assistant* < = >	*Manager* < = >
Class I: Startup to	Bonus %					4.0%–4.5%	5.0%–5.5%
2 years	Salary					$21.6K	$25.8K
Class II: $250,000–$900,000	Bonus %					4.0%–4.5%	5.0%–5.5%
annual sales	Salary					$21.6K	$25.8K
Class III: $901,000–$1,140,000	Bonus %	None	None	OR	0.5%–1.0%	3.5%–4.0%	4.5%–5.0%
annual sales	Salary	$12K	$14.4K		$21K	$24K	$28.8K
Class IV: $1,141,000–$1,490,000	Bonus %	None	None	AND	0.5%–1.0%	3.5%–4.0%	4.5%–5.0%
annual sales	Salary	$12K	$14.4K		$21K	$26.4K	$31.8K
Class V: $1,491,000–$1,650,000	Bonus %	None	None	0%–0.5%	0.5%–1.0%	3.5%–4.0%	4.5%
annual sales	Salary	$14.4K	$16.8K	$21K	$22.8K	$28.8K	$34.8K
Class VI: $1,651,000–$1,840,000	Bonus %	None	None	0%–0.5%	0.5%–1.0%	3.5%–4.0%	4.5%
annual sales	Salary	$16.8K	$19.2K	$21K	$22.8K	$31.2K	$38.4K
Class VII: $1,841,000–Plus	Bonus %	None	None	0%–0.5%	0.5%–1.0%	3.5%–4.0%	5.0%
annual sales	Salary	$19.2K	$21.5K	$24K	$26K	$34.2K	$42.5K

■ Measurement Systems

De la Monte's motivational philosophy of "goals and controls" underpins Qwik Paint's systems for measuring operations performance. Although both he and Luneson maintain that the only "true" profit center is that of the corporation as a whole, both center and regional managers are responsible for attaining sales and gross margin "targets." Independent of the goals established in the annual planning process, these performance targets are viewed by senior executives as "fixed operating standards."

To determine merit increases (the sole form of annual increments in salary), center managers are evaluated semiannually by their regional managers on such criteria as shop cleanliness, recordkeeping, safety, and the like, while regional managers are evaluated by the vice president of operations on parameters such as leadership, customer complaints, and other administrative aspects of their jobs.

The annual corporate planning and budgeting process consists of a meeting between de la Monte and Luneson, where Luneson reviews the previous year's financial results, projects operating and corporate expenses for the upcoming year, and applies a "growth factor" to arrive at sales and profit targets for the upcoming year. Subsequently broken down by individual center, these projections are neither shared with center managers nor used to evaluate center managers' performance, as Luneson deems it "distracting" for managers to concern themselves with "financial analysis." Aside from these corporate projections, all managers are expected to set challenging daily, weekly, monthly, and quarterly sales and margin goals. Occasionally, de la Monte randomly calls centers to inquire about their goals for a given time period, as well as their progress in meeting them.

■ Reward Systems

Center management personnel are compensated via a combination of salary and a triple-tiered incentive bonus, with the bonus incentives designed to contribute approximately 60% of the effective manager's annual compensation. As of early 1991, the average salary for all class 1 center managers was approximately $30,000, while the average salary for all class 7 center managers was about $45,000.

The quarterly sales bonus is calculated by combining the quarterly salaries of a center's management personnel (including the salary of the secretary, if any) and multiplying that sum by a factor of ten, the result being the "sales bogey." A 10% bonus is paid on the difference between actual sales (minus parts and sublet sales) and the "bogey." For example, if a center's total management salaries for a given quarter were $17,499, the bogey would be $174,990, and the sales bonus would be determined as follows:

Sales Assumptions: (for 1 quarter):	Total sales:	$300,000
	Parts and sublet sales:	– 45,000
	Adjusted sales:	$255,000
Calculation of Sales Bonus:	Adjusted sales:	$255,000
	Sales "bogey":	– 174,990
	Residual:	$ 80,010
	Sales bonus (10%):	**$ 8,001**

A quarterly parts and sublet bonus, equal to 5% of parts and sublet sales and earned when the center attains a 30% markup on vehicle parts, based on a sliding scale, is paid upon achievement of specified gross margin percentage results. (See Exhibit 5 for an illustration of how the Gross Margin is calculated.) Each of these bonuses is divided among center personnel as follows: manager, 50%; outside salesperson, 40%; and production manager, 10%. With the regional manager's approval, a center manager can effect minor adjustments in these bonus-plan allocations to reward particularly outstanding performances during a given quarter.

A noteworthy element of the incentive system is the imposition of penalties if the utilization of direct labor or supplies exceeds established standards. For example, given the output standard of $1\frac{1}{2}$ cars per person per day, a 10-member crew center is expected to produce 15 cars a day. If the center, during a given quarter, falls below this standard, the dollar amount of the "excess" direct labor and supplies is subtracted from whatever bonuses were otherwise payable.

Luneson, vice president of finance, who designed the bonus system in 1981, deems the penalties "an absolute necessity"; they reduced the magnitude because of excess labor and materials costs. He explained:

> Before the penalties, whole *buckets* of paint were just getting up and "walking out" of the shops—*15 or 20 gallons at a shot*—because of "repaints," wastage, and (I suspect) employee theft. So, I devised the standards and went to Ricardo and said, "I will not be responsible for the company's financial health, unless I can zap these guys when they fail to meet any of these standards." "OK," he said, "do it." By golly, now when they hang on to excess crew, or tolerate such poor quality that they end up doing lots of repaints, or whatever—it comes right outta their hides. Yessirree!

Regional managers can earn a maximum $8,000 annual sales bonus and a maximum $27,000 gross margin bonus if their assigned regions achieve specified sales increases and gross margin percentage targets, respectively. Prior to 1989, these bonuses averaged 35%–40% of their total annual compensation. In 1989, however, declining sales and gross margins resulted in comparatively meager bonuses. No regional bonuses were paid in 1990, and early 1991 operating results indicated the improbability of bonuses in 1991.

■ Selection and Retention Issues

With few exceptions, the company develops its own managers in-house. Newspaper advertisements, augmented by referrals from current center managers, are the primary means of attracting future managerial talent. Applicants who pass an initial screening, a series of interviews at corporate headquarters and an aptitude test, are put through a two-week training class covering all aspects of center operations and management. Successful trainees are assigned to the centers as assistant production managers, from which they progress to production manager, then outside salesperson, and eventually to center manager. Prior to 1989, the typical management trainee reached center management grade in approximately three years.

Two recent trends are cause for concern. First, according to the regional managers, outside salespeople are increasingly resisting promotions to center manager jobs. Given the high managerial turnover of 1990, this is alarming, prompting concerns about what can be done to "restore [their] ambition." Second, there are increased center manager "grumblings" about limited opportunities for further advancement. "We are in something of a double-bind," Brent McAvoy, training director, opined. "We cannot expand until we stabilize and stop losing experienced people, but we cannot stabilize unless we are growing and giving managers advancement opportunities."

■ Production Shop Operators

A medium-sized center (e.g., class 4) employs a shop crew of 12 to 15 people—four or five bodymen, three or four sanders, two or three maskers, a pre-detailer, a painter, and a detailer/driver. (It might also have a full-time spotman, if required by the volume of partial paint jobs.) Stationed by task specialty within the shop, these employees are supervised by the production manager—aided, in a larger center, by either an assistant production manager (i.e., a trainee) or a "shop foreman" (usually a senior sander).

Smooth running of the production line entails tracking customer vehicles, monitoring individual task groups, and controlling labor and materials usage. To facilitate vehicle tracking, centers maintain a large "production board" indicating the whereabouts of each vehicle within the production line. To facilitate production control, managers are expected to compare regularly the performance of each task team against established output and quality standards (e.g., the paint usage standard of one gallon per vehicle). Close monitoring of team performance permits ready assessments of the center's progress in attaining desired operating results.

With the exception of bodymen, all production workers are paid hourly wages. The painter is the highest paid (at an average rate of $9.50 an hour), while the pre-detailer or detailer usually earns the lowest wage (averaging approximately $5 an hour). Additionally, each task group can earn a bonus upon attainment of specified performance levels. For example, painters receive a $5.50/car bonus after painting the first 60 cars in a week, while sanders earn a $1.75/car bonus after sanding the first 20 vehicles in a day.

Bodymen, considered to be akin to "independent contractors," are paid a straight 40% commission on the bodywork portion of the job estimate. Top management feels that this system simplifies daily staffing decisions and eliminates "freeloading," as the bodymen control their own work pace and are free to leave upon completion of a day's work. "Being on commission," Upshaw stated, "they have no reason to drag out the work, but if there is lots of work they go at it like madmen because the more they do, the more they make."

VIEWS FROM "THE TRENCHES": CENTER MANAGER PERSPECTIVES

Center managers confront a variety of challenges in achieving and sustaining acceptable center performance levels—that is, those that triggered the desired financial and career rewards. The following comments capture their views on various aspects of their task responsibilities.

■ Views of the Manager's Job

Beyond voicing the widespread belief that they are "the real pros in the industry" and that their managerial effectiveness is "unsurpassed," nearly all center managers acknowledge the reasons for their high "burnout" rate, as captured in these comments by an 11-year veteran manager:

> It takes a certain kind of breed to deal with these constant, daily pressures. We get to our centers at about seven every morning, Monday through Saturday. Aside from Saturday (which is just a half-day), it is usually around eight o'clock when we get home (later on Fridays, because that is our big day in terms of customers picking up their cars). Weeks can pass where you literally do not see any daylight hours; you are driving to and from work in the dark. Home is basically a place to sleep and, maybe on the weekends, to eat. . . . I have to believe that all the intensity—the pressures—has to have some effect on the quality of home life a manager can have. I know I sometimes take these frustrations home with me. And sometimes I see some of our managers who are married at one point, and then you see them a few months later, and they are divorced or something. So at times, I wonder, "is this what the job is doing to us?"

The manager of another center describes his job as "a continuous juggling act inside [of] a pressure-cooker environment." The "normal pressures" (e.g., to meet sales targets, control costs, and keep the crew intact) have become even more intense of late, he explained, due to low interest rates on new-car loans which are dampening consumer interest in "fixing up the old clunker." Stating that managers are scrambling just to attain results comparable to those of the previous year, he admits that "at times, you almost reach a point of saying, 'I cannot take it any more, let me out!' "

Further complications in the process of maintaining effective management teams are personnel transfers to fill vacancies created by resignations and promotions. "As soon as you get a good team going," complained one manager, "the supervisor comes along and reassigns a team member to another center. This is happening now about every three months."

■ View of the Production Crew

The maintenance of a skilled, motivated crew is a major challenge for managers. Highly skilled painters and bodymen are always in demand, and filling vacancies in these categories often requires the regional manager's assistance. Further, at certain centers, even the sourcing of less-skilled people (e.g., sanders) is problematic, as these physically demanding, low-paying jobs are unattractive to many American workers. Hence, immigrant workers hold the majority of the production jobs.

Crew retention is most frequently cited by managers as the most challenging aspect of the job. "Turnover in the shop just destroys a center," stated one class 7 manager. "To avoid ruining our P&L's with a lot of repaints, we have to keep quality up and turnovers down," he said, noting that as "the key" to building a center's reputation for quality workmanship.

Minimizing production-crew turnover is particularly difficult during the winter months because production costs and margins can be greatly affected by decisions about the number of employees to retain for a relatively brief span of time. During this season, managers constantly walk a thin line between retaining too many and too few crew members. Although margins can be maintained by running the shop with a skeletal crew, this tactic entails the risk of not having a crew to call upon when the sales volume increases. "They [crew members] do not sit around waiting for you to call them back," explained one manager. "They leave town."

Given the crew's critical role in determining a center's long-term viability, managers emphasize the importance of a "people-oriented" approach to motivating production personnel. It is important, they feel, to make the crew's job as pleasant as possible. "Let's face it," one allowed, "their jobs are not the easiest in the world. Otherwise, folks would be standing in line to be hired." In addition to listening to the crew's concerns, managers emphasize the importance of monetary rewards for exceptional performance. Occasionally, these rewards are given from the manager's own pocket. "Yeah, I could put it on my payroll," acknowledged one manager, "but it might be just enough to screw up car costs—in which case, there goes my gross margin bonus."

Even managers who deem their crews among the best in the company wonder what might be done to heighten their employee's shop-wide focus and team spirit. Admitting that vehicles are sometimes "lost in the line," one such manager lamented that when each team finished its own task, "they are finished, as far as they are concerned." How to make crew members more attentive to the whole series of tasks performed on vehicles is the perennial challenge of every manager.

■ Views of Customer Relations

Despite the company's commitment to the maintenance of excellent customer relations, managers acknowledge that rarely a week passes without the occurrence of a customer complaint—a few of which end up in small claims court. Most of these problems can be attributed to (1) not "qualifying" the written estimate—that is, not specifying items to be excluded in the contracted job; (2) "overselling" the quality of work to be performed—for example, representing that the finished vehicle would look "brand new"; (3) not following through with the crew on promises made to the customer; and (4) not inspecting the completed vehicle prior to its presentation to the customer.

In selling, it is sometimes wiser to forego a sale rather than make inappropriate promises. However, much "overselling," as well as failure to qualify estimates, stem from pressures to meet quotas. "We will tell the customer anything he wants to hear [in order] to make the sale," confessed one seasoned manager. "Then, as the day gets hectic, you forget that one promise out of dozens made that day, even though, initially, you had every intention of following through."

Managers agree that limited selling time tends to increase the incidence of customer relations problems. "Sometimes I feel I am cheating customers by only giving them five or ten minutes of my time," stated a recently appointed manager. "When you are charging someone maybe $750 for a paint job, you would like to be able to spend more time with him, to fully understand his needs. But, with my other responsibilities, I just cannot spend too much time with any one customer."

The tendency to "get [customers] in and get them out as fast as possible" is confirmed by several veteran managers. "When they come back to get their car," explained one, "you do not have time to do the proper presentation. You usually end up saying something like, 'Hi, Mr. Customer, here is your car. That will be $900, please. Thank you, see you later!' "

Agreeing with this view of the origins of many customer relations problems, another manager cites a recent example of a customer complaint created by managerial time pressures:

> If I had had more time to spend with this guy, I would have discouraged him from leaving the car in the first place [because] he was being just too precise about every little thing. Anyhow, after taking the car in, I tried to follow it in the production line to make sure that we did everything called for in the contract. But, somehow, somewhere along the way, his bumper got a tiny little scratch on it. I personally did not have time to do the final inspection, so the scratch was not spotted before he came back for the car. When he saw it, he came completely unglued. I offered to repair, or even replace, the bumper and [to] pay for a rental car for him. But, he arrived that day in such a negative mood [that] there was just no pleasing him. . . . The last I heard, he is suing us.

■ Views of Recent Company Performance

In addition to their view that instability "at the top" has contributed to Qwik Paint's loss of ground, managers attribute the decline in performance to several sources. Foremost among these is the intense competition. "The competition gets stronger each year," asserted a long-time veteran. "We cannot match their prices, so we have to compete on quality and service."

Second, regarding the managerial turnover, managers complain that bonus earnings in 1990 deteriorated to the point where a few managers were experiencing financial difficulty. "If you are used to living off $60,000 a year," commented one manager, "it is a shock to discover that this year you are going to have to 'make do' with $45,000."

Finally, a sizable number of managers complain of a "lack of support" and "hostile attitudes" from their regional managers. One veteran manager offered graphic citations of the kind of supervisory behaviors displayed during his regional manager's periodic visits: "surprise visits at seven o'clock in the morning, ten-minute 'tongue-lashings' for minor infractions, intense 'grillings' for failing to meet sales targets and for running a 'disaster-zone' shop area, and other conduct which has the effect of 'demoralizing the whole team' in the space of a two-hour visit."

The following comments by a newer manager, supervised by a different regional manager, are indicative of what center managers mean by "lack of [regional manager] support":

> He is always saying, "No excuses, just results." Yet, if you ask him for help, he will say, "Oh, come on, you know how to do that!" And you know you had better say, "Oh, yeah, I do—sorry." Yet, all the time you know you do not know how to do that; you need help. So, what do you do? You try not to give him any bad news—even if it means sometimes being a little "creative" when he asks how many cars you have taken in. You just hope to make the numbers before he gets your P&L sheet.

VIEWS FROM THE MIDDLE: REGIONAL MANAGER PERSPECTIVES

According to regional managers, the decline in performance and the recent high turnover among center managers spring from a common set of problems: "unrealistic" performance expectations and increasingly intense competition. Additionally, top management's "interference" in operations, "nondisclosure" of certain financial data, and "infighting" among themselves are seen as contributing factors.

■ Performance Targets

Given that low interest rates are negatively impacting sales throughout the industry, regional managers view top management's expectation of annual increases in sales and the 48% gross margin target as totally unrealistic. "Last year, the companywide gross margin was just 45%," fumed one of the relatively new regional managers. "Ricardo and Luneson are still living in the past, when interest rates were high and we had no real competition."

Contending that "some centers have simply 'maxed' out," regional managers argue that the bonus system should be revised in order to eliminate a major source of disgruntlement—that is, the fact that few center managers and no regional managers qualified for bonuses in 1990. "There has got to be some recognition of the increased difficulty of attaining the bonuses," reasoned a newer regional manager.

■ Operational Autonomy

A second concern is that of perceived interference in the supervisory role of the regional managers. Pointing out that de la Monte's tendency to maintain active involvement in operations eviscerated their authority and credibility, one particularly outspoken regional manager complained: "Certain managers—Ricardo's 'pets'—know as well as we do that they can always appeal to de la Monte and get whatever decision we make reversed."

■ Financial Data

Another concern involves the type, amount, and timeliness of financial data shared with regional managers and their center managers. In particular, the absence of pricing information on supplies (from the company's warehouse) at the time of order is viewed as impeding center cost control. ["Hogwash," Luneson had exclaimed, when approached about the issue. "If a guy needs 'X' gallons of paint at the time of his order, how would price data make him a 'better' manager?" Pointing out that managers are responsible for controlling supplies usage, not prices, he bristled: "If they keep this in mind, they will do just fine on their P&L's."]

Cost allocation methods are another source of discontent. In particular, the allocation to individual centers of a pro rata share of supplies cost (based on the total supplies costs incurred by all centers in a given month)—in lieu of providing center-specific, precise cost data—is viewed by regional and center managers alike as penalizing the efficient manager. Labeling this aspect of the accounting system "a joke," one regional manager stated: "When we go over the P&L's with our managers, they say, 'Geez, but, I did not use that much paint last month!' And, they are right."

Although the company began obtaining paint in $\frac{3}{4}$-gallon containers in 1989 (the amount required for the average paint job), centers were still being charged for a full gallon on their P&L's. For these reasons, all quickly agreed when one regional manager declared: "None of us has an ounce of faith in the P&L's."

■ Intragroup Relations

The final vexing concern of regional managers is the lack of cooperative teamwork among themselves. They individually decry their constant "political" behaviors, conduct motivated, they agree, by the desire to "look better than the other guy." Cited examples include the nonsharing of information about operations innovations, personnel availability, and other matters of potential benefit to the entire group. Yet, given both the continued mutual recriminations between Lazulli and Bravo and the majority perception of the fourth regional manager as "a one-man team [who was] strictly out for himself," none foresee a near-term change in their strained relationships.

■ Bravo and Lazulli Concerns

Additionally, the two regional managers have their own particular complaints, largely centering on the evolution of their relationship with de la Monte. In particular, both men perceive a loss of the "one-for-all, all-for-one family spirit" that prevailed in earlier times. Stating that de la Monte is "not the same caring, generous person" of years past, Lazulli traced this perceived change to the arrival of "that shiny-pants accountant, the so-called 'financial genius' ":

> That is when [de la Monte] started coming down hard on Bravo and me with stuff like: "You are not managing properly, you are driving me to ruin!" Yet, he [Luneson] has never once set foot in one of our centers—not once!

Finally, both men blame de la Monte for the bitter rivalry that led to their 1990 demotions. With Lazulli vigorously concurring, Bravo asserts that de la Monte himself declared that the "winner" of the 1989 wholesale-retail competition would become the next vice president of operations. "Then he sacks us," continued Bravo, "when I became so successful in increasing wholesale business that our overall margin dropped—because Victor here just could not keep on the retail side." [Victor: "No. Emilio, you sabotaged my efforts on the retail side, and you know it!"]

VIEWS FROM THE TOP: SENIOR MANAGER PERSPECTIVES

Within senior management, there exists two divergent sets of views on the causes of the company's deteriorating performance. De la Monte, Upshaw, and Luneson describe the problem as a "lack of motivation" among regional managers and a neglect of the "basic fundamentals" of managing the business by center managers. This trio subscribe to a view best captured by de la Monte's succinct pronouncement that "there is nothing wrong with our management systems; they have proven their effectiveness through time." Increased emphasis on operating goals and controls is their proposed remedy.

More compelling to Cordova, Vernon, and McAvoy are center and regional manager complaints of a lack of both operating autonomy and effective levers with which to obtain consistently high levels of performance from their respective teams. Along with diminishing bonuses, these dissatisfactions are seen as driving the high turnover rate among center managers. This troika deems it of paramount importance to "tackle the underlying problem, not just the symptoms."

Additionally, Cordova and others are uncomfortable with the "assumptions" underlying some of the administrative systems. The penalties, in particular, are seen as "perpetuat[ing] an adversarial relationship," thereby contributing to the mistrust with which many center managers view corporate actions. Describing Luneson's approach to motivation as being "straight out of the Dark Ages," Vernon prefers "positively [motivating] people, not pouncing on them with these 'Gotcha!' kinds of controls at every opportunity." This trio desires changes that will reduce top management's "having to play 'cop' day in and day out."

Luneson, however, as the originator of the penalties, is adamantly opposed to their removal. Describing the penalty system as "just great," he argues that it "made the fellas much better managers, despite what some 'newcomers' may think." In his view, the penalties are precisely the kind of "strict control" required "to avoid financial disaster." "You cannot go pussyfooting around in this business," he warned. "Nosirree! This is no Nordstrom's!"

Another divergence in views among senior managers concerns their perceptions of the causes of the two veteran regional managers' "negativity." While most executives tend to dismiss Lazulli and Bravo as "chronic malcontents," Cordova surmises that at the crux of their disaffection was an abiding belief that the promises made when they initially joined Qwik Paint—promises about becoming "wealthy" when the company went public—have not been kept. However, with de la Monte's having heatedly dismissed Cordova's suggestion that he (de la Monte) seek to resolve the matter directly with Lazulli and Bravo, Cordova foresees a continuation of the current impasse and friction.

This prognosis is shared by Vernon, operations vice president, who has grown weary of attempting to effect changes in Lazulli and Bravo's outlook and attitudes. Stating that de la Monte has only "vacillated" each time the subject of terminating the two men has been broached, Vernon confesses that the impasse has begun to give him "nightmares." "After all," he asked rhetorically, "where else on this planet can those two 'birds' go, with their high school educations, and draw their $90,000-a-year salaries?"

THE IMMEDIATE CHALLENGE

Given the severity of the array of problems confronting Qwik Paint & Body Centers, Cordova believes that central to any actions to be taken is the overriding objective of bolstering the company's competitive position by stabilizing the operations area. Thus, it is imperative, he concludes, that he soon determine what, if any, changes are needed in the organization and management of operations to enhance the company's ability to deliver consistently high quality and customer service at each center.

CASE 21

Spec's Music

Carol A. Reeves, University of Arkansas

Ann Spector Lieff, CEO of Florida-based Spec's Music and Video, was proud of her company's accomplishments since she had become CEO 10 years ago, but she felt some concern as she looked over the company's financial statements. After years of growth in revenues and earnings, Spec's had experienced its first earnings decline in 1990. Although the company's revenues increased by 23 percent to $49 million, earnings fell by 11 percent to approximately $2 million. Management had expected a decline in performance due to a rapid expansion in the number of Spec's stores and was convinced that in future years earnings would return to their old rates as new stores became profitable. However, the music and video retailing industries were experiencing some decline that had troubled all of retailing during the recession that began in 1990, and it was uncertain when this decline would end. Ms. Lieff was faced with difficult choices regarding whether the company should continue its past growth given this tough economic environment.

SPEC'S HISTORY

After practicing law for a few years in the late 1920s, Martin Spector became a talent agent in the entertainment industry, a career that culminated with a two-year stint as head of talent for Universal Pictures after World War II. In 1948, Mr. Spector moved to Miami with his wife and young son and opened a retail store that sold records, cameras, and televisions. The store, which bore his nickname, Spec, provided a solid means of support for the growing Spector family, which soon included two sons and two daughters.

All of the Spector children worked at Spec's on the weekends and during the holidays when they were growing up. The two sons worked for the com-

Copyright © 1991 by Carol A. Reeves. This case is intended for classroom discussion only, not to depict effective or ineffective handling of administrative situations. All rights reserved to the authors and the North American Case Research Association.

pany for a short period of time after school, but neither decided to pursue a career with Spec's. Roz, the oldest daughter and second child, began working for Spec's full-time after graduating from Washington University with a degree in English in 1972. She has served as Treasurer since 1979 and executive vice president since 1980. Ann, the third child, earned a degree in sociology from the University of Denver in 1974 and has been working for the company since that time. She worked in a variety of positions from 1974 to 1980, including buyer, store manager, regional supervisor, and vice president.

Martin Spector called his daughters into his office in 1980 and transferred all of his stock to them, primarily for estate planning purposes. In addition, Ann assumed the roles of president and CEO from her father. The stock transfer had little impact at the time; the stock was not traded and Mr. Spector retained preferred stock, which gave him considerable decision-making power in the company. However, in 1984, the Spectors decided that the company had to expand if it was to remain competitive with the national chains that were beginning to enter the Florida market. Since 1948, the chain had grown gradually, and by 1985 had sales of $16 million from its 16 stores. All Spec's stores had been financed from the operations of the company, but new growth would require the use of outside funds.

An initial public offering (IPO) of stock in Spec's was made in October 1985. The offering was oversubscribed, with 660,000 shares being sold at $6.00 each. The net proceeds from the sale were $3,457,254, which were used to finance the company's expansion outside of South Florida.[1] Over the next five years the chain grew rapidly, and by the end of 1990, the company operated 57 stores and had revenues of over $50 million.

Although Mr. Spector was 85 years old in 1990, he was still very active in the business. He served as chairman of the board and his daughters still consulted him on major decisions. Ann and Roz still follow the business practices that their father established with his first store. Spec's is known in the industry for its high ethical standards, a trait regarded as rare in the music business. Mr. Spector has attributed the growth of the company to a philosophy based on paying the bills on time, taking care of key employees, and treating the customers well so they will tell others about the store and become frequent customers. According to Ms. Lieff, "We don't take short cuts and we aren't greedy. We're more concerned about being ethical and profitable than with getting big."

PRERECORDED MUSIC INDUSTRY

The year 1990 marked the eighth consecutive year of growth in the prerecorded music industry. Unit shipments increased 8.1 percent to 865.7 million units. Dollar volume, calculated by suggested retail price, rose 16.7 percent to $7.54 billion. Exhibit 1 contains a recording industry sales profile from 1980 to 1990.

Although past growth in the industry has been favorable, the outlook for the near future is less optimistic. Retailers reported dismal sales for the first six

[1]Ann Lieff and Rosalind Zacks each owned 700,000 of the 1,400,000 shares of stock in the company at the end of 1985. After an additional 660,000 shares were purchased in the IPO, the daughters each controlled 35 percent of the stock of the company.

Exhibit 1 **Recording Industry Sales Profile**

	Units		Value of Shipments		% of $ Value, by Format				
Year	*Mil.*	*% Change*	*Mil.$*	*% Change*	*Cassettes*	*CDs*	*LPs/EPs*	*Singles*	*8-Track*
1990*	865.7	+8.1	$7,541.1	+16.7	46.0	45.8	1.1	4.8	Nil
1989	800.7	+5.1	$6,464.1	+3.3	51.7	40.0	3.4	4.8	Nil
1988	761.9	+7.8	$6,254.8	+12.3	54.1	33.4	8.5	4.0	Nil
1987	706.8	+14.3	$5,567.5	+19.7	53.2	28.6	14.2	3.9	0.1
1986	618.3	–5.4	$4,651.1	+6.4	53.7	20.0	21.1	4.9	0.2
1984	679.8	+17.6	$4,370.4	+14.6	54.5	2.4	34.4	6.8	0.8
1983	578.0	+0.1	$3,814.3	+4.7	47.5	NM	44.3	7.1	0.7
1982	577.7	–9.1	$3,641.6	–8.3	38.0	NM	52.9	7.8	1.3
1981	635.4	–7.1	$3,969.9	+2.8	26.8	NM	59.0	6.5	7.8
1980	683.7	–2.5	$3,862.4	+4.8	20.1	NM	59.3	7.0	13.6

Source: Adapted from the Recording Industry Association of America.

Note: Sales represent manufacturer shipments, net of returns; dollar values based on suggested retail prices, which often exceed actual prices. NM = not meaningful.

*Estimated.

months of 1991. The industry's two largest competitors, Musicland and Trans World Music, had chainwide sales decreases of 5 percent and 7 percent, respectively, for the first quarter (Verna & Christman, 1991). Trans World's sales increased 11 percent for the second quarter, but some store sales decreased 8 percent. Analysts believe that the rest of the industry has experienced a similar decline, which has been attributed to the recession, a decrease in mall traffic, and lack of blockbuster hits.

In the past, the music industry has been considered recession-proof because of the low prices of its products. However, the demographic makeup of the country is changing, making the industry more vulnerable to economic downturns. Buyers under 30 years of age purchased 65 percent of all music in 1988. The growth rate of this segment has been declining and will continue to decline through the year 2000. Conversely, the 35–54 age group is expected to grow substantially, and this group must increase its music purchases if the industry is to grow at previous rates. As detailed below, several other issues are currently confronting the music industry.

■ Technological Changes

Technological changes have accounted for much of the growth in the music industry. When superior recording and playback technologies are introduced, music buyers begin to replace their old collections with the new format. Vinyl albums, which accounted for most music sales in 1982, are practically nonexistent now, comprising less than 1 percent of sales. CDs, which were nonexistent in 1982, now account for 45 percent of sales and are still growing in popularity. Only 25 percent of U.S. households own a CD player, and as they become more accepted, the music industry expects sales to increase as individuals replace their vinyl albums with CDs.

A few years ago, it was expected that digital audio tape (DAT) would replace CDs as the music medium of choice. DAT offers the advantage of digital sound while allowing users to record music onto the tape. However, DAT machines are expensive ($1000) and music producers declined to record music on DAT because of concerns with noncompensated reproduction.

A more promising technology, the digital compact cassette (DCC), was unveiled by Philips Electronics in April 1992. DCC players, unlike DAT machines, can play both analog and digital tapes. This will allow consumers to continue to listen to their old tapes but buy new music in the digital format. All of the DCC machines have the Serial Copy Management System (SCMS) to prevent multiple digital copies from being made. The DCC machine will retail initially for approximately $600, and prices are expected to drop fairly quickly, making DCC much more affordable than the DAT machines.

Sony announced in 1992 that it will introduce a new CD player that can record. Sony's CD player will use a 2.5-inch disc that won't work on current CD players, tempering optimism about the new format. Most experts believe that a recordable CD player that is compatible with current CD players will be available within a few years.

■ Longbox

Increasing concern about the environment has created pressure on the music industry to eliminate wasteful packaging on CDs, which are packaged in 6 × 12 inch boxes (longboxes). Retailers like the longboxes because the length facilitates displays, the size makes shoplifting more difficult, and old LP fixtures can be used to display them. However, environmentalists and lawmakers have chosen the longbox to illustrate the problem with wasteful packaging in this country. Although retailers had been adamant in their support of the longbox, in 1991 the National Association of Record Merchandisers (NARM) agreed to support a 5 × 11 inch version of the longbox, which has no cardboard or jewel box (plastic case). This version has yet to be adopted and it remains unclear whether the reduced size will satisfy critics.

■ Label Stickering

In early 1990, the music industry was deluged with complaints about the lyrics on "As Nasty As They Want to Be," an album by rap group 2 Live Crew. In several states, sales clerks and store managers were arrested and charged with distribution of obscenity for selling the album. Bills restricting sales of obscene music were introduced in 15 states. In response, many record merchandisers placed stickers on music that was judged to contain offensive lyrics and adopted a voluntary 18-to-buy policy for this music. Retailers then came under attack for not protecting First Amendment rights to freedom of speech.

The state bills were defeated and the furor over obscene lyrics has diminished, at least for the present. Some merchandisers have rescinded their 18-to-buy policies, but in more conservative parts of the country, including Florida, most retailers have continued restricting sales of stickered products. Although it has hurt sales, Spec's has continued its 18-to-buy policy because management believes that its customers desire the policy.

■ Shrinkage

One of the most persistent problems for retailers is shrinkage, or theft by customers and employees. In the industry, an average of 3 percent of a store's inventory will be lost due to shrinkage. For a medium-sized firm like Spec's, every percentage point in shrinkage can mean losses of up to $500,000. For a large chain, a percentage point in shrinkage can result in losses of up to $3 million. Merchants estimate that internal theft accounts for approximately half of shrinkage.

The most common methods used to reduce shrinkage include electronic article surveillance gates, two-way mirrors, video cameras, and increased customer service. A good point-of-sale (POS) system, which can track returns, voids, and inventory, is very effective at preventing internal pilferage. Spec's has installed an advanced POS system and hired a director of loss prevention to combat theft, which is a particular problem in the Miami area.

■ Record Manufacturers

Six record manufacturers and distribution companies dominate the prerecorded music business. They are Time-Warner of the United States, Bertelsmann AG (RCA/Ariola) of West Germany, Sony Corp. (CBS–Columbia and Epic) of Japan, Matsushita Electric Industrial, Ltd. (MCA and Geffen) of Japan, Thorn-EMI (EMI and Capitol) of Britain, and the Netherlands' Dutch Philips Industries (Polygram). Matsushita's purchase of MCA and Sony's purchase of

CBS Records has resulted in the joining of music hardware and software for these Japanese firms, causing concern among music retailers that the companies will give away their software to promote their hardware.

Effective advertising campaigns are critical to bringing customers into record stores. To promote their albums, record producers engage in cooperative advertising with retailers. However, cooperative advertising dollars go to larger retailers because of their ability to advertise on a large scale and reach more customers. Larger accounts are also able to participate in promotional appearances by recording stars. Smaller accounts do not enjoy these benefits, making it much more difficult for them to compete with regional and national chains.

The six music manufacturers accounted for 95 percent of the sales of pop music in 1990. The last major independent record producer, Geffen Records, was sold to MCA for $545 million in 1990. The consolidation in the industry and dominance of six firms worry many insiders, who fear that creativity in the industry will decline. Independents have traditionally been the source of most new trends in the music industry but now have minimal clout. Industry experts are concerned that if it had not been for the boost in sales provided by CDs, retail sales would have declined precipitously in the late 1980s, due to a lack of exciting recordings from new and existing artists. Music manufacturers and retailers depend on blockbuster hits for a substantial portion of their sales, but without the innovative sounds that are often discovered and developed by independent manufacturers, there is concern whether new music interesting enough to stimulate substantial sales will be forthcoming.

The gross margins on cassettes average 5 percent higher than for CDs. In 1990, music retailers complained to manufacturers that CD prices should be lowered to encourage more purchases of this format. In response, music manufacturers raised the price of cassettes, thus decreasing the price differential between the two formats. The average list price for CDs is $11.53 and for tapes, $7.46. However, popular tapes have been listing for $10.98, while popular CDs list for $15.98.

Music retailers are allowed to return products ordered from the record manufacturers but are charged a "disincentive fee," which is generally 5 percent, for returns. When music is ordered, retailers are granted a 1 percent incentive on their total purchases, making the breakeven point for returns 20 percent. If fewer titles are returned, the retailer makes money; if more titles are returned, the retailer loses money. Thus, careful inventory management can result in significant savings for retailers. Spec's returned 11 percent of its inventory to manufacturers in 1990, but the figure for 1991 was higher.

VIDEO INDUSTRY

The video rental industry grew sharply in the 1980s, with consumer expenditures on videocassette rentals and sales reaching an estimated $10–$12 billion in 1990. However, growth slowed dramatically in 1989 to 7 percent, and a 6 percent growth rate is projected through 1993. The slowdown in video sales and rentals has been attributed to the declining number of homes acquiring VCRs for the first time. Approximately 70 percent of U.S. homes own VCRs, and sales and rentals of videotapes decline significantly after the first year of ownership.

As most consumers want to rent hit movies, video stores that have the resources to stock an adequate number of hits have a tremendous advantage over competitors who must rely on older movies supplemented by a few copies of hit movies. The "mom-and-pop" rental stores that dominated the video rental industry in its infancy have largely been pushed out by national and regional chains because of the high capital expenditures needed to stock hot titles, advertise effectively, and install sophisticated computerized inventory systems.

Many music retailers, including Spec's, have found synergy with video rentals. Virtually all stores that are part of the major music chains sell prerecorded videos. In addition, many of these stores rent videos.

The largest national video competitor is Blockbuster Video, based in Ft. Lauderdale, Florida. Blockbuster had sales of $633 million and controlled 11 percent of the national video market in 1990. With 1600 stores, CEO H. Wayne Huizenga claims that Blockbuster is 17 times larger than its next largest competitor and is bigger than the next 99 of its competitors combined (Altaner, 1991). Blockbuster owns approximately half of its stores and operates the other half under franchise agreements. Huizenga predicted that Blockbuster would have 2000 stores by the end of 1991 and grow at a rate of 20–30 percent in future years.

■ The Future of Video

A current concern of many video rental outlets is the declining price studios are charging for new video film releases. Films intended to go to the rental market retail for $90 and smash hits, such as *Ghost*, carry a $99 price tag. At this price, most consumers opt to rent the movie rather than purchase it. However, several hit movies, including *E.T.*, *Roger Rabbit*, and *Home Alone*, have been priced at $24.95 or less, which has prompted consumers to purchase the films rather than rent them. The volume generated by lower-priced films has made it lucrative for the film studios to release films for the consumer rather than the rental market, and the price for some of these films has now dropped to $14.95.

At $10 billion, revenues from home videos are twice the revenues movie studios receive from movie theaters. This gives video stores clout with the studios and they have pressured the studios to change their low-price policies. In response, some studios are discontinuing mass market pricing on new releases or are granting a two- to three-week window before releasing tapes at volume prices. However, if the revenues from sales at the lower prices prove substantial, movie studios may increase their efforts at selling films to consumers.

The evolution of pay-per-view (PPV) technology may have a dramatic effect on the video rental industry in the future. Time-Warner, Inc., is experimenting with a 150-channel fiber-optic cable system that would allow consumers to order movies into their homes for $4.95. Users would have access to 10 different titles running continuously with start times staggered every 30 minutes. AT&T recently announced that it is teaming up with TCI cable and US West phone company for the first large-scale test of video-on-demand. Their project, called Viewer Controlled Cable Television (VCCTV), consists of two services. One would allow customers to choose from 1000 theatrical and special-interest titles that they can watch at any time. The other service would allow customers to select from approximately fifteen features, scheduled to start every 15 minutes, on a pay-per-view basis. Although a price for the service has not been disclosed, officials say it will be competitive with rentals (Verna, 1991a).

These cable systems go a long way toward overcoming the main disadvantage of pay-per-view, the lack of choice regarding programming and timing. However, they are still not true video-on-demand systems and some experts believe that the technology for this is still 15 to 20 years away. Other experts believe that the advances in video compression capabilities are progressing rapidly enough to make pay-per-view a formidable competitor to video rentals within 5 years.

The key to the feasibility of pay-per-view and video-on-demand systems may be the movie studios. If the studio cannot realize sufficient revenues from the new systems, they may continue to delay releases of hot titles to cable companies until their movies are no longer generating a large volume of video sales and/or rentals. Without attractive movies to show, the cable companies are unlikely to attract enough viewer interest to make the systems cost effective.

COMPETITION

Three trends have dominated the retail music industry since 1985: consolidation, public firms being acquired and taken private, and a growth in the number of retail outlets. Many regional companies have been bought out by the major players in the industry, who have grown much larger through these acquisitions and store openings. Three major music retailers, The Musicland Group, Wherehouse Entertainment, and Sound Warehouse, have been taken private since the beginning of 1988. The top 25 music chains by store count at the end of 1990 are presented in Exhibit 2.

Competition in the Florida area has become intense over the past decade as national chains recognized that Florida has a very favorable demographic base. The state's population grew by more than three million persons, an increase of 32.7 percent, during the 1980s (Smith and Shahidullah, 1991). Although the state has a large retirement community, it also has a rapidly growing younger population. As all music retailers sell the same basic product, only stores that are able to differentiate themselves on location, price, selection, and/or customer service will prosper. Information on Spec's major competitors follows.

■ The Musicland Group

Musicland, operating under the names Musicland, Sam Goody, and Discount Records, has 805 stores and is the largest music retailer in the United States. In addition, Musicland has been expanding its presence in video retailing and by the end of 1990 had 135 Suncoast Motion Picture video stores, which were engaged exclusively in video sales. Eighty-seven percent of Musicland's stores are located in mall locations. Although all of the stores sell videotapes, only 40 of them rent videos.

In mid-1990, Musicland's management filed to take Musicland public. The proceeds from the sale, expected to be $78–$96 million, were to be used to reduce debt and finance growth. At the end of 1989, Musicland's debt totaled $266 million, most of which was incurred when management led a leveraged buyout of Musicland from Primerica for $410 million in 1988. This debt burden

Top 25 Music Chains by Store Count: Number of Locations as of 12/31/90 **Exhibit 2**

Chain	***Headquarter Location***	***Total Locations***	***Est. Revenues for Selected Chains, 1990 (millions)***
Musicland Stores Corp.	Minneapolis, MN	805	836
Trans World Music Corp.	Albany, NY	485	357
Target Stores Inc.	Minneapolis, MN	420	—
Wherehouse Entertainment, Inc.	Torrance, CA	283	328
Camelot Music	North Canton, OH	281	550
Record Bar Inc.	Durham, NC	182	230
Live Specialty Retail Group	Milford, MA	144	150
Sound Warehouse	Dallas, TX	142	142
Waxworks	Owensboro, KY	140	—
Hastings Books & Records Inc.	Amarillo, TX	123	—
Turtle's Music and Video	Marietta, GA	115	153
National Record Mart	Pittsburgh	111	—
Record World	Port Washington, NY	92	—
Wee Three Record Shops	Philadelphia, PA	84	—
Show Industries	Los Angeles, CA	82	—
Central South Music Sales	Nashville, TN	70	—
Tower Records/Video	West Sacramento, CA	61	—
Best Buy Co. Inc.	Bloomington, MN	58	—
Spec's Music Inc.	Miami, FL	57	49
Harmony House Records & Tapes	Troy, MI	33	—
Kemp Mill Music	Beltsville, MD	33	—
RecordShop Inc.	Sausalito, CA	33	—
Nobody Beats the Wiz	Brooklyn, NY	31	—
Entertainment Enterprises	Carmel, IN	25	—

has resulted in three years of net income decreases for the company, and for the six months ended June 31, 1990, the company reported losses of $3.79 million on sales of $318 million. Same-store sales for the period were up 6 percent, compared to 3.3 percent in 1989. The downturn in the stock market following Iraq's invasion of Kuwait prompted management to delay the stock offering, leaving Spec's and Trans World Music as the only publicly owned music and video retail chains.

■ Trans World Music Corp.

The second largest music retailer is Trans World Music Corp, which runs stores under 22 logos, including Record Town, Tape World, Great American Music,

Coconuts, Good Vibrations, Midland Records, and the Music Co. Trans World grew from 64 stores in 1984 to 546 outlets in 32 states by March 1991. The company financed its initial growth with a public offering of its stock in 1986.

Trans World has followed Musicland's lead and opened 50 Saturday Matinee Videos, which sell videos (no rentals). Similar to Musicland's Suncoast Motion Picture stores, these stores average 2000 square feet and carry 6000 titles. Although the sales per square foot have not been as high as those for mall record stores, which are expected to average $350–$400, both Musicland and Trans World expect sales to pick up as consumers become more familiar with this type of store.

Trans World's music stores are operated under four basic formats, 2 for mall locations (1200 and 2700 square feet), one for free-standing or strip stores (1400 to 18,000 square feet), and one for licensing agreements with other retailers. Trans World's Florida stores include four full-line mall stores, seven specialty mall stores, and 10 free-standing stores. Approximately two-thirds of the company's stores nationwide are located in malls. Although almost all of the stores sell videotapes, few rent them.

Trans World experienced financial difficulties in 1989. Blame for the decline was placed on several factors. The company was criticized for paying too much to rent space and acquire companies and for failing to stock a broad enough selection in its stores. Critics contended that Trans World's centralized buying staff led to cookie cutter stores that were insensitive to the regional differences in buyers' tastes. The company also became embroiled in a bitter trademark infringement suit with Peaches Records, which was settled for $2.5 million.

After internal restructuring, Trans World rebounded in 1990, earning $13.3 million on revenues of $312.8 million. In the 1991 fiscal year, which ended in March, Trans World reported an increase of 8.5 percent in net income, to $14.4 million, on sales of $365.5 million. Same-store sales increased 3 percent for the year. Trans World's long-term debt was $31.1 million. In 1991, management plans to slow its growth rate and open 70–80 stores.

■ Super Club

In October 1989, after studying the U.S. market for three years, Belgium-based Super Club N.A. (50 percent of which is owned by Philips N.V.) bought two major music chains, the 114-unit Atlanta-based Turtle's chain and the 167-unit Durham, N.C.-based Record Bar. In the same month, they also acquired the Video Towne and MovieTime/Alfalfa video chains. These acquisitions were quickly followed by the purchases of two additional video chains and a video wholesaler, Best. By mid-1991, the company had become the fourth largest music store retailer, with 300 outlets, and also operated 180 video stores.

Super Club has attempted to achieve synergies with its approach to the entertainment business. Super Club has drawn on the expertise of Record Bar and Turtle's and has begun stocking music in more than 100 of Super Club's video stores. Company officials hope that adding music will generate an additional $40–$50 million per year in sales.

For the fiscal 1991 year, which ended in March, Super Club reported a loss of $426 million, which the CEO attributed to inefficiencies in the acquired companies. To combat this, in mid-1991 Super Club combined the operations of Record Bar and Turtle's and began moving the headquarters of the chain to

Atlanta. The combination was made to allow the company to achieve economies of scale and invest in more advanced operating systems. Chief Operating Officer Bill Shepard stated that the goal of Super Club is to become a national player. "Now, we are ganging up so we can take on the Camelots and Trans Worlds in the business" (Christman, 1991: 1).

■ Camelot Music

Camelot Music experienced the most aggressive growth in its history in the 1990 and 1991 fiscal years. During this time, Camelot acquired 61 music stores, bringing its total to 292 stores operating in 32 states. Sales for the 1990 fiscal year approached $300 million. Although Camelot has expanded aggressively, management of the privately owned company plans to emphasize quality rather than quantity. Paul David, president and founder of Camelot, stated, "We have no illusions to be the biggest. We just want to be the best" (Christman, 1990: 38). David expects competition to be much stiffer in the 1990s and believes that Camelot will be successful because of its emphasis on customer service and the caliber of people employed in the organization.

Camelot has three basic store configurations: a 2400–3600-square-foot mall store, a 4000–6000-square-foot super mall format, and a 10,000–12,000-square-foot superstore. Eighty to eighty-five percent of Camelot's sales come from music products, but video sell-through is becoming an increasingly important part of Camelot's product mix. Camelot is currently expanding its distribution center to 280,000 square feet so that it can continue to serve all of its stores. It is also investing $5 million in POS, merchandising, and inventory management systems.

■ Sound Warehouse

Sound Warehouse, headquartered in Dallas, is the eighth largest retailer, with 142 stores in 15 states, including Florida. Sound Warehouse stores average 10,800 square feet and sell and rent videos in addition to traditional music software. Sound Warehouse's new stores are even larger, with an average retail space of 12,000 square feet. With a few exceptions, these stores are free-standing or are the anchors in strip malls.

In May 1989, Sound Warehouse was acquired by Shamrock Holdings, an entertainment concern controlled by the family of Roy Disney. Shamrock had bought the 60-unit Music Plus chain, which operates in California, in 1988 but the two chains are run separately. Shamrock is trying to increase its presence in the entertainment field and has provided the capital necessary for further expansion in the Midwest, Southeast, and Detroit. Shamrock has targeted Florida for expansion of the Sound Warehouse chain.

■ Record Clubs

An increasing amount of competition for retail music stores is coming from record clubs, which sell their products by mail. It is estimated that the record clubs accounted for 7.9 percent of music sales in 1989. (Record stores accounted for 71.1 percent, other stores for 15.6 percent, and mail order, 4.5 percent.) BMG Record Club has approximately 38 percent of these sales, while Columbia House has the rest. Retailers were not concerned with record clubs when they offered competitive prices for music and targeted rural customers or those who didn't like to go to music stores. However, in recent years the clubs have begun to offer 8 CDs for the price of one or 8 CDs for a penny if 6 additional CDs are bought over the next three years. They have also broadened their customer base and are now going after mainstream customers. This has resulted in a drain on customers going to music stores.

The clubs' aggressive marketing has led to charges by retailers that the record clubs are causing a credibility gap with their consumers, who see music being offered at rock bottom prices by the clubs but at $15.98 or $16.98 in the stores. In response to complaints from retailers, some music manufacturers are changing their policies. Geffen Records has decided to quit licensing music to the clubs. EMI and Polygram are considering withdrawing their licenses or increasing the length of time before clubs get labels. Neither Time-Warner nor Sony have responded to retailers' concerns, which might be expected since each of these companies owns half of Columbia House.

■ General Merchandisers

In addition to the competitors above, Spec's and other retailers face competition from general merchandisers like Target and Wal-mart. Although these stores do not typically offer the selection to be found in record stores, they often offer their music and video products at very low prices to draw customers into the stores. One video chain owner complained that he was selling *Batman* at 11 cents above cost to match the prices offered by local mass merchant chains.

SPEC'S MUSIC

Spec's Music is the largest specialty retailer of prerecorded music and video products in Florida. The company sells cassettes, compact discs, records, video movies, music videos, blank audio and video tapes, and audio and video accessories. Thirty-seven of the company's 57 stores rent video movies.

The company's basic strategy has remained the same since Mr. Spector founded the firm—good service, extensive selection at competitive prices, and a pleasant shopping environment. The company clusters its stores within a geographic area to take advantage of economies of scale in advertising, distribution, and administration. Currently, Spec's stores are clustered around 3 hubs—Southeast Florida, Central Florida (other than Orlando), and the Tampa/St. Petersburg area. Spec's does not have a strong presence in Orlando and has no stores in the Tallahassee or Jacksonville areas. Exhibit 3 illustrates the locations of Spec's stores. With the exception of the original Spec's store in Coral Gables, which is owned by a Spector family trust, all of Spec's locations are leased.

The company's strategy for the types of stores it is opening has changed, and most new stores are freestanding or located in strip shopping centers and contain 7000 to 10,000 square feet, as opposed to mall stores, which have from 2500 to 3500 square feet. Of the 12 new stores opened in fiscal year 1990, eight were superstores. In October 1990, Spec's opened the largest music and video store in Florida, a 20,000-square-foot store in a 2.2-million-square-foot outlet

Spec's Locations

Exhibit 3

North Central
Gainesville (2)
Ocala (2)

South Central
Lakeland (3)
Plant City (1)
Sebring (1)
Winter Haven (2)

Tampa Bay
Bradenton (1)
Brandon (1)
Clearwater (2)
Seminole (1)
St. Petersburg (2)
St. Petersburg Beach (1)
Tampa (3)

Southwest
Ft. Meyers (1)
Naples (1)
Sarasota (2)

Central
Daytona Beach (2)
Deland (1)
Kissimmee (1)
Melbourne (1)
Sanford (1)
St. Cloud (1)
Winter Park (1)

Treasure Coast
Boynton Beach (1)
Jensen Beach (1)
Palm Beach (1)
Stuart (1)
Vero Beach (1)
West Palm Beach (1)

Southeast
Boca Raton (1)
Coconut Grove (1)
Coral Gables (1)
Coral Springs (1)
Ft. Lauderdale (1)
Hialeah (1)
Hollywood (2)
Homestead (1)
Key West (1)
Miami (4)
North Miami (2)
North Miami Beach (1)
Plantation (1)
Pompano (1)
South Miami (1)
Sunrise (1)

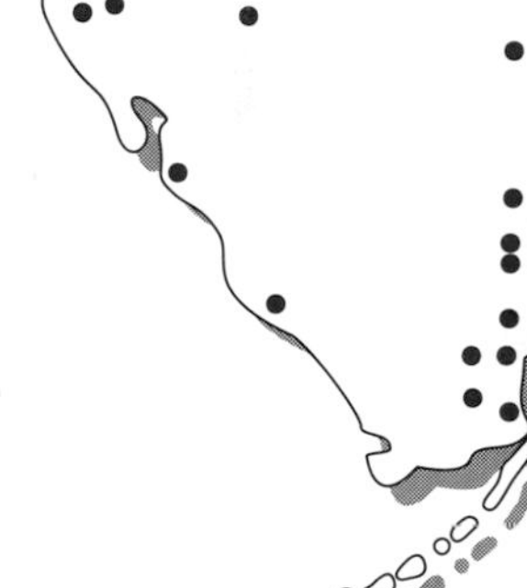

mall. In mid-1991, Spec's operated 17 superstores, 16 stores in enclosed shopping malls, and 24 stores in strip shopping centers.

Free standing and strip stores allow Spec's to rent videos, which does not work well in mall stores because of parking limitations. An additional advantage of free standing and strip stores is that they are cheaper to lease than mall locations. Rents for superstores average $8–$15 per square foot as opposed to $20–$40 for mall locations (Sternberger, 1991). However, sales per square foot tend to be higher in malls and mall stores tend to become profitable in months, whereas superstores may take 1 to 2 years to break even. The breakeven point in the industry for a smaller store is $250–$300 per square foot, and for a large store, $150 per square foot.

Spec's warehouse and corporate offices were expanded in 1988 and 1991 and contain 56,000 square feet. All stores are stocked once or twice times weekly from the warehouse in west Miami, from which 90 percent of new products are shipped. Stores in southeast and southwest Florida are stocked by two company trucks, while delivery outside these areas is made by common carriers providing next-day service. The proximity of the warehouse and the sophistication of the company's computer systems have allowed it to build stores in the last three years without backroom storage. This decreases store costs and encourages staff to put new products on the shelves as soon as they arrive.

Management

The top management at Spec's has changed somewhat in recent years as the company has brought on additional managers to help with the rapid growth of the company. In addition, the board of directors has added two outside directors to the four Spector family members. A leading investment firm has referred to Spec's management as "not just family management, (but) really good family management" (Bibb, 1991: 7).

Two vice presidents, three district managers, and one merchandiser supervise the operation of Spec's stores and visit stores within their territories regularly to provide on-site management. The company has a "Manager-in-Training" program for promising associates and hires experienced managers from outside sources. Spec's stresses promotion from within and several of the company's officers began their careers as customer service associates. One of the primary concerns of Ms. Lieff is making sure that existing personnel are able to handle their positions in the larger company and that capable outside management personnel can be identified and integrated as the company grows.

Personnel

Spec's has approximately 700 employees, 375 of whom work full-time. The company hires temporary employees during peak sales periods, such as Christmas. Retail sales clerks, who are referred to as customer service associates, are compensated on an hourly basis and do not receive sales commissions. Employees are evaluated every 6 months, and receive raises depending upon responsibility, tenure, and merit. All employees receive 30 percent discounts on store products and health insurance if they work more than 30 hours per week. The company has also made a profit-sharing plan available to all full-time employees who have completed 18 months of continuous service. Management believes that it has good relations with its employees. However, the shrinking labor market has made the hiring of good associates a primary concern of management.

Product/Market Mix

Although cassettes had been Spec's largest product line, CDs, video rentals, and video sales have become increasingly important. CDs are the company's fastest-growing product category, accounting for 38 percent of sales in 1991. The company has eliminated the vinyl record collection in its stores over the past 2 years. Exhibit 4 shows the changes in Spec's product mix over the past four years.

Because the video rental business is driven by hit movies, the company is emphasizing them and decreasing the number of standard (catalog) selections in new stores. Daily rental fees for videos range from $.49 to $2.50. The average number of rental videos in the company's stores is 6,500, with the largest store offering a selection of 11,000 videotapes. The store's automated systems have been crucial in allowing the store to keep a sufficient stock of demanded videos in the stores.

The company has changed its amortization schedule for new videotapes to more accurately reflect the tapes' useful product life. New titles are now depreciated on a 24-month accelerated schedule, with 70 percent being amor-

Changes in Spec's Product Mix **Exhibit 4**

	1990	*1989*	*1988*	*1987*
Audio products				
Cassettes	34%	36%	35%	34%
CDs	31	28	26	20
LPs	3	7	10	19
Video products				
Video rentals	16	14	12	11
Video sales	8	6	4	4
Other products	8	9	10	12

tized in the first year and 30 percent in the second year, with no salvage value. This accounting change should reduce pre-tax income by $300,000–$400,000 in the 1991 fiscal year.

■ Advertising and Promotion

Spec's promotional attack includes radio, newspaper and TV ads, direct mail, and community-oriented contests. The company's advertising stresses promotional pricing, a broad assortment and depth of merchandise, and the convenience of store locations. In recent years, direct mail has become an important component of the company's advertising mix. Direct mail advertising was not possible before the company expanded enough to warrant the costs associated with this type of campaign.

■ Finance

Spec's growth has been financed primarily from current operations but the company plans to take advantage of debt as needed in financing future growth. At the end of the 1990 fiscal year, the company carried $1.8 million of long-term debt on its balance sheet. Spec's conservative use of debt has made it popular with the investment community and may give it a strong competitive advantage in the coming year. With the downturn in the real estate market, developers are giving preference to debt-free companies, which may enable Spec's to lease very attractive store sites on favorable terms.

■ Management Information Systems

Spec's management information systems continue to impress analysts and investors. The company replaced hand-held optical scanners with a point-of-sale system in 1990. Prior to the installation of this system, employees had to remove inventory tags that had been scanned with a hand-held optical scanner. The point-of-sale system represented a significant investment for the company, but management feels that the new system will help decrease check-out time, control inventory, increase margins at the stores, and help buyers in their ordering. Daily sales from each store are automatically transmitted to the company's central computer, allowing management to keep a close tab on sales in each store and throughout the entire organization.

Spec's is preparing to initiate computer-to-computer transactions with vendors that have established such systems. This will allow the company to expedite return authorizations, orders, and invoices.

RECENT FINANCIAL RESULTS

With the exception of 1990, earnings and revenues for Spec's increased at five-year annually compounded rates of 37 percent and 22 percent, respectively. As a result of these numbers, the company was referred to as a "darling of Wall Street." It made *Forbes* list of the 200 best small companies in the United States in 1987 and 1988 and was cited as one of Florida's top 100 companies from 1987 to 1989. However, 1990 was a year of mixed results for the company.

Spec's revenues increased by 23 percent in 1990, but net income was down 11 percent. Exhibits 5 and 6 present recent financial results for the company and Exhibit 7 compares Spec's with other music retailers. Company management had expected earnings to go down and had warned the investment community that short-term earnings would fall because of the costs associated with the introduction of the POS system, the rapid expansion in the number of stores, and the costs associated with opening larger stores. In 1990, Spec's opened twelve stores, renovated and relocated five, and closed two stores. The square footage of company stores increased 88 percent in eighteen months.

Wall Street did not respond favorably to Spec's 1990 results. Spec's announced its results at a time when the stock market was declining in general and hitting retailers especially hard. Spec's stock price, which increased 68 percent in 1989, fell 65 percent in 1990, to $3\frac{3}{16}$. At one point Spec's stock was trading at just 25 percent above its IPO price in October 1985. Management offered to buy back 300,000 shares, giving the Spector family control of 51 percent of the stock. By mid-1991, the stock had rebounded to $4\frac{3}{4}$, but management, and many in the investment community, believe that the company is undervalued.

In the first quarter of the 1991 fiscal year, Spec's experienced its first loss since becoming a public company. Although revenues increased 25 percent to $12.3 million, the company experienced a net loss of $29,000. The results included a one-time charge of $78,000 for the closing of three stores and an additional write-off of $120,000 for the new video amortization policy. For the first nine months of fiscal year 1991, revenues rose by 22 percent to $45.2 million, while earnings were $1.5 million, a decline of 6 percent from 1990.

THE COMPANY'S FUTURE PLANS

As the outlook for growth in Florida is positive, Spec's plans to concentrate its sales efforts in Florida for the immediate future. The Miami area is expected to grow 9 percent over the next five years, the Orlando area 15 percent, the Jacksonville area 7 percent, and the Tallahassee area 10 percent (Smith and

Spec's Music: Consolidated Balance Sheets

Exhibit 5

	July 31		
	1990	*1989*	*1988*
Assets			
Current assets			
Cash and equivalents	$ 412,555	$ 342,684	$ 365,890
Receivables	239,625	211,905	172,003
Inventories	11,914,011	9,139,138	7,538,320
Video rental inventory, net	5,641,158	3,968,012	3,083,106
Prepaid expenses	620,524	698,858	450,417
Prepaid income taxes	31,020	—	—
Deferred tax asset	219,000	242,000	—
Total current assets	19,077,893	14,602,597	11,609,736
Equipment and leasehold improvements, net	6,497,410	5,022,850	4,298,580
Other assets	445,104	269,915	415,545
Total assets	$26,020,407	$19,895,362	$16,323,861
Liabilities and Stockholders' Equity			
Current liabilities			
Accounts payable	$ 7,338,935	$ 4,249,659	$ 4,397,205
Accrued expenses	1,214,399	1,059,929	931,796
Income taxes payable	—	22,000	168,999
Preferred dividends payable	—	22,540	22,540
Total current liabilities	8,553,334	5,354,128	5,520,540
Long term debt	1,800,000	1,000,000	—
Deferred income taxes	745,000	942,000	617,988
Stockholders' equity			
$8 cumulative preferred stock, par value $1.00; 5,635 shares authorized, 5,635 issued and outstanding in 1989; redeemed and cancelled in 1990.	—	5,635	5,635
Common stock, par value $.01; 10,000,000 shares authorized; 5,326,941 and 5,158,242 shares issued and outstanding as of July 31, 1990 and 1989, respectively.	53,270	51,583	38,643
Additional paid-in capital	3,805,594	3,462,720	3,453,170
Retained earnings	11,063,209	9,079,296	6,687,885
Total stockholders' equity	14,922,073	12,599,234	10,185,333
Total liabilities and stockholders' equity	$26,020,407	$19,895,362	$16,323,861

Bayva, 1991). Other locations will be considered as the Florida market becomes saturated. In particular, management plans to capitalize on its expertise in the Hispanic market and expand to Puerto Rico. However, for the moment, management has decided to concentrate on digesting the rapid growth it has experienced over the last two years, delaying movement into the Orlando, Tallahassee, and Jacksonville areas.

Exhibit 6 **Spec's Music: Consolidated Income Statements**

	Years Ended July 31		
	1990	*1989*	*1988*
Revenues			
Product sales	$41,506,970	$34,604,504	$28,640,793
Video rentals	7,852,427	5,547,404	3,890,276
	49,359,397	40,151,908	32,531,069
Cost of goods sold	30,427,649	24,545,110	19,755,800
Gross profit	18,931,748	15,606,798	12,775,269
Store operating, general, and administrative expenses	15,916,590	12,228,544	10,088,864
Operating income	3,015,158	3,378,254	2,686,405
Other income (expense)			
Commissions and other	166,380	204,787	272,810
Interest income	18,245	41,969	25,185
Interest expense	(98,600)	(54,107)	(22,470)
Recovery of related party advances	—	—	6,288
	86,025	192,649	281,813
Earnings before income taxes and cumulative effect of a change in accounting principle	3,101,183	3,570,903	2,968,218
Income taxes	1,106,000	1,340,400	1,153,000
Earnings before cumulative of a change in accounting principle	1,995,183	2,230,503	1,815,218
Cumulative effect of a change in accounting principle	—	205,988	—
Net earnings	$ 1,995,183	$ 2,436,491	$ 1,815,218
Earnings per Common Share			
Before cumulative effect of a change in accounting principle	$.37	$.42	$.35
From a cumulative effect of a change in accounting principle	—	—	—
Net earnings	$.37	$.46	$.35
Weighted average number of common shares outstanding	5,364,000	5,299,000	5,152,000

According to Peter Blei, Spec's chief financial officer, Spec's will weather the tough times confronting the industry. "I'm optimistic because . . . the economy will improve, we're doing all right, we're profitable, we're surviving, and we're paying our bills on time. We're a strong company" (Verna, 1991b: 43). However, several problems confront Ms. Lieff. How long will the economic downturn last, and does this situation present an expansion opportunity for Spec's, a threat, or both? If the company does not expand to all areas of Florida, will the national chains lock up the attractive retail sites? If the company does

Company Results, 1989–1990 Fiscal Year **Exhibit 7**

	Spec's	*Trans World*	*Musicland*	*Wherehouse*	*Sound Warehouse*	*Average*
Revenues (000,000)	$49	$313	$695	$388	—	—
Five-year revenue growth	24.2%	37.6%	17.2%	25.7%	—	26.1%
Gross margin ex. video rental	35.4%	37.8%	41.5%	32.3%	32.0%	35.8%
Operating margin	6.1%	8.9%	9.3%	2.3%	4.0%	6.1%
Five-year operating earnings growth	26.1%	40.3%	36.9%	4.6%	—	24.7%
Net margin	4.0%	4.3%	0.9%	1.4%	nml	2.12%
Inventory turnover ex. video	2.6	1.8	2.9	2.9	2.5	2.5
Return on equity	14.42%	25.70%	9.76%	nm	—	16.6%
Debt/capital	10.76%	33.94%	85.93%	98.16%	—	57.2%
Total stores at year end	55	442	825	263	123	—
Net addition of stores, 12 months	10	5	143	42	19	—
Percentage change in stores	18.2%	1.1%	17.3%	16.0%	8.5%	15.4%
Sales per average store (000)	$959	$713	$960	$1,603	—	$1,031
Sales per square foot	$239	$261	$284	$ 256	$162	$ 240
Comp store sales gain	3.9%	3.1%	3.3%	6.9%	1.0%	3.64%

Sources: Company reports and Paine Webber.

expand, does it have the financial strength, systems, management, and store personnel needed for the expansion? Are the recession and the large number of store openings responsible for the company's recent downturn, or has management failed to implement necessary changes to keep the firm's profits growing? What changes, if any, should the company make to best position it for the increasingly competitive environment in which it operates?

REFERENCES

Altaner, P. 1991. Blockbuster continues efforts to quell skeptics. *Billboard,* May 18: 9, 86.

Bibb, C. 1991. Spec's Music, Inc.: Uncertainty creates opportunity. *Paine Webber,* January 22: 7.

Christman, E. 1990. Camelot conquers new territories. *Billboard,* September 15: 38.

Christman, E. 1991. Record Bar, Turtle's united under Super Club Music shell. *Billboard,* May 4: 1, 86.

Smith, S.K., & Bayva, R. 1991. Projections of Florida population by county 1990–2020. *Population Studies,* University of Florida Bureau of Economic and Business Research, 24 (2).

Smith, S.K., & Shahidullah, M. 1991. Revised annual population estimates by county in Florida, 1980–1990, with components of growth. *Special Population Studies,* University of Florida Bureau of Economic and Business Research, May.

Standard and Poor's Industry Surveys. 1991. Leisure time. March 14: L43.

Sternberger, S. 1991. Spec's Music, Inc. (SPEK). *Ladenburg, Thalman & Co. Inc.,* February.

Verna, P. 1991a. AT&T, cable co. link for vid. test. *Billboard,* May 18: 8, 85.

Verna, P. 1991b. Trans World, Spec's results reflect cool retail climate. *Billboard,* June 15: 43.

Verna, P., and Christman, E. 1991. Music biz dismal, retailers report. *Billboard,* June 8: 4, 85.

Wall Street Journal. Philips' Super Club sees "sizable loss" for its current year. September 14: B3.

Ward's Business Directory of U.S. Private and Public Companies. 1992. Detroit: Gale Research.

CASE 22

Phoenix Holdings' Troubled Acquisition

Joseph Wolfe, Bradley W. Miller, University of Tulsa

By early 1992 it was obvious to J. "Mike" Miller, president and CEO of Phoenix Holdings, Inc. that something had gone wrong with his company's purchase of the Western Aero Supply Corporation; a San Antonio aircraft parts wholesaler. His banks were wondering about Western Aero's low performance, many of his suppliers had frequently placed it on a COD-only delivery basis, and employee morale had deteriorated. More importantly, the San Antonio operation, which was the foundation for a newly created regional wholesale branch, had been discontinued for over a year, thus destroying one of the acquisition's key assets and much of the synergies Mike wanted for the two additional branches he had created. Although it was known that numerous short-term transition costs would be involved with the March 1989 acquisition, he now wondered into what kinds of mess he had gotten Phoenix Holdings.

After collecting various internal reports and his thoughts on the company's situation, Mike wanted to bounce his ideas off some of his top executives. As a result of these discussions, Western Aero's ultimate future was to be decided, as it was now May 1992 and some type of action had to be taken. Would a little more "fine tuning" in the company's San Antonio and Dallas branches and of its new catalog sales operation turn this acquisition around or was the purchase of Western Aero basically a flawed idea? Should Phoenix "hang tough" a little longer, or should basic changes be set into motion?

GENERAL AVIATION INDUSTRY

The aviation industry's customers can be divided into two major categories comprising military and civilian sales. Within the civilian category, there exist the broad categories of commercial and general aviation. General aviation is

This case is intended for classroom discussion only, not to depict effective or ineffective handling of administrative situations. All rights reserved to the authors and the North American Case Research Association.

comprised of all civil flying excluding certificated route air carriers, supplemental operators, large-aircraft commercial operators, and commuter airlines. This aviation group is made up mostly of privately owned aircraft, but a small proportion consists of light-demand air taxis, agricultural applications of insecticides and fertilizers, and powerline patrols and observation.

For a number of business cycles, the demand for general aviation equipment appeared to be tied to the nation's Gross National Product (GNP). If GNP increased 1%, general aviation shipments increased 4%, and this relationship held true until the late 1970s. Thereafter, despite a relatively robust economy from 1983 to 1989, general aviation shipments fell during the same period. For example, from 1978 to 1979 real GNP rose about 3.2%, while general aviation shipments fell 1.1%. Exhibit 1 demonstrates the previous and current relationships between GNP and general aviation aircraft shipments. The Federal Aviation Administration (FAA) believes the industry's departure from its historic demand relationship can be attributed to a number of price and operating expense factors: higher prices charged for new airplanes, raising fuel and maintenance costs for owners and operators, and increased product liability by the manufacturers.

Between 1972 and 1987, the purchase price of a single-engine airplane rose 240%, and multiengined and turboprop airplane prices rose 300% and 220%, respectively, from 1972 to 1989. While these price increases dampen the demand for new aircraft, which ultimately have to be serviced, the absolute size and cost of operating and maintaining America's fleet of active general aviation aircraft, as well as the number of pilots available and their number of logged flight hours, have the most direct effect on the aircraft service industry. Exhibit 2 provides information on the value of all civil aeronautic shipments made in the United States for selected years from 1972 to 1991. Exhibit 3 gives various measures of flying activity, such as the number of airports available, the number and classes of pilot licenses held and general aviation-type airplanes being flown, and the number of flight hours recorded and airplane fuel consumed, for the years 1983 to 1989. Exhibit 4 displays the FAA's forecasts of flying activity for the years 1993 to 2001.

Regarding the variable costs associated with private flying, Exhibits 5 and 6 reveal the historical cost trends for general aviation's two largest airplane

Exhibit 1 **GNP Levels and General Aviation Aircraft Shipments**

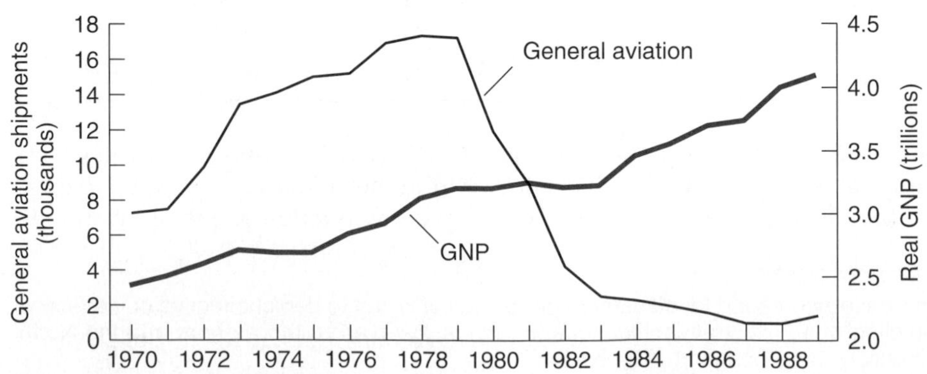

Exhibit 2

Civil and Military Aerospace Industry Sales, 1975 to 1991 (in billions of current dollars)

Group	*1975*	*1980*	*1985*	*1989*	*1990*	*1991*
Civil	6.5	16.3	13.7	22.1	31.4	38.1
Military	10.0	15.2	36.8	38.9	38.3	32.1
Total	16.5	31.5	50.5	61.0	69.7	70.2

Source: Statistical Abstract of the United States 1991 (Washington, D.C.: Bureau of the Census, U.S. Department of Commerce), Table 1086.

Note: Preliminary data for 1990 and estimated data for 1991.

Exhibit 3

Civil Flying, 1983 to 1989

Item	*Unit*	*1983*	*1985*	*1987*	*1988*	*1989*
Public airports	1,000	4.8	5.9	5.0	5.0	5.1
Private airports	1,000	11.2	10.5	12.0	12.3	12.4
Total	2,000	16.0	16.4	17.0	17.3	17.5
Fixed-wing aircraft	1,000	200.8	198.0	204.1	197.0	204.5
Multiengine	1,000	34.5	33.6	33.0	32.2	33.2*
Single-engine						
4-place and over	1,000	107.2	105.6	107.5	105.2	108.5*
3-place and less	1,000	59.2	58.8	63.5	59.6	62.8*
Rotorcraft	1,000	6.5	6.4	6.3	6.4	7.5
Pilot licenses						
Commercial	1,000	159	152	144	143	145
Private	1,000	319	311	301	300	293
Student	1,000	147	147	146	137	143
General aviation						
Hours flown	Million	35.2	34.1	33.4	33.6	35.0
Fuel consumed						
Gasoline	Mil. gal.	428	420	402	398	418*
Jet fuel	Mil. gal.	613	691	672	746	741*

Sources: Statistical Abstract of the United States 1991 (Washington, D.C.: Bureau of the Census, U.S. Department of Commerce), Table 1081; and *FAA Statistical Handbook of Aviation: Calendar Year 1989* (Washington, D.C.: U.S. Department of Transportation), Tables 8.2 and 8.3.

*Estimated by the case writers.

categories. In constant 1972 dollars, the operating costs of flying a single-engine piston airplane peaked in 1983 and then fell about 10% to a fairly constant rate from 1987 to 1989. Maintenance costs, however, for this same type of airplane have risen almost constantly since 1971, although the overall increase has been less than the aircraft's operating costs.

Although many relatively low-growth indicators exist for this industry, the FAA notes a number of encouraging signs. In recent years, the cost of purchasing turbojet aircraft has actually fallen and only moderate price increases for

Exhibit 4

Selected FAA General Aviation Forecasts for 1993–2001

Item	*Unit*	*1993*	*1995*	*1997*	*1999*	*2001*
Active aircraft	Thousands	220.0	220.5	223.5	225.0	227.0
Hours flown	Millions	35.0	36.5	38.0	38.5	39.7
Private pilots	Thousands	305.0	306.0	307.0	308.0	310.0
Student pilots	Thousands	145.0	148.0	149.0	149.5	150.0

Source: Interpreted from graphs found in *FAA Aviation Forecast Fiscal Years 1990–2001* (Washington, D.C.: Department of Transportation, FAA-APO 90-1, March 1990), pp. 100, 102, 103.

Exhibit 5

Single-Engine Operating and Maintenance Costs

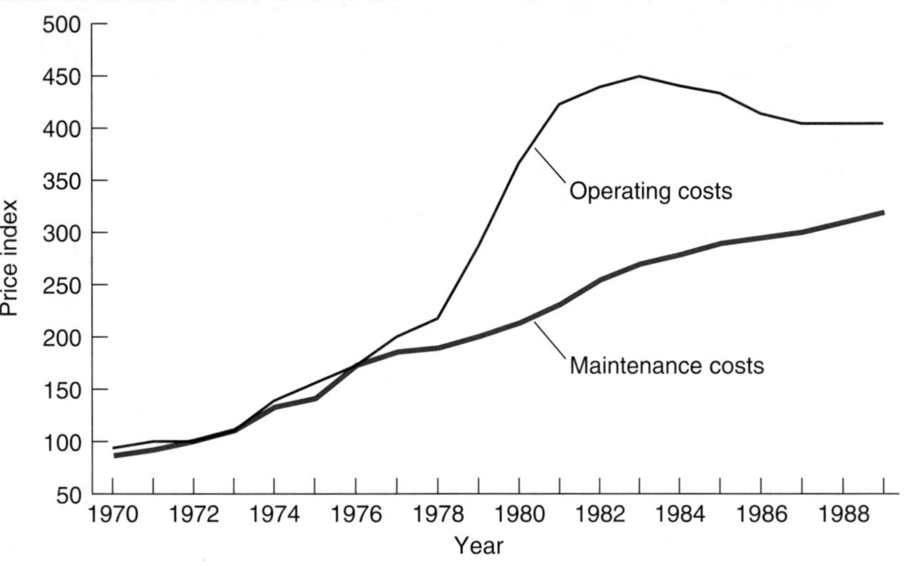

Source: Adapted from *FAA Statistical Handbook of Aviation: Calendar Year 1989* (Washington, D.C.: U.S. Department of Transportation), p. 95.

multiengine piston and turboprop aircraft have been experienced. This has resulted in an annual growth rate of 3.6% for turbine-powered aircraft from 1989 to 2001 and an annual increase of 4.3% for turbine rotorcraft. Respective annual flight hour increases of 3.8% and 6.5% for these aircraft have been forecasted by the FAA for the same time period. Additional encouraging signs for the industry have appeared. Based on marketing research, it has been estimated that 3.6 million American households have a family member who wants to learn how to fly and can afford to do so. Sales of business-type jets should accelerate by 1995 as deliveries of the new Cessna CitationJet and Swearingen SJ-30 begin in 1992 and 1993. Learjet, Inc. expects to deliver thirty new aircraft in 1993, with four Model 60s and twenty-six 30-Series being planned for production. The piston-powered, single-engine aircraft segment, however, is expected to experience little if any growth for the rest of the 1990s.

Multiengine Operating and Maintenance Costs **Exhibit 6**

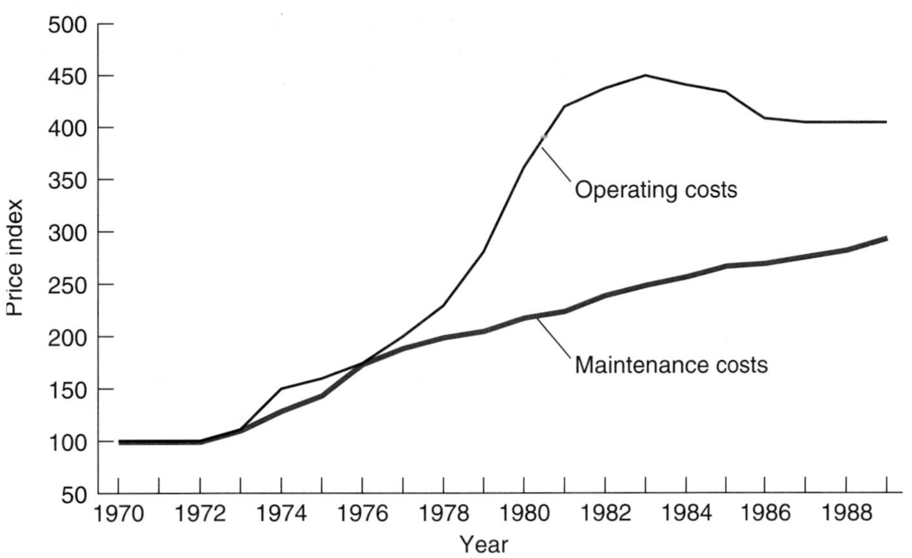

Source: Adapted from *FAA Statistical Handbook of Aviation: Calendar Year 1989* (Washington, D.C.: U.S. Department of Transportation), p. 96.

WHOLESALE GENERAL AIRCRAFT PARTS INDUSTRY STRUCTURE

The manufacturers of general aviation aircraft use a large number of American parts suppliers when they make their airplanes. These suppliers, in turn, contract with a number of local distributors/wholesalers to make their parts and supplies available for aftermarket repairs and maintenance that inevitably follow from the use of the aircraft in which their parts are used. Of the two groups, commercial versus general, the latter market is the largest, broadest, most fragmented, and more easily entered. If the requisite distributorships can be obtained, a local wholesaler can supply the complete overhaul servicing needs of one single-engined airplane with a parts inventory amounting to between $8,000 to $10,000; an inventory of about $2,000 can overhaul the typical small airplane engine. Given that parts manufacturers will directly air-ship parts to end users under emergency aircraft-on-the-ground situations (AOG orders), a wholesale distributor does not even need a complete inventory to still obtain credit for customer purchases and to service the majority of that customer's needs. Accordingly, a wholesale distributor can enter this industry with a relatively small capital investment in a minimum-sized inventory, depending on the number of customers and competitors in a given market area.

Until 1986, the wholesale airplane industry was dominated by two key players—Aviall, Incorporated and Van Dusen Air, Incorporated. Between them they garnered about 40% of the industry's $500 million to $600 million in annual sales. In November 1985, Aviall was acquired by Ryder System, Inc. for $149.0 million, and in 1986 it purchased Van Dusen Air's aircraft parts distribution business. In its newly combined form, Aviall operates over 80 stocking locations with 700 employees throughout the world. It has over 65,000 active parts numbers, represents over 200 major product lines and 1,000 suppliers, and possesses a working base of more than 25,000 customers. Despite its size and supposed economies of scale, Ryder System's aviation businesses experienced losses in 1989, while in 1990, they accounted for 23.3% of the company's overall sales but only 17.6% of its operating profits.

In late 1989, Global Aircraft Parts, Ltd., a new entrant in this industry, estimated the annual domestic sales and the number of locations for this industry's major participants, as shown in Exhibit 7. Industry experts have noted the constant dilemma faced by those in the distribution channels for general aviation parts and supplies. The typical wholesaler employs a "hub-and-spoke" distribution system. In this type of operation, a central warehouse or distribution center is created along with a number of "spokes," or local branch offices, which take and solicit orders from regional customers. Each local branch also maintains inventories for making immediate deliveries. Should a branch be out of stock on specific items, sometimes amounting to 25% to 30% of the customer's original order, those items that are available are delivered immediately, and the branch attempts to provide the remaining items from inventories held at the company's "hub," or other branches. To be financially successful, a parts wholesaler must minimize inventory levels both at each branch and within its overall system to maximize the return on its major assets while providing optimal "fill rates" for its customers. Although a typical branch might obtain five to seven stock turns a year, an overall system with many branches might obtain less than three turns a year. If a low fill rate is the result of inadequate inventory levels, but a higher stock turn and lower inventory investment for the wholesaler, customers must pay for additional delivery costs on back-ordered items while having their important revenue-producing airplane on the ground for an unnecessarily long time period. In this regard, while customers are generally price sensitive, immediate and complete deliveries are the deciding factor in emergency, nonscheduled repair situations. For scheduled maintenance checks and overhauls, where parts can be ordered many weeks in advance, price is a greater factor than speedy and complete deliveries.

Exhibit 7 **Major Domestic Participants, Late 1990**

Company	*Annual Sales*	*Locations*
Aviall, Inc.	$370,000,000	70
Piedmont Aircraft Supply	35,000,000	18
Cooper Aircraft Supply	35,000,000	7
Atlantic Aviation	15,000,000+	1
Less than $15 million annual sales		
AAR Western Skyways		2
Aircraft Service		1
Cosgrove Aircraft Service		1
Omaha Airline Supply		3
Precision Aeromotive		1
Western Aero Supply		2

At one time, competition in this industry's parts segment was waged at the local level between isolated local participants. With the advent of telemarketing and fast overnight deliveries provided by carriers such as Federal Express, United Parcel Service, and DHL Worldwide Express, national catalog wholesalers have entered the scene. Working from one large and efficient "paper-free" warehouse using highly automated inventory tracking systems and very accurate sales forecasting techniques, they compete by offering very low prices on what are basically commodity-type items while simultaneously providing relatively speedy deliveries. They accomplish this while maintaining minimum inventory levels for both themselves and their customers, although some feel their service is very impersonal and unsupportive.

Service is another key to success in this industry. While service is a function of the distributor's in-stock position, service is also dependent on how well the company relates to its customers. For most transactions, this is manifested in the knowledge the company's salespeople possess when taking orders or suggesting parts and supplies that should be purchased. This translates into customer loyalty that can partially offset a competitor's lower prices. A good salesperson knows engines, can help customers with superseded parts numbers, is knowledgeable about FAA regulations regarding parts and component upgrades, and can quickly locate information in the numerous parts reference manuals that must be employed. Over the years, a person of this type can cultivate a following among purchasing agents, mechanics, and engineers in the local area, and this service aspect frequently influences the distributor chosen by the industry's service stations, known as fixed-base operators (FBOs).

Although many wholesalers have attempted to improve their service levels while implementing operating efficiencies so they can be profitable with lower margins, many FBOs are unhappy with the overall distribution system they must use. First, although fill rates have often been low, wholesalers typically provide little information regarding what parts ordered will be shipped immediately and what parts are back-ordered for what time period. The back order itself causes an inordinate amount of down time on an aircraft, while the lack of shipping information wastes mechanics' time and interferes with the rational scheduling of aircraft maintenance and service. Second, because back-ordered items must be shipped separately, the FBO must pay freight charges on each separate shipment. For a typical order, this could result in four or five separate shipments. And third, the frequency of back orders and out-of-stock situations frustrates the FBO's desires to implement just-in-time (JIT) inventory systems. Although the use of JIT exacerbates the problem caused by the wholesalers, it is a viable way to lower the service station's inventory investment. Any wholesaler that could help the FBO accomplish a reasonable JIT inventory system would prove to be a strong partner in containing overall airplane service costs.

WESTERN AERO SUPPLY CORPORATION

Western Aero Supply is a $5.5-million-a-year company engaged in the wholesale distribution of new aircraft parts (SIC 5088, CLs 2612 and 2613). It was incorporated in San Antonio, Texas, in late 1946 by William B. Matthews. For almost 40 years, it had been a good performer at its single location. By the early

1980s, however, its profitability began to suffer due to Matthews' declining interest and advancing age and the competitive pressures exerted by Aviall's San Antonio branch. Aviall, Inc. featured a complete line of parts and supplies, had lower prices, and provided superior service by maintaining a better systemwide in-stock position.

Mike Miller purchased Western Aero for $650,000. At the time of purchase, Western's year-to-date losses had amounted to about $20,000, with the year's projected losses amounting to over $45,000. He believed that the price was justified based on the company's assets, the distribution rights it held, and the goodwill it had created over the years. About two-thirds of Western's value consisted of its parts inventories, about $30,000 worth of office equipment, and its receivables less payables. The remainder of the purchase price was based on the value of goodwill, a noncompetitive covenant on William Matthews, and the exclusive right to distribute various manufacturers' products in the San Antonio area. In negotiating Western Aero's price, it was believed that about 75% of the receivables would be collected and that about 20% of the inventory was almost worthless, while another 20% could only be sold at prices substantially below original cost. As part of the final agreement, Matthews was allowed to keep his former office and retain the use of his telephone and secretary. Additionally, the company's name could not be changed while he was still alive, and two of his favorite employees received guaranteed employment at Western Aero.

As soon as the deal had been closed, Western Aero's headquarters were moved to Tulsa, Oklahoma, where the new wholly owned subsidiary shared office space and expected synergies with Phoenix Holdings' two other operations. As shown in Exhibit 8, all subsidiaries serviced the general aviation industry, with Mid-States Aircraft repairing and overhauling general aircraft engines and Precision Hose Technology servicing the end user's needs for flexible tubing and hoses. A number of internal benefits were anticipated. Mid-States Aircraft, Phoenix's largest subsidiary with about 60% of its total sales, could have about 40% of its parts supplied by Western Aero. Although

Exhibit 8 **Corporate Structure**

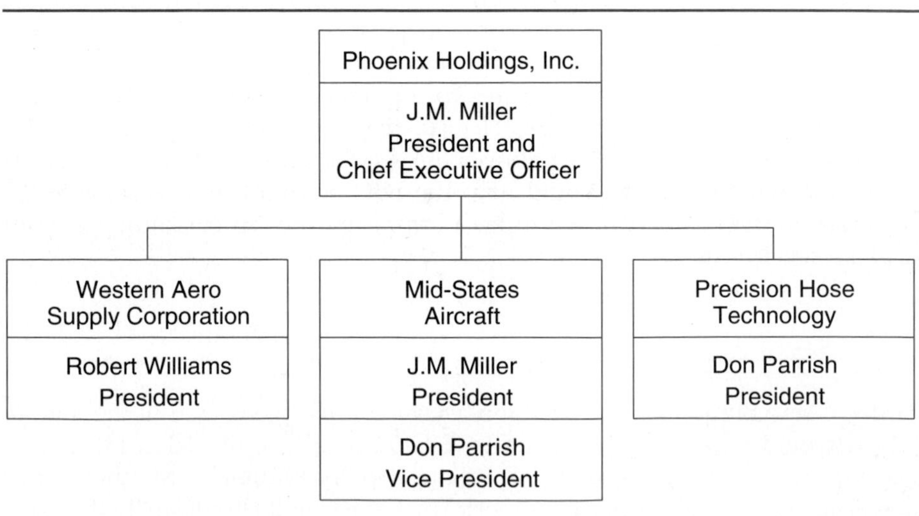

Precision Hose Technology already had a Stratoflex hose distributorship, it could now combine its purchases with those of Western, thereby obtaining a larger volume discount. In addition to moving Western's headquarters to Tulsa, branch operations were begun in that city as well as in Dallas in September 1988. With these additions, Phoenix Holdings, Inc. became a company with revenues amounting to $15–$16 million per year.

At the time of the Dallas branch's creation, numerous attractions appeared to exist. Inexpensive office and warehouse space was available, and the logistics were good. Dallas was a major market, only a 50-minute flight from Tulsa, so the inventories from both branches could service each other, and it was a market midway between Tulsa and San Antonio. Additionally, Western Aero had the chance to hire two people with business dealings in the Dallas market: John Henderson was hired from Aviall, and John Hassel was engaged after having worked for Omni Air, an insolvent Dallas parts distributor. It was believed that through their hiring, a number of major accounts would automatically be brought to the new branch. In justifying the Dallas operation, Mike Miller said, "I was led to believe by the two Aviall people I had hired that customers were so displeased with Aviall's service we would be successful with any branch we opened against them."

Others in the company were less confident about the operation's chances for success. Daus Decker, Western's San Antonio manager, thought that Western Aero's overall priorities were wrong. He argued "Before going blindly to the wind in Dallas, we should rebuild San Antonio. It will take over a year to build up San Antonio with only one manager there all the time. We don't have enough resources to build a branch in Dallas while trying to make San Antonio successful at the same time. What's worse, we'll be fighting Aviall in its own hub city." Exhibit 9 presents various market and population statistics associated with cities located in the Southwest.

Statistics for Selected Cities **Exhibit 9**

City	*Metropolitan Population (1,000s)*	*10-Year Growth (Percent)*	*Local Airports (Number)*	*Local Wholesalers (Number)*	*Aircraft Schools (Number)*
Austin	782	45.6	4	8	14
Dallas	3,885	32.6	11	137	42
Houston	3,302	20.7	11	26	25
Kansas City	1,566	9.3	12	34	17
Little Rock	513	8.1	2	6	8
Oklahoma City	959	11.4	9	21	18
San Antonio	1,302	21.5	4	44	13
Tulsa	709	7.9	6	28	17

Sources: Statistical Abstract of the United States 1991 (Washington, D.C.: Bureau of the Census, U.S. Department of Commerce), Tables 36 and 38 for population statistics; 1991 respective city telephone directory *Yellow Pages* for all remaining information.

Notes: Population reported for 1990; population growth from 1980 to 1990.

With branch operations in San Antonio, Dallas, and Tulsa at the end of 1988, Western Aero had created a regional hub-and-spoke distribution system, and Phoenix Holdings was expecting a large turnaround in the following year. Management thought that work force reductions, efficiencies brought about through the use of a new automated system, and more branches to cover the company's higher fixed costs would be reflected in profitable returns. Western Aero also invested money in marketing efforts and in the hiring of skilled salespeople and managers to handle the new computerized system in the two additional branches. Five new people were hired and three others transferred from the company's Mid-States Aircraft operation.

As shown in the company's 1989–1991 income statements and balance sheets in Exhibits 10 and 11, J.M. Miller's expected turnaround did not materialize. To become more competitive, Western Aero continued its membership in the National Aircraft Parts Distribution Association (NAPDA), spent more on advertising, and began catalog sales, in late December 1991, with full-page parts listings in *Trade-A-Plane,* a trimonthly "Yellow Pages" newspaper. NAPDA is a voluntary association which, for a $1,000 monthly fee, allows its members to fill one another's stockouts at 5% above cost, thereby ensuring the complete shipment of any customer's order. With Western Aero's use of catalog sales, it entered a hotly contested, price competitive arena, while also angering many of its local customers. Its goal was to undersell all competitors on the industry's most visible items. Exhibit 12 displays Western Aero's quoted prices in *Trade-A-Plane* on a sample of airplane parts and supplies versus prices of its two major full-line catalog competitors—Chief Aircraft, Inc., set in Oregon on California's northern border, and San-Val Discount located in Van Nuys, California. Exhibit 13 lists the major product categories carried by Western Aero and the typical markups recently obtained on those goods.

Exhibit 10 **Western Aero Supply Income Statements**

	Year Ending December 31		
	*1989**	*1990*	*1991*
Customer sales**	$ 810,845	$5,056,108	$4,314,106
NAPDA sales	240,834	1,476,331	1,216,000
Total sales	$1,051,679	$6,532,439	$5,530,106
Cost of sales	781,902	5,331,491	4,766,055
Gross profit on sales	$ 269,777	$1,200,948	$ 764,051
Selling and general administrative expense	279,084	1,095,819	763,926
Income from operations	$ (9,307)	$ 105,129	$ 125
Net other expense	(2,973)	(85,700)	(56,641)
Income before taxes	$ (12,280)	$ 19,429	$ (56,516)
Taxes/tax recovery	(1,200)	3,475	(3,500)
Net income	$ (11,080)	$ 15,954	$ (53,016)

Source: Audited company reports.

*Results for the year's last eight months.

**Includes transfer sales to affiliates at 5% over cost.

Western Aero Supply Balance Sheets

Exhibit 11

	Year Ending December 31		
	*1989**	*1990*	*1991*
Assets			
Current			
Cash	$ 103,007	$ —	$ —
Trade accounts receivable	197,834	430,402	385,580
Parts inventories	517,621	960,818	1,037,848
Due from parent and affiliates	—	403,523	478,051
Covenant not to compete, current	43,729	43,729	43,729
Prepaid expenses and other	9,355	10,757	12,573
Total current assets	$ 871,546	$1,849,229	$1,957,781
Net property and equipment	$ 56,958	$ 32,747	$ 16,229
Other			
Unamortized covenant not to compete	$ 145,764	$ 102,035	$ 58,306
Other assets	3,872	7,480	9,513
Total other assets	$ 149,636	$ 109,515	$ 67,819
Total assets	$1,078,140	$1,991,491	$2,041,829
Liabilities and Stockholders' Equity			
Current liabilities			
Notes payable	$ —	$ 445,770	$ 645,770
Accrued expenses	3,187	—	—
Due to affiliate	95,634	—	—
Accounts payable and accrued expenses	236,419	881,110	844,194
Current maturities of long-term debt	77,529	60,730	57,888
Total current liabilities	$ 412,769	$1,387,610	$1,547,852
Long-term debt, less current maturities	236,684	159,240	102,352
Total liabilities	$ 649,453	$1,546,850	$1,650,204
Stockholders' equity			
Preferred stock, 5%, cumulative $5.00 par	$ 15,500	$ 15,500	$ 15,500
Common stock, $.50 par	37,187	37,187	37,187
Additional paid-in capital	30,410	30,410	30,410
Retained earnings	390,721	406,675	353,659
	$ 473,818	$ 489,772	$ 436,756
Less: Treasury stock, at cost	(45,131)	(45,131)	(45,131)
Total stockholders' equity	$ 428,687	$ 444,641	$ 391,625
Total liabilities and stockholders' equity	$1,078,140	$1,991,491	$2,041,829

Source: Audited company reports.

*Liabilities and equity created and held during the time of possession of Western Aero by Phoenix Holdings, Inc.

Exhibit 12

Sample of Catalog Items and Prices

Items	*Listed Price* Western Aero	San-Val Discount	Chief Aircraft
Assets			
Lord Engine Mount—Cessna 180-182	$ 180.00	$ 186.00	$ 204.95
Alcor Single CHT set	175.00	179.95	172.95
Concorde Battery CB25 (12-9)	73.00	75.00	75.00
Cleveland Conversion Kit—Piper J-3	445.00	454.95	499.95
4522 Landing Lights	21.00	22.50	22.25
RN-2100 Scott oil pressure gauge	22.00	24.95	22.95
McCreary Tire—600-6 4 Ply Air-trac	43.00	45.00	45.00
Goodyear Tire—650-8 8 Ply Special II	91.00	95.00	106.00
Slick Magneto—4271	275.00	283.95	279.95
Slick Harness—6 cylinder	190.00	185.00	196.00
Concorde Battery—CB24-11 (G242)	158.00	164.00	157.00
O-Ring sets	50.00	56.95	64.95
Totals	$1,723.00	$1,773.25	$1,846.95

Exhibit 13

Product Categories and Expected Gross Margin Ranges

Product Category	*Gross Margin Percent*
Pilot supplies	35 – 45
Engine parts	10 – 20
Engines	5 – 10
Ignition products	15 – 20
Pumps and filters	15 – 25
Tires and tubes	25 – 35
Navigation and communication	25 – 30
Batteries	20 – 30
Harnesses and accessories	25 – 35
Hardware	50 – 70
Lighting systems	30 – 40
Lights	35 – 45
Paint, chemicals, and lubricants	30 – 40
Wheels and brakes	15 – 30
Heating and exhaust systems	20 – 30
Miscellaneous	30 – 35
Average	15 – 20

Source: Management's estimates.

Note: The proportion of engine sales made during a period is the major contributor to the range in obtained margins.

CLOSE THE SAN ANTONIO BRANCH?

As branch operations settled down, Mike Miller almost immediately became concerned about the poor monthly sales and gross profits being generated in San Antonio. Given its high wage costs, this branch was selling too few big-ticket items such as engines and cylinders and too many high-margin but low-ticket items such as masking tape, paint cans, hose fittings, and sectionals. Daus Decker, the branch's manager, started off well by selling old inventory purchased at comparatively low costs given their current inventory replacement value. The operation's gross profits started to decline, however, as soon as he had to work with fresh, high-cost inventories. In November 1990, Daus was transferred to Dallas as a salesman, and Paul Feltes was sent from Tulsa's branch to San Antonio, where he served as branch manager until March 1991.

Paul experienced only limited success at selling the company's bigger-ticketed items, although he had been very successful doing so in Tulsa. When the operation showed no real profit improvement, Mike Allen was hired to replace Paul Feltes, in April 1991. Given monthly losses ranging from $5,000 to $10,000, and Mike's cumulative branch tallies on their profits and losses as summarized for the year in Exhibit 14, it was concluded in September that the San Antonio sales force lacked both the product and customer knowledge, as well as the necessary charisma, to make the branch a success. Additionally, the branch had become a joke within the company, and most customers in the San Antonio area itself felt Western Aero was more a hardware vendor than an engine and airframe supplier.

Branch Income Statements, Year Ending December 31, 1991 **Exhibit 14**

	Dallas	*San Antonio*	*Tulsa*
Sales	$1,054,345.78	$ 614,625.57	$2,862,947.07
Cost of Sales	892,774.92	498,034.02	2,288,939.92
Gross Profit	$ 161,570.86	$ 116,591.55	$ 574,007.15
Direct Expenses			
Wages	$ 92,417.06	$ 122,739.34	$ 195,068.82
Automobile	5,959.61	2,833.48	13,084.61
Discounts taken	7,795.28	4,144.26	16,024.15
Benefits	n.a.	820.48	1,568.82
Telephone	16,517.94	23,529.04	35,821.26
Freight	10,017.02	22,626.26	43,671.26
Office supplies	579.73	n.a.	8,932.94
Rent	15,600.00	3,273.50	6,000.00
Employee insurance	4,428.72	20,850.05	15,436.90
Utilities	1,355.00	(3,681.89)	1,897.29
Warehouse	1,944.83	2,759.36	9,055.78
Operating expenses	$ 156,615.19	$ 199,893.88	$ 346,561.83
Overhead contribution	$ 4,955.67	$ (83,302.33)	$ 227,445.32

Source: These data were compiled by Mike Miller personally for use in his analysis of the three branch operations.

Once Mike had made the shutdown decision, Robert Williams was dispatched to San Antonio in December to make the pronouncement to its employees. All were given four weeks' severance pay. Although not the reflective type, Mike Miller exclaimed in the aftermath, "If I had it to do all over again, I would have hired a whole new staff right away in the very beginning." Certainly, this move might have minimized the effects of William Matthews' habit of coming to the office every day and reminiscing about the "good old days," acting like he still owned the business.

REFERENCES

Business plan. Global Aircraft Parts, Ltd., March 1990.

FAA Aviation Forecasts Fiscal Years 1990–2001. Washington, D.C.: U.S. Department of Transportation, FAA-APO 90–1, March 1990.

FAA Statistical Handbook of Aviation: Calendar Year 1989. Washington, D.C.: U.S. Department of Transportation.

"A Flying Start." *Express Magazine,* Winter, 1990, p. 8.

Kolcum, Edward H. "Ryder Managers Predict Aviation Units Will Show Moderate Growth in 1990." *Aviation Week & Space Technology,* 26 March 1990, p. 77.

Newitt, Jane. "Gray Skies Forever?" *American Demographics,* November 1989, pp. 36–39.

1987 Census of Wholesale Trade: Commodity Line Sales, United States. Washington, D.C.: Bureau of the Census, U.S. Department of Commerce.

Phillips, Edward H. "Business Aircraft Sales Linked to Global Economic Recovery." *Aviation Week & Space Technology,* 16 March 1992, pp. 136–138.

Statistical Abstract of the United States 1991. Washington D.C.: Bureau of the Census, U.S. Department of Commerce.

CASE 23

Circus Circus Enterprises, Inc.

John K. Ross, III, Mike Keefe, Bill Middlebrook, Southwest Texas State University

Although Circus Circus Enterprises, Inc. (hereafter Circus) describes itself as a merchant and compares its stores to supermarkets and shopping malls, its products are hardly those one finds on typical store shelves. The merchandise of Circus is "entertainment," and the stores are huge pink-and-white striped concrete circus tents, a 600-foot-long riverboat replica, and a giant castle. Their areas of operation are the glitzy vacation and convention meccas of Las Vegas, Reno, and Laughlin, Nevada. Circus's marketing of its products has been called "right out of the bargain basement" and caters to low rollers and family-oriented vacationers wanting more than a conventional gambling-oriented vacation.

Circus was purchased in 1974 for $50,000, as a small and unprofitable casino operation by partners William G. Bennett, an aggressive cost-cutter who ran furniture stores before entering the gaming industry in 1965, and William N. Pennington (see Exhibit 1 for board of directors and top managers). The partners were able to rejuvenate Circus back to profitability, went public with a stock offering in October 1983, and have since averaged a growth rate in earnings per share of more than 30% per year. Today, Circus operates 10% of the hotel rooms and 11% of the total casino space in Las Vegas, while it operates 52% of rooms and 35% of total casino space in Laughlin. Casino operations provide over half the total revenue for Circus (see Exhibit 2). In 1990, Circus reported a net income of more than $75 million and employed more than 13,000 people. Circus management projects it will earn more than $100 million in fiscal year 1992.

This case is intended for classroom discussion only, not to depict effective or ineffective handling of administrative situations. All rights reserved to the authors.

Exhibit 1 **Circus Circus Enterprises, Inc., Board of Directors and Top Management**

Directors			
William G. Bennett	65	Chairman	
William N. Pennington	67	Nominee	
Richard P. Banis	45	Nominee	
Glenn W. Schaeffer	37	Nominee	
Melvin L. Larson	60	Nominee	
Arthur M. Smith, Jr.	68	Nominee	
Carl F. Dodge	74	Nominee	
Top Management			
William G. Bennett	65	CEO	25 years
Glenn Schaeffer	37	President/CFO	13 years
James Muir	37	Executive VP & COO	10 years

Source: 1990 Annual Report and correspondence with Glenn Schaeffer.
Note: Of the other seven general managers, only one is age 50 or older.

Exhibit 2 **Circus Circus Enterprises, Inc., Sources of Revenue**

Casinos	57.9%
Food and beverage	15.7%
Hotel	15.3%
Other	11.1%

CIRCUS CIRCUS OPERATIONS

Circus defines entertainment as pure play and fun, and it goes out of its way to see that customers have plenty of opportunity for both. Each of Circus's "stores" has a distinctive personality. Circus Circus–Las Vegas is the world of the Big Top, where live circus acts perform free every 30 minutes. Kids may cluster around video games, while the adults migrate to nickel slot machines and dollar game tables. At the Excalibur, visitors are transported back in time to a medieval castle, where they may watch a joust, mingle on a medieval street with costumed jugglers and jesters, shop, dine at a feast, play blackjack, cheer in the hofbrau, bet on a sporting event, see a sword fight, dance in a medieval village, swim, get married, or play the slot machines. All of Circus's operations and entertainment are continuous year round.

Circus operates seven properties in all (see Exhibit 3). At one end of the Vegas strip is Circus Circus–Las Vegas, a circus big top that covers 795 hotel rooms, shopping areas, two specialty restaurants, a buffet with seating for 1,100, fast-food shops, cocktail lounges, video arcades, 110,000 square feet of casino, and live circus acts. Guests who stay in the facility's other 1,998 rooms

Circus Circus Enterprises, Inc., Holdings **Exhibit 3**

Location	*Properties*	*Percent Revenues By Market*
Las Vegas	Circus Circus–Las Vegas Excalibur Silver City Casino Slots-A-Fun	49.9%
Laughlin	The Colorado Belle The Edgewater	29.6
Reno	Circus Circus–Reno	20.5

travel by elevated monorail from the adjacent Circus Skyrise and Circus Manor or from the nearby Circusland RV Park.

Excalibur, Circus's latest and biggest venture, anchors the other end of the Las Vegas strip. It is the first sight travelers see as they exit Interstate 15. (Management was confident that the sight of a giant, colorful medieval castle would make a lasting impression on mainstream tourists and vacationing families arriving in Las Vegas.) Guests cross a drawbridge, with moat, onto a cobblestone walkway where multicolored spires, turrets, and battlements loom above. The castle walls are four 28-story hotel towers containing a total of 4,032 rooms. Inside is a medieval world complete with a Fantasy Faire inhabited by strolling jugglers, fire eaters, and acrobats, as well as a Royal Village complete with peasants, serfs, and ladies-in-waiting around medieval theme shops. The 100,000-square-foot casino encloses 2,600 slot machines, more than 100 game tables, a sports book, and a poker and keno area. There are 12 restaurants, capable of feeding more than 20,000 people daily, and a 900-seat amphitheater. Excalibur, which opened in June 1990, was built for $294 million, primarily financed with internally generated funds.

Situated between these two anchors on the Las Vegas strip are two smaller casinos, also operated by Circus. The Silver City Casino and Slots-A-Fun primarily depend upon the foot traffic along the strip for their gambling patrons.

All of Circus's operations do well in the city of Las Vegas. Circus Circus–Las Vegas's 1990 operational earnings were flat, due to the openings of Excalibur and the Mirage, but the company fared well overall. In its first 43 days of operation, Excalibur added $11 million in operating income to offset the lack of growth elsewhere and is expected to add $100 million at the end of the first 12 months. Circus's hotel room occupancy rates in Las Vegas are typically 98%–100%, and prior to the opening of Excalibur, Circus referred nearly one million "room nights" to other hotels each year. Seating over 3,000, the restaurants at Excalibur alone are able to offer more meals per day than any other single-site commercial establishment in the world. Although Circus loses fifty cents on each meal it serves, the popular buffets generate enough cash flow each year to cover debt obligations nearly six times.

The company's other big top facility is Circus Circus–Reno. With the addition of Skyway Tower in 1985, this big top now offers a total of 1,625 hotel rooms, 60,000 square feet of casino, a buffet that can seat 800 people, shops, video arcades, cocktail lounges, midway games, and circus acts. As a project, Circus Circus–Reno had several marginal years, but has had a more solid performance recently.

The Colorado Belle and the Edgewater Hotel are located in Laughlin, Nevada, on the banks of the Colorado River, a city 90 miles south of Las Vegas. The Colorado Belle, opened in 1987, features a huge paddle wheel riverboat replica, a 64,000-square-foot casino, a buffet, cocktail lounges, and shops. Adjacent hotel towers provide a total of 1,234 guest rooms.

The Edgewater, acquired in 1983, has a southwestern motif and offers 595 guest rooms, a 57,000-square-foot casino, a bowling center, a buffet, and cocktail lounges. Renovations to the Edgewater and the addition of 1,000 more guest rooms was completed in February 1991.

Circus has achieved success through an aggressive growth strategy. Since 1984, Circus increased its available hotel rooms from approximately 2,500 to more than 11,000. Casino space has increased from 165,000 square feet to more than 427,000 square feet during the same period. A strong cash position, innovative ideas, and attention to cost control have allowed Circus to satisfy the bottom line during a period when competitors were typically taking on large debt obligations to finance new projects (see Exhibits 4, 5, 6, and 7).

Circus's projects have been tailored to attract mainstream tourists, approximately 25% of which are family vacationers. Prices and credit limits are low, while the diversity of potential entertainment activities is substantial.

Exhibit 4

Circus Circus Enterprises, Inc., Selected Financial Information

Measure	***FY91***	***FY90***	***FY89***	***FY88***
Earnings per share	$2.78	$2.60	$2.58	$1.48
Current ratio	.88	.66	1.12	2.34
Total liabilities/total assets	.77	.76	.72	.47
Operating profit margin	26.1%	28.7%	28.6%	27.6%

Exhibit 5

Circus Circus Enterprises, Inc., Five-Year Summary

	Sales (in 000s)	***Net Income (in 000s)***	***EPS***
FY '91	$692,052	$76,292	$2.78
FY '90	522,376	76,064	2.60
FY '89	511,960	81,714	2.58
FY '88	458,856	55,900	1.48
FY '87	373,967	28,198	0.75
FY '86	306,993	37,375	1.00

Circus Circus Enterprises, Inc., Annual Income (in 000s) **Exhibit 6**

Fiscal Year End	*1/31/91*	*1/31/90*	*1/31/89*	*1/31/88*
Net sales	$ 692,052	$ 522,376	$ 511,960	$ 458,856
Cost of goods	364,552	227,942	217,891	200,005
Gross profit	$ 327,500	$ 294,434	$ 294,069	$ 258,851
Selling, general, and administrative expenses	128,026	124,228	125,380	113,361
Income before depreciation and amortization	$ 199,474	$ 170,206	$ 168,689	$ 145,490
Depreciation and amortiziation	40,998	31,216	31,800	29,134
Nonoperating income	(570)	1,030	1,493	4,113
Interest expense	42,048	26,818	28,425	19,733
Income before taxes	$ 115,858	$ 113,202	$ 109,957	$ 100,736
Prov. for income tax	39,566	38,138	37,478	38,809
Net income before expenditure items	$ 76,292	$ 75,064	$ 72,479	$ 61,927
Expenditure items and discontinued items	0	0	9,235	(6,027)
Net income	$ 76,292	$ 75,064	$ 81,714	$ 55,900
Outstanding shares	27,443,165	28,532,324	37,907,346	37,907,346

MARKETPLACES

Laughlin

Laughlin represents a market quite distinct from that of Las Vegas and Reno. Laughlin is a city with a population of 4,400, as compared with 650,000 in Las Vegas and 119,000 in Reno. Laughlin caters to single-day travelers from nearby Arizona and southern California population centers and, at present, has 4,000 hotel rooms and 5,500 more under construction or in the planning stage. Nine casinos opened in Laughlin during the period between 1986 and 1990. Such construction activities have been, at times, a disruptive factor to the tourism business, due to the strain placed on the city's housing, schools, and water supplies. Laughlin has been described as the industry's fastest-growing market, but its future depends on the extent to which it becomes a destination resort, as contrasted to a day-trip resort. Although Circus's facilities must compete with six major casinos such as Harrah's Del Rio, in fiscal year 1989, Circus's facilities here produced between 40% to 50% of the Laughlin market's operating profits.

Las Vegas

Las Vegas is a more established gambling market, although recently growth has been quite explosive. Twenty well-known casinos, such as Caesar's World, Harrah's, and the Golden Nugget, cater to the upscale gambler, offering big-name entertainment, free drinks for gamblers, easy credit, and glamorous surroundings. Las Vegas draws clientele largely from southern California and

Exhibit 7

Circus Circus Enterprises, Inc., Balance Sheet ($ in 000's)

Fiscal Year End	*1/31/1991*	*1/31/1990*	*1/31/1989*	*1/31/1988*
Annual Assets				
Cash	$ 18,134	$ 19,411	$ 20,667	$ 14,212
Marketable securities	0	0	0	60,097
Receivables	5,977	2,156	3,197	3,319
Inventories	16,573	9,337	15,714	10,861
Other current assets	13,601	10,323	8,212	8,734
Total current assets	$ 54,285	$ 41,227	$ 47,790	$ 97,223
Property, plant, and equipment	$728,756	$612,905	$455,074	$413,745
Net property, plant, and equipment	$728,756	$612,905	$455,074	$413,745
Deferred charges	0	$ 9,252	0	0
Intangibles	0	$ 11,654	$ 12,328	$ 11,198
Deposits and other assets	$ 9,438	0	$ 8,920	$ 6,891
Total assets	$792,479	$675,038	$524,112	$529,057
Annual Liabilities				
Notes payable	$ 0	$ 0	$ 0	$ 0
Accounts payable	16,048	23,690	9,578	7,177
Current long-term debt	938	935	1,485	2,053
Accrued expenses	43,652	35,104	29,326	30,822
Income taxes	818	2,345	2,168	1,420
Total current liabilities	$ 61,456	$ 62,074	$ 42,557	$ 41,472
Deferred charges/income	48,209	42,586	38,933	39,529
Long-term debt	496,750	408,314	296,316	168,339
Noncurrent capital leases	0	0	0	485
Other long-term liabilities	1,221	1,340	1,394	1,174
Total liabilities	$607,636	$514,314	$379,200	$250,999
Common stock net	1,571	1,912	1,907	1,903
Capital surplus	52,302	47,376	43,273	42,035
Retained earnings	281,587	205,295	130,370	237,290
Treasury stock	(150,617)	(93,859)	(30,638)	(3,170)
Shareholder equity	184,843	160,724	144,912	278,058
Total liabilities and net worth	$792,479	$675,038	$524,112	$529,057

the rest of the southwestern United States. It ranks as the fifth most popular convention location in the nation and is becoming more popular for tours from Asia and Europe.

Several new casino-hotels, including the Mirage, Excalibur, and O'Shea's, have opened in Las Vegas during 1989–1990. Additionally, MGM has begun development of the MGM Grand Hotel and Theme Park scheduled for opening in 1993. This rapid growth in Las Vegas has some observers worried; however, most expect it to be readily absorbed by the current market and increased tourism. The expected increase in family vacationers may end up exerting pressures on the more traditional "gambling only" casino operations, forcing them to compete with the theme resorts.

■ Reno

In Reno, recent growth has been modest. Bad weather in the first half of 1989 kept "walk-in" traffic low, causing revenues for all tourist-based businesses to be flat. Like Las Vegas, Reno is a relatively established gaming market, with ten major casinos catering to the upscale gambler. It draws clientele largely from northern California and the rest of the northwestern United States. Circus Circus–Reno generates the highest profit margins of any major Reno gaming property and expects to be the leader in absolute profits in the near future.

THE GAMING INDUSTRY

The gaming industry captures a large amount of vacation/leisure time dollars spent in the United States. Gamblers lost nearly $28 billion in 1988 on legal and illegal wagering, including wagers at racetracks, at bingo parlors, in lotteries, and at casinos. This figure does not include dollars spent on lodging, food, transportation, and other related expenditures associated with visits to gaming facilities. Casino gambling accounts for 33% of all legal gambling expenditures, second only to lotteries at 39%. The popularity of casino gambling may be credited to more frequent and somewhat higher payout, as compared to lotteries and racetracks; however, as winnings are recycled, the multiplier effect restores a high return to casino operators.

Two geographical areas—the state of Nevada and Atlantic City, New Jersey—dominate the gaming industry, being the only areas allowing full-fledged casino gambling. Nevada accounted for 62% of the industry's revenues in 1989. Higher profitability in Nevada is believed due to two factors: lower interest expense because of old debt and lower regulatory and labor costs. Circus Circus is ranked first in annual sales volume among gaming companies and casinos that have properties in Nevada (see Exhibit 8). Limited gaming activity

Gaming Companies Located in Nevada, by Annual Sales Volume (000s) **Exhibit 8**

Circus Circus Enterprises, Inc.	$522,000
Mirage	500,000
Desert Palace Inc.	498,000
Showboat Inc.	342,000
California Hotel & Casino	332,000
Golden Nugget Inc.	300,000
Las Vegas Hilton Corp.	200,000
Hotel Ramada of NV	175,000
Holiday Casino Inc.	171,000
Sahara Casino Partners LP	165,000
MGM Desert Inn Inc.	135,000
Harvey's Wagon Wheel Inc.	100,000
Imperial Palace Inc.	100,000
Mare-bear Inc.	92,200

Source: 1991 Dun's Business Rankings, by sales volume within Nevada.

(such as floating casinos, bingo, poker parlors, video gambling, lotteries, and parimutuel betting) is allowed in other states, but significant expansion beyond these two areas is expected to be slow due to legal constraints in these jurisdictions.

Besides geographical separation, the primary differences in the two markets reflect the different types of consumers frequenting these markets. While Las Vegas attracts overnight resort-seeking vacationers, Atlantic City's clientele are predominantly day-trippers traveling by automobile or bus. According to the Las Vegas Convention and Visitor Authority, Las Vegas is a destination market, with most visitors planning their trip more than a week in advance, (81%), arriving by car (47%) or airplane (42%), and staying in a hotel (72%). Gamblers are typically return visitors (77%), averaging 2.2 trips per year, and like playing the slots (65%).

Development of new and existing markets will determine the industry's future. New theme resorts are being introduced to differentiate the market and are expected to capture most of the increase in gaming revenues. Atlantic City is expanding transportation and lodging accommodations to better enable it to attract resort and convention-related business, but it will be some time, if ever, before it can compete with Nevada. Casino operations account for 67% of net revenue for companies that have gaming facilities in Nevada, as compared to 88% for Atlantic City, showing Atlantic City's stronger dependence on gambling (legislation currently under consideration in New Jersey may make the Atlantic City gaming industry more competitive in the future).

The gaming industry is led by eight companies that account for more than half of total casino revenues. According to Standard and Poor's Industry Surveys, the Trump Organization, Caesar's World, and Promus were the leaders in gaming revenues in calendar year 1990 (see Exhibit 9). Other revenue leaders were Bally Manufacturing, Golden Nugget, Circus Circus, Aztar, and Hilton Hotels. All of the top eight companies have casino operations in Nevada except for Trump.

MAJOR INDUSTRY PLAYERS

■ Bally Manufacturing Corporation

Bally Manufacturing Corporation is a diversified organization that operates casinos and fitness centers and produces and distributes gaming products. Bally is one of the largest casino operators in the world, with 268,000 square feet of casino space and 4,800 guest rooms in four casinos: Bally's–Las Vegas and Bally's–Reno in Nevada; Bally's Park Place and Bally's Grand in Atlantic City, New Jersey. In 1989, casino hotel operations had sales of $949 million, which was more than half of Bally's total sales. Bally's has pursued a growth strategy through acquisitions over the last five years. It owns several hotels in Las Vegas and in Reno and the former Golden Nugget in Atlantic City. Unable to make debt payments, Bally announced in 1991 that both Nevada and New Jersey casino operations were being restructured.

In addition to casinos, Bally's Scientific Games offers gaming equipment and services. This segment produces German wall machines and coin-operated gaming equipment and recently was the first to sell slot machines to the former Soviet Union. Producing and selling paper ticket lottery games is

Major U.S. Casino Operators **Exhibit 9**

	Gaming Revenues (in millions)		
Company	*Fiscal 1988*	*Fiscal 1989*	*Fiscal 1990*
Caesar's World	636	698	673
Promus Companies	631	680	E690
Bally Manufacturing	671	674	E646
Trump Organization	548	571	818
Aztar	358	410	401
Circus Circus	320	324	E410
Hilton Hotels	320	314	E370
Showboat	244	292	E290
Resorts International	243	227	205
Pratt Hotels	206	219	230
Golden Nugget	113	207	593
Clairidge	133	129	135
MGM Grand	129	119	E83
Sahara Casinos LP	47	95	99
Totals	4,599	4,959	E5,643

Source: Standard & Poor's Industry Surveys, October 1991.
E = Estimated.

another of Bally's gaming segments, with customers in the United States as well as Costa Rica, Guatemala, and Venezuela. Finally, Bally operates 315 fitness centers and manufactures exercise bicycles, among other items, for the health club market.

■ Caesar's World, Inc.

In 1989 Caesar's World was listed as the top revenue-producing casino operator (in absolute dollars) in the United States. Caesar's owns and operates three casino-hotels: Caesar's Palace in Las Vegas, Caesar's Tahoe, and Caesar's Atlantic City (87% ownership). Altogether, these properties offer 223,000 square feet of casino space and 2,600 rooms with an average 84% occupancy (86 percent in Las Vegas). Caesar's revenues were adversely impacted by the opening of Golden Nugget's Mirage in Las Vegas and Trump's Taj Mahal in Atlantic City. Caesar's reacted to competitive pressures by renovating and adding on to its properties in all three locations. In addition, it began operation of its first cruise/casino called "Caesar's Palace at Sea," aboard a Japanese-owned luxury cruise liner. Another cruise/casino is already under construction and should be operating in the near future.

Capitalizing on the Caesar's name are two other subsidiaries, Caesar's World Resorts and Caesar's World Merchandising. Caesar's World Resorts owns and operates four nongaming resorts in the Pocono Mountains, Pennsylvania. In addition, Caesar's has an agreement with a Japanese firm to manage a new noncasino resort, scheduled to open in 1992 in Henderson, Nevada. Caesar's World Merchandising, Inc. markets private-label apparel, accessories, gifts, and fragrances.

■ Golden Nugget Inc.

All of Golden Nugget's gaming operations are located in Nevada. It owns and operates the Golden Nugget–Downtown, Las Vegas, the new Mirage on the strip in Las Vegas, and the Golden Nugget–Laughlin. The Mirage, an extremely ambitious resort venture with 3,056 hotel rooms and 95,000 square feet of casino space, became Vegas's top attraction when it opened in 1989. Constructed around a tropical theme, it offers a 20,000-gallon aquarium, a 54-foot-high volcano that erupts with piña colada scented fumes every fifteen minutes, rare white tigers in a jungle scene, tropical gardens, a multitude of restaurants, bars, shops, and an adjacent 16,000-seat outdoor sports arena. The Mirage was the first of the tourist-family-oriented theme resorts in Las Vegas. The project cost more than $615 million and was largely financed with borrowed money.

Formerly known as the Nevada Club, Golden Nugget–Laughlin was purchased in 1988 and is currently expanding its room capacity, casino space, and parking services. A combined total of 155,500 square feet of casino space and 5,037 guest rooms are offered by Golden Nugget's three operations.

When Golden Nugget sold its Atlantic City casino to Bally Manufacturing, it retained $14\frac{1}{2}$ acres of prime real estate on the Boardwalk. Golden Nugget owns 300 acres of property near Las Vegas, on which it developed a world-class golf course and clubhouse. The company is still uncertain about future plans for its New Jersey acreage.

■ Hilton Hotels Corporation

The Hilton family name is well known around the world for fine hotels. Hilton owns four casino-hotels: the Las Vegas Hilton and a Flamingo Hilton in Las Vegas, in Reno, and in Laughlin, Nevada. These casino-hotels have 6,602 guest rooms with 86% average occupancy rate. Additionally, Hilton opened two new theme casinos in 1989, O'Shea's in Las Vegas and Paco's in Reno. Casinos and casino-hotels brought in revenue of $545 million in 1989, 57% of which was derived from gaming.

Producing slightly less revenue are the 271 other hotels and inns owned, managed, or franchised by Hilton. In 1989, Hilton's U.S. operations opened five new hotels and scheduled the opening of two all-suite hotels. The Conrad Hilton subsidiary, operating hotel and gaming properties outside the United States, opened two new hotels in 1989 and has three more scheduled for opening during the early 1990s.

■ Promus Companies Inc.

A relatively new company, Promus is a spin-off of Holiday Corporation (the transaction occurred in February 1990). Promus has both casino-hotel and hotel-only operations. Promus operates Harrah's casino-hotels in Reno, Lake Tahoe, and Laughlin, Nevada; Harrah's in Atlantic City; Holiday Casino and Holiday Inn Hotel in Las Vegas; and Bill's in Lake Tahoe, Nevada. The casinos and casino-hotels have a total of 315,000 square feet of casino space and 4,500 rooms. In 1989, gaming operations contributed $846 million to sales, compared to $94 million contributed by hotel operations. Harrah's leads the gaming industry in net profitability and is the only casino gaming company operating in all five domestic markets.

Promus's hotel segment develops real estate for the purpose of selling it, while retaining franchise and management contracts. It operates 336 hotels under the names of Embassy Suites, Hampton Inn, and Homewood Suites. While only 23 hotels are wholly owned, 71 are managed through a management contract, and the remaining 242 are licensed to franchise owners and other investors.

■ MGM Grand Inc.

MGM Grand Inc. has been a low-key player in the gaming industry since the MGM Grand, Las Vegas, fire and its sale of two Nevada properties to Bally. MGM Grand Inc. owns the subsidiaries MGM Desert Inn Inc., MGM Grand Hotel, Inc., MGM Marina Inc., and MGM Grand Air Inc. In early 1990, the company purchased the Marina Hotel and Casino and the Tropicana Country Club in Las Vegas. Together, the two properties constitute 115 acres on which the MGM Grand Hotel and Theme Park will be erected, with expected completion in 1993. The $910 million complex will be the world's largest hotel, with 5,011 rooms, a 170,000-square-foot casino, and a 35-acre theme park. Built around the Wizard of Oz theme, visitors walk under a 109-foot-tall gold lion and up the yellow brick road into Emerald City, an entertainment area. Staged performances on three levels will entertain visitors riding the 50-passenger elevator. The MGM Desert Inn was sold in 1991 for $130 million to help finance the project.

THE LEGAL ENVIRONMENT

Within the gaming industry, all current operations must consider compliance with extensive gaming regulations as a primary concern. Gambling operations are subject to regulatory control by the Nevada State Gaming Control Board, by the Clark County Nevada Gaming and Liquor Licensing Board, and by city governments. Gaming companies must submit detailed operating and financial reports to authorities. Nearly all financial transactions, including loans, leases, and the sale of securities, must be reported. Some financial activities are subject to approval by regulatory agencies.

Although Circus can expect to exert only limited influence on regulatory matters, it took a step in 1989 to strengthen its ability to deal with regulatory concerns by electing Carl F. Dodge to its board of directors. Dodge is a former chairman of the Nevada Gaming Commission.

THE FUTURE FOR CIRCUS CIRCUS

Circus intends to continue its growth in the Nevada markets by further innovation in theme-oriented entertainment. Both Excalibur and Circus–Las Vegas have room for expansion (the company owns substantial excess land), and Circus management has expressed intent to launch new projects at one or both sites.

Circus has done well by introducing theme-oriented entertainment "megastores" and can be expected to innovate further on that concept. Likewise, its focus on serving middle-income tourists by delivering family entertainment at relatively low prices (room prices range from $28 to $110) has been effective in capturing market share. Excalibur represents a move upscale in the clientele income target, and it is not clear yet whether future projects will cater to the lower- or upper-middle-class tourists. Circus believes that customer loyalty in the gaming industry is closely tied to the merchant's ingenuity, and management believes that the philosophy that brought them this far can be expected to carry them into the future. Circus will consider ventures outside Las Vegas and Nevada as they arise. Circus has set aggressive performance targets for itself, including exceeding by 20% both the average annual growth rate in earnings per share and return on equity, as well as sustaining its industry-leading profit margin and return on invested capital.

CASE 24

Taurus Hungarian Rubber Works

Joseph Wolfe, University of Tulsa; Gyula Bosnyak, Taurus Hungarian Rubber Works; Janos Vecsenyi, International Management Center, Budapest

Although Taurus had adjourned the three-day top management planning session conducted at its Lake Balaton retreat less than two years ago, many major company decisions had been made since that time. Still the basic implementation of the company's diversification strategy had not been accomplished. As director of the company's Corporate Development Strategic Planning Department, Gyula Bosnyak recognized both the timing and the enormity of the events and issues involved. In early 1988, the Hungarian government had passed its Corporation Law, which put all state-owned firms on notice to re-privatize and recapitalize themselves. Not only did the firm have to deal with the mechanics of going public, it had to obtain the ideal mix of debt and equity capital to ensure solid growth for a company that was operating in a stagnant economy and a low-growth industry. Top management was also concerned about the route they should follow in their attempts to invigorate the company. It was an accepted fact that Taurus had to maintain or even improve its international competitiveness, and that it had to diversify away from its traditional dependence on the manufacturing of truck and farm tires.

Rather than viewing this situation as a bothersome threat, Gyula had seen this as an opportunity for Taurus to deal with its working capital problem as well as to begin serious diversification efforts away from its basically noncom-

© 1990 University of Tulsa, Tulsa, USA. Distributed by the European Case Clearing House Ltd, Cranfield Institute of Technology, Cranfield, Bedford MK43 OAL, England. This publication may not be reproduced, stored, transmitted or altered in any way without the written consent of the copyright owner, except as permitted under the Copyright, Designs and Patents Act 1988. It is outside the scope of licenses issued by the Copyright Licensing Agency. All rights reserved to the contributors. Printed in England. The European Case Clearing House Limited is a registered charity.

This case is intended for classroom discussion only, not to depict effective or ineffective handling of administrative situations. All rights reserved to the authors.

petitive and highly threatened commercial tire manufacturing operation. Now, in spring 1990, he was beginning to sort out his company's options before making his recommendations to both Laszlo Geza, vice president of Taurus's Technical Rubber Products Division, and Laszlo Palotas, the company's newly elected president.

RUBBER AND RUBBER PRODUCTION

Christopher Columbus was probably the first European to handle rubber. Haitian natives had used it for centuries as a football-sized sphere that they threw into a hole in the wall of a playing field. These balls were derived from a dried milky liquid obtained by cutting the bark of a "weeping wood" or cauchuc tree. While the natives also used this substance to make shoes, bottles, and waterproof cloth, the Western world's commercial use of the product was limited until two discoveries greatly expanded rubber's usefulness and properties. In 1819, Thomas Hancock discovered latex rubber could be masticated, which allowed it to be converted into products of different shapes by the use of pressure and the addition of other materials. Unfortunately, mastication deprived rubber of its elastic qualities.

The discovery of vulcanization by Charles Goodyear in 1839 solved this problem and also kept rubber products from becoming tacky. Goodyear found the addition of sulphur to crude rubber at a temperature above its melting point improved its mechanical properties and its resistance to temperature changes. After these twin discoveries, the commercial uses of rubber multiplied greatly with the greatest impetus coming from J.B. Dunlop's rediscovery of the pneumatic tire which he applied to his son's bicycle in 1888. Shortly thereafter, the rise of the automobile industry at the century's turn resulted in a tremendous increase in the demand for rubber and its principle application in the manufacture of automobile and truck tires. The world's long ton consumption of rubber prior to World War II in approximate thirty-year periods was as follows:

1840–1872	150,000
1873–1905	1,000,000
1906–1940	18,850,000

The production of natural rubber entails collecting the juice of the 60 to 80 foot high Hevea brasiliensis tree, which is now plantation grown in such tropical countries as Brazil, Malaysia, and Indonesia. The trees are tapped by cutting through the tree's bark, which contains latex tubes. A flow of liquid amounting to about five pounds per year can be obtained from each tree. The milky substance is dehydrated for shipment by spraying and drying, by acidification, coagulation, washing and rolling, or by drying it with smoke. Natural rubber is usually transformed into sheet or crepe. Sheet rubber is smoke-dried and obtains a dark brown color while crepe is air-dried, is much lighter in color, and is passed through heavy rollers at the beginning of the drying process.

As shown in Exhibit 1 a wide range of rubber applications can be obtained through the addition of various ingredients to latex rubber during its masticating or compounding manufacturing stages. Carbon black is added for high abrasion resistance, oils for making the material more workable, and paraffin for better light resistance. Other ingredients, such as antioxidant, activators,

Major Nontire Rubber Uses **Exhibit 1**

Mechanical goods	Hard rubber products
Latex foam products	Flooring
Shoe products	Cements
Athletic goods	Drug sundries
Toys	Pulley belts
Sponge rubber	Waterproof insulation
Insulated wire and cable	Conveyor belts
Footwear	Shock absorbers and vibration dampeners
Waterproofed fabrics	

and various organic and inorganic coloring substances are also employed and various accelerators are used to (1) hasten the vulcanization process, (2) allow it to occur at room temperatures, and (3) improve the product's ultimate quality.

Because of the tremendous increase in the need for natural rubber in the early 1920s, and the realization of its strategic importance by both Germany and Russia from their World War I experiences, vigorous research into the creation of a synthetic rubber was conducted in the 1930s. The first butadiene-styrene copolymer from an emulsion system (Buna S) was prepared at the research laboratories of I.G. Farbenindustrie, followed shortly thereafter by the analogous butadiene-acrylonitrile copolymer (Buna N). By 1936, Germany was able to produce 100 to 200 tons of synthetic rubber a month while by 1939, the factories at Schkopau and Hüls could produce 50,000 tons per year.

The family of "Buna" rubbers are produced by polymerizing butadiene, with sodium (natrium) acting as a catalyst. This process was originally conducted at a temperature of about 50° centigrade, but the copolymerization of butadiene and styrenes is now usually done in aqueous phase.[1] In an emulsion copolymerization process carried out at 50° centigrade, so-called cold rubber, the hydrocarbons to be polymerized are in emulsion and contain a constituent of the activator system dissolved in them. The second part of the activator system is present in the watery medium of the emulsion. The combined activator system initiates the process of polymerization and the polymer's molecule size is regulated by adding various substances. The entire process is stopped after about 60.0% of these substances have reacted. The resulting product is very much like latex rubber and from this phase on can be treated like the natural substance. A large variety of other synthetic rubbers can be produced in addition to the Buna rubbers. Exhibit 2 presents a forecast of the demand for these rubbers for the year 1992.

Combining both natural and synthetic rubbers, it has been estimated that world consumption of these substances will be about 15.9 million metric tons in 1992. According to William E. Tessmer, managing director of the Interna-

[1]Polymerization is a reaction involving the successive addition of a large number of relatively small molecules (monomers) to form a final compound or polymer. A polymer is a giant molecule formed when thousands of molecules have been linked together end to end. A copolymer is a giant molecule formed when two or more unlike monomers are polymerized together.

Exhibit 2

Predicted Demand for Synthetic Rubbers in 1992 (nonsocialist countries, in thousands of metric tons)

Synthetic Rubber	*Forecast*
Styrene-butadiene[a]	2819
Carboxylated styrene-butadiene	1015
Polybutadiene	1142
Ethylene-propylene diene	556
Polychloroprene	268
Nitrile	238
All others[b]	1025
Total	7063

Source: Adapted from International Institute of Synthetic Rubber Producers; Bruce F. Greek, "Modest Growth Ahead for Rubber," *Chemical & Engineering News,* Vol. 66, No. 12, March 21, 1988, p. 26.

[a]In both liquid and solid forms.
[b]Includes polyisoprene and butyl.

tional Institute of Synthetic Rubber Producers, this is an 11.0% increase from the 14.4 million tons estimated for 1987. As shown in Exhibit 3, about 70.0% of the world's rubber consumption is in the form of synthetic rubber. Exhibits 4 and 5 show the predicted geographic distribution of rubber demand for the year 1992.

WORLDWIDE RUBBER COMPANY COMPETITION

Rubber firms now compete on the international level because of a number of driving forces. Automobiles and trucks, which are the major users of tire and rubber products, are ubiquitous; the high operating scales required for efficient plant operations compel manufacturers to find markets that can support them; and growth opportunities no longer exist in many of the manufacturers' home countries. As has been the case within its domestic automobile industry, the United States has been invaded by a number of very competitive and efficient foreign tire and rubber manufacturers. Those foreign competitors in turn have

Exhibit 3

Predicted World Consumption of Rubber (in millions of metric tons)

Type	*1986*	*1987*	*1988*	*1989*	*1990*	*1991*	*1992*
Synthetic	9.5	9.8	9.8	9.9	9.9	10.0	10.0
Natural	4.5	4.6	4.9	5.1	5.4	5.7	5.9
Total	14.0	14.4	14.7	15.0	15.3	15.7	15.9

Source: Based on Bruce F. Greek, "Modest Growth Ahead for Rubber," *Chemical & Engineering News,* Vol. 66, No. 12, March 21, 1988, pp. 25–26.

Note: One metric ton equals 2,204.6 pounds.

Exhibit 4

Predicted Changes in Rubber Demand by Geographic Area (in thousands of metric tons)

Geographic Area	*1987*	*1992*	*Change*
North America	3,395	3,432	1.09
Latin America	788	944	19.80
Western Europe	2,460	2,953	20.04
Africa & Middle East	259	324	25.10
Asia & Oceania	3,060	3,541	15.72
Socialist countries	4,057	4,706	16.00
Total	14,019	15,900	13.42%

Source: Based on Bruce F. Greek, "Modest Growth Ahead for Rubber," *Chemical & Engineering News,* Vol. 66, No. 12, March 21, 1988, p. 26.

acquired firms or have entered into joint ventures on a global scale, thereby increasing their penetration into a number of countries. Exhibit 6 displays the financial results that have been obtained by the major world rubber manufacturers for 1984 and 1988, while Exhibit 7 reviews the alternative strategies and recent actions taken by the industry's principal actors. As best as can be determined, Exhibit 8 demonstrates that Michelin has recently become the world's largest tire manufacturing firm with a worldwide market share of 21.3%, with Goodyear and Bridgestone basically tied for second place in world sales.

TAURUS HUNGARIAN RUBBER WORKS

Today's Taurus Hungarian Rubber Works has an ancestry dating back more than a century. From its earliest days with the founding of the factory of Erno

Exhibit 5

Predicted Demand for Rubber in Socialist Countries (in millions of metric tons)

Socialist Group	*1987*	*1992*
East European		
Synthetic	2.90	3.30
Natural	.40	.37
Total	3.30	3.67
Asian Socialist		
Synthetic	.30	.43
Natural	.46	.61
Total	.76	1.04

Source: Based on Bruce F. Greek, "Modest Growth Ahead for Rubber," *Chemical & Engineering News,* Vol. 66, No. 12, March 21, 1988, pp. 25–26.

Exhibit 6

Selected Company Sales and Profits (in U.S. dollars)

Company	1984 Sales (billion)	1984 Profits (million)	1988 Sales (billion)	1988 Profits (million)
B.F. Goodrich (U.S.)	3.40	60.6	n.a.[a]	n.a.
Bridgestone (Japan)	3.38	65.1	9.30	310.2
Cooper (U.S.)	.56	23.9	.73	35.0
Firestone (U.S.)	4.16	102.0	n.a.[b]	n.a.
GenCorp (U.S.)	2.73	7.2	.50	n.a.[c]
Goodyear (U.S.)	10.24	391.7	10.90	330.0
Michelin (France)	5.08	(256.5)	8.70	397.4
Pirelli (Italy)	3.50	72.0	7.01	172.1
Taurus (Hungary)	.26	11.5	.38	9.0
Uniroyal (U.S.)	2.10	77.1	2.19	11.8

Sources: Akron Beacon Journal, January 13, 1986, p. B8, "Powerful Profits Around the World"; *Fortune*, Vol. 120, No. 3 (July 31, 1989), pp. 292, 294, Gary Levin, "Tire Makers Take Opposite Routes"; *Advertising Age*, Vol. 60, No. 6 (February 6, 1989), p.34.

[a]Merged with Uniroyal in 1987.
[b]Acquired by Bridgestone in 1988.
[c]Acquired by Continental in 1987.

Schottola, it has been Hungary's most important rubber producer. In growing to its current size, Taurus has both grown internally and has acquired several smaller manufacturers.

The first Hungarian rubber factory was established in 1882, and in 1890, it became a public company under the name Magyar Ruggyantaarugyar Rt. Because Hungary lacked a domestic producer of automobiles at the century's turn, the company supported the creation of an automobile plant, which was ultimately located in Arad, and the formation of the Autotaxi company in Budapest. During the period before World War I, Magyar Ruggyantaarugyar grew rapidly and was soon exporting between 30.0% and 35.0% of its products outside Hungary. Its rubber balls, toys, asbestos-rubber seals, and Palma heels gained a worldwide reputation for quality.

During the interwar period, the Hungarian rubber sector declined dramatically with its export sales dropping to 15.0%–18.0% of total production. Its factory equipment deteriorated and only its lines of rubber yarns and latex products could remain internationally competitive. Pre-World War I global market shares of 0.6% fell to 0.3% and its annual sales growth rates dropped to 1.5%–2.0% per year.

Upon the nationalization of all rubber firms after World War II, the Hungarian government pursued a policy of extensive growth for a number of years. From 1950 to 1970, annual production increases of 12.5% a year were common while the rubber sector's employment and gross fixed asset value increased a respective average of approximately 6.2% and 15.7% per year. Although growth was rapid, great inefficiencies were incurred. Plant utilization rates were low and productivity ratios lagged by about 1.5 to 3.0 times that obtained by comparable socialist and advanced capitalist countries. Little attention was paid to rationalizing either production or the product line as sales to the

Recent Activities of Various Tire and Rubber Companies — Exhibit 7

Bridgestone Corporation: Bridgestone's acquisition of the Firestone Tire & Rubber Company in 1988 for $2.6 billion vaulted it into a virtual tie with Goodyear as the world's second largest tire company. The acquisition has been a troublesome one for Bridgestone, with Firestone losing about $100.0 million in 1989, causing the parent company's 1989 profits to fall to about $250.0 million on sales of $10.7 billion. Bridgestone has already invested $1.5 billion in upgrading Firestone's deteriorated plants and an additional $2.5 billion will be needed to bring all operations up to Bridgestone's quality standards. Last year's North American sales were $3.5 billion, and the firm plans to quadruple the output of its La Vergne, Tennessee, plant. Currently, Bridgestone is attempting to increase its share of the American tire market while slowly increasing its share of the European market as Japanese cars increase their sales in that area. In mid-1989, nine top executives were forced to resign or accept reassignment over disputes about the wisdom of the company's aggressive growth goals. Bridgestone is a major factor in Asia, the Pacific, and South America, where Japanese cars and trucks are heavily marketed.

Continental Gummi—Werke AG: Continental is West Germany's largest tire manufacturer and is number two in European sales. It purchased General Tire from Gencorp in June 1987 for $625.0 million and is basically known as a premium quality tire manufacturer. Continental entered a $200.0 million joint radial tire venture in December 1987 with the Toyo Tire & Rubber Company and Yokohama Rubber Company for the manufacture of tires installed on Japanese cars being shipped to the American market. Another part of the venture entails manufacturing radial truck and bus tires in the United States.

Cooper Tire and Rubber Company: This relatively small American firm has been very successful by specializing in the replacement tire market. This segment accounts for about 80.0% of its sales and nearly half of its output is sold as private-labeled merchandise. Cooper has recently expanded its capacity by 12.0% with about 10.0% more capacity scheduled for completion in late-1990. About 60.0% of its sales are for passenger tires while the remainder are for buses and heavy trucks. The company is currently attempting to acquire a medium truck tire plant in Natchez, Mississippi to enable it to cover the tire spectrum more completely.

Goodyear Tire and Rubber Co.: The last of two major rubber companies left in the United States. Goodyear has diversified itself into chemicals and plastics, a California to Texas oil pipeline, as well as into the aerospace industry. Automotive products, which include tires, account for 86.0% of sales and 76.0% of operating profits. Its recent sales growth has come from African and Latin American tire sales where the company has a dominant market share. Additional plant expansions have been started in Canada and South Korea (12,000 tires daily per plant) and will be available in 1991 although they should not produce significant revenues until 1992. Goodyear is attempting to sell off its All America pipeline for about $1.4 billion to reduce its $275.0 million per year interest charges on $3.5 billion worth of debt.

Michelin et Cie: Although it lost $1.5 billion between 1980 and 1984, Michelin has become profitable again. In late 1988, the company acquired Uniroyal/Goodrich for $690.0 million, which made it the world's largest tire company. Uniroyal had merged in August 1986 with the B.F. Goodrich Co., creating a company where 29.0% of its output was in private brands. Passenger and light truck tires were sold in both the United States and overseas, and sales grew 44.5% although profits fell 11.1%. Michelin has entered a joint venture with Okamoto of Japan to double that company's capacity to 24,000 tires a day. While a large company, Michelin is much stronger in the truck tire segment than it is in the passenger tire segment.

Pirelli: After having been frustrated in its attempts to acquire Firestone, Pirelli purchased the Armstrong Tire Company for $190.0 million in 1988 to gain a foothold in the North American market. Armstrong, under the guise of Armtek Corporation, was attempting to diversify out of the tire industry by selling off its industrial tire plant in March 1987. Pirelli, which is strong in the premium tire market, obtained a company whose sales are equally divided between the original equipment and replacement markets and one that has over 500 retail dealers. In the acquisition process Pirelli obtained a headquarters building in Connecticut, three tire plants, one tire textile plant, and one truck tire factory. Armstrong's 1988 sales were $500.0 million.

Exhibit 8

Top Market Shares in World Tire Market

Company	*1985*	*1990*
Goodyear	20.0%	17.2%
Michelin	13.0	21.3
Bridgestone	8.0	17.2

Source: Adapted from Stuart J. Benway, "Tire & Rubber Industry," *The Value Line Investment Survey*, December 22, 1989, p. 127.

Hungarian and Eastern bloc countries appeared to support the sector's activities. At various times, the nationalized firm produced condoms, bicycle and automobile tires, rubber toys, boots, and raincoats.

During this period, the government also restructured its rubber industry. In 1963, Budapest's five rubber manufacturers—PALMA, Heureka, Tauril, Emerge, and Cordatic—were merged into one company called the National Rubber Company, and new locations in Vac, Nyiregyhaza, and Szeged were created. Purchasing, cash management, and investment were centralized, and a central trade and research and development apparatus was created. Contrary to the normal way of conducting its affairs, however, the company pioneered the use of strategic planning when the classic type of centralized planning was still the country's ruling mechanism.

In 1973, the company changed its name to the Taurus Hungarian Rubber Works, and it currently operates rubber processing plants in Budapest, Nyiregyhaza, Szeged, Vac, and Mugi as well as a machine and mold factory in Budapest.

As shown in Exhibits 9 through 12, Taurus operates four separate divisions while engaging in a number of joint ventures. Sales have increased annually to the 20.7 billion Forint mark with an increasing emphasis on international business.

■ Tire Division

The tire division manufactures tires for commercial, nonpassenger vehicles after having phased out its production of automobile tires in the mid-1970s. Truck tires, as either bias-ply or all-steel radials, account for about 34.0% of the division's sales. Farm tires are its other major product category as either textile radials or bias-ply tires. Farm tires were about 20% of the division's sales in 1988. A smaller product category includes tire retreading, inner tubes, and fork lift truck tires. About 58.0% of the division's volume is export sales, of which the following countries constituted the greatest amounts (in millions of Forints):

United States	351.7	West Germany	183.5
Algeria	298.2	Yugoslavia	172.0
Czechoslovakia	187.3		

The division has recently finished a World Bank-financed capacity expansion in the all steel radial truck tire operation. This project was begun in

Taurus Hungarian Rubber Works Organisation Structure **Exhibit 9**

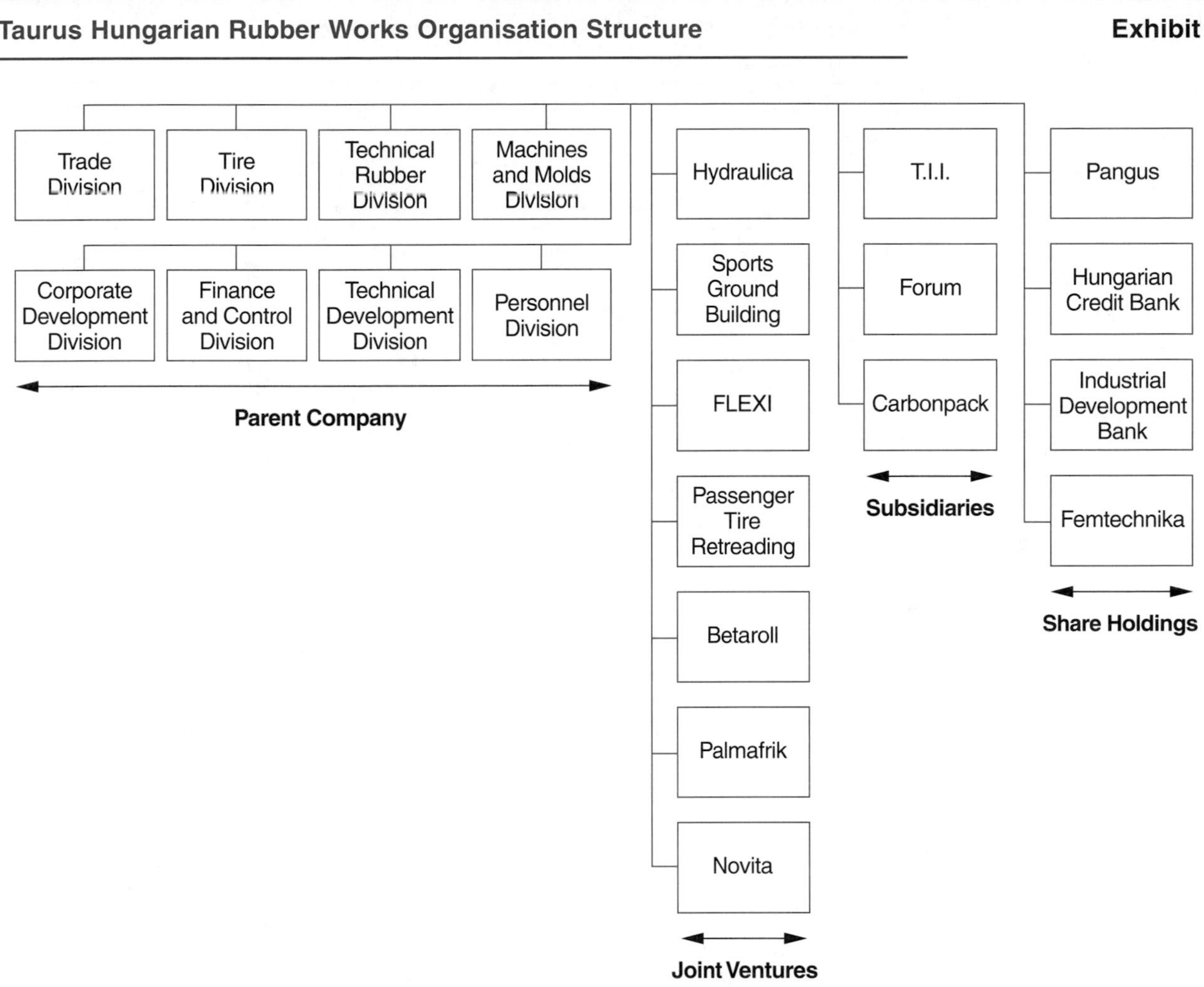

Source: 1988 Annual Report, p. 17

December 1986. Eleven new tires within the Taurus Top Tire brand have been scheduled for the market of which two were completed in 1988 and another three in early 1990. The division is also developing a new supersingle tire under a licensing agreement with an American tire manufacturer.

Total Company Sales (selected years; in millions of Forints) **Exhibit 10**

Market	***1981***	***1983***	***1985***	***1986***	***1987***	***1988***	***1989***	***1990***
Export	2,560	2,588	3,704	4,055	4,517	5,349	6,843	7,950
Domestic	7,890	9,024	9,381	9,979	11,174	12,255	12,056	12,716
Total	10,450	11,612	13,085	14,034	15,691	17,604	18,899	20,666

Source: 1988 Annual Report and internal company data.

Exhibit 11

Selected 1988 Division Performance Information (in millions of Forints)

	Division			
Item	*Tires*	*Technical Rubber*	*Machines & Molds*	*Trade*
Revenues	6,591	6,484	212	5,612
Assets				
Gross fixed assets	5,201	2,756	268	—
Net fixed assets	2,934	1,199	123	—
Inventories	1,024	601	100	—
Employees	3,987	3,912	557	208

Note: Machine and mold sales include output used in-house.

Exhibit 12

Selected 1989 Division Performance Information (in millions of Forints)

	Division			
Item	*Tires*	*Technical Rubber*	*Machines & Molds*	*Trade*
Revenues	8,547	7,183	242	4,694
Assets				
Gross fixed assets	5,519	2,787	292	—
Net fixed assets	3,016	1,120	135	—
Inventories	1,126	545	104	—
Employees	4,021	3,851	552	198

Note: Machine and mold sales include output used in-house.

▪ Technical Rubber Division

This division manufactures and markets an assortment of rubber hoses, air-springs for trucks and buses, conveyor belts, waterproof sheeting, and the PALMA line of camping gear. The PALMA camping gear line has a 15.0% world market share while the company's rotary hose business is a world leader with 40.0% of all international sales. The demand for high pressure and large bore hoses is closely related to offshore drilling activity while the sale of air-springs for commercial vehicles is expected to increase as this technology gains increasing acceptance with vehicle manufacturers. The former Soviet Union is this division's largest customer with 1989 sales of 380.0 thousand

Forints. In recent years, sales within the division have been distributed in the following fashion:

Large bore high pressure hoses	6.7%
Rotary hoses	27.1
Hydraulic hoses	14.7
Camping goods	18.0
Waterproof sheeting	13.9
Air springs	5.3
Conveyor belts	14.3

■ Machine and Molds Division

This division manufactures products that are used in-house as part of Taurus's manufacturing process as well as products used by others. About 70.0% of its sales are for export, and its overall sales were distributed as follows in 1988:

Technical rubber molds	24.0%
Polyurethane molds	17.0
Machines and components	25.0
Tire curing molds	34.0

■ Trade Division

The Trade Division conducts Eastern European purchases and sales for Taurus as well as performs autonomous distribution functions for other firms. Its activities serve both Taurus's other divisions as well as those outside the company. It is expected that this division will continue to function as Taurus's purchasing agent while increasing its outside trading activities; its status with regard to trading in the former Eastern bloc is in a state of flux.

IMPLEMENTING TAURUS'S STRATEGY OF STRATEGIC ALLIANCES

Immediately after returning from his company's top management conference, Gyula began collecting materials to confirm the tentative decisions that had been made at Lake Balaton. Based on secondary data collected and assembled into Exhibits 13 and 14 he could see the general rubber industry had fallen

Comparative Average Annual Growth Rates **Exhibit 13**

Period	*Rubber Sector*	*All Industry*
1960–1970	8.3%	6.8
1970–1980	4.0	4.1
1980–1990	1.7	4.3
Average	4.7%	5.1%

Source: Internal company report.

Exhibit 14 **10-Year Growth Rates for Selected Industries (1977 to 1988)**

Sector	*Annual Growth Rate*
Data processing equipment	21.0
Transistors	17.0
Aircraft	16.0
Medical equipment	15.0
Measuring and control equipment	13.5
Electronic games	13.2
Telecommunication equipment	12.9
Metal processing equipment	10.4
Synthetic fibres	7.8
Steel	7.4
Building materials	7.3
Fertilisers	7.0
Agricultural equipment	4.5
Coal	3.2
Passenger cars	2.5
Crude oil	0.5

Source: Internal report.

from a better than average industry growth performance in the 1960–1970 period to one that was far inferior to the industrial average during the 1980–1990 period. He also saw that other industries, such as data processing, aircraft, medical equipment, and telecommunication equipment, had obtained sizeable growth rates from 1977 to 1988. Moreover, he was extremely aware of the increasing concentration occurring in the tire industry through the formation of joint ventures, mergers, cooperative arrangements, and acquisitions. It was obvious that at least the rubber industry's tire segment had passed into its mature stage. In response to this, most major rubber companies had obtained diversifications away from the heavy competition within the industry itself, as well as attempted to find growth markets for their rubber production capacity. For the year 1988 alone, Gyula listed the various strategic alliances shown in Exhibit 15, while Exhibit 16 reviews the diversification activities of Taurus's major tire competitors in 1990.

Within the domestic market, various other Hungarian rubber manufacturers had surpassed Taurus in their growth rates as they jettisoned their low profit lines and adopted newer ones possessing greater growth rates. Taurus's market share of the Hungarian rubber goods industry had slowly eroded since 1970, and this erosion increased greatly in the decade of the 1980s due to the creation of a number of smaller start-up rubber companies encouraged by Hungary's new private laws. While the company's market share stood at about 68.0% in 1986, Gyula estimated Taurus's market share would only fall another 4.0% by 1992. Exhibit 17 displays the figures and estimates he created for his analysis.

Strategic Alliances in 1988

Exhibit 15

Goodrich (USA) and Uniroyal (Great Britain) operate as a joint venture.

Pirelli (Italy) acquired Armstrong (USA).

Firestone (USA) acquired by Bridgestone (Japan), which has another type of alliance with Trells Nord (Sweden).

General Tire (USA) acquired by Continental Tire (West Germany), which, in turn operates in cooperation with Yokohama Tire (Japan). Continental also owns Uniroyal Englebert Tire.

Toyo (Japan) operates in cooperation with Continental Tire (West Germany), while also operating a joint venture in Nippon Tire (Japan) with Goodyear (USA).

Michelin (France) operates in cooperation with Michelin Okamoto (Japan).

Sumitoma (Japan) operates in cooperation with Nokia (Finland), Trells Nord (Sweden), and BTR Dunlop (Great Britain).

Source: Corporate annual reports.

Rubber Company Diversifications

Exhibit 16

Rubber Company	*Nontire Sales %*	*Major Diversification Efforts*
Goodyear	27.0	Packing materials Chemicals
Firestone	30.0	Vehicle service
Cooper	20.0	Laser technology
Armstrong	n.a.	Heat transmission equipment
General Tire	68.0	Electronics Sporting goods
Carlisle	88.0	Computer technology Roofing materials
Bridgestone	30.0	Chemicals Sporting goods
Yokohama	26.0	Sporting goods Aluminum products
Trelleborg	97.0	Mining Ore processing
Aritmos	n.a.	Food processing
Nokia	98.0	Electronics Inorganic chemicals

Note: Major diversifications as of 1990.

With the aid of a major consulting firm, Taurus had recently conducted the in-depth analysis of its business portfolio shown in Exhibit 18. It was concluded that the company operated in a number of highly attractive markets, but that the firm's competitive position needed to be improved for most product lines. Accordingly, the firm's emphasis was to be placed on improving

Exhibit 17

Distribution of Rubber Goods Production Between Taurus and All Other Hungarian Rubber Manufacturers

	Percent of Market			
Manufacturer	*1970*	*1980*	*1986*	*1992*
Taurus	95.0	80.0	68.0	65.0
All others	5.0	20.0	32.0	35.0

Source: Internal company data for years 1970 to 1986 and personal estimate for 1992.

the competitiveness of the company's current product lines and businesses. In 1991 Taurus was to implement two types of projects—software projects dealing with quality assurance programs, management development, staff training efforts, and the implementation of a management information system and hardware projects dealing with upgrading the agricultural tire compounding process as well as upgrades in the infrastructures of various plants.

Fundamental to Taurus's desire to be more growth oriented was its newly enunciated strategy shown in Exhibit 19. As formally stated, the company was seeking strategic alliances for certain business lines rather than growth through internal development which had been its previous growth strategy.

Exhibit 18

The Taurus Portfolio

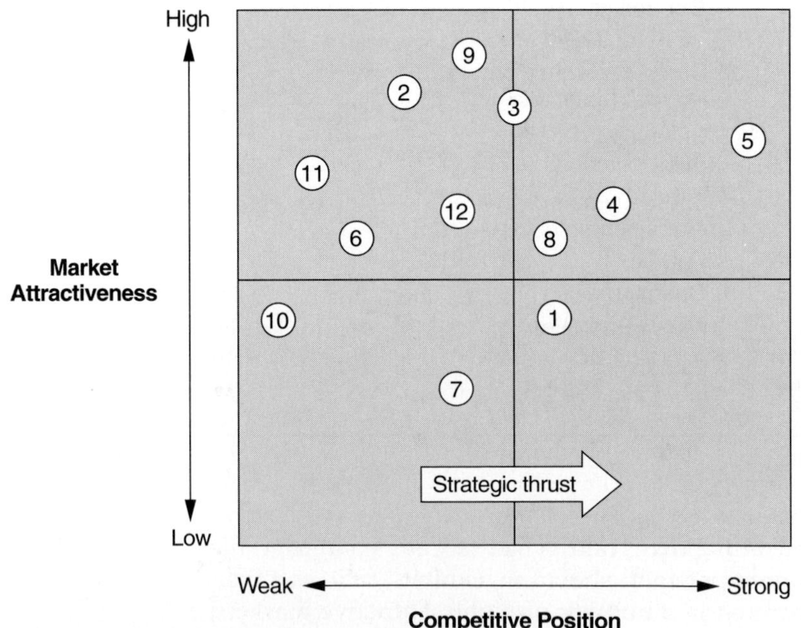

1. Bias tires
2. Steel radial truck tires
3. Agricultural tires
4. Rotary hoses
5. Special hoses
6. Conveyor belts
7. Camping mattresses
8. Rubber sheets
9. Air springs
10. V-belts
11. Precision technical rubber
12. Machines and molds

Source: Company documents and consulting group's final report.

Taurus' Strategy for the 90's **Exhibit 19**

The decade of 1990 is predicted to be a busy stage of the rubber sector worldwide.

There are strong factors of concentration in traditional manufacturing business[es] and particularly in tire operations. The role of substitute products is growing in several areas. On the other hand, the fast end-of-century growth of industrial sectors is expected to stimulate the development of sophisticated special rubber products. In the face of these challenges, Taurus bases its competitive strategy on the following:

A continuous structural development program has been started aimed at *increasing the company's competitive advantage,* with scope to cover a range from manufacturing processes, through quality assurance, to the reinforcement of strengths and elimination of weaknesses.

Efficiency is a prerequisite of any business activity. The company portfolio must be kept in good balance.

Associated with profitability, the company keeps developing its sphere of operations, determining the direction of diversification according to the criteria of potential growth and returns.

Our pursuit of competitive advantages and diversification must be supported by a powerfully expanding *system of strategic alliance and cooperation.*

Source: Taurus's Annual Report.

While it was felt that internal development possessed lower risks, as it basically extended the company's current areas of expertise, benefitted the various product lines already in existence, and better served its present customer base while simultaneously using the company's store of management knowledge and wisdom, internal development possessed a number of impediments to Taurus's current desires for accelerated growth. Paramount was its belief that management was too preoccupied with its current activities to pay attention to new areas outside its specific areas of expertise.

Now ranked at thirtieth in size in the rubber industry, Taurus found it was facing newly formed international combinations with enormous financial strength, strong market positions, and diverse managerial assets. Given the high degrees of concentration manifesting themselves in the rubber industry, and that even the largest firms have had to accomplish international cooperative relationships, Taurus determined that it too should seek cooperative, strategic alliances. In seeking these affiliations, the company would be very open and responsive to any type of reasonable alternative or combination that might be offered. These alliances could include participating with companies currently in operation or the creation of new, jointly held companies, whether they are related or unrelated to the rubber industry. The only real criteria for accepting an alliance would be its profitability and growth potential.

In pursuing strategic alliances, Gyula notes that Taurus's bargaining position differs greatly between the various business lines in its portfolio. As an aid to understanding its bargaining strategy with potential allies, Taurus's businesses are placed into one of three categories as shown in Exhibit 20. Category I types are those where Taurus's bargaining position is relatively weak as it feels it has little to offer a potential suitor. Category II types are those where Taurus can contribute a sizable "dowry" and has much to offer the potential

Exhibit 20 **Cooperation Potentials by Product Line**

	Cooperation Category		
Product Lines	*I*	*II*	*III*
Truck tires	*		
Farm tires			*
Rotary hoses		*	
Specialty hoses			*
Hydraulic hoses	*		
Waterproofing sheets		*	
Belting	*		
Camping goods			*
Air springs			*
Machines and molds		*	
Precision goods			*

Source: Internal company report.

ally, while Category III types are those businesses with mixed or balanced strengths and weaknesses.

The problem now comes to the restructuring of the company's current divisions to make them into rational and identifiable business units to outside investors, as well as serving Taurus's own needs for internal logic and market focus. Which product lines should be grouped together and what should be the basis for their grouping? Gyula saw several different ways to do this. Products can be grouped based on a common production process or technology. They can be based on their capital requirements, grouped by markets served, or trade relations that have already been established by Taurus. Depending on how he defines the company's new SBUs, he knows he will be making some major decisions about the attractiveness of the company's assets as well as defining the number and the nature of Taurus's potential strategic alliances. As he explained:

> If I create an SBU which manufactures hoses a good joint venture partner might be someone who manufactures couplings for hoses—this would be a match that would be good for both of us and it would be a relatively safe investment. If, on the other hand, I create a business which can use the same hoses in the offshore mining and drilling business, and this is a business that is really risky but one that could really develop in the future, what do I look for in partners? I need to find an engineering company that's creating large mining exploration projects. For every type of combination like this I can create, I have to ask myself each time "What are the driving questions?"

In reviewing the company's portfolio, he immediately saw three new SBUs he could propose to Laszlo Geza, vice president of the Technical Rubber Division. One SBU will serve the automobile industry through the manufacture of rubber profiles (rubber seals and grommets that provide watertight fits for car windows, V-belts for engines and engine components such as their air conditioning, power steering, and electrical units, and special engine seals. Another unit would serve the truck and bus industry by manufacturing the bellows for articulated buses, and air springs for buses, heavy-duty trucks, and long-haul trailers. The last newly created SBU will target the firm's adhesives and rubber sheeting at the construction and building industry where the products can be used to waterproof flatroofs as well as serve as chemical-proof and watertight liners in irrigation projects and hazardous waste landfill sites.

Although top management knows "the house is not on fire" and that a careful and deliberate pace can be taken regarding the company's restructuring, Gyula wants to make sure the proposals he is about to make are sound and reasonable. Moreover the success or failure of this restructuring will set the tone for Taurus's future diversification efforts.

REFERENCES

Benway, S.J., "Tire & Rubber Industry," *The Value Line Investment Survey,* December 22, 1989, p. 127.

Garvey, B.S., Jr., "History and Summary of Rubber Technology," in M. Morton (Ed.), *Introduction to Rubber Technology,* New York: Reinhold, 1959, pp. 1–43.

Greek, B.F., "Modest Growth Ahead for Rubber," *Chemical & Engineering News,* Vol. 66, No. 12, March 21, 1988, pp. 25–29.

Thompson, A.A., Jr., "Competition in the World Tire Industry," in A.A. Thompson, Jr., and A.J. Strickland, *Strategic Management: Concepts and Cases,* Homewood, Ill. R.D. Irwin, 1990, pp. 518–548.

APPENDIX 1: FINANCIALS

Exhibit 21

Taurus Hungarian Rubber Works Income Statements for 1988–1990 (in millions of Forints; year ended December 31)

	*1988**	*1989*	*1990*
Basic activities	10,637.7	12,193.4	14,918.6
Nonbasic activities	6,270.0	6,705.5	5,747.0
Total revenues	16,907.7	18,898.9	20,665.6
Direct costs	12,022.1	13,095.0	13,819.6
Indirect costs	4,235.6	4,963.3	5,714.8
Production and operating costs	16,257.7	18,058.3	19,534.4
Before tax profit	650.0	840.6	1,131.2
Taxes	290.0	386.0	491.4
After tax profit	360.0	454.6	639.8

*1988 data adjusted for better comparability to reflect the effects of tax changes initiated in 1989.

Taurus Hungarian Rubber Works Balance Sheets for 1988–1990 (in millions of Forints; year ended December 31)

Exhibit 22

	*1988**	*1989*	*1990*
Assets			
Cash, bank deposits, and receivables	2,491.1	3,157.0	3,763.2
Inventories	2,749.6	2,803.8	2,888.3
Other current assets and capital investments	577.4	739.7	938.6
Current assets	5,818.1	6,700.5	7,590.1
Property	2,480.7	2,772.0	3,008.6
Machines and equipment	4,718.2	6,202.6	6,357.9
Fleet	46.3	46.4	48.6
Other	27.9	25.9	25.6
Fixed asset value	7,273.1	9,046.9	9,440.7
Accumulated depreciation	3,977.0	4,303.8	4,687.7
Unaccomplished projects	541.4	272.2	541.6
Total fixed assets	3,837.5	5,015.3	5,294.6
Total assets	9,655.6	11,715.8	12,884.7
Liabilities			
Short-term loans	1,531.7	1,684.3	1,444.0
Accounts payable	922.7	1,378.5	2,072.8
Accrued expenses	95.8	141.4	151.6
Provisions for taxes	(274.1)	195.0	34.7
1989 long-term debt service	267.0	129.9	314.3
Other liabilities due within 12 months	58.0	5.4	242.1
Total current liabilities	2,601.1	3,534.5	4,259.5
Provisions and noncurrent liabilities	61.4	335.1	.4
Long-term loans	725.4	1,453.1	1,815.7
Equities and funds reserves	5,907.7	5,938.5	6,169.2
Current year after-tax profit	360.0	454.6	639.8
Total equity and funds	6,267.7	6,393.1	6,809.0
Total liabilities	9,655.6	11,715.8	12,884.6

*1988 data adjusted for better comparability to reflect the effects of tax changes initiated in 1989.

CASE 25

Rimeda

J.P. Kairys, Jr., Steven Cox, University of Western Ontario

In May 1992, Stasys Mezhonis, general director of Rimeda, was contemplating a strategy for his enterprise to prosper through the tough economic restructuring currently underway in Lithuania, Eastern Europe, and the Republics of the Commonwealth of Independent States (CIS), and the economic recession underway in most Western countries. Rimeda was experiencing enormous uncertainty caused by the changeover from the old centralized system of the former USSR to a new market system and was preparing plans to privatize the company soon.

Moreover, the company was being forced to adapt from manufacturing the majority of its production output for military defense needs to becoming a company that would survive only if markets for civilian uses of its products could be found and effectively sold to. It was facing a similar situation to that of American defense manufacturers that in the past had to shift production from military to civilian uses.

BUSINESS ENVIRONMENT

The changeover of the economic system from socialism to capitalism was underway simultaneously in the 15 independent republics of the former Soviet Union, as well as within the formerly socialist states of Eastern Europe. As different countries had arrived at differing stages of changeover, the same was true of companies operating within this environment. Suppliers, producers, consumers, and governments were all experiencing the effects of these changes.

Certain names and other identifying information may have been disguised to protect confidentiality. Preparation of this case was funded in part by the government of Canada.

This case is intended for classroom discussion only, not to depict effective or ineffective handling of administrative situations. This case was prepared by J.P. Kairys, Jr. and Steven Cox of the Western Business School. Copyright © 1992, The University of Western Ontario. All rights reserved to the authors and the University of Western Ontario.

In May 1992, the currency of the former Soviet Union was still the official currency of the republics of the former USSR, although all the republics were formulating plans to issue their own currency (the *litas* in Lithuania). The ruble currently had a market-set valuation of approximately R120 = US$1.00. However, the ruble was experiencing rapid inflation that had not been quantified by the government, but which seemed to be in the 100% to 300% per annum region, with the inflation rate differing for materials, products, and wages. Deposit interest rates offered by the banks were in the 40% to 50% per annum range, while lending rates were in the 100% region (although private lender rates could be as high as 200% to 300%).

There was also political uncertainty within the region caused not only by the suddenness of the upheaval of the former system to the new one but also by the possibility that some form of the former system might attempt a comeback. This uncertainty was a major reason holding back potential Western joint venture partners and was also an underlying factor for much of the short-term behavior of some businesses and consumers (i.e., lack of saving and investment, trading instead of production, and so on).

COMPANY HISTORY

Rimeda was one of Lithuania's oldest enterprises. The company was established in 1934 as a radio sets manufacturer, but had become a producer of military electronic equipment in the period following World War II. Because of its highly sensitive military production mandate, the enterprise's very existence was considered classified and it was referred to only by its project number. All products carried product model numbers, but otherwise carried no marking of their origin of manufacture. Products were shipped to Moscow or specified transhipment points for distribution.

In September 1991, ownership of Rimeda had transferred from the Soviet Central Ministry of Radio Industry to the Ministry for Economics, Government of Lithuania. After the unsuccessful putsch in Moscow, agreements had been reached transferring ownership of all enterprises that belonged to Moscow with no compensation required, although some issues had been left for later negotiation. Prior to the change in ownership, Rimeda had operated together with four other partner enterprises in Byelorussia and Russia. All five companies were now separate legal entities, and Rimeda currently cooperated with these enterprises through contracts. Even though Rimeda had made investments in some of these related companies, all assets were now the property of the domestic country.

OVERVIEW OF PRODUCTS

In 1991, Rimeda manufactured a diverse mix of electrical products according to the following broad product lines:

Product Line	*Percent of Sales*
Medical equipment	40
Consumer goods	30
Radio measurement devices	28
Cable equipment	2

Medical equipment included products such as an echotomoscope (an ultrasound device used in diagnostics of various internal human diseases) and the Urat-2 (a diagnostic device for crushing kidney stones). Both of these products were offered for sale in the West, with prices ranging from US$5,000 for the Urat-2 to US$30,000 for the echotomoscope.

Consumer goods included products such as TV antennas, oil heaters, charging devices (boosters) for automobiles, burglary alarm systems for flats, and antihijacking systems. These products were sold or bartered quite extensively in states of the former Soviet Union, but were not offered for Western sale because of differing standard requirements and/or lesser quality than Western competition.

Radio measurement devices included a wide range of normal and high-speed oscilloscopes, frequency generators, complex meters, and microwave generators. These devices had been designed to the specification of the former USSR Defense Ministry and were rapidly declining as a percentage of sales due to the cessation of defense-related orders. However, future sales to former Soviet Union countries or Soviet client states (i.e., Iran, Iraq, India, Pakistan, Turkey, Afghanistan) were possible as equipment breakdowns occurred or spare parts were needed. The electrical units were integrated into complete electronic systems that were interdependent upon one another, so that it was not possible to change easily to a new or different electronic technology. The various devices sold had a price range from US$80 to US$40,000, and the oscilloscopes were considered inexpensive by Western standards (roughly one-third the price of comparable Western models).

Cable equipment was a new, emerging product line for the company. There was currently the possibility of introducing the fiber system of communications in Eastern Europe, although this would require Western partners. Other potential applications for this cable product line included transmission of cable signals on 30 channels of satellite TV, and also as connectors for computer and video systems. The technology also had application in electricity, gas, and water measurement devices and in information systems (such as train and airline scheduling). High-quality cable equipment could find markets in Baltic, Eastern Europe, and CIS countries and in countries in the West.

PRODUCTION

The enterprise's plant occupied several large buildings near downtown Vilnius, and included over 50,000 square meters of plant space and 25,000 square meters of production space. The plant currently operated one shift eight hours a day, five days a week, although it had once operated two production shifts.

Most of the basic production equipment was between 5 to 12 years old, but there was older equipment. The equipment was well maintained. The general director recognized that even the newest equipment was in some cases outdated because of older technologies, and pointed to comparisons in countries like Finland where equipment might be old (25 years) but still useful.

Rimeda's equipment was designed to be universally used, especially the metal-working equipment. This gave it high flexibility of use, which had been a requirement under the former production system of multiple product production, and nonuse of continuous methods. Product throughput time varied, depending upon products: A magnetic lock could be manufactured in one week, most consumer products could take two months, and medical equipment could experience a four-month production cycle. The throughput time was increasing because of longer customs and transport delays from suppliers.

Rimeda employed over 4,000 people spread over management, engineering, technical, and production worker functions. The qualifications and skills needed to work at the plant were highly dependent upon the job function. Some workers had only a high school education. However, most of the management, engineering, and technical staff were highly qualified and trained. The majority had been trained at the St. Petersburg (formerly Leningrad) Polytechnical Institute and at other well-known universities in the area. There was some flexibility in the organization, as about 15% of the work force possessed multiple skills (e.g., could work as tool and die cutter, but also work as turning operator or finisher of metal).

Rimeda used different production methods, depending upon the product. For most products, production was either project/job shop or batch method. Rimeda recognized that there could be advantages in increased batch, or even continuous production, but realized that such a changeover required major investments. The enterprise formerly had a complex range of production tasks, and batch or mass production techniques did not always apply.

CHANGE IN CORPORATE CULTURE

The general director was in the process of effecting change in the corporate culture of Rimeda—changing over the system of accounting to the Western philosophy of profit orientation. Training courses had commenced for the managers within the firm, and it was planned that this training would eventually broaden to include all employees. But the director general was aware of the enormity of the changes that were being attempted; under the previous system, employees had been motivated to produce maximum output without the goal of making a profit. Now the firm was faced with situations where products might have to be curtailed at the height of their production due to lack of demand, but the managers in the system were not equipped with the analytical tools to make such decisions.

INVENTORY

The general director estimated that R100 million of unsold, finished goods inventory was currently held in stock by the enterprise. Rimeda was attempting to shift its production toward only the goods that were selling, but it was still producing certain finished goods for inventory in the hope that customers could be found, and management was researching all market opportunities very thoroughly. The general director felt that if he did not take this risk, half of the employees might have to be fired. In the director's estimation, the company could theoretically stop production and sell from present inventories for four months. The present cost to keep the plant operating (accounts payable, payroll, utilities) and make ongoing capital improvements was R35 million/month.

The inventory consisted mainly of radio measurement equipment. There was also some medical equipment that was frozen in inventory because it was being upgraded to improve its quality and raise its competitiveness in the marketplace.

COST AND PRICING

Inventory was at present accounted for on the LIFO system, and it was costed by the standard cost method for determining the cost of goods sold. The technology department established the average length of time needed to produce a good and the resource material inputs. Previously, there had been separate departments designing technology and establishing standard costs, but recently these departments had been integrated.

For example, the total cost of one of the enterprise's medical equipment products was as follows:

Labor	10–15%
Raw materials	60–65%
Overhead	20–25%

Prices for products were then established, taking into account the standard cost of the product, an allowance for overhead such as sales, finance, and other general and administrative expenses. The senior management of Rimeda then looked at the market prices that their products could obtain and the costs of producing them, then made their pricing decisions and/or cost reduction decisions from this information. Establishing a profitable price was made trickier by the time lapses involved and by the rapid inflation of the ruble, which wreaked havoc with input costs (i.e., one ton of copper had increased from R2,000 to R300,000, and the production worker salary had increased from R350/month to R2,500/month). It was very difficult to establish prices when the cost of materials and components increased almost daily.

Rimeda was currently achieving a minimum of 10% gross margin on its sales, but even this was difficult to achieve in an inflationary environment. As recently as January 1992, Rimeda was obtaining a 60% margin on medical equipment, but this margin had subsequently fallen to the 10% level. The general director was very aware that if costs escalated faster than prices, Rimeda would be losing money on its sales.

RESEARCH AND DEVELOPMENT

Under the former ownership structure, there were two separate enterprises: the Design Institute (employing 1,500 people) and the Production Enterprise (now Rimeda). The Ministry of Defense ordered the Institute to develop projects and provided full financing; the ministry then ordered the Enterprise to produce the products. Now, there were no ministry orders, and the Institute and Enterprise were separate legal organizations that cooperated by way of contracts (but without exclusive rights).

The general director thought it was necessary to effect a merger of the two organizations, so that Rimeda would have an R&D department and a production department. The general director also recognized that there were not quite enough skilled people to fully staff such an R&D department and that further hiring and/or training might be required. He was especially interested in education opportunities for Rimeda's engineers and technical specialists with foreign teachers; this would be very important in the transformation to a market economy.

One important issue for Rimeda was patent protection. For instance, Rimeda produced a microwave therapy device that was capable of curing 87 illnesses, such as stomach ulcers, diabetes, and cerebral palsy. The product had been awarded two gold medals by the Belgian king. However, the patent for the technology was held by a Ukrainian firm that wished to monopolize the technology, and Rimeda was unable to produce it.

Another problem could arise if a designer working for Rimeda sold the rights for his or her medical equipment to another enterprise. That enterprise could create the product and market it, while Rimeda would have no recourse since there were no laws guaranteeing rights for intellectual property.

SUPPLIERS

As a former military supplier, Rimeda had received priority allocations of resources: the best technical people, the highest-quality raw materials, and superior life-style conditions for its employees. Now, Rimeda was faced with problems in securing reliable supplies, because the former system that served it was breaking down due to the lack of an efficient payments settlement system. This breakdown of the financial system was felt through all stages of the production system, as raw material suppliers or manufacturers that had once granted credit or relied on the state for payment were now requiring upfront payments for goods.

Most of Rimeda's 700 suppliers were located outside Lithuania, so that establishing commercial links with them was problematic. Supplies were delivered by contracts, but prices were established by clauses that allowed prices to be determined on an ad hoc basis. Before product components or materials were actually supplied, the prices were corrected. Certain materials (copper) could not be sold by contract (prohibited by the Russian government), and these materials were purchased instead at Trade Exchanges of the former almagamated enterprises operated by the Soviet Union.

Terms of trade for suppliers usually mandated prepayment. Seventy percent of Rimeda's raw material and component supplies were purchased prepaid, sometimes using bank credit. Certain suppliers were also monopoly producers, so that Rimeda had no choice but to take their components because Western companies required hard currency payments.

QUALITY

Rimeda's management acknowledged that their product quality was not up to Western standards, but the enterprise was rapidly restructuring to improve quality on all fronts.

Rimeda produced very precise equipment, and while it was mechanically sound, it suffered from quality problems. Many of these problems emanated from poor quality or unreliable components supplied from the CIS countries. Poor-quality components were only discovered after they were installed in a device and it was tested. Although the quality of supplies was of concern, there was little recourse for poor-quality goods that were shipped. The rejection rate for faulty parts as a rule was about 3% to 5% for components, although it was higher for some components. There was no mechanism to sue suppliers or to return defective components or raw materials.

Under the previous system, the quality of products was monitored by the deputy director of quality, who had a special "police" office responsible for monitoring quality. Now, the general director supervised quality through the technical director, who in turn managed the quality manager, who had a small staff that checked products for quality. The technical director could then effect improvements where needed. If quality problems were determined, the quality department had the right to stop production to correct the flaw.

The general director had made it clear to the production managers for each of the various product groups that if a bad-quality product were made, it could not be sold. According to the general director, "the persons responsible for quality have to have their behavior changed to view sales, not production, as paramount. Education is underway to change the psychology and behavior, and production managers are responsible for their own quality. This is risky, but there is no other way."

One additional group subordinate to the technical director was in charge of ensuring standards throughout the production process. If the technical director changed the product, he was responsible for ensuring that the changes were followed through all the production processes. For instance, the Soviet electrical requirements were not the same as in the West. Rimeda was implementing Systems for International Standards (ISO 8000), under which technical parameters were being changed, but also certificates for international standards were being issued.

TERMS OF SALE

This year, Rimeda expected total sales of roughly R700 million. Rimeda's quantity and terms of sale varied according to the consumer. Under an ideal situation, Rimeda wanted upfront payment for goods, but obtained this in only 5% of its sales. Upfront payments came for goods that were highly marketable.

For the remaining 95% of sales, Rimeda offered credit terms, and accounts receivable totaled R37 million. The enterprise's normal credit terms were payment within one month, but they had many accounts receivable that were almost one year old.

When a receivable went unpaid over one month, a manager was sent to collect the money in person. In some cases, the account was settled by the bartered exchange of goods or raw materials. In cases of very old receivables, there was no mechanism available to take the money from the customer. If Rimeda sued through the legal system, decisions took a long time. Even if successful, there was no way to get money from a company that was in a huge cash deficit. There was no bankruptcy law that gave creditors access to assets of debtors in default.

TRANSPORTATION

Lithuania had good transportation systems internally, but such was not the case throughout the CIS. Goods moving between Vilnius and Moscow took roughly one to two weeks to be received; if received sooner, they usually sat on loading docks until the consumer obtained the bills of lading and started searching out the goods. Most goods were shipped by rail and truck.

MARKETING

The marketing area of Rimeda was divided into two departments: the pre-project marketing development (PPMD) department and the marketing-sales (MS) department. Both departments worked in conjunction with the R&D department.

The PPMD department was a strategic product development group and was managed by the technical director. The department was constantly searching for new products, seeking out potential Western partners, and delegating the task of developing the appropriate product technology to the R&D department. The technical director was responsible for the profitability of future sales and for telling the production director about upcoming changes in products so that the sales staff could be informed and be able to prepare the market for the new products.

The MS department, responsible for sales, was managed by the production director. He was supposed to estimate production based on sales estimates. The production director also regularly analyzed the market and was responsible for the delivery of quality product services. If improvements were required in a particular product, the technical director was responsible for telling the R&D department so that improvements could be made.

The general director felt it was very important for the production director to manage the sales because the importance of marketing had been underlined to him. Because the production director had to prepare a marketing plan (revised monthly), only products that were demonstrated to be salable were produced. This sales focus prevented him from producing products for stock.

SALES FORCE

Rimeda sold to 400 clients on a fairly regular basis, but estimated that the total size of its client base could easily reach 10,000 if all clinics, hospitals, technical facilities, and enterprises were included.

Under the former system, there were no salespeople working for Rimeda. All orders were issued by the military. Rimeda now employed a sales force of 17 sales agents spread across the Baltic states, CIS republics, Eastern Europe, and a few selected Western markets (Holland, Germany, and others). The general director wanted to orient Rimeda's sales to serve Scandinavia and the countries of the former COMECON trading block, and he had placed great priority on further developing and expanding his sales team. The sales agents were responsible for preparing and signing contracts with consumers.

One sales channel for Rimeda was Mashpriborintorg, a centralized enterprise of the former USSR that sold to Western markets a catalog of electronic products. Rimeda was still making some sales through this organization, although it was collapsing due to the restructuring. As well, it sold the products as "Made in the USSR" and did not identify Rimeda as the manufacturer.

The sales team were very new in their roles, and those selected were people who had been involved in demonstrating the product around the former Soviet Union. The current sales force used the same offices that had been used before to demonstrate and service Rimeda's devices. The big advantage offered by these offices was that the sales force already knew many of the acquaintances and contacts from the former system of demonstrating the product. Sales agents were not exclusive to Rimeda and were paid a commission of 3% of the value of the sale.

Rimeda had begun offering broader services to its clients for installation or repair, depending upon the terms of the contract. The enterprise was preparing to offer a guarantee of repair for its products.

The enterprise was also investigating engaging retired Western business executives who provided marketing advice to companies around the world through a nonprofit firm (the International Executive Service Corps—IESC).

COMMUNICATION

The general director was aware that some Western firms spend between 7% and 10% of their sales on marketing expenses to find a place in the market. Rimeda had started advertising to Western markets. For instance, Rimeda had spent UK2,000 pounds sterling to run a half-page advertisement in the *International Finance Journal* (published by Sterling Publications). So far, the advertisement had not generated sales, but it was a first step toward establishing Rimeda's name in Western markets.

One major hurdle that Rimeda was attempting to overcome was establishing its corporate name in the markets that had used its products under Soviet Defense Ministry issue. Rimeda did not possess full lists of Defense Ministry customers, and since the devices did not state origin of manufacture, many potential consumers did not know where to reorder the products.

Rimeda was also in the process of rewriting/developing new sales brochures for its products, especially to show to potential Western consumers. Together with this, the enterprise was developing product brand names for its devices, which previously had been referred to only by their model serial number.

COMPETITION

Rimeda was marketing select models of its medical and radio measurement equipment to the West, but was not selling consumer goods or cable equipment to Western markets because the differing technical standards made them incompatible. Rimeda faced differing competition for each of its product line as follows:

Product Line	*Eastern Europe/ CIS Competition*	*Western Competition*
Medical equipment	Baltic, 0 CIS, 5	Toshiba, Siemens American Laboratories Aloka, Fukuda
Consumer goods	Many	Not sold in West
Radio measurement equipment	Baltic, 0 CIS, 0	Marconi Hewlett-Packard Rohde & Schwartz
Cable equipment	Baltic, 0 CIS, 0	French and Danish competition

Rimeda also knew that it possessed several competitive advantages. Rimeda had established access to suppliers and to certain Eastern and CIS markets. Rimeda had examined its competitors' products for comparison purposes and knew that it possessed some unique technologies such as galvanized plastics.

Rimeda also had the capability to produce microwave equipment for uses such as private communications and thought it had an opportunity to sell to Eastern European and CIS states that were in the process of changing over their telephone technology. Rimeda knew that its microwave technology was inexpensive by Western standards at $\frac{1}{10}$th to $\frac{1}{15}$th the Western price, but this was offset by the lack of comparable service support that Rimeda could offer and by the use of older-generation parts and components. However, Rimeda planned to make initial sales at low prices to obtain hard currency that would be invested toward reconstructing the product and improving its quality.

In the cable equipment market, Rimeda had no CIS competitors. It planned to manufacture a system similar to Western cable TV systems.

FINANCE

As seen in the financial statements of Exhibits 1 and 2, Rimeda had total assets of R233 million as of April 1, 1992, which represented a growth of roughly R55 million in just three months. Much of the growth was attributable to the rapid inflation being experienced by the ruble.

Rimeda was also facing a severe financial crunch caused by the inability of its clients to pay for goods and by the lack of credit terms from suppliers. The banking system of the former Soviet Union had disintegrated, and there were enormous problems in making settlements with CIS countries. The banking system lacked liquidity; at times just obtaining enough ruble banknotes to meet a payroll was a very difficult exercise, caused by a deficiency of banknotes, even though Rimeda had positive current account balances (at times, the payroll could be paid up to two weeks late). Although Lithuania was still using the currency of the former USSR (the ruble), it was planning to issue the *litas* in 1992.

Balance Sheets (rubles in 000s)

Exhibit 1

	January 1, 1992	April 1, 1992
Assets		
Fixed capital and WIP inventory		
Fixed capital—depreciation	$ 74,390	$ 70,193
Investments in fixed capital in process	5,848	8,644
Total	$ 80,238	$ 78,837
Long-term investments		
Credits (personal loans)	392	58
Total	$ 392	$ 58
Goods and inventory		
Raw materials, components	$ 44,214	$ 63,870
WIP inventory	6,721	7,296
Finished goods	16,237	37,719
Total	$ 67,172	$108,885
Cash and accounts receivable		
Cash		
Money in cash, bank deposits, and current accounts	$ 857	$ 3,007
Hard currency deposits and curr. accts.	11	11
Subtotal cash	$ 868	$ 3,018
Accounts receivable		
Accounts receivable and goods supplied in transportation	$ 22,994	$ 30,045
Payments in advance	33	483
Other accounts receivable	6,775	11,820
Subtotal accounts receivable	29,802	42,348
Total	30,670	45,366
Total assets	$178,472	$233,146
Equity and Liabilities		
Equity		
Nominal state-owned capital	$116,415	$113,578
Nominal stock capital	3,516	3,516
State-owned capital reserve	2,040	3,975
Total	$121,971	$121,069
Retained earnings and reserves		
Current earnings		$ 6,867
Compulsory earnings reserves	1,317	2,183
Other earnings reserves	4,128	1,738
Total	$ 5,445	$ 10,788
Long-term liabilities		
Bank loans to employees of company	62	35
Total	$ 62	$ 35
Short-term liabilities		
Short-term bank loans (notes)	$ 29,833	$ 67,011
Accounts payable to suppliers	6,009	13,105
Taxes accrued payable	3,210	4,803
Wages accrued payable	3,209	5,753
Social insurance payments accrued	1,093	2,009
Others	7,152	7,606
Total	$ 50,506	$100,287
Reserves	488	967
Total equity and liabilities	$178,472	$233,146

Exhibit 2 **Income Statement for the First Quarter of 1992 (rubles in 000s)**

Product sales	50,230
Production cost	30,618
	+19,612
Various sales income	9,826
Various losses	9,082
	+744
Income from nonproduction services sales	233
Nonproduction services costs	2,550
	–2,317
Sales profit	+18,039
Taxable nonsales income	+136
Nontaxable losses	–3,172
Total profit	+15,003
Taxable profit	18,175
Nontaxed expenditures from profit (charity, culture, etc.)	75
Taxable profit	+18,100

Of pressing concern to the company was nonpayment of accounts receivable. By May 1992, the accounts receivable were R37 million, but payments were slowed by lack of money on the consumers' part and the absence of fresh lending to companies.

PREPARING FOR PRIVATIZATION

By Lithuanian law, Rimeda was soon due to be privatized. The general director knew that the tough part of this task would be to ensure that the organization adjusted quickly to the new market-oriented realities. He was trying to create the concept of a new enterprise, recognizing that the structure of the plant was not flexible in terms of equipment and the mindset of the staff.

Under the "law of primary privatization," every citizen of Lithuania had been issued a passbook that contained an amount of "accounting rubles" that was determined by the age of the citizen. Citizens over 35 years old received the maximum allocation, younger ones less. The rubles had gone through two upward indexations (to account for inflation), and citizens were allowed to contribute real rubles on a matching basis. If a 35-year-old person had contributed the maximum, it was possible to have R80,000 for his or her account. These rubles could then be used to purchase shares in privatized companies, to purchase the flat in which the citizen was living, or to invest in agricultural and/or industrial enterprises. If none of the three options were selected, the government of Lithuania planned to issue long-term bonds in *litas*, the new Lithuanian currency, for the face value amount.

Because of the rapid inflation of the ruble, the government had indexed various asset classes for privatization purposes. For instance, Rimeda's fixed assets were R78 million and the state capital was R120 million. Both classes of assets were scheduled to be indexed at a multiple of five for valuation purposes. The privatization law next allowed up to 30% of the shares of this revalued company to be sold to the public, with the remaining 70% to be withheld for further privatization issues and/or sale to Western joint venture partners. The initial offering of 30% was to be targeted toward employees of the enterprise.

To prepare for privatization, Rimeda was placing values on extraneous assets owned by the company that were destined to be sold off. For instance, the enterprise owned a resort property (R0.5 million), a canteen (R3 million), a vacation property on the Baltic coast (R2.5 million), and other social welfare assets.

Another organizational change that Rimeda was undertaking was to split the company into a holding company with four subsidiaries according to product line (see Exhibit 3). Because Rimeda recognized that some product lines might grow while others might decline, separating them would make this process clearer. Each subsidiary would have its own management, technical engineers, workers, and service force, and would be charged a pro rata rent for the plant space it occupied. The holding company would provide head office support (sales, transportation, utilities, accounting, and computer and management information systems), as well as some overall strategic, financial, and marketing direction. This structure of ownership would potentially allow the enterprise to select different joint venture partners for each of the subsidiary divisions.

The general director believed that sales of medical equipment were currently the most profitable, and he expected healthy future growth from this product line. Radio measurement was currently the least profitable, even though it was a high-quality product. Radio measurement equipment sales required further research of new markets, including those in the West.

ORGANIZATION

Stasys Mezhonis, Rimeda's general director, had graduated from Kaunas Polytechnical Institute in 1964, with a specialization in machine building technology (metal working). Stasys was sent to Rimeda's former enterprise

Rimeda Organization **Exhibit 3**

Private ownership 30%

Government ownership 70%

Rimeda "holding company" 100%

Medical equipment

Consumer equipment

Radio measurement equipment

Cable equipment

as a foreman, then went on to hold a variety of positions such as technologist, chief of shop division in technology, chief of shop, and deputy technical director. In 1979, Stasys was moved to work for Sigma Enterprise (a computer and information systems enterprise) as the deputy technical director. In September 1991, Stasys returned to Rimeda as general director—"I came back home."

Stasys had graduated from a Lithuanian business program ($1\frac{1}{2}$ years of study in the evenings), and had studied psychology and teaching to earn his degree from Kaunas. During his work at Sigma, Stasys had the opportunity to communicate with many foreign partners regarding strategic tasks and obtaining new technologies and new products.

Stasys had a positive vision for the enterprise: "The future of Rimeda will see a flourishing prosperity together with the assistance of foreign partners." He believed that within five years Rimeda would become a dominant competitor in medical equipment, information systems, and communication systems.

The former organization had been very hierarchical, with all orders received from Moscow. The former general director had 12 directors reporting to him. Stasys had changed the upper management structure of Rimeda to the organizational design shown in Exhibit 4.

The management hierarchy in place reporting to these six directors was based on the former management structure, and Stasys was considering whether to further change the organizational structure. The new structure under consideration was to develop a matrix form of organization, with each division having a general manager and with functional specialists within each division reporting to the "head office" holding company directors. Each division/subsidiary would operate as a separate profit center separated into strategic business units.

SEARCHING FOR NEW MARKETS AND PARTNERSHIPS

Rimeda was now actively seeking joint venture partnerships for each of the different product lines that it planned to split off into separate subsidiaries. Rimeda was seeking a partnership where it held a minimum of 51% of the equity and majority control of the venture.

Exhibit 4 **RIMEDA: Upper Management Structure**

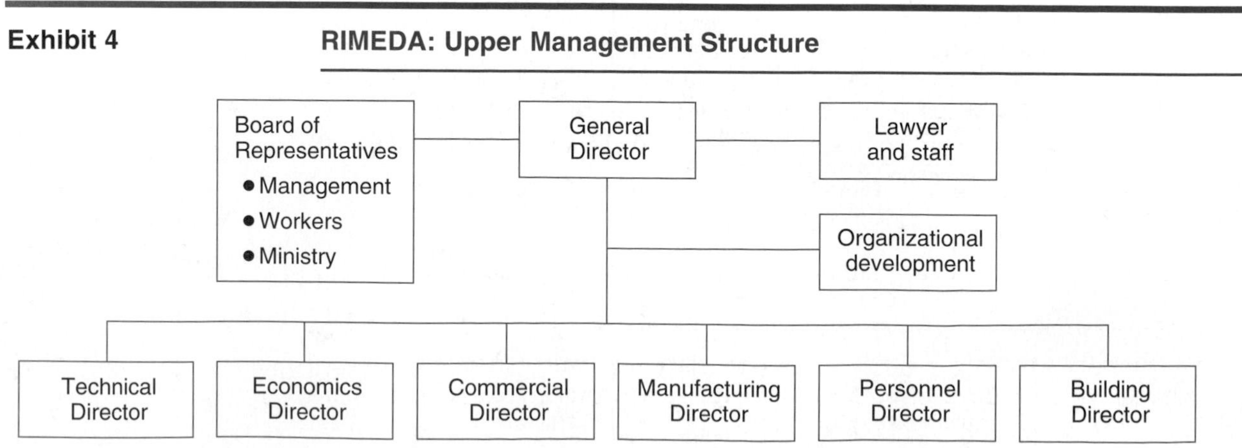

Just a few years previously, no one in the Soviet Union would have thought the opportunity existed to export products to the West or to engage in partnerships with Western companies. Within the Soviet Union, trade was established directly between the producer and the consumer, with no intermediaries other than the state. Now, commercial structures were rapidly developing to facilitate trade, but there were still problems with the settlements/payments system.

Rimeda currently sold 98% of its production to states that made up the former COMECON trading block, but it had started making sales to Western countries, such as Holland and Germany, which accounted for 2% of sales. Rimeda wanted to increase sales to Western countries as fast as possible because such sales offered solid future prospects and hard currency payment.

Rimeda had received overtures from several Western companies but found the process of selecting reliable, credible partners to be difficult. The general director postulated that "some firms are coming to the Baltic market because of their own bad financial condition—they are looking for cheap labor and high technical levels of proficiency, which we possess because we used to work for the military with its high technical requirements." For example, one American firm had approached Rimeda with a proposal to purchase some equipment to manufacture optical fiber systems for communications, which was an unknown technology in Eastern Europe and the CIS. The upfront capital required was US$12 million, and the joint venture proposal estimated ultimate annual sales of up to US$100 million.

The general director noted how difficult it was to establish the credibility of the many firms that approached him with a joint venture proposal. In his opinion, the main obstacles to joint ventures were problems created by the turbulent economic environment (i.e., the banking system). However, he recognized that the quickest way to enter Western markets was through such a joint venture because of the hard currency that it would bring, and that with that hard currency would come greater access to Eastern European markets first and Western markets second. If Rimeda could find a serious partner, the general director knew that it would increase the overall technical level of expertise within Rimeda and would give the enterprise a heightened profile when competing within the markets of the former Soviet Union. But the window of opportunity would not last forever, as wage levels and costs of production began to adjust to market levels and the competitive advantage that these factors provided began to narrow.

One important advantage cited by the general director that gave Western companies an advantage over Rimeda was that many Western companies had government defense funding available that acted as subsidies to the development of new technologies or applications. The general director planned to develop communication systems because it was one of the priority fields of the government of Lithuania, and it might be possible to obtain investment credits from that government at some future time.

DECISION AT HAND

The situation facing the general director was serious. If new orders were not received within the next month, it was possible that scaled-back production might have to be considered. In his words, "we are facing complex problems caused by the death of the old socialist system."

CASE 26

The Swatch

Arieh A. Ullmann, SUNY-Binghamton

THE SWISS WATCH INDUSTRY IN THE LATE 1970s

In 1978 when Dr. Ernst Thomke became managing director of ETA after a 20-year leave of absence from the watch industry, the position of this Swiss flagship industry had changed dramatically. Just like other industries suffering from the competitive onslaught from the Far East, the Swiss watch industry faced the biggest challenge in its four hundred years of existence. Once the undisputed leaders in technology and market share—which the Swiss had gained thanks to breakthroughs in mechanizing the watch manufacturing process during the nineteenth century—the Swiss had fallen on hard times.

In 1980, Switzerland's share of the world market, which in 1952 stood at 56%, had fallen to a mere 20% of the finished watch segment while world production had grown from 61 million to 320 million pieces and movements annually. Even more troubling was the fact that the market share loss was more pronounced in finished watches compared to nonassembled movements (Exhibit 1). Measured in dollars, the decline was not quite as evident because the Swiss continued to dominate the luxury segment of the market while withdrawing from the budget price and middle segments.

The Swiss, once the industry's leaders in innovation, had fallen behind. Manufacturers in the United States, Japan, and Hong Kong had started to gain share especially since the introduction of the electronic watch. Although in 1967 the Swiss were the first to introduce a model of an electronic wristwatch at the Concours de Chronometrie of the Neuchatel Observatory (Switzerland), smashing all accuracy records, they dismissed the new technology as a fad and continued to rely on their mechanical timepieces where most of their research efforts were concentrated.

This case is intended for classroom discussion only, not to depict effective or ineffective handling of administrative situations. All rights reserved to the authors and the North American Case Research Association.

Exhibit 1

World Watch Production and Major Producing Countries (1980)

Country	*Production (million pieces)*			*Market Share (%)*
	Electronic	*Mechanic*	*Total*	
Switzerland: watches	10.4	52.6	63.0	20
incl. nonassembled movements	13.0	83.0	96.0	30
Japan: watches	50.4	17.1	67.5	21
incl. nonassembled movements	53.8	34.1	87.9	28
United States: watches & movements	2.0	10.1[1]	12.1[1]	
Rest of Europe: watches & movements	4.5	57.2[1]	61.7[1]	42[2]
Rest of Asia: watches & movements	76.0	31.3[1]	113.0[1]	
Latin America: watches & movements	—	2.7[1]	2.7[1]	

Source: Swiss Watchmanufacturers Federation (FH).
[1]Includes unassembled movements.
[2]Without unassembled movements.

While the Swiss dominated the watch segments based on older technologies, their market shares were markedly lower for watches incorporating recently developed technologies (Exhibit 2). Thus, when electronic watches gained widespread acceptance, the Swiss watch producers found themselves in a catch-up race against the Japanese, who held the technological edge (Exhibit 3).

The situation of the industry which exported more than 90% of its production was aggravated by adverse exchange rate movements relative to the U.S. dollar, making Swiss watches more expensive in the United States—then the most important export market. Until the early 1970s, the exchange rate stood at US$1 = SFr. 4.30; by the end of the decade it had dropped to about US$1 = SFr. 1.90.

Threat

STRUCTURAL CHANGE IN THE INDUSTRY

Throughout its history, the Swiss watch industry was characterized by an extreme degree of fragmentation. Until the end of the 1970s, frequently up to

Exhibit 2

Switzerland's 1975 Share of World Production by Type of Technology

Technology	*Year of Introduction*	*Stage of Product Life Cycle*	*Swiss Share (%)*
Simple mechanical	Pre-WWII	Declining	35
Automatic	1948	Mature	24
Electric	1953	Declining	18
Quartz (high freq.)	1970	Growing	10
Quartz (solid state)	1972	Growing	3

Source: Swiss Watchmanufacturers Federation, Bulletin No. 13, Bienne, June 30, 1977.

Share of Annual Output of Electronic Watches **Exhibit 3**

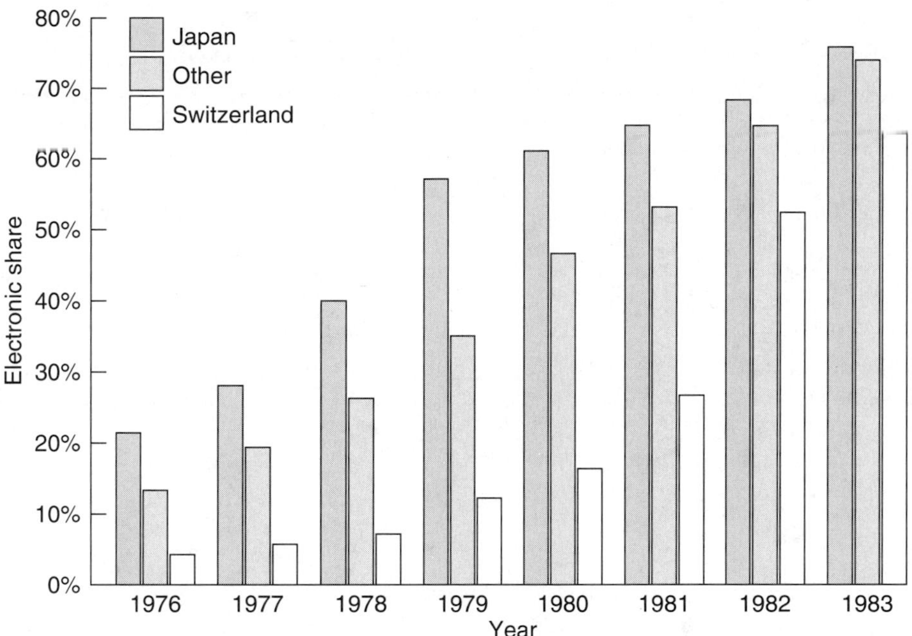

thirty independent companies were involved in the production of a single watch. Skilled craftsmen called suppliers manufactured the many different parts of the watch in hundreds of tiny shops, each of them specializing in a few parts. The movements were either sold in loose parts ("ebauche") or assembled to "chablons" by "termineurs," which in turn supplied the *etablisseurs,* where the entire watch was put together. In 1975, 63,000 employees in 12,000 workshops and plants were involved in the manufacture of watches and parts. Each etablisseur designed its own models and assembled the various pieces purchased from the many suppliers. Only a few vertically integrated manufacturers existed that performed most of the production stages in-house (Exhibit 4). The watches were either exported bearing the assembler's or manufacturer's brand name (factory label) via wholly owned distributors and independent importers, or sold under the name of the customer (private label). By the late 1970s, private label sales comprised about 75% of Swiss exports of finished watches. In addition, the Swiss also exported movements and unassembled parts to foreign customers (Exhibits 5a and 5b).

This horizontally and vertically fragmented industry structure has developed over centuries around a locally concentrated infrastructure and depends entirely on highly skilled craftsmen. Watchmaking encompasses a large number of sophisticated techniques for producing the mechanical watches, and this complexity is exacerbated by the extremely large number of watch models. The industry is highly specialized around highly qualified labor, requiring flexibility, quality, and first-class styling at low cost.

This structure is, however, poorly suited to absorb the new electronic technology. Not only do electronics render obsolete many of the watchmaker's skills that had been cultivated over centuries, it also requires large production volumes to take advantage of the significant scale and potential experience effects.

Exhibit 4 **Traditional Structure of Swiss Watch Industry**

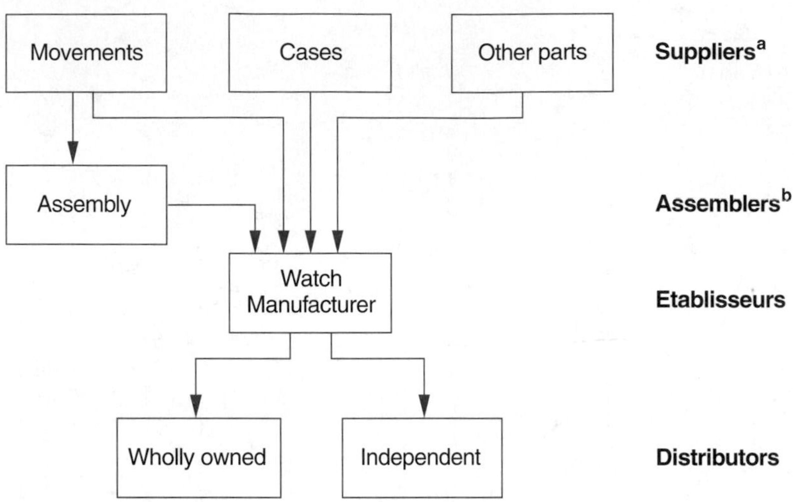

Source: Based on Bernheim, 1981.

[a]1975: 5,500 plants

[b]1975: 6,500 assemblers and etablisseurs combined

Whereas the traditional Swiss manufacturing methods provided few benefits from mass production, the extreme fragmentation from the suppliers to the distributors prevented even these. Furthermore, the critical stages in the value added chain of the watch shifted from parts and assembly—where the Swiss had their stronghold—to distribution where the Japanese concentrated their efforts. Encasement, marketing, and wholesale and retail distribution, which the Japanese producers emphasized, represented over 80% of the value added.

Sales of mechanical watches in the budget and middle price segments dropped rapidly when electronic watches entered the market. Initially these were Texas Instruments, Inc., National Semiconductor Corp., Hughes Aircraft, Intel, and Time Computer. Due to rapidly rising production and sales volumes of electronic watches, prices dropped dramatically from $1000 to $2000 in 1970 to $40 in 1975 and less than $20 by the end of the 1970s. At this time, most of the early American digital watch producers had started to withdraw from the watch business and it was the cheap digital watch from Hong Kong that flooded the market. As an indication of the eroded market power of the Swiss, the sale of assembled and unassembled movements had started to rise while exports of finished watches declined (Exhibit 5a)—a trend that negatively affected domestic employment.

The industry's misfortune caused large-scale layoffs, and bankruptcies started to increase steeply in the 1970s. Since the watch industry was concentrated around a few towns in the western part of Switzerland, the ensuing job losses led to regional unemployment rates unknown in Switzerland since the 1930s (Exhibit 6).

ETA, where Dr. Thomke became managing director, was a subsidiary of Ebauches SA which in turn was a subsidiary of ASUAG (General Corporation of Swiss Horological Industries Ltd.). ASUAG had been created in 1931 during the first consolidation period in the industry. It was Switzerland's largest

Swiss Exports of Watches, Movements, and Parts — Exhibit 5

(a) 1960–1980

Year	*Finished Pieces*[1]	*Watches Francs*[2]	*Assembled Pieces*[1]	*Movements Francs*[2]	*Unassembled Pieces*[1]	*Movements Francs*[2]
1960	16.7	767.2	8.2	192.7	n.a.	n.a.
1965	38.4	1334.4	14.8	282.7	n.a.	n.a.
1970	52.6	2033.8	18.8	329.5	n.a.	n.a.
1975	47.2	2391.2	18.6	329.1	5.4	44.0
1976	42.0	2262.4	20.0	343.0	8.0	54.2
1977	44.1	2474.5	21.9	381.3	15.8	94.8
1978	39.7	2520.0	20.6	380.3	18.7	103.5
1979	30.3	2355.6	18.6	371.1	20.2	121.0
1980	28.5	2505.8	22.5	411.8	32.7	189.2

(b) 1981–1990

Year	*Finished Pieces*[1]	*Watches Francs*[2]	*Assembled Pieces*[1]	*Movements Francs*[2]	*Unassembled Pieces*[1]	*Movements Francs*[2]
1981	25.2	2880.2	19.9	382.5	27.5	160.5
1982	18.5	2754.6	12.7	256.4	14.5	81.0
1983	15.7	2676.6	14.6	247.1	12.7	76.8
1984	17.8	3063.9	14.5	235.0	14.6	98.5
1985	25.1	3444.1	13.4	220.4	18.8	138.9
1986	28.1	3391.0	13.3	213.4	19.4	133.3
1987	27.6	3568.0	11.1	179.4	20.9	122.8
1988	28.0	4128.8	12.2	202.8	31.9	162.1
1989	29.9	5080.0	12.6	217.7	28.4	136.3

Source: Swiss Watchmanufacturers Federation.
[1]In millions.
[2]In millions of current Swiss Francs.

watch corporation (total sales 1979: SFr. 1,212 million) and combined a multitude of companies under its holding structure including such famous brands as Certina, Eterna, Longines, and Rado. Ebauches, of which ETA was part, was the major producer of watch movements for ASUAG and most of the other Swiss etablisseurs. The other large Swiss manufacturer was SSIH (Swiss Watch Industry Corporation, Ltd.), which also was a creation of the same 1931 consolidation and whose flagships were Omega and Tissot. During the second half of the 1970s, ASUAG suffered from declining profitability and cash flow, poor liquidity, rising long-term debt, and dwindling financial reserves due to sluggish sales of outdated mechanical watches and movements which comprised about two thirds of ASUAG's watch sales. Diversified businesses outside the watch segment contributed less than 5% of total sales.

TURNAROUND AT ETA

Ernst Thomke grew up in Bienne, the Swiss capital of watchmaking. After an apprenticeship in watchmaking with ETA, he enrolled in the University of

Exhibit 6 **Swiss Watch Industry: Companies and Employment**

Year	*Number of Companies*	*Employment*
1960	2,167	65,127
1965	1,927	72,600
1970	1,618	76,045
1975	1,169	55,954
1976	1,083	49,991
1977	1,021	49,822
1978	979	48,305
1979	867	43,596
1980	861	44,173
1981	793	43,300
1982	727	36,808
1983	686	32,327
1984	634	30,978
1985	634	31,949
1986	592	32,688
1987	568	29,809
1988	562	30,122

Source: Swiss Watchmanufacturers Federation.

Berne where he first studied physics and chemistry and later medicine. After his studies, he joined Beechams, a large British pharmaceuticals and consumer products company as a pharmaceutical salesman. In 1978, when his old boss at ETA asked him to return to his first love, he was managing director of Beecham's Swiss subsidiary and had just been promoted to Brussels. However, his family did not wish to move and so, after 18 years, he was back in watches.

When he took over, morale at ETA was at an all-time low due to the prolonged period of market share losses and continued dismissals of personnel. ETA's engineers and managers no longer believed in their capabilities of beating the competition from Japan and Hong Kong. Although ETA as the prime supplier of watch movements did not consider itself directly responsible for the series of failures, it was equally affected by the weakened position of the Swiss watch manufacturers. When Thomke assumed his role as managing director of ETA he clearly understood that, for a successful turnaround, his subordinates needed a success story to regain their self-confidence. But first a painful shrinking process had to be undertaken in order to bring costs under control. Production, which used to be distributed over a dozen factories, was concentrated in three centers and the number of movement models reduced from over 1000 to about 250.

As a first step, a project called "Delirium" was formulated with the objective to create the world's thinnest analogue quartz movement—a record which at that time was held by Seiko. When Thomke revealed the idea to ETA's engineers they were quick to nickname it "Delirium Tremens" because they considered it crazy. But Thomke insisted on the project despite his staff's doubts. To save even the tiniest fraction of a millimeter some watch parts were for the first time bonded to the case instead of being layered on top of the watch back. Also, a new extra thin battery was invented. In 1979, the first watch was launched with the Delirium movement and ETA had its first success in a long time. In that year, ASUAG sold more than 5,000 pieces at an average price of $4,700 with the top model retailing for $16,000.

The Delirium project not only helped to boost the morale of ETA's employees, it also led to a significant change in strategy and philosophy with ETA's parent, Ebauches SA. No longer was Ebauches content with its role as the supplier of movement parts. In order to fulfill its primary responsibility as the supplier of technologically advanced quality movements at competitive prices to Switzerland's etablisseurs, Ebauches argued, it was necessary to maintain a minimum sales volume that exceeded the reduced domestic demand. Therefore, in 1981 ETA expanded its movement sales beyond its then current customers in Switzerland, France, and Germany. This expansion meant sales to Japan, Hong Kong, and Brazil. Ebauches thus entered into direct international competition with Japanese, French, German, and Soviet manufacturers. In short, ETA claimed more control over its distribution channels and increased authority in formulating its strategy.

As a second step, the organizational culture and structure were revamped to foster creativity and to encourage employees to express their ideas. Management layers were scrapped and red tape reduced to a minimum. Communication across departments and hierarchical levels was stressed, continued learning and long-term thinking encouraged, playful trial-and-error and risk taking reinforced. The intention was to boost morale and to create corporate heroes.

The third step consisted of defining a revolutionary product in the medium- or low-price category. By expanding even farther into the downstream activities, Thomke argued, ETA would control more than 50% instead of merely 10% of the total value added. Since 1970 the watch segments below SFr. 200 had experienced the highest growth rates (Exhibit 7). These were the segments the Swiss had ceded to the competitors from Japan and Hong Kong. As a consequence, the average price of Swiss watch exports had steadily risen, whereas the competitors exported at declining prices. Given the overall objective to reverse the long-term trend of segment retreat, it was crucial to reenter one or both of the formerly abandoned segments. Thomke decided to focus on the

World Watch Production by Price Category, 1970 vs. 1980 **Exhibit 7**

	Sales (million pieces)		
Price Category	*1970*	*1980*	***Growth %***
Less than 100 SFr.	110	290	264
100–200 SFr.	33	50	52
200–500 SFr.	20	20	0
More than 500 SFr.	7	10	43

Source: Adapted from Thomke (1985).

low price segment. "We thought we'd leave the middle market for Seiko and Citizen. We would go for the top and the bottom to squeeze the Japanese in the sandwich."[1] The new concept was summarized in four objectives:

1. Price: Quartz-analogue watch, retailing for no more than SFR. 50.
2. Sales Target: 10 million pieces during the first three years.
3. Manufacturing Costs: Initially SFr. 15—less than those of any competitor. At a cumulative volume of 5 million pieces, learning and scale economies would reduce costs to SFr. 10 or less. Continued expansion would yield long-term estimated costs per watch of less than SFr. 7.
4. Quality: High quality, waterproof, shock resistant, no repair possible, battery only replaceable element, all parts standardized, free choice of material, model variations only in dial and hands.

The objectives were deliberately set so high that it was impossible to reach them by improving existing technologies; instead, they required novel approaches. When confronted with these parameters for a new watch, ETA's engineers responded with "That's impossible," "Absurd," "You're crazy." Many considered it typical of Thomke's occasionally autocratic management style which had brought him the nickname "Ayatollah." After all, the unassembled parts of the cheapest existing Swiss watch at that time cost more than twice that much! Also, the largest Swiss watch assembler—ETA's parent ASUAG—sold 750,000 watches annually scattered over several hundred models. In an interview with the *Sunday Times Magazine,* Thomke told the story: "A couple of kids, under 30, said they'd go away and look at the Delirium work and see if they could come up with anything. And they did. They mounted the moving parts directly on to a molded case. It was very low cost. And it was new, and that is vital in marketing."[2] The concept was the brainchild of two engineers. Elmar Mock, a qualified plastics engineer, had recommended earlier that ETA acquire an injection molding machine to investigate the possibilities of producing watch parts made of plastic. Jacques Muller was horological engineer and specialist in watch movements. Their new idea was systematically evaluated and improved by interdisciplinary teams consisting of the inventors, product and manufacturing engineers, specialists from costing, marketing and accounting as well as outside members not involved in the watch industry.

The fourth step required that ETA develop its own marketing. In the 1970s and early 1980s, it did not have a marketing department. Thomke turned to some independent consultants and people outside the watch industry with extensive marketing experience in apparel, shoes, and sporting goods to bring creative marketing to the project. Later, as Swatch sales expanded worldwide, a new marketing team was built up to cover the growing marketing, communications, and distribution activities.

PRODUCT AND PROCESS TECHNOLOGY

A conventionally designed analogue watch consists of a case in which the movement is mounted. The case is closed with a glass or crystal. The move-

[1]Moynahan, Brian, and Andreas Heumann, "The Man Who Made the Cuckoo Sing," *The Sunday Times Magazine,* August 18, 1985, p. 25.

[2]Moynahan/Heumann, op. cit.

ment includes a frame onto which the wheels, the micromotor needed for analogue display, other mechanical parts, as well as the electronic module are attached with screws. First the movement is assembled and then mechanically fixed in the case. Later the straps are attached to the case.

The Swatch differs both with regard to its construction as well as the manufacturing process.

■ Construction

First, the *case* is not only an outer shell, it also serves as the mounting plate. The individual parts of the movement are mounted directly into the case—the Delirium technology was perfected. The case itself is produced by a new very precise injection molding process that was specifically developed for this purpose. The case is made of extremely durable plastic that created a super-light watch.

Second, the number of *components* is reduced significantly from 91 parts for a conventional analogue quartz watch to 51 (Exhibit 8). Unlike in conventional watch assembly, the individual parts of the movement—the electronic module and the motor module—are first assembled in subgroups before mounting and then placed in the case like a system of building blocks.

Third, the *method of construction* differs in that the parts are no longer attached with screws. Components are riveted and welded together ultrasonically. This eliminates screws and threads and reduces the number of parts and makes the product rugged and shock-resistant. As the crystal is also welded to the case, the watch is guaranteed water resistant up to 100 feet.

Fourth, the tear-proof *strap* is integrated into the case with a new, patented hinge system that improves wearing comfort.

Fifth, the *battery*—the only part with a limited life expectancy of about three years—is inserted into the bottom of the case and closed with a cover.

Swatch Components **Exhibit 8**

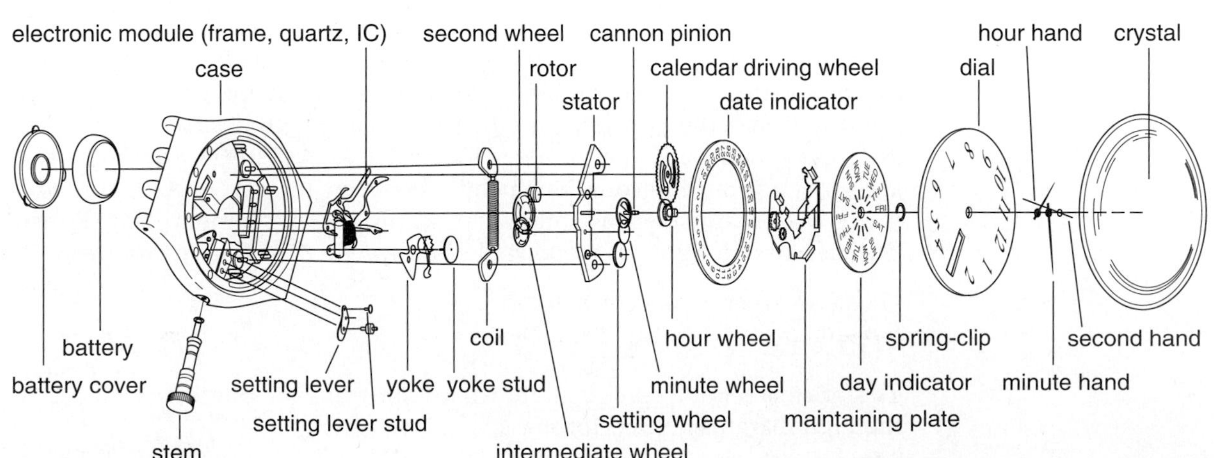

■ Production

First, as a special advantage the Swatch can be assembled from one side only.

Second, because of this, it is possible to fully automate the watch mounting process. Ordinary watches are assembled in two separate operations: the mounting of the movement and the finishing. The Swatch, however, is produced in one single operation (Exhibit 9). According to representatives of the Swiss watch manufacturers, this technology incorporates advanced CAD/CAM technology as well as extensive use of robotics and is the most advanced of its kind in the world.

Third, due to the new design, the number of elements needed for the Swatch can be significantly reduced and the assembly process simplified. As a prerequisite for incorporating this new product technology, new materials have to be developed for the case, the glass and the micro motor. Also, a new assembly technology was designed and the pressure diecasting process perfected.

Fourth, quality requirements have to be tightened, because the watch can not be reopened and therefore, except for the battery, not be repaired. Given these constraints, each step in the manufacturing process has to be carefully controlled including the parts, the preassembled modules, the assembly process itself as well as the final product. This is especially important because in the past high reject rates of parts and casings indicated that many Swiss manufacturers had difficulties with quality control, which damaged their reputation.

Overall, the new product design and production technology reduces the costs significantly and raises product quality above watches in the same price category produced by conventional technology.

MARKETING

The new marketing team came up with an approach that was unheard of in this industry dominated by engineers.

■ Product Positioning

Contrary to the conventional wisdom in the industry, it is not the product, its styling and technical value that are emphasized but its brand name. Quality attributes such as waterproofness, shock resistance, color, preciseness are less important than the association of the brand name with positive emotions such as "fun," "vacation," "joy of life." The watch is positioned as a high-fashion accessory for fashion conscious people between 18 and 30. As it turned out, many people outside this range started buying the Swatch. Jean Robert, a Zurich-based designer, is responsible for Swatch's innovative designs.

■ Pricing

The price is set at a level that allows for spontaneous purchases yet provides the high margins needed for massive advertising.

Swatch Assembly Process **Exhibit 9**

1 A new kind of injection molding, employing high-strength plastic, produces the case and mounting plate in one piece, through a single molding step.
2 The electronic module is built in and riveted ultrasonically in place. It contains the quartz-integrated circuit, the coil connector and the battery contacts.
3 The hand-setting mechanism and coil are assembled.
4 The motor module is inserted. For the first time in the history of watchmaking, the second wheel is driven directly.
5 The train wheel and maintaining plate are riveted.
6 Assembly of the date indicator.
7 Mounting of the day indicator.
8 The dial and hands are put in place and welded to the case to seal out water.

■ Distribution

As a high-fashion item competing in the same price range as some Timex and Casio models, the Swatch is not sold through drugstores and mass retailers. Instead, department stores, chic boutiques, and jewelry shops are used as distribution channels. Attractive distributor margins and extensive training of the retailers' sales personnel combined with innovative advertising ensure the unique positioning of the product.

■ Brand Name

In 1982, 20,000 prototypes of 25 Swatch models were pretested in the United States, which was viewed as the toughest market setting the trend for the rest of the world. The unisex models only differed in color of the cases and straps and the dial designs. It was during these pretests that Franz Sprecher, one of the outside consultants of the marketing team, came up with the name "Swatch" (Swiss + Watch = Swatch) during a brainstorming session with the New York–based advertising agency concerning the product's positioning and name. Up until then, Sprecher's notes repeatedly mentioned the abbreviation S'Watch. During this meeting, Sprecher took the abbreviation one step further and created the final name.

THE SWATCH TEAM

Besides Thomke, three individuals were crucial for the successful launching of the Swatch: Franz Sprecher, Max Imgrueth, and Jacques Irniger.

Franz Sprecher obtained a masters in economics and business from the University of Basle. Following one year as a research assistant and Ph.D. student, he decided to abandon academia and to enter the international business world as a management trainee with Armour Foods in Chicago. After six months, he returned to Switzerland and joined Nestlé in international marketing. Two years later, he became sales and marketing director of a small Swiss/Austrian food additives company. Later Sprecher moved to the position of international marketing director of Rivella and then account group manager at the Dr. Dieter Jaeggi Advertising Agency in Basle. Sprecher took a sabbatical at this point in his career and planned to return to the international business world as a consultant within a year. Towards the end of this period while thinking of accepting a position as a professor at the Hoehere Wirtschafts und Verwaltungschochschule in Lucerne, he received a phone call from Dr. Thomke concerning the new watch. Thomke told Sprecher: "You've got too much time and not enough money, so why don't you come and work for me." Sprecher then took over the marketing of the, as yet unnamed, product as a freelance consultant. Today, he continues to consult for Swatch as well as for other brands such as Tissot and Omega.

Another important person involved in the creation of the Swatch is Max Imgrueth. Max Imgrueth was born in Lucerne, Switzerland. Following graduation from high school in St. Maurice, a small town in the Valais surrounded by high mountains, he went to Italy and studied art history in Florence and fashion and leather design in Milan. After a brief stint in linguistics, he enrolled in business courses at the Regency Polytechnic in England and the New York University. In 1969, he left the United States because he had difficulties in obtaining a work permit and started to work in a women's specialty store in Zurich, Switzerland. Two years later, he switched to apparel manufacturing and became manager for product development and marketing.

In 1976, he was recruited by SSIH, owners of the Omega and Tissot brands. From 1976 to 1981, he was in charge of product development and design at Omega's headquarters in Bienne. Conflicts with the banks—which at that time de facto owned SSIH due to continued losses—over Omega's strategy led him to resign from his job and to start a consulting business. One of his first clients was ETA Industries, which were just getting ready to test market the Swatch in San Antonio, Texas. He succeeded in convincing ETA that San Antonio was the wrong test market and that the Swatch as a new product required other than the traditional distributors. As a consequence, New York and Dallas were chosen as primary test sites, and TV advertising and unconventional forms of public relations were tried out. While working on debugging the introduction of the Swatch, he was offered the position of President of Swatch USA, a job that initially consisted of an office on Manhattan's Fifth Avenue and a secretary.

The third individual involved in the early phase of the Swatch is Jacques Irniger who joined ETA in 1983 as Vice-President of Marketing and Sales for both ETA and Swatch worldwide. In 1985, he was a board member of the Swatch SA, Vice-President of Marketing-Sales of ETA SA Fabriques d'Ebauches and President of Omega Watch Corp., New York. Irniger received his doctorate in economics from the University of Fribourg, a small city located in the French speaking part of Switzerland. After training positions in marketing research and management at Unilever and Nestlé, he became marketing manager at Colgate Palmolive in Germany. After Colgate, he moved on to Beecham Germany as Vice-President of Marketing. Before joining ETA, he was Vice-President of Marketing and Sales for Bahksen International.

MARKET INTRODUCTION

The Swatch was officially introduced in Switzerland on March 1, 1983—the same year that ASUAG and SSIH merged after continued severe losses that necessitated a SFr. 1.2 billion bailout by the Swiss banks. During the first four months, 25,000 Swatch pieces were sold—more than a third of the initial sales objective of 70,000 for the first twelve months. According to some distinguished jewelry stores located in Zurich's famous Bahnhofstrasse where Switzerland's most prestigious and expensive watches were purchased by an endless stream of tourists from all over the world, the Swatch did not compete with the traditional models. On the contrary, some jewelers reported that the Swatch stimulated sales of their more expensive models. The success of the Swatch encouraged other Swiss manufacturers to develop similar models which, however, incorporated conventional quartz technology.

Subsequent market introductions in other countries used high-powered promotion. In Germany, the launching of the Swatch was accompanied by a huge replica of a bright yellow Swatch that covered the entire facade of the black Commerzbank skyscraper in Frankfurt's business district. The same approach was used in Japan. On Christmas Eve, 1985, the front of a multistory building in Tokyo was decorated with a huge Swatch that was 11 yards long and weighed more than 14,000 pounds. Japan, however, turned out to be a difficult market for the Swatch. The 7,000 Yen Swatch competed with domestic plastic models half the price. Distribution was restricted to eleven department stores in Tokyo only and carried out without a Japanese partner. After six months, it became obvious that the original sales target of SFr. 25 million for the first year could not be reached. The head of the Japanese Swatch operation, the American Harold Tune, resigned. His successor was a Japanese.

In the United States, initial sales profited from the fact that many American tourists coming home from their vacation in Switzerland helped in spreading the word about this fancy product which quickly became as popular a souvenir as Swiss army knives. U.S. sales of this $30 colorful watch grew from 100,000 pieces in 1983 to 3.5 million pieces in 1985—a sign that Swatch USA, ETA's American subsidiary, was successful in changing the way time pieces were sold and worn. No longer were watches precious pieces given as presents on special occasions such as confirmations, bar mitzvahs, and marriages and to be worn for a lifetime. "Swatch yourself" meant wearing two, three watches simultaneously like plastic bracelets. Swatch managers traveling back and forth between the United States and Switzerland wore two watches, one showing EST time, the other Swiss time.

The initial success prompted the company to introduce a ladies' line one year after the initial introduction, thus leading to 12 models. New Swatch varieties were created about twice a year. Also, special models were designed for the crucial Christmas season: In 1984 scented models were launched, a year later a limited edition watch called Limelight with diamonds was sold at $100. The Swatch was a very advertising-intensive line of business. For 1985, the advertising budget of Swatch USA alone was $8 million, with U.S. sales estimated at $45 million (1984 sales: $18 million). In 1985, Swatch USA sponsored MTV's New Year's Eve show; the year before it had sponsored a breakdancing festival offering $25,000 in prizes, and the Fresh Festival '84 in Philadelphia.

Swatch managers were, however, careful not to flood the market. They claimed that in 1984 an additional 2 million watches could have been sold in the United States. In England, 600,000 watches were sold in the first year and the British distributor claimed he could have sold twice as many.

CONTINUED GROWTH

The marketing strategy called for complementing the $30 time piece with a range of Swatch accessories. The idea behind this strategy was to associate the product with a lifestyle and thereby create brand identity and distinction from the range of look-alikes that had entered the market and were copying the Swatch models with a delay of about three months. In late 1985, Swatch USA introduced an active apparel line called Funwear. T-shirts, umbrellas, and sunglasses should follow in the hope of adding an extra $100 million in sales in 1986. Product introduction was accompanied by an expensive and elaborate publicity campaign including a four-month TV commercial series costing $2.5 million, an eight-page Swatch insert featuring a dozen Swatch accessories in *Glamour, GQ, Vogue,* and *Rolling Stone,* a $2.25 million campaign on MTV. In January 1985, Swatch AG was spun off from ETA. The purpose of the new Swatch subsidiary was to design and distribute watches and related consumer goods such as shoes, leather and leather imitation accessories, clothes, jewelry and perfumes, toys, sports goods, glasses and accessories, pens, lighters and cigarettes. Swatch production, however, remained with ETA. Furthermore, licenses were being considered for the distribution of the products. All of these products as well as the watches were designed in the United States with subsequent adaptations for European markets.

This strategy of broadening the product line is, however, not without risks, because it could dilute the impact of the brand name. *Forbes* mentioned the examples of Nike, which failed miserably when it tried to expand from runningwear to leisure wear, and so did Levi when it attempted to attach its brand recognition to more formal apparel.[3] Yet Max Imgrueth was quick to point to other examples such as Terence Conran, a designer and furniture maker who succeeded in building a retail empire ranging from kitchen towels to desk lamps around his inexpensive, well-designed home furnishings aimed at the young.

ENSURING SUCCESS

At the end of 1985, Swatch annual sales were expected to reach 8 million pieces (1984: 3.7 million). The Swatch was so successful that by the end of 1984 Swatch profits exceeded all product related investments and expenditures contributed significantly toward ETA's overhead. The Swatch represented 75% of SMH's unit sales of finished watches and made it SMH's number one brand in terms of unit sales and the number two brand in terms of revenues, topping such prestige brands as Longines and Rado. SMH (Swiss Corporation for Microelectronics and Watchmaking Industries, Ltd.) was the new name of the Swatch parent after the ASUAG-SSIH merger in 1983. Thanks to the Swatch, SMH was able to increase its share of the world market (1985: 400 million units) from 1% to 3% within four years. The success also invigorated the Swiss industry at large (Exhibit 5b). Despite this success, the managers at Swatch continued to perfect and expand the Swatch line.

In 1986 the Maxi-Swatch was introduced which was ten times the size of the regular Swatch. Before the start of the ski season during the regular year, the Pop-Swatch was launched which could be combined with different color wristbands. As a high-technology extravaganza the Pop-Swatch could also be worn in combination with a "Recco-Reflector" which had been developed by another SMH subsidiary. The Recco reflected radar waves emitted from a system and thus helped to locate skiers covered by avalanches.

In 1987, Swatch wall models and the Swatch Twinphone were introduced. The latter was not just colorful. It had a memory to facilitate dialing and, true to its origin, provided an unconventional service in that it had a built-in "party-line," so that two people could use it simultaneously.

The year 1988 saw the successful introduction of the Twinphone in the United States, Japan, and the airport duty-free business as well as the expansion of the Pop-Swatch product line. The Swatch accessories line was discontinued due to unmet profit objectives and negative impact on the Swatch brand image.

[3] Heller, Matthew, "Swatch Switches," *Forbes*, January 1986, p. 87.

In its 1989 annual report, SMH reported cumulative sales of over 70 million Swatch pieces. Over 450 models of the original concept had been introduced during the first 7 years (Exhibit 10). The Swatch had also become a collector's item. Limited edition models designed by well-known artists brought auction prices of SFr. 1,600, SFr. 3900, and SFr. 9,400—about 25 to 160 times the original price!

In 1990, the "Swatch-Chrono" was launched to take advantage of the chronometer fashion. Except for the basic concept—plastic encasement and battery as the only replaceable part—it has little in common with the original model and represents a much more complex instrument. It has four micromotors instead of only one due to the added functions and is somewhat larger in diameter. Despite the added complexity it claims to be as exact and robust as the original Swatch. As a special attraction, the watch, which is available in six models, retails for only SFr. 100. The company is also experimenting with a mechanical Swatch to be marketed in developing countries where battery replacement poses a problem. In this way, the company hopes to boost sales in regions that represent only a minor export market for the Swiss.

The success of the Swatch at the market front is supported by a carefully structured organization. Just like the other major brands of SMH, the Swatch has its own organization in each major market responsible for marketing, sales, and communication. These regional offices are supported by SMH country organizations that handle services common to all brands such as logistics, finance, controlling, administration, EDP, and after-sales service.

Exhibit 10 **Swatch Sales (millions of units)**

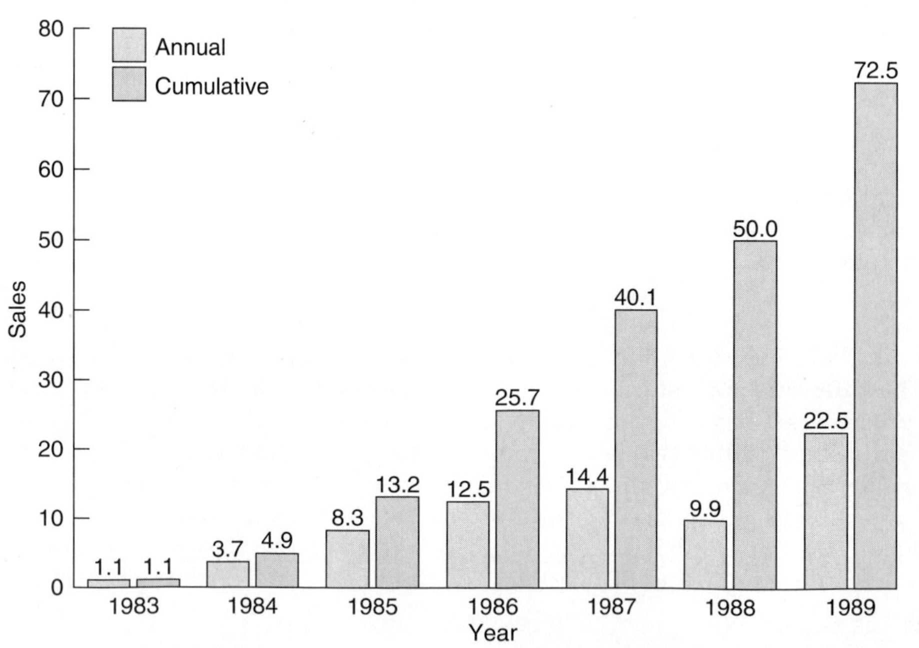

The Swatch also meant a big boost for Dr. Thomke's career. He was appointed general manager of the entire watch business of the reorganized SMH and became one of the key decision makers of the new management team that took over in January 1985. The "Swatch Story" was instrumental in the turnaround of SMH, which only six years after the merger of two moribund companies showed a very healthy bottom line (Exhibit 11).

SMH: Financial Data **Exhibit 11**

	1989	*1988*	*1987*	*1986*	*1985*	*1984*
Income Statement Data						
Sales Revenues						
Gross sales	2,146	1,847	1,787	1,895	1,896	1,665
Costs						
Of which: Materials	793	681	670	759	812	714
Personnel	646	580	577	593	556	541
External services	346	331	335	356	360	286
Depreciation	80	71	73	68	61	60
Total operating costs	1,865	1,663	1,655	1,776	1,789	1,601
Operating profit (loss)	281	142	117	103	66	51
Income before taxes	209	126	90	82	72	38
Net income	175	105	77	70	60	26
Balance Sheet Data						
Assets						
Current assets	1,194	1,065	1,103	1,080	1,070	1,049
Of which: Inventories	602	562	528	568	513	524
Fixed assets	529	510	533	507	456	451
Total assets	1,723	1,575	1,636	1,587	1,526	1,500
Liabilities and Stockholders' Equity						
Short-term debt	367	384	442	503	524	501
Long-term debt	295	302	798	801	862	898
Total liabilities	662	686	1,240	1,304	1,386	1,399
Total shareholders' equity	892	760	697	648	490	420
Total liabilities & shareholders' equity	1,723	1,575	1,636	1,587	1,526	1,500
Other Data						
Personnel: in Switzerland	8,822	8,385	8,526	9,323	9,173	8,982
Personnel: abroad	2,963	2,893	2,597	2,611	2,353	2,311
Personnel: total	11,785	11,278	11,123	11,934	11,526	11,293
Stock price*—High	560	395	490	700**	410	***
Low	378	178	150	375	127	

Note: All monetary values in million SFr.

* Nominal value SFr./share.

** Trading moved from Basle to Zurich on 7/17/1986.

FUTURE

Despite the smashing success of the Swatch and its contribution to the reinvigoration of the Swiss watchmaking industry, future success is by no means guaranteed.

First, competition remains as fierce as ever. The 1980s were characterized by an oversupply of cheap watches because many manufacturers had built capacity ahead of demand. Prices dropped, especially for the cheapest digital watches, a segment that the Swiss avoided. However, several competitors switched to the more sophisticated analogue models and thus created competition for the Swatch. Many look-alikes with names such as Action Watch, A-Watch, and the like, flooded the market.

Second, the Swiss have to guard their brand recognition—not just because of the diversification of the Swatch line. It is not clear whether the Swatch brand name is strong enough to create a sustainable position against imitations. Also, the quality advantage of Swatch is neither evident to the consumer nor a top priority for the purchasing decision.

A third issue is for how long the Swatch can maintain its technological advantage. By the late 1980s, all imitations were welded together. In addition, many competitors, especially the Japanese, were larger than SMH and therefore able to support larger R&D budgets.

A fourth threat is market saturation. While countries with a gross domestic product per capita of over $5000 comprise only 17% of the world's population, they absorb 87% of Swiss watch exports. The changes in watch technology and pricing during the last 10 years have increased watch consumption. In England, consumption grew from 275 watches per 1000 inhabitants in 1974 to 370 watches 10 years later. In the United States, the respective figures were 240 and 425 units of which 90% were made up of low-price electronic models. While the average life of a watch is much shorter today and consumers have started to own several watches, market saturation cannot be ruled out. Also, given the trendy nature of the Swatch, it can fall out of fashion as quickly as it had conquered the market. For this situation SMH is not as well prepared as, say, Seiko or Casio, whose nonwatch businesses are much stronger and contribute more in terms of overall sales and profits.

A fifth threat is the continued rapid development of technology especially in the field of communications. Increasingly, time measurement is evolving into one of several features of an integrated communication system. Watches are already integrated into a wide variety of products including household durables, computers, telephones. Several SMH subsidiaries involved in microelectronics, electronic components, and telecommunications are busy developing products in this area and searching for applications in other markets as well. In the late 1980s, SMH started to test prototypes of a combined watch/pager. In late 1990, Motorola introduced a combined watch/pager. It was not clear how SMH and its Swatch subsidiary will fare in this evolving era despite its high-technology sector which, however, is smaller than that of its competitors (Exhibit 12).

Finally, despite the success of the Swatch and of several mid-priced models under other brand names such as Tissot, the Swiss continue to experience higher than average unit prices for their watches. This is partially due to the success of their luxury mechanical watch pieces, which are frequently encased in precious metal and adorned with precious stones. However, executives of Swiss companies express concern about this trend.

SMH Subsidiaries (1990) **Exhibit 12**

Company Name, Registered Offices	*Field of Activity*	*Shareholding SMH Direct or Indirect in %*
Omega SA, Bienne	Watches	100
Compagnie des montres Longines, Francillon SA, Saint-Imier	Watches	100
SA Longines pour la vente en Suisse, Saint-Imier	Distribution	100
Columna SA, Lausanne	Distribution	100
Longines (Singapore) PTE Ltd. Singapore (SIN)	Distribution	100
Longines (Malaysia) Sdn., Kuala Lumpur (MAL)	Distribution	100
Montres Rado SA, Lengnau	Watches	100
Tissot SA, Le Locie	Watches	100
Certina, Kurth Freres SA, Grenchen	Watches	100
Mido G. Schaeren & Co SA, Bienne	Watches	100
Mido Industria e Comercio de Relogios Ltda. Rio de Janeiro (BRA)	Distribution	100
Swatch SA, Bienne	Watches	100
ETA SA Fabriques d'Ebauches, Grenchen	Watches, movements, electronic components and systems	100
ETA (Thailand) Co. Ltd. Bangkok (THA)	Watches and movements	100
Leader Watch Case Co. Ltd. Bangkok (THA)	Watch cases	100
Endura SA, Bienne	Watches	100
Lascor SpA. Sesto Calende (ITA)	Watch cases	100
Diantus Watch SA, Castel San Pietro	Watches and movements	100
Societe Europeenne de Fabrication d'Ebauches d'Annemasse (SEFEA) SA. Annemasse (FRA)	Watch components and electronic assembly	100
Ruedin Georges SA, Bassecourt	Watch cases	100
EM Microelectronic-Marin SA, Marin	Microelectronics	100
SMH Italia S.p.A. Rozzano (ITA)	Distribution (Omega, Rado, Tissot, Swatch, Flik Flak)	100
SMH (UK) Ltd. Eastleigh (GBR)	Distribution (Omega, Tissot)	100
SMH Australia Ltd. Prahran (AUS)	Distribution (Omega, Tissot, Swatch, Flik Flak)	100
SMH Belgium SA. Bruxelles (BEL)	Distribution (Omega, Tissot, Flik Flak)	100
SMH Ireland Ltd. Dublin (IRL)	Distribution (Omega)	100

REFERENCES

Bernheim, Ronnie A., *Koordination in zersplitterten Maerkten*. Berne, 1981: Paul Haupt Publ.

ETA S.A., "SWATCH. The Revolutionary New Technology." company brochure.

Federation de l'industrie horlogere Suisse (Swiss Watchmanufacturers Federation), *Annual Reports*, 1983–1989, Bienne.

Heller, Matthew, "Swatch Switches," *Forbes*, January 27, 1986, pp. 86–87.

Hieronymi, O. et al., *La diffusion de nouvelles technologies en Suisse.* Saint-Saphorin, 1983: Georgi.

Hill, Wilhelm, *Die Wettbewerbsstellung der schweizerischen Uhrenindustrie.* Report for the Swiss Federal Department of Economics, mimeo., Basle 1977.

Ludwig, Benoit D., "Innovation is mehr als neue Produkte," *io Management-Zeitschrift,* no. 2 (1985), pp. 54–59.

Moynahan, Brian, and Andreas Heumann, "The Man Who Made the Cuckoo Sing," *The Sunday Times Magazine,* August 18, 1985, pp. 23–25.

Mueller, Jacques, and Elmar Mock, "Swatch. Eine Revolution in der Uhrentechnik," *Neue Zuercher Zeitung,* Fernausgabe Nr. 50, March 2, 1983.

Neue Zuercher Zeitung, various issues 1980–1990.

SMH Swiss Corporation for Microelectronics and Watchmaking Industries Ltd., annual reports 1984–1989.

Swiss American Review, "Swatch-Chef in Japan hat den Hut genommen," July 2, 1986, p. 9.

Thomke, Ernst, "In der Umsetzung von der Produktidee zur Marktreife liegt ein entscheidender Erfolgsfaktor," *io Management-Zeitschrift,* no. 2 (1985), pp. 60–64.

Union Bank of Switzerland, *The Swiss Watchmaking Industry.* USB Publications on Business, Banking and Monetary Topics No. 100, Zuerich, March 1986.

CASE 27

Deli Rockwool Corporation in the People's Republic of China

James A. Brunner, Mao Jianhua, University of Toledo

Prior to President Nixon's historic visit to China and the signing of the Shanghai Communiques in February 1972, trade between the United States and the People's Republic of China (PRC) was negligible. For 1972, total trade between the two countries was only $95.9 million. The normalization of diplomatic and economic relations, the Chinese open-door policy since 1978, and especially the passage by the U.S. Congress on January 24, 1980, of the U.S.–China Trade Agreement granting most-favored nation status to China, provided great momentum to the development of trade between the two countries. According to U.S. statistics, bilateral trade reached $20 billion in 1990, making the United States China's third largest trading partner, exceeded only by Hong Kong and Japan.

Since China, a country with documented history of 4,000 years, was closed to the outside world prior to 1972, it is a newcomer in the international business world. China's way of doing business, though now changing gradually, has been influenced greatly by its culture, history, customs, values, and ethics, as well as by the political and economic climate and management and foreign trade administration systems. China and the United States had been isolated from each other for nearly 30 years, since 1949. Thus, the development of understanding and appreciation of the differences in culture, values, and customs is very helpful in developing business relationships between the two countries.

What follows is a narrative of one U.S. firm's attempt to enter the Chinese market and, hopefully, to create for itself a whole new path of growth, after several years of stagnant sales. As is made clear in the case, doing business in the PRC is very different from doing so in the United States, and, as one group of American businesspeople discovered, attempting to reach new horizons in the PRC can be quite challenging.

This case is intended for classroom discussion only, not to depict effective or ineffective handling of administrative situations. All rights reserved to the authors.

BACKGROUND

Shenyang Building Materials Corp. (hereafter referred to as the End User), headquartered in Shenyang in the northeast of China, produces different types of building materials, such as bricks, concrete elements, and sanitary wares. It employed 1,000 people and had sales of $7 million in 1989. Supported by the local government, the management wanted to go ahead with an investment in a rockwool* production factory, after a preliminary study. The project proposal had been approved by the local economic and planning commissions. As China's economy is centrally planned and foreign trade is monopolized by the government, the End User has no authority to import the machinery and technology directly to produce rockwool.

Yanjing Building Materials Machinery and Technology Import & Export Corp. (hereafter called the Buyer), headquartered in Beijing, is one of the organizations authorized by the Ministry of Foreign Economic Relation and Trade (MOFERT) to engage in the import and export business with foreign countries. The Buyer specializes in the import and export of building materials, machinery, and technology and is responsible for organizing and conducting the technical and commercial negotiations as well as signing and executing contracts on behalf of end users. It sent inquiries to three different foreign suppliers for bidding: Deli in the United States, Toya in Japan, and Horri in Sweden. The preliminary technical discussions had been conducted during a visit by a Buyer delegation to the United States, Japan, and Sweden in January 1989. Commercial negotiations were scheduled to take place in Beijing from November 12 to December 23, 1989, with these three suppliers.

Shenyang is a major city in China and has a population of 5 million. The city is well known for its heavy industry and building materials industries. Located in the northeast of China, Shenyang has long winters, when the temperature can drop as low as -30°F. With the rapid growth of the local population, the local government worked out a massive construction program to ease the housing shortage. All the buildings were constructed of brick and concrete elements, without the use of any insulation materials, which caused a huge waste of heat energy. Considering the rich resources of feldspar, dolomite, and slag in the surrounding areas, the necessary raw materials for rockwool production, the local government realized the demand from local and neighboring provinces for this product was enormous. The local government had listed the development of the insulation industry as one of the priorities in the local development program.

Deli Rockwool Corp., headquartered in West Virginia, is the biggest U.S. company specializing in the design and delivery of rockwool machinery and production technology. The company was founded in 1967 and employed 500 people. Its worldwide sales in 1989 were $37.2 million (see Exhibit 1). It had supplied more than 30 complete rockwool production lines all over the world, but none in the PRC (see Exhibit 2). Exhibit 2 shows that Asia was an emerging area. Recent market research indicated that with the fast development of China's economy, there would be a huge demand for insulation material for the building construction, insulation, and oil-refinery industries. However,

*_Rockwool:_ Mineral wool made by blowing a jet of steam through molten rock (such as limestone or siliceous rock) or through slag and used chiefly for thermal and sound insulation.

Exhibit 1

Deli Rockwool Corporation: Worldwide Sales

Year	Sales ($ in millions)	Profit ($ in millions)
1986	$41.3	$2.29
1987	40.8	2.22
1988	38.4	2.19
1989	37.2	2.17

Exhibit 2

Deli Rockwool Corporation: Sales Volume Distribution (by percentage of sales)

Year	North America	South America	Europe	Asia
1986	52.4%	23.0%	14.8%	10.0%
1987	40.8	15.0	22.2	22.0
1988	40.7	11.9	19.8	27.6
1989	32.3	13.0	19.9	34.8

China lacked the advanced technology and machinery to produce rockwool. Deli management had defined this factor as one of the firm's key objectives for entering this market. New strategies were to be developed to position the firm to capture the Chinese market in the future and stimulate the otherwise declining sales volumes and revenues of the company. Deli management was also aware that the Japanese firm Toya and the Swedish company Horri, Deli's main competitors in this industry, were also trying to enter the PRC market.

In late 1989, Deli received an inquiry from the Buyer for a rockwool production line with an annual designed capacity of 15,000 tons. In January 1990, the company received a visit from a Chinese delegation headed by Xin Xiaming for a plant tour and detailed technical discussions. Following the visit, an exchange of information was conducted through fax, telex, and mail, and progress was very encouraging. At the invitation of the Buyer, Deli sent a team of four to China in December 1990 for formal commercial negotiations.

On December 16, 1990, the Deli group arrived at Beijing airport. The group consisted of John Gross, vice president of the Marketing Department; Richard Wolf, chief engineer; Arthur Miller, a lawyer; and Tony Shen, a recently hired marketing assistant who was born in China and moved to the United States in 1978, after the Chinese Cultural Revolution. At the airport, the Deli group was met by Wang Hai, director of the Import Department, and Miss Chen Ling, a young interpreter from Yanjing Building Materials Import and Export Corp. Wang Hai expressed his warmest welcome to the arriving Deli group. "Mr. Xin wants me to convey his apologies to you for not being able to pick you up at the airport himself. He is at a meeting with the Japanese Toya representatives, but he is looking forward to seeing you at a welcoming banquet this evening."

Before the Deli group's visit, John had learned that Japanese Toya and Swedish Horri were also bidding for this project, but John did not expect the Chinese to arrange negotiations with other suppliers simultaneously. John had met Xin at an exhibition in Hannover, Germany, two years previously, and both had become very interested in each other's business activities. In the preceding year, John had invited and sponsored the visit of Xin's delegation to Deli's rockwool manufacturing facilities and research center in West Virginia. Xin and his delegation had been greatly impressed by Deli's state-of-the-art technology and grateful for the hospitality John extended to them. The two men had developed a close relationship and expressed a strong mutual interest in developing China's rockwool insulation industry.

On the way to the hotel, Wang Hai enthusiastically recalled the history of Beijing and noted such historical sites as the Great Wall, the Summer Palace, and the Forbidden City. "It is your first time here, you must see the Wall. Do you know in China there is a saying, 'You are not a hero unless you have climbed the Wall.'" The Deli group was amused by this expression.

Half an hour later, the Deli group arrived at the Great Wall–Sheraton Hotel, a five-star hotel in Beijing managed by the Sheraton group. Located in the eastern part of Beijing, the hotel was not far from the American Embassy. John was surprised to find the hotel very typically American, and it had built up a part of the Great Wall in its backyard. After check-in, Wang Hai kindly escorted the Deli group to their rooms; after five minutes, their luggage was sent to their rooms. Pleased by the good service, John offered a $3 tip to the bellboy, but he said, "No, thank you." John was obviously puzzled and embarrassed by his refusal and thought the amount might not be adequate. Wang Hai saw this and explained in a friendly way, "China is a socialist country. To serve guests is his duty. Tipping is not allowed here. He will be disgraced if he accepts your tip." After the Deli group had been settled, Wang Hai wished them a good rest and said that Xin would come to pick them up at 7:00 P.M. to take them to the banquet.

WELCOMING BANQUET

Punctually at 7:00 P.M., Xin arrived at the hotel with a large delegation of 15 Chinese. John knew two of them from the Shenyang Building Materials Corp., but the rest were new to him. After shaking hands and exchanging greetings, Xin introduced each of them to the Deli group. They were officials from the Shenyang Economic Commission; the Shenyang Planning Commission; and the Bank of China, Shenyang Branch; and mechanical, electrical, civil, and process engineers from the Shenyang Designing Institute. As China is a socialist country characterized by central planning, the foreign trade system functions as an integral part of the national and local economic planning mechanism. An end user has to initiate a project proposal and a feasibility study for approval by the local government authorities, such as the already-mentioned commissions, before the import of a proposed project. The commissions are responsible for planning, executing, financing, and supervising the local economic development program. They also evaluate the priority and feasibility of a proposed project according to the local development program and then grant or deny the project accordingly.

A few minutes later, Xin drove the Deli group to a downtown restaurant famous for Chinese Cantonese delicacies. Entering the dining room, the Deli group was surprised to notice not only place cards on the tables but also Maotai, wine, beer and cold foods (appetizers). According to a Chinese custom, Xin, the host, was seated facing north, while John was seated opposite him. The remaining Americans were interspersed among the Chinese.

After tea was served, the tiny cups were filled with Maotai, a premium Chinese drink containing 60% alcohol and normally used to entertain old friends or distinguished guests. To demonstrate the strength of the Maotai, Xin held a lighted match near his cup, and the Maotai immediately ignited. John thought to himself, "Wow, this stuff could fuel a car!" Following this, Xin gave a welcoming speech expressing his warmest welcome to the Deli group on behalf of his company and lauding the friendship between the two countries. "I hope the negotiations will be conducted in a spirit of friendship and on the basis of mutual benefit and equality, and we wish the negotiations to be successful. Let's *Ganbei* [bottoms-up]," Xin enthusiastically proposed. All the Chinese applauded, then rose, touched their cups with those of the Deli people, and emptied their drinks.

Encouraged by Xin's warm speech, John sensed it was his turn to give a responding speech expressing his appreciation for their invitation to China and the excitement in seeing many old and new Chinese friends at the banquet. John enthusiastically said: "We believe Deli has the best technology and machinery in the world, and with all this and our best service, we will no doubt turn your plant into one of the best in the world." All the Chinese applauded, saying, "Yes, yes." Following the applause and toasts, the representatives from the Shenyang Economic Commission, the Shenyang Planning Commission, the Bank of China, the Designing Institute, and the End User proposed *Ganbei* in turn to the Deli group. Aware of the 60% alcohol content, the Deli people tried to use wine instead, but were dissuaded, in a friendly manner, by the Chinese.

After the fifth course of food was served and numerous *Ganbeis*, John felt he had had enough and thought there would be only a few courses left. Out of curiosity, he picked up the menu and to his surprise, there would be seven more courses and what astonished him was that these seven courses included dog's meat, duck's paw, and snake soup. John carefully asked Xin whether these foods were normal Cantonese food. Xin smiled and replied affirmatively. He then started explaining the varieties and differences in Chinese foods from different regions. "I think the Cantonese food tastes best. The dog's meat is very good during the winter, as it produces more heat than any other meat. Have you heard such a saying? 'Cantonese eat all flying animals except airplanes and all climbing animals except a table.'" Everyone around the table laughed at his humorous comments.

The Deli team were very impressed by the rich varieties of the Chinese delicacies. After the seventh course was served, the food on the plates before the Deli group resembled a hill, but the Chinese continued to persuade them by saying, "Qiang, Qiang, please eat more, more, please." As it might be impolite to stop eating and drinking while the Chinese were continuing, the Deli representatives tried to follow the protocol and tasted a bit of every course at the urging of the Chinese.

After the fruit was served, which indicated the end of the banquet, John expressed his thanks to Xin for his kind invitation to this wonderful banquet and said this was the most delicious food he had ever had. To his surprise, Xin replied humbly, "No, no. It is only a simple dinner. Hope you don't mind." John, confused by his reply, saw that the two tables being cleared by the waitresses were full of unfinished foods. "This much food would feed my family for a week," John murmured to himself.

TECHNICAL MEETING

The next day, a meeting was scheduled at the Buyer's headquarters. The Deli group was greeted by Xin at the entrance. Entering the room, the Deli group was surprised to find the flags of both countries on the table. The Chinese arranged themselves on one side of the table, and the Deli group was seated opposite them. After tea was served, Xin proposed the initiation of the meeting. As he had other important matters to attend to, he stated, he could not participate in every meeting but had authorized Wang Hai to handle the negotiations. After shaking hands with the Deli people, Xin left the conference room.

As Deli's technology was new to many of the Chinese present at the meeting, Wang Hai suggested Deli give a technical presentation first. Richard, Deli's chief engineer, started the presentation, which would cover raw materials preparation, feeding, melting, spinning, curing, forming, and packaging. He emphasized the advantages of Deli's melting and spinning technology and how this technology could benefit the End User in terms of raw materials' consumption and labor costs in the long run.

Apparently, due to a lack of technical background, the interpreter had difficulty in translating the technical terms used to explain the process and the machinery. Many times, she had to consult the dictionary or ask Richard to repeat the technical terms. The questions asked by the Chinese engineers also revealed her inadequate translation. The presentation proceeded slowly. John thought to himself, "What can we do? It is just a start. The tough part comes later. How can the poor girl handle the translation of commercial and legal jargon later on? How can the ideas of both parties be communicated correctly?" John started to worry. During the break, he asked Tony whether he could do the translation. Tony was disinclined, saying that would not only embarrass Wang, but also cause the girl to lose face. Besides, seldom did the Chinese use or trust a foreign interpreter, and they always relied on the translation of their own interpreter. "Then what proposal can I make to carry on the negotiation smoothly so as not to embarrass or offend the Chinese?" John asked himself.

FIRST ROUND PRICE NEGOTIATIONS

The negotiations continued in the afternoon and immediately turned to the most sensitive issue—price. To the surprise of every Deli team member, they found the competitors' quotations on the table before the Chinese negotiators. Wang Hai pointed out that according to Chinese trade practice, quotations from different suppliers shall be fully compared before a contract is signed. "The Swedish and Japanese suppliers have agreed to reduce their prices by 20% and 15%, respectively. We have reviewed Deli's prices and found them on the high side, and the technology transfer fee is unreasonable and especially overvalued. You have already recovered your development costs in your previous machinery and product sales, and we think the technology transfer fee is far greater than is justified. It is unfair that Deli wishes to charge us for both the machinery and technology. We hope Deli can reduce the prices to a competitive level!" Wang Hai remarked.

John then endeavored to explain Western business practices and how his company had been investing money for the research and development of new technology. "The technology and machinery offered in the quotation represent the latest innovations and would greatly reduce the End User's labor and raw materials usage and thereby reduce production costs. That is why our fee is different from others, and it would be valued at this level on the world market." The Chinese seemed passive and unenthusiastic with John's explanation and argued that labor and raw materials were not their major concerns, as they were cheap in this area. What concerned them most was that Deli's prices greatly exceeded their approved foreign currency budget.

They also explained the difficulties they would have in applying for any additional hard foreign currency and that it might take up to six months to get this application approved. If Deli could not reduce its prices to their budget level, they would have to buy from another source. John was disappointed not only that the Chinese did not evaluate the technology in terms of economic efficiency and the benefits it would bring to them in the long run, but also by the Chinese bureaucracy and red tape to get any additional funds approved. The discussion continued for another hour, and John learned this project had only a $4.2 million foreign currency budget. "We hope you will reconsider the price and quote a more favorable one. As we will have a meeting with the Japanese supplier tomorrow morning, we have arranged for you to visit the Great Wall and Ming Tombs, and our interpreter will accompany you. Our negotiations are scheduled for the day after tomorrow," Wang said. John was obviously not happy with this arrangement, as his group was here for business and not sightseeing. He was also frustrated over the absence of a time schedule, as the Chinese had not yet discussed the time frame for the negotiations. His team had to leave China on December 23 to be home for the Christmas holidays.

Back at the hotel, Miller expressed his worry that price was so transparent in China, as there were almost no commercial secrets here. He doubted whether the Chinese side would keep their promise and commitment in the contract to protect Deli's technology. As China had neither the laws nor regulations to protect industrial properties, nor was it a member of the Convention for the Protection of Industrial Property (Paris Convention), he pondered what remedies Deli could seek if the Chinese violated the confidentiality clause. If the Chinese copied the technology, not only would Deli's long-term strategy in this market not be realized, but also all of its effort to enter the PRC market would be for naught. Tony told John that he shared this view, but at the same time, the Chinese negotiators regarded a price concession from Deli as a face-giving act and an indication of its willingness to continue the cooperation on this project. A price concession from Deli would be necessary.

SIGHTSEEING TOUR

The Chinese had arranged for the Deli group to visit Baidaling, the best preserved part of the Great Wall, and the Ming Tombs. As they are located to the northwest of Beijing, about 75 kilometers away from the hotel, the trip started early in the morning. On the way to the Wall, the interpreter proudly lectured on the history of the Wall: "The Great Wall is more than ten thousands li long [one kilometer for two lis], and it is one of the few man-made objects which can be observed from the moon." The Wall turns and twists on the mountain ridges, and it has a magnificent view. It is difficult to imagine how the ancient Chinese built it during a time when there were neither modern transportation facilities nor lifting devices. After they descended from their climbing of the Wall, their young interpreter kindly bought for each Deli member a certificate proclaiming that he had climbed the Wall. "All of you are heroes now," she laughed. The Deli people were pleased with this interesting gift.

SECOND ROUND PRICE NEGOTIATION

All parties returned to the negotiating table the next morning. Mr. Wang first asked John about his team's visit to the Wall and then immediately went to the price issue. The room became very silent. Obviously, the Chinese were expecting new prices from John. John proposed a 3% reduction on the machinery, a 5% on the technology, and gave Wang a copy of the new quotation, as shown in Exhibit 3.

To his dismay, the Chinese looked very quietly at his new quotations and then responded. "We appreciate your price cuts, but they are still far higher than we expected. For your information, your Japanese competitor agreed to further reduce their price yesterday. To be very honest with you, you are in a disadvantageous position. Please reconsider your price. We should resolve this issue before we proceed on the contract negotiations. Let's have a break," Mr. Wang said.

John was afraid that if he gave the Chinese a new quotation that day, the Chinese might use the concessions won from him to wrest further concessions

Exhibit 3 **Deli Rockwool Corporation: Revised Price Quotation**

Machinery	$3,900,000
Technology transfer	280,000
Installation and erection	270,000
Training	100,000
Spare parts for 2 years	250,000
	$4,800,000*

*The price is FOB New York Port, USA, including seaworthy packing. The quotation is valid until February 20, 1991.

from the Japanese supplier, then use the Japanese concessions to bargain with him again the next day. He was also afraid that if the negotiations continued in this way, it would become a time-consuming and weariful marathon. His team might still be sitting here at Christmas time. He also started wondering whether the Chinese were really intending to buy his technology and machinery or were simply using Deli to get a better deal from the competitors. The meeting was adjourned for half an hour. To break this deadlock and give the Chinese face to move on with negotiations, John promised Wang to try his best to help him with price, but as the final price would depend very much on the payment terms and other contract terms, he suggested both parties continue the negotiations. Wang exchanged his views with his group and then replied, "We will study your proposal, and let's meet in the afternoon." John noticed the Chinese wished to avoid direct confrontation with him and also wanted to solicit comments from their superiors.

CHINESE CONTRACT VERSUS AMERICAN CONTRACT

The negotiations continued in the afternoon. Before the negotiations started, Wang Hai distributed to John and Arthur Miller each a Chinese contract form and said, "Our leader has agreed to your proposal, so let's start discussing the contract terms. This is our standard commercial contract form." After a quick skimming, Miller found the form was exactly the same as the one he had seen three years previously. "But your standard is too simple and outdated and does not incorporate any of the needed adaptations and changes in it. Besides, there are many ambiguities in it. For example, the rights and obligations are too general and uncertain for the guarantee of the acceptance test; your arbitration clause, letter of credit, and remedy for a breach of contract must be renegotiated. This contract cannot be used for our project. I have prepared the contract from our side, and we can negotiate on this form." Miller then gave Wang two copies of his contract drafts. But the Chinese were very adamant and refused to accept Deli's contract form. Wang Hai replied, "I am sorry, our contract form is not negotiable, otherwise our relevant authorities will not approve it. We have signed many agreements on this form. If you have any objection to some terms, we can negotiate these later on."

As the contract form was an important issue, Miller did not give up. He still attempted, by asking questions, to elicit the Chinese reasoning behind this position and intended to persuade the Chinese to change their minds. To his disappointment, Wang continually repeated the same statement, but he was unwilling to provide any enlightenment on this issue. John and Miller observed that the Chinese were very sensitive about the contract form. Later on, they learned that as the Chinese negotiators were unfamiliar with the U.S. legal system and laws, they were afraid they might be given unfavorable terms or taken advantage of if they accepted a foreign contract form. Besides, as the signed contract would be subject to reviews by the government, Chinese negotiators were afraid that the signed contract would not be approved by the authorities if a foreign contract form were used. So they normally insist firmly on using their own standard contract form, even though it might not incorporate some necessary adaptations or changes to reflect the rights and obligations of both parties.

IRREVOCABLE LETTER OF CREDIT VERSUS CONFIRMED IRREVOCABLE LETTER OF CREDIT

Miller was uncertain of the Chinese political stability and its continuing foreign trade policy. He also had read recently in a U.S. newspaper that some Chinese companies delayed payments due to the shortage of hard currency. Miller thus proposed that the irrevocable letter of credit issued by the Bank of China should be confirmed by a third designated bank. Miller explained how this type of letter of credit worked in Western countries and tried to convince the Chinese to accept it. Wang Hai politely rejected the proposal and said, "According to our rules, the confirmed letter of credit is not applicable in China. The Bank of China is owned by our government, and, of course, its financial standing can't be questioned. Our bank, unlike the banks in capitalist countries, will not go bankrupt. We have never issued this kind of letter of credit."

Miller was surprised by the different trade practices here. There were many internal rules and regulations, often contradicting international business practices, that the Chinese negotiators had cited but could not back with documentation. In the United States, parties to a contract are only bound by the laws and regulations that are published and to which the parties have access prior to their decisions. Miller also found the Chinese organizations had much less independent decision-making power than Western organizations had, and many of their decisions would be subject to the time-consuming government approvals.

GUARANTEE

At this point, the negotiations shifted to the next topic, the guarantee. The Chinese asked for assurances that Deli would guarantee to do everything possible to ensure that the final product would meet the contract specifications, even if repeated and time-consuming tests involving the presence of Deli's technicians in China were required. Miller observed that the guarantee clause the Chinese proposed was too general and uncertain, that the language used was too vague and ambiguous. He demanded specificity concerning the rights and obligations under the guarantee; otherwise, this clause would create for Deli a continuing and vague obligation to repair a bad situation. Such language could serve as a basis for the Chinese to make a claim, even though unsatisfactory products might have resulted from a failure of the Chinese to follow technical instructions carefully or to provide a sufficient power supply and appropriate raw materials for test runs. "Yes, of course, we will be responsible for our deficiencies from our side, but Deli should be responsible for its faults," Wang Hai said, stressing that, "Deli must provide the best machinery and technology, as stipulated in the contract, and produce the contract products." Obviously, the Chinese misunderstood Miller's position and perceived it as an attempt from Deli's side to avoid any responsibility for a lack of quality control. Tony Shen explained to Miller and John that given the high costs of failure and limited reward for success in the Chinese system, Chinese negotiators are generally reluctant to assume what would be seen as normal entrepreneurial risks in the West. So during the contract negotiations, the Chinese emphasized the need for positive outcomes of the project and tried to make the foreign supplier assume most of the risks inherent in the venture, as well as stand as the sole guarantor of the technology.

DISCUSSION, ARBITRATION VERSUS LITIGATION

The negotiations proceeded to the solution of disputes. On the fourth day, Miller suggested that all disputes or claims arising relating to this contract should be settled through litigation, but his proposal was immediately declined by the Chinese. Wang insisted that all disputes should be settled through friendly discussion and reconciliation. In case no settlement could be reached, the case would be submitted to the China Council for Promotion of International Trade for arbitration in Beijing.

Afraid that the Chinese arbitration organization might act partially, or in favor of the Chinese side, Miller proposed using a third country, such as the Stockholm Commercial Chamber, for arbitration. After a quick exchange with other Chinese, Wang agreed. "We prefer arbitration. No matter what happens, we can always sit down and solve the disputes through friendly discussion or reconciliation. Between friends, everything can be negotiated." John noticed that the Chinese were exceptionally cautious with every position and proposal Miller had made. John was puzzled by this. Tony explained that the Chinese stress the ethical and moral obligation rather than the legal obligation. The Chinese traditionally and culturally distrust lawyers, whom they call troublemakers or pettifoggers. Therefore, they are adverse to litigation, a face-losing and humiliating act, and are of the opinion that discussion and negotiation can avoid loss of face by either party and maintain the self-respect as well as the friendship between the two sides. Therefore, the Chinese were reluctant to consider the possibility of a breakdown in the relationship.

ALTERNATIVES

It was already December 21. After four days of negotiations, both groups had gone through most of the contract terms, but the resolution of the pricing issue was still pending. John asked Tony, "The Chinese know we have to go back for Christmas soon, and I am wondering whether they are using a stalling tactic to get the best out of us." Tony suggested, "Since the Chinese place a great deal of importance on personal relationships *(Buangxi)* and you have a good relationship with Xin, why don't you invite Xin and Wang to a dinner and settle the price problem face-to-face at the dinner table?" John appreciated his suggestion. He had learned before coming to China that *Buangxi* is a very prevalent cultural phenomenon in this country, and it is very essential to establish and cultivate *Buangxi* and use it in order to get business accomplished.

At 7 P.M., Xin, Wang, and the interpreter punctually arrived at the hotel. During the course of dinner, John turned the conversation to the price issue. Xin said he had been aware of the progress of the negotiations, and he appreciated John and his team's sincere efforts in the previous days. "Though we admit to some extent your technology is better than that of the Japanese, their prices are much lower. For your information, the End User has only $3 million for this project, but the Japanese have agreed to further reduce their prices below the budget level. China is huge, and the potential market is very big. This project is very important both to you and your competitors. In China, there is a saying, 'Less profits, more projects.' I hope through this project, Deli can build up a good reputation in China and our two companies can develop a long-term cooperative relationship. As we are old friends, and as long as you can reduce your prices to our budget level, I will try to persuade [the End User] to order the machinery and technology from you. The president of [the End User] was my classmate in high school, and we have a very close relationship."

John realized Xin was giving him a favor and face. "What face can I give to him in return? What concession can I make from my side?" To reduce the price to their budget level would mean a negative profit margin for Deli on this project. To insist on the present prices would most probably cause the company to lose this project to its competitor and eventually let the Japanese establish the first foothold in this market. Should Deli go back and wait until the End User's budget is increased, even though that would take months or even longer? Should John suggest that the Chinese buy the key machinery instead of the whole line in order to meet the budget? However, Deli's reputation in this market would be at risk if the machinery from the Chinese did not perform well with Deli's machinery. John recalled the high hopes everyone at Deli had for the Chinese project. In a way, the future of the firm seemed to be riding on this deal. Deli's plans called for dominating the market in China. Were those plans sound in the first place, or even realistic? Should the company sacrifice now for future growth, or go home and forget the whole thing?

John found himself in a dilemma with these alternatives. "Doing business in China is more difficult than building the Wall!" John murmured.

CASE 28

Cognex Corporation

Don Hopkins, Temple University

In 1981, Dr. Robert Shillman, a professor at MIT, formed a company called Cognex Corporation, located in Needham, Massachusetts. It was intended to build customized machine vision systems. These systems were meant to serve as inspection systems and be the "eyes" for industrial robots. The firm's first five years were a disaster.

Cognex got off to a rough start, but learned from its early experiences. It had to walk away from some early contracts because it could not solve the customers' problems. For example, in 1985, American Cynamid wanted Cognex to build a vision system to read expiration dates on packs of surgical sutures. The firm got the system to work in the lab, but it failed on site in Cyanamid's plant in Puerto Rico.

The fatal problem was the strong tropical sun: The light in the plant was too bright. The Cognex system used a strobe light to freeze an image of the product. However, this system required that the surrounding light be significantly weaker than the strobe. This was not the case at mid-day in the Puerto Rican plant. The problem could have been solved by putting a cover over one part of the manufacturing floor, but the firm's specialized software engineers did not think of simple solutions like this.

"We had a bunch of people who knew a lot about software processing, but not much about conveyor belts," noted Allan Wallack, a consultant brought into Cognex to change its strategy. Cognex had to refund Cyanamid's money and walk away. Errors like this resulted in $5 million in total losses by 1986.

Wallack and Shillman soon decided that Cognex would have a hard time making a profit on customized systems like the one designed for Cyanamid. Instead, Cognex decided to focus on standardized, proprietary vision systems for OEMs (original equipment manufacturers) in the electronics and semiconductor markets. The primary customer would not be the end users who pro-

---

This case is intended for classroom discussion only, not to depict effective or ineffective handling of administrative situations. All rights reserved to the author and the North American Case Research Association.

duce the chips or electronic devices but the firms that sold robots and testing equipment to the end user.

In 1986, Cognex implemented this new strategy. This required new products and restructured management, sales, marketing, manufacturing, and engineering departments. However, the strategy allowed the company to focus on new product development, rather than on the intensive service support required for customized systems sold to end users. In 1987, Cognex began shipping its new products.

Now the company thrives, growing about 50% a year. Most significantly, the bulk of its growth comes from Japan, where Japanese companies have a tradition of shunning American suppliers in favor of dealing with other Japanese companies. Shillman says, "In 10 or 15 years, we'll have hundreds of millions of dollars in revenue."[1] How was this turnaround possible in an industry where virtually every other American producer of robots or robotic subsystems has been driven out of business? The robot business is now one of a long list of industries dominated by the Japanese. How did this aberration come about, and will it continue?

THE INDUSTRIAL ROBOT INDUSTRY

The robotics business once was seen as having great potential. Two big mistakes happened along the way. First, the market was overestimated, resulting in vast overcapacity in the 1980s. Second, the industry was lost to the Japanese. American firms bet on the wrong technology, and the large American firms exited the industry. Westinghouse, GE, IBM, and Cincinnati Milacron have all left the business after being beaten by the Japanese. Many smaller American firms, such as Prab and Graco, have stopped making robots.

Westinghouse acquired Unimation Inc., the American firm that first developed industrial robots, in 1963. Westinghouse planned to build a billion-dollar business in factory automation. "It's absolutely sick. It breaks my heart to think of how we lost the industrial robot industry," said George Munson, former marketing vice president at Westinghouse Unimation. "Our basic approach was wrong. It was a classic case of trying to merge an entrepreneurial organization into a relatively slow-moving, large American corporation," commented Thomas Murrin, the manager in charge of Westinghouse's advanced technology group, which includes Unimation.[2]

In 1983, there were 62 American firms producing complete robots. Unimation was the leader with its Unimate hydraulic robot and had over 40% of the U.S. market. Unfortunately, Unimation and other U.S. firms bet on hydraulic robots, whereas the industry ultimately would be dominated by electric robots. Japanese firms, like Kawasaki Heavy Industries Ltd., hedged their bets and developed both hydraulic and electric robots.

"Unimate suffered from a design flaw that caused it to vibrate. Consequently, a coupling in the fluid line had to be left slightly loose, lest it burst under pressure. The dripping that resulted couldn't be fixed, short of redesigning the robot at prohibitive expense. So, the devices were equipped with drip pans that overflowed unpredictably, sometimes halting the assembly lines where they were in use. When a robot broke down, it took two people to work on it—a plumber and an electrician."[3]

But Westinghouse liked its product because it could sell drip pans as options. "Our guys said why fix it when we were making money on the drip pan, not to mention the extra hydraulic fluid," said Mr. Weisel, a former Unimation manager.[4] However, customers like Chrysler started replacing hydraulic robots with electric ones. Out of the 2,000 robots now at the car company that weld, stamp, and assemble parts, only 15% are still hydraulic.

Westinghouse introduced PUMA in 1985. PUMA was a large electric robot capable of replacing Unimate, but the company was too late. In 1985, Unimation sales dropped 40%. PUMA was a me-too robot, too late to compete with the Japanese. Additionally, by the mid-1980s, customers were less interested in robots because these firms started to comprehend that their products would have to be extensively redesigned in order to effectively incorporate robots into the manufacturing process. Manufacturing and product development would have to work together in designing new products. This was not typical for many American firms at the time. Japanese robot makers aided their customers in redesigning their products to be "robot friendly." The Japanese stressed simple robots, keeping fixed costs low and in line with JIT (just-in-time) production. American firms stressed high-cost "smart" machines, exploiting their firms' software skills. For example, GE designed a four-arm robot that did many things simultaneously, but the machine was so taxed that it broke down frequently. One reason U.S. manufacturers were not in love with robots is because keeping them from breaking down was so much work. In some operations, American companies that have once used robots have eliminated them completely.

The Japanese were able to build on their experience and develop comparable robots with 30% fewer components. Partly as a result, their robots have lower maintenance costs and are more reliable.

THE VISION THING

In spite of the failure of these large American firms, some small entrepreneurial firms were successful in certain niches. One of these niches was machine vision systems. Machine vision systems are used for machine guidance, part sorting, inspection, and gauging. For example, the inspection of package labels or semiconductor chips is a tedious, labor-intensive process that can be replaced with the use of a vision system, resulting in higher productivity. IBM has replaced its chip inspectors with a vision system made by Cognex. Many industry experts predict that robots with vision capability will be the "next generation" of robots as they become more sophisticated. Already, Ford and GM use vision systems to install auto windshields.

The basic idea behind a vision system is to digitize a picture and interpret its meaning through computer software. Systems range in complexity from simple camera-computer hookups to units with laser controls. Machine vision comes in uni-dimensional, two-dimensional, and three-dimensional forms. Pictures are made up of elements called "pixels." The pixels are digitized and interpreted by a customized software package.

THE VISION SYSTEM INDUSTRY

In 1985, there were probably about 100 vision system firms (this number includes manufacturers and systems houses; systems houses combine hardware from different companies, design the software, install and debug the system, and then provide service). Today there are many fewer vision firms, probably about 20. Between 1985 and 1990, there was a huge shake-out as a result of too many firms entering the business because of overly optimistic forecasts and low entry barriers. Only the firms with a strategic commitment remained.

The industry was easy to enter. An industry expert commented: "There is no barrier to entry. None. Any halfway bright person could go to Digital Equipment Corporation and buy an original equipment manufacturer's (OEM) computer, say, for about $5,000, and from any number of companies buy an interface board that lets a camera 'talk' to the computer, and go to any video store and buy an off-the-shelf camera that's used for security surveillance or something, put it all in a cabinet that costs a couple hundred bucks, and he's got a vision system. It doesn't do much, and it's not very sophisticated, but he's a player in the market!"[5] As a result, the market was full of "mom and pop" companies, small players operating out of their garages.

Vision systems have been easier to sell than robots because unions apparently do not feel as threatened by them. Purchase decisions for vision systems are thus made at lower levels of management than for other robots. Part of this acceptance is because the vision systems do a better job than manual labor can. A manager with a vision firm noted: "A good example is label inspection. Picture dishwashing liquid bottles coming by. You are sitting in a chair in front of a conveyor and the bottles are coming by at a rate of five a second, 300 a minute. On the other side of the conveyor is a mirror, and your job is to look at both the front of the bottle, and in the mirror, at the back of the bottle. You are supposed to identify those bottles that have torn labels or labels that are misplaced by more than a sixteenth of an inch. That's a lousy job, and you probably aren't doing it very well."[6]

By 1988, machine vision sales were only $196 million, and about half of the firms making systems made them for their own use. By 1990, nearly half of the entire market was represented by the electronics and automotive industries. According to Bader Associates, the entire 1990 market was $477.8 million, broken down as follows: 10% from electronics, 38% from autos, 10% from machinery, 8% from fabricated metal products, 6% from fabricated commodities, and 28% from various small users (see Exhibit 1).

Competition between companies is based on software, computing speed and power, product functionality and performance under "real-world conditions," flexibility, programmability, and on-site engineering expertise and service.

Vision systems are used in two main ways. One is to recognize an object or pattern. An example would be the system used to scan bar codes on items at grocery store checkouts. The second is to measure specific characteristics of an object. This second function is more important to manufacturing operations. Systems that assess depth, surface orientation, and position are key to guiding robotic devices. This visual guidance is called "visual serving." For example, a camera may be placed on the end of a robotic arm and used to guide the arm to its destination. An example would be the SMD (surface mount device) industry where a vision system guides a robot in mounting an electronic component on the surface of a circuit board.

THE ROBOTICS INDUSTRY

In a technical sense, vision systems are not robots but are often a major robotic subsystem, so the success of the two industries is strongly linked. A robot,

Exhibit 1

Forecasted Robot Use and Sales in the United States and Application by Industry

Industry	***1985***	***1990***	***1995***
Agriculture	1%	1%	1%
Mining and extractive	1	2	2
Construction	0	1	1
Electricity generation	1	1	1
Consumer consumables	2	5	5
Nonmetal commodities	2	4	5
Primary metals	3	4	5
Fabricated commodities	5	6	6
Fabricated metal products	10	8	8
Machinery	8	10	11
Electronics	8	10	16
Automotive	51	38	26
Aerospace	6	6	8
Other transport equipment	2	3	4
Total	100%	100%	100%

Forecasted Robot Sales in the United States, by Application

	1985	1990	1995
Machine tending	16%	15%	15%
Material transfer	16	15	15
Spot welding	26	15	10
Arc welding	10	10	9
Spray painting/coating	10	10	7
Machining	5	7	7
Electronic assembly	6	12	14
Other assembly	5	8	12
Inspection	5	7	10
Other	1	1	1
Total	100%	100%	100%

	1985		***1990***		***1995***	
Application	*Units*	*Sales*	*Units*	*Sales*	*Units*	*Sales*
Machine tending	800	$ 28.0	1,650	$ 61.1	2,250	$ 69.8
Material transfer	800	28.8	1,650	62.7	2,250	78.8
Spot welding	1,300	78.0	1,650	95.7	1,500	75.0
Arc welding	500	30.0	1,100	66.0	1,350	78.3
Spray painting	500	30.0	1,100	66.0	1,050	63.0
Electronics assembly	300	10.5	1,320	52.8	2,100	66.4
Other assembly	250	8.8	880	30.8	1,800	63.0
Inspection	250	13.0	770	38.5	1,500	75.0
Other	50	2.0	110	4.2	150	6.0
Total	4,750	$229.1	10,230	$477.8	13,950	$575.3

Source: Robotics in Service, Joseph F. Engelberger, MIT Press, 1989. (He criticizes the above forecasts for excluding service robots.)

according to the Robot Institute of America (RIA), is a "reprogrammable multifunction manipulator designed to move material, parts, tools, or specialized devices through variable programmed motions for the performance of a variety of tasks." *Programmable* is the key word in this definition. Thus, a complicated but single-use piece of factory equipment would not qualify as a robot.

Robots were invented in the United States over 30 years ago. Significant growth in installation started in the 1980s. Forecasters had optimistically predicted sales of $2 billion by 1990. During the middle of the 1980s, it became clear that the industry would not live up to these expectations. In 1984, shipments by U.S.-based robot suppliers were 5,136 units and $332.5 million in sales. The U.S.-installed base was 14,500 units, mostly in the auto industry, as of 1984. Sales and units, respectively, were $443 million and 6,209 in 1985 and $441 million and 6,219 in 1985. RIA reported booked orders of about $500 million in 1990. Robotic exports equaled $100 million in 1990 and represented 6,000 complete units. This is twice the unit volume exported in 1989. Orders for 1991 were level, but shipments were expected to increase as the backlog was reduced.

The auto industry absorbs about 50% of the industry's sales, mostly by buying spot welders. As such, the bulk of U.S. robotic producers are located in the midwestern states of Illinois, Indiana, Iowa, Michigan, and Wisconsin, but particularly in Michigan, where about one-sixth of all U.S. robot producers are located.

The auto industry is, of course, very cyclical. The robotics industry is starting to diversify its customer base, however. Other applications include heavy machinery, aerospace, electronics, food, drugs, and service industries. Other applications include arc welding, spray painting, loading and unloading, machining, material transfer, assembly operations, and inspection. Almost 37,000 robots had been installed in the U.S. by 1990, and another 20,000 more by the end of 1991. Trends aiding this growth are an increasing labor shortage, a growing market for used robots, more emphasis on manufacturing, miniaturization in the electronics industry, the potential for service robots (for security, cleaning, and use in health care), and the new importance of product integrity in the pharmaceutical industry.

The advantage of a robot comes primarily from its ability to work at a constant pace and with high accuracy throughout a work shift. This results in lower hourly costs for the operation of an industrial robot relative to a blue-collar worker. In 1981, the direct hourly labor cost was about $17 in the auto industry, compared to a robot's hourly cost of about $5. Robots also increase flexibility, allowing plants to work on a batch basis involving a variety of products at the same site.

Growth in the market for robots is likely to be affected by several factors. First, the cost of robots may decrease as they slide down the experience curve. The average cost of a robot in 1990 was either $40,000 or $110,000, depending on whose estimate you accept. These figures are expected to decline significantly in the next ten years. Second, sensing devices may improve. "Blind robots" are adequate only in very orderly manufacturing environments (not the norm), and thus the large amount of research being conducted on visual and tactile sensing devices may lead to a broader market. Third, robot size might be reduced. The size of robots has started to decline, increasing the potential for placing them in preexisting plants. Finally, systems integration and "building block designs," now being emphasized in the robotics industry, is moving away from individual robots and toward complete systems of flexible manufacturing and modules that comprise them.

THE JAPANESE ROBOTICS INDUSTRY

Japan is the leading producer, exporter, and market and has the largest installed base of robots in the world. However, it may also be the most saturated market for robots. There are about 300 Japanese robot firms, which provide about 50% of the world's demand for robots and generate sales of about $2.1 billion. Exhibit 2 shows the number of robots installed by country for 1980, 1984, 1989, and 1992.

Kawasaki Heavy Industries became the first Japanese entrant, in 1968, when it signed a licensing agreement with Unimation. Kawasaki improved on the Unimation design, and other firms soon entered the market, including Hitachi, Toshiba, and Ishikawajima-Harima Heavy Industries. Many important competitors entered in the middle 1970s. Fanuc (pronounced "fan-nuke") entered in 1974 and is now considered the world's dominant robot firm. Their first units were made for their own use. Fanuc is well known for the totally automated noodle factory it produced and for its use of robots to build its own robots.

Robots using the Panasert brand name, produced by Matsushita, were critical in America's loss of the consumer electronics industry. The robots automated the insertion of components onto circuit boards for TVs. Matsushita sells products under the Panasonic brand name and is known for its world-class manufacturing expertise.

Japanese competitors can be placed into several strategic groups including steel makers (e.g., Kobe Steel and Daido Steel), machinery producers (e.g., Fanuc, Toyoda Machine Works, Komatsu, and Toshiba Seiki), electronics firms (e.g., Hitachi, Matsushita, NEC, Toshiba, Fuji Electric, and Mitsubishi Electric), and transportation equipment firms (e.g., Kawasaki and Mitsui Engineering

Robots Installed by Country **Exhibit 2**

Country	*1992*	*1989*	*1984*	*1980*
Japan	274,000	220,000	67,300	15,250
United States	40,000	37,000	14,500	4,700
Germany	28,120	22,400	6,600	1,255
Italy	24,268	9,500	2,585	353
France	11,917	7,063	2,700	580
United Kingdom	9,634	5,908	2,623	371
Spain	5,476	2,000	516	284
Sweden	5,297	3,800	2,400	940
Belgium	3,221	1,800	775	58
Total	401,933	309,471	99,999	23,791

Source: Adapted from Japan Industrial Robot Association, July, 1985.

Note: Does not include manual manipulators and fixed-sequence control machines.

and Shipbuilding). Japanese firms often utilized their robots in their own manufacturing process, perfecting them in the process before putting them on the market. Some Japanese firms also have the advantage of being in the electronics industry, allowing them to easily incorporate electronic components into their robots. However, the Japanese have a definite disadvantage in software, which partly explains their emphasis on simpler robots.

There are several reasons that Japan became the biggest and earliest market for robots, including global dominance of the Japanese electronics industry, growth of their auto industry, a pronounced labor shortage, lifetime employment practices, a high proportion of engineers in management, less short-term financial pressure, emphasis on energy conservation, cooperation of unions, development of many Japanese companies as the premier manufacturing firms in the world, and government assistance and encouragement.

Japan represented 60% of the total installed base of robots by the early 1970s. In 1984, it represented 66% versus North America's 14.9%—and where the customers are, the producers are likely to be. "The total populations of robots in the U.S. is around 37,000," says John O'Hara, president of RIA. "The Japanese add that many in one year."[7]

Why have U.S. firms been so slow to incorporate robots into their manufacturing operations? "The companies selling robots plain lied about the capabilities of their equipment and the circumstances under which they could perform," says Roger Nagel, a former manager of automation technology at International Harvester.[8] "U.S. companies made robot hands that were so ungodly complex that in many cases, they had no chance of standing up in a real industrial environment," says Dennis Wisnosky, former vice president of GCA Industrial Systems Group, previously the second leading robot firm in the United States.[9] The Japanese started with simple machines and then used their experience to make more advanced robots.

The industries in Japan with the heaviest use of robots are as follows: electronics industry (36% of installed base), automotive industry (29%), plastic processing industry (10%), general machinery industries (7%), and the metalworking industry (5%).

Japanese robotics firms held the dominant position in the 1980s by a large margin. As a spokesman for the Long Term Credit Bank stated, "It's only a matter of time before the industrial robot becomes one more piece of merchandise which symbolizes Japan."[10]According to Andrew Tanzer and Ruth Simon, writing in *Forbes* magazine, "It happened in consumer electronics, memory chip production, and machine tools. Now it's happening in robotics."[11]

Robots can make flexible manufacturing and JIT production and inventory easier to achieve. Japan's firms are in the forefront of these "lean" production methods. For example, though U.S. carmakers have robotized, they have done so mainly in the area of spot welding and spray painting. Japanese carmakers, on the other hand, have robotized in a way that allows them to shift quickly from the production of one model to another. In the United States, robots have not spread much beyond carmakers and their suppliers.

In 1991, America imported $300 million in robots and parts as part of a total demand of $350 million. The United States exported $210 million in robots or parts in 1991, mostly to Europe and Canada. America imports approximately 55% of its complete robot systems, 80% of them from Japan. Many American robotics firms produce entirely offshore, often in Japan.

The Japanese market has become highly saturated. It has been estimated, for example, that as much as 90% of Japan's auto assembly lines have already been automated. Japanese electronics firms are also considered to be highly saturated. Most electronics firms moved to automatic insertion in the early 1970s. Also, many of the electronic firms, like Matsushita, produced their own robots and were among the first to automate. But as electronic components are miniaturized further, a new wave of automation may develop in this industry. Saturation is leading to increased pressure to export and to find new applications.

GMF

The largest seller of robots in the United States was the joint venture between General Motors and Fanuc known as GMF. This venture had about 27% of the U.S. robot market in 1985. GMF produced painting and laser robots used for welding and cutting. It had 1991 sales exceeding $250 million. Fanuc altogether has about half the U.S. market, although it imports twice as many robots as it makes in the United States, and its U.S.-produced units are designed in Japan. Fanuc also entered a joint venture with GE. Many other Japanese companies forged links with U.S. firms mainly to provide distribution of Japanese hardware or gain access to U.S. software. Many U.S. robotics firms buy basic Japanese robot units and add refinements and peripherals such as software and vision systems. No Japanese firms, other than GMF, set up manufacturing in the United States. Japanese robot makers are making modest profits, at best, because of the intense competition, but most remain in robotics to help maintain their own manufacturing capability.

Fanuc is the world's leading producer of industrial robots. It is reported to be consistently profitable. Fanuc is the lowest-cost producer and yet has very high quality. Controls and robots account for about 75% of its business. The company believes in "Weniger Teile" (German engineering slogan for reducing the number of parts) as a way of driving down costs.

Since GM and GE threw in the towel and linked up with Fanuc, the company has had the U.S. market handed over to it. GM was the industry's single biggest customer. Says consultant Gordon Richardson, "U.S. manufacturers were caught napping. They were trumpeting all sorts of advances, but they had not done the underlying job of making reliable systems."[12] Fanuc has a reputation for making reliable systems. There is speculation that Fanuc will one day abandon its U.S. partners.

COGNEX CORPORATION

Cognex has managed to prosper, along with a few other machine vision firms such as Allen-Bradley and Itran in the United States and Israeli-based Optrotech and Orbot. Although about 100 firms have attempted to develop profitable machine vision businesses, Cognex is one of only a few to make it a viable business. Cognex earned $6.5 million on sales of $21 million in 1990. For the past several years, it has grown about 50% a year. Cognex had installed more than 7,500 vision systems by the end of July 1991, more than anyone else. Cognex management claims to have 10% to 20% of the machine vision market.

Cognex's focus on proprietary machine vision systems for the electronics industry struck gold when it began selling to General Signal's Electroglas division, which produces equipment to check the silicon wafers used for semiconductor chips (i.e., wafer probers). However, Cognex's strategy makes it highly dependent on a small number of specialized products in cyclical, closely related industries.

■ Customers

Cognex's U.S. customers include AT&T, Digital Equipment, Electro Scientific Industries, GE, Hughes Aircraft, Merck Pharmaceuticals, Polaroid, Teradyne, Texas Instruments, Xerox, IBM, Hewlett-Packard, and General Signal. Their Japanese customers include Ando, Micronics, Seiko Seiki, Shinkawa, Suzuki, Tenryu, Toray, TSK, Yamaha, NEC, Tokyo Seimitsu, Matsushita, Sanyo, and Komatsu. Other international customers include Alphasem, Bobst, Elektronik und Technik, Fraunhofer Institut, Intertrade Scientific, Hiltcroft, Rolex, SGS-Thomson, and Trident Micro Systems.

However, in 1990, Cognex's top three customers represented 47% of its net revenues. In 1988, Cognex had two main customers: General Signal, representing 18% of total sales, and IBM, representing 9%. Its third major customer is Japan's Shinkawa Ltd., with whom Cognex signed a contract in 1989 for $9 million in products to be delivered over two years. Shinkawa is a leader in the manufacture of wire bonding equipment (wire bonding machines attach chips to the ceramic packages inserted onto printed circuit boards) and in the use of machine vision systems. Shinkawa replaced its own vision systems with those of Cognex. Cognex is providing it with the Cognex 2000, as well as wire bonding software, and has given Shinkawa the right to manufacture the 2000 and its software under "certain circumstances."

In fact, most of Cognex's recent growth has come from Japan. For example, during the first quarter of 1991, sales grew 8% domestically, but 59% in Japan, compared to the same quarter of 1990. "In a world where companies are reporting earnings decreases, we're ecstatic. Compared to the general economy, we're doing extremely well," commented Shillman.[13]

Cognex has won about two-thirds of the business for vision systems of semiconductor and electronic equipment firms (excluding captive sales). Shillman says, "We really are the market leader in the country and maybe the world. It's still a small business, but we're growing nicely."[14] Cognex thinks of itself as being in the electronics and semiconductor business, rather than in the robotics industry.

Trends in the electronics industry (i.e., semiconductor chips, consumer electronics, and computers) favor machine vision, due to smaller components and higher-density circuits requiring accurate alignment, inspection, and placement. Cognex vision systems guide the placement of components onto integrated circuits (for instance, as applied in the SMD market) that go into consumer electronic products. A majority of these customers are in Japan and Korea. In 1990, Cognex signed sales agreements with leading manufacturers of SMD assembly equipment. Probably the biggest producer of SMD (or automatic insertion) equipment is Matsushita with its Panasert line. Other Japanese producers of SMD assembly equipment include Sanyo, TDK, and Fuji. Surface mounting is a new technology used in making circuit boards; the old approach, called "through-the-hole," involved placing a component in an opening in the circuit board. With surface mounting, the component sits on top of the board, and thus no holes are needed in the board. Other Cognex OEM markets include laser memory repair systems, package printers for integrated circuits, printing systems for the production of printed circuit boards, wire bonders, die bonders, semiconductor wafer dicers, and probers. In many of these applications, a vision system is used to locate the item accurately so it can be processed (e.g., probers rely on a vision system to align each chip prior to testing).

Cognex also sells to advanced manufacturing engineering companies that purchase multiple systems for internal use in their own manufacturing processes and to systems houses that package complete production systems.

■ Products

Customers pay for each system they buy from Cognex, as well as a licensing fee per system for each software module. The software comes in modules organized by three function levels and according to tasks: (1) system software (tasks: image acquisition, compilation, communication, control, and math functions); (2) image processing (tasks: filtering, histogramming, projecting, spatial averaging, transforming coordinates, edge detecting, morphology, and auto-focus); and (3) image analysis software (tasks: search, reference feature selection, character recognition, inspection, and scene angle finder). Customers can build their own systems by using the C programming language to interconnect each of the three levels of software.

The firm also sells what it calls VAP (vision application programs). These are complete vision systems for targeted vision problems. For example, the company offers VAPs for high-speed character verification and for the SMD market.

Cognex's products include the Cognex 2000, 3000, 3100, 3200, 3400, and 4000. Introduced in 1990, the 4000 is a vision system that can be plugged into a customer's computers. These products are designed to perform automatically inspection, identification, guidance, and gauging tasks. Of the $7.6 million increase in sales from 1989 to 1990, 66% came from growth of the 3000 and 17% from growth of the 2000. Income is also generated by such services as software development and licensing fees.

An advanced Cognex system sells for about $20,000. It typically includes a circuit board and vision software. The heart of its product consists of a printed circuit board run by a Motorola microprocessor (68000 or 68020) and a proprietary coprocessor that Cognex refers to as its "vision engine" (a coprocessor is not included in the 2000 model). This hardware is controlled by proprietary software. Its model 2000 has 2 MB of memory, and its family of 3000 models have 2–8 MB.

■ Competition

Cognex has little real competition in Japan from the Japanese because of their disadvantages in software. Customers want a minimum of hardware and a maximum of software, because it saves space. Space is very expensive in manufacturing environments requiring absolute cleanliness, such as in a semiconductor fabrication facility. Cognex has a one-board system that saves space, compared to the multiboard systems of competitors. The Japanese use primitive "binary" vision systems (black and white) compared with the better "gray-scale" vision systems used by Cognex. Gray-scale systems are more accurate and result in higher yields (i.e., fewer defective circuit boards). In some product types, Cognex competes against the Japanese firms Yaskawa and CSC (Creative Systems Corp.). But Cognex is pressured more by American firms, such as Itran, AISI, Imaging Technology Inc. (ITI), ICOS, View Engineering, International Robomation Intelligence (IRI), and Adept Technology. One of Cognex's main competitors, Intellidex, went bankrupt in 1991. Cognex has three types of competitors: other firms like itself that produce machine vision systems, firms that produce them for their own needs (and who might sell to the external market in the future), and producers of "board-level" processing systems, some of which have developed machine vision software recently. Several machine vision companies are profiled next.

- *Intelledex.* Founded in 1981, it was the number two U.S. firm in the niche of assembly robots for the electronics and semiconductor industries. But sales have been small and profits elusive. Sales were about $15 million in 1990. The firm went bankrupt in May 1991.

- *Adept Technology.* Intelledex's main competitor. The firm was formed when a group of West Coast engineers left Unimation. The firm has 70% of the market for small assembly robots. Sales have stagnated at about $40 million for several years. The company says it is profitable but will not talk about a rumor that it will delay going public because of a weak balance sheet.

- *Robotic Vision Systems.* Like many vision system survivors, RVS is focused on one narrow niche. It emphasizes the guidance of robots that apply sealants. The company has posted modest profits in the past but recently won a $3.6 million sale to Ford Motor for a system that sprays coatings on the lower part of car bodies to help them resist scratching from stones or other road debris.

- *Perceptron.* This firm makes sheet metal checking devices for the auto industry. Its latest generation is named Veristar. Sales were $10 million in 1988. Sales to European carmakers have skyrocketed, and Ford recently bought a new system. Foreign sales were about 35% of total sales in 1989.

- *Hitachi.* Hitachi America Ltd. manufactures robots for arc welding, material handling, and assembly; vision technology for robot guidance, product inspection and flow control, measurement, and security. However, it has not emphasized the external market for vision systems.

- *Panasonic Factory Automation.* PFA offers four distinct automation product lines: Panarobo assembly robots, welding equipment, Panasert electronic circuit assembly equipment, and Panasonic test and measurement instrumentation. This Japanese firm also has not emphasized the external market for vision systems.

- *Sony Corp. of America Factory Automation Equipment Division.* Sony Factory Automation Division provides robots, vision systems, compact tabletop assembly units, odd-form component insertion and surface mount machines, flexible precision assembly cells, and systems integration services. An integrated robot vision system is available, as well as a stand-alone high-speed, gray-scale vision system, but it makes vision systems mainly for its own use.

• *Applied Intelligent Systems Inc.* AISI designs and manufactures a family of machine vision computers and software for automated recognition, measurement, and inspection tasks. The AISI computers, combined with applications and development software, provide OEMs, system integrators, and others with machine vision systems.

• *Itran Corp.* (pronounced "i-train"). Itran Corp. manufactures machine vision systems for the inspection and process control needs of manufacturers. Applications include pharmaceuticals, electronics, high-speed packaging, and automotive. Its products include I-Pak, a label verification system designed for the pharmaceutical market, and the MVP series, used for a wide variety of manufacturing applications.

■ The Japanese Threat

One main concern is how long large Japanese electronic companies will refrain from entering or emphasizing Cognex's markets (the top 11 Japanese electronic firms are Matsushita, NEC, Toshiba, Hitachi, Fujitsu, Sony, Mitsubishi Electric, NTT, Canon, Sharp, and Sanyo). Sony and Hitachi already supply their own needs for advanced vision systems and might be the first to challenge Cognex's dominant position in its markets.

Cognex protects its technology mainly by keeping "trade secrets," rather than by patenting. The company's software is copyrighted, and the firm uses a number of security measures to protect its intellectual property. For example, Cognex uses nondisclosure agreements with employees, suppliers, consultants, and customers. However, "reverse engineering" is a constant threat for Cognex, and the firm's *Prospectus* (from when it went public in 1989) notes, "Effective patent, copyright and trade secret protection may be unavailable in certain foreign countries."

Japanese customers are a major part of Cognex's sales, totaling about 40%. Revenues grew in Japan by 103% in 1990. The company's attitude is that by doing business in Japan, it "becomes Japanese." In 1990, Cognex established a Tokyo subsidiary, Cognex K.K., and terminated its relationship with its previous Japanese distributor.

In December 1990, Cognex signed its first contract with a Korean customer, a major Korean conglomerate. Cognex expects this agreement to lead to the use of Cognex vision systems in this customer's integrated circuit manufacturing plant.

Sales in Europe were up 191% in 1990, compared to 1989. European sales represented 7%, 5%, and 9% of total sales in 1988, 1989, and 1990, respectively. Domestic sales, as a percent of total sales, have been declining, with 79%, 64%, and 49% of total sales being domestic in 1988, 1989, and 1990, respectively. Japanese sales, as a percent of total, have been increasing, with 13%, 29%, and 40%, respectively, in 1988, 1989, and 1990. Cognex has offices in California, Germany, and now Tokyo, in addition to its headquarters in Massachusetts.

Manufacturing

In-house manufacturing at Cognex includes final assembly, quality control, and final testing, as well as shipment of systems and board-based products. Parts for components are purchased from suppliers and sent to subcontractors for assembly and testing. Some subassemblies are made in-house. All commodity items like electronic parts and sheet metal are purchased, inspected, and warehoused. The firm has its own quality control inspectors, materials personnel, and purchasing agents. Some components are available only from a single source. Some final assembly of systems level products is done outside by third parties. The third-party contractor assembles and does initial testing of the product, using fixtures and programs owned by the company, and returns the product to Cognex for quality inspection and final testing.

Technology

"Engineers designing automated equipment demand machine vision technology that is extremely flexible, accurate, and easy to integrate. They also demand products that provide a well-planned growth path so that they can solve new and more difficult problems without completely re-engineering their systems. Cognex Corporation is unique in offering a complete, compatible family of single-board vision systems designed for the OEM, system integrator, and advanced engineer. It offers a family of systems that provide accuracy, flexibility, and a range of performance levels in various industrial applications."[15]

Cognex's systems require that factory engineers use the C programming language. "You get eight ring-bound books of documentation with their systems. For somebody who's not a programmer, it's overwhelming," comments Jeffrey Johnson, who works for Square D Company as an expert in manufacturing engineering.[16]

Cognex plans to simplify the programming requirement by using a system of English phrases on a Macintosh computer. This new system, called "On-Sight," has been sold on a test basis to several firms (known as beta sites) since October 1990. The company plans to incorporate customer comments into the product design process.

Also in development is the VC-2, a vision chip intended to detect visual defects in manufactured products. This chip is known as an "ASIC" (application-specific integrated circuit). The VC-2, which will be proprietary, was expected to be completed in 1991. This chip, according to Cognex, will perform vision detection of flaws at a high-rate of speed in new and more difficult applications such as finding cracks on semiconductor dies and unintended ink streaks in printing processes. The VC-1, an earlier version, the firm believes was the world's first ASIC able to run both image analysis and image-processing functions at high speeds. A patent was applied for in 1987. All Cognex's vision chips are produced by outside contractors.

Finances and Management

In spite of its rapid growth, the company has no outstanding long-term or short-term debt (though in August 1990, the firm was granted a line of credit equal to $1 million, or 80% of its receivables, whichever is less). It went public in the summer of 1989, offering shares at $11 and raising $6.6 million in this offering. As of August 16, 1991, its stock sold over the counter for $57 per share.

In a news release, Cognex announced net income of $4.3 million or $.99 per share for the first six months of 1991, compared to $2.9 million for the same period of 1990. Revenue was $14.5 million, compared to $10.9 million for the same period in 1990. Chairman Shillman said, "Business remains strong in our two principal markets, the U.S. and Japan. Shipments of our newest product, the Cognex 4000, increased from 2% of revenue in the first quarter to 15% in the second quarter, evidence of the growing acceptance and demand for this product."[17] See Exhibits 3 and 4 for financial statements.

Cognex's management consists of Shillman, four vice presidents, and a director of marketing. Shillman is a Ph.D. and former professor who wrote his thesis on how people recognize written characters. The board of directors consists of Shillman, two representatives of venture capital firms, and two outsiders. The company had 224 common shareholders of record as of December 31, 1990, with 4,341,756 shares outstanding. It earned $1.50 per common share in 1990. One of its customers, General Signal, invested $3 million to ensure access to its technology.

Cognex has about 100 employees. The firm has 16 direct sales and service employees, 14 engineers involved in software development and four involved in hardware projects, and the balance of its employees are involved in product documentation, customer training, administration, and engineering support.

THE FUTURE

Cognex management summarizes its approach to the business in the following way: "What's the key to our success? We believe it's innovation . . . our willingness and, oftentimes, our eagerness to do things differently than they have been done before. We don't want to be the same as everyone else. We want to be better."[18]

Exhibit 3

Cognex Income Statements

	1991	*1990*	*1989*
Revenue			
Product	$28,959,000	$20,932,995	$14,524,594
Other	2,589,000	2,624,774	1,385,701
Total	$31,548,000	$23,557,769	$15,910,295
Costs			
Product	$ 5,338,000	$ 3,977,884	$ 3,741,173
Other	541,000	308,683	222,208
Total	$ 5,879,000	$ 4,286,567	$ 3,963,381
Gross profit	$25,669,000	$19,271,202	$11,946,914
R&D and engineering expense	4,362,000	3,778,786	2,507,532
Selling, general, and administrative expense	8,694,000	6,768,649	4,873,359
Income from operations	12,613,000	8,723,767	4,566,023
Interest income	1,401,000	1,329,563	699,322
Interest expense	2,000	66,577	81,551
EBIT	14,012,000	9,986,753	5,183,794
Tax	4,520,000	3,466,000	1,469,000
Net income	$ 9,492,000	$ 6,520,753	$ 3,714,794

Exhibit 4

Cognex Balance Sheets

	1991	1990	1989
Assets			
Current assets			
Cash and equivalents	$13,449,000	$ 4,062,074	$ 5,973,139
Short-term investments	20,015,000	17,221,524	8,081,762
Accounts receivable less reserve	4,152,000	2,701,976	1,743,767
Other receivables	—	628,390	145,462
Inventories	1,051,000	944,501	854,497
Other current assets	764,000	208,989	80,431
Total current assets	$39,431,000	$25,767,454	$16,879,058
Equipment, furniture, and leaseholds at cost			
Machinery and equipment	$ *	$ 3,531,991	$ 2,461,365
Furniture and fixtures	*	280,044	272,370
Leasehold improvements	*	268,361	260,511
	$ 3,925,000	$ 4,080,396	$ 2,994,246
Less accumulated depreciation and amortization	1,914,000	2,362,729	1,885,548
	$2,011,000	$ 1,717,667	$ 1,108,698
Other assets	270,000	333,655	174,239
Total assets	$41,712,000	$27,818,776	$18,161,995
Liabilities and Equity			
Current liabilities			
Current par of LT Debt		$ —	$ 21,395
Current part of deferred revenue	$ 258,000	683,825	369,200
Deferred credits		—	584,150
Accounts payable	303,000	295,458	173,699
Accrued expenses	2,626,000	1,095,818	764,143
Accrued income taxes	389,000	—	306,603
Customer deposits	1,682,000	1,907,805	1,627,758
Total current liabilities	$ 5,258,000	$ 3,982,906	$ 3,846,948
Stockholders' investment			
Common stock, $.002 par value—Authorized 10,000,000 shares—Issued 4,075,903 and 4,051,642 shares in 1990 and 1989, respectively	17,000	8,152	8,103
Additional paid in capital	19,269,000	16,172,746	15,246,529
Deferred compensation	—	—	(15,000)
Cumulative translation adjustment	(1,000)	(22,508)	(21,312)
Accumulated earnings	17,169,000	7,677,480	1,156,727
Treasury stock, at cost, 250,000 shares in 1989		—	(2,060,000)
Total stockholders' investment	36,454,000	23,835,870	14,315,047
Total liabilities and equity	$41,712,000	$27,818,776	$18,161,995

*Exact breakdown of equipment, furniture, and leaseholds at cost is not available.

In terms of customer relations, Cognex pledges, "We will do whatever it takes to satisfy each customer. In return, we require the customer's firm commitment to an ongoing and profitable relationship." On corporate culture: "We have created an innovative corporate culture that is responsive to employees' needs, both personal and professional. We encourage creative dissent, and we reward both talent and perseverance in all aspects of our employees' daily endeavors."[19]

Cognex's goals for 1991 include:

1. Initiate development of the next generation of vision engine.
2. Ship VC-2, proprietary vision chip.
3. Continue development of "On-Sight."
4. Expand participation in the SMD market.
5. Sign at least one OEM in a new market or application.
6. Expand sales in Japan and Korea.
7. Continue growth in revenues and profits.

Robert Shillman's letter to stockholders concludes:

> Cognex's second decade promises to be as exciting as the first. The need for Cognex products is expected to grow in order to satisfy the increasing demand, worldwide, for highest quality goods selling at the lowest possible price. Faced with this demand, manufacturers of all kinds of products . . . from the simplest light bulb to the most complex computer chip . . . are increasingly turning to automated manufacturing, and, in many cases, automated manufacturing means machine vision.
>
> To continue to dominate the market for vision systems in this next decade, Cognex will focus its team on creating machine vision systems with the following four attributes:
>
> 1. Capability: Our products must be capable of solving a broad range of problems in a wide variety of industries. Our vision systems must be equally proficient in guiding robots inserting windshields at an automative plant as they are in inspecting microscopic wire bonds in an integrated circuit.
> 2. Reliability: Our products must work reliably under difficult, factory-floor conditions, where everyday problems can include uncontrolled part placement, poor lighting and noisy electrical environments.
> 3. Useability: Our products must be useable by a wide range of customers, from the experienced design engineer at an OEM to his factory-floor counterpart who oftentimes has no knowledge of machine vision or computer programming.
> 4. Affordability: Our products must be priced so that our customers can readily realize their payback potential.
>
> As we enter our second decade, we will continue the Cognex tradition of working hard, working smart and using innovation whenever possible. We look forward to the challenges, and to the successes that are on the road ahead. And look forward to sharing the rewards of the journey with you.[20]

A key question is, Should Cognex try to expand its product line and target market? At present it is dependent on two closely linked, cyclical industries and is dependent on three major customers for 49% of its business. New industries or applications would reduce this dependence. Or should Cognex make a thrust into the broader robotics market?

Can the firm successfully make the transition from an entrepreneurial firm to one that is professionally managed? At present, the firm is made up mostly of engineers. As the firm grows, its administration may require professional management. History is replete with firms whose founders hung on too long in trying to manage their creations themselves (e.g., Ford Motor). On the other hand, is Cognex vulnerable to losing key employees?

Another question for this successful firm is, Can it continue to be successful in markets where the bulk of the customers are Japanese and where it has to compete against Japanese firms selling vision systems? Will customers, like NEC, which uses Cognex systems in the production of semiconductors and incorporates these systems into its own robots, continue to buy from Cognex as Japanese firms start to emphasize machine vision products? How well will Cognex be able to compete if Sony and Hitachi start to focus on the external machine vision industry? How well are they protected from "reverse engineering," something the Japanese excel at?

Apparently, the firm thinks it will continue to succeed. It survived the huge shakeout of 1985–1990 because, according to Shillman, "Our technology was better."[21] Cognex believes it can continue to win the Japanese market by "becoming Japanese."

ENDNOTES

1. *Forbes,* 10 December 1990, p. 284.
2. *Wall Street Journal,* 6 November 1990, p. A1.
3. Ibid.
4. Ibid.
5. Multicon, Inc., . . . , Robotics, David W. Rosenthal, NACRA, 1984.
6. Ibid.
7. *Forbes,* 16 April 1990, p. 150.
8. Ibid.
9. Ibid.
10. Daniel Hunt, *Industrial Robotics Handbook,* 1983, p. 298.
11. *Forbes,* 16 April 1990, p. 150.
12. *Fortune,* 25 May 1987, p. 56.
13. *Wall Street Journal,* 12 February 1990, p. B4B.
14. *Electronic Business,* 5 February 1990, p. 26.
15. Cognex product literature.
16. *Forbes,* 10 December 1990.
17. News release, 23 July 1991.
18. Cognex, *Annual Report,* 1990.
19. Ibid.
20. Ibid.
21. *Fortune,* 13 August 1990.

CASE 29

Cadbury Schweppes, PLC

Franz T. Lohrke, James Combs, Gary J. Castrogiovanni,
Louisiana State University

All large (food) companies have broken out of their product boundaries. They are no longer the bread, beer, meat, milk or confectionery companies they were a relatively short time ago—they are food and drink companies.—Sir Adrian Cadbury, Chairman, (retired) Cadbury Schweppes, PLC. (Smith, Child, & Rowlinson, 1990: 9)

In the early 1990s, Cadbury Schweppes, PLC, embodies the archetypical modern food conglomerate. With extensive international operations in confectionery products and soft drinks, the company maintains a diversified global presence. Although Cadbury has enjoyed a relatively stable competitive environment through much of the company's history, contemporary developments in the international arena present Cadbury management with many diverse and critical challenges.

THE HISTORY OF CADBURY

The company began in 1831 when John Cadbury began processing cocoa and chocolate in the United Kingdom (U.K.) to be used in beverages. In 1847, the company became Cadbury Brothers, and in 1866, it enjoyed its first major achievement when the second generation of Cadburys found a better way to process cocoa. By using an imported cocoa press to remove unpalatable cocoa butter from the company's hot cocoa drink mix instead of adding large quantities of sweeteners, Cadbury capitalized on a growing public concern for adulterated food.

The company further prospered when it later found that cocoa butter can be used in recipes for edible chocolates. In 1905, Cadbury introduced Cadbury

This case is intended for classroom discussion only, not to depict effective or ineffective handling of administrative situations. All rights reserved to the authors.

Dairy Milk (CDM) as a challenge to Swiss firms' virtual monopoly in British milk chocolate sales. A year later, the firm scored another success with the introduction of a new hot chocolate drink mix, Bournville Cocoa. These two brands provided much of the impetus for Cadbury's early prosperity (Jones, 1986).

Cadbury faced rather benign competition throughout many of the firm's early years. In fact, at one point, Cadbury provided inputs for the U.K. operations of the American firm, Mars, Inc. (Smith, Child, & Rowlinson, 1990). Cadbury also formed trade associations with its U.K. counterparts, J. S. Fry and Rowntree & Co., for the purpose of, among other things, reducing uncertainty in cocoa prices. The company later merged financial interests with J. S. Fry, but spurned offers in 1921 and 1930 to consolidate with Rowntree (Jones, 1986).

Facing growing protectionist threats in overseas markets following World War I, Cadbury began manufacturing outside the U.K., primarily in Commonwealth countries (see Exhibit 1). This international growth was also prompted by increasing competition. For example, by 1932 Cadbury management considered the Swiss company, Nestlé, as their primary competitor in the international arena (Jones, 1986).

In 1969, Cadbury merged with Schweppes, the worldwide maker of soft drinks and mixers. The merger offered both companies an array of advantages, both defensive and offensive. First of all, both companies faced potential takeover threats from larger firms, so the merger placed the new company in a better defensive posture to ward off unwanted suitors. On the offensive side, the marriage allowed the new company to compete better on a worldwide scale. Cadbury had invested primarily in Commonwealth countries, and Schweppes had branched out into Europe and North America, so the new company enjoyed greater geographic dispersion. The increased international presence also allowed the company to defray product development costs over a wider geographic base. Furthermore, the new company enjoyed greater bargaining power with suppliers. For example, following the merger, Cadbury Schweppes became the largest U.K. purchaser of sugar (Smith, Child, & Rowlinson, 1990).

The British confectionery companies historically pursue a different strategy than their American counterparts. While U.S. companies, such as Mars, Inc., manufacture narrow product lines and employ centralized production, Cadbury maintained 237 confectionery products until World War II forced the company to scale back to 29. While faced with a lack of intense competition, Cadbury's brand proliferation strategy could be undertaken. As rivalry heated up in the mid-1970s, though, Cadbury's share of the U.K. chocolate market fell from 31.1 to 26.2 percent between 1975 and 1977. Management then began to realize that the lower-cost, American-style strategy of rationalized product

Exhibit 1 **Cadbury's Foreign Direct Investment**

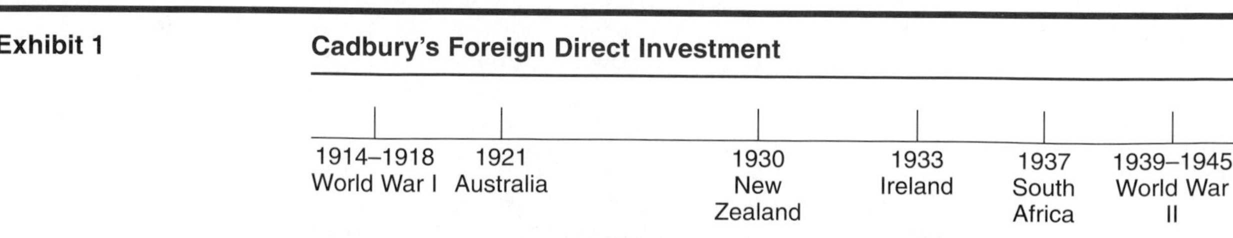

Source: Adapted from Jones, 1986.

lines and centralized production provided the only viable means to compete (Child & Smith, 1987).

Along with its many leading products, Cadbury had also become famous for its unique management style. "Cadburyism," which drew influence from the founders' Quaker heritage, included providing for worker welfare and cultivating harmonious community relations. Following Cadbury's reorientation toward core products and rationalized production, though, the company's old management style underwent a transformation. Confectionery manufacturing personnel were reduced from 8565 to 4508 between 1978 and 1985 (Child & Smith, 1987). In the process, management's traditional close relationship with workers, which had been built through years of maintaining employment stability, began to erode as worker reduction became an explicit goal of Cadbury executives.

THE ENVIRONMENT

As is the case with several products in the food industry, many of Cadbury's product lines enjoy very long product life cycles. (See Exhibit 2 for assorted confectionery products of Cadbury and its rivals.) Food and beverage companies derive substantial benefit from their long-established products, such as Cadbury's CDM bar, and the occasional new product introductions often require little in the way of technological investment. The food companies, therefore, compete primarily by seeking cost reduction through process improvements such as automation, by finding alternative inputs to replace expensive cocoa, and by introducing creative packaging and marketing (Child & Smith, 1987).

Successful new product introductions remain sporadic, though, and many of the most successful confectionery products, such as Mars Bar and Rowntree's Kit Kat, have been around since the 1930s (Tisdall, 1982). Some unsatisfied demand seems to persist, however, as is evidenced by Rowntree's successful 1976 launch of its Yorkie bar, Mars' profitable introduction of Twix a few years later, Cadbury's notable 1984 launch in the U.K. of its Whispa bar, and Hershey's 1988 introduction of Bar None (Weber, 1989).

Nevertheless, new brand introductions require immense investments in development and marketing costs with only limited possibilities for success. For instance, various research suggests that approximately 60 percent of new food product introductions have been withdrawn inside of five years, and this figure may be an underestimate (Smith, Child, & Rowlinson, 1990). Consequently, established brands with customer loyalty represent crucial assets for food and beverage companies.

MODERN CADBURY SCHWEPPES

Expansion is key to Cadbury's plans to improve its international position. Chief Executive Officer Dominic Cadbury commented, "If you're not operating in terms of world market share, you're unlikely to have the investment needed to support your brands" (Borrus, Sassen, & Harris, 1986: 132). In 1986,

Exhibit 2

Assorted Major Brand Names of Cadbury Schweppes and Its Confectionery Competition

Cadbury Schweppes

Cadbury Dairy Milk (CDM)	Roses
Milk Tray	Whole Nut
Crunchie	Fruit and Nut
Whispa	Trebor

Nestlé

Nestlé Crunch bar	Polo
Kit Kat	Quality Street
Smarties	Yorkie
After Eight	Aero
Rolo	Black Magic
Dairy Box	Fruit Pastilles
Butterfinger	Baby Ruth

M&M/Mars, Inc.

Mars Bar	Galaxy
Twix	Maltesers
Bounty	Milky Way
M&Ms	Snickers

Hershey

Hershey Bar	Reece's Peanut Butter Cup
Hershey Kisses	Reece's Pieces
Mounds	Almond Joy
Bar None	

Phillip Morris

Milka
Toberlone
E. J. Brachs candy

Cadbury shared third place in the world with Rowntree and Hershey, each having approximately 5 percent of the market. Nestlé held second place with about 7.5 percent, while Mars dominated internationally with approximately 13 percent (van de Vliet, 1986: 44–45).

To generate its necessary worldwide expansion, Cadbury has two primary markets in which to gain positions. Enjoying a dominant position in its home market, the company realized that the United States and the remaining countries of the European Economic Community (those besides the U.K.) provided critical markets for a worldwide standing. According to Terry Organ, director of international confectionery, "Rightly or wrongly . . . we decided to tackle the U.S. first" (van de Vliet, 1986: 45). Earlier, Cadbury had taken steps toward competing more vigorously in the United States by acquiring Peter Paul in 1978. By 1980, however, the company still controlled only about 3.5 percent of the U.S. confectionery market, far eclipsed by its bigger rivals, Hershey and Mars.

In the United States, Cadbury did not have sufficient size to employ the sales force of its competitors. The company, therefore, had to rely on food brokers to push products to wholesalers, which left the firm far removed from the consumer. Further, the company could be easily outspent in advertising by its two larger rivals (Borrus et al., 1986).

To compound problems, the company also committed two marketing blunders in the U.S. market. When Cadbury introduced Whispa, the company's marketing success of the decade in the United Kingdom, management did not realize that distribution channels in the United States were much longer than in the United Kingdom. Consequently, the candy bars aged seven to nine months by the time they reached test markets in New England, and consumers reacted accordingly.

The company's second mistake occurred following an effort to standardize its candy bar size across countries. When Cadbury first introduced its CDM bar in the United States, the bar commanded a higher price than its U.S. rivals. Since CDM was also larger than U.S. competitors' regular bars, consumers often were willing to pay a little extra. When Cadbury reduced the size, however, management soon discovered that given the choice between CDM and American confectionery products of equal size and price, U.S. consumers usually chose the more familiar American products (van de Vliet, 1986). According to one former Cadbury executive, "What happened in the United States was a gigantic, gargantuan cock-up, and the fact that London (Cadbury headquarters) did not know what was happening is a sheer disgrace" (Gofton, 1986: 20).

Not all the news from the other side of the Atlantic is bad for the U.K. company, however. Although Peter Paul Cadbury only controlled a small piece of the U.S. chocolate market, some products such as Coconut Mounds and York Peppermint Patties dominated their segments. Cadbury's Creme Eggs also enjoyed seasonal success. Moreover, the company's acquisition of Canada Dry from R. J. Reynolds provided Cadbury Schweppes with a strong position in the carbonated mixers market in the United States and many other countries (see Exhibit 3 for U.S. market shares). For example, although Cadbury Schweppes only commanded about a 3 percent market share in the $43 billion U.S. soft drink industry, the company sold Canada Dry, the number one ginger ale and club soda in the United States, and Schweppes, the leading tonic water in the American market (Winters, 1990). Additionally, the cola giants, Coca-Cola and PepsiCo, did not (as yet) vigorously market products in segments dominated by Cadbury Schweppes. Overall, though, the company faced an uphill struggle in many segments of the U.S. market.

In an effort to remedy some of the company's problems in the U.S. confectionery market, Cadbury decided to sell its manufacturing assets to Hershey in 1988, catapulting the Pennsylvania company to the dominant position in the U.S. market (see Exhibit 4). Cadbury also granted Hershey licenses to manufacture and sell its Peter Paul products including Mounds, Almond Joy, and York Peppermint Patties. Under this arrangement, Cadbury gained the benefit of Hershey's marketing muscle behind the Peter Paul products (Swarns & Toran, 1988).

Cadbury also faced challenges to building market share across the Atlantic in the European Economic Community (EEC). Similar to the United States,

Exhibit 3

Top Five Soft Drink Companies in the US (percent of total market)

	1986	*1987*	*1988*	*1989*	*1990*
Coca-Cola, Co.	39.8	39.9	39.8	40.0	40.4
Classic	19.1	19.8	19.9	19.5	19.4
Diet Coke	7.2	7.7	8.1	8.8	9.1
Sprite	3.6	3.6	3.6	3.6	3.6
PepsiCo	30.6	30.8	31.3	31.7	31.8
Pepsi-Cola	18.6	18.6	18.4	17.8	17.3
Diet Pepsi	4.4	4.8	5.2	5.7	6.2
Mountain Dew	3.0	3.3	3.4	3.6	3.8
Dr. Pepper	4.8	5.0	5.3	5.6	5.8
Dr. Pepper	3.9	4.0	4.3	4.6	4.8
Diet Dr. Pepper	.4	.4	.4	.4	.4
7-Up	5.0	5.1	4.7	4.3	4.0
7-Up	3.5	3.4	3.1	3.0	2.9
Diet 7-Up	1.4	1.0	1.0	.9	.9
Cadbury Schweppes	4.2	3.7	3.5	3.1	3.2
Canada Dry	1.4	1.4	1.4	1.3	1.2
Sunkist	.9	.7	.7	.7	.7
Schweppes prod.	.5	.5	.5	.6	.6
Crush	1.4	1.0	.8	.6	.6
Total market share of top five	84.4	84.5	84.6	84.7	85.2

Sources: Standard and Poor's Industry Surveys, 1991; company reports.

Schweppes' beverages enjoyed success on the continent (Borrus et al., 1986), but Europe's confectionery industry proved difficult to break into, since the market remained dominated by family-owned firms and suffered from overcapacity (van de Vliet, 1986). Successful expansion in the EEC, however, was crucial to Cadbury's remaining a dominant player in the worldwide food and beverage industries.

CONTEMPORARY CHALLENGES

The 1990s has brought about radical shifts in the industries in which Cadbury Schweppes competes. First, corporate leaders (and stock markets) discovered that food and beverage enterprises with established brand names are not mundane investments offering only lackluster financial returns. Purchasing popular brands or taking over companies that have portfolios full of well-known products often provides a safer and more economical avenue for growth than attempting to develop entirely new products. In 1985, for instance, Phillip Morris acquired General Foods for $5.75 billion, approximately three times book value, while R. J. Reynolds laid out $4.9 billion for Nabisco Brands (van de Vliet, 1986).

These attempts to acquire popular brands are also dictated by dramatic industrywide changes that alter the nature of competition faced by the inter-

Exhibit 4

Top Five Companies in the $8 Billion US Confectionery Market

1980		1988	
Company	*Market Share*	*Company*	*Market Share*
Mars	17.0	Hershey	20.5
Hershey	15.3	Mars	18.5
Nabisco	7.1	Jacobs Suchard	6.7
E. J. Brachs	6.4	Nestlé	6.7
Peter/Paul Cadbury	3.5	Leaf	5.6

Sources: Weber, 1989; company reports.

national food and beverage enterprises. First, the push by the 12 countries of the European Economic Community to remove trade barriers among the member nations by 1992, sparked a buying frenzy of European food companies with established brand names (see Exhibit 5 for a comparison of the North American and EEC markets). Many non-European companies fear that the EEC will eventually increase tariff barriers for products from outside the Community, which could effectively close foreign companies out of the European market. This anticipation of "Fortress Europe" sent companies without EEC operations scurrying to acquire European enterprises.

Second, the common perception that only the largest companies could survive over the long term in most European and global industries also contributes to the takeover hysteria. To become big quickly, companies began aggressively acquiring rival food companies. For example, Nestlé scored a major victory in July 1988, when it outbid its Swiss counterpart, Jacobs Suchard, to acquire Cadbury's long time U.K. competitor, Rowntree. In the process, Nestlé moved from a minor status in the EEC confectionery market into a first place duel with Mars. In the U.K. market, Nestlé's acquisition

Exhibit 5

The United States and the European Economic Community

	US	EEC
Population	243.8 million	323.6 million
Gross national product (GNP) (in 1987 $US)	4.436 trillion	3.782 trillion
Per capita GNP	$18,200	$11,690
Inflation	3.7%	3.1%
Unemployment	6.1%	11.0%

Sources: House, 1989; U.S. Bureau of the Census.

Note: EEC members include the U.K. (England, Scotland, Wales, Northern Ireland), Ireland, Denmark, Germany, France, Belgium, the Netherlands, Luxembourg, Portugal, Spain, Italy, and Greece.

positioned the company in a second place battle with Mars and within striking distance of first place Cadbury (*Mergers and Acquisitions*, 1989). In January 1992, Nestlé attempted to continue its acquisition binge by launching a hostile takeover bid for the French mineral water company, Source Perrier.

Other major food conglomerates, such as Phillip Morris (U.S.) and Unilever Group (U.K./Netherlands), are also rumored to be on the prowl for acquisitions in Europe (Browning & Studer, 1992). These heavyweights not only present medium-sized food and beverage companies like Cadbury with increased competition in the marketplace, they also represent potential bidders in any acquisitions attempted by Cadbury. This increased competition threatens to drive up acquisition prices through cutthroat bidding for popular brand names. In fact, as the takeover battles become more heated, stock market analysts speculate that Cadbury and other medium-sized companies could find themselves targets of acquisition attempts (Browning & Studer, 1992).

The European food and beverage industries are undergoing other changes along with the acquisition binges. At the end of the food and beverage distribution pipeline, for example, many European supermarkets are also consolidating. In April 1990, eight EEC grocery chains formed an alliance to combine buying power and promote house brands. As these supermarket companies combined forces, they greatly enhanced their bargaining power against the food and beverage companies. This increased power threatens future profits of food and beverage companies since the grocery chains' ability to demand price concessions from the companies is enhanced by the stores' consolidation. Furthermore, since supermarkets only want to carry the top two or three brands for each product type, food and beverage companies face the option of acquiring popular brands or risking lost shelf space in stores (Templeman & Melcher, 1990).

In response to these massive changes in the industry (see Exhibit 6 for food sales in Europe), Cadbury also began acquiring name brand products and searching for strategic alliances. In 1986, for example, the company decided to end its bottling agreement with Pepsi to form a joint venture with Coca-Cola in the United Kingdom (Gofton, 1986). In 1990, Cadbury purchased the European soft drink operations of Source Perrier (Templeman & Melcher, 1990), and in 1991, the company formed a joint venture with Appolinarus Brunnen AG, a German bottler of sparkling water (see Exhibit 7 for Cadbury Schweppes worldwide sales figures).

Exhibit 6 **Food Sales: Europe (including the U.K.)**

Nestlé	$15.1 billion
Unilever	12.2
Phillip Morris*	8.0
BSN	7.8
Mars	4.1
Cadbury Schweppes	3.1

Source: Adapted from Templeman & Melcher, 1990.

*Includes Jacobs Suchard.

Exhibit 7

Cadbury Schweppes' 1990 Worldwide Sales (in £ million*)

Region	*Total Sales*	*Confectionery*	*Beverages*
United Kingdom	1,476.0	715.4	760.6
Continental Europe	638.0	195.6	442.4
Americas	403.7	18.3	373.5
Pacific Rim	495.5†	N/A‡	N/A‡
Africa and other	132.9	91.2	38.8

Sources: Adapted from Compact Disclosure; *Wall Street Journal.*

Note: Total sales will not always equal confectionery plus beverages. In the U.S. (Americas region), for example, Cadbury Schweppes also generated sales from its Mott's subsidiary.

*1 £ = $1.93
†Sales primarily in Australia/New Zealand
‡N/A: not available

With the competitive environment heating up, Cadbury management faces a number of crucial questions. Can the company continue to compete independently against the food and beverage mega-corporations that are forming, or should Cadbury merge with another company before being faced with a hostile takeover attempt? Does Cadbury have the resources to acquire more brand names, or should management continue to investigate the joint venture route? Should Cadbury continue its emphasis on Europe, or should the company's attention shift to possible opportunities in the underdeveloped Asian market? Whatever Cadbury Schweppes' management decides to do, they have to move quickly. The choices of popular name brand food and beverage products on the table are being cleared away fast (Templeman & Melcher, 1990).

REFERENCES

Borrus, A., Sassen, J., & Harris, M. A. 1986. Why Cadbury Schweppes looks sweet to the raiders. *Business Week,* January 13: 132–133.

Browning, E. S., & Studer, M. 1992. Nestlé and Indosuez launch hostile bid for Perrier in contest with Agnellis. *Wall Street Journal,* January 21: A3.

Child, J., & Smith, C. 1987. The context and process of organizational transformation—Cadbury Limited in its sector. *Journal of Management Studies,* 24: 565–593.

Gofton, K. 1986. Has Cadbury got his finger on the button? *Marketing,* July 31: 20–25.

House, K. E. 1989. The 90's & Beyond: The U.S. stands to retain its global leadership. *Wall Street Journal,* January 23: A8.

Jones, G. 1986. The chocolate multinationals: Cadbury, Fry and Rowntree 1918–1939. In G. Jones (Ed.), *British Multinationals: Origins, Management and Performance:* 96–118. Brookfield, VT: Gower Publishing Co.

Mergers and Acquisitions. 1989. The Nestlé–Rowntree deal: Bitter battle, sweet result. September/October: 66–67.

Smith, C., Child, J., & Rowlinson, M. 1990. *Reshaping work: The Cadbury experience.* Cambridge: Cambridge University Press.

Standard and Poor's Industry Surveys. 1991. Food, beverages, and tobacco. June 27: F23–F27.

Swarns, R. L., & Toran, B. 1988. Hershey to buy U.S. business from Cadbury. *Wall Street Journal,* July 25: 30.

Templeman, J. & Melcher, R. A. 1990. Supermarket Darwinism: The survival of the fattest. *Business Week,* July 9: 42.

Tisdall, P. 1982. Chocolate soldiers clash. *Marketing,* July 29: 30–34.

van de Vliet, A. 1986. Bittersweet at Cadbury. *Management Today,* March: 42–49.

Wall Street Journal. Various issues.

Weber, J. 1989. Why Hershey is smacking its lips. *Business Week,* October 30: 140.

Winters, P. 1990. Cadbury Schweppes' plan: Skirt cola giants. *Advertising Age,* August 13: 22–23.

APPENDIX 1: FINANCIALS

Balance Sheet (in £ 000)

Exhibit 8

	Fiscal Year Ending		
	12/29/90	*12/30/89*	*12/31/88*
Assets			
Cash	62,600	57,400	41,300
Marketable securities	118,000	33,300	200,700
Receivables	554,100	548,200	434,500
Inventories	328,200	334,800	253,400
Total current assets	1,062,900	973,700	929,900
Net property, plant, and equipment	978,800	822,500	602,200
Other long-term assets	320,700	332,600	20,700
Total assets	2,362,400	2,128,800	1,552,800
Liabilities			
Notes payable	60,100	57,400	92,200
Accounts payable	272,100	263,900	409,500
Current capital leases	76,200	76,300	21,900
Accrued expenses	320,900	305,900	52,100
Income taxes	78,200	95,800	81,800
Other current liabilities	154,700	143,600	118,800
Total current liabilities	962,200	942,900	776,300
Long-term debt	407,900	381,400	124,700
Other long-term liabilities	108,401	124,000	74,600
Total liabilities	1,478,501	1,448,300	975,600
Preferred stock	300	N/A	3,300
Net common stock	174,400	173,600	150,400
Capital surplus	95,800	36,700	33,000
Retained earnings	115,799	167,600	88,800
Miscellaneous	381,600	217,400	210,500
Total shareholders' equity	767,899	595,300	486,000
Minority interest	116,000	85,200	91,200
Total liability and net worth	2,362,400	2,128,800	1,552,800
1 £ =	$1.93	$1.61	$1.81

Exhibit 9 **Income Statement (in £ 000)**

	Fiscal Year Ending		
	12/29/90	*12/30/89*	*12/31/88*
Net sales	3,146,100	2,766,700	2,381,600
Cost of goods sold	1,738,400	1,596,900	1,365,000
Gross profit	1,407,700	1,169,800	1,016,600
Sell general and administrative expense	1,074,700	907,500	787,800
Income before interest and taxes	333,000	262,300	228,800
Nonoperating income	3,800	3,100	4,400
Interest expense	57,200	31,100	17,500
Income before taxes	279,600	234,300	215,700
Taxes and miscellaneous expenses	100,200	85,500	75,200
Income before expense items	179,400	148,800	140,500
Extraordinary items	N/A	15,200	28,400
Net income	179,400	164,000	168,900
1 £ =	$1.93	$1.61	$1.81

Sources: Adapted from Compact Disclosure; *Wall Street Journal.*

Note: N/A = not applicable.

CASE 30

The Blockbuster Video Challenge

John Dunkelberg, Tom Goho, Wake Forest University

When Mike Gibbons picked up the morning newspaper, the headline got his immediate attention: Blockbuster Video Opens in September 1990. As he read the article under the headline, he learned that Blockbuster Video was planning to open a 6,500-square-foot video tape rental store within 50 yards of his own 5,000-square-foot video rental store. Although he heard that Blockbuster had done a market survey in the early spring and that it had inquired about leasing two different pieces of commercial property, Mike had not expected them to come to a town as small as Lumberton.

As he finished the article, he started making notes on the possible consequences of the arrival of Blockbuster on his business and to map a strategy for the four-month period before the proposed opening. Since Mike had visited Blockbuster stores to learn as much about their operation as possible, he felt like he knew the volume of sales they needed to be profitable and that it would be very hard for both he and Blockbuster to be profitable in the limited (population was 26,000) Lumberton market.

BACKGROUND

Mike Gibbons and a partner started Video Station three years ago when Mike was 21 years of age with $22,000 in startup capital. The basic concept was to deliver rental videos to customers, homes just like pizza was delivered. Customers could order from a video library of just over 500 tapes and for $2.99, Video Station would deliver the requested tape to a customer's home. The next day the tape could be dropped in one of four drop boxes located throughout Lumberton. Since opening the store, Mike had lowered the price to $1.99 for

This case is intended for classroom discussion only, not to depict effective or ineffective handling of administrative situations. All rights reserved to the authors and the North American Case Research Association.

one night. The business quickly outgrew the original 143-square-foot room, and Video Station expanded into an adjacent room that was remodeled to handle walk-in business. During the first year of business, Mike's partner ran the day-to-day business while Mike finished his last year of college and worked at Video Station on the weekends. Revenues that first year were $64,000 with all surplus cash flows being used to purchase additional tapes.

During the second year, Mike's partner, who had finished college the previous year, decided to enter law school, so Mike bought out his partner. Video Station expanded to a second store located in a small shopping mall. The 1,200-square-foot store contained about 1500 video tapes. To finance this expansion required additional capital, which was obtained by a $100,000 loan based on Mike's personal assets. The money was used to remodel the second store, purchase the initial inventory for the second store, increase the inventory in the first store, and to purchase a general-purpose vehicle for use in deliveries. Revenues during the second year were $173,000. Mike received an annual salary of $12,000 and all other profits were used to purchase additional tapes.

During the third year, Video Station opened a third store that had 5,000 square feet of retail floor space plus additional space for offices. This store contained over 12,000 tapes and required an additional $200,000 loan for the remodeling and the purchase of tapes. Revenues grew each month and the total revenue for the year was $278,000. Video Station was just beginning its fourth year when Mike read the announcement of the planned arrival of Blockbuster Video.

PRESENT POSITION

The growth of Video Station had come partly at the expense of some of the smaller video rental stores and, over the past two years, ten had gone out of business leaving nine smaller competitors. Mike estimated that his remaining competitors had an average of less than 1,000 video tapes each and combined had less than half the total video rental business in Lumberton. He also estimated that the present annual revenues from video rentals in Lumberton was about $600,000. This does not seem to be enough business for two big stores (Video Station and Blockbuster) to both be profitable.

While the growth of Video Station had been phenomenal, it had not been profitable. The sales mix had been 90 percent in store rentals and 10 percent delivery. The cost of furnishing the last two stores plus the cost of purchasing a large inventory of tapes required Mike to borrow almost $300,000. The growth of revenues, however, had been up to Mike's expectations, and he expects Video Station to become profitable this year. The income statement for the first six months indicates that his estimates are on target. (See Exhibit 1.)

Although the income statement indicated a healthy firm, Mike knew that what would be more important in the next few months would be cash flows, for cash would be needed to keep the business afloat during a period of time after Blockbuster opened when sales may be greatly reduced due to the high promotional campaign that Blockbuster normally used to open new stores. His cash flows for the past three months were positive (see Exhibit 2), although he

Video Station, Inc.: Income Statement, Six Months Ending June 30, 1990 **Exhibit 1**

Revenues		$167,842
Expenses		
Salaries	$41,743	
Payroll taxes	3,848	
Depreciation	46,102	
Utilities	7,301	
Rent	11,514	
Sales taxes	8,873	
Office expenses	12,661	
Maintenance	838	
Interest expense	14,558	
Total expenses		$147,438
Income before taxes		$ 20,404

had purchased slightly more video tapes than usual. Finally, he looked at his most recent balance sheet to see what his financial position was going into a period of tough competition. (See Exhibit 3.) Two items looked ominous: notes payable and retained earnings.

The notes payable, which had been used to purchase the tape inventory, to make leasehold improvements, and to purchase fixtures and office furniture for the last two stores, required only interest payments for the next three years. The other item, retained earnings, was negative because during the first three years of operation, Video Station had large depreciation expenses. Before Blockbuster had announced its opening Mike had felt like Video Station had gone through its growth period okay and was poised to finally be a profitable operation. The profitable time now seemed far away.

Video Station, Inc.: Cash Flow, Three Months, April–June 1990 **Exhibit 2**

Cash received		$85,774
Cash expenditures		
Purchases	$26,308	
Salaries	22,768	
Payroll taxes	2,391	
Utilities	3,614	
Rent	5,754	
Maintenance	395	
Other taxes	4,353	
Office expenses	7,876	
Interest expense	7,279	
Total cash expenditures		$80,738
Net cash inflows		$ 5,036

Exhibit 3 **Video Station, Inc.: Balance Sheet, June 30, 1990**

Cash	$ 5,264	Accounts payable	$ 15,429
Inv.	3,700	Withholding/FICA payable	2,270
Prepaid exp.	1,390	Notes payable	257,518
Total cur. assets	$ 10,354	Total cur. liabilities	$275,217
Office equip.	$ 48,409	Common stock	$ 10,400
Furniture & fixtures	53,400	Retained earnings	(25,409)
Video tapes	223,068		
Leasehold improv.	39,800		
Acc. dep.	(114,823)		
Total assets	$260,208	Total liabilities & equity	$260,208

BLOCKBUSTER VIDEO

Blockbuster Entertainment Corporation operates and licenses Blockbuster Video stores that rent video tapes. The firm has grown from 19 stores in 1986 to 1,934 stores (1,010 company-owned and 924 franchises) in 44 states, Washington, D.C., Puerto Rico, Canada, the United Kingdom, and Guam, as of September 1991. The typical Blockbuster store carries 7,000 to 13,000 tapes and the stores range in size from 4,000 to 10,000 square feet. In 1989 the 301 company-owned stores that had been in operation for more than a year were averaging monthly revenues of approximately $69,000.

Although the growth in the United States in consumer spending on rentals seems to have slowed, Blockbuster Video believes it has the opportunity to take market share away from smaller competitors through its strategy of building large stores with a greater selection of tapes than most of its competitors. As the largest video chain in the United States, Blockbuster Video also has advantages in marketing and in the purchase of inventory. Blockbuster Video's pricing is $3.50 per tape for two nights. However, there apparently has been some discussion within the organization to give local stores some pricing discretion.

According to a prospectus, Blockbuster plans to purchase a vacant lot for about $310,000 and then lease a 6,400-square-foot building that is being built to their specifications, under a long-term lease agreement for $8.50 per square foot per year for the first three years. The cost of completely furnishing the building, including the video tapes, will be approximately $375,000 and Blockbuster plans to spend over $150,000 on the grand opening promotions. Blockbuster's operating costs are very similar to Video Station's since the computer checkout equipment is similar and both firms have approximately the same personnel costs. Both firms depreciate their tapes over 12 months.

EFFORTS TO NEGOTIATE

After analyzing Blockbuster's plans, Mike called Mr. George Atkins, the president of SEC Video, who had the Blockbuster Video licensee agreement for Virginia and South and North Carolina. Mike thought that a meeting with Mr.

Atkins could be beneficial to learn more about Blockbuster's plans and to see if Blockbuster was interested in purchasing Video Station. Video Station had about the same size store that Blockbuster was planning to build, used the same type computer checkout system and many of the same fixtures, and had the same open store layout. Mike's thinking was simple: there was not enough business for both stores to be profitable. Blockbuster would save a lot of money by moving into his store and needed only to make minor changes to have a store that looked just like all other Blockbuster stores. Mike had not thought about owning a video store all his life, and he had been thinking of returning to graduate school even before the Blockbuster announcement.

Mr. Atkins seemed very happy to meet with Mike and invited him to his office in Sumter, SC. During the meeting Mr. Atkins made a tentative offer to purchase Video Station for 40 percent of current sales plus the value of the existing tapes, and he seemed willing to purchase the leases on Mike's two stores. He did state that he would not consider a move into Mike's store because there was not enough parking area. In addition, all Blockbuster stores were to be new and the company had a policy against moving into existing stores. Interestingly, during the meeting, in which Mr. Atkins tried very hard to learn what Video Station's revenues were, he stated that he thought the potential video rental market in Lumberton was about $1,000,000 per year. Mike thanked Mr. Atkins for his time and agreed to think about his offer.

After calculating what he thought was a reasonable point to start negotiating, Mike met with Mr. Atkins about one month later. Mike opened the meeting with a brief statement of what had transpired in the last meeting and again asked if Blockbuster would not consider using Video Station's existing building, as the cost saving to Blockbuster would be enormous. Mr. Atkins again stated that Blockbuster had a policy about new stores due to the image the company wished to maintain. He then reminded Mike that Video Station was worth more right now than it would ever be again, about how large Blockbuster was compared to Video Station, and how they would soon be able to take Mike's customers through promotions like giving away a Blazer or a popular sports car each month until they had the market share they wanted.

He then offered to purchase Video Station for 40 percent of MIke's last twelve months' sales. This figure included all of Video Station's assets but none of its liabilities. This offer was so far from the previous offer that Mike did not attempt to negotiate, but he did leave the possibility of future talks open. Mr. Atkins stated that this was his final offer and he told Mike that "I will not call you again." He then hurried off to his waiting private plane to fly to a similar size town about forty miles away to discuss the purchase of that town's largest video store. As the plane taxied from the control tower, Mike began mentally analyzing his options and wondering about the future of Video Station when Blockbuster Video opened its store in less than three months.

CASE 31

Gal-Tech and Melanin: A Case of Technology Transfer

John P. McCray, Juan J. Gonzalez, University of Texas at San Antonio

INVENTION AT ITS BEST

It had been a rough day. Jim Gallas leaned back in his office chair and tried to relax, but thoughts of his current research problems kept plaguing him. For more than five years now, he had been trying to develop an efficient solar energy heat exchanger. To do this, he needed a near-perfect solar energy absorber. His efforts had met with frustration. Then he had decided to try melanin.

Melanin is a natural substance found in the skin and eyes of most animals. In humans, melanin darkens the skin when exposed to the sun, thus protecting us from the sun's radiation. In the back of the eye, melanin forms a "black box" that absorbs much of the harmful radiation coming into the eye.

Gallas hoped that melanin would prove to be the perfect energy absorber, so he began to research melanin extensively. After several experiments, he found that while melanin absorbed light, it did not generate enough heat for practical energy production. These experiments revealed, however, that melanin had some interesting properties; it absorbed the sun's rays that were most damaging to the human eye. Melanin absorbed virtually all of the ultraviolet light, much of the blue light, and some of the blue-green light. As a result of these experiments, melanin's solar energy prospects did not look good, but Gallas wondered if melanin could be useful in another way.

As Gallas tried unsuccessfully to push the frustration of not finding a good energy absorber out of his mind, he glanced down at his desk at some glass slips with melanin on them. The thought struck him that melanin might make a good sunglass coating. The glass, if covered with melanin, would protect the

---

This case is intended for classroom discussion only, not to depict effective or ineffective handling of administrative situations. All rights reserved to the authors.

human eye by absorbing the harmful radiation of the sun. The phone rang, and he was jarred back to more pressing problems. The following week, he continued his search for a perfect solar absorber. Then while he was working, the thought of coating sunglasses with melanin surfaced again. Where had this idea come from? Oh, yes, he remembered, he had thought of it the prior week! The thought dwelled with him; melanin did have exactly the right properties to block the harmful rays of the sun. Maybe melanin could be a commercial product. But how could melanin be coated onto something like glass or plastic?

Gallas's interest in melanin increased. It seemed to have more potential as a filter against harmful sunlight than as a heat absorber within solar heaters. Although there are substances other than melanin that will block some of the harmful effects of the sun, none are natural, and none will do the job as efficiently or effectively as melanin does. Other substances block the ultraviolet or blue or green or red light, but none block the harmful effects of the sun in the optimum proportion and over the entire light spectrum, as melanin does.

Wherever it is important to block the harmful effects of the sun, melanin can be useful. Some of the products that might utilize melanin came immediately to mind: sunglasses, eyeglasses, contact lenses, and protective coatings for auto, home, and office windows, even paint. Also, Gallas hypothesized that adding melanin to plastics will help protect the plastic from the sun's damage and keep it from decomposing. He believed in melanin's great potential, so he continued his research.

Gallas set about the task of mixing melanin, a water soluble substance, with plastic. First he tried to melt the plastic and mix it with melanin, but this only resulted in a messy glob. Using various techniques, he tried for six months to mix melanin and plastic, but was unsuccessful. As a result of these experiments, Gallas realized that melanin and plastic would have to be mixed at the molecular level.

Mel Eisner, a fellow physicist, became interested in the problem and began to work with Gallas. Mel suggested that a melanin precursor might mix with with a plastic monomer. Gallas conducted several more experiments with the advice and help of a chemist, Frank Feldman, and eventually the process worked. He had invented a melanin concentrate that would mix with plastic or could be formed into a film and applied to glass. For their help in developing the process, and with the understanding that they would continue to be active in the development of melanin concentrate into a commercial product, Gallas promised Eisner and Feldman each 15 percent of the future business income from the invention.

GOING FOR A PATENT

Gallas prepared a detailed description of his process and applied for a U.S. patent. The patent authorities rejected his application because they did not believe that the process he described constituted a true discovery. Gallas rewrote his request and resubmitted, again with no success.

Gallas now wondered what to do. He had a process that he had discovered, and he was convinced the process was unique and therefore patentable. Also, he knew that a patent was absolutely necessary for his invention to become a successful product.

Determined to get a patent, Gallas decided to use a patent attorney. He wanted a law firm with experienced patent attorneys, an excellent reputation, and offices in both Houston and Washington, D.C. He also wanted a firm that believed he could obtain the patent and would fight to get it. He decided to use a well-known patent law firm in Houston, Texas. Besides meeting all of his requirements, he was impressed that several attorneys on the staff of the firm were former attorneys at the U.S. patent office.

Since Gallas could not afford to pay the fees that the patent attorneys required in order to file the patent request, he convinced them to accept as payment 15% of the final benefits that would be derived from the patent. The patent attorneys accepted his offer and a staff attorney from the firm was assigned to file the patent request. The application was filed for the third time, but the request was again rejected by the U.S. patent office, this time on the basis of "obviousness" because another patent had been recently been awarded for putting melanin into a skin cream.

Another year passed, but Gallas did not give up. He decided that if he gave a senior attorney at the law firm, Mr. Barnes, a 5% interest in the patent, Barnes would be more motivated to get the application accepted. The patent application was rewritten again. A clear description of the Gallas process showed that melanin-treated lenses designed to protect the human eye were significantly different from melanin-treated skin cream, and that no one had a patent to incorporate melanin onto transparent plastic or glass. This argument convinced the examiner, and the patent was granted October 6, 1987.

The patent abstract reads: "Optical lens system incorporating melanin as an absorbing pigment for protection against electromagnetic radiation." The patent protects the process of applying melanin to surfaces such as plastic and glass from duplication. Gallas retained the patent attorneys to protect and defend his new patent. Knowing how important the patent was, he estimated an expense of $10,000 per year for attorney fees to protect the patent once the product was commercialized.

BECOMING A BUSINESSMAN

Once he had a patent which would protect his invention, Gallas went about developing his new technology into a business. The patent was owned by a "partnership" of Gallas, 50%; Eisner, 15%; the law firm, 15%; Mr. Barnes, 5%; and Feldman, 15%.

The patent attorneys helped Gallas to incorporate under the name of Gal-Tech Corporation, which was chartered in December 1987 as a C corporation. Two thousand shares of stock were authorized and one thousand issued. Stock was to be divided using the same percentages as the patent ownership, with each of the final stockholders receiving their stock at $1.00 par value. However, Gallas recognized that rights to the patent did not necessarily carry over to the corporation.

The attorneys had talked of giving their top partner, Mr. Sliplock, 5%, which Gallas assumed would come out of the firm's 15%. Only later, when negotiations were under way to develop the actual production company, Gal-Tech, did he discover that the attorneys had meant an additional 5%. Gallas argued that since Mr. Barnes would receive 5% of the company, Mr. Sliplock's percentage should be included with the law firm's 15%; they agreed. Because Frank Feldman could no longer give time to the project, Gallas felt that his percentage should be lowered. Feldman agreed to trade his 15% of the patent for 2% ownership in Gal-Tech. Another chemist was brought in, Robert Williams, who was given 3% of the stock, and Feldman's remaining 10% was given to Gallas. Gallas was uncomfortable with the Houston law firm owning such a large percentage (10%) of the company, and offered to pay them $65,000 for their remaining ownership, payable as soon as the corporation was capitalized. This stock was then divided between Gallas (7%) and Eisner (3%). In addition, Gallas had promised Mel Eisner $20,000 and Frank Feldman $10,000 for their past work. Eisner and Feldman were willing to take notes with interest-only annual payments at 10%, and the principal due at the end of five years. Gallas, who had invested several years and a great deal of his own money, was willing to take a similar note for $100,000. In this way, the patent became the property of Gal-Tech Corporation and could be amortized over its remaining life. The final stock ownership was Gallas, 67%; Eisner, 18%; Barnes, 5%; Sliplock, 5%; Feldman, 2%; and Williams, 3%.

Gallas knew that before anyone would invest in Gal-Tech, he would have to develop a market for melanin concentrate. While he was applying for the patent, he had been contacted by the television network CNN. Not wanting to discuss his discovery before receiving the patent, he had put them off. Once tha patent was issued, he contacted them and arranged for a television interview. After the interview aired, several other media representatives contacted him for interviews and/or articles. While visiting Monterrey, Mexico, Gallas read an article about himself and his process in a local newspaper and realized that his discovery was beginning to gain widespread press coverage. Prompted by the publicity about melanin and its potential, several large companies contacted Gallas about the process, but because he did not have a marketing strategy nor a definite commercialization plan, few maintained their interest.

Gallas began to research possible markets for his discovery. He quickly learned that the ophthalmic industry includes eyeglasses, sunglasses, contact lenses, and surgically implanted intraocular lenses. However, FDA approval would be needed before contact lenses and intraocular lenses could use melanin. The most obvious potential user of the melanin concentrate seemed to be the sunglass industry. He manufactured a few pairs of melanin treated sunglasses as prototypes. With their amber colored lenses, the glasses made eye-catching samples to show to prospective investors.

THE SUNGLASS MARKET

The sunglass market is composed of three basic components: prescription sunglasses, high-end sunglasses (over $20.00 per pair), and low-end sunglasses (under $20.00 per pair). The nonprescription sunglass market is growing steadily. In 1985, 160 million pairs were sold and 175 million were sold in 1986. Bausch and Lomb's Consumer Products Division estimates that total sales for the industry were $1.3 billion in 1987, a 16% increase over 1986. From 1986 to 1987, the under-$20 market segment increased 9% and the over-$20 market segment, which accounts for 40–45% of the total sunglass market, increased

22%. There are over 250,000 locations that sell sunglasses in the United States, according to Bausch & Lomb, with nearly 55,000 locations selling sunglasses that retail at $20 or over. Many traditional optical retailers are now displaying sunglasses separately and setting up kiosks from which to sell sunglasses.

Brand awareness and glamour are important factors in the sunglass business, and sales are often influenced by celebrities' use of a particular brand. The perception of value by the consumer is also important in the marketing of sunglasses. Vuarnet, a major producer, claims its sunglasses "not only protect your eyes and make a fashion statement, they also help your visual performance and through that your physical performance." This perception of quality is apparently well received by consumers, who purchased $50 million in sunglasses from Vuarnet in 1987.

An ophthalmic industry report (1988) showed the average price for a pair of sunglasses at $13.55, according to a survey of 80,000 families. Substantial action in the "higher-end" product (sunglasses of over $20) was implied by a near 45% market share. Some of the more traditional optical retailers were reported as trying to capture a share of the nonprescription sunglass market by enhancing their in-store displays and planning sunglass fashion departments. Others, like D.O.C., the large Michigan-based optical chain, began pursuing a different strategy by opening kiosks, primarily in or adjacent to malls. Lens Crafters opened its Goggles prototype sunglass store in the spring in Sacramento, California. The sunglasses-only retail concept seemed to be catching on with traditional retailers since ophthalmic frame distributors were promoting signature and designer lines of sunwear. Sunglass stores such as the 157-store Sunglass Hut chain appeared to be the fastest-growing segment of the market. Bausch and Lomb celebrated the 50th anniversary of its Ray Ban line with sales running at an all time record of 5.5 million pairs worldwide.

ENVISIONING A FIRM

Gallas learned that the sunglass industry already offered lenses that block a specific portion of the light spectrum. Ultraviolet absorbers block a significant percentage of the UV range. Nationwide, optical labs report coating 13% of eyeglasses with UV protection, which is the state of current technology for eye protection. Blue-blockers blocked out all of the blue light but sacrificed color vision. Gallas felt that melanin would be the logical next step because melanin would block the harmful effects of UV, blue, and blue-green light.

Convinced more and more of the commercial significance of his discovery, Gallas began contacting firms that he thought would be interested in melanin. As a physicist, he would ask to speak to the person in charge of technical development and proudly explain his discovery and its uses to this person. Time after time, he was surprised to hear negative comments about incorporating melanin into their products using his process. Perhaps the greatest turning point in the development of his product was when he realized that the real value of the melanin process was not its technical attributes but the perception of value by the consumer. This led Gallas to talk to the marketing departments of the companies that he was contacting. He was surprised when he received a much stronger response from the marketing managers than he had from the scientists.

Also, instead of contacting only manufacturers, he began to contact distributors and those companies that manufacture and market their own sunglasses. Visiting with the marketing managers in these firms brought much more positive responses, and a few firms began to show genuine interest in using melanin.

After many interesting inquiries, two large sunglass manufacturer/distributors began serious talks with Gallas. One represents the high end of the market, the other represents the low end. Gallas believes that the high end producer will offer a contract before the end of the first year, paying a licensing fee of $200,000 and a 50 cent royalty per pair sold. Because the low-end company's sales are more seasonal, they will probably not produce melanin sunglasses until the second year. Gallas estimates that they will then pay a licensing fee of $100,000 and also pay a 50 cent royalty per pair sold. The high-end distributors estimate that they can sell 1,140,000 pairs of melanin-treated sunglasses the first year. Between the two distributors, sales will double the second year and increase by 50% the third. Sales will be recorded at the time the concentrate is shipped; receivables can be expected to equal six weeks' sales.

The sunglass firms that have contacted Gallas have excellent name recognition, well-established distribution channels, and promotional and advertising capabilities that little Gal-Tech cannot possibly match. Because of this, Gallas has decided that he should negotiate an agreement to let the sunglass firms advertise his product along with their own, instead of attempting to reach the consumer himself. Still, Gallas knows that advertising, promotion, travel, and entertainment will consume $100,000 of Gal-Tech's first-year budget and at least 10% of gross income thereafter.

The closer Gallas gets to commercializing his product, the more questions he has concerning the structure of his company and the manufacture of melanin concentrate. He initially planned to license the manufacture of the melanin concentrate, but he realizes that allowing others to produce the concentrate might endanger his control of the process and weaken his patent. Gallas has decided that Gal-Tech will have to produce the melanin concentrate itself. He has reviewed the manufacturing operations of his company. The sunglass lenses will be coated with 10 microns of the melanin concentrate. Assuming the average diameter of a lens is about 6 centimeters, each pair of sunglasses will require .085 gram of melanin concentrate. It will therefore require about 85 kilograms of melanin to produce the tint for 1 million pairs of sunglasses. Actual production of concentrate should include an additional 20 percent to account for losses and defects in the process of coating the lenses, plus 10% to be used for internal research and development. Therefore, it will take about 115 kilograms of melanin concentrate to support the sales of one million pairs of melanin coated sunglasses.

The melanin concentrate can initially be produced in 20-liter containers in a batch process that takes place over a 24-hour period and yields about 75 grams of melanin per container. Assuming 250 days of production per year, each 20-liter vessel will yield about 19 kilograms of melanin per year. Because of this short production cycle, only a two weeks' supply of chemicals will be kept on hand; also, a finished inventory of two weeks' sales will be kept.

The raw materials used in the production of melanin concentrate are peroxides such as benzol peroxide, solvents such as chloroform and methanol, and the melanin precursors such as catechol and L-Dopa. These raw materials are readily available from several suppliers in quantities necessary to produce all projected requirements. Substitute raw materials are also available. The raw materials cost approximately $1.00 per gram of melanin concentrate produced, a cost that is not expected to change within the next three years.

There are no physical properties of melanin concentrate that limit transportation or distribution. Shipping expenses will be about $4,000 the first year.

Personnel will be divided into three functional areas at Gal-Tech: production, sales and marketing, and administration and finance. Each function needs a director; production also requires two technicians and a shipping clerk, and administration requires a secretary/bookkeeper. The production chief will be in charge not only of production, but also research and development, and will need to have a Ph.D. in physics or chemistry. His or her salary will be included in cost of sales. Gallas estimates that the kind of people necessary to make Gal-Tech a success would require annual salaries of: Chairman of the Board, $20,000; President, $55,000; Production Chief, $40,000; Sales and Marketing Chief, $30,000; Administrator, $25,000; Shipping Clerk, $15,000; production technicians (each), $20,000; and Secretary/Bookkeeper, $15,000. Individual salaries are not expected to change over the following three years, but Gallas estimates that at the beginning of the third year, they will have to hire two more technicians, one more shipping clerk, and one more secretary to help the marketing chief. Gallas budgets an additional 9% for payroll taxes, up to the legal limits. Health and workmen's compensation insurance should be about $8,000 per employee for the first year of operations and increase 5% each year.

Dr. Gallas feels that the firm will need room to grow. Five thousand square feet of office/warehouse space is available at 50 cents per square foot, which includes common area maintenance and property taxes. Finish out will be accomplished by the landlord, including inside walls and HVAC. One month's rent is required as a deposit. Annual insurance should be about one dollar per square foot of space. Furniture and fixtures required and their costs are: lab furniture and fixtures, $12,000; vent hoods (2), $18,000; scale, $10,000; microscope, $10,000; ovens, $10,000; chemicals, $10,000; glassware, $5,000; lab computers, $5,000; office furniture and equipment, $20,000; office computer, software, $6,000; and office supplies, $2,000. These costs will be depreciated over five years, using straight-line depreciation. If sales increase according to plan, $100,000 will have to be borrowed at the beginning of the third year to purchase additional equipment. Dr. Gallas hopes to then negotiate a note to be payable over five years, at an interest rate of 12%. He knows that any investors will require audited financial statements, and he is prepared to pay $5,000 per year for this and other accounting services.

In order to stay a viable company, Gal-Tech will have to invest in itself through research and development. The first year of operation, $200,000 will need to be spent, and 20% of gross revenue thereafter for R&D.

BECOMING A GOING CONCERN

Dr. Gallas has made an appointment with a venture capitalist and plans to ask for $250,000 to capitalize Gal-Tech. James Gallas has the vision needed to make his discovery a profitable company. He has a patent and a solid knowledge of how his business will operate. What he doesn't have is the formal structure and financial projections required to attract the capital necessary to bring his vision to life. He needs a formal plan, incorporating all that he knows about his target markets, proposed operations, and financial commitments, including pro forma financial statements for three years.

CASE 32

Hickory Ridge Golf Club

James J. Chrisman, Harold Valentine, Louisiana State University

Greg Hamilton, owner of Hickory Ridge Golf Club (HRGC), a modest nine-hole public golf course in Columbia, South Carolina, nursed his first cup of coffee of the day lost in thought. Normally, Hamilton would have been bustling around the course, preparing for the day's business. Play was generally brisk in the mornings on warm, spring days, and the morning of May 3, 1989, promised to be no exception. In spite of this, Hamilton knew he had to make a decision that could have an important short- and long-term impact on the profitability, and perhaps even the survival, of his business.

In 1988, his first year of business, HRGC's revenues exceeded $116,000, although the firm suffered a loss of $17,000 (see Exhibit 1 for 1988 profit and loss statement). Cart rentals accounted for over 19 percent of revenues, second only to greens fees (see Exhibit 2 for 1988–1989 sales breakdowns). However, his fleet of nine electric carts had not been sufficient to meet 1988 demand, much less the increase in cart usage expected in 1989. Furthermore, the carts he did have were old and in need of frequent repair, which further aggravated the situation. Hamilton knew that he needed to decide whether or not to purchase or lease a new fleet of carts or additional carts and, if so, from whom. However, he was unsure of where to begin. He wondered how much revenue he had previously lost due to his inadequate fleet. More importantly, he wondered how his decision might affect revenues in 1989. As he finished his coffee he vowed to bring up the subject with his course architect/mechanic, Harold Valentine, a friend as well as trusted confidant. Hamilton knew he could count on Valentine to help him solve his dilemma.

This case was prepared by Harold Valentine, OC(SS), USN, under the direction of James J. Chrisman, Associate Professor of Management at Louisiana State University. The case was based on field research.

This case is intended for classroom discussion only, not to depict effective or ineffective handling of administrative situations. All rights reserved to the authors.

Exhibit 1

Hickory Ridge Golf Club: Profit and Loss Statement, 1989 (from IRS Schedule C)

Sales	$116,270	
Cost of goods sold	–21,079	
Gross profit	95,191	
Salaries & administrative	–112,801	
Expenses		
Wages & salaries		36,327
Repairs		7,532
Supplies		13,885
Utilities & telephone		7,549
Advertising		900
Car & truck expenses		2,353
Insurance		6,411
Dues & publications		693
Rent on business property		1,338
Taxes		4,905
Interest expense		13,459
Depreciation		13,590
Other		3,859
Net profit	–$17,610	

Exhibit 2

Hickory Ridge Golf Club: Revenues, 1988–1989

	Greens Fees	*Golf Carts*	*Pull Carts*	*Snack Bar Pro Shop*	*Beer*	*Total Revenues*
1988						
January	$ 1,069	$ 290	$ 38	$ 280	$ 800	$ 2,476
February	2,906	833	92	360	1,920	6,110
March	4,601	1,728	127	997	2,400	9,852
April	7,713	2,773	271	2,337	1,380	14,474
May	6,463	2,236	252	1,443	1,960	12,354
June	5,193	1,866	210	1,116	1,880	10,264
July	5,665	2,436	204	1,691	2,000	11,996
August	5,811	2,657	188	1,242	1,900	11,798
September	5,616	2,382	204	465	1,800	10,467
October	5,024	1,943	201	864	1,100	9,132
November	4,969	1,762	190	883	1,000	8,804
December	4,925	1,664	210	748	996	8,543
Total	$59,955	$22,570	$2,187	$12,426	$19,136	$116,270
1989						
January	$ 5,497	$ 1,803	$ 206	$ 665	$ 1,680	$ 9,851
February	3,700	1,023	163	853	800	6,539
March	7,472	2,404	338	1,347	2,040	13,601
April	10,531	3,297	509	2,511	2,080	18,928
Total	$27,200	$ 8,527	$1,216	$ 5,376	$ 6,600	$ 48,919

HAMILTON'S BACKGROUND

For Hamilton, the purchase of HRGC was an important step in fulfilling a lifelong dream—to own and run a public golf course. Born on May 18, 1950, and raised in the Columbus, Ohio, area, Hamilton was introduced to golf by Arnold Adams, owner of Possum Run Golf and Swim Club. Adams gave Hamilton his first job but was far more than just an employer. He passed on his love of golf, including the conviction that it should be a game easily accessible to the general public. For several years Hamilton spent nearly every spare moment with Adams on the course.

Marriage at age 21 brought many changes to Hamilton's life, including three children, but his dream to own a golf course was unchanged. His wife, Dr. Cynthia Hamilton, supported Hamilton not only emotionally, but also financially through her psychiatry practice. In 1978 the couple moved to Columbia, South Carolina, and Hamilton took on the position of assistant pro at Linrick Golf Club on Monticello Road. While at Linrick, Hamilton earned his PGA assistant's license and hoped to eventually earn his PGA pro's license.

BACKGROUND OF HICKORY RIDGE GOLF CLUB

HRGC opened in 1957 as an 18-hole, par-71 golf course. It was built on a very modest budget by the Williams family, who owned that particular tract of land. The Williams family operated the course for less than a decade before selling it in 1964. Several owners followed during the next 15 years, before the McAlister family bought it in 1978. Almost immediately the McAlisters, who were in the construction business, cut the golf course to nine holes and built a housing development on what had been the "back nine." During their ownership, only a minimal amount of money was invested in maintaining the course and it gradually fell into the state of disrepair in which Hamilton found it in 1988.

■ Conditions at Purchase

When Hamilton bought HRGC there was little reason to believe that it had ever been a pleasant, well-kept golf course. The clubhouse and equipment shed were filled with garbage that had accumulated over the years. There was almost no equipment, and what remained was virtually unusable. One old tractor represented the only piece of heavy equipment, and it needed to be jump-started before it was used. The gang mower and greens mower were almost beyond repair and were unable to perform the functions for which they had been designed. There was also an ancient fairway aerator and a fleet of fourteen 1976 E-Z-GO carts. Of these, only six carts worked at all, and they were extremely dangerous to use; some were without brakes or a reverse gear.

The condition of the course was not much better than the equipment. The grounds were generally overgrown, and the encroaching bushes, weeds, and trees gave the course an air of abandonment. There was a significant amount of grass in the sand traps, and the sand that had escaped discouraged grass from growing where it was needed. The greens were receding from lack of care and were being eaten away by fungus and weeds. The tees were eroding noticeably due to improper cart path management and design. Due to lack of aeration the ground was hard, thereby preventing the grass from infiltrating the topsoil for proper growing conditions. Finally, the pond on the course was an eyesore, filled with floating and submerged garbage. The pond was overgrown and has less than three feet of water at its deepest point, making it unsuitable to use for irrigation.

▪ Improvements and Changes

Needless to say, Hamilton's refurbishing effort encompassed every facet of the course's buildings, equipment, and grounds. Hoping to keep the transition of ownership smooth, Hamilton sought to retain those employees who had worked under the McAlisters. There were frequent disagreements between the workers and Hamilton in the early months due to improper communication and personal conflicts. In July 1988 the course superintendent was fired and most of Hamilton's other personnel problems were resolved. Johnny Clayton was hired as greenskeeper and Valentine as architect/mechanic to round out the work force.

As noted above, the clubhouse and shop areas were nearly inaccessible because of the accumulated trash. This was removed and trucked away, clearing the way for several improvements. Hamilton's original office was a 50-foot square closet that he unwillingly shared with the pesticides and herbicides. To solve this problem, Hamilton had a larger office built on the back of the clubhouse and recarpeted the adjoining apartment. He installed a pro shop and built up its inventory from scratch, to be able to provide golfers with desired supplies and accessories. He also improved the snack bar, buying some new tables and chairs, a refrigerator, and a hot dog machine.

In addition to these improvements, Hamilton made numerous capital equipment acquisitions. Although he was able to repair the gang mower, the other pieces of equipment, including the greens mower and tractor, had to be replaced. He also purchased twelve used (1984 model) Club Car electric carts to bolster the pathetic cart fleet in May 1988. Two of the older carts had been junked, giving HRGC a total of sixteen carts at that point in time.

The other major capital expenditure Hamilton made was the purchase of a new irrigation system, an absolute necessity in maintaining a quality golf course. The irrigation system was installed on all greens and tees, and on five of the nine fairways. Hamilton installed a 30-horsepower pump to drive the irrigation system itself, and a submersible pump which kept the pond filled from a newly dug quartz aquifer well. The pond then became the reservoir for the irrigation water. To keep it both attractive and useful, it was stocked with fish to reduce algae and aquatic weed growth.

The holes themselves required a great deal of attention. Eroded areas were filled in and turf grass and greens were revamped. Fairways were aerated and brush was cut away from the roughs, widening every hole. New tee markers and flags for the greens were purchased. Areas that might be damaged by the carts were roped off, and cables were installed along the road to prevent vandals from driving their cars on the fairways and greens, as had previously occurred.

Finally, Hamilton took action to ensure that the course met the needs and preferences of his customers. A University of South Carolina marketing research project was completed in April of 1989 to better define these needs. Price structuring at the course was changed, and alcohol use was restricted to that which was purchased on the course.

INDUSTRY ENVIRONMENT

Golf had become a booming business and was expected to grow rapidly in the final decade of the twentieth century. Nearly every authority agreed that the number of players was steadily increasing, as were the revenues these additional golfers brought in. According to *Golf Market Today* (1989), there were approximately 11.2 million golfers in the United States in 1970. As of the beginning of 1989, that figure had nearly doubled to 21.7 million, with the rate of growth accelerating over each of the past four years. Researchers from the National Golf Foundation estimated that over 30 million people would be golfing in this country by the year 2000.

This explosive growth was attributed, in large part, to the increased interest in golf on the part of women, the elderly, and the "Baby Boomers" (*PGA Magazine*, 1989). Of particular importance was the impact women were likely to have on the future of the game. In 1989 around 25 percent of all golfers were women, yet 40 percent of all new players were women. Many of them had careers and found golf an excellent way to relax and to conduct business (*Savvy*, 1989).

The growth of golf also attracted the attention of the business world. *Business Week* (1989) called golf "a global phenomenon" and a "$20 billion industry with a growth rate that is nothing short of phenomenal." The golf boom had been felt in the stock market too, with many corporations—such as Emhart Industries, a maker of club shafts, and American Brands, a maker of golf shoes—seeing significant changes in their stock quotes (*Research Recommendations*, 1989). This growth was leading to increased corporate involvement, something that had become evident on the PGA tour, where corporate sponsorship, not to mention purses, were up (*Golf Digest*, 1989).

Although the possibilities for growth seemed limitless, it appeared unlikely that supply could keep up with demand even though both the number of courses opened and those under construction rose significantly from 1987 to 1988 (*Golf Market Today*, 1989; *Golf Digest*, 1989). In 1987, there were 145 new courses opened and 513 under construction or in the planning stage; in 1988, 211 opened and 662 were being constructed or planned. South Carolina was tied for fifth in the nation in terms of the number of new courses opened (12), and ranked 16th overall in total golf courses (280). Nevertheless, the situation in some areas was becoming serious, with overcrowding becoming more and more common (*Business Week*, 1989). Even planning for 50 percent growth over the next decade—and some believed this growth would be closer to 100 percent (*Golf Digest*, 1989)—the golf industry estimated that 4,000 new facilities, or an average in excess of one new course opening per day, would be necessary within the next ten years (*Golf Market Today*, 1989).

The Golf Course Superintendents Association singled out the lack of public golf courses as especially distressing in the overall facility shortage (*Golf Course Management*, 1989). Over 80 percent of all golfers used public courses, and this figure was expected to increase. For this reason *Golf Market Today* estimated that at least 60 percent of all new courses needed to be public.

■ Keys to Success

Certain aspects of running a successful course had not changed; for example, it was still important to have a clean, well-maintained course and polite, well-trained employees. Nevertheless, in 1989 golf was becoming more and more a common man's game. It had become more important for the golf course owners to understand the needs and habits of a more diverse group of customers. For example, some courses in Florida sought to lure in the seniors with special senior citizens discount packages, failing to consider the fact that most of their golfers were already seniors. Most of these courses were driven out of business because they failed to consider who their golfers were.

Diversity was also a watchword within the industry. Golfers had a fascination with gadgets: the newer, the more innovative, the more original, the better. Therefore, it was becoming more and more likely to find golf-related novelty items and gadgets in the pro shop. Along the same line, golfers were more likely to remain satisfied with their course if they were given a variety of views and shots. Courses with all or most of their holes constructed with a consistent layout bored the average golfer.

LOCAL ENVIRONMENT

Located in the middle of the state, Columbia was the capital of South Carolina. The state government and the University of South Carolina (1987 enrollment of approximately 24,000) were the major employers in the area. With an unemployment rate of only 3.9 percent, Columbia was prosperous compared to the state in general. The average per capita income of the area was $13,795 in 1987 compared to $12,036 in the state.

The population of the Columbia area (Lexington and Richland counties) was approximately 453,000 in 1990; it had grown an estimated 10.4 percent between 1980 and 1990. The majority of the existing population was distributed in the areas north, west, and east of downtown, extending out about 15 miles. New residential development was concentrated primarily in the northeast and northwest quadrants of the city. A large portion of the area's growth was expected to be centered in these regions. Furthermore, in 1987 there were approximately 34,000 students enrolled in the nine colleges and universities in the area. Exhibit 3 provides selected demographic data on the Columbia SMA.

■ Columbia's Golf Industry

The local golf scene was changing and growing with the Columbia community. The Columbia by-pass—Interstate 326—was expected to be completed by late 1990. The by-pass would make most public golf courses in the region more accessible to local golfers (within a thirty-minute drive). There also was the possibility of new competition in the local industry. Four syndicates—two from Florida, and one each from Texas and California—were analyzing the potential profitability of constructing major 27- or 36-hole golf complexes in Columbia. Among local groups, Fort Jackson had received approval for an additional 18 holes, Richland County was seeking to obtain grants to build an 18- or 27-hole course southeast of Columbia, and Charwood Country Club in West Columbia was considering whether to construct nine additional holes to complement the nine holes that were recently completed. If it did so, Charwood would offer customers a total of 27 holes of golf. Generally, there was a regional trend toward clubs offering a combination of memberships and pay-for-play options. Golf was also becoming more accessible to the public because prices were rising slower than the cost of living.

Demographic Characteristics of the Columbia, South Carolina, SMA **Exhibit 3**

	Population (000s)		*Estimated Average Household Effective Buying Income*		*Estimated Retail Sales per Household*	
	1990	*Estimate 1993*	*1988*	*1993*	*1988*	*1993*
Lexington County	168	190	$31,251	$44,888	$12,532	$17,729
Columbia SMA	453	496	$32,602	$46,758	$17,026	$24,153
South Carolina	3,487	3,687	$27,058	$38,954	$15,932	$22,761
South Atlantic Region	43,575	46,830	$31,915	$45,074	$18,252	$25,918
United States	248,710	260,094	$33,198	$46,997	$17,745	$24,989

Population Breakdowns by Age, Sex, and Race

	Total	*< 5 Yrs*	*5–17 Yrs*	*18–64 Yrs*	*≥ 65 Yrs*	*Median*	*% Male*	*% White*
Columbia SMA								
1980 act.	410,088	28,510	86,026	265,429	30,123	27.3	49.2%	69.9%
1990 proj.	472,800	34,570	82,820	312,570	42,890	31.0	NA	NA
South Carolina								
1980 act.	3,121,820	238,516	703,450	1,892,526	287,328	28.0	48.6%	68.8%
1990 proj.	3,622,000	272,600	619,200	2,248,700	409,500	32.0	NA	NA

Source: South Carolina Statistical Abstract 1989, South Carolina Budget and Control Board, pp. 288–289, 297.

▪ Study on Golf in Columbia

A study completed for Hickory Ridge Golf Club on April 20, 1989, served to further explain local conditions. This study targeted 210 golfers both familiar and unfamiliar with HRGC and had a margin of error of plus or minus 2 percent (see Exhibit 4). The following summarizes the findings of the study:

> Hickory Ridge Golf Club, as well as Columbia area public golf courses, have a clientele that consists mainly of twenty to forty year old males who prefer to play eighteen holes of golf per day. These individuals play more than fifteen times per year. Of these players almost 43 percent are college students. We believe that the level of college play can be increased by sponsoring a student/professor day early during each semester. It is our finding that lower green fees coupled with good greens and fairways are the most important factors to the public golfer. Financial records revealed that weekdays hold the greatest opportunity for increased profitability. This may be accomplished by increasing league play. It should be noted that in order to avoid simply shifting weekend play to weekday play, Hickory Ridge should refrain from lowering weekday rates.
>
> Our study has determined that the public golfer seeks a greater selection of golf balls and hot food. While riding carts are most preferred, a ratio of seven pull carts to ten riding carts should be maintained in future purchases. Word of mouth

Exhibit 4 **The Columbia Public Golfer: Market Survey Results, 1989**

The survey summarized below was based on the responses of 210 individuals in the Columbia, South Carolina, SMA.

1. Sixty-eight percent of the respondents were from 20 to 40 years old.
2. Fifty-six percent of the respondents drove between 5 and 15 miles to play golf.
3. Thirty-eight percent of the respondents' income was below \$10,000; 28 percent of the respondents' income was between \$20,000 and \$30,000.
4. Eighty-three percent of the respondents located new golf courses through word of mouth.
5. Fifty-one percent of the respondents would play more golf if lower greens fees were available.
6. Sixty-five percent of the respondents play golf more than fifteen times per year.
7. Sixty-two percent of the respondents that were pro shop customers said that their most frequent purchase was golf balls.
8. Fifty-seven percent of the respondents said that they would prefer food items such as hot dogs and hot sandwiches offered in the clubhouse.
9. Seventy-two percent of the respondents prefer to play eighteen holes of golf per outing.
10. Eighty-seven percent of the respondents prefer to ride in a cart or walk with a pull cart while golfing.
11. Sixty-two percent of the respondents said that the primary determinant in the selection of a golf course is the condition of the fairways and greens.
12. Sixty percent of the respondents said that they expect to pay between \$4 and \$6 per round.
13. Ninety-seven percent of the respondents prefer to play with a friend or a foursome.
14. Twenty-seven percent of the respondents prefer to play on Saturdays.
15. Eighty percent of the respondents were male.
16. Thirty-four percent of the respondents were college students; forty-nine percent were in the work force.

Source: Postich, Miller, & Valentine, 1989.

is by far the most prevalent manner in which golfers learn about new courses. Therefore road signs should be used for directional purposes only, keeping all forms of advertising within a fifteen mile radius. By following these recommendations, Hickory Ridge Golf Club should continue to have a substantial increase in play.

COMPETITORS

In 1989 HRGC had twenty competitors in the Columbia area, of which ten were public and ten private (see Exhibit 5). Among those courses, only one—Sedgewood Golf Course—was located within 4 miles of HRGC. Exhibit 6 shows locations, and Exhibits 7–9 provide information on the characteristics of each golf course in the Columbia area.

Columbia Area Golf Courses: May 1989 — Exhibit 5

Private	*Public*
1. Coldstream Country Club Inc., Irmo, SC	11. Charwood Country Club, West Columbia, SC
2. Columbia Country Club, Columbia, SC	12. Coopers Creek Golf Club, Pelion, SC
3. Crickentree Golf Club, Columbia, SC	13. Hickory Ridge Golf Club, Columbia, SC
4. Forest Lake Country Club, Columbia, SC	14. Hidden Valley Country Club, West Columbia, SC
5. Golden Hills Golf and Country Club, Lexington, SC	15. Lake Marion Golf Club, Santee, SC
6. Mid Carolina Club Inc., Prosperity, SC	16. Linrick Golf Course, Columbia, SC
7. Timberlake Plantation, Chapin, SC	17. Paw Paw Country Club, Bamberg, SC
8. Wild Wood Country Club, Columbia, SC	18. Persimmon Hill Golf Club, Johnston, SC
9. The Windermere Club, Blythwood, SC	19. Pineland Plantation Golf Club, Sumter, SC
10. Woodlands Country Club, Columbia, SC	20. Sedgewood Country Club, Hopkins, SC
	21. White Pines Country Club, Camden, SC

Locations of Columbia Area Golf Courses — Exhibit 6

Exhibit 7 **Characteristics of Columbia Area Golf Courses: Dues, Greens Fees, and Hours**

Private Courses

#	*Dues/Fees*	*Open Hours*	*Closed*	*Tee Time*
1.	$77/month, $210 initiation	7:30 am–6:00 pm	Thanksgiving & Xmas	8 am
2.	Not available (NA)	Not available	Not available	NA
3.	$9,500 equity	8:30 am–dark	Mondays	NA
4.	$2,500 equity	8:00 am–6:30 pm		9 am
5.	$75/month, $2187 initiation	8:00 am–6:30 pm	Monday, Thanksgiving, Xmas, & New Years	8 am
6.	$30/month, $750 initiation	8:00 am–8:00 pm	Xmas	8 am
7.	$90/month, $2500 initiation*	8:00 am–7:00 pm	Xmas	9 am
8.	$100/month, $7500 initiation	7:30 am–8:00 pm	Xmas & New Years	8 am
9.	$100/month, $2500 initiation	8:00 am–8:00 pm	Monday, Thursday, Friday, Thanksgiving, Xmas, & New Years	10 am
10.	$105/month, $2000 initiation	8:00 am–7:00 pm		8 am

Public Courses

#	*(9/18) Dues/Fees Weekdays, Weekends*	*Open Hours*	*Closed*	*Tee Time*
11.	$6.00/10.00, $8.00/12.00	7:30 am–9:30 pm		8 am
12.	$9.00/11.00, $9.00/11.00	7:00 am–dark		10 am
13.†	$4.50/7.00, $6.00/8.50	8:00 am–dark		Open
14.	$6.00/8.00, $12.00/12.00	8:00 am–dark		8 am
15.	$15.00/25.00, $15.00/25.00	Daylight–dark		7 am
16.	$5.50/8.50, $6.50/10.50	7:30 am–dark	Xmas	8 am
17.	$10.50/16.80, $13.65/21.00	8:00 am–dark	Xmas	10 am
18.	$5.50/11.00, $8.00/16.00	8:00 am–7:00 pm	Xmas	8 am
19.	$5.00/10.00, $8.00/12.00	7:00 am–dark	Xmas	8 am
20.	$7.00/11.00, $11.00/13.00	7:30 am–dark	Xmas	10 am
21.	$8.00/8.00, $10.00/10.00	7:30 am–dark		Open

*Property ownership required.
†Nine-hole course.

■ Sedgewood Golf Course

Sedgewood Golf Course, HRGC's only local competitor, was very different in significant ways. Located 4 miles from HRGC, it was an 18-hole, 6,810-yard, par-72 course with restricted tee times on weekends and holidays. The most noticeable difference was in the price structure. A round of nine holes costs

Exhibit 8

Characteristics of Columbia Area Golf Courses: Amenities and Special Rates

Private Courses

#	*Pro Shop*	*Senior Rate (9/18)*	*Student Rate (9/18)*	*Restaurant*	*Snack Bar*	*Lockers*
1.	Yes	No	No	Yes	No	No
2.	NA	NA	NA	NA	NA	NA
3.	Yes	No	No	Grill	Yes	Yes
4.	Yes	No	No	Yes	Yes	Yes
5.	Yes	No	No	Yes	Yes	Yes
6.	Yes	No	No	Yes	Yes	Yes
7.	Yes	No	No	Grill	No	Yes
8.	Yes	No	No	Grill	No	Yes
9.	Yes	No	No	Yes	Yes	Yes
10.	Yes	No	No	Yes	Yes	Yes

Public Courses

#	*Pro Shop*	*Senior Rate (9/18)*	*Student Rate (9/18)*	*Restaurant*	*Snack Bar*	*Lockers*
11.	Yes	$5.00/$6.00	$5.00/$6.00	No	Yes	No
12.	Yes	No	No	No	Yes	Yes†
13.*	Yes	$4.50 weekday	$4.50 weekday	No	Yes	Yes
14.	Yes	$6.00	$6.00	No	Yes	No
15.	Yes	No	No	No	Yes	No
16.	Yes	$4.50/$6.00	$4.50/$6.00	No	Yes	No
17.	Yes	No	No	No	Yes	No
18.	Yes	No	No	Yes	No	No
19.	Yes	Varies	No	No	Yes	No
20.	Yes	$1 off	$1 off	No	Yes	No
21.	Yes	Varies	No	Yes	Yes	Yes

*Nine-hole course.
†Yes, also indicated if plans have been set in motion to install lockers within the next year.

$7–$11, depending on the day it was played, and a round of eighteen holes costs $11–$13. A riding cart costs an additional $9 per person for nine holes and $18 per person for eighteen holes. In comparison, on weekdays HRGC charges $4.50 for nine holes, $7 for eighteen, and $8 for the entire day; its rates were $1.50 higher on weekends and holidays. Furthermore, at HRGC it costs only $6.50 per nine holes per cart regardless of the time of week. One noticeable similarity between the two courses, however, was that they both suffered from erosion and lack of complete course maintenance.

Exhibit 9

Characteristics of Columbia Area Golf Courses: Course and Cart Information

Private Courses

#	Yardage	Par	Cart Fees (9/18)
1.	6,155	71	$4.75/$8.40 per person
2.	NA	NA	NA
3.	6,471	72	$8.00/$16.00 per cart
4.	6,450	72	$2.50/$5.00 per person
5.	6,461	71	$5.00/$8.00 per person
6.	6,600	72	$3.50/$7.00 per person
7.	6,703	72	$4.75/$8.50 per person
8.	6,726	72	$9.05 + tax per person for 18 holes
9.	6,900	72	$5.25/$10.50 per person
10.	6,786	72	$4.00/$8.00 per person

Public Courses

#	Yardage	Par	Cart Fees (9/18)
11.	6,100	72	$4.00/$8.00 per person
12.	6,550	72	$4.00/$8.00 per person
13.*	2,807	35	$6.50 per cart
14.	6,700	72	$4.00/$8.00 per person
15.	6,615	72	Included in greens fee
16.	7,080	73	$6.00/$12.00 per cart
17.	6,700	72	Included in greens fee
18.	7,050	72	$4.50/$9.00 per person
19.	7,084	72	$4.00/$8.00 per person
20.	6,810	72	$9.00/$18.00 per cart
21.	6,400	72	$4.00/$8.00 per person

*Nine-hole course.

■ Other Facilities at Local Golf Courses

Also noteworthy were the facilities of the other competitors. All courses had pro shops on the premises, and there were a total of twenty-nine pro shops in the Columbia area. These ranged from discount shops, such as Nevada Bob's, to extremely exclusive shops, such as the one at Forest Lake Country Club. Most of these shops were run by sales representatives. The biggest money tended to come from club repair and sales of golf balls, tees, and golf gloves. The average shop was likely to stock around thirty sets of clubs, although in extreme cases local shops were known to stock in excess of one hundred sets. Most stocked golf clothing such as socks, shoes, and hats, and many also carried shirts and pants. Certain pro shops, particularly those in country clubs, stocked extremely large inventories of clothing items.

Only three courses offered full restaurant/dining facilities, all of them private courses. The remaining private courses had limited restaurant facilities and many also operated snack bars. The operators of the public courses felt the profit potential of a restaurant was limited. Only two had grills. These offered hot sandwiches, hamburgers, and so on, as well as drinks and snacks, and were open during lunch and dinner hours. Almost all of the public courses had simple snack bar facilities, however, offering hot dogs, cold drinks, chips, and candy.

Another thing many public courses lacked was locker areas, including shower facilities. These were especially appealing to the blue collar workers, who would often golf on the way to or from work. Although eight of the ten private courses offered locker areas, only two of the eleven public courses did so.

CURRENT OPERATIONS

In practical terms, Hamilton and Valentine believed that HRGC was without any direct competition because of several distinctive characteristics. First, it was the only nine-hole golf course in the Columbia area. It was also unusually level and short (2807 yards, compared to an average of 3313 yards for nine holes in the area) for a par-35, nine-hole course, making it especially suitable for elderly and young players. Its length, the absence of hills, the wide fairways, and the lack of water (which only came into play on one hole) made HRGC a good course for the beginning golfer. Furthermore, besides Hickory Ridge, only six of the other area courses were open 365 days per year, and only one of them had entirely unrestricted tee times. Overall, these factors attracted many beginners, senior citizens, and blue collar customers to HRGC.

■ Sales and Fees

Sales were broken down into five areas. (For a complete sales breakdown, see Exhibit 2.) During the first four months of 1989, course revenues totaled $48,911. Of this amount, 55.6 percent came from greens fees, 17.4 percent came from cart rentals, 11.0 percent came from snack bar and pro shop sales, 13.5 percent came from beer sales, and 2.5 percent came from pull cart rentals.

The marketing survey conducted by the University of South Carolina provided the impetus for many changes, especially in pricing and advertising. The price structure was entirely revamped based on the survey's findings. Greens fees were raised from $4.00 for nine holes, $6.50 for eighteen holes, and $7.50 for the entire day to $4.50, $7.00, and $8.00 during weekdays. Rates increased from $5.00, $7.50, and $8.50 to $6.00, $8.50, and $9.50 during weekends and holidays. The cart rates were raised from $6.00 per nine holes to $6.50 per nine holes and senior citizens and student discount fees were restricted to weekdays.

The new fee structure was designed with two purposes in mind. First, it was intended to underprice the competition while allowing HRGC to maintain an acceptable profit margin (between 2.5 and 4 percent). Second, it was intended to make golf accessible to as many residents of the Columbia area as possible.

■ Course Operations

Despite all the improvements, HRGC still suffered from problems with erosion, especially in the tee areas, and inconsistent conditions on the greens. Course conditions, however, were steadily improving, with new equipment allowing for more efficient use of working hours.

HRGC's facilities had not changed much since Hamilton's purchase of the course. The only additions were the office built in the clubhouse and the pump house constructed near the pond. However, the existing facilities had taken on a markedly different appearance as a result of the extensive clean-up efforts. Hamilton made no change in tee times, keeping them entirely open and making the course available on a first-come-first-served basis 365 days a year. His reason for this was to allow the greatest number of people to tee off in the shortest amount of time possible while providing the maximum number of tee-off hours; he did not want any unnecessary restrictions on the golfers.

HRGC sold a full line of golf balls, a moderate selection of golf clubs (as well as some rentals), golf gloves, and other complementary items such as socks. The shop did not carry golf shoes or clothes. After a round of golf, players could also sit back with a chili dog and a cold drink at the snack bar and watch the PGA tour or a ballgame on television before making the long trip back home.

In conjunction with the increase in prices, Hamilton continued his efforts to make the course more playable. Clean-up was continued both on the course and in the clubhouse, and the pro shop inventory was greatly expanded to include a full line of golf balls as well as a limited selection of clubs. HRGC kept approximately six sets in stock, at a value of approximately $2,000.

■ Advertising

The survey had also recommended that Hamilton target certain groups, such as the elderly and the student golfer. As a result, Hamilton formulated a new advertising strategy designed to entice a greater number of college students to golf at HRGC. In hopes of catching the eye of new students, Hamilton concentrated his advertising efforts at the beginning of each semester, reducing his efforts as final exams neared. He advertised in the *State,* and planned to advertise in the *Gamecock.* The *State* newspaper, a statewide publication, charged $85.50 for one weekend advertisement. The *Gamecock,* the University of South Carolina's student newspaper, was only published during the spring and fall semesters; it charged $25.00 per week for advertisements. Billboards were also employed along the main roads to bring in golfers who might not have otherwise known about HRGC. In addition, because the survey indicated that the vast majority of golfers (more than four-fifths) try out new courses as a result of word of mouth, Hamilton concentrated on promoting a friendly atmosphere at HRGC and rejected both radio and television advertising, which he had previously been considering.

■ Employees

Hamilton continued to employ Jim Alsing and Pete Peterson to operate the counter while hiring John Clayton as grasskeeper, and Harold Valentine as course architect and mechanic. He also billeted himself to work at the course as projects and schedules required.

Counter work consisted of collecting greens and cart fees, controlling cart usage, managing the snack bar and pro shop, keeping the area clean, and some miscellaneous administrative duties. The bulk of the maintenance work fell upon Valentine and Clayton. Valentine, along with being the course agronomist and chemical specialist, worked as part-time mechanic, bringing with him ten years of experience in that field with the navy, as well as years of experience as a young man growing up on his father's farm in Tennessee. Clayton's primary job was to maintain the greens, fairways, and roughs, along with a host of other special projects. Clayton's father, an employee at HRGC many years previous, had helped him to develop an understanding of, and devotion to, the golf industry. Most special projects were contracted out to hired individual consultants as needed.

THE CART DECISION

In May 1989 Hamilton's cart fleet was sorely depleted. Out of the original fourteen E-Z-GO carts, only two were still running. The brakes on one of those were irreparably damaged and unlikely to last much longer. Nine of the twelve recently acquired Club Car carts were also usable. The other three had been rendered completely useless by cracks in the transaxles and main drive gears. The nine still in use, however, suffered from various mechanical problems. The fusible links on two of the carts—parts that normally last for years—were burning out about every two weeks. On a third cart, the rear support bracket for one of the shock absorbers had broken. Because the frame to which the bracket was attached was constructed of aluminum, it required a special type of welding service not available at a reasonable cost in the Columbia area.

There were other problems that pointed to the general deterioration of the fleet. Hamilton was beginning to recognize that extensive body damage could occur to fiberglass carts on a heavily wooded course such as HRGC, and that fiberglass repairs were extremely expensive. On several carts, the batteries were no longer holding their charges all day, and tires were beginning to lose air overnight. Both of these problems were becoming progressively worse. Three of the twelve battery chargers had suffered complete failures in the power supply units, rendering them completely useless. In addition, none of the replacement parts that had been ordered from Club Car had arrived, making it necessary to cannibalize parts from the three useless carts to keep the rest of the fleet operational.

These mechanical problems were causing trouble for Hamilton. For one thing, he had a contract to supply fifteen carts for thirty people in a golf league. On any given day he could be certain of only six to nine working carts. Even more significant was the fact that the proportion of golfers at HRGC who desired to use riding carts (the cart-rental ratio) had increased from 26 to 30.6

percent. Likewise, while the level of play had increased by 35.7 percent over the previous year, the number of cart rentals had increased by 41.7 percent over the same period. More than ever, Hamilton's customers wanted to use his carts; but Hamilton had fewer and fewer carts available.

■ Alternatives

Hamilton and Valentine began to investigate the various options available to alleviate the cart crisis at HRGC. There were several options, each with its own set of questions to consider.

The first alternative considered was to repair the current fleet with borrowed funds. If HRGC went this route, the cost of repairs and the remaining life of the used carts would be important. Valentine believed that repairing the current fleet would provide no more than four years of extended operation with minimum visible improvement in the overall situation.

A second alternative was to purchase an entirely different fleet or a fleet of used ones, as they had in 1988. Either option would require Hamilton to borrow additional funds. With the prime rate at 11.5 percent, HRGC's ability to obtain and repay such a loan was open to debate.

A third alternative was to lease a fleet, which would require no additional borrowing. If this alternative was selected, Hamilton would need to decide whether or not to purchase a maintenance agreement along with the leased fleet. Under a lease agreement, Hamilton would control the number of carts to be maintained by the course, but not how they could be used. For example, some leases prohibit the use of carts to do maintenance work.

There were several other factors that Hamilton and Valentine needed to consider regardless of whether they fixed the old fleet, bought a new or used fleet, or leased a new one. First, they had to consider what types of options would be necessary to meet the expectations of the customers. Do customers want sun roofs, full cart enclosures for winter golf, and sweater baskets? Second, they needed to decide if they wanted to use three-wheel or four-wheel carts. Four-wheelers cause less turf damage and have a lower insurance cost because of their greater riding stability. Third, they had to decide if they wanted gas or electric carts. Gas-powered carts required the purchase of fuel and oil, and needed more daily maintenance. They were also noisier, gave off fumes, and did not ride as smoothly. Electric-powered carts were heavier, caused greater soil compaction and grass deterioration, but provided a smoother ride. Because they ran on electricity, they required the purchase of battery packs, which needed replacement about every three years. Finally, they had to determine how many carts would be needed.

■ Visiting the Cart Companies

There were four regional companies that Hamilton and Valentine investigated: Melex, Yamaha, Club Car, and E-Z-GO. Each of these companies provided carts for lease and purchase. Valentine visited each of these firms for Hamilton in late May, seeking a four-year term agreement without maintenance agreements. He visited Melex in North Carolina first, then traveled to Yamaha, Club Car, and E-Z-GO in Georgia.

Melex

Melex had the lowest selling price: $2,800 for a gasoline-powered cart and $2,580 for the electric. Its lease cost was $59 per month with a residual value of $675. In addition, Melex had an outstanding distribution system and was staffed by kind and gracious sales representatives. Melex kept a full maintenance facility at Raleigh, North Carolina. The company had over ten years of experience in the United States. However, the carts themselves, as well as all parts, were manufactured in Yugoslavia. Its carts were metal and extremely similar in design to the previous year's model of E-Z-GO.

Yamaha

Yamaha's carts were more expensive: $3,500 for gasoline, $3,200 for electric. Lease prices were $72.00 per month with a residual value of $1,400. The Yamaha carts were not as aesthetically pleasing as the other models. According to one of the local courses, they had fairly poor records of holding up on rough, hilly terrain. Valentine found that the Yamahas also had fiberglass bodies similar to those of Club Car. The company had served the American golf industry eight years yet seemed to lack adequate maintenance facilities and trained mechanical personnel in the southeastern United States. Newnan, Georgia, was the closest maintenance facility for Yamaha. The carts and parts were manufactured in Japan.

Club Car

Club Car had been in operation for about thirty years under various forms of management and ownership. The company was well established in the U.S. golf industry, and its carts and parts were made in the United States. Club Car has a service facility located only about 70 miles away in Augusta, Georgia. Its prices were higher than Melex at $3,250 for the gasoline models, $2,800 for the electric, and lease prices of $71 per month with a residual value of $450. The carts themselves showed design flaws in the differentials and electrical systems. The bodies were fiberglass. Club Car also appeared to have a serious problem with parts availability. According to Valentine, the company was generally uncooperative; an abrupt cessation of communications occurred after it was discovered that HRGC was also considering E-Z-GO carts.

E-Z-GO

E-Z-GO was very experienced in the U.S. golf industry with thirty-five years already under its belt. Its carts and parts were manufactured in this country. All parts were in stock at its Augusta, Georgia, facilities. The company made a very sturdy cart with a full sheet metal body and tubular frame designed to stand up to years of use and abuse. Their gas carts cost $2,900, the electric carts cost $2,680, and leasing was $59 per month with a residual value of $675. According to Valentine the carts themselves seemed to be mechanically sound in every area, corrosion resistant, and eye-appealing. The electric models held their charges better than those from the other three companies, and their battery chargers were the only ones that showed how long it took for batteries to charge, making it possible to predict battery replacement needs.

OTHER ISSUES

In addition to the decision regarding the cart fleet, Hamilton had several other pressing issues to consider. Each issue would likely need to be resolved before Hamilton's goals regarding HRGC could be attained.

When Hamilton bought HRGC, the only cooler in the snack bar was half of a whiskey barrel filled with ice. Although it made an adequate cooler, it was inefficient. Each time a drink was ordered the attendant had to reach down into the ice to find the desired brand of beer. Furthermore, the attendant had to keep track of how much of each brand was on ice to be sure that he did not run out of cold cans of any one brand. The cost of replacing the cooler was estimated at $1,585.

The clubhouse was still in need of significant renovation. Furthermore, as the ratio of revenues from clubhouse activities (pro shop and snack bar) to revenues from the golf course increased, the need to renovate became more pressing. Renovation costs were expected to be approximately $8,000.

With no mower for the rough, Hamilton was trying to use the fairway mower. This, however, did not work well on the higher, thicker rough grass. A new mower would cost $1,150.

A new rotivator would allow HRGC to use more efficient aeration techniques. The rotivator cut thin slices in the ground and was usable year round. By contrast, the old aerator made large holes in the turf and could only be used once per year to minimize interference with play. Rotivators cost $3,000.

The irrigation system reached all tees and greens but only five of the nine fairways. Hamilton wanted to add irrigation to the other four fairways even though he knew its installation would cause considerable interruption in play. Building the addition to the irrigation system would cost $6,000.

A temperature-controlled workshop was needed adjacent to the clubhouse. Because of the extreme temperatures in the metal cart shed, repair work there was almost impossible. If a new fleet of carts were bought or rented, or if the old fleet were repaired, this workshop would be mandatory. Its cost would amount to $1,000.

Hamilton also owned a 15-acre, pie-shaped plot of ground adjacent to the golf course. He was considering adding a nine-hole, par-27 course there; however, construction costs would be $75,000 at the minimum.

CONCLUSION

All of these issues weighed upon Hamilton's mind as Valentine concluded his report about the cart companies. He knew that he would need to spend money in order to turn Hickory Ridge Golf Course into the kind of facility he wanted it to be. He accepted that. But there were so many areas that needed attention. What should come first?

Again, his thoughts returned to the cart dilemma. Everything seemed to revolve around his making a correct decision about the carts. If he repaired what he had, he might risk continued problems. If he leased or bought, well, that seemed like such a big step! One thing was certain: he could not ignore the problem. Every day he waited meant lost revenues and lost golfers. A golfer who decided to go somewhere else to play might never bother coming back. He had all the information he needed. Hamilton was determined to make a decision based upon this information as soon as possible, then act upon his choice, for the good of his business.

REFERENCES

Business Week, "Golf: Business Challenges and Opportunities." March 27, 1989.

Golf Course Management, 1989.

Golf Digest, "The Explosive Future of Golf." March/April 1989.

Golf Market Today, "Course Development on the Upswing in the U.S." Volume 28, No. 3 (May/June 1989), pp. 3–5.

PGA Magazine, "Wanted: More Golf Courses." March 1989.

Postich, Miller, & Valentine, "Hickory Ridge Golf Club." University of South Carolina, 1989.

Research Recommendations, February 20, 1989.

Savvy, "Taking a Swing at Success." April 1989.

U.S. Department of the Census, *State and Metropolitan Area Data Book 1991*, Washington, D.C.

CASE 33

NSP Corporate Graphics, Inc.

Sharon L. Oswald, Mary Astone, Auburn University

Price is long forgotten when quality and service are long remembered. . . .—Babe McGehee

Looking back on his first year as president of NSP Corporate Graphics, Inc. (NSP), Michael Plumb recalled a promise he made to the board of directors four months earlier. He told the board that if he had not turned the company around by the completion of 1992, his second year as president, he would agree to resign. With one year under his belt, and one more year to go before his self-imposed deadline, Michael was pleased with the changes he had made and anticipated the challenges that lie ahead. Michael saw his major problem to be how to survive in what he classified as a mature industry.

THE FOUNDING OF NSP

C.H. "Babe" McGehee and Tom Edwards became friends in the fifth grade after Babe's family moved to the small town of Auburn, Alabama. As Babe recalled, the early days were trying. As a "preacher's kid," Babe had to fight all of the boys in his class just to be accepted. After he beat up Tom, one of the larger boys in his class, he never had further problems. Instead, Babe and Tom became best friends, a friendship that was to last a lifetime. Their friendship grew in college where they pledged with the same fraternity at Auburn University. They lost touch for a while during the war, but after World War II were reunited. Babe was working in construction in Mobile, Alabama, and Tom was back in Auburn building houses with his father. Tom convinced Babe to join him in the construction business in Auburn. A very enterprising team, they were always in search of new opportunities. Tom found a plant for sale that produced wooden ammunition boxes for use in the Korean Conflict. Seeing

---

This case is intended for classroom discussion only, not to depict effective or ineffective handling of administrative situations. All rights reserved to the authors and the North American Case Research Association.

future opportunities, they bought the plant and moved it from Columbus, Mississippi, to Auburn in 1952. The end of the conflict brought a significant decrease in the demand for ammunition boxes. Tom decided to modify the business to produce returnable wooden soft drink containers to meet the increasing demands of that industry. By 1962, Tom again recognized that the returnable glass bottle was losing ground and the future for the container company looked grim. He began looking to diversify into new ventures. When the container plant was closed in 1990, it was the last remaining plant of its type in the United States.

Tom became interested in the screen printing business and began looking for viable prospects (see Exhibit 1). He identified Dixie Printing in nearby Opelika as their next business opportunity. Screen printing was a natural choice because the company's current skill in cutting special angles for wooden soft drink containers was readily transferred to Dixie Printing's production of plywood shapes for highway traffic signs. After cutting the plywood base the firm then applied the sign front. The partners bought Dixie Printing, convinced the former owner, Jim Crawford, to join them, and moved their new business to Auburn directly across the street from the container plant. The newly formed firm, National Screen Printers (later changed to NSP Corporate Graphics, Inc.), incorporated as a closely held corporation in 1962 with 30,000 shares of stock selling at a par value of $10 per share.

The first meeting of NSP's board of directors was held on February 2, 1962, at a local motel. The company had approximately 60 original stockholders, primarily from the Auburn/Opelika area. Less than two-thirds of the stock was sold with the rest retained by the company. During the early days, Tom and Babe offered to work for free until the firm was profitable. The board of directors refused this offer and insisted that they take a salary of $250 per month. Within three years, NSP reached its goal of profitability. In 1985 the firm declared its first dividends at 50 cents per share.

Shortly after the formation of NSP, the 3M Corporation effectively put them out of the sign business with their development of a "do it yourself" sign that could be made by prison inmates or municipality employees. NSP diversified again, this time into water-applied decals, and later into pressure sensitive decals. As a result, NSP turned its attention to fleet graphics (decals on the side of semi-trucks).

In 1989, NSP was ranked in the top 15 percent (in terms of size) of all screen printing firms in the country. That same year the company was a semi-finalist for the state of Alabama U.S. Senate Productivity Award. Currently, while still involved in fleet graphics, NSP has expanded its services to include all aspects corporate graphics, signage and design.

Exhibit 1

Screen Printing

Screen printing is one of the oldest forms of printing. It began with the printing of silk. Areas of the silk were blocked out to make an impression on the material. This process involved depositing ink through a screen mesh. Today, photographic and chemical agents are used to screen out color. Screen printing is superior to some other forms of printing because it allows heavier deposits of ink onto a surface resulting in a more vibrant, longer-lasting finish.

■ Succession of Management

Tom became president of the newly formed National Screenprinters, and Babe was the secretary-treasurer. During the early days, Babe spent most of his time running the container factory while Tom took over the operations of the screen printing business. Tom was the driving leader of the new corporation. It was his expertise in machinery and equipment that created the spirit of strong manufacturing and commitment to quality for which the company has always been recognized by its customers. NSP is one of the few companies in the industry that is almost entirely automated, a tribute to the solid foundation established by Tom. Tom and Babe occupied a single office at NSP that was equipped with two desks and a manual Royal typewriter. While Tom was overseeing manufacturing, Babe handled most of the personnel issues. In 1979, Tom died unexpectedly and Babe assumed the position of firm president. A portrait of Tom (and Babe) in the lobby of NSP signified Tom's continued presence in the company.

As president, Babe had a much different management style from his predecessor. By self-admission, Babe was a laissez-faire administrator who believed in the talents and capabilities of his employees and therefore did not interfere with their work. Babe attributed the success of NSP to the theme of one of his favorite sayings: "No amount of planning will replace dumb luck." He admitted that during the 1970s the firm did nothing to position itself in the market. NSP operated in a very conservative manner, taking few risks. The company had a debt to equity ratio of about 10 to 15 percent when the rest of the industry was operating at ratios in excess of 50 percent. As a result, Babe felt inactivity was the best strategy the company could have taken. Many of its competitors chose an aggressive approach and ended up losing money or closing their doors. Babe let the plant manager, comptroller, and sales manager act as a triumvir for the firm. He exercised his administrative authority only when the three disagreed on the direction the firm should take.

In 1982, Michael Plumb joined NSP as sales manager, working out of his home in Atlanta, Georgia. Michael, originally from the Northeast, attended the University of Vermont, where he obtained a degree in history. Michael's northeastern work ethic was considered by fellow employees to be quite foreign to the NSP style, and he was often described by others as an "aggressive Yankee." His previous experience and training at 3M, Creatist, and Kux Manufacturing, coupled with his "slick" appearance and natural gift of gab and knowledge of the product, made him an accomplished salesman. In 1987 his position was upgraded in title to vice president of sales. This gave him more leverage with customers. Michael came to NSP with high goals—he wanted to be more than vice president of sales, he wanted to be president. When he informed Babe of his plan he was advised to show his true commitment to the firm by moving to Auburn. Michael made the move.

Not only was Michael determined to move to Auburn, he was committed to becoming a good corporate citizen. He joined Rotary. He and his family became active in the Presbyterian church. Finally, he became a Crisis Center telephone volunteer. The latter was an eye-opening experience for Michael. As he put it, he grew up with the "silver spoon" in his mouth and has lived an almost idyllic life. He was unaware of the everyday problems that many other people encountered, such as marital problems, drug abuse, and delinquency. The Crisis Center not only taught him to effectively listen and empathize (through 40 hours of intense training), but also made him more aware of the problems that could be affecting his employees.

In 1989, on his 70th birthday, Babe stepped down as president of the corporation but remained involved as the chairman of the board of directors. Babe envisioned another in-house candidate as his heir apparent, but in one of the few instances of disagreement with Babe, the board of directors chose Michael, who better fit the image that they wanted to project as the company's chief executive. The board wanted someone with new visions—someone with a well-rounded background in the screen printing industry. Michael best met that need. He had experience in all three levels of screen printing—he sold to screen printing companies, he worked for an installation company, and he sold screen printing.

■ Michael Plumb

As CEO of NSP Michael's management philosophy paralleled that of Alvin Toffler's, "dare to imagine the future." Toffler suggested that managers look for "big chances," be willing to work toward these goals, and dare to differ from conventional wisdom. Michael believed in this philosophy without taking it to extremes. One example was when he assumed the position of president of NSP. The employees in the firm were surprised when Michael decided not to move to the largest office in the firm and, instead, stayed in his smaller inner office.

Another of his personal philosophies was to "do what you do well and do it often." Michael's talent was sales—so, he spent at least one-quarter of his time making new contacts and servicing old accounts, particularly the Federal Express account, and another quarter of his time managing sales. He also spent some of his time working in the plant because he felt the only way to keep current on the business was to do the job. The remainder of his time was spent in new market development and performing the normal duties of a corporate executive.

Michael was considered to be a challenging person, very demanding of the people around him. He set high standards for himself and expected others to have equally high goals for themselves. He was a tried and true person and let no obstacles get in his way. As a result, he seldom allowed himself time to relax. While he was very family-oriented and concerned about spending quality time with his family, he often found himself thinking of business during family vacations or other outings. One of his greatest obsessions was his determination to be fair. In both his work and his home life he was careful to look at all situations in terms of the fairness of the outcome.

His management style was open, but he also felt the need to get involved with day-to-day plant operations. Part of this involvement meant keeping the employees fully appraised of the firm's position in the industry. In fact, he took every available moment to update the employees on NSP progress. On one occasion when the city was under a tornado alert and all employees were gathered in the basement for safety, Michael announced the previous quarter's earnings and updated all employees on new accounts. All meetings were not spontaneous, however; Michael held monthly meetings with all employees—always just prior to breaktime so as to never cut into their free time. Seldom, if ever, was there a written, pre-established agenda. His meetings were informal and light-hearted, yet he was always in control. Still, he was quick to compliment the employees for their part in any financial or productivity improvements, or to answer any question pertaining to company operations. The format of all meetings were in Michael's head. His monthly meetings with management personnel were run quite the same. However, while ideas for new ventures surfaced for discussion, the direction the company would take was usually predetermined by Michael.

■ The Screen Printing Industry

Large-format screen printing in the United States was about a $750 million industry. Recently two of the largest competitors—Ariston and Screen Art—merged, placing the new company in a position of dominance. Despite the merger, the screen printing industry was primarily comprised of many small to mid-sized firms. Very little capital is required (about $10,000) to get started in screen printing. For this reason the industry is flooded with "mom and pop" operations. The business is largely regionalized with few national firms. The flooded market and steep competition results in characteristically low operating margins and low switching costs to the buyer of screen printing services. This is compounded by the fact that most of the larger screen printing clients use more than one vendor, making it difficult for any one company to solely maintain a major corporate account. The competition is so intense that an exclusive account today could be subdivided or retracted tomorrow. Survival in the industry is dependent on a firm's ability to diversify its business among a large number of companies.

Two types of screen printing businesses exist. Firms such as National ScreenPrinters specialize in fleet and large graphics, and silk-screen shops concentrate on t-shirts and specialty advertising items (such as coffee cups).

Fleet Graphics

Fleet graphics is a successful means of corporate exposure. A 1977 study conducted by the American Trucking Association, Inc., showed that an over-the-road tractor-trailer combination made 101 visual impressions per mile during the daylight hours. Assuming an average annual mileage of 100,000, this totaled 10.1 million impressions. The study further measured the visual impact of local delivery vans, for a total of 16 million visual impressions per year. Nighttime use of trucks added another 37.5 percent to the previous numbers. Statistics showed that over two-thirds of the motorists favored the use of fleet graphics as a means of advertising.

In response to the positive appeal of fleet graphics, much of the industry has focused on "spicing up" the distribution fleets. One company, Eastern Foods Inc., changed its trucks and tractors for their Naturally Fresh salad dressings from brown and white with yellow stripes to an elaborately produced full color rolling billboard of tantalizing vegetables and salad dressings. The fleet graphics business was highly dependent on the truck-trailer market. The truck-trailer market is a mature market, considered by some to be in a state of crisis. Trailer manufacturers are cutting capacity, consolidating production into fewer manufacturing plants, and finding ways to create long-term business partnerships with motor carrier customers. The financial demands on the industry heightened since 1975 as a result of leveraged buyouts on the part of the five major trailer manufacturers. Typically, the trucking industry had been restrictive in the amount of money the companies allocated toward advertising, and this has become more pronounced in recent years. Economic predictions saw some improvements for the trailer business as a result of the continued decline of foreign trade deficits.

■ The Federal Express Account

When Michael joined NSP, he brought with him the Federal Express account, having first called on them in 1978. After 13 years of a close working relationship that was uncharacteristic of the industry, Michael still felt the need to nurture them as if they were a new account, while, at the same time, not rely too heavily on their business. Federal Express comprised 18 percent of the company's annual sales. Consequently, Michael and the entire NSP staff were very aware of the importance of Federal Express to their bottom-line. Of the six staff artists at NSP, one was fully devoted to the Federal Express account. Michael felt that quality and value-added service have been the reasons they have maintained this important account. "While everyone in the business can produce a good decal, it is the quality of our art department that has made the difference," he explained. Because of their reputation with Federal Express officials, NSP has received more than just their fleet graphics business, they have focused on an entire corporate identity program.

■ Employee Stock Ownership Program

The heart of NSP was in Babe's pet project—the employee stock ownership program (ESOP). Getting the employees involved in the profitability of the company was an idea that he and Tom shared from the early days of operation. In 1973, he attempted to get approval to offer stock to the employees at 75 percent of book value. Through his investigation, he found that the Securities and Exchange Commission would not approve informal offerings of this nature, so he temporarily dropped the idea.

In early 1981, Babe became interested in a simplified employee pension plan (SEP) and operationalized it in 1983, the same year the company's net profit first broke $100,000, and dividends of $2 per share were declared. Babe still was not completely satisfied with the SEP because he wanted the employees to feel more of a tie to the company. He soon became convinced that an employee stock ownership program (ESOP) was what his company needed. He felt that if employees were given the opportunity to buy into their own company, they would take a greater interest in the business and the company would benefit. In 1985 NSP became one of the first small firms in America to bring the ownership concept to its employees.

The company, which is about 30 percent employee-owned, revolved around the ESOP program. (No stockholder has a controlling interest in NSP. Babe, who is the largest stockholder, maintains about 12 percent of the stock.) This is very apparent by the slogan on each employees' nametag "If it has to be, it is up to me." The importance of the ESOP program is even proudly displayed in all advertisements about NSP. Under the terms of the plan, employees become eligible to participate after reaching the age of 18 and after completing 12 consecutive months of employment. Contributions to the plan are based on a percentage of the salaries of the participants, and the rate is set by the board of directors annually. Vesting in the program takes five years.

Each year since 1985, employees have received a record of their ownership and each year a distribution has been made. "Even in years when we didn't do well, we gave about an 8 percent distribution. We are committed to making distributions," Babe explains. Babe feels the ESOP encourages quality and service because it motivates the employees to work harder. "We all have to have the profit motive to work a little harder." As a result, it is a universal belief among management and staff that their quality and service is superior because they, as owners of the company, cared about the products they produce—craftsmanship, detail, timely delivery, and precise installation.

PRESENT OPERATIONS—1990

■ Strategic Planning

The firm previously was not involved in formal strategic planning; instead planning was based on Babe's "dumb luck." Consequently, from the inception of NSP, planning was always "seat-of-the-pants" or whatever seemed right at the time. For example, the decision to get into interior design graphics came with the addition of a staff member, Jeff Hill, who had previous experience in the field—no market research was conducted.

Michael's most recent concern was to be "everything" to 300 top customers. Everything meant doing all corporate graphics for the client—from letterhead design to interior signage to fleet graphics. There was no magic associated with the number 300, no breakeven point, no market research. His only rationale for this number was to take an average of his 5.5 salespeople (including himself) and multiply that times servicing the needs of about 50 to 60 accounts each. Michael did not see NSP as ever being a large company; consequently he set his goals accordingly.

Formal planning seemed to be on the horizon for NSP. Prior to 1990, the company's one attempt at formal planning came quite by accident. At a scheduled meeting between key management personnel and a major supplier, the supplier failed to show up. Consequently, the managers found themselves at loose ends and began talking about future directions. Upon reflection Michael said those were the best two hours they had ever spent. Michael believed planning was a necessary evil. He admitted that the company existed for a number of years without any interaction with the outside world—existing in a vacuum. His recent attempts at formalizing ideas brought a full-day management retreat where the mission statement and objectives presented in Exhibits 2 and 3 were formalized.

■ Organizational Structure

The organizational structure of National ScreenPrinters is depicted in Exhibit 4. Babe serves as chairman of the board, and Michael as president. Jim Davis

Exhibit 2

Mission Statement: National ScreenPrinters, Inc.

NSP will provide our customer with high-quality products and service to enhance their corporate image. Long-term enduring relationships will be developed with our customers and suppliers.

A consistent, caring, and conscientious posture with all our contacts will be maintained through motivated co-owners in our ESOP company. NSPeople will keep a clear focus to provide integrity and responsiveness to our customers.

A reasonable profit will be reinvested equally to our shareholders and employees, knowing that NSPeople are the driving force behind our product and service.

Note: The mission statement is included in all corporate literature. The ESOP logo is proudly embossed in the middle of the mission statement on all official documents.

Exhibit 3

Long-Term Goals

At the one-day planning meeting held in the summer of 1990, the following long-term goals were established for NSP.

1. Establish market niche(s)/areas of diversification.
2. Strive for 100 percent UV printing, if profitable.
3. Establish the art department as a profit center.
4. Expand the CAMGraphix (computerized graphics).
5. Purchase a new die cut machine or a TA 41 machine.
6. Determine the feasibility of establishing an in-house advertising agency.
7. Provide a computer station for each artist.
8. Perfect the accounting system to trace costs.
9. Establish a positive working environment.
10. Examine the employee benefits program.

is plant manager. Jim, a member of Babe's early triumvir, has been with NSP about 14 years. Betty Stallings, comptroller and business manager, has been with NSP about 12 years. Michael rounded out the early management team established by Babe. A 26-year veteran of NSP, Larry Long serves the company as production manager.

Richard Syler joined NSP six years ago as marketing manager. Richard, who had no formal training in marketing, held a degree in fine art/sculpture from a small local college, but recently enrolled in an introductory marketing class to learn the basics of his profession.

Jeff Hill came to NSP about one year ago as research and development manager. He had previous experience with Madix, a store fixture company, and brought new expertise to the company in terms of interior decor. The most recent member of the management staff, Ken Roberts, also joined NSP about a year ago as sales manager. Ken, who came to the company from Avery, a decal-related business, works out of his home in Atlanta.

One position that received recent visibility at NSP, because of an emphasis on staffing and job descriptions, was that of personnel specialist, presently

Organizational Structure

Exhibit 4

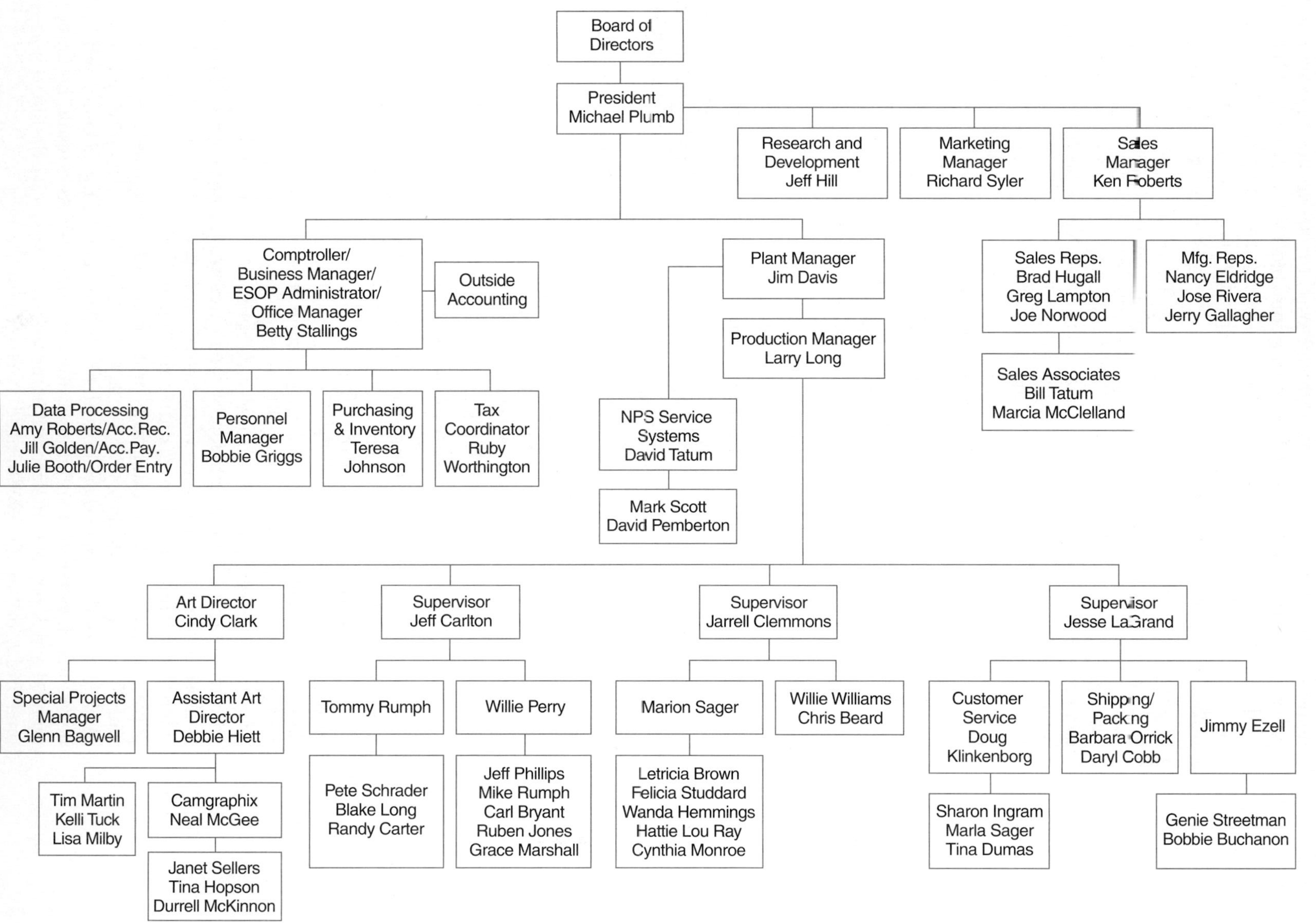

held by Bobbie Griggs. She came to the job from the production area with no previous personnel experience. In selecting someone for this position, Michael said he was looking for someone with intelligence and initiative and Bobbie seemed to fit that description. She has been with the company for approximately four years.

■ Personnel

The soul of NSP's operations are its 75 full-time employees. But no one in the company reflected the friendly, warm attitude of the NSPeople (as they fondly refer to themselves) more than Ruby Worthington. Known to employees and clients alike as "Miss Ruby," she has been receptionist and tax coordinator for the company for the past 13 years. Miss Ruby, according to Michael, kept the "southern warmth" in the business, something that despite its "Yankee" leader NSP ever strived to retain.

Personnel activities, like most other aspects of NSP, were not formalized. Until recently, there were no employee job descriptions. While job descriptions seemed to Michael to be a necessary evil, his recent attempt to formalize the planning procedure extended to the development of descriptions for all NSP jobs to coincide with a proposed merit system of performance evaluation. Still, Michael believes that every employee should be able to do many jobs—cross training, he feels, is the key to successful operations. This belief is carried into the office. For example, Bobbie Griggs continues to work half-time in the production area, and Larry Long doubles in sales. In order to achieve a completely cross-trained organization, Michael is content to keep his operation relatively small. He feels if everyone knows several jobs they will never lose sight of why they are in business. The job descriptions are expected to set standards upon which to judge performance, something that previously was nonexistent at NSP.

Almost since its beginning, NSP operated one 10-hour shift four days per week. No one, with the exception of management and the office staff, was regularly scheduled to work on Friday. The company ran about 20 percent overtime hours. Michael's philosophy is that he will always opt for overtime rather than hiring new employees. A team of graduate students who analyzed NSP operations for a class project suggested that the company implement staggered shifts. Staggered shifts would allow employees to continue working four days, while at the same time cover the entire week. Staggered shifts began at NSP in November 1990. Concurrently, approximately 70 percent of the employees opted to work five 8-hour days. This resulted in key equipment and departments being staffed for 50 straight-time hours per week.

Employees are on the honor system in regard to time worked. There are no time cards. Recently, the use of time cards became an issue among employees who feel that the implementation of time cards would benefit the company because too many employees were taking advantage of the honor system. Interestingly, most employees didn't find time cards to be an invasion of privacy, but found wearing uniforms problematic. One area where Michael has had some problem dealing with the honor system is in relation to sick days. Michael is seldom sick; therefore, he has little tolerance for sickness and believes sick days taken are often used for extra time off. As a result, he implemented a sick policy that stated that anyone who missed work due to illness on a Friday or Monday would need a doctor's excuse.

NSP is not unionized and Michael wants it to stay that way. Monthly meetings are his way of allowing employees to voice concerns before problems got out of hand.

■ Sales Force

Michael is aware of the importance of a good sales force. "It used to be that if you were ethical and a nice guy you could keep jobs—this is no longer the case—today you have to be all that and good," Michael explained. "Today the three p's of sales are price, product, and personality." Three sales representatives and two sales associates report to Ken Roberts. One of the sales representatives, Brad Hugall, operates out of the Auburn office, while the others operate primarily out of Georgia and Mississippi. The three manufacturers representatives extend the business into New York, Florida, and Texas. Much of their day-to-day selling is conducted by telephone. Michael gave financial constraints as the reason for keeping the sales force small and relatively immobile. Since the business is market driven, he feels it is too costly to "go out and drum up business." Instead, Michael has elected to further develop existing accounts. By further development, he intends to provide all the corporate graphics, fleet and decor, for his select 300 accounts. This goal would be met without increasing the current size of the sales force. "If you develop a unique enough relationship with the customer, you can differentiate yourself from the masses."

NSP sales representatives operate in designated territories. The sales goal for all representatives is $1 million annually; however, most have averaged about $600,000. Commissions are generally not affected by the profit margin on the specific sales. Compensation is based on a commission of 5 percent after a base level of $30,000 in sales is met. According to Michael, while manufacturers representatives have added to the business, the company could not survive without full-time salespeople. "It's the nature of the business—you can only count on your internal salesforce," he explained.

■ Financial Performance

NSP's current balance sheet, statement of income and retained earnings, and statement of cash flows are displayed in Exhibits 5–7, respectively. In a comparison to 1988, costs of goods sold increased by .5 percent, operating expenses increased by 20 percent, and gross profits decreased by 20 percent in 1989. This resulted in a net loss for the year. Michael partially attributed the loss to serious inefficiencies that he believes will be corrected with the staggered work week. He also admits that profits were overstated in previous years because "goods in process" were counted at 100 percent. With the implementation of a new form of inventory accounting (LIFO), Michael feels that some of the previous problems will be corrected.

The company recently began to take a closer look at where the true costs of the business exist. In 1989 it implemented a "Covalent System" used for cost recovery, cost estimating, cost tracking, and cost inventory. The focus of this system was to make NSP a more profitable business. "We have been behind the eight ball in technology particularly in the plant. Until recently we kept labor figures by hand on manilla cards," Michael explained. As a result, it was discovered that 43 percent of their sales dollars were spent on raw materials.

Exhibit 5

Schedules of Cost of Goods Sold, Years Ended December 31, 1990, 1989, and 1988

	1990	*1989*	*1988*
Inventory, beginning of year	$ 768,470	$ 794,757	$ 578,398
Production department			
Purchases	1,869,483	1,848,928	1,889,213
Salaries	612,266	493,199	423,359
Application labor expenses	1,878	24,659	30,304
Depreciation	126,272	93,672	71,016
Freight	3,133	7,470	4,484
Insurance	112,428	99,556	51,248
Taxes	49,626	50,666	39,746
Supplies	91,353	79,570	59,114
Repairs and maintenance	30,819	34,382	34,254
Utilities	45,855	46,644	39,372
Contract labor	52,529	48,427	44,143
Uniforms	9,355	10,704	8,067
Rent	6,000	7,533	2,000
Refunds	140	6,787	—
Travel	7,176	4,290	1,818
Miscellaneous	107,997	9,521	4,227
Total costs—production	3,126,310	2,866,008	2,702,365
Art department			
Salaries	136,195	114,365	111,908
Supplies	12,440	25,840	23,968
Contract labor	20,010	21,811	39,138
Insurance	11,215	10,522	7,272
Taxes	10,900	9,330	8,160
Repairs and maintenance	3,176	3,089	1,326
Miscellaneous	5,055	910	949
Total cost—art	198,991	185,867	192,721
Application department			
Salaries	61,898	83,921	43,739
Supplies	1,899	1,030	413
Contract labor	361	7,450	—
Taxes	5,069	5,398	2,872
Travel	16,568	22,538	16,765
Repairs and maintenance	4,999	2,468	4,207
Insurance	14,681	20,216	3,968
Depreciation	3,072	3,071	3,071
Miscellaneous	7,244	2,120	630
Total costs—application	115,791	148,212	75,665
Goods available for sale	4,209,562	3,994,844	3,549,149
Less—inventory, end of year	764,356	768,470	794,757
Cost of goods sold	$3,445,206	$3,226,374	$2,754,392

Consequently maintaining good vendor relations became as important to their bottom line as increasing sales. The Covalent System also helped NSP identify product lines and markets which were not showing an adequate return. For example, the system indicated a poor return on their metal plate printing operations. As a result, they discontinued the service and sold the equipment. Inefficiencies in machine operations have also been identified through the Covalent System, as well as duplication of efforts. The latter became apparent in the supervision of four-color printing. Formally, during the printing of four-color jobs an employee from the art department and the printing department would supervise the work. This unnecessary duplication increased job costs. The Covalent System has allowed NSP employees to know exactly where they were in the production process in order to better keep the client informed as to the status of their project.

Pension Plan

The primary investment to the ESOP, according to the terms of the plan, was NSP stock. The contribution rates for 1989 and 1988 were set at 6 percent and 15 percent of covered salaries and wages and amounted to $50,412 and $106,304, respectively.

Balance Sheets, December 31, 1990, 1989, and 1988 **Exhibit 6**

	1990	*1989*	*1988*
Assets			
Current assets			
Cash	$ 29,249	$ —	$ 10,503
Trade accounts receivable (net)	981,550	675,790	1,056,839
Other receivables	1,656	2,610	3,710
Inventories	790,665	768,470	794,757
Prepaid expenses	43,190	177,226	64,166
Total current assets	1,846,310	1,624,096	1,929,975
Property, plant, and equipment			
Land	10,613	10,613	10,613
Land improvements	6,031	25,013	25,013
Buildings and improvements	645,242	617,379	512,665
Furniture, fixtures, and equipment	1,112,099	947,509	743,035
Vehicles	36,492	42,881	36,881
	1,810,477	1,643,395	1,328,207
Less accumulated depreciation	764,356	678,317	557,011
Net property, plant, and equipment	1,046,121	965,078	771,196
Other assets			
Deposits	—	22,559	—
Total assets	$2,892,431	$2,611,733	$2,701,171

(Continued)

Exhibit 6

Balance Sheets, December 31, 1990, 1989 and 1988 (continued)

	1990	*1989*	*1988*
Liabilities and Stockholders' Equity			
Current liabilities			
Line of credit	$ 268,035	$ —	$ —
Bank overdraft	—	$ 628	$ —
Current portion of notes and capital leases payable	62,013	190,067	52,900
Current portion of ESOP note payable	—	46,093	—
Accounts payable	235,677	195,236	345,600
Accrued salaries and wages	32,256	9,710	37,008
Accrued interest	5,953	4,110	—
Deferred revenue	4,875	—	119,297
Payroll and sales taxes payable	66,063	14,074	20,755
Pension plan contribution payable	—	44,571	106,304
Total current liabilities	674,872	504,489	681,864
Long-term liabilities			
Notes and capital leases payable, net of current portion	59,293	—	258,058
ESOP note payable	307,947	308,254	—
Deferred income taxes	95,780	95,780	81,926
Total long-term liabilities	463,020	404,034	339,984
Less current portion	(62,013)		
Total liabilities	1,075,879	908,523	1,021,848
Stockholders' equity			
Common stock—authorized 30,000 shares; $10 par value per share; issued 27,134 shares at December 31, 1989 and 22,665 shares at December 31, 1988	271,344	271,344	226,652
Additional paid-in capital	575,324	575,324	164,154
Retained earnings	1,305,919	1,244,587	1,322,215
Less			
Treasury stock at cost, 3,163 shares at December 31, 1989 and 1988	(32,945)	(33,698)	(33,698)
ESOP contra account	(303,090)	(354,347)	—
Total stockholders' equity	1,816,552	1,703,210	1,679,323
Total liabilities and stockholders' equity	$2,892,431	$2,611,733	$2,701,171

Income Statement, December 31, 1990 **Exhibit 7**

	1990	*1989*	*1988*
Sales	$4,484,290	$4,191,169	$3,960,962
Cost of goods sold	3,440,092	3,226,374	2,754,392
Gross profit	1,044,198	964,795	1,206,570
Operating expenses			
General and admin.	304,724	391,561	326,838
Sales	518,511	475,716	365,729
	823,235	867,277	692,567
Income from operations	220,963	97,518	514,003
ESOP contribution	—	—	—
Other income and (expenses)	(50,797)	(103,889)	(121,979)
Net income (loss)	$ 170,166	(6,371)	$392,024

Inventories

Inventories were previously stated at the lower of cost or market on a first-in, first-out (FIFO) basis. In 1990, this system was changed to a last-in, first-out (LIFO) system.

Excess inventory has been an area of concern for Michael. A normal production run includes a 10 percent overrun as a control for error. Historically these extra finished goods do not get sold and end up as inventory costs.

■ Production Services

NSP billed itself as a company dedicated to fleet graphics and visual marketing programs. The services provided by the company could be divided into eight categories: Truckgraphix, Creative Design Systems, Durabanners, Architectural and Environmental Graphics, Decor, Corporate Graphics, Original Equipment Manufacturers and Service Systems. Michael believes the industry was currently working at 75 percent of capacity. Because of this, he feels it is important to completely service his accounts. This means that, if a client wants something and NSP cannot provide it, NSP will find someone who can. An example of this was storefront awnings. NSP had the screen printing capabilities but did not supply awnings. Management found a small "mom and pop" operation that could and the job went to NSP.

The glut in the industry is also a reason Michael decided to expand his operations to include services such as interior decor. This particular move was augmented by the addition of Jeff Hill, who had prior experience in that type of design. A natural extension of their business would have been in the screen printing of specialty products such as shirts and coffee cups. While some of the managers wanted to choose this option, Michael disagreed. He felt NSP could make a bigger impression in the market by expanding to more types of services rather than scaling down present operations to a smaller medium. In fact, he was so committed to the concept that he proposed and ultimately changed the name of the company in 1990 from National ScreenPrinters, Inc., to NSP Corporate Graphics, Inc. While most of their graphics work is done by computer, Michael is quick to point out that the art department is capable of producing work far beyond computer graphics—whatever the client wants.

NEW VENTURES

One venture that Michael recently entertained was the production and sale of a lighted table. Because of the size of their graphic work, lighted tables large enough to accommodate their work were not available. Michael commissioned two engineering professors at Auburn University to design and build a table for their use. Because the resulting table was perfectly suited for their large-scale graphic work, Michael considered producing and selling the table to competitors. "Someone is going to eventually build such a table and market it, why shouldn't it be us?" he asked. However, members of his management staff convinced him that their time would be better served concentrating on their primary business. As a result, the company is investigating obtaining and then selling the patent for the table, another idea suggested to Michael by the MBA student team. Back-lighted signs are the newest NSP venture. Through a working agreement with the 3M Corporation, NSP implemented a "Roll N' Ship" program that allows them to design signage on one of 3M's translucent films that can be rolled into easily transportable tubes for damage-free shipping. This program allows firms with multilocation back-lighted signs to portray a consistent image.

CONCLUSION

Michael sees a bright future for NSP. Unlike his predecessors, he does not plan to move conservatively. He sees himself as a risk-taker, full of new ideas for NSP. He sees his company on the brink of a new era and he wants to move quickly. Changes are inevitable. He is convinced that the only way to survive is to diversify; to concentrate on his chosen 300 accounts and provide any service they request. Since his product is homogeneous, the extra service he feels is his only competitive edge. If this idea doesn't work, he is confident that he will find one that will.

Michael believes in NSP and he believes in the concept of ESOP. With the employees in command of the company he feels the company can only get better. As he puts it, "We control our own destiny because we own our own destiny."

APPENDIX 1: NSP SERVICES

A brief explanation of each NSP service follows.

- *Truckgraphix.*® Truckgraphix® is the trademark name for NSP's larger-than-life decals for the side of company vehicles. The decals offer a more cost-effective method of identification than paint and are used by more than 85 percent of trucks on the road today. Additionally, the decals last almost four times longer than paint. NSP's capabilities span from a simple one-color mark to full-color photographic reproductions, and are light-reflective for easy visibility at night. Truckgraphix® is used by such customers as Eastern Foods (Naturally Fresh), Food World, and Delta Airlines (ground equipment).

- *Creative Design Systems.* The company boasts of a staff of professionally trained graphic designers that can revise and update an existing logo or create a total corporate identity program.

- *Durabanners.*® Durabanners® is the registered name of NSP's posters and banners of the business. Using state-of-the-art equipment to produce their pressure-sensitive vinyl banners, the end products are created to last up to seven years.

- *Architectural and Environmental Graphics.* A new service offered by NSP, architectural and environmental graphics includes design services for both internal and external "re-imaging." This includes signage and other graphics, such as color bars, geometric shapes and symbols, and worded messages, developed to modernize a facility.

- *Decor.* The Decor Group deals with internal signage for supermarkets, drug and soft goods retailers, hardware and auto parts stores, and convenience and department stores. This includes such things as banners, aisle markers, shelf talkers, and displays.

- *Corporate Graphics.* Another new venture for NSP is corporate graphics. For interested customers, NSP will design a complete graphics package for a company that includes logos and letterhead paper.

- *Original Equipment Manufacturers.* NSP produces decals for installation by the manufacturers for such products as lawn mowers, ladders, boats, trailers, and snowmobiles. This market is considered a difficult one to break into because manufacturers rarely change this type of graphics and their current suppliers.

- *Service Systems.* Installation is a final step to NSP's graphics. The company either offers personal installation, or provides the customer with a detailed how-to book for easy application.

CASE 34

St. Charles Transfer Company Dilemma

Lynda L. Goulet, University of Northern Iowa; Jeffery Foulk,
Vice President of an affiliated moving agency

THE INITIAL MEETING IN JANUARY

On a sunny but bone-chilling January morning, Bert Christensen, president of the New Meadows Transfer Company, passed the coffee and donuts to Scott Sorenson, president of S&S Transfer Company, and Ted Thompson, president of St. Charles Transfer Company. All three owned and operated moving company agencies that were affiliated as agent representatives of Mayflower Transit Company, the fourth largest nationwide household goods carrier in the United States. Ted, Scott, and Bert had known each other for a very long time. Their relationship had evolved from many years of late nights at Mayflower conventions and family weekends at Bert's cabin. In fact, the friendship was such that other Mayflower agents and Mayflower Transit personnel referred to them as "The Three Musketeers."

Ironically, the Mayflower agents had gathered at the request of Joe Stavely, agent/recruiter for Allied Van Lines, another major nationwide household goods moving carrier. Joe arrived at the New Meadows Transfer Company office just as Bert was pouring the next round of coffee. After congenial introductions and a few good-natured barbs regarding the condition of each van line's equipment, the meeting commenced.

"Gentlemen, it's no secret that Allied Van Lines has a serious problem in your part of the state," Joe announced quite earnestly. "In less than two months Ajax Transfer Agencies will close their doors and leave Allied without any

---

This case is intended for class discussion, not to illustrate either effective or ineffective handling of an administrative situation. The names of the local firms, owners, and locations have been disguised to preserve the firms' desire for anonymity.

Presented to and accepted by the Midwest Society for Case Research. All rights reserved to the authors and the MSCR. Copyright 1992 by Lynda Goulet and Jeffery Foulk.

representation in numerous market areas within the state. Allied is most anxious to replace the agencies it will lose in the four larger cities—New Meadows, Grandview, Hill City, and St. Charles—by the end of March."

■ The Situation at Ajax

Ajax Freight, Inc. consisted of two businesses: the Ajax Freight Company and the Ajax Transfer Company. The freight line business accounted for over half of the firm's total sales and virtually all of its profits. Ajax Transfer Company had been affiliated with Allied Van Lines for over twenty years and, in the late 1970s and early 1980s, developed a network of nine Allied-affiliated moving agencies statewide. Ajax's larger agencies were located in New Meadows, Grandview, Hill City, and St. Charles. (Refer to Exhibit 1.) These agencies were neither the largest nor the smallest moving agencies in their respective local markets. In terms of equipment, facilities, and personnel, the agencies in these four cities were approximately half the size of their Mayflower counterparts.

The household goods moving business was developed by the president and founder of Ajax Freight, Arnie Jackson. He devoted almost all his time to this business, leaving his sons to operate the freight business. During the past year, Arnie Jackson had been killed in an auto accident and his sons assumed control of the firm. Since that time, the Jackson brothers instituted numerous personnel and policy changes in the household goods moving business to streamline operations and reduce operating costs. In spite of these changes, the Ajax Transfer Company was unable to sufficiently improve its profitability, and the brothers decided to eliminate the business unit and, with it, Ajax's affiliation with Allied Van Lines. Household goods moving operations would cease at all locations by April 1. Ajax Freight, Inc., however, would continue to operate. The freight side of the business operated in almost all of the same markets as the household goods moving business and, in most locations, shared some of the facilities such as the office and warehouse. Any assets of the Ajax Transfer Company that were unnecessary for the continued operation of the freight business would be liquidated.

Joe Stavely was a very good judge of human nature and a shrewd businessman. He knew what it might cost Allied to start up new agencies from scratch and decided it would be more beneficial to recruit existing agents of other carriers in the target markets. Joe was also aware of the reputation for quality and service of the three Mayflower agents to whom he was speaking, as well as their close personal relationship. He felt that a mass switch to Allied was possible and that such a move would provide substantial benefits to Allied.

■ Household Goods Moving

The household goods moving industry generates sales from local, intrastate, and interstate moving operations. Based upon estimated total revenues for household goods moving of $6.5 billion in 1990, the five largest nationwide moving companies and their agents control about 30% of the total moving revenues in the United States. The leaders include North American Van Lines, Allied Van Lines, United Van Lines, Mayflower Transit Company, and Bekins Van Lines. (Refer to Exhibit 2 for information on revenues and shipments.) These five "mother van lines" and approximately one hundred other firms are designated by the Interstate Commerce Commission as class I movers, each

Map of Local Moving Agencies **Exhibit 1**

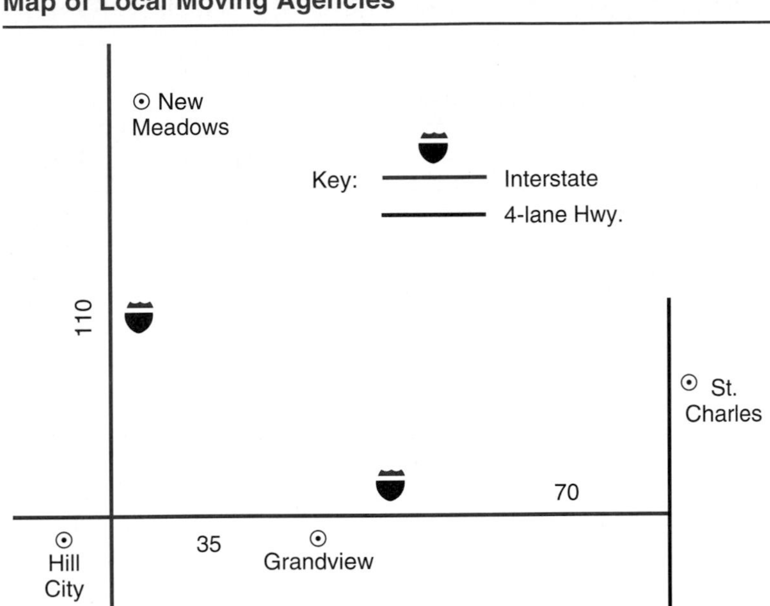

New Meadows
Population = 355,000
Estimated size of moving market:
$6.5 million
Local moving agents:
New Meadows (Mayflower)
Ajax Transfer (Allied)
10 other affiliated moving agents
7 local moving agencies

Grandview
Population = 170,000
Estimated size of moving market:
$2.2 million
Local moving agents:
S & S Transfer (Mayflower)
Ajax Transfer (Allied)
4 other affiliated moving agents
3 local moving agencies

Hill City
Population = 95,000
Estimated size of moving market:
$1.65 million
Local moving agents:
S & S Transfer (Mayflower)
Ajax Transfer (Allied)
3 other affiliated moving agents
1 local moving agency

St. Charles
Population = 140,000
Estimated size of moving market:
$1.25 million
Local moving agents:
St. Charles Transfer (Mayflower)
Ajax Transfer (Allied)
2 other affiliated moving agents
2 local moving agencies

producing over $5 million in annual revenues. Approximately 3,100 other interstate movers are designated as either class II or class III, with annual revenues less than $5 million. Class II or III movers may perform some level of nationwide moving. However, due to a smaller agency network, or no agency network at all, the majority of the business generated by firms in these classes is regional or local. Approximately 2,000 of the interstate carriers are members of the Household Goods Carrier's Bureau (HHGCB).

The larger class I carriers have extensive agency representation in local markets either through privately owned local moving companies that have a

Exhibit 2

Comparative Analysis of the Five Largest and Other Major Interstate Household Goods Carriers*

	Revenues (in millions of dollars)				
Year	*North American*	*Allied*	*United*	*Mayflower*	*Bekins*
1980	259.0	291.9	239.6	181.6	125.8
1981	297.5	302.6	259.7	192.5	153.8
1982	298.4	273.9	239.7	192.9	168.0
1983	343.2	300.3	262.2	213.6	165.8
1984	403.0	353.9	328.4	261.9	203.3
1985	428.8	370.4	351.1	291.8	199.7
1986	458.0	376.9	382.9	299.0	197.6
1987	507.8	382.7	404.5	300.3	207.1
1988	540.4	383.6	425.6	309.8	203.8
1989	559.5	406.0	452.7	320.4	202.2
1990	549.2	398.6	457.3	305.9	202.3

	Number of Shipments (in thousands)				
Year	*North American*	*Allied*	*United*	*Mayflower*	*Bekins*
1980	213.3	270.2	194.7	149.1	106.1
1981	220.2	267.1	203.0	141.2	119.1
1982	217.1	232.8	182.9	136.4	133.3
1983	243.5	258.1	194.6	144.2	134.9
1984	271.3	265.7	214.4	164.5	163.8
1985	272.1	263.7	228.9	179.8	169.1
1986	293.5	249.3	228.7	180.5	164.5
1987	349.8	261.5	242.3	187.6	185.6
1988	371.4	252.0	246.3	193.6	173.1
1989	369.1	256.4	234.4	193.8	170.3
1990	378.3	243.0	237.1	176.0	172.2

	Annual Shipments (in thousands)		
Other Major Household Goods Carriers	*1980*	*1985*	*1990*
Burnham Service Company	39.0	73.6	156.9
Atlas Van Lines	92.3	90.2	93.0
Global Van Lines	59.6	41.9	26.4
Graebel Van Lines		11.8	25.3
Wheaton Van Lines	29.5	22.0	23.3
Paul Arpin Van Lines	6.5	17.1	20.7
Pan American Van Lines	17.5	18.8	18.5
National Van Lines	11.1	11.3	18.3
American Red Ball	20.7	13.1	12.4

Sources: Household Goods Carrier's Bureau, *Moving Industry Financial Statistics,* 1990, pp. 32, 44; Household Goods Carrier's Bureau, *Quarterly Operating Statistics,* 1980 through 1990.

*Total revenue (shipments) reflects all revenues (shipments) generated by the firms above, including both long-distance and local household goods moving, for the national carrier, as well as the carrier's affiliated agents.

contractual agreement to represent the "mother van line" or through carrier-owned agencies. Together, these agencies provide the mother van line (class I carrier) with long-distance moving orders, perform various local services for the carrier, and provide other local moving and related services.

When a privately owned, affiliated agency "sells" a long-distance moving order, the charges for the move are paid by the customer directly to the mother van line, who in turn pays the local agency a writing commission from the revenues received. When the local agency transports goods long distance for the carrier, the agency receives a base-hauling commission from the revenues received by the carrier. The local agencies are also reimbursed, in full, for any revenues received by the mother van line that represent charges for local packing, storage, or other services associated with a long-distance move that were performed by the local agency. In contrast, local moves sold by the privately owned local agency do not directly involve the "mother van line." The charges for such local moves are paid by the customer directly to the local agency.

The nationwide class I carriers also maintain their own carrier fleet (truck-tractors and trailer units), in addition to having carrier-owned local agencies. However, some of the carriers, such as Allied, operate a relatively small carrier fleet, relying on their local affiliated agencies to perform the majority of long-distance hauling within the moving system. Thus, the actual hauling of household goods by the major carriers is performed by either agency-operated or carrier-operated vehicles. Furthermore, the drivers are either employees of the local agency, contract drivers who have an arrangement with the local agency or the national carrier or its carrier-owned local agencies, or drivers employed by the national carrier. Contract drivers own their own truck-tractors, and pull trailers (vans) are owned by the local agency or national carrier. They pay their own expenses associated with a move and receive their revenue from the agency or carrier with which they have a contract. When such contract drivers perform long-distance moving services for which the local agency receives a base-hauling commission from the national carrier, the contract driver is paid a percentage of the base-hauling commission received by the local agency.

■ Joe Stavely's Presentation

Recognizing that the decision to switch affiliation was likely to hinge on a comparison of the economic benefits between the local agency's present affiliation and Allied's compensation package, Joe Stavely continued his presentation to the three agency owners.

"Allied is committed to improving its leadership position in the household goods moving industry by developing quality agents and recruiting only those agents that exhibit a first-class image. In order to attract agents like yourselves, Allied has an outstanding compensation schedule related to long-distance moves.

"The compensation program Allied offers has two features that should be of interest to you. First, Allied pays you $50 for each customer visit under its exclusive Welcome Home™ program. When Allied moves a [long-distance] shipment into your area, just have one of your reps stop at the house and have the customer verify the visit with a signature. In addition to your regular writing commission [for long-distance moves originating in the local market], if you increase your quarterly sales from one year to the next, Allied will pay you a bonus based on your improvement. Now I won't mislead you, the writing commission itself for a long-distance move order may be slightly less than with Mayflower, but when you combine the writing commission, the Welcome Home™ fee, and the sales bonus, you can easily exceed your current writing commissions.

"Second, we encourage our agents to haul shipments and reflect this with a base-hauling commission 2% more than what you are getting with Mayflower. To enhance the ability for local Allied agencies [or their contract drivers] to haul the majority of Allied shipments, we have instituted a computer link between our central dispatching department at Allied headquarters and the majority of Allied's local agents. The system allows the local agents an option of constructing their own backhauls [loads originating in the shipment's destination area] from registered Allied loads from around the country. A local agent could deliver a shipment to a distant location, knowing there would be a very good chance of getting at least a partial load back to the local area. Also, let me assure you that the Allied policy has always allowed our agents to haul the vast majority of tonnage. Of course, Allied does have a few contract drivers operating directly through Allied Van Lines, but unlike Mayflower's own sizable contract fleet, Allied's contract drivers will not compete with you for existing shipments within our dispatch system. [Their loads are arranged from new move orders before the new orders are entered into the dispatch system.]

"Gentlemen, you understand my predicament and what Allied has to offer as a mother van line. I am interested in each of you becoming Allied representatives in your respective cities, but please understand that I need commitments very shortly. In the meantime, I will be working with other prospects in the event you choose to remain with Mayflower. I will contact each of you individually in the next few days."

Although commissions and hauling policy were major concerns to the three Mayflower agents, there were many other issues to consider with a change of affiliation. All three agents had been associated with Mayflower for many years, and all agency insignias, uniforms, and equipment would need to be reidentified in accordance with Allied Van Lines' specifications. Joe assured the owners that these and other factors would be dealt with on an individual basis. He added that Allied would also provide training support for introducing all agency personnel to Allied's policies and procedures.

THE SITUATION AT ST. CHARLES TRANSFER IN EARLY MARCH

Subsequent to the January meeting, Ted Thompson, the owner of the St. Charles Transfer Company, had begun to explore the potential of expanding his own agency into other cities. Since New Meadows was geographically too far from St. Charles, the only logical expansion alternatives worth considering were Grandview and Hill City. If Scott's S&S Transfer, with locations in both of these communities, remained with Mayflower, then Ted's firm could switch to Allied and expand into either or both of these locations. Of course, it would be even better if Scott changed affiliations, because then Ted could consider expansion without all the hassle. Ted also considered the personal relationship aspect of the decision. What would happen to them if they didn't all do the same thing? Because they were all Mayflower agencies in different cities, they really didn't compete with one another. But if their affiliations differed, the temptation to expand into each other's territory could significantly alter that relationship and have tremendous implications for their friendship. On the other hand, business was business and each had to do what he thought best for his own company.

By the end of February it was clear that the other two men had made their decisions. Bert (New Meadows Transfer) had accepted the offer from Allied, but Scott (S&S Transfer) had turned Joe, and Allied, down. The eraser on the end of the pencil tapped on the desk pad while Ted stared out the window of his office at the St. Charles Transfer truck yard. He noticed water from melting snow had filled tracks in the lawn left by someone's truck turning the corner too short. Every year it was the same problem and the thought had always been the same: "I ought to sink a couple of posts at the edge of the curb to provide markers for the drivers." This springlike day, however, that thought never came to mind. Ted was contemplating the events of the past few weeks and had only three days, until Friday, to decide whether to commit to major changes in the family-owned business.

■ Allied's Final Offer to St. Charles Transfer

Joe Stavely and two other representatives from Allied had flown into St. Charles to present their final offer to Ted. Allied would prefer to see St. Charles Transfer operate agencies for them in all three markets to be vacated by Ajax's dissolution, but would be satisfied if the firm expanded only into Grandview at the present time. As Ted pointed out to them, he would not switch if he weren't going to expand, so at least they agreed on the expansion point. However, Ted did not see how it would be possible to expand into both locations at once. Since the prime moving months would be starting in a matter of a few weeks, St. Charles Transfer would have to act quickly. Opening one new location and changing over everything in St. Charles to meet Allied requirements would be enough of a problem. Since Allied had no other "nibbles" for an agency in Hill City at the present time, it would be willing to give Ted the option of expanding into Hill City later in the year. Beyond that, Allied would give Ted the right of first refusal if another firm were interested in becoming an Allied agent in Hill City. Of course, that would require Ted to open up an agency immediately if he accepted.

In St. Charles the switch to Allied would be relatively simple compared to the time and effort required to establish a new office, acquire the necessary equipment, and hire and train personnel for Grandview. Additionally, Ted would have to consider changing the name of the firm, since it would be inappropriate to use the current name in Grandview. Allied's offer included the repainting of all St. Charles's equipment to Allied specifications at no charge. Allied would also provide a three-month supply of sales literature at no cost. Further, to help provide cash flow for the transition period, Allied agreed to provide a no-interest, six-month loan amounting to 80% of the firm's current accounts receivable balance from Mayflower. Ted had anticipated that possible delays in payments from Mayflower were likely and would create a severe cash shortage for St. Charles Transfer at the time it would be in the most need of funds. Allied also agreed to place temporarily in the firm's two offices the phone lines of Ajax's offices in St. Charles and Grandview when they closed. This could be very important since new phone books would not be available until the summer. Potential customers attempting to reach Allied's agents, through Ajax's listings, would be able to get through to St. Charles Transfer.

The last item that Allied's offer included was two free ALLFAX™ electronic estimators, one for each office, with a value of around $5,000. Allied was the leader in the implementation of electronic estimating. Their estimator calculated, stored, and produced hard-copy moving estimates based upon information fed into the unit by the agent sales representative. St. Charles Transfer did not use any kind of electronic system for estimation and had not perceived the need to do so, but admitted that it would be very helpful.

■ Conversation at St. Charles Transfer's Office

"Well, they're on their way back to Chicago," Bill Robertson, operations manager for St. Charles Transfer, announced as he stepped into Ted's office. Bill had just returned from driving the Allied Van Lines recruiters to the airport. He planted himself in the chair across from Ted's desk. "What do you think? Do we switch and open up in Grandview or not? It's hard to imagine Bert went with Allied without Scott doing the same." Bill shook his head. "I suppose it's because New Meadows is more of a commercial account town [company-paid moves rather than personal moves] and Allied seems to have an edge in that market. [The mother van lines have 'national commercial accounts' with large, multilocation businesses. When such firms transfer their management personnel from one location to another, they use the van line with which they have a contractual arrangement.] We don't have all that much commercial business here, and neither does Grandview, so I'm not sure if it'll make any difference if we stay with Mayflower or go with Allied. Both are well-known national movers. Who's gonna care if we drive orange or green trucks!"

Ted leaned back in his chair. "I wouldn't think it'd make that much difference, but let's face it, we've got Allied beat by a long shot for long-distance moves originating here. We've been with Mayflower ever since the business was founded, and they have the most recognized name in the moving business. You've read the marketing surveys. Unfortunately, this town isn't growing all that much. That's why opening up elsewhere is attractive. But it's not just giving up the Mayflower name that I'm worrying about. What about Leon? Leon's the best contract driver we've ever had. He's been with us for 20 years and, as you know, is really proud of being a member of Mayflower's Elite Fleet. [A group consisting of contract drivers who have exhibited exceptional performance ratings in the areas of low-damage claims, on-time delivery, and traffic safety.] He consistently earns 20% to 30% more in revenues than the average contract driver and gets preference for backhauls as well. [Leon's recent revenue was $130,000, compared to the average of $103,000 for owner-operator drivers under contract to Mayflower or local agencies affiliated with Mayflower.] Unless Allied can guarantee at least as much transportation revenue with them as he gets from Mayflower, Leon may tell us to go fly a kite. With his reputation, Mayflower headquarters would gladly sign him up as a full-time contract driver for them! As hard as it is to find drivers, especially good ones, we can't afford to lose him."

The two thought for a moment, then Ted broke the silence. "I just wish Grandview were 20 miles closer. I don't like the idea of having to hire and train people when you can't keep tabs on them. What do you do when Grandview is over an hour away? I'd certainly have to find an office manager I could trust."

Bill instantly thought of Ace. Ace was John Samuels, the former sales manager for St. Charles Transfer. His first few years with St. Charles had been very successful, but when the local economy experienced a recession and his sales commissions fell, he resigned. "What about Ace? I know it sounds crazy, but he knows the business and is good at selling. Sales will be what we need if we expand. He wasn't a detail man, but he was very good with people and knew how to sell moves, probably as a result of an earlier career of selling used cars."

Ted responded immediately. "I don't think so. He's now working for one of our unaffiliated competitors, and I can't believe he's making any more money than he was with us. I don't really know why he left, but somehow I'm convinced the money was just an excuse. Besides, we probably ought to give serious consideration to the Ajax people, but I don't know any of them. They should be willing to listen since they'll be out of jobs by April, but I don't think they will. From everything I've heard, Ajax pays its management a lot more than we do. They can afford to since they're not unionized like we are and their labor costs are much lower. What I really can't understand is why the company wasn't profitable."

After a brief pause, Ted continued. "At the last Mayflower convention, I spoke with an agent from another state who had multiple locations in separate cities. He had opened a nonunion operation within 120 miles of his unionized agency a year before. So far he hadn't had any big problems, but each agency was set up as an independent company and operated completely separately. I don't know if I'd want that kind of complicated arrangement just to minimize the union threat. There are times, I'd imagine, when it would be helpful to send extra trucks and people over to Grandview and vice versa. But we can't do that if Grandview's nonunion. And I'd certainly prefer to have it that way, to keep costs down. Between their hourly wage and fringes, our people are costing us nearly $20 an hour. As near as I can figure it, a nonunion operation would cost us only half of that."

After pausing a couple of minutes to let all that Ted had said sink in, Bill responded to some issues Ted had raised. "If we kept the operations in the two cities separate, we probably could avoid being unionized in Grandview, just as your friend from the convention managed to do. The extra profit might be worth all the extra red tape. But as far as the Leon problem goes, to my way of thinking, it's not just Leon that's an issue, but getting drivers, period. We still have a problem getting good drivers here, in spite of the relatively high unemployment rate. Those who can drive don't like the idea of loading and unloading furniture as well. And those who apply don't seem to have the kind of driving records we need to keep our reputation up and insurance rates down. Since the economy's better in other parts of the state, we could really have problems recruiting."

"You know, Bill," continued Ted, "I imagine Scott is thinking along the same lines we are. He's now got an excellent chance to expand into New Meadows and, if we switch, he could open up here, too. He knows he'd have to deal with the union situation and the lack of drivers if he opened up here, so I'm not sure he'd be so eager to move into St. Charles. But someone probably would. Mayflower wouldn't be happy to lose us. We've got too big a share of the long-distance market here. They'd be real anxious to find a new agent, fast."

As Ted stared out of the office window, another truck turned the corner too sharply, deepening the rut in the lawn. Ted didn't even notice. "Bill, as I see it the easiest thing to do would be forget about it and stay with Mayflower. But having this type of opportunity to grow, to open new agencies, comes along only once in a while. Darn it, I just wish I had more time to consider alternatives. And I sure wish it weren't so critical to get set up in Grandview before the end of the month!"

THE HOUSEHOLD GOODS MOVING INDUSTRY

Prior to the turn of the twentieth century, the belongings of most families were few enough that, when it was time to relocate, the family made their own arrangements and moved by whatever means were available. As possessions and home size increased, so did the demand for a moving service industry. By the 1920s, the moving and storage industry was comprised of many multistory warehouses and local drayage services utilizing horse teams, wagons, and occasionally, motorized vehicles. The local warehouse firm would pack smaller items in boxes at the customer's residence. The warehouse firm would then arrange to move all items out of the home to the warehouse, where the entire shipment would be crated in wooden containers. This was accomplished either through the use of a drayage firm or with the warehouse firm's own drayage equipment, if the firm had such equipment. Once the goods were crated, it would then be the responsibility of the person moving to arrange and coordinate the goods shipment, usually by rail, and the required warehousing and drayage service at the destination.

The inconvenience of this process created the opportunity for firms to assume all aspects of a relocation. By the mid-1920s, both Red Ball Transit Company and Mayflower Transit Company had opened company booking offices in selected cities for the purpose of arranging moving services involving any of the cities in which they had offices, using company-owned moving vans. Any storage services would be provided by local warehouses as needed, by transit company arrangements. Then in 1930 the Baltimore Storage Company approached Mayflower Transit with a proposal to represent Mayflower as an agent/booker. Since Mayflower did not have a location in Baltimore, this arrangement permitted Mayflower to geographically expand its services without having to open a new office. It did not take long for other local warehouses and long-distance moving companies to recognize the efficiencies of this type of cooperative effort between the van line and its warehouse agents. These associations have continued to the present time in almost the same form as when they were originally conceived. The local warehouse/agent firm performs local packing, storage, and local moving services. Long-distance moves are arranged through the affiliation with the "mother van line."

Both Mayflower and Allied were original innovators in developing agency networks. Many agents that signed on at the outset of nationwide expansion of these two carriers have retained their affiliation for over half a century. Mayflower's local agents have even formed their own association, apart from the mother van line. This association addresses business concerns, presents new ideas, and promotes relationships among the various agents.

■ Regulation of the Motor Carrier Industry

The Motor Carrier Act of 1935 brought under regulation all forms of motor carrier transportation that operate on public highways and designated the Interstate Commerce Commission (ICC) as the regulatory body for the interstate motor carrier industry. The ICC supervised the operating procedures of carriers and reserved the authority to dictate the scope of operations and service levels a carrier would be required to provide to a market. Additionally, the ICC authorized only certain numbers and type of carriers to operate within a given market. Price differentiation for identical services was very rarely allowed, and competition was based upon the quality of service, which was closely monitored by the ICC.

The Motor Carrier Act of 1980 and the Household Goods Act of 1980 initiated a change in the previous regulation. Entry regulations were eased, allowing easier entry into interstate trucking. The change in regulation also permitted greater price competition. Instead of having set rates charged by all movers for the same service, price and service option discounts, commercial contracts with negotiated prices, and other options were permitted. The greater number of interstate carriers, coupled with the carriers' ability and need to price competitively, put a great deal of downward pressure on freight rates and on profits. This trend of declining profits can be seen in Exhibit 3. Both sampled groups of household goods carriers recorded profit margins of only 1% in 1989, compared to margins of almost 3% in 1980. Actual net income in dollars was at its lowest level by the end of the decade for both groups, despite growing revenues over the period.

Average Revenue and Net Income for Selected Household Goods Carriers* **Exhibit 3**

	Class I & II Carriers		*Class III Carriers*	
Year	*Revenue*	*Net Income*	*Revenue*	*Net Income*
1980	$2,662,200	$ 77,200	$383,900	$11,000
1981	2,864,200	76,800	408,500	7,200
1982	2,900,900	61,500	404,500	5,500
1983	3,341,700	72,800	437,600	16,700
1984	3,846,300	107,400	464,600	26,600
1985	4,202,500	74,100	503,700	17,500
1986	3,897,700	84,300	461,200	13,800
1987	4,252,300	90,500	444,200	16,900
1988	4,301,900	82,400	446,600	3,900
1989	4,542,100	48,500	501,400	5,200

Source: Household Goods Carrier's Bureau, *Moving Industry Financial Statistics*, 1990.

*Figures reflect averages based on sample data collected by the Household Goods Carrier's Bureau; sample size for class I (revenue over $5 million) and class II (revenue between $1 million and $5 million) carriers was over 500 firms; sample size for class III (revenue less than $1 million) carriers was approximately 2,700 firms.

The deregulation of the industry also created a driver shortage. Since more motor carriers entered the industry, driver demand increased more rapidly than the supply of qualified drivers. This shortage caused some trucking companies to actually lower their driver qualification standards and hire personnel with poor driving records and little experience. Furthermore, the downward pressure on rates and profits resulted in lower pay rates for drivers, though this trend has begun to turn around as firms work to retain their driver fleet. Many trucking firms have instituted driver recognition and safety programs to show appreciation for driver achievement and to improve the image of the driver and the industry.

A related problem involves insurance. The trucking industry has experienced a crisis involving the cost and availability of liability coverage for its truck fleets. A combination of overall increases in insurance premiums and a perception of increased risks associated with underwriting trucking company insurance has left many trucking firms with doubled or tripled premiums, increased deductibles, or no insurance coverage at all. Truck liability insurance is not the only insurance protection that has increased. Workmen's compensation insurance has risen, attributed primarily to greater exposure to back injuries. Cargo coverage, for protection against damage to transported goods, has also significantly increased. Many carriers are now self-insuring their cargoes for all but catastrophic events. St. Charles Transfer experienced first-hand the insurance problem in 1985 when the company's insurance agent for the past 25 years notified the firm that the underwriting insurance carrier would not renew coverage. Negotiations with another insurance firm produced less coverage and a higher premium.

■ The Process of Household Goods Moving

Trucks and trailers used to move household goods constitute the major investment for local moving agencies. A truckload of household goods will weigh in the vicinity of 18,000 to 24,000 pounds, compared to a load of freight goods weighing in excess of 50,000 pounds. For this reason, the equipment used in household goods transport has different characteristics from typical truck-tractors and trailer units. The truck-tractor used to pull furniture trailers does not need to possess the power and structural capacity of a large general freight type unit. Many moving agencies will use smaller, single-drive axle tractors, which are adequate for the lesser weight associated with household goods. These tractors initially are less costly to purchase and are also less expensive to operate, considering fuel, licensing costs, and insurance costs. The price of such new tractors, however, ranges from $50,000 to $65,000, depending on features.

The majority of trailers (vans) used for transporting household goods are specially equipped, high-volume trailers. A 48-foot furniture trailer will have nearly 4,200 cubic feet of space and be equipped with over 200 quilted pads for wrapping furniture, dollies and carts for carrying large items, ladders for stacking to the full ten-foot-plus inside height, and a ramp for loading from ground level. The total cost of such a fully equipped trailer is about $35,000. An innovative feature that nearly all household goods movers have adopted is the addition of air-cushion bags used as shock-absorption devices between the trailer "box" and the axle assembly. "Air-ride suspension" gives the loaded items a much smoother ride and has allowed moving companies to haul items of a more fragile nature, such as artwork and electronics.

Household goods moving services consist of packing, loading, driving, and delivery. Packing service entails wrapping and packing into cardboard containers such items as clothes, pictures, dishes, books, and knick-knacks. Once the goods are prepared for moving, whether packed by the customer or the moving agent, the goods must be loaded onto the trailer, padded, and strapped into place. In some moves the belongings must be unloaded into the agent's warehouse for a period of time, before being again loaded and driven to the destination. At the destination site, the household goods would be unloaded from the trailer, placed in the home as requested, and unpacked by either the customer or the moving agent at the destination location.

Moving services are labor intensive. Packing, for example, is time consuming and commands a high profit margin. The amount of labor required to fully pack an average three-bedroom home will total 24 to 32 man-hours and cost the customer $1,500 to $2,000. Full packing service of a one- or two-bedroom apartment may cost the customer $400 to $700, while a large home may generate packing revenues in excess of $3,000. Charges are usually assessed by the number and size of cartons required, including costs for the materials and a per-carton labor rate for packing service. Material cost is approximately 15% to 20% of the total packing cost for the customer.

The major portion of a customer's moving expense is, nevertheless, transportation related, comprised of loading, transporting, and unloading services. Labor for loading the average three-bedroom home can amount to 24 to 30 man-hours, while unloading will typically require only three-fourths of the loading time. Because local moves are labor intensive and the mileage involved is generally low, local moving transportation charges are generally assessed on an hourly basis. Long-distance moving charges are assessed on a combination of shipment weight and mileage moved and are in addition to any packing or miscellaneous service rendered. For comparison, the contents of a one- or two-bedroom apartment, weighing 3,000 pounds, to be moved 450 miles can cost the consumer $1,100 to $1,300 in transportation charges; the contents of an average three-bedroom home, weighing 10,000 to 14,000 pounds, to be moved the same distance would result in transportation charges in the $2,500 to $3,500 range; and the contents of a larger dwelling, weighing 18,000 to 22,000 pounds, would involve transportation charges from $4,000 to $4,600.

In addition to charging for any requested packing and unpacking services and loading, driving, and unloading services, a household goods moving agency may generate revenues from other services provided. Customers who wish to do their own packing may purchase cardboard containers from the agent. The handling and disassembly/reassembly of large items may also result in an additional charge. Transit insurance coverage is chargeable to the customer. A customer may also desire storage services, in the event the family is not ready to move into the destination dwelling when their present dwelling must be vacated. A customer may also be willing to pay extra for a guaranteed pickup and delivery schedule. Alternatively, a mover may self-impose a penalty amounting to a cash reimbursement to a customer if pickup and delivery time frames are not met. It is customary for a mover to provide a customer with a two- or three-day window for pickup and a one-week to ten-day window for long-distance delivery. Some movers will also guarantee that an experienced, top-performing driver will be assigned to larger move orders.

■ Consumers of Household Goods Moving

A study conducted in 1986 by the Household Goods Carrier's Bureau revealed that nearly 43% of all household goods moving occurs in the four-month period between June and September. Considering that a majority of moves are performed for families with adults between 25 and 45 years old, it stands to reason that the busiest moving times would be during the summer, when their children are not in school. About 45% of long-distance moves are paid for by employers; 35% to 40% are individual (personal or COD) moves; and the remaining 15% to 20% involve military or civilian governmental personnel.

A majority of employer-paid moves are "full-service" moves in which the moving agencies provide packing and unpacking service, as well as transportation service. Many of these moves are made under contractual arrangements between the move-paying employer and the national carrier (national commercial accounts). COD moves are generally one-time arrangements between an individual and the agent/carrier. As might be expected, less service is usually performed by the carrier in this type of move. In the beginning of the 1980s, the average revenue for a national account move was about 1.6 times the average revenue for a COD move. However, by the end of the decade this ratio had dropped to below 1.4, indicating the gap between the two types of moves was narrowing.

In 1988, 17.6% of the U.S. population changed residency, up from 16.8% in 1984. (Data on mobility patterns, along with other demographic information related to household goods moving, appear in Exhibit 4.) Increased mobility, coupled with the consumer information movement, has resulted in more knowledgeable customers concerning the operations and services of moving

Exhibit 4

Demographic Information Related to Household Goods Moving

Demographic	*1980*	*1990*
U.S. population (in millions)	227.7	250.0
No. households (in thousands)	80,776	93,347
Average household size	2.76	2.63
Median income of households	$17,710	$28,906 (1989)
% of households by size of household		
1 person	22.7%	24.6%
2 people	31.4%	32.3%
3 people	17.5%	17.3%
4 people	15.7%	15.5%
5 or more	12.8%	10.4%
% of households by age of householder		
15–24	8.1%	5.5%
25–34	23.0%	21.9%
35–44	17.3%	22.0%
45–54	15.7%	15.5%
55–64	15.5%	13.4%
65+	20.3%	21.6%

(Continued)

Demographic Information Related to Household Goods Moving (continued)

Exhibit 4

Consumer Price Index (all items)

1980:	82.4	1983:	99.6	1986:	109.6	1989:	124.0
1981:	90.9	1984:	103.9	1987:	113.6	1990:	130.7
1982:	96.5	1985:	107.6	1988:	118.3		

Demographic	***1983***	***1987***
U.S. population (in millions)	234.3	242.8
No. households (in thousands)	83,918	89,479
No. housing units (in thousands)	93,519	102,652
% of housing units by size		
1–3 rooms	14.5%	13.0%
4 rooms	19.1%	21.2%
5 rooms	23.5%	22.8%
6 rooms	19.6%	19.2%
7 or more	21.4%	23.8%
% of U.S. population moving		
Within same county	10.4%	11.3%
Same state, different county	3.6%	3.6%
Different state	2.8%	2.7%
Total in U.S. moving	16.8%	17.6%
from abroad	.5%	.5%
% of population moving by age group		
less than 19	18.0%	19.4%
20–24	34.1%	35.2%
25–29	30.0%	31.8%
30–44	16.9%	17.9%
45–54	8.7%	10.2%
55+	5.4%	5.8%

Money Income of Households (1986) (average median income: $28,168)

Income Levels	*% of Households*	*Average Disposable Income*
under $15,000	30.2%	$ 1,014
$15,000–$20,000	10.4	2,304
$20,000–$25,000	9.6	3,438
$25,000–$30,000	8.6	3,737
$30,000–$35,000	7.9	4,700
$35,000–$40,000	6.8	5,841
$40,000–$50,000	9.7	6,746
$50,000–$75,000	11.3	11,493
$75,000–$100,000	3.3	22,818
over $100,000	2.2	47,320

Source: U.S. Department of Commerce, *U.S. Statistical Abstract,* 1991, Tables 2, 25, 56, 59, 721, 770,1282.

companies. Further, a reduction in governmental regulation in the motor carrier industry has given the customer a great deal more leverage in negotiating the moving contract. Household goods carriers have responded to the deregulated environment by offering price discounts, service guarantees, and highly advertised quality control programs. The major carriers have all responded similarly to the changing marketplace. Thus, the primary source of differentiation in the moving marketplace is the local moving agency. While there are many agents who provide quality, professional service, some agents lack a well-trained sales force, employ inexperienced labor, use inadequate equipment, and have unsecured warehouse facilities. From the consumer's point of view, it is preferable to employ a local agent who can fulfill the need for a safe, well-arranged transfer of household possessions.

The local agent at the origination point is the key component in the long-distance moving chain. It is the local origin agent who provides the cost estimate, writes the contract, does any requested packing and/or warehousing, provides the loading personnel, and usually provides the drivers and equipment to move the goods to the destination. This agent also dispatches the move information to the national carrier, works with the national carrier to arrange the details of the move, and acts as a liaison between the customer and the national carrier. When the shipment arrives at the destination city, the driver obtains assistance to do the unloading from the local agency at or nearby the destination site. These arrangements will have been made by the origin agent. The destination agent, however, will provide any unpacking services that are requested and handle any problems that arise as a result of the move (such as a damage claim).

ST. CHARLES TRANSFER COMPANY OPERATIONS

St. Charles Transfer has been in the moving and storage business for over sixty years and has served as an agent for Mayflower Transit Company for nearly fifty years. The major lines of business for St. Charles Transfer consist of a storage warehouse for both household goods and commercial items; a local and statewide delivery service of commercial freight; local moving of household goods, offices, and industrial equipment; packing service; and long-distance moving. Exhibit 5, the recent income statement for the firm, identifies the sales contribution for each of these services. St. Charles Transfer's operating revenues have remained fairly stable over the past several years. Its income from operations has gradually deteriorated, however, reflecting increased transportation-related expenses, insurance costs, and the inability to raise prices on local moves. Prices on long-distance moves, based on a combination of shipment weight and mileage, are established by Mayflower and are competitive with other nationwide household goods carriers' prices. The firm's investment income normally is sufficient to more than offset its interest expense. However, during the past year St. Charles Transfer sold two truck-tractors and replaced them with newer equipment, as well as purchased an additional small van. This created an unusual gain on the sale of assets and additional long-term debt. The firm also pays out about half of its net income as dividends to stockholders, who are mostly family members.

St. Charles Transfer Company, Income Statement for Recent Year Ending December 31 **Exhibit 5**

Operating revenues			
Goods moving			
Long distance[1]	$313,900		
Local	15,500	$329,400	
Writing commissions		33,800	
Packing			
Long distance	$ 98,500		
Local	24,600	123,100	
Storage			
Long distance	$ 32,000		
Local	8,000		
Commercial	40,100	80,100	
Freight hauling		42,200	
Total operating revenue			$608,600
Operating expenses			
Salaried personnel[2]		$112,000	
Wages[2]		206,600	
Packing materials		23,500	
Depreciation		32,600	
Fuel, oil, repairs, etc.		36,600	
Taxes, income expense		42,900	
Leasing expense		21,800	
Insurance (all types)		93,700	
Other administrative expense		26,000	
Total operating expenses			(595,700)
Income from operations			$ 12,900
Other income[3]		$ 36,200	
Interest expense		(17,600)	
Other income, net			18,600
Income before taxes			$ 31,500
Taxes			(6,800)
Net income			$ 24,700

[1]St. Charles received $235,900 in base-hauling commissions from Mayflower from revenues generated by St. Charles's drivers and $78,000 in commissions from revenues generated by St. Charles's contract drivers for hauling shipments.

[2]Includes fringes.

[3]Two-thirds of other income reflects a gain on the sale of two used truck-tractors; one-third reflects dividend and interest income from the firm's investments.

St. Charles Transfer operates a 50,000-square-foot, single-story steel and concrete warehouse, the most modern warehouse in the area. Approximately half of the storage revenue each year is generated from commercial warehousing. Through state permits, the firm operates as an intrastate contract freight carrier. Since the truck-tractors used for household goods moving are quite suitable for use in lighter-weight freight hauling, the firm only needed to acquire freight trailers to engage in this line of activity. The freight business also complements the warehousing of commercial goods, since St. Charles Transfer has the ability to move products from a manufacturer to the warehouse and from the warehouse to the purchaser of the goods, as long as both the manufacturer's plant and the purchaser's location are within the state. Such commercial activity does not involve packing.

Although the firm has the equipment and personnel to move office equipment and some industrial products that require sensitive handling, its main business is the servicing of household goods moving, especially long-distance moving. Three other long-distance-affiliated agents operate within the St. Charles market, including Ajax. Nevertheless, St. Charles Transfer dominates this part of the market, writing approximately 40% of the long-distance moves originating in its metropolitan area. In contrast, Ajax's share of the long-distance market is 15%. Long-distance goods-moving revenue, as shown in Exhibit 5, reflects the base-hauling commissions St. Charles Transfer receives from Mayflower. Approximately $78,000 of these commissions represents St. Charles Transfer's share of transportation revenues generated by the firm's contract drivers. The remainder are revenues generated by the agency's own drivers.

Unlike its contract drivers, who actively seek backhauls on long-distance moves, St. Charles Transfer is more concerned with having its drivers return to St. Charles as soon as possible, to minimize the firm's need for additional labor. This means that the firm's trailers are usually empty one way of every trip. Thus, of the 70,000 long-distance miles driven last year to make the 100 long-distance moves, only half reflect mileage associated with moving revenue. Because of the firm's desire to limit its drivers' time on the road, the firm's customers tend to be those who are anxious to have immediate delivery service, rather than have the agency schedule the move for when it can arrange backhauls. This approach to doing business is somewhat unusual, and Ted considered it to be one of the main reasons why the firm had a strong market share.

Writing commissions are also received from Mayflower as payment for obtaining a long-distance move originating within the St. Charles area. The writing commission and base-hauling revenue from long-distance moves are typically received from Mayflower one to two months after the services have been provided. For this reason, the firm's accounts receivable balance is typically large, especially during the height of the moving season. This is fairly standard within the industry and reflects the fact that the customer of the long-distance move makes payment directly to the national carrier, who must then remunerate the local agencies that participated in the move, according to the national carrier's agent compensation program. When St. Charles Transfer provides packing, storage, or other special services (not transportation related) for a long-distance move, such revenues are 100% reimbursed by Mayflower after the customer makes payment. About 80% of the firm's packing revenues and 40% of the total storage revenues derive from long-distance moves.

In addition to St. Charles Transfer's three rivals in long-distance moving, two other firms in the area compete exclusively in the local moving market. St. Charles Transfer has approximately a 20% share of the local moving market, while Ajax and one of the independent local agencies each have a 25% share. The other three firms have about equal shares of the remaining market. (The other independent agency is mainly involved in commercial freight hauling.) In local moves, the customer pays St. Charles Transfer directly for all services rendered. Ten percent of the firm's total storage revenue and 20% of the packing revenue is derived from local moving business. Revenue from local moves associated with the actual loading, transportation, and unloading is recorded on the firm's income statement as local goods moving revenue. St. Charles Transfer's approach to the local moving market is somewhat selective, preferring to bid on moves that involve packing services.

St. Charles Transfer also owns four truck-tractors, four trailers, and three small van/trucks. The firm also leases four trailers on a long-term basis, a common practice within the trucking industry. The annual cost of such arrangements appears as rental expense in the income statement. Recent equipment purchases are responsible for the majority of the firm's long-term debt and interest expense, as shown in Exhibits 5 and 6.

St. Charles Transfer employs the equivalence of five full-time nonoffice employees, who are paid on a time-and-mileage basis. These people are primarily occupied with packing, loading, and driving, as well as maintaining the

St. Charles Transfer Company, Balance Sheet for Recent Year Ending December 31 **Exhibit 6**

Assets		
Current assets		
Cash	$ 25,300	
Accounts receivable[1]	51,200	
Warehouse supplies	13,000	
Prepaid expenses	26,600	
Total current assets		$116,100
Fixed assets		
Land and buildings	$311,000	
Equipment	363,400	
Accumulated depreciation	(336,600)	
Net fixed assets		337,800
Other assets		
Investments		136,400
Total assets		$590,300
Liabilities and Equity		
Current liabilities		
Accounts payable	$ 34,000	
Notes payable	35,900	
Accrued expenses	49,200	
Total current liabilities		$119,100
Long-term liabilities		
Mortgage debt	$ 19,400	
Other debt[2]	133,400	
Total long-term liabilities		152,800
Total liabilities		$271,900
Equity		
Common stock	$ 86,000	
Retained earnings	232,400	
Total equity		318,400
Total liabilities and equity		$590,300

[1]$39,100 of the accounts receivable outstanding are owed by Mayflower for base-hauling and writing commissions.

[2]Debt recently acquired to purchase two new truck-tractors and a van.

equipment and warehouse. In addition to Ted Thompson and Bill Robertson, the firm employs a full-time secretary/bookkeeper. Bill, as operations manager, is responsible for most of the management activities associated with the terminal and warehouse, including dispatching, claims work, and coordination with Mayflower. Ted devotes most of his time to sales, moving estimate preparation, and order writing. The firm also has arrangements with four contract drivers, including Leon, who own their own truck-tractors and pull trailers owned by St. Charles Transfer. All of these contract drivers are approved by Mayflower Transit to haul long-distance orders generated by any of Mayflower's agencies, now numbering approximately 800, in the United States.

St. Charles Transfer's own equipment and personnel are used to pack, load, transport, unload, and unpack for nearly all moves originating in the St. Charles area with a destination within the state. When the destination is out of state, but within 450 miles of St. Charles, St. Charles Transfer performs the packing and loading services, while the firm's contract drivers provide the transportation service. Furthermore, when St. Charles is the destination city, the firm's contract drivers make nearly all the long-distance moves for Mayflower. This arrangement with Mayflower is the result of St. Charles Transfer's long-standing affiliation with Mayflower and the superior services provided by the firm and its contract drivers. This ability of St. Charles Transfer to be personally involved in almost all moves within a 450-mile radius provides it with a major advantage in the marketplace. Such service is particularly attractive to employer-paid relocations, for which employer corporations expect and need trouble-free transfers for their employees.

Moves greater than 450 miles are coordinated through the Mayflower Transit Company. The actual transportation service for such longer moves is done by either Mayflower's own employees, Mayflower's own contract drivers, or the employees or contract drivers of Mayflower's local agency network (including private agencies and Mayflower-owned local agencies). The local agency at the point of origination receives the writing commission for selling the order and receives revenue for performing any packing and related services for the customer. The local agency at the point of destination receives revenue for performing unpacking services. The destination agent is also responsible for coordinating any damage claims and resolving other problems the customer may have.

This arrangement for long-distance moves involving multiple Mayflower agencies may be illustrated with the following example of the Johnson family relocation from Boston to St. Louis. The Bunker Hill Storage Company, an agent for Mayflower in Boston, wrote the order for the Johnson move and performed the majority of the packing service, readying the household possessions for shipment. Meanwhile, Leon Busch, a contract driver for St. Charles Transfer, was in the process of delivering a shipment in Buffalo, New York. By previous arrangement with Mayflower, Leon then drove from Buffalo to Boston to load the Johnson's shipment. Leon hired loading help from Bunker Hill Storage. The following day Leon drove to Syracuse to load another shipment, also by prearrangement with Mayflower, hiring loading assistance from the Syracuse Mayflower agency. The second shipment filled the remainder of Leon's trailer. Two days later Leon arrived in Lexington, Kentucky, to unload the Syracuse move, leaving the next morning for St. Louis, Missouri. In both destination cities, Leon stopped at the local Mayflower agency to hire labor to unload the shipments. Since St. Louis was less than a day's drive from St.

Charles and there were no shipments from St. Louis in that direction at that time, Leon drove home empty.

Both origination agencies received revenues for their packing services, remunerated in full from Mayflower. Both received a writing commission from Mayflower. Both also received revenue from Leon for loading services performed by their agency employees. Both destination agencies received revenues for any unpacking services they may have performed, remunerated in full from Mayflower, and revenue from Leon for unloading services performed by their agency employees. St. Charles Transfer received 10% of the base-hauling commission from Mayflower as its share of the revenue generated by Leon to cover Leon's use of St. Charles Transfer's trailer and for other services the agency provided to assist Leon, such as record keeping and coordination with Mayflower to obtain the Buffalo shipment and the two backhauls. Leon received approximately 50% of the transportation revenues as his base-hauling commission from Mayflower, out of which he paid his own expenses, including the loading and unloading services he had hired. (It may be noted that any revenues St. Charles Transfer receives for contract drivers' hiring loading/unloading services is minimal and is recorded as part of the long-distance packing revenue.)

■ The Household Goods Moving Market

The primary factors that influence the demand for moving services from firms in this industry include number of households, size of household possessions, mobility patterns, and economic considerations. Recent trends in these variables are shown in Exhibit 4. The cost of utilizing the services provided by this industry is typically not a consideration for the individual consumer when the employer is paying for the move, although in poorer economic times the employer may not be willing to pay for the employee's packing and unpacking. When one considers the average cost of a long-distance move, such a personal expenditure is likely to represent a significant proportion of a household's disposable income for all but the wealthiest of households.

Smaller households with fewer possessions and lower income levels, that move shorter distances and must bear the moving cost themselves, are less likely to utilize the services provided by this industry. Instead, many such potential customers move their own possessions by renting equipment from U-Haul or Ryder. Many others move locally with their own trucks or those borrowed from friends. This practice is more prevalent in rural areas and in certain regions of the country. The transportation cost for a 17-foot rental van, appropriate for moving the normal possessions in a smaller-sized home, for 450 miles, one-way, would cost the householder about $425, plus fuel. Renting the same size van for a local move would cost $35 per day, plus $.50 per mile, plus fuel.

Given a population (or household) base and growth rate for a community, community population demographics, the overall economic health of the community, the growth in local residential building, the size and mix of existing dwellings, and the presence (or absence) of many large employers that are likely to transfer personnel, the size of the local moving market can be estimated. The estimated sizes of the moving markets in the four metropolitan areas are shown on the map in Exhibit 1. These estimates include transportation revenues from local moves, transportation revenues from long-distance moves originating in the local area, and associated loading, packing, and storage services. These estimates do not include revenues from the following sources: commercial freight hauling and commercial warehousing; transportation revenues generated by agency drivers or contract drivers not originating in the local area; and revenue from unpacking, unloading, and warehousing of goods not originating in the local area. Approximately 80% of the total market revenue estimates are attributable to long-distance moves.

The St. Charles metropolitan area, consisting of a population base of about 140,000, is estimated to represent about a $1.25 million yearly demand for the services of the household goods moving industry. During the 1980s, especially the early part of that decade, the local economy faced a severe recession. Many labor and management jobs were lost, and families left the area in search of employment elsewhere. Population declines created a softening of property values, retail business sales, and new residential construction. However, as the 1990s approached, the community's economy began to rebound as economic development efforts within the community were beginning to attract new employers. Overall, there are positive feelings regarding the future growth of the community, but there is a general consensus among community leaders that the St. Charles area has a long way to go to match the prosperity of the late 1970s and that population expansion will be a slow process.

Grandview and Hill City were somewhat affected by the same general environmental conditions that devastated St. Charles. However, each of those communities has a more diversified local economy, being significantly less dependent on any particular industry's health. As a result, both communities have been more able to cope with upswings and downturns in various segments of the economy. Further, both communities are experiencing population and economic growth. Grandview has a population of 170,000 and an estimated moving market of nearly $2.2 million, with good future growth prospects. Its economic base reflects the presence of major employers in packaged foods, electronics, and communications. The Hill City area has a population base of 95,000, but is estimated to generate moving market revenues of $1.65 million annually and also is experiencing growth, though somewhat less than that expected for Grandview as a result of state budget cuts for the university system. Its economic base includes the largest university in the state, a very large university-related hospital complex, a large private research center, and a diverse mix of manufacturing and service businesses. The city is located at the junction of two major interstate highways (refer to Exhibit 1). This location may be viewed as providing advantages and disadvantages to the local moving agencies in Hill City. Transportation of goods is facilitated by access to the interstate system. However, much moving industry activity is channeled through the area. As a result, Hill City is a prime target for providing drivers with backhauls. Grandview also suffers in a similar manner from its proximity to Hill City and the interstate highway junction. St. Charles, however, is a much more limited source of backhauls.

■ St. Charles Transfer's Operating Projections for Grandview

Ted Thompson based his operating projections for Grandview on several assumptions. He believed that the operation would require, at the very minimum, a sales office, enough storage space to hold several bundles of packing materials and two to three household shipments, a parking area for vehicles, a small packing van or pickup truck, and three tractor/trailer rigs. After a visit to Grandview to look over Ajax's equipment, Ted located a small building that could be rented relatively inexpensively and would suit his requirements very nicely, at least for the first year. The liquidation of the Ajax Transfer Companies would provide a convenient opportunity to obtain used equipment. This would be especially advantageous since the equipment would not have to be entirely repainted. Ted estimated that his vehicular needs for Grandview could be purchased used from Ajax for about $110,000 at the liquidation sale.

Financing for the equipment purchases and to provide working capital would be obtained through additional stockholder investment of $80,000, a 36-month bank note for $100,000 and a 6-month, interest-free loan from Allied of $30,000. After visiting his banker, Ted felt fairly confident he could arrange the three-year loan as soon as he made the decision to expand, with approximately $12,000 in interest payments the first year and equal principal repayments in each of the three years. Ted had considered liquidating about half of the firm's investments, rather than relying on family members to personally invest in the firm, but decided the income generated by the investments was necessary to defray existing interest expenses from the St. Charles operation. Between his personal ability to obtain a second mortgage on his home and funds available for investment by family members, Ted felt confident of raising the needed equity. Refer to Exhibits 7 and 8 showing the Grandview pro forma income statement and estimated cash flow.

The Grandview location would require an agency manager who would be expected to act as part-time salesperson, public-relations person, claims handler, and dispatcher. The new manager's salary would be $35,000, comparable to Bill's salary. Since it would be very important to engage in as much marketing as possible during the switch-over to Allied, a full-time, straight-commission salesperson would also be needed to perform move estimating and sales call duties. Based on revenue estimates, the standard commission rate used by most of the local moving agents in the area, and the proportion of sales likely to be generated by the agency manager and the full-time salesperson, Ted estimated the salesperson would receive about $25,000 in commissions. A part-time secretary-bookkeeper would also be needed and paid a salary of $10,000. The salary and commission expense estimate in the pro forma statement includes fringes for these personnel. In addition to these expenses, Ted allocated $20,000 for the officers of St. Charles Transfer and the office personnel at the St. Charles location for their increased responsibilities associated with the new location. The benefits to be received by the firm's officers would be in lieu of dividends; the office personnel would receive bonuses.

Pro forma revenues for the proposed Grandview location were based on sales levels and a sales mix comparable to the Ajax agency's current sales in Grandview. This information was provided by Allied, with the consent of the Ajax brothers. Since Ajax would still be operating its freight and commercial warehousing business in Grandview, no revenues from either of these two sources were included in Ted's forecast.

Ajax's share of the long-distance market in Grandview was about 15% of the estimated moving revenues, derived from hauling about 65 shipments from Grandview to other locations. The firm, however, did attempt to obtain backhauls whenever possible, so additional revenues could be derived from this source. Ajax's contract drivers were under contract to the Ajax parent com-

Exhibit 7 **St. Charles Transfer Company, Pro Forma Income Statement for Proposed Grandview Agency**

Operating revenues			
Goods moving			
Long distance[1]	$235,000		
Local	55,000	$290,000	
Writing commissions[2]		25,000	
Packing			
Long distance	$ 72,000		
Local	18,000	90,000	
Storage			
Long distance	$ 16,000		
Local	4,000	20,000	
Total operating revenue			$425,000
Operating expenses			
Salaried personnel[3]		$ 85,000	
Wages[3]		100,000	
Officers/management		20,000	
Packing materials		17,000	
Depreciation		22,000	
Fuel, oil, repairs, etc.		32,000	
Taxes, income expense		24,000	
Leasing expense		25,000	
Insurance (all types)		55,000	
Other administrative expense		18,000	
Total operating expenses			(398,000)
Income from operations			$ 27,000
Interest expense			(12,000)
Income before taxes			$ 15,000
Additional taxes			(2,500)
Net income			$ 12,500

[1]$180,000 in base-hauling commissions from the firm's drivers and $55,000 in commissions from contract drivers.

[2]Includes Welcome Home™.

pany, rather than any given agency, so no local agency revenues were reported from revenues generated by the contract drivers. Ted based his long-distance revenue projections on the number of shipments Ajax had made, plus one more shipment per month. No backhauling was included, but Ted hoped to convince two or three of Ajax's contract drivers to work for his new agency. Ted estimated the long-distance mileage at about 52,000 miles.

Ajax's share of the local moving market was greater than average, at about 20% of the estimated local moving revenues, derived from over 100 moves within the county. Because this was significantly more local business than St. Charles Transfer was doing, Ted's mileage estimates for this part of the operation had to be much greater than in the St. Charles market. Approximately 3,000 miles were required for the relocations, each involving three distinct "legs" of the trip: from the office to the present dwelling, from the present dwelling to the new dwelling, and back to the office. Based on 100 relocations, the mileage was expected to increase proportionally. Ted himself drove about

St. Charles Transfer Company, Estimated Cash Flow for Proposed Grandview Agnecy **Exhibit 8**

	1st Quarter	*2nd Quarter*	*3rd Quarter*	*4th Quarter*
Sales	$ 85,000	$150,000	$110,000	$ 80,000
Revenue collections[1]	$ 40,000	$145,000	$105,000	$ 90,000
Cash expenses				
Equipment purchase	$110,000	$ 0	$ 0	$ 0
Salaries/wages/other	45,000	60,000	50,000	50,000
Leasing expense	7,000	6,000	6,000	6,000
Packing material	10,000	4,000	2,000	1,000
Fuel, oil, repairs	7,000	11,000	9,000	5,000
Taxes (all)	7,000	7,000	7,000	5,500
Insurance	18,000	14,000	14,000	9,000
Other administrative expenses	6,000	5,000	4,000	3,000
Interest	3,000	3,000	3,000	3,000
Total expenditure disbursement	$213,000	$110,000	$ 95,000	$ 82,500
Principal repayment	8,340	38,340	8,340	8,320
Total disbursements	$221,340	$148,340	$103,340	$ 90,820
Beginning cash balance[2]	$210,000	$ 28,660	$ 25,320	$ 26,980
Plus collections[1]	40,000	145,000	105,000	90,000
Cash available	$250,000	$173,660	$130,320	$116,980
Less disbursements	(221,340)	(148,340)	(103,340)	(90,820)
Net cash balance	$ 28,660	$ 25,320	$ 26,980	$26,160
Desired cash balance	$ 25,000	$ 25,000	$ 25,000	$ 25,000

[1]Revenue collections are based on a 40-day collection period.

[2]Beginning cash: $100,000 bank loan; $80,000 stockholders; $30,000 Allied loan.

7,000 miles in the past year, making sales calls throughout the county in which St. Charles was located, as well as in several adjacent counties. In the Grandview operation, Ted believed, the new salesperson's efforts could initially be restricted to within the county to offset somewhat the greater number of calls required, and he estimated the mileage required to be around 8,000 miles.

Total storage and packing revenue estimates were assumed to be proportionally similar to those in the St. Charles operation: 80% for long-distance, 20% for local moving services. However, because the warehouse space initially would be somewhat limited in Grandview, total storage revenues were based on a comparison of the relative size of the storage area compared to the size of the warehouse allocated to household goods moving in St. Charles.

Based on the time drivers would be required to be on the road for long-distance hauling, the amount of time and number of people needed to load a long-distance move, the amount of time and number of people required for a local move, and the number of each kind of move anticipated in Grandview, Ted believed that five full-time employees would be needed, the same number as he now employed in St. Charles. Ted's estimate for wages was based on the current wage rate for nonunion employees in the Ajax agency: $10 per hour, including fringes, a figure which would be attractive to any of the agencies operating in St. Charles!

Other expense projections in the pro forma were based on comparisons to the St. Charles operation. The significantly lower cost of insurance and the lower taxes were a result of Ted's plan to purchase used equipment and the fact that the building would be rented. At the present time Ted anticipated leasing two trailers for use in Grandview.

THE DAY OF RECKONING

Friday had arrived and Ted was again sitting at his desk, looking vacantly out the window. In a few minutes he was to make the phone call that would determine the future direction of St. Charles Transfer. Two major thoughts were in his mind, pulling him in different directions. On the one hand, he was anxious to do something new, take on a challenge. His dad had wanted to expand the business twenty years earlier, but had had a mild heart attack. In fact, Ted was to be the manager at the new location, a city about 100 miles southeast of St. Charles. During his dad's recovery, however, the agency had been opened by someone else. Ted knew his dad really favored the opportunity to expand into Grandview and, maybe, Hill City in the future. On the other hand, Ted knew he wouldn't have a free minute to himself for at least the next six months. His kids were growing up and soon would be leaving the "nest." Neither of them was particularly interested in the moving business, so he didn't have the same motivation to expand as his father did. Spring and summer involved enough work as it was, without having to face the problems that would surely arise in a new agency in a new town. Just then Bill stuck his head in the office and asked, "Well, what are you going to tell Joe?"

CASE 35

Crowley Inn: "Un Bon Place Pour Rester"

Arthur Sharplin, McNeese State University

Crowley, Louisiana, hometown of colorful Louisiana governor Edwin "Fast Eddie" Edwards, is in the heart of Cajun country, 60 miles west of Baton Rouge. Crowley Inn—with 59 rooms, a restaurant, and a bar—is at the intersection of Louisiana Highway 13, the main north–south route through Crowley, and Interstate Highway 10. Also at that intersection are a Texaco and an Exxon station, a Kentucky Fried Chicken, and a Burger King restaurant. But, as Mayor Bob Istre states, "Crowley Inn is the first business you see, and it is the only one out there that calls itself 'Crowley' anything. We are proud of it, warts and all." Inn manager Shirley Miller puts it more strongly, "C'est pour du monde de la village au Crowley [It is for the people of the Village of Crowley]."

The inn was completed in 1973; its owner defaulted on his $800,000 loan in 1986, resulting in seizure by the lender, a savings and loan company. The S&L was taken over by the Resolution Trust Company (RTC) in 1990. Then, on May 21, 1991, the RTC sold the inn to Art and Kathy Sharplin of Lake Charles, 45 miles to the west. Art taught business at McNeese State University in Lake Charles.

They formed Crowley Motel, Inc. (CMI) to hold the property and assigned Art's associate, Debbie King, to manage the investment with the help of an on-site manager. The RTC's manager, Pam Potts, soon quit without notice. Debbie promoted Shirley Miller, who was daytime front-desk clerk, to manager.

The bar, called Martin's Tavern, had been rented to Burnell Martin, a local barber, and CMI assumed that lease, which was to expire at the end of 1992. The tavern had become a popular night spot for Crowleyites, frequented by the mayor, the sheriff, and other leading citizens, as well as by rice farmers, crawfishers, and oilfield hands. A true Cajun, Martin had talked of setting up an off-track betting parlor and then arranged to get two of Louisiana's first

---

This case is intended for classroom discussion only, not to depict effective or ineffective handling of administrative situations. All rights reserved to the author.

video poker machines, which were to be legal beginning in June 1992. In February 1992, famous Cajun chef Roy Lyons agreed to lease the restaurant for two years, naming it Chef Roy's Cafe Acadie. Debbie breathed a sigh of relief. She remarked, "The restaurant has been one big headache. It required more employees than the motel, took most of our management time, ate us alive with repairs, and lost money every month." Art had helped his brother build and operate several other motels years earlier and knew that motel restaurants typically lose money.

The Sharplins had intended to sell the motel after fixing it up, and that was still a possibility. However, Art asked Debbie and Shirley to assume a ten-year holding period in management decisions. So they were looking for ways to improve motel operations and to implement a marketing plan that they had helped develop.

FACILITIES

The physical plant had presented quite a challenge to Debbie, who said she knew "less than nothing" about running a motel, let alone fixing one. Most of the rooms were distinctly substandard—sagging and stained bedding; broken furniture; 20-year-old TVs and room air conditioners; ceilings despackled and discolored by leaks; faded curtains hanging loose at one end; plumbing fixtures pitted and coated with white scum; washroom counters spotted with cigarette burns; mice holes in walls; and tacky traps behind credenzas, each holding a grizzly menagerie of dehydrated bugs and roaches. It all seemed even worse in the dim hue cast by cheap old incandescent lamps with their yellowed and tattered shades.

Outside, water seeped through a cracked pavement from a broken underground pipe, nurturing a patch of green slime. The clack, clack, clack of the sewer plant blower gave notice of imminent failure in that vital system. From the sewer plant, it was possible to see into the small equipment room, where an aging boiler had piled clumps of damp rust on the floor. Past the dumpster, overflowing with customer and trespasser refuse, a pothole in the truck parking area had grown to become a muddy pond.

The lobby building was little better. Art discovered the heating, ventilating, and air conditioning system heated and cooled the void above the hung ceilings, in addition to the usable space. However, one of the two main condenser units had been inoperative for months. Someone had poured tar on the leaks in the roof overhang, and the black goo hung in stringy drops from the pegboard soffit and the shrubs beneath. In the restaurant kitchen, only one of the overhead exhaust systems worked; an oven door was tied shut with a stocking; cold air leaked from the walk-in freezer through a cocked door; and a long-disabled deep fryer held its last charge of grease, stale and mantled with scorched meal.

However, the inn had originally been well built. Though 20 years old, it was still attractive. The guest room building was made of concrete blocks and steel-reinforced slabs, with front and back walls of wood paneling. Piping was copper and cast iron, not plastic. One wall in each room was latex enameled and the others had vinyl wall covering, torn and unglued in a few places, but of good quality. The lobby building, of brick veneer, was shrouded with 90-

year-old live oaks and much younger pines, giving a sense of homeyness and comfort. The neat grey and blue decor, though not striking, added a subdued welcomeness.

From May 1991 to February 1992, Crowley Inn's cash flow was applied to upgrading the property. Art and Kathy bought 60 rooms of used furniture, drapes, lamps, and bedspreads from the refurbishment contractor for a Holiday Inn in Beaumont, Texas. Debbie purchased 60 each of new RCA TVs with remote controls, GE clock radios, and chrome clothes racks with hangers. She also acquired new shower rods and curtains, bed linens, pillows, and a full complement of new beds and foundations. Kathy modified and helped install the drapes, advised on aesthetics, and livened the lobby with greenery and art work. Shirley arranged for several local men, unemployed artisans she could hire for minimum wage, to help as needed. As each shipment arrived, they would come in to take out the old and install the new. They did much more—sanding the cigarette burns off the washroom counters, painting, stopping mice holes, patching concrete, and so on. An air-conditioning contractor replaced or repaired over twenty room air conditioners, renovated the lobby building heating, ventilating, and air conditioning system, and worked long hours on the restaurant coolers and freezers. A roofer replaced the leaky third of the motel roof and put proper patches on that of the lobby building. Total cost of the renovations: about $130,000.

Two prospective franchisors were asked to inspect the property. Best Western identified about $120,000 in needed improvements—more modern room lights and furniture, new carpeting, vinyl covering for the concrete block walls, and so on—but seemed anxious to do the deal. Red Carpet Inns was ready to franchise immediately, suggesting only minor changes. Debbie concluded the inn was then nearly up to standard for low-end franchises, such as Day's Inns, Comfort Inns, Scottish Inns, and Red Carpet, but not for lower–mid-range ones like Best Western and Quality Inns. Front-desk clerk Josie Forrestier put it differently: "Crowley Inn used to be just a dump. Now, it is *'un bon place pour rester'* [a good place to stay]."

PERSONNEL AND ORGANIZATION

When Pam Potts resigned, the motel employed six housekeepers plus a supervisor, a maintenance man, and five front-desk clerks, all at minimum wage. There were no written job descriptions. The RTC had balked at paying overtime, and it had become standard practice to show eight-hour shifts on time cards, although employees often worked more or fewer hours. A housekeeper explained, "Pam gives us more than we can do. So we have to punch out and then go back and finish the work."[1] In fact, most time cards for that period show handwritten checkout times, with no indication of who had made the entries. This was allegedly done because Pam could not keep the time clock working properly.

However much time the housekeepers actually spent, the rooms stayed dirty. Two large dogs, or maybe camels, had been left alone in room 112. Pale spots in the soiled mauve carpet marked where they had done their "business," and the fetor gushed out to greet new guests. One such guest, a nurse from Florida, chose another room. She later wrote Mayor Istre:

> I am writing to express my concern regarding the deplorable condition of the Crowley Inn. The mattresses and springs in our room would probably have been rejected by the worst flophouse in the country. The mattresses had a permanent swag, not to mention, sir, a URINE STAIN about 36 inches in length. The tub has mildew all around the caulking. The drapes and spreads haven't seen a laundry in years, it appears. The carpet has stains. The pillows also are stained, not to mention lumpy. Neither mattresses nor pillows have protective covers that can be wiped down between customers. The swimming pool looked cloudy and green our entire stay, and though the desk clerk assured us it was okay, we declined.

No housekeeper, not even the head one, had worked at any other motel. Each was left to decide the best way to clean rooms. Also, there was no regular inspection by any manager. During that period, two or three people a night refused to stay after seeing their rooms.

Had the offended nurse seen more rooms than two, she might have suffered even greater dissonance. In one room, toilet paper came off the bottom of the roll—in another, off the top. Another room had a bed with a small, flowered pillow and a large, white one—next door was an identical set. In room 124, a double bedspread was stretched to half cover a king-sized bed, while a king-sized spread in room 122 fell in clumps around a double bed. Also in this room, were five tiny bars of soap, while in another, none at all. There were waste baskets of various sizes and amounts in each guest room, pint freezer boxes for ice buckets, shower curtains loose from hanger rings, stiff bath cloths behind a commode or hung on a shower curtain rod, a KFC box, with dehydrated chicken parts, peeping out from under a bed. The furniture, old, cheap, and stained though it was, need not have been so misdistributed. Chair counts ranged from four to none. In one instance, an orange sled chair was paired with a puce overstuffed one. There were chairs with no tables, and tables with no chairs.

Wallace Mayer, the maintenance man, was responsible for cleaning the parking areas, mowing the lawn, taking waste to the dumpster, making bank deposits, moving heavy items, adding chlorine to the sewer plant, maintaining the swimming pool, and fixing anything broken. Sixty-seven, but physically strong and unfailingly good-natured, Wallace went about his tasks with consistency, if not speed. A motel begets refuse, and the housekeepers often stacked bulging bags of it in the vending machine areas until Wallace could take them to the dumpster, 50 feet away. It was just as well; the bags hid the grey-matted residue next to the machines, and the cans and candy wrappers cast behind them by long-forgotten guests. Wallace kept the lawn and shrubs trimmed, but dairy cups and flattened cans were often left for another day. And six packs of empty beer cans could sometimes be seen standing at the parking lot curb in mute, noontime tribute to Bacchus, whom the Cajuns place just above Zeus.

The province of neither housekeeping nor maintenance, room windows and screens suffered from evasion. Rain splatter had formed rivulets on the dusty panes, and layers of ancient cobwebs gave the half screens a fuzzy translucence.

As the renovation progressed, Debbie and Shirley began frequent, though sporadic, inspections. Art decreed, "No employee walks past a piece of trash. Nobody!" Cards saying "It was my pleasure to clean your room" were given to housekeepers to sign and leave on credenzas. Debbie obtained videos on proper bed making and room cleaning. She asked the head housekeeper to train her charges and to inspect all guest rooms daily. Of the six housekeepers, only Sandra Guillotte adapted—and survived. The head housekeeper soon decided she, too, could not meet Shirley's and Debbie's escalating demands. The new one, Carol Hoffpauir, promised she could. In February 1992, Shirley told of the improvement:

> We're getting compliments. We used to be afraid to ask if a guest enjoyed their stay. But today, at least five people commented on how nice the rooms were. Carol checks every room every day, and I do twice a week. We set a new record last week, a whole week without a complaint. The housekeepers still miss things—a bath cloth, or something left in a drawer—but they are doing so much better.

Art asked Shirley, "Why are the housekeepers doing better?" "Because we keep demanding more," she replied. "If we didn't demand it, they wouldn't do it." Carol Hoffpauir agreed, adding:

> I write them up every day, which rooms they clean and what they do wrong. We talk, and they can all read my notes on the clipboard, which I leave on the desk. If they do good, I tell them and I tell Shirley.
>
> I wish I could find five workers who take pride in cleaning the way I do. Two of the girls do, but the others seem to just tolerate it. I can hire and fire; I just have to tell Shirley my reasons. But I would rather just get them out of their old routine.

Art asked, "Doesn't the improved situation here inspire them?" "I reckon so," Carol replied, "but you have to tell them when they mess up." Debbie added, "We know that new surroundings don't motivate."

Exhibit 1 shows the organization and employees at the end of February 1992. The desk clerks and Wallace were paid $5 an hour; the housekeepers, minimum wage; Shirley, $300 a week; and Carol, $200. Art had instituted one-week paid vacations, but there was no company medical insurance nor retirement plan. Shirley talked about her job:

> I have a little problem supervising these people. You see, going from housekeeper, to the front desk, to being a manager—I was one of them; I can't come out and fuss at them. It was really hard at first. I called them together and told them it was business for eight hours. After that, we can go have a beer together. I told

Crowley Inn Organization and Employees **Exhibit 1**

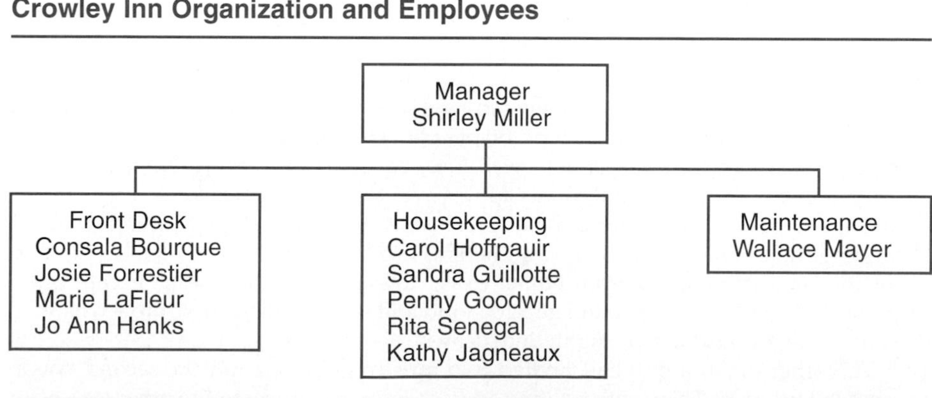

them, "I don't demand respect—don't call me 'Ma'am' or screen my calls. But when I say I want this done, I want it done. I don't want to stay on your butt." They are not kids. And I'm not running an old folk's home or a community center.

Everybody is from Crowley or Church Point, all Cajun. They take things very lightly. They are all struggling, but they leave their problems at home, unless they get too big. Sometimes, you just need to talk. I listen. I cried when I had to fire Joanne (the former head housekeeper). She's happier though, drinking and trying to get unemployment. Marie works in the restaurant after she finishes here, because she needs the money. Her mother is sick—over 90% stoppage in her heart. I could go on and on. This is a second home, for all of us.

Mr. Wallace is part of the furniture. He has been here six, seven, maybe eight years. He does not want 40 hours—says it will cut his social security. Takes off Friday noon. He is good; you just have to point it out. He loves his job, and we all depend on him. We took a poll the other day on what Mr. Wallace enjoys most; we think he likes blowing off the parking lot best.

You get to know the customers. We talk; give them a little Cajun flavor: "Oh, you're from Texas. Well, we went to San Antonio last year . . . blah, blah, blah." It makes them come back. The truck drivers and oilfield hands holler at us when they come in the door. Whether we use the right English, they don't care. It's like being a bartender. Our regular guests will just about tell you their life story. You even get to know the ones who come here for a couple of hours. They trust us, park their girlfriend right here in front. Some men leave women behind here. The other day, one stood on the interstate an hour with her thumb up, until somebody stopped.

Cajuns may seem a little standoffish at first. Not at the front desk; this is *our* territory, and we feel secure. The girls always have a smile and gab for a guest. But at other places you're afraid to say the wrong thing. I was in Wisconsin with Byron [Shirley's son, a priest] last year and I told someone, "Catch me a Coke." They kidded me about it. Byron took me aside and said, "Mom, you don't *catch* a Coke; you just get one." He used to bring his priest friends home. I would beg him, "Byron, don't bring these educated people here." But, once I get to know them I get the biggest kick when they come. And I can't get them out of the house. We shouldn't be ashamed of our language, anyway. Listen to Governor Edwards: "Dis, dat, and dem." And he's a lawyer, definitely an educated man.

Jo Ann and Josie were at the front desk, just outside Shirley's office, and stopped at the door to listen. Jo Ann said, "All the improvements make us proud and we want to do it better—makes me smile more. We bring a problem to Shirley and it gets taken care of, immediately. If it is a big one, Shirley gets on the phone with Debbie and it gets solved." Josie added, "It's exciting. Every day, I look forward to coming to work." Jo Ann's shift was over, and she excused herself.

Josie continued:

Customers like to hear us talk. They can't get over how friendly we are. Some say they expected to see a mean type of people. They think Cajuns are ignorant, uneducated, barefoot people with web toes. We are different. But we're Americans—Texas is over here and Mississippi is over there. I tell customers everybody around here is friendly. I make people feel welcome. I want them to feel they are getting their money's worth. I want them to know I am their friend and to think of this as a home away from home. I say, "It's a quiet little place," except on Saturday night, when the band gets too loud and some of the people are—what's a nice way of putting it?—highly intoxicated.

The other night, a guy had invited two girls to his room and the second one showed up early. They were fighting and screaming, disturbing the other guests.

> So I called the sheriff. The one in the room reached right over the deputy and, "Pow!" laid the other one out. The deputy brought her up here in handcuffs and threw her in the car.
>
> The inn is like my home, too. When Kenny and the Jokers [a Lafayette, Louisiana, band] play in the bar, I come about an hour early to hear them. And my kids [17, 15, 14, and 13 years old] love to come here, sometimes to go swimming. There is nowhere else to do that. We eat in the restaurant sometimes. When I worked in housekeeping, I would come by sometimes just to visit. I always try to be here thirty minutes early, and I usually hang around that long after my shift.

During the annual rodeo and the monthly horse show, the inn's regular guests merged with equestrians—from spirited barrel racers to wrinkled Marlboro men. Drowsy tourist's senses were jostled by the too-metallic jangle of spurs on concrete stairs and the too-earthy aroma of a dozen horse trailers. Wide-brimmed hats were worn everywhere—at restaurant tables, on the crowded dance floor in the tavern, even in the bathroom. One inebriated cowboy thought his bed was a dance floor, until it collapsed. Another, dispirited by lost love, conjectured to aim at his head but blew just his palm away, spraying scraps of flesh and bone onto a new mattress. And a famous Cajun musician, held hostage during a drug withdrawal by two burly friends, broke a table and ripped a chrome fixture from the wall.

Mostly, though, Crowley Inn was, as Josie said, a quiet little place, a place where Texaco could house visiting executives and straying locals could enjoy secret liaisons. And it seemed so much a part of the employees' and townspeople's lives that Art wondered whether he and Kathy had title in fee so simple as they had supposed.[2]

Ninety-two-year old retired Catholic priest Msgr. Jules O. Daigle, of nearby Welsh, Louisiana, would agree with Shirley that Cajuns should not be ashamed of the way they talk. He insisted that Cajun was a true language, saying, "To call Cajun bad French is to call French and Italian bad Latin." Father Daigle fought for years to preserve the Cajun language and culture. In the preface to his Cajun language dictionary, he wrote:

> Historically, the Cajuns are the descendants of the French people who colonized the general area of ancient Acadia, now known as Nova Scotia, beginning in 1604. . . . In 1755, the British began a cruel, systematic program of deportation of our ancestors. . . . Penniless, ill-clad and, worst of all, being both French and Catholics, nothing but scorn and hatred awaited them in the colonies. . . . After serving their indenture to the British colonists, some of them made their way back to Acadia or to Canada. Others found refuge in the French islands of Martinique, Guadaloupe, St. Dominque, etc. In the meanwhile, many of the Acadians who had evaded capture by the British sought refuge in the forests among the friendly Indians of the north. Of all the Acadians deported by the British, a considerable number were brought to England as prisoners: eventually, most of these found their way into France. . . . It was from all the above groups that many of the Acadians came to Louisiana, beginning in the early 1760s. Free at last, they had to begin a totally new and different kind of life, in a strange land. . . . The Acadians had to invent a new vocabulary, find new types of foods, develop a new cuisine and a whole new way of life. Thus was born the Cajun language and Cajun culture. . . .
>
> To some, a Cajun is a crude, ignorant, backward person who speaks little or no English. . . . His principal interest in life is boozing, eating and having a good time. To be sure, there are such Cajuns, but they are an infinitesimal minority and are in no way characteristic of the Cajun people.[3]

Father Daigle went on to write that the Cajuns are our bishops, judges, lawyers, contractors, college professors, beauticians, bricklayers, farmers, teachers, and so forth. He concluded, "Yes, and sure enough, some of them are lazy, ignorant bums and drunks: all in about the same proportion as the rest of the American population."

MARKETING

Art and Kathy had initially been inclined to seek a franchise. Best Western was the leading candidate, Quality Inns a close second, but the urge ebbed and flowed. Debbie and Shirley also expressed ambivalence about franchising, but both were excited about promotion and other aspects of marketing.

■ Crowley Best Western?

Most motels are franchised. Franchisors typically provide a reservation system, advice on pricing, national advertising, a franchisee directory showing locations and amenities, quality control standards, yearly inspections, training, informational services, design help, and an approved-supplier catalog. Best Western's 1992 charge for all this was about $350 per room initially plus a similar amount annually. Other franchisors get a certain percentage of room revenue. For example, Red Carpet quoted 4.5% for Crowley Inn, with no initial fee. Holiday Inns was collecting as much as 7% then.

Art believed Crowley Inn could qualify for a Best Western franchise within six months by making the following expenditures (in addition to the annual fee):

Initial franchise fee	$21,000
Best Western signs	12,000
Reservation and accounting system	15,000
Required renovations	96,000
Total	$144,000

Debbie, Shirley, and Art reached consensus that this would allow hiking the average daily rate (ADR) by $4.00 or increasing average occupancy by 15% or some combination of the two. Art concluded, "Assuming 64% occupancy, which I think is about the industry average, the added revenue would be $56,000 a year, a good return on $144,000."

Debbie objected,

> Well, 68% has been about our average. Even that should jump this year with or without a franchise. We have really improved this property since last summer, when we ran 76%. Besides, some of the renovations Best Western requires won't improve customer service—things like covering the concrete-block wall with vinyl and replacing the two-by-four ceiling tiles in the baths and lobby with two-by-two squares. I'll bet we could do the worthwhile renovations, which would cost maybe $60,000, and raise ADR by $3.00, without a franchise.

"What about Red Carpet?" asked Art. "We can have their sign up in a month."

"I don't think they add a thing," replied Debbie. Shirley nodded in concurrence.

Art said, "Okay, but you know there has been talk of a Day's Inn just seven miles away, in Rayne. If we were Best Western, no one would dare do that."

After a few more minutes of discussion, they all agreed to defer the decision on franchising for at least six months. "We haven't taken a cent out of this thing," said Art. "And I would like for you to produce some cash before we reinvest any more big chunks."

■ The Marketing Plan

Art asked Debbie to help prepare a marketing plan. "What should be our main objective?" she asked. "What's wrong with 'maximize shareholder wealth'?" he replied. A few days later, Debbie brought Art her rough draft. The final version is presented in the final section.

Debbie and Shirley were in essential agreement about each element of the marketing plan. During the last week of February 1992, they met to discuss both the process and the time frame for implementing the plan.

FINANCE

Art and Kathy paid $475,000 for the inn. They advanced another $21,000 then and more later for working capital. CMI gave the Sharplin's demand notes earning 10% interest for all but $1,000 of their investment and issued common stock for that. Exhibits 2 and 3 provide financial reports for CMI.

■ The Bank Loan

After buying Crowley Inn, Art and Kathy applied for a $380,000 loan from Evangeline Bank, in Crowley, to partly reimburse themselves and to fund improvements. The bank offered .5% under bank prime (then 10.5%) for a seven-year loan with 15-year amortization. But the bank's attorney delayed approving the title, noting that the inn sign and the sewer plant encroached over the adjacent property and that ten guest rooms had been built over an existing servitude. Art knew this when he bought the inn and thought it a small matter, since the problem had existed without complaint for 20 years. However, he suggested the loan amount be cut to $200,000 in view of the title problems.

The bank continued to delay closing, and after a few weeks Art and Kathy resolved not to bother with the loan. Art explained:

> We might be happier taking eight or ten thousand a month in interest, principal, and fees than we would getting, say, $380,000, at once. I never have believed this "optimum debt ratio" stuff anyway. Of course, having the inn financed might make it easier to sell. But we will cross that bridge if we come to it.

Besides, Art acknowledged, there was no certainty they could get the loan anyway.

■ Cost Structure

The motel business typically involves high fixed costs, partly because of the capital required. For example, Holiday Inns claimed its cost for a new motel

Exhibit 2

Income Statements

	May–December 1991	January 1992
Revenue		
Room revenue[a]	$272,011	$ 48,770
Telephone revenue	7,351	1,334
Restaurant revenue[b]	136,977	18,085
Rental income[c]	5,400	1,120
Miscellaneous revenue	9,218	637
Total revenue	$430,957	$ 69,946
Expenses		
Food purchases	$ 45,994	$ 5,857
Telephone	11,789	1,224
Salaries and wages	128,029	16,101
Payroll tax expense	14,478	3,085
Operating supplies	11,147	2,376
Office supplies	4,209	127
Taxes, licenses, and fees	6,755	1,709
Credit card fees	1,348	715
Professional fees	14,529	1,520
Travel and entertainment	1,199	0
Advertising	12,223	4,984
Repairs and maintenance	14,707	7,447
Miscellaneous	1,358	440
Utilities	36,285	6,655
Cable television	1,307	148
Insurance	15,293	2,002
Interest	31,487	6,344
Depreciation	23,100	3,300
Total expenses	$375,237	$ 64,034
Income before taxes	$ 55,720	$ 5,912
Income taxes (22%)	12,258	$ 1,301
Net income	$ 43,462	$ 4,611

[a]Monthly room revenue for May 21, 1991, through December 1991 was as follows: May, $16,648; June, $36,941; July, $46,720; August, $48,303; September, $38,240; October, $40,221; November, $38,738; and December, $23,364.

[b]The restaurant was leased beginning February 1, 1992, for $2,300 a month, including utilities (estimated at $600 a month). Up to that point, it had accounted for about 60% of salaries and wages, food purchases, and shares of several other expense items.

[c]This includes $900 a month for the bar. The remainder is for rental of the banquet room.

averaged $65,000 per room. And Art's brother, Jerry, said a new 60-room Best Western would cost about $22,000 a room, including land cost.

The problem was not severe for CMI. Its debt was held by its owners, and interest charges had been accrued rather than paid. But Art directed Shirley to pay interest out, along with half the cash flow (which would be treated as payment of principal), beginning in April 1992.

Balance Sheets **Exhibit 3**

	May 21, 1991	*December 31, 1991*	*January 31, 1992*
Assets			
Cash	$ 7,745	$ 12,007	$ 9,389
Accounts receivable		17,274	12,277
Land	40,000	40,000	40,000
Improvements	358,728	438,963	441,963
Furniture and fixtures	75,647	132,269	133,069
Accumulated depreciation		(23,100)	(26,400)
Security deposits	11,930	11,930	11,930
Total assets	$494,050	$629,343	$622,228
Liabilities			
N/P, A&K Sharplin	$493,050	$570,969	$555,700
Accrued and withheld tax		13,913	17,455
Total liabilities	$493,050	$584,882	$573,155
Equity			
Common stock	$ 1,000	$ 1,000	$ 1,000
Retained earnings		43,461	48,073
Total equity	$ 1,000	$ 44,461	$ 49,073
Total claims	$494,050	$629,343	$622,228

Debbie calculated the variable cost per room-night at Crowley Inn as follows:

Housekeeping labor	$3.21
Supplies	2.61
Laundry	.80
Avoidable utilities and telephone	1.70
Total	$8.32

Debbie had been keeping close tabs on room cleaning costs, supplies, and other variable items. After studying CMI's cost structure, she decided to concentrate more on marketing. Debbie explained:

> At a $32.50 ADR, each extra room-night produces $24.18 for fixed costs and profit. That's $725 a month, about $8,700 a year, almost enough to pay for two billboards on I-10. If we raise prices, rather than let occupancy rise, the result may be even better. At 72% occupancy, we sell about 1,275 room-nights a month. So anything that lets us raise rates by $1 produces $15,000 a year.

To Art's chagrin, Shirley also became less tight-fisted. On February 21, 1992, Debbie called from Crowley to say she was excited about all the nice improvements Shirley was making. "The oak trees have been pruned and fertilized, she got someone to mow the lawn, and there is new paint all around," said Debbie. Later that day, Kathy told Art she had learned that Shirley wanted to paint the entire motel and lobby building.

■ Possible Sale of the Inn

In February 1992, Art was approached by two prospective buyers: Mahesh Patel, who owned an Econo-Lodge motel in Huntsville, Texas, and Fred Gossen, Jr., a businessman from Rayne, Louisiana, seven miles east of Crowley.

Art convinced Kathy they should offer to sell the inn real estate, chattels, and leases to Gossen for $800,000, with $200,000 down and seller financing of the remainder at 12% for seven years, with 180-month amortization. They made a similar offer to Patel, but at $900,000 with $250,000 down and a five-year balloon.

Kathy had changed her mind by the next day. "Why don't we take out, say, $10,000 a month for a couple of years," she said, "We can probably still sell the motel for $800,000."

Art called Debbie to meet them at his campus office. "If we refuse an $800,000 offer," he began, "it is as if we just bought the inn for that amount." Debbie and Kathy agreed.

"Assuming Kathy is right," Art continued, "what discount rate should we use to settle the question?"

After a moment's thought, Debbie said, "This is effectively an equity investment in an entrepreneurial business. So I would suggest something like 40%."

"But can't we treat the project as a normally financed one; that is, say, $600,000 in 12% debt and $200,000 in equity?" Art asked, "If you stick with your 40% for equity, that gives a discount rate of 19%."

Kathy interjected, "I don't understand this discount rate stuff, Art. But if we get $200,000 in cash, we will have to put it in the Merrill Lynch account at about 5%. That's a far cry from 19%."

"Instead of doing that, we could pay off the 11% debt on the Pepsi building [a building Art and Kathy owned in Pineville, Louisiana]," said Art.

After a few minutes more discussion, Art promised to fax a note to Gossen, withdrawing the offer. "What about Patel?" asked Kathy. "That offer is not in writing," replied Art. "Besides, there is zero chance Patel is going to accept without negotiating. And when he makes the first counter, the law deems my offer withdrawn. Besides, real estate deals have to be in writing to be enforceable."

"By the way," Debbie asked, "why did you quote $100,000 higher to Patel?"

"Three reasons: I think Fred will treat our people better, I would not be as confident of getting paid, and a broker is involved on that deal," answered Art.

The next day, Art asked Shirley, "What do you think about the sale idea?"

She replied, "It's your decision, but $800,000 is a lot of money." Art knew Shirley hoped he would not sell. She had often said she loved her job; a sale would put it at risk.

He asked, "Do you know that if I put $800,000 in the bank at 6% it would only draw $4,000 a month?" "Is that all?" exclaimed Shirley, "Debbie and I can get you a lot more than that without selling."

Art stopped by to see Chef Roy and get his input about a possible sale. Roy said, "I personally hope you keep the motel. But I can't advise you to turn down a profitable deal."

When Art saw Burnell Martin, Burnell volunteered, "I hear you are thinking about selling. Art, keep this place. It's a gold mine."

THE MARKETING PLAN

■ Mission

The mission of Crowley Inn is to maximize return on invested capital by providing quality lodging and related services delivered by competent and enthusiastic employees operating a clean, well-maintained facility—at prices fully reflecting the quality of service.

■ Marketing Objective

The objective of the marketing plan is to maximize motel revenue while keeping expenses low. Revenue targets for 1992 are:

Room revenue ($33.00 ADR; 72% occupancy)	$512,000
Telephone revenue (1991 rate + 10%)	24,453

■ Target Market

Our current guests are mostly blue-collar persons on business travel, about 20% from Louisiana and the rest from all regions of the country. About 45% pay with cash or check, 36% use credit cards, and 19% have us bill a third party. Here are data taken from 247 folios completed in February 1992:[4]

Purpose of Travel		*Home Address*		*Payment*	
Work crew	48	Lousiana	52	Employer	47
Truck driver	38	Northeast	27	Credit card	89
Local	15	Southeast	17	Cash	111
Tourist	10	Northwest	13		
Business	38	Southwest	21		
Military	2	Foreign	11		
Cannot tell	96	Cannot tell	106		

With average occupancy of 41 rooms, we serve a tiny percentage of those who pass our door. Daily traffic counts near the inn during 1990 were as follows:[5]

I-10 east of Crowley (both directions)	29,530
I-10 west of Crowley (both directions)	26,600
Hwy 13 north of I-10 (both directions)	7,570
Hwy 13 south of I-10 (both directions)	18,430

Visitors to families and businesses in Crowley (1990 population, 14,038) and surrounding Acadia Parish (1990 population, 55,882) may also be potential new customers. The Cajun tradition of *fais-dodo*[6] and family togetherness in general pull many who leave the area back to it frequently.

In addition to our present customer base described earlier, we will seek to attract and serve more up-scale guests, including (1) white-collar business travelers, (2) tourists, (3) sojourners in the local area.

■ Product

Our main product is a room-night, which includes the elements listed below.

1. An attractive, comfortable, secure room—well-supplied, clean, and with all amenities in good order.
2. Attractive, functional vending machines.
3. Attractive, clean, neat grounds and paved areas.
4. Easy access to good food, drink, and entertainment.
5. Daily servicing of room by neat, well-dressed personnel to exceed standards set by Best Western or comparable franchisors.
6. Guest services provided by enthusiastic, competent, neat, articulate, well-dressed personnel who reflect the local culture.

A room-night is more perishable than a bruised tomato. We accept delivery of 59 room-nights every day, and unsold ones spoil sometime around midnight.

Shirley and Debbie plan to enhance the value and salability of room-nights in 1992 by:

1. Aggressive training and supervision of housekeepers.
2. Aggressive training of front-desk clerks, including role-playing of common types of guest contacts.
3. Inspections of all rooms daily by the head housekeeper.
4. Aggressive training and supervision of the maintenance person.
5. Inspection of all room and facilities at least weekly by Shirley, and at least monthly by Debbie.
6. Setting up of control systems to assure creative compliance with vital policies.
7. Upgrading of the work team, through training, supervision, and/or replacement of employees.

■ Price

Current prices at Crowley Inn are shown below. Pricing of room-nights is done by front-desk clerks, who have a list of "approved" commercial customers.

1. Basic room night	$31.00 ($29 commercial)
2. Each guest above one/room	$ 4.00/night
3. Local telephone calls	$ .50
4. Long-distance calls	AT&T rates plus 40%
5. Facsimile transmissions	$ 2.00/page
6. Rollaway bed or crib	$ 5.00/night

Members of the American Association of Retired Persons and others over 65 are eligible for commercial rates. ADR has been about $32.50 since a $2 per room-night price increase in July 1991. Two factors tend to pull ADR down. First, few customers are charged the $4 per extra guest. In fact, only about one in 20 (based on a check of February 1991 folios) completes the "number of persons in room" blocks on the folio. Second, front-desk clerks give commercial rates to most who ask for a discount. Shirley says pricing policies are clear and understood by all front-desk clerks, but they do not follow policies well.

Shirley and Debbie plan to:

1. Review pricing policies and change them or enforce them.
2. Set up control systems to identify and correct improper pricing practices.
3. Ensure that telephone billing equipment and practices are correct.
4. Price room-nights at no less than the double-occupancy rate during special events, when the inn normally fills up.
5. Price room-nights at no less than the double-occupancy rate whenever as many as 40 rooms are reserved.
6. Review pricing frequently, and quickly implement justified changes, as when occupancy moves reliably above 75%.

■ Promotion

Crowley Inn relies primarily on billboards for advertising. For eastbound traffic, there are two signs, on the left 16 miles out and on the right 4 miles out. For westbound traffic, signs are on the left at 13 miles and on the right at 7 miles. The signs carry the slogan, "Comfort you can afford," and have a large inset saying, "24 hr. Grill." They are yellow and white on a black background.

Debbie is developing an image, involving a slogan, a logo, and sign designs. A consultant is helping. The new slogan is "Comfortable, caring, and Cajun." This is intended to suggest comfortable lodging supplied by caring personnel with a Cajun flair. The logo is a large C containing a rice design, used alone or in spelling "Crowley Inn."

Debbie plans to rent two additional billboards on I-10, one in each direction, and have all billboards repainted. Chef Roy agreed to pay a fifth of the cost, and a fifth of the sign space will be devoted to advertising Cafe Acadie. A "board" across the bottom of each sign will announce special features such as HBO-Showtime, Martin's Tavern, and live entertainment. Each billboard costs about $400 to repaint and about $400 per month.

Debbie also plans to place two signs along Highway 13, a few miles on either side of the inn. Each of these is expected to cost about $300 to paint and $200 per month.

Debbie just purchased space on electronic bulletin boards at the Tourist Information Centers at the east and west I-10 entry points to Louisiana. Users will dial a two-digit code to connect them to the front desk at the inn.

Crowley Inn will join the Louisiana Travel Promotion Association (LTPA). LTPA publishes the *Louisiana Tour Guide* annually and helps members with advertising, printing, and the like.

Though the inn is right beside I-10, an informal survey suggests many people pass without noticing it. So Kathy and Shirley plan to have the guest-room doors painted a noticeable color, such as burgundy, and to use bright colors elsewhere to make the inn more conspicuous.

Shirley and Debbie plan to start making sales calls on present and prospective direct-bill customers and sending them direct-mail advertisements from time to time. They also are seeking ways to entice tour groups to the inn.

■ Place

Crowley Inn is 16 miles east of its nearest competitor, a TraveLodge in Jennings. The Jennings Holiday Inn is three miles further west. East of Crowley, the larger town of Lafayette has a Holiday Inn, a La Quinta Inn, a Motel 6, and several other motels and hotels.

Crowley is home to the Louisiana Rice Festival and nearby towns sponsor festivals celebrating crawfish, frogs, ducks, and other animals and plants. During the days surrounding each festival, the inn normally is booked solid. The inn also fills up during the monthly horse show in Crowley and during the annual rodeo.

Crowley is the seat of Acadia Parish (county) and Art suggested that this makes it the "Capital of Acadiana" (Cajun country is often called Acadiana). A famous Cajun restaurant, Belizaires', is a half mile south of the Crowley Inn, and its signs attract many visitors. Debbie and Shirley plan to feature the "Capital of Acadiana" theme in ads and signs and to encourage the Crowley Chamber of Commerce to do so. Mayor Istre concurred.

ENDNOTES

1. The industry standard for room cleaning time is about a half-hour per room, including laundering. Of course, expensive hotels allow more, inexpensive ones less.
2. "Fee simple" title, in legal jargon, means absolute title.
3. Jules O. Daigle, *A Dictionary of the Cajun Language* (Ann Arbor: Edwards Brothers, 1984), pp. viii–x.
4. Folios are the forms guests fill out upon check-in. Marie LaFleur, who knows most regular inn guests, sorted the folios by purpose of travel. The "local" category, she said, mainly involved romantic liaisons.
5. Provided by the Louisiana Department of Transportation.
6. A country dance, usually involving an overnight stay. Cajun families tend to be close-knit and children usually come along to a *fais-dodo,* bedding down on quilts when they get sleepy.

CASE 36

The YWCA of Black Hawk County

Lynda L. Goulet, Peter G. Goulet, University of Northern Iowa

In 1991, the YWCA of Black Hawk County began its eighth decade of operation. Through most of the 1980s, the YWCA flourished in spite of an unfavorable local economic environment. Its facilities were renovated and its programs expanded. However, by the end of the decade some problems were beginning to become evident.

In late 1989, the YWCA developed its initial budget for 1990, which showed a budgeted deficit of slightly over $24,000 based on estimated direct (annual fundraising) support revenues of $20,000. This estimated level of direct support was below the actual support funds raised in 1989. However, memberships declined after membership and program fees were raised in the last quarter of 1989 and it was believed that these fee increases might also lead to lower levels of direct support. (Exhibits 1 through 4 present revised revenue and expense budgets, based on the increased direct support revenues required to balance the budget.)

The initial budget developed for 1991 projected a somewhat larger deficit than that originally projected for 1990. The executive director recognized that the organization could no longer continue operating as it had in the past. If the organization was to avoid "red ink," it would have to raise revenues from program and fee income or an increase in direct support fundraising, or it might have to consider cutting its level of service. The executive director realized that the organization's environment had changed and to prosper in this environment the YWCA would have to differentiate itself by providing programs and services that met unfilled community needs.

The organization requests that no users of this case make inquiries relating to the YWCA's activities or performance because of time and work constraints of the organization's directors, officers, and staff. The case authors wish to sincerely thank the Executive Director for her valuable assistance in preparing this case.

This case is intended for classroom discussion only, not to depict effective or ineffective handling of administrative situations. All rights reserved to the authors and the Midwest Society for Case Research.

Exhibit 1 YWCA Sources of Revenue

	1988		1989		1990		1991
	Budget	*Actual*	*Budget*	*Actual*	*Budget*	*Actual*	**Budget**
Program service fees	$120,000	$112,020	$120,000	$120,140	$133,700	$123,040	$150,000
United Way allocation	94,030	94,035	97,665	97,670	99,075	99,080	100,485
Membership dues	42,350	40,350	45,000	42,000	45,000	42,685	51,750
Invest. inc. & interest	19,200	27,400	30,500	32,870	32,400	33,060	32,400
Direct support	43,400	14,035	29,000	27,380	44,160	21,650	59,420
Tours	10,500	13,950	11,500	18,000	14,000	15,650	14,000
Building use fees	8,000	9,320	8,000	8,530	9,000	7,870	8,500
Special events	5,000	11,160	7,000	4,355	6,000	6,025	1,500
Camperships	5,000	4,715	5,000	3,755	5,000	4,530	5,000
Salable supplies	4,500	5,250	5,200	4,620	4,600	4,570	4,600
Government grants	1,265	1,225	1,000	1,075	4,000	8,050	22,700
Other	3,450	2,460	3,800	360	925	800	5,025
Total revenue	$356,695	$335,920	$363,665	$360,755	$397,860	$367,010	$455,380
Total expenses (Exhibit 2)	$356,695	$340,120	$363,665	$354,505	$397,860	$366,160	$455,380
Excess or (deficit)	0	($4,200)	0	$6,250	0	$850	0

Exhibit 2 YWCA Expenses

	1988		1989		1990		1991
	Budget	*Actual*	*Budget*	*Actual*	*Budget*	*Actual*	**Budget**
Salaries and wages							
Professional	$ 73,870	$73,245	$85,475	$ 82,870	$ 85,945	$ 82,700	$ 87,885
Clerical, office	51,590	50,600	55,270	55,620	60,220	60,525	72,250
Program staff	48,270	44,215	42,700	43,660	64,725	55,060	85,790
Payroll tax & fringes	32,115	31,895	31,620	30,480	35,115	33,005	40,245
Total salaries/wages	$205,845	$199,955	$215,065	$212,630	$246,005	$231,290	$286,170
Building expenses							
Utilities	$ 32,000	$24,295	$26,000	$ 23,260	$ 32,000	$ 22,660	$ 32,000
Janitorial	23,000	22,465	23,000	22,495	26,955	22,490	24,000
Insurance	14,950	17,180	17,400	14,575	13,075	10,225	12,915
Supplies/maint./other	14,200	14,835	15,700	14,460	16,700	17,825	18,100
Total building exp.	$ 84,150	$78,775	$82,100	$ 74,790	$ 88,730	$ 73,200	$ 87,015
Prof./audit/legal fees	$20,500	$16,020	$ 18,800	$ 19,370	$ 11,910	$ 15,100	$ 20,180
Dues, travel, conferences	10,200	10,580	9,200	9,310	10,350	9,940	11,450
Fin. assist. to individ.	10,000	9,380	10,000	8,070	8,000	3,140	5,000
Goods for resale	4,200	4,160	4,000	3,990	4,000	4,710	4,000
Program suppl./transpor.	4,900	4,585	4,850	4,925	7,065	7,800	15,905
Print/advert./mailing	10,400	10,485	13,000	13,810	14,000	14,805	18,160
Office suppl./telephone	6,500	6,180	6,650	7,610	7,800	6,175	7,500
Total other expenses	$ 66,700	$ 61,390	$ 66,500	$ 67,085	$63,125	$ 61,670	$ 82,195
Total expenses	$356,695	$340,120	$363,665	$354,505	$397,860	$366,160	$455,380

YWCA Budgeted Sources of Revenue by Program Category — Exhibit 3

	Residence		*Day Care*		*Youth*		*Adult HP*		*Spec. Serv.*	
	1990	*1991*	*1990*	*1991*	*1990*	*1991*	*1990*	*1991*	*1990*	*1991*
Program fees	12,000	12,500	41,200	62,900	29,000	28,400	48,000	43,500	3,500	2,700
United Way	15,170	15,340	13,250	13,300	25,170	25,845	11,235	12,000	34,250	34,000
Membership	0	0	760	1,600	7,230	6,800	28,150	27,000	3,490	4,000
Invest. income	0	0	0	0	0	0	0	0	0	0
Direct support	0	0	0	0	0	0	0	0	0	0
Tours	0	0	0	0	0	0	0	0	14,000	14,000
Building use	0	0	0	0	2,750	1,800	3,950	4,900	0	0
Special events	0	0	0	0	500	0	0	550	2,000	950
Camperships	0	0	5,000	5,000	0	0	0	0	0	0
Salable suppl.	0	0	0	0	0	0	1,500	1,500	0	0
Govt. grants	0	0	2,200	0	1,800	11,280	0	0	0	11,420
Other	325	325	0	0	500	0	0	0	0	4,600
Direct revenue	27,495	28,165	62,410	82,800	66,950	74,125	92,835	89,450	57,240	71,670
Allocation of other revenue	13,400	15,835	27,050	34,000	11,395	13,900	19,320	24,260	19,765	21,175
Total revenue	40,895	44,000	89,460	116,800	78,345	88,025	112,155	113,710	77,005	92,845
Total expense (Exhibit 4)	40,895	44,000	89,460	116,800	78,345	88,025	112,155	113,710	77,005	92,845

	1990	*1991*		*1990*	*1991*
Total budgeted direct rev.	$306,930	$346,210	Total estimate direct. exp.	$346,525	$395,840
Allocation of other rev.	90,930	109,170	Allocation of other exp.	51,335	59,540
Total budgeted revenue	$397,860	$455,380	Total estimated expenses	$397,860	$455,380

THE YOUNG WOMEN'S CHRISTIAN ASSOCIATION

The YWCA has its roots in England in the middle of the nineteenth century. Two groups—one a Prayer Union to pray for women and the other which founded Christian homes for women—merged to form the first YWCA. In 1894, the World YWCA was organized in London and headquartered in Geneva. By the turn of the 20th century, hundreds of local YWCA organizations had been established in the United States, and in 1906 the national United States YWCA was formed. Local YWCA organizations are affiliated with their national organization. Local YWCA organizations are, in turn, members of the World YWCA.

The symbol of the world YWCA is a blue triangle, the three sides of which stand for body, mind, and spirit, referring to the recreational, educational, and spiritual aspects of the programs provided by the organization. Beginning with its response to the Industrial Revolution's effect on women, the organization has attempted to help girls and women, without regard to economic, religious, or racial background, move into the mainstream of society by providing safe, comfortable, and inexpensive housing, as well as numerous other programs. The purpose and primary imperative of the YWCA of the United States of America are presented in Exhibit 5. All local YWCA affiliates must adhere to this mission. However, at a conference during the summer of 1991, the national (U.S.A.) YWCA had a planned program agenda that includes a

Exhibit 4 **YWCA Estimated Expenses by Program Category**

	Residence		*Day Care*		*Youth*		*Adult HP*		*Spec. Serv.*	
	1990	*1991*	*1990*	*1991*	*1990*	*1991*	*1990*	*1991*	*1990*	*1991*
Salaries/wages										
Professional	6,075	6,470	14,505	17,735	14,280	12,420	14,700	13,975	27,315	29,130
Cler./office	6,570	7,585	8,175	10,300	11,655	13,700	17,155	20,115	8,130	8,720
Prog. staff	4,290	4,505	26,560	42,705	10,905	11,970	15,925	17,210	7,045	9,400
Tax/fringes	2,660	3,565	6,570	9,440	5,850	5,825	7,850	7,630	8,830	9,475
Total S&W	19,595	22,125	55,810	80,180	42,690	43,915	55,630	58,930	51,320	56,725
Building exp.										
Utilities	6,400	6,400	3,200	3,200	5,760	5,760	9,600	9,600	4,800	4,800
Janitorial	5,390	4,800	2,695	2,400	4,850	4,320	8,085	7,200	4,045	3,600
Insurance	2,060	2,000	3,810	3,750	1,775	1,775	2,990	2,945	1,595	1,595
Supp./maint.	1,400	1,800	850	1,050	3,550	3,850	7,795	7,500	950	1,300
Total bldg.	15,250	15,000	10,555	10,400	15,935	15,705	28,470	27,245	11,390	11,295
Fees	0	0	0	0	2,705	7,530	4,990	3,160	0	3,260
Dues/travel	100	100	300	300	175	1,175	350	350	175	175
Fin. assist	200	200	5,800	2,500	1,100	1,200	800	1,000	100	100
Goods: resale	0	0	0	0	0	0	1,600	1,600	0	0
Prog. supplies	0	0	3,500	6,100	1,840	2,980	560	780	985	5,600
Print/adv./mail	20	20	1,200	1,360	2,920	3,490	4,180	4,560	2,680	3,180
Office & phone	600	600	480	480	720	720	1,200	1,200	600	600
Total other	920	920	11,280	10,740	9,460	17,095	13,680	12,650	4,540	12,915
Direct expense	35,765	38,045	77,645	101,320	68,085	76,715	97,780	98,825	67,250	80,935
Allocated exp.	5,130	5,955	11,815	15,480	10,260	11,310	14,375	14,885	9,755	11,910
Total expense	40,895	44,000	89,460	116,800	78,345	88,025	112,155	113,710	77,005	92,845

Exhibit 5

Young Women's Christian Association of the United States: Purpose and Primary Imperative

The Young Women's Christian Association of the United States of America, a movement rooted in the Christian Faith as known in Jesus and nourished by the resources of that faith, seeks to respond to the barrier-breaking love of God in this day.

The Association draws together into responsible membership women and girls of diverse experiences and faiths, that their lives may be open to new understanding and deeper relationships and that together they may join in the struggle for peace and justice, freedom and dignity for all people.

The One Imperative—To thrust our collective power toward the elimination of racism wherever it exists and by any means necessary.

discussion of whether the national organizational should revise its purpose to state that while its roots are in Christianity, the organization is committed to serving all women.

THE YWCA OF BLACK HAWK COUNTY

The YWCA of Black Hawk County, established in 1911, is a nonprofit organization consisting of a board of trustees (11 members of which 5 are men); a board of directors (28 members, all women); numerous committees; an executive director; 4 full-time program directors; 2 full-time office personnel; and 60 part-time or hourly staff. Further the organization relies on the services of approximately 350 volunteers.

The board of directors is composed of women with strong, diverse backgrounds of professional, business, and community service. Almost all board members are career women (active or recently retired), and the few that are homemakers are actively involved in serving their community. The professionals represented include: a veterinarian, a nursing home administrator, a shopping center manager, several teachers (university, elementary, and technical school), secretaries, a stockbroker (president of the board), social workers, a nurse, managers in various local businesses and government, and entrepreneurs. There are now eight African-American women serving on the board, an increase of three from the YWCA's board during the late 1980s. Almost all members of the board of directors serve on one or more of the following committees: Finance, Financial Development, Planning, Personnel, Membership, Building, Special Services, Health Promotion Services, Youth, Nominating, and the One Imperative Committee.

The president of the board is an ex-officio member of the board of trustees, which meets quarterly to monitor the management of the YWCA's Endowment Fund (consisting of slightly over $400,000). The majority of the members of the board of trustees have expertise in finance and law. The executive director and the four program directors of the YWCA are not members of the board of directors. The executive director began working for the YWCA in April 1989, having served for 9 years as director of the Family and Children's Council (an organization focusing primarily on child abuse issues). The local YWCA's mission is presented as Exhibit 6.

FACILITIES, PROGRAMS, AND SERVICES

The Black Hawk County YWCA is located in a three-story brick building in the downtown area of Waterloo, Iowa. The building, built in 1924, was renovated in 1984–1985 following a $1 million fundraising drive. The facility contains several large meeting rooms, a gymnasium, a weight room, a year-round heated pool, residential rooms, and several kitchens. Its facilities are accessible to the handicapped and ample free parking is adjacent to the building. In 1940, a 130-acre site about a half-hour drive from the YWCA was purchased for a camp site. During the 1950s a pool was constructed, the lodge was winterized, a new dining hall was built, and accommodations for campers were expanded at Camp Wahpaton. Further renovations were made in 1984–1985.

Exhibit 6

Young Women's Christian Association of Black Hawk County: Mission Statement

The Young Women's Christian Association of Black Hawk County serves women and their families within Black Hawk County and surrounding areas. Services are provided for individuals of all ages, races, creeds, and socioeconomic backgrounds.

The YWCA works to promote individual growth and development and to strengthen good community relations.

Promotion of individual growth and development is accomplished through education and training, health and fitness activities, recreation, support services, and other organized efforts designed to develop skills for daily living.

Efforts to strengthen good community relations include both cooperative efforts with other organizations to address community needs, and actions and advocacy on selected current issues consistent with the National YWCA Statement of Purpose and The One Imperative.

Therefore, we determine, as members of the YWCA of Black Hawk County, to thrust our collective power toward the elimination of racial injustice in our unremitting effort to establish peace, justice, freedom, and dignity for all.

The programs and services offered by the YWCA are divided into five major categories: residential, elementary day care, youth development, adult health promotion, and special services. Each of these is described below.

- *Residential Program*—The YWCA provides 10 rooms (one has handicapped access) for women in transition who need a place to stay while they attend school, seek employment, or resolve personal problems. Most of the women served may be categorized as having very low income levels. Rates are $120 or $140 per month with kitchen and laundry facilities available. In the last three years the program has experienced occupancy rates exceeding 85%.

- *Elementary Day Care*—The YWCA provides state-licensed child care before and after school hours and during the summer. Child care is provided at several sites, including elementary schools and a local church from 6:30 a.m. until school begins and after school until 6 p.m. The cost is $3 per session, including a breakfast or afternoon snack and tutoring and other activities. Summer day care is provided for a 10-week period, 7 or 9 hours per day, for $42 per week, including breakfast and lunch. In addition, child care is provided during school holidays. A new three-week summer program for 9- to 12-year-olds is in the planning stage for 1991. The first week will focus on cultural awareness; the second week the children will participate in a community service project; and the third week will focus on environmental awareness. Whether this program will be offered depends upon the availability of staff personnel.

- *Youth Development*—A variety of programs and activities are available for children and young adults. Classes are held in swimming, Tae Kwon Do, gymnastics, and dance. Special classes are also held on various topics including babysitting, cooking, art, and other recreational activities. "Fit Kids" is a special health program for overweight children that stresses exercise, self-esteem building, and nutrition education. A new program is "Mother-Daughter Choices," which teaches goal setting and problem solving to sixth-grade girls and their mothers.

- *Adult Health Promotion*—Activities focusing on health and fitness for adults include swimming, fitness, scuba, massage, gymnasium activities, weight room training, and aerobics. In addition, special programs are offered in such areas as nutrition, weight loss, breast self-examination, and cholesterol and blood pressure measurement. "Applause" is an exercise program serving women who have undergone breast cancer surgery. "Super Unique Moms" is a new program aimed at teenage mothers to help them learn parenting skills and socialize with other teen mothers. Their children are cared for by the staff during the program periods.

- *Special Services*—Included in this program category are: classes in prenatal care, crafts, cooking, wardrobe, personal growth, and leadership; advocacy classes to educate people in areas of public policy such as sexual harassment, affirmative action, and discrimination; conferences and seminars on diverse topics such as balancing work and family, African history, and substance abuse; club groups including hiking and book discussions; and tours, one to three day trips within the state or in nearby surrounding states. In 1988, there were 27 tours with 1550 total boardings. In both 1989 and 1990, the tour program's boardings were close to 2000. In the first few months of 1991, the tour program set attendance records. Several tours have been arranged to Dubuque, Iowa, where tour participants spend an afternoon or evening on a riverboat cruise that features low-stakes gambling. Iowa law permits riverboat gambling with a loss limit of $200 per individual. It should also be noted that the tour program's reported revenue (refer to Exhibit 1) is net of all costs except the YWCA's personnel involved in arranging the tours.

Exhibit 7 identifies the number of individuals served by each of the five program categories. One of the major difficulties with program participant data is that they do not show total service levels, but are based on an unduplicated count of participants in each program. A participant who uses a given program more than once, or multiple programs within a given category, is still only counted once. Records of attendance are maintained manually, with each person's participation in a program category reported on a different file card. Thus, the data in Exhibit 7 essentially reflect the number of file cards for the year. The managers recognize that this manual system is inefficient, but at the

Program Participants **Exhibit 7**

	1988	*1989*	*1990*
Residential	35	32	40
Elem. day care	116	136	159
Youth devel.	1938	1412	1303
Adult health prom.	2057	1748	1911
Special serv.	2224	2797	1852
Total	6370	6125	5265

present time the staff does not have the time, expertise, or funds to computerize the system.

YWCA LOCATION AND BLACK HAWK COUNTY DEMOGRAPHICS

Between 1980 and 1990, the population of Black Hawk County declined about 11%, from about 140,000 to slightly under 125,000. This was approximately the same level as the county's 1960 population. Waterloo is the county's main city with a population of about 66,500 (down from about 76,000 in 1980). Cedar Falls, adjacent to the western boundary of Waterloo, has a population of 34,300 (down from 36,300 in 1980) and is the site of the University of Northern Iowa with a growing student population of 13,000. Several other small cities are located within the county, three of which are adjacent to Waterloo's city limits. Exhibit 8 identifies the composition of the population by age, race, and household characteristics.

Exhibit 8 **Black Hawk County Demographics**

Age Distribution of Population

Under 15 years	22.9%
15–19	10.8%
20–24	11.9%
25–34	16.9%
35–44	10.1%
45–54	8.9%
55–64	8.3%
65 and over	10.2%

Racial Groups and Their Labor Force Participation Rate

	% of Population	*Labor Participation %*
White	92.3%	63.2%
Black	6.3%	63.5%
Other	1.4%	63.7%

Household Characteristics

1 person	21.4%
2 persons	32.3%
3 persons	17.4%
4 persons	16.4%
5 or more persons	12.5%
Average persons per household	2.72
Average persons per family	3.21

Source: Cedar Falls Chamber of Commerce; U.S. Bureau of the Census.

The area's population decline can be attributed to the agricultural crisis in the early 1980s and the resulting decline in employment by farm-related businesses. One of Waterloo's major employers, Deere and Company, reduced local employment by about 10,000 during the 1980s. However, both population and employment levels have again begun to increase as new employers from diverse industries have moved into the area. Residential housing construction has been experiencing a boom in the last three years, confirming the area's economic recovery.

The YWCA is located about four blocks from the central downtown area of Waterloo. The YW is approximately a 15-minute drive from Cedar Falls and a 10-minute drive from most residential areas in Waterloo. Waterloo's downtown area includes shopping, office complexes, and numerous governmental offices.

SOURCES OF REVENUE

As a nonprofit organization, the YWCA of Black Hawk County receives revenues from a variety of sources. (See Appendix 1 for a brief description of the characteristics of nonprofit organizations.) Its primary sources are program service fees, United Way allocations, membership dues, investment income from the Endowment Fund, direct support, tours, building use fees, special event fees, "camperships," salable supplies, and government grants. These revenue sources are identified in Exhibits 1 and 3.

Even though the allocation from the United Way has recently increased annually (refer to Exhibit 1), there is no guarantee this trend will continue. The United Way conducts its annual fundraising campaign each fall. The amount of money raised, less expenses, is then available for allocation among *all* United Way affiliated organizations. The number of organizations receiving funds from the United Way in Black Hawk County exceeds 50 and has been increasing. Each year each organization seeking United Way funds submits a request for a certain level of funding and makes presentations to the United Way to explain and justify the request. Allocations are based on the comparative merit of the requests and the total amount of funds available. Allocations are determined in the first quarter of the year and are based on the funds raised in the previous year's campaign.

Currently, when the YWCA submits its request to United Way, the request must be made by program. Documents must be presented showing the number of participants served by each program, including the number of "new" participants served by each program. United Way, in turn, makes its allocations to the YWCA by program, as shown in Exhibit 3. It may be noted that in 1983 revenues received from the United Way totaled $144,000 and constituted 48% of the YWCA's operating budget. This may be contrasted to the 1990 allocation of slightly less than $100,000, representing about 25% of the YWCA's budget revenues.

The United Way is not the only organization supplying funds to human service providers in Black Hawk County. A major foundation and several other agencies also provide significant funds. To coordinate the allocation of these scarce resources more effectively an organization known as the Metro Fund Distribution Coordination Council was recently established. This organization is intended to support the standardization of funding requests and to develop independent research in support of regional human service needs to make the distribution of funds more effective. Beginning in 1991 this organization will receive all funding requests and provide these requests to all funding agencies along with its needs research information. To initiate its activities the coordinating council commissioned the Center for Social and Behavioral Research at the University of Northern Iowa to conduct a community needs survey in December, 1990. The results of that survey identified the major problems/needs within the community to be: substance abuse, employment, housing, family services (child abuse and teen pregnancy), and child care. The implication of this new structure is that to obtain funds human service providers will have to make their human service activities consistent with the needs identified by the coordinating council. The YWCA's executive director will serve on several of the coordination council's research committees.

Twice a year the YWCA's financial development committee has a fund raiser that generates support revenue and also serves a public relations function, creating awareness of the YWCA's activities in the community. Interest earned on the YWCA Endowment Fund is another major source of revenue. In an emergency the organization may also borrow money from the fund. The YWCA provides several kinds of memberships, identified in Exhibit 9. Membership fees were raised in the last quarter of 1989. Supporting, sustaining, and sponsoring memberships help the YWCA serve those persons less able to afford its services. The YW offers financial aid for memberships, programs, and activities. A YWCA membership provides: quarterly program brochures; free weight training instruction; a voice in determining YW policies and programs; and access to facilities, classes, clubs, support groups, programs, and special services for which fees are charged. For example, for adults unlimited use of the pool, gymnasium, and weight room is $14 per month or $125 per year. Access to the gym only is $75 per year (or $7 per month or $.75 per visit); access to the pool only is $110 per year (or $12 per month or $1 per visit). The Body Shop (weight room) is restricted to persons 15 years or older, while the use of the whirlpool requires anyone under the age of 12 to be accompanied by an adult. A life guard is on duty at all times when the pool is open. It may be mentioned that the World and National YWCA organizations' charters restrict voting membership to women and teenage girls. Thus, none of the local YWCA's male members may vote.

Exhibit 9(a) identifies the trend in voting members (female adults and teen girls). The large increase in memberships in 1985 may be attributed to curiosity associated with building renovation following the fundraising campaign. The decline in membership in 1990 may be attributed to the increase in membership fees. Exhibit 9(b) identifies recent membership trends, by type of membership, based on calendar years. Exhibit 9(c) presents the same membership data calculated for the period October through September to show the change in membership before and after the increase in fees.

COMMUNITY IMAGE

In 1982, prior to the major fundraising effort to renovate the YWCA's building and Camp Wahpaton, a consulting firm from Chicago was hired. The consulting firm's primary tasks included: determining the attitudes of community leaders to the proposed fundraising program, identifying community leaders capable and willing to assume a major role in the campaign, and developing

YWCA Memberships **Exhibit 9**

(a) Types of Memberships and Prices as of Fall 1989

Sponsoring	$250	Adult	$25 (was $20)
Sustaining	$100	Sr. citizen and teens	$15 (was $10)
Sustaining	$ 50	Youth (under 12)	$ 8 (was $4)

Adult Women and Teen Girl Memberships (voting members)

1983	*1984*	*1985*	*1986*	*1987*	*1988*	*1989*	*1990*
1686	1628	1917	1641	1662	1706	1717	1484

(b) Membership Count for Calendar Years (Jan. through Dec.)

	1987	*1988*	*1989*	*1990*
Adult women	1100	1084	1088	871
Women senior citizens	496	550	565	561
Teen girls	66	72	64	52
Youth: girls	486	541	499	379
Adult men	221	239	211	188
Men senior citizens	52	67	57	51
Teen boys	40	60	64	40
Youth: boys	413	440	377	329
Total	2874	3053	2925	2471

(c) Memberships—Oct. Previous Year Through Sept. Current Year

	1988	*1989*	*1990*
Adult women	1059	1135	900
Women senior citizens	525	579	553
Teen girls	66	73	47
Youth: girls	524	488	418
Adult men	233	239	202
Men senior citizens	71	56	53
Teen boys	47	74	41
Youth: boys	414	380	348
Total	2939	3024	2562

an appropriate timing and strategy for the campaign. To these ends, the firm conducted approximately 50 interviews with corporate and community leaders whose opinions and support were considered vital to the success of the YWCA's fundraising efforts. Several findings from this survey are shown in Exhibit 10.

As a result of the survey the YWCA made a concerted effort to carefully select members for the board of directors who have business experience and visibility in the community. Members of the board who are not actively involved with the organization during their three-year term are replaced.

As a result of its 1982 survey, the consulting firm recommended that the YWCA conduct an awareness program prior to the fundraising campaign, that the objective of the fundraising campaign be scaled down from $1.75 million to $1 million, and that the campaign be planned for 1983. The campaign was, in fact, a success, raising slightly more than the $1 million established goal. The

Exhibit 10 **Consultant's Report from Interviews**

Perceived Image of the YWCA	
Good	68%
Fair	19%
Poor	9%
Unaware	4%
Belief in Attainability of the $1.75 Million Objective	
Attainable	30%
Possibly attainable	23%
Unattainable	32%
No response	15%
Willingness to Make a Personal Contribution to the Campaign	
Yes	64%
Maybe	21%
No	15%
Willingness to Work on Fundraising Campaign	
Yes	34%
Maybe	19%
No	47%
Perceived Strength of YWCA Board to Raise Funds	
Good	13%
Average	25%
Weak	49%
No response	13%

Source: Adapted from "A Planning Study Program Prepared for the YWCA of Black Hawk County." June 17, 1982. Ketchum, Inc.

awareness campaign and the subsequent building renovation resulted in a substantial increase in membership. However, this increase was not permanent.

At the end of the 1980s, there was some indication that the YWCA's image had become less clear. Many new programs had been added, making it difficult for the general public to understand the organization's primary purpose. Further, many new competitors had entered the local area, providing programs that overlapped considerably with the YWCA's offerings.

COMPETITION

The YMCA may be considered the closest competitor to the YWCA. During 1980, the YMCA had a fundraising effort that raised $2.7 million for the construction of a new YMCA facility. The new YM was opened in 1982 on a site on the western edge of Waterloo, adjacent to Cedar Falls. The old YM, located in downtown Waterloo, was subsequently converted into office space, an eating club, and a private health club. The juxtaposition of the two fundraising efforts within a three-year period resulted in a wide variety of responses from the general public. On the positive side, many people felt that it was important to the community to have a Y facility in downtown Waterloo and supported the YWCA's campaign. On the other hand, some citizens believed that having two separate Y organizations was unnecessary. The new central location of the YMCA made it more attractive to Cedar Falls residents. The YMCA's membership totals almost 5000 and membership fees are more expensive than membership in the YWCA. For example, adult memberships cost $216 per year, youth memberships are $78 for ages 13–18 or $66 for ages 7–12, and family memberships run $384 per year. (However, membership at the YMCA entitles the member to use the weight room, gym, and pool at no extra cost.) Many of the adult members of the YWCA are especially attracted to the YW because of its downtown location and because the facilities are not usually full.

The YWCA's primary competition for youth and teens are the Boy Scouts, the Girl Scouts, the Camp Fire Girls, the Boys/Girls Club, and the Big Brothers and Big Sisters organizations. Recently all seven of these United Way agencies have formed a Youth Development Association to share ideas and to focus attention on the need for youth development programs throughout the area. All of these organizations face common difficulties: lack of funds and a reliance on volunteer workers.

The YWCA has identified numerous other local organizations that provide competition for one or more of the other four categories of its programs/services. These include the following:

- Area hospitals that permit the public to use their physical fitness facilities for a modest fee and provide wellness and other educational programs at a low cost;
- Waterloo and Cedar Falls city recreational facilities;
- Private recreation and fitness centers in the area;
- Private day care facilities (the average cost for elementary day care before and after school and during holidays is $1.50 per child per hour);
- Local hotels/motels that permit the public to utilize their pool facilities for a small fee;
- Public schools that permit the use of their recreational facilities, including indoor pools, for a small fee or for free and also provide educational programs/services;
- Senior citizens centers that have facilities that may be rented and provide activities and programs for senior citizens as well as the general public;
- Local churches that have facilities and provide activities and programs for various age groups; and
- Other social service organizations (both nonprofit and governmental) providing programs and activities for various groups, such as the Martin Luther King Jr. Center, the Family Service League, Goodwill Industries, and so forth.

THE PROBLEM

As 1991 approached, the executive director viewed the deteriorating, although not yet critical, budget situation and realized that some action was required if the YWCA was to avoid cutting its services. Increased competition, potential complications in obtaining funds from county funding agencies, the need to differentiate its programs, increasing competition for the scarce time of willing, experienced volunteers, the need to find additional revenues, and other problems all needed to be addressed if the YWCA of Black Hawk County was to continue to serve its constituents effectively.

APPENDIX 1: CHARACTERISTICS OF NONPROFIT ORGANIZATIONS

Nonprofit organizations may be termed nonstock corporations because, although they receive a state charter, there are no owners and, hence, there is no stock. A board of trustees is established to oversee the organization's activities to protect the interests of the groups that the organization is chartered to serve. Nonprofit organizations are exempt from federal and state taxes on income derived as a result of activities related to the organizations' social welfare purpose. Nonprofits may also engage in activities unrelated to their purpose. However, revenues from such unrelated purposes must be less than half of the organization's total revenue and any profit earned on such activities is taxed at the corporate rate. Any profit (or deficit) generated (after any applicable tax) from the nonprofit's activities is recorded in a "fund balance" account similar to the retained earnings account for a for-profit business. Nonprofits may borrow funds and even issue corporate bonds. When a nonprofit operates at a deficit, however, creditors may not force the organization into bankruptcy. If a nonprofit chooses to terminate its operations, assets are sold to pay creditors. If insufficient funds exist, then creditors will not receive the full amount owed to them. However, if extra assets or funds remain after creditors have been paid in full, such assets or funds are "gifted" to another nonprofit with a similar purpose.

CASE 37

The Metropolitan Museum of Art

Marilyn M. Helms, Paula J. Haynes, Tammy L. Swenson, University of Tennessee at Chattanooga

The New York Metropolitan Museum of Art, or Met, ended the 1990–1991 fiscal year with an operating deficit of $2 million. The deficit occurred in part because of decreases in auxiliary revenue, increases in operation expenditures, and decreases in admissions revenue. Even though the base museum attendance figures exceeded those of previous years, the absence of large-scale ticketed exhibitions or "blockbusters" curtailed admissions revenue in 1990. During 1991, however, admissions revenues increased due to rising admission prices and the return of large-scale exhibitions.

The Met is dependent on external sources of revenue including interest on endowments, gifts, governmental appropriations, and grants as well as internal sources of revenue from merchandising operations, auditorium rental, parking garage fees, restaurants, admissions, memberships, royalties, and fees. Operating expenses include costs of the curatorial departments, providing educational programs and libraries, providing public information, costs associated with development including marketing research, stocking merchandise inventories for auxiliary operations, and various additional administrative costs.[1] Because total expenditures are rising at a faster rate than total revenues, future deficits are predicted. Management of the museum must find creative and effective ways to sustain financial stability.

HISTORY

The state of New York established the museum on April 13, 1870, by granting a charter to a group forming a corporation in the name of the Metropolitan Museum of Art. The corporation was formed for the purpose of "establishing

This case is intended for classroom discussion only, not to depict effective or ineffective handling of administrative situations. All rights reserved to the authors.

and maintaining in the city of New York a museum and library of art, of encouraging and developing the study of the fine arts, and the application of arts to manufacturing and practical life, of advancing the general knowledge of kindred subjects, and, to that end, of furnishing popular instruction and recreation."[2] The mission remains unchanged to date with one exception, the word "recreation" has been removed.[3]

CITY SUPPORT

The city of New York owns the building housing the museum, but the collections are the property of the corporation operating the Met. The city continues to appropriate funds to the museum to be used for maintaining the building as well as providing utilities at no charge to the Metropolitan. The allocations in 1991 totaled $15,633,609 which is 9.3 percent of the total operating revenue for the year; however, the allocations are increasing at a decreasing rate due to the fiscal instability of the city of New York. A history of support from the city of New York is included in the five-year summary shown in Exhibit 1.[4]

COLLECTIONS

The Met is a nonprofit, tax-exempt [501(c) (3)] organization located on the east side of Central Park. Museum collections include ancient and modern art from

Exhibit 1 **The Metropolitan Museum of Art: Five-Year Summary**

	1991	*1990*	*1989*	*1988*	*1987*
Operating Fund: Revenue and Support					
Total income from endowment including The Cloisters	$ 14,169,461	$ 12,815,529	$ 10,838,371	$ 10,849,935	$ 9,912,411
City of New York					
Funds for guardianship and maintenance	9,645,657	10,193,481	9,892,601	9,970,936	8,339,423
Values of utilities provided	6,068,111	5,398,227	5,489,227	4,910,772	4,768,439
Memberships	11,723,453	10,809,726	10,557,710	9,732,467	9,674,124
Gifts and grants					
Education, community affairs, and special exhibitions	5,784,889	5,921,025	4,419,936	2,481,572	3,852,564
General-purpose contributions	15,864,740	14,126,525	11,492,125	9,862,288	9,596,497
Income for specified funds utilized	439,330	539,539	403,308	323,237	360,722
Admissions	8,621,001	7,304,343	10,032,361	6,588,169	8,343,996
Royalties and fees	1,814,579	1,222,951	1,438,572	878,547	838,063
Other	3,817,124	4,941,078	4,393,423	4,737,758	2,241,464
Gain on partial termination of pension plan				7,828,874	
Income before auxiliary activities	77,948,345	73,272,424	68,957,634	68,164,555	57,927,703
Revenue of auxiliary activities	90,154,977	79,565,366	78,480,090	64,967,946	61,088,135
Total revenue and support	168,103,322	152,837,790	147,437,724	133,132,501	119,015,838

(Continued)

The Metropolitan Museum of Art: Five-Year Summary (continued) **Exhibit 1**

Expenses					
Curatorial					
Curatorial departments, conservation and cataloguing	16,617,016	15,091,929	14,921,578	13,266,536	12,724,858
Operation of The Cloisters	3,253,558	2,913,132	2,801,680	2,404,003	2,322,191
Special exhibitions	5,789,990	6,242,448	5,061,807	3,407,668	5,056,044
Education, community programs, and libraries	5,300,858	5,104,734	5,700,470	4,351,743	3,641,121
Financial, legal, and other administrative functions	6,084,069	5,542,451	5,046,463	4,646,079	4,483,464
Public information, development, and membership services	5,431,390	6,649,179	5,398,638	4,809,956	5,259,375
Operations					
Guardianship	15,404,915	14,981,129	13,497,933	12,305,602	12,434,875
Maintenance	9,994,162	8,460,979	8,075,233	7,284,095	6,721,522
Operating services	5,359,190	4,870,045	4,572,179	3,870,884	3,586,939
Value of utilities provided by the city of New York	6,068,111	5,398,227	5,489,227	4,910,772	4,768,439
Nonexhibition capital construction and renovation	2,088,713	2,530,557	1,163,930		
Expenses before auxiliary activities	81,391,972	77,784,810	71,729,138	61,337,338	60,998,828
Cost of sales and expenses of auxiliary activities	88,672,214	77,647,773	72,223,048	61,555,170	53,968,101
Total expenses	170,064,186	155,432,583	143,952,186	122,892,508	114,966,929
Revenue and support (under) over expenses	(1,960,864)	(2,594,793)	3,485,538	10,239,993	4,048,909
Transfer of gain on partial termination of pension plan and net pension income to endowment funds				9,195,557	
Net (decrease) increase in operating fund balance	$(1,960,864)	$(2,594,793)	$ 3,485,538	$ 1,044,436	$ 4,048,909
Additional information					
Endowment funds balance	$450,890,594	$425,725,761	$396,149,106	$331,790,406	$353,836,762
Capital construction expenditures	$ 22,978,339	$ 20,434,301	$ 15,476,598	$ 30,866,842	$ 22,299,538
Acquisitions of art	$ 16,945,340	$ 18,259,644	$ 17,107,754	$ 15,845,522	$ 7,000,695
Full-time employees	1,627	1,659	1,568	1,542	1,503
Visitors to the Main Building and The Cloisters	4,702,078	4,558,560	4,816,388	3,978,404	4,859,522

Source: The Metropolitan Museum of Art, *Annual Reports.*

Egypt, Greece, Rome, the Near and Far East, pre-Columbian cultures, and the United States. The Cloisters, a branch museum, houses the European medieval art collection. This gallery is located in Fort Tryon Park on the far north tip of Manhattan Island.[5] The structure is constructed from parts of five European monasteries. Opened in 1938, the land and the building were donated to the city of New York and much of the art within was donated by John D. Rockefeller, Jr. (see Exhibit 2 for the area map).[6]

Exhibit 2
The Metropolitan Museum of Art: Floor Plan

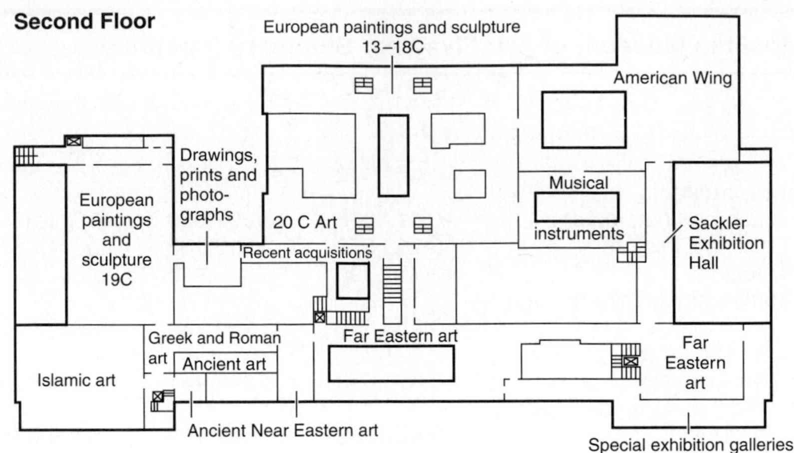

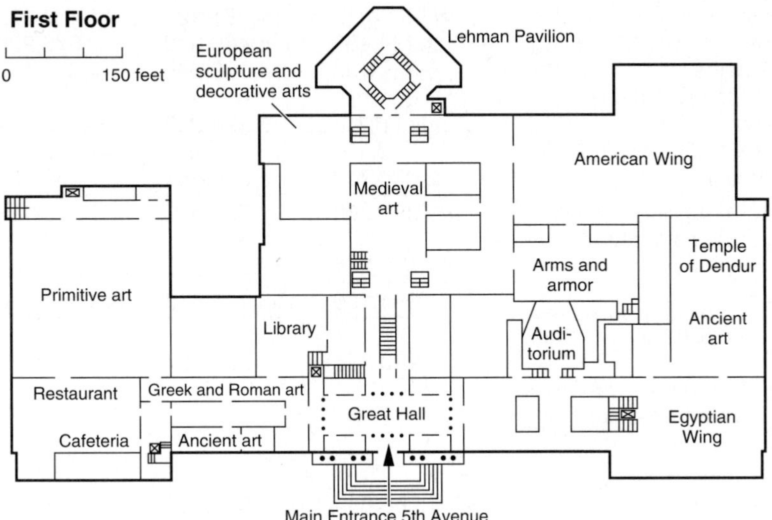

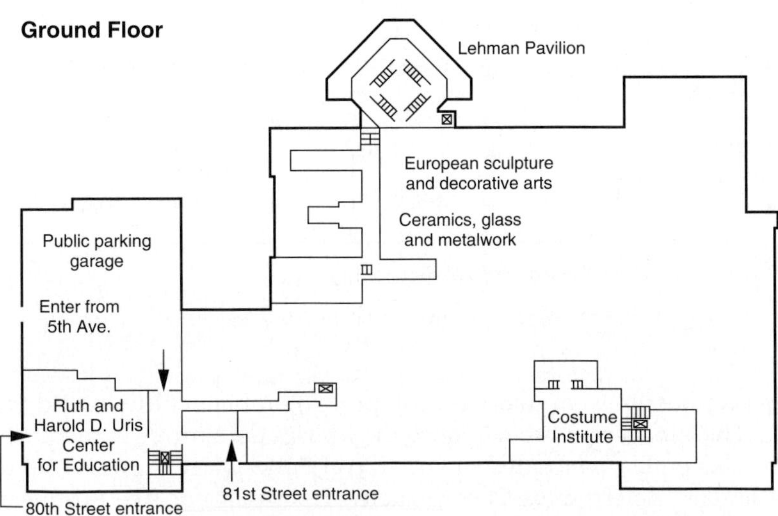

Courtesy of the Metropolitan Museum of Art. All rights reserved.

FACILITIES

The museum consists of many gallery wings, a 250,000 volume library of art and reference materials, used by graduate students in accordance with the museum's affiliation with New York University; a 708- and a 246-seat auditorium; 3 classrooms; a restaurant and cafeteria; a parking garage; and a museum store (as is shown in Exhibit 3). Ten other museum stores are operated by the Metropolitan off-site in New York City, Connecticut, California, Ohio, and New Jersey.[7]

ACTIVITIES

Activities at the museum include guided tours, lectures, gallery talks, concerts, formally organized educational programs for children, inter-museum loans, and permanent, temporary, and travelling exhibitions.[8]

MANAGEMENT

Currently, the Met is operated by a dual management system, as shown in Exhibit 4. The president and the director report directly to the board of trus-

The Cloisters: Floor Plan **Exhibit 3**

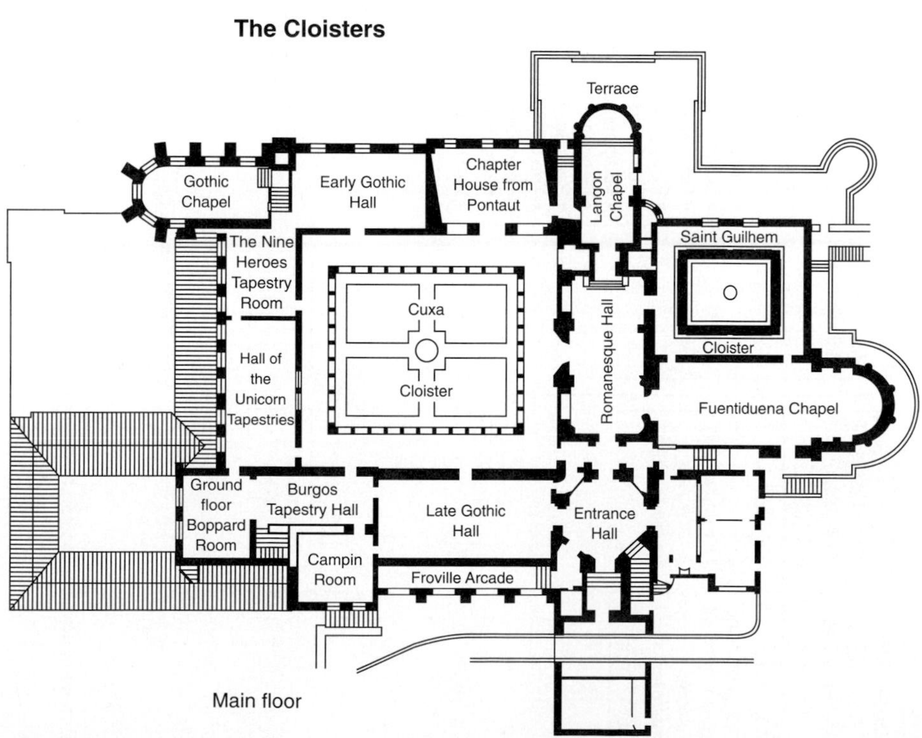

Courtesy of the Metropolitan Museum of Art. All rights reserved.

Exhibit 4 **The Metropolitan Museum of Art: Organization Chart, October 1990**

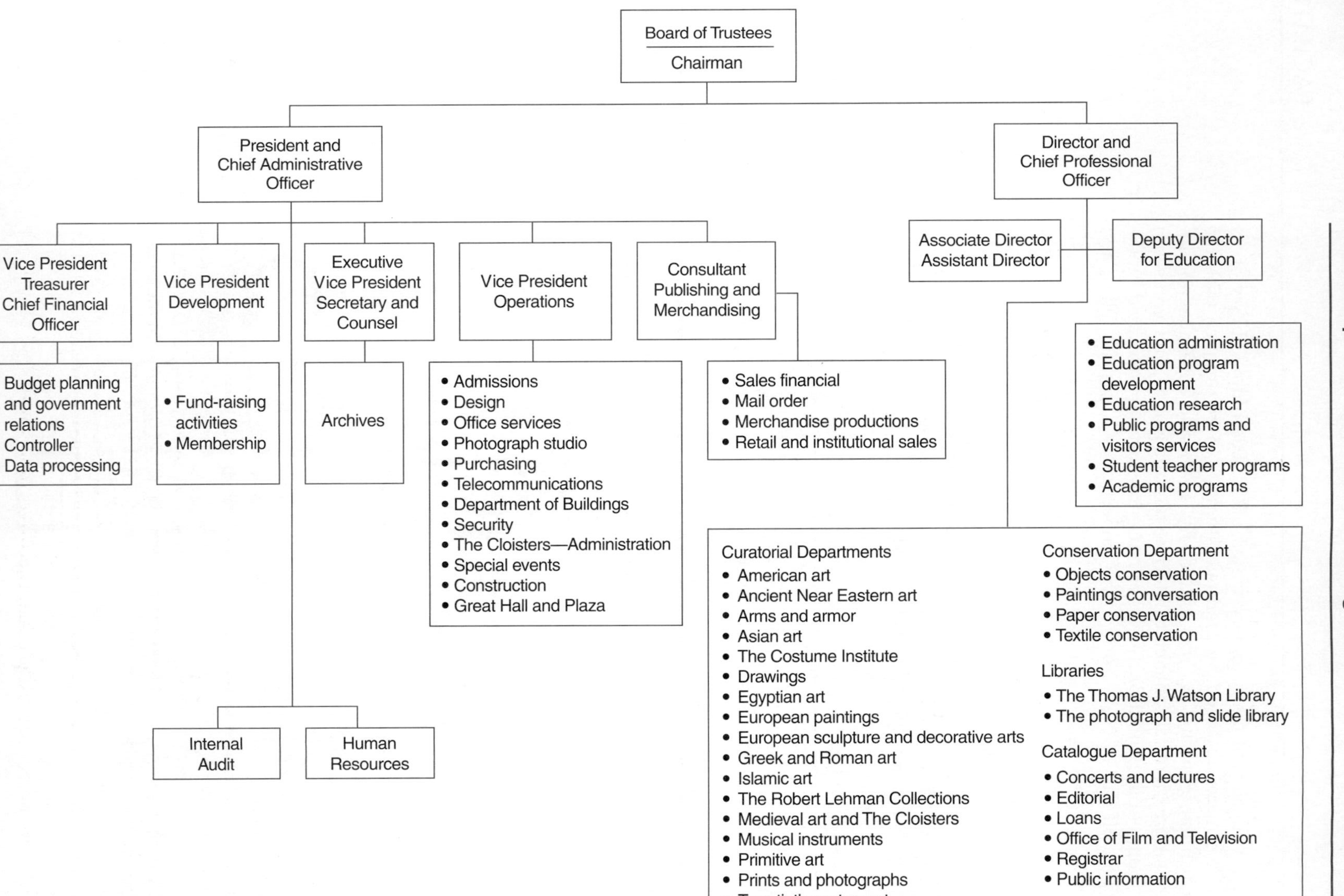

Courtesy of the Metropolitan Museum of Art. All rights reserved.

tees. The dual management system was started in 1978, when the board decided the museum was too complex and large for one person to manage.[9] Prior to the board's action in 1978, Thomas Hoving had been the chief executive at the museum since 1967. Often disparaged as a publicity-seeking showman, by 1971, Hoving had brought the museum to a fiscal crisis through his excessive acquisitions and expansion projects.[10] Some of these included the addition of the Lehman Wing, a glass-covered garden court in 1975; the Sackler Wing, a climate-controlled glass-roofed room, housing the Temple of Dendur in 1978; and the American Wing in 1980. Major renovations of the Great Hall and Costume Institute were completed in 1970 and 1971.[11]

Most of the controversy surrounding Hoving's tenure was due to his role in institutionalizing the "blockbuster" event at the Metropolitan as an answer to the financial crisis. Because the public is most attracted to temporary events, attendance figures were high at the large-scale ticketed events.[12] Examples of these types of events were the "Treasures of Tutankhamen" show in 1978 and 1979 in which 1.2 million tickets were sold. Other examples of large-scale ticketed events include "The Great Age of Fresco," "Mexico: Splendors of Thirty Centuries," and the controversial "Harlem on my Mind."[13] The "blockbuster" issue has been intensely debated, however. Supporters of these events say the attraction of new audiences will diminish the elitist image of museums. While those against such exhibitions, such as Sherman Lee, director of the Cleveland Museum, feel the values of the marketplace, if applied carelessly, may undermine public confidence in the museum's integrity.

Both of these views aside, the revenue earned from additional attendees has helped support all the museum's activities in the last ten years. Since Lee's retirement from the Cleveland Museum, Philippe de Montebello, the current director of the Metropolitan and Hoving's successor, has taken on the responsibility of the "anti-blockbuster" cause. Mr. de Montebello's position is to "lament the cost-effective mentality that places any museum activity that does not generate attendance or immediate income in jeopardy."[14] For the year ended June 30, 1990, there were no large-scale ticketed events at the Metropolitan, and the total revenue from admissions decreased by 27 percent.[15] However, during 1991 the museum's increased admission prices and large-scale exhibition offerings increased total admission revenues.

Currently, de Montebello and William H. Luers, the president, share the responsibility of managing the Met. Philippe de Montebello, a graduate of Harvard and New York University, is primarily responsible for all curatorial functions, conservation departments, libraries, and educational activities. William H. Luers, a former U.S. Ambassador to Czechoslovakia, is responsible for the business side of the Metropolitan. His basic responsibilities include daily operations, merchandising, development, human resources, internal auditing, and all financial matters including budgeting. Even though the president is responsible for development of the Metropolitan including fund raising, de Montebello is also involved heavily in this activity as well as acquiring donations of works of art and money. Mr. Luers stated, "Phillippe should be perceived as the man who gives esthetic and artistic vision to the museum. And I am the manager, diplomat, executive, fund-raiser, and basically a communicator."[16]

FUND-RAISING

In 1982, the Met began a public campaign to raise $150 million to offset operating deficits and enhance the endowment. Even though large gifts have been solicited for specific projects on several occasions, this campaign was the first formal fund-raising drive ever conducted. These funds were supposed to help the Metropolitan Museum achieve financial stability, to allow all galleries to stay open when the museum is open, to finance the existing educational programs, the work of curatorship, and the conservation library.[17] This five year drive was completed in 1987 and was successful in meeting the $150 million goal; however, the Metropolitan has experienced an operating deficit of $2.6 million for the 1989–1990 fiscal year and a $2.0 million deficit for 1990–1991 with future deficits predicted. The development staff at the Metropolitan has implemented the following fund-raising techniques in an attempt to offset deficits.

■ Endowed Chairs

An effective fund-raising technique, borrowed from universities and hospitals, has been soliciting funds for existing curatorships in the form of endowed chairs. All major art dealers in New York as well as industry leaders are approached to solicit endowments. These chairs would carry the name of the donor who would add to the endowment indefinitely. This drive was the first attempt to raise the salaries of curators so the Metropolitan could be competitive within the job market by attracting the best people and retain the people they already have by increasing their existing salaries. Raises of this type would have not otherwise been possible due to the operating fund shortfalls.[18, 19]

■ Corporate Sponsorship

As governmental funding decreases, corporations have come under increasing pressure to take the lead in funding social and community programs. Based on a 1991 study performed by *American Demographics,* the largest share of corporate support goes to education (38 percent) with health and human services (34 percent) following. The results of this survey do not present a promising future in corporate sponsorship of the arts because most corporations practice "strategic philanthropy" focusing philanthropic efforts to maximize their returns.[20] At the Metropolitan, great effort is given to matching the 30 annual special exhibits to corporations' activities to entice them to fund the exhibit; otherwise the exhibit might not be shown.[21] One example of matching a corporation's activities to an exhibit was a gift of $500,000 from the Hunting World Group of Companies to maintain a gallery displaying American Arms.[22]

A corporate patron program is also available and requires an annual donation of $30,000. This membership level allows companies the right to have one party a year, at their own expense, in the Temple of Dendur, the American Wing, or in the Medieval Sculpture Hall. Proceeds from this technique cover operating costs. Even though private use of public space is a controversial issue, it has proved to be a successful way to generate funding. Phillippe de Montebello said, "There is no ministry of culture in the United States. We don't receive a check from Washington, so we have to seek ways to provide revenues."[23]

■ Memberships

The museum has various levels of membership and councils. The chair's council members donate $25,000 annually and are included in the governance of the museum. Membership in this council is by invitation only. The Real Estate Council is responsible for raising money for special showings not fully financed. Each member is given 15 invitations to a special showing.[24] There are many memberships available to the public. Members enjoy free admission and receive the *Bulletin*, a quarterly magazine, and the bimonthly events listing, the *Calendar*. Also they receive catalogues of the museum at no cost and are given 10 percent off all merchandise. The Metropolitan Museum's membership is now over 100,000. In addition, the contribution levels required for all categories of membership were increased in 1991. See Exhibits 5 and 6 for a comparison of the number of members by category for 1987 through 1991.

Annual Members — Exhibit 5

*Current Prices**	*1991*	*1990*	*1989*	*1988*	*1987*
Student ($30)	1,557	1,575	1,517	1,309	1,381
Individual ($70)	29,175	33,054	34,548	30,425	32,379
Dual ($125)	21,261	23,299†	24,485‡	22,440	23,826
Sustaining ($300)	6,539	7,329	7,729	6,486	7,047
Supporting					
Contributing ($600)	1,547	1,671	1,885	1,798	1,773
Donor ($900)	555	611	634	562	581
Sponsor ($2,000)	507	521	541	524	577
Patron ($4,000)	156	182	175	142	82
Upper patron ($6,000)	51	62	51	45	36
Nat'l asso. ($35)*	32,848	31,555	29,777	31,058	27,189
Total	94,196	99,859	101,342	94,789	94,871

Source: The Metropolitan Museum of Art, *1991 Annual Report.*

*Rates for all membership categories were increased an average of 21 percent in 1991.
†Includes life members.
‡Nonresident membership.

Members of the Corporation — Exhibit 6

	1991	*1990*	*1989*	*1988*	*1987*
Honorary fellows for life	3	3	3	3	4
Fellows for life	873	901	911	936	965
Fellows in perpetuity	329	336	342	349	357
Benefactors	355	389	372	364	334
Total corporation members	1,560	1,629	1,628	1,652	1,660
Total annual members	95,756	99,859	101,342	94,789	94,871
Grand total	97,316	101,488	102,970	96,441	96,531

Source: The Metropolitan Museum of Art, *1991 Annual Report.*

■ Government Grants

For the year ended June 30, 1991, the Met received funding from the local, state, and federal governments. The city of New York provides the building that houses the museum, the utilities, and appropriate funds for maintaining the building. The state of New York provides an annual allocation from the New York State Council on the Arts for general operating and program support. Special capital funds from the Natural Heritage Trust were received for support of the special exhibitions programs. Federal agencies such as the National Endowment for the Arts and the Institute of Museum Services provided support for specific projects and general operations. Funds provided from governmental sources amounted to $17,059,604 for the year ended June 30, 1991. Most governmental support is appropriated on an annual basis; therefore, during recessionary periods this external funding is uncertain.[25]

■ Gifts

The 1986 Tax Reform Act (TRA86) curtailed donations of works of art to the Metropolitan and other museums. The change in the tax law reduced the tax deduction donors could take for appreciated art objects. This move resulted in many of these objects being sold to the highest bidder in auction houses.[26] A survey conducted by *American Demographics* found that charitable giving by corporations fell by 12 percent after the 1986 Tax Reform Act became effective.[27] In March 1991, the Metropolitan received the largest gift it had received in over 50 years, probably due to a temporary "tax window," a one-year restoration of tax deductions for the full market value of art donated in 1991. Valued at $1 billion, the paintings donated by Walter Annenberg will not become the property of the Metropolitan until Mr. Annenberg's death.[28]

■ Admissions

The Met is the number one tourist attraction in New York City. For the year ended June 30, 1991, there were 4,702,078 visitors to the museum and the Cloisters. (Refer again to Exhibit 1 for attendance figures from 1987 through 1991.) Attendance decreased in 1990 because there were no large-scale ticketed exhibitions like the two in 1989. Because of this, revenue from admissions decreased by $2,728,000 (27 percent). This decrease is 3.7 percent of the total revenue before auxiliary operations. The management of the museum has decided to veer away from ticketing exhibitions in an effort to make special exhibitions more spontaneous and more rewarding for the frequent visitor.[29]

HOURS OF OPERATION

Evening hours were added on Friday and Saturday nights in place of opening on Tuesday evening in an attempt to increase attendance. Attendance on Tuesday evening averaged 2,500, while attendance on Friday and Saturday evenings is averaging between 3,500 and 5,000.[30] See Exhibit 7 for the hours of operation and the suggested donations for admission to the museum.

Museum Hours and Admission Charges **Exhibit 7**

Hours of Operation	
Sunday, Tuesday–Thursday	9:30 a.m.–5:15 p.m.
Friday, Saturday	9:30 a.m.–8:45 p.m.
Monday	Closed
Donation for Admission	
Adults	$5.00
Students and seniors	2.50
Children under 12	Free

Source: The Official Museum Directory 1990. National Register Publishing Company.

TARGET CUSTOMER

Many surveys are conducted by the Metropolitan each year to determine the key demographics of their visitors. See Exhibit 8 for the demographics of the average visitor to the Met. The Met's management feels that understanding the demographics of the current average visitor is the key to effectively marketing the museum's services. Of the 1,357 surveyed, 48 percent were New York City residents, 39.6 percent were residents in other areas of the United States, and 12.4 percent were foreign residents.[31]

VOLUNTEERS

Approximately 800 volunteers work at the Metropolitan Museum. Three hundred of these are docents, or volunteers, who lead tours of school children and other groups.[32] Unfortunately, the Met's traditional volunteer pool is shrink-

Customer Demographics **Exhibit 8**

Demographics	*Data*	*Percent*
Number of visits within 1 year	1–3 visits	32.8
Time spent in museum	2 hours	36.0
Primary reason for visiting museum	Special exhibition	51.1
Median age of visitors	Age 38	
Sex of visitors	Female	57.0
Education of visitors	Baccalaureate	33.5
Occupation of visitors	Teachers/other professionals	47.5
Ethnicity of visitors	Caucasian	76.1
Museum membership	Member	15.5

Source: The Metropolitan Museum of Art, January 1991.

ing. According to a Census Bureau study conducted in 1989, 59 percent of the women in the United States are now employed. As women continue to enter the work force, nonprofit organizations are finding it difficult to attract volunteers to work during the daytime hours.[33]

AUXILIARY OPERATIONS

Today, at the Metropolitan there are a growing number of business executives on the board because of the recognition that the museum has evolved into a big enterprise with an investment portfolio and business activities such as a reproduction studio and retail outlets. Because external funds can no longer be relied on, greater emphasis must be placed on the generation of internal sources of revenue.

■ Museum Shops

Retail shops are operated within the museum and at the Cloisters and in ten off-site locations. Four of these satellite shops are in New York: Rockefeller Center, New York Public Library, the Americana at Manhasset, and Macy's. Two are in Connecticut: Stamford Town Center and Westfarms Mall. Two are in California: Century City Shopping Center in Los Angeles and Southcoast Plaza in Costa Mesa. One is in Ohio at Columbus City Center, and one is in New Jersey at the Mall at Shorthills.[34] Because the Met is a tax-exempt, nonprofit organization, it does not have to pay taxes on profits realized from any retail operations, therefore, some feel it has an unfair advantage over other retailers selling similar goods.[35] The museum is only required to pay income taxes on all retail items unrelated to its mission, in accordance with section 511 (imposition of tax on unrelated business income of charitable organizations) of the *Internal Revenue Code.*

The purpose of the unrelated business income tax is to prevent tax-exempt organizations from competing unfairly with businesses whose earnings are taxed. Unrelated business income is any income derived from any unrelated trade or business. The term unrelated trade or business is defined in section 513 of the *Internal Revenue Code* as "the case of any organization subject to the tax imposed by section 511, any trade or business the conduct of which is not substantially related (aside from the need of such organization for income or funds or the use it makes of the profits derived) to the exercise or performance by such organization of its charitable, educational, or other purpose or function constituting the basis for its exemption under section 501."[36] The stores sell greeting cards, posters, calendars, postcards, sculptures, glass, and jewelry. Nearly all the items offered are reproductions or adaptations from the museum's collections. These items are not available for sale at any other retail location. Items are sold in the museum shops or through mail order. The museum management contends the sale of the items in the shops falls within the mission of the museum in that the sale of an item makes people think about the museum outside its walls and it serves as an extension of their visit. Groups who represent small businesses are lobbying for changes in the tax code because some commercial ventures undertaken by nonprofit institutions compete unfairly with private companies who are selling nearly the same merchandise. These groups want the tax code rewritten detailing specifically which items would be considered tax-exempt.

The Metropolitan's merchandising activities resemble those of commercial businesses in some ways but are unique in others. The resemblances include the Met's desire to introduce such technology as a point of sale (POS) computerized inventory system into its stores. The differences include the requirement that all merchandise sold in the museum must reflect the permanent collection to preclude assessment of taxes on the earnings. Therefore, the decision on the types of items to sell do not necessarily reflect customer wants. Marketing research consists of showing pictures of items in the permanent collection to randomly selected customers in the museum shop to determine if the items should be reproduced for sale.

The museum almost never advertises except to invite people to join their catalog mailing list. Six catalogs per year are mailed out to members and other customers on the mailing list. The Christmas catalog is mailed out to 3 million people and the others are mailed to a smaller number. Some of the merchandising policies, such as buying large quantities of an item to get it at a lower price, have led to inventory storage problems. It is not unusual for an item to remain in the inventory for up to two years. The museum manufactures the molds to make the actual copies of art in its own reproduction studio. The art books are printed in the United States and around the world.[37]

The museum leases space for offsite retail stores and for the warehouse which serves as the headquarters for the mail order business and a storage facility for inventory. Lease costs for all rented spaces used solely for the retail operation amounted to $1,456,295 and $1,675,519 for the years ended June 30, 1990 and 1991, respectively.[38]

■ Restaurants

The museum operates a restaurant, cafeteria, and bar. The restaurant and bar are open to accommodate the evening hours on Fridays and Saturdays. The museum has received approval to open a new restaurant to replace the current restaurant and cafeteria so that the space can be used for additional galleries.[39]

■ Other Auxiliaries

Other auxiliary operations at the Metropolitan are the parking garage and the auditorium. The parking garage is located adjacent to the museum for use by its patrons at the rate of $8.50 for the first hour, $1.00 for each additional hour up to the fifth, $17.50 for five to ten hours, and $19.50 beyond ten hours.[40]

■ Auxiliary Results of Operations

Net income from merchandising operations was $787,852 for the year ended June 30, 1991. Though sales from mail orders were up 4 percent, the total revenue was less than forecasted. A general softening of the retail industry was thought to be the reason for this shortfall. The net contribution to the museum's operations from auxiliaries totaled $1.48 million in 1991. See Exhibit 9 for the balance sheet and Exhibit 1 for the five-year summary.[41]

Exhibit 9 **The Metropolitan Museum of Art: Balance Sheet, for the Years Ended June 30, 1991, 1990, 1989, 1988, 1987**

	1991	*1990*	*1989*	*1988*	*1987*
Assets					
Cash	$ 606,396	$ 907,578	$ 395,529	$ 1,237,648	$ 1,915,744
Investments, at market	531,292,293	521,786,251	500,028,584	425,091,168	444,762,386
Receivables	41,046,111	33,443,105	34,426,235	26,112,389	13,697,322
Merchandise inventories	18,019,006	19,710,828	15,528,500	13,110,043	10,848,449
Fixed assets, at cost, net	18,609,096	13,413,486	9,953,319	8,580,484	8,548,091
Deferred charges, prepaid expenses, and other assets	7,042,756	5,622,154	4,092,675	4,900,913	4,510,822
Total assets	$616,615,658	$594,883,402	$564,424,842	$479,032,645	$484,282,814
Liabilities and Fund Balance					
Accounts payable	$ 21,631,963	$ 27,182,146	$ 27,075,186	$ 23,926,641	$ 16,527,236
Accrued expenses, primarily payroll, annual leave, and pension	14,112,100	14,363,817	13,080,930	9,636,881	6,003,065
Deferred income, principally memberships, gifts, and grants	11,038,712	10,700,500	9,801,820	8,716,301	7,533,288
Notes payable	15,800,000	7,750,000	8,000,000	10,400,000	8,000,000
Loan payable	46,915,000	47,655,000	48,260,000	48,260,000	44,990,000
Total liabilities	$109,497,775	$107,651,463	$106,217,936	$100,939,823	$ 83,053,589
Fund (deficit) balance	507,117,883	487,231,939	458,206,906	378,092,822	401,229,225
Total liabilities and fund balance	$616,615,658	$594,883,402	$564,424,842	$479,032,645	$484,282,814

Source: The Metropolitan Museum of Art, *Annual Reports.*

FUTURE OUTLOOK

The future financial stability of the Met is the key concern of management. The fiscal instability of the city of New York could lessen future city support. Threatened reductions in federal funding could also have an adverse effect on the museum's operations. The national recession could also effect the museum in terms of attendance and retail sales.

According to the book *Megatrends 2000,* researchers predict the arts will begin to replace sporting events as society's primary leisure activity. The authors cite a 1988 report by the National Endowment of the Arts calculating Americans spend $28 billion on sports events compared to $3.7 billion on art events. However, more than 500 million people visited American museums last year, far more than attended professional sporting events.[42]

Growth in the future must continue to come from individual and corporate donors. Statistics from *The Economist* show that while the French government spends approximately $30 per capita on the arts, the British $9, the U.S. federal and state governments together spend only about $2. This means others, including corporate America, will be required to help reduce this differential.[43]

Many believe the resurgent interest in the arts will bring success for the museum shops. Patrons want to support local culture and are spending generously on books, maps, models, posters, replicas, and other museum shop items. The Metropolitan sold more products than any other museum in 1991 and remains the only museum manufacturing its own line of merchandise. Second in sales was the Smithsonian Institution in Washington, D.C., which sells through its nine museum shops and catalog. Other shops with a minimum of $1 million in annual sales include the Museum of Modern Art and Whitney Museum of American Art in New York, Boston's Museum of Fine Art, the San Francisco Museum of Modern Art, the Art Institute of Chicago, the Los Angeles County Museum of Art, the Philadelphia Museum of Art, and the San Diego Museum of Art.[44]

Competition for museum shops is not solely limited to museum locations. The Museum Company, a retailer based in East Rutherford, New Jersey, has opened stores in seven states in two years and sells merchandise from the Louvre in Paris, the British Museum, and other art institutions and pays royalties to the museums. Its first year revenues topped $10 million.

OTHER MUSEUM COMPETITION

Because there are multiple demands for the free time of museum visitors, many activities, outings, and other forms of recreation and leisure are potential substitutes. The direct competitors, or other museums, are plentiful and many are in the New York area. These include the American Museum of Natural History, the Museum of Modern Art, the Whitney Museum, and the Museum of the city of New York.

Other activities and forms of available recreation range from sporting events to theatrical presentations. The New York metropolitan area is the home of two National Basketball Association teams; three National Hockey League teams; two National Football League teams; two baseball teams; and two race tracks. Broadway, the most celebrated street in America, offers daily productions in forty theaters and numerous off-Broadway shows for the tourist or resident of New York.

In addition, each of the five New York boroughs has many attractions to choose from including the Statue of Liberty, the Bronx Zoo, the National Historic Landmark district on Staten Island. Central Park and the World Trade Center are easily accessible to all visitors via the New York City subway.

ENDNOTES

1. The Metropolitan Museum of Art, *1990 Annual Report.*
2. Howe, W. *A History of the Metropolitan Museum of Art.* Arno Press, New York, 1913, p. 125.
3. The Metropolitan Museum of Art—Charter, Constitution, and By-Laws, p. 3.
4. The Metropolitan Museum of Art, *1990 Annual Report.*

5. *The Official Museum Directory 1990.* National Register Publishing Company, 1990, p. 581.
6. *Collier's Encyclopedia,* 1981, Volume 16, p. 70f.
7. *The Official Museum Directory 1990.* National Register Publishing Company, 1990, p. 581.
8. Ibid.
9. Glueck, G. "The Metropolitan Museum's Diplomat at the Top," *The New York Times,* May 2, 1988.
10. Conforti, M. "Hoving's Legacy Reconsidered," *Art in America,* June 1986, pp. 19–23.
11. Collier's Encyclopedia, 1981, Volume 16, p. 70f.
12. Conforti, M. "Hoving's Legacy Reconsidered," *Art in America,* June 1986, pp. 19–23.
13. Tomkins, C. "The Art World," *The New Yorker,* February 28, 1983, pp. 94–97.
14. Conforti, M. "Hoving's Legacy Reconsidered," *Art in America,* June 1986, pp. 19–23.
15. The Metropolitan Museum of Art, *1990 Annual Report.*
16. Glueck, G. "The Metropolitan Museum's Diplomat at the Top," *The New York Times,* May 2, 1988.
17. Russell, J. "Met Museum Opens 5-Year Drive for $150 Million," *The New York Times,* October 26, 1982.
18. Glueck, G. "A Raise for Met's Curators," *The New York Times,* November 14, 1990.
19. Glueck, G. "Met Museum Seeks Endowed Chairs," *The New York Times,* March 15, 1983.
20. O'Hare, B. "Good Deeds Are Good Business," *American Demographics,* September 1991, pp. 38–42.
21. Salmans, S. "The Fine Art of Museum Fund Raising," *The New York Times,* January 14, 1985.
22. "$500,000 to Met Museum," *The New York Times,* December 20, 1990.
23. Taylor, J. "Party Palace," *New York,* January 9, 1989, pp. 20–30.
24. Salmans, S. "The Fine Art of Museum Fund Raising," *The New York Times,* January 14, 1985.
25. The Metropolitan Museum of Art, *1990 Annual Report.*
26. Glueck, G. "For Two Museums, a Very Good Week," *The New York Times,* March 1, 1991.
27. O'Hare, B. "Corporate Charitable Gifts Reached 5.9B in 1990," *American Demographics,* September 1990, p. 38.
28. Glueck, G. "For Two Museums, a Very Good Week," *The New York Times,* March 1, 1991.
29. The Metropolitan Museum of Art, *1990 Annual Report.*
30. Smith, "Weekends at Dusk, A New Met Museum," *The New York Times,* March 30, 1990.
31. The Metropolitan Museum of Art, Survey, December 1990 and January 1991.
32. The Metropolitan Museum of Art, *1990 Annual Report.*
33. Mergenbagen, P. "A New Breed of Volunteer," *American Demographics,* June 1991, pp. 54–55.
34. The Metropolitan Museum of Art, *1990 Annual Report.*
35. Honan, W. "Deciding Which Profits Should Be Tax Exempt," *The New York Times,* May 15, 1988.
36. Internal Revenue Code, Section 511.

37. Feder, B. "Metropolitan Museum Shows Retailing Bent," *The New York Times,* May 27, 1988.
38. The Metropolitan Museum of Art, *1990 Annual Report.*
39. Ibid.
40. Ibid.
41. Ibid.
42. Naisbitt, J., and Aburdene, P. *Megatrends 2000.* New York: Wm. Morrow & Co, 1990.
43. David, L. "Picture of Success: National Gallery of Art Celebrates 50th Anniversary," *International Washington Flyer,* V1, pp. 70–74.
44. Soltis, S. "Retailing Rodin: Museum Shops Carve a Profitable Niche," *International Washington Flyer,* 1992, V1, p. 73.

CASE 38

University of Texas Health Center at Tyler

Mark J. Kroll, University of Texas at Tyler; Vickie Noble, University of Texas Health Center at Tyler

The health care industry in the United States is in a state of crisis. Evidence of this crisis is apparent in spiraling health insurance premiums and health care costs, rural hospital closings, governmental reimbursement funding reductions, increasing liability litigation, and rising levels of indigent care loads. Compounding the problem further are a nationwide nursing shortage, rapidly advancing and costly technology, and increasing competition among health care providers.

Against this backdrop, the University of Texas Health Center at Tyler attempts to fulfill its mission of providing patient care, conducting research, and providing education related to cardiopulmonary diseases. Since the Health Center receives a percentage of its operating resources from the state of Texas, it must provide indigent health care to the poor in its region. It must also provide care to indigents with tuberculosis from anywhere in the state. However, the center has not refused services to any Texas indigents, regardless of the nature of their illness. As health insurance premiums have risen, more and more people have lost their coverage. As a result, private hospitals frequently refuse treatment and refer patients to state-supported institutions. This trend, in conjunction with the closing of many of the region's rural hospitals, as well as federal reimbursement reductions, compel many individuals to seek care at the Health Center under indigency charity status.

Unfortunately, state funding levels for this type of care have not kept pace with demand, seriously undermining the financial base of the institution.

This case is intended for classroom discussion only, not to depict effective or ineffective handling of administrative situations. All rights reserved to the authors and the North American Case Research Association.

However, the Health Center must provide competitive wages in order to attract nursing and select allied health personnel who are in short supply. Additionally, the Health Center must operate in the competitive local hospital market for a paying patient base while providing costly technology and instrumentation. Most of the major strategic issues confronting the Health Center are ultimately related to the dilemmas faced by the health care industry. Compounding the Health Center's problems, however, have been reductions in state general revenue appropriations as a percentage of the total operating budget for research, operations, and maintenance.

The center is experiencing critical shortages of clinic treatment facilities that are needed to meet changing modes of care and reimbursement bases (more out-patient versus in-patient care). And local competition for specific patient groups has increased.

In addition to the issues just mentioned, there is the unique issue of the hospital's research mandate. While the Health Center has successfully increased levels of grant-funded research, inadequate research laboratory facilities could potentially choke off further progress.

HISTORY

The Health Center was established in 1947 as a state turberculosis sanatorium. It operated under the State Board of Control by act of the 50th Texas Legislature. Over the years, the institution has changed in a number of ways. Its role and scope was expanded to adapt to new medical technology and to the changing health care needs of the state and region.

The institution was established at the site of a deactivated World War II army infantry training base, Camp Fannin, and is located eight miles northeast of Tyler, Texas. The state acquired 614 acres and the existing facilities of the base hospital from the federal government. Most of the base's 1,000 beds were in rows of wooden barracks, with each barrack accommodating 25 beds in an open ward. The first patients were accepted in 1949.

Supervision of the East Texas Tuberculosis Sanatorium was later transferred to a newly formed Board of Texas State Hospitals and Special Schools. In 1951, the Texas Legislature changed the hospital's name to the East Texas Tuberculosis Hospital. Its role and scope were changed from simple custodial care to treatment using newly developed drugs.

Although several legislative acts passed during the 1940s and 1950s changed the institution's governing authority, it was not until 1969 that its scope was expanded beyond the care and treatment of tuberculosis patients. In that year, the legislature authorized the institution to develop pilot programs aimed at treating other respiratory diseases, such as asthma, lung cancer, chronic bronchitis, emphysema, and occupational diseases related to asbestos. In 1971, the Texas Legislature gave the institution a broader mission of education and research as well as patient care. The name was changed to the East Texas Chest Hospital, to be operated under the Texas Board of Health. This program expansion into education and research reflected the increasing stature of the facility and its scientific capabilities.

In 1977, Tyler senator Peyton McKnight introduced legislation transferring control of the hospital to the board of regents of the University of Texas system. This legislation authorized the regents to use the institution as a teaching hospital and to change its name to the University of Texas Health Center at Tyler. It also reaffirmed the institution's role and scope as a primary state referral center for patient care, education, and research in the diseases of the chest.

The physical face of the institution has also changed dramatically over the years. In 1957, the state completed a 320-bed, six-story brick and masonry structure, which allowed for removal of most of the wooden barracks. A few of these structures still remain and have been renovated for use as research laboratories. Other major building programs were initiated in the late 1960s and early 1970s. An outpatient clinic was added to the hospital in 1970. In 1976, the state appropriated $17 million for construction of a completely modern hospital facility. A six-story 320-bed hospital annex was built adjacent to the original structure, doubling the size of the complex. At the same time, the lower three floors of the old hospital building were renovated to house additional offices and allow for expansion of programs in cardiac and pulmonary rehabilitation and cancer treatment.

The Watson W. Wise Medical Research Library was dedicated in 1984, giving support to an expanded research faculty and the addition of new departments such as biochemistry, microbiology, and physiology. In 1987, the Health Center's Biomedical Research Building was completed. In 1991, construction began on an $11 million expansion of its ambulatory care facilities designed to house and expand the clinical laboratory, radiology, and surgical facilities. This change facilitates delivery and efficient handling of ambulatory patient services. The facility also provides space for the Family Practice Residency Program and other clinics, as well as space for clinical research.

In carrying out its mission, the institution has evolved from a custodial-care facility only to an institution with the threefold purpose of patient care, education, and research. Open heart surgery became available in 1983, and the Health Center was designated as one of the state's regional cystic fibrosis centers. In 1985, the Health Center was designated as a national cystic fibrosis satellite center. The first postgraduate medical education program in east Texas, residency training in family practice, was launched in 1985 in cooperation with two Tyler hospitals. By the end of the 1986 fiscal year, the Health Center had 11 resident physicians in training.

Grant research funding has increased dramatically in recent years. In 1983, funding was $78,347; by 1985, funding reached $808,836; and in 1986 research funding was more than twice the 1985 level, with a total of $1,931,427. In 1988, $2,896,061 in research grant monies were received, while the center spent $4,819,343 on research-related activities. This research funding was, and continues to be, from external sources such as the National Institutes of Health, the Texas Affiliate of the American Heart Association, the American Lung Association of Texas, the Muscular Dystrophy Foundation, private medical-research foundations, and several industrial and pharmaceutical firms. Completion of the Biomedical Research Building in 1987, followed by the recruitment of research scientists, has helped the institution to aggressively pursue the research component of its mission.

COMPETITION

Competition for paying customers between the two local general hospitals is intense. Each of the two major private hospitals averages between 12,000 and

16,000 inpatient admissions annually. Each also has an operating budget of approximately $100 million and a medical staff of about 300 physicians. As a state agency that specializes in the treatment of cardiopulmonary diseases, the Health Center does not compete directly with these local hospitals. However, the institution competes indirectly for market share for specific patient groups, such as those with cardiopulmonary diseases.

It is important to recognize that the center's operating budget is comprised of general revenue appropriations from the state, research grant funding, and locally generated revenues from services rendered to patients who are able to pay. During the period 1981 to 1989, the percentage composition of the operating budget coming from appropriated versus generated funds has changed significantly. General revenue appropriations have decreased from 66% of the operating budget for fiscal year 1982 to 38% of the operating budget for fiscal year 1990. Consequently, the Health Center has been forced to generate local funds through the paying patient base (see Exhibit 1).

Complicating matters is the fact that the Health Center's operating budget must support educational programs as well as some of the research done. State appropriations for indigent patient care, in actual dollars, have remained relatively constant over the 1983–1990 period (see item 12 of Exhibit 1, General Revenue Appropriations). However, indigent and charity care levels provided rose dramatically until 1988, at which point they leveled off. See item 5 of Exhibit 1, Subtotal, Revenue Reduction. Exhibit 2 illustrates the rapid growth in charity care during the 1980s.

The net result has been a large gap between funds received from the state to provide indigent care and the amount actually provided by the Health Center. In total dollars, indigent care services averaged $12 million per year from 1983 to 1985; however, indigent care services averaged approximately $18 million per year from 1986 to 1990. To help make up the difference the institution must compete for paying patients in service areas offered by other local hospitals. Currently, for each dollar of health care services the center provides, on average 50% is reimbursed through Medicare, approximately 6% is repaid through Medicaid, and 5% is paid by private insurers or patients. That leaves almost 40% to be borne by the center.

The two major competing hospitals offer similar health care programs in cardiology and cardiovascular surgery; therefore, competition for market share exists. They both aggressively advertise and promote their image, services, and facilities. One of the two hospitals has recently completed a modernization and expansion project for cardiovascular surgery and intensive care units. It has also been able to keep its profitability up and mortality rate down for cardiovascular services.

By law, however, the Health Center does not directly advertise in a manner competitive or comparative with that of the local hospitals. The organization limits its promotional efforts to presentations of programs and health care services as community service efforts. Ironically, the local hospitals could be in a position to claim unfair competition and disadvantage because the Health Center is partially funded by legislative appropriations. Further, a higher mortality rate exists at the Health Center because higher-risk patients are treated. High-risk status generally accompanies indigency status because patients have not received basic health care and wait longer before seeking medical attention. At this point, the disease process is advanced.

University of Texas Health Center at Tyler: Financial Information

Exhibit 1

	FY 1990	FY 1989	FY 1988
1. Patient service revenue (gross)	$38,536,820	$33,642,732	$34,408,785
Annual percent increase	14.55%	(2.23%)	4.15%
2. Revenue adjustments			
(excluding bad debts, charity)	$ 6,932,712	$ 4,797,391	$ 4,525,220
Percent of patient revenue	17.99%	14.26%	13.15%
3. Charity	$ 9,172,281	$ 9,184,960	$12,947,936
As percent of gross revenue	23.8%	27.3%	37.6%
4. Bad debts	$ 2,795,851	$ 1,904,750	$ 1,984,674
As percent of gross revenue	7.3%	5.7%	5.8%
5. Subtotal, revenue reduction			
(adjustments, charity, and bad debts)	$18,900,844	$15,887,101	$19,457,830
As percent of gross revenue	49%	47%	57%
6. Net patient service revenue	$19,635,976	$17,755,631	$14,950,955
Annual percent increase	10.59%	18.76%	(8.84%)
7. Total patient cash collections	$19,546,082	$16,513,679	$15,694,463
8. Collection rate (#7/#6)	99.5%	93.0%	105.0%
9. Cost to charge ratio	97.4%	92.0%	86.1%
10. Collection by source			
Medicare	$11,071,994	$ 9,194,415	$ 9,529,772
Medicaid	1,645,293	1,347,954	860,152
Insurance	5,371,077	4,768,401	4,365,443
Private/self-pay	1,457,718	1,202,909	939,096
Total (same as #7)	$19,546,082	$16,513,679	$15,694,463
11. Budgeted operating revenue			
(as originally approved)	$36,892,387	$34,316,301	$36,331,730
12. Statement of revenue and expenses			
Net patient service revenue	$19,635,976	$17,755,631	$14,950,955
General revenue appropriations	13,296,372	12,209,063	12,209,063
Appropriations related to overhead	n/a	n/a	n/a
Other operating revenue	2,115,611	2,090,823	2,329,976
Total operating revenue	$35,047,959	$32,055,517	$29,489,994
Operating expenses			
Direct			
Salaries and wages	$17,381,939	$16,687,738	$16,332,959
Supplies and other	12,452,104	12,127,114	11,167,801
Depreciation	3,325,503	2,142,208	2,142,208
Total operating expenses	$33,159,546	$30,957,060	$29,642,968
Excess of revenues over expenses	$ 1,888,413	$ 1,098,457	$ (152,974)
Extraordinary items			
Interest	182,427	145,482	180,673
Medicare/Medicaid retroactive settlements	0	1,752,308	227,061
Total excess of revenues and extraordinary items over expenses	$ 2,070,840	$ 2,996,247	$ 254,760

Exhibit 2 **University of Texas Health Center at Tyler: Indigent Care Versus State Appropriations for Patient Care**

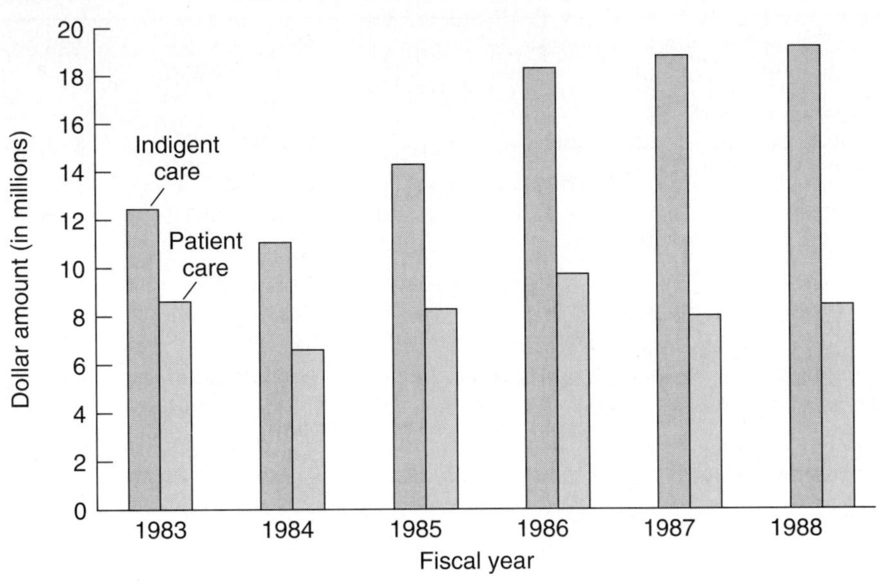

Given the Health Center's mission of patient care, education, and research, the focus of the institution is not one of direct competition with local hospitals. In effect, while the Health Center is a hospital in the traditional sense, it is also much more. To achieve all three dimensions of its mission, the hospital's resources must be divided, and it is the three elements combined that comprise the Health Center's "product." For example, in the treatment of asbestos-related disease, the patient benefits significantly through specialized treatment that is unavailable at the local hospitals. Grant-funded research provides the combined efforts of a clinical researcher, who works at the molecular level of the disease, with an experienced pulmonary disease physician specialist. The patient can participate in clinical trials, such as new drug therapy, which may lead to improvements in treatment of the disease. Further, the Health Center's advanced technology instrumentation base, which includes three electron microscopes, improves diagnostic capabilities. These microscopes provide ultra-high magnification for enhanced research studies and patient care. Therefore, the Health Center provides specialized products for research and patient care.

CUSTOMERS (MARKET)

The Health Center is located in the middle of Smith County, Texas, in an area known as east Texas. The hospital's primary patient base is derived from the surrounding population of its 24 county service area. It bases its forecasts for future patient loads and program implementation on the demographics of this region. East Texas, like the rest of the state, is increasing in population. The Health Center service area had a population of approximately 1,155,317 in

1988. Analysts project a 1.4% to 2.1% annual population increase through the year 2000 (see Exhibit 3). Age is another important factor in the analysis of the Health Center service area demographics. Percentages of the state population by age group are provided in Exhibit 4.

For the years 1985–2025, the 0–17-year-old age group of the Texas population will decline 3.7%, while the 45–64 group will increase 6%. The 65 and older group of the Texas population will increase from 9.65% to 16.24%. Therefore, the population in Texas is both aging and growing. These trends are apparent in the average ages of the Health Center's patients (see Exhibit 5 for by-county patient ages). Such a demographic profile will obviously have an impact on the direction of patient care for the elderly at the Health Center as well as on Texas and the nation.

Many hospitals and physicians statewide refer patients to the Health Center for diagnosis and treatment, especially when pulmonary problems are suspected. However, the bulk of patients come from the surrounding east Texas area. Patient admission data for the fiscal years 1988–1990 are provided in Exhibit 6, while Exhibit 7 lists admissions by county in the service area.

University of Texas Health Center at Tyler: Service Area Population, 1990–2000 **Exhibit 3**

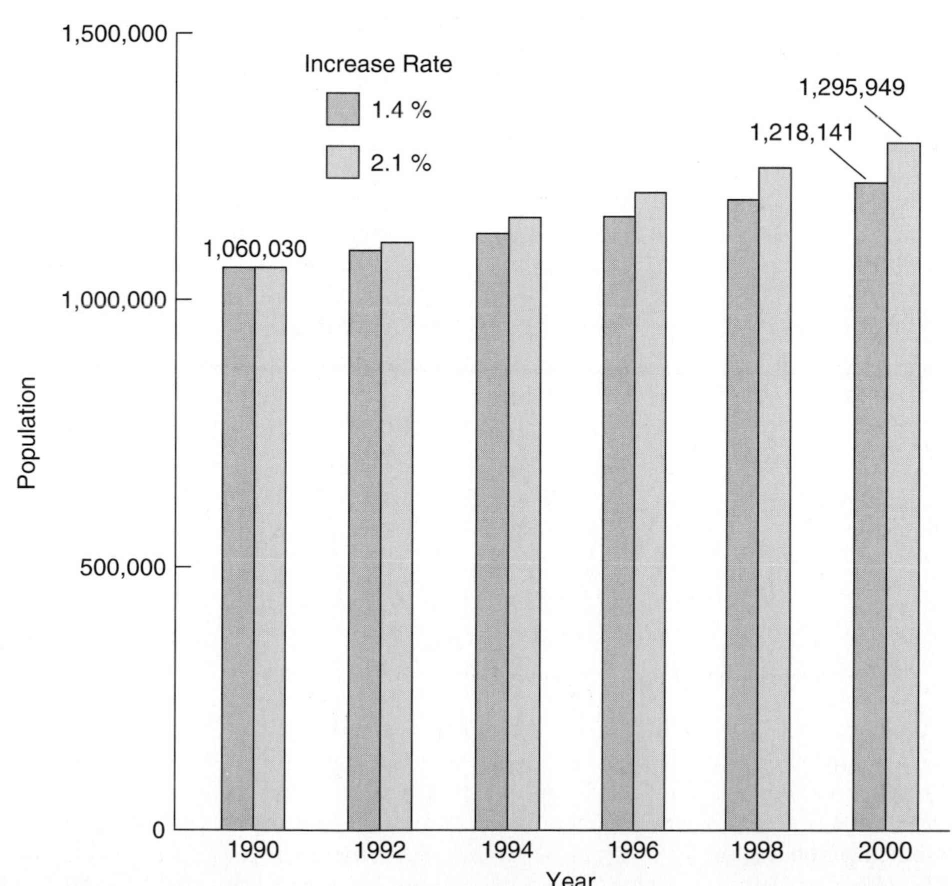

Exhibit 4 **Texas Population by Age, 1985 and 2025**

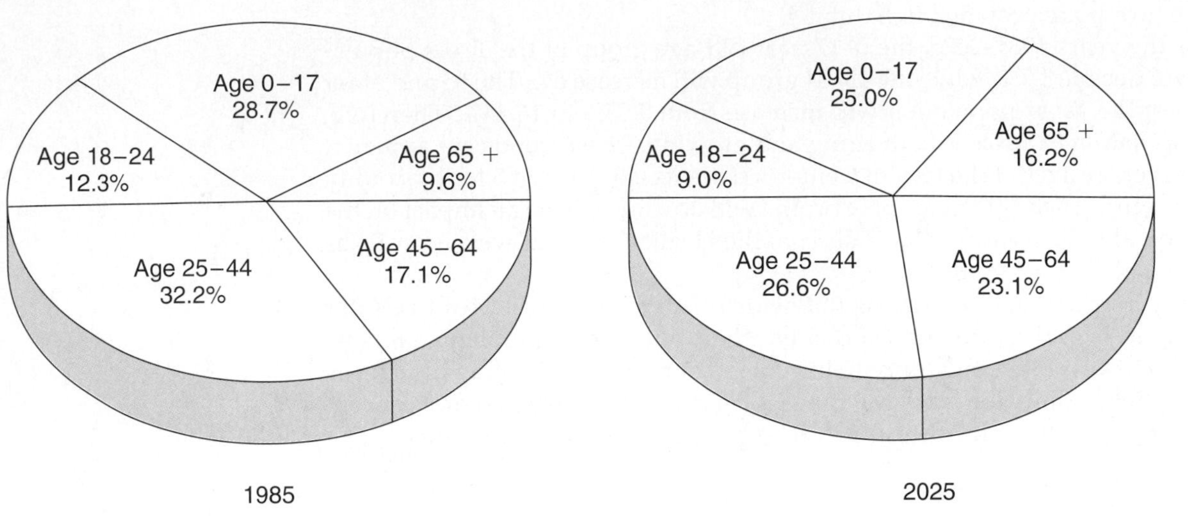

Exhibit 5 **University of Texas Health Center at Tyler: Average Age for Patients, East Texas Service Area (24 counties)**

County	*Average Age*
Anderson	55
Angelina	52
Bowie	48
Camp	51
Cass	51
Cherokee	52
Gregg	48
Harrison	55
Henderson	57
Hopkins	54
Houston	62
Hunt	57
Kaufman	60
Marion	53
Morris	57
Panola	53
Rains	63
Rusk	57
Shelby	54
Smith	51
Titus	51
Upshur	55
Van Zandt	58
Wood	57
Unknown	47
Total average age	57

University of Texas Health Center at Tyler: Statistical Information

Exhibit 6

	FY 1990	*FY 1989*	*FY 1988*
1. Average Number of Beds in Operation			
Adult and pediatric	100	198	204
Infant	n/a	n/a	n/a
Special care bassinets	n/a	n/a	n/a
Total	199	198	204
2. Inpatients			
Total admitted	3,528	3,827	4,244
Adult and pediatric	3,528	3,827	4,244
Newborn	n/a	n/a	n/a
Total days	40,120	39,639	46,695
Adult and pediatric	40,120	39,639	46,695
Newborn	n/a	n/a	n/a
Average inpatients per day	110	109	127.6
Adult and pediatric	110	109	127.6
Newborn	n/a	n/a	n/a
Average stay (Day) per patient	11.0	10.0	12.0
Adult and pediatric	11.0	10.0	12.0
Newborn	n/a	n/a	n/a
3. Outpatients			
Number of clinic visits	59,942	50,695	46,092
Average clinic visits per day	240	203	184
Number of emergency room visits	n/a	n/a	n/a
Average emergency room visits per day	n/a	n/a	n/a

Patient referrals are from group practices, physicians, hospitals, governmental agencies, and self-referrals (Exhibit 8 illustrates a recent increase in referring physicians). Most patients admitted for diagnosis and treatment are referred because their clinical problems require specialized diagnosis and treatment provided by the Health Center. Exhibit 9 reports the percentages of outpatients admitted for treatment in each of the specialty areas. Many times, referrals are made for acutely ill pulmonary patients requiring longer than average intensive care.

It is important to recognize that the Health Center has an unusual patient population because of its broader service area, commitment to indigent care, and aging population. These factors have resulted in increasing demands on the center for medical services. Indigent care provided by the hospital has increased from $10.9 million to $18.9 million in the 1982–1990 period. Beginning in 1988, a great deal of indigent care was provided not only to people in counties within the service area but also to a large number of Texans outside the east Texas service area. At present, approximately 28% of the indigent care the Health Center provides is to patients residing outside the immediate east

Exhibit 7 **University of Texas Health Center at Tyler: Admissions—Inpatients and Outpatients, East Texas Service Area (24 counties)**

County	*Inpatient Admissions*	*Outpatient Visits*	*Admissions Total*
Anderson	78	1,061	1,139
Angelina	28	272	300
Bowie	21	175	196
Camp	19	325	344
Cass	23	473	496
Cherokee	119	2,295	2,414
Gregg	305	7,503	7,808
Harrison	66	899	965
Henderson	198	3,169	3,367
Hopkins	24	348	372
Houston	5	153	158
Hunt	14	175	189
Kaufman	24	199	223
Marion	14	186	200
Morris	13	485	498
Panola	23	306	329
Rains	14	187	201
Rusk	209	2,571	2,780
Shelby	24	322	346
Smith	1,051	25,779	26,830
Titus	22	487	509
Upshur	288	6,707	6,995
Van Zandt	143	2,264	2,407
Wood	244	3,927	4,171
Unknown	15	2,760	2,775
Total admissions	2,984	63,028	66,012

Texas service area. This accounts for $5,371,000 of the total $18,926,403 of indigent care services provided in 1990. In one attempt to rein in indigent care costs, recently the center has started limiting the prescription drugs it provides free of charge and has placed limits on the amount of indigent care provided by the general medicare clinic and the family practice clinic. Exhibit 10 provides forecasts for Health Center financial operations data.

REGULATION AND ECONOMICS

In the health care field, regulations are an integral part of the economics that drive the industry. Regulations are promulgated by numerous government and industry agencies. These include the Healthcare Financing Administration (HCFA), the Department of Health and Human Services, the American Hospital Association, the Food and Drug Administration (FDA), the Texas Department of Health, and the Joint Commission on Accreditation of Hospitals Organization (JCAHO).

Operational regulations for the Health Center are imposed by the state of Texas and the University of Texas System. While these entities prescribe the operational parameters, the Prospective Payment System for Federal Medi-

University of Texas Health Center at Tyler: Referring Physicians, Fiscal Year 1990 to Fiscal Year 1991 **Exhibit 8**

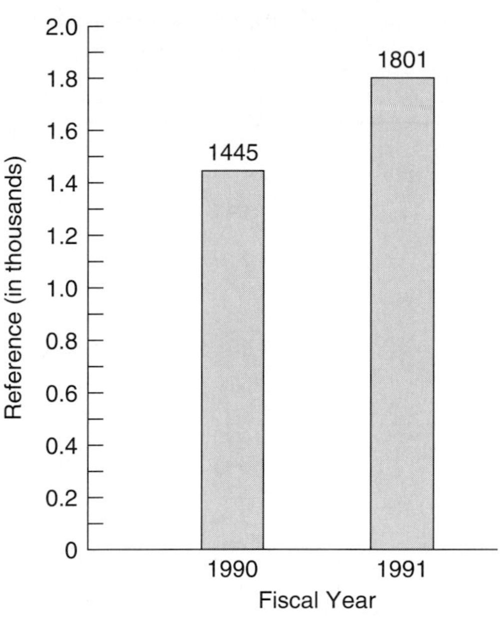

University of Texas Health Center at Tyler: Outpatient Clinic Admissions **Exhibit 9**

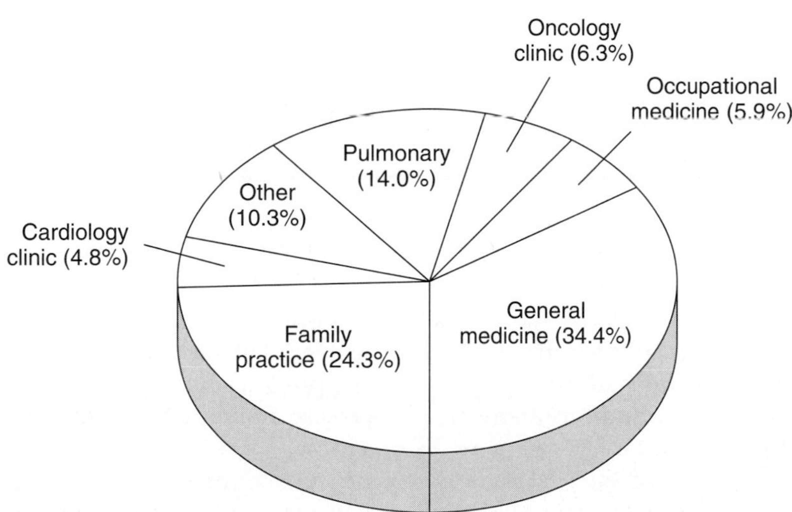

care/Medicaid reimbursement has had the most significant impact on the health care industry and the Health Center in recent years. Enacted in October 1984, the system established "Diagnosis Related Groups" (DRGs), whereby Medicare/Medicaid reimbursement payments to hospitals are based primarily on the diagnosis of the patient. This system does not reimburse for actual costs

Exhibit 10

University of Texas Health Center at Tyler: Strategic Plan—Financial Analysis (current operation)

	Projected Increments (or decrements)	
	1990–1991	*1993–1994**
Projected Income (1985–1986 constant dollars)		
General revenue	$17,266,989	$1,500,000
Net student fees		
Income from patients	22,345,719	2,750,000
Available balances		
Other	3,310,123	300,000
Subtotal education and general funds	$42,922,831	$4,550,000
Contract and grant funds	$ 3,449,012	$ 275,000
PUF funds[a]		
Restricted funds	1,662,830	100,000
MSRDP (net)[b]	5,762,583	275,000
Auxiliary enterprises	152,817	10,000
Service department funds	2,311,614	15,000
Subtotal non E&G	$13,338,856	$ 675,000
Total	$56,261,687	$5,225,000
Projected Expenditures (1990–1991 constant dollars)		
Planned changes		$5,066,948
Projected increment available for general growth improvement		$ 158,052

Note: *All of these values (except 1990–1991) represent the anticipated annual "changes" in each of the items.

(Continued on facing page)

[a]"PUF": Permanent university funds allocation—funds received from earnings on investments and assets.

[b]Medicare standard reinbursement fee amount.

incurred for patient care if the required treatment varies from the average costs related to the "normal" treatment routine. The system pays the hospital only the average costs associated with a particular course of treatment. In other words, a given rate and length of hospital stay is established for reimbursement payment, and any additional costs over the predetermined rate are borne by the hospital. In addition, many treatments are reimbursable only as an outpatient charge.

The initial intent of the system was to standardize rates, force efficiency, reduce utilization rates among Medicare patients, and shift some of the health care cost burden from the federal to state level. Cost control became a real objective for the health care industry. The Health Center has monitored the progress of the new system and tried to anticipate its impact on the institution. As a result, inpatient hospital rooms were converted to outpatient clinics. The center's plans include the construction of additional ambulatory care clinic space.

(Continued) **Exhibit 10**

Projected Increments or (decrements)				
1994–1995	*1995–1996*	*1996–1997*	*1997–1998*	*1998–1999*
$2,000,000	$3,000,000	$3,500,000	$3,500,000	$3,500,000
2,750,000	2,750,000	2,750,000	3,000,000	3,000,000
300,000	300,000	300,000	350,000	350,000
$5,050,000	$6,050,000	$6,550,000	$6,850,000	$6,850,000
$ 275,000	$ 275,000	$ 275,000	$ 275,000	$ 300,000
100,000	100,000	100,000	150,000	200,000
275,000	275,000	275,000	300,000	300,000
10,000	10,000	10,000	12,500	15,000
15,500	16,000	16,500	17,000	17,500
$ 675,500	$ 676,000	$ 676,500	$ 754,500	$ 832,500
$5,725,500	$6,726,000	$7,226,500	$7,604,500	$7,682,500
$5,397,128	$2,628,386	$2,107,956	$2,742,821	$ 0
$ 328,372	$4,097,614	$5,118,544	$4,861,679	$7,682,500

In addition, the industry will be impacted by another reduction in federal reimbursements that appears to be on the way. The Federal Budget Committee Agreement of 1990 has targeted approximately $2 billion in Medicare spending reductions. These reductions specifically affect reimbursement adjustment factors for indirect medical education, such as the residency program at the Health Center. As a teaching facility that receives this factor benefit, the Health Center obviously would be impacted negatively, though the magnitude has not yet been assessed. The economic implications of all the factors mentioned are enormous for the Health Center. Currently, 50% of the institution's patients are covered by Medicare. This percentage is projected to increase significantly, based on an industry projection that the Medicare patient base will double by the year 2025.

GOVERNANCE

The Health Center's education mission has been impacted by both federal and state funding reductions as well. It receives no funding from the University of

Texas system for salaries of physician residents. The federal government has also reduced special funding for physician residents.

The UT system is presided over by a board of regents, made up of members from diverse professions and backgrounds, including businessmen, educators, and physicians. Each is considered to be knowledgeable and successful in a given field. They are external to the University of Texas system and typically have significant positions of power and influence in their chosen career field. In addition, the members usually have political and persuasive powers with the Texas Legislature in order to secure funding and associated legislation for the system.

The board of regents sets the financial and operating guidelines of the University of Texas system through operating budgets, capital expenditure approvals, program implementation, and related activities confirmations. The board essentially supports or rejects recommendations from the administrators of the universities and medical centers in the system. The board of regents implements its decisions through the chancellor of the University of Texas system. The Health Center's top management is organized along functional lines according to business, research, and medical classifications. The organization chart for the Health Center is illustrated in Exhibit 11. The medical and research divisions are directed by the executive associate director, who is a physician as well as a research scientist. He is highly regarded for his skills as an administrator, physician, and researcher, as evidenced by his membership on national and international committees in his fields. He is supported by assistant administrators along functional lines such as the chief of staff and the associate director for patient services. The business division is directed by the executive associate director for administration and business affairs who holds a master's degree in health care administration. He is supported by assistant administrators along functional lines.

This group of directors, administrators, and assistant administrators comprises the administrative staff. They meet weekly to develop policy and to implement strategic plans and to perform various administrative functions.

The strategic plans developed by the directors are distributed to administrators and to the next management level, the department heads. Based on input from these groups, the plan is revised by a committee that includes representation from the medical, research, and education divisions. The strategic plan that emerges forms part of the basis for budget requests for special programs, operating funds, equipment, and personnel.

Strategic decision-making authority is vested in the administrative staff. Both the department heads and administrative staff are responsible for making operational decisions. Most routine operations are managed by department heads who control departmental budgets. Accountability at each managment level is maintained through a criteria-based job performance evaluation system.

Information at the Health Center is distributed through a communications channel. The organizational chart outlines the primary formal channels of communication. Memos and formal meetings are the primary means of formal communication. In addition to the weekly administrative staff meetings, task- or subject-specific meetings are held among the various administrators.

Standing committees form another formal communication channel. These committees utilize several techniques to communicate with employees at various levels of the organization. Formal meetings, hearings, interviews, ques-

Exhibit 11 Organization Chart: The University of Texas Health Center at Tyler

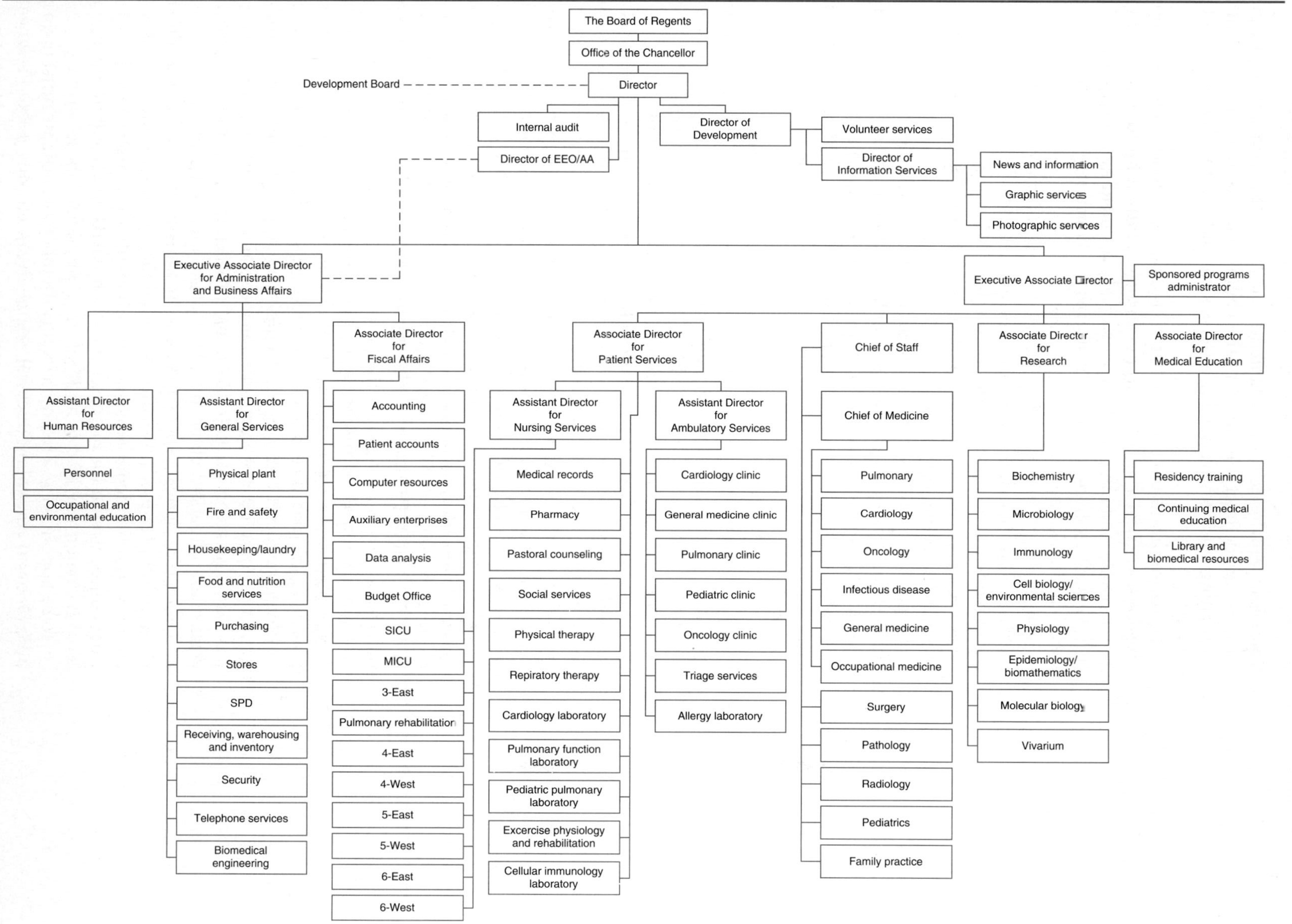

tionnaires, and review of documentation enable the committees to perform their assigned functions. Most of the committees are required by health care accrediting and governmental agencies as well as the University of Texas system.

The communication network between management levels varies among the divisions. Medical management divisions generally communicate through formal meetings and memos. Weekly medical staff meetings are conducted by the chief of staff to discuss medical concerns, to distribute policy changes, and to solicit feedback from the staff.

Monthly department head meetings provide for communication among the medical, educational, business, and research groups. This is a critical network communication link because of the complex and unique nature of a university health center. In addition, routine informal information exchange occurs at all levels in managing operations.

Given the Health Center's threefold mission, faculty members are appointed to positions in either research or clinical areas. Members may be appointed as an instructor, assistant professor, associate professor, or professor. Positions are also defined by a specialty field of practice. All new faculty members initially receive one-year appointments, which are reviewed annually for renewal.

Clinical and research faculty are recommended for promotion by their respective department heads to the Faculty Promotion Committee. Assuming the Health Center director and associate directors concur with a promotion recommendation, it is submitted to the University of Texas system vice chancellor for health affairs and board of regents for final approval.

To join the Health Center's clinical faculty, a candidate must have at least a medical doctorate degree from an accredited school and be licensed to practice medicine in Texas. To be considered for promotion, the clinical faculty member must demonstrate competence in four areas: clinical practice, service to the institution, research, and teaching. A physician who recently has completed a residency program or fellowship initially is appointed as an instructor and usually serves in that position for two years before being considered for promotion to assistant professor. Promotion from assistant to associate professor requires five years of experience and evidence of performance in the four areas just mentioned. Promotion to professor also usually requires five years of service. Elements that go into the promotion decision include peer evaluation and recognition as an authority in a specialty through lecturing and publication in medical journals. Additionally, for promotion from instructor to a professorial rank, board certification in a specialty is desirable but not mandatory.

Physician-faculty are in effect employed by the Health Center full time; therefore, they do not have private medical practices. To fulfill the clinical practice dimension of their positions, physicians are provided with private offices; an outpatient clinic area; laboratory, radiology, and ancillary services; and nursing, clerical, and support staff personnel. In addition, the Health Center provides medical malpractice liability insurance and legal assistance, along with retirement plans and other benefits. Although physicians are salaried, compensation for increases in patient visits and resultant income for the Health Center may lead to additions to a physician's base salary.

To be appointed as a research faculty member, a candidate must have at least a Ph.D. or an equivalent doctoral degree in a medically related science. Here, too, new faculty members begin as instructors. Promotion to assistant professor typically requires postdoctoral training, publication in scientific journals, receipt of research grant funding, and an independent scientific reputation. Promotion to associate professor requires a minimum of four years of significant publishing, lecturing, and receipt of grant funding, as well as the attainment of an international scientific reputation.

CURRENT SITUATION

The Health Center at Tyler has made significant progress in the implementation of its threefold mission to provide patient care, conduct research, and provide education. Patient care services include inpatient and outpatient (ambulatory care) services provided by nationally recruited, full-time clinical physicians and consulting staff. The Health Center has acquired additional medical and surgical intensive care suites, a heart catheterization laboratory, and an open heart operating room. The Health Center provides a full range of services for cardiovascular diagnosis, treatment, and rehabilitation, including coronary angioplasty. Coronary angioplasty, a new, advanced treatment for cardiovascular disease, eliminates the need for open heart surgery in selected patients. Nationally known for its pulmonary disease capabilities, the Health Center has the most highly developed program for comprehensive evaluation and treatment of occupational lung diseases in Texas.

In fiscal year 1990, hospital admissions were 3,528 and the total number of patient days was 40,120, with an average length of stay of 11.0 days (see Exhibit 6). As a result of the decline in state funding, the Health Center has been forced to rely on its local income budget for capital expenditures. State funding reductions for research have also resulted in recruitment delays for scientists.

However, changing economic conditions, reductions in both state and federal funding, and the increasing costs of providing health care programs present both opportunities and challenges. Being partially state funded requires the Health Center to provide indigent health care. In fact, the Health Center has had to absorb large increases in indigent care, since many private hospitals in the region refuse to treat the indigent and instead refer them to state institutions. State and federal funding, however, have not kept pace with the increases in recent years nor does it appear that adequate funding for future indigent care will be forthcoming. Improving its services to paying patients and increasing that portion of the center's business has become a key element of the Health Center's strategic plan to offset indigent care losses.

The Health Center has continued to work on carrying out its threefold mission of patient care, research, and education despite the economic pressures felt by the health care industry. It has just graduated the first class of resident physicians completing the three-year Family Practice Residency Program. Four of its research investigators received awards, and the number of postdoctoral fellows coming on board to conduct research last year totaled 12. The Health Center was reaccredited in 1991, for three years, by the Joint Commission on Accreditation of Hospitals. Exhibit 10 provides an outline of the anticipated changes in the sources of funds and expenditures for the Health Center in the coming years.

There has been an enormous increase in the number of ambulatory care patient visits. The Health Center is trying to address these needs through the construction of a new ambulatory care center, enabling the staff to take care of more patients with greater efficiency. Pursuit of additional research grants will also be a key component in the center's ability to build its status as a research institution. Given the decline in state support for research, attracting other funds will become more and more critical. Additionally, if the hospital is to keep its head above water financially, it will have to attract more paying customers, even though it does not promote itself in direct competition with regional private hospitals. As a result, the years ahead present both opportunities and threats to the center's ability to continue to build quality services in patient care, research, and education.

REFERENCES

The University of Texas Health Center at Tyler. *Annual Hospital Report for 1983.* Tyler: University of Texas Health Center at Tyler, 1983, p. 41.

The University of Texas Health Center at Tyler. *Annual Hospital Report for 1984.* Tyler: University of Texas Health Center at Tyler, 1984, p. 4.

The University of Texas Health Center at Tyler. *Annual Hospital Report for 1985.* Tyler: University of Texas Health Center at Tyler, 1985, p. 2.

The University of Texas Health Center at Tyler. *Annual Hospital Report for 1986.* Tyler: University of Texas Health Center at Tyler, 1986, p. 33.

The University of Texas Health Center at Tyler. *Annual Hospital Report for 1988.* Tyler: University of Texas Health Center at Tyler, 1988, p. 11.

The University of Texas Health Center at Tyler Fiscal Affairs. *A Position Paper on the Aspects of Indigent Care Given.* Tyler: University of Texas Health Center at Tyler, October 1988, p. 18.

The University of Texas Health Center at Tyler. *Strategic Plan Through 1996–1997, Volume 1.* Tyler: University of Texas Health Center at Tyler, 1984, p. 4.

CASE 39

BASF's Proposed Paint Plant

Max E. Douglas, Indiana State University

INTRODUCTION

In early 1988, BASF Corporation, a member of the international German-based BASF Group, released plans for a five-year, $2 billion capital expansion program. BASF Corporation is one of the largest chemical companies in North America. In 1988, net sales equaled $5 billion, while net income amounted to $149 million. Nearly 22,000 people are employed by the four divisions of BASF Corporation. Its diversified product mix includes the following: basic, intermediate, and specialty chemicals; colorants; dispersions; fiber raw materials; fibers; automotive coatings; printing inks; urethane specialties and chemicals; plastics; advanced composite materials; antifreeze; crop protection products; pharmaceuticals; vitamins; fragrances; and audio, video, and computer recording media.

On March 10, 1988, BASF officials announced that the company intended to build a manufacturing facility somewhere in the American Midwest. Three cities were selected as finalists: Terre Haute, Indiana (located in Vigo County); Evansville, Indiana; and Portsmouth, Ohio. Terre Haute's drawing card was an undeveloped county industrial park comprised of 1,476 acres. Terre Haute has a population of roughly 57,483 and is located in the West Central part of Indiana. As a community, Terre Haute was in dire need of expanded employment opportunities since several major companies had exited the area over the past decade. Statistics published by the local Chamber of Commerce showed that between 1979 and 1987, the community suffered a net loss of 6,062 jobs. However, data published by the local Democratic Party reported that 6,102 jobs had been created in the community between 1986 and 1991. (See Exhibits 1–3.)

On March 28, 1988, the Vigo County commissioners signed a licensing agreement with BASF, allowing the company to inspect and conduct soil tests

---

This case is intended for classroom discussion only, not to depict effective or ineffective handling of administrative situations. All rights reserved to the author and the Midwest Society for Case Research.

Exhibit 1 **Major Industrial Development Activity, Terre Haute, Indiana, 1986–1991**

Company	*New Investment ($ in millions)*	*New Jobs*
*Accurate Glass	$ 4.0	20
*ALCAN	95.0	0
*Ampacet	25.5	130
*Avganics	3.0	20
*Bemis	71.0	300
*BF Goodrich	19.0	50
*CBS	24.9	150
Coca-Cola	2.0	0
*DADC	30.0	125
*Distr. Term. Corp.	.4	2
*Donnelley	2.0	65
General Housewares	.4	20
Green Leaf	1.3	35
*Hercules	30.0	90
*Ivy Hill	5.0	125
Jadcore	7.0	75
*Kyoto Foods	4.0	100
*Numerical Concepts	1.7	45
Pfizer	55.0	0
*Pillsbury	4.0	0
*Pitman-Moore, Inc.	60.0	0
*Shenango	4.0	125
*Snacktime	6.0	170
*Specialty Blanks	2.5	34
Standard Register	3.0	9
*Tredegar	14.4	60
*Tri Industries	4.5	205
*Wabash Fiber Box	3.0	0
Western Tar	.5	5
Weston Paper	30.0	5
Winslow Scale	.4	12
Totals	$513.5	1,977

*Denotes companies assisted by the city of Terre Haute.

at the county industrial park located south of Terre Haute. Approximately a month later, BASF released more precise information regarding the nature of the plant facility. Tentative plans called for a $150 million automotive paint plant that would employ approximately 500 local people. These economic data encouraged city and county government officials to court BASF Corporation. In mid-June, an entourage of local government officials and business leaders visited a BASF plant in Gainsville, Ohio. On July 6, 1988, BASF announced that the soil tests at the industrial park were affirmative and that the company was initiating procedures to "option" land at the Vigo County Industrial Park. Further discussion between company and county government officials revealed that a small 30-acre parcel of land within the industrial park was still owned by the federal government. BASF stressed that the company would need this 30 acres to develop its plant operations. The Vigo County Commissioners eventually purchased this acreage from the General Services Administration in order to accommodate BASF.

Major Commercial Development Activity, Terre Haute, Indiana, 1986–1991

Exhibit 2

Company	*New Investment (in millions)*	*New Jobs*
*Boston Connection	$ 2.0	144
*Conway Trucking	2.5	22
*Farmer's Market(s)	.8	48
Honey Creek Square	2.5	0
*IBM	2.0	0
Indiana-Am. Water Co.	.8	0
Merchants National Bank	3.0	18
*Miller Business Forms	.4	9
*MRI	2.8	5
Osco (Ft. Harrison)	1.3	22
Pharmor	.9	71
*Plaza No. Shopping Ctr.	1.6	125
Sam's Wholesale	2.2	120
*T.H. First Natl. Bank	10.0	65
T.H. Savings Bank	.9	6
Toys "R" Us	2.0	75
*Tribune Star	1.0	10
*Wabash Commission	.5	0
Walmart	1.6	175
Totals	$38.8	915

*Denotes companies assisted by the city of Terre Haute.

Major Institutional Development Activity, Terre Haute, Indiana, 1986–1991

Exhibit 3

Company	*New Investment ($ in millions)*	*New Jobs*
*A.P.&S. Clinic	$ 5.5	20
Charter Hospital	4.6	120
*Hamilton Center	2.7	0
*Regional Hospital	21.2	244
*Union Hospital	20.1	400
*ISU	51.4	0
Ivy Tech	5.0	56
Rose Hulman Inst.	14.0	122
St. Mary's/Woods	2.0	0
*Vigo Co. School Corp.	30.0	0
*Airport Auth.	13.5	0
Federal Penitentiary	1.4	41
Army Reserve	3.0	0
Natl. Guard–Air	4.0	230
VFW Post 972	.6	0
Totals	$179.0	1,233

*Denotes companies assisted by the city of Terre Haute.

Note: New investment and new jobs total, from Exhibits 1–3, $731.3 million and 4,125, respectively.

CONTROVERSY DEVELOPS

On August 10, 1988, Jack Wehman, Midwest venture director for BASF, announced that the company planned to build a hazardous waste incinerator and establish a landfill in addition to building its paint manufacturing plant. The proposed incinerator and landfill would handle on-site wastes and imported wastes trucked to the site from other BASF plants. Following this news release, Evansville mayor Frank McDonald indicated that his city would no longer pursue the BASF plant. Terre Haute mayor Pete Chalos and Portsmouth mayor Roger Bussey indicated that their communities were still positive about the BASF plant, regardless of the implications of the incinerator and landfill.

In contrast to the favorable reception to the August 10 BASF announcement by Terre Haute's mayor and other BASF supporters, a local community action group, Citizens for a Clean County (CCC), organized to begin an anti-BASF campaign. The initial purpose of the CCC was to stop BASF from building the waste treatment facility on the site and from importing waste to the incinerator/landfill. The CCC eventually became the primary opponent to BASF, although other BASF adversaries expressed their opposition regarding the importation of toxic wastes. For example, one local entrepreneur, Jim Shanks, mailed 8,000 letters, maps of the "Fallout Zone," and petitions to Vigo County residents living in the southern and eastern parts of the county, enlisting their opposition to BASF. In reaction to the growing anti-BASF sentiment, BASF Corporation hired Fleishman Hilliard, a St. Louis opinion research firm, to conduct community focus groups to solicit views regarding the proposed automotive paint plant, hazardous waste incinerator, and landfill.

In his November 8 letter, Shanks explained why he felt BASF should not be allowed to proceed with the project. Shanks praised the 1500-acre tract Vigo County set aside for industrial development and its potential for eliciting long-term economic growth for the region. However, he expressed three primary concerns over BASF's plans. First, BASF planned to hire only 400 new employees. Second, since BASF would be exempt from local property taxes, Shanks argued that Vigo County residents would end up subsidizing the BASF toxic waste operation. Finally, Shanks noted environmental concerns. BASF would initially process 36 million pounds of hazardous waste, placing both residents and businesses at risk in the event of an environmental disaster. Shanks' enclosed map illustrated the potential impact such a disaster could have on the entire city of Terre Haute. He urged community members to sign a petition; write or call their county councilmen, commissioners, and mayor; and attend an informational meeting on November 12 featuring an environmental protection specialist with the EPA.

On November 18, BASF responded with the first of three letters over a six-week period. In these letters, BASF officials stressed the economic benefits the plant would bring to the community as well as BASF's concern for the environmental impact of their proposed facility. In the first letter, BASF Venture Director Jack M. Wehman noted the following benefits to Vigo County as a result of the facility:

- the potential for additional BASF facilities,
- $150 million immediate capital investment,
- at least 400 new skilled jobs hired locally,
- 3500 new construction jobs created during the erection of the facility,

- 1000 new jobs available to the community to serve BASF's ongoing operation.
- Benefits to other sectors of the local economy, including expansion of the tax-base.

In his December 5 letter, Wehman emphasized several additional points, most notably that:

- There is great potential for various future installations beyond the initial paint plant.
- Storage of hazardous wastes will only require 25 of the 1000 acres purchased, and no more than 50 acres during the next 100 years.
- BASF will maintain about 200 of the 1000 acres as a wildlife preserve, as well as a 300–500 foot setback from the perimeter property as a green buffer zone.
- BASF will only treat its own hazardous waste. Treatment presents no hazards to the local community.

Reply cards were enclosed to solicit community reaction to the BASF proposal.

On December 24, Wehman mailed the third letter, thanking residents for returning their reply cards, mostly in favor of the BASF plant. In this letter, Wehman purported to answer some of the key questions asked on the cards. He reiterated many of the previous assertions, but also made three additional points:

- Residents can expect a rollback in taxes as a result of the $150 million commitment by BASF. The increase in the tax-base will improve funding for all local public-supported institutions such as schools, libraries, hospitals and clinics, as well as additional highway projects.
- BASF expects to increase employment—at competitive wages and with an extensive benefits plan—in the area from 500 to about 1500 in the coming years. BASF plans to share the cost of skill training with the State of Indiana.
- BASF is an equal opportunity firm.

ECONOMIC DEVELOPMENT PLAN STIRS PUBLIC DEBATE

While this controversy was dominating the community news, the local government officials continued to pursue a plan for the economic development of the industrial park. The Vigo County Council created the Vigo County Redevelopment Commission to oversee the development of the 1,505-acre industrial park. The County Redevelopment Commission hired the Terre Haute Department of Redevelopment to draw up a detailed economic development plan for the industrial park. The existence of an economic development plan for the park was a prerequisite for qualifying for federal funds to underwrite the development of infrastructure such as sewer and water lines. The final economic development plan proposal called for $6 million in improvements to the property in order to make it suitable for industrial development. On November 28, 1988, the Vigo County Redevelopment Commission declared that the industrial park was an economic development and tax allocation area, despite opposition from area residents. Following this official declaration, the Redevelopment Commission submitted the proposed economic development plan to the Vigo County Area Planning Commission. The Area Planning Commission was charged with determining whether the proposed economic development plan conformed with the comprehensive land usage plan for the entire county. On December 7, 1988, a public meeting at a local high school was conducted by the Area Planning Commission. Despite much opposition from the audience, the economic development plan was approved by this commission 11 to 3.

Following this vote of approval by the Area Planning Commission, the Redevelopment Commission scheduled public hearings regarding the industrial park economic development plan. Some 30 hours of testimony was heard over three days. Spearheading the anti-BASF forces was the Citizens for a Clean Community. Members of the CCC hired outside consultants to speak at the hearings.

One spokesperson, Hugh Kaufman, an employee of the Environmental Protection Agency, expressed concerns about the BASF incineration/hazardous waste landfill proposal. According to Kaufman, hazardous waste facilities inhibit industrial and economic growth, rather than promote it. Costs and burdens fall on local governments, which may have additional liabilities if waste from incinerators enters public water and sewage systems. Kaufman further stressed that increased industrial traffic and repairs, chemical spills, and the expanded need for continual training of emergency response teams add additional concerns and costs for taxpayers.

Another environmentalist, John Blair, gave testimony during the marathon hearings. Blair was paid $125 per diem by the Oil, Chemical, and Atomic Workers (OCAW) local in Giesmar, Louisiana, to help promote opposition to the BASF plant. OCAW had been engaged in a bitter four-year lockout with BASF at the Giesmar plant. Blair said evidence suggests that BASF often acts in an immoral fashion. He claimed that BASF's real intentions were to locate a hazardous treatment plant using the paint plant as a carrot. Blair further charged that the economic development plan under consideration had no enforcement provisions. Blair claimed that Terre Haute would become a "national sacrifice zone" if it began accepting hazardous waste from other areas.

In addition to the "expert" testimony, several citizens presented personal position statements. One opponent, Eva Kor, a survivor of Nazi Germany's World War II Auschwitz concentration camp, claimed that BASF was one of three companies formed out of the ashes of the German company I.G. Farben. Kor claimed that Farben used slave labor from the Auschwitz camp until "they were used up." She opposed BASF locating in Terre Haute and suggested a referendum be held to resolve the issue. CCC member Harold Cox reported that more than one-half of the polled respondents in a local survey opposed a hazardous waste facility. Although in the minority, BASF supporters cited the tremendous economic boost that the company would provide for the community. In addition, BASF advocates labeled the CCC as a biased group more interested in protecting their property values than in stopping the importation of toxic waste. Nevertheless, the majority of statements presented during the 30 hours of public hearings conducted by the Vigo County Redevelopment Commission demonstrated opposition to the establishment of an incinerator and landfill adjacent to the automotive paint plant, as well as to the importation of hazardous wastes from other BASF plants for disposal in Terre Haute.

Subsequent to the public hearings, the Redevelopment Commission reviewed all written testimony regarding the economic development plan. On

January 19, 1989, the Redevelopment Commission conducted its final session to determine the fate of the proposed plan for the industrial park. One of the commissioners, Linda Burger, expressed concern that this plan would allow the importation of several truckloads of hazardous wastes into the community. Burger indicated further concern about the high cancer rates that already existed in Vigo County. She proposed an amendment to the economic development plan that would ban the importation of toxic wastes into Vigo County. The amendment was rejected 3 to 2. The economic development plan was finally approved 4 to 1.

LEGAL ACTION TAKEN

Shortly following the approval of the economic development plan by the Redevelopment Commission, the CCC and 16 other people living near the industrial park filed a legal petition for judicial review against the Redevelopment Commission, the Vigo County Commissioners, and Vigo County. The petition made the following charges:

1. The economic development plan was adopted by using impermissible procedures alleged to be (a) inadequate notice of when the Redevelopment Commission would meet; (b) holding meetings in rooms too small to accommodate interested parties; and (c) curtailment of public comment.
2. The Redevelopment Commission was wrong to meet during regular business hours because that precluded some people from attending.
3. Four out of five commission members had conflicts of interest.
4. The economic development plan jeopardized the public health, safety, and welfare of the community.

Coinciding with the filing of the legal petition by the CCC and others was the public introduction of a BASF visitation team. The team consisted of employees from various areas of the company such as human resources, operations, and plant safety. BASF provided biographical sketches of each member and indicated that they were sent to discuss the quality of work life at BASF and to share their experience concerning environmental safety of BASF at other plant locations. Jack Wehman, Midwest venture director for BASF, indicated that the presence of this team did not mean BASF had decided on Terre Haute. That decision, according to Wehman, depended on the outcome of the litigation over the industrial park. Wehman stressed that the visitation team's purpose was to gather and disseminate information pertaining to the proposed paint plant.

Shortly after the preceding two events (CCC's legal petition and the arrival of BASF's visitation team), the mayor of Terre Haute, Pete Chalos, expressed displeasure that a legal petition had been filed to disaffirm the economic development plan for the county industrial park. Mayor Chalos stated:

> I think that there are some people on the loose here that want to take us back 20 years and put Terre Haute in the position of being called an injunction city. I certainly hope cooler heads and wiser people take a leading role in making sure BASF comes here.

During March 1989, the litigation and personal charges filed to disaffirm the approved economic development plan intensified. On March 1, the coalition of the CCC and local property owners filed an amended court petition claiming that the adoption of the economic development plan by the Redevelopment Commission on January 19, 1989, should be canceled because county commissioners failed to adopt an ordinance establishing the Redevelopment Commission. Hugh Kaufman, an EPA employee, charged that the purchase of the 30-acre tract of land for the Vigo County Industrial Park from the GSA was fraudulent. Kaufman contended that the GSA should have determined the environmental impact of potential development before selling federal land. He further implied that a new impact study should have been conducted rather than to rely on the original assessment covering the 1,476 acres sold to Vigo County in 1986. County government officials responded that they had followed appropriate legal advice in purchasing the additional 30 acres for $50,000 at a public auction held on August 19, 1988.

ECONOMIC DEVELOPMENT PLAN DECLARED NULL AND VOID

By mid-March 1989, Judge Frank Nardi conducted a pretrial conference in an attempt to resolve questions and issues raised by the plaintiffs. Judge Nardi indicated that he would review all inclusive evidence about the way the Vigo County Redevelopment Commission was formed and the procedures used to reach its decision. Following federal court hearings, Judge Nardi gave the CCC and Vigo County adequate time to file written briefs. The core of the plaintiffs' position was as follows: The Economic Development Plan was written especially for BASF, was adopted in violation of certain aspects of state law, and was approved by government officials without giving proper consideration to all factors, including environmental impact issues. The defendants (county officials) testified that plaintiffs were given full rein during public hearings and that the plan was a reasonable one, designed with BASF in mind, seeking economic development by attracting not only BASF but other industry as well to the industrial park. Defendants also contended that monitoring the environment was a state and federal responsibility and that the incineration of waste from other BASF plants was permissible as part of the industrial park. On July 1, 1989, Judge Nardi ruled that the economic development plan approved by the Redevelopment Commission was null and void. Nardi cited the following reasons:

1. Questions of propriety regarding payments and alliances that suggested possible conflicts of interest among the commissioners.
2. Prejudgement of the decision before the Vigo County Redevelopment Commission was formed.

As a result of these findings, the economic development plan was remanded to the Vigo County Commissioners for further action.

MEANWHILE BACK AT THE RANCH

While Judge Nardi was analyzing the data contesting the approval of the economic development plan (approximately April 1–July 1, 1989), another controversy was brewing. BASF opponents expressed concern that the company had not produced a complete list of chemicals that would be imported, burned, and/or buried at its selected Midwest facility. Company officials indicated that the amount of waste handled, if Vigo County were selected, would be strictly limited by the redevelopment plan. BASF stressed that it would act responsibly and show concern for the short-run and long-run impact on the environment. BASF officials reassured the community that no third-party wastes would be imported. It was also pointed out that BASF was following common corporate practice, in that partial lists were seldom released. According to BASF management, most large companies do not release lists of chemicals until they apply for a state permit for incineration operations.

Unfortunately for BASF officials, their responses were jaded by an analysis of data conducted by a local Indiana State University chemistry professor, Dr. John Corrigan. A reporter of the *Sullivan Daily Times* (a local community newspaper 30 miles south of Terre Haute) asked Professor Corrigan to analyze some unpublished BASF documents. Data revealed that BASF intended to incinerate up to 152 chemicals—waste residues from 33 plants in 14 states in 1991–1992. Corrigan reported that metals for incineration included cadmium, chromium, lead, and barium, among others; these chemicals cannot be destroyed or rendered harmless by incineration. BASF officials responded that the data were not current and were subject to revision. Jack Wehman, Midwest venture director for BASF, responded to the community concern by saying that following Judge Nardi's decision, BASF would begin the permit process and make a full disclosure of chemicals to be disposed of at the Vigo County facility. The controversy over the chemical list at this point remained unresolved. A major factor contributing to the impasse was the ruling by U.S. District Court Judge Nardi, declaring the economic development plan null and void.

POST–ECONOMIC DEVELOPMENT PLAN

Subsequent to Judge Nardi's ruling declaring the economic development plan for the industrial park null and void, controversy continued regarding the possible sale of industrial park land to BASF. A joint meeting of the Vigo County Commissioners, seven county councilmen, and the five members of the Redevelopment Commission resulted in a consensus not to appeal Judge Nardi's ruling on the plight of the economic development plan. County commissioners expressed concern that deed restrictions might have to accompany the sale of industrial park acreage in order to protect the environment. Special concern about importation of hazardous waste was expressed. John Scott, president of the commission, indicated that he was worried that BASF had not yet published a list of what wastes would be imported. On July 15, 1989, anti-BASF groups met with county commissioners to share their views about the future of the industrial park. Harold Cox, representative of the CCC, said that a new economic development plan should be written to attract a wider spectrum of potential buyers. It was stressed that Vigo County needed to market to industries that do not present environmental health risks. The commissioners responded that they welcomed ideas for marketing the land, but emphasized that the industrial park was still for sale but that no specific time frame had been established to offer the property for public bid. About a month after this meeting, the Vigo County Commissioners sought legal advice regarding the disposal of the industrial park. The commissioners also stated that public hearings would be conducted. BASF opponents hoped that the new hearings would result in a plan restricting activities that are ecologically unsound, while promoting safe economic development of the industrial park.

BASF MODIFIES PLANS

On August 31, 1989, BASF Midwest venture director Jack Wehman announced that his corporation would be scaling down its plans for an industrial plant in Vigo County. He stated:

> Our new plan calls for the construction of a stand-alone automotive plant with the necessary waste-management facilities for only the paint plant. This means that the waste-management facility will handle only the waste from the site's paint plant. These are on-site generated wastes.

Wehman further explained that the waste-management operations would include a wastewater treatment facility, an incinerator system, and a landfill for the incinerated ash, all of which would dispose of on-site wastes. These revisions would require only 200–300 acres of land and about 300 local employees at a cost of roughly $100 million. Wehman further projected that these 300 local employees would complement 100 "imported" workers, each earning about $10.15 per hour, or about $8.4 million in annual income. In addition, Wehman estimated that the 2,000 construction workers employed for the two-year project would generate about $40 million per year in payroll. Wehman concluded by stressing the need to negotiate the sale of needed land in the park within the next six weeks, so that the plant could be operational by the end of 1992.

The Vigo County Commissioners reacted favorably to BASF's revised plan and indicated that selling appropriate acreage with a clear title within six weeks seemed feasible. At this point, the commissioners stated that public hearings regarding the sale of the land seemed unnecessary, especially since wastes would not be imported into the community.

On the flip side, however, many community members still questioned the integrity of BASF's proposed revision. A member of one anti-BASF coalition, Mothers Against Toxic Chemical Hazards, indicated that opposition to BASF continued because the revision still proposed a toxic waste incinerator and landfill for the site. Harold Cox, president of the CCC, stated that the proposed landfill was not allowed according to Vigo County's comprehensive land use plan. Other opponents voiced concern that the industrial park had not been appropriately marketed. BASF adversaries stressed the previous "bait and switch" tactics in which the company initially announced plans for a paint plant and later added the hazardous waste facilities to its agenda. A staunch critic of BASF opponents was Terre Haute mayor Pete Chalos. Chalos criticized environmental groups who had previously said they would accept BASF if toxic waste was not imported. Mayor Chalos indicated he had studied BASF's new proposal and was optimistic that the county commissioners would accommodate BASF.

Two days after announcing their revised plan for the paint plant operations, BASF released two bound volumes of printed material explaining in detail the list of chemicals that could be treated and disposed of at its midwestern paint plant. BASF officials assured the community that all of the tested materials would be handled using procedures that protect the safety, health, and environmental welfare of the citizens.

BASF'S BID FOR INDUSTRIAL PARK LAND APPROVED BY COUNTY

On October 27, 1989, approximately six weeks following its announced plant revision, BASF submitted a bid of $500,000 for 296.7 acres of industrial park land. Jack Wehman expressed hope for a successful culmination of the sale and stated that his company would begin a skills inventory of the local work force. The skills inventory was quite successful, as 1,836 people completed surveys. BASF officials emphasized that the survey was not a job application; it was a tool to give BASF an idea of what skills local people have and what training would be needed.

At first, it appeared that BASF was on the road to Terre Haute. But on November 2, 1989, four local anti-BASF groups united to form the Terre Haute Environmental Rights Coalition (TERC). TERC's attorney, Mike Kendall, wrote a letter to the county attorney, Robert Wright, advising him that the terms of the BASF bid for the 296 acres of industrial park were extremely biased in favor of the company. Kendall said the county should reject the conditions of the BASF offer; Kendall reinforced TERC's opposition by stating that they would take whatever legal steps were necessary to prevent the sale.

Controversy heightened because BASF filed an amendment to its original bid that had substantial changes regarding its property rights at the industrial park if the sale were consummated. TERC's legal counsel indicated that BASF's amended bid may have violated the public bid law and expressed concern that the substantive changes made by the amendment might be a de facto new bid. Kendall also pointed out that the original bid was the only one available to the public from October 30 to November 14.

On November 20, 1989, a public hearing on the BASF bid proposal sparked heated debate. Several BASF officials made presentations of the company plans and fielded questions from the public and county officials. TERC's attorney, Mike Kendall, stated the following summary position:

> We are not against having a facility such as the one described per se, but BASF's revised bid is not enough. We question the legality of negotiating a revised bid and the granting of easements which the BASF facility would require. County commissioners do not have the authority to accept an amended bid, except one that raises the price and then only after certain other notice provisions have been complied with.

Other BASF adversaries continued to remind county officials that the industrial park had never been properly marketed and that no such plan existed. Advocates of BASF stressed that the Vigo County area was in desperate need of jobs.

Despite the threats of TERC and other sundry opponents, on November 22, 1989, the Vigo County Commissioners and Vigo County Council voted unanimously to accept BASF's bid for 296.7 acres of land in the industrial park. Selected parts of the sale order were as follows:

1. The Board of Commissioners finds that the county has no other need for the real estate; Vigo County has severe economic stagnation; the use of real estate for industrial development would help alleviate problems of unemployment and economic stagnation; the soil conditions of the real estate are appropriate for the manufacturing facility, incinerator, and landfill.
2. The Commissioners are satisfied that the proposed facility will not threaten the health of local residents as long as the incinerator and landfill are operated in accordance with federal, state, and local laws, rulings, ordinances, and regulations.

A few days after Vigo County approved the sale of land to BASF, the company announced formation of a Community Awareness Panel to provide information to the Vigo County region about BASF's plans and actions. Jack Wehman reported that the panel would meet monthly to discuss topics such as plant facilities, environmental standards, safety and emergency procedures, employment training, and social commitments. Wehman stressed that the agenda was open and that panel members were their own people—not expected to be ambassadors for BASF. Although Wehman claimed that the Awareness Panel was a balanced representation of the community, he pointed out that anti-BASF people declined to serve. Two prominent leaders of the CCC, Harold Cox and John Strecker, rebutted Wehman's comments, stating they had not been asked to serve. Cox pointed out that the makeup of the Awareness Panel was skewed in favor of BASF.

TERC FILES LAWSUIT

On April 10, 1990, the Terre Haute Environmental Rights Coalition filed a lawsuit in U.S. district court stating the following:

1. The Government Services Administration violated the National Environmental Policy Act by selling land to Vigo County without requiring an environmental impact study before each of two land sales to the county. TERC requested that the sale be declared null and void and that the title to the industrial park land revert back to the U.S. government. The suit also requested that the GSA be required to conduct an environmental impact study in light of the intended use of the land—e.g., a hazardous waste landfill and incinerator.
2. TERC also filed a motion for an injunction stopping the county from selling the 296 acres to BASF until the lawsuit was resolved.

TERC legal counsel, Mike Kendall, also stated that the lawsuits would be filed against county officials for failing to disclose the true use of the property to the GSA—a violation of the Racketeer and Corrupt Organizations Act. In response to the charge that GSA was negligent in failing to conduct an environmental impact study, assistant U.S. attorney Sue Bailey filed a motion to dismiss the TERC lawsuit based on the position that the action taken by the federal government was several years old and the property no longer belonged to the federal government. Jack Wehman, Midwest venture director for BASF, issued a position statement:

> The frivolous filing of two federal lawsuits against the county and federal government by the Environmental Rights Coalition brings into question whether this group is concerned about the health and economic welfare of the citizens of Vigo County. BASF is not a defendant in either of the two lawsuits but, as a partner in the economic development of the community, we are disappointed in these self-serving delaying tactics. BASF is steadfast in its interest to invest more than $100 million in an automotive plant facility which will bring new jobs to Vigo County. BASF remains confident that the county and federal attorneys will resolve this matter to the satisfaction of the great majority of Vigo County residents.

Continued debate followed TERC's legal action. A countersuit was eventually filed by Vigo County Commissioners charging that TERC's complaint was "frivolous, unreasonable, and groundless." The countersuit further claimed that members of TERC were negligently and maliciously interfering with a contractual relationship simply to fulfill a goal of stopping the sale of land to BASF.

TERC responded with the following position statement:

> Some local government officials put all the public's marbles in one basket with BASF for less than 300 jobs. Instead of going after BASF, the commissioners should have spent the last two years enticing good corporate citizens with sound environmental records that would have provided hundreds of additional jobs. Having evaded the requirement for an environmental impact study and faced with a fickle BASF, the Vigo County Commissioners are in danger of being left with an empty plot of land, legal fees, and no jobs for our people.

In response to this legal impasse, Jack Wehman stated in mid-June, 1990, that if the federal lawsuit were not settled by September 1, 1990, BASF may decide to locate elsewhere. Wehman stressed that BASF must get its plant on line by the end of 1992.

BASF BREAKS OFF COURTSHIP

On September 4, 1990, Jack Wehman announced that BASF corporate officials in Germany decided the corporation would no longer consider land at the Vigo County industrial park as an option for its automotive plant. A big stumbling block to the marriage of BASF and Vigo County was the unresolved litigation filed by TERC claiming that the original sale of federal land by the GSA to Vigo County failed to comply with environmental regulations. Mixed emotions were recorded in the community, ranging from bitter disappointment to jubilation. City and county officials faced the dilemma of developing a new marketing plan for the industrial park in order to attract new companies and create jobs. BASF executives wondered what they could have done to avoid the confrontation and how their location strategy should be changed in the future. TERC's legal counsel, Michael Kendall, stressed that BASF's decision was not an issue about a group of people who allegedly kept a company out of Vigo County. It was about a victory for environmental integrity.

BIBLIOGRAPHY AND REFERENCES

"A Company at Work." BASF Corporation, January 1, 1989.

"An Economic Development Plan for the Vigo County Industrial Park." Vigo County Redevelopment Commission, November 1988.

Annual Report, BASF Corporation, 1988.

"BASF Pulls Out of Wabash Valley." *Terre Haute Tribune Star,* 10 September 1990.

"BASF Corporation: Proposed Midwest Facility for Terre Haute." BASF Corporation.

"BASF Corporation: Proposed Midwest Facility for Terre Haute." BASF Corporation, January 1989.

Cox, Harold, and Pat Duffy. "Court Rules Against Plan." *CCC Newsletter,* Fall, 1989.

"GSA Disputes Kaufman's Claim." *Terre Haute Tribune Star,* 14 March 1989.

Halladay, John. "BASF Lawsuit Gaining Weight." *Terre Haute Tribune Star,* 15 March 1989.

Halladay, John. "BASF's Efforts to Avoid Court Stopped by Judge." *Terre Haute Tribune Star,* 16 March 1989.

Halladay, John. "Testimony Ends in BASF Lawsuit." *Terre Haute Tribune Star,* 24 March 1989.

Halladay, John. "BASF Hearings Sham, Foes Charge in Post-Trial Brief." *Terre Haute Tribune Star,* 24 May 1989.

Halladay, John. "BASF Battle Heats Up Again." *Terre Haute Tribune Star,* 6 July 1989.

Halladay, John. "Development-Environmental Tie Possible." *Terre Haute Tribune Star,* 13 July 1989.

Halladay, John. "Officials Schedule New Hearings on Industrial Park." *Terre Haute Tribune Star,* 26 August 1989.

"Hazardous Waste Incineration: Questions and Answers." U.S. Environmental Protection Agency, 5 April 1988.

"Hazard Waste Incinerators." Greenpeace, 1987.

Heldman, Deborah D. "BASF Breaks Off Courtship with Vigo." *Terre Haute Tribune Star,* 5 September 1990.

Igo, Becky. "Chalos Says BASF Loss Could Hurt." *Terre Haute Tribune Star,* 20 June 1990.

Igo, Becky. "Counterclaim Filed on BASF Land Sale." *Terre Haute Tribune Star,* 23 June 1990.

Igo, Becky. "BASF Foes Call County's Legal Retaliation Intimidation." *Terre Haute Tribune Star,* 26 June 1990.

Igo, Becky. "TERC Files Opposition to Dismissal Request." *Terre Haute Tribune Star,* 24 July 1990

LeBar, Gregg. "Chemical Industry: Regulatory Crunch Coming." *Occupational Hazards,* November 1988.

Loughlin, Sue. "BASF Foes Ask Delay in Sale." *Terre Haute Tribune Star,* 16 July 1989.

Loughlin, Sue. "Several Foes Remain Opposed to BASF's Plans." *Terre Haute Tribune Star,* 31 August 1989.

Loughlin, Sue. "Community Leaders Beaming: Mayor Critical of Environmental Groups." *Terre Haute Tribune Star,* 31 August 1989.

Loughlin, Sue. "Federal Judge Thinking over TERC Request." *Terre Haute Tribune Star,* 13 April 1990.

Petiprin, Amy. "More Than 1800 Fill Out Survey: BASF Completes First Step in Hiring Process." *Terre Haute Tribune Star,* 5 November 1989.

Porter, Kelley. "Too Secret or Just Not Ready?" *Terre Haute Tribune Star,* 25 June 1989.

Porter, Kelley. "BASF's Chemicals List Still Not Complete." *Terre Haute Tribune Star,* 7 April 1989.

Porter, Kelley. "Prof More Worried Now After Studying Incineration Data." *Terre Haute Tribune Star,* 26 June 1989.

Porter, Kelley. "Judge Voids Economic Plan; Cites Conflicts." *Terre Haute Tribune Star,* 1 July 1989.

Porter, Kelley. "Wright's Statements Labeled Speculative." *Terre Haute Tribune Star,* 12 July 1989.

Porter, Kelley. "BASF Scales Back Its Plant Plans." *Terre Haute Tribune Star,* 31 August 1989.

Porter, Kelley. "BASF Releases Chemical List in Continued Spirit of Sharing Facts." *Terre Haute Tribune Star,* 2 September 1989.

Robinson, Dick. "Commissioners Confident They Can Meet Land Deadline." *Terre Haute Tribune Star,* 31 August 1989.

Shanks, Jim. Personal letter, November 8, 1988.

Walters, Gordon. "BASF Submits $500,000 Bid for Industrial Land." *Terre Haute Tribune Star,* 28 October 1989.

Walters, Gordon. "Environmentalist Form Anti-BASF Coalition." *Terre Haute Tribune Star,* 3 November 1989.

Walters, Gordon. "BASF Bid Meeting Postponed." *Terre Haute Tribune Star,* 15 November 1989.

Walters, Gordon. "Coalition Promises to Sue Commissioners." *Terre Haute Tribune Star,* 21 November 1989.

Walters, Gordon. "County Approves Offer to Sell Land to BASF." *Terre Haute Tribune Star,* 23 November 1989.

Walters, Gordon. "BASF Fulfills Panel Promises." *Terre Haute Tribune Star,* 29 November 1989.

Wardell, George. "Loss of Jobs Hurts Local Businesses." *Terre Haute Tribune Star,* 26 February 1989.

Wehman, Jack M. Personal letter, December 24, 1988.

Wehman, Jack M. Personal letter, December 5, 1988.

Wehman, Jack M. Personal letter, November 18, 1988.

CASE 40

Hoechst-Roussel Pharmaceuticals, Inc.: RU 486

Jan Willem Bol, David W. Rosenthal, Miami University of Ohio

By the end of 1992, the management of Hoechst-Roussel Pharmaceuticals had, as yet, made no public announcement as to their plans for marketing RU 486 in the United States. While the product had been available for testing in very limited quantities, the steps necessary to bring the new drug to market had not yet been undertaken.

RU 486 is a chemical compound that is commonly referred to as "the morning after pill" in the press. The compound has the effect of preventing a fertilized egg from attaching to the uterine wall or to ensure that a previously attached egg would detach. The pill has been thoroughly tested in several European countries with significant success.

The compound has also become the focus for a great amount of publicity, press coverage, and industry speculation. RU 486 was also the center of a series of U.S. Senate hearings. Activists, both in support of the product and in opposition to the product, have sought to influence the company's course of action since the product's inception.

Pharmaceutical industry observers suggest that the company is not marketing the product aggressively in order to "maintain a low profile." It is clear that the Hoechst-Roussel management has an ongoing and very complex issue to resolve as to the disposition of RU 486.

HISTORY

In 1980, Dr. Etienne-Emile Baulieu of Roussel-Uclaf developed RU 486, trade name Mifepristone, as an alternative to surgical abortion. The company re-

---

This case is intended for classroom discussion only, not to depict effective or ineffective handling of administrative situations. All rights reserved to the authors and the North American Case Research Association.

ferred to the product as a "contragestive," something between a contraceptive and an abortifacient. Like birth control, it could prevent a fertilized egg from implanting on the uterine wall and developing. It could also ensure that an implanted egg "sloughed off" or detached, making the product more like a chemical abortion. Its use was primarily intended for first trimester pregnancies, because if taken up to 49 days after conception, it was 95% successful. If the ferilized egg is not completely expelled, surgical abortions are then available with no complications. Researchers believe that the success rate will approach 100% when dosage levels are more defined. RU 486 is a synthesized steroid compound that induces bleeding comparable to that of a menstrual period for approximately one week. A few patients have reported slight nausea and cramps. Complications are rare, but it is recommended that the drug be taken under a physician's care because of the potential for heavy bleeding or the failure to abort.

The drug was first offered to the French market in September of 1988 and during the time it was on the market, 4,000 women used the drug and reported a 95.5% success rate. However, during this time strong protests and proposed worldwide boycotts of Hoechst products (Roussel's West German parent company) brought about the removal of RU 486 from the market and all distribution channels. Dr. Baulieu said the company's decision was "morally scandalous." At this point the French government, which owns 36% of Roussel-Uclaf, intervened. Two days after the pill's removal, Health Minister Claude Evin ordered RU 486 back into production and distribution in France, saying, "The drug is not just the property of Roussel-Uclaf, but of all women. I could not permit the abortion debate to deprive women of a product that represents medical progress." Since then, the product has been sold only to authorized clinics. Over 100 French women take the drug each day. Thus, approximately 15% of all French abortions are conducted through the use of RU 486.

Because it triggered such strong emotion for and against its use, Roussel management was hesitant to make it available to the world. Dr. Eduoard Sakiz, of Roussel, commented, "We just developed a compound, that's all, nothing else. To help the woman. . . . We are not in the middle of the abortion debate." Roussel holds the patent to the compound, but willingly supplies it for investigations around the world. The only American study was done by the Population Council, a nonprofit research organization in New York City, in connection with the University of Southern California. The study showed a 70% efficacy rate. Shortly after the drug became legal in France, China was able to officially license the use of the drug and by 1991 was close to manufacturing the drug itself. In 1990, Roussel management decided to market RU 486 to Great Britain, Sweden, and Holland as well.

It is generally believed that groups opposed to abortion under any circumstances have been largely responsible for keeping the drug out of the United States. Similarly, interest in research on the drug in the United States has apparently been curtailed by the intimidating tactics of the anti-abortion groups. No U.S. drug maker has sought a license from Roussel. However, other compounds, similar to RU 486, are in the process of development by pharmaceutical companies both in the United States and worldwide.

No long-term risks or effects have been found to result from continuous use of the drug, nor are any problems expected from brief, intermittent use. There is no information about how the drug might affect a fetus if the woman decided to continue her pregnancy after RU 486 failed, because the limited number of reported failures have all been followed by surgical abortions. Some studies reported that the drug seemed to suppress ovulation for 3 to 7 months after use. One medical journal did report that use of the drug created birth defects in rabbits, but the results could not be duplicated in rats and monkeys (known to be more similar to human make-up).

RU 486's primary function is obviously that of chemical abortions. It is thought that the drug could be especially important in the developing nations, where many women lacked access to medical facilities and anesthetics needed for surgical abortion. The drug would be particularly beneficial for three segments of the population. It would help in developing countries where maternal mortality is high. It would be useful among teenagers whose use of contraceptives is erratic at best. Thirdly, it would be useful for women who for various reasons are unable to use other methods successfully. Secondary markets are potentially available as well because RU 486 functions by inhibiting progesterone. The drug could, therefore, be beneficial in the treatment of Cushing's disease, in which an overactive adrenal gland releases too much of a steroid similar to progesterone. The drug could also be used to treat types of cancer that depend on progesterone for growth, such as tumors of the breast and endometriosis (abnormal growth of uterine lining), and other cancers of the reproductive system. In addition, RU 486 could potentially treat the nearly 80,000 women yearly who have ectopic pregnancies, a dangerous condition in which the egg develops outside the uterus.

In France, the availability of RU 486 is limited and the product is used only under medical supervision. Because of these conditions the price is high, about $100 (U.S.). It is estimated that on a larger production scale with increasing markets, the cost of the drug could be reduced in the United States. Industry consultants believe that when drug companies identify the large profit potential associated with RU 486 interest in the drug will strengthen in the United States.

POLITICAL AND LEGAL ENVIRONMENT

The management of Hoechst-Roussel faces considerable problems with the introduction of RU 486 into the U.S. The process of obtaining FDA approval is not likely to begin without the vocal support of American women who see the drug as an important means to achieve more personal and political control over their fertility. The process is likely to require considerable time and expense in order to satisfy the requirements of the FDA. Despite criticisms of its speed and process, the FDA has shown little inclination to reduce the time required for licensing new drugs. The politically sensitive nature of RU 486 is unlikely to speed the process.

While the approval process for RU 486 could probably be significantly shortened because of the test data already generated by foreign researchers, no American company has as yet petitioned the FDA to even begin the process. The standards required by the FDA for approval of a new drug are safety for the recommended use and substantial evidence of efficacy. The clinical trials and testing occur in three phases. Of twenty drugs that enter clinical testing under the FDA, only one will ultimately be approved for the market. It frequently costs a pharmaceutical company up to $125 million and 15 years to move a contraceptive from the lab to approval for the market.

With RU 486, the FDA has apparently resolved to be more restrictive than usual. Special policies and exceptions to their normal FDA rules have been enacted. Under normal circumstances the FDA allows patients to ship unapproved drugs into the country if the drugs are to treat life threatening conditions. The agency refused to apply these rules to RU 486. The FDA commissioner, Frank Young, has written to a Congressional representative that the FDA would not permit the drug to be imported into the United States for personal use, something it has allowed for certain other unapproved drugs.

One exception was not removed by the FDA. Because American doctors are able to prescribe an FDA approved drug for a use other than the use approved, there is a possibility RU 486 may enter the United States through this secondary market. Even though the FDA does not have jurisdiction to regulate the administration of a drug by a physician, the potential liability of a physician who chooses to prescribe RU 486 for abortions is probably sufficient to render this possibility remote.

RU 486 is not without its advocates. If RU 486 were to become available in the United States, the National Academy of Sciences reported that the FDA must streamline its stringent rules for the approval of new contraceptives. It also recommended that pharmaceutical companies must be given federal protection from liability suits so they would be encouraged to resume the contraceptive business.

If the Federal Government approved the pill, an individual state could not limit a doctor's decision to prescribe it. The fundamental tenet of the U.S. Supreme Court decision, *Roe* v. *Wade,* was that abortion in the first trimester should remain free from intrusive regulation by the state. Under this precedent, the most likely use of RU 486 in the United States was confirmed as an abortifacient to be administered under close medical supervision. The remote possibility of RU 486's introduction as a monthly antifertility drug would also be well within abortion law, and perhaps would allow RU 486 to be treated under law as a contraceptive.

Paradoxically, some observers argue that the United States is most likely to witness the appearance of RU 486 if the *Roe* v. *Wade* decision were overturned, and abortion again became illegal. It is suggested that a black market for the pill would evolve to meet the need for illegal abortions. Dr. Sheldon Siegel of the Rockefeller Foundation stated, "If there is a serious attempt to constrain further progress and further knowledge about RU 486, then it is likely that a black market manufacturer and supply system would develop." In this scenario, the pill might pose very serious health risks for women, since many could suffer side effects, especially in the absence of medical supervision. Still more frightening is that women ingesting the pill illegally would no longer have access to the backup of safe surgical abortion.

DRUG INDUSTRY

The drug industry consists of three primary segments: biological products, medicinals and botanicals, and pharmaceutical preparations. Pharmaceuticals were generally classified into one of two broad groups:

- Ethical pharmaceuticals—available only through a physician's prescription;
- Over-the-counter (OTC) and proprietary drugs—sold without prescription.

The pharmaceutical industry has grown steadily since 1970 as a result of rising health care spending throughout the world and the continuing product innovations from manufacturers. From 1970 to 1980 worldwide sales grew at an average of 10%–12%, in real dollars. In the 1980s growth was slightly lower at 7% and real growth rates are expected to decrease slightly during the early 1990s, ranging from 6% to 8%. The growth rates vary considerably among countries and product categories. An estimated breakdown of worldwide ethical sales by countries or regions with projected growth rates is shown in Exhibit 1.

SIZE AND COMPOSITION

The industry is not particularly concentrated; the top four firms comprise slightly less than 10% of the market. Within specific product categories, however, there is much higher concentration, the top four competitors often sharing 40%–70% of total sales. Exhibit 2 lists the pharmaceutical sales of the leading global pharmaceutical companies.

RESEARCH AND DEVELOPMENT

The overall health of the pharmaceutical industry is measured by the number of products it develops, the value of its exports, and the level of its profits.

Leading Pharmaceutical Markets **Exhibit 1**

Country	*1987 Sales (U.S. $MM)*	*Percent of Total*	*1990–1995 Growth Potential*
United States	$23,979	22.0	Moderate
Japan	15,690	14.4	Moderate
West Germany	6,527	6.0	Moderate
France	5,992	5.5	Moderate
China	4,890	4.5	Low
Italy	4,690	4.3	High
United Kingdom	3,370	3.1	Low
Canada	1,710	1.6	Moderate
South Korea	1,500	1.4	High
Spain	1,480	1.4	Moderate
India	1,400	1.3	High
Mexico	1,300	1.2	Declining
Brazil	1,180	1.1	Declining
Argentina	856	0.8	Declining
Australia	685	0.6	Moderate
Indonesia	590	0.5	Moderate
Others	33,200	30.4	High
Totals	$109,039	100.0	

Source: Adapted from Thompson from Arthur D. Little Inc.

Exhibit 2

20 Leading Global Pharmaceutical Companies

Company	*Country*	*1987 Sales (U.S. $000)*
Merck & Co., Inc.	U.S.A.	$5,060,000
American Home Products Corp.	U.S.A.	5,020,000
Pfizer Inc.	U.S.A.	4,910,000
Hoechst Corp.	West Germany	4,610,000
Abbott Laboratories	U.S.A.	4,380,000
SmithKline Beckman Corp.	U.S.A.	4,320,000
American Cyanamid Co.	U.S.A.	4,160,000
Eli Lilly & Co.	U.S.A.	3,640,000
Warner-Lambert Co.	U.S.A.	3,480,000
Schering Plough Co.	U.S.A.	2,690,000
Upjohn Co.	U.S.A.	2,520,000
Sterling Drug Inc.	U.S.A.	2,300,000
Squibb Corp.	U.S.A.	2,150,000
Schering Corp.	U.S.A.	1,900,000
E.R. Squibb & Sons Inc.	U.S.A.	1,800,000
Hoffman-LaRouche Inc.	Switzerland	1,500,000
Miles Inc.	U.S.A.	1,450,000
Glaxo Inc.	U.S.A.	937,000
Rorer Group Inc.	U.S.A.	928,000
A. H. Robins	U.S.A.	855,000

Source: Estimates based on various industry sources. The figures should be regarded as approximations due to differences in fiscal years of companies, and variations in data due to different definitions of pharmaceutical sales.

These factors are, in turn, directly affected by the amount of dollars spent on research and development.

The U.S. drug industry spent some $6 billion on R&D in 1988, up from $5.4 billion in 1987 and $4.7 billion in 1986. As a percentage of sales, the drug industry spent more on R&D than any other major industry group. In 1988 research accounted for more than 15% of revenues. Exhibit 3 lists research and development expenditures for some of the leading pharmaceutical companies.

THE OUTLOOK IN 1992

There are a number of positive factors affecting the industry at the beginning of the 1990s. The demographic growth trend in the over-65 segment of the population presents both a larger and more demanding market. The nature of the pharmaceutical business tends to make sales and revenues recession-resistant. High and increasing profit margins tend to attract capital in order to support the ambitious research and development needs of the industry.

However, all conditions are not positive for the industry. Pharmaceutical firms have been increasingly criticized for their drug pricing policies. Critics argue that relatively low manufacturing costs should be reflected in the pricing of drugs, and that high profit levels prove their point. Generic (unbranded) drugs continue their trend of high growth, supplanting the higher profit

Research and Development Expenditures (million $ and % of sales by year) **Exhibit 3**

	1986		1987		1988	
Abbot	$295	8%	$361	8%	$455	8%
Bristol-Myers	311	8	342	8	394	7
Johnson & Johnson	521	7	617	8	674	7
Hoechst Group	395	10	540	10	608	10
Eli Lilly	429	13	466	13	541	13
Merck	480	12	566	11	669	11
Rorer Group	70	8	82	9	103	10
Schering-Plough	212	9	251	9	298	11
SmithKline	377	10	424	10	495	10
Squibb	163	9	221	10	294	11
Syntex	143	15	175	16	218	17
Upjohn	314	14	356	14	380	14
Warner-Lambert	202	7	232	7	259	7

Source: Annual Reports.

branded segment of the market. Liability costs and the costs associated with compliance with increasingly complex and restrictive regulation continue to soar.

Drug companies in the United States essentially have a free reign to price their companies as they wish. This is contrary to the policies in many countries outside the United States where pharmaceutical prices are strictly regulated by governmental agencies. However, as a result of the rapid increase of healthcare costs during the 1970s and 1980s, there is a movement toward a more restrictive pricing environment at the state and federal level. In order to make their operations more efficient and acquire economies of scale, many companies have chosen to form alliances with other firms. A trend toward consolidation through merger and acquisition has resulted.

The growth of the generic drug segment poses a significant problem for the industry because these products are priced much lower than branded products. Prices of generic goods are often as much as 50% lower than the same branded drug. All 50 states have laws that permit substitution of generic drugs for branded drugs. As a result, the generic drug market doubled in sales from 1983 to 1987.

Pharmaceutical companies face extensive product liability risks associated with their products. This is especially true for "high risk" products such as vaccines and contraceptives. The cost of liability insurance to cover these adverse effects has forced many companies to co-insure or curtail their research efforts in these areas. In 1991 liability insurance coverage for the manufacture and sale of contraceptives was in most cases impossible to obtain. As a result of the "insurance crunch" the industry has become polarized. Only small companies with few assets and large corporations with the ability to self-insure tended to be marketers of contraceptives.

The pharmaceutical industry's high profit levels, and "heavy" expenditure on marketing, make it a frequent target for attack by political figures and consumer advocates. Critics suggest that the pharmaceutical companies price drugs so high that only wealthy patients can afford treatment. Marketing expenditures are blamed for "overprescribing," or the tendency for physicians to rely too heavily on drugs for treatment. Marketing is also blamed for hiding information regarding side effects and contra-indications from physicians in order to boost sales.

OUTPATIENT DRUG COVERAGE

Regulation of health care plays an important role in the pharmaceutical industry. Increasingly complex regulations both at the state and federal level require corresponding increases in costs of compliance. Further, the political nature of the regulatory system often creates uncertain conditions for the industry. The outpatient drug coverage provision of the Medicare catastrophic health insurance bill is an example of the uncertainty in the regulatory environment. This bill is expected to have both a positive and negative impact on the U.S. market. Scheduled to begin a three-year phase-in period in 1991, the plan is to cover 50% of Medicare beneficiaries' approved drug expenditures, after an annual deductible of $600 is met. Although the new coverage is expected to expand the overall market, it also makes the industry more dependent on the federal government, whose reimbursements are increasingly affected by cost constraints. Further, policies regarding other social issues, such as race or sex discrimination, abortion, and even environmental protection, come into play for those health care facilities that deal with Medicare recipients. The documentation necessary to show compliance with the relevant regulation encompasses an increasing cost for facilities. Pharmaceutical company managers are uncertain what effect such regulation will have on specific products.

CONTRACEPTIVE INDUSTRY

As of 1991, there were nearly 6 million unwanted pregnancies each year in the United States, and as a result, there were 1.6 million surgical abortions. Yearly, there are an estimated 500,000 pregnancy-related deaths worldwide, 200,000 from improperly performed abortions. Up to half of these unwanted preganancies and deaths could be prevented if women had more birth control options. In 1991, American contraceptive research came to a virtual halt, causing the United States to fall far behind other countries in developing new techniques. In the early 1980s, eleven companies in the United States did research in the contraceptive field, but by 1991 only two continued such studies. Political opposition and the potential danger of large liability suits appear to be the most important reasons for the decline in focus on these drugs.

In 1991, there were several "morning after" or abortion-inducing drugs that had been approved by the FDA for use in the United States. These abortifacients are distributed only to hospitals approved by the manufacturer, the Upjohn Company. The compounds are based on prostaglandins, which are powerful hormones that could cause serious side effects. These abortion-inducing drugs are only available by prescription and under the most controlled conditions. The FDA allows these drugs to be used only for second trimester pregnancies and only in certain hospitals. The drugs are neither advertised to the public nor promoted to physicians by company sales representatives. Likewise, samples of the drugs are not provided to the medical profession. Jessyl Bradford, spokeswoman for Upjohn, stated, "We believe that our commitment to provide a safe and effective alternative to saline and surgical procedures is a responsible one. However, we do not promote abortion. It is an individual decision, made in consultation with a physician. We make no effort to influence such decisions."

The contraceptive market is relatively small, its value being about $1 billion yearly worldwide. Within this market, $700 million is accounted for by the use of oral contraceptives. There are, however, nearly 3 million women in the United States alone who use nonoral methods. The profit margin of contraceptives is very high. To illustrate, the U.S. government, buying in bulk for shipment overseas, is able to buy a monthly supply of birth control pills for about 18 cents, whereas, the average consumer pays about $12 a month. The leader in the contraceptive field is a company named Ortho, which sells contraceptive pills, diaphragms, spermicides, and other products for family planning (i.e., home pregnancy kits). Ortho is continuing to develop improved oral contraceptives that provide better cycle control and reduced side effects; however, the estimated cost of contraceptive development from the laboratory to the market is estimated at $125 million. Contraceptive development in the United States is slowing. Although pro-life forces attribute the decline to their efforts, companies and outside experts argue that the reduction is the result of three main factors: high research costs, relatively low potential profit, and the enormous risk that liability suits present. Robert McDonough, spokesman for Upjohn Company, said, "(Upjohn) terminated its fertility research program in 1985 for two reasons. There was an adverse regulatory climate in the United States. It was increasingly difficult to get fertility drugs approved. And there was a litigious climate. . . . Litigation is terribly expensive, even if you win."

Recently, an $8.75 million judgment was granted against GD Searle to a woman injured by the company's Copper-7 intrauterine device. Similarly, Dalkon Shield cases forced the AH Robbins Company into bankruptcy. In the late 1980s, AH Robbins was forced to establish a $615 million trust fund to compensate victims of IUD caused pelvic infections and deaths. Such settlements made liability insurance for contraceptive manufacturers nearly impossible to obtain.

One of the few organizations in the U.S. that has continued research on contraceptives is the Population Council, a $20 million nonprofit organization backed by the Rockefeller and Mellon foundations. The Population Council had been conducting U.S. studies of RU 486 on a license from the French developer. Additional support for contraceptive development is evident in legislation to provide a $10 million grant for the "development, evaluation, and bringing to the marketplace of new improved contraceptive devices, drugs, and methods." If passed the grant would put the federal government into the contraceptive marketing business for the first time.

HOECHST CELANESE

Hoechst Celanese is a wholly owned subsidiary of Hoechst AG of Frankfurt, West Germany. Hoechst AG and its affiliates constitute the Hoechst Group, one of the world's largest multinational corporations, encompassing 250 companies in 120 nations. The Hoechst companies manufacture and conduct research

Exhibit 4 **Hoechst-Roussel's Prescription Drugs**

Lasix (furosemide)	A widely prescribed diuretic
Clarofan (cefotaxime)	One of the largest selling third-generation cephalosporin antibiotics used to treat infections
Topicort (desoximetasone)	A steroid applied to the skin
Streptasea (streptokinase)	A product used to dissolve clots in blood vessels, e.g., in the treatment of heart attack
Trental (pentoxifylline)	Improves arterial blood flow and is used to treat intermittent claudication (leg pain associated with arteriosclerosis)
Diabeta (glyburide)	An oral antidiabetic agent used in the treatment of non-insulin-dependent diabetes.

Source: Hoechst AG *1988 Annual Report.*

on chemicals, fibers, plastics, dyes, pigments, and pharmaceuticals. The United States is the largest and fastest growing segment for the Hoechst product lines and is often the key point for establishing worldwide marketing capability.

Within its Life Sciences Group, Hoechst Celanese, in affiliation with Roussel-Uclaf (a French pharmaceutical company), provide leading products to the prescription-drug markets in the United States. The division is referred to as Hoechst-Roussel Pharmaceuticals Incorporated (HRPI) and its primary prescription drugs provided to the U.S. health care market are explained in Exhibit 4.

The company also markets directly to consumers stool softener/laxatives, including Doxidan and Surfak, and is developing potential drugs for many indications, including Alzheimer's disease, cardiovascular disease, tumors, and diabetes. HRPI had not previously invested research into the contraceptive or abortion drug categories.

ROUSSEL-UCLAF

Roussel-Uclaf, founded in Paris, France, is engaged in manufacturing and marketing chemical products for therapeutic and industrial use, perfumes, eyeglasses, and nutritional products. In addition, Roussel is one of the world's leading diversified pharmaceutical groups. Within its pharmaceutical group, Roussel invests its research into a wide range of product categories including antibiotics, diuretics, steroids and laxatives.

Roussel employed over 14,759 individuals and its 72 subsidiaries yielded a total net income of over $84 million dollars in 1988. Ownership was held by two groups: the German company Hoechst AG with 54.5% of common stock and the French government with 36%.

In 1979, George Teutsch and Alain Belanger, chemists at the French drug company, synthesized chemical variations on the basic steroid molecule. Some of the new chemicals blocked receptors for steroids, causing inhibition of the effects of the steroids, including the hormones involved in sexual reproduction. Because of the controversy surrounding birth control, Roussel did not want to study these hormones and had always maintained a company policy not to develop drugs for contraception or abortion. However, after much persuasion by consultant Baulieu discussing the other revolutionary effects the compounds might have besides those with sexual reproduction, Roussel continued its research and eventually began manufacturing RU 486 in the early 1980s.

TECHNICAL ISSUES

RU 486 acts as an antiprogesterone steroid. Progesterone is a hormone that allows a fertilized embryo to be implanted on the inner wall of the uterus. Progesterone also reduces the uterus' responsiveness to certain contractile agents that may aid in the expulsion of the embryo. Additionally, progesterone helps the cervix to become firm and aids in the formation of a mucous plug that maintains the placental contents. All of these steps are necessary for an embryo to properly develop into a fetus. Without progesterone initiating the chain of events, an embryo cannot mature.

RU 486 masks the effects of progesterone by binding to the normal receptors of the hormone and prohibiting a proper reaction. The embryo cannot adhere to the uterine lining, so the subsequent changes do not occur and the normal process of menstruation (shedding of the uterine wall) begins.

The Population Council sponsored two studies (1987 and 1988) at the University of Southern California (USC) that examined the efficacy of RU 486. The results from the two studies were as follows:

1987	100 mg. a day for 7 days: 73% effective
	50 mg. a day for 7 days: 50% effective
1988	600 mg. tab: 90% effective

The studies were conducted without prostaglandin, a compound that drastically increases RU 486's effectiveness. With prostaglandin, RU 486 was tested at 95.5% efficacy.

The conclusions reached from the USC experiments were that RU 486 was more effective with a higher dose and that the earlier it was administered in the gestational period, the greater its efficacy. The tests were all conducted on women within 49 days of their last menstrual cycle.

OPPOSITION

The National Right-to-Life Committee of the United States played an important role in keeping RU 486 from being introduced into the United States. Their convictions stem from their belief that a human life begins at conception, at which point RU 486 intervenes. According to Jim McDonald, former vice president of Students United for Life, "RU 486 is a poison just like cyanide or other poisons. Poisons are chemicals that kill human beings . . . RU 486 is such a poison which kills the growing unborn human being."

Abortion opponents also resisted the marketing of RU 486 because in clinical testing, women were required to agree to surgical abortions if the drug was unsuccessful. Prevention of abortions is the primary focus of the right-to-life group. Pro-lifers also suggest that by simply taking a pill to end a pregnancy, the moral significance of the act is eliminated. A right-to-life advocate, Congressman Robert Dornan, wrote a letter to his colleagues in 1986 to gain support to curtail federal funding for the testing of the pill. He states his concern that, "The proponents of abortion want to replace the guilt suffered by women who undergo abortion with the moral uncertainty of self-deception. Imagine with the 'Death Pill,' the taking of a pre-born life will be as easy and as trivial as taking aspirin."

Pro-life groups reacted strongly and even violently to prevent the drug's introduction into the U.S. market. The U.S. right-to-life group began its campaign by pressuring the French company that originated the pill, Roussel-Uclaf. As a result of the efforts and the influence of this group, which included bomb threats on Roussel executives, the company discontinued its production of RU 486 until the French government demanded its redistribution. Subsequently the strategy of the group has focused on preventing the drug's introduction in the United States. The transfer of pressure to the U.S. domestic market occurred as a result of RU 486's expansion into the British and Chinese markets and the resultant fear that the United States was the next logical market for introduction.

Pro-life groups continued their letter writing campaign to Roussel and extended the campaign to Roussel's parent company, Hoechst AG. Further, they threatened to boycott Hoechst's American subsidiary, Hoechst-Celanese. The right-to-life campaign has been successful to date, as Hoechst placed a "quarantine" on the drug, limiting its distribution to current markets.

Another strategy used by abortion opponents included putting pressure on the U.S. Congress to limit federal funding for research on the drug. Such limitations could strongly impede the Food and Drug Administration approval process. In 1991 the only U.S. testing of the drug was being conducted by the Population Council. At the same time, pro-life congressmen lobbied for legislation to prohibit further testing. The position of the president and the increasingly conservative character of the Supreme Court suggested that the introduction of RU 486 would meet stiff resistance.

In addition to the anti-abortion concerns, pro-life and some feminist groups were concerned over the short- and long-term physical dangers associated with the use of the drug. Advocates for the pill stress that a main advantage of the drug is that it is a "safe" method of abortion as compared to the probabilities of injury associated with surgical abortion. The safety claim is largely unsubstantiated, however, due to the lack of available objective test results. According to the *Yale Journal of Law and Feminism,* "The level of ignorance about the long-term effects of RU 486 makes it premature to apply the adjective 'safe.' . . ." Although Dr. Baulieu stated that studies had been performed using rabbits and immature human eggs, no direct objective evidence from these tests has been provided to substantiate his claims of safety.

There are additional concerns that the drug could harm subsequent offspring or cause malformation in unsuccessful abortions. Baulieu admitted that there had been cases where the drug was unsuccessful in causing the abortion and the women had foregone surgical abortion. He indicated that there had been no evidence of maldevelopment. RU 486 was said to be "quickly flushed from a woman's system, making long-term effects less likely." This claim has not yet been proven through empirical evidence.

Although the efficacy of RU 486 is increased significantly when used in conjunction with a prostaglandin, the possibility of incomplete abortion remains. Such a condition is dangerous because of the potential for the tissue remaining in the uterus to cause infection. The threat to the health and life of the woman is, therefore, a reasonable concern.

The final concern that pro-life advocates have about the dangers of RU 486 is that it has been proven to be ineffective on ectopic pregnancies, pregnancies that occur in the fallopian tubes or the ovary rather than in the uterus. The concern is that the number of ectopic pregnancies in the United States has increased and by using RU 486, "the woman would believe that she was no longer pregnant until her fallopian tube burst and endangered her life."

Gynecologists and obstetricians are mixed in their views toward the introduction of RU 486 into the United States. Pressure from doctors belonging to the World Congress of Obstetrics and Gynecology forced the French government to demand the redistribution of the product previously. However, some doctors consider the product to be unnecessary. Dr. Jettinger, a gynecologist and obstetrician, believes that there are other chemical alternatives available and stated, "The drug will be a fiasco for whoever decides to market it due to the stink from Right to Life groups." Dr. Jettinger stated:

> We already have similar forms of chemical abortifacients that are legal and are used in the U.S. For example, Ovral is used as a "morning after" pill. In residency . . . when a rape victim came into the emergency room, she was given one dose of Ovral then and another one in the morning. This makes the uterus incapable of conception which is similar to the effects of RU 486. This method is 95.5% effective whereas RU 486 alone [without prostaglandins] is only up to 90% effective. Not many people are aware that this goes on so there is not much publicity.

PROPONENTS

RU 486 is not without supporters. The controversy surrounding the drug elicited the attention of many consumer and political groups. Family planning establishments such as Planned Parenthood Federation of America, World Health Organization, and the Population Council and feminist groups such as the Committee to Defend Reproductive Rights, Boston Women's Health Book Collective, and the National Women's Health Network all support the drug. During the period that Roussel had stopped production and sale of RU 486, the World Congress of Gynecology and Obstetrics had planned to ask physicians to boycott Roussel products if the company's decision was not reversed. Kelli Conlin, president of the National Organization for Women in New York, called for a campaign urging U.S. pharmaceutical companies to test abortion drugs such as RU 486. "Companies cannot let these (anti-abortion) groups push them around. And that group is really a minority."

Right to life groups consider RU 486 to be a particular threat because one of their main avenues of action has been picketing abortion clinics and making the process more difficult for those people who choose to abort their pregnancies. RU 486 could be used in a doctor's office, thus making such action less useful to influence patients. Further, because the drug is to be used within the first seven weeks of pregnancy, the emotional appeal of showing developed fetuses in danger of abortion would be limited since all that is observed is bleeding similar to menstruation. One fear of pro-life groups was that if RU 486 became common the whole term "abortion" could become obsolete. Dr. Baulieu told the *MacNeil/Lehrer NewsHour* in September 1986 that "abortion, in my opinion, should more or less disappear as a concept, as a fact, as a word in the future. . . . "

If the pill were authorized for use, it would be possible for a woman to take the pill safely and privately very soon after missing her period without ever knowing whether she was actually pregnant or not. In fact, if used monthly, there was some question whether it should actually be labeled an *abortion drug*. Depending on when it was taken, RU 486 worked virtually the same way as the "pill" or IUD. Normally, the pill prevented pregnancy by suppressing ovulation, but certain forms (containing lower doses of hormones to reduce the side effects) occasionally failed to suppress ovulation and instead prevented the fertilized ovum from implanting in the uterus. The IUD, too, worked by irritating the uterus and preventing implantation. If RU 486 was used within 8 days of fertilization it brought about the same effect.

One of the most basic reasons given in support of RU 486 is safety. The United States has one of the highest percentages of accidental pregnancies in the industrialized world. According to the World Health Organization, "Surgical abortions kill 200,000 women each year. Companies are retreating from research in abortion for fear of controversy, special interest pressure, and product liability questions—creating a major health care crisis." Likewise, there are increased safety problems when the abortion is postponed until later stages of pregnancy. Women facing an unwanted pregnancy often attempt to avoid the physically and emotionally painful abortion decision by ignoring it. If the abortion options were less harsh, it is thought that many women would face their situations more immediately and, therefore, safely. Polls indicated that "Americans tend to oppose early abortions much less fervently and in fewer numbers than late abortions."

Pro-life groups argue that conception equates to fertilization, thus making RU 486 a form of chemical abortion. However, the Federal Courts and the American College of Obstetrics and Gynecology defined "conception" as implantation. In 1986, the Federal Appeals Court overturned an Illinois law using the pro life definition as statute. The implantation definition is based on the fact that 40%–60% of all fertilized ova fail to implant. Some pro-choice advocates suggest therefore, that according to the pro-life argument, women should be required to take progesterone to encourage implantation and prevent accidental death of the fertilized ova.

One of the most significant reasons for support for the introduction of RU 486 is the improvement it provides over other abortion options. With RU 486, there would be "no waiting, no walking past picket lines, no feet up in stirrups for surgery." In many cases, abortion clinics would be unnecessary. The clinics, instead, could be replaced by a few 24-hour emergency clinics that would treat any potential complications. It would make the abortion decision much more a personal matter. In some cases it would remove the psychological agony of deciding on an abortion at all. Women who took the pill just a few days after missing their period would never even know if they had been pregnant. Considering the extreme emotional trauma an abortion often causes, this is considered by supporters to be a great benefit. Finally, the cost of RU 486 would make it much more attractive than other methods. According to a *Newsweek* article, "if RU 486 is approved, Planned Parenthood plans to make it available free or 'at cost' at its family planning centers."

A number of industry observers suggest that the availability of RU 486 in the U.S. market is inevitable. They argue that there are enough people who support RU 486 for a black market to develop. It is even more likely because it is already legal and available in other countries. Some radical groups even call for their members to support its illegal use. Norma Swenson, of the Boston Women's Health Book collective, argues that RU 486 would save so many women from death by "botched abortions" that it would be worth it for women's groups to organize its underground use. "Using RU 486 . . . would be a type of civil disobedience."

CONCLUSION

The management of Hoechst-Roussel hold the legal and moral responsibility for the decision regarding introduction of RU 486 to the United States. It is clear that, regardless of its direction, the decision will have far reaching implications for a variety of people, including its stockholders and customers, but also the U.S. society as a whole. It is evident that the pressures being brought to bear will continue to build.

REFERENCES

"A Pill That May Diffuse the Abortion Issue," *Business Week,* April 1, 1985.

"Abortion Pill Expected to Be Sold in Europe," Editorial, *The New York Times,* December 18, 1986.

Allen, Charlotte Low. "RU 486, the French Abortion Pill: What Is Safe?" *Science,* September 22, 1989, volume 245, pp. 1319–24.

Baulieu, Etienne-Emile. "Contragestion and Other Clinical Applications of RU 486, an Antiprogestrin at the Receptor," *Science,* September 22, 1989, volume 245, pp. 1351–56.

Bradford, Jessye. "Letter to Columbia from Upjohn," 1987.

Bradley, Ed. *60 Minutes,* 1989.

"Changing the Whole Abortion Debate," *Washington Post,* March 1, 1986.

Cole, Leonard. "Abortions Will Be Moot Soon," *The New York Times,* October 9, 1989.

"Conception of a Controversy: The French Doctor and His Pill to Prevent Pregnancy," *Washington Post,* December 1986.

DeWitt, Phillip E. "A Bitter Pill to Swallow," *Time,* February 26, 1990, p. 44.

Fraser, Laura. "Pill Politics: A New Drug Makes Abortion More Personal, Private and Convenient. So Why Do We Have to Fly to France to Get It?" *Mother Jones,* June 1988, volume 13, pp. 30–35.

Greenhouse, Steven. "A New Pill, a Fierce Battle," *The New York Times Magazine,* February 12, 1989.

Greenhouse, Steven. "Drug Maker Stops All Distribution of Abortion Pill," *The New York Times,* October 27, 1988.

Kolata, Gina. "Any Sale in U.S. of Abortion Pill Still Years Away," *The New York Times,* October 30, 1988.

Palca, Joseph. "The Pill of Choice?" *Science,* September 22, 1989, volume 245, pp. 1319–24.

Ricks, Sarah. "The New French Abortion Pill," *Yale Journal of Law and Feminism,* 1989.

Smith, Emily T., et al. "Abortion: A Vocal Minority Has Drugmakers Running Scared," *Business Week,* November 14, 1988, p. 59.

Standard and Poors Industry Surveys. July 13, 1989, "Healthcare," p. 17.

Verity, C. William. U.S. Department of Commerce. *Industrial Outlook—Drugs.* January 1989, p. 16.

Company Index

Name Index

Page numbers followed by n indicate material in notes.

Subject Index

Headings in bold type indicate cases.

Instructions for Using CASE ANALYST

Strategic and Financial Analysis Software to Accompany

Strategic Management: Text and Cases, Second Edition

Prepared by Marshall Schminke, Thomas J. McAlister, and Patrice Beck

of Creighton University

CASE ANALYST is an easy-to-use interactive spreadsheet template that helps you better understand and interpret the financial information from cases in the text. It consists of five parts:

1. A guide to generating your case analysis.
2. A financial growth and ratio template that allows you to calculate and analyze the key growth statistics and financial ratios of the firm.
3. A graphics component that allows you to visually inspect multiple ratios over time.
4. A "what if"component that lets you make projections about the future of the firm and assess the impact of these projections.
5. A printing option that allows you to generate hard copy output of these analyses.

Hardware and Software Requirements

CASE ANALYST will operate on any IBM PC or PC-compatible computer with at least 512K of memory and DOS 2.1 or later. It requires that you have access to Lotus 1-2-3, Version 2.01 or later.

Before you begin, you should make backup copies of the CASE ANALYST disks, and use these backups when performing your analyses; store the originals for safe keeping. You should be sure to save your working files on a separate disk under a new name, to prevent accidentally copying over the original files.

How to Use CASE ANALYST

CASE ANALYST files behave just like any other Lotus 1-2-3 worksheet files. They contain much of the financial information you see in the cases in the text (balance sheets and income statements). All of this data has been entered for you, and the package calculates a wide variety of financial ratios and compound growth statistics for you.

For a single or dual floppy disk system:

1. Insert your DOS disk in Drive A (usually the top drive of the two) and turn on the computer.
2. At the A> prompt, remove the DOS disk and insert your Lotus 1-2-3 system disk into Drive A.
3. Type: 123
4. Press the [return] or [enter] key. (The Lotus spreadsheet will appear on the screen.)
5. Remove the Lotus system disk and insert the CASE ANALYST disk that contains the case you wish to analyze into Drive A.
6. Type: /FR (AUTO123.WK1 should be highlighted at this point. If it is not, press the space bar until it is highlighted.)
7. Press the [return] or [enter] key, and the main menu will appear. From this point, follow the instructions on the screen.
8. You are now ready to use the CASE ANALYST software.

For a hard drive system:

1. Be sure the Lotus 1-2-3 system program is installed on your hard drive. If it is not, consult your Lotus installation manual for instructions.
2. The first time you use CASE ANALYST you will need to create a subdirectory on your hard drive to store the files. The next steps create this subdirectory, named ANALYST.
3. Turn on the computer. At the C:\> prompt:
4. Type: MD C:\ANALYST
5. Press the [return] or [enter] key. Copy the CASE ANALYST files from the single 3.5" disk or both 5.25" disks to your hard drive, using standard DOS commands, as follows.
6. Type: COPY A:*.* C:\ANALYST
7. Press the [return] or [enter] key. If you are using the 5.25" disks, repeat step 6 with the second CASE ANALYST disk.
8. Run the Lotus system program. When Lotus is loaded:
9. Type: /FD C:\ANALYST\
10. Press the [return] or [enter] key.
11. Type: /FR (AUT0123.WK1 should be highlighted at this point. If it is not, press the space bar until it is highlighted.)
12. Press the [return] or [enter] key, and the main menu will appear. From this point, follow the instructions on the screen.
13. You are now ready to use the CASE ANALYST software.

Note: If you are using LOTUS 123 from a menu-driven network, you may be able to auto-load the CASE ANALYST software by placing the CASE ANALYST disk in the default drive and loading 123 as per your system's instructions. Consult your network advisor to see whether this is feasible with your system.